D1387671

TERRELL

ON THE

LAW OF PATENTS

AUSTRALIA
The Law Book Company
Brisbane ∗ Sydney ∗ Melbourne ∗ Perth

CANADA
Carswell
Ottawa ∗ Toronto ∗ Calgary ∗ Montreal ∗ Vancouver

AGENTS:
Steimatzky's Agency Ltd., Tel Aviv;
N.M. Tripathi (Private) Ltd., Bombay;
Eastern Law House (Private) Ltd., Calcutta;
M.P.P. House, Bangalore;
Universal Book Traders, Delhi;
Aditya Books, Delhi;
MacMillan Shuppan KK, Tokyo;
Pakistan Law House, Karachi, Lahore.

TERRELL

ON THE

LAW OF PATENTS

FOURTEENTH EDITION

BY

DAVID YOUNG, M.A.
One of Her Majesty's Counsel

ANTONY WATSON, M.A.
One of Her Majesty's Counsel

SIMON THORLEY, M.A.
One of Her Majesty's Counsel

RICHARD MILLER, B.Sc.
of the Middle Temple, Barrister

LONDON
SWEET & MAXWELL
1994

First Edition	(1884)	By Thomas Terrell
Second Edition	(1889)	By Thomas Terrell
Third Edition	(1895)	By W.P. Rylands
Fourth Edition	(1906)	By Courtney Terrell
Fifth Edition	(1909)	By Courtney Terrell
Sixth Edition	(1921)	By Courtney Terrell and A.D. Jaffe
Seventh Edition	(1927)	By Courtney Terrell and D.H. Corellis
Eighth Edition	(1934)	By J.R. Jones
Ninth Edition	(1951)	By K.E. Shelley, K.C.
Tenth Edition	(1961)	By K.E. Shelley, Q.C.
Eleventh Edition	(1965)	By Guy Aldous, Q.C., Douglas Falconer and William Aldous
Twelfth Edition	(1971)	By Douglas Falconer, Q.C., William Aldous and David Young
Thirteenth Edition	(1982)	By William Aldous, Q.C., David Young, Q.C., A. Watson and S. Thorley.

Published in 1994 by
Sweet & Maxwell Limited, of South Quay Plaza, 183 Marsh Wall, London E14 9FT
Typeset by Tradespools Ltd., Frome
Printed and bound in Great Britain by Hartnolls Ltd., Bodmin

A catalogue record for this book is available from the British Library

ISBN 0 421 40890 1

U.K. statutory material and extracts from *Reports on Patent, Design and Trademark Cases* in this publication are acknowledged as Crown copyright; extracts from Law Reports, King's Bench Division and Chancery Division are reproduced with the permission of the Incorporated Council of Law Reporting for England and Wales, the copyright holder.

No natural forests were destroyed to make this product.
Farmed timber was used and replanted.

PREFACE

The last edition of this book was more than 12 years ago at which time case law relating to the Patents Act 1977 was still fairly sparse. Since then the 1977 Act has been amended by the Copyright, Designs and Patents Act 1988 and the Patents County Court has been in operation since 1990. Furthermore the impact of the Patents Act 1949 is less marked today, although it still remains with us. Thus, since the last edition there has been a considerable development of the law.

As a consequence of such changes we have reformulated the book so that generally for each subject the provisions of the 1977 Act (as amended) are addressed first and have been largely rewritten. As regards the 1949 Act we have endeavoured to bring up-to-date those parts of the old edition which are still relevant to existing old Act patents, but have omitted those provisions which no longer seem to be relevant such as the provisions of the 1949 Act relating to extensions of patent term and licences of right. Generally we have endeavoured to state the law as at the end of May 1994.

As this book is intended for those practising in the U.K. courts whilst covering the law regarding applications for and oppositions to European patents it does not deal with detailed European Patent Office practice and procedure. On the practical side we have re-introduced precedents and pleadings to be found in Chapter 14.

In the preparation of this edition we are very grateful for the help given by Guy Burkill, Andrew Waugh, Colin Birss and in particular David Votier of Carpmaels and Ransford for his assistance on the chapter on Applications for European Patents.

D.Y.
A.W.
S.T.
R.M.

July 1994.

TABLE OF CONTENTS

Para.

1. PATENTS

2. THE NATURE OF PATENTABLE INVENTIONS

3. THE APPLICANT AND APPLICATION

4. THE SPECIFICATION

5. GROUNDS OF REVOCATION

6. INFRINGEMENT OF LETTERS PATENT

7. AMENDMENT OF SPECIFICATIONS

8. DEVOLUTION, ASSIGNMENTS AND LICENCES, CO-OWNERSHIP AND REGISTRATION

9. COMPULSORY LICENCES (ABUSE OF MONOPOLY) AND LICENCES OF RIGHT

10. REVOCATION PROCEEDINGS

11. ACTION TO RESTRAIN THREATS

12. ACTION FOR INFRINGEMENT

13. USE BY THE CROWN, INCOME TAX, STAMPS, ETC.

14. PRECEDENTS AND PLEADINGS

APPENDICES

TABLE OF CASES

(References are to Paragraph number)

xi

TABLE OF EUROPEAN PATENT OFFICE DECISIONS

(References are to Paragraph number)

xlv

TABLE OF EUROPEAN COMMISSION DECISIONS

(References are to Paragraph number)

TABLE OF STATUTES

(References are to Paragraph number)

1

TABLE OF STATUTORY INSTRUMENTS

(References are to Paragraph number)

On pp. lxiii–lxviii, the heading should read
"Table of **International Treaties and** E.C. Legislation".

TABLE OF EC LEGISLATION

(References are to Paragraph number)

RULES OF THE SUPREME COURT

(References are to Paragraph number)

RULES OF THE COUNTY COURT

(References are to Paragraph number)

CHAPTER 1

PATENTS

Introduction and History

Definition

The grant of a patent for an invention is the grant to the patentee for a **1.01**
limited period of a monopoly right in respect of that invention, *i.e.* the
right to exclude others from using that invention. The term "patent" is
derived from "Letters Patent" and indeed in statutes prior to the Patents
Act 1977 "patent" was defined as meaning "Letters Patent for an
invention".

Letters Patent

"Letters Patent," that is, open letters, *literae patentes*, are so called **1.02**
"because they are not sealed up, but exposed to view, with the Great
Seal pendant at the bottom, and are usually addressed by the Sovereign
to all the subjects of the Realm".[1] They are the common form of making
grants of dignities, appointments to certain offices of state and grants of
privilege of various kinds, including, until the coming into operation of
the Patents Act 1977, monopoly rights in inventions. They derive their
authority from the fact that they are issued under the Great Seal, "for all
the King's subjects are bound to take notice of the King's Great Seal".[2]

In the case of letters patent for inventions the seal of the Patent Office
had, since 1883,[3] been substituted for the Great Seal, and by section 21 (1)
of the Patents Act 1949:

> "A patent sealed with the seal of the Patent Office shall have the same
> effect as if it were sealed with the Great Seal of the United Kingdom,
> and shall have effect throughout the United Kingdom[4] and the Isle of
> Man".

---

[1] 2Bl.Comm., c.21, s.2.
[2] *East India Co. v. Sandys* (1684) Skin. 224.
[3] 46 & 47 Vict., c.57, s.12.
[4] This includes Northern Ireland, but not the Channel Islands.

Modern form of Patent

1.03   Since the coming into operation (on June 1, 1978) of the Patents Act 1977, Letters Patent are no longer issued to patentees on the grant of a patent. Instead, the Comptroller sends to the proprietor a certificate in the prescribed form stating that the patent has been granted to him.[5]

The following short outline of the history of the growth of the law and practice may perhaps be of service as an introduction to present practice and legislation.

Early industrial grants

1.04   It has been recognised from the earliest times that the regulation of trade lay within the prerogative of the Crown. The charters and patents granted to the trade guilds and corporations are well known. Grants of special privileges were, however, also made to individuals from time to time. Thus, between 1331 and 1452 various letters of protection were issued to foreign weavers and other craftsmen.[6] In 1347 there was a complaint in Parliament that an alien merchant had a monopoly of exporting Cornish tin;[7] while in 1376 John Peeche, Alderman of Walbrook Ward, was impeached in respect of a patent giving him the right to sell sweet wines in the City of London contrary to an ordinance of Parliament.[8]

The origin of the present patent system is to be found, however, in the "Monopoly System" inaugurated by Cecil in the reign of Queen Elizabeth I. While originally designed to encourage the setting up of new industries,[9] it became in fact a method of farming out the powers of the Crown. In the last parliament of the reign two Bills were introduced with the object of reforming the system, but were not proceeded with[10] as the Crown promised to recall some of the patents and that none "should be put in execution but such as should first have trial according to law".

The Case of Monopolies

1.05   The only patent which was in fact tried in the courts was Darcy's Patent for the monopoly of importing, manufacturing and selling playing cards, which was the subject of the famous *Case of Monopolies*.[11]

---

[5] P.A. 1977, s.24(2), Patents Rules 1990 (S.I. 1990 No. 2384), r.38 and Sched. 3.
[6] See, *e.g. Cal.Pat. Rolls* (1330–34) 161; (1967–70) 105; Rymer, x, 761; xi, 317.
[7] Tydman of Lynnburgh, who had liberty to export tin without paying the customary tax: see *Rot.Parl.* ii, 168; *Cal. Close Rolls* (1346–49) 328.
[8] The facts are obscure: see *Rot.Parl.* ii, 328; *Cal.Pat. Rolls* (1374–77) 448, 457; *Cal Fine Rolls*, viii, 225, 227.
[9] For the provisions of the early patents see Hulme, 12 L.Q.R. 145.
[10] There is no record of their provisions.
[11] Otherwise *Darcy v. Allein* (1602) 1 W.P.C. 1; Noy 173; Moore K.B. 671; 11 Co.Rep. 84b. See the composite report in J. W. Gordon, K.C., *Monopolies by Patent*, London, 1897. There had been a previous action on the patent before the Privy Council: see Hulme, 16 L.Q.R. 51.

This patent was held invalid as being a monopoly illegal at common law, and also as being a licence for importation of playing cards contrary to certain statutes. The judgment[12] deals in some detail with the characteristics of illegal monopolies, and the conclusions to be drawn from it are that a monopoly was illegal at common law:

(a) if it prevented a craftsman from carrying on his ordinary trade,[13] or

(b) if it tended to raise the price of a commodity and lower its quality, or

(c) if the Crown was deceived in its grant, intending the grant to be for the public good, whereas it was in fact not so.[14]

No mention was made of patents for new trades and inventions, but they were expressly admitted to be valid by the defendant's counsel during the course of the case.[15]

The Book of Bounty

In 1610 the proclamation usually known as "The Book of Bounty"   **1.06** was issued. This set forth "monopolies" as the first of the "special things for which We ... command no suitor presume to move Us". Projects for new inventions were, however, excepted from this prohibition, provided they were not contrary to law or hurtful to the state and trade, or generally inconvenient.

The first judicial pronouncement on the legality of patents for inventions occurs, however, in 1614, when the following statement is to be found in the report of the *Clothworkers of Ipswich Case*[16]:

"But if a man hath brought in a new invention and a new trade within the kingdom in peril of his life and consumption of his estate or stock, etc., or if a man hath made a new discovery of anything, in such cases the King of his grace and favour in recompense of his costs and travail may grant by charter unto him that he shall only use such a trade or trafique for a certain time, because at first people of the kingdom are ignorant, and have not the knowledge and skill to use it. But when the patent is expired the King cannot make a new grant thereof".

Statute of Monopolies, section 6

The abuses of the monopoly system finally became so scandalous that   **1.07** the agents most concerned in enforcing certain patents were impeached.

---

[12] It only appears in Co.Rep. at p.86.
[13] Citing *Davenant v. Hurdis (Merchant Taylor's Case)* (1599) Moore K.B. 576.
[14] Citing *Earl of Kent's Case*, 21 Edw. 3, 47. The grant was also said to be *primae impressionis*.
[15] See the report in Gordon, *op. cit.* p.205, at 219; Noy at 182.
[16] Godbolt 252.

Some 20 patents were thereupon revoked by proclamation, and others left for trial in the courts. At the same time a joint committee of both Houses of Parliament agreed a Bill which was finally passed on May 25, 1624.

This Act is the Statute of Monopolies. It recited the publication and effect of the Book of Bounty and declared all monopolies, dispensations, and grants to compound penalties void. All such grants were to be tried at common law; and by section 6 the foundations of modern patent law were laid down in the following terms:

"Provided also (and be it declared and enacted)[17] that any declaration before mentioned shall not extend to any letters patent and grants of privilege for the term of fourteen years or under, hereafter to be made, of the sole working or making of any manner of new manufactures within this realm, to the true and first inventor and inventors of such manufactures which others at the time of making such letters patent and grants shall not use, so as also they be not contrary to the law or mischievous to the state, by raising prices of commodities at home, or hurt of trade, or generally inconvenient".

1.08 The statute was intended to be declaratory of the common law.[18] For various reasons, but probably mainly on account of the exception in favour of corporations made by section 9, the Act had little practical effect for many years, and the Age of Monopolies did not finally come to an end until the outbreak of the Great Rebellion. Patents for inventions continued to be granted under the Commonwealth; and the law and practice remained almost unchanged until long after the Restoration.

In the early days of the patent system the greater part of all patent litigation had been conducted before the Privy Council.[19] All patents contained a proviso for revocation by that body, and questions of validity were normally tried before it. After the Restoration the Privy Council continued for some time to exercise this jurisdiction but from about 1753 onwards patent litigation (with the exception of petitions for extension[20]) has been conducted in the Court of Chancery and Queen's Bench.

Prior to 1795 there were practically no reported cases on the construction of the Statute of Monopolies.[21] The statute was in fact virtually in the position of a new Act; and the development of modern patent law can be said to date, for practical purposes, from this period.

---

[17] Words in brackets repealed by the Statute Law Revision Act 1888 (S.L.R.A. 1988), s.1, Sched., P.I.

[18] See Co.Inst. III, c.85; *Feather v R.* (1865), 6 B. & S. 257, at p.285; *Australian Gold, etc., Co. v. Lake View, etc., Ltd* [1901], 18 R.P.C. 105, at p.114.

[19] For an account of the practice at this date, see Hulme, 33 L.Q.R. 65.

[20] Introduced by 5 & 6 Will. 4, c.83.

[21] See Eyre L.C.J. in *Boulton v. Bull* (1795), 2 H.Bl. 463.

Patent Legislation 1852 to 1949

Important changes in the procedure for obtaining the grant (includ- **1.09**
ing provisional protection) were introduced by the 1852 Act, and by the
Acts of 1883 to 1888[22] there came into being the system that existed until
June 1, 1978, when substantially the whole of the 1977 Act[23] came into
operation. The law and practice under that system was amended and
developed from time to time in various statutes. Thus, until the 1932
Act[24] the grounds upon which a patent could be revoked (*i.e.* the
grounds of invalidity) had remained those available at common law,
but that Act, while retaining the grounds at common law, introduced a
number of specific statutory grounds. The 1949 Act[25] abolished the
grounds available at common law leaving the statutory grounds
specified in that Act[26] as constituting the complete code of grounds upon
which a patent could be revoked.[27] The 1949 Act was also noteworthy as
providing, for the first time, for the appointment of specialist patent
judges to hear patent matters.[28] The 1977 Act effected far-reaching
changes in our patent system and law, but a number of the provisions of
the 1949 Act (as amended) remain since the 1977 Act enacted that certain
provisions of the 1949 Act should continue to apply to existing patents
and patent applications,[29] *i.e.* patents granted and applications for
patents in being before June 1, 1978, the last of which will not expire
until 1998. Such provisions of the 1949 Act which continue to apply in
respect of existing patents and patent applications are considered more
fully hereafter, but it may be noted here that they include, for instance,
the grounds of revocation by the Court under that Act (with one minor
amendment) while the grounds under that Act upon which a patent
may be revoked by the Comptroller are extended to be the same as those
for revocation by the Court.

Patents Act 1977

The statute is divided into three parts: **1.10**

Part I, sub-titled "New Domestic Law," enacts a code of domestic
patent law changed in many significant respects from that developed
and existing under previous legislation.

Part II of the Act enacts provisions intended to meet the United
Kingdom's obligations under three international conventions, the
Patent Co-operation Treaty of 1970 (P.C.T),[30] the European Patent

---

[22] 46 & 47 Vict. c.57; 48 & 49 Vict. c.63; 49 & 50 Vict. c.37; 51 & 52 Vict. c.50.
[23] 25 & 36 Eliz. 2, c.37.
[24] 22 & 23 Geo. 5, c.32.
[25] 12–14 Geo. 6, c.87.
[26] P.A. 1949, s.32.
[27] *American Cyanamid Co. (Dann's Patent)*, [1971] R.P.C. 425.
[28] P.A. 1949, s.84(1).
[29] P.A. 1977, s.127 and Scheds. 1, 2, 3 and 4.
[30] Cmnd. 4530.

Convention of 1973 (E.P.C.)[31] and the Community Patent Convention of 1975 (C.P.C.).[32]

Part III deals with miscellaneous and general matters including provisions as to legal proceedings and the creation of the Patents Court.

Copyright, Designs and Patents Act 1988

1.11   Prior to the Act, actions for infringement of patents could not be brought in the County Court.[33] Whilst there was a provision for infringement issues to be determined by agreement in the Patent Office, the procedure was seldom invoked.[34] Due to concern about the high cost of patent litigation in the High Court provision was made for patent infringement and revocation actions to be brought in a County Court having special jurisdiction.[35] The designated court has jurisdiction throughout England and Wales and has no financial limitation.[36] Special provisions are made with regard to transfer between the High Court and the Patents County Court.[37]

International Conventions

1.12   Some brief reference should be made at this point to the international conventions referred to above, for not only is Part II of the Act directed to meeting the United Kingdom's obligations under them but many of the changes effected in the domestic patent law are intended to assimilate that law to that of the European patent system established by the E.P.C.

Paris Convention

1.13   The International Convention for the Protection of Industrial Property (signed in Paris in 1883 and revised on a number of occasions, the last revision being in 1967) provides that, as regards the protection of industrial property, each member country shall afford to nationals of other member countries the same protection as it affords to its own nationals and that the filing of an application for a patent in one member country gives a right of priority to the date of that filing in respect of corresponding applications filed in other member countries within 12 months of that date. Since the Act of 1883[38] United Kingdom patent legislation has provided for such "convention applications" from

---

[31] Cmnd. 5656.
[32] Cmnd. 6553.
[33] P.A. 1977, s.61(1) and s.130(1).
[34] P.A. 1977, s.61(3).
[35] Copyright, Designs and Patents Act 1988 (C.D.P.A. 1988), s.287 and s.291.
[36] C.D.P.A.1988, s.287(2) and s.288. Patents County Court (Designation and Jurisdiction) Order 1994, see S.I. 1994 No. 1609.
[37] C.D.P.A.1988, s.289 and *Memminger v. Trip-Lite* [1992]R.P.C.227.
[38] Patents, Designs and Trade Marks Act 1883, s.103.

nationals of other convention countries and the Act of 1977 retains such provision.[39]

Patent Co-operation Treaty

The P.C.T., has as one of its objects "to simplify and render more **1.14** economical the obtaining of protection for inventions where protection is sought in several countries", but is not intended to diminish rights under the Paris Convention.[40] Under the Treaty, where patent protection for an invention is sought in a member of the contracting states, a single "international application" may be filed at one of the "receiving offices" (which will usually be the applicant's local national office) and the application will have a right of priority from the date of such filing. The Treaty, which is more fully considered later in this work,[41] also makes provision for an international search for prior art to be made in respect of each such international application. To meet the United Kingdom's obligations under this Treaty the 1977 Act provides that such an international application which designates the United Kingdom as a country for which patent protection is sought is to be treated as an application for a patent under the Act, with the date of its international filing as its filing date under the Act and, if published in accordance with the Treaty, is to be treated as published under the Act provided certain conditions are fulfilled.[42]

European Patent Convention

The E.P.C. established a European patent organisation with its own **1.15** European Patent Office (EPO), situated in Munich for the granting of European patents under the system of law set out in the Convention. This Convention is expressed to be a special agreement within the Paris Convention,[43] as indeed is the C.P.C. Under the system of the European Convention a patent application must designate in which of the Contracting States of the Convention patent protection is desired and if, after the examination by the EPO, the application is accepted, a European patent is granted for each of the designated states, the patents having the same specification and claims. Any such European patent is to be treated in the state for which it is granted as having "the effect of and be subject to the same conditions as are national patents granted by that state".[44] The 1977 Act meets that obligation by providing that any European patent granted for the United Kingdom (a "European patent

---

[39] P.A. 1977, s.5 and s.90.
[40] P.C.T. Art. 1(2).
[41] See *post* §3.04
[42] P.A. 1977, s.89.
[43] Paris Convention, Art. 19.
[44] E.P.C., Art. 2.

(U.K.)'') shall be treated as if it were a patent granted under the Act,[45] so that questions of infringement and validity of European patents (U.K.) will be for United Kingdom courts and the Comptroller in cases where his jurisdiction under the 1977 Act is involved. The validity of the patent in all designated states can additionally be challenged in opposition proceedings at the EPO for a limited period after grant.[46]

Community Patent Convention

1.16   The C.P.C., to which the member states of the European Community (EC) are signatories, constitutes a special agreement within the E.P.C.[47] and has as its object the creation of a Community patent system for the EC with a view to ensuring the free movement within the EC of goods protected by patents. Although signed in December 1975 the Convention is still not yet in force, and there are no indications as to when it will come into force.

Under this Convention an application for a European patent which designates any EC country will be deemed to have designated all EC countries and, if the application proceeds to grant, a single "unitary" Community patent will be granted for the whole of the EC instead of separate European patents for each of the EC countries. Such Community patents are to be of "equal effect" throughout the EC and may be granted, transferred, revoked or allowed to lapse only in respect of the whole of the EC.[48] Under the transitional provisions of the Convention, during the transitional period (as yet unspecified in duration) an applicant will be able to opt for separate European patents for designated countries of the EC instead of a Community patent, but after the termination of such transitional period the only European patents which may be granted in respect of the United Kingdom will be Community patents.

1.17   Community patents are to be subject only to the provisions of the C.P.C. and those provisions of the E.P.C. which are binding upon every European patent.[49] Accordingly the 1977 Act provides that:

> "all rights, powers, liabilities, obligations and restrictions from time to time created or arising by or under the Community Patent Convention and all remedies and procedures from time to time provided for by or under that Convention shall . . . have legal effect in the United Kingdom",[50]

thus making the C.P.C. part of our law. The Convention provides that a

---

[45] P.A. 1977, s.77(1).
[46] E.P.C., Art. 99.
[47] E.P.C., Art. 142.
[48] C.P.C., Art 2.
[49] C.P.C., Art. 1(3).
[50] P.A. 1977, s.86(1). (Not yet in force).

national patent is to be ineffective to the extent that it covers the same invention as a Community patent.[51]

Relationship Between Domestic Patent Law and the International Conventions

One of the Resolutions annexed to the C.P.C. states the intention of **1.18** the signatories to work "to bring their laws into conformity, as far as is practicable, with corresponding provisions of the E.P.C., C.P.C. and the Patent Co-operation Treaty." Many of the changes in United Kingdom law relating to national patents brought about by the 1977 Act are intended to assimilate our national patent law to the system of law of the E.P.C. and also, at least in some respects, to that of the C.P.C., as the Act itself states.[52]

Thus, as will be developed more fully in the next chapter, a statutory **1.19** definition of patentability has been introduced and its language closely parallels that of the definition in the E.P.C.[53] The new statutory definition replaces the law which had been developed as to what constituted patentable inventions. Again, while it has long been a requirement of English law that to be patentable an invention should be new and should have involved an inventive step (*i.e.* should not have been obvious), the 1977 Act now contains provisions as to novelty and inventive steps which follow corresponding provisions in the E.P.C.[54] Further, whereas previously the law as to what constituted infringement of a patent had been built up around the language contained in the form of Letters Patent granted for inventions, in the Act there is a statutory definition of infringement which follows, with some differences of wording, the corresponding provisions as to infringement in the C.P.C.[55] The term of the national patent has been increased from 16 years to 20 years in line with the term of a European patent.

Present Position

At the present time the United Kingdom law and practice as to **1.20** patents is regulated by:

(a) the 1977 Act, as the principal statute;
(b) The Copyright Designs and Patents Act 1988, sections 287 *et seq.*;
(c) a number of the provisions of the 1949 Act, as amended by the 1977 Act, which provisions continue to apply to "existing" patents and patent applications (*i.e.* those patents granted and those patent applications made before June 1, 1978);

---

[51] C.P.C., Art. 80.
[52] P.A. 1977, s.130(7).
[53] *Ibid.* s.1 and *cf.* E.P.C., Arts. 52 and 53.
[54] *Ibid.* s.2(1),(2) and (3); *cf.* E.P.C., Art. 54, and see Chap. 5, *post*, para. 5.20.
[55] *Ibid.* s.60; *cf.* C.P.C., Arts 29, 30, 31, and see Chap. 6, *post*, para. 6.06.

(d) the Patents Rules 1990[56] (being rules made pursuant to powers in the 1977 Act);[57]

(e) certain of the rules of the Patents Rules 1968 (rules made pursuant to powers in the 1949 Act),[58] as amended, continue to apply to "existing" patents and patent applications;

(f) Rule 104 of the Rules of the Supreme Court[59]

Requirements of a Valid Patent

1.21   The primary requirements of a valid patent effective in the United Kingdom at the present time may be summarised as follows:

(a) Patents under the 1977 Act and the E.P.C.

Any person may apply for a patent but a patent may only be granted to the inventor, or a person entitled to the whole property in the invention by operation of law or prior agreement, or the successor in title to the inventor or such person. The applicant must make a proper disclosure of his invention and must clearly specify the limits of the monopoly claimed. The invention must be "patentable", *i.e.* be new, not obvious to those skilled in the art to which it relates, and be capable of industrial application. Further it must not be one the publication or exploitation of which would be generally expected to encourage offensive, immoral or anti-social behaviour. The patent may be granted by the U.K. Patent Office following an application made in accordance with procedure laid down in the 1977 Act, and the 1990 Rules.[60] Alternatively, the application may be prosecuted pursuant to the E.P.C. by an application made to the EPO designating the United Kingdom.[61] Once granted the European Patent (U.K.) has the same effect in this country as though it had been granted by the U.K. Patent Office.[62] Prior to grant the application equates with an application made under the 1977 Act.[63]

(b) Patents under the 1949 Act

1.22   Existing patents under the 1949 Act (*i.e.* patents granted before June 1, 1978, and patents granted since that date but upon existing applications under the 1949 Act) continue to be governed by the requirements as to validity in the 1949 Act (as amended by the 1977 Act). For such patents the applicant was required to be the true and first inventor or his

---

[56] (S.I. 1990 No. 2384.)
[57] P.A. 1977, s.123.
[58] P.A. 1949, s.94.
[59] (S.I. 1978 No. 579) (6–11).
[60] P.A. 1977, ss.14–21; Patents Rules 1990, rr. 16–38.
[61] E.P.C., Arts. 75–85 and 90–98; E.P.C. Rules 24–37 and 39–54.
[62] P.A. 1977, s.77(1).
[63] P.A. 1977, s.78.

personal representative or be an assignee deriving title from the first and true inventor. He must have made a proper disclosure of his invention and have clearly specified the limits of the monopoly claimed. The subject of the invention must be a "manufacture" (as to which see Chapter 2, *infra.*), or a method of controlling manufacture, which was new, useful, and not obvious to those skilled in the art to which it relates. Further, it must not be for an illegal purpose and no valid patent must have previously been granted for it.

The grounds upon which such an existing patent may be revoked are set out in section 32 of the 1949 Act (as amended by the 1977 Act).

CHAPTER 2

THE NATURE OF PATENTABLE INVENTIONS

Contents

Historical definitions of patentable inventions

2.01   The Statute of Monopolies declared all grants of monopoly rights to be void at common law, but excepted letters patent and grants of privilege in respect of any "manner of new manufactures".[1] Under the 1949 Act an invention, to be patentable, had either to be a "manner of new manufacture the subject of letters patent and grant of privilege within section 6 of the Statute of Monopolies", or be a new method or process of testing applicable to the improvement or control of manufacture.[2]

  This definition was not re-enacted in the 1977 Act which defines inventions differently and in similar, though not identical, terms to those used in the E.P.C. to define patentable inventions under that Convention. Since the validity of "existing patents" continues to be governed by the 1949 Act (as amended by the 1977 Act), it is considered that this work should still retain an account of the law as to the nature of patentable inventions under the 1949 Act as being the law which still applies to existing patents, (see part 2 below).

1. Patentable Inventions under the 1977 Act

2.02   The former definition of an invention as a "manner of new manufacture" and the body of case law which interpreted that definition have been replaced by a statutory codification of the requirements of patentability based upon and intended to have the same effect as[3] the corresponding provisions of Articles 52 to 57 of the E.P.C.

  The term "patentable invention" is now defined in section 1(1) of the

---

[1] See *ante*, §1.07.
[2] P.A. 1949, s.101(1).
[3] P.A. 1977, s.130(7).

1977 Act as an invention which satisfies the four conditions laid down in that section. These are that:

(a) the invention is new,
(b) it involves an inventive step,
(c) it is capable of industrial application and
(d) the grant of a patent is not excluded by subsections 2 and 3 of subsection 1.

The first two, that the invention be novel and that it involve an inventive step, are explained in sections 2 and 3 of the Act and equate to the objections to validity of anticipation and obviousness under the old law. They are more fully discussed in Chapter 5 below.

The third and fourth conditions are discussed below.

The third condition: Industrial Applicability

Industrial Applicability is defined in section 4 of the Act in the following terms: **2.03**

"Subject to subsection (2) below, an invention shall be taken to be capable of industrial application if it can be made or used in any kind of industry, including agriculture."

Dealing first with the generality of subsection (1), presumably "industry" will be construed in the widest possible sense, as including almost any commercial enterprise, just as "manufacture" was broadly construed under the old law. The specific inclusion of agriculture points towards such a construction. It is accordingly submitted that the old case law can still be of guidance, in that anything which was a "manner of manufacture" under the old law must be capable of industrial application under the new. The requirement that the invention can be "made or used" in industry is apt to cover both product and process claims, and also methods of testing and other applications where no vendible product results.

Subsection (1) is, however, subject to subsection (2), which together with subsection (3) provides: **2.04**

"(2) An invention of a method of treatment of the human or animal body by surgery or therapy or of diagnosis practised on the human or animal body shall not be taken to be capable of industrial application.

(3) Subsection (2) above shall not prevent a product consisting of a substance or composition being treated as capable of industrial application merely because it is invented for use in any such method."

Further, section 4 is one of the sections referred to in section 130(7) of the

Act and is thus to be interpreted, if possible, in the same way as the corresponding articles of the E.P.C., Articles 52(1) and (4) and Article 57.

The exclusion thus covers methods of treatment involving surgery, methods of treatment involving therapy and methods of diagnosis. It is an exclusion which should be narrowly interpreted,[4] but therapy has been interpreted to have the wide meaning of any medical treatment of disease whether preventative or curative.[5]

It is, however, only claims to methods that are exempted, not claims, for example, to surgical instruments, or therapeutic or diagnostic apparatus.

2.05 Historically the first inventor of a new product suitable for use in medical treatment was entitled to a claim to the product *per se*. This remains the case. Difficulties arise where the product is already known and the invention resides in the discovery of a novel medical use (first medical use), or where, although known for medical use, the invention resides in the discovery of a novel second medical use.

2.06 First medical use is covered by section 2(6) of the Act. The fact that the product forms part of the state of the art does not prevent the invention from being taken to be new if any medical use of the product does not form part of the state of art.[6] Providing, therefore, the use is otherwise inventive, a claim to the product for use in the medical application is permissible.

2.07 The permissibility of second medical use claims has been considered both in the EPO[7] and in the Patents Court.[8,9,10]

In the former it was held that whilst a claim to the method of use could not be permitted, a claim to the use of a product for the manufacture of a medicament for a specified new and inventive medical use could be permitted (the so-called Swiss type of claim).

This reasoning was approved in the *Wyeth* case where the Patents Court sat en banc. Falconer J., giving the judgment of the Court stated:

"The approach of the Enlarged Board of Appeal to the question of the novelty requirement in a Swiss type use claim directed to a second or subsequent medical use may be summarised, it seems, as follows:
   (1) Because of the provisions of Article 52(4) (first sentence) (which corresponds to section 4(2) of the 1977 Act), the normal type of use claim, whereby a new use of a known product may be protected, is not open to pharmaceutical inventions directed to the use of medicaments in a method of medical treatment.
   (2) However, no intention to exclude second (and subsequent)

---

[4] G05/83 *EISAI/Second medical indication*: [1985] O.J. EPO 64, [1979–85] EPOR B:241.
[5] *Unilever (Davis') Appn.* [1983] R.P.C. 219, and see T19/86 *DUPHAR/Pigs II*: [1989] O.J. EPO 24, [1988] EPOR 10.
[6] *Sopharma S.A.'s Appn.* [1983] R.P.C. 195.
[7] G05/83 *EISAI/Second medical indication*: [1985] O.J. EPO 64, [1979–85] EPOR B:241.
[8] *Wyeth's Appn.* [1985] R.P.C. 545.
[9] *Ibid.* at p.567.
[10] T144/83 DU PONT/*Appetite suppressant*: [1986] O.J. EPO 301, [1987] EPOR 6.

medical indications from patent protection, other than by a purpose-limited claim (under the provisions of Article 54(5), corresponding to section 2(6) of the 1977 Act), is to be deduced from the terms of the E.P.C. or the legislative history of the material articles thereof.

(3) In that regard the Swiss type of use claim now being considered is not prohibited by Article 52(4) and is capable of industrial application.

(4) As to novelty, the Board consider that in the type of claim specifically provided for in Article 54(5), namely, a purpose-limited product claim to a known substance or composition for a first (and, therefore, novel) pharmaceutical use, the required novelty for the claim is to be found in the new pharmaceutical use.

(5) Similarly, in the Swiss type of use claim directed to use of a known pharmaceutical in the manufacture of a medicament, not novel in itself, for a novel second (or subsequent) therapeutic use, the required novelty of the claimed process may be found in the new second (or subsequent) therapeutic use.

That approach to the novelty of the Swiss type use of claim directed to a second, or subsequent, therapeutic use is equally possible under the corresponding provisions of the 1977 Act and, notwithstanding the opinion expressed earlier as to the better view of the patentability of such a Swiss type claim under the material provisions of the Act considered without regard to the position, as it has developed, under the corresponding provisions of the E.P.C., having regard to the desirability of achieving conformity, the same approach should be adopted to the novelty of the Swiss type of claim now under consideration under the material provisions of the Act."

Second medical use claims can, therefore, be obtained providing they are drafted appropriately.

Furthermore, the exemption only applies to methods which fall within the exempted categories. Claims directed to cosmetic treatment will be susceptible of industrial application providing the treatment does not involve surgery since surgery must relate to the method of treatment and not its purpose. The same will presumably apply to contraceptive methods[11] and methods of harming the body[12] which under the old law were not regarded as methods of treatment of the body and were consequently patentable.

As for methods of treatment practised on the animal body, it is **2.08** submitted that a distinction should be drawn between veterinary and farming techniques. To the veterinary surgeon, the animal body is a recipient of medical treatment; to the farmer it is a vendible product. The

---

[11] *Schering A.G.'s Appn.* [1971] R.P.C. 337.
[12] *Palmer's Appn.* [1970] R.P.C. 597.

Solicitor-General contemplated such a distinction in *C. & W.'s Application*[13] a case decided under the 1907 Act, when he said:

"if it were an Application simply for the use of the process for the purpose of removing lead from animals in order to make them better marketable products, it might be that different considerations would apply".[14]

The practical difficulties in drawing such distinctions may well be considerable, but this can be no ground for depriving the "factory farmer" of protection for his techniques altogether.

The fourth condition: Excluded Inventions

2.09   Section 1(2) sets out a list of items which are declared not to be inventions for the purposes of the Act. The subsection provides:

"It is hereby declared that the following (among other things) are not inventions for the purposes of this Act, that is to say, anything which consists of —
   (a) a discovery, scientific theory or mathematical method;
   (b) a literary, dramatic, musical or artistic work or any other aesthetic creation whatsoever;
   (c) a scheme, rule or method for performing a mental act, playing a game or doing business, or a program for a computer;
   (d) the presentation of information;
but the foregoing provision shall prevent anything from being treated as an invention for the purposes of this Act only to the extent that a patent or application for a patent relates to that thing as such."

2.10   A number of matters arise. First, the list is not an exhaustive one, for "other things" may still be included. It is not clear whether this is a reference to the power to vary section 1(2) given to the Secretary of State by section 1(5), or whether it contemplates the list being extended by a new body of case law. It is submitted that the correct view is that the court retains a discretion to exclude other forms of innovation from the category of patentable inventions, for otherwise the parenthesised words would be superfluous. Accordingly the old law on what was not a "manner of manufacture" can still be of guidance.

2.11   Secondly, it is necessary to consider the effect of the words "only to the extent that a patent or application for a patent relates to that thing as such".

---

[13] (1914) 31 R.P.C. 235, at p.236.
[14] See also *U.S. Rubber Co.'s Appn.* [1964] R.P.C. 104.

In *Merrill Lynch Inc.'s Application*,[15] Falconer J. held, that if anything in the excluded categories constituted the inventive step then no patent could be granted regardless of how the claim was drafted. This reasoning was subsequently rejected in the Court of Appeal.[16] The matter was considered further in *Gale's Patent Application*[17] when Nicholls L. J. stated the law to be:

"Section 1(2) comprises a non-exhaustive catalogue of matters or things, starting with 'a discovery', which as such are declared not to be inventions. Thus, a discovery as such is not patentable as an invention under the Act. But when applied to a product or process which, in the language of the 1977 Act, is capable of industrial application, the matter stands differently. This was so held in *Genentech Inc.'s Patent* [1989] R.P.C. 147. There, this court by a majority decision held that section 1(2) did not depart from the established principle mentioned above. Purchas L. J., at page 208, and also Dillon L. J., at page 240, decided that the quotation from Whitford J. set out above[18] still represented the law. Dillon L. J. said:
  'In so far as a patent claims as an invention the practical application of a discovery, the patent does not, in my judgment, relate only to the discovery as such, even if the practical application may be obvious once the discovery has been made, even though unachievable in the absence of the discovery'."

Accordingly, providing the claim is, in substance as well as form, a claim to a product or process embodying or employing the excluded matter, a patent can validly be granted even if the inventiveness resides in the incorporation of the excluded matter into the product or process.

Thirdly, it is necessary to consider the ambit of the excluded **2.12** categories which occur also in Article 52(2) E.P.C..[19] These are all abstract matters which are thought to be better protected under other areas of industrial property law, particularly copyright.

Subsection 1(2)(*a*) excludes any discovery, scientific theory or math- **2.13** ematical method. This follows the old law, which distinguished between an invention and a mere disclosure of a principle.

Subsection 1(2)(*b*) excludes any literary, dramatic, musical or artistic **2.14** work or any other aesthetic creation whatsoever. Again there is no change from the old law.[20] Such things are regarded as more properly the subject of copyright protection, which protects only the form of expression and not the underlying idea.

---

[15] [1988] R.P.C. 1.
[16] [1989] R.P.C. 561 following *Genentech Inc.'s Patent* [1989] R.P.C. 147, see Fox L.J. at pp.563–569.
[17] [1991] R.P.C. 305 at 324.
[18] See *Genentech Inc.'s Patent* [1987] R.P.C. 553 at 566:
[19] S.130(7) of P.A. 1977 applies to s.1(2) of P.A. 1977.
[20] *Nelson's Appn.* [1980] R.P.C. 173.

2.15   Subsection 1(2)(*c*) excludes any scheme, rule or method for performing a mental act, playing a game or doing business,[21] or a program
for a computer. The first part of this exclusion is stated in curiously
limited terms. Under the old law it was not possible to patent "an idea or
a scheme or a mere method"[22] of any type; the rule was not confined to
the limited category of mental acts, playing of games and doing
business. Each case was decided on its own merits. Thus, even methods
of performing physical acts, such as the method of flying an aeroplane in
Rolls-Royce Ltd.'s Application,[23] were not patentable. Such an application
might be accepted today, unless the court ruled that such a method fell
among the "other things" referred to in section 1(2).
     Computer programs have created particular difficulties and are,
therefore, considered below under a separate heading.

2.16   Subsection 1(2)(*d*) excludes from the class of inventions anything
which consists of the presentation of information. This may go further
than the old law, which distinguished between novelty in the information itself, which was unpatentable as being a mere discovery,[24] and
novel methods of presenting information, which were patentable.[25] It is
submitted that the wording of the subsection is capable of covering both
of these categories. However, where the presentation serves a technical
purpose the claim amounts to more than presentation as such, and
should be allowed.[26]

Computer programs

2.17   Under the old law, computer programs as such were not patentable;[27]
however, a claim to a computer when programmed in a particular way
was acceptable,[28] as was a method of conditioning a computer to operate
in a particular way.[29]
     The new Act declares in section 1(2) that computer programs as such
are not inventions and in consequence not patentable. No direct
reference is made to the two formerly acceptable forms of claim referred
to above.

2.18   In the Guidelines for Examination in the EPO it is stated:

"A computer program claimed by itself or as a record on a carrier, is
not patentable irrespective of its content. The situation is not normally

---

[21] *Merrill Lynch Inc.'s Appn.* [1989] R.P.C. 561.
[22] *Ward's Appn.* (1912) 29 R.P.C. 79; *D.A. & K.'s Appn.* (1926) 43 R.P.C. 155.
[23] [1963] R.P.C. 251.
[24] *Ciba-Geigy A.G. (Dürr's) Appn.* [1977] R.P.C. 83.
[25] *Rhodes' Appn.* [1973] R.P.C. 243; *Kessler's Appn.* [1973] R.P.C. 413.
[26] Compare *Pitman's Appn.* [1969] R.P.C. 646; *Gever's Appn.* [1970] R.P.C. 91. Contrast
     T163/85 *BBC/Colour television signal:* [1990] O.J. EPO 379, [1990] EPOR 599, and T119/88
     FUJI/Coloured disk jacket: [1990] O.J. EPO 395, [1990] EPOR 615.
[27] *Slee and Harris's Appn.* [1966] R.P.C. 194.
[28] *Badger Co. Inc.'s Appn.* [1970] R.P.C. 36.
[29] *Burrough's Appn.* [1974] R.P.C. 147; *I.B.M. Corp.'s Appn.* [1980] F.S.R. 564.

changed when the computer program is loaded into a known computer. If however the subject-matter as claimed makes a technical contribution to the known art, patentability should not be denied merely on the ground that a computer program is involved in its implementation."

This reasoning was applied by the Technical Board of Appeal in *Vicom System Inc.'s Application*[30] and this decision was approved by the Court of Appeal in *Merrill Lynch Inc.'s Application*.[31]

Offensive, immoral, and anti-social inventions

Subsection 1(3)(*a*) provides that a patent should not be granted for an **2.19** invention the publication or exploitation of which would be generally expected to encourage offensive, immoral, or anti-social behaviour. This is qualified by section 1(4), which provides that behaviour shall not be considered objectionable in those ways merely because it is prohibited by domestic law. This contrasts with the provisions of the old Act, under which a ground of revocation was that the primary or intended use or exercise of the invention was contrary to law.[32] Additionally, the Comptroller had a power to refuse applications for immoral inventions,[33] and the Royal Prerogative was sometimes exercised against offensive ones[34]; however, neither the Comptroller's power nor the prerogative could be invoked after grant.

The new provisions of sections 1(3)(*a*) and 1(4) are based upon Article **2.20** 53(*a*) of the E.P.C., and are intended to ensure that differences in national laws do not lead to anomalies in the patentability of inventions as between different states. Thus, in applying them, the court becomes an arbiter of morals but not law. Whether or not the morality of different states is any more consistent than their law is questionable. However, given the paucity of reported cases under the old law, these subsections are unlikely to receive much judicial attention particularly having regard to the apparently liberal approach to morality currently being demonstrated by the courts.[35]

Animal and plant varieties

Subsection 1(3)(*b*) provides that a patent shall not be granted for "any **2.21** variety of animal or plant or any essentially biological process for the production of animals or plants, not being a micro-biological process or the product of such a process". The old law is in substance retained;

[30] T208/84 *VICOM/Computer-related invention*: [1987] O.J. EPO 14, [1986] EPOR 74.
[31] [1989] R.P.C. 561.
[32] P.A. 1949, s.32(1)(*k*).
[33] P.A. 1949, s10(1)(*b*).
[34] P.A. 1949, s.102(1).
[35] See *Masterman's Appn.* [1991] R.P.C. 89.

plant varieties may be protected only by the provisions of the Plant Varieties and Seeds Act 1964, as amended by the Plant Varieties Act 1983, and animal varieties are not protectable. It is not clear what is contemplated by an "essentially biological process"; the phrase may well be given a narrow and restricted meaning in view of the broad definition of "industrial application" in section 4(1) which includes inventions in the field of genetic engineering. The equivalent provision of the E.P.C., Article 53(b) has been narrowly interpreted.[36] Note the special provisions of the Act as to disclosure relating to inventions which require for their performance the use of a micro-organism.

2. Patentable Inventions under the 1949 Act

2.22   The current relevance of the question "what is a patentable invention under the 1949 Act" lies in section 32 of that Act which provides a ground of invalidity that "the subject of any claim is not an invention within the meaning of this Act".[37]

Some existing patents will remain in force until 1998 and even after that date their validity could still be challenged on this ground.

Manner of new manufacture

As indicated above, under the 1949 Act an invention to be patentable had either to be a manner of new manufacture which was the subject of letters patent and grant of privilege within section 6 of the Statute of Monopolies, or be a new method, or process of testing, applicable to the improvement or control of manufacture.

2.23   This requirement involves two separate considerations, *viz.*, Is it a manner of manufacture? Is it new? The first of these considerations is dealt with in this chapter and the second, that of novelty, is dealt with in Chapter 5.

2.24   In order to ascertain what is a "manner of manufacture" under the Act of 1949, it is necessary to consider what has been decided by the courts, the question in essence being: "Is this a proper subject of letters patent according to the principles which have been developed for the application of section 6 of the Statute of Monopolies?"

Processes

2.25   It is evident that if the construction of the words "new manufacture" were limited to the production of new articles, to the exclusion of the

---

[36] See Guidelines for Examination in the EPO, Part C, Chap.IV at 27; and T49/83 *CIBA-GEIGY/Propagating material*: [1984] O.J. EPO 112, [1979–85] EPOR C:758.
[37] P.A. 1949, s.32(1)(d).

process of manufacturing old articles by cheaper, better and improved methods, the inducement which the common law intended to give to inventors would be curtailed to very narrow limits. Passages in the judgments in some of the early cases seem to throw doubt on the validity of patents for processes,[38] but we find that the courts gradually extended the meaning of the word "manufacture" to include improvements in manufacture and changes in method which though small in themselves have great economic importance.[39]

A discovery not a "manufacture"

A mere discovery is not proper subject-matter for a patent. In *Reynolds* **2.26** *v. Herbert Smith & Co. Ltd.*[40] Buckley J. explained the distinction between a discovery and an invention in the following terms:

"Discovery adds to the amount of human knowledge, but it does so only ... by disclosing something ... Invention also adds to human knowledge, but not merely by disclosing something. Invention necessarily involves also the suggestion of an act to be done, and it must be an act which results in a new product, or a new result, or a new process, or a new combination for producing an old product or an old result".[41]

A bare principle not a "manufacture"

Nor can a claim be made for the monopoly of a natural principle, since **2.27** that would be to claim the laws of nature, which have always existed. Man merely discovers the principle; but if, in addition to discovering it, he can describe a method of utilising that principle so as to make it applicable to the production of a new manufacture, he can obtain a patent for the method, and to this extent will be protected in the application of the principle itself.

Test to be applied

There have been many instances in which the Patent Office have **2.28** received applications for patents for ingenious ideas, but have refused

---

[38] *e.g. Hornblower v. Boulton* (1799), 8 T.R. 95.
[39] *R. v. Wheeler* (1819), 2 Barn. & Ald. 345, at p.349; see also *Ralston v. Smith* (1865), 11 H.L.C. 223. 1 W.P.C. 627, at p.633. And see *Boulton v. Bull* (1795), 2 H.Bl. 463, at p.468; *Crane v. Price* (1842), 1 W.P.C. 393, at p.409.
[40] (1903) 20 R.P.C. 123, at p.126.
[41] And see *Lane-Fox v. Kensington & Knightsbridge Electric Lighting Co.* (1892) 9 R.P.C. 413, at p.416; *Chamberlain and Hookham Ltd. v. Mayor, etc., of Bradford* (1903) 20 R.P.C. 673, at p.687 (H.L.); *British Thomson-Houston Co. Ltd. v. Charlesworth Peebles & Co.* (1923), 41 R.P.C. 180, at p.209 (H.L.); *Heap v. Bradford Dyers' Association Ltd.* (1929) 46 R.P.C. 254, at p.264; *Reitzman v. Grahame-Chapman and Derustit Ltd.* (1950) 67 R.P.C. 178; *Magnatex Ltd. v. Unicorn Products Ltd.* (1951) 68 R.P.C. 117, at p.122.

these on the ground that they could not be classed as "manufactures". It is possible that some of the applications that have been refused in the past might at a later date have been considered as allowable. However, it was well settled that one could not get patent protection for a mere idea.[42]

2.29   In *G.E.C.'s Application*,[43] which was for a method of extinguishing incendiary bombs, Morton J. put forward the "vendible product test":

> "In my view a method or process is a manner of manufacture if it
>   (a) results in the production of some vendible product, or
>   (b) improves or restores to its former condition a vendible product, or
>   (c) has the effect of preserving from deterioration some vendible product to which it is applied.
> In saying this I am not attempting to cover every case which may arise by a hard and fast rule."

The application was refused. The fact that this test is not a "hard and fast" rule was emphasised in a number of subsequent cases. Further, in applying the test the word "product" must be given a wide meaning.[44]

2.30   In *Elton and Leda Chemicals Ltd.'s Application*,[45] which was for a method of fog dispersal, and was allowed, Lloyd-Jacob J. said:[46]

> "Although an inventor may use no newly devised mechanism, nor produce a new substance, nonetheless, he may, by providing some new and useful effect, appropriate for himself a patent monopoly in such improved result by covering the mode or manner by means of which his result is secured. Seeing that the promise which he offers is some new and useful effect, there must of necessity be some product whereby the validity of his promise can be tested."

2.31   Referring to this passage, the High Court of Australia in *N.R.D.C.'s Application* (in a judgment referred to with approval in *Swift's Application*)[47] said:[48]

> "... the tenor of the passage seems to be that what is meant by a 'product' in relation to a process is only something in which the new and useful effect may be observed. Sufficient authority has been cited to show that the 'something' need not be a 'thing' in the sense of an article; it may be any physical phenomenon in which the effect, be it

---

[42] *I.B.M. Corp.'s Appn.* [1980] F.S.R. 564, at 568.
[43] [1961] R.P.C. 21.
[44] See, *e.g. Cementation Co. Ltd.'s Appn.* (1945) 62 R.P.C. 151; *Rantzen's Appn.* (1947) 64 R.P.C. 63; *Reizmann v. Grahame-Chapman and Derustit Ltd.* (1950) 67 R.P.C. 25, at p.32.
[45] [1957] R.P.C. 267.
[46] [1957] R.P.C. 267, at p.268.
[47] [1962] R.P.C. 37.
[48] [1961] R.P.C. 134, at p.145.

creation or merely alteration, may be observed: a building (for example), a tract or stratum of land, an explosion, an electrical oscillation. It is, we think, only by understanding the word 'product' as covering every end produced, and treating the word 'vendible' as pointing only to the requirement of utility in practical affairs, that the language of Morton J.'s 'rule' may be accepted as wide enough to convey the broad idea which the long line of decisions on the subject has shown to be comprehended by the Statute."

Biochemical and microbiological processes

Prior to the decision in *American Cyanamid v. Berk Pharmaceuticals*,[49] **2.32** there were doubts as to whether biochemical processes constituted a manner of new manufacture.[50] In that case the patent was for a method of producing tetracycline by cultivation of a certain strain of micro-organism. Whitford J. said at page 253 of the report:

> "It appears to me . . . that the work of Dr. Growich and his assistant in the production of mutant strains . . . was as much, and the use of the specific strains in a process such as is claimed by the subsidiary claims of the Growich patent can be considered as much, a method for producing a new and salutary effect intimately connected with trade and manufacture as was the method involving the operation of James Watt's condenser."[51]

Agriculture

Likewise methods of agricultural cultivation were generally refused **2.33** patent protection, an exception being made for a method of mushroom cultivation in which the methods specified differed entirely from natural conditions.[52] However, the law may have been changed by the decision in *Swift's Application (R. v. Patents Appeal Tribunal)*,[53] following which it was held, in *U.S. Rubber Co.'s Application*,[54] that a method of medically treating an animal would be acceptable.

Medical treatment

A method of medical treatment of human beings to cure or prevent **2.34** disease is not a manner of manufacture.[55] There was, however, difficulty in drawing the line between what was, and what was, not medical

---

[49] [1976] R.P.C. 231.
[50] See, *e.g. General Electric Co.'s Appn.* [1961] R.P.C. 21.
[51] See also *Commercial Solvents Corp. v. Synthetic Products Ltd.* (1926) 43 R.P.C. 185.
[52] *Szuec's Appn.* [1956] R.P.C. 25.
[53] [1962] R.P.C. 37.
[54] [1964] R.P.C. 104.
[55] *Schering A.G.'s Appn.* [1971] R.P.C. 337; *Upjohn Co. (Roberts') Appn.* [1977] R.P.C. 94.

treatment.[56] Thus, applications were refused for a method of treating dental caries[57] and a method of inducing loss of pain sensibility by sound recording.[58] A method of sealing pits and tissues in teeth in order to prevent possible future caries was also held to be unpatentable on the ground that the purpose of the treatment was therapeutic.[57] However, a method of cleaning teeth was held to be acceptable if limited to the cosmetic effect only.[59]

2.35   In *Bio-Digital Science's Application*,[60] a method of screening to detect disease was held not to be a method of medical treatment. Whitford J. said at page 674:

> "I do not think it would be right to regard the method of claim 1 here as falling within the term 'medical treatment' in that sense. In fact the whole process covered by the claim is carried out before the question of whether medical treatment is necessary or not is considered at all. Furthermore, in the case of those whose slides are below the reaction limit no medical treatment is in fact necessary or applied. I do not think it would be right to regard this method as 'medical treatment' in the sense referred to just because it may in appropriate cases be a preliminary step leading to subsequent medical treatment if decided upon."

2.36   In *Eli Lilly & Co.'s Application*,[61] a claim to the "commercial application" of known compounds as drugs was refused, as in effect it sought to protect a method of treatment. The court looked behind the form of the claim to its intention, the two patents judges sitting en banc saying at page 445:

> "It seems to us therefore that in a case where the alleged invention is based on the discovery of unexpected curative properties of known compounds care must always be taken to examine the form of claim actually made. The matter must be looked at as one of substance and if the conclusion is that whatever the precise form of words used the true effect of the claim will be to prevent the manufacture or supply of the compounds in question for the purpose of treating illness or disease in human beings, then the claim must be refused."

2.37   A method of preventing conception was not considered to be a form of medical treatment[62]; however, a method of inducing an abortion is so

---

[56] *Stafford-Miller's Appn.* [1984] E.S.R. 258.
[57] *Lee Pharmaceuticals Appn.* [1978] R.P.C. 51.
[58] *Neva Corp.'s Appn.* [1968] R.P.C. 481.
[59] *Oral Health Products Inc. (Halstead's) Appn.* [1977] R.P.C. 612.
[60] [1973] R.P.C. 668.
[61] [1975] R.P.C. 438.
[62] *Schering A.G.'s Appn.* [1971] R.P.C. 337.

regarded,[63] on the grounds that it must be carried out and notified by a registered medical practitioner.

Packages of known substances

In order to overcome the difficulties of patenting methods of medical **2.38** treatment by the use of known compounds, and also to avoid the problems of making out a case of indirect infringement against the suppliers of these compounds, applicants have attempted to claim compounds or collections of compounds when packaged in a particular way. Again the courts found difficulty in determining when such a claim genuinely constituted a manner of new manufacture and when it did not.

In *L'Oreal's Application*,[64] the claim was held to be unpatentable on the **2.39** grounds that any member of the public might want to make up such a package for many other purposes besides the one contemplated by the applicants. The two patents judges sitting en banc said at page 571:

"The applicants claim a pack consisting of two known ingredients suitable for producing a known compound. The ingredients and their product being known, the applicants have added nothing whatever to human knowledge and have not given the consideration necessary to support a grant of letters patent in the form which they seek. The proposed claim covers no more than another example of a form of combined package in itself well known. It would be an unwarranted restriction upon the freedom of the public to grant a monopoly which would prevent them buying or producing such a package."

However, the *L'Oreal* case was distinguished in *Organon Laboratories'* **2.40** *Application*[65] in a decision delivered on the same day. This application related to a package of two kinds of known pill arranged on a card in a particular order so that they could be taken in accordance with a new method of contraception. Graham J. allowed the application to proceed, observing that:

"though the truth may be that the basic discovery lies in the method of treatment and not in the arrangement of the pills on the card and though the arrangement itself is not in any way a guarantee that the treatment must or will be followed, the card itself cannot unequivocally be said to be obvious if no-one would be likely to want to make it except for the treatment in question . . ."

A package containing a known compound together with instructions **2.41**

---

[63] *Upjohn Co. (Kirton's) Appn.* [1976] R.P.C. 324.
[64] [1970] R.P.C. 564; See also *London Rubber Industries Patent* [1968] R.P.C. 31.
[65] [1970] R.P.C. 572; See also *Blendax-Werke's Appn.* [1980] R.P.C. 491.

for its use in some novel way is not a patentable invention.[66] In *Ciba-Geigy A.G. (Dürr's) Applications*,[67] the Court of Appeal held that the instructions did not make the contents of the container a manner of new manufacture, as there was no interaction between the two. A claim to the process specified in the instructions was accepted but the court expressly declined to comment on whether sale of the package with instructions would indirectly infringe the process claim or would in any other respect be tortious.

Presentation of information

2.42   A distinction was drawn between mere novelty in information, which did not constitute a manner of manufacture, and novel methods or articles for presenting information, which did. In *Kessler's Application*,[68] Whitford J., after reviewing the authorities, explained that:

> "a distinction is drawn between, for example, a printed book, a book being a manner of manufacture where the only novelty is in the literary content, which it is said cannot on any basis be patentable, and, for example, the first book ever printed in Braille, which it is said would have been, as at its date, a manner of new manufacture, whatever the nature of the literary content of the work in question."

2.43   Thus, applications in respect of a speedometer calibrated in a novel manner,[69] and a document facilitating the periodical payment of fees[70] were accepted. A claim to a recorded sound having certain physiological properties was refused in *Neva Corp.'s Application*,[71] it being an "essay in the fine and not in the applied arts," for which copyright was the appropriate form of protection.

2.44   Applications in respect of inventions relating to printed sheets and the like were refused if the arrangement of printed words or pictorial matter was directed to a purely visual or intellectual purpose, but were allowable if the printed or pictorial content was so arranged as to effect some mechanical operation.[72] Cases which were refused include a system of printed envelopes,[73] new systems of indexing,[74] a printed explanation of the music on the back of a gramophone record,[75] a scheme for colouring camouflage,[76] a new system of musical notation,[77]

---

[66] *Dow Corning Corp. (Bennett's) Appn.* [1974] R.P.C. 235.
[67] [1977] R.P.C. 83.
[68] [1973] R.P.C. 413.
[69] *Rhodes' Appn.* [1973] R.P.C. 243.
[70] *Kessler's Appn.* [1973] R.P.C. 413.
[71] [1968] R.P.C. 481.
[72] *Virginia-Carolina Chemical Corp.'s Appn. and other Appns.* [1958] R.P.C. 35, at p.36.
[73] *Johnson's Appn.* (1902) 19 R.P.C. 56.
[74] *Ward's Appn.* (1912) 29 R.P.C. 79; *R.'s Three Appns.* (1923) 40 R.P.C. 465.
[75] *S.'s Appn.* (1923) 40 R.P.C. 461.
[76] *L.T.'s Appn.* (1920) 37 R.P.C. 109.
[77] *M.'s Appn.* (1924) 41 R.P.C. 159; *C.'s Appn.* (1920) 37 R.P.C. 247.

architects' plans,[78] a navigational chart to enable the ascertainment of the position of an aircraft in flight,[79] a medium carrying an instructional message,[80] and others.[81] Cases which were allowed included a newspaper page,[82] a device to enable a ship to navigate a channel,[83] a printed ticket designed to serve a mechanical purpose,[84] a printed sheet for teaching pronunciation and which could be used in a speaking machine[85] and time recording cards.[86] This principle has been extended to other articles, *e.g.* cinematograph films and gramophone records.[87]

Schemes and plans

A scheme or plan was not a manner of manufacture on the ground   **2.45** that it was a mere idea.[88] However, a mode of carrying a principle or idea into practical effect could be patentable.[89] In *Otto v. Linford,*[90] claim 1 of the plaintiff's specification ran as follows:

"Admitting to the cylinder a mixture of combustible gas or vapour with air, separate from a charge of air or incombustible gas, so that the development of heat and the expansion or increase of pressure produced by the combustion are rendered gradual substantially as and for the purposes set forth."[91]

Jessel M. R. in the Court of Appeal said:

"It is said that what is claimed is a principle ... or, as it is sometimes termed, the 'idea' of putting a cushion of air between the explosive mixture and the piston of the gas motor engine, so as to regulate, detain, or make gradual, what would otherwise be a sudden explosion. Of course, that could not be patented. I do not read the patent so; I read the patent as being to the effect that the patentee tells us that there is the idea which he wishes to carry out; but he also

---

[78] *E.S.P.'s Appn.* (1945) 62 R.P.C. 87.
[79] *Kelvin and Hughes Ltd.'s Appn.* (1954) 71 R.P.C. 103.
[80] *Nelson's Appn.* [1980] R.P.C. 173.
[81] *W.R.'s Appn.* (1924) 41 R.P.C. 216; *D.A. & K.'s Appn.* (1926) 43 R.P.C. 154; *R.P.C.'s Appn.* (1924) 41 R.P.C. 156; *P.'s Appn.* (1924) 41 R.P.C. 201; *A.E.W.'s Appn.* (1924) 41 R.P.C. 529; *Johnson's Appn.* (1930) 47 R.P.C. 361.
[82] *Cooper's Appn.* (1902) 19 R.P.C. 53.
[83] *Loth's Appn.* (1924) 41 R.P.C. 273.
[84] *Fishburn's Appn.* (1940) 57 R.P.C. 245.
[85] *Pitman's Appn.* [1969] R.P.C. 646.
[86] *Alderton and Barry's Appn.* (1941) 58 R.P.C. 56.
[87] See, *e.g. W.R.'s Appn.* (1924) 41 R.P.C. 216; *F.'s Appn.* (1954) 72 R.P.C. 127; *American Optical Co.'s Appn.* [1958] R.P.C. 40; *C.M.'s Appn.* (1944) 61 R.P.C. 63; *Huber's Appn.* [1956] R.P.C. 50.
[88] *D.A. & K.'s Appn.* (1926) 43 R.P.C. 154; *Hiller's Appn.* [1969] R.P.C. 267; *I.B.M. Corp.'s Appn.* [1980] F.S.R. 564.
[89] *Househill Co. v. Neilson* (1843) 1 W.P.C. 673; *Neilson v. Harford* (1841) 1 W.P.C. 295; *British Thomson-Houston Co. Ltd. v. Corona Lamp Works Ltd.* (1921) 38 R.P.C. 49, at p.70.
[90] (1882) 46 L.T. (N.S.) 35.
[91] *Ibid.* at 39.

describes other kinds of machines which will carry it out; and he claims to carry it out substantially by one or other of these machines. That is the subject of a patent."

2.46   However, this case was distinguished in *Rolls-Royce Ltd.'s Application*,[92] which was for a novel method of operating a known type of jet aircraft using known controls. The application was refused on the ground that such a method was a mere flight plan; the *Otto* case differed in that there were no already-provided operator controls and the invention had to be put into practice by means of workshop adjustment and tuning at the least.

2.47   A method of collating statistical data using known means operating in its normal manner was not a manner of manufacture;[93] however, claims to methods of operating a computer involving the use of apparatus modified, or programmed to act in a particular way were accepted.[94]

Computer programs

2.48   Claims to computer programs and algorithms as such were refused by the Patent Office on the grounds that these amounted to no more than mere schemes or plans, and this reasoning was taken as correct in the decided cases.[95] However, claims to computers when programmed in particular ways, and to methods of operating or programming computers, were held to be acceptable, as were claims to the physical embodiment on cards or tape of programs.

2.49   Claims to computers when programmed to operate in a particular manner were accepted on the ground that although the machine itself was known it was regarded as having been temporarily modified.[96] In *Gever's Application*,[97] Graham J. explained:

"The invention as proposed to be claimed is not a scheme or plan but a piece of apparatus which it is admitted, as I understand it, can only function in a certain way when it has the appropriate series of cards appropriately punched and inserted into it."

2.50   A claim to a method of programming a computer was rejected in *Slee and Harris's Application*,[98] on the ground that the results obtained therefrom did not constitute a vendible product, but this decision was doubted in *Burroughs' Application*,[99] in which Graham J. said:

---

[92] [1963] R.P.C. 251.
[93] *Stahl and Larsson's Appn.* [1965] R.P.C. 596.
[94] *Burroughs Corp. (Perkin's) Appn.* [1974] R.P.C. 147; *I.B.M. Corp.'s Appn.* [1980] F.S.R. 564.
[95] See, *e.g. I.B.M. Corp.'s Appn.* [1980] F.S.R. 564, at p.568.
[96] *Slee and Harris's Appn.* [1966] R.P.C. 194, at p.198.
[97] [1970] R.P.C. 91, at p.97.
[98] [1966] R.P.C. 194.
[99] [1974] R.P.C. 147, at p.158.

"If, however, in practice the method results in a new machine or process or an old machine giving a new and improved result, that fact should in our view be regarded as the 'product' or the result of using the method, and cannot be disregarded in considering whether the method is patentable or not."

A claim to the physical embodiment of a program was accepted in *Slee* **2.51**
and Harris's Application,[1] on the grounds that the card or tape upon which the program was recorded was analogous to a cam which physically co-operated with a machine so as to control its operation. A similar decision was reached in *Gever's Application*.[2] In that case, Graham J. drew an analogy with the notation on a printed sheet which could be used with a speaking machine in *Pitmans Application*,[3] and said at page 97:

"So here in my judgment it would not be right to class the information or directions which are contained in the punched cards which are inserted into the applicant's machine as being purely intellectual, literary or artistic. The object of the cards is amongst other things to ensure that the old machine functions in a particular way which it is alleged is new."

The distinction between these acceptable forms of claim and a claim **2.52**
to a mere program as such was a fine one, but it was one which the court was both willing and able to draw in practice. The Patents Appeal Tribunal (P.A.T.), consisting of Graham and Whitford JJ. sitting en banc, explained in *Burroughs' Application*:[4]

"If a claim, whatever words are used, namely, whether the claim is for example for 'a method of transmitting data ...', 'a method of controlling a system of computers' or 'a method of operating or programming a computer ...', is clearly directed to a method involving the use of apparatus modified or programmed to operate in a new way, as the present claims are, it should be accepted. This may conveniently be done by using some such words as 'a method of transmitting data over a system of computers (or of controlling a system of computers) consisting in programming such computers so that ...' ... From what has been said it follows that, in our judgment, the actual words used are not important provided they delimit something more than a mere method or mere idea or mere desideratum, and whether this is so or not must be judged by looking at all the matters and apparatus in question."

---

[1] [1966] R.P.C. 194.
[2] [1970] R.P.C. 91.
[3] [1969] R.P.C. 646.
[4] [1974] R.P.C. 147, at 160.

2.53   This decision was followed with approval by the same court in *I.B.M. Corp.'s Application*,[5] where the judgment concludes with the following words:

> "We agree with the superintending examiner that under the Act of 1949 and the decided cases, the law is that an inventive concept, if novel, can be patented to the extent that claims can be framed directed to an embodiment of the concept in some apparatus or process of manufacture."

Method of testing

2.54   An important enlargement of the field of patentable invention made by the 1949 Act was the inclusion in section 101(1) of "any new method or process of testing applicable to the improvement or control of manufacture." However, there was authority to the effect that a method of testing might be patentable even though it did not fall within the provisions of this passage.[6]

> "It is trite law that you cannot patent a discovery, but if on the basis of that discovery you can tell people how it can be usefully employed, then a patentable invention may result. This in my view would be the case, even though once you have made the discovery, the way in which it can be usefully employed is obvious enough."

---

[5] [1980] F.S.R. 564.
[6] *Bio-Digital Sciences Appn.* [1973] R.P.C. 668.

CHAPTER 3

THE APPLICANT AND APPLICATION[1]

Contents	Para.

1. General Introduction

3.01 Under the 1977 Act at present one of two types of patent may be applied for, namely:

(a) a national patent granted by the U.K. Patent Office and restricted in territory to the United Kingdom; or

(b) a European patent granted by the European Patent Office (EPO)[2] which so far as it is a European Patent (U.K.) is from the date of grant (when published in the *European Patent Bulletin*) to be treated as if it were a national patent under the 1977 Act.[3]

These patents may be applied for either by application made directly to the U.K. or European Patent Offices, or indirectly by means of the P.C.T.[4]

3.02 An applicant may apply for both a European patent (U.K.) and a national patent in respect of the same invention in order to safeguard

---

[1] This chapter relates to all applications made on or after June 1, 1978 (the appointed day), and any applications made under the 1949 Act which in respect of which a complete specification has not been filed by such date and were abandoned in accordance with the provisions of s.127(4) of the 1977 Act. For applications made under the 1949 Act see *Terrell* (12th ed.), Chap. 3.

[2] In accordance with the provisions of the E.P.C.

[3] P.A. 1977, s.77(1).

[4] See *post*, § 3.04.

the possibility of not obtaining a patent by one of the two methods. A consequence of this approach is that assuming both national and European patent (U.K.) are granted for the same invention the Comptroller must revoke the national patent.[5] The amendments to section 73(2) do however, give the applicant the opportunity of awaiting the outcome of opposition proceedings in the EPO before making an election.

The choice between the national patent office route and the EPO route will depend to some extent on how many countries in Europe the applicant wishes to seek protection in. Clearly if protection is only desired for the United Kingdom a national patent should be applied for as it will be cheaper to obtain than a European Patent (U.K.) and once granted will have the same effect. If protection is desired for a number of European countries, the European route will become more attractive from a cost point of view but the decision to use the EPO (as opposed to the national patent offices) may then depend on weighing up the probability of obtaining the patent in the desired form via the EPO as opposed to via the various national patent offices, including the U.K. Patent Office. Another factor which may influence the choice of route is whether the patent is likely to be opposed. The E.P.C. provides that a person may oppose the grant of a European patent retrospectively provided opposition is entered within nine months from the publication of the grant in the *European Patent Bulletin*.[6] Opposition will apply to all the contracting states in which the European patent has effect[7] and such oppositions may therefore be attractive to a third party as a cheap and convenient way of seeking to challenge a patentee's patent.

3.03   An application for a European Patent (U.K.) will be converted to a national (British) application in accordance with the provisions of section 81 of the 1977 Act[8] if under the E.P.C. the application is deemed to be withdrawn for any reason.

The Patent Co-operation Treaty (P.C.T.)

3.04   In addition to a national application or a European Patent (U.K.) application in the manner mentioned above, sections 89A and B of the 1977 Act[9] give effect to the P.C.T. under which, on the basis of a single application called an international application, an applicant may acquire a number of national patents of the applicant's choice in any of the contracting states and/or regional European patents in any such contracting state that has also ratified the E.P.C.

The P.C.T. was ratified by this country on October 24, 1977, and the

---

[5] P.A. 1977, s.73(2) and (3) as amended with effect from January 1, 1991, by C.D.P.A. 1988, Sched. 5, para.19, and see *Maag Gear Wheel and Machine Co. Ltd.'s Patent* [1985] R.P.C. 572; *Marley Roof Tile Co. Ltd.'s Patent* [1994] R.P.C. 231, C.A.
[6] See E.P.C., Arts. 99, 100; and *post* Chap. 3, §3.55.
[7] E.P.C., Art. 99(2).
[8] See also E.P.C., Arts 135–137.
[9] As amended by the C.D.P.A. 1988, Sched. 5, para.25.

starting date for filing international applications was June 1, 1978. The manner of operation of the P.C.T. is laid down in the treaty itself and in the Regulations under the P.C.T. (P.C.T. Rules).[10] The benefit of an application made under the P.C.T. is that a single application can be made seeking protection in a number of convention countries.

In outline the Treaty works in the following way: an applicant (who **3.05** must either be a national, or resident of a P.C.T. contracting state) may make his international application either to his local patent office or, in those contracting states that have also ratified the E.P.C., to the EPO.

To comply with national security requirements a resident of the United Kingdom must file a P.C.T. application at the U.K. Patent Office unless permission to do otherwise is obtained in advance from the Patent Office.[11] The local patent office (referred to as the receiving office) will check the application for formalities and provide the application with its international filing date.[12] The receiving office then will forward a copy of the application to the International Bureau and to the International Searching Authority[13] which may either be a national office (if of sufficient size) or an intergovernmental organisation such as the International Patent Institute.[14] Such Searching Authority will carry out an international search which is sent to the International Bureau and to each of the designated offices for which the applicant seeks a patent. The international application and the international search[15] are published by the International Bureau. They are also communicated to the patent offices of each of the contracting states designated in the application- "a designated office". If the applicant wishes to proceed further he must ensure that the application has been sent to the designated offices and the required fees paid in general within 20 months of the priority date of the application.[16] The remainder of the prosecution to grant is carried out in the designated offices.

Chapter II of the P.C.T. additionally provides for an international preliminary examination on the demand of the applicant—the objective of such provisions being to formulate a "preliminary and non-binding opinion of the questions whether the claimed invention appears to be novel, to involve any inventive step (to be non-obvious) and to be industrially applicable".[17] Chapter II is not applicable to all contracting states. The procedures and time limits for making an application under

---

[10] P.C.T., Art 58. The Regs. can be and are amended by the Assembly and serve as the means for regulating the manner of operation of the Treaty.
[11] P.A. 1977, s.23.
[12] P.C.T., Art. 11.
[13] P.C.T., Art. 12; the International Bureau is the International Bureau of the World Intellectual Property Organisation the International Searching Authority for P.C.T. applications filed at the U.K. or European Patent Office is the novelty investigation branch of the EPO (in the Netherlands).
[14] P.C.T., Art. 16.
[15] P.C.T., Arts. 20 and 21.
[16] P.C.T., Arts. 20, 22 and 39(1)(*a*)—or if applicable up to 25 months if there is an international preliminary examination.
[17] P.C.T., Art. 33.

the P.C.T. are complex. They are supervised by the International Bureau who publish a Gazette and other advisory material relating to the operation of the P.C.T.[18]

3.06   The relationship between an international application and the grant of a patent (U.K.) is regulated by sections 89, 89A and 89B of the 1977 Act as amended.[19] Up until the expiry of the prescribed period the application is deemed to be in the International phase.[20] Thereafter, it is deemed to be in the national phase.[21] The prescribed period is, in general, 20 months from the priority date although it is 30 months in the case where the United Kingdom has been elected in accordance with Chapter II of the P.C.T.[22] In order to enter the national phase all necessary fees must be paid, and translations filed at the Patent Office[23] and provided copies of any amendment effected during the international phase (and any translation) are filed at the Patent Office, the amendment is treated as though made under the 1977 Act.[24] Whilst in the international phase, the provisions of the P.C.T. relating to publication, search, examination and amendment apply and not those of the Act.[25] In all other respects the Act applies.[26] Once in the national phase, only the provisions of the Act apply.[27] Further, during the international phase, the application is treated as a foreign or convention application for the purpose of determining questions about entitlement. Section 12 of the 1977 Act thus applies. Once the national phase is entered, section 8, rather than section 12, applies.[28]

When the national phase begins, the Comptroller considers the international search report and refers the application for so much of the examination and search required in the case of a national application under sections 17 and 18 of the 1977 Act as he sees fit.[29] Thereafter, the application proceeds in the same way as a national application.

So far as the relationship between an international application and the grant of a European Patent (U.K.) is concerned, if the international application contains an indication that only a European patent is required and not also a United Kingdom patent, section 89 does not apply.[30] The EPO acts as the receiving office,[31] International Searching

---

[18] P.C.T., Art. 55. See also *Brossmann's Appn.* [1983] R.P.C. 109, and *Matsushita Electric Work's Appn.* [1983] R.P.C. 105.
[19] C.D.P.A., Sched. 5, para.25.
[20] P.A. 1977, s.89A(2).
[21] P.A. 1977, s.89A(3).
[22] Patent Rules 1990., r.85.
[23] P.A. 1977, s.89A(3).
[24] P.A. 1977, s.89A(5).
[25] P.A. 1977, s.89A(1).
[26] P.A. 1977, s.89(1); *Prangley's Appn.* [1988] R.P.C. 187, and *Vapocure Technologies Appn.* [1990] R.P.C. 1.
[27] P.A. 1977, s.89(1).
[28] P.A. 1977, s.89B(4).
[29] P.A. 1977, s.89B(5).
[30] P.A. 1977, s.89(4).
[31] E.P.C., Arts. 151, 152.

Authority[32] and International Preliminary Examining Authority.[33] The EPO may also act as a designated office to receive the international search report and process the application to grant if an international application seeks a European patent designating one or more contracting states which have also ratified the E.P.C.[34] In such cases the EPO will adopt the international search report in lieu of the European search report subject to any supplementary European search reports deemed necessary by the Administrative Council.[35] In addition the EPO may act as an elected office for the purposes of using an international preliminary examination.[36]

2. Application for National (U.K.) Patent

A. The Applicant

Who may apply

Section 7(1) of the 1977 Act enables any person to make an application **3.07** for a patent either alone or jointly with another. This should be contrasted with section 7(2) as to who is entitled to be granted a patent. Prima facie the inventor, or joint inventors are the persons to whom a patent may be granted and such persons are defined as the "actual deviser" of the invention.[37] However, such right is subject to any assignment by the deviser before[38] or after[39] the making of the invention or to any other enactment, rule of law, foreign law, treaty or international convention.[40] The successors in title of an inventor, or assignee, or person otherwise entitled to the patent are entitled to the grant of the patent.[41] It should be noted that a patent is no longer validly granted to the first importer of the invention into this country as had been the case prior to the 1977 Act. Prima facie a person who applies for a patent is deemed to be the person who is entitled to be granted a patent.[42] However, the importance of the right persons applying for the grant of the patent cannot be overemphasised in view of the power to revoke the patent if such persons are not granted the patent.[43] Machinery exists

---

[32] E.P.C., Art. 154.
[33] E.P.C., Art. 155.
[34] E.P.C., Art. 153.
[35] E.P.C., Art. 157.
[36] E.P.C., Art. 156.
[37] P.A. 1977, s.7(3).
[38] P.A. 1977, s.7(2)(*b*).
[39] P.A. 1977, s.7(2)(*c*).
[40] P.A. 1977, s.7(2)(*b*).
[41] P.A. 1977, s.7(2)(*c*)
[42] P.A. 1977, s.7(4).
[43] See P.A. 1977, ss.72(1)(*b*) and 72(2) as amended by the C.D.P.A. 1988, Sched. 5, para.18.

both before the grant[44] and after the grant[45] of a patent for the determination by the Comptroller or the High Court as to whether any other person is entitled to the patent either alone or jointly.

Employee Invention

3.08   As between employer and employee section 39(1) enacts that an invention made by an employee shall be taken to belong to the employer if, but only if:

> (1) it was made in the course of the normal duties of the employee or outside such duties but specifically assigned to him and the circumstances (in either case) were such that an invention might reasonably be expected to result therefrom; or
> (2) it was made in the course of duties of the employee which duties were of such a nature giving rise to such a responsibility that the employee had a special obligation to further the interests of the employer.

In *Harris' Patent*, Falconer J. considered the ambit of section 1 and its relationship to the pre–existing common law. He entertained doubts as to whether the section was declaratory of the common law, but reached no decision on the point. He held that the correct question to ask as regards "normal duties" was to enquire whether designing, or inventing formed part of the employee's duties. If it was part of the employee's duties to turn his mind to problems as they arose then the requirements of subsection 1(*a*) were satisfied. With regard to subsection (*b*) he went on to state, at page 37:

> "Under paragraph (*b*), the question is whether Mr Harris's duties were such as to place him under such 'a special obligation to further the interests of this employer's undertaking', in this case the valve business of Reiss Engineering. The wording of the paragraph, under condition (ii), clearly envisages that the extent and nature of the 'special obligation to further the interests of the employer's undertaking' will depend upon the status of the employee and the attendant duties and responsibilities of that status. Thus, plainly the position in this regard of a managing director whose obligation to further the interests of his employer's undertaking of which he is the managing director will, no doubt, extend across the whole spectrum of the activities of the undertaking, will differ from that of, say, a sales manager."

3.09   Where the invention belongs to the employer it should normally

---

[44] P.A. 1977, s.8. See *post*, § 3.21.
[45] P.A. 1977, ss.9, 37.

apply for the grant of the patent in its own name, the employee inventor having a right to be mentioned in any patent granted thereon.[46] Such an application must be accompanied by a statement of the employer's right to the grant of a patent and the name of the inventor(s).[47] If the employee applies for the patent in his own name, he will hold it on trust for the employer and can be ordered to transfer the same to the employer.[48] Alternatively the employer may within two years[49] of the grant of the patent apply to revoke the same and make a fresh application for a patent which will be treated as having been filed on the date of filing of the earlier patent.[50] Application may be made in the joint names of inventor and employee—however this may encourage employees to seek compensation.[51]

By section 39(2)[52] of the 1977 Act where an invention belongs to an employee, any exploitation of that invention by the employee enjoys immunity from suit by the employer in respect of infringement of any copyright, or design right vested in the employer.

Convention application

A patent may also be applied for under the 1977 Act by a person   **3.10**
resident abroad who has made an application in a convention country[53] for protection in respect of an invention equivalent to such application, and if such application is made within a period of 12 months from the date of the application in the convention country, the priority date of that invention will be the date of filing of the convention application provided it is supported by matter disclosed in the earlier convention application.[54]

However, the persons entitled to the grant of such a patent are the same as a non-convention application under the 1977 Act.

A person resident in the United Kingdom cannot file, or cause to be   **3.11**
filed a patent application for a patent outside the United Kingdom unless that person has filed an application in this country not less than six weeks beforehand and no secrecy restrictions[55] have been imposed on such application.[56]

---

[46] P.A. 1977, s.13(1).
[47] P.A. 1977, s.13(2); Patents Form Nos. 1/77 and 7/77.
[48] *Amplaudio Ltd. v. Snell* (1938), 55 R.P.C. 237; *Forte v. Martinex* (1947) 64 R.P.C. 26.
[49] The period of two years does not apply if the person registered as proprietor of the patent knew he was not entitled to the patent—s.37(5) of the 1977 Act.
[50] P.A. 1977, s.37(5), s.72(1)(*b*).
[51] As to compensation of employees see s.40 and 41 of the 1977 Act and *post* § 3.73 *et seq.*
[52] Introduced by C.D.P.A. 1988, Sched. 5, para.11.
[53] A convention country is one declared as such by Order Council—see s.90 of the 1977 Act; Sched. 4, para.9 continues the 1949 Act conventions countries—see also para.1.13.
[54] P.A. 1977, s.5(2), (4), (5).
[55] Secrecy restrictions: see P.A. 1977, s.22.
[56] P.A. 1977, s.23(1).

Mention of inventor

3.12 The inventor(s) have the right to be mentioned as such in any granted patent or published application for a patent.[57] The counterpart of this is that an applicant who is not the sole/joint inventor(s) must make a statement on Patents Form No. 7/77 identifying the inventor(s) and the derivation of the applicant's right to be granted the patent.[58] Such a statement must be made within 16 months after the declared priority date or, where there is no declared priority date, the date of filing the application.[59] Failure to make such a statement within the 16 month period will mean that the application will be taken to be withdrawn.[60]

Machinery exists for disputing inventorship and the Comptroller has power to certify that any person was wrongly named as an inventor on an application by the true inventor or joint inventor.[61]

Applicant may act by agent

3.13 Provided the Patent Office received an express authorisation signed by the applicant before the expiration of three months from the filing date of the application, an agent may sign Patents Form No. 1/77 on behalf of the applicant and any notice or other documents under the 1977 Act.[62]

Such an agent need not be a patent agent,[63] but he must be an agent duly authorised to the satisfaction of the Comptroller who may refuse to recognise certain persons for reasons related to their conduct or status as agents.[64]

B. Procedure on Application

3.14 In accordance with section 14(1) of the 1977 Act, every application for a patent shall be made in the prescribed form[65] and shall be filed at the Patent Office in the prescribed manner,[66] accompanied by the filing fee. Furthermore, every application shall contain a request for the grant of a patent, a specification containing a description of the invention, a claim or claims and any drawing referred to in the description or claims and

---

[57] P.A. 1977, s.13(1).
[58] P.A. 1977, s.13(2); Patents Rules 1990, r.15.
[59] Patents Rules 1990, r.15(1).
[60] P.A. 1977, s.13(2).
[61] P.A. 1977, s.13(3); Patents Rules 1990, r.14.
[62] Patents Rules 1990, r.90(1).
[63] P.A. 1977, s.130(1) for definition of patent agent.
[64] P.A. 1977, s.115; Patents Rules 1990, r.90.
[65] Patents Form No. 1/77; see Patents Rules 1990, r.16.
[66] Patents Rules 1990, r.18–28.

an abstract.[67] The purpose of the abstract is to give technical information, and on publication does not form part of the state of the art.[68]

Date of filing

If a declaration of priority pursuant to section 5(2) of the 1977 Act[69] is   **3.15**
made it must be made on Patents Form No. 1/77 at the time of filing the
application and must state the date of filing of any application specified
in the declaration and the country in or for which it was made.[70] Section
15(1) of the 1977 Act defines the date of filing the application as the
earliest date on which the following conditions are satisfied, namely:

(a) the documents filed at the Patent Office contain an indication that
a (U.K.) patent is sought
(b) the documents identify the applicant(s)
(c) the documents contain a description of the invention (this
description does not have to comply with the Act or Rules) and
(d) the applicant pays the filing fee.

Priority

Section 15, however, merely fixes the filing date, it does not deal with   **3.16**
the priority which can be claimed as a result. Hence, to secure the
earliest priority date the application must either be based upon an
application for protection in respect of the invention in or for a
convention country, or upon an application for a patent under the 1977
Act provided the date of filing of the later application is made during the
period of 12 months following the date of the earlier (or earliest)
application, and provided the invention of the later application is
supported by matter disclosed in the earlier application.[71] The priority
document does not, however, form part of the application.[72]

In view of the power to revoke a patent if the matter disclosed in the
specification extends beyond that disclosed in the application for a
patent[73] it is of great importance that the description of the invention
included with the application corresponds to that of the specification as
filed.

---

[67] P.A. 1977, s.14(2); see also s.15(5) and Patents Rules 1990 r.25(2) for time for putting in
order.
[68] P.A. 1977, s.14(7); see Patents Rules 1990, r.19.
[69] Or s.127(4) of the 1977 Act in the case of applications under the 1949 Act which are taken
to be abandoned.
[70] Patents Rules 1990 r.6(1).
[71] P.A. 1977, s.5(2); see *post*, § 4.26.
[72] *Mitsui Engineering and Shipbuilding Co.'s Appn.* [1984] R.P.C. 471.
[73] P.A. 1977, s.72(1)(*d*), see *post*, § 5.96.

The Specification

3.17   In accordance with section 14(3) and (5) of the 1977 Act the specification must disclose the invention in a manner "which is clear enough and complete enough for the invention to be performed by a person skilled in the art."[74] The claim or claims must:

(a) define the matter for which protection is sought;
(b) be clear and concise;
(c) be supported by the description; and
(d) relate to one invention or to a group of inventions which are so linked as to form a single inventive concept.[75]

The specification must state the title of the invention[76] and the description must include a list briefly describing the figures in the drawings (if any).[77]

The Drawings

3.18   The detailed requirements for the drawings forming part of the application are set out in rule 18 of the Patents Rules 1990.

There are, however, special provisions in relation to late filed drawings. Drawings cannot be filed after the date which is treated as being the date of filing without altering that date to the date on which the drawing is filed.[78] However, the severity of this provision has been mitigated by the enactment of section 15(3A) of the 1977 Act.[79] Where errors, or mistakes with regard to the filing of drawings have been made, sections 15(2) and (3) do not prevent the Comptroller's power to act under section 117(1) of the Act. Where, therefore, the failure to file the right drawings is due to a clerical error, or mistake, the discretion to correct the error arises. In this respect the decision in *Antiphon A.B's Application*[80] is not now good law.

Micro-organisms

3.19   In accordance with section 14(4) of the 1977 Act,[81] rule 17 of the Patents Rules 1990, and Schedule 2 thereto, lays down the requirements

---

[74] See P.A. 1977, s.72(1)(*c*) where the same test is to be applied for revocation of the granted patent, and see *post*, § 5.03.
[75] Pursuant to P.A. 1977, s.14(6), Patent Rules 1990, r.22 provides three classes of when an application is to be treated as relating to a group of inventions linked to form a single inventive concept.
[76] Patents Rules 1990, r.16(2), 16(3); the title must be short and indicate the matter to which the invention relates.
[77] Patents Rules 1990, r.16(4).
[78] P.A. 1977, s.15(2) and (3) and see *Antiphon A.B.'s Appn.* [1984] R.P.C. 1, and *V.E.B. Kombinat Walzlager und Normteile's Appn.* [1987] R.P.C. 405.
[79] C.D.P.A. 1988, Sched. 5, para.2 which came into effect January 7, 1991.
[80] See fn.77.
[81] See also P.A. 1977, ss.72(1)(*c*); 72(3).

for making available to the public the micro-organism used in the performance of the invention, including the deposit of the micro-organism in a culture collection not later than the date of filing the application and the supplying, either in the specification as filed, or within a prescribed period therafter,[82] the name of such collection, the date upon which the culture was deposited and the accession number of the deposit.

Single Invention

An application must relate to one invention or to a group of inventions so linked as to form a single inventive concept.[83] No definition can be given as to what constitutes a single invention. But it is submitted that if a novel general principle is disclosed, any machine or process which embodies that general principle can be regarded as an embodiment of a single invention, notwithstanding that there may also be disclosed additional optional details or non-fundamental variants which are claimed in subsidiary claims. But the mere fact that all the new disclosures relate to the same machine or process, which is not itself the invention claimed in that specification, does not make all such disclosures one invention.[84] Claims to intermediate and final chemical products do not necessarily relate to a single invention.[85]   **3.20**

Guidance as to what constitutes a group of inventions so linked as to form a single inventive concept can be obtained from Patents Rules 1990, rule 22. To avoid the objection of multiplicity of inventions, an applicant may divide out the inventions to form separate applications and the new application(s) may be entitled to the original filing date. A divisional application of this nature is, however, only permitted to retain the original filing date if there is no new matter added in the new application.[86] The test for new matter is the test laid down in section 76(1).[87] If the divisional application does contain new matter, it can be amended, prior to grant, to exclude that matter. In this respect *Hydroacoustics Inc.'s Application* is no longer good law.[88]

It should be noted that the contents of the claims form part of the disclosure in addition to the material in the body of the specification.[89] A divisional application can only be made before a patent is granted on the original application, or before that application is withdrawn.[90] Once

---

[82] Patents Rules 1990, Sched. 2, para.1(3); see *Chinoin's Appn.* [1986] R.P.C. 39.
[83] P.A. 1977, s.14(5)(*d*).
[84] *J.'s Appn.* (1925) 42 R.P.C. 1; *Z's Appn.* (1910) 27 R.P.C. 285. See also *Jones's Patent* (1885) Griff.P. C. 285; *Robinson's Patent* (1886) Griff.P.C.267.
[85] *Celanese Corporation of America's Appn.* (1952) 69 R.P.C. 227.
[86] P.A. 1977, s.15(4).
[87] C.D.P.A. 1988, Sched. 5, para.20.
[88] [1981]F.S.R. 538.
[89] P.A. 1977, s.130(3) and see *Van der Lely's Appn.* [1987] R.P.C. 61.
[90] Patents Rules 1990, r.24 and see *Ogawa Chemical Industries Appn.* [1986] R.P.C. 106.

granted no objection can be taken to the validity of the patent on grounds of lack of unity of invention.[91]

Disputes before grant as to entitlement to application or grant of patent[92]

3.21   Section 8 of the Act provides the means for resolving disputes as to the entitlement to patents which arise before grant, and even before application. It is one of a number of sections by which questions of entitlement can be resolved.[93] Under section 8, if the Comptroller or Patents court[94] is satisfied that a person other than the applicant or applicants is entitled to be granted (alone or with any other person including one or more of the joint applicants) a patent for an invention or has, or would have any right in or under any patent so granted or any application for such a patent in accordance with section 8(1) of the 1977 Act, the Comptroller has wide powers under section 8(2) of the 1977 Act to substitute one name of an applicant for another, refuse the application, require appropriate amendments or make an order transferring or granting any licence or other right in or under the application.[95] In addition to such powers, in accordance with section 8(3) and subject to the limitations imposed therein, the Comptroller may by order permit the person who is held to be entitled to a part or the whole of the patent when granted to make a new application in respect thereof within three months from the expiry of time for appealing from the Comptroller's order or where appeal is brought from the day on which it is finally disposed of.[96] Furthermore, there are provisions for safeguarding those original applicants (and licensees of the original applicants) who are held not to be entitled to the grant of the patent, but who before registration of a reference under section 8 in good faith worked the invention in this country or made effective and serious preparations to do so.[97]

Whilst a reference under section 8 is made at any time before a patent has been granted, the fact that the reference has not been determined before the time when the application is in order for grant will not hold up the grant; rather the reference will on the grant of the patent be treated as a reference under section 37.[98]

3.22   If any dispute arises between joint applicants, the Comptroller after

---

[91] P.A. 1977, s.26.
[92] Generally Patents Rules 1990, r.7 to 13 for the regulations relating to such disputes.
[93] See section 37, Determination of Right to Patent After Grant; section 12, Determination of Questions about Entitlement to Foreign and Convention Patents, and see *Cannings United States Appn.* [1992] R.P.C. 459; section 82, Jurisdiction to Determine Questions as to right to a European Patent.
[94] P.A. 1977, s.8(7); s.130(1), and see *Brockhouse PLC's Patent* [1984] R.P.C. 332.
[95] See *Norris' Patent* [1988] R.P.C. 159, and *Viziball's Appn.* [1988] R.P.C. 213.
[96] Patents Rules 1990, r.10, and see *Amateur Athletic Association's Appn.* [1989] R.P.C. 717.
[97] P.A. 1977, s.11 which corresponds in part to s.64, see *post* § 6.67.
[98] P.A. 1977, s.9.

giving all parties an opportunity of stating their case[99] may give such directions as he thinks fit.[1]

Preliminary Examination and Search

Within 12 months of the date of filing (or from the declared priority **3.23** date whichever is appropriate) an applicant must request a preliminary examination and search[2] to determine whether the application complies with the formal requirements of the Act.[3] Failure to make such a request will mean that application is taken to be withdrawn.[4] If the examiner concludes that the application relates to more than one invention he shall only conduct a search into the first invention.[5]

Publication of application

Except for those applications containing matter which might be **3.24** prejudicial to the defence of the realm or the safety of the public,[6] the Comptroller shall publish the application as soon as possible after a period of 18 months from the declared priority date or where there is no declared priority date, the date of filing the application.[7] Preparations for publication are normally completed when the specification has been allocated to a printing contractor.[8] After this time, publication cannot be avoided by seeking to withdraw the application.

Substantive Examination

Either at the time of requesting a preliminary examination or in any **3.25** event no later than six months from the date of publication[9] an applicant must request a substantive examination.[10]

Such an examination involves a consideration as to whether the invention is new *and* involves an inventive step in the light of the documents resulting from such search. Further, the application is examined to ensure that it complies with all the requirements of the Act and the rules.[11] The Comptroller is obliged to provide the applicant with

---

[99] Patents Rules 1990, r.12.
[1] P.A. 1977, s.10.
[2] P.A. 1977, ss.15(5)(*b*) and 17(1); Patents Rules 1990, r.25(2).
[3] P.A. 1977, ss.15(3) and 17(2); Patents Rules 1990, rr.28(2) and 31.
[4] P.A. 1977, s.15(5).
[5] P.A. 1977, s.17(6) and see *Mollister's Appn.* [1983] R.P.C. 10.
[6] P.A. 1977, s.22.
[7] P.A. 1977, s.16; Patents Rules 1990, r.27.
[8] *Intera Corp.'s Appn.* [1986] R.P.C. 459.
[9] P.A. 1977, s.18(1), Patents Rules 1990, r.33; except for those cases falling within s.22 where, in general, the period is two years from the declared priority or filing date (whichever is the case).
[10] P.A. 1977, s.17(4), (5) and 18(2).
[11] P.A. 1977, s.17(5).

a copy of the search report[12] and the examiner's report after substantive examination.

Amendment prior to grant

3.26   On receipt of the examiner's search report under section 17(5) or the examiner's report after substantive examination, an applicant has the opportunity to amend the specification of his own volition and without the consent of the Comptroller.[13] Any further amendment requires the consent of the Comptroller.[14] No amendment is permissible which results in the application or specification disclosing matter which extends beyond that disclosed before amendment.[15]

Failures in the Course of Prosecution

3.27   The 1977 Act, and the Patents Rules 1990 lay down a number of specific time limits which have to be met and other requirements which have to be fulfilled in order for a patent to be granted. Inevitably there will be failures in meeting those time limits and requirements.

Corrections of Errors in Documents

3.28   Section 117(1) of the Act provides that:

> "The comptroller may, subject to any provision of rules, correct any error of translation or transcription, clerical error or mistake in any specification of a patent or application for a patent or any document filed in connection with a patent or such an application".

The breadth of this discretion is, however, limited in two ways. First, the subsection cannot be invoked to circumvent other mandatory statutory requirements. Whilst section 15 has been amended[16] to allow such a correction in relation to section 15 itself, the expression of principle will remain good law.

Secondly, in so far as the correction is a correction to the specification, it can only be made if the correction is obvious in the sense that it is immediately evident that nothing else would have been intended than what was offered as the correction.[17]

The Comptroller is entitled to require the proposed correction to be advertised and opposition can be entered to the correction.[18]

---

[12] P.A. 1977, s.18(3) and (4).
[13] Patents Rules 1990, r.36(3), (4).
[14] Patents Rules 1990, r.36(5).
[15] P.A. 1977, s.19(1); s.76; s.72(1)(*d*).
[16] CDPA Sched. 5, para.2.
[17] Patents Rules 1990, r.91(2); see *Antiphon A.B.'s Appn.* [1984] R.P.C. 1; *Dukhorskoi's Appn.* [1985] R.P.C. 8, and G11/91 CELTRIX/Correction of errors: [1993] O.J. EPO 125.
[18] Patents Rules 1990, r.91(3)–(6).

Alteration of Time Limits

The degree of flexibility to extend time limits depends upon the   3.29
nature of the time limit which has been missed. These are dealt with by
rule 110 of the Patents Rules 1990. An automatic extension of one month
is available in many cases.[19] Further extensions are available in the
exercise of the Comptroller's discretion.[20] In other cases no extension is
permitted.[21]

Correction of Irregularities

In addition to the above, the Comptroller has a general discretion   3.30
under rule 100 of the Patents Rules 1990 to allow any document to be
amended, or any irregularity in procedure to be rectified on such terms
as he shall direct.[22] In the case of time limits which cannot be altered
under rule 110, alteration is only permissible if the irregularity is
attributable wholly or in part to an error, default, or omission on the part
of the Patent Office.[23]

Hearing and appeal

If the applicant and Comptroller disagree on any matter, the   3.31
Comptroller must give the applicant an opportunity of a hearing[24] and
an appeal lies from the Comptroller's decision to the Patents Court.[25]
Subject to any appeal, the time for putting the application in order is
three and a half years from the declared priority date or date of filing
whichever is appropriate.[26]

Third Party Objections

Between publication and grant a third party may make observations   3.32
in writing to the Comptroller on the question whether the invention is a
patentable invention.[27] There is no mechanism by which a third party
can oppose the grant of a U.K. patent. In this respect the procedure for
obtaining a U.K. patent differs significantly from an equivalent European patent. Making observations under section 21 is thus the only way
by which a third party can seek to influence the grant, or refusal, of a

---

[19] Patents Rules 1990, r.110(3), and see *Aisin Seikikik's Appn.* [1984] R.P.C. 191.
[20] Patents Rules 1990, r.110(4).
[21] Patents Rules 1990, r.110(2).
[22] See *E.D.F's Patents* [1992] R.P.C. 205.
[23] Patents Rules 1990, r.100(2), and see *E's Appn.* [1983] R.P.C. 231; *Hill's Appn.* [1985]
R.P.C. 339; *Mitsubishi Jidosha Kogyo K.K.'s Appn.* [1987] R.P.C. 449.
[24] P.A. 1977, s.101; Patents Rules 1990, r.88.
[25] P.A. 1977, s.97.
[26] P.A. 1977, s.20; Patents Rules 1990, r.34.
[27] P.A. 1977, s.21; and Patents Rules 1990, r.37.

patent. The third party's rights are limited to making written observations. He has no right to be heard, or to be informed of the Examiner's, or Applicant's reaction to the observations.

Grant of patent

3.33   The Comptroller must publish a notice of the grant of the patent in the Official Journal as soon as is practicable after grant[28] and a patent takes effect on the date on which such notice is published.[29]

3. Application for European Patent (U.K.)

A. The Applicant

Who may apply

3.34   A European patent application may be filed by any natural or legal person or anybody equivalent to a legal person[30] either alone or jointly or by two or more applicants designating different contracting states.[31]

In contrast the right to the grant of a European patent belongs to the inventor or his successor in title or, if the inventor is an employee, the right to the grant shall be determined in accordance with the law of the State in which the employee is mainly employed or, if not known, then the law of the State in which the employer has his place of business.[32] There is a presumption before the EPO that the applicant is entitled to the grant of the patent.[33]

Disputes as to Entitlement

3.35   The EPO does not decide who is entitled to the grant of the patent. Section 82 of the 1977 Act which follows the E.P.C. Protocol on Recognition confers jurisdiction on the Patents Court and Comptroller to determine whether a person has a right to be granted a European patent if any of the following conditions apply:

(a) the applicant has his residence or principal place of business in the United Kingdom, or

(b) the other party claims that the patent should be granted to him

---

[28] P.A. 1977, s.24(1).
[29] P.A. 1977, s.25(1).
[30] E.P.C., Art. 58.
[31] E.P.C., Art. 59; see Art. 79 as to the need to designate the contracting state or states in which protection is desired, and see Art. 118 as to requirement for unity of application where applicants are not the same.
[32] E.P.C., Art. 60; for U.K. position see P.A. 1977, s.39.
[33] E.P.C., Art. 60(3).

and he has his residence or place of business in the United Kingdom and the applicant does not have his residence or place of business in any of the relevant contracting states.

In the case of an employee/employer dispute the conditions to be satisfied are:

(a) the employee is mainly employed in the U.K., or
(b) the employee is not mainly employed anywhere or his place of main employment cannot be determined but the employer has a place of business in the U.K. to whcih the employee is attached.

In either case it is possible for the parties to agree to submit to the jurisdiction of a contracting state other than the U.K..[34]

By section 12 of the 1977 Act (which is subject to section 82) the Comptroller is given jurisdiction to decide the right to grant, not only European patents, but other foreign patents provided the question is referred before grant.[35]

Once a dispute has arisen as to the person entitled to the grant of a European patent, the EPO has power to stay the prosecution of the European application.[36] If before grant by a final decision it is adjudged that a person other than the applicant is entitled to the grant, the EPO has power to substitute the successful claimant as applicant, or allow him to file a new application or refuse the existing application.[37]

B. Procedure on Application

The procedure for applying, and the manner in which European patents are prosecuted to grant are covered in detail in the publication *Guidelines for Examination in the European Patent Office* published by the EPO. There follows a brief discussion on the procedure designed primarily to contrast that procedure with the procedure for obtaining a U.K. patent.

Language

There are three official languages of the EPO, English, French and German, and European patent applications must be filed in one of these

3.36

---

[34] See *Kakkar v. Szelke* [1988] F.S.R. 97 and [1989] F.S.R. 225, but also see *Duijnstee v. Lodeewijk Goderbauer* [1985] F.S.R. 221 (ECJ), [1985] 1 C.M.L.R. 220. The two decisions cannot be easily reconciled.

[35] See, *e.g. Canning's U.S. Appn.* [1992] R.P.C. 459.

[36] E.P.C. rules, r.13(1).

[37] E.P.C., Art. 61.

languages.[38] The selected official language is used in all subsequent proceedings[39] subject to certain exceptions.[40] The authentic text of a European patent or patent application, is the language used in the proceedings before the EPO.[41] Where the language of the proceedings is French or German, a translation into English of the specification or the claims is to be treated as the authentic text for the purposes of domestic proceedings in the United Kingdom other than proceedings for revocation if as translated the scope is narrower than that of the original language.[42] Subject to safeguarding provisions, a proprietor or applicant may file a corrected translation.[43]

Where to apply

3.37   An application for a European patent (U.K.) can either be made at the U.K. Patent Office or with the EPO in Munich or the Hague—British applicants must normally file through the Patent Office[44] for security reasons.[45]

A European divisional application must however be filed with the EPO.[46]

Where a European application (U.K.) is made at the Patent Office, the Patent Office must forward all applications, other than for secret patents, to the EPO in the shortest time compatible with the secrecy provisions of section 22 of the 1977 Act.[47] An application which does not reach the EPO before the end of the fourteenth month after filing (or if priority claim, after the date of priority) shall be deemed to be withdrawn.[48] Such an application can be converted to a national application.[49]

How to apply

3.38   A European patent application shall contain:

(a) a request for the grant
(b) a description of the invention
(c) one or more claims

---

[38] E.P.C., Art. 14(1).
[39] E.P.C., Art. 14(3).
[40] E.P.C. Rules, rr.1–2.
[41] E.P.C., Art.70, P.A. 1977, s.80(1).
[42] P.A. 1977, s.80(2).
[43] P.A. 1977, s.80(3) to (4).
[44] P.A. 1977, s.23; E.P.C., Art. 75(1).
[45] P.A. 1977, , s.22; E.P.C., Art. 75(2).
[46] E.P.C., Art. 76.
[47] E.P.C., Art. 77; within 6 weeks where clearly no secrecy problems, within four months (or 14 months if priority claimed from priority date) where further examination required.
[48] *Ibid.*
[49] P.A. 1977, , s.81; E.P.C., Art. 135(1)(*a*).

(d) any drawings and
(e) an abstract.[50]

The request for the grant shall contain the designation of the contracting state or states in which protection is sought.[51] To secure a date of filing documents filed must contain:

(a) an indication that a European patent is sought
(b) the designation of at least one contracting state
(c) information identifying the applicant and
(d) a description and one or more claims in an official language such as English.[52]

Specifications

The application must: 3.39

(a) relate to one invention only or to a group of inventions so linked as to form a single general inventive concept[53]
(b) disclose the invention in a manner sufficiently clear and complete for it to be carried out by a person skilled in the art[54] and
(c) the claims must define the matter for which protection is sought, be clear and concise and be supported by the description.[55]

The abstract should be drafted so as to constitute an efficient instrument for the purpose of searching.[56]

Micro-organisms

Special requirements for deposit of the culture of the micro-organism   **3.40** are laid down in the E.P.C. Rules.[57]

---

[50] E.P.C., Art. 78; the abstract merely serves for use as technical information, in particular as an aid during search and examination—see E.P.C., Art. 85.
[51] E.P.C., Art. 79; E.P.C. Rules, r.26.
[52] E.P.C., Art. 80; this differs from a national application where claims are not required, see *ante*, § 3.10.
[53] E.P.C., Art. 82; E.P.C. Rules, r.30; same as under 1977 Act except for word "general"; see *ante* § 3.15.
[54] E.P.C., Art. 83; E.P.C. Rules, r.27, which provides a list of matters to be included in the description unless a different manner or order would be better. See also r.34 which relates to prohibited matter.
[55] E.P.C., Art. 84; E.P.C. Rules, r.29. Where appropriate the claims should first define the subject matter by reference to features which are part of the prior art followed by a characterising portion; claims shall not rely on references to the drawings or description except where absolutely necessary and the old "omnibus claim" is prohibited.
[56] E.P.C. Rules, r.33.
[57] E.P.C. Rules, rr.28 and 28(a).

Mention of Inventor

3.41   The inventor shall have the right *vis-à-vis* the applicant or proprietor to be mentioned[58] and the European patent application shall designate the inventor.[59] An incorrect designation can be corrected.[60]

Priority right

3.42   An applicant may claim priority in respect of an earlier application for a patent in a state which is a party to the Paris Convention if the later European application is made within 12 months of the earlier application.[61]

An applicant desiring to take advantage of the priority of an earlier application must file a declaration of priority[62] and the earlier priority will only be accorded to those elements of the European application which are included in the application or applications whose priority is claimed.[63]

Formal Examination of application and Search

3.43   The receiving section[64] examines the application to make sure the correct fee has been paid and the application is generally in order[65] so that a date of filing may be accorded the application.

Once a date of filing has been accorded, the Receiving Section further examines the application to make sure the detailed formal requirements of the E.P.C. have been complied with.[66]

Deficiencies may be corrected within specified time limits which vary according to the nature of the deficiency.[67]

At the same time the Search Division draws up a European search report.[68] The search report shall mention those documents which may be taken into consideration in deciding novelty and inventive step. In all these reports the procedure at the EPO is analogous to the procedure at the U.K. Patent Office.

---

[58] E.P.C., Art. 62; E.P.C. Rules, r.18; see *ante* § 3.14.
[59] E.P.C., Art. 81; E.P.C. Rules, r.17 and 18.
[60] E.P.C. Rules, r.19.
[61] E.P.C., Art. 87; such earlier application may be another E.P.C. application (see E.P.C., Art 66) or a P.C.T., application (see P.C.T., Art. 11); or a utility model, but not an industrial design.
[62] E.P.C., Art. 88; E.P.C., Rules, r.38.
[63] E.P.C., Art. 88(3) and (4); disclosure of the elements is sufficient even though not claimed.
[64] E.P.C., Art. 16.
[65] E.P.C., Art. 90; E.P.C. Rules, r.39.
[66] E.P.C., Art. 91; E.P.C. Rules, rr.40–43.
[67] See, *e.g.* E.P.C. Rules, rr.31, 41(3), 43(2), 84 and 85*a*.
[68] E.P.C., Art. 92; E.P.C. Rules, rr.44–47.

Publication of application

A European application must be published as soon as possible after   **3.44**
the expiry of the period of 18 months from the date of filing or date of
priority whichever is the appropriate date.[69] It is contemplated that the
European search report and the abstract will generally be published at
the same time. An application, or a claim to priority, can be withdrawn
at any time up to the date when the technical preparations for
publication have been completed.[70] This date is deemed to be 10 weeks
before the expiry of the relevant period.[71]

Substantive Examination

A request for examination must be filed not later than six months   **3.45**
from when the *European Patent Bulletin* has mentioned the publication of
the European search report[72] (extendible for one month on payment of a
surcharge).[73] For an international application under the P.C.T. the six
months is taken from the publication of the P.C.T. search report.[74] An
examining division consisting of three technical examiners[75] is responsible for the examination of each European patent application. Examination prior to a final decision will as a general rule be entrusted to one
member of the division (the substantive examiner) but oral proceedings
will be before the division itself which may be enlarged by the addition
of a legally qualified examiner.[76]

Besides considering the application for novelty and inventive step,
the examiner will be concerned with the sufficiency of description,
clarity of claims and whether there is unity of invention. The examiner
must invite the applicant to file his observations to any objections that
the examiner may have[77] and such objections shall be contained in a
reasoned statement.[78]

Amendment before grant

An applicant can freely amend the description, claims and drawings   **3.46**
of his own volition after receiving the European search report and
before receipt of the first communication from the examining division.[79]
After receipt of such communication the applicant may only amend
once without the consent of the examining division.[80] No amendment is

---

[69] E.P.C., Art. 93; E.P.C. Rules, rr.48–50.
[70] E.P.C. Rules, r.48.
[71] [1987] O.J.EPO 312, Statement by President of EPO July, 1978.
[72] E.P.C., Art. 94(2).
[73] E.P.C. Rule, r.85*b*.
[74] E.P.C., Art. 157(1).
[75] E.P.C., Art. 18.
[76] *Ibid.*
[77] E.P.C., Art. 96(2).
[78] E.P.C. Rules, r.51(3).
[79] E.P.C. Rules, r.86(2).
[80] E.P.C., Art. 123; E.P.C. Rules, r.86(3).

permissible by which an application in its amended form contains subject matter which extends beyond the content of the application as filed.[81]

Where there is more than one invention an applicant may file a divisional application in respect of subject matter that does not extend beyond the content of the earlier application[82] thereby retaining for the divisional the filing date of the earlier application. Again these provisions are analogous to the procedure at the U.K. Patent Office.

Observations by third parties

3.47   Following publication of the European patent application any person may present observations to the EPO concerning the patentability of the invention—such person shall not become a party to the proceedings before the EPO. As with the position under the 1977 Act, this procedure suffers from the disadvantage that whilst observations can be made, the person making them does not know what effect the observations have on the Examiner or the applicant.[83]

Grant of the patent

3.48   If the examining division decides to grant the European patent, it will do so only if the applicant's approval of the text of the patent is first obtained, all fees due are paid[84] within three months and translations of the claims into the two other official languages of the EPO are filed. The grant will not take effect until mention of the fact has been made in the *European Patent Bulletin*.[85] At the time of such mention the EPO must publish a specification of the European patent.[86]

As from the publication of such mention, a European patent (U.K.) shall be treated for the purposes of Parts I and III of the 1977 Act as if it were a patent granted under the 1977 Act,[87] provided the appropriate translations into English have been filed at the Patent Office if the patent was published in French or German.[88]

Conversion of a European patent applciation (U.K.) to an application under the 1977 Act

3.49   The Comptroller may direct that an application for a European patent (U.K.) be treated as an application under the 1977 Act where the application is deemed to be withdrawn due either to restrictions on

---

[81] E.P.C., Art. 123(2).
[82] E.P.C., Art. 76; E.P.C. Rules, r.25.
[83] E.P.C., Art. 115l see *ante*, § 3.32.
[84] E.P.C., Art. 97(2) and (3); E.P.C. Rules, r.51(4).
[85] *Ibid.*
[86] E.P.C., Art. 98; E.P.C. Rules, r.53.
[87] P.A. 1977, s.77(1); E.P.C., Art. 64.
[88] P.A. 1977, s.77(6) and (7); E.P.C., Art. 65.

processing of applications under the E.P.C. or where a European application has not been forwarded to the EPO within the 14 months allowed by the E.P.C.[89]

Effect of filing an application for a European patent (U.K.)

An application for a European patent (U.K.) having a date of filing **3.50** under the E.P.C. shall be treated for the purposes of certain provisions of the 1977 Act as an application under the 1977 Act.[90]

Representation

Natural or legal persons having either a residence or their principal **3.51** place of business within the territory of one of the contracting states do not have to be represented by a professional representative but other persons, except for filing an application, must be represented professionally.[91]

There is a list of professional representatives who have all either passed the European qualifying examination[92] or under the transitional provisions were entitled automatically to be representatives because of their previous experience as a patent agent in a contracting state.[93]

In addition to the list, professional representation may also be undertaken by any legal practitioner qualified in one of the contracting states and having his place of business within such state to the extent that he is entitled, within the state, to act as a professional representative in patent matters.[94]

Oral hearings

Oral proceedings may take place either at the instance of the EPO if it **3.52** considers this to be expedient or at the request of any party to the proceedings.[95] However, oral proceedings before the receiving section will only take place at the request of the applicant where the receiving section considers this to be expedient or where it envisages refusing the application. Further requests for oral proceedings by the same parties on the same subject will generally not be allowed.[96]

Such proceedings are not in public except when before the board of

---

[89] P.A. 1977, s.81.
[90] P.A. 1977, s.78(1) as amended by the C.D.P.A. 1988, Sched. 5, para.22, and see *L'Oreals Appn.* [1986] R.P.C. 19; the same provisions apply to an international application for a European Patent (U.K.) see P.A. 1977, s.79; *cf.* P.A. 1977, s.89 for an international application for a patent.
[91] E.P.C., Art. 133; E.P.C. Rules, r.101, authorisation.
[92] E.P.C., Art. 134; E.P.C. Rules, r.102; see also P.A. 1977, s.84.
[93] E.P.C., Art. 163; E.P.C. Rules, r.106.
[94] E.P.C., Art. 134(7); see also P.A. 1977, s.84(2).
[95] E.P.C., Art. 116(1); E.P.C. Rules, r.71.
[96] E.P.C., Art. 116(2).

appeals and the enlarged board of appeals after publication of the application.[97]

At the pre-grant stage, the hearing will usually be an informal discussion with the receiving section or examining division. Written evidence and documents will normally be used and only in exceptional cases will oral evidence be adduced. The rules, however, require that minutes be kept and be provided to the parties.[98]

Appeals

3.53   Certain decisions of the receiving section and examining divisions are appealable to a board of appeal.[99] However, unless the decision indicates an appeal is permissible therefrom, it may only be appealed either if it is a final decision or together with a final decision.[1] Notice of appeal must be filed at the EPO within two months of the date of notification of the decision.[2] A statement of grounds must be filed within four months.[3] In *ex parte* proceedings the notice of appeal is first considered by the receiving section or examining division who may in clear cases allow the appeal.[4] This procedure is called an interlocutory revision. If the appeal is not allowed within one month it must be remitted to the board of appeal[5] without delay and without comment.

On appeal the board of appeal must invite the party or parties to file observations on points raised by another party or by the board itself[6]

As a result of such exchange of views it may be necessary or desirable to request an oral hearing.[7]

Inspection of files

3.54   Subject to certain exceptions the files are not open to inspection without the consent of the applicant prior to the publication of the application.[8] After publication the files may be inspected on request but subject to certain exceptions.[9]

---

[97] E.P.C., Art. 116(3) and (4).
[98] E.P.C. Rules, r.76(1).
[99] E.P.C., Art. 106(1).
[1] E.P.C., Art. 106(3).
[2] E.P.C., Art. 108; see E.P.C. Rules, r.64 for content of the notice of appeal.
[3] *Ibid.*
[4] E.P.C., Art. 109.
[5] See E.P.C., Art. 21 for constitution of Board of Appeals.
[6] E.P.C., Art. 110(2).
[7] See *ante* § 3.49.
[8] E.P.C., Art. 128; see *ante* § 3.31.
[9] E.P.C., Art. 128(4); E.P.C. Rules, r.93.

4. Opposition to the Grant of a European Patent (U.K.)

Introduction

As from the publication of the mention of its grant in the *European* **3.55**
Patent Bulletin, a European Patent (U.K.) is treated as if it were a patent
granted by the U.K. Patent Office[10] , subject to a translation into English
being filed at the U.K. Patent Office within three months of grant if the
specification is in French or German.[11] However, a European Patent
(U.K.) remains subject to the E.P.C. and in particular to that part of the
Convention providing for opposition proceedings in the EPO after
grant.[12]

Grounds of opposition

Once granted the validity of grant in all designated states can be **3.56**
opposed by an opposition lodged at the EPO. In this respect the validity
of a European patent can be challenged whereas that of a U.K. patent
may not.

Opposition may only be filed on the grounds that:[13]

  (a) the subject matter of the European patent is not patentable within
the terms of Articles 52–57;[14]

  (b) the European patent does not disclose the invention in a manner
sufficiently clear and complete for it to be carried out by a person
skilled in the art;[15]

  (c) the subject matter of the European patent extends beyond the
content of the application as filed, or, if the patent was granted on
a divisional application or on a new application filed in accordance with Article 61, beyond the content of the earlier application
as filed.[16]

Time for opposition

Notice must be given to the EPO within nine months from the **3.57**
publication of the mention of the grant of the European patent in the
European Patent Bulletin,[17] and the opposition fee must be paid within
the same period. An opposition may be filed even if the European patent
has been surrendered or has lapsed for all designated states.[18]

---

[10] P.A. 1977, s.77(1).
[11] P.A. 1977, s.77(6).
[12] E.P.C., Part V.
[13] E.P.C., Art. 100.
[14] Equivalent to PA 1977 ss. 1–3. See (ante § 2.02 *et seq.* and *post* § 2.20 *et seq.* and 5.65 *et seq.*
[15] Equivalent to PA 1977 s.72(1)(c). See *post* § 5.03 *et seq.*
[16] Equivalent to PA 1977 s.72(1)(d). See *post* § 5.96 *et seq.*
[17] E.P.C., Art. 99(1).
[18] E.P.C., Art. 99(3).

The opponent

3.58   Any person may oppose a European patent.[19] "Any person" is to be construed in line with Article 58 of E.P.C. as meaning any natural person (private individual, self–employed persons, etc.), any legal person or any body associated to a legal person under the law governing it.[20] However, a professional representative may not file an opposition in his own name (other than on his own behalf), unless the party whom he represents is identified before the end of the opposition period.[21] Opposition may be filed by a proprietor against his own patent, for the purposes of making amendments in the EPO, rather than in the national Patent Offices of the designated states.[22]

Intervention

3.59   If an opposition is filed, any third party who proves that proceedings for infringement of the same patent have been instituted against him may intervene in the proceedings. Notice of the intervention must be given within three months of the date on which the infringement proceedings were instituted.[23]

Similarly any third party may also intervene if he proves:

(a) that the proprietor of the patent has requested that he cease alleged infringement of the patent, and

(b) that he has instituted proceedings for a court ruling that he is not infringing the patent.[24]

Territorial effect of opposition

3.60   Article 99(2) of the E.P.C. provides that the opposition shall apply to the patent in all contracting states in which the patent has effect. Where the opposition is filed in respect of only some of the designated states it will be treated as if it were in respect of all the designated states.[25]

---

[19] E.P.C., Art. 99(1).

[20] EPO Guidelines D. I. 4.

[21] T10/82 *BAYER/Admissibility of opposition:* [1983] O.J.EPO 407, [1979–85] EPOR:B:381; T25/85 *DEUTSCHE GELATINE-FABRIKEN, STOESS & CO./Opponent-identifiability:* [1986] O.J.EPO81, [1986] EPOR 158.

[22] Decision G1/84 MOBIL OIL/Opposition by proprietor: [1985] O.J.EPO 299, [1986] EPOR 39.

[23] E.P.C., Art. 105(1).

[24] *Ibid.*

[25] EPO Guidelines D. I. 3.

Procedure

Notice of opposition
The Notice of opposition must contain[26]   **3.61**

(a) the name and address of the opponent and the state in which his residence, or principal place of business is located;[27]
(b) the number of the patent against which opposition is filed, and the name of the proprietor and title of the invention;
(c) a statement of the extent to which the patent is opposed and of the grounds on which the opposition is based as well as an indication of the facts, evidence and arguments presented in support of these grounds;
(d) if the opponent has appointed a representative, his name and the address of his place of business.[28]

If the notice is defective, the opponent will be invited to remedy the deficiency. Where the notice fails to comply with E.P.C. Article 99(1), E.P.C. rule 1(1) or rule 55(c) or does not provide sufficient identification of the patent against which opposition has been filed, the deficiency must be remedied before expiry of the opposition period.[29] In other cases, the opposition division shall specify an appropriate period (usually two months) for remedying the deficiency.[30] If the opponent fails to remedy the deficiency the opposition will be rejected as inadmissible or, in certain cases,[31] the opposition will be deemed not to have been filed.

The requirement of rule 55(c) for the notice of opposition to contain "an indication of the facts, evidence and arguments presented in support of" the opposition is fulfilled only if the contents of the notice are sufficient to enable the opponent's case to be properly understood by both the opposition division and the proprietor.[32] Merely citing a prior art document, without identifying the relevant passage within it, may not be adequate.[33]

Substantive examination
Examination is conducted by an opposition division in accordance   **3.62**
with the provision of the implementing regulations.[34] An opposition

---

[26] E.P.C. Rules, r.55 and see *EPO Guidelines* D. III. 6.
[27] See E.P.C. Rules, r.26(2)(c).
[28] *Ibid.*
[29] E.P.C. Rules, r.56(1).
[30] E.P.C. Rules, r.56(2).
[31] *EPO Guidelines* D. IV. 1.2.1.
[32] Decision T222/85 *PPG/Ungelled polyesters:* [1988] O.J.EPO. 128, [1987] EPOR 99.
[33] *Ibid.*
[34] E.P.C., Art. 101; the Implementing Regulations are r.55–63 of E.P.C.

division is made up of three technical examiners at least two of whom shall not have taken part in the proceedings for grant of the patent to which the opposition relates.[35] Normally an opposition division will entrust one of its members with examination of the opposition (but not with the conduct of oral proceedings) up to the time of the final decision of the opposition.[36]

As a general rule the opposition division confines its examination to those grounds of opposition relied upon by the opponent.[37] However, the opposition division is not restricted to those grounds and may of its own motion broaden the inquiry.[38] Like the examination procedure, opposition proceedings are based on the investigative principle, but they are not to be treated as a continuation of the examination proceedings.[39] In particular, it is not open to the opposition division to consider whether a claim is "clear" and supported by the description, as required by Article 84, unless an amendment to the claims is offered during opposition proceedings.[40] Even then, the opposition division is confined to the question whether the amendment itself causes the claim to be unclear or lacking in support.[41]

In preparation of the examination the proprietor of the patent is invited to file his observations on the opposition and to file any amendments he may wish to make.[42] The observations and amendments are communicated to the other parties to the opposition and, if the opposition division considers it expedient, they will be invited to reply.[43] This whole step may be dispensed with in the case of an intervention.[44] Further rounds of observations are possible,[45] but are not usual.

Amendment may be offered at virtually any stage, even during the course of oral proceedings. Amended claims may be put forward in the form of one or more "auxiliary requests", which will be considered only if the opposition division finds the main set of claims not to be valid.

The parties may submit evidence in support of alleged facts.[46]

Evidence may be given or obtained by:

(1) requests for information,
(2) production of documents,
(3) written opinions by experts,

---

[35] E.P.C., Art. 19(2).
[36] E.P.C., Art. 19(2) and see *EPO Guidelines* D. II. 5.
[37] *EPO Guidelines* D. V. 2.
[38] E.P.C., Art. 114(1).
[39] Decision T23/86 *NAIMER/Computer-controlled switch:* [1987] O.J.EPO 316, [1987] EPOR; 383.
[40] *Ibid.*
[41] Decision T301/87 *BIOGEN/Alpha-interferons:* [1990] O.J.EPO 335, [1990] EPOR:190.
[42] E.P.C. Rules, r.57(1).
[43] E.P.C. Rules, r.57(3).
[44] E.P.C. Rules, r.57(4).
[45] E.P.C., Art. 101(2).
[46] *EPO Guidelines* E. IV. 1.2.

(4) inspection,

(5) sworn statements in writing, or

(6) oral hearings.[47]

Although evidence may be submitted at any time, this should be done at the earliest opportunity. Evidence submitted late may not be admitted.[48] If oral proceedings have been requested, the parties will usually be invited by the opposition division to submit any further observations or evidence no later than four weeks before the oral proceedings are scheduled to take place. Evidence filed later will normally be admitted only if it is considered to be determinative of the outcome of the opposition.

In exceptional cases (*e.g.* where the scope of the main claim is narrowed by amendment to a dependent claim originally thought to be of minor importance) the opposition division may carry out an additional search and cite new material.[49] However, as the grant of the patent will have been preceded by a search by the search division, cases involving additional searches are very rare.

The opposition division will first of all endeavour to reach a decision in written proceedings.[50] However, if the division considers it expedient or if any party requests it, oral proceedings will be held.[51] At the oral proceedings the parties may state their cases and put forward and argue submissions. Members of the opposition division may put questions to the parties. If the opposition division considers it necessary, the oral proceedings will include the taking of oral evidence.[52] However, there is no obligation upon the division to take oral evidence, even if a party has requested it.

The decision

The decision of the opposition division may be: **3.63**

(a) to revoke the patent,

(b) to reject the opposition or

(c) maintain the patent as amended.[53]

The decision may only be based on the grounds or evidence on which the parties have had an opportunity to present their comments.[54]

Before deciding to maintain the patent in amended form, the opposition division must inform the parties of its intention and invite

---

[47] *Ibid.*
[48] E.P.C., Art. 114(2).
[49] *EPO Guidelines* D. VI. 5.
[50] *EPO Guidelines* D. VI. 1.
[51] E.P.C., Art. 116.
[52] E.P.C. Rules, r.72(1).
[53] E.P.C., Art. 102.
[54] E.P.C., Art. 113(1).

them to state their observations within two months if they disapprove of the text in which it is intended to maintain the patent.[55] However, the practice of the EPO is to regard this requirement as fulfilled if the amendment is requested during oral proceedings, and the opponent has been given a reasonable opportunity during the oral proceedings to comment on the amendment.[56] The opposition division will then deliver an interlocutory decision, against which an appeal may be lodged.

Costs

3.64   The general rule is that each party pays its own costs. In cases where there have been oral proceedings or evidence has been taken orally, the opposition division may "for reasons for equity" order a different apportionment.[57] For example, costs may be awarded against a party which requests oral proceedings, if no new arguments are raised during the oral proceedings,[58] or which fails to inform the EPO of facts which would have rendered oral proceedings unnecessary if disclosed earlier.[59] Costs may also be awarded against a party which produces new facts or evidence after the end of the opposition period.[60] The apportionment of costs is dealt with in the decision on the opposition although the actual amount to be paid is fixed upon request to the registry of the opposition division at a later date.[61] The fixing of costs by the registry is subject to review by a decision of the opposition division.[62] Any final decision of the EPO fixing the amount of costs may be enforced in the U.K. by the procedure set out in section 93 of the 1977 Act.

Appeal

3.65   An appeal lies from all final decisions of the opposition division to the Board of Appeal. Interlocutory decisions may only be appealed together with the final decision unless the decision allows separate appeal.[63] An appeal has suspensive effect.[64] Notice of Appeal must be filed in writing at the EPO within two months after the date of notification of the decision appealed from.[65] Within four months after the date of

---

[55] E.P.C. Rules, r.58(4).
[56] Decisions T219/83 *BASF/Zeolites:* [1986] O.J.EPO 211, [1986] EPOR 247 and T185/84 *BASF/Paint line supply system:* [1986] O.J.EPO 373, [1987] EPOR 34 and Guideline D. VI 6.2.1.
[57] E.P.C., Art. 104(1).
[58] Decision T167/84 *NISSAN/Fuel injectorvalve:* [1987] O.J.EPO 36, [1987] EPOR 344. (1987/8, 369).
[59] Decision T10/82 *BAYER/Admissibility & opposition:* [1983] O.J.EPO407, [1979–85] EPOR:B:381. (1983/10, 407).
[60] Decision T117/86 *FILMTEC/Costs:* [1989] O.J.EPO 40, [1989] EPOR: 504. (1989/10, 401).
[61] E.P.C., Art. 104(2).
[62] *Ibid.,* for the procedure see E.P.C. Rules, r.63(3).
[63] E.P.C., Art. 106(1) and (3).
[64] E.P.C., Art. 106(1).
[65] E.P.C., Art. 108.

notification, a written statement setting out the grounds of appeal must be filed.[66]

The opposition division has power to rectify its decision if it considers the appeal to be admissible and well–founded.[67]

In general, the provisions relating to the proceedings before the opposition division apply to the appeal proceedings *mutatis mutandis*.[68] Following examination the board may either exercise any power within the competence of the opposition division or remit the case for further consideration.[69]

5. Miscellaneous

Term of patent

Under the 1977 Act the maximum term of a patent is 20 years from the date of filing the application.[70] As regards the transitional provisions for patents granted under the 1949 Act,[71] patents are classified into "new existing patents" and "old existing patents"—*viz* those with more than five years to run as on June 1, 1978, and those with five years or less to run. All old existing patents have now expired. As regards new existing patents the maximum term of such patents is extended from 16 to 20 years from the date of the patent so that the last will expire in 1998.

3.66

Supplementary Protection Certificates

For the special case of pharmaceutical products (which, in general, require extensive testing before marketing approval is granted) Supplementary Protection Certificates were introduced under EEC Regulation No 1768/92 of June 18, 1992.[71a] The certificate is intended to extend the period of protection initially conferred by a patent, once that patent has expired, to compensate to an extent for the patent life lost in obtaining such approval. The duration of the certificate reflects a compromise between the interests of patentees and generic producers and is therefore equal to the patent life lost between patent filing date and the date of first marketing approval in the Community, minus five years, subject to a long stop of five years. The certificate's effects are stated to

3.67

---

[66] *Ibid.*
[67] E.P.C., Art. 109.
[68] E.P.C. Rules, r.66(1).
[69] E.P.C., Art. 111(1).
[70] P.A. 1977, s.25(1).
[71] P.A. 1977, Sched. 1. paras.3 and 4.
[71a] The Regulation has direct effect in the laws of all Member States and the relevant provisions applied from January 2, 1993. The Regulation has been further implemented by the Patents (Supplementary Protection Certificate for Medicinal Products) Regulations 1992 (SI 1992 No. 3091) which allow extension of the 1977 Act to cover certificates by means of the Patents (Supplementary Protection Certificate for Medicinal Products) Rules 1992 (SI 1992 No. 3162).

be the same as the patent on which it is based save that the protection conferred extends only to the product covered by the marketing approval. Drugs which received marketing authorization after January 1, 1985 in the United Kingdom are eligible for a certificate.

Restoration of lapsed patents

3.68   Renewal fees have to be paid annually to maintain a patent in force so that failure to pay the appropriate renewal fees on time will lead to the patent ceasing to have effect.[72] By section 25(4) a period of grace of six months is allowed providing the renewal fee and a supplementary fee is paid within that period. Thereafter restoration of the patent for failure to pay the renewal fees can only be obtained if the requirements of section 28 of the 1977 Act as amended are met.[73] As amended the section provides:

> **28.**—(1) Where a patent has ceased to have effect by reason of a failure to pay any renewal fee, an application for the restoration of the patent may be made to the comptroller within the prescribed period.
>
> (1A) Rules prescribing that period may contain such transitional provisions and savings as appear to the Secretary of State to be necessary or expedient.
>
> (2) An application under this section may be made by the person who was the proprietor of the patent or by any other person who would have been entitled to the patent if it had not ceased to have effect; and where the patent was held by two or more persons jointly, the application may, with the leave of the comptroller, be made by one or more of them without joining the others.
>
> (2A) Notice of the application shall be published by the comptroller in the prescribed manner.
>
> (3) If the comptroller is satisfied that the proprietor of the patent took reasonable care to see that any renewal fee was paid within the prescribed period or that that fee and any prescribed additional fee were paid within the six months immediately following the end of that period, the comptroller shall by order restore the patent on payment of any unpaid renewal fee and any prescribed additional fee.
>
> (4) An order under this section may be made subject to such conditions as the comptroller thinks fit (including a condition requiring compliance with any provisions of the rules relating to registration which have not been complied with), and if the proprietor of the patent does not comply with any condition of such an order the comptroller may revoke the order and give such directions consequential on the revocation as he thinks fit.

---

[72] P.A. 1977, s.25(3).
[73] P.A. 1977, s.28 as amended by C.D.P.A. 1988, Sched. 5, para.6.

Rule 41 of the Patents Rules 1990 currently provides a period of 19 months from the date on which the patent ceased to have effect as being the prescribed period for the purposes of section 28(1). Thus, a proprietor can overlook two annuity payments and still be able to apply to restore the patent. In order to obtain restoration the proprietor must show that he took reasonable care to see that the renewal fee was paid. Prior to amendment section 28(3) required also that he should show that the fees were not paid due to circumstances beyond his control. The combined effect of the amendment to the Act and the rules should ensure that the hardship and confusion created by the old law is mitigated.[74]

What is reasonable care will depend upon the circumstances of the case and will be a question of fact. Evidence must be filed.[75] Where a patentee pays renewal fees himself, as opposed to such fees being paid by a patent agent on his behalf it has been held that he is entitled to rely on the notice from the Patent Office under section 25(5) of the 1977 Act and make the late payment together with the additional fee for late payment. Thus, failure by the Patent Office through no fault of the patentee to send the statutory notice in time will not disentitle the patentee from having his patent restored to him.[76]

Where the proprietor reasonably delegates responsibility for payment of renewal fees to a Patent Agent or a corporate patent department, reasonable care must in general also be demonstrated on the part of the responsible officers. If they take reasonable care, negligence of a properly instructed employee will not prevent restoration.[77]

Section 28A of the 1977 Act[78] makes provision for regulating acts done in the period of lapse where a patent is subsequently restored. Anything done in relation to the patent in that period (*e.g.* assignments or licensing) is valid.[79] An infringing act is actionable providing it took place during the six month period of grace or was the continuation or repetition of an earlier infringing act.[80] Further there are provisions for safeguarding those persons who began in the lapsed period in good faith to do or make effective and serious preparations to do an act which would otherwise have been an infringing act had the patent not lapsed.[81] These provisions equate to the protection given by section 64 of the Act to a person who has secretly, prior, used an invention.[82]

---

[74] Patents Rules 1990, r.41(1)(b).
[75] See *Textron Inc.'s Patent* [1989] R.P.C. 441.
[76] *Ling's Patent* and *Wilson and Pearce's Patent* [1981] R.P.C. 85.
[77] *Textron INC's Patent* [1989] R.P.C. 441; *Frazer's Patent* [1981] R.P.C. 53; *Sony Corporation's Patent* [1990] R.P.C. 152.
[78] Inserted by C.D.P.A. 1988, Sched. 5, para.7.
[79] P.A. 1977, s.28A(2).
[80] P.A. 1977, s.28A(3).
[81] P.A. 1977, s.28A(4)–(7).
[82] See *post*, § 6.67.

The restoration provisions apply to existing patents as well as patents created under the 1977 Act.[83]

Secret patents

3.69   Where application is made for a patent in respect of either:

(a) a class that has been notified to the Comptroller by the Secretary of State as containing information the publication of which might be prejudicial to the defence of the realm, or

(b) a class that contains information the publication of which might be prejudicial to the safety of the public, the Comptroller may give directions for keeping secret any information concerning the invention.[84]

As regards (b), directions can only be given by the Comptroller for a period of up to three months after what would have been the date for publication;[85] however, such time can be extended by the Secretary of State if he considers the safety of the public is at risk.[86] While directions are in force the application may only proceed up to the stage where it is in order for grant but it is not published and no patent is granted thereon.[87] If the application is for a European patent or an international application for a patent, it is not to be sent to the relevant processing institution.[88] The position must be reviewed within the first nine months from the date of filing of the application and thereafter at least once in every period of 12 months.[89] Once secrecy directions are revoked, the Comptroller may extend the time for doing anything required to be done in connection with the application.[90] If any use of a secret invention is made by a government department after the application had been brought into order for grant (and after the period for publication has expired) or if the applicant suffers hardship by reason of the secrecy directions, compensation may be claimed.[91] No renewal fees are payable during the period of secrecy.[92]

---

[83] P.A. 1977, Sched. 2, para.1.
[84] P.A. 1977, s.22(1), (2).
[85] P.A. 1977, s.22(2).
[86] P.A. 1977, s.22(5).
[87] P.A. 1977, s.22(3).
[88] *Ibid.*; in the case of the European patent, to the EPO; in the case of the international application to the International Bureau.
[89] P.A. 1977, s.22(5).
[90] *Ibid.*
[91] P.A. 1977, s.22(7).
[92] P.A. 1977, s.22(8).

Disclosure between earlier and later applications

The use or publication of any matter described in an earlier **3.70** application which forms the basis of a claim to priority[93] shall not invalidate the later application or any patent granted thereon.[94] Thus, an applicant after complying with the minimum of formalities has a limited period within which he can freely disclose the invention, *e.g.* for the purpose of obtaining financial assistance without adversely affecting his rights.

Rights on publication of application

From the date of publication of the application until the grant of the **3.71** patent, an applicant has the same right as he would have had if the patent had been granted on the date of publication, except that he cannot institute proceedings for infringement until the patent has been granted.[95] However, in order to obtain relief for infringement in respect of acts committed prior to grant it must be established that the allegedly infringing act infringes the claims of the application (in the form they were just prior to publication) as well as the claims of the patent as granted.[96]

Abandoned applications

In the event of an application being abandoned or becoming void **3.72** before publication the application, specification, drawings, specimens and samples left in connection with the application are not thereafter published nor are they open to public inspection.[97] This general position is subject to certain exceptions,[98] one of which is where the applicant later applies for a new application relating to the subject-matter of the earlier abandoned application, if the later application is published.

6. Employee's Rights to Compensation

Where an invention is made after June 1, 1978,[99] by an employee who **3.73** is employed or mainly employed in the United Kingdom or, if not mainly employed anywhere and his place of employment cannot be determined, then if his employer has a place of business in the United

---

[93] Under the 1977 Act s.5(2) and (5), the relevant application.
[94] P.A. 1977, s.6.
[95] P.A. 1977, s.69(1), (2); corresponding provisions apply to European patent applications—see E.P.C., Art. 67.
[96] P.A. 1977, s.69(2)(*b*).
[97] P.A. 1977, s.118(2); this provision together with s.118(3) also applies to existing patents.
[98] P.A. 1977, s.118(3) to (5).
[99] P.A. 1977, s.43(1).

Kingdom to which the employee is attached,[1] then the employee may have a claim against his employer for compensation in respect of a patent granted for such invention. Patent is defined as a patent or other protection and references to its being granted mean references to its being granted whether under the law of the United Kingdom or the law in force in any other country or under any treaty or international convention.[2] Whether an employee has such a claim will be considered under two separate categories, first where the employee has made an invention belonging to the employer, and secondly where the invention belongs to the employee.

Inventions belonging to employer

3.74   Where it can be established by an inventor-employee that a patent (of which he is the inventor) is of outstanding benefit to the employer, and that it is just that the employee should be awarded compensation, the court or Comptroller may award such compensation to secure for the employee a fair share of the benefit which the employee has derived or may reasonably be expected to derive from the patent.[3]

Outstanding benefit

3.75   The onus is on the employee to show outstanding benefit, and that the benefit was derived from the patent rather than the invention.[4] The aims may shift to the employer, but this will depend upon the evidence before the court, there is no presumption that returns obtained from the sales of goods or services, the subject of a patent, were due in part to the patent.[4a]

Whether any benefit is outstanding is a question of fact, but the Act directs that both the size and nature of the employer's undertaking are relevant considerations. The word outstanding indicates actual, and not potential benefit. It implies a superlative and means something out of the ordinary which would not be expected to arise from the results of the duties for which the employee was paid.[4b] Benefit is defined as being benefit in money or moneys worth.[5] Regard must be had to the costs of any investment of resources or any investment in marketing incurred by the employer. Hence there is a similarity to the inquiry as to whether a patentee would have been entitled to an extension of the term of a patent under the 1949 Act for inadequate remuneration.[6]

---

[1] P.A. 1977, s.43(2).
[2] P.A. 1977, s.43(4), and see *Menco-Med Ltd's Patent* [1992] R.P.C. 403; *G.E.C. Avionic's Patent* [1992] R.P.C. 107; *British Steel PLC's Patent* [1992] R.P.C. 117.
[3] P.A. 1977, s.40(1) and s.41(1).
[4] *Menco-Med Ltd.'s Patent* [1992] R.P.C. 403; *G.E.C. Avionics Patent* [1992] R.P.C. 107; *British Steel Plc's Patent* [1992] R.P.C. 117.
[4a] *Menco-Ltd.'s Patent* [1992] R.P.C. 403 at p.415, not following on this part of the decision *G.E.C. Avionics Patent* [1992] R.P.C. 107.
[4b] See note 4.
[5] P.A. 1977, s.43(1).11.
[6] P.A. 1949, s.23; see in particular s.23(5) the profits made by the patentee "as such."

Fair Share (Inventions belonging to employer)

3.76 In determining the fair share of the benefit the court or Comptroller shall take the following matters into account:[7]

(a) the nature of the employee's duties, his remuneration and the other advantages he derives or has derived from his employment or the invention

(b) the effort and skill which
   (i) the employee has devoted to making the invention and
   (ii) any other person has devoted including advice or other assistance by any other employee not a joint inventor[8] and

(c) the contribution made by the employer to the making, developing and working of the invention.

Inventions belonging to the employee

3.77 The court or the Comptroller will award compensation where it can be established that:

(a) a patent has been granted for an invention made by and belonging to an employee

(b) his rights in the invention, application or patent have been assigned to the employer or an exclusive licence has been granted to the employer,

(c) the benefit derived by the employee from the assignment or licence is inadequate in relation to the benefit derived by the employer from the patent; and

(d) it is just that the employee should be awarded compensation in addition to the benefit already received.[9]

Once more it is the benefit that the employer derives from the patent, not the invention, that has to be considered and in this case measured against the benefit derived by the employee from the assignment of his rights in the invention.

Fair Share (Inventions belonging to employee)

3.78 The court or Comptroller must consider the following matters[9a]

(a) any conditions in any licence granted in respect of the invention or patent

(b) the extent to which the invention was made jointly by the employee with any other person and

---

[7] P.A. 1977, s.41(4).
[8] See P.A. 1977, s.43(3) where making an invention excludes merely contributing advice or other assistance and see *British Steel PLC's Patent* [1992] R.P.C. 117.
[9] P.A. 1977, s.40(2).
[9a] P.A. 1977, s.41(5).

(c) the contribution made by the employer to the making, developing and working of the invention.

For employees' inventions the nature of the employee's duties and his remuneration are not to be taken into account, whilst terms in any licences granted by the employer are. In other respects the matters to be taken account of are the same as for employer's inventions.

Claims procedure[10]

3.79   A claim may be made at any time after the patent is granted and prior to the expiration of one year after it ceases to have effect.[11] The claimant will generally be the employee but where he dies before an award is made his personal representatives or their successors in title may exercise his right to make or proceed with an application.[12]

The fact that a claimant has made an earlier application for an award (whether successful or not) will not prevent a further application in respect of the same invention.[13] Equally once an order has been made it can be subsequently varied or discharged, suspended or revised as the case may be.[14]

Contracting out of the awards provisions

3.80   Rights to compensation will be substituted where there is a collective agreement between a trade union to which the employee belongs and the employer or an employers' association.[15] Apart from this, in the case of employees' inventions it is not possible for an employer to compromise the employee's right to compensation.[16]

As regards an employers' invention it is possible to compromise a claim to compensation once the invention has been made; in the case of prospective inventions however it is not possible to diminish an employee's right to compensation.[17]

An employer can not avoid the claim to compensation where he assigns the patent or application for the patent to a person connected with the employer.[18] In such a case to determine the benefit derived by the employer the court will assess the amount that could reasonably be expected to have been derived if the transaction had been an arms length one.[19]

---

[10] See Patents Rules 1990, r.59 for detailed procedure.
[11] Patents Rules 1978, r.60(2); special provisions related to where a patent has lapsed.
[12] P.A. 1977, s.43(6).
[13] P.A. 1977, s.41(7)
[14] P.A. 1977, s.41(8) and Patents Rules 1990, r.60.
[15] P.A. 1977, s.40(3) and (6).
[16] P.A. 1977, s.40(4).
[17] P.A. 1977, s.42(1) and (2).
[18] P.A. 1977, s.41(1).
[19] P.A. 1977, s.41(2).

6. Marking

Marking article "patented," "patent applied for"

If any person falsely represents that anything disposed of by him for **3.81** value is a patented product he is liable on summary conviction to a fine.[20]

To dispose of an article for value having stamped, engraved or impressed on it or otherwise applied to it the word "patent" or "patented" or anything expressing or implying that the article is a patented product will be taken to represent that the article is a patented product.[21] Patent includes a European patent (U.K.).[22] Similar provisions apply to where a person falsely represents that a patent has been applied for or that a patent is pending.[23] Application includes an application for a European patent (U.K.).[24] It is no offence, however, to describe an article as patented or patent applied for after the patent or application for a patent relating thereto has expired or has been revalued or withdrawn within a period thereafter not reasonably sufficient to enable the accused to take steps to ensure the representation is not made or continued to be made.[25]

It is a defence for the accused to prove that he used due diligence to prevent the commission of the offence.[26] If there is a patent it is only a defence if it can be established that the claims of the patent relied upon, on a proper construction, cover the article sold as "patented".[27]

Marking article "licensed"

In a case where a licence had been revoked and the former licensees **3.82** were sued for infringement, the words "manufactured under licence form the P.C. Co". were, upon a motion for an interlocutory injunction, ordered to be removed.[28] But where "made under Ormond patent" appeared on the goods, the patentee failed in an action for passing off.[29]

---

[20] P.A. 1977, s.110(1); this applies to new and existing patents. The maximum fine is not exceeding level 3 on the standard scale (£1000), see Criminal Justice Act 1982, s.37(2) as substituted by Criminal Justice Act 1991, s.17.

[21] P.A. 1977, s.110(2).

[22] P.A. 1977, s.77(1)(*b*).

[23] P.A. 1977, s.111.

[24] P.A. 1977, s.78(1).

[25] P.A. 1977, s.110(3), s.111(2).

[26] P.A. 1977, s.110(4), s.111(4).

[27] *Esco Ltd. v. Rolo Ltd.* (1923) 40 R.P.C. 471.

[28] *Post Card Automatic Supply Co. v Samuel* (1889) 6 R.P.C. 560; See *Austin Baldwin, etc. v. Greenwood etc.* (1925) 42 R.P.C. 454; *British and International Proprietaries Ltd. v. Selcol Products Ltd.* [1957] R.P.C. 3.

[29] *Ormond Engineering Co. v. Knopf* (1932) 49 R.P.C. 634.

CHAPTER 4

THE SPECIFICATION

Contents   *Para.*

1. History

History of the specification

4.01   In the early days of the patent system the working of the invention was part of the consideration for the grant; and in many cases provisions were inserted in the patent requiring the instruction of apprentices.[1] In the case of one invention only was the grantee required to publish a description of his invention,[2] and there is some reason for supposing that this was done at the instance of the patentee himself.[3]

The requirement of a specification appears to have been introduced originally merely as a means of ascertaining the ambit of the monopoly claimed, and not with a view to ensuring that the public were placed in possession of the invention, though this naturally followed. The original practice was merely to state the subject-matter of the invention in very general terms in the patent itself.[4] It was thus open to the patentee to allege that anything which fell within this general description was an infringement of the patent. The difficulties caused by this practice were met to a limited extent by introducing into the recitals technical details of the invention.[5] In 1711, however, we find it stated in Naismith's Patent No. 387 that the patentee "has proposed to ascertain" the details of his invention "in writing under his hand and seal to be enrolled in our Court of Chancery" within six months after the date of the patent. And

---

[1] See Hulme, 12, 13 L.Q.R.; Co.Inst. 3.
[2] *Sturtevant and Rovinson's Patents* (1611–12); see Supplement to Patent Office Series of Specifications.
[3] See Hulme, 16 L.Q.R.
[4] *E.g.* 1 W.P.C. 9; Gordon 240 (Gilbert's "Water Plough" Patent).
[5] *E.g.* Pownall's Patent No. 391 (1712).

after 1716 a proviso requiring this to be done was inserted in every patent.

The Form

Until 1852 patents were granted in all cases upon applications which **4.02** specified the "title" only of the invention, and no obligation to file a specification arose until the patent was sealed. The period of six months, allowed for furnishing the description, was to ensure that the inventor should not be forestalled before he could complete the invention and bring it to a practical form. It was, however, necessary that the specification should not be inconsistent with or wider than the "title" (which still continued to form the basis of the grant), and patents were frequently held invalid on the ground of variance between the title and the specification as constituting a "fraud on the Crown".[6] The 1852 Act effected a change in the procedure on application, and an inventor had thereafter to file either a "provisional" or a "complete" specification at the time he made his application. This practice has continued ever since.

Under the 1949 Act, every non-convention application had to be accompanied by either a complete specification or a provisional specification (followed by a complete specification within a period of 15 months) and every convention application had to be accompanied by a complete specification.[7] Under the 1977 Act an application for a patent must contain a specification.[8]

2. Existing Specifications Under the 1949 Act

Provisional Specifications

Under the 1949 Act a patentee could apply for a patent by either filing **4.03** a provisional or complete specification. The primary object of the legislature in providing for the filing of a provisional specification was to enable the inventor to improve and perfect the invention during the period of "provisional protection"[9] and at the same time maintain as the priority date of the later filed "complete specification" the date of the earlier filed provisional specification.

In *Newall v. Elliott*[10] Byles J. said:

"The office of the provisional specification is only to describe

---

[6] See *Brunton v. Hawkes* (1821), 4 Barn. & Ald. 541; see also *Cochrane v. Smethurst* (1816), Dav. P.C. 354; *R. v. Else* (1785), 1 W.P.C. 76; *Bloxam v. Elsee* (1827), 6 Barn. & Cress, 169; *Croll v. Edge* (1850), 9 C.B. 479.
[7] P.A. 1949, s.3(1).
[8] P.A. 1977, s.14(2).
[9] See Terrell (13th ed.), §3.10.
[10] (1858) 4 C.B.(N.S.) 269 at p.293.

generally and fairly the nature of the invention, and not to enter into all the minute details as to the manner in which the invention is to be carried out."

In *Stoner v. Todd*[11] Jessel M. R. said:

"A provisional specification was never intended to be more than a mode of protecting an inventor until the time of filing a final specification; it was not intended to contain a complete description of the thing so as to enable any workman of ordinary skill to make it, but only to disclose the invention, fairly no doubt, but in its rough state."

and, as explained by Lloyd–Jacob J., sitting as the Patents Appeal Tribunal, in *Glaxo Group Ltd.'s Application*:[12]

"The interval of time between the filing of the two specifications [*i.e.* the provisional and the complete] is intended to provide an opportunity for the development and precise expression of the invention foreshadowed in the provisional..."

In *I.C.I. (Clark's Application)* Lloyd–Jacob J.[13] stated that all the provisional specification needed to contain was "a description of the general nature of the invention, its field of application and the anticipated result".

Effect of provisional specification on "priority date"

4.04   Since the 1977 Act the only relevance of a provisional specification is to establish the "priority date" of the claims of an existing patent. No publication, use, or claiming in another patent, which occurs after the priority date of a claim, can affect its validity. In the case of an application accompanied by a provisional specification, the priority date of a claim will be the date of the application if (but only if) the claim is "fairly based on the matter disclosed in that specification",[14] otherwise the priority date is the date of filing of the complete specification.[15] This is still the law relating to existing patents under the 1977 Act. Where there is conflict on priority date between a patent granted under the 1949 Act and the 1977 Act, section 128 of the 1977 Act may be relevant.

---

[11] (1876) 4 Ch.D. 58.
[12] *Glaxo Group Ltd.'s Appn.* [1968] R.P.C. 473 at p.480.
[13] [1969] R.P.C. 574 at 583.
[14] P.A. 1949, s.5(2).
[15] P.A. 1949, s.5(6).

Rules to determine whether "fairly based"

In *Mond Nickel Co.'s Application*[16] Lloyd–Jacob J., sitting as the Patents   **4.05**
Appeal Tribunal, said:

"It seems to me that there is a threefold investigation which is called
for. First, one has to inquire whether the alleged invention as claimed
can be said to have been broadly described in the provisional
specification, and only if an affirmative answer is given to that
question does one proceed to the second question, which is: Is there
anything in the provisional specification which is inconsistent with
the alleged invention as claimed? If it is found, upon examination,
that the invention as characterised in the claim includes something
which is inconsistent with that which is described in the provisional
specification, as at present advised I should think that it would be
right to conclude that the claim could not have been fairly based upon
the disclosure; but, assuming that those two burdens are satisfactorily
surmounted, there is, I think, a third matter for inquiry: Does the
claim include as a characteristic of the invention a feature as to which
the provisional specification is wholly silent?"

In *Imperial Chemical Industries Ltd.'s Application*[17] Lloyd–Jacob J. said   **4.06**
that in his above statement:

"the word 'broadly' was used in respect of the description and carried
the meaning of 'in a general sense', such as would be exemplified by a
statement in the provisional specification that reaction products were
dissolved in hot water, where the complete specification introduced a
specific temperature range ... The function of the provisional
specification is to provide a description of the alleged invention, and,
if such description includes as essential a requirement for its
performance [three specified chemical substances] as does this
provisional specification, a claim which does not require one such
essential requirement to be adopted is neither logically nor legitim-
ately founded upon it."

Whilst the rules set out by Lloyd–Jacob J. have been accepted as   **4.07**
assisting in the decision whether or not a claim is fairly based on a
provisional specification, they should not be treated as a substitute for
the words of the Act.

The fact that a provisional specification is in wide general terms will
not prevent a claim in a complete specification drafted in more precise
and restricted claims being fairly based on such disclosure.[18] The third
test in the *Mond Nickel Case, see supra* is not applicable where the

---

[16] [1956] R.P.C. 189 at p.194.
[17] [1960] R.P.C. 223 at p.228.
[18] *British Drug Houses Ltd.'s Appn.* [1964] R.P.C. 237; *Glaxo Group Ltd.'s Appn.* [1968] R.P.C.
473.

characteristic as to which the provisional specification is wholly silent, necessarily results from matters disclosed in such specification.[19]

4.08   The Court of Appeal in *Stauffer Chemical Co.'s Application*[20-22] (a case concerned with the fair basis of a complete specification founded on a convention application) made it clear that the word "fairly" does not take account of the applicants' conduct, but depends upon the contents and language of the priority documents. As Roskill L. J. said:

> "If the other conditions are satisfied, the entitlement to the earlier priority date is unconditional and not the subject of judicial discretion founded upon some subjective concept of good behaviour. A claim otherwise well-founded under section 5(4) does not become ill-founded because it may lead to a result which some might consider unfortunate or morally wrong."

However, the Court did go on to point out that developments and additions may be incorporated providing the additional features do not involve inventive steps or a departure from the idea described in the convention application.

4.09   All that has been said above in relation to the claim being fairly based on a prior provisional specification is equally applicable to the case where what purported to be a complete specification was filed with the application and was subsequently treated as a provisional specification.[23]

Convention application priority

4.10   The 1949 Act sets out three requirements for a claim, in a complete specification filed pursuant to a convention application, to have the priority date of the convention application. First, the application must be for an invention in respect of which protection has been applied for in a convention country.[24] Secondly, the complete specification must be filed in pursuance of such appliation and thirdly, the claim must be "fairly based" on the disclosure in the relevant foreign application.

The first requirement involves a comparison of the inventions disclosed in the British and foreign applications, and the third, the matters considered above in respect of whether claims are fairly based upon a provisional specification.[25]

4.11   Section 69(2) provides that:

---

[19] *Letraset Ltd. v. Rexel Ltd.* [1974] R.P.C. 175 at 197.
[20-22] [1977] R.P.C. 33.
[23] P.A. 1949, s.3(5).
[24] *Polaroid Corp.'s Patent* [1981] R.P.C. 111.
[25] *Kopat's Patent* [1965] R.P.C. 404; *Stauffer Chemical Co.'s Appn.* [1977] R.P.C. 33; *Polaroid Corporation's Patent* [1980] R.P.C. 441.

"matter shall be deemed to have been disclosed in an application for protection in a convention country if it was claimed or disclosed (otherwise than by way of disclaimer or acknowledgment of prior art) in that application or in documents submitted by the applicant for protection in support of and at the same time as that application."

In *E. I. du Pont de Nemours and Co.'s Application*[26] Lloyd–Jacob J., sitting as the P.A.T., said:

"It will be observed that this subsection specifically constitutes the claims a disclosure, but in doing so it expresses a distinction between matter claimed and matter disclosed … It is not that the claims in a convention application are assimilated to the general disclosure in the body of the specification, but that they are deemed to constitute a disclosure of their own, so that, if another claim may be fairly based upon them, the applicant is entitled to priority therefor. This he secures in addition to his right to seek claims fairly based upon the disclosure in the body of the specification, for which he may claim the date to which his original application for patent protection entitled him."

If the complete specification is filed pursuant to two or more applications accompanied by provisional specifications or two or more convention applications, and a claim (being fairly based on the disclosure in more than one prior specification) might otherwise have more than one priority date, the earlier or earliest is the effective one.[27]

Reference to provisional specification

The provisional specification can also be referred to for any admissions that it may contain as to the prior art.[28]　　　　　　　　　　　**4.12**

Lord Esher stated in *Parkinson v. Simon*:

"How are we to get at what is the real object of the plaintiffs' patent? I think it is true to say that you may look for that purpose at the provisonal specification. For the object of the complete specification is to carry out in detail that which is more generally expressed in the provisional specification."[29]

Although this statement may be open to criticism, it has been followed.[30] But if the provisional specification contains a description of the manner

---

[26] [1979] 71 R.P.C. 263.
[27] P.A. 1949, s.5(5).
[28] *British Celanese Ltd. v. Courtaulds Ltd.* (1933) 50 R.P.C. 259 at p.270.
[29] *Parkinson v. Simon* (1894) 11 R.P.C. 493 at p.503.
[30] *Chapman and Cook v. Deltavis Ltd.* (1930) 47 R.P.C. 163 at p.171; *British Celanese Ltd. v. Courtaulds Ltd.* (1932) 49 R.P.C. 63 at p.84.

in which the invention may be carried into effect, it does not follow that, if the complete specification describes a better method, the earlier method is thereby disclaimed.[31] There is no such doctrine as "file wrapper" estoppel as exists in the United States and generally the court will not look beyond the complete specification in construing the ambit of its claims.

"Disconformity" abolished

4.13   An allegation of "disconformity" between the invention claimed in the complete specification and that disclosed in the provisional can no longer be relied on. Under the 1949 Act every claim has its own priority date. Where a claim includes a number of alternatives, there is no provision in the Act for attributing different priority dates to the different alternatives, and the claim as a whole will have the latest priority date to be attributable to any one of the alternatives.[32] However, in certain circumstances such a claim may be split so as to maintain the earliest priority date in respect of one claim.[33] If there was no disclosure of the invention the subject of the claim, by the applicant or a person from whom he derives title, in a provisional specification, or, in the case of a convention application, in the relevant foreign application, prior to the date when the claim itself was filed (it being part of the complete specification) the priority date of the claim will be the date of its filing.[34] In that case it can be attacked by reason of any disclosure occurring prior to that date irrespective of whether other claims have an earlier priority date or not.

The Complete Specification

4.14   By sections 4(3) and 4(4) of the 1949 Act a complete specification shall:

    (a) particularly describe the invention and the method by which it is to be performed;

    (b) disclose the best method of performing the invention which is known to the applicant and for which he is entitled to claim protection;

    (c) end with a claim or claims defining the scope of the invention claimed;

    (d) have a claim or claims which;

        (i)   relate to a single invention,

---

[31] *Sandow Ltd. v. Szalay* (1905) 22 R.P.C. 6 at p.14; *Furr v. Truline (C.O.) (Building Products)* [1985] F.S.R. 553.

[32] *Thornhill's Appn.* [1962] R.P.C. 199.

[33] *Farbenfabriken Bayer A.G.'s Patent* [1966] R.P.C. 278; *Anderson's Appn.* [1966] F.S.R. 218; *Bristol Myers Co.'s Appn.* [1966] F.S.R. 223; *Wellcome Foundation Ltd.'s Appn.* [1968] R.P.C. 107.

[34] P.A. 1949, s.5(6).

(ii) are clear and succinct,
(iii) are fairly based on the matter disclosed in complete specification.

All but d(i) above of these positive requirements are reflected in the provisions for revocation of an old existing patent once granted and will be considered in the next chapter together with the other grounds of invalidity.

3. Specifications Under the 1977 Act

Filing
The date of filing an application is the date when:[35]   **4.15**

(a) the documents filed contain an indication that a patent is sought;
(b) the documents identify the applicants;
(c) the documents contain a description of the invention; and
(d) the filing fee is paid.

This enables a specification to be filed to claim priority rather like a provisional specification under the 1949 Act. Claims and an abstract can be filed later.[36] Provision is also made[37] for filing a further application in respect of any part of the matter contained in an earlier application and for such further application to have the date of filing of the earlier application.[38] It should be noted that the further application can only have the filing date of the earlier application if it is in respect of any part of the matter contained in the earlier application. The filing date is important as it determines the priority date as discussed below.

The Specification
Although section 15 of the Act enables provisional documents to be   **4.16**
filed to secure an early filing date, section 14 of the Act requires that every application for a patent must be made in the prescribed form,[39] must contain a request for grant of a patent, a specification and an abstract. All documents, except drawings, should be in English.[40]
The specification must disclose the invention in a manner which is clear enough and complete enough for the invention to be performed by

---

[35] P.A. 1977, s.15(1).
[36] P.A. 1977, s.15(5).
[37] P.A. 1977, s.15(4).
[38] P.A. 1977, s.5(2).
[39] Patents Rules 1990, r.16 *et seq*.
[40] Patents Rules 1990, r.20. *Rohde and Schwarz's Appn.* [1980] R.P.C. 155.

a person skilled in the art.[41] What is disclosed is a question of construction for the Judge when properly instructed. It should be noted that it is not necessary to describe the best method known to the applicant.

4.17   The specification must also end with a claim or claims which must[42] define the matter for which the applicant seeks protection, be clear and concise, be supported by the description and relate to one invention or to a group or inventions which are so linked as to form a single inventive concept. The requirement of clarity is similar to that of the 1949 Act,[43] and the requirement that the claim must be "supported" by the description whilst worded differently from the 1949 Act requirement that the claim must be "fairly based" is probably in substance very similar.[44]

In *Genentech Inc. v. Wellcome Foundation* the Court of Appeal held that the width of claim is not a ground of revocation under section 72(1) of the 1977 Act nor under Article 100 of the E.P.C. (the *Grounds for Opposition*). Indeed it should be noted that the only ground of revocation relating to the content of the specification is that of failure to disclose the invention clearly or completely enough for it to be performed by the person skilled in the art.[45]. It is therefore incumbent on the Patent Office to ensure that, prior to the grant of the patent, claims are properly supported by the description and are clear and concise. In *Glatt's Application*[46] on a fair reading of the specifications as a whole it was held that the claims could not be supported by the description in that they were not limited to air permeable conditioning fabrics which formed the basis of the invention as described. Whitford J. went on to state that had such claims been allowed in the wide form a court might well in infringement proceedings have construed them as being limited to air permeable fabrics.

In *Protoned BV's Application*[47] an amendment was sought to delete from the claim the word "compression" in the expression "mechanical compression spring". Whitford J. held not only would such an amendment result in "added matter" of other types of spring contrary to section 76(2)(*a*) but also such a claim would not be supported by the description and therefore would be contrary to section 14(4)(*c*).

---

[41] P.A. 1977, s.14(3).
[42] P.A. 1977, s.14(5).
[43] P.A. 1949, s.4.
[44] *Glatt's Appn.* [1983] R.P.C. 122.
[45] P.A. 1977, s.72(1)(*c*).
[46] See n.44.
[47] [1983] F.S.R. 10.

Micro-organism patents

The general provisions of the 1977 Act apply, but specific provision is **4.18** made for deposit and availability of the organism.[48] Section 14(3) requires the specification to disclose the invention in a manner which is clear enough and complete enough for the invention to be performed by a person skilled in the art.

Where a patent relates to an invention which requires the use of a micro-organism which is not available to the public at the date of filing, section 14(3) is satisfied if, at the date of filing, a culture of the micro-organism is deposited in a recognised depository institution and the name of such institution, the date when the culture was deposited and the number of the deposit are provided either in the application as filed or are added thereto within the time limits specified in Schedule 2, paragraph 1(3) of the 1990 Rules; paragraph 1(5) of Schedule 2 also requires the specification to mention any international agreement under which the micro-organism is deposited.

In *Chinoin's Application*[49] Falconer J. held that Rule 17 did not require the deposit of every strain of a new species to support a claim relating to that species but that the deposit of one strain would only support that strain and strains derived therefrom.

The abstract

The abstract is intended to give technical information and may be **4.19** reframed by the Comptroller.[50] The abstract when published does not form part of the "state of the art".[51]

European Patents

Under section 77 of the 1977 Act, European patents are treated as **4.20** patents granted in pursuance of applications under the 1977 Act.

Priority date

The priority date of an invention to which an application for a patent **4.21** relates and any matter contained in an application is the date of filing the application;[52] subject to the right of an applicant to claim by way of declaration the date of filing of an earlier application. This right applies to applications filed in convention countries.[53]

---

[48] P.A. 1977, s.125(a) (as from 7th Jan. 1991) and Patents Rules 1990, r.17 and Sched.2. See also § 3.19.

[49] *Chinoin's Appn.* [1986] R.P.C. 39; see also *Genentech Inc. v. The Wellcome Foundation* [1989] R.P.C. 147 where *Chinoin's Appn.* is considered.

[50] P.A. 1977, s.14(7).

[51] P.A. 1977, s.2(3).

[52] P.A. 1977, s.5(1).

[53] P.A. 1977, s.5(4).

4.22 To enable a successful claim to be made to the filing date of an earlier application, the following formal conditions must be satisfied:

(a) the claim by declaration must be made by the applicant or a predecessor in title of his;

(b) the declaration must specify one or more earlier relevant applications, each having a date of filing during the period of 12 months immediately preceding the date of filing of the application in suit.[54]

4.23 Providing the above formal conditions are satisfied, then any invention to which the application in suit relates, which is supported by matter disclosed in the earlier relevant application or applications, will be entitled to the priority of the earliest relevant application containing such disclosure.[55] Further the priority date of any matter contained in the application in suit which was disclosed in an earlier application will be the earliest relevant application containing such disclosure.[56] The determination of the priority date not only of the invention, but also of the matter contained in the specification is important for the purpose of the date at which the state of the art is to be determined for anticipation,[57] obviousness[58] and also as a disclosure against other patents.[59] It is sensible therefore that the required declaration should be made wherever possible.

4.24 In the case where an invention or other matter was disclosed in two earlier applications by the same applicant, then priority can only be claimed from the first and the second will be disregarded, unless the second application was filed in the same country as the first and before the second was filed the first was withdrawn, abandoned or refused without having been made available to the public, without leaving any rights outstanding and without serving to establish a priority date for any other application.[60] These provisions are to prevent applications extending the period of 12 months provided in the Act.[61]

4.25 Section 125(2) provides that where more than one invention is specified in any claim, each invention may have a different priority date. This provision should be read together with section 14(5) which states that the claim or claims shall relate to one invention or a group of inventions which are so linked to form a single inventive concept. Thus, a single claim can contain more than one invention and each invention may have a different priority date. However the word "specified"

---

[54] P.A. 1977, s.5(2).
[55] P.A. 1977, s.5(2)(a).
[56] P.A. 1977, s.5(2)(b).
[57] P.A. 1977, s.2(1), (2).
[58] P.A. 1977, s.3.
[59] P.A. 1977, s.2(3).
[60] P.A. 1977, s.5(3).
[61] P.A. 1977, s.5(2).

in section 125(2) suggests that such can only occur where both inventions are set out and not where a wide claim encompasses two inventions.[61a]

Priority date—the test

If a priority date earlier than the date of filing is sought pursuant to **4.26** section 5(2), then the earlier priority will be obtained if the invention "is supported by matter disclosed in the earlier relevant application". These words are similar to those in section 14(5)(c) in respect of support of the claims. It is submitted that disclosure can be explicit or implicit and will be a matter of construction by the court when properly instructed.

The requirement under the 1977 Act that the invention must be "supported by matter disclosed" should be contrasted with the requirement under the 1949 Act that the claim must be "fairly based on the matter disclosed".[62] Two differences are apparent; first, there is no explicit requirement in the 1977 Act that the support should be "fair" and secondly, the change from "basis" to "support". It is submitted that despite these two apparent differences there is little difference in practice. To construe the word "supported" as not requiring a fair or proper support would be inconsistent with the purpose of the section. However, the change from "basis" to "supported" may require a more detailed disclosure under the 1977 Act than under the 1949 Act. The word "basis" suggests that it is sufficient to disclose the main principles or features; whereas "supported" indicates a more detailed disclosure which would include supplying all the necessaries of the invention.

By virtue of section 130(7), section 5 is to be construed as to have "as nearly as practicable the same effects in the U.K. as the corresponding provisions of the E.P.C. have".

Article 88(3) requires the elements of the European Application to be included in the application or applications whose priority is claimed.

Article 88(4) of the E.P.C. states that if certain elements of the invention for which priority is claimed do not appear among the claims formulated in the previous application, priority may, nonetheless, be granted provided that the documents of the previous application as a whole specifically disclose such elements. EPO Guidelines (C–V, 2.1–2.5) specify that an element may be a feature disclosed or it may be the combination of certain features. The basic test is that the subject-matter of the claim must be derivable directly and unambiguously from the disclosure of the invention in the priority documents when account is taken of any features implicit to a person skilled in the art in what is expressly mentioned in the document.

[61a] See also *Hallen Co. v. Brabantia* [1990] F.S.R. 134 where Aldous J. tested for the presence of a number of discrete claims by applying the old law of prior claiming.
[62] P.A. 1949, s.53(3).

Divisional Patents

4.27   Whilst section 15(4) of the 1977 Act permits an applicant to file a divisional application, to maintain the earlier date of the parent patent, no new matter may be added as this would be contrary to section 76(1).[63] Thus, in contrast to the 1949 Act, it is no longer possible to have a series of divisionals relating to added matter with cascading priorities.[64]

4. General Principles of Construction

4.28   Patent specifications are construed like other documents and the normal rules of construction of documents apply. This is so whether the patents were granted under the 1949 Act or the 1977 Act. Thus, the cases decided under the previous Patents Acts still apply.

4.29   In *Catnic Components Ltd. v. Hill & Smith*,[65] a case of infringement under the 1949 Act, Lord Diplock stated:

> "a patent specification is a unilateral statement by the patentee, in words of his own choosing, addressed to those likely to have a practical interest in the subject matter of his invention (*i.e.* 'skilled in the art'), by which he informs them what he claims to be the essential features of the new product or process for which the letters patent grant him a monopoly ... A patent specification should be given a purposive construction rather than a purely literal one derived from applying to it the kind of meticulous verbal analysis in which lawyers are too often tempted by their training to indulge ..."

Lord Diplock's exposition of the law has been approved of and frequently applied in respect of the construction of patent claims under the 1977 Act.[66]

The person to whom the specification and the claims is addressed may be a team "whose combined skills would normally be employed in that art"[67] depending on the subject matter in question.

Origin of the claim

4.30   In *British United Shoe Machinery Co. Ltd. v. A. Fussell & Sons Ltd.*[68] Fletcher Moulton L. J. dealt with the history of distinct claims as part of specifications. After mentioning the proviso (formerly inserted in the

---

[63] See *Hydroacoustics Inc.'s Appn.* [1981] F.S.R. 538.
[64] *Ibid.*
[65] [1982] R.P.C. 183 at 242–243.
[66] *A.C. Edwards Ltd. v. Acme Signs & Displays Ltd.* [1992] R.P.C. 131 at 136; *Southco Inc. v. Dzus Fastener Europe* [1992] R.P.C. 299 at 312.
[67] See *General Tire and Rubber Co. v. Firestone Tyre and Rubber Co. Ltd.* [1972] R.P.C. 457 at 485.
[68] (1908) 25 R.P.C. 631 at p.650.

patent itself), which required the patentee to state in writing the nature of his invention and the method of performing the same, he said:

"These two things—the delimitation of the invention and full practical directions how to use it—are in their nature almost antagonistic. As it is the duty of the inventor to give the fullest practical information to the public, he is bound to put in, if, for instance, the invention is a process, quantities and times which are the best he knows. But it would be very cruel to hold him to the invention when carried out only with those best quantities and times, because a person could then take his invention in substance if he did not take it in quite the best way, and the value of the grant would be practically nothing. Hence inventors, in their own protection, took to introducing into their specifications language intended to distinguish between that which was there for the practical information of the public, and that which was there for delimitation of the invention. Out of that has arisen the practice, which originally was perfectly optional, of having a separate part of the specification primarily designed for delimitation. That is what we call the claim."

Construction is for court alone

The construction of the specification is for the court alone when **4.31** properly instructed as the notional skilled addressee. Lindley L. J. in *Brooks v. Steele and Currie*,[69] said:

"The judge may, and indeed generally must, be assisted by expert evidence to explain technical terms, to show the practical working of machinery described or drawn, and to point out what is old and what is new in the specification. Expert evidence is also admissible, and is often required to show the particulars in which an alleged invention has been used by an alleged infringer, and the real importance of whatever differences there may be between the plaintiff's invention and whatever is done by the defendant. But, after all, the nature of the invention for which a patent is granted must be ascertained from the specification, and has to be determined by the judge and not by a jury, nor by any expert or other witness. This is familiar law, although apparently often disregarded when witnesses are being examined."[70]

Under the 1949 Act the form of the patent provided "that these our **4.32**

---

[69] (1896) 13 R.P.C. 46 at p.73.
[70] And see *Neilson v. Harford* (1841), 1 W.P.C. 331 at p.370; *Seed v. Higgins* (1860), 30 L.J.Q.B. 314 at p.317; *Hill v. Evans* (1860), 31 L.J.Ch. 457 at p.460; *Kaye v. Chubb & Sons Ltd.* (1886), 4 R.P.C. 289 at p.298; *Gadd & Mason v. Mayor, etc. of Manchester* (1892) 9 R.P.C. 516 at p.530; *British Dynamite Co. v. Krebs* (1896) 13 R.P.C. 190 at p.192; *Nestlé & Co. v. Eugene* (1921) 38 R.P.C. 342 at p.347; *Canadian General Electric Co. v. Fada Radio* (1930) 47 R.P.C. 69 at p.90; *Glaverbel SA v. British Coal Corp. (No. 2)* [1993] R.P.C. 90.

letters patent shall be construed in the most beneficial sense for the advantage of the patentee", but these words apply to the patent grant itself and have no relation to the words of the specification. In construing a specification there is no special rule of benevolent interpretation other than as applies to all documents. In *Needham and Kite v. Johnson & Co.*[71] Lindley L. J. said:

"I do not like the expression 'benevolent interpretation.' I do not believe in it. The question is whether a given construction is the true construction; but, of course, if any patent is capable of more constructions than one, the general rule would be applied that you would put upon it that construction which makes it a valid patent rather than a construction which renders it invalid."[72]

In *British Thomson-Houston Co. Ltd. v. Corona Lamp Works Ltd.*[73] Lord Shaw said:

"I think there is no rule, whether of benevolent or malevolent construction, which should apply to patent specifications. A specification must take its rank among all ordinary documents which are submitted to a reader for his guidance or instruction, and a reader ordinarily intelligent and versed in the subject-matter. Such a reader must be supposed to bring his stock of intelligence and knowledge to bear upon the document, not unduly to struggle with it, but anyhow to make the best of it; if, as the result, he understands what the invention is, can produce the object and achieve the manufacture by the help of the written and drawn pages, then the subject-matter of the invention cannot fail on the head of vagueness."[74]

Construction of the claims

4.33   It is the normal principle of construction of a document that it should be construed as a whole so as to give a sensible consistent meaning to every part of it. The question as to the extent to which the body of the

---

[71] (1884) 1 R.P.C. 49 at p.58.
[72] See also *Parkinson v. Simon* (1895) 12 R.P.C. 403 at p.411; *Submarine Signalling Co. v. Henry Hughes & Son Ltd.*(1932) 49 R.P.C. 149 at p.174; *Henriksen v. Tallon* [1965] R.P.C. 434 at p.443.
[73] (1921) 38 R.P.C. 49 at p.89.
[74] See also *Plimpton v. Spiller* (1876), 6 Ch.D. 412 at p.422; *Otto v. Linford* (1882), 46 L.T.(N.S.) 35 at p.39; *Cropper v. Smith & Hancock* (1884) 1 R.P.C. 81 at pp.88, 89; *Automatic Weighing Machine Co. v. Knight* (1889) 6 R.P.C. 297 at p.307; *Edison Bell Phonograph Co. Ltd. v. Smith* (1894) 11 R.P.C. 389 at p.400; *Benno Jaffé, etc., Fabrik v. Richardson* (1893) 10 R.P.C. 261 at p.271; *Nobel's Explosives Co. Ltd. v. Anderson* (1894) 11 R.P.C. 519 at p.523; *Tolson v. Speight* (1896) 13 R.P.C. 718 at p.721; *E.M.I. v. Lissen* (1939) 56 R.P.C. 23 at p.46.

specification can be used to interpret the claims was canvassed in the House of Lords in *Electric and Musical Industries Ltd. v. Lissen Ltd.*,[75] a case in which there was a division of opinion. The statement as to the construction of the claims by Lord Russell is frequently cited, but in fact, as appears from Lord Macmillan's speech, there was no majority of the House in favour of his views. It can, however, be stated that it was accepted that "if the claims have a plain meaning in themselves, then advantage cannot be taken of the language used in the body of the specification to make them mean something different"[76] (*per* Lord Porter), but the case is not a conclusive authority for any wider principle as to the construction of a specification. The following extract[77] from the speech of Lord Russell is often cited, although perhaps without it always being fully appreciated that it was not as a whole accepted by a majority of the House of Lords, but has been frequently accepted as an accurate statement of the law:

"The Court of Appeal have stated that in their opinion no special rules are applicable to the construction of a specification, that it must be read as a whole and in the light of surrounding circumstances; that it may be gathered from the specification that particular words bear an unusual meaning; and that, if possible, a specification should be construed so as not to lead to a foolish result or one which the patentee could not have contemplated. They further have pointed out that the claims have a particular function to discharge. With every word of this I agree; but I desire to add something further in regard to the claim in a specification.

"The function of the claims is to define clearly and with precision the monopoly claimed, so that others may know the exact boundaries of the area within which they will be trespassers. Their primary object is to limit and not to extend the monopoly. What is not claimed is disclaimed. The claims must undoubtedly be read as part of the entire document, and not as a separate document; but the forbidden field must be found in the language of the claims and not elsewhere. It is not permissible, in my opinion, by reference to some language used in the earlier part of the specification, to change a claim which by its own language is a claim for one subject-matter into a claim for another and a different subject-matter, which is what you do when you alter the boundaries of the forbidden territory. A patentee who describes an invention in the body of a specification obtains no monopoly unless it is claimed in the claims. As Lord Cairns said, there is no such thing as infringement of the equity of a patent.[78]

4.34

---

[75] (1939) 56 R.P.C. 23.
[76] *Ibid.*, at p.39.
[77] See n.75.
[78] *Dudgeon v. Thomson* (1877) 3 App.Cas. 34.

"I would point out[79] that there is no question here of words in Claim 1 bearing any special or unusual meaning by reason either of a dictionary found elsewhere in the specification or of technical knowledge possessed by persons skilled in the art. The prima facie meaning of words used in a claim may not be their true meaning when read in the light of such a dictionary or of such technical knowledge; and in those circumstances a claim, when so construed, may bear a meaning different from that which it would have borne had no such assisting light been available. That is construing a document in accordance with the recognised canons of construction. But I know of no canon or principle which will justify one in departing from the unambiguous and grammatical meaning of a claim and narrowing or extending its scope by reading into it words which are not in it; or will justify one in using stray phrases in the body of a specification for the purpose of narrowing or widening the boundaries of the monopoly fixed by the plain words of a claim.

4.35   "A claim is a portion of the specification which fulfils a separate and distinct function. It, and it alone, defines the monopoly; and the patentee is under a statutory obligation to state in the claims clearly and distinctly what is the invention which he desires to protect. As Lord Chelmsford said in this House many years ago: 'The office of a claim is to define and limit with precision what it is which is claimed to have been invented and therefore patented.'[80] If the patentee has done this in a claim the language of which is plain and unambiguous, it is not open to your lordships to restrict or expand or qualify its scope by reference to the body of the specification. Lord Loreburn emphasised this when he said: 'The idea of allowing a patentee to use perfectly general language in the claim and subsequently to restrict or expand or qualify what is therein expressed by borrowing this or that gloss from other parts of the specification is wholly inadmissible.'[81] Sir Mark Romer expressed the same view in the following felicitous language: 'One may and one ought to refer to the body of the specification for the purpose of ascertaining the meaning of words and phrases used in the claims, or for the purpose of resolving difficulties of construction occasioned by the claims when read by themselves. But where the construction of a claim when read by itself is plain, it is not, in my opinion, legitimate to diminish the ambit of the monopoly claimed merely because in the body of the specification the patentee has described his invention in more restricted terms than in the claim itself.'"[82]

---

[79] (1936) 53 R.P.C. at p.41.
[80] *Harrison v. Anderston Foundry Co.* (1876), 1 App.Cas.574.
[81] *Ingersoll Sergeant Drill Co. v. Consolidated Pneumatic Tool Co.* (1907) 24 R.P.C. 61 at p.83.
[82] *British Hartford-Fairmont Syndicate Ltd. v. Jackson Bros. (Knottingley) Ltd.* (1932) 49 R.P.C. 495 at p.556. See also *Minerals Separation North American Corporation v. Noranda Mines Ltd.* (1952) 69 R.P.C. 81.

But, as Lord Evershed M.R. stated in *Rosedale Associated Manufacturers*   **4.36**
Ltd. v. Carlton Tyre Saving Co. Ltd.[83] :

"It is no doubt true and has been well established (see, for example, the speech of Lord Russell of Killowen in the *E.M.I. v. Lissen* case) that you must construe the claims according to their terms upon ordinary principles, and that it is not legitimate to confine the scope of the claims by reference to some limitation which may be found in the body of the specification, but is not expressly or by proper inference reproduced in the claims themselves. On the other hand, it is clearly no less legitimate and appropriate in approaching the construction of the claims to read the specification as a whole. Thereby the necessary background is obtained and in some cases the meaning of the words used in the claims may be affected or defined by what is said in the body of the specification."

An example of how the body of the specification may affect the meaning of the claims is to be found in *British Thomson-Houston Co. Ltd. and Others v. Guildford Radio Stores*[84] where the body of the specification stated that:

"one feature of the invention consists in an effective means for smoothing out the rectified current supplied to the amplifying apparatus to such an extent that no disagreeable noise will be produced in the circuits by reason of the fact that an alternating source of supply is employed",

and Claim 1 contained the words "the field-winding of the sound-reproducing device is employed to smooth out fluctuation in the rectified current". It was argued that the claim was too wide in that it covered any degree of "smoothing", including cases which fell far short of the elimination of the objectionable noise, but Luxmoore J. held that the claim should be construed as limited to that degree of smoothing.

The case of *E.M.I. v. Lissen (supra)* has also to be read in the light of *Catnic Components Ltd. v. Hill & Smith*[85] where Lord Diplock posed the question as:

"whether persons with practical knowledge and experience of the kind of way in which the invention was intended to be used, would understand that strict compliance with a particular descriptive word or phrase appearing in a claim was intended by the patentee to be an essential requirement of the invention so that *any* variant would fall outside the monopoly claimed, even though it could have no material effect upon the way the invention worked."

---

[83] [1960] R.P.C. 59 at p.69.
[84] (1938) 55 R.P.C. 71.
[85] [1982] R.P.C. 183 at 243.

Lord Diplock went on to emphasise that such "broadening" of a claim only arises where the immaterial variant would be one that was obviously so at the date of publication of the specification.

The 1977 Act

4.37   Section 125(1) of the 1977 Act specifies that "unless the context otherwise requires" an invention shall be taken to be "that specified in a claim ... as interpreted by the description and any drawings ... and the extent of the protection conferred by a patent (or application for a patent) shall be determined accordingly".

The approach to such interpretation is stated (section 125(3)) to be that of the Protocol on the Interpretation of Article 69 of the E.P.C., namely, that the extent of protection is not to be defined:

"by the strict, literal meaning of the wording used in the claims, the description and drawings being employed only for the purpose of resolving an ambiguity found in the claims. Neither should it be interpreted in the sense that the claims serve only as a guideline and that the actual protection conferred may extend to where, from a consideration of the description and drawings by a person skilled in the art, the patentee has contemplated. On the contrary, it is to be interpreted as defining a position between these extremes which combines a fair protection for the patentee with a reasonable degree of certainty for third parties."

4.38   In a number of cases[86] the courts have regarded these provisions as not differing from Lord Diplock's criteria set out ante. The case of *Improver Corporation v. Remington Inc.*[87] is instructive in this regard as illustrating how the United Kingdom and German Courts can still come to different conclusions as to the protection to be afforded to a patentee in respect of the same patent both countries purporting to apply the Protocol—the German Court adopting a much broader protection to the patentee.

Construction as at date of publication

4.39   A specification is to be construed with reference to the state of knowledge at the time it is published.[88] Lord Esher M. R. in *Nobel's Explosives Co. Ltd. v. Anderson*[89] said: "Now what is the very first canon

---

[86] See n.66.
[87] *Improver Corp. v. Remington Consumer Products* [1989] R.P.C. 69.
[88] *Badische Anilin und Soda Fabrik v. Levinstein* (1887) 4 R.P.C. 449 at p.463; *Lane-Fox v. Kensington and Knightsbridge Electric Lighting Co. Ltd.* (1892) 9 R.P.C. 413 at p.417; *Presto Gear Case, etc., Co. v. Orme, Evans & Co. Ltd.* (1901) 18 R.P.C. 17 at p.23; *Marconi's Wireless Telegraph Co. v. Mullard Radio Valve Co.* (1923) 40 R.P.C. 323 at p.334.
[89] (1894) 11 R.P.C. 519 at p.523.

of construction of all written business documents? Why, that the court ought to construe them as if it had to construe them the day after they were published."[90]

Construction of amended specification

Where an amendment has been made after the date of publication of a **4.40** complete specification, the amendment is for all purposes deemed to form part of the specification[91] and, therefore, the specification is to be read in the form in which it appears after amendment. In construing an amended specification under the 1949 Act, reference may be made to the specification as originally published.[92]

"Substantially as described"

The claims at the end of a specification frequently end with the words **4.41** "as herein described", or "substantially as herein described". The effect of these words on the ambit of the claim, both as regards novelty and infringement, is to be ascertained by reading the specification as a whole. It is an unprofitable exercise to attempt to reconcile the very large number of decisions that have been given as to the meaning of these words.[93]

Lord Morton in *Raleigh Cycle Co. Ltd. v. H. Miller & Co. Ltd.*,[94] expressed the majority opinion of the House of Lords as follows:

"For many years it has been a common practice to insert as the last claim in a patent specification, a claim on the same lines as Claim 5[95] in the present case. I think that the reason why such a claim has been

---

[90] And see *Ore Concentration Co. (1905) v. Sulphide Corporation* (1914) 31 R.P.C. 206 at p.224. See *American Cyanamid Co. v. Upjohn Co.* [1970] 1 W.L.R. 1507, *per* Lord Diplock.

[91] P.A. 1949, s.31(2) and P.A. 1977, s.75(3).

[92] P.A. 1949, s.31(2), proviso. And see *Tecalemit Ltd. v. Ewarts* (1927) 44 R.P.C. 488 at p.500; *Multiform Displays Ltd. v. Whitmarley Displays Ltd.* [1957] R.P.C. 260.

[93] See, *e.g. Curtis v. Platt* (1863), 3 Ch.D. 135n.; *Westinghouse v. Lancashire and Yorkshire Ry.* (1884) 1 R.P.C. 229 at p.241; *Young and Neilson v. Rosenthal* (1884) 1 R.P.C. 29 at p.33; *Easterbrook v. Great Western Ry.* (1885) 2 R.P.C. 201 at p.208; *United Telephone Co. v. Bassano* (1886) 3 R.P.C. 295 at p.315; *Proctor v. Bennis* (1887) 4 R.P.C. 333; *Lyon v. Goddard* (1893) 10 R.P.C. 354 at p.362; *Cassel Gold Extracting Co. Ltd. v. Cyanide Gold Recovery Syndicate* (1894) 11 R.P.C. 232 at p.257; *Parkinson v. Simon* (1894) 11 R.P.C. 403 at p.408; *North British Rubber Co. v. Gormully* (1894) 11 R.P.C. 283; *Brooks v. Lamplugh* (1898) 15 R.P.C. 33 at p. 49; *Welsbach Incandescent Gas Light Co. Ltd. v. New Incandescent, etc., Co. Ltd.* (1900) 17 R.P.C. 237 at p.250; *Ackroyd & Best Ltd. v. Thomas and Williams* (1904) 21 R.P.C. 737 at pp.749, 750; *Holmes v. Associated Newspapers Ltd.* (1910) 27 R.P.C. 136; *Bonnard v. London General Omnibus Co. Ltd.* (1921) 38 R.P.C. 1 at p.9; *Thomas v. South Wales, etc., Co. Ltd.* (1925) 42 R.P.C. 22; *Tecalemit Ltd. v. Ewarts Ltd.* (1927) 44 R.P.C. 488; *Wright and Eagle Range Co. Ltd. v. General Gas Appliances Ltd.* (1927) 44 R.P.C. 169; *Rose Street Foundry Ltd. v. India Rubber, etc., Ltd.* (1929) 46 R.P.C. 294 at p.311; *Wanganui v. Maunder and Beavan* (1930) 47 R.P.C. 395; *Walsh v. Albert Baker & Co. Ltd.* (1930) 47 R.P.C. 458; *Cincinnati Grinders Inc. v. B.S.A. Tools Ltd.* (1931) 48 R.P.C. 33 at pp.69, 82; *de Havilland's Appn.* (1932) 49 R.P.C. 438; *Crabtree & Sons Ltd. v. Hoe & Co. Ltd.* (1936) 53 R.P.C. 443.

[94] (1948) 65 R.P.C. 141 at p.157.

[95] See *ante*.

inserted, in the present case and countless other cases, is as follows. The patentee fears that his earlier claims may be held invalid, because they cover too wide an area or fail sufficiently and clearly to ascertain the scope of the monopoly claimed. He reasons as follows: 'If I have made a patentable invention and have described the preferred embodiment of my invention clearly and accurately, and without any insufficiency in the directions given, I must surely be entitled to protection for that preferred embodiment, and that protection may fairly extend to cover anything which is substantially the same as the preferred embodiment.'

4.42 "This reasoning seems sound to me, and I cannot doubt that if Claim 5 had read 'an electric generator for lighting a pedal cycle, constructed and arranged substantially as described herein and shown in the accompanying drawings,' it would have been a valid claim ... So far as I can see, there is no insufficiency or ambiguity in their description of the preferred embodiment of that invention, or in the accompanying drawings. In these circumstances, the patentees must surely be entitled to obtain at least this measure of protection ... [It is objected that] Claim 5 is not a narrow claim, but a very wide one, at least as wide as Claim 1. It claims the invention 'as described' and the drawings are referred to in the claim merely as an illustration of one form which the invention may take. This argument is based upon certain decided cases and in particular upon *Tucker v. Wandsworth Electrical Manufacturing Co. Ltd.*[96]

"Before turning to the authorities, I would point out that this is a strange construction to place upon the last of five claims in a specification. Is it really to be supposed that in this last claim the patentee merely intends to echo his first claim, adding a reference to the drawings which seems, on this footing, to be needless and possibly confusing? It is surely more likely that the last claim, referring to the drawings, is intended to be a narrow claim, incorporating the drawings as part of the description, and directed to saving the patent from revocation, if all wider claims are held to be bad.

4.43 "In *Hale v. Coombes*[97] Claim 1 was as follows: 'A projectile of the type herein referred to provided with a device which (etc., etc.) ... substantially as described.' Claim 6 was as follows: 'Projectiles of the type herein referred to ... constructed and arranged and adapted to operate substantially as hereinbefore described with reference to and shown respectively in Figs. 1 to 4 inclusive, in Figs. 5 and 6, in Figs. 7 and 8 and in Figs. 9 and 10 of the drawings.' The majority of the House of Lords held that Claim 6 was a good claim. Lord Sumner, after expressing the view that the words 'substantially as described' in

---

[96] (1925) 42 R.P.C. 531.
[97] (1925) 42 R.P.C. 328.

Claim 1 did not serve to restrict that claim within patentable limits, expressed himself[98] as follows: "Claim 6, however, stands on a somewhat different footing, for, after the words 'constructed and arranged and adapted to operate substantially as hereinbefore described' the inventor continues 'with reference to and as shown respectively in' certain annexed figures. I think that this addition bringing in the figures, which are clear in themselves, does limit Claim 6 to a contrivance which follows the figures and does not go beyond them. It virtually directs that the drawings are to be read into and as part of this claim, an unusual but permissible form to adopt (*Hattersley v. Hodgson*[99]). Thus Claim 6 does not merely stand or fall with the construction of Claim 1 . . .''

The conclusion would appear to be that the words "substantially as described" are insufficient by themselves to limit a claim to the preferred embodiment described, but that if some reference to the drawings is also to be found in the limiting words, even though it is only by reason of the use of expressions such as "as shown" or "as illustrated", the claim is limited to something which is substantially that which is described and depicted in the accompanying figures.[1] **4.44**

This view was taken by the House of Lords in the case of *Deere & Co. v. Harrison McGregor & Guest Ltd.*[2] when considering a claim to a device "constructed substantially as described and with reference to, or as illustrated by [certain drawings]". Lord Reid said,[3] referring to the *Raleigh* case, "That case appears to me to be ample authority for holding this patent valid, but it also shows that a claim of this kind cannot have a wide scope".

It is desirable for the patentee to include a claim of this character, because it may result in his succeeding in an action and obtaining an injunction, where otherwise he would have failed altogether.[4] Moreover, such a claim is not limited to precisely what is illustrated in the drawings, but includes mechanism which, while differing in immaterial respects, adopts all the essentials of that illustrated, even though it may not fall within some of the other subsidiary claims.[5] **4.45**

Duplication of claims

The court will if possible construe the claims so as to give a different meaning to different claims. In *Parkinson v. Simon*[6] Lord Esher M. R. said: **4.46**

---

[98] (1925) 42 R.P.C. 328 at p.346.
[99] (1906) 23 R.P.C. 192.
[1] See *R. W. Crabtree & Sons Ltd. v. R. Hoe & Co. Ltd.* (1936) 53 R.P.C. 443.
[2] [1965] R.P.C. 461.
[3] At p.476.
[4] *Raleigh v. Miller* (1948) 65 R.P.C. 141; *Surface Silos Ltd. v. Beal* [1960] R.P.C. 154.
[5] *Raleigh v. Miller* (1948) 65 R.P.C. 141 and case cited under note 96.
[6] (1894) 11 R.P.C. 493 at p.502.

"When you find a patent with several claims in it, you must, if you can, so construe those claims as to give an effective meaning to each of them. If there are several claims which are identical with each other, then some of them have no effect at all. It follows from the ordinary rules of construction that you must construe the different claims so as to make them effective if possible, to be different from each other in some respects, or else they are not effective."[7]

But if after properly construing the specification and claims, little or no difference can be found between two of the claims, "this circumstance affords no ground for departing from the reasonable and natural meaning of the language"[8] and the fact that one claim is practically a repetition of another will not render the patent invalid.[9]

Effect of disclaimers

4.47   The inventor is to be presumed not to claim things which he must have known perfectly well were not new if a reasonable alternative construction is possible.[10]

The effect of a common form of specific reference was discussed in *Société, etc., Dewandre v. Citröen Cars Ltd.*[11] where one of the patents contained the following disclaimer: "I am aware of Patent 223214 [*i.e. Godeau*] and do not claim anything claimed therein." Romer L. J. said: "We are, therfore, invited by the patentee himself so to construe his claims as to exclude anything claimed by *Godeau*, and this we must do whether *Godeau's* claims be good or bad".[12]

It is to be observed that the effect of a specific reference (in the above form) may be to render the ambit of the claims vague or doubtful, and in such a case the patent would be bad for ambiguity.[13]

Previous constructions binding

4.48   When a specification has once received a judicial construction the court, in a subsequent action in respect of the same invention, will hold

---

[7] See also *Mergenthaler Linotype Co. v. Intertype Ltd.* (1926) 43 R.P.C. 239 at p.289; *Samuel Parkes & Co. Ltd. v. Cocker Bros. Ltd.* (1929) 46 R.P.C. 241 at p.247.

[8] *Per* Tomlin J. in *Brown v. Sperry Gyroscope Co. Ltd.* (1925) 42 R.P.C. 111 at p.136.

[9] *Per* Lindley L. J. in *Wenham Co. Ltd. v. Champion Gas Lamp Co.* (1890) 7 R.P.C. 49 at p.55; see also *New Vacuum, etc., Ltd. v. Steel & Wilson* (1915) 32 R.P.C. 162 at p.171; *Samuel Parkes & Co. Ltd. v. Cocker Bros. Ltd.* (1929) 46 R.P.C. 241 at p.247.

[10] *Haworth v. Hardcastle* (1834), 1 W.P.C. 480 at p.484; *Cropper v. Smith & Hancock* (1884) 1 R.P.C. 81 at p.85; *Lyon v. Goddard* (1893) 10 R.P.C. 121 at p.133; *Tubes Ltd. v. Perfecta Seamless Steel Tube Co. Ltd.* (1903) 20 R.P.C. 77 at p.97.

[11] (1930) 47 R.P.C. 221 at p.275.

[12] *Cf. Pugh v. Riley Cycle Co. Ltd.* (1913) 30 R.P.C. 514 at p.524.

[13] See *British Celanese Ltd. v. Courtaulds Ltd.* (1932) 49 R.P.C. 259 at pp.273, 284, and *post*, § 5.113 *et seq.*

itself bound on that point by such previous decision,[14] but fresh evidence may be adduced in a subsequent action for the purpose of showing that that which before was not regarded as an anticipation is so in fact.[15]

European Patents

The authentic text of a European patent is the language of prosecution **4.49** before the EPO.[16] The only exception is where the language of such proceedings is French or German and in such case the English translation is used if the English translation confers protection which is narrower than that conferred by it in French or German.[17]

If the authentic text is in a foreign language then the English courts will consider an English translation. Any disputes as to the correct translation is a question of fact to be decided by the court on evidence.

---

[14] *Edison v. Holland* (1886) 3 R.P.C. 243 at p.276; *Automatic Weighing Machine Co. v. Combined Weighing Machine Co.* (1889) 6 R.P.C. 367 at p.370.
[15] *Shaw v. Day* (1894) 11 R.P.C. 185 at p.189; *Edison v. Holland* (1886) 3 R.P.C. 243 at p.277; *Flour Oxidizing Co. Ltd. v. Carr & Co. Ltd.* (1908) 25 R.P.C. 428 at p.448; *Higginson and Arundel v. Pyman* (1926) 43 R.P.C. 291 at p.300.
[16] P.A. 1977, s.80(1).
[17] P.A. 1977, s.80(2).

CHAPTER 5

GROUNDS OF REVOCATION

5.01 The validity of all "existing" patents (*i.e.* those granted under the 1949 Act and still in force) is governed by the 1949 Act and the revocation provisions of the 1977 Act only relate to patents granted under that Act. Both the Court and the Comptroller have power to revoke a patent at the suit of any person. The Comptroller also has power on his own initiative to revoke a patent on the ground of lack of novelty or duplication of patenting under the 1977 Act and the E.P.C.[1]

Under the 1949 Act the grounds upon which a patent can be revoked for invalidity are set out in section 32(1)(*a*) to (*l*) and by section 32(4) each of these grounds of invalidity can be relied upon as a defence to an action for infringement without the necessity of seeking revocation of the patent. The grounds of invalidity there set out follow to a large extent the grounds of invalidity introduced into the 1907 Act by section 3 of the 1932 Act as a codification of the grounds of invalidity previously established by the common law. The grounds of invalidity in the 1949 Act are a complete code and whatever flexible powers the Court had under the common law have been absorbed into the Act.[2] It is, therefore, desirable that one should have regard to the language of the Act in considering whether or not any particular ground of invalidity is made out, although, of course, the old authorities are binding where the law is unchanged. Furthermore, as Lord Diplock stated in *Bristol Myers Co. (Johnson's) Application*:[3]

> "where any doubt has arisen as to the meaning of expressions used in the sections of those statutes which set out the grounds of invalidity of a patent, recourse has been had to the earlier decisions of *scire facias* and any ambiguity has been resolved in favour of the meaning that is more consistent with the principles that underlay them."

Under the 1977 Act the grounds upon which a patent may be revoked **5.02** are set out in section 72. Section 74 sets out the various proceedings in which the validity of a patent may be put in issue. The 1977 Act is a new and complete code and there has been a marked change in language and indeed in the actual grounds of revocation. Nevertheless (subject to the state of the art by which the invention is to be adjudged), there are certain grounds, namely insufficiency, novelty and obviousness in respect of which many of the authorities under the 1949 Act are relevant to.[4] It is proposed, therefore, to deal with such common grounds first, and thereafter to deal with the separate grounds under the 1977 Act and 1949 Act respectively thus avoiding any overlap.

1. Insufficiency

P.A. 1977, section 72(1)(*c*): "the specification of the patent does not **5.03** disclose the invention clearly enough and completely enough for it to be performed by a person skilled in the art".

P.A. 1949, section 32(1)(*h*): "the complete specification does not

---

[1] P.A. 1977, s.73. And see *Morley Roof Tile Co. Ltd.'s Patent* [1994] R.P.C. 231, C.A.
[2] *American Cyanamid Co. v. Upjohn Co.* [1971] R.P.C. 425.
[3] [1975] R.P.C. 127 at 156.
[4] See Aldous J. in *Mentor Corp. v. Hollister Inc.* [1991] F.S.R. 557 at 561 re treatment of insufficiency under the 1977 Act.

sufficiently and fairly describe the invention and the method by which it is to be performed".[5]

The inventor is entitled to assume that the person to whom the specification is addressed will be in possession of the common knowledge in the art at the date of the specification. The language in which the invention is described and the extent to which details need to be given will, therefore, depend upon such common knowledge and upon the class of person who will have to act upon the directions given in the specifications.

5.04   Whilst under the 1949 Act the objections of insufficiency, ambiguity, inutility and false suggestions have in some cases overlapped,[6] it is clear that there is no such overlap under the 1977 Act. Sections 14(3) and (5) provide as follows:

"(3) The specifications of an application shall disclose the invention in a manner which is clear enough and complete enough for the invention to be performed by a person skilled in the art.
(5) The claim or claims shall—
  (a) define the matter for which the applicant seeks protection,
  (b) be clear and concise,
  (c) be supported by the description; and
  (d) relate to one invention or to a group of inventions which are so linked as to form a single inventive concept"

Section 14(3), but not section 14(5), is mirrored in section 72. In *Genentech Inc.'s Patent*[7] the Court of Appeal decided that the 1977 Act provided a complete code so that it was not open to the court to revoke a patent on the ground that the claim was not supported by the description. Likewise, ambiguity is not a ground of revocation under the 1977 Act save in so far as it can be brought under sections 72(1)(c) and 14(3).

Prior to the 1977 Act it had been said that the directions should be sufficient to enable "a workman of competent skill in his art," or a "competent engineer" to carry the invention into effect.[8] This is now expressly stated in the 1977 Act. It is clear, however, that the class of persons comprised in the words "skilled in the art" must depend upon the subject-matter with which the invention is concerned. For example, a workman, or even a foreman, in a chemical works might not possess the technical skill and knowledge to understand a new chemical process which the manager would have no difficulty in directing them to put in practice.

Thus, in *Incandescent Gas Light Co. v. De Mare Incandescent Gas Light*

---

[5] See also P.A. 1977, s.14(3), and P.A. 1949, s.4(3).
[6] See *Summers v. Cold Metal Process* (1948) 65 R.P.C. 75 at pp.101 to 105.
[7] [1989] R.P.C. 147, see also *Mölnlycke A.B. v. Procter & Gamble* [1992] F.S.R. 549 at 584.
[8] See, *e.g. Morgan v. Seaward* (1836) 1 W.P.C. 170 at p.174; *Plimpton v. Malcolmson* (1876) 3 Ch.D. 531.

System Ltd.[9] Wills J. said: "The subject-matter of the specification is such that no one but a person possessing a very considerable amount of chemical knowledge could, at the date of the specification, be considered a competent workman."

Under the 1949 Act the date at which the patent specification must be tested for sufficiency is the date of publication of the specification and this applies even if the specification is amended. If the specification is amended, it is the amended specification that must be considered.[10] However, the whole scheme of the 1977 Act requires the specification to be sufficient as of the date of filing. Thus, by reason of section 76, no added matter may be introduced by amendment after such date. Also, there is the provision for micro-organisms that they must be deposited in a culture collection not later than the date of filing (see Rule 17(1)(*a*)). In *Asahi Kasei Kogyo U.K.'s Application*,[10a] Lord Oliver referred to the requirement of section 14(3) as the need to contain an "enabling disclosure" as of the filing date.

More than one addressee

The complexity of the problems arising in modern industries may necessitate more than one "addressee" of the specification. In *Osram Lamp Works Ltd. v. Pope's Electric Lamp Co.*[11] Lord Parker said: **5.05**

> "A specification may be considered as addressed, at any rate primarily, to the persons who would in normal course have to act on the directions given for the performance. These persons may be assumed to possess not only a reasonable amount of common sense, but also a complete knowledge of the art or arts which have to be called into play in carrying the patentee's directions into effect. I say arts because in carrying out the directions given by the patentee it may well be necessary to call in aid more than one art. Some of the directions contained in a specification may have to be carried out by skilled mechanics, others by competent chemists. In such a case, the mechanic and chemist must be assumed to co-operate for the purpose in view, each making good any deficiency in the other's technical equipment. The specification cannot be considered insufficient merely because the mechanic without the aid of the chemist, or the chemist without the aid of the mechanic, would be unable to comprehend the meaning of, or to carry into effect, the direction given by the patentee."

---

[9] (1896) 13 R.P.C. 301 at p.327.
[10] *Anxionnaz v. Rolls Royce Ltd.* [1967] R.P.C. 419 at pp. 471–472. See *American Cyanamid Co. v. Upjohn Co.* [1971] R.P.C. 425, *Illinois Tool Works Inc. v. Autobars Co. Ltd.* [1974] R.P.C. 337 at 369, *Standard Brand Inc.'s Appn.* [1981] R.P.C. 499 at 530.
[10a] [1991] R.P.C. 485 at 536.
[11] (1917) 34 R.P.C. 369 at p.391.

Degree of sufficiency required

5.06   The general principles by which the "sufficiency" of the specification should be determined were stated by Lindley L.J. in *Edison and Swan Electric Co. v. Holland*[12] in the following way:

> "... in describing in what manner the invention is to be performed, the patentee does all that is necessary, if he makes it plain to persons having reasonable skill in doing such things as have to be done in order to work the patent, what they are to do in order to perform his invention. If ... they are to do something the like of which has never been done before, he must tell them how to do it, if a reasonably competent workman would not himself see how to do it on reading the specification...."

As Lloyd L.J. said in *Mentor Corp. v. Hollister Inc.*:[13]

> "The question for decision in the present case is whether the specification discloses the invention clearly enough and completely enough for it to be performed by a person skilled in the art. This obviously involves a question of degree. Disclosure of an invention does not have to be complete in every detail so that anyone, whether skilled or not, can perform it. Since the specification is addressed to the skilled man it is sufficient if the addressee can understand the invention as described and can then perform it. In performing the invention the skilled man does not have to be told what is self evident or what is part of common general knowledge that is to say what is known to persons versed in the art. But the difficulty. How much else may the skilled man be expected to do for himself?"

Lloyd L.J. went on to state that each case will turn on its own facts depending on the nature of the invention and cited, with approval as a working definition, the following words of Buckley L.J. in giving the judgment of the Court of Appeal in *Valensi v. British Radio Corporation*:[14]

> "...the hypothetical addressee is not a person of exceptional skill and knowledge and he is not to be expected to exercise any invention or any prolonged research, enquiry or experiment. He must, however, be prepared to display a reasonable degree of skill and common knowledge of the art in making trials and to correct obvious errors in the specification, if a means of correcting them can readily be found... Further, we are of the opinion that it is not only inventive steps that can not be required of the addressee. While the addressee must be taken as a person with a will to make the instructions work, he is not

---

[12] (1889) 6 R.P.C. 243 at p.289.
[13] [1993] R.P.C. 7 at p.10; see also *Helitune Ltd. v. Steward Hughes Ltd.* [1991] F.S.R. 171 at 201, 202; *Chiron Corp. v. Organon Teknika Ltd.* [1994] F.S.R. 202.
[14] [1973] R.P.C. 337.

called upon to make a prolonged study of matters which present some initial difficulty: and in particular, if there are actual errors in the specification—if the apparatus really will not work without departing from what is described—then unless both the existence of the error and the way to correct it can be quickly discovered by an addressee of the degree of skill and knowledge which we envisage the description is insufficient."

In *Genentech Inc.'s Patent*[15] relating to the field of synthesis of a human tissue plasminogen activator in recombinant DNA technology, the Court of Appeal considered in such a field involving intellectual gifts and ingenuities of approach, the person skilled in the art for the purpose of insufficiency must have a degree of inventiveness.

Generally speaking, therefore, the inventor is not required to give **5.07** directions of a more minute nature than a person of ordinary skill and knowledge of the art might fairly be expected to need.[16] If, for example, the specification directs that a certain substance is to be used, it will be sufficient if the invention can be carried out with the substance sold commercially under that name even though the substance if chemically pure would be inoperative. Thus, in *"Z" Electric Lamp Co. v. Marples, Leach & Co.*[17] the specification prescribed the use of a substance known as "phospham" in the manufacture of incandescent electric lamps for a particular purpose. The defendants showed that "phospham" in the strictest chemical sense would not operate in the manner desired. The plaintiffs on the other hand, showed that the substance as obtained from chemical manufacturers was not quite pure and that it would work satisfactorily. It was held that the addressee was the lamp manufacturer, and that he would in the ordinary course of business procure his "phospham" from the chemical manufacturer.

Again if it is necesary to use some old or well-known apparatus, the specification need only refer to the apparatus by the name by which it is generally known. But should the success of the invention depend particularly on the manner in which a well-known apparatus is to be used, the directions must lay stress on this point, if it would not be obvious to the skilled man.

In *Badische Anilin und Soda Fabrik v. La Société, etc., du Rhône*[18] the **5.08** specification directed (in an example) that two substances were to be heated together "in an autoclave". It was proved that in similar operations the trade frequently made use of the autoclaves which were not made of iron, and that in many such operations enamelled

---

[15] [1989] R.P.C. 147 at 215.
[16] See also *Boulton v. Bull* (1795), 2 H.Bl. 463 at p.478; *Morgan v. Seaward* (1836), 1 W.P.C. 170 at p.174; *Gaulard and Gibb's Patent* (1889) 6 R.P.C. 215 p.224; *Miller v. Clyde Bridge Steel Co.* (1892) 8 R.P.C. 198 at p.201; *Hopkinson v. St. James's and Pall Mall Lighting Co.* (1893) 10 R.P.C. 46 at p.61; *Kane & Pattison v. Boyle* (1901) 18 R.P.C. 325 at p.336.
[17] (1910) 27 R.P.C. 305 at p.316; 737 at p.744.
[18] (1898) 16 R.P.C. 359.

autoclaves had advantages. The success of the paintiff's process entirely depended, however, upon the use of an *iron* vessel, and the specification was declared insufficient.[19]

In the case of a chemical process, it is not permissible, by using general words such as "treating", "converting", or "replacing", to attempt to cover all possible methods, whether then known or subsequently to be discovered.[20]

Necessity for disclosure of more than one embodiment

5.09   In *Mölnlycke A B v. Procter & Gamble*[21] Morrit J. following a decision of the Technical Board of Appeal in *Genentech I/Polypeptide Expression*[22] rejected a submission by the defendants that to comply with section 72(1)(c) of the 1977 Act a skilled man should be able to make all embodiments falling within the claimed monopoly. Thus, an invention is sufficiently disclosed if at least one way is described which enables the skilled man to carry out the invention.

However by virtue of sections 125(2) and 14(5) and (6) a claim under the 1977 Act can contain more than one invention and if, when properly construed, two or more inventions are claimed, no doubt the specification to be sufficient must contain clear directions to enable the skilled person to perform each of the inventions claimed. Such an argument may in certain circumstances be used successfully to contend that the width of the claims is not properly supported by the description, a contention which is not itself a ground of invalidity.

Limits of necessary experiments

5.10   The directions given must be such as to enable the invention to be carried into effect without an excessive number of experiments.

In *Plimpton v. Malcolmson*[23] Jessel M.R. said: "You must not give people mechanical problems and call them specifications". But the inventor cannot be expected to relieve the "competent workman" from all obligation to take trouble in carrying into effect the description in the specification. For example, in modern engineering practice no one would think of treating the drawings of a machine in a specification as working drawings: a certain amount of designing and calculation has to be carried out before a machine can be built, and the degree of knowledge requisite to perform such operations must be presumed in the person to whom the specification is addressed.

---

[19] See also *Wallace v. Tullis, Russell & Co. Ltd.* (1922) 39 R.P.C. 3; *John Summers & Sons Ltd. v. The Cold Metal Process Co.* (1948) 65 R.P.C. 75.

[20] *British Celanese Ltd.'s Appn.* (1934) 51 R.P.C. 192.

[21] [1992] F.S.R. 549 at 594; accepted as correct and followed in *Chiron Corp. v. Organon Teknika Ltd.* [1994] F.S.R. 202 at 241, Aldous J.; see also *Quantel v. Spaceward Microsystems* [1990] R.P.C. 83 at 136.

[22] T292/85 GENENTECH/Polypeptide Expression: [1989] O.J. EPO 275, [1989] EPOR 1.

[23] (1876) 3 Ch.D. 531 at p.576.

In *Edison and Swan Electric Light Co. v. Holland*[24] Cotton L.J. said: **5.11**

"The objection taken as a whole, was that the specification did not sufficiently show how the invention is to be carried into effect. It is necessary that this should be done so as to be intelligible, and to enable the thing to be made without further invention by ... a person conversant in the subject. But in my opinion it is not necessary that such a person should be able to do the work without any trial or experiment, which, when it is new or especially delicate, may frequently be necessary, however clear the description may be."[25]

The degree of experiment which will be permissible is a question of **5.12** fact in each case. In *Leonhardt v. Kallé*[26] the inventor had given six examples of the use of oxidisable substances in the process claimed, and one of the objections raised was that the specification showed no means for ascertaining what oxidisable substances were not suitable. Romer J. said:

"Now, with reference to that, what has the patentee done, and what really could he do more? He has pointed out numerous oxidisable substances, and admittedly those oxidisable substances he mentioned are as good, if not better, and are more easily dealt with than the other oxidisable substances which are not specifically mentioned. Was it reasonable to suppose that the patentee ought to set himself down as a sort of dictionary to specify every known oxidisable substance, and to point out which of those could not give very useful results, or which might be disregarded? ... I think, seeing what numerous examples are given, that it would be easy to a chemist ... to ascertain in which one of the examples ... the substance he is dealing with falls and apply that example".[27]

No need to state advantages
In general it is not necessary for the inventor to state the advantages of **5.13** the invention. In *Badische Anilin und Soda Fabrik v. Levinstein*[28] the

[24] (1889) 6 R.P.C. 243 at p.277.
[25] And see *Morgan v. Seaward* (1836) 1 W.P.C. 170 at p.176; *Otto v. Linford* (1882) 46 L.T.(N.S.) 35 at p.40; *British Dynamite Co. v. Krebs* (1896) 13 R.P.C. 190 at p.192; *Osram Lamp Works Ltd. v. Pope's Electric Lamp Co.* (1915) 32 R.P.C. 369 at p.391; *Watson, Laidlaw & Co. v. Pott & Others* (1910) 27 R.P.C. 541 at p.588; (1911) 28 R.P.C. 565 at p.580; *Aktiengesellschaft für Anilin, etc. v. Levinstein Ltd.* (1921) 38 R.P.C. 277 at p.291; *No-Fume Ltd. v. Frank Pitchford & Co. Ltd.* (1935) 52 R.P.C. 231 at p.243; *International de Lavaud Manufacturing Corporation Ltd. v. Clay Cross Co. Ltd.* (1941) 58 R.P.C. 177; *John Summers & Sons Ltd. v. The Cold Metal Process Co.* (1948) 65 R.P.C. 75; *Valensi v. British Radio Corp.* [1973] R.P.C. 337; *Mentor v. Hollister Corp.* [1993] R.P.C. 7.
[26] (1895) 12 R.P.C. 103 at p.116.
[27] See also *Wegmann v. Corcoran* (1879) 13 Ch.D. 65, and cases cited *ante*, note 25.
[28] (1887) 4 R.P.C. 449.

specification described four processes for the production of sulpho acids of oxynaphthaline applicable to dyeing and printing, and varying in colour from brown to red. All these processes were claimed, although only one of the shades was proved to have any practical value, and it was argued that the patent was bad on the ground that no description was given of the relative advantages of each particular shade of colour. It was held by the House of Lords that to require such discrimination was to insist upon what was really impracticable; Lord Halsbury L.C. said:

> "Upon the principle contended for, each shade must not only be shown, but its excellence or popularity must be distinguished separately by the patentee. This, as it appears to me, reduces the obligation supposed to press upon the patentee to an absurdity".[29]

Advantage whole essence of invention

5.14   Where the attainment of a particular advantage constitutes the whole essence of the invention it may be necessary to state this advantage and to confine the claims to apparatus or processes that will achieve it in order properly to delimit the invention.[30]

Drafting of a "selection" patent

5.15   In the case of a "selection" patent,[31] *i.e.* one in which the inventive step resides in the discovery that one or more members of a class have some special advantage for some particular purpose, the following requirements as to drafting were laid down by Maugham J. in *I.G. Farbenindustrie A.G.'s Patents*[32]

> " . . . it is necessary for the patentee to define in clear terms the nature of the characteristic which he alleges to be possessed by the selection for which he claims a monopoly. He has in truth disclosed no invention whatever if he merely says that the selected group possesses advantages. Apart altogether from the question of what is called sufficiency, he must disclose an invention; he fails to do this in the case of a selection for special characteristics, if he does not adequately define them".

---

[29] 4 R.P.C. 449 at p.464. See also *Keith and Blackman Co. Ltd. v. Tilley, etc., Gas Syndicate* (1913) 30 R.P.C. 537 at p.546; *Roth v. Cracknell* (1921) 38 R.P.C. 120 at p.128.

[30] *Clay v. Allcock & Co. Ltd.* (1906) 23 R.P.C. 745; *Clyde Nail Co. Ltd v. Russell* (1916) 33 R.P.C. 291 at p.306; *Contraflo Condenser, etc., Co. Ltd. v. Hick, Hargreaves & Co. Ltd.* (1920) 37 R.P.C. 89 at p.103; *Thomas v. South Wales, etc., Engineering Co. Ltd.* (1925) 42 R.P.C. 22 at p.27; *I.G. Farbenindustrie A.G.'s Patents* (1930) 47 R.P.C. 289 at p.323.

[31] See *post* § 5.59.

[32] (1930) 47 R.P.C. 289 at p.323. See also *Esso Research and Eng. Co.'s Appn.* [1960] R.P.C. 35; *E.I. Du Pont de Nemours & Co. v. AKZO*, [1982] F.S.R. 303.

Micro-organisms

5.16 Failure to make micro-organisms available by their deposit in a relevant culture collection is treated as not sufficiently disclosing the invention.[33]

Alloys

5.17 In *Mond Nickel Co. Ltd.'s Application*[34] the Appeal Tribunal said:

"an applicant who claims an alloy must follow one of these courses:
 (1) he can claim an alloy by specifying all the ingredients of which it is composed, together with the range of proportions in which they are to be present, but he need not exclude impurities;
 (2) he can claim an alloy where it is to be used in connection with a well-known and understood commercial process, such as the manufacture of steel, by making it consist of the specific ingredients ... stating the range of their respective proportions, together with the whole or any part of a class of incidental ingredients which are used in the particular trade at the date of the claim and which together with their respective ranges of proportions are well known in the particular trade;
 (3) he can claim an alloy where it is to be used in connection with a well-known and understood commercial process, such as the manufacture of steel, by making it consist of the specified ingredients together with one or more of a specified number of the incidental ingredients (using that phrase in the sense in which I have used it in the preceding paragraph) specifying the respective ranges of the proportions of such incidental ingredients.
"Further, in the case of a well-known and understood commercial process, in which all or any of a number of incidental ingredients (using the phrase as I have used it above) may be added at the option of the manufacturer, I am further of the opinion that, if he so desires, an applicant, instead of claiming an alloy, can claim a method of manufacture consisting, for instance, of the addition for a stated purpose (*e.g.* as an inoculant in the manufacture of cast iron) of specific ingredients, the range of the proportions of such respective ingredients being stated, and can state both in the body of the specification and in the claim that in carrying out his invention all or any of the incidental ingredients (using that phrase as I have used it above) may be added. In certain circumstances such a course may be found to be preferable to a claim for an alloy, and I see no objection to it in principle."

---

[33] See P.A. 1977, s.125A(4); see Chap. 4, §§ 4.18.
[34] (1948) 65 R.P.C. 123 at p.125.

Essential material

5.18   "What the section requires is a sufficient description. This suggests in the context of a specification a number of words, illustrations, diagrams or symbols. It does not include an obligation to make available with the specification any particular substance."[35]

Provided that all the materials and the process are sufficiently and fairly described then the requirements of the section are met.

Effect of errors

5.19   An error in a specification which may be said, in a sense, to be a technical error, will not render the patent invalid, although it be an error in description or drawing, provided it be such an error as the skilled addressee would at once observe and be in a position to correct.[36] If, however, experiments would be required to show that there was an error, the patent will be invalid.[37] It frequently occurs that the inventor states an erroneous theory as to the operation of the machine or process, the subject of the invention. This will not invalidate the patent[38] unless it amounts to a statement that would in practice be misleading, or amounts to a false suggestion.[39]

2. Lack of Novelty

5.20   **P.A. 1977, section 72(1)(a):** "the invention is not a patentable invention" which by virtue of section 1(1) requires the invention to be new.

   P.A. 1949, section 32(1)(e): "the invention, so far as claimed in any claim of the complete specification, is not new having regard to what was known or used before the priority date of the claim in the United Kingdom".

   Under the 1977 Act an invention is to be taken to be novel if it does not form part of the state of the art.[40] The state of the art comprises all matter (whether a product, process or any information relating to either) which has been made available to the public whether in the United Kingdom

---

[35] *Per* Lord Guest in *American Cyanamid v. Upjohn Co.* [1970] 1 W.L.R. 1507 at p.1520.

[36] *No-Fume Ltd. v. Frank Pitchford & Co. Ltd.* (1935) 52 R.P.C. 231 at p.243; see also *Valensi v. British Radio Corp.* [1973] R.P.C. 337 and *ante* § 5.06.

[37] *Simpson v. Holliday* (1866) L.R. 1 H.L. 315 at p.321; *Otto v. Linford* (1882) 46 L.T. (N.S.) 35 at p.40; *Miller v. Scarle* (1893) 10 R.P.C. 106 at p.111; *British United Shoe Machinery Co. v. A. Fussell & Sons Ltd.* (1908) 25 R.P.C. 368 at p.385; *True and Variable Electric Lamp Syndicate v. Bryant Trading Syndicate* (1908) 25 R.P.C. 461; *Knight v. Argylls Ltd.* (1913) 30 R.P.C. 321 at p.348.

[38] See *"Z" Electric Lamp Co. v. Marples, Leach & Co.* (1910) 27 R.P.C. 737 at p.746.

[39] As in *Monnet v. Beck* (1897) 14 R.P.C. 777 at p.847. See also *"Z" Electric Lamp Co. v. Marples, Leach & Co.* (1910) 27 R.P.C. 737; *Le Rasoir Apollo's Patent* (1932) 49 R.P.C. 1.

[40] See P.A. 1977, s.2(1).

or elsewhere prior to the priority date of the invention by written or oral description, by use or in any other way.[41] It also includes matter contained in applications for patents and patents of earlier priority date which are published after the priority of the patent under attack.[42]

What constitutes being made available to the public

The words "made available to the public" are not new to patent law in   **5.21**
that they formed part of the definition of "published" in the 1949 Act.[43]
The distinction between availability and publication was abolished by the definition of publication in the 1949 Act. The definition of "published" in the 1977 Act equates it with being made available to the public.[44] Although the Act does not use the word published in respect of the novelty provisions, Aldous J. in *P.L.G. Research Ltd. v. Ardan International Ltd.*[45] stated that "made available to the public" should be given the same meaning as those words used in the definition of "published" in section 101 of the 1949 Act:

> "Thus, to form part of the state of the art, the information given (by the user) must have been made available to at least one member of the public who was free in law and equity to use it."[46]

The two major differences between novelty under the 1977 Act and the 1949 Act are; firstly, matter available in any part of the world is relevant as opposed to purely United Kingdom knowledge. Secondly, subject to section 64 of the 1977 Act (vested rights in respect of earlier use), user, including secret user, which does not make available the necessary information to enable a third party to adopt the same cannot be relied upon to invalidate a 1977 Act patent. There is also the further difference to be borne in mind, which is implicit in the concept of making matter available to the public, namely, that such matter must constitute what has been referred to as an enabling disclosure,[47] in other words that the information which can be obtained from the prior matter is sufficient for the man skilled in the art to implement such disclosure.

Thus, when considering the question of novelty two quite separate   **5.22**
questions have to be considered *viz.*

(1) whether any particular document or act, having regard to its history and circumstances, is such as can be relied on against

---

[41] P.A. 1977, s.2(2).
[42] P.A. 1977, s.2(3).
[43] P.A. 1949, s.101(1); see also P.A. 1907–1919, s.11.
[44] P.A. 1977, s.130(1).
[45] [1993] F.S.R. 197 at 226.
[46] *Genentech Inc.'s Patent* [1989] R.P.C. 147 at 204.
[47] See *Asahi Kasei Kogyo K.K.'s Appn.* [1991] R.P.C. 485, 539; and *Quantel Ltd. v. Spaceward Microsystems Ltd.* [1990] R.P.C. 83; and *Genentech Inc. (Human Growth Hormone) Patent* [1989] R.P.C. 613.

the validity of a claim having a later priority date[48] and, if the answer be Yes,

(2) whether the contents of the document or the details of the act are such as to invalidate the claim on the ground of lack of novelty.

Question (1) will be considered first.

A. Making available by oral disclosure

5.23   An invention can become "known" by a prior oral disclosure equally as by a prior published document or by a prior user. As Bowen L.J. said in *Humpherson v. Syer*:[49]

"I put aside questions of public use and treat this as a question of whether there has been a prior publication: that is, in other words, had this information been communicated to any member of the public who was free in law and equity to use it as he pleased. ... If so, the information had been given to a member of the public and there was nothing further to serve as consideration for any patent."

The disclosure in the above case was by the defendant and it was accepted, and it is submitted it is the law, that the mere knowledge by a third party unaccompanied by a disclosure free of conditions of secrecy does not make an invention "known". Publication by oral description is now explicitly included in section 2(2) of the 1977 Act.

B. Making available by documents

5.24   A claim is invalidated if the invention claimed in it was previously "known", and, accordingly, the nature of the document which made it known is immaterial.

What constitutes a written disclosure

In the case of a book or other document containing a description of the invention it is not necessary that it should have been sold in order to constitute disclosure. Mere exhibition in a bookseller's window for sale,

---

[48] See P.A. 1977, s.2(1).
[49] (1887) 4 R.P.C. 407 at p.413; and see *Dollond's Case* (1766) 1 W.P.C. 43.

or sending it to a bookseller in this country to be sold, is sufficient disclosure.[50]

It is the practice for the Patent Office library to receive copies of foreign specifications from abroad which are open to public inspection. A British patent may be invalidated by the fact that such a specification, or any other document containing a description of the invention claimed, was on view before the priority date of the British application.[51] Prior publication in a foreign journal and in a foreign language (if commonly understood) will invalidate a British patent if it can be shown that a single copy was deposited in Great Britain in a public place, and was open to public inspection.[52]

Where a book, written in French, was in the British Museum in a room **5.25** not ordinarily accessible to the public and only its title appeared in the catalogue in the public reading room, this was held not to be sufficient publication.[53] Whether or not the document is ordinarily accessible to the public appears to be the crucial test.[54] Where a German specification, six weeks earlier in date, was placed on the shelves of the Patent Office library in a place where members of the public in search of information of the kind in question would normally go, this was sufficient publication.[55] Where a document had been obtained from South Africa by an employee of a company, it was held that it had been published as the document had been communicated to a single member of the public without inhibiting fetter.[56] .

A claim to a chemical substance cannot be sustained, notwithstanding that the substance may be put to novel use, when it has been disclosed in a prior publication.[57]

Interference

The 1977 Act does not contain any ground of prior claiming, but **5.26** provides in section 2(3) that the state of the art shall be taken to comprise matter contained in an application for another patent which was published on, or after the priority date of that invention if such matter was contained in the application for that other patent both as filed, and as published, and the priority date of that matter was earlier. This subsection was designed to prevent double patenting of the same invention or interference between patents.

---

[50] *Lang v. Gisborne* (1862) 31 Beav. 133 at p.136; 31 L.J.Ch. 769.
[51] *Harris v. Rothwell* (1886) 35 Ch.D. 416; (1886) 3 R.P.C. 383; (1887) 4 R.P.C. 225 (C.A.); *Pickard v. Prescott* (1892) 9 R.P.C. 195.
[52] *V. D. Ltd. v. Boston Deep Sea Fishing Co. Ltd.* (1935) 52 R.P.C. 303 at p.328.
[53] *Otto v. Steel* (1885) 31 Ch.D. 241; (1886) 3 R.P.C. 109.
[54] See also *Plimpton v. Malcolmson* (1876) 3 Ch.D. 531; *Plimpton v. Spiller* (1876) 6 Ch.D. 412.
[55] *Harris v. Rothwell* (1887) 4 R.P.C. 225 at p.232; 35 Ch.D. 416 at p.431; and see *Humpherson v. Syer* (1887) 4 R.P.C. 407 at p.415.
[56] *Bristol-Myer's Co. Appn.* [1969] R.P.C. 146.
[57] *Gyogyszeripari Kutato Intezet's Appn.* [1958] R.P.C. 51.

Fifty year old specifications

5.27   Under the 1949 Act a claim in a complete specification is not invalidated by prior publication of the invention in a specification filed in pursuance of a United Kingdom application dated more than 50 years before the date of filing of such complete specification,[58] or in a specification describing the invention for the purposes of a foreign application made more than 50 years before that date.[59] Nor is it invalidated by publication in an official abridgment or extract of such a 50 year old specification.[60] A mere reference to an earlier specification by its number is not a fresh publication of the earlier specification; but republication may occur if there is a description and reference to the earlier specification.[61]

It is submitted, however, that a 50 year old specification could be used as evidence to support an allegation of prior user.[62] In the case of an abandoned application no specification relating to it is published,[63] yet the court has power to order the production of a specification filed on an abandoned application, not as an anticipation, but as evidence of collateral facts, and in the interests of justice.[64]

Admission by patentee as to prior publication

5.28   In *Chapman and Cook v. Deltavis Ltd.*[65] Clauson J. said:

"...if a patentee, though entirely erroneously, does state by way of... recital in his specification that a particular form of thing is common... he will have, so to speak, recited himself out of court and I venture to doubt whether he could possibly maintain any claim to a monopoly in a thing which he has recognised to be something which existed."

Such an admission may be binding on the patentee even though made only in the provisional specification.[66]

5.29   But this principle must not be taken too far, as was pointed out by the Court of Appeal in *Sonotone Corporation v. Multitone Electric Co. Ltd.*[67] where, after referring to the above observations of Clauson J., Sir Raymond Evershed M.R. stated:

"But the case supposed by Clauson J. was, in our judgment, wholly different from the present. It may well be that as between a patentee

---

[58] P.A. 1949, s.50(1)(*a*).
[59] P.A. 1949, s.50(1)(*b*).
[60] P.A. 1949, s.50(1)(*c*).
[61] *AMP Inc. v. Hellerman Ltd.* [1962] R.P.C. 55 at p.183.
[62] *AMP Inc. v. Hellerman Ltd.* [1962] R.P.C. 55 at p.183.
[63] P.A. 1949, s.79(1).
[64] See *Pneumatic Tyre Co. Ltd. v. English Cycle Co.* (1897) 14 R.P.C. 851.
[65] (1930) 47 R.P.C. 163 at p.173.
[66] *British Celanese Ltd. v. Courtaulds Ltd.* (1933) 50 R.P.C. 259 at p.270.
[67] (1955) 72 R.P.C. at p.140.

and the Crown, at any rate, clear admission of the state of the prior art on the basis of which a particular monopoly had been claimed and granted could not subsequently be withdrawn or modified. But it does not seem to us necessarily to follow that in a case like the present where, we are assuming, an admission is made as regards some integers of a combination for which a monopoly is claimed, the patentee could not in an infringement action resile from his admission to the extent of attempting to show that some particular feature or integer or some particular combination which on this view he must be taken to have included in the known prior art was in fact not old or known at all."

C. Making available by prior use

Prior to the coming into force of the 1977 Act it had been the law that **5.30** no patent could be validly granted to prevent the public in the United Kingdom doing either that which was done in public or in secret before the priority of the patent applied for.[68] For patents granted under the 1977 Act that has now changed. Patents may now be granted for an invention covering a product that has been put on the market provided the product does not provide an enabling disclosure of the invention claimed—this may particularly be the case where the invention relates to the method of making the product which may not be discernable from the product itself.[69]

In *Bristol–Myers Co. Application*[70] (a 1949 Act patent) the House of Lords held that there was a use of the antibiotic, the subject of the invention by its sale, as part of a mixture of compounds even though its presence could not have been detected by analysis. Such cases no longer apply to patents granted under the 1977 Act.

It is submitted, however, that those cases which required means of knowledge to be provided by use, do accord with the requirement of making the matter available to the public. Thus, in *Stahlwerk Becker A.G.*[71] it was held by the House of Lords that to establish prior use it was enough to prove that the steel had been manufactured and sold before the patent was taken out and that any person who had purchased the steel could by analysis have known what the composition was. It was not necessary to establish that the composition had been in fact ascertained by analysis to show there was a public knowledge.

---

[68] See *post*.

[69] See *P.L.G. Research Ltd. v. Ardon International Ltd.* [1993] F.S.R. 197 at 225.

[70] [1975] R.P.C. 127; See also *W.L. Gove & Associates Inc. v. Kimal Scientific Products Ltd* [1988] R.P.C. 137.

[71] (1919) 36 R.P.C. 13; See also Chapter V, Part D of Guidelines for Examination in EPO, para 3.1.3.1 referred to in *Pall Corp v. Commercial Hydraulics (Bedford) Ltd.* [1990] F.S.R. at 347.

In *Merrell Dow Pharmaceuticals Inc. v. Norton & Co. Ltd.*,[71a] Aldous J. held that the prior use of a product was to be considered in the same way as a prior published document. In both cases it was necessary to ascertain what was the disclosure and whether it had made the product available to the public. Prior public use did not invalidate a patent for a product in a case where the product which was being used was incapable of analysis and an examination would have disclosed nothing as to its composition or manufacture.

Samples

5.31   The gift of a sample of the invention will invalidate a 1977 Act patent applied for subsequently if it provides the means of knowledge.[72]

Whilst dealing commercially with samples of an invention before the priority date of the patent constitutes a prior use under the 1949 Act,[73] to constitute matter made available to the public such use must be of one which enables the recipient of the sample to ascertain the invention in a manner which he is free in equity and law to use.[74]

D. Exceptions as to what constitutes the state of the art under the 1977 Act

5.32   Disclosure of any matter constitutes the invention made within six months prior to the date of filing the application is to be disregarded if:

(a) the matter was obtained unlawfully or in breach of confidence either from the inventor or any third party who had obtained it in confidence from the inventor[75]

(b) the disclosure was due to or made in consequence of the inventor displaying the invention at an international exhibition.[76]

A special exception is also provided for substances to be used for medical or veterinary use where the substance or composition already forms part of the state of the art but it's new use does not.[77]

As regards what constitutes exceptions to prior disclosure under the 1949 Act see *post* § 5.43.

[71a] [1994] R.P.C. 1.

[72] See *Fomento Industrial S.A. v. Mentmare Manufacturing Co. Ltd.* [1956] R.P.C. 87 at 105.

[73] See *Wheatley's Application* [1985] R.P.C. 9; *W.L. Gove Associates v. Kimal Scientific Products Ltd.* [1988] R.P.C. 137.

[74] See *Quantel Ltd. v. Spaceward Microsystems Ltd.* [1990] R.P.C. 83 and *P.L.G. Research Ltd. v. Arden International Ltd.* [1993] F.S.R. 197.

[75] P.A. 1977, s.2(4)(*a*) and (*b*).

[76] P.A. 1977, s.2(4)(*c*).

[77] P.A. 1977, s.2(6).

E. Prior user relating to 1949 Act patents

The prior user which will invalidate a patent under section 32(1)(e) of **5.33** the 1949 Act must be such as will make the invention "not new" and must, therefore, be "public use". As to the circumstances under which secret prior use will invalidate a patent under section 32(1)(l), see *post*. However, Lord Diplock said in *Bristol-Myers Appn.*

> "To sell the product by way of trade is to 'use' it, notwithstanding the seller's ignorance of its identity or his lack of knowledge of its composition or his uncertainty as to how and where further supplies of it could be obtained."[78]

In *Dollands* case,[79] which is usually assumed to be a case of prior user, **5.34** the objection to Dolland's patent was that he was not the inventor of the method of making new object-glasses, but that Dr. Hall had made the same discovery before him. It was held that inasmuch as Dr. Hall had confined it to his closet, and the public were not acquainted with it, Dolland was to be considered the inventor. This appears to be a case where the prior user was both secret and experimental.

In *Carpenter v. Smith*[80] the patent sued on was for a lock. The defendant **5.35** called a witness who proved that a similar lock had been used on a gate adjoining a public road for 16 years prior to the patent. It was held that this invalidated the patent. Lord Abinger C.B. analysed the meaning of the words "public use". "Public use does not mean a use or exercise by the public, but a use or exercise in a public manner". In *Taylor's Patent*[81] the patent was for a fire-grate. It was revoked on the ground that a similar grate had been used in a private house in the ordinary way and under no conditions of secrecy.

In *Stead v. Anderson*[82] the alleged prior user consisted in the use on a **5.36** private carriage-drive, the principal approach to a private house, of the kind of paving for which the patent was granted. Parke B. said:

> "If the mode of forming and laying blocks at Sir W. Worsley's had been precisely similar to the plaintiff's, that would have been sufficient user to destroy the plaintiff's patent, though put in practice in a spot to which the public had not free access."[83]

---

[78] [1975] R.P.C. 127 at p.157.
[79] (1766) (unrep.) but mentioned in 1 W.P.C. at p.43.
[80] (1841) 1 W.P.C. 530; 9 M. & W. 300.
[81] (1896) 13 R.P.C. 482.
[82] (1847) 2 W.P.C. 151.
[83] And see *Humpherson v. Syer* (1887) 4 R.P.C. 407 (C.A.).

5.37   Even an admittedly experimental prior public working of the invention is sufficient to invalidate the patent (for the invention is thereby made known) unless such experimental working necessarily takes place in public, having regard to the nature of the invention.[84] It is submitted that "public working" in this connection means a user of the invention in such a manner that a skilled person present can see or deduce the details of the invention. In *Boyce v. Morris Motors Ltd.*,[85] where the alleged prior user related to a thermometer used on a motor car during tests, Sargant L.J. said (distinguishing *Carpenter v. Smith*):

> "But here, the mere fact that these cars were driven on the public highway did not give anybody the opportunity of stopping the car and asking to have a look into the top of the radiator to see what was there . . . there was no greater public user . . . than if the cars had been driven on a private testing ground . . . "

A prior exhibition of a machine which is a failure will not affect the validity of a patent for a successful machine, even though there may be considerable similarity between the machines.[86]

Three mile limit for ships

5.38   It was held in 1935 that in order to be available against validity an alleged prior user taking place in a ship must occur within the three mile limit.[87]

Secret use

5.39   The law is unclear as to what the words "secret use" mean. In *Bristol-Myers Co.'s Application*,[88] Lord Diplock and Kilbrandon agreed with the Court of Appeal and held that the word "secret" meant "Done with an intention of being concealed; clandestinely", Lords Reid and Morris held that the test was objective and that "secret" means what is concealed in fact. Lord Cross leaving the point open, stated that whatever else "secret" meant, a user which puts it out of the inventor's power to prevent the purchaser discovering, if he can, the manner in which the invention works cannot be termed a "secret user" whatever be the state of mind of the inventor.

Offer to sell

5.40   The fact that there was no demand for the article is irrelevant.[89] Deposit in a warehouse for the purposes of sale, but not amounting to a public exhibition as in a shop, has been held to be prior user.[90] An offer for sale in a foreign periodical which was circulated in this country has

---

[84] P.A. 1949, s.51(3). *Cave-Brown-Cave's Appn.* [1958] R.P.C. 429.
[85] (1926) 44 R.P.C. 105 at p.149.
[86] *Murrary v. Clayton* (1872) 7 Ch.App. 570 at pp. 581–582.
[87] *V.D. Ltd. v. Boston, etc., Ltd.* (1935) 52 R.P.C. 303 at p.331.
[88] [1975] R.P.C. 127.
[89] *Losh v. Hague* (1838) 1 W.P.C. 530 at p.536.
[90] *Mullins v. Hart.* (1852) 3 Car. & Kir. 297.

been held not to be an offer for sale made in this country.[91] It is suggested that an oral or written offer for sale unaccompanied by the good themselves would not of itself constitute a prior user, but could provide evidence that a particular user was public and not secret.

Experiments and trials

An experiment in the course of making the invention is not a prior **5.41** publication by user.[92] The effect of experiments by way of reasonable trial of the invention made before the priority date of the claim was clearly laid down in the 1949 Act,[93] and it is submitted that many of the dicta in cases dealing with this subject[94] prior to the 1949 Act are not now good law. The law in respect of the 1949 Act patents may be summarised as follows:

Any such trial which constitutes a disclosure in public of the invention or of information which renders the invention obvious will invalidate a patent of subsequent priority date unless:

(a) (i) The invention is of such a nature that it is reasonably necessary for such trial to take place in public; and

    (ii) (a) the trial is reasonable;

        (b) takes place within one year before the priority date; and

        (c) is by or with the consent of the patentee or applicant or a person from whom he derives title[95]; or

(b) the trial is secret.[96]

The mere fact that the user amounts to a "commercial working" of the invention does not necessarily make such user other than by way of "reasonable trial".[97] It must be a question of fact and degree in each case and whether or not it is done for the patentee is irrelevant.[98]

F. Exceptions to prior disclosure under the 1949 Act

Under the 1949 Act an invention claimed in a complete specification is **5.42** deemed not to be "anticipated" if the invention was published before

---

[91] *Cincinnati Grinders (Inc.) v. B.S.A. Tools Ltd.* (1931) 48 R.P.C. 33 at p.51.

[92] *Housefill Co. v. Neilson* (1843) 1 W.P.C. 673 at p.708.

[93] P.A. 1949, ss.32(2), 50(2), 51(3).

[94] *Morgan v. Seaward* (1836) 2 M. & W. 544 at p.557; 1 W.P.C. 167 at p.187; *Newall v. Elliott* (1858) 4 C.B. (N.S.) 269 at p.295; *Cornish v. Keene* (1835) 1 W.P.C. 501 at p.508; *Croysdale v. Fisher* (1884) 1 R.P.C. 17 at p.21; *Germ Milling Co. v. Robinson* (1886) 3 R.P.C. 254, 399; *Morgan v. Windover* (1888) 5 R.P.C. 295 at p.302; *Elias v. Grovesend Tinplate Co.* (1890) 7 R.P.C. 455 at p.466; *Electrolytic Plating Apparatus Co. v. Holland* (1901) 18 R.P.C. 521 at p.526; *Robertson v. Purdey* (1907) 24 R.P.C. 273.

[95] P.A. 1949, s.51(3).

[96] P.A. 1949, s.32(2).

[97] See P.A. 1949, s.50(2), proviso. And see *Newall v. Elliott* (1858) 4 C.B.(N.S.) at p.295.

[98] *Perard Engineering Ltd.'s Appn.* [1976] R.P.C. 363.

the priority date of the claim in certain circumstances.[99] It is further provided that the Comptroller shall not refuse to accept a complete specification or to grant a patent, and a patent shall not be revoked or invalidated, by reason only of any circumstances which, by virtue of these provisions of the Act, do not constitute an anticipation of the invention.[1] For example, in these cases a patent cannot be invalidated on the ground that the invention has been rendered obvious. The cases are:

(a) Prior publication in a patent specification, or an abridgment of a patent specification, relating to a patent specification more than fifty years old.[2-3]

(b) If the matter published
   (i)   was obtained from the applicant or from some person from whom he derives title,
   (ii) was published without the consent of the person entitled,
   (iii) is the subject of a British or (in a convention case) of a foreign application made as soon as reasonably practicable after the applicant learned of the publication, and
   (iv) had not been commercially worked in the United Kingdom before the priority date of the claim (otherwise than for the purpose of reasonable trial) with the consent of the person entitled.[4]

    The word "obtained" includes matter obtained abroad.[5]

(c) If the publication took place pursuant to a patent application made in contravention of the rights of the person entitled, or by such wrongful applicant, or someone authorised by him, subsequent to such wrongful application.[6] This provision will apply both where the wrongful application is fraudulently made and where it is made pursuant to a genuine misapprehension as to his rights by the applicant. If the prior application is refused, or any patent granted is revoked, or the offending claims are excised by amendment, the subsequent rightful application can be ante dated to the date of the earlier wrongful application for the purposes of the provisions of the Act relating to the priority date of the claims.[7]

(d) If the publication took place because the invention was communicated to a government department or any person authorised by a government department, for investigation as to its merits.[8]

(e) If the publication took place for the purposes of an exhibition

---

[99] P.A. 1949, ss.50, 51, 52.
[1] P.A. 1949, ss.50(4), 51(4), 52(1).
[2-3] P.A. 1949, s.50(1). See *ante*, § 5.27.
[4] P.A. 1949, s.50(2).
[5] *Ethyl Corp.'s Patent* [1966] R.P.C. 205.
[6] P.A. 1949, s.50(3).
[7] P.A. 1949, s.53.
[8] P.A. 1949, s.51(1).

certified by the Department of Trade and Industry, or in a paper
read by the inventor before a learned society,[9] provided that a
patent is applied for in the United Kingdom[10] not later than six
months after the opening of the exhibition, or the reading or
publication of the paper.

(f) Where a complete specification is filed pursuant to an application
accompanied by a provisional specification, or pursuant to a
convention application, no publication of any matter contained in
such provisional specification or such convention application
after the date of such provisional specification or convention
application will invalidate the patent.[11]

G. Distinction between novelty and obviousness

The law draws a distinction between "novelty" (the absence of **5.43**
novelty being commonly referred to as "anticipation") and "obviousness" (commonly referred to in the older decided cases as "lack of
subject-matter"). This latter phrase is nowhere used in the Act in this
sense and is more appropriate to express the absence of any quality of a
nature such as to make the invention inherently patentable than the
absence of the quality of "inventiveness". For example, a new filing
system or a new game of cards, however ingenious, is not patentable
and could appropriately be described as lacking in subject-matter for
invention.[12] Accordingly the expression "subject-matter" is never used
in this book, except in quotations from judgments, in the sense of
possessing the quality of inventiveness.

In *Gadd and Mason v. Mayor etc. of Manchester*[13] Lindley L.J. said: **5.44**

"... In considering subject-matter, novelty is assumed; the question is
whether, assuming the invention to be new, it is one for which a
patent can be granted. In considering novelty, the invention is
assumed to be one for which a patent can be granted if new, and the
question is whether on that assumption it is new. Has it been
disclosed before? If there is an earlier specification for the very same
thing, the second invention is not new; but if the two things are
different, the nature and extent of the difference have to be considered. The question becomes one of degree. But unless it can be said that
the differences are practically immaterial, that there is no ingenuity in
the second invention, no experiment necessary to show whether it can

---

[9] P.A. 1949, s.51(2).
[10] *Ethyl Corp's. Patent* [1963] R.P.C. 155.
[11] P.A. 1949, s.52.
[12] See *ante*, Chap. 2.
[13] (1892) 9 R.P.C. 516 at p.525.

be successfully carried out or not, the second cannot be said to have been anticipated by the first ... "

5.45   The above statement of Lindley L.J. has been frequently cited for the purpose of contrasting "novelty" and "obviousness", but the distinction between these is better illustrated by *Molins v. Industrial Machinery Co. Ltd.*[14] The patentee had discovered that in a high-speed cigarette-making machine the filling of the cigarettes tended to become irregular, which defect was not apparent in earlier low speed machines. The trouble was cured by imparting to the shower of tobacco falling upon the travelling band of paper in the machine a component of velocity in the direction of horizontal movement. Claim 1 of the patent was as follows:

> "A cigarette-making machine of the continuous rod type wherein the tobacco showered into the trough of the machine is given a movement in the direction of movement of the cigarette rod prior to the same engaging with the band or web of cigarette paper".

5.46   An earlier specification of one *Bonsack* disclosed a machine which was not capable of being run at any speed at which this particular defect would manifest, but for some reason, which none of the experts were able to explain satisfactorily, *Bonsack* had provided an inclined shute for the tobacco which would necessarily impart a movement to it of the kind in the claim. Lord Greene M.R. said:[15]

> "I am satisfied that the discovery of the causes of the defect was by no means obvious and that an act of invention was necessary. The same remark applies to the realisation that the defect could be remedied by imparting to the falling tobacco a component of movement in the direction of the moving band ... (But) the claim includes every cigarette-making machine in which a component of movement in the direction of the travelling band or web is imparted to the shower of tobacco at whatever speed the machine runs or is capable of running. If the claim ... covers a machine which is the subject-matter of an earlier patent, it is necessarily void. In the present case there is such an earlier patent and ... the existence of that earlier patent is fatal to its validity ... But here an argument is put forward which I have some difficulty in following ... *Bonsack's* specification does not explain for what purpose in the construction of his machine the trough is to be inclined ... It is said, as I follow the argument, that *Bonsack* cannot be an anticipation because it does not appear and ought not to be assumed that, in giving directions for the invention of his trough, he was envisaging the same problem as that with which the present

---

[14] (1938) 55 R.P.C. 31.
[15] (1938) *Ibid.* at p.38.

inventor was concerned, and that if the problems were not the same, the validity of the present claim is not affected by the fact that this particular element is to be found inserted for no apparent purpose in *Bonsack's* machine ... (But) *Bonsack's* instruction is to make a machine of a particular kind ... The inclination which he gives to his trough is a physical part necessarily present in each machine made in accordance with his specification and is as much a part of the true nature of that machine as any other element in it"

and the claim, as originally drafted, was held invalid for lack of novelty.

5.47 An amendment was asked for and permitted by which the opening words of the claim were made to read: "A cigarette-making machine of the continuous rod type capable of moving at a speed of more than 900 cigarettes per minute ... " Lord Greene M.R. said:[16]

"Now if the specification is amended in this way there can, in my opinion, be no suggestion that it is anticipated by *Bonsack*. A cigarette-making machine capable of running at a rate of 900 cigarettes a minute or more is a different machine from *Bonsack's* since *Bonsack's* machine could not run at anything approaching that speed."

5.48 Therefore, anticipation is established if the claim, when properly construed, includes something which has previously been published.[17] If the prior disclosure does not fall within the words of the claim the latter is not invalid on the ground that the invention claimed is not new. The different question then has to be considered whether it was obvious and did not require any inventive step to reach the invention claimed from the general field of prior knowledge. In most cases this latter question is the one that gives rise to difficulty, for it is rare to find a prior disclosure that falls strictly within the wording of a claim since every claim has been the subject of careful investigation in the Patent Office before it has been allowed.

Test to be applied to prior document

5.49 In *P.L.G. Research Ltd. v. Ardon International.*[18] Aldous J. stated as follows:

"Novelty has been a requirement of patent law for hundreds of years and there are a number of well-known authorities which help to illustrate what must be established. They are still good law. It is sufficient for me to refer to the judgment of the Court of Appeal in the *General Tire & Rubber Co. v. Firestone Tyre & Rubber Co. Ltd.* [1972]

---

[16] (1938) 55 R.P.C. 31 at p.43.
[17] See *Electric and Musical Industries Ltd. v. Lissen Ltd.* (1937) 54 R.P.C. 307 at p.324.
[18] [1993] F.S.R. 197 at 218.

R.P.C. 457 at 485.

In that case, the Court of Appeal stated:

5.50   'The earlier publication and the patentee's claim must each be construed as they would be at the respective relevant dates by a reader skilled in the art to which they relate having regard to the state of knowledge in such art at the relevant date. The construction of these documents is a function of the court, being a matter of law, but, since documents of this nature are almost certain to contain technical material, the court must, by evidence, be put in the position of a person of the kind to whom the document is addressed, that is to say, a person skilled in the relevant art at the relevant date. If the art is one having a highly developed technology, the notional skilled reader to whom the document is addressed may not be a single person but a team, whose combined skills would normally be employed in that art in interpreting and carrying into effect instructions such as those which are contained in the document to be construed. We have already described the composite entity deemed to constitute the notional skilled addressee.'

'When the prior inventor's publication and the patentee's claim have respectively been construed by the court in the light of all properly admissible evidence as to technical matters, the meaning of words and expressions used in the art and so forth, the question whether the patentee's claim is new for the purposes of section 32(1)(*e*) falls to be decided as a question of fact. If the prior inventor's publication contains a clear description of, or clear instructions to do or make, something that would infringe the patentee's claim if carried out after the grant of the patentee's patent, the patentee's claim will have been shown to lack the novelty, that is to say, it will have been anticipated. The prior inventor, however, and the patentee will have approached the same device from different starting points and may for this reason, or it may be for other reasons, have so described their devices that it cannot be immediately discerned from a reading of the language which they have respectively used that they have discovered in truth the same device; but if carrying out the directions contained in the prior inventor's publication will inevitably result in something being made or done which, if the patentee's patent were valid, would constitute an infringement of the patentee's claim, this circumstance demonstrates that the patentee's claim has in fact been anticipated.'

'If, on the other hand, the prior publication contains a direction which is capable of being carried out in a manner which would infringe the patentee's claim, but would be at least as likely to be carried out in a way which would not do so, the patentee's claim will not have been anticipated, although it may fail on the ground of obviousness. To anticipate the patentee's claim the prior publication must contain clear and unmistakable directions to do what the patentee claims to have invented: *Flour Oxidizing Co. Ltd.*

v. Carr & Co. Ltd. (1908) 25 R.P.C. 428 at 457, line 34, approved in *B.T.H. Co. Ltd. v. Metropolitan Vickers Electrical Co. Ltd* (1928) 45 R.P.C. 1 at 24, line 1. A signpost, however clear, upon the road to the patentee's invention will not suffice. The prior inventor must be clearly shown to have planted his flag at the precise destination before the patentee.'[th]"

The test whether the disclosure contained in a prior document is such as **5.51** to invalidate a subsequent invention was stated by Lord Westbury L.C. in *Hills v. Evans*[19] in the following terms:

"The antecedent statement must, in order to invalidate the subsequent patent, be such that a person of ordinary knowledge of the subject would at once perceive and understand and be able practically to apply the discovery without the necessity of making further experiments ... the information ... given by the prior publication must, for the purposes of practical utility, be equal to that given by the subsequent patent."

As Lord Reid stated in *C. Van der Lely N.V. v. Bamfords Ltd.*[20]: **5.52**

"There are two branches of this statement. The first is that a 'person of ordinary knowledge of the subject would at once perceive and understand and be able practically to apply the discovery without the necessity of making further experiments' ... Lord Westbury must have meant experiments with a view to discovering something not disclosed. He cannot have meant to refer to the ordinary methods of trial and error which involve no inventive step and generally are necessary in applying any discovery to produce a practical result ... The other requirement is that 'the information given by the prior publication must for the purpose of practical utility be equal to that given by the subsequent patent.' There may be cases where the skilled man has to have the language of the publication translated for him or where he must get from a scientist the meaning of technical terms or ideas with which he is not familiar, but once he has got this he must be able to make the machine from what is disclosed by the prior publication."

The "person of ordinary knowledge"

The "person of ordinary knowledge" referred to by Lord Westbury is **5.53** the typical addressee of the plaintiff's patent specification, the kind of person who would be expected to make a machine or carry out the

---

[19] (1860) 31 L.J. Ch. 457 at p.463. Also reported (1862) 4 De G. F. & J. 288, 45 E.R. 1193. See also *Armstrong Whitworth & Co. Ltd. v. Hardcastle* (1925) 42 R.P.C. 543 at p.555.
[20] [1963] R.P.C. 61 at p.71.

process of the kind in question (see, *per* Lord Reid in *C. Van der Lely N.V. v. Bamfords Ltd.*).[21] The dicta of Lord Watson in *King, Brown & Co. v. Anglo-American Brush Co.*[22] does not, it is submitted, mean in its context that the "persons of ordinary knowledge" are not the persons who would make the machine or carry out the process but are persons of superior knowledge such as "men of science and employers of labour", but, if it should have this meaning, then it is submitted that it is not good law. The correct statement of the law on this point is that set out in the last sentence of the above quoted extracts from Lord Reid's speech in *C. Van der Lely N.V. v. Bamfords Ltd.*[23] The "person of ordinary knowledge" may be a team combining the knowledge of more than one art.[24]

5.54   In *Kaye v. Chubb & Sons Ltd.*[25] Lord Esher M.R. said:

> "I quite agree with what has been stated as to the law by Lord Westbury. If in the first patent which is thus alleged there is a general statement which gives no clear intimation either by its own construction or ... by considering what would be the effect of it upon a hypothetical workman of ordinary skill ... and if some other person coming with great skill and great care should, out of the general words, really produce something not inconsistent with them, but which is not disclosed by them, I quite agree that he can take out a patent, and he cannot be defeated, because that which is really his invention can be got within general words which describe nothing."[26]

In *Gillette Safety Razor Co. v. Anglo-American Trading Co. Ltd.*[27] Lord Moulton said:

> "In ascertaining its effect the court must consider what it (the prior document) would convey to the public to whom it was addressed, *i.e.* to mechanicians. I recognise that it would be most unfair to subsequent patentees if we tested this by what it would convey or suggest to a mechanical genius; but, on the other hand, it would be equally unjust to the public to take it as though it were read only by mechanical idiots".

5.55   In *British Thomson-Houston Co. Ltd. v. Metropolitan-Vickers Ltd.*,[28] where the question was whether *Rosenberg's* invention (which was concerned with the bringing of synchronous electric machines into exact synchronism before establishing the electric connection) was anticipated by a prior specification of *Tesla*, Lord Dunedin said: "Would a man

---

[21] *Ibid.*
[22] (1892) 9 R.P.C. 313 at p.320.
[23] [1963] R.P.C. 61 at p.71. See also *Ransberg Co. v. Aerostyle Ltd.* [1968] R.P.C. 287 at p.299.
[24] *Tetra Molectric Ltd. v. Japan Imports* [1976] R.P.C. 547 at 583.
[25] (1887) 4 R.P.C. 289 at p.298.
[26] Cited by Lord Upjohn in *Ransberg Co. v. Aerostyle Ltd.* [1968] R.P.C. 287.
[27] (1913) 30 R.P.C. 465 at p.481.
[28] (1928) 45 R.P.C. 1.

who was grappling with *Rosenberg's* problem ... and had *Tesla's* specification in his hand have said: 'That gives me what I wish'?" These words have been frequently quoted and cited as providing a test by which inventiveness can be established. But, it is submitted, they are quite unhelpful for this purpose. In the first place the meaning of the words "what I wish" is not clear. They presumably do not mean "a solution of the problem" because one previously published solution cannot anticipate or render obvious an alternative solution which required a further act of invention to produce. It would seem that the words mean "the solution which the patentee subsequently disclosed and claimed". But in that case this is merely putting into different (and more obscure) words the very question that the test is supposed to give assistance in answering. *British Thomson-Houston Co. Ltd. v. Metropolitan-Vickers Ltd.*[29] has been lucidly explained by Lord Greene M.R. in *Molins v. Industrial Machinery Co. Ltd.*[30]

"Mosaic" of publications not legitimate

It is not legitimate to piece together a number of prior documents in   **5.56** order to produce an anticipation of the invention. In *Von Heyden v. Neustadt*[31] the defendants pleaded anticipation, and put in evidence a mass of paragraphs extracted from a large number of publications. James L.J. in his judgment, said:

"We are of opinion that if it requires this mosaic of extracts, from annuals and treaties spread over a series of years, to prove the defendants' contention, that contention stands thereby self-condemned ... And even if it could be shown that a patentee made his discovery of a consecutive process by studying, collating and applying a number of facts discriminated in the pages of such works, his diligent study of such works would as much entitle him to the character of an inventor as the diligent study of the works of nature would do."[32]

And in *Lowndes' Patent*[33] Tomlin J. said:

"It is not open to you to take a packet of prior documents and ... by ... putting a puzzle together produce what you say is a disclosure in the nature of a combination of the various elements which have been contained in the prior documents. I think it is necessary to point to a

---

[29] *Ibid.*
[30] [1937] 55 R.P.C. 31.
[31] (1880) 50 L.J. Ch. 126 at p.128.
[32] And see *Rondo Co. Ltd. v. Gramophone Co. Ltd* (1929) 46 R.P.C. 378 at p.391; *Pope Appliance Corpn. v. Spanish River, etc., Ltd.* (1929) 46 R.P.C. 23; [1929] A.C. 269.
[33] (1928) 45 R.P.C. 48 at p.57.

clear and specific disclosure of something which is said to be like the patentee's invention."

A series of papers which form a series of disclosures and refer to each other, so that "anyone reading one is referred by cross-references to the others", do not, however, form a mosaic.[34]

Construction of prior documents

5.57   The general rule for the construction of prior documents is the same as that for any other documetns, *viz* "that the document should be construed as if the court had to construe it at the date of publication, to the exclusion of information subsequently discovered".[35] In determining the meaning of the document regard may be had only to what is stated in the document itself, and parol evidence can be admitted merely "for the purpose of explaining words or symbols of art . . . and . . . of informing the court of relevant surrounding circumstances".[36]

5.58   But this does not apply to photographs, or presumably to drawings, as appears from the speech of Lord Reid in *C. Van der Lely N.V. v. Bamfords Ltd.*:[37]

"There is no doubt that, where the matter alleged to amount to anticipation consists of a written description, the interpretation of that description is, like the interpretation of any document, a question for the court assisted where necessary by evidence regarding the meaning of technical language. It was argued that the same applies to a photograph. I do not think so. Lawyers are expected to be experts in the use of the English language, but we are not experts in the reading or interpretation of photographs. The question is what the eye of the man with appropriate engineering skill would see in the photograph, and that appears to me to be a matter of evidence. Where the evidence is contradictory the judge must decide. But the judge ought not in my opinion to attempt to read or construe the photograph himself; he looks at the photograph in determining which of the explanations given by the witnesses appears to be most worthy of acceptance."

The intention of the author of the document is not material.[38]

---

[34] *Sharpe & Dohme Inc. v. Boots Pure Drug Co. Ltd.* (1927) 44 R.P.C. 367 at p.402; (1928) 45 R.P.C. 153 at p.180.

[35] *Ore Concentration Co. (1905) Ltd. v. Sulphide Corporation Ltd.* (1914) 31 R.P.C. 206 at p.224; *Nobel's Explosives Co. Ltd. v. Anderson* (1894) 11 R.P.C. 519 at p.523; see also *British Thomson-Houston Co. Ltd. v. Metropolitan-Vickers etc. Ltd.* (1928) 45 R.P.C. 1 at p.20.

[36] *Canadian General Electric Co. Ltd. v. Fada Radio Ltd.* (1930) 47 R.P.C. 69 at p.90.

[37] [1963] R.P.C. 61.

[38] *Ibid*; and see *Kaye v. Chubb & Sons Ltd.* (1887) 4 R.P.C. 289 at p.298.

Selection patents

The House of Lords in *E.I. Du Pont De Nemours And Company v. Akzo*   **5.59**
N.V.[39] drew a distinction between the degree of information necessary
to enable a product to be made and the information that is necessary to
anticipate a claim to a selected member of a class. Where the inventive
step lies in the selection of a member having special advantages from a
previously disclosed class there will be no anticipation of a claim to the
product *per se* unless the selected member has been made and the special
advantages ascertained.

Common general knowledge

Prior knowledge sufficient to invalidate a patent need not be found in   **5.60**
a particular document but may be common general knowledge, *i.e.*,
such as every worker in the art may be expected to have as part of his
technical equipment.[40] The relevant date at which the state of common
general knowledge is to be considered is immediately before the
priority date of the patent.[41] However any document relied on as a prior
publication must be construed as of its date of publication to the
exclusion of information subsequently discovered.[42] It is submitted that
it is not legitimate to invalidate a claim for a new combination or a new
process by showing that some of the integers or steps are to be found in a
prior disclosure while the remainder are matters of common knowledge, unless it can be proved that it would be obvious to combine all
such features. If such be the case then the ground of invalidity is
obviousness.

"Mere paper anticipation"

It has sometimes been said that if a prior disclosure is contained only   **5.61**
in a document and there is no evidence that such disclosure has given
rise to any practical result, this is "mere paper anticipation" and must be
appraised in some specially strict manner.[43] It is difficult to understand
the relevance of this observation. If the document in fact discloses the
invention and is to be found in a place (*e.g.* a public library) to which the
public have access, it is wholly immaterial that in fact no one has ever
read it. From one point of view a well-known document which has not
actually led to the invention should be regarded with much greater
suspicion as an anticipation, for the failure of an obscure document to

---

[39] H.L., [1982] F.S.R. 303.
[40] *Automatic Coil Winder, etc., Co. Ltd. v. Taylor Electrical Instruments Ltd.* (1944) 61 R.P.C. 41
at p.43.
[41] See *British Thomson-Houston Co. Ltd. v. Stonebridge Electrical Co. Ltd.* (1916) 33 R.P.C. 166
at p.171.
[42] *Ore Concentration Co. v. Sulphide Corporation Ltd.* (1914) 31 R.P.C. 206; *Minnesota Mining
and Manufacturing Co. v. Bondinn Ltd.* [1973] R.P.C. 491.
[43] See *Metropolitan-Vickers, etc. Ltd. v. B.T.-H. Co. Ltd* (1926) 43 R.P.C. 76 at p.93.

lead to a useful manufacture may be explained by the fact that no one having both the means and the inclination to put it into practice has ever seen it. It is submitted that any alleged prior disclosure in a document must be assessed on its own language, irrespective of how many or how few people may have seen it and how little action may have resulted from its publication.

Disclosure of machine processes

5.62   Under the 1949 Act if a prior document disclosed a machine which could operate only in a particular way, or if the document gave directions that the machine should be operated in that way, a subsequent patent claiming a method or process consisting merely of that way of operation is invalid, notwithstanding that the actual machine disclosed in the prior document is impractical.[44] Similarly a claim for a chemical substance is invalid if that substance is disclosed in a prior published document even if the method of preparation disclosed in the prior document is erroneous.[45] However, under the 1977 Act it is a necessary requirement that the prior disclosure enables the skilled reader to make the product or substance in question.[46]

The prior disclosure of a machine will not invalidate a claim for a process for which the machine is suitable unless the process as well as the machine is specifically disclosed. In *Flour Oxidizing Co. v. Carr & Co.*[47] Parker J. said:

> "When the question is solely one of prior publication it is not, in my opinion, enough to prove that an apparatus described in an earlier specification could have been used to produce this or that result. It must also be shown that the specification contains clear and unmistakable direction so to use it."

The publication of a device provided with an adjustment is a complete publication of the device without the adjustment, because an ordinary mechanician would appreciate that the provision of the adjustment was optional.[48]

Inevitable result

5.63   In *General Tire & Rubber Co. v. Firestone Tyre & Rubber Co. Ltd.*[49] the Court of Appeal stated:

---

[44] *Otto v. Linford* (1882) 46 L.T. (N.S.) 35 at p.44.
[45] *Smith Kline & French Laboratories' Appn.* [1968] R.P.C. 415.
[46] *Asahi Kasei Kogyo KK's Appr.* [1991] R.P.C. 485.
[47] (1908) 25 R.P.C. 428 at p.457.
[48] *Gillette Safety Razor Co. v. Anglo-American Trading Co. Ltd.* (1913) 30 R.P.C. 465 at p.481.
[49] [1972] R.P.C. 457 at p.486. See also *Quantel Ltd. v. Spaceward Microsystems Ltd.* [1990] R.P.C. 83 at 112.

" ... if carrying out the directions contained in the prior inventor's publication will inevitably result in something being made or done which, if the patentee's patent were valid, would constitute an infringement of the patentee's claim, this circumstance demonstrates that the patentee's claim has in fact been anticipated.

"If, on the other hand, the prior publication contains a direction which is capable of being carried out in a manner which would infringe the patentee's claim, but would be at least as likely to be carried out in a way which would not do so, the patentee's claim will not have been anticipated, although it may fail on the ground of obviousness. To anticipate the patentee's claim the prior publication must contain clear and unmistakable directions to do what the patentee claims to have invented: *Flour Oxidizing Co. Ltd. v. Carr & Co. Ltd.* (1908) 25 R.P.C. 428 at 457, line 34, approved in *British Thomson-Houston Co. Ltd. v. Metropolitan-Vickers Electrical Co. Ltd.* (1928) 45 R.P.C. 1 at 24, line 1). A signpost, however clear, upon the road to the patentee's invention will not suffice. The prior inventor must be clearly shown to have planted his flag at the precise destination before the patentee."

Publication by drawing or photograph

A patent for a machine may be anticipated by a drawing or photograph of it unaccompanied by explanatory letterpress if published in a book or elsewhere so that it could become generally known, provided that any machinist would understand it, and could make the machine from the drawing without any further information, and without the exercise of ingenuity,[50] but making such inferences as the skilled addressee would make.[51]   **5.64**

3. Obviousness

P.A. 1977, section 72(1)(a): the invention is not a patentable invention which by virtue of section 1(1) requires the invention to involve an inventive step. Section 3 provides that an invention shall be taken to involve an inventive step if it is not obvious to a person skilled in the art having regard to any matter which forms part of the state of the art by virtue of section 2(2).   **5.65**

P.A. 1949, section 32(1)(f): "the invention, so far as claimed in any

---

[50] *Herrburger, Schwander et Cie v. Squire* (1889) 6 R.P.C. 194 at p.198; *Electric Construction Co. Ltd. v. Imperial Tramways Co. Ltd.* (1900) 17 R.P.C. 537 at p.550; *C. Van der Lely N.V. v. Bamfords Ltd.* [1963] R.P.C. 61.
[51] *Lightning Fastener Co. Ltd. v. Colonial Fastener Co. Ltd.* (1934) 51 R.P.C. 349 at p.367; *Howaldt Ltd. v. Condrup Ltd.* (1937) 54 R.P.C. 121 at p.133.

claim of the complete specification, is obvious and does not involve any inventive step having regard to what was known or used, before the priority date of the claim, in the United Kingdom.''

In considering whether or not an invention is obvious, the way in which the inventor arrived at the invention may well be relevant in support of its unobviousness.[52] However, such evidence can rarely be used to attack the obviousness of a patent.[53] Patents have been held valid for inventions that have been the result of the merest accident,[54] and for inventions imported from abroad. But in considering whether any given invention can be considered obvious or not having regard to prior knowledge or prior user it is necesary to inquire whether in fact the new contrivance would be indicated to the class of persons to whom the prior documents are addressed, and who are concerned in the art with which the invention deals, by an examination of the available prior knowledge.[55] It has been suggested that the only relevant documents are those that a diligent searcher would know about.[56] However it is submitted that the correct view is that all published documents are relevant and that these should be considered as read carefully and completely.[57]

Approach to obviousness

5.66   A useful approach adopted by Oliver L.J. in *Windsurfing International Inc. v. Tabur Marine (Great Britain) Ltd.*[58] and which has been followed in other cases[59] is as follows:

(a) First the court identifies the inventive concept embodied in the patent in suit.

(b) Next the Court will assume the mantle of the normally skilled but unimaginative addressee in the art at the relevant date and will impute to him what was at that date, common general knowledge in the art in question.

(c) The Court should then identify what, if any differences exist between the matters cited as being "known or used" and the alleged invention.

(d) Finally the court has to decide whether, viewed without any

---

[52] *SKM S. A. v. Wagner Spraytech (U.K.)* [1982] R.P.C. 497 at 505 applied in *P & G Coy v. Peaudouce (U.K.) Ltd.* [1989] F.S.R. 180 at 190.
[53] *Crane v. Price* 1 W.P.C. 393 at 411.
[54] *Liardet v. Johnson* (1883) 1 W.P.C. 53.
[55] See *Martin v. H. Millwood Ltd.* [1956] R.P.C. 125 at p.139.
[56] *Techograph Printed Circuits Ltd. v. Mills & Rockley (Electronics) Ltd.* [1972] R.P.C. 346 at p.355.
[57] *Ibid.* at p.361.
[58] [1985] R.P.C. 59 at 73–74.
[59] See *P&G Coy v. Peaudouce (UK) Ltd* [1989] F.S.R. 180; *Fairfax (Dental Equipment) v. Fihol (S.J.)* [1986] R.P.C. 499 at 510–512; *3 M v. Rennicks (UK) Ltd.* [1992] R.P.C. 331: *Chiron Corp. v. Organon Tekniva Ltd.* [1994] F.S.R. 202; *Mölnlycke AB v. Proctor & Gamble Ltd.* [1994] R.P.C. 49.

knowledge of the alleged invention, those differences constitute steps which would have been obvious to the skilled man or whether they required any degree of invention.

How obviousness to be judged

In *Allmanna Svenska Elektriska A/B v. The Burntisland Shipbuilding Co.* **5.67** *Ltd.*[60] it was stated by the Court of Appeal:

"The matter of obviousness is to be judged by reference to the 'state of the art' in the light of all that was previously known by persons versed in that art derived from experience of what was practically employed, as well as from the contents of previous writings, specifications, textbooks and other documents ... When the relevant facts (as regards the state of the art) are known, the question: Was the alleged invention obvious? must in the end of all be as it were a kind of jury question. The relevant question to be asked and answered is in form and substance the question formulated by Sir Stafford Cripps and cited by the Master of the Rolls in *Sharpe and Dohme Inc. v. Boots Pure Drug Co. Ltd.*:[61] 'The real question is: Was it for all practical purposes obvious to any skilled chemist in the state of chemical knowledge existing at the date of the patent, which consists of the chemical literature available ... and his general chemical knowledge, that he could manufacture valuable therapeutic agents by making the higher alkyl resorcinols ...'

"It only remains to say that the question must be answered objectively, for it is immaterial that ... the invention claimed was in truth an invention of [the inventor] in the sense of being the result of independent work and research on his part—without knowledge on his part of many of the matters which must, on any view, be taken into account by the court."

This statement of the law was approved by the House of Lords in *Martin v. H. Millwood Ltd.*[62] Lord Morton said:

"I entirely agree with the reasoning of the Court of Appeal and would only add that the court did not, of course, throw any doubt upon the principle that there may be invention in a 'combination'; see, for instance, *British Celanese v. Courtaulds Ltd., per* Lord Tomlin".[63]

The Cripps form of question was adopted, in a modified form, by the Court of Appeal in *Killick v. Pye.*[64]

---

[60] [1951] 68 R.P.C. 63 at p.69.
[61] (1928) 45 R.P.C. 153 at p.173.
[62] [1956] R.P.C. 125 at p.139.
[63] (1935) 52 R.P.C. 171 at p.193.
[64] [1958] R.P.C. 366 at p.377.

5.68   But it is submitted that the "Cripps" form of question really does no more than reduce the question "was the invention obvious?" into the context of the particular case. It does not set any standard or test by which obviousness is to be judged. However, the required standard has been made clear in a number of cases. Thus, in *Siddell v. Vickers & Sons Ltd.*[65] Lord Herschell stated it as "so obvious that it would at once occur to anyone acquainted with the subject, and desirous of accomplishing the end". A much quoted test in similar terms enunciated by Lopes L.J. in *Savage v. Harris & Sons*[66] was:

> "The material question to be considered in a case like this is, whether the alleged discovery lies so much out of the track of what was known before as not naturally to suggest itself to a person thinking on the subject; it must not be the obvious or natural suggestion of what was previously known."

It is submitted that in that test the "person thinking on the subject" must be the notional skilled person in the particular field.

In *Mölnlycke AB v. Proctor & Gamble Ltd.*[66a] the Court of Appeal in the judgment of the court have recently stated:

> "the criterion for deciding whether or not the claimed invention involves an inventive step is wholly objective. It is an objective criterion defined in statutory terms, that is to say whether the step was obvious to a person skilled in the art having regard to any matter which, forms part of the state of the art as defined in section 2(2). We do not consider that it assists to ask whether 'the patent discloses something sufficiently inventive to deserve the grant of monopoly'. Nor is it useful to extract from older judgments expressions such as 'that scintilla of invention necessary to support a patent'. The statute has laid down what the criterion is to be. It is a qualitative not a quantitative test."

The Court of Appeal went on to state that in applying the statutory criterion the primary evidence will be that of properly qualified expert witnesses who will say whether or not, in their opinions, the relevant step could have been obvious to a skilled man having regard to the state of the art. All other evidence is secondary to that primary evidence. The importance of secondary evidence such as the contemporary events as to what persons in the art were doing and evidence of the commercial success of the invention will vary from case to case, but (so the Court of Appeal have stated) it must be kept firmly in its place and not allowed to

---

[65] (1890) 15 App. Cas. 496; (1890) 7 R.P.C. 292 at p.304.
[66] 13 R.P.C. 364 at p.370.
[66a] [1994] R.P.C. 49, leave to appeal to H.L. refused.

obscure the fact that it is no more than an aid in assessing the primary evidence. In so stating the Court of Appeal appears at least in part to have abrogated its role of judging obviousness and to have given expert testimony an unwarranted status of assessing what is obvious which is a matter for the court.

Quantum of Invention

In its judgment in the case of *Martin and Biro Swan Ltd. v. H. Millwood Ltd.*[67] (subsequently affirmed by the House of Lords), the Court of Appeal said "obviousness denies the presence of any inventive step whatever".[68] However, while some exercise of the inventive faculty is required, the *quantum* of invention necessary to support a patent is small. Thus, Ormerod L.J., delivering the judgment of the Court of Appeal in *Killick v. Pye*[69] stated:

5.69

"It is well settled that the validity of a patent, challenged on the ground of inventiveness, may be established though the inventive step represent a very small advance."

In considering whether the invention claimed is obvious, the relevant comparison is not between the preferred embodiment of the invention claimed and the prior art. If any embodiment within the scope of the claim is obvious, then the claim is invalid.[70]

5.70

If the alleged invention is in fact obvious, it is not any the less so because it was not obvious to an expert called at the trial.[71]

5.71

Simplicity no objection

In *Siddell v. Vickers & Sons Ltd.*[72] Lord Herschell said:

5.72

"If the apparatus be valuable by reason of its simplicity there is a danger of being misled by that very simplicity into the belief that no invention was needed to produce it. But experience has shown that not a few inventions ... have been of so simple a character that once they have been made known it was difficult ... not to believe that they must have been obvious to everybody."[73]

There may be invention in what is merely simplification.[74] But matters

---

[67] (1954) 71 R.P.C. 458.
[68] *Ibid.* at p.466.
[69] [1958] R.P.C. 366 at p.377.
[70] *Woodrow v. Long Humphreys & Co. Ltd.* (1934) 51 R.P.C. 25; *Non-Drip Measure Co. Ltd. v. Strangers Ltd.* (1942) 59 R.P.C. 1 at p.23 (reversed in H.L. on other grounds).
[71] *John Wright and Eagle Range Ltd. v. General Gas Appliances Ltd.* (1929) 46 R.P.C. 169 at p.178; *Automatic Coil Winder etc. Co. Ltd. v. Taylor Electrical Instruments Ltd.* (1943) 60 R.P.C. 111 at p.119.
[72] See n.65.
[73] See also *Thierry v. Riekman* (1897) 14 R.P.C. 105.
[74] *Pope Appliance Corp. v. Spanish River etc. Mills Ltd.* (1929) 46 R.P.C. 23 at p.55 (P.C.).

of ordinary skilled designing or mere workshop improvements cannot be considered as requiring the exercise of invention.[75]

Ex Post Facto Analysis

5.73   In *Non-Drip Measure Co. Ltd. v. Strangers Ltd.*[76] Lord Russell said:

"Whether there has or has not been an inventive step in constructing a device for giving effect to an idea which when given effect to seems a simple idea which ought to or might have occurred to anyone, is often a matter of dispute. More especially is this the case when many integers of the new device are already known. Nothing is easier than to say, after the event, that the thing was obvious and involved no invention. The words of Moulton L.J. in *British Westinghouse v. Braulik*[77] may well be called to mind in this connection: 'I confess' (he said) 'that I view with suspicion arguments to the effect that a new combination, bringing with it new and important consequences in the shape of practical machines, is not an invention, because, when it has once been established, it is easy to show how it might be arrived at by starting from something known, and taking a series of apparently easy steps. This *ex post facto* analysis of invention is unfair to the inventors and, in my opinion, it is not countenanced by English patent law ...' It is always pertinent to ask, as to the article which is alleged to have been a mere workshop improvement, and to have involved no inventive step, has it been a commercial success? Has it supplied a want? Some language used by Tomlin J. in *Samuel Parkes & Co. Ltd. v. Cocker Bros. Ltd*[78] may be cited as apposite: 'Nobody, however, has told me, and I do not suppose that anybody ever will tell me, what is the precise characteristic or quality the presence of which distinguishes invention from workshop improvement.... The truth is that when once it has been found ... that the problem had awaited solution for many years and that the device is in fact novel and superior to what had gone before and has been widely used in preference to alternative devices, it is, I think, practically impossible to say that there is not present that scintilla of invention necessary to support the patent.' "

5.74   In *Technograph Printed Circuits Ltd. v. Mills & Rockley (Electronics) Ltd.*[79] Lord Diplock said:

"The cross-examination of the respondents' expert followed with

---

[75] See *Safveans Aktie Bolag v. Ford Motor Co. (Eng.) Ltd.* (1927) 44 R.P.C. 49 at p.61; *Curtis & Son v. Heward & Co.* (1923) 40 R.P.C. 53, 183; *Shaw v. Burnet & Co.* (1924) 41 R.P.C. 432.
[76] (1943) 60 R.P.C. 135 at p.142.
[77] (1910) 27 R.P.C. 209 at p.230.
[78] (1929) 46 R.P.C. 241 at p.248.
[79] [1972] R.P.C. 346 at p.362.

customary skill the familiar 'step by step' course. I do not find it persuasive. Once an invention has been made it is generally possible to postulate a combination of steps by which the inventor might have arrived at the invention that he claims in his specification if he started from something that was already known. But it is only because the invention has been made and has proved successful that it is possible to postulate from what starting point and by what particular combination of steps the inventor could have arrived at his invention. It may be that taken in isolation none of the steps which it is now possible to postulate, if taken in isolation, appears to call for any inventive ingenuity. It is improbable that this reconstruction *a posteriori* represents the mental process by which the inventor in fact arrived at his invention, but, even if it were, inventive ingenuity lay in perceiving that the final result which it was the object of the inventor to achieve was attainable from the particular starting point and in his selection of the particular combination of steps which would lead to that result.''

Commerical success

While, as pointed out above, the practical utility and commercial success of the invention may be a material factor in determining whether the new result was obvious or not,[80] it is always necessary to consider whether any commercial success is due to the patented invention or to extraneous causes. In the latter event commercial succes is quite irrelevant when deciding whether the invention is obvious. **5.75**

In *Longbottom v. Shaw*[81] Lord Herschell said:

"Great reliance is placed upon the fact that when this patent was taken out and frames were made in accordance with it, there was a larger demand for them ... I do not dispute that that is a matter to be taken into consideration; but, again, it is obvious that it cannot be regarded in any sense as conclusive ... If nothing be shown beyond the fact that the new arrangement results in an improvement, and that this improvement causes a demand for an apparatus made in accordance with the patent, I think that it is of very little importance."

And in *Wildey and White's Mfg. Co. Ltd. v. Freeman and Letrik Ltd.*,[82] Maugham J. said: **5.76**

"In my opinion commercial success which is shown to be due to the precise improvement the subject of the specification ought to have considerable weight ... and, *a fortiori*, if it is shown that there is a

---

[80] See *Hinks & Son v. Safety Lighting Co.*, 4 Ch.D. 607; see also n. 66a, *supra*.
[81] (1891) 8 R.P.C. 333 at p.336.
[82] (1931) 48 R.P.C. 405 at p.414.

long-felt want ... In the case, however, of such an article as we have here, a comb, ... questions of price, form, colour and design, quite apart from the question of clever advertising, may well conduce to, or indeed, be completely responsible for, the commercial success of the article."[83]

However, even if an invention is commercially successful and the step taken was not an obvious commercial step to take, if the invention is obvious, from a technical or practical point of view, it will be held to be invalid. See *Hallen Company v. Brabantia (U.K.) Ltd.*[84]

New use of old material or contrivance

5.77   In *Gadd and Mason v. Mayor etc. of Manchester*[85] the plaintiff's invention was to keep gasometers vertical by means previously described. Lindley L. J., after a review of the authorities, expressed the law upon this subject by the two following propositions:

"1. A patent for the mere new use of a known contrivance, without any additional ingenuity in overcoming fresh difficulties, is bad, and cannot be supported. If the new use involves no ingenuity, but is in manner and purpose analogous to the old use, although not quite the same, there is no invention: no manner of new manufacture within the meaning of the statute of James.

"2. On the other hand, a patent for a new use of a known contrivance is good, and can be supported if the new use involves practical difficulties which the patentee has been the first to see and overcome by some ingenuity of his own. An improved thing produced by a new and ingenious application of a known contrivance to an old thing, is a manner of new manufacture within the meaning of the statute. If, practically speaking, there are no difficulties to be overcome in adapting an old contrivance to a new purpose, there can be no ingenuity in overcoming them, there will be no invention, and the first rule will apply. The same rule, will, I apprehend, also apply to cases in which the mode of overcoming the so-called difficulties is so obvious to everyone of ordinary intelligence and acquaintance with the subject-matter of the patent, as to present no difficulty to any such person. Such cases present no real difficulty to people conversant with the matter in hand, and admit of no sufficient ingenuity to

---

[83] And see *Gosnell v. Bishop* (1888) 5 R.P.C. 151 at p.158; *Haskell Golf Ball Co. Ltd. v. Hutchinson (No. 2)* (1906) 23 R.P.C. 301 at p.313; *Thermos Ltd. v. Isola Ltd.* (1910) 27 R.P.C. 388 at p.398; *Erickson's Patent* (1923) 40 R.P.C. 477 at p.487; *B.T.-H. v. Charlesworth, Peebles & Co.* (1925) 42 R.P.C. 180 at p.195; *British United Shoe Machinery Co. Ltd. v. E. A. Johnson & Co. Ltd.* (1925) 42 R.P.C. 243 at p.252; *Wright and Eagle Range Ltd. v. General Gas Appliances Ltd.* (1929) 46 R.P.C. 169 at p.179; *Paper Sacks Proprietary Ltd. v. Cowper* (1936) 53 R.P.C. 31 at p.54; *E.M.I. (Clarke's) Appn.*, [1970] R.P.C. 5.
[84] [1989] R.P.C. 307 at 327.
[85] (1892) 9 R.P.C. 516.

support a patent. If, in these two classes of cases, patents could be supported, they would be intolerable nuisances, and would seriously impede all improvements in the practical application of common knowledge ... But unless an invention can be brought within one or other of the above classes, a patent for it cannot be held bad on the ground of want of subject-matter."[86]

Although this judgment of Lindley L.J. must not be read as if it were a statute,[87] it has frequently been applied.[88]

Analogous user

In *Morgan & Co. v. Windover & Co.* the invention amounted to the use   **5.78**
in the front part of a carriage of springs of a type formerly used in the rear part. The patent was held invalid in the House of Lords, Lord Herschell said:

"... the mere adaptation to a new purpose of a known material or appliance, if that purpose be analogous to a purpose to which it has already been applied, and if the mode of application be also analogous so that no inventive faculty is required and no invention is displayed in the manner in which it is applied, is not the subject-matter for a patent ... once it is admitted that all that can be claimed as new is the idea of putting it (the springs) in the front instead of at the back and that when once that idea was entertained, any workman told to do it would, without any instructions or any special mechanical skill, be able at once to do it, it seems to me that really concludes the case ..."[89]

In *Harwood v. Great Northern Ry.*,[90] the patentee used a "fish plate" for   **5.79**
joining together the ends of rails. The evidence showed that this particular form of joint had been applied in various mechanical contrivances and notably in the joining together of pieces of timber used in bridge building, but not exactly the same kind of strains were involved. Lord Westbury L.C. said:[91]

---

[86] See also *Hayward v. Hamilton* (1881) Griff, P.C. 115; *Blakey & Co. v. Latham & Co.* (1889) 6 R.P.C. 29, 184; *Morgan & Co. v. Windover & Co.* (1890) 7 R.P.C. 131; *Lane-Fox v. Kensington & Knightsbridge Electric Lighting Co. Ltd.* (1892) 9 R.P.C. 413 at p.416; *Savage v. Harris & Sons* (1896) 13 R.P.C. 90, 364; *Brooks v. Lamplugh* (1898) 15 R.P.C. 33; *British Liquid Air Co. Ltd. v. Brit. Oxygen Co. Ltd.* (1908) 25 R.P.C. 218, 577 at p.601; *British Vacuum Cleaner Co. Ltd. v. L. & S.W. Ry.* (1912) 29 R.P.C. 309; *Merten's Patent* (1914) 31 R.P.C. 373; *Bonnard v. London General Omnibus Co. Ltd.* (1921) 38 R.P.C. 1; *Auster Ltd. v. Perfecta Motor Equipments Ltd.* (1924) 41 R.P.C. 482.
[87] *Lister & Co. Ltd.'s Patent* [1966] R.P.C. 30.
[88] E.g. by the House of Lords in *Benmax v. Austin Motor Co. Ltd.* (1955) 72 R.P.C. 39 at p.44 and *Parks-Cramer Co. v. Thornton & Sons Ltd.* [1969] R.P.C. 112 at p.128.
[89] (1890) 7 R.P.C. 131 at pp.137, 138.
[90] (1864) 35 L.J.Q. B.27.
[91] *Ibid.* at p.38.

"Then the question is whether there can be any invention of the plaintiff in having taken that thing, which was a fish for a bridge, and having applied it as a fish for a railway. Upon that I think that the law is well and rightly settled, for there would be no end to the interferences with trades, and with the liberty of any mechanical contrivance being adopted, if every slight difference in the application of a well-known thing were held to constitute a patent ... No sounder or more wholesome doctrine, I think, was ever established by the decisions which are referred to in the opinions of the four learned judges, who concur in the second opinion delivered to your lordships, namely, that you cannot have a patent for a well-known mechanical contrivance, merely because it is applied in a manner, or to a purpose which is analogous to the manner, or to the purpose in or to which it has been hitherto notoriously used."[92]

Limits of doctrine of analogous user

5.80   The decision in *Harwood v. Great Northern Ry.* was considered in *Pope Appliance Corporation v. Spanish River etc. Mills Ltd.*[93] and Lord Dunedin said:

"Analogous user is what its name denotes, something which has to do with user. He [*i.e.* the trial judge] has applied the doctrine not to things used, but to things described ... The doctrine of analogous user only applies to cases as to things in actual use."

Nevertheless, the question remains in every case whether the invention claimed is or is not obvious, having regard to what was previously known.[94] If the the manufacture with which the claim is concerned is of a different kind from that of the prior disclosure this will, of course, be an important circumstance to be taken into account, but it does not necessarily follow that the invention claimed has sufficient of the inventive quality.

Invention may lie in the idea

5.81   However, if the idea of using the known contrivance for the new purpose was not an obvious idea, but involved some degree of ingenuity, the patent may well be valid, notwithstanding that once the

---

[92] And see *Blakey & Co. v. Latham & Co.* (1889) 6 R.P.C. 184; *Singer v. Rudge Cycle Co.* (1894) 11 R.P.C. 463; *Dredge v. Parnell* (1899) 16 R.P.C. 625; *Acetylene Illuminating Co. Ltd. v. United Alkali Co.* (1904) 21 R.P.C. 145 at p.155; *British Oxygen Co. v. Maine Lighting Co.* (1924) 41 R.P.C. 604; *Harris v. Brandreth* (1925) 42 R.P.C. 471; *Magnatex Ltd. v. Unicorn Products Ltd.* (1951) 68 R.P.C. 117; and *Benmax v. Austin Motor Co. Ltd.* (1955) 72 R.P.C. 39.
[93] (1929) 46 R.P.C. 23 at p.56.
[94] P.A. 1949, s.32(1)(*f*); and see *Allmanna Svenska Elektriska v. Burntisland Shipbuilding Co. Ltd.* (1951) 68 R.P.C. at pp.69, 70.

idea of the new application is conceived no further act of invention is required to put it into practice.[95] It has been said

> "a man who discovers that a known machine can produce effects which no one knew could be produced by it before may make a great and useful discovery, but if he does no more his discovery is not a patentable invention."[96]

It is submitted that in its context this passage means

(a) that a patent cannot be granted for a known machine or process merely because the applicant has discovered that such known machine or processes can be used for a novel purpose and
(b) that if the new "effects" are not a manner of manufacture (or, under the present law, a method of testing for purposes of manufacture)[97] no patent can be granted.

It does *not* mean that a new process of manufacture is necessarily not patentable if it is to be effected by a machine or process known in itself.[98]

In *Hicktons Patent Syndicate v. Patents etc. Ltd.,*[99] the invention involved **5.82** a conception by no means obvious. Once it had been conceived, however, it could not be denied that the application was obvious, and the trial judge had held the patent invalid on this ground. In the Court of Appeal Fletcher Moulton L.J. said:[1]

> "The learned judge says, 'an idea may be new and original and very meritorious, but unless there is some invention necessary for putting the idea into practice it is not patentable.' With the greatest respect for the learned judge, that, in my opinion, is quite contrary to the principles of patent law, and would deprive of their reward a very large number of meritorious inventions that have been made. I may say that this dictum is to the best of my knowledge supported by no case, and no case has been quoted to us which would justify it ... To say that the conception may be meritorious and may involve invention, and may be new and original, and simply because when you have once got the idea it is easy to carry it out, and that that deprives it of the title of being a new invention according to our patent law, is, I think, an extremely dangerous principle, and justified neither by reasons, nor authority ... In my opinion, invention may lie in the idea, and it may lie in the way in which it is carried out, and it may be in the combination of the two; but if there is invention in the

---

[95] See *Muntz v. Foster* (1843) 2 W.P.C. 93.
[96] *Lane-Fox v. Kensington etc. Co. Ltd.* (1892) 9 R.P.C. 413 at p.416.
[97] See *ante*, Chap. 2; P.A. 1949, s.101(1).
[98] See *Otto v. Linford* (1882) 46 L.T. (N.S.) 35 at p.39.
[99] (1909) 26 R.P.C. 339.
[1] *Ibid.* at p.347.

idea plus the way of carrying it out, then it is good subject-matter for letters patent."[2]

By the last sentence, having regard to its context, the learned Lord Justice plainly means that if there is invention either in the idea itself, or in the means by which it is utilised, or in a combination of the two, then the patent cannot be invalid for lack of the inventive quality.

5.83   In *Olin Mathieson Chemical Corporation v. Biorex Ltd.*[3] Graham J. said:

" ... the invention may lie in the idea of taking the step in question. Why should anyone want to take this step unless he had first appreciated that such a step might give him a useful product? ... and it is in my judgment not obvious to take the step in question unless and until it has been conceived that the idea of doing so might lead to a useful result. Of course, once one has the idea of doing so it is perfectly obvious how to do it but that is not the material question."

Likewise invention may also lie in finding out the problem.[4]

Automaticity

5.84   There cannot be invention in the mere idea of doing automatically anything that was previously done manually.[5] A claim which "is in effect a claim for the principle of automaticity ... is not a claim that any patentee can make".[6]

However, as was pointed out by Whitford J. in *S. p. A. Virginio Rimoldi & Co.'s Patent,*[7]

"one has to be careful about making,...too broad a pronouncement on questions such as 'there is nothing patentable in automation,' becomes whether there is or not must I think depend upon the circumstances of each case ..."

Chemical cases

5.85   In the case of patents for chemical and metallurgical processes the principles applicable are precisely similar, and in the application of an

---

[2] And see *Benton & Stone Ltd. v. Thomas Denston & Son* (1925) 42 R.P.C. 284 at p.297; *Teste v. Coombes* (1924) 41 R.P.C. 88 at p.105; *Wright & Eagle Range Ltd. v. General Gas Appliances Ltd.* (1927) 44 R.P.C. 346 at pp.362, 363.
[3] [1970] R.P.C. 157 at p.192.
[4] See *Beecham Group Ltd.'s (Amoxycillin) Appn.* [1980] R.P.C. 261 at 291, Buckley L.J.
[5] *British United Shoe Machinery Co. Ltd. v. Simon Collier Ltd.* (1909) 26 R.P.C. 21 at pp.48–50; *Submarine Signal Co. v. Henry Hughes & Son Ltd.* (1932) 49 R.P.C. 149 at p.175; *Parks-Cramer Co. v. Thornton & Sons Ltd.* [1969] R.P.C. 112 at p.128.
[6] *Per* Romer L.J. in *Submarine Signal Co. v. Henry Hughes & Son Ltd (1932) loc. cit.* [1971] R.P.C. 44 at p.53.
[7] [1971] R.P.C. 44.

old and well-known process to a new material the same question arises, that is to say, "was the new application obvious in view of the common knowledge?" Some years ago a distinguished chemist stated, when giving evidence in such a case, that "there is no prevision in chemistry". this phrase having been often repeated has given rise to the belief that the law applicable to chemical cases is peculiar. This is not the case. The unexpected nature of chemical reactions may make a chemist, who is aware that things may and do occur contrary to expectation, distrustful of his own belief in what to anticipate.[8] The question of obviousness, however, has to be decided on the evidence in each particular case.

In *Osram Lamp Works Ltd. v. Pope's Electric Lamp Co.*,[9] Lord Parker said: **5.86**

> "I agree that the invention consists merely in the application to tungsten and its compounds of a process (previously) invented and disclosed by Dr. Welsbach for making filaments of osmium or other metals of the platinum group. This is good subject-matter, unless, having regard to what was generally known at the date of the patent sued upon, it was obvious without experiment or research that the process invented by Welsbach could be applied to tungsten and its compounds as well as to osmium or other metals of the platinum group. I an not prepared to hold that this was obvious. Indeed, all the facts appear to point to the contrary conclusion."

The patent was held valid. On the other hand, in *British Thomson-Houston Co. Ltd. v. Duram Ltd.*[10] the patentees stated that they had discovered that tungsten became ductile if the coherent metal (rendered coherent by any suitable method) were heated, and claimed broadly, "The method of working tungsten which consists in subjecting the metal in a coherent form to the action of heat while it is being operated on or manipulated." It was proved to be the common practice of metallurgists to work metals hot either to test their properties or in the course of industries, and that to apply such a process to tungsten was obvious. The patent was held invalid.[11]

Verification

If the alleged inventive step consists in fact merely in a verification of **5.87** the published statements of other workers in the art, that will not be proper subject-matter for a patent. In *Sharpe & Dohme Inc. v. Boots Pure*

---

[8] *Cf. Sharpe & Dohme Inc. v. Boots Pure Drug Co. Ltd.* (1928) 45 R.P.C. 153 at p.173.
[9] (1917) 34 R.P.C. 369 at p.396.
[10] (1918) 35 R.P.C. 161.
[11] See also *Aero Carbon Light Co. v. Kidd* (1887) 4 R.P.C. 535; *McLay v. Lawes & Co. Ltd.* (1905) 22 R.P.C. 199; *Reitzman v. Grahame-Chapman* (1950) 67 R.P.C. 178; *Magnatex Ltd. v. Unicorn Products Ltd.* (1951) 68 R.P.C. 117.

Drug Co. Ltd.,[12] Astbury J., referring to certain of the documents cited, said:

"If the statement is there, ... it is a disclosure of a fact, and even if no chemist would have appreciated that it was right, if it turns out that it is right, you cannot take a patent out for verifying a prior statement."

He held the patent to be invalid. The judgment was confirmed by the Court of Appeal.

In *Aktiengesellschaft für Aluminium Schweissung v. London Aluminium Co. Ltd. (No. 2)*,[13] the patentee claimed a process for autogenously welding aluminium by the use of a very high temperature oxy-hydrogen blowpipe and a flux of a certain composition. It was proved that an identical flux was commonly known for soldering aluminium at a much lower temperature, but that no one would have suspected that this flux would have remained stable and unvolatilised at the higher temperature of the oxy-hydrogen blowpipe, although in fact its action as a flux to dissolve the oxide of aluminium was the same in both cases. It was held that in face of the unforeseen behaviour of the flux at the higher temperature there was invention in its use and a new process was made available to the public and that the patent was valid.

In the last-mentioned case, the basis of the invention was the discovery of a previously unknown characteristic of the flux. But there is no inventive step in merely appreciating that a known characteristic, previously regarded as a defect, could be an advantage. Thus, in *Reymes-Cole v. Elite Hosiery Co. Ltd.*,[14] Diplock L.J. said:

"It would seem an odd result of patent law if the plaintiff, by patenting as he has purported to do in the product claims of the specification stockings containing small tucks of this kind, could prevent manufacturers from continuing a process of manufacture which they had previously used in which such tucks were produced accidentally, and from marketing the products of such process which contained an unintentional tuck. In my view, the law does not entail this consequence. The plaintiff may have been the first to recognise that a physical characteristic which was already well known, but regarded as an accidental imperfection in a stocking, was an advantage, but such recognition, without more, is not an invention, and does not involve any inventive step."

---

[12] (1927) 44 R.P.C. 367 at p.390.
[13] (1920) 37 R.P.C.
[14] [1965] R.P.C. at p.117.

Combinations

In *British Celanese Ltd. v. Courtaulds Ltd.*[15] Lord Tomlin said: **5.88**

"It is accepted as sound law that a mere placing side by side of old integers so that each performs its own proper function independently of any of the others is not a patentable combination, but that where the old integers when placed together have some working interrelation producing a new or improved result then there is patentable subject-matter in the idea of the working interrelation brought about by the collocation of the integers."[16]

The "Sausage Machine Case"

The principle is illustrated by the well-known case of *Williams v. Nye*[17]   **5.89**
(the "Sausage Machine Case"). The patent was for a machine for mincing meat and filling the minced meat into skins so as to make sausages. In fact it consisted of a well-known filling machine so as to combine in one apparatus two machines which had formerly been used separately. The mincing part performed no more than its already well-known functions, and the same remark is true of the filling part. The ultimate result was novel and useful, but there was no difficulty to be overcome and no invention.[18]

The principles to be applied in considering whether an invention consisting of a combination of old integers was obvious were stated in *Wood v. Gowshall Ltd.*[19] by Greene L.J. as follows:

"The dissection of a combination into its constituent elements, and the examination of each element in order to see whether its use was obvious or not, is ... a method which ought to be applied with great caution since it tends to obscure the fact that the invention claimed is the combination. Moreover, this method also tends to obscure the facts that the conception of the combination is what normally governs and precedes the selection of the elements of which it is composed, and that the obviousness or otherwise of each act of selection must in general be examined in the light of this consideration. The real and ultimate question is: is the combination obvious or not?"

---

[15] (1935) 52 R.P.C. 171 at p.193.
[16] See also *Klaber's Patent* (1906) 23 R.P.C. 461 at p.469; *British United Shoe Machinery Co. Ltd. v. A. Fussell & Sons Ltd.* (1908) 25 R.P.C. 631 at p.657.
[17] (1890) 7 R.P.C. 62.
[18] See also *Wood v. Raphael* (1897) 13 R.P.C. 730; 14 R.P.C. 496; *Layland v. Boldy & Sons Ltd.* (1913) 30 R.P.C. 547.
[19] (1937) 54 R.P.C. 37 at p.40.

Labour-saving machinery

5.90 In certain classes of invention, such as automatic labour-saving machinery, a very small alteration in the selection and arrangement of the parts may produce an important result. In *British United Shoe Machinery Co. Ltd. v. A. Fussell & Sons Ltd.*[20] the patent was for a high-speed machine for screwing the soles of boots to the welts. Fletcher Moulton L.J. said:[21]

> "Its merit is that it does this operation at a high speed, and with unvarying accuracy, so that you can work these machines so as to yield a huge output without making wasters ... When you come to a machine of this type, you have to alter very seriously the canons which influence you in deciding such questions as novelty. In the case of operations which have to be done under normal circumstances, in the absence of any special difficulties arising from speed, small and trivial alterations in the apparatus are viewed with suspicion, as possibly being idle variants; but when you come to machines which with this demand upon them still give uniform success, I think any tribunal will be very careful before it applies its ordinary ideas of what are mere idle and trivial changes to those alterations which have resulted in a success so triumphant. So that I approach the consideration of novelty in this case, *i.e.* of the importance of apparently slight variations in the combination, in a very humble spirit, willing to be taught by those who know the practical performance of the machine, and are able to judge of the means which render that practical performance so successful."

Selection

5.91 A selection from possible alternatives for the solution of a problem may afford subject-matter for a patent, but:

> "a mere selection among possible alternatives is not subject-matter. A selection to be patentable must be a selection in order to secure some advantage or avoid some disadvantage. It must be an adaption of means to ends impossible without exercise of the inventive faculty. It follows that in describing and ascertaining the nature of an invention consisting in the selection between possible alternatives, the advantages to be gained, or the disadvantages to be avoided ought to be referred to."[22]

The general principles governing the validity of such patents were

---

[20] (1908) 25 R.P.C. 631.
[21] (1908) 25 R.P.C. 631 at p.646.
[22] *Per* Lord Parker in *Clyde Nail Co. v. Russell* (1916) 33 R.P.C. 291 at p.306; and see *Thomas v. South Wales Colliery etc. Co. Ltd.* (1925) 42 R.P.C. 22 at p.27; *Safveans Aktie Bolag v. Ford Motor Co. (Eng.) Ltd.* (1927) 44 R.P.C. 49 at p.61.

discussed in *I.G. Farbenindustrie A.G.'s Patents*[23] by Maugham J., who pointed out that the following conditions must be fulfilled:

(a) The selection must be based on securing some advantage (or avoiding some disadvantage) by the use of the selected members;
(b) all the selected members must possess the required advantage; but a few exceptions here and there would not be sufficient to make the patent invalid;
(c) the selection must be for "a quality of a special character" which is peculiar to the selected group, and this quality must not be one which would be obvious to an expert.

Selection patents are usually concerned with chemical processes, but the question of obviousness is not essentially different from that which arises in other kinds of inventions. As Maugham J. pointed out:

"If the selected compounds being novel, possess a special property of an unexpected character ... I cannot see that the inventive step essentially differs from the step in producing a new result by a new combination of well-known parts or indeed from using the common and well-known factors (cranks, rods, toothed wheels and so forth) employed in mechanics in the construction of a new machine."[24]

Evidence

In coming to a conclusion as to whether or not a claim contains a real **5.92** inventive step over what was previously known or used, the court in the past has attached considerable weight to the evidence of the inventor himself.[25] Evidence which shows that the invention was not obvious to the defendants at the priority date will be of considerable weight if the defendants were persons skilled in the art, *e.g.*

(a) where the defendants at first contended that they had made the invention and offered to help the plaintiff to get a patent if they were granted a free licence,[26] or
(b) where the defendants introduced into a subsidiary claim of a patent specification of theirs the feature alleged to be obvious.[27]

The evidence of a director of the defendant company that the invention was new to him has been held to be relevant on the issue of

---

[23] (1930) 47 R.P.C. 289 at pp.322, 323.
[24] (1930) 47 R.P.C. 289 at p.321. See also *E.I. Du Pont v. Akzo N.V.* (H.L.), [1982] F.S.R. 303 and *supra* §5.15.
[25] Lightning Fastener Co. Ltd. v. Colonial Fastener Co. Ltd. (1934) 51 R.P.C. 349 at p.367; *Howaldt Ltd. v. Condrup Ltd.* (1937) 54 R.P.C. 121 at p.133, *SKM S.A. v. Wagner Spraytech (U.K.) Ltd.* [1982] R.P.C. 497.
[26] *Siddell v. Vickers* (1890) 7 R.P.C. 293 at pp.304, 305.
[27] *C. Van der Lely N.V. v. Bamfords Ltd.* [1961] R.P.C. 296 at p.316.

obviousness.[28] However, in the recent case of *Mölnlycke AB v. Proctor & Gamble*[29] the Court of Appeal has held that under the 1977 Act such secondary evidence should be kept firmly in its place. Obviousness being an objective test, the primary evidence is that of the expert's view as to the man skilled in the art having regard to the state of the art relied upon. An *ad hoc* expert, however, may not give evidence that the invention is, or is not, obvious, that being a matter for the court itself to decide.[30]

4. Other Grounds of Invalidity Under the 1977 Act

A. "Not a patentable invention"

P.A. 1977, section 72(1)(*a*): "the invention is not a patentable invention."

By Section 1(1)(c) a patentable invention is required to be capable of industrial application.

5.93   Section 4(2) proscribes a method of treatment of the human or animal body by surgery or therapy or of diagnosis practised on the human or animal body. However, a product consisting of a substance or composition to be used for any of such purpose is not so proscribed.[31]

Such exemption from patentable subject matter is similar to that which appertained under the 1949 Act as to whether a method or treatment of humans and animals was an invention, *i.e.* a manner of manufacture. Reference should be made to Chapter 2 where such cases are discussed.

Subject to Section 4(2) an invention is to be taken to be capable of industrial application if it can be made or used in any kind of industry including agriculture.[32] Such an objection cannot be used to argue that the claims are not fairly based or lacking utility.[33]

Other exclusions from patentability: P.A. 1977, section 1(1)(*d*)

5.94   The following are excluded from being patented:[34]

(a) A discovery, scientific theory or mathematical method;

---

[28] *McGlashan v. Gaskell & Chambers (Scotland) Ltd.* (1952) 69 R.P.C. 43.
[29] [1994] R.P.C. 49; see also § 5.68, *supra*.
[30] *British Celanese Ltd. v. Courtaulds Ltd.* (1935) 52 R.P.C. 171 at p.196.
[31] P.A. 1977, s.4(3).
[32] P.A. 1977, s.4(1).
[33] See *Chiron Corp. v. Organon Teknika Ltd.* [1994] F.S.R. 202.
[34] See P.A. 1977, s.1(2), (3) and (4); See *ante* Chap. 2.

(b) a literary, dramatic, musical or artistic work or any other aesthetic creation whatsoever;

(c) a scheme, rule or method for performing a mental act, playing a game or doing business, or a program for a computer;

(d) the presentation of information;

(e) an invention the publication or exploitation of which would be generally expected to encourage offensive, immoral or anti-social behaviour;

(f) any variety of animal or plant or any essentially biological process for the production of animals or plants, not being a micro-biological process or the product of such a process.

In *Genentech Inc's Patent*[35] the Court of Appeal stated a patent which claimed the practical application of a discovery did not relate to the discovery as such and patentability was therefore not excluded by section 1(2) even though the practical application might be obvious once the discovery had been made. However, it was held that the claims in question were not claims for the practical application of the discovery.

B. "Grantee not entitled to be granted the patent"

P.A. 1977, section 72(1)(b): "the patent was granted to a person who   **5.95** was not entitled to be granted that patent."

This ground of revocation (as amended by the C.D.P.A. 1988, Schedule 5, paragraph 18 as from January 7, 1991) is only open to a person who has established his right to be entitled to be granted the patent or a patent for part of the patent sought to be revoked[36] and in any case cannot be made if the attempt to establish his right was started after two years from grant unless, it is proved that the registered proprietor at the time of grant or when the patent was transferred to him knew he was not entitled to the patent.[37]

As to the persons entitled to the patent on grant, section 7(2) should be read in conjunction with section 39(1) and (2) regarding whether an employees invention belongs to the employee or the employer.

C. Unlawful extension of disclosure

P.A. 1977, section 72(1)(d): "the matter disclosed in the specification   **5.96** of the patent extends beyond that disclosed in the application for the

---

[35] [1989] R.P.C. 147; See also *Merrill Lynch's Application* [1989] R.P.C. 561.
[36] P.A. 1977, s.72(1).
[37] P.A. 1977, s.72(2).

patent, as filed, or, if the patent was granted on a new application filed under section 8(3), 12 or 37(4) above or as mentioned in section 15(4) above, in the earlier application as filed."

Whilst this subsection provides a new ground of revocation, it is based on an old concept embodied in section 76[37a] that an amendment to a specification (whether pre or post grant) cannot add new matter.[38]

In *Bonzel (T.) v. Intervention (No.3)*[39] Aldous J. in holding a patent for a dilation catheter to be invalid on the grounds of added subject matter stated that:

"the decision as to whether there was extension of disclosure must be made on a comparison of the two documents (application as filed, patent as granted) read through the eyes of a skilled addressee. The task of the court is threefold:

   (a) to ascertain through the eyes of a skilled addressee what is disclosed, both explicitly and implicitly in the application

   (b) to do the same in respect of the patent as granted

   (c) to compare the two disclosures and decide whether any subject matter relevant to the invention has been added whether by deletion or addition. The comparison is strict in the sense that subject matter will be added unless such matter is clearly and unambiguously disclosed in the application either explicitly or implicitly."

In *A.C. Edwards Ltd. v. Acme Signs & Displays Ltd*[40] in considering whether matter was implicitly disclosed by the contents of the specification as filed Fox L.J. applied the test set out by the Technical Board of Appeals in the EPO in THOMSON-CSF/Collector for high-frequency tube,[41]

"In order to determine whether or not the modification made to a claim extends the subject matter of a patent application beyond the contents of the application as filed, it is necessary to find out whether the resulting overall modification to the contents of the application (whether by addition, modification or withdrawal) is such that the information presented to the skilled man is not derived directly and unambiguously from that which the application contained previously, even taking account of the elements which are implicit to the skilled man (Guidelines for Examination of the EPO C-vi, 5.4)".

[37a] As amended by C.D.P.A. 1988, Sched. 5, para. 20.

[38] See Chap. 7, § 7.18; *cf* P.A. 1949, s.31(1).

[39] [1991] R.P.C. 553 at 574.

[40] [1990] R.P.C. 131 at 147; See also T194/84 *GENERAL MOTOR/Zinc electrodes*: [1990] O.J.EPO 59, [1989] EPOR 351.

[41] T151/84 THOMSON-CSF/Collector for high-frequency tube: [1988]EPOR 29.

In *Southco Inc. v. Dzus Fasteners Europe Ltd*,[42] a case concerning the pre-grant broadening of a claim, Purchas L.J. considered the Technical Board of Appeals' decision in HOUDAILLE/Removal of feature[43] where the board held that the deletion of a certain claimed feature may not violate Article 123(2) E.P.C. (Extending subject matter) provided the skilled person would

"directly and unambiguously recognise that
   (*a*) the feature was not explained as essential in the disclosure,
   (*b*) it is not, as such, indispensible for the function of the invention in the light of the technical problem it serves to solve and
   (*c*) the replacement or removal requires no real modification of other features to compensate for the change."

D. Unlawful extension of protection by amendment

P.A. 1977, section 72(1)(*e*): "the protection conferred by the patent has   **5.97**
been extended by amendment which should not have been allowed."

This subsection also provides a new ground of revocation.

Prior to grant an amendment may extend the protection conferred by the application for a patent provided subject matter thereby is not added (see *ante*). However, after grant no amendment to a claim is allowable if it extends the protection conferred by the patent.[44] This restriction is similar to that under the 1949 Act.[45]

Two criteria are necessary. First, that the protection conferred by the patent has been extended by amendment and secondly, that such amendment should not have been allowed, *i.e.* is contrary to section 76(3)(*b*) which only applies to a granted patent.

The amendment of a granted claim to replace a restrictive term (which in its strict literal sense does not clearly embrace a particular described embodiment of the invention) by a less restrictive term (which obviously embraces the embodiments) is permissible under Article 123(3) of the E.P.C. provided that

(a) the restrictive term in the granted claim is not so clear in its technical meaning that it could be used to determine the exact protection without reference to the description and drawings; and

(b) that it is clear from the description and drawings and from the

---

[42] [1992] 299 at 319 and 324; See also T136/88 VAN DER LELY: October 11, 1989 where the HOUDAILLE decision was confirmed.
[43] T331/87 HOUDAILLE/Removal of feature: July 6, 1989 *Houdaille Industries Inc.* [1991] O.J. EPO 1-2 at 22.
[44] See P.A. 1977, s.76(3)(*b*) as amended by C.D.P.A. 1988, Sched. 5, para. 20; see Chap. 7, § 7.64.
[45] P.A. 1949, s.31(1).

prosecution of the examination proceedings that it was never intended to exclude such embodiment.[46]

5. Grounds of Invalidity Peculiar to Old Act Patents

A. Non-disclosure of best method known to applicant

5.98   **P.A. 1949, section 32(1)(*h*):** "the complete specification ... does not disclose the best method of performing it (the invention) which was known to the applicant for the patent and for which he was entitled to claim protection."

The applicant must disclose the best method of performing the invention which was known to him and for which he was entitled to claim protection.[47] Under the 1932 Act the patent was invalid if "the complete specification does not disclose the best method known to the applicant for the patent at the time when the complete specification was left at the Patent Office",[48] whether that method was a matter of public knowledge or not.[49] It is submitted, that by reason of the words, see *ante* in the present Act "and for which he was entitled to claim protection", the patentee is now relieved from this burden and need only disclose the best method known to him if it is something which could form the subject-matter of a patent application by him, *i.e.* something which is not publicly known and constitutes a patentable advance on anything previously published. The relevant date of knowledge has been held to be shortly before the filing of the complete specification in the United Kingdom.[50] In *Du Pont de Nemuors v. Enka BV*[51] Falconer J. held that the defendants could only succeed if they established that the better method of performing the invention was the work of the inventor or one of the inventors. He also went on to hold that knowledge of the company was the knowledge of the person who gave instructions for and controlled the application properly instructed as to be in possession of the relevant information.

At common law a patent has always been held to be invalid if the inventor in his specification did not communicate all his knowledge regarding the invention, or if he misled the public.

---

[46] See *Steyr-Daimler-Puch v. Fuji Jukagyo KK. T371/88 FUJI/Transmission apparatus*, May 29, 1990 [1992] O.J.EPO 157.
[47] P.A. 1949, s.32(1)(*h*).
[48] 1932 Act, s.3, amending s.25(2) of 1907 Act.
[49] *Norton and Gregory v. Jacobs* (1937) 54 R.P.C. 271 at p.277.
[50] See *Monsanto Co. v. Maxwell Hart (London) Ltd.* [1981] R.P.C. 201.
[51] [1988] F.S.R. 69.

Invention communicated from abroad

In *Wagmann v. Corcoran*[52] the patent had been granted on a commun-   **5.99**
ication from abroad. The rollers prescribed by the specification for use in
the machine were obtained by the plaintiff from Italy, where the process
of their manufacture was kept secret, but the specification did not
mention this fact, and they could not be made from the description
given. The specification was held to be insufficient and misleading. Fry
J. held that

> "though the grantee of a patent for an invention communicated to
> him by a foreign resident abroad is only bound to tell the public all
> that he himself knows, yet if the original inventor has not told him
> enough to enable him so to describe the invention as that it can be
> constructed by the aid only of the specification, the patent will be
> invalid."[53]

The above case is distinguishable from the case of *Plimpton v.
Malcolmson*,[54] where the question was whether the patentee, having
disclosed a useful invention, was bound to disclose some fact more
useful than the description actually given, which he himself did not
know, but which was within the knowledge of the person communicating from abroad. It was properly held that he was not so bound, but it is
obvious that he was bound to describe an invention in itself useful, and
that he was bound to disclose all that he himself knew, and to give a
sufficient description to work the invention.

Misleading description

It has been held that if the patentee gives details in his specification   **5.100**
which are not necessary to the invention, which of themselves do not
constitute an invention, and which are merely put in for the purpose of
misleading the public either as to the nature of the invention or as to
how it is to be carried into effect, then the patent will be void.[55]

Good faith of applicant

The requirement that the best method known must be disclosed is not   **5.101**
so much for perfection of detail as to ensure good faith on the part of the
applicant. In *Tetley v. Easton*[56] Pollock C.B. said; "A man has no right to
patent a principle and then give to the public the humblest instrument

---

[52] 13 Ch.D. 65.
[53] As stated in the headnote, p.66; see the judgment at p.77 and 39 L.T. (N.S.) at p.568. See
  also *Sturtz v. De la Rue* (1842) 1 W.P.C. 83.
[54] (1876) 3 Ch.D. 531 at p.582.
[55] See *Lewis v. Marling* (1829) 1 W.P.C. 490 at p.496.
[56] (1853) Macr.P.C. 48 at p.76.

that can be made from his principle, and reserve to himself all the better part of it." And in *Heath v. Unwin*[57] Coleridge J. said:

> "If the inventor of an alleged discovery, knowing two equivalent agents for effecting the end, could, by the disclosure of one, preclude the public from the benefit of the other, he might, for his own profit, force upon the public an expensive and difficult process, keeping back the simple and cheap one, which would be directly contrary to the good faith required from every patentee in his communication with the public."[58]

5.102   In *British Dynamite Co. v. Krebs*[59] the inventor, Nobel, described a new explosive (dynamite) which, the specification stated, was to be made by causing nitro-glycerine (*per se* a dangerous liquid) to be absorbed by a porous unexplosive substance. He gave a list of such substances which were shown to be more or less useful. The resulting mass was safe and could be stored. He found subsequently that a well-known silicious earth ("kieselguhr") possessed the requisites of porosity and power of absorption to a very high degree, and the dynamite actually manufactured was, in consequence, always produced by the aid of this material. Lord Hatherley, restoring the judgment of Fry J., said:

> "If it had been proved that the inventor, Nobel, knew the best material, which turned out to be a material called 'kieselguhr,' a silicious earth; if he had known of the existence of 'kieselguhr' at the time, and that it would take up 75 per cent. of the nitro-glycerine, whereas some other materials specified by the patentee took up only 25 to 50 per cent., it would have been an objection to his patent to say that he, being in possession of the best mode of producing the most valuable dynamite, had not informed the public of that method."

In *Du Pont de Nemours v. Enka BV*[60] it was held that the nondisclosure of best method was not restricted to cases of dishonest conduct in withholding information from the public, it covers any case in which the applicant has not disclosed the best method known to him of performing the invention whatever the reason for that omission.

In each of the cases quoted above it would seem that the information that was withheld, or assumed to have been withheld, amounted to a patentable invention and, therefore, the principle of those decisions is still applicable.

---

[57] (1855) 2 W.P.C. 236 at p.243.
[58] And see *Wood v. Zimmer* (1815) 1 W.P.C. 44n.; *Crossley v. Beverley* (1829) 1 W.P.C. 112 at p.117; *Morgan v. Seaward* (1836) 1 W.P.C. 167 at p.174; *Franc-Strohmenger & Cowan Inc. v. Peter Robinson Ltd.* (1930) 47 R.P.C. 493 at p.501.
[59] (1896) 13 R.P.C. 190 at p.195.
[60] [1988] F.S.R. 69.

B. Claim not fairly based

P.A. 1949, section 32(1)(i): " . . . any claim of the complete specification   **5.103**
is not fairly based on the matter disclosed in the specification."
It was always a requirement at common law that the claim should not
be more extensive than the invention.[61]
In *C. Van der Lely N.V. v. Ruston's Engineering Co. Ltd*[62] Oliver L.J.   **5.104**
stated that:

> "in order that a claim is fairly based on the disclosure in the
> specification one has at least to find that that invention for which
> monopoly is claimed is disclosed as an invention in the specification.
> The inventor is, *in fairness* to the public, entitled only to monopolise
> that which, fairly read, he has disclosed as his invention."

Neil L.J. in the same case stated,[63] in seeking an answer to the question
one must first construe the specification itself to discover the nature of
the invention and where stated the problem with which the invention is
intended to deal. To decide whether a claim is fairly based on the
specification, Neil L. J. adopted as correct the statement of Dillons L.J. in
Therm-a-Stor v. Weatherseal Windows (No.2),[64] *viz* "The claims in a patent
must not go beyond the disclosure in the specification".

The notion of the court holding a balance as between the public and
the patentee which has been suggested[65] does not, it is submitted assist
in determining the issue. However, in chemical, or drug cases a useful
test first propounded by Sir Lionel Heald and adopted by Mr Justice
Graham in *Olin Mathieson Chemical Corporation v. Biorex Laboratories*[66] is
whether it is possible to make a "sound prediction" about a certain area,
then *prima facie* it would be reasonable that the monopoly claimed
should extend to such area.

In *Mullard Radio Valve Co. Ltd. v. Philco Radio and Television Corpora-*   **5.105**
tion[67-68] the invention was concerned with obviating a defect which
occurred in the use of a four-electrode thermionic valve when placed in
the final amplifying stage and arranged so that the grid nearest the
cathode was the "control" grid and the grid between the "control" grid
and the anode was the "screening" grid; the invention consisted in
inserting an additional "suppressor" grid between the "screening" grid

---

[61] *Hill v. Thompson and Forman* (1817) 1 W.P.C. 235. And see *Gandy v. Reddaway* (1885) 2
R.P.C. 49; *Dick v. Elloms* (1900) 17 R.P.C. 196 at p.200; *Woodrow v. Long Humphreys & Co.
Ltd.* (1934) 51 R.P.C. 25; *Gill's Appn.* (1937) 54 R.P.C. 119.
[62] *Lancer Boss Ltd. v. Henley Forklift Co. Ltd.* [1975] R.P.C. 307 at p.314, and *C. Van der Lely
N.V. v. Rustons Engineering Co. Ltd.* [1985] R.P.C. 495 (May L.J.).
[63] 53 R.P.C. 323.
[64] 53 R.P.C. 323 at p.345.
[65] *Van der Lely v. Rustons Engineering Co. Ltd.* [1985] R.P.C. 461 at 474.
[66] [1970] R.P.C. 157 at p. 182.
[67-68] [1984] F.S.R. 323 at 339.

and the anode, which "suppressor" grid was maintained at a relatively low potential. Whether a grid was the "control" grid or the "screening" grid or the "suppressor" grid depended not on its construction but on the external electric potentials applied to the electrodes. The claim in question was for "a discharge tube having at least three auxiliary electrodes between the cathode and the anode, characterised in that the auxiliary electrode nearest to the anode is directly connected to the cathode so as to be maintained continuously at the cathode potential." Lord Macmillan said

"Is the patentee entitled to such a monopoly? He is entitled to say that a discharge tube so constructed is new, for discharge tubes with such a connection were not previously known or made; and he is entitled to say that such a discharge tube has patentable utility in the sense that it can be used and will work as a discharge tube. But is the claim justified by the inventive idea which the patentee has disclosed? . . . It was submitted that in a claim for an article it is sufficient to establish that the article is capable of being used to perform the invention, and that it is nothing to the purpose to show that it may also be used or abused in ways which do not perform the invention or which achieve some other and different results, unless, it can also be shown that the article claimed will not in certain circumstances work at all. But when an article is claimed its virtue must reside in itself. It must always be capable of giving the advantages which the patentee has told you may be expected from its use. A discharge tube having three or more electrodes of which the one nearest the anode is directly connected with the anode will not give the advantage which the patentee discovered and described unless the electrodes in its vicinity are used to perform particular functions in a particular order of arrangement. The article claimed is a discharge tube in which by virtue of its construction the grid nearest the anode will always be kept at the same potential as the cathode, and its construction will no doubt always ensure this. But the inventor's purpose was not to invent a discharge tube which should have this feature. If his problem had been to invent a tube in which the grid nearest the anode should always be at cathode potential, his problem could have been easily and obviously solved. Anyone could have told him that all he had to do was to establish a physical connection between the grid nearest to the anode and the cathode. His problem was to obviate disadvantages which arose when a screening grid was interposed between the control grid and the anode, a quite special and definite problem. I do not think that he is entitled to prevent anyone in future from making a valve in which the grid nearest to the anode is connected with the cathode merely because he has discovered that in a valve in which the other grids are utilised in a particular way this connection will give the special advantage which he discovered. It is because he has sought to do so that the claim is, in my opinion, too wide. The fact that an article of obvious construction is discovered to give a valuable and new benefit if employed in a particular way does not entitle the discoverer to prevent everyone else from making that article. A patentee is granted his monopoly in order to protect the invention which in his specification he has communicated to the public. He is not entitled to claim a monopoly more extensive than is necessary to protect that which he has himself said is his invention … If an inventor claims an article as his invention but the article will only achieve his avowed object in a particular juxtaposition and his inventive idea consists in the discovery that in that particular juxtaposition it will give new and useful results, I do not think that he is entitled to claim the article at large apart from the juxtaposition which is essential to the achievement of those results. It was argued for the appellants that if an article is new, is useful and has subject-matter, then it is necessarily patentable and entitled to protection. But a claim may be for an article which is new, which is useful and which has subject-matter, yet it may be too wide a claim because it extends beyond the subject-matter of the invention. The consideration which the patentee gives to the public disclosing his inventive idea entitles him in return to protection for an article which embodies his inventive idea but not for an article which, while capable of being used to carry his inventive idea into effect, is described in terms which cover things quite unrelated to his inventive idea, and which do not embody it at all.''

This case has given rise to considerable discussion and it has even been suggested that in consequence of the passage referring to ''juxtaposition'' quoted above it has now become difficult to formulate a valid claim for an article *per se*. It is argued, for example, that a new and ingenious sparking plug cannot be claimed by itself, as it lies on sale in its carton on a shop counter, because it is of no value for the purpose for which it was invented until it has been suitably fixed in an internal combustion engine, and even then a motive fluid must be supplied to the engine and an electric current to the sparking plug. Accordingly, it has been questioned whether a claim to the sparking plug can be valid unless it be limited by reference to its use in an engine coupled with the provision of a suitable motive fluid and electric current. Obviously, only a user would infringe a claim so restricted, so that the manufacture and sale of the sparking plug could not be prevented and in practice the patentee's monopoly would be worthless. It is submitted that this view is based on an entire misconception of *Mullard v. Philco*, the reasoning in which can be simply expressed as follows. A claim for a combination of integers, even though some or all are old, is permissible if a novel result is achieved by the combination.[69] But the claim must include (and, **5.106**

---

[69] See § 5.88.

therefore, be limited by) all the necessary integers. In the case under discussion some of the necessary integers for the invention were the electric potentials to be applied to the electrodes. It was essential, therefore, that these electric potentials should be specified in the claim. As they were not, the claim was invalid. The actual article in question was held to be of an obvious and non-inventive character, the real invention requiring that it should be used in a particular way. The case has no application where the article itself requires an act of invention to produce it and is itself the subject-matter of the invention.

Mullard v. Philco has been further explained in the course of the proceedings in which an unsuccessful attempt was made to amend the claim mentioned above.[70]

The Comptroller wil not accept broad and indeterminate claims of a speculative character covering fields which the patentee has done nothing to explore.[71]

Wide claims for new "principles"

5.107   Where the patentee has disclosed a method of applying what is sometimes inaccurately referred to as "a new principle", *i.e.* a new general method of achieving some result, a wide claim is permissible. "Such a claim ought probably to be construed as a claim of monopoly for that arrangement carried out by any means substantially similar to those disclosed in the specification."[72]

Claim for a "principle"

5.108   In *Ridd Milking Machine Co. Ltd. v. Simplex Milking Machine Co. Ltd.*,[73] Lord Shaw said:

"It might be possible in very many cases of a claim for apparatus—if the argument presented were sound—to evolve a claim for a principle from a description given of the results achieved, and to maintain accordingly that it was the principle of the invention in that sense which was the real subject of the claim. This is, in their Lordships' opinion, a method of construction of patent claims which is accompanied with serious danger ... if any claim for a principle is made it must undoubtedly appear in the claim as that claim is stated, and must not

---

[70] *Mullard Radio Valve Co. Ltd. v. British Belmont Radio Ltd. and Others* (1939) 56 R.P.C. 1 at p.10. See also *American Optical Co.'s Appn.* [1958] R.P.C. 40; *Mergenthaler Linotype Co.'s Appn.* [1958] R.P.C. 278; *Letraset Ltd. v. Dymo Ltd.* [1976] R.P.C. 65. C *Van der Lely N.V. v. Rustran's Engineering Co. Ltd.* [1985] R.P.C. 461 at 494.

[71] *Esan's Appn.* (1932) 49 R.P.C. 85 at p.87; *Shell Devlopment Co.'s Appn.* (1947) 64 R.P.C. 151; *Pottier's Appn.* [1967] R.P.C. 170.

[72] Per Wright J. in *Edison Bell Phonograph Co. Ltd. v. Smith* (1894) 11 R.P.C. 148 at p.163. And see *Automatic Weighing Machine Co. v. Knight* (1889) 6 R.P.C. 297 at p.304 (C.A.); *Ashworth v. English Card Clothing Co. Ltd.* (1903) 20 R.P.C. 790.

[73] (1916) 33 R.P.C. 309 at p.317.

be left to an inference resting on a general review of the specification, or a general search among the language employed therein for the meritorious element of principle or idea."[74]

In *Jupe v. Pratt.*,[75] in the course of the argument, Alderson B. said:

"You cannot take out a patent for a principle. You may take out a patent for a principle coupled with the mode of carrying the principle into effect, provided you have not only discovered the principle but invented some mode of carrying it into effect. But then you must start with having invented some mode of carrying the principle into effect. If you have done that, then you are entitled to protect yourself from all the other modes of carrying the principle into effect, that being treated by the jury as a piracy of your original invention."

These words have been commented on in *R.C.A. Photophone Ltd. v. Gaumont British Picture Corporation Ltd.*[76] Lord Wright said:[77]   **5.109**

"It is true that what is often, very inaptly, called a principle, by which is meant some general method of manufacture, may be validly claimed, so long as it is new, and the inventor describes one mode of carrying it into effect (*Jupe v. Pratt* (1837)); still, even in such a case, the precise ambit of the claim must depend on the language used."

And Greene L.J. said:[78] " ... the words are not 'you are entitled to protection,' but 'you are entitled to protect yourself,' which appear to me clearly to mean that you are entitled to draft your claim in words wide enough to secure the protection desired."[79]

Nevertheless, a wide claim to a "principle" must not be so extensive   **5.110** as to amount to a claim to *any* method of solving a particular problem, and this is clearly illustrated by *British United Shoe Machinery Co. Ltd. v. Simon Collier Ltd.*,[80] where the patent was for a machine for performing some of the operations involved in bootmaking, more particularly trimming the edge of the sole. The position of the trimming knife at any

---

[74] And see *Dudgeon v. Thomson* [1877] 3 App.Cas. 34 at p.44; *Incandescent Gas Light Co. Ltd. v. Sunlight Incandescent Gas Lamp Co. Ltd.* (1896) 13 R.P.C. 333; *Presto Gear Case Co. v. Orme Evans & Co.* (1901) 18 R.P.C. 17 at p.23; *Ackroyd and Best Ltd. v. Thomas & Williams* (1904) 21 R.P.C. 737 at p.750; *Marconi's Wireless Telegraph Co. v. Mullard Radio Valve Co. Ltd.* (1924) 41 R.P.C. 323 at p.334; *British United Shoe Machinery Co. Ltd. v. Gimson Shoe Machinery Co. Ltd. (No. 2)* (1928) 46 R.P.C. 137 at p.159.
[75] (1837) 1 W.P.C. 144 at p.146.
[76] (1936) 53 R.P.C. 167.
[77] (1936) 53 R.P.C. 167 at p.186.
[78] (1936) 53 R.P.C. 167 at p.205.
[79] And see *Neilson v. Harford* (1841) 1 W.P.C. 331 at p.355; *Automatic Weighing Machine Co. v. Knight* (1889) 6 R.P.C. 297 at p.304; *Nobel's Explosives Co. v. Anderson* (1894) 11 R.P.C. 519 at pp.525, 527; *Ashworth v. English Card Clothing Co. Ltd.* (1903) 20 R.P.C. 790 at p.797; *British Vacuum Cleaner Co. Ltd. v. J. Robertshaw & Sons Ltd.* (1915) 32 R.P.C. 424 at p.435.
[80] (1909) 26 R.P.C. 21.

moment was automatically governed by the position of a guide which bore upon another portion of the boot so that the width of the sole was varied in relation to that other portion. One of the patentee's claims was as follows: "In a sole trimming machine, a trimming knife, a guide, support therefor, and automatic means for automatically varying the relative positions of the knife and guide during the trimming operation for the purpose described." One method of effecting such automatic variation (by means of a cam) was described and made the subject of other claims.

5.111   Parker J. said:[81]

> "If on the true construction of the specification, the claim is as wide as the defendants contend, the validity of the patent depends upon whether an inventor, who discloses one way of doing automatically for a particular purpose what, in existing machines, could be done for the same purpose, not indeed, automatically, but by the service or skill on the part of the workman, can obtain the grant of letters patent for all means of doing the same thing automatically for the same purpose. It appears from the judgment of Alderson B. in *Jupe v. Pratt*[82] ... that though you cannot take out a patent for a principle, yet if the principle is new, and you show one mode of carrying it into effect, you may protect yourself against all other modes of carrying the principle into effect. If, however, the principle is not new, you can only protect yourself against those modes of carrying it into effect which are substantially the same as the mode you have yourself invented, the question being in each case what is the pith and marrow of the invention sought to be protected, and it being impossible to treat any principle already known as part of such pith and marrow. Thus, where the principle is old, a claim to all modes of carrying it into effect will avoid the patent as in *Patterson v. Gas Light and Coke Co.*[83] ... In the present case, considering that in existing machines the relative position of knife and guide could be varied (though not automatically) ... the problem was simply how to do automatically what could already be done by the skill of the workman. On the other hand, the principle which the inventor applies for the solution of the problem is the capacity of a cam to vary the relative position of two parts of a machine while the machine is running. Assuming this principle to be new, it might be possible for the inventor, having shown one method of applying it to the solution of the problem, to protect himself during the life of his patent from any other method of applying it for the same purpose, but I do not think the novelty of the principle applied would enable him to make a valid claim for all means of solving the problem

[81] (1909) 26 R.P.C. at p.49.
[82] (1837) 1 W.P.C. 144 at p.146. Approved, *Chamberlain & Hookham Ltd. v. Mayor etc., of Bradford* (1903) 20 R.P.C. 673 at p.684; and see *British United Shoe Machinery Co. v. Standard Rotary Machine Co.* (1917) 34 R.P.C. at pp.46 and 47.
[83] (1875) 2 Ch.D. 812.

whether the same or a different principle were applied to its solution. If he could do so, it would seem to follow that the invention of one means to secure a particular end would entitle an inventor to protection against all means of attaining the same end. If, therefore, the claim be construed as including all automatic means of solving the problem (the learned judge held that it had this meaning), I am of opinion it is too wide, and is not proper subject-matter for letters patent."[84]

No need to "distinguish new from old"

There is no need to discriminate in the claims themselves between the   **5.112** prior state of the art and the new features in fact introduced by the inventor. The reason for this was stated by Fletcher Moulton L.J. as follows:[85]

"In the Act of 1883, for the first time, it was made a statutable duty to insert claims to define the invention, and that has been continued up to the present time; but the language of the statute follows that of the old proviso and leaves no doubt that the duty is only to define the invention for which the monopoly is claimed. The justice and sufficiency of that requirement is obvious ... A patentee often works solitarily. He has very little idea of what others are doing ... and much of his work ... has been to re-invent that which others, without his knowledge, have invented. The consequence is that the inventive act of the inventor can have no relevance or effect; ... Then are we to say that he is to state what would have been the inventive act, supposing him to know the whole knowledge of the world? ... Of course, if his ignorance has led him to claim something which is not novel he has to take the penalty ... But to say that he must also ascertain, under the penalty of his patent being bad, everything that preceded his invention, every approach from every side that persons have made to it, and must correctly indicate the little step which he has made in addition to these, ... would be to require something of him which would be perfectly idle so far as regards utility to the public, and grossly unjust so far as the patentee is concerned ... A man must distinguish what is old from what is new *by* his claim; but he has not got to distinguish what is old from what is new *in* his claim. If the combination which he has claimed, and for which he asks a monopoly, is novel, that is sufficient. There is no obligation to go further and to state why it is novel, or what in it is novel."[86]

---

[84] And see *Submarine Signal Co. v. Hughes & Sons Ltd.* (1932) 49 R.P.C. 149 at p.175; *Automatic Weighing Machine Co. v. Knight* (1889) 6 R.P.C. 297 at p.308; *R.C.A. Photophone Ltd. v. Gaumont British Picture Corporation Ltd.* (1936) 53 R.P.C. 167 at p.186.

[85] *British United Shoe Machinery Co. Ltd. v. A. Fussell & Sons Ltd.* (1908) 25 R.P.C. 631 at p.651.

[86] And see *Jackson v. Wolstenhulmes* 1 R.P.C. 105 at 108; *Fellows v. T.W. Lench Ltd.* (1917) 34 R.P.C. 45 at p.55; *Marconi's Wireless Telegraph Co. Ltd. v. Mullard Radio Valve Co. Ltd.* (1924) 41 R.P.C. 323 at p. 334; *Sonotone Corporation v. Multitone Electric Co. Ltd.* 72 R.P.C. 131 at p.140.

C. Ambiguity

5.113   **P.A. 1949, section 32(1)(*I*):** "the scope of any claim of the complete specification is not sufficiently and clearly defined."
This has been a requirement of patent law for many years.[87] However in recent times the Courts have been more lenient in the standard of definition required. Modern claims are difficult to formulate and decisions have reflected this difficulty.

5.114   In *General Tire & Rubber Co. v. Firestone Tyre & Rubber Co. Ltd.*[88] the Court of Appeal stated:

> "it is clear in our judgment that the question whether the patentee has sufficiently defined the scope of his claims is to be considered in relation to the facts of each case, that allowance is to be made for anydifficulties to which the circumstance give rise, and that all that is required of the patentee is to give as clear a definition as the subject matter admits of. It is also clear that in our judgment that, while the court is to have regard to all the relevent facts, the issue of definition is to be considered as a practical matter and little weight is to be given to puzzles set to a manufacturer wishing to satisfy himself that he is now infringing the patent."

5.115   Nevertheless in defining the scope of the claims it is the duty of the patentee to mark out his territory clearly and without any ambiguity. In *Natural Colour Kinematograph Co. Ltd. v. Bioochemoo Ltd. (Smith's Patent),*[89] Lords Loreburn L.C. said:

> "this patent is bad for ambiguity in the specification. There seems to be some danger of the well-known rule of law against ambiguity being in practice invaded. Some of those who draft specifications and claims are apt to treat this industry as a trial of skill, in which the object is to make the claim very wide upon one interpretation of it, in order to prevent as many people as possible from competing with the patentee's business, and then to reply upon carefully prepared sentences in the specification which, it is hoped, will be just enough to limit the claim within safe dimensions if it is attacked in court. This leads to litigation as to the construction of specifications which could generally be avoided, if at the outset a sincere attempt were made to state exactly what was meant in plain language. The fear of a costly law-suit is apt to deter any but wealthy competitors from contesting a patent. This is all wrong. It is an abuse which a court can prevent, whether a charge of ambiguity is or is not raised on the pleadings,

---

[87] Philpott v. Hanbury (1885) 2 R.P.C. 33 at p.38; *Edison and Swan Electric Co. v. Holland* (1889) 6 R.P.C. 243 at p.280.
[88] *General Tire & Rubber Co. v. Firestone Tyre & Rubber Co. Ltd.,* [1972] R.P.C. 457 at p.514 & 515.
[89] (1915) 32 R.P.C. 256 at p.266.

because it affects the public by practically enlarging the monopoly, and does so by a kind of pressure which is very objectionable. It is the duty of a patentee to state clearly and distinctly, either in direct words or by clear and distinct reference, the nature and limits of what he claims. If he uses language which, when fairly read, is avoidably obscure or ambiguous, the patent is invalid, whether the defect be due to design, or to carelessness, or to want of skill. Where the invention is difficult to explain, due allowance will, of course, be made for any resulting difficulty in the language. But nothing can excuse the use of ambiguous language when simple language can easily be employed, and the only safe way is for the patentee to do his best to be clear and intelligible. It is necessary to emphasise this warning."[90]

In *P & G Coy v. Peaudouce (U.K.) Ltd.*,[91] where the claims were to a disposable nappy having *inter alia* a semi-rigid absorbant body defined by reference to a Taber stiffness as measured by a specified TAPPI standard requiring five test specimens to be taken from each sample unit, the Court of Appeal held that the claims were invalid for ambiguity because five test readings were not determinative of whether the absorbant body had a value above or below the required Taber value of 7, but due to the scatter of such readings may require as many as 100 or possibly even 200 test specimens for a would be infringer to ascertain whether or not he fell within the claim.

In *British Ore Concentration Syndicate Ltd. v. Minerals Separation Ltd.*,[92] **5.116**
Lord Halsbury said:

"The statute requires it [the specification] to be a distinct statement of what is the invention ... If he [the applicant] designedly makes it ambiguous, in my judgment the patent would undoubtedly be bad on that ground; but even if negligently and unskilfully he fails to make distinct what his invention is, I am of opinion that the condition is not fulfilled, and the consequence would be that the patent would be bad."[93]

In examining a specification against which a plea of ambiguity is raised it is necessary that the wording of the claim should be interpreted according to the general principles of construction and in the light of the common knowledge of the art. Thus, when there is a choice between

---

[90] See also *Franc-Strohmenger and Cowan Inc. v. Peter Robinson Ltd.* (1930) 47 R.P.C. 493 at p.501.
[91] [1989] F.S.R. 180.
[92] (1910) 27 R.P.C. 33 at p.47.
[93] And see *Linotype and Machinery Ltd. v. Hopkins* (1910) 27 R.P.C. 109 at p.112; see also, *e.g. Taylor's Patent* (1916) 33 R.P.C. 138; *White v. Todd Oil Burners Ltd.* (1929) 46 R.P.C. 275; *Rose Street Foundry, etc., Co. Ltd. v. India Rubber, etc. and Telegraph Works Co. Ltd.* (1929) 46 R.P.C. 294; *Cincinnati Grinder Inc. v. B.S.A. Tools Ltd.* (1931) 48 R.P.C. 33; *British Celanese Ltd. v. Courtaulds Ltd.* (1933) 50 R.P.C. 259; *Minerals Separation North American Corporation v. Noranda Mines Ltd.* (1952) 69 R.P.C. 81.

two meanings, one should if possible reject that meaning which leads to an absurd result and construe the claim with the knowledge of the skilled addressee.[94] In *British Thomson-Houston Co. Ltd. v. Corona Lamp Works Ltd.*,[95] the patent had been granted in respect of gas-filled incandescent lamps, and the inventor had discovered that new and valuable results were obtained by making the filament of the lamp of "large" diameter. The claim was as follows:

> "An incandescent electric lamp having a filament of tungsten or other refractory metal of large diameter or cross section or of concentrated (*i.e.* coiled) form and a gas or vapour of low heat conductivity at relatively high pressure, the combination being such that the filament may be raised to a much higher temperature than is practicable in a vacuum lamp without prohibitive vaporisation or deterioration or excessive shortening of useful life, substantially as set forth."

It was not denied that the invention was valuable or that the directions in the body of the specification were sufficient to enable the invention to be carried into effect according to the examples given, but it was argued that the word "large" was not sufficiently clear in its meaning to define the ambit of the monopoly and that a manufacturer would have to experiment with filaments of varying relative dimensions before he could ascertain whether or not he was within the monopoly claimed— the attainment of the stated advantages being the only criterion of infringement. The House of Lords, however, held that there was no valid objection to the claim; that the experiments necessary were clearly within the competence of the manufacturers; that numerical definition of the limits of "largeness" was unnecessary having regard to the common knowledge of the dimensions used in practice and under varying conditions, and that to require such a definition would be to open the door to evasion. And in the somewhat similar case of *Watson, Laidlaw & Co. Ltd. v. Potts, Cassels and Williamson*[96] Lord Shaw pointed out that it was important "not to permit a mathematical analysis to empty a description in plain language of its practical merit."

5.117   On the other hand, where a word or phrase of a somewhat vague character is used in the claim and is not defined in the body of the specification, it is a question of fact, to be determined on the evidence, whether the use of such word or phrase renders the claim invalid for ambiguity.[97] The fact that some part of a claim is capable of more than one construction does not necessarily mean that the claim is ambiguous.[98] It frequently happens that a patentee who is plaintiff in an action

---

[94] *Henriksen v. Tallon Ltd.* [1965] R.P.C. 434 at p.443.
[95] (1922) 39 R.P.C. 49.
[96] (1911) 28 R.P.C. 565 at p.581.
[97] *Unifloc Reagents Ltd. v. Newstead Colliery Ltd.* (1943) 60 R.P.C. 165; *Martin v. Selsdon Fountain Pen Co. Ltd.* (1949) 66 R.P.C. 193.
[98] See n.94.

for infringement of the patent is forced to contend that some part of the claim has a meaning other than its ordinary or natural meaning in order to embrace the alleged infringement[99] or to save the claim from invalidity for some other reason, *e.g.* inutility,[1] with the consequence that the claim is ultimately held to be ambiguous. But a claim is not necessarily invalid for ambiguity merely because the patentee contends for a construction which the court is not prepared to adopt.[2]

A claim may be limited by the result to be attained and if so limited is not invalid for ambiguity,[3] provided that in, for instance, a claim for an article, the limitation is "sufficient to characterise the construction of the article claimed."[4]

The use of the word "substantially" in the claim, in phrases such as **5.118** "substantially as described", or "substantially as described and shown in the drawings" does not render the claim invalid for ambiguity.[5] On the other hand, if the monopoly should be defined by reference to such general terms as "known methods" or "general methods", or equivalent phrases, this may lead to ambiguity.[6]

Discrepancies in drawings

The result of there being a discrepancy between the printed matter **5.119** and the drawings depends upon whether the discrepancy produces ambiguity sufficient to mislead. If what is meant is clear to persons skilled in the art, then the specification is not ambiguous, and it is immaterial from which part of the specification they have drawn their information. If there is material ambiguity, the patent is invalid.[7]

D. Inutility

P.A. 1949, section 32(1)(g): "the invention, so far claimed in any claim **5.120** of the complete specification, is not useful."

Utility at common law

In *Elias v. Grovesend Tinplate Co.*,[8] Lindley L.J. said:

---

[99] *Pathé Cinema S.A. v. Coronel Camera Co.* (1940) 57 R.P.C. 48.
[1] *Raleigh Cycle Co. Ltd. v. H. Miller & Co. Ltd.* (1948) 65 R.P.C. 141; and see *E.M.I. Ltd. v. Lissen Ltd.* (1939) 56 R.P.C. 23 at p.40.
[2] *Slumberland Ltd. v. Burgess Bedding* (1951) 68 R.P.C. 87 at p.98.
[3] *No-Fume Ltd. v. Frank Pitchford & Co. Ltd.* (1935) 52 R.P.C. 231.
[4] *Mullard Radio Valve Co. Ltd. v. British Belmont Radio Ltd.* (1939) 56 R.P.C. 1 at p.16.
[5] *Raleigh Cycle Co. Ltd. v. H. Miller & Co. Ltd.* (1948) 65 R.P.C. 141 at p.159. And see *ante* § 4.41.
[6] *British Celanese Ltd.'s Appn.*, (1934) 51 R.P.C. 192.
[7] See *e.g. Knight v. Argyll's Ltd.* (1913) 30 R.P.C. 321 at p.348.
[8] (1890) 7 R.P.C. 455 at p.467.

"It is very singular that the Statute of James says nothing whatever about utility, but utility has been engrafted into it because of the words to which I have called attention; that is to say, it has been found mischievous to the State to grant patents which are not useful as well as new."[9]

The test of utility

5.121   Inutility, in the sense in which that word is used in modern patent law and practice, is concerned solely with the scope of the claim, and means that the claim covers a mechanism or a process which is useless for the purposes indicated by the patentee, *i.e.* which does not produce the result or one of the results claimed in the specification. A patent would also be void for utility if the invention was useless for any purpose whatsoever, but this is a circumstance which is unlikely to occur in practice.

In *Lane-Fox v. Kensington and Knightsbridge Electric Lighting Co. Ltd.*[10] the relevant claim was as follows: "The employment as described of secondary batteries as reservoirs of electricity in combination with a mode or system of distribution such as is hereinbefore explained". Lindley L.J. said:[11]

"The utility of the alleged invention depends not on whether by following the directions in the complete specification all the results now necessary for commercial success can be obtained, but on whether by such directions the effects which the patentee professed to produce could be produced and on the practical utility of those effects ... to judge of utility the directions in the specification obtained can be attained, and is practically useful at the time when the patent is granted, the test of utility is satisfied ... 'Useful for what?' is a question which must always be asked, and the answer must be useful for the purposes indicated by the patentee."[12]

5.122   In *Vidal Dyes Syndicate Ltd. v. Levinstein Ltd.*[13] Fletcher Moulton L.J. said:

"By his specification, and the claim with which it concludes, the patentee delimits the area of his monopoly. If the validity of his patent is challenged, he has to show that all within that area is novel and

---

[9] See also 3 Co.Inst. 181.
[10] [1892] 3 Ch.424; (1892) 9 R.P.C. 413.
[11] [1892] 3 Ch. at p.431; (1982) 9 R.P.C. at p.417.
[12] See also *Mullard Radio Valve Co. Ltd. v. Philco Radio and Television Corporation* (1935) 52 R.P.C. at p.287.
[13] (1912) 29 R.P.C. 245 at pp.268, 271.

useful ... It is a question involving the area of monopoly claimed, and if, on the proper construction of the specification, the court holds that the patentee has claimed a process which is so dangerous that an expert chemist would avoid it, or even a process which an expert chemist would take to be impossible, the consequence is ... that his patent is invalid."[14]

In *Alsop's Patent*,[15] Parker J. said: **5.123**

"In considering the validity of a patent for a process it is, therefore, material to ascertain precisely what the patentee claims to be the result of the process for which the patent has been granted; the real consideration which he gives for the grant is the disclosure of a process which produces a result, and not the disclosure of a process which may or may not produce any result at all. If the patentee claims protection for a process for producing a result and that result cannot be produced by the process, in my opinion the consideration fails. Similarly, if the patentee claims a process producing two results combined and only one of these results is in fact produced by the process, there is a partial failure of consideration ... and such partial failure of consideration is sufficient to avoid the patent ... Objections to patents on the grounds above referred to are sometimes treated as objections for want of utility, and when so treated the well known rule is that the utility of an invention depends upon whether, by following the directions of the patentee, the result which the patentee professed to produce can in fact be produced (see Lindley L. J. in *Lane-Fox v. Kensington, etc., Co., supra*). Want of utility in this sense must, however, in my opinion, be distinguished from want of utility in the sense of the invention being useless for any purpose whatsoever. In the case of an invention not serving any useful purpose at all, the patent would no doubt be void, but not entirely for the same reason. It would probably be void at common law on the ground that the King's prerogative could not be properly exercised unless there were some consideration moving to the public, and the public could not be benefited by the disclosure of something absolutely useless. It would certainly be avoided as mischievous to the State and generally inconvenient within the Statute of Monopolies. But it may well be that an invention, which is void because it does not produce the result or one of the results claimed, may, nevertheless, be useful as producing other results."[16-17]

---

[14] See also *Simpson v. Holliday* (1866) L.R. 1 H.L. 315, quoted in *Vidal Dyes Syndicate Ltd. v. Levinstein Ltd.* (1912) 29 R.P.C. at p.271.

[15] (1907) 24 R.P.C. 733 at p.752.

[16-17] Quoted with approval by Lord Birkenhead L.C. in *Hatmaker v. Joseph Nathan & Co. Ltd.* (1919) 36 R.P.C. 231 at p.237; see also *Raleigh Cycle Co. Ltd.v. H. Miller & Co. Ltd.*, (1948) 65 R.P.C. at p.154.

Two classes of promise

5.124   A distinction was, however, drawn by Parker J. in *Alsop's Patent*,[18] between two kinds of promise as follows:

> "There may be cases in which the result which the patentee claims to have produced can in fact be produced, but the patentee has gone on to detail the useful purposes to which such result can be applied, and that in fact the result produced cannot be applied to one or more of such purposes. In such a case I do not think the patent is necessarily void, provided there are purposes for which the result is useful. If it be avoided it can only be because it contains a misrepresentation so material that it can be said the Crown has been deceived. The importance of drawing a distinction between what the patentee claims to have effected by the invention for which he claims protection, and a statement of the additional purposes to which the invention can be applied is well illustrated by the case of *Lyon v. Goddard*."[19]
>
> In the latter case, the patentee claimed a disinfecting apparatus enabling the use of steam at high pressure in an inner chamber, but also pointed out that his apparatus could be used for disinfection by dry heat without steam, which second method did not differ from that of a previously known apparatus. The patent was held valid.)

5.125   In *Norton and Gregory Ltd. v. Jacobs*[20] Lord Greene M.R. said:

> "A claim made in language which upon its true construction would be wide enough to cover the use of reducing agents which are not effective to produce the desired result would be bad for inutility ... But it is said that the language of the claim must be construed so as to exclude any reducing agent which a chemist of ordinary skill would know, with or without experiment, to be unsuitable in view of the result to be achieved. We are unable to accept this argument. The fact that a skilled chemist desiring to use the invention would reject certain reducing agents as being unsuitable is one thing; it is quite a different thing to say that a claim must in point of construction be cut down so as to exclude those reducing agents because a skilled chemist would not use them. To adopt the latter proposition would be not to construe the specification but to amend it."[21]

5.126   The nature of the promise is also important in that it is addressed to the skilled man and the Courts will not accept that such a man will, in

---

[18] (1907) 24 R.P.C. 733 at p.753.
[19] (1894) 11 R.P.C. 354.
[20] (1937) 54 R.P.C. 271 at pp.275, 276.
[21] See also *Raleigh Cycle Co. Ltd. v. Miller & Co. Ltd.* (1948) 65 R.P.C. 141 at p.155; *Minerals Separation North American Corporation v. Noranda Mines Ltd.*, (1952) 69 R.P.C.81; *Henriksen v. Tallon Ltd.* [1965] R.P.C. 434.

carrying out the promise, act without common sense.[22] However, where the claim covers perfectly proper and not unskilled or mistaken applications of a device for purposes not fulfilling the promise, the claim will be invalid for inutility.[23]

It is immaterial to the question of inutility that no one expert in the art **5.127** would be misled by the promise of the result, as was pointed out by Sir Raymond Evershed in *Sonotone Corporation v. Multitone Electric Co. Ltd.*:[24]

"As regards inutility . . . the argument upon it turned largely upon the suggestion or promise implicit, as in our judgment it was, in page 2, lines 115 to 126, which relate most particularly to Claims 1 and 4. It is true, as the judge pointed out, that no one expert in the art might or would be misled by the promise. But in our judgment that fact does not of itself provide an answer to the objection, if the promise was made as we hold, and is unfulfilled . . . (See, for example, *Osram Lamp Works Ltd. v. Pope's Electric Lamp Co. Ltd.*,[25] per Lord Haldane.) This is not the kind of case in which, for the purposes at any rate of considering the validity of Claims 1 and 4, the promise made is fulfilled in fact though the reason assigned for the result is erroneous. (See, for example, *"Z" Electric Lamp Co. Ltd. v. Marples.*)[26] We, therefore, think, if it were necessary, that the objection of inutility would prevail to invalidate Claims 1 and 4 and consequentially Claims 2, 3 and 5 also. But, in our opinion, the objection ought not to prevail against Claim 6 (the claim to the drawings). The principle that the promise forms, or forms part of, the consideration for the monopoly does not appear to us, as we construe the specification, to be applicable to Claim 6. Alternatively, if the promise be properly related, as it were, to Claim 6, then, as we have already said, the promise seems to us to have been fulfilled though not for the reason exclusively assigned in the promise."

Commercial success not necessary

Utility in the patent law sense is in no way related to commercial **5.128** success. In *Badische Anilin und Soda Fabrik v. Levinstein*[27] Lord Halsbury L.C. said:

"The element of commercial pecuniary success has, as it appears to me, no relation to the question of utility in patent law generally,

---

[22] *Martin and Miles v. The Selsdon Fountain Pen Co.* (1949) 66 R.P.C. 193 at p.214; *Vaisey v. Toddlers Footwear* [1957] R.P.C. 90 at p.100.
[23] *Horville Engineering Co. Ltd. v. Clares (Engineering) Ltd.* [1976] R.P.C. 411 at p.445.
[24] (1955) 72 R.P.C. at p.146.
[25] (1917) 34 R.P.C. at p.390.
[26] (1910) 27 R.P.C. at p.737.
[27] (1887) 4 R.P.C. at p.462.

though, of course, where the question is of improvement by reason of cheaper production, such a consideration is of the very essence of the patent itself, and the thing claimed has not really been invented unless that condition is fulfilled."

Subsequent improvement immaterial

5.129   It is not an objection to the patent that the original form of the invention has been superseded by later improvements. In *Edison & Swan Electric Light Co. v. Holland*[28] Lindley L.J. said:

"Edison's patent is said to be of no use, and the proof of this statement is said to be furnished by the fact that lamps are not made according to the patent, even by Edison himself. The utility of the patent must be judged by reference to the state of things at the date of the patent; if the invention was then useful, the fact that subsequent improvements have replaced the patented invention and rendered it obsolete and commerically of no value does not invalidate the patent."[29]

E. False suggestion

5.130   **P.A. 1949, section 32(1)(j):** " the patent was obtained on a false suggestion or representation."

These words are wide enough to cover any false statement made by an applicant by which the Crown is deceived, but in a majority of cases such a false statement results also in some additional ground of invalidity which is separately defined, such as inutility (false promise) and/or insufficiency. It is irrelevant whether or not there was deliberate falsehood by the patentee if the Crown was in fact misled, but "if false suggestion is alleged, it must be established on the basis of the documents in which the alleged false suggestion was made—the onus being, of course, on the objector."[30] The false statements could be made either in the application forms or in the complete specification. In *Intalite International N.V. v. Cellular Ceilings Ltd. (No. 2)*[31] Whitford J. held that the mere fact that a misleading statement might be found in the body of a specification was not sufficient to establish invalidity on the ground of false suggestion. The statement must have misled the Comptroller into granting the patent. The patent is obtained upon the suggestions or representations set out in the recitals to the patent grant itself (see *ante*,

---

[28] (1889) 6 R.P.C. 243 at p.283.
[29] See also *Aktiengesellschaft für Autogene Aluminium Schweissung v. London Aluminium Co. Ltd. (No. 2)* (1920) 37 R.P.C. 153; (1921) 38 R.P.C. 163 (C.A.); (1922) 39 R.P.C. 296 (H.L.).
[30] *Kromschröder's Patent* [1960] R.P.C. 75 at p.83. *Martin v. Scribal Pty. Ltd.* [1956] R.P.C. 215 at p.224. See *Patent Concern N.V. v. Melotte Sales Co. Ltd.* [1968] R.P.C. 263.
[31] [1987] R.P.C. 532; following *Valensi v. British Radio Corp. Ltd.* [1973] R.P.C. 337 at 381.

§§ 13–15) and falsity in any of them will be sufficient to invalidate the patent, if the false statement is of such materiality that the patent can be said to be "obtained" on it.[32] In paragraph 6 of Schedule 1 of the 1977 Act it is stated that it shall not be a ground of revocation that the patent was obtained on a false suggestion or representation that a claim of the complete specification had a priority date earlier than the date of filing the application for the patent. The paragraph goes on to state that if such a suggestion or representation was made, the priority date of the claim shall be taken to be the date of filing the application of that patent.

F. Prior grant

P.A. 1949, section 32(1)(a): "the invention, so far as claimed in any claim of the complete specification, was claimed in a valid claim of earlier priority date contained in the complete specification of another patent granted in the United Kingdom."   **5.131**

It has always been the law that a patent will be invalidated if the invention is shown to have been the subject of a valid prior grant.[33] Prior claiming is also a ground of opposition to the grant.[34]

The fact that there has been no prior publication is not material in this connection. It has been said that in order to render the second grant invalid, there must be proof "not only of similarity in essentials, but of identity."[35] If such be the law it would follow that the subsequent claim cannot be invalidated on the ground of prior claiming unless the two claims are for substantially the same invention, *i.e.* if one is larger or smaller in its scope than the other this ground of invalidity is inapplicable, even where the later claim is the larger.[36] Some decisions, discussed in the succeeding paragraphs, seem to point to a contrary conclusion, but it is submitted that the above is a correct summary of the law.   **5.132**

In *Kromschröder's Patent (Revocation)*,[37] the Court of Appeal held that: **5.133**

(a) Claim 1 of the patent in suit, 755462, claimed a gas meter of a certain construction,

(b) this same gas meter was claimed under the description "through flow appliance" in Claim 1 of a prior patent specification 716771 in combination with certain "fittings for pipe lines", but that

(c) as the monopolies claimed in the two claims were different in that

---

[32] *Parry Husband's Appn.* [1965] R.P.C. 382; *Muccino's Appn.* [1968] R.P.C. 307.
[33] 1 W.P.C. 15, note (*h*).
[34] P.A. 1949, s.14(1)(*d*).
[35] *Per* Lord Guthrie in *Blackett v. Dickson and Mann Ltd* (1909) 26 R.P.C. 73 at p.82. *Comptroller's Ruling* (1912) 29 R.P.C. (D).
[36] *Comptroller's Ruling* (1922) 39 R.P.C. (C); but *cf. Carpmael's Appn.* (1927) 46 R.P.C. 321.
[37] [1960] R.P.C. 75.

in 755462 there was no limitation to the "fittings for pipe lines", there was no prior claiming.

It will be observed that Claim 1 of the later patent 755462 could be said to be wider in scope that that of the earlier in that it contained no limitation to the "fittings for pipe lines", and that the decision of the Court of Appeal appears to have established that in such a case there is not need for the later claim to be so worded as to disclaim the invention claimed in the earlier claim. The material passage of the judgment of the court is as follows:

"We will assume that the invention claimed in Claim 1 of Patent 755462 is included in Claim 1 of Patent 716771. But it is not, as an invention, itself the subject of a distinct claim in the latter patent. In our judgment, the language of paragraph (*a*) of section 32 (1) of the Act requires that it should be and the words 'claimed in a valid claim' are not satisfied if the invention in question is only covered or comprehended by the claim as being a part or integer (however important) of some wider combination or 'arrangement' which and which alone is the subject-matter of the claim. The words at the beginning of the paragraph—'the invention so far as claimed in any claim'—seem to us to postulate that the suject-matter contemplated must itself be that for which protection is claimed; and we think the same sense should be given to the later words—'claimed in a valid claim.' "[38]

5.134   The decision in *Kromschröders Patent* was followed in *Daikin* Kogyo Co. Ltd.'s Application.[39] Buckley L.J. said:

"It is not, in my opinion, sufficient to show that operations or methods which would fall within an earlier claim would amount to infringements of a patent granted in respect of a later claim. Section 14(1)(*c*) requires the invention so far as claimed in the later specification is claimed in a claim of the earlier specification.
Where an earlier claim is wider in its scope than a later claim and there is no separate claim in the earlier specification restricted to the subject-matter of the later claim, the claimant of the earlier claim cannot, in any judgment, assert that he has made a prior claim to the subject-matter of the later claim."[40]

5.135   It is submitted that the passages quoted above mean that identity of claims is required. This has been accepted in some cases.[41] But in the

---

[38] [1960] R.P.C. 75 at p.82.
[39] [1974] R.P.C. 559.
[40] *Ibid.* at p.580.
[41] [1963] R.P.C. 271.

cases of *Syntex S.A.'s Application*[42] and *Merck & Co. (Macek's) Patent*[43] (both cases concerned with prior claiming as a ground of opposition under section 14(1)(c) of the Act) the Tribunal has held prior claiming to be established where the earlier claim was narrower in scope but for an invention falling within the monopoly claimed by the later (and wider) claim. In the latter case the Tribunal (Lloyd-Jacob J.), after referring to the judgment of the Court of Appeal in the *Kromschröder* case, said,[44]

> "The 1949 Act introduced this phrase 'the invention so far as claimed in any claim' not only in section 14(1)(c) but elsewhere in the Act and in particular in section 14(1)(b) (prior publication), section 14(1)(d) (prior user) and section 14(1)(e) (obviousness) ... So far as concerns prior publication and prior user, if a claim to a manner of manufacture includes one embodiment of it which is not new, that claim has always been regarded as invalid whatever novel and ingenious embodiments the claim also covers (see *Molins v. Industrial Machinery Co. Ltd.*, 55 R.P.C. 31). So too, with obviousness (*Woodrow v. Long Humphrey & Co.*, 51 R.P.C. 25); and unless and until the patentee has been able, by suitable amendment, to exclude from the claim the invalid portion of the monopoly, the taint of invalidity attaches to it in its fullness and deprives it of monopoly effect.
>
> "There would appear to be no ground for construing the phrase 'the invention so far as claimed in any claim' in different senses in the sub-divisions of section 14(1), so that, if the cited prior claim on its fair construction can be seen to grant as a manner of manufacture that which the later claim on its fair construction would re-monopolise, the objection of prior claiming is established, and this despite the inclusion in the later claim of variants of the manner of manufacture to which no objection can properly be raised."

The decision in the *Merck* case was held in *Daikin Kogyo* not to be in conflict on the basis that the claim was of a comprehensive type which was a convenient summation of what was in effect a number of separate claims to different compositions.   **5.136**

The test for prior claiming enunciated in the *Merck* case has been applied by the Patents Appeal Tribunal in subsequent cases.[45] In *Wilkinson Sword Ltd.'s Application*[46] the applicants' claim was held to be prior claimed although wider in scope than the cited prior claim. However, it is submitted that this decision is of doubtful authority as it is difficult to see how the wider claim could be construed as a number of   **5.137**

---

[42] [1966] R.P.C. 560.
[43] [1967] R.P.C. 157.
[44] *Ibid.* at pp.162, 163.
[45] See, *e.g. Pittsburgh Plate Glass Co.'s Appn.* [1969] R.P.C. 628; *Union Carbide Corporation's Patent* [1971] R.P.C. 81; *Allen & Hanbury's Appn.*, [1977] R.P.C. 113; but see *I.C.I. Ltd. (Howe's) Appn.*, [1977] R.P.C. 121 and *Westinghouse Electric Corporation (Frost's) Appn.*, [1973] R.P.C. 139.
[46] [1970] R.P.C. 42.

separate claims. In *Ethyl Corporation's Application*[47] the Patents Appeal Tribunal (Graham J.) held that when the earlier claim is broader than the later claim and includes within it the area covered by the later claim, the later claim is prior-claimed unless the later claim can be justified on the basis of a selection patent as to which see *ante*, § 5.91.

5.138   In considering prior claiming, confusion is sometimes created by the consideration that manufacture according to the second claim may constitute an infringement of the earlier claim, and manufacture according to the earlier claim may equally be an infringement of the later. This, it is submitted, is wholly irrelevant in either case.

5.139   There appears to be only one reported case where a patent has been clearly held by a court to be invalid on the ground of prior grant.[48] In order to be an effective prior grant the prior claim must be valid.[49]

5.140   Applications for patents have from time to time been refused on the ground of prior claiming where the invention claimed is in substance the same in both claims.[50] Where the later claim differed from the earlier only by the introduction of a feature that was a matter of common knowledge at the priority date of the earlier claim, the later claim was disallowed on opposition.[51] In *Commercial Solvent Corporation's Application*[52] Lloyd-Jacob J., sitting as the Patents Appeal Tribunal, said:

"When the objection which is being considered is prior claiming, what the Patent Office and this Tribunal have to determine is whether such difference as appears between the two claims as a matter of language imports any real differentiation as a matter of inventive step",[53]

but it is submitted that is this no longer good law having regard to the *Kromschröder* and *Daikin Kogyo* decisions *ante*.

5.141   Where a chemical substance has been claimed in an earlier claim, an applicant who devises some new process of making the same chemical substance is not entitled to claim that substance *per se*, but he is not, of course, debarred from claiming the new process which he has devised, subject to a proper acknowledgment of the earlier patent.[54] A claim to the use of intermediates was held to be a prior claim to a claim to the intermediates.[55]

Where an application is divided into more than one application, no

---

[47] [1970] R.P.C. 227.
[48] *Rowland and Kennedy v. The Air Council* (1927) 44 R.P.C. 433.
[49] See *Mica Insulator Co. v. Electric Co.* (1898) 15 R.P.C. 489; *Robertson v. Purdey* (1907) 24 R.P.C. 273 at p.297.
[50] *I.G. Farbenindustrie's Appn. for Revocation* (1934) 51 R.P.C. 53; *Carpmael's Appn.* (1929) 46 R.P.C. 321.
[51] *Babcock and Wilcox Ltd.'s Appn* (1952) 69 R.P.C. 224.
[52] (1954) 71 R.P.C. 143.
[53] See also *Imperial Chemical Industries Ltd.'s Appn.* [1957] R.P.C. 12; *Standard Telephones and Cables Ltd.'s Appn.* [1958] R.P.C. 108; *Kromschröder's Patent* [1960] R.P.C. 75.
[54] *Macfarlan (J.F.) and Co. Ltd.'s Appn.* (1954) 71 R.P.C. 429.
[55] *Merck & Co.'s Appn.* [1973] R.P.C. 220.

complete specification must include a claim for matter claimed in another, in the sense that no two claims must be coterminous.[56]

G. Applicant not entitled to apply

P.A. 1949, section 32(1)(b): "the patent was granted on the application of a person not entitled under the provisions of this Act to apply therefor." **5.142**

Section 1 of the 1949 Act limited the class of persons who were entitled to apply for a patent. In general, the applicant was required to be either the inventor or his assignee.[57] If the person who applied was not the person entitled to apply, then the patent is invalid. This ground of invalidity can be raised by any person and is not limited to the person who should have been the proper applicant; compare section 32(1)(c), set out below.

H. Patent obtained in contravention of the rights of the petitioner

P.A. 1949, section 32(1)(c): "the patent was obtained in contravention of the rights of the petitioner or any person under or through whom he claims." **5.143**

There is an overlap between this and the preceding ground of revocation in that, where the applicant is not the "true and first inventor" but has "obtained" the invention in this country from the petitioner for revocation, then the patent would be invalid both under section 32(1)(b) and under section 32(1)(c). But it appears that under section 32(1)(c) a petitioner can seek the revocation of a patent where the "obtaining" from him had taken place abroad and the patentee had applied, in contravention of the petitioner's rights (e.g. of confidence), for a patent in the United Kingdom. In such a case the patentee could properly claim to be the "true and first inventor", being the "importer" of the invention and, therefore, no case for revocation could be made under section 32(1)(b), but, nevertheless, the patent could apparently be revoked under section 32(1)(c) at the instance of the person from whom the invention had been obtained. There are, no doubt, other cases than the above where there will be no overlap, e.g. where a servant makes an invention and applies for a patent for it contrary to his conditions of employment. This ground of invalidity can only be alleged by the

---

[56] Patent's Rules 1968, r.13(3); *Arrow Electric Switches Ltd.'s Appn.* (1944) 61 R.P.C. 1.
[57] For a full treatment of the law on this subject, now no longer relevant save in relation to this section, see Terrell (12th ed.), Chap.3; *cf.* P.A. 1977, see *ante* § 5.95.

persons whose rights have been contravened by the obtaining of the grant of the patent.[58]

I. Invention not a manufacture

5.144   **P.A. 1949, section 32(1)(d):** "the subject of any claim of the complete specification is not an invention within the meaning of this Act."

Having regard to the definition of "invention" in section 101(1) of the Act and the inclusion of lack of novelty as a separate ground of revocation in section 32(1)(e), it appears that this ground relates solely to whether the claim relates to a "manner of manufacture" or a "method or process of testing" as defined above. These requirements have been fully dealt with in Chapter 2, to which the reader is referred.

J. Use of invention illegal

5.145   **P.A. 1949, section 32(1)(k):** "the primary or intended use or exercise of the invention is contrary to law."

It will not be sufficient to establish invalidity on the above ground to prove that the invention could be used for purposes contrary to law (*e.g.* gaming).[59] In order to establish this ground of revocation it must be proved that the "primary or intended" use is illegal. This ground of invalidity is to be found in section 6 of the Statute of Monopolies, but it does not appear that any patent has been held invalid upon this ground.

K. Prior secret use

5.146   **P.A. 1949, section 32(1)(l):** "the invention, so far as claimed in any claim of the complete specification, was secretly used in the United Kingdom, otherwise than as mentioned in subsection (2) of this section, before the priority date of that claim."

Not every case of secret prior user will invalidate the claim, because certain kinds are excluded by section 32(2). Accordingly, if the secret prior user is only for the purpose of reasonable trial and experiment or is by or by authority of a government department to whom the applicant for a patent has disclosed the invention, or is by a third person to whom the applicant has disclosed the invention and takes place without the

---

[58] See *Patent Concern N.V. v. Melotte Sales Co. Ltd.* [1968] R.P.C. 263.
[59] *Pessers & Moody v. Haydon & Co.* (1909) 26 R.P.C. 58; *Walton v. Ahrens* (1939) 56 R.P.C. 193 at p.203.

applicant's consent or acquiescence, then such secret prior user does not affect the validity of the claim.[60] Further, although a claim will be invalid for obviousness if it contains no inventive step over a public user, such is not the case with secret user, which cannot be relied upon in support of the plea of obviousness.[61] There is often considerable difficulty in deciding whether or not a user was "for the purpose of reasonable trial or experiment only" (see under "Experiments and Trials" at § 5.41).

---

[60] P.A. 1949, s.32(2).
[61] P.A. 1949, s.32(1), (e)(f).

CHAPTER 6

INFRINGEMENT OF LETTERS PATENT

Introduction

6.01   In the 1949 Act as in past legislation, there was no definition of infringement. The infringement of a patent was instead the doing, after the date of publication of the complete specification,[1] of that which the patent had prohibited being done. The words of the Royal Command were as follows:

> "We do by these presents for Us, our heirs and successors, strictly command all our subjects whatsoever within our United Kingdom of Great Britain and Northern Ireland, and the Isle of Man, that they do not at any time during the continuance of the said term (sixteen years from the date hereunder written of these presents) either directly or indirectly make use of or put in practice the said invention, nor in anywise imitate the same, without the consent, licence or agreement of the said patentee in writing under this hand and seal, on pain of incurring such penalties as may be justly inflicted on such offenders for their contempt of this our Royal Command, and of being answerable to the patentee according to the law for his damages thereby occasioned."[2]

6.02   The 1977 Act has now codified the law of infringement by providing a complete definition in section 60 (necessarily so, since the patent no longer contains any Royal Command). Section 60(1) specifically pro-

---

[1] P.A. 1949, s.13.
[2] See Patents Rules 1968, Sched. 4.

vides that (subject to the provisions of section 60) a person infringes a patent for an invention *if, but only if* he performs the acts there specified. Thus, subject to the law of joint tortfeasors,[3] and to the transitional provisions in the Act,[4] section 60 is exhaustive of what constitutes infringement.

However, although the law as to infringement has not only been codified but also altered and extended in part, many of the principles developed under the 1949 Act will continue to apply. The old law as such applies only by reason of transitional provisions[5] to a now vanishing, if not extinct, number of cases where infringement of an existing patent was begun prior to the coming into force of the 1977 Act; under those transitional provisions, where the infringement began after the coming into force of the 1977 Act, then it is the new law of infringement which applies, even for old Act patents. This chapter will therefore not deal independently with the law under the 1949 Act; for a comprehensive discussion of the old law, and the transitional provisions, reference may be made to previous editions of this work.

The definition of infringement contained in section 60 of the 1977 Act **6.03** arises out of the C.P.C. wherein it was resolved that the Member States should adjust their patent laws so as to bring them into conformity with the corresponding provisions of the E.P.C., the C.P.C. and the P.C.T. As a result there is a striking and unusual[6] provision in section 130(7) of the 1977 Act specifying that certain sections of the Act (including sections 60 and 69) are so framed as to have as nearly as practicable the same effect in this country as the corresponding provisions of the E.P.C., C.P.C. and P.C.T. have in the territories to which they apply. Thus, not only are the provisions as to infringement different in the 1977 Act but also regard has to be had in interpreting those provisions to the intentions of the draftsman.

"Infringement" of invalid patent

It has been said that there cannot in any event be an infringement of an **6.04** invalid patent,[7] but the word "infringement" is used in the statutes and has been used in many judgments as meaning "within the scope of the monopoly claimed." It will be used in this chapter in that sense.

---

[3] See 6.56 *et seq.*
[4] P.A. 1977, Sched. 4, para. 3.
[5] P.A. 1977, Sched. 4, para. 3.
[6] *Per* Oliver J. in *Smith Kline & French Laboratories v. R. D. Harbottle (Mercantile) Ltd.* [1980] R.P.C. 363 at 372.
[7] See *Pittveil & Co. v. Brackelsberg Melting Processes Ltd.* (1932) 49 R.P.C. 23 p.32; *Van der Lely (C.) N.V. v. Maulden Engineering Co.* [1984] F.S.R. 157.

Ascertainment of whether there is infringement

6.05   In order to determine whether there has been infringement of a patent, it is necessary:

(a) To decide whether the acts alleged to have been done by the Defendant were of such a nature that they fell within the statutory definition of infringement.

(b) To construe the specification and claims so as to determine whether those acts fell within the claims.

(c) To determine who is liable for those acts.

(d) To decide whether such acts are excused by any statutory exceptions or rule of law, or

(e) whether the relief available to the patentee is restricted.

Each of these questions will be considered in turn under headings 1–5 below, and thereafter additional rights against non-infringers and the right of third parties to seek a declaration of non-infringement will be discussed.

1. Nature of the Infringing Act

Jurisdiction

6.06   The 1977 Act extends to the United Kingdom, the Isle of Man, the territorial waters and any area designated by order under section 1(7) of the Continental Shelf Act 1964 or section 22(5) of the Oil and Gas (Enterprise) Act 1981[8].

Infringement under section 60

6.07   The ambit of infringement is defined by section 60 and in so far as any difficulties in construction arise reference is to be had to section 130(7).[9] Acts which (subject to the other provisions of section 60) constitute infringing acts are set out in section 60(1) and (2). Subsection (1) applies to acts done in relation to patented products or processes whereas subsection (2) applies to acts which do not involve patented products or processes which nonetheless constitute infringement. The former can be considered as direct infringing acts and the latter as indirect.

---

[8] P.A. 1977, s.132(2)–(4).
[9] See *ante*, §6.03.

Damage

Damage is not and has never been an essential of the cause of action. **6.08**
In *Smithkline Corp. v. D.D.S.A. Pharmaceuticals*,[10] Buckley L.J. said:

"So it seems to me ... that it is not incumbent to show that he has suffered commercial loss. It is an infringement if his monopoly has been infringed, and he is entitled to a remedy."

Of course, even once liability has been established, the nature of the remedy may depend upon the nature of the loss sustained; see generally Chapter 12 §§12.208 *et seq.*

Direct infringement without knowledge

With one exception (offer of a process for use)[11] it remains the law in **6.09** relation to direct infringement that the knowledge or intention of the infringer is irrelevant. In *Proctor v. Bennis*[12] Cotton L.J. said:

"The right of the patentee does not depend on the defendant having notice that what he is doing is an infringement. If what he is doing is in fact an infringement, even although the defendant acts in the way which ... was bona fide or honest, he will not be protected from an injunction by that. It does not depend on notice."

Thus, there was no duty cast upon a patentee to inform persons that what they were doing amounted to an infringement of his patent; and if he knew of the infringement and omitted to give a warning, he was not stopped from subsequently bringing an action, but he would be denied relief if his conduct amounted to acquiescence.[13]

In *Stead v. Anderson*[14] Wilde C.J. said: "We think it clear that the action is maintainable in respect of what the defendant does, not what he intends."[15] Equally, if a person intending to infringe a patent did not in fact do so, he would not be taken to have infringed.[16]

Innocence may, however, provide an answer to a claim for damages.[17]

Proof of an intention to infringe, apart from actual infringement, may justify an injunction to restrain infringement.[18]

---

[10] [1978] F.S.R. 109 at p.144.
[11] See *post*, §6.28.
[12] (1887) 4 R.P.C. 333 at p. 356.
[13] *Ibid.*
[14] (1847) 2 W.P.C. 151 at p.156.
[15] And see *Wright v. Hitchcock* (1870) L.R. 5 Ex. 37 at p.47; *Young v. Rosenthal* (1884) 1 R.P.C. 29 at p.39.
[16] *Newall v. Elliott* (1864) 10 Jur. (N.S.) 954 at p.958.
[17] See *post*, §6.89.
[18] See *post*, §12-209 *et seq.*

Where the invention is a product

6.10   Where the invention is a product, section 60(1)(*a*) provides that the patent will be infringed by any person who:

    (a) makes
    (b) disposes of
    (c) offers to dispose of
    (d) uses or
    (e) imports the product or
    (f) keeps the product whether for disposal or otherwise.

It is submitted that the expression "where the invention is a product" is not a reference to a patented product as defined in section 130(1) of the 1977 Act. This would have the effect of making all products obtained directly by means of a patented process "products" within the meaning of section 60(1)(*a*) and hence section 60(1)(*c*) would become otiose.[19] It therefore appears that the expression "where the invention is a product" means no more than where the allegedly infringed claim is a product claim.

(a) Makes

6.11   No difficulty should arise with the word "makes" as it is an ordinary English word with wide meaning; it also formed part of the old Royal Command in the grant of Letters Patent and thus the law developed under the 1949 Act and earlier statutes will continue to apply.

Making and selling all of the constituent parts of a machine as a collection or kit so that they may easily be put together might amount to direct infringement under this head,[20] such a kit amounting in substance to the complete article. Further, unless the kit is made only for export, liability is also likely to arise in repeat of such acts as indirect infringement under section 60(2),[21] and the vendor may also be a joint tortfeasor with the person who assembles the parts.[22]

Repairing a patented article may fall within the scope of an implied licence from the patentee, although it is not permissible to make a new article under the guise of repair.[23]

(b) Disposes of

6.12   "Disposes" is a word not used in earlier statutes or in the Royal

---

[19] See also "where the invention is a process", *post*, para. 6.23.
[20] See *United Telephone Co. v. Dale* (1884) 25 Ch.D. 778 at p.782; *Dunlop Pneumatic Tyre Co. Ltd. v. David Moseley & Sons Ltd.* (1904) 21 R.P.C. at p.280; and *cf. Cincinnati Grinders (Inc.) v. B.S.A. Tools Ltd.* (1931) 48 R.P.C. 33 at pp. 46–48, 58, 76; *Rotocrop Corp. v. Genbourne* [1982] F.S.R. 241 at 259.
[21] See *post*, §6.29.
[22] See *Rotocrop Corp. v. Genbourne* [1982] F.S.R. 241 at 258–9, and *post*, §6.56.
[23] See *post*, §6.62.

Command. In its widest meaning it would cover any loss of physical possession including destruction. The C.P.C., however, does not use the word "dispose" but instead refers to putting on the market. "Dispose" therefore has a more limited meaning covering only loss of physical possession by transferring that possession to another in the course of trade (*e.g.* by way of sale). This will, it appears, extend also to lending[24] but delivery to or by a warehouseman or carrier will not amount to disposal.[25]

In the case of goods manufactured abroad, the goods themselves had   **6.13** to come into this country to constitute infringement under the old law, and the same is now required by section 60. In *Badische Anilin und Soda Fabrik v. Johnson and the Basle Chemical Works*[26] a trader in England ordered goods from the defendant in Switzerland to be sent by post to England. The defendant addressed the goods to the trader in England and delivered them to the Swiss Post Office, by whom they were forwarded to England. The goods were manufactured according to an invention protected by the plaintiff's patent. It was held by the House of Lords that, since the contract of sale was completed by the delivery to the Post Office in Switzerland, and since the Post Office was the agent of the buyer and not of the vendor, the vendor had not made, used, exercised or vended the invention within the ambit of the patent, and that the patentee had no right of action against the vendor for an infringement of the patent.[27]

In *Badische Anilin und Soda Fabrik v. Hickson*[28] it was argued on behalf   **6.14** of the plaintiff that as the vendor had set aside the goods in the foreign country, the property in them had passed, and there was a complete sale. Lord Loreburn said that although there was appropriation to the purchaser and a completed sale, the operation of completing the sale had not taken place in this country, and consequently there had been no infringement.

However, although in the circumstances the vendor may not have been liable as a primary infringer he might have been liable as a joint tortfeasor.[29]

(c) Offers to dispose of

This expression is apt to cover in particular an offer for sale. It is   **6.15** doubtful whether a mere advertisement, being an invitation to treat, rather than an offer, amounts to an offer to dispose, but it will probably

---

[24] Under the old law, lending was not an infringement: *United Telephone Co. Ltd. v. Henry & Co.* (1885) 2 R.P.C. 11.

[25] See *Smith Kline French Laboratories v. R. D. Harbottle (Mercantile) Ltd.* [1980] R.P.C. 363; *Kalman v. Packaging (U.K.)* [1982] F.S.R. 406.

[26] (1897) 14 R.P.C. 919.

[27] See also *Morton Norwich Products Inc. v. Intercen Ltd.* [1978] R.P.C. 501 at p.516; *Saccharine Corp. Ltd. v. Reitmeyer* (1900) 17 R.P.C. 606.

[28] (1906) 23 R.P.C. 149.

[29] See *post*, §6.56 *et seq.*

amount to a threat to dispose of the products being advertised and thus injunctive relief may be obtained on a *quia timet* basis. The offer must be an offer within the jurisdiction to dispose of infringing products within the jurisdiction.[30]

(d) Uses

6.16   Again, the word "use" was included in the old Royal Command and the law as developed thereunder will continue to apply.

6.17   In the case of *Neilson v. Betts*[31] the facts were as follows: Betts (the plaintiff) was the patentee of an invention for the manufacture of capsules for the purpose of covering bottles of liquid and protecting the contents from the action of the atmosphere. The patent did not extend to Scotland. Neilson and his co-appellants (the defendants) were persons who bottled beer in Glasgow for the Indian market. They bottled the beer and covered it with capsules, which were apparently made in Germany in accordance with Betts' specification. The beer was shipped by the appellants in vessels which called at Liverpool to complete their cargoes; on some occasions the beer was transhipped in England, but no cases of beer were opened, nor was any of the beer sold in this country.

It was held by the House of Lords (affirming the judgments in the courts below) that as the object of Betts' invention was to make a capsule that would preserve beer, whilst the beer was in England it was being preserved by the use of Betts' invention, and consequently that there was an infringement of the patent.

Lord Chelmsford, in giving judgment in the court below, said:[32]

"It is the employment of the machine or article for the purpose for which it was designed which constitutes its active use, and whether the capsules were intended for ornament, or for protection of the contents of the bottles upon which they were placed, the whole time they were in England they may be correctly said to be in active use for the very objects for which they were placed upon the bottles by the vendors. If the beer, after being purchased in Glasgow, had been sent to England, and had been afterwards sold here, there can be no doubt, I suppose, that this would have been an infringement, because it would have been a profitable user of the invention, and I cannot see how it can cease to be a user because England is not the final destination of the beer."[33]

---

[30] *Kalman v. PCL Packaging (U.K.)* [1982] F.S.R. 406 at 417–8.
[31] (1871) L.R. 5 H.L. 1.
[32] L.R. 3 Ch.App. 429 at p.439.
[33] See also *Nobel's Explosives Co. v. Jones, Scott & Co.* (1881) 17 Ch.D. 721; *Universities of Oxford and Cambridge v. Richardson* 6 Ves 689; *Dunlop Pneumatic Tyre Co. Ltd. v. British and Colonial Motor Car Co. Ltd.* (1901) 18 R.P.C. 313; *Hoffman-La Roche & Co. A.G. v. Harris Pharmaceuticals Ltd.* [1977] F.S.R. 200; *Morton Norwich Products Inc. v. Intercen Ltd.* [1978] R.P.C. 501; *Smith Kline Corp. v. D.D.S.A. Pharmaceuticals Ltd.* [1978] F.S.R. 109.

In the case of *Adair v. Young*[34] certain pumps, which were an **6.18**
infringement of the plaintiff's patent, were fitted on board a British ship.
There was no evidence of their having been used. It was held by the
Court of Appeal that there had been no infringement, but as there was
evidence of an intention to use the pumps, an injunction was granted
against the use of the pumps.

The section is directed to commercial use; an application to regulatory **6.19**
authorities to sell a product in the United Kingdom, even though
accompanied by data relating to the patented product, is not "use" of
the product in the United Kingdom.[35]

Similarly, under the old law, taking out a patent for a process or
machine that infringed a prior patent did not amount to infringement,[36]
nor did the granting of a licence to manufacture under a subsequent
patent constitute infringement.[37]

(e) Imports

Importation by way of trade of patented goods, or goods made **6.20**
abroad by a patented process was an act of infringement under the old
law, and it is submitted that the authorities decided thereunder will
continue to apply. It was decided in *Pfizer Corporation v. Ministry of
Health*, as stated by Lord Upjohn,

> "that where an importer imports into this country articles made
> abroad, but in accordance with a British patent, for the purpose of
> distributing and selling them in this country, he quite plainly is using
> and exercising the patent, and he thereby infringes the patent the
> moment he introduces them into this country."[38]

(f) Keeps . . . whether for disposal or otherwise

The term "keeping, whether for disposal or otherwise" again prima **6.21**
facie extends to all forms of keeping including warehousemen and
carriers. The question arose in *Smith Kline French Laboratories v. R. D.
Harbottle (Mercantile) Limited*[39] where British Airways were alleged to
have infringed the plaintiffs patent by keeping a product covered by
that patent in their capacity as warehousemen. Oliver J. held that having
regard to section 130(7) and the words of the C.P.C., the word "keeping"
did not extend to the activities of mere warehousemen and carriers such
as British Airways.[40] He favoured construing the term in the sense of

---

[34] (1879) 12 Ch.D. 13.
[35] *Upjohn v. Kerfoot* [1988] F.S.R. 1 at 7; compare *Smith Kline & French Laboratories v. Douglas*
[1991] F.S.R. 522.
[36] *Tweedale v. Ashworth* (1890) 7 R.P.C. 426 at p.431.
[37] *Montgomery v. Paterson* (1894) 11 R.P.C. 221, 663.
[38] [1965] R.P.C. 261.
[39] [1980] R.P.C. 363.
[40] *Ibid.* at pp.371–4; see also *Nobel's Explosives v. Jones, Scott & Co.* (1881) 17 Ch.D.721.

"keeping in stock", although as this was an interlocutory application he expressly declined to arrive at a definitive interpretation.

6.22 Under the old law, once goods had been imported, mere purchase, ownership, possession, or transport did not amount to infringement although an injunction could be justified on the ground that it was strong evidence of a threat to use. On the other hand, where such purchase, ownership, possession or transport involved use of the invention, there was infringement.[41]

In *Smith Kline Corp. v. D.D.S.A. Pharmaceuticals Ltd.*[42] the defendants imported infringing goods into this country for the purpose of exporting the same to Nigeria. Buckley L.J. said:[43]

> "It seems to me that in the light of these authorities, Whitford J. was fully justified in saying, as he did in the course of his judgment in the *Hoffman–La Roche* case[44] at page 207: 'I entirely agree with the views which have been expressed that possession with the intention of using the articles for trade purposes and for the securing of a profit amounts to an infringement: whether the dealing which you are proposing to carry on is a dealing with a customer in this country or with an export customer.' "

Where the invention is a process

Use of a process

6.23 By section 60(1)(*b*), regardless of knowledge, a person who uses a patented process in the United Kingdom without the consent of the proprietor infringes that patent.

Dealing in the products of a process

6.24 Section 60(1)(*c*) further provides that it is an infringement where the invention is a process, if a person disposes of, offers to dispose of, uses or imports any product obtained directly by means of the process or keeps any such product whether for disposal or otherwise. Again, this is so regardless of knowledge. The expressions "uses", "disposes", "imports", and "keeps" will be construed in the same manner as in section

---

[41] *Moet v. Pickering* [1878] 8 Ch.D. 372; *Adair v. Young* (1879) 12 Ch.D.13; *Pressers etc. Ltd. v. Newell & Co.* (1914) 31 R.P.C. 51 (disapproving *United Telephone Co. v. London Globe etc. Co.* (1909) 26 Ch.D. 766); *British Motor Syndicate v. John Taylor & Sons Ltd.* (1900) 17 R.P.C. 723; *British United Shoe Machinery Co. v. Simon Collier Ltd.* (1909) 26 R.P.C. 21 at p.534 and (1910) 27 R.P.C. 567; *Non-Drip Measure Co. Ltd. v. Strangers Ltd.* (1942) 59 R.P.C. 1; and see note 33 *ante*.
[42] [1978] F.S.R. 109.
[43] [1978] F.S.R. 109 at p.113.
[44] [1977] F.S.R. 200.

60(1)(a).[45] Thus, the subsection assimilates dealings in the products of a process invention with product inventions and no distinction is to be drawn between a process used in this country or abroad.

The extent to which the words of the subsection "obtained directly by   **6.25**
means of that process" have amended the previous law remains uncertain. Two particular problems arise: first, what limitation is to be imported by the use of the word "directly", and secondly, what, if any limitation is to be imported by the word "process"?

As to the first, under the old law, providing the product was   **6.26**
produced as a direct result of the use of a process substantially the whole of which was the subject of a patent, the sale of that product in this country was an infringement, and this was so even though the manufacture took place abroad.[46] However, if the patent covered only a minor improvement upon a machine or a process already known, the importation of the product would not be held to constitute infringement. Thus, in *Wilderman v. F. W. Berk & Co. Ltd.*[47] the patent related to an improvement in a part of an electrolytic machine for making caustic potash. The defendants had imported caustic potash from abroad and the plaintiff proved that this had been made in Germany by means of an electrolytic cell fitted with the improvement which was the subject of his patent. No evidence was adduced as to the materiality of the improvement in enabling the production of the caustic potash. Tomlin J. said:[48]

"It is urged on the plaintiff's behalf that once I am satisfied that there has been used in connection with the manufacture of an imported article, in however an unimportant or trifling respect, some apparatus or material in respect of which there is a subsisting patent, the importation of the article manufactured is necessarily an infringement. I do not think that the cases to which I have been referred compel me to accept so wide a proposition, and I do not accept it. I cannot think, for example, that the employment of a patented cutting blowpipe or a patented hammer in the manufacture of some part of a locomotive would necessarily render the importation of the locomotive an infringement. In my judgment, each case must be determined on its own merits by reference to the nature of the invention, and the extent to which its employment played a part in the production of the article the importation of which is complained of . . . I do not think that the plaintiff has proved, and I am not prepared to hold, that the device the subject-matter of the invention was of such a character, or was so used, in relation to the manufacture of the caustic potash in question,

---

[45] See *ante*, § 6.10 *et seq.*
[46] *Wright v. Hitchcock* (1870) L.R. 5 Ex.37; *Elmslie v. Boursier* (1869) L.R. 9 Eq. 217; *Townsend v. Haworth* (1875) 12 Ch.D. 831; *Von Heyden v. Neustadt* (1880) 14 Ch.D. 230; *Neilson v. Betts* (1871) L.R. 5 H.L. 1 at p.11; *Beecham Group Laboratories Ltd. v. Bristol Laboratories Ltd.* [1978] R.P.C. 153.
[47] (1925) 42 R.P.C. 79.
[48] *Ibid.* at p.88.

as to render the importation of such potash an infringement of the patent."

Where a patented process had been used in the course of manufacture of the article or substance which had been imported, the stage at which such process has been used was immaterial; and in *Saccharin Corporation Ltd. v. Anglo-Continental Chemical Works*[49] it was held that the importation was equally an infringement whether the process was used in the production of some intermediate substance or in effecting the final transformation into the substance imported. This decision was considered by the House of Lords in *Beecham Group Laboratories Ltd. v. Bristol Laboratories Ltd.*[50] Whilst the principle of the Saccharin doctrine was approved, no decision was reached on the extent thereof.

Although there is no guidance to be derived from the 1977 Act or the instruments referred to in section 130(7), it is submitted that since there is no reason in logic for altering the existing law, the word "directly" in section 60(1)(c) should not be given a narrow meaning so as to alter that law.

6.27   As to the second problem, that of whether the use of the word "process" imports any limitation, under the old law products of a patented machine were deemed to be infringements of a patent for that machine. In *Townsend v. Haworth*,[51] Jessel M. R. said:

"What is every person prohibited from doing? He is prohibited from making, using or vending the prohibited articles, and that, of course, includes in the case of machinery the product, if I may say so, of the machinery which is the subject of a patent. It is what is produced by the patent."[52]

Again, such a sale was an infringement even where the manufacture took place abroad.[53] Section 60(1)(c) however refers specifically only to the case where the invention is a process and thus it is submitted that prima facie dealings in products produced by a patented machine are not covered by section 60(1)(c). However, under modern drafting practice most patents for such a new machine will include both product and process claims.

Offer of a process for use
6.28   The only form of direct infringement where knowledge is a prerequisite to liability is when the invention is a process and the infringing act

---

[49] (1900) 17 R.P.C. 307.
[50] [1978] R.P.C. 153 at p. 203. See also pp. 184 and 199.
[51] 12 Ch.D. 831.
[52] See also *United Horse Shoe v. Stewart* (1885) 2 R.P.C. 122; *Wilderman v. F. W. Berk* (1925) 42 R.P.C. 79.
[53] See *ante*, §6.13.

consists of offering the process for use. In this case, section 60(1)(*b*) provides that the offer is only an infringement if the person offers it for use in the United Kingdom when he knows, or it is obvious to a reasonable person in the circumstances, that its use there without the consent of the proprietor would be an infringement of the patent. There is thus a subjective and an objective test for knowledge, only one of which has to be satisfied for infringement to occur. This provides additional protection for an innocent infringer[54] providing his innocence is reasonable.

The nature of the knowledge required may be contrasted with that required by section 60(2).[55] Section 60(1)(*b*) requires knowledge that use would be "an infringement of the patent", whereas section 60(2) only requires knowledge of suitability and intention to put "the invention into effect". The former appears to require knowledge not only that the use involves applying the inventive concept in question, but also that that inventive concept is protected by the patent in suit.

It is not yet clear what acts are encompassed by "offering a process for use", in particular in the case of dealings in machinery which is capable of operating using an infringing method. Unless the machine is incapable of operating in any other way, it is submitted that more than the mere supply of the machine will be required. In view of the new statutory definition of this type of infringement, the old law appears to offer little guidance; it may be found in the previous edition of this work.[56]

Indirect infringement

Under the old law, indirect infringement had been held to occur in certain circumstances where a person made and sold elements of a combination which was patented, but the law was far from clear.[57] This type of infringement is now covered by section 60(2) of the 1977 Act which provides that a person (other than the proprietor of the patent) infringes a patent for an invention if, while the patent is in force, and without the consent of the proprietor, he supplies or offers to supply in the United Kingdom a person other than a licensee or other person entitled to work the invention with any of the means, relating to an essential element of the invention, for putting the invention into effect when he knows, or it is obvious to a reasonable person in the circumstances, that those means are suitable for putting, and are intended to put, the invention into effect in the United Kingdom.

6.29

It is therefore now an infringement to supply or offer to supply "means relating to an essential element of the invention" with the requisite knowledge.

---

[54] See also P.A. 1977, s.62 and *post*, §6.89.
[55] See *post*, §6.32.
[56] Terrell (13th ed.), §§ 6.22–23.
[57] See Terrell (13th ed.), §§ 6.19 *et seq.*

Supply or offer to supply

6.30   These words are not used in section 60(1) which refers instead to "disposal". Supply however contemplates a transfer to a third party, whereas disposal does not necessarily do so; subject to this difference, it is submitted that the meaning is the same.

Means relating to an essential element

6.31   Whether or not any particular means is an essential element of a given invention will be a question of fact in each case. It will clearly cover the supply of a product in kit form to be assembled by the purchaser into an infringing item but the dividing line between essential and inessential elements is not clear. Under the old law the question of whether or not an integer of a claim was essential was often considered for the purpose of the so-called doctrine of pith and marrow,[58] and the reasoning in those old cases may be of some assistance in determining what is an essential element. In general, however, it is suggested that better guidance would be obtained by considering the element in question and determining whether without that element the invention could be put into effect.

Knowledge

6.32   The knowledge required may be contrasted with that required in the case of offering a patented process for use.[59] Actual knowledge or the objective knowledge of a reasonable man will suffice and the knowledge must be not only that the means is suitable for putting the invention into effect but also that it is intended to put the invention into effect in the United Kingdom. It is submitted that section 60(2) does not require that the infringer be aware that the inventive concept in question is covered by any patent.

Persons entitled to work the invention

6.33   This expression does not extend to persons protected from infringement by virtue of section 60(5)(a), (b) or (c).[60] It does however extend to a Crown user[61] and to uses authorised by section 28(6)[62] (use or preparation for use commenced during a period when the patent had lapsed)[63] or section 64[64] (use or preparation for use commenced before the priority date).[65]

---

[58] See *post* 6.36.
[59] See *ante*, § 6.28.
[60] P.A. 1977, s.60(6), and see *post*, § 6.81 *et seq.*
[61] P.A. 1977, s.60(6)(a).
[62] See *post*, §6.80.
[63] P.A. 1977, s.60 (6)b.
[64] *See post,* § 6.67 *et seq.*
[65] P.A. 1977, s.60(6)(b).

Staple commercial products

Special protection against infringement under section 60(2) of the Act **6.34** is however given to suppliers of staple commercial products. Section 60(2) does not apply to the supply or offer of such a product unless the supply or the offer is made for the purpose of inducing the person supplied to do an act which constitutes infringement by virtue of section 60(1).[66] There is no definition of a staple commercial product in the 1977 Act and the expression does not appear in the instruments referred to in section 130(7). The use of the word staple is presumably a reference to raw materials or other basic products commonly available and the purpose of the subsection is to protect the supplier of such products even if he has knowledge that they are to be put to an infringing purpose. The scope of the words is far from clear and the dividing line between protecting the supplier of raw materials on the one hand and giving a fair monopoly to the patentee must be a question of fact in each case.

As to the inducement given by the supplier of a staple commercial product which renders him subject to the provisions of section 60(2), no limitation is placed on the wording so that any inducement whether oral or written, express or implied will suffice. The test, however, is a subjective one.

2. Ascertainment of the Monopoly and Infringement

The principles applicable to the construction of the specification and **6.35** its claims have already been fully dealt with in Chapter 4, § 4.33 *et seq.* A claim is to be construed without reference to the alleged infringement; it should be construed "as if we had to construe it before the Defendant was born".[67] Once the true scope of the monopoly has been determined, the question of whether the alleged infringement falls within its scope will depend upon the facts proved.

Although the construction has to be determined without reference to the infringement in practice the Court does, and must know what the alleged infringement is. Only then does it become possible to isolate what are the material points of construction which actually arise for decision. Thus, Aldous J. approached construction in *Lux Traffic Controls v. Pike Signals*[68] as follows:

> "A claim of a patent should be construed as at the date of publication of the patent and without reference to the alleged infringement.

---

[66] P.A. 1977, s.60(3).
[67] *Nobel v. Anderson* (1894) 11 R.P.C. at 523.
[68] [1993] R.P.C. 107 at 126.

However, it is convenient to consider the questions of construction in the context in which they arise and therefore I pass to infringement."

Further, the doctrine of "purposive construction" as described below, and the requirements of section 125 of the 1977 Act and the Protocol on the Interpretation of E.P.C. Article 69, will apply and these also give rise to questions of fact which may involve consideration of the nature of the alleged infringement. Nevertheless, the objective of the exercise is to determine the true scope of the claims as they would have been read at the date of publication of the specification without knowledge of particular allegedly infringing acts.

6.36   Before the landmark decision of the House of Lords in *Catnic v. Hill & Smith*,[69] infringement was approached in two ways. First, if the alleged infringement fell within the strict literal meaning of the claims and embodied every integer there recited, there was said to be "textual infringement". However, the law never restricted the patentee's monopoly to the strict language of the claims so as to enable a potential infringer to avoid infringement by incorporating immaterial variations. This led to the development of the so-called "Pith and Marrow" doctrine, which was established through the cases and is charted at §§ 6.52 *et seq.* of the Thirteenth Edition of this work. In view of the comments of the Court of Appeal in *Codex Corp. v. Racal-Milgo*,[70] it is not thought necessary to deal with them here.

6.37   In *Catnic* at page 242, Lord Diplock said:

"My Lords, in their closely reasoned written cases in this House and in the oral argument, both parties to this appeal have tended to treat 'textual infringement' and infringement of the 'pith and marrow' of an invention as if they were separate causes of action, the existence of the former to be determined as a matter of construction only and of the latter upon some broader principle of colourable evasion. There is, in my view, no such dichotomy; there is but a single cause of action and to treat it otherwise, particularly in cases like that which is the subject of the instant appeal, is liable to lead to confusion."

He then went on to set out the proper approach to purposive construction, and hence to the determination of infringement, as follows:

"My Lords, a patent specification is a unilateral statement by the patentee, in words of his own choosing, addressed to those likely to have a practical interest in the subject matter of his invention (*i.e.* 'skilled in the art'), by which he informs them what he claims to be the essential features of the new product or process for which the letters

---

[69] [1982] R.P.C. 183.
[70] [1983] R.P.C. 369; quoted *post*, §6.37.

patent grant him a monopoly. It is those novel features only that he claims to be essential that constitute the so-called 'pith and marrow' of the claim. A patent specification should be given a purposive construction rather than a purely literal one derived from applying to it the kind of meticulous verbal analysis in which lawyers are too often tempted by their training to indulge. The question in each case is: whether persons with practical knowledge and experience of the kind of work in which the invention was intended to be used, would understand that strict compliance with a particular descriptive word or phrase appearing in a claim was intended by the patentee to be an essential requirement of the invention so that *any* variant would fall outside the monopoly claimed, even though it could have no material effect upon the way the invention worked.

"The question, of course, does not arise where the variant would in fact have a material effect upon the way the invention worked. Nor does it arise unless at the date of publication of the specification it would be obvious to the informed reader that this was so. Where it is not obvious, in the light of then-existing knowledge, the reader is entitled to assume that the patentee thought at the time of the specification that he had good reason for limiting his monopoly so strictly and had intended to do so, even though subsequent work by him or others in the field of the invention might show the limitation to have been unnecessary. It is to be answered in the negative only when it would be apparent to any reader skilled in the art that a particular descriptive word or phrase used in a claim cannot have been intended by a patentee, who was also skilled in the art, to exclude minor variants which, to the knowledge of both him and the readers to whom the patent was addressed, could have no material effect upon the way in which the invention worked."

The true question to be asked is thus, in summary, whether strict compliance with the particular piece of claim language was intended to be an essential requirement of this invention. The final paragraph quoted above provides tests by which the answer to this question may be obtained. The word "this" at the end of its second sentence refers back to the qualification "even though it could have no material effect upon the way the invention works", rather than to its immediately preceding sentence. The tests in that paragraph have been analysed by Hoffman J. in *Improver v. Remington* as follows:[71]

"If the issue was whether a feature embodied in an alleged infringement which fell outside the primary, literal or acontextual meaning of a descriptive word or phrase in the claim ('a variant') was nevertheless within its language as properly interpreted, the court should ask itself the following three questions:

---

[71] [1990] F.S.R. 181 at 189.

(1) Does the variant have a material effect upon the way the invention works? If yes, the variant is outside the claim. If no—

(2) Would this (*i.e.* that the variant had no material effect) have been obvious at the date of publication of the patent to a reader skilled in the art. If no, the variant is outside the claim. If yes—

(3) Would the reader skilled in the art nevertheless have understood from the language of the claim that the patentee intended that strict compliance with the primary meaning was an essential requirement of the invention. If yes, the variant is outside the claim.

"On the other hand, a negative answer to the last question would lead to the conclusion that the patentee was intending the word or phrase to have not a literal but a figurative meaning (the figure being a form of synecdoche or metonymy)[72] denoting a class of things which included the variant and the literal meaning, the latter being perhaps the most perfect, best-known or striking example of the class."[73]

In *Codex v. Racal*,[74] the Court of Appeal considered it unnecessary to consider in detail the authorities on construction prior to *Catnic*, and said at page 380:

"In the light of the clear and authoritative summary of the relevant law in the speech of [Lord Diplock], we think that it will henceforth be unnecessary, and usually undesirable, for counsel to take the court through the previous decisions referred to in the speech and to which our attention was drawn in detail."

Statutory Provisions as to Construction

6.38   The 1977 Act for the first time contains and incorporates by reference a number of principles relating to construction of claims. Section 125 of the 1977 Act (which corresponds to Article 69 of the E.P.C.) provides:

"125.—(1) For the purposes of this Act an invention for a patent for which an application has been made or for which a patent has been granted shall, unless the context otherwise requires, be taken to be that specified in a claim of the specification of the application or patent, as the case may be, as interpreted by the description and any drawings contained in that specification, and the extent of the protection conferred by a patent or application for a patent shall be determined accordingly.

---

[72] **Synecdoche:** "a figure of speech in which a part is made to represent the whole or vice versa (*e.g.* new faces at the meeting)"; **Metonymy:** "the substitution of the name of an attribute or adjunct for that of the thing meant (*e.g.* Crown for the king)" (Concise Oxford Dictionary).

[73] See also the similar approaches by Aldous J. in *Southco v. Dzus* [1990] R.P.C. 587 at 606 in *Lux Traffic Controls v. Pike Signals* [1993] R.P.C. 107 at 126.

[74] [1983] R.P.C. 369 at 380.

(2) . . .

(3) The Protocol on the Interpretation of Article 69 of the European Patent Convention (which Article contains a proviso corresponding to subsection (1) above) shall, as for the time being in force, apply for the purposes of subsection (1) above as it applies for the purposes of that Article."

The Protocol referred to provides as follows:

"Article 69 should not be interpreted in the sense that the extent of the protection conferred by a European patent is to be understood as that defined by the strict, literal meaning of the wording used in the claims, the description and drawings being employed only for the purpose of resolving an ambiguity found in the claims. Neither should it be interpreted in the sense that the claims serve only as a guideline and that the actual protection conferred may extend to what, from a consideration of the description and drawings by a person skilled in the art, the patentee has contemplated. On the contrary, it is to be interpreted as defining a position between these extremes which combines a fair protection for the patentee with a reasonable degree of certainty for third parties."

Although *Catnic* was concerned with a patent granted under the 1949 Act, it is now well settled that its approach is also the proper one to be adopted in applying the above statutory provisions of the 1977 Act.[75] There has thus been no change as to the principles of patent construction; the approach is precisely the same for both 1949 Act and 1977 Act patents. In the absence of ambiguity as a ground of revocation for new Act patents, questions of construction may sometimes prove more difficult, although it is submitted that it would be open to the Court to hold that infringement was not proven in a case where the language of the claim is so obscure that its boundary could not be determined with any proper precision.

Application of the Principle of Purposive Construction

It does not necessarily follow that because the variant works in a different way or has advantages of its own, the variant therefore has a material effect on the way in which the invention as such works.[76]

6.39

---

[75] *Improver v. Remington* [1989] R.P.C. 69 (C.A.); *A.C. Edwards v. Acme* [1992] R.P.C. 131 (C.A.); *Southco v. Dzus* [1992] R.P.C. 299 (C.A.); and see *Improver v. Remington* [1990] F.S.R. 181 at 197–198, where Hoffman J. at first instance explains why he reached a different conclusion from that in parallel proceedings before the German court.

[76] *Insituform v. Incliner* [1992] R.P.C. 83 at 92. Compare Bowen L.J.'s famous dictum in *Wenham Co. v. Champion Gas* (1890) 7 R.P.C. 49 at 56: "The superadding of ingenuity to a robbery does not make the operation justifiable", and *British Liquid Air v. British Oxygen* (1909) 26 R.P.C. 509 at 528.

Purposive construction is a principle of construction of the claim language, and does not entitle the Court to rewrite or amend the claim in the guise of construing it.[77] Thus, in *Codex v. Racal*,[78] the Court of Appeal said:

> "there is no suggestion in Lord Diplock's speech that one should look only to the essence or principle of a patent in suit and hold there to have been an infringement merely because that essence or principle has been made use of by the alleged infringer. There may have been, or there may not. The question to be asked is one of construction, but of purposive or realistic construction through the eyes and with the learning of a person skilled in the art, rather than with the meticulous verbal analysis of the lawyer alone."

In *Step v. Emson*[79] , Hoffman L.J. said:

> "The well known principle that patent claims are given a purposive construction does not mean that an integer can be treated as struck out if it does not appear to make any difference to the inventive concept. It may have some other purpose buried in the prior art and even if this is not discernible, the patentee may have had some reason of his own for introducing it."

6.40   In *Codex*,[80] the Court of Appeal upheld the trial judge's finding that there had been infringement, in spite of the very different digital technology used in the infringing device, and declined to give the claims a narrow reading so as to limit them to embodiments using older analogue technology as described in the specification itself and in relation to which the literal language of the claim was more readily suited. At first instance,[81] Whitford J. had held:

> "The advance of technology has led, so far as the alleged infringement is concerned, to a device which presents differences over the techniques described in the patent; techniques which were in themselves old at the date of the patent. These new techniques no doubt have their own advantages. No instructed reader considering the *Codex patent* would in my judgment have thought that strict compliance with the techniques of application, which in a field like this are forever rapidly changing, was an essential requirement of the invention."

---

[77] *Cf. Norton & Gregory v. Jacobs* (1937) 54 R.P.C. 271 at 276, where the Court of Appeal rejected a similar approach.
[78] [1983] R.P.C. 369 at 381.
[79] February 19, 1993, (C.A.), (Unrep.).
[80] [1983] R.P.C. 369.
[81] 1981, (Unrep.).

Similarly, in *Societé Nouvelle des Bennes Saphem v. Edbro*,[82] Lawton L.J. said that:

"In my judgment the specification in suit does not purport to describe a design for a device but what the invention will do when used on a vehicle. The language used is that showing function . . . I am unable to accept Whitford J.'s finding that the plaintiffs have chosen to claim their monopoly in terms of apparatus rather than function. In my judgment the claim, when construed, was for a device that had three functional features."

He went on to construe the language of the claim more broadly than it had been below, a construction with which the other members of the Court of Appeal agreed.

In contrast, an example of a case where the plaintiff sought to extend **6.41** the principle of purposive construction too far was *W. Houdstermaatschappij v. Madge Networks*,[83] where the plaintiff's approach was criticised as involving an attempt to distil the essence or principle of the patent in suit (and to do so in the light of the alleged infringement), contrary to the dictum in *Codex* quoted above.

Where the claim was for a mechanical combination of selected parts arranged in a particular way so as to have a particular functional interaction, that particular selection, arrangement and interaction of parts constituted the essence of the invention. In such a case those parts and the particular arrangement and functional interaction would all be essential features of the claimed combination and for infringement one had to find those selected parts arranged and interacting in that way.[84] In principle this would appear still to be so, although much will turn on the language actually used.

"Combination" does not protect integers individually

A patent for a combination is not infringed by taking separately the **6.42** integers which were comprised in that combination. In *Clark v. Adie*[85] Lord Cairns said:

"Suppose, my lords, that in a patent you have a patentee claiming protection for an invention consisting of parts which I will designate as A, B, C, and D; he may at the same time claim that as to one of those parts, D, it is itself a new thing, and that as to another of those parts, C, it is itself a combination of things, which possibly were old in themselves, but which, put together and used as he puts them

---

[82] [1983] R.P.C. 345 at 361.
[83] [1992] R.P.C. 386.
[84] See *Rodi & Weinberger A.G. v. Showell (Henry) Ltd.* [1969] R.P.C. 367 at 391; and *Birmingham Sound Reproducers Ltd. v. Callaro Ltd.* [1956] R.P.C. 232 at p.246.
[85] (1872) 2 App.Cas. 315.

together and uses them, produce a result so new that he is entitled to protection for it as a new invention. In a patent of that kind the monopoly would or might be held to be granted, not only to the whole and complete thing described, but to those subordinate integers entering into the whole which I have described. But then, my lords, the invention must be described in that way; it must be made plain to ordinary apprehension, upon the ordinary rules of construction, that the patentee has had in his mind, and has intended to claim, protection for those subordinate integers; and moreover he is, as was said by the Lord Justices, at the peril of justifying those subordinate integers as themselves matters which ought properly to form the subject of a patent of invention."[86]

This approach of course remains the law.

Evidence relating to Construction

6.43   As a result, mere colourable evasions of the strict language of the claims will not avoid infringement. The question whether an evasion is colourable or material will be a question of fact in each case. The evidence of a skilled man can therefore be received as to the materiality of any variant and as to his understanding of the meaning to be given to various words or phrases appearing in the claim.

The *Catnic* decision, therefore, resolves the dilemma that had arisen over the years as to whether evidence as to the meaning of words and phrases appearing in patent specifications was admissible or whether, on the ground that construction of the claims was a matter of law for the Court alone, it was not.[87]

Thus, in *Unilever v. Schöler Lebensmittel,*[88] Aldous J. said:

"I believe that there should be relevant evidence as to the background against which this specification should be construed. The claim must, in my view, be interpreted as part of the whole document; it must be given a purposive construction read through the eyes of the skilled man in the art and in the light of what has been done before.

"On that basis it is possible that any prima facie view that I have arrived at could in fact be changed by evidence as to what was on the market and what the skilled man would have in his mind when reading this patent."

---

[86] (1908) 25 R.P.C. 361 at 654–655.
[87] Contrast *British Celanese v. Courtaulds* (1935) 52 R.P.C. 171 at 195; *Allmanna Svenska Electriska A/B v. The Burntisland Shipbuilding Co. Ltd.* (1951) 68 R.P.C. 63 at 76; *American Cyanamid Co. v. Ethicon Ltd.* [1979] R.P.C. 215 at 249.
[88] [1988] F.S.R. 596.

However, there are still limits to such evidence. In *Glaverbel v. British* **6.44**
Coal (No.2),[89] Mummery J. said:

"In the *Catnic* case (*supra* at page 243) Lord Diplock held that a patent
specification should be given a purposive construction rather than a
purely literal one. This approach is the same as that which the courts
have adopted to the construction of documents generally, as ex-
pounded in statements of Lord Wilberforce in his well-known
speeches in *Prenn v. Simmonds*, [1971] 1 W.L.R. 1381 at 1384 and 1385,
and in *Reardon Smith Line Ltd. v. Yngvar Hansen-Tangen*, [1976] 1
W.L.R. 989 (see also the comments of the Court of Appeal on these
decisions in *Rabin v. Gerson Berger Association Ltd.*, [1986] 1 W.L.R. 526
at 533). According to these cases, the court, as part of the process of
construction, should look beyond 'internal linguistic considerations'
to the object of the document under scrutiny and to its surrounding
circumstances or 'matrix of fact', which provide the context in which
the language of the document is used.
    "In aid of the construction of a patent specification extrinsic
evidence of relevant circumstances surrounding the preparation of
the specification is therefore admissible. For example, there is no
doubt that evidence can be given of the state of the art at the time of
the specification among those to whom the teaching in the specification is addressed. Evidence may be given explaining the meaning at
that time of scientific and technical terms, words and phrases used in
the specification and in the relevant art.
    "A relevant expert is entitled to give evidence of what the
specification would have taught him and whether what is described
in the specification could be carried into effect by workers skilled in
the art (see *British Thomson-Houston Co. Ltd. v. Charlesworth, Peebles &
Co.*, (1925) 42 R.P.C. 180 at 208, and *British Celanese Ltd. v. Courtaulds
Ltd.*, (1935) 52 R.P.C. 171 at 196.
    "There are, however, clear limits to the evidence which the court
will admit in aid of construction of a patent specification or of any
other document. The meaning of the specification must be ascertained
from the particular language in which it is expressed, as seen in its
objective factual setting. Consistently with this approach, the courts
have refused to admit the following evidence either to enlarge or
restrict the ordinary meaning of the language of the specification ...
    "(c) The opinion of expert witnesses on the construction of the
specification (or of any other document) will not be admitted by the
court. The position was stated as clearly as it can be by Lord Tomlin in
the *British Celanese* case (*supra*) at page 196 in these terms:
        'He [that is, an expert witness] is not entitled to say nor is Counsel
        entitled to ask him what the specification means, nor does the

---

[89] [1993] R.P.C. 90 at 93 (appeal pending).

question become any more admissible if it takes the form of asking him what it means to him as an engineer or as a chemist.'

"The cases constantly emphasise that it is for the court, and not for an expert witness, to construe the specification and the ambit of the claims made in it."

He did, however, in that case allow part of the disputed evidence to be taken *de bene esse* pending appeal. In practice, it is submitted, that there may be difficult grey areas between evidence of construction of the claim as a whole, and evidence of the meaning of words and phrases found within it (for the latter have to be read in their context), and disputes may arise as to whether the words in question have a technical meaning at all. The court has in the past tended to be lenient in admitting such evidence, and the modern practice of preparing and exchanging witness statements in advance has led to parties taking a broad view as to how far witnesses may go on this issue.

"Suitable for"

6.45   A claim to an article "suitable for" a particular purpose is a claim to that article, whatever its intended purpose, so that the intended use need not be shown.[90]

Substance available in nature

6.46   Under the old Act, where a complete specification claimed a new substance, the claim was to be construed as not extending to that substance when found in nature.[91] The section has no equivalent in the 1977 Act for new Act patents.

Subsidiary claims

6.47   Where the specification contains a number of claims, the subsidiary claims will often be drafted so as to add one integer to the combinations claimed in previous claims. In these circumstances it is submitted that the added integer would be likely to be the only inventive idea of that subsidiary claim and that a purposive construction could not, therefore, be applied to that subsidiary claim so as to extend its scope to combinations not having that integer.[92] The decision of the House of Lords in *Catnic*, however, does leave scope for argument based on the facts of each case.

---

[90] *Adhesive Dry Mounting Co. Ltd. v. Trapp & Co.* (1910) 27 R.P.C. 341; *Furr v. Truline (C.D.) (Building Products)* [1985] F.S.R. 553.

[91] P.A. 1949, s.4(7).

[92] See *C. Van der Lely N.V. v. Bamfords Ltd.* [1963] R.P.C. 61 at 78; *Submarine Signal Co. v. Henry Hughes & Son Ltd.* (1932) 49 R.P.C. 149 at 175.

Omnibus claims: "substantially as described"

If a claim alleged to be infringed contains the word "substantially" or **6.48** the phrase "substantially as described" it is for the court to decide whether infringement has taken place, though it may be a difficult question.[93]

Onus of proof

The onus of proving infringement lies in general on the Plaintiff. **6.49** However, in relation to new Act patents by section 100(1) of the 1977 Act, if the invention is a process for obtaining a new product, the same product produced by a person other than the proprietor of the patent, or a licensee of his, shall, unless the contrary is proved, be taken in any proceedings to have been obtained by that process. Thus, in this case the onus is shifted to the Defendant. It is however provided that in considering whether a party has discharged the burden imposed on him, the Court shall not require him to disclose any manufacturing or commercial secrets if it appears to the Court that it would be unreasonable to do so.[94] It is anticipated that in most cases the Court will order limited disclosures as has been done in the past.[95]

The section would, however, appear to have little practical importance, in those cases concerning a "new product" the main claims will be product claims; and in other cases the section will not apply, in which case the previous law as set out below will become pertinent.

In general, the onus of proving infringement under the 1949 Act lay **6.50** on the plaintiff even where the defendant had used or sold articles alleged to have been made by a patented process, whether in this country or abroad.

In *Cartsburn Sugar Refining Co. v. Sharp*, Lord Kinnear said:[96] **6.51**

"No witness has been examined of sufficient skill as a mechanic to give a detailed description of the machine in question. All that is proved is that it does not correspond in all respects, though in some respects it does correspond, to the description in Hersey's patent. It is said that as the manufacture complained of had taken place in America, it was incumbent on the respondents, upon the principle which received effect in the case of *Neilson v. Betts*,[97] to prove by negative evidence that it was not maufactured according to the specified process. I think no such onus lies upon the respondents in the present

---

[93] *Raleigh Cycle Co. Ltd. v. Henry Miller & Sons Ltd.* (1946–48) 65 R.P.C. at p.160; and see *Surface Silos Ltd. v. Beal* [1959] R.P.C. 154; *Deere & Co. v. Harrison, McGregor & Guest Ltd.* [1965] R.P.C. 461; *Daikin Koygo's App.* [1974] R.P.C. 559; *Lancer Boss Ltd. v. Henley Forklift Co. Ltd.* [1975] R.P.C. 306; *Rotocrop International v. Genbourne* [1982] F.S.R. 5.
[94] P.A. 1977, s.100(2).
[95] See, *e.g. Warner-Lambert v. Glaxo* [1975] R.P.C. 101; *Cera v. Centri Spray* [1979] F.S.R. 175; *Roussel Uclaf v. I.C.I.* [1990] R.P.C. 45 (C.A.), affirming [1989] R.P.C. 59.
[96] (1884) 1 R.P.C. 181 at p.186.
[97] (1871) L.R. 5 H.L. 1.

case, because there can be no question on the evidence that such articles as were sold by the respondents may have been produced by machinery which involved no infringement of the complainers' patent. That being so, it lay upon the complainers to prove their case, and as they took a commission to America for the purpose of proving it, there could have been no difficulty in their obtaining a sufficient description of the machine to which it is alleged they have traced the cubes of sugar sold by the respondents to enable them to establish the infringement, if infringement there was."

But where the articles were made abroad, and the plaintiffs in consequence could not be afforded full opportunity of inspecting the machinery by which they were made, it was held that it lay with the defendants to rebut a prima facie case made out by the plaintiffs.[98]

6.52   In the various *Saccharin* cases,[99] the plaintiffs were the owners of patents which covered all known processes of making saccharin. They were able to produce evidence to the effect that although it was conceivable that saccharin might be made in some other way, no other processes were then known to the scientific world. The defendants, who imported saccharin, could not give any satisfactory account of the way in which the imported substance was actually made. It was held that infringement had been established.

3. Who is liable for the Infringing Acts?

6.53   As a basic principle the person or persons who actually performed the infringing acts are liable to the patentee. However, the rights of the patentee are not restricted merely to an action against the actual infringer.

Section 60(1) provides that a person infringes *if, but only if* he performs the acts there set out. However, it is submitted that section 60, which relates essentially to the types of act which constitute infringement, does not limit the liability of persons for the commission of those acts. Accordingly, liability may arise where a person commits an infringing act through the agency of another; or where the relationship between two people is such as to constitute a common design so as to make them liable as joint tortfeasors and one infringes a patent, then both will be liable. In this respect it is submitted that the pre-1977 law will continue to apply. But the suggestion that there might have been a quite separate

---

[98] *Saccharin Corp. v. Dawson* (1902) 19 R.P.C. 169; *Saccharin Corp. v. Jackson* (1903) 20 R.P.C. 611; *Saccharin Corp. v. Mank & Co.* (1906) 23 R.P.C. 25; *Saccharin Corp. Ltd. v. National Saccharin Co. Ltd.* (1909) 26 R.P.C. 654; and see *British Thomson-Houston Co. v. Charlesworth, Peebles & Co.* (1923) 40 R.P.C. 426 at p.456.
[99] *Ibid.*

tort of procuring infringement by others[1] is no longer good law, except where section 60(2) applies.[2]

Infringement by agents and servants

A person could infringe a patent by making the article himself, or by **6.54** his agent, or by his servants. The agent and servants themselves could infringe the patent, and actions could be brought against them individually, but that did not absolve the person who employed them for that purpose. In *Sykes v. Howarth*[3] the invention consisted in the application of cards or strips of leather covered with wire to rollers at "wide distances". A person who contracted to clothe rollers and supplied to a "nailer" cards of such width that when applied to the rollers they must of necessity leave wide spaces, and who himself paid the nailer, was held to have infringed the patent, though he alleged that his business was that of a card-maker only, and did not include the nailer's work. Fry J. said:

> "I have come to the conclusion that the nailer must be deemed to have been the agent, for the purpose of nailing on, of the defendant . . . there is a contract to clothe in the manner prescribed by the particulars given to the defendant, and that contract was carried into effect by a person paid by the defendant—the defendant himself receiving the total amount for which he contracted. The consequence is that in my judgment all the defences fail."

In *Gibson and Campbell v. Brand*,[4] it was held that an order given by the defendant for the making of silk by a process which infringed the plaintiff's patent, which order was executed in England, was sufficient to satisfy the allegation that the defendant made, used, and put in practice the plaintiff's invention, although the silk was in fact made through the agency of others. Sir N. C. Tindal C.J. said: "This is quite sufficient to satisfy an allegation that he made those articles, for he that causes or procures to be made, may well be said to have made them himself."

But actions against mere workmen who innocently helped in an infringement and were not the really guilty persons, were not encouraged.[5]

---

[1] Which was sometimes put forward under the old law; see *e.g. Belleging v. Witten* [1979] F.S.R. 59 at 66, citing *Lumley v. Gye* (1853) 2 E&B 216; *Rotocrop v. Genbourne* [1982] F.S.R. 5 at 260; *Dow v. Spence Bryson* [1982] F.S.R. 598 at 626–630.
[2] See *ante*, § 6.29 *et seq.*
[3] (1879) 12 Ch.D. 826 at p.832.
[4] (1841) 1 W.P.C. 631.
[5] See *Savage v. Brindle* (1896) 13 R.P.C. 266.

Company directors

6.55   Directors of a limited liability company would only be liable for infringements committed by the company if it is proved that the company acted as their agent, or that they expressly authorised the infringement.[6]

Joint Tortfeasorship

6.56   Persons may be liable for infringement if their acts are such as would make them joint tortfeasors under the general law.[7] The general law is as stated by Scrutton L.J. in *The Koursk*[8] when he said:

"Certain classes of persons seem clearly to be joint tortfeasors: the agent who commits a tort in the course of his employment for his principal, and the principal; the servant who commits a tort in the course of his employment and his master; two persons who agree on common action, in the course of, and to further which, one of them commits a tort. These seem clearly joint tortfeasors; there is one tort committed by one of them on behalf of, or in concert with, another."

But before a person can be said to be a joint tortfeasor, he must have acted in concert with another person in the commission of the tort.[9] The mere sale in the ordinary way of business of goods, which the vendor is entitled to sell, is not tortious, even though the purchaser may subsequently use the goods wrongly. Thus, the mere sale of articles which are not themselves protected by a patent, but which can be used for the purposes of infringement, will not amount to an infringement,[10] even if the seller knows the articles will be used for this purpose.[11] But as

---

[6] *British Thomson-Houston Co. Ltd. v. Sterling Associates Ltd.* [1924] 2 Ch. 33; (1924) 41 R.P.C. 311; see also *Cropper Minerva Machines Co. Ltd. v. Cropper, Charlton & Co. Ltd.* (1906) 23 R.P.C. 388 at p.392; *Pritchard and Constance (Wholesale) Ltd. v. Amata Ltd.* (1925) 42 R.P.C. 63; *Reitzman v. Grahame-Chapman and Derustit Ltd.* (1950) 67 R.P.C. 178 at p.185. *T. Oertli A.G. v. E. J. Bowman Ltd.* [1956] R.P.C. 282. P.L.G. v. Ardan [1992] F.S.R. 59. Compare also decisions on infringement of other intellectual property rights: *P.R.S. v. Cyril* [1924] 1 K.B. 1; *Walker (John) & Sons v. Ost (Henry) & Co.* [1970] R.P.C. 489; *Hoover v. Hulme* (STO) [1982] F.S.R. 565; *White Horse Distillers v. Gregson Associates* [1984] R.P.C. 61; *Evans (C.) & Son v. Spritebrand* [1985] F.S.R. 267; *Besson (A.P.) v. Fulleon* [1986] F.S.R. 319.
[7] *Morton-Norwich Products Inc. v. Intercen Ltd.* [1978] R.P.C. 501.
[8] [1924] P. 140 at p.155.
[9] *Innes v. Short* (1898) 15 R.P.C. 449; *Morton-Norwich Products Inc. v. Intercen Ltd.* [1978] R.P.C. 501; *Belegging-En Exploitatiemaatschuppig Lavender B.V. v. Witten Industrial Diamonds Ltd.* [1979] F.S.R. 59 at 66. *Rotocrop International Limited v. Glenbourne Limited* [1982] F.S.R. 241.
[10] *Sykes v. Howarth* (1879) 12 Ch. 826; *Townsend v. Howarth* (1875) 48 L.J. Ch. 770; *Dunlop Pneumatic Tyre Co. Ltd. v. David Moseley & Sons Ltd.* (1904) 21 R.P.C. 274 at p.278; *Adhesive Dry Mounting Co. v. Trapp & Co.* (1910) 27 R.P.C. 341 at p.353; *White v. Todd Oil Burners Ltd.* (1929) 46 R.P.C. 275 at p.293. *Belegging-En Exploitatiemaatschappig Lavender B.V. v. Witten Industrial Diamonds Ltd.* [1979] F.S.R. 59 at 64.
[11] *Townsend v. Howarth* (1875) 48 L.J. Ch. 770; *Kalman v. Packaging (U.K.)* [1982] F.S.R. 406.

noted above[12] sale of a kit of parts intended to be assembled into a patented product may make the seller a joint tortfeasor with the purchaser.

The distinction between conduct which does or does not create liability as a joint tortfeasor will depend on the facts of each case but guidance can be obtained from the judgment of Graham J. in *Morton Norwich Products Inc. v. Intercen Ltd.* when he referred to "a concerted design"[13] and from the judgment of Buckley L.J. in the *Belegging* case when he said:[14] "Facilitating the doing of an act is obviously different from procuring the doing of the act."[15]

Dillon L.J. explained this latter dictum in *Mölnlycke v. Procter & Gamble*,[16] in which he said:

"A person who merely facilitated but did not procure the infringement, was not a joint tortfeasor with the infringer and so was not liable if, for instance, he sold articles which could be used for infringing or non-infringing purposes even though he knew that they would probably be used and were intended to be used for the infringing purposes. More recently however a new concept has been developed. Parties will be regarded as joint tortfeasors if on the facts they had a common design to market in the United Kingdom articles which in truth infringe a United Kingdom patent."

The authorities were reviewed by the Court of Appeal in *Unilever v. Gillette*[17] in which the plaintiff applied to amend its pleadings to allege joint tortfeasorship by the American parent company of the defendant. Mustill L.J. said:[18] **6.57**

"As to the authorities on this subject, if I am right in the view just expressed that they are really cases on the facts, I suggest that little is to be gained by matching the circumstances of each case against each of the allegations in the draft amended statement of claim. For my part I prefer to take the relevant part of the amendment as a whole, and to ask whether, if the allegations therein are proved to be true (and there seems no dispute that they will be), and if they are set in the context of the relationship between the companies in the Gillette Group, when that has emerged at the trial, a judge directing himself correctly could reasonably come to the conclusion that:

---

[12] See *ante*, §6.11; see also *Incandescent Gas Light Co. v. New Incandescent Mantle Co.* (1898) 15 R.P.C. 81.

[13] [1978] R.P.C. 501 at 513.

[14] [1979] F.S.R. 59.

[15] See *Dow Chemical A.G. v. Spence Bryson & Co.* (No.2) [1982] F.S.R. 397 and 598 at 626–630; *Kalman v. Packaging (U.K.)* [1982] F.S.R. 406; *Rotocrop International v. Genbourne* [1982] F.S.R. 241 at 260.

[16] [1992] R.P.C. 21 at 29.

[17] [1989] R.P.C. 583.

[18] *Ibid.* at 608.

(a) there was a common design between Boston and G.U.K. to do acts which, if the patent is upheld, amounted to infringements, and

(b) Boston has acted in furtherance of that design.

"I use the words 'common design' because they are readily to hand, but there are other expressions in the cases, such as 'concerted action' or 'agreed on common action' which will serve just as well. The words are not to be construed as if they formed part of a statute. They all convey the same idea. This idea does not, as it seems to me, call for any finding that the secondary party has explicitly mapped out a plan with the primary offender. Their tacit agreement will be sufficient. Nor, as it seems to me, is there any need for a common design to infringe. It is enough if the parties combine to secure the doing of acts which in the event prove to be infringements."

A "good arguable case" was held established on the facts of that particular case, and amendment of the pleading was allowed.

Similarly, in *Mölnlycke v. Procter & Gamble*,[19] the Court of Appeal declined to strike out an action against the third defendant, a member of the same group as the other defendants, against all of whom a good arguable case of joint tortfeasorship had been pleaded. The stated only purpose for joinder of the third defendant was in order to obtain discovery. The Court of Appeal held that common design may be pleaded in such circumstances without being an abuse of the process of the Court, even though the effect of the concept of common design was that discovery in cases involving multinational companies could become burdensome. Dillon L.J. referred to the power of the Court to control discovery so as to prevent oppression, and said:

"It is a long–established rule that a plaintiff who has been injured by a number of joint tortfeasors can choose which he will sue. But the defendants have no right whatsoever to dictate which the plaintiff shall sue or make the choice for him."[20]

As the pleading supported an arguable case of joint tortfeasorship in that case, on the principles of *Unilever v. Gillette*,[21] the action was allowed to proceed.

---

[19] [1992] R.P.C. 21.
[20] *Ibid.* at 35. See also *Lubrizol v. Exxon* [1992] R.P.C. 281 at 296 (affirmed on appeal on other grounds, [1992] R.P.C. 467).
[21] See *ante*. See also *Puschner v. Palmer* [1989] R.P.C. 430, another case where the Court declined to strike out an allegation of common design.

4. Defences and Statutory Exceptions to Infringement

Consent of the proprietor of the patent

It is a prerequisite of infringement under section 60(1) and (2) of the 1977 Act that the act complained of should be done without the consent of the proprietor of the patent. There is no requirement that this consent should be express and the normal rules of law will apply to determine whether consent is to be implied. **6.58**

Express instructions by patentee

Express instructions given by the patentee, or on his behalf, negatived infringement if they were specific directions to do that which was claimed in the specification, such directions amounting in effect to a licence. **6.59**

In *Kelly v. Batchelar*[22] the plaintiff's patent was for a telescopic ladder, being two ladders joined together, the inner being raised or lowered by means of an endless cord. The plaintiff, for the purpose of adducing evidence of infringement, instructed an agent to order from the defendant an adjustable ladder with the endless cord. The defendant made a ladder to this order, but without a cord. The agent of the plaintiff said that it would not do, but must have a cord with pulleys, whereupon the defendant added the cord as instructed. In the action for infringement brought against the defendant, North J. held that the defendant acted upon the express instructions of the plaintiff's agent, who had power and authority to give such instructions, and, consequently, that making this ladder did not amount to an infringement of the plaintiff's patent.[23]

In *Dunlop Pneumatic Tyre Co. v. Neal*[24] the agent of the plaintiffs was sent to the defendant to ask him to repair an old tyre, the subject of the plaintiff's patent, with a view to ascertaining whether the defendant was infringing the patent by purporting merely to repair tyres. The agent gave no express instructions as to what was to be done to the worn tyres beyond saying that they were to be repaired. It was held that what was done by the defendant amounted to infringement, and that in such a case he could not shelter himself behind the instructions of the plaintiff's agent.

Effect of sale by patentee

Where a patentee by himself, or by his agent, sold the patented article without limitation, he sold the right of free disposition as to that article, **6.60**

---

[22] (1893) 10 R.P.C. 289.
[23] See also *Henser & Guignard v. Hardie* (1894) 11 R.P.C. 471.
[24] (1899) 16 R.P.C. 247.

and if he sold the article abroad, the purchaser could import and sell it in England. Lord Hatherley, in *Betts v. Willmott*,[25] said:

> "Unless it can be shown, not that there is some clear injunction to his agents, but that there is some clear communication to the party to whom the article is sold, I apprehend that inasmuch as he had the right of vending the goods in France, or Belgium or England, or in any other quarter of the globe, he transfers with the goods necessarily the licence to use them wherever the purchaser pleases. When a man has purchased an article he expects to have control of it, and there must be some clear and explicit agreement to the contrary to justify the vendor in saying that he has not given the purchaser his licence to sell the article, or to use it wherever he pleases as against himself."

Where, however, goods are made under licence abroad, it is a question of fact in each case whether the licence implies permission to sell the licenced product in this country in violation of the patent.[26] Similarly if the patentee has assigned his patent rights in this country, prima facie, he cannot then manufacture infringing articles abroad and seek to sell them in this country.[27]

However, any sale in this country under such circumstances may not be a violation of the patent either under the doctrine of Exhaustion of Rights[28] or by reason of an Implied licence or consent.[29]

Limited licence

6.61   If a person acquired goods covered by a patent and at the time when he acquired those goods he had knowledge that a restrictive condition has been imposed in relation to them, any dealing with the goods in breach of such restrictive condition, constituted an infringement.[30] The restrictive condition was not effective if such person gained knowledge of it only after he had acquired the goods, even though he might receive such knowledge before reselling the goods.[31]

---

[25] (1871) L.R. 6 Ch.App. 239 at p.245.
[26] See *Societe Anonyme des Manufactures de Glaces v. Tilghman's Patent Sand Blast Co.* (1883) 25 Ch.D. 1; *Beecham Group Ltd. v. International Products Ltd.* [1968] R.P.C. 129; *Beecham Group Ltd. v. Shewan Tomes (Traders) Ltd.* [1968] R.P.C. 268 at p.284; *Minnesota Mining & Manufacturing Co. v. Geerpres Europe Ltd.* [1974] R.P.C. 35.
[27] *Betts v. Willmott* (1871), L.R. 6 Ch.App. 239.
[28] See *post*, § 6.63.
[29] See *Revlon Inc. v. Cripps & Lee Ltd.* [1980] F.S.R. 85.
[30] *National Phonographic Co. of Australia Ltd. v. Menck* (1911) 28 R.P.C. 229; *Columbia Graphophone Co. Ltd. v. Murray* (1922) 39 R.P.C. 239; *Columbia Graphophone Co. Ltd. v. Thoms* (1924) 41 R.P.C. 294; *Sterling Drug Inc. v. C. H. Beck Ltd.* [1973] R.P.C. 915.
[31] *Gillette Industries Ltd. v. Bernstein* (1942) 58 R.P.C. 271 at 282.

Repairing

Difficult questions of fact may arise where it is alleged that the patent **6.62** has been infringed by what amounts to the manufacture of a new article under the guise of repairing an old article which had been made under the patent. In *Sirdar Rubber Co. Ltd. v. Wallington, Weston & Co.*,[32] Lord Halsbury said: "The principle is quite clear, although its application is sometimes difficult; you may prolong the life of a licensed article, but you must not make a new one under cover of repair."

In *British Leyland Motor Corp. v. Armstrong Patents Co.*,[33] Lord Bridge cited the above passage with approval, and said:

"Letters patent, on their face, always granted to the patentee the exclusive right 'to make, use, exercise and vend' the invention. A literal application of this language would lead to the absurdity that a person who acquired the patented goods would infringe the patent if he used or resold them. To avoid this absurdity the courts had recourse to the doctrine of implied licence. In the field of repair it is clear that a person who acquires a patented article has an implied licence to keep it in repair, but must stop short of renewal."

In *Solar Thompson Engineering Co. Ltd. v. Barton*[34] Buckley L.J. expressed the law as follows:

"The cardinal question must be whether what has been done can fairly be termed a repair, having regard to the nature of the patented article. If it is, any purchaser of such an article, whether from the patentee or from a licensee of the patentee or from a purchaser from the patentee or such a licensee or purchaser, is impliedly licensed to carry it out or to contract with someone else to carry it out for him; for clearly the implied licence must be as transferable as the patented article and must include permission to authorise an agent or contractor to carry out whatever the owner of the article could himself do under the licence, had he the required skill and equipment."

Exhaustion of Rights under European Law

It was established by the European Court in *Parke Davis v. Probel*[35] that **6.63** the mere existence and exercise of patent rights does not of itself infringe Articles 85 or 86 of the Treaty of Rome.

However, the doctrine of exhaustion of rights developed under EC law serves to restrict the right of a patentee to bring proceedings for

---

[32] (1907) 24 R.P.C. 539 at p.543.
[33] [1986] R.P.C. 279 at 358.
[34] [1977] R.P.C. 537 at p.555. See also *Dellareed v. Delkim Developments* [1988] F.S.R. 329.
[35] [1968] C.M.L.R. 47; [1968] F.S.R. 393, European Ct.; see also [1989] *Thetford Corp. v. Fiamma S.p.A.* F.S.R. 57.

infringement in this country where the patentee has already received compensation for the marketing of the infringing goods in another Member State. The principle of the free movement of goods must then prevail.

Section 60(4) of the 1977 Act, which contains an express reference to the doctrine of exhaustion of rights as set out in Article 81(1) of the C.P.C. has not yet been brought into force. However, the doctrine is well-established by decisions of the European Court of Justice under Articles 30 and 36 of the Treaty of Rome, which is part of United Kingdom domestic law by virtue of the European Communities Act 1972.

The doctrine takes its name from the concept that once a patentee has dealt in or consented to dealings in the goods within the EC, his patent rights are exhausted and he cannot then seek to revive them to prevent further circulation. Its application can be seen from two landmark decisions of the European Court.

In *Centrafarm v. Sterling*[36] the E.C.J. held that it was incompatible with the rules of the EC treaty concerning free movement of goods for a patentee to seek to exercise his rights to prevent sale in a Member State of products originally marketed in another Member State by the patentee or with his consent. The fact that the defendants, parallel importers, were able to profit from price differences between the states concerned as a result of different national legislation was irrelevant. The Court held:

"As a result of the provisions in the Treaty relating to the free movement of goods and in particular of Article 30, quantitative restrictions on imports and all measures having equivalent effect are prohibited between Member States.

"By Article 36 these provisions shall nevertheless not include prohibitions or restrictions on imports justified on grounds of the protection of industrial or commercial property.

"Nevertheless, it is clear from this same Article, in particular its second sentence, as well as from the context, that whilst the Treaty does not affect the existence of rights recognized by the legislation of a Member State in matters of industrial and commercial property, yet the exercise of these rights may nevertheless, depending on the circumstances, be affected by the prohibitions in the Treaty.

"Inasmuch as it provides an exception to one of the fundamental principles of the Common Market, Article 36 in fact only admits of derogations from the free movement of goods where such deroga-tions are justified for the purpose of safeguarding rights which constitute the specific subject matter of this property.

"In relation to patents, the specific subject matter of the industrial property is the guarantee that the patentee, to reward the creative

---

[36] Case 15/74, [1974] E.C.R. 1147, [1974] 2 C.M.L.R. 480, [1975] F.S.R. 55.

effort of the inventor, has the exclusive right to use an invention with a view to manufacturing industrial products and putting them into circulation for the first time, either directly or by the grant of licences to third parties, as well as the right to oppose infringements.

"An obstacle to the free movement of goods may arise out of the existence, within a national legislation concerning industrial and commercial property, of provisions laying down that a patentee's right is not exhausted when the product protected by the patent is marketed in another Member State, with the result that the patentee can prevent importation of the product into his own Member State when it has been marketed in another State."

"Whereas an obstacle to the free movement of goods of this kind may be justified on the ground of protection of industrial property where such protection is invoked against a product coming from a Member State where it is not patentable and has been manufactured by third parties without the consent of the patentee and in cases where there exist patents, the original proprietors of which are legally and economically independent, a derogation from the principle of the free movement of goods is not, however, justified where the product has been put onto the market in a legal manner, by the patentee himself or with his consent, in the Member State from which it has been imported, in particular in the case of a proprietor of parallel patents."

"In fact, if a patentee could prevent the import of protected products marketed by him or with his consent in another Member State, he would be able to partition off national markets and thereby restrict trade between Member States, in a situation where no such restriction was necessary to guarantee the essence of the exclusive rights flowing from the parallel patents."

In *Merck v. Stephar*[37] a similar result was reached in a case in which it had been impossible for the patentee to obtain a patent in the other Member State; he had nevertheless placed the relevant goods on the market there himself. The Court there held:

"It is for the proprietor of the patent to decide, in the light of all the circumstances, under what conditions he will market his product, including the possibility of marketing it in a Member State where the law does not provide patent protection for the product in question. If he decides to do so he must then accept the consequences of his choice as regards the free movement of the product within the Common Market, which is a fundamental principle forming part of the legal and economic circumstances which must be taken into account by the proprietor of the patent in determining the manner in which his exclusive right will be exercised."

---

[37] Case 187/80, [1981] E.C.R. 2063, [1981] 3 C.M.L.R. 463, [1982] F.S.R. 57.

The doctrine does not apply to goods placed on the market pursuant to a compulsory licence,[38] for in view of the compulsory nature of the licence, such goods cannot be considered to have been marketed with the consent of the proprietor. It does not apply to goods modified to such an extent as no longer to be in substance the patentee's goods.[39] The doctrine does not apply to goods placed on the market outside the EC.[40] In addition, the Treaties of Accession of Spain and Portugal contain provisos limiting the application of the doctrine in certain cases (notably in respect of pharmaceuticals).[41]

Abuse of Dominant Position as a Defence

6.64　It has been held arguable that where the patentee's attempt to enforce his monopoly constitutes an abuse of a dominant position contrary to Article 86 of the Treaty of Rome, this may constitute a defence to an infringer sued under the patent. In *Pitney-Bowes v. Francotyp-Postalia GmbH*,[42] Hoffman J. reviewed the authorities and said:

"It is sufficient that the existence of the intellectual property right creates or buttresses the dominant position which the plaintiff is abusing. The remedy contemplated by the court is that the plaintiff may have to be deprived of the means of maintaining his dominant position."

However, in that case he struck out a number of the pleaded allegations of abuse; and as for the rest, the decision merely determined that they were arguable.

Similarly in *Chiron v. Murex*[43] the Court of Appeal upheld the decision of Aldous J. that a number of alleged abuses should be struck out; but an allegation of abuse by charging excessive prices for patented products was held arguably to constitute an abuse which might give rise to a defence to the action, in that the grant of an injunction in the action could buttress the ability of the plaintiff to continue their abusive conduct by continuing to charge high prices. However, the allegation was struck out on the ground that no effect on inter-state trade was shown.

In both of the above cases, the Court did not give strong encouragement even in relation to those abuses which it considered in principle might amount to arguable defences. However, clearly the strength of such a defence will depend on the particular facts which a defendant is

---

[38] Case 19/84, *Pharmon v. Hoechst* [1985] E.C.R. 2281, [1985] 3 C.M.L.R. 775, [1986] F.S.R. 108.

[39] *Dellareed v. Delkim Developments* [1988] F.S.R. 329 at 347.

[40] Case 51/75, *EMI v. CBS* [1976] E.C.R. 811, [1976] 2 C.M.L.R. 235.

[41] See also *Smith Kline & French Laboratories (Cimetidine)* Patent [1990] R.P.C. 203 (C.A.); Case C191/90 *Generics (U.K.) Ltd. v. Smith Kline & French Laboratories Ltd.* [1993] R.P.C. (E.C.J.); *Wellcome v. Discphasm Ltd.* [1993] F.S.R. 433.

[42] [1991] F.S.R. 72.

[43] [1994] F.S.R. 187; see also *Digital Equipment Corporation v. LCE Computer Maintenance* (Mervyn Davies J., May 22, 1992, (Unrep.) a copyright case), and *IBM v. Phoenix* [1994] R.P.C. 251.

able to establish and it is not possible from the authorities to date to categorise those types of allegation which may or may not give rise to a successful defence, save to say that it seems clear that the mere refusal to grant licences, either at all or on reasonable terms, is not an abuse.[43a] At present there is no United Kingdom case in which a defence under Article 86 to a patent infringement action has succeeded, and the point remains for decision.

"Infringement not novel" (Gillette Defence)

Since no relief could be obtained in respect of an invalid patent, if the **6.65** defendant could prove that the act complained of was merely what was disclosed in a publication which could be relied on against the validity of the patent, without any substantial or patentable variation having been made, he had a good defence. This is the so-called Gillette defence arising out of the words of Lord Moulton in *Gillette Safety Razor Co. v. Anglo-American Trading Co.*[44] where he said:

> "I am of opinion that in this case the defendant's right to succeed can be established without an examination of the terms of the specification of the plaintiff's letters patent. I am aware that such a mode of deciding a patent case is unusual, but from the point of view of the public it is important that this method of viewing their rights should not be overlooked. In practical life it is often the only safeguard to the manufacturer. It is impossible for an ordinary member of the public to keep watch on all the numerous patents which are taken out and to ascertain the validity and scope of their claims. But he is entitled to feel secure if he knows that that which he is doing differs from that which has been done of old only in non-patentable variations such as the substitution of mechanical equivalents or changes of material, shape or size. The defence that 'the alleged infringement was not novel at the date of the plaintiff's letters patent,' is a good defence in law, and it would sometimes obviate the great length and expense of patent cases if the defendant could and would put forth his case in this form, and thus spare himself the trouble of demonstration on which horn of the well-known dilemma the plaintiff had impaled himself, invalidity or non-infringement."[45]

Lord Moulton's dicta in the Gillette case were, however, considered **6.66** and explained in *Page v. Brent Toy Products Ltd.*,[46] where the prior

---

[43a] Case 238/87 *Volvo v. Erik Verg (U.K.) Ltd.* [1988] E.C.R. 6211; [1989] 4 C.M.L.R. 122.
[44] (1913) 30 R.P.C. 465 at 480.
[45] See also *Proctor v. Bennis* (1887) 4 R.P.C. 333 at p.351; *Cincinnati Grinders (Inc.) v. B.S.A. Tools Ltd.* (1931) 48 R.P.C. 33 at p.58; *Merrell Dow v. H.N. Norton* [1994] R.P.C. 1 at p. 13 (under appeal).
[46] (1950) 67 R.P.C. 4.

document in question was more than fifty years old and, therefore, could not be relied on as destroying novelty.[47] Evershed M.R. said:[48]

> "Lord Moulton was not stating that this plea, that the infringement was not novel, was a separate defence against a claim of infringement, but was confining himself to the case where the alternatives of invalidity or non-infringement were open to the defendant. He was stating 'This is a convenient brief form of raising, by way of pleading, the whole case. If the allegation is made good, then where the dilemma is present, the result must be that the plaintiff fails by being impaled on one horn or the other . . . in this case . . . there is no dilemma for the plaintiff; the plea of invalidity is not open to the defendants on this particular matter.' And, in my judgment, the language of Lord Moulton does not entitle the defendants here to raise as a separate defence this form of words."

Such a defence was argued in *Hickman v. Andrews*,[49] and although it failed on the facts of the case, Graham J. said of it: "It is a good defence if it is strictly proved."[50]

The principle was again considered by the Court of Appeal in *Windsurfing v. Tabur Marine*[51] in which Lord Oliver explained that the policy behind the invalidity ground of obviousness was that it would be: "wrong to prevent a man from doing something which is merely an obvious extension of what he has been doing or what was known in the art before the priority date of the patent granted " The defendant's obviousness attack succeeded (the other horn of the dilemma, no-infringement, apparently did not need to be considered).

It is submitted that although Lord Moulton's test may be helpful in assisting a manufacturer to decide whether or not to proceed with some art which may appear to fall within the claim of a patent, it does not provide any additional defence to an infringement action. It is in reality an attack on validity which invokes the policy underlying the grounds of anticipation and obviousness.

Right to continue use begun before priority date

6.67   Under the 1949 Act no protection was given to an infringer who commenced his infringing activity before the priority date of the patent. However, secret use was a ground for revocation of a patent and thus secret use was protected. Under the 1977 Act secret use no longer invalidates a patent but rights are given under section 64 to any person who in the United Kingdom before the priority date of the invention

---

[47] See *ante*, §5.27.
[48] (1950) 67 R.P.C. at p.13.
[49] [1983] R.P.C. 147.
[50] [1983] R.P.C. at 172.
[51] [1985] R.P.C. 59.

does in good faith an act which would constitute an infringement of the patent if it were in force, or makes in good faith effective and serious preparations to do such an act.

In the United Kingdom

Although the Act specifies that the act in question must be in the **6.68** United Kingdom, it is submitted that this will extend to all forms of potentially infringing acts including importation.

In good faith

The act or preparations must be in good faith and thus use of an **6.69** invention in contravention of the inventor's rights, for example in breach of confidence, will be excluded.

Which would constitute an infringement

It is necessary that the act in question would, if the patent had been **6.70** granted, have constituted infringement. Thus, if the act in question was one for which protection was given by the Act (*e.g.* private or experimental use) the user will not be able to benefit from the rights granted by section 64. However, experimental use may constitute effective and serious preparations to do an "infringing" act.

Effective and serious preparations

This concept was new in the 1977 Act and occurs in both section 64 **6.71** and section 28. Whether preparations have become effective and serious will be a question of fact in any given case, and in view of the wide range of possible circumstances that could arise, it is difficult to predict what extent of protection the section will afford. In *Helitune v. Stewart Hughes*,[52] the defendant had produced prototypes of the products in issue, but at the priority date had not sold any and instead was concentrating on producing a different "non-infringing" product. It was held that the stage of making effective and serious preparations had not been reached. Similarly, it is possible to envisage other factual circumstances where it is difficult to identify the moment when activities move to a stage of being effective and serious preparations to infringe; for example, as a product moves from a paper proposal to a commercial trial, or where negotiations, *e.g.* to import an article in confidence move from mere preparatory discussions to contractual negotiations. Once the contract is concluded, it is submitted that the preparations will have been completed, but before then the position is less clear.

---

[52] [1991] F.S.R. 171.

The Court will have to decide the question on the basis of the user's evidence and the onus will be on him to show the necessary preparations.

The rights given

6.72   The rights given are set out in section 64 (1) and (2) of the 1977 Act (as amended by C.D.P.A. 1988), which provide that any person who has in good faith done the necessary act or preparations shall have the right:

(1) to continue to do or, as the case may be, to do that act (but not to grant a licence to another person to do the act); and
(2) if it was done, or the preparations were made, to do it in the course of a business, to
    (a) authorise the doing of that act by any partners of his for the time being in that business, and
    (b) assign that right, or transmit it on death (or in the case of a body corporate on its dissolution), to any person who acquires that part of the business in the course of which the act was done or the preparations were made.

Continue to do that act

6.73   The meaning to be given to the word "act" presents considerable difficulties. Clearly the word covers a single infringing act which extends over a period of time (for example the building of a ship), but it is submitted that it is also intended to cover a situation in which infringing acts are repeated, for example, by the use of a machine which repeatedly produces infringing products day after day, even though the making of each individual article will be a separate act of infringement for the purposes of damages and of the Limitation Acts. It is submitted that the right to continue is therefore not limited merely to completing one infringing act.[53]

6.74   The Act, however, gives no guidance as to what, if any, quantitative or qualitative restrictions are to be placed on the right to repeat the prior act. It is submitted that there are no quantitative restrictions. If a person has manufactured one potentially infringing product he should be at liberty to repeat that act as and when he pleases even if this involves the purchase of new plant since any quantitative restriction would be inconsistent with one of the objects of Patent Law which is to contribute to the increase of knowledge without fettering the right of others to use their pre-existing knowledge.

The right is restricted to continuing to do *that* act and not any infringing act. Thus, if the potentially infringing act was making (which no doubt would be effective and serious preparations also for disposal)

---

[53] See *Rotocrop International v. Genbourne* [1982] F.S.R. 241 at 262.

this would not entitle the person in question instead of making to import. Such a conclusion is consistent with the provisions of section 64(3).

An as yet unresolved difficulty is the question of to what extent the **6.75** section permits any qualitative change in the act to be repeated. In *Helitune v. Stewart Hughes*,[54] Aldous J. said (obiter) that:

"Section 64(1) relates to acts which constitute an infringement and not to any particular product or process. As I have stated the acts are those covered by a patent as set out in section 60. Thus, provided a person has carried out an infringing act before the priority date, he can continue to carry out that act even though the product or process may be different to some degree. This can be illustrated by considering a person who uses an infringing process. The fact that he alters that process after the priority date does not matter. The section states that the doing of that act, namely using an infringing process, shall not amount to an infringement."

However, this view was doubted in *Lubrizol v. Exxon*,[55] in which the deputy judge said:

"The act which the alleged infringer is entitled to continue to conduct by virtue of section 64(2) is the act which he was committing before the priority date. It was not an infringement then. It was an act of commerce. It is that specific act of commerce which he is entitled to continue. I have difficulty in accepting that by, for example, manufacturing product A before the priority date, he was thereby given a right to manufacture any product after the priority date. In my view, section 64 is intended to safeguard the existing commercial activity of a person in the United Kingdom which is overtaken by the subsequent grant of a patent. It is not meant to be a charter allowing him to expand into other products and other processes."

At one extreme, the construction suggested in *Helitune* would permit a prior user who had fortuitously done an act falling within the scope of one of the claims thereafter to take advantage of the patentee's most favoured embodiment. That would give the prior user an unfair advantage as regards development of the invention. But at the other extreme, the *Lubrizol* construction could be excessively restrictive, in preventing no qualitative change in the act to be repeated. However, it is submitted that some measure of freedom to incorporate qualitative changes must properly be given to the prior user, and it cannot have been the intention of the legislature to restrict a manufacturer to making precisely the same product right down to such details as colour and

---

[54] [1991] F.S.R. 171.
[55] [1992] R.P.C. 281.

markings. It is submitted that the prior user will be permitted to modify his prior use in ways that do not affect the essential nature of his product or process, but not in ways that materially alter and improve its nature; for the prior user should generally be able to show that the placing of a product on the market in itself involved an intention to make modifications of the former kind during the lifetime of the product.

Right to assign to successors

6.76 Section 64(2) provides a right to assign the right to continue to do the prior use to successors and to authorise business partners to do the prior use. The right is limited to cases where the prior use or preparation was done in the course of a business and the assignment is to a person acquiring that part of the business.

No right to grant licences

6.77 A prior user obtaining rights under section 64 cannot licence another to exercise those rights.[56]

Protection on disposal

6.78 Where a patented product is disposed of by any person to another in exercise of a right conferred by section 64(2), that other and any person claiming through him shall be entitled to deal with the product in the same way as if it has been disposed of by a sole registered proprietor.[57]

Old Act patents

6.79 By Schedule 4, paragraph 3(2) of the 1977 Act, section 64 will apply in relation to existing patents granted under the 1949 Act, as a defence to allegations of infringement by acts done after the coming into force of the 1977 Act. Of course, *ex hypothesi* those acts contemplated by section 64(1) performed before the priority date of an old Act patent will have been done before the coming into force of the 1977 Act. It is submitted that there is however no inconsistency here, as there are two different acts to be considered. First, the act (or preparation) which provides a defence under the section: by section 64(1), this had to be an act which would have infringed the patent if it had been in force; for old Act patents, this would have to have been an infringement under the old law.[58] Secondly, the act alleged by the patentee to have been an infringement; *ex hypothesi* this will have had to have been committed after the date of publication of the patent application; for any action not

---

[56] P.A. 1977, s.64(4).
[57] *Ibid.*
[58] By reason of P.A. 1977, Sched. 4, para. 3(1).

now barred under the Limitation Acts, the provisions of Schedule 4, paragraph 3(2) will apply in relation to that (and paragraph 3(3) may provide a yet further defence). Of course, under the old law prior secret use was also a ground of invalidity[59] and it is, therefore, possible that both prior secret use and section 64 can be relied upon in appropriate cases.

Right to continue use commenced while patent has lapsed

Although a patent may lapse by reason of failure to pay renewal fees, **6.80** section 28 of the 1977 Act[60] contains provision for the restoration of the patent under certain circumstances. The section also contains provision for the protection of persons who may have begun to use the invention in the meantime.[61] Provided such acts, or serious and effective preparations to do such acts, are begun not less than six months after the date of lapse, then similar protection is provided as under section 64. However, if such acts were begun before the end of the period of six months after lapse[62] (*i.e.* were either begun before lapse, or begun less than six months after lapse), then they are treated as infringements.[63]

Private use

Under section 60(5)(*a*), an act which would otherwise infringe a **6.81** patent will not do so if it is done privately and for purposes which are not commercial. But if there is a dual purpose and one of those purposes is commercial, then this exemption will not apply.[64]

Experimental Use

Similarly, under section 60(5)(*b*), an act done for experimental **6.82** purposes relating to the subject matter of the action will not be an infringement.

The subsection was considered by the Court of Appeal in *Monsanto Co. v. Stauffer Chemical Co.*,[65] where Dillon L.J. held that the word "experiment" was to be given its ordinary meaning, and in view of the statutory history of the section, decisions under the old law as to what constituted "experimental purposes" were not of assistance. (These were, however, reviewed in the judgment of Falconer J. in the same report).

He went on to hold that, although experimental purposes could have

---

[59] See *ante*, Chap. 5, § 5.146.
[60] Which applies to old and new Act patents; see P.A. 1977, Sched. 2.
[61] P.A. 1977, s.28(5)–(9).
[62] P.A. 1977, s.28(5)(*a*).
[63] *Ibid.*
[64] *Smith Kline & French v. Evans* [1989] F.S.R. 513.
[65] [1985] R.P.C. 515; compare also *Monsanto v. Stauffer (New Zealand)* [1984] F.S.R. 559; *Smith, Kline & French v. Evans* [1989] F.S.R. 513.

an ultimate commercial end in view (hence the difference in wording between subparagraphs 60(5)(a) and (b)),

> "Trials carried out in order to discover something unknown or to test a hypothesis or even in order to find out whether something which is known to work in specific conditions, *e.g.* of soil or weather, will work in different conditions can fairly, in my judgment, be regarded as experiments. But trials carried out in order to demonstrate to a third party that a product works or, in order to amass information to satisfy a third party, whether a customer or a body such as the PSPS or ACAS [regulatory bodies], that the product works as its maker claims are not, in my judgment, to be regarded as acts done 'for experimental purposes'. The purposes for which tests or trials are carried out may in some cases be mixed and may in some cases be difficult to discern; indeed, in the present case, if fuller evidence is given at the trial, a different result may then be reached. On the affidavit evidence before this court, it is not clear to me what the defendants are still wanting to find out about TOUCHDOWN. On that evidence, if I ask, in relation to the defendants' proposed field trials of category (2) to be carried out by the second defendant's personnel on land rented on other farms, the broad question whether those trials would be carried out, or done, for experimental purposes, my answer is that they would not; they would be carried out in order to obtain the approval of the PSPS and ACAS."[66]

6.83   Under the old law, use of the invention for the purpose of bona fide experiment was not an infringement and, it is submitted, that the old decisions on the limit of this principle may still be of value.

In *Frearson v. Loe*[67] Jessel M.R. (after referring to the defendant's acts) said:

> "He said he did this merely by way of experiment, and no doubt if a man makes things merely by way of bona fide experiment, and not with the intention of selling and making use of the thing so made for the purpose of which a patent has been granted, but with a view of improving upon the invention, the subject of the patent, or with a view of seeing whether an improvement can be made or not, that is not an invasion of the exclusive rights granted by the patent. Patent rights were never granted to prevent persons of ingenuity exercising their talents in a fair way. But if there be neither using nor vending of the invention for profit, the mere making for the purpose of experiment and not for a fraudulent purpose ought not to be

---

[66] *Ibid.* at p.542.
[67] (1878) 9 Ch.D. 48 at p.66.

considered within the meaning of the prohibition, and if it were, it is certainly not the subject for an injunction."[68]

Where, however, an infringing product was sold for experimental use by another, the vendor was liable for infringement;[69] again it is submitted that the same result would follow under the 1977 Act. To purchase and use infringing articles for the purpose of instructing pupils and to enable them to pull them to pieces and put them together again was not mere experimental use, and amounted to an infringement.[70]

Extemporaneous preparation on prescription

6.84 The extemporaneous preparation in a pharmacy of a medicine for an individual in accordance with a prescription given by a registered medical or dental practitioner is excluded by section 60(5)(c) from infringement, as are all dealings with medicines so prepared. The provision is new in the 1977 Act; it is consistent with the policy of section 4(2).

Vessels, vehicles and aircraft

Ships

6.85 An act which consists of the use, exclusively for the needs of a relevant ship, of a product or process in the body of such a ship or in its machinery, tackle or apparatus or other accessories in a case where the ship has temporarily or accidentally entered the internal or territorial waters of the United Kingdom does not constitute infringement.[71] Relevant ship is defined in section 60(7); the definition expressly excludes ships registered in the United Kingdom, and the protection extends only to uses exclusive to the needs of that ship so that a distinction is to be drawn between a use which is exclusive for such needs and one which is not. Difficulties may therefore arise where the ship is a specialist ship, for example adapted for containers, and the use in question relates to the handling of the containers. It is submitted that the dividing line is to be ascertained by asking whether, with the equipment possessed by the ship, it could operate without using the product or process in question. The protection extends both to temporary and accidental entry into the territorial waters which are not themselves defined in the 1977 Act. Reference must therefore be had to

---

[68] See also *Muntz v. Foster* (1843) 2 W.P.C. 93 at p.101; *Jones v. Pearce* (1832) 1 W.P.C. 122 at p.125; *Proctor v. Bayley & Son* (1889) 6 R.P.C. 106, 538; *Pessers etc. Ltd. v. Newell & Co.* (1914) 31 R.P.C. 51.
[69] *F. Hoffmann-La Roche & Co. A.G. v. Harris Pharmaceuticals Ltd.* [1977] F.S.R. 200.
[70] *United Telephone Co. v. Sharples* (1885) 2 R.P.C. 28.
[71] P.A. 1977, s.60(5)(d).

the prevailing Crown Declarations as to territorial waters at the time of the infringement. By section 132(4), the 1977 Act and the protection of this subsection will also apply to use on the Continental Shelf where appropriate.

Aircraft, hovercraft and vehicles

6.86   Use of a product or process in the body or operation of a relevant[72] aircraft, hovercraft or vehicle which has temporarily or accidentally entered or is crossing the United Kingdom (including the airspace above it and its territorial waters) or the use of accessories for such aircraft, hovercraft or vehicle is also protected.[73] In this subsection there is no requirement of "exclusive use" but otherwise the protection is complementary to that for ships. Further protection is given in respect of the use of exempted[74] aircraft which are lawfully entering or crossing the United Kingdom (as defined above) and of the importation into the United Kingdom or the use or storage there of any part or accessory for such an aircraft.[75]

Breach of restrictive conditions

6.87   Under section 44(3), in any proceedings for infringement of a patent it is a defence to prove that at the time of infringement there was in force a contract or licence relating to the patent made by or with the consent of the Plaintiff containing a condition or term void by virtue of section 44 of the 1977 Act.[76] The defence is a complete one, but falls to be construed strictly given its highly penal nature.[77]

5. Limitation on Patentees' Rights and other Protection for Infringers

6.88   The 1977 Act makes a number of provisions to safeguard an infringer against damages or otherwise to restrict a patentee's rights against an infringer. In addition an infringer may also be able to seek protection by seeking an indemnity or compensation from a third party.

---

[72] Defined in P.A. 1977, s.60(7).
[73] P.A. 1977, s.60(5)(*e*).
[74] Defined in P.A. 1977, s.60(7).
[75] P.A. 1977, s.60(5)(*f*).
[76] See *post*, § 8.65.
[77] *Fichera v. Flogates* [1983] F.S.R. 198.

Restrictions on damages

Innocent infringement

By section 62(1), an infringer is not liable for damages or an account if he **6.89** proves that at the date of infringement he was not aware, and had no reasonable ground for supposing, that the patent in suit existed.[78] The marketing of an article with the word "patent" or "patented" is not sufficient notice to make an infringer liable in damages unless the number of the patent accompanies such words. But this special defence is not available to an infringer who has been informed of the existence of a patent application in respect of the article in question.[79] Given that it is generally possible to conduct patent searches, one cannot specify in what circumstances the Court may hold that an infringer had no reasonable grounds for supposing that the patent existed. The onus is on the infringer. However, the proviso to the section suggests that a liberal approach is contemplated. Section 62 re-enacts section 59(1) of the 1949 Act with minimal differences so that the old law will continue to apply.

Infringement after failure to pay renewal fee

Under section 62(2), the Court or Comptroller has a discretion to **6.90** refuse to award any damages or to make any order for an inquiry as to damages in respect of infringements committed during the six-month grace period provided by section 25(4) of the 1977 Act but prior to the date on which the renewal fee and additional fee are paid.[80]

Infringement before amendment

Section 62(3) provides that no damages are to be awarded in respect of **6.91** infringements occurring before the date of a decision allowing amendment unless the Court is satisfied that the specification as originally published was framed in good faith and with reasonable skill and knowledge.[81] This re-enacts section 59(3) of the 1949 Act. Section 62(3), unlike sections 62(1) and (2), makes no reference to an account of profits. In *Codex Corp. v. Racal-Milgo*[82] the patentee was held entitled to an account without having to establish good faith or reasonable skill and knowledge.

---

[78] *Wilderman v. F. W. Berk & Co. Ltd.* (1925) 42 R.P.C. 79 at p.90; *Lancer Boss Ltd. v. Henley Forklift Co. Ltd.* [1975] R.P.C. 307 at p.314 (decisions under the equivalent P.A. 49, s.59(1).
[79] *Wilbec Plastics v. Wilson Dawes* [1966] R.P.C. 513.
[80] See also "Restoration of Lapsed Patents", *ante*, §3.67.
[81] P.A. 1949, s.59(3).
[82] [1983] R.P.C. 369.

Partially Valid Patent

6.92   Section 63 of the 1977 Act contains provisions limiting relief where a patent is found at trial to be only partially valid; these are discussed *post*, Chapter 12, §12.251.

Non-registration of a change in proprietorship or of an exclusive licence

6.93   Section 33 of the 1977 Act applies to a number of transactions, instruments or events,[83] in particular to assignments of patents or applications and to the grant or assignment of any licence under the patent. Provision is made in the Act for the entry on the Register of Patents of details of these transactions, instruments and events.[84] Infringement proceedings can be brought by a subsequent proprietor and also, if the assignment to him conferred on him the right, for infringements committed before that date.[85] An exclusive licensee is, subject to the provision of section 67 of the Act, given like rights to bring proceedings for infringement as a patentee.[86]

However, where by virtue of a transaction, instrument or event to which section 33 applies a person has become the proprietor or exclusive licensee of a patent and the patent is subsequently infringed, he shall be awarded neither damages nor an account of profits in respect of such a subsequent infringement occurring before the transaction, instrument or event is registered unless:

(a) it was registered within the period of six months beginning with its date or

(b) the Court or the Comptroller is satisfied that it was not practicable to register it before the end of that period and that it was registered as soon as possible after that date.[87]

The restriction on the right to claim damages or an account applies only to subsequent infringements and thus any right to recover damages for earlier infringements which may have been transferred by virtue of section 30(7) or section 32(7) is unaffected.

The policy of the section was held in *Mölnlycke v. Procter & Gamble*[88] to be to protect the infringer from a claim at the suit of someone whose interest he could not have ascertained from an inspection of the register, and not merely to punish the applicant for delay. Where a first licence is unregistered, but a second one is granted which constitutes a fresh

---

[83] See P.A. 1977, s.33(3); see also Chap. 8, §8.27.
[84] See P.A. 1977, s.32 and s.33.
[85] See P.A. 1977, s.30(7) and s.31(7).
[86] P.A. 1977, s.67(1).
[87] P.A. 1977, s.68; see also Chap. 8, §8.28.
[88] [1994] R.P.C. 49 at 109.

agreement, damages may be awarded from the date of the second licence.[89]

Infringement before grant

The right to bring proceedings in respect of infringements of a patent **6.94** occurring subsequent to the date of publication but prior to grant is provided for in section 69 of the 1977 Act. As with section 60,[90] section 69 is to be construed as to have as nearly as practicable the same effect in the United Kingdom as the corresponding provision of the E.P.C., C.P.C. and P.C.T. have in the territories to which those conventions apply.[91]

It is provided that subsequent to publication and prior to grant, **6.95** subject to two restrictions, an applicant for a patent shall have the same right to bring proceedings before the Court or the Comptroller in respect of acts which would have infringed the patent if granted as he would have had if the patent had been granted on the date of publication.[92] The first restriction is that no proceedings can be brought until the patent is granted.[93] Secondly, the onus is on the applicant to show that the alleged infringing act would, if the patent had been granted on the date of publication of the application, have infringed not only the patent, but also the claims (as interpreted by the description and any drawings referred to in the description or claims) in the form in which they were contained in the application immediately before the preparations for its publication were completed by the Patent Office. This latter requirement is new and takes account of the fact that it may be possible before grant to obtain claims wider in scope than the published claims provided that the claims as amended do not extend the scope of the disclosure of the application.[94] Thus the second restriction requires the ambit of the claims[95] both as published and as granted to be ascertained and no infringement prior to the grant will occur unless the infringing act would infringe both sets of claims.

Even if the two requirements above are satisfied, the Court or **6.96** Comptroller is given a discretion as to whether to reduce any award of damages for infringements occurring before grant.[96] The Court or Comptroller is directed to consider whether it would have been reasonable to expect from a consideration of the application as published that a patent would be granted conferring on the proprietor of the patent protection against the infringing act.[97]

---

[89] *Minnesota Mining v. Rennicks* [1992] F.S.R. 118.
[90] See *ante*, §6.03.
[91] P.A. 1977, s.130(7).
[92] P.A. 1977, s.69(1).
[93] P.A. 1977, s.69(1)(*a*).
[94] See P.A. 1977, s.76(2).
[95] See *post*, §6.35.
[96] P.A. 1977, s.69(3).
[97] *Ibid.*

Sections 62(2) and (3) of the 1977 Act[98] do not apply to infringements before grant.[99]

The cause of action accrues for the purposes of the limitation Acts when the infringement takes place, in spite of the statutory bar on commencement of proceedings until after grant.[1]

Warranty under Sale of Goods Act

6.97   On the sale of an article there is an implied warranty[2] that the purchaser will enjoy quiet possession of the goods and this possession is disturbed when the goods infringe a patent, whether or not that patent was in force at the date of sale.[3] Accordingly where an infringer has obtained the infringing items under a contract to which the Sale of Goods Act applies, although he will have no defence to the infringement action, he will be entitled to be indemnified by the vendor.

6. Patentees' Rights Against Non-Infringers

6.98   Whilst a mere carrier, warehouseman or agent for transhipment was not liable for infringement,[4] an action could properly be brought against them for an injunction to restrain them from dealing with or disposing of infringing articles in any way.[5] Further, an action for discovery lies against a non-infringer in order to identify infringers or infringing goods.[6]

Nothing in the 1977 Act is inconsistent with the continuation under the protective jurisdiction of equity of these rights and, as is implicit in *Smith Kline French Laboratories v. R. D. Harbottle (Mercantile) Ltd.*[7] they remain good law.

7. Right of Non-Infringer to Seek Declaration

Declaration of non-infringement

6.99   Under section 71 of the 1977 Act, any person doing or proposing to do

---

[98] See *ante*, §6.90 and §6.91.
[99] P.A. 1977, s.69(3).
[1] *Sevcon v. Lucas CAV* [1986] R.P.C. 609.
[2] Sale of Goods Act 1979, s.12(2)(*b*).
[3] *Niblett v. Confectioner's Materials Co.* [1921] 3 K.B. 387; *Microbeads A.G. v. Vinhurst Road Markings* [1976] R.P.C. 19.
[4] See §6.22 *ante* and *Nobel's Explosives Co. v. Jones, Scott & Co.* (1894) 17 Ch.D. 721.
[5] *Washburn and Moen Manufacturing Co. v. Cunard Steamship Co.* (1889) 6 R.P.C. 398 at p.403. See also *Upmann v. Elkan* (1871) L.R. 7 Ch.App. 130.
[6] *Norwich Pharmaceutical Co. v. Commissioners of Customs & Excise* [1974] R.P.C. 101.
[7] [1980] R.P.C. 363.

any act may seek a declaration from the Court or from the Comptroller that that act is not or would not be an infringement of a patent. The Defendant to the action will be the Patentee who need not have asserted that the act in respect of which the declaration is sought is or would be an infringement. It is however a prerequisite of bringing an action for a declaration that the person has applied in writing to the patentee for a written acknowledgement to the effect of the declaration claimed, furnishing him also with full written particulars of the act in question and that the Patentee has failed to give the acknowledgement. The subsection only refers to patents and it therefore appears that it cannot be invoked in respect of an application for a patent. However, since the subsection is expressed as being without prejudice to the Courts jurisdiction to make a declaration, it is submitted that in an appropriate case this jurisdiction could be invoked. Other than this no restriction is placed upon the right to seek a declaration. Thus, a declaration can be sought, for example, to the effect that the act is not an infringement by reason of the provisions of section 64 of the 1977 Act[8] as well as the more conventional type of declaration.

No special provisions are made as to costs and therefore the normal **6.100** principles under which costs are awarded both in the Courts and before the Comptroller will apply.[9] In a declaration action, the validity of the patent may be put in issue[10] and thus it is now possible for a potential defendant in a patent action to raise as a plaintiff issues of infringement and validity in one action.

In the case of a declaration action brought in the High Court no exceptional procedure is laid down so the ordinary Supreme Court Rules of procedure will apply. Where the action is brought before the Comptroller, rules of procedure are laid down,[11] but such an action cannot be brought when proceedings relating to the patent are pending in the Court without leave of that Court.[12] A declaration made by the Comptroller has the same effect as a declaration by the Court save that a decision by the Comptroller or on appeal from him on validity does not create an estoppel in a subsequent attack on validity in civil proceedings where infringement is an issue.[13] It is therefore submitted that a declaration whether made by the Court or Comptroller would be binding against the Patentee and all successors in title.

---

[8] See *ante*, §§ 6.99 *et seq.*
[9] *Mölnycke v. Procter & Gamble* [1990] R.P.C. 267; P.A. 1949, s.66(2) had special provisions but has not been re-enacted.
[10] P.A. 1977, s.72(1)(*c*), reversing P.A. 49, s.66(s).
[11] Patent Rules 1990, r.74.
[12] P.A. 1977, s.74(7).
[13] P.A. 1977, s.71(2).

8. Infringement Under the E.P.C., C.P.C. and P.C.T.

The European Patent Convention

6.101   Any infringement of a European patent is to be dealt with by national law.[14] The 1977 Act[15] provides that as from publication[16] of the mention of its grant in the European Patent Bulletin a European patent shall be treated as if it were a patent granted under the 1977 Act.

Accordingly infringement will be considered under the law applicable to patents granted under the 1977 Act and, in particular, express provision is made to cover cases where the European Patent is found partially valid after commencement of infringement proceedings.[17] Provisions are also made to deal with amendment and revocation generally.[18]

The law relating to actions for infringement of European patent applications before grant but after publication will be the same as national law.[19]

The Community Patent Convention

6.102   As the C.P.C. is not in force, there are no patents granted under it. As and when it does come into force, the provisions relating to infringement of Community Patents are set out in Articles 29–32 of the C.P.C. Whilst there are differences in wording between these articles and the coresponding provisions of the 1977 Act[20] it is submitted that having regard to the provisions of section 130(7)[21] there will be no difference in practice.

Legal effect is to be given in this country to rights arising under Community Patents[22] and in so far as infringement is not governed by the convention, natural law shall apply.[23] The forum for infringement proceedings is laid down by Article 69.[24]

The Patent Co-Operation Treaty

6.103   In essence the P.C.T. provides a convenient method of applying for national patents in a multitude of countries (see *ante* §1.14). National patents are thereby obtained and the question of infringement will be decided in respect of a patent granted pursuant to a P.C.T. application in the same way as a patent granted pursuant to an ordinary application.

---

[14] E.P.C. Art 64(3).
[15] P.A. 1977, s.77(1).
[16] For special provisions as to publication see P.A. 1977, s.77(6) and (9).
[17] P.A. 1977, s.77(3).
[18] P.A. 1977, s.77(4) and (5).
[19] P.A. 1977, s.78.
[20] P.A. 1977, ss.60 and 64.
[21] See *ante*, §6.03.
[22] P.A. 1977, s.86 (not brought into effect).
[23] C.P.C. Art 36.
[24] See also P.A. 1977, s.88.

CHAPTER 7

AMENDMENT OF SPECIFICATIONS

History of law

During the period when specifications were filed or enrolled in the **7.01** Court of Chancery, the Master of the Rolls, as Keeper of the Records, had power at common law to correct errors in a specification, but this power was strictly limited to the correction of verbal or clerical errors arising from mistake or inadvertence.[1]

A patent may, however, be rendered invalid by reason of the patentee claiming something which is not new or not useful, or through some innocent misdescription or misrepresentation, and it had long been recognised that an opportunity to amend should be available to the patentee to cure such invalidity.[2]

Statutory powers of amendment

The common law power of amendment was too restricted to be of use **7.02** in such cases and by the Acts of 1835 and 1844[3] the patentee was given power to file a disclaimer or a memorandum of alteration provided that by so doing he did not extend the ambit of his monopoly. Any such disclaimer or amendment, however, was made at the patentee's own peril, and, in a subsequent action involving the validity of the patent, objection might be taken on the ground that it in fact extended the monopoly.

Section 18 of the 1883 Act permitted, in cases where there were no legal proceedings relating to the patent pending, amendments by disclaimer, correction or explanation. Where there were such legal proceedings pending the patentee had by section 19 to apply to the court for permission to apply to the Comptroller, only amendments by disclaimer being allowed in this case. Section 18(9), also provided that

---

[1] *Sharp's patent* (1840) 1 W.P.C. 641 at p.649; *Gare's Patent* (1884) 26 Ch.D. 105.
[2] See *May and Baker Ltd. v. Boots Pure Drug Co. Ltd.* (1950) 67 R.P.C. 23 at 40.
[3] 5 & 6 Will 4 c.83 and 7 & 8 Vict. c.69.

the granting of leave to amend should be conclusive as to the permissibility of the amendment, save in cases of fraud, though this provision was not given its full effect until the decision of the House of Lords in *Moser v. Marsden*.[4]

The Act of 1907 by section 21 substantially re-enacted section 18 of the Act of 1883, and by section 22 (corresponding in other respects to section 19 of the Act of 1883) conferred upon the court itself power to allow amendments by way of disclaimer in any action for infringement or proceeding for revocation. This power was extended to cases of amendments by way of correction or explanation by the alteration effected in section 22 of the 1907 Act by the Act of 1919.

Under the acts prior to the 1949 Act it was a requirement that the amended specification should not claim an invention "substantially larger than or substantially different from" the invention previously claimed. The latter provision was interpreted in a manner which in many cases rendered the ostensible right of a patentee to amend largely illusory and the omission of this provision in the 1949 Act was a great advantage to patentees. The many reported cases on the topic of "substantially different" are not now applicable.

1949 Act

7.03   Except as mentioned above, the 1949 Act generally contained the same provisions as to amendment as its predecessor, the 1907 Act. As discussed in greater detail below, the provisions of this Act dealing with amendment are still in existence and have not been repealed by the 1977 Act. They continue to govern amendment of patents granted under the 1949 Act.

1977 Act

7.04   The 1977 Act which only applies to patents granted under that Act has adopted a quite different manner of setting out what amendments are permissible. The most fundamental alteration to the law introduced by the 1977 Act is that the correctness of a decision allowing amendment either before or after grant can be challenged at a later date and if, in revocation proceedings, the court is satisfied that the protection conferred by a patent has been extended by an amendment which should not have been allowed, the patent will be revoked. Under the 1949 Act, a decision allowing an amendment could not be challenged in subsequent proceedings. The 1977 Act also differs from the 1949 Act in that amendments of applications before grant are now covered by the same provisions as amendments after grant. Under the 1949 Act, amendments of specifications prior to acceptance was not governed by the same provisions as those covering amendment after acceptance.

---

[4] (1892) 9 R.P.C. 24.

Application of 1949 and 1977 Acts

7.05 The relevant sections of the 1949 Act continue to govern amendment to patents granted under that Act and to applications made under the 1949 Act, that is to say applications made prior to June 1, 1978. All applications made on or after this date and patents granted on such applications are governed by the 1977 Act. It will be convenient to consider the provisions of the two Acts separately.

Since much of the case law established under the 1949 Act is still applicable to the 1977 Act, in this Chapter the 1949 Act is considered first.

1. Amendment Under the 1949 Act

7.06 Under the 1949 Act an applicant for a patent or a patentee may at any time after acceptance of the complete specification apply to amend by way of disclaimer, correction or explanation. Unless the amendment is for the purpose of correcting an obvious mistake,[5] the following conditions must be fulfilled, *viz.*

(a) the amended specification must not claim or describe matter not in substance disclosed in the specification before the amendment; and

(b) everything covered by an amended claim must have fallen within the scope of at least one claim prior to the amendment.[6]

It is submitted that the effect of the 1949 Act is, in general terms, that the Comptroller or the court has jurisdiction to make any amendment in the body of the specification which does not involve the introduction of new matter and that any amendment can be made to claims, including the introduction of one or more new claims, provided that the claims as amended are fairly based[7] on the complete specification as accepted and that the amendments do "not make anything an infringement which is not an infringement already".[8] The most important exception to the above concerns amendment of obvious mistakes.

The Act contains separate provisions for the correction of clerical errors. See *post* § 7.60.

Disclaimer

7.07 Amendments by way of disclaimers can take three forms: limitation of what is claimed, deletion of matter contained in the body of the

---

[5] See *post* §7.16.
[6] P.A. 1949, s.31(1).
[7] See *post*, §7.18.
[8] *The Distillers Co. Ltd.'s Appn.* (1953) 70 R.P.C. 221 at p.223, *per* Lloyd-Jacob J.

complete specification and a specific abandonment to a monopoly which covers a certain piece of prior art (a specific disclaimer).

Limitation of the Claim

7.08   As stated by Fox L.J.

"any reduction in the scope of the claims is a disclaimer: it will take out of infringement something which otherwise would be an infringement."[9]

The amendment takes the form of adding extra integers into the claim or where a range is specified by reducing the range.
As Lord Denning stated in *AMP. Inc. v. Hellerman Ltd*:[10]

"A disclaimer takes place whenever the patentee reduces the ambit of his monopoly, for he thereby renounces his previous claim in its fullest scope. This renunciation need not, however, be done in express terms. It is sufficient if it is done impliedly ... once you add another essential feature to a combination, you produce a sub-combination: and amendment so as to limit the scope of the specification to a sub-combination which was within the original claim is disclaimer."

Whatever amendment is made to a claim it cannot be a disclaimer unless the amendment has taken out of infringement something which infringed the unamended claim.
As is dealt with below, cutting down the scope of the monopoly in one respect does not provide a justification for its extension in other respects.[11]

Deletion of matter

7.09   It is sometimes necessary for the patentee to seek to delete passages from the body of the complete specification either by way of consequential amendment following limitation of the claims or to remove passages which cause difficulties of interpretation or lead to possible attacks of invalidity. Such amendments are often put forward as being by way of disclaimer on the basis that they constitute an abandonment of part of the original disclosure. While an amendment which is merely disclaiming some part of the original invention claimed[12] or assists in the

---

[9] *Corning Glass Works Appn.* [1984] R.P.C. 459 at p.463 and see also *May and Baker Ltd. v. Boots Pure Drug Co. Ltd.* (1950) 67 R.P.C. 23 at p.40; *Antiference Ltd. v. Telerections Installations (Bristol) Ltd.* [1957] R.P.C. 31; *Schwank's Patent* [1958] R.P.C. 53; *Baker Perkins Ltd.'s Appn.* [1958] R.P.C. 267.
[10] [1962] R.P.C. 55 at p.71.
[11] See *post*, §7.21.
[12] *Amp. Inc. v. Hellerman Ltd.* [1962] R.P.C. 55.

interpretation of the disclosure[13] is allowable, amendment will not be allowed if it results in the disclosure of a new invention.[14] Deletion of factual statements such as the state of the prior art is not a disclaimer and the Court may not allow amendment by way of disclaimer if the main reason is to remove matter which might give rise to an attack on validity.[15]

Specific disclaimer

It not infrequently occurs that a claim is anticipated by the disclosure **7.10** of an earlier patent or other publication in circumstances where the prior publication can fairly be regarded as accidental or fortuitous in the sense that the publication merely discloses something which falls within the claims of the later patent rather than disclosing the basic invention contained in the patent. It is often impossible to amend the claims to avoid anticipation by such prior art without unduly narrowing the scope of the claims and it is a convenient way to avoid anticipation merely to disclaim what is specifically disclosed in the prior publication. Such an amendment, known as a specific disclaimer, is normally inserted in the body of the complete specification just before the claims. Because such an amendment merely disclaims what is specifically disclosed it will not prevent the patent being found invalid for obviousness unless the nature of the prior disclosure is such that it would not be obvious to modify what is disclosed in any material way. The court will not allow an amendment of this type if it is clear that the amended specification is still invalid for obviousness.[16]

A disclaimer of this type is rarely appropriate to distinguish prior **7.11** publications which are not so old or obscure as to be of no practical relevance. In the early part of the century a specific reference took the form of a statement that the grantee was aware of a particular patent, and did not claim what was therein claimed (or described).[17] A disclaimer, however, is to be regarded as an exception from the monopoly granted and the above form of reference was frequently open to the objection that it introduced ambiguity into the specification.[18] It has, therefore, been the practice for many years to require a precise and accurate statement of what is disclaimed.[19] An example of a typical disclaimer is set out in the report of Official Ruling 1922 (C).[20]

---

[13] *Wilkinson Sword Ltd. v. Gillette Industries Ltd.* [1975] R.P.C. 101.
[14] *Bristol Myers (Johnson & Hardcastle's) Appn.* [1974] R.P.C. 389.
[15] See *post*, §7.24.
[16] See *Esso Research and Engineering Co.'s Appn. for Revocation of Shell's Patent* [1960] R.P.C. 35 and *Holliday & Company Ltd.'s Appn.* [1978] R.P.C. 27.
[17] See, *e.g. Lynde's Patent* (1888) 5 R.P.C. 663.
[18] See *Societe etc. Rhone-Poulenc's Appn.* (1933) 50 R.P.C. 230; see also *British Celanese Ltd. v. Courtauld's Ltd.* (1933) 50 R.P.C. 259 at p.284.
[19] *Societe etc. Rhone-Poulenc's Appn.* (1933) 50 R.P.C. 230; see also *Baker's Appn.* (1934) 51 R.P.C. 145.
[20] 39 R.P.C. Appendix V; see also *Rhone-Poulenc Appn.* (1933) 50 R.P.C. 230.

Correction

7.12   "Correction is to be interpreted as 'a putting right of some mistake that had been made in the preparation of the specification ... ' There are, therefore, two requirements to be met: (1) A mistake must be shown to have been made; (2) The proposed amendment must provide the proper substitute for the mistake so as to insure correctness. So far as the first of these is concerned, a mistake may be so obvious on the face of the document that no evidence would be required to establish its existence. But ... unless and until the court is satisfied by perusal of the documents or by evidence that a mistake has occurred, the right to amend on this ground has not arisen."[21]

7.13   There are a number of ways in which the preparation of a patent specification can go wrong but not all such "mistakes" can be corrected. There have been a number of decisions in which the Courts have attempted to define the type of "mistakes" which can be corrected, and at present the position is not wholly clear. It is however, established that errors of transcription, namely where the words do not express the intention of the inventor or draftsman, are mistakes which can be corrected. On the other hand it has been said that "mistakes" which are essentially errors of judgment cannot be corrected. Thus, a failure to include a particular claim could not be corrected[22] and a wrong formula could not be corrected when it was clear that at the time the specification was drafted the patentee knew it might be incorrect.[23] In the *Distillers* and *Tee-Pak* cases[24] it was suggested that "mistakes" could be divided into errors of transcription and errors of judgment of which only the former could be amended. The accuracy of this classification has been doubted[25] and in at least two cases not followed.[26]

7.14   In the case of *Holtite Ltd. v. Jost (Great Britain) Ltd.*[27] the House of Lords did not deal in the leading opinion with the relevance of how the mistake occurred. It is however clear from the evidence filed and the decisions of the lower courts that in that case there was no error of transcription and the wording of the claim accurately expressed the draftsman's intention. It is submitted that deliberate decisions taken with full knowledge of material facts cannot later be corrected on the ground that they were mistakes. However, only further decision of the courts will clarify the position with regard to mistakes falling between errors of judgment of this nature and pure errors of transcription. Many

---

[21] *Distiller & Co. Ltd.'s Appn.* (1953) 70 R.P.C. 221 at p.223 quoting *National School of Salesmanship v. Plomien Fuel Economiser Ltd.* (1942) 59 R.P.C. 95 at 107.

[22] *Ibid.* and *Tee-Pak Inc.'s Appn.* [1958] R.P.C. 396.

[23] *Zambon S.P.A.'s Patent* [1971] R.P.C. 95.

[24] (1953) 70 R.P.C. 221 and [1958] R.P.C. 396.

[25] *General Tyre & Rubber (Frost's) Patent* [1974] R.P.C. 207 at 228.

[26] *Pittsburg Plate Glass Co. Patent* [1971] R.P.C. 55 and *Holtite Ltd. v. Jost (Great Britain) Ltd.* [1979] R.P.C. 81.

[27] *Ibid.*

of the above mentioned cases were cases concerned with obvious mistakes. This is discussed further *post* § 7.16.

Explanation

As regards "explanation," in *Beck and Justice's Patent*,[28] Sir R. Webster **7.15**
A.-G. said; "My idea of the function of an explanation ... is to explain more clearly what is necessary to understand the meaning of the patentee at the time he patented the invention."

In *Johnson's Application*,[29] Sir S. T. Evans S.-G. said:

> "If a man uses a word in an ordinary sense—using it fairly—and if he finds that by some people ... that word is taken to mean something that he did not intend it to mean, I think ... that it is one of the cases intended to be covered by the first subsection under the word 'explanation'."

In more recent cases, amendment by way of explanation has been allowed to remove possible ambiguity,[30] and to define more clearly what the court held to be the proper construction of a contentious phrase.[31]

Deletion of passages in the body of the complete specification can be allowed as being by way of explanation.[32]

Obvious mistake

As dealt with in more detail below[33] section 31(1) of the 1949 Act **7.16**
prohibits any amendment which has the effect of widening the scope of the patent unless the amendment is by way of amendment of an "obvious mistake". In the leading Opinion in *Holtite v. Jost*, Lord Diplock reviewed the law as follows:[34]

> "The policy of the section is clear. A major purpose of a patent specification is to define the scope of the invention claimed (section 4(3)(c)), so as to give public notice of the limits of the monopoly claimed. An amendment, if allowed, is retrospective to the date of filing the complete specification. So, with one exception, an amendment which enlarged the limits of the scope of the invention claimed would make actionable, *ex post facto*, what at the time when it was

---

[28] Griff. L.O.C. 10.
[29] (1909) 26 R.P.C. 780 at p.783. See also *Merck & Co. Inc.'s Appn.* (1952) 69 R.P.C. 285.
[30] *Polymer Corporation Patent* [1972] R.P.C. 39.
[31] *General Tyre and Rubber Plant* [1974] R.P.C. 207 and *J. Lucas (Batteries) Ltd. v. Gaedor* [1978] R.P.C. 297 at pp.346–350; see also *Roussel Uclaf V.I.C.I.* [1991] R.P.C. 51.
[32] *Polymer Corporation Patent* [1972] R.P.C. 39, but see *Corning Glass Works Appn.* [1984] R.P.C. 459 at p.466; and see *ante*, §7.09.
[33] See *post*, §7.21.
[34] [1979] R.P.C. 81 at p.91.

done the doer had no reason to suppose amounted to an infringement of the patentee's rights. An amendment that would have this effect is what is forbidden by the section. The one exception is where the amendment is for the purpose of correcting an 'obvious mistake'; but this exception is not in conflict with the policy disclosed by the remainder of the section, since if the mistake was obvious, it cannot have misled. In the context of correcting it, the natural meaning of the expression 'obvious mistake' is that: what must be obvious is not simply that there has been *some* mistake but also what the mistake is and what is the correction needed. But the correction needed does not fail to be obvious merely because, as a matter of drafting, there is more than one way of expressing it without affecting its meaning. Furthermore, having regard to the function of the specification as a warning to the public of the limits of the monopoly claimed, the mistake must be apparent on the face of the specification itself to an instructed reader versed in the particular art to which the invention relates. If beyond such evidence of the relevant art as may be needed to equip the court with the knowledge that would be possessed by the instructed reader, some other evidence extraneous to the specification is required to show that there has been a mistake in expressing the real intention of the inventor, the mistake is not an 'obvious mistake' within the meaning of the section."

7.17   It follows from the above that, apart from the fact that the "mistake" must be one that can be regarded as a mistake within the meaning of the section,[35] if the amendment is a widening amendment not only the mistake but also the necessary correction must be obvious to the skilled reader. The application of these requirements is illustrated in a number of cases.[36] The knowledge and diligence which must be attributed to the hypothetical skilled reader is considered in *P.P.G. Industries Inc.'s Patent*.

Not in substance disclosed in specification before amendment

7.18   As previously stated, by virtue of section 31(1) of the 1949 Act, an amendment is not allowable (except by way of correction of an obvious mistake) the effect of which would be that the specification would claim or describe matter not in substance disclosed in the unamended specification. While there have been many cases where there has been a dispute as to whether the matter sought to be added by amendment was disclosed in the unamended specification, the general principle is clear.

---

[35] See *ante*, §7.12.

[36] *Pittsburg Plate Glass Co.'s Patent* [1971] R.P.C. 55; *Zambon, S.P.A.'s Patent* [1971] R.P.C. 95; *Chevron Research Co.'s Patent* [1970] R.P.C. 580; *Union Carbide Corporation Appn.* [1969] R.P.C. 362; *General Tyre & Rubber Co. Patent* [1972] R.P.C. 259; *Farmhand Inc. v. Spadework Ltd.* [1975] R.P.C. 617; *Holtite v. Jost* [1979] R.P.C. 81; and *P.P.G. Industries Inc.'s Patent* [1987] R.P.C. 469.

A patentee cannot after acceptance of his complete specification seek to improve the patent by adding matter which was not in fact originally disclosed. Were this not the case a patentee might add matter devised a long time after the priority date of his patent. The requirement of section 31(1) is often referred to as a requirement that there must be a fair basis for the amendment of the unamended specification. These words in fact are contained in the 1949 Act in one of the grounds of invalidity[37] and in the requirement that the complete specification must be fairly based on the original provisional specification or convention document.[38] As a result, there has been a tendency to cite cases on whether complete specifications were fairly based on provisionals or convention documents[39] as authorities relevant to "fair basis" for amendments and it has been recognised by the Court of Appeal that the tests are basically the same.[40] The tendency of the Courts in older cases was to apply the requirement for "fair basis" strictly against the patentee. However, this approach has become progressively relaxed and it was stated by the Court of Appeal in *Ethyl Corporation's Patent*: (*per* Salmon, L.J.),

"From 1883 until after the end of the last war, the courts tended to regard patent monopolies with some disfavour as being generally contrary to the public interest. Since, at any rate, 1949, the climate of opinion has changed. It is now generally recognised that it is in the public interest to encourage inventive genius. Accordingly the modern tendency of the courts has been to regard patent claims with considerably more favour than formerly,"[41]

and (*per* Denning, M.R.): "Section 31(1) should be given a liberal interpretation so as to permit any fair amendment which has already been in substance disclosed."[42]

Whether or not a feature sought to be added is in substance disclosed **7.19** turns on the facts of the particular case, and reference to other decisions is often not very helpful. Reference should, however, be made to *Windsurfing International Inc. v. Tabur Marine (G.B.) Ltd.*[43] where the Court of Appeal refused to allow an amendment limiting the monopoly claimed in the broadest claim to a feature claimed in a subsidiary claim. This was on the grounds that the particular feature was disclosed as being non-essential and the proposed amendment would not simply "amend the specification but turn it on it's head".[44]

The main area of difficulty arises out of amendments known as **7.20**

---

[37] s.32(1)(*b*).
[38] s.5(2).
[39] See *e.g. Mond Nickel Co.'s Appn.* [1956] R.P.C. 189; *I.C.I.'s Appn.* [1960] R.P.C. 223 and *Hercules Inc.'s Appn.* [1968] R.P.C. 203.
[40] *Ethyl Corporation's Patent* [1972] R.P.C. 169 at 194.
[41] [1972] R.P.C. 169 at 193.
[42] *Ibid.* at p.195.
[43] [1985] R.P.C. 59.
[44] *Ibid.* at p.82.

"intermediate generalisations". Such an amendment was the subject of the *Ethyl* case quoted above. In the claim sought to be amended a compound was merely required as being present in the combination. By the amendment, the patentees sought to limit the presence of the compound to a given numerical range of 20 per cent. to 80 per cent. of another constituent. In the unamended specification the range as such was not specified but examples were given having percentages falling within the range. The court held that the unamended disclosure could be regarded as fairly disclosing the whole range and that it was therefore permissible to disclaim down to such a limited range. This decision has made it much easier for patentees to reduce their monopoly by reference to a generalisation of some specific examples given in the unamended specification.[45] Although the amendment must be based on the disclosure, it need not be derived from features stated to be inventive.

Within scope of one claim of unamended specification

7.21   Save for an amendment to correct an obvious mistake, the amended claim must be within the scope of at least one unamended claim. This means that the amendment must only add limitations to the claim. The fact that several limitations have been added to a claim does not justify removal of a limitation in the unamended claim.[46]

Discretion

7.22   Both the court and the Comptroller have a discretion to refuse to allow amendment by virtue of the word "may" in sections 29 and 30 of the 1949 Act. The court's discretion is generally exercised taking into account two factors, the effect of the amendment on the validity or intelligibility of the patent and the conduct of the patentee.

Vagueness or ambiguity

7.23   Where an amendment is of a vague nature and would create uncertainty as to what the new claim really means it will be refused.[47] If the original claim is ambiguous and susceptible of two interpretations, no amendment will be permitted which gives the patentee the benefit of

---

[45] See, *e.g. Matbro Ltd. v. Michigan (G.B.) Ltd.* [1973] R.P.C. 823; *Screen Printing Machinery Ltd.'s Appn.* [1974] R.P.C. 628 as compared to older view of law set out in *Rose Bros. (Gainsborough) Ltd.'s Appn.* [1960] R.P.C. 247. See also *Stauffer Chemical Co.'s Appn.* [1977] R.P.C. 33.

[46] *Sinkler's Appn.* [1967] R.P.C. 155.

[47] *Parkinson's Patent* (1896) 13 R.P.C. 509 at 514. See also *J. Lucas (Batteries) Ltd. v. Gaedor Ltd.* [1978] R.P.C. 297 at p.350; *I.C.I. Ltd. (Whyte's) Patent* [1978] R.P.C. 11, *Beloit Corporation's Appn.* (No.2) [1974] R.P.C. 478 and see *Hauni-Werke Korber & Co. K.G.'s Appn.* [1982] R.P.C. 327.

the wider interpretation,[48] as this may result in enlarging the scope of the monopoly. Amendment will also be refused if the amendment might affect the construction of some other claim.[49]

Curing invalidity

If the amendment is made to avoid anticipation, obviousness or prior **7.24** claiming, it is not an objection that the amendment will validate the patent and indeed that it is the whole purpose of the amendment. The law is, however, not wholly clear as to whether amendments can be made to cure false suggestions, inutility, failure to disclose best method and insufficiency where the basis of the objection is that the patentee, when making the application, has not been frank or has not given the fullest disclosure required by the Act. In principle it would seem wrong that at least in the more serious cases the patent should be saved by amendment. The court is of course exercising a discretion and it is submitted that minor errors or mis-statements which do not vitiate the whole basis on which the patent was granted should be allowed to be corrected but that no amendment should be allowed to cure cases where there has been a serious failure to comply with the requirements of the Act.[50] This would appear to be supported by what authority there is. Where a patent was revocable on the grounds of fraud, amendment was not allowed to disclaim the parts fraudulently claimed[51] and in another case leave was refused to remove a false suggestion.[52] It has been held that a passage in a specification which is a "definite affirmation of utility" of the invention claimed cannot be removed on the basis that it is a disclaimer[53] and in a more recent case[54] amendment was refused where the patentee sought to delete matter which was embarrassing and might have assisted an attack on the validity of the patent.

Amendment does not cure invalidity

While it is not the normal procedure to attack the validity of a patent **7.25** as it is proposed to be amended (other than in the course of revocation proceedings, see *post* § 7.47) the court or Comptroller will not allow an amendment which still clearly leaves the patent invalid or if what remains is so small as not to warrant the grant of a patent.[55]

---

[48] *Chain Bar Mill Co. Ltd.'s Appn.* (1941) 58 R.P.C. 200 at p.205 and *Union Carbide Corp.'s Appn.* [1969] R.P.C. 530 at p.543.
[49] *Plastic S.A.'s Patent* [1970] R.P.C. 22.
[50] See *Kromschröder's Patent* [1959] R.P.C. 309 and *Great Lakes Carbon Corp.'s patent* [1971] R.P.C. 117 at p.125.
[51] *Ralston's Patent* (1908) 25 R.P.C. 13.
[52] *Parry Husbands Appn.* [1965] R.P.C. 382.
[53] *Antiference Ltd. v. Telerection Installations Ltd.* [1957] R.P.C. 31.
[54] *Union Carbide Corporation's Appn.* [1972] R.P.C. 854.
[55] See (1911) 28 R.P.C. Comptroller's Ruling A; *Great Lakes Carbon Corp.'s Patent* [1971] R.P.C. 117 at p.123; *V.E.B. Pentacon Appn.* [1971] R.P.C. 368 at p.373; *Bristol Myers Co.'s Appn.* [1979] R.P.C. 450 and *Ministry Agriculture's Patent* [1990] R.P.C. 61; see also

Conduct of patentee

7.26   The conduct of the patentee will be taken into account in deciding whether leave to amend should be granted and the merit of the invention is not a relevant consideration.[56] In considering the principles which generally apply a distinction should be made between cases where the amendment is merely to delete invalid claims and cases where the amendment is sought to cure otherwise invalid claims.

Amendment of partially valid patent

7.27   In *Van der Lely (C) N.V. v. Bamfords Ltd.*, the difference between the two types of amendment was stated to be as follows:

"Where a claim has been found to be valid, the patentee has made good his claim to monopoly rights to that extent. But where a claim has been found to be invalid, the patentee has failed and it may well be said that no good reason exists why he should be accorded a second chance."[57]

Section 63 of the 1977 Act[58] provides that relief can be granted in an action in respect of a patent which is "only partially valid" and infringed.[59] Accordingly, where section 63 applies, the court will normally be inclined to permit amendment, at least to the extent of deleting the invalid claims with the necessary consequential amendments unless the patentee's conduct has been such that he ought to be "driven from the judgment seat". In the *Van der Lely* case, Pearson L.J. said:

"The court has to consider and decide whether any, and if so what, amendments should be allowed; and, therefore, if it be shown that the applicant's behaviour in relation to the patent has been so bad that he ought to be driven from the judgment seat, the court can refuse to allow any amendment at all to be made. On the other hand, the court should have regard to the direction given (usually by the same court) under section 62 and would naturally be inclined to allow the amendments necessary for correction of the specification by striking out the invalid claims and making the consequential amendments in the body of the specification and in the valid claims ... I think the

---

Armstrong's Patent, (1896) 13 R.P.C. 501 at p.508; (1897) 14 R.P.C. 747; *Hennebique's Patent*, (1911) 28 R.P.C. 41; *Unifloc Reagents Ltd. v. Newstead Colliery Ltd.*, (1943) 60 R.P.C. 165 at p.178; *Parks-Cramer Co. v. G. W. Thornton & Sons Ltd.* [1966] R.P.C. 99 at p.134.

[56] *Smith Kline & French Lab. Ltd. v. Evans Medical Ltd.* [1989] F.S.R. 561; *Autoliv Development A.B.'s Patent* [1988] R.P.C. 425; *Hsiung's Patent* [1992] R.P.C. 497 (C.A.).

[57] [1964] R.P.C. 54 at p.76.

[58] By Sched. 4(3) of the 1977 Act it is provided that s.63 of the 1977 Act, not s.62 of the 1949 Act, applies to acts carried out after the appointed day.

[59] As to a "partially valid patent" see *Hallen v. Brabantia* [1990] F.S.R. 134.

court should prima facie be disposed to allow such amendments, because if they are not made, the invalid claims will remain in the patent as a potential 'nuisance to industry' as it has been called."[60]

In the *Van der Lely* case the patentee persisted up to the House of Lords in maintaining invalid claims knowing the grounds on which the claims were attacked. It was held, however, that amendment limited to allowing deletion of invalid claims was allowable even after the decision of the House of Lords holding those claims invalid. Recent cases allowing deletion of invalid claims are set out in the footnote.[61] Leave to amend by deleting invalid claims may be granted subject to conditions see *post* § 7.33.

Amendment of invalid patent

Where the amendment is sought to validate claims, the court will   7.28
refuse amendment if they consider the patentee's conduct has been such that as a matter of discretion they should refuse to allow amendment. In earlier cases the court was comparatively strict and would refuse leave to amend if the patentee had shown any lack of diligence or had originally made unduly wide claims.[62] For the last 20 years, however, the courts have been much more liberal in the exercise of their discretion and, as a general rule, the discretion will not be adversely applied unless the patentee had deliberately elected to maintain invalid claims which he knew or should have known required amendment "covetous claiming".[63] The modern attitude was set out by Graham J. in *Matbro Ltd. v. Michigan (G.B.) Ltd.*,[64] " ... mere delay is not, of itself, necessarily sufficient to justify refusal of amendment. There must have been or be likely to be some detriment to the respondents or to the general public caused by such delay before it can be an effective bar to relief." The Learned Judge also stated that there was:

"a clear distinction between instances where a patentee knows of prior art which he genuinely, and quite properly in the circumstances, thinks is irrelevant, and other instances where, though he learns of or has been warned of objections which are available against his patent as a result or prior art, yet he takes no steps to put his specification right by way of amendment, or still worse, knowingly persists in

---

[60] [1964] R.P.C. at pp.73 and 74. See also *Bentley Engineering Co. Ltd.'s Patent* [1981] R.P.C. 361.
[61] *Hallen v. Brabantia* [1990] F.S.R. 134 and *Chiron v. Organon* (Amendment) [1994] F.S.R. 458. See also Chap. 12, §12.251.
[62] See, *e.g. Howlett's Appn.* (1941) 58 R.P.C. 238 (explained in *I.C.I.'s Appn.* [1978] R.P.C. 11) and *Ludington Cigarette Machine Co. v. Baron Cigarette Machine Co.* (1900) 17 R.P.C. 745.
[63] *Smith Kline & French Lab. Ltd. v. Evans Medical Ltd.* [1989] F.S.R. 561; see also *Bentley Engineering Co. Ltd.'s Patent* [1981] R.P.C. 361, *Donaldson Co. Inc.'s Patent* [1986] R.P.C. 1 and *Autoliv Developments A.B.'s Patent* [1988] R.P.C. 425.
[64] [1973] R.P.C. 823 at 833–834.

retaining it in the unamended and suspect form. In the latter cases delay is culpable because potential defendants and the general public are entitled to plan their activities on the assumption that the patentee, though warned, has decided not to amend. If the patentee, by his conduct, lulls the public into a false sense of security he cannot thereafter be allowed to change his mind and ask for amendment, or at any rate without adequate protection being granted to the public."

7.29   This attitude is shown in the cases set out in the footnote[65] and a helpful review of the authorities is set out in *Smith Kline and French Lab. Ltd. v. Evans Medical Limited.*[66] In this case the Court held that even though no member of the public had suffered detriment due to the failure to amend the patent in issue, leave to amend should be refused since it was in the public interest that patents should be amended promptly. In an earlier case,[67] where the patentees persisted up to the House of Lords in seeking to make their claim cover as wide a field as possible and issued advertisements as to a decision of the court which were held to be misleading, permission to amend was refused. It is suggested that such conduct would still lead to refusal of leave. Where a patentee persisted in submitting, on several occasions, amendments which did not distinguish the prior art, as a matter of discretion, leave to make any amendment was refused.[68] It is probably unlikely that amendment will be refused solely because of the original width of the claim unless the patentee had clear knowledge that it could not be supported.[69]

Amendment after Judgment to validate patent other than by deleting invalid claims

7.30   Although by virtue of section 30(1) of the 1949 Act the Court may allow amendment "at any time" and this includes the situation where all claims of the patent in suit have been held invalid there are no recent cases where amendment has been allowed in these circumstances. In *Windsurfing International Inc. v. Tabur Marine (G.B.) Ltd.*[70] the Court of Appeal refused to allow the patentees an opportunity to attempt to amend their patent to produce a valid claim. The Court held that the amendment sought would not be allowable but also indicated that since

---

[65] *Bristol Myers Co. v. Manon Freres Ltd.* [1973] R.P.C. 823; *American Cyanamid's Patent* [1974] R.P.C. 349; *J. Lucas (Batteries) Ltd. v. Gaedor Ltd.* [1978] R.P.C. 301; *General Tyre's Appn.* [1974] R.P.C. 207; *Wilkinson Sword Ltd. v. Gillette Industries Ltd.* [1975] R.P.C. 101; *Bentley Engineering Co. Ltd's Patent* [1981] R.P.C. 361.
[66] [1989] F.S.R. 513.
[67] *British Thomson-Houston Co.'s Patent* (1919) 36 R.P.C. 251.
[68] *Scholl Manufacturing Co. Ltd.'s Appn.* [1974] R.P.C. 383.
[69] *American Cyanamid's Patent* [1977] R.P.C. 349; *Wilkinson Sword Ltd. v. Gillette Industries Ltd.* [1975] R.P.C. 101; *I.C.I.'s Patent* [1978] R.P.C. 11; *Zambon S.P.A.'s Patent* [1971] R.P.C. 95.
[70] [1985] R.P.C. 59.

considering a newly formulated monopoly would require effectively a new trial, the Court "would require considerable persuasion that the imposition upon a successful defendant of such a manifestly inconvenient and oppressive course would be a proper exercise of discretion in an otherwise strong case". In another case[71] the Court of Appeal who had held the patent in suit invalid refused an application to allow the patentees to formulate amendments which might validate the patent. The Court indicated that a question concerning amendment should have been raised earlier than after judgment in the Court of Appeal. It would seem therefore that, except perhaps in a case where there is an obvious amendment which clearly would validate the patent, the Court of Appeal will not entertain an application to amend. It is uncertain whether this attitude will be adopted by the Patents Court but it is very possible that if the amendment proposed would require effectively a new trial the Court might also in its discretion refuse the patentee an opportunity to amend. It follows that Patentees who feel that their existing claims might be found invalid should raise the possibility of Amendment before the trial.

Appeal on discretion

Where discretion has been exercised by a judge, the Court of Appeal will not interfere unless the discretion has been wrongly exercised.[72] But if the judge has attached insufficient weight to any relevant considerations, or has erred in principle or come to a conclusion unsupported by the evidence, then an appellate court will exercise its own discretion which may be in the contrary sense.[73]   **7.31**

Adequacy of original drafting

There is no burden on an applicant in an amendment proceeding affirmatively to establish either good faith, or reasonable skill and knowledge in the original drafting of the complete specification, as an essential pre-requisite for the grant of leave to amend.[74] Although as a matter of discretion leave might be refused where the original drafting was grossly incompetent. The question of the good faith, reasonable skill and knowledge of the original drafting is, however, relevant to the   **7.32**

---

[71] *Proctor & Gamble Co. v. Peaudouce [U.K.] Ltd.* [1989] F.S.R. 614 and see also *British Thomson-Houston Co.'s Patent* (1919) 36 R.P.C. 251.
[72] *Allen v. Doulton* (1887) 4 R.P.C. 377 at p.383; *Lang v. Whitecross Wire & Iron Co. Ltd.* (1889) 6 R.P.C. 570; *Armstrong's Patent* (1897) 14 R.P.C. 747 at p.754 (C.A.); *Ludington Cigarette Machine Co. v. Baron Cigarette Machine Co.,* (1900) 17 R.P.C. 745 (H.L.); *British Thomson-Houston Co.'s Patent* (1919) 36 R.P.C. 251; *Holtite Ltd. v. Jost (Great Britain) Ltd.* [1974] R.P.C. 81.
[73] *Raleigh Cycle Co. Ltd. v. H. Miller & Co. Ltd.* (1950) 67 R.P.C. 226; *Van der Lely (C) N.V. v. Bamfords Ltd.* [1964] R.P.C. 54. *General Tyre (Frost's) Patent* [1974] R.P.C. 207.
[74] *Schwark's Patent* [1958] R.P.C. 53.

question of whether damages will be awarded in respect of any infringement occurring prior to a decision allowing amendment.[75]

Impositions of conditions

7.33   Both the Comptroller and the court have power to impose conditions when granting leave to amend. Although conditions have been imposed[76] (for example, preventing suing for infringements committed prior to the application to amend) this is rarely done and has not occurred in recent cases. As was stated by Graham J. in *Wilkinson Sword Ltd. v. Gillette Industries:*[77]

> "In general, it requires a special case before conditions should be imposed—see *General Tire & Rubber Co. (Frost's) Patent* [1974] R.P.C. 207 at 22. Infringers are normally sufficiently protected by the provisions of section 59(3)[78] which prohibits the award of damages in respect of infringements committed before the date of the amendment, unless the court is satisfied that the original claims were framed with reasonable skill and knowledge. To justify conditions there must therefore be present something abnormal such as, perhaps, acquiescence or bad faith of some kind by the patentee."

In *Hallen v. Brabantia*[79] Aldous J. stated:

> "In my view it is for a defendant to establish that special conditions exist before terms will be imposed or a patentee will be deprived of part of his damages. A patentee who has made an invention, disclosed it to the public in his specification and established that his specification was framed in good faith and with reasonable skill and knowledge is entitled to the full rewards provided by the law unless some special circumstances exist. For instance, it would be right to safeguard a person who has been led by a defect in a patent specification to act to his detriment. Where an amendment is to be made and a defendant establishes no more than he received reasonable advice that a patent was not infringed or was invalid, no limitation on damages or conditions should be imposed. It seems to me that a defendant must also establish that he acted on the advice to his detriment and that the advice given was based in some way upon the defect to be cured by the amendment."

---

[75] s.59(3). See *post* §7.56.
[76] See, *e.g. Dorr Co. Inc.'s Appn.* (1942) 59 R.P.C. 113 at p.118; *Bray v. Gardiner* (1887) 4 R.P.C. 40; *Deeley v. Perkes* (1896) 13 R.P.C. 581; *Ludington Cigarette Machine Co. v. Baron Cigarette Machine Co.* [1900] 17 R.P.C. 214, 745; *Geipel's Patent* (1903) 20 R.P.C. 545; (1904) 21 R.P.C. 379; *Gillette Safety Razor Co. v. Luna Safety Razor Co. Ltd.* (1910) 27 R.P.C. 527; *White's Patent* [1958] R.P.C. 287.
[77] [1975] R.P.C. 101 at p.105.
[78] Now s.62(3) of the P.A. 1977. See *post*, §7.56.
[79] [1990] F.S.R. 134 at p.149.

Further amendments

The fact that an amendment has already been made is not of itself an objection to a subsequent application for a further amendment.[80]

7.34

Amendment after expiry

A patent can be amended after it has expired.[81]

7.35

Amendment to subsidiary claims

Where the broadest claim is amended by disclaimer it may be permissible to add further limitations not added to the broadest claim into dependent subsidiary claims.[82]

7.36

Practice

If an action for infringement or revocation of the patent is pending before the Court an application to amend must be made to the Patents Court.[83] If no such action is pending, the application must be made before the Comptroller.[84] The procedure is different depending on whether the application is made under section 29 or section 30 of the 1949 Act, this is set out below. The general principles set out in § 7.45 *et seq.*, however, apply equally whether the application is before the court or the Comptroller.

7.37

Practice under section 29 of the 1949 Act

The application to amend is advertised by the Comptroller and any person may oppose within one month (with the possibility of an extension of time up to a further three months) from the date of the advertisement.[85] Under the former law an opponent had to establish his locus standi, but this is not required by the 1949 Act.[86] An appeal from the Comptroller lies to the Patents Court.[87]

7.38

Reasons for amendment must be given under section 29(2) which places on the applicant an obligation of revealing fully why he wishes to alter his specification, and an application will be refused for failure to disclose these reasons.[88] It is not the practice to require the reasons for amendment to be inserted in the statutory advertisements.

---

[80] *Chatwood's Patent Safe and Lock Co. v. Mercantile Bank of Lancashire Ltd.* (1900) 17 R.P.C. 23.
[81] *Bristol Myers Co. v. Manon Freres Ltd.* [1973] R.P.C. 823.
[82] *I.C.I.'s Patent* [1978] R.P.C. 11.
[83] P.A. 1949, s.30.
[84] P.A. 1949, s.29.
[85] Patents Rules 1968, r.91(1).
[86] P.A. 1949, s.29(4) but see *Ibid.* r.91(2). And *Braun A.G.'s Appn.* [1981] R.P.C. 21.
[87] P.A. 1949, s.29(5).
[88] *Clevite Corpn.'s Patent* [1966] R.P.C. 100. See also *Waddington Ltd's Patent* [1986] R.P.C. 158.

Where an error in the advertisement was corrected in a subsequent advertisement, the time for entering opposition was held to run from the date of the second advertisement.[89]

Evidence

7.39 The Comptroller normally decides the question upon evidence by statutory declaration, but where necessary takes evidence viva voce.[90] The Comptroller also has power to order discovery, but will not usually do so as the patentee is under a duty to make full and frank disclosure and failure to give voluntary discovery of relevant documents could lead to the amendment being refused as a matter of discretion.[91]

When legal proceedings are pending

7.40 The Comptroller cannot entertain an application to amend the specification while any action for infringement or any proceeding for revocation is pending before the court,[92] although he may correct clerical errors in a specification at any time under section 76 of the 1949 Act.

In *Brooks & Co. Ltd. v. Lycett's Saddle and Motor Accessories Co. Ltd.,*[93] notice of trial in an action for infringement had been given. An order was obtained for the action to stand over generally, with liberty to either party to restore, for a settlement to be arrived at. The negotiations proved abortive, but nothing more was done for two years, when the plaintiffs applied to the Comptroller for leave to amend their specification under section 18 of the Act of 1883, which leave was granted. The defendants afterwards applied to restore the infringement action to the list. On the trial of the action it was contended that this amendment was invalid, as the action had been "pending" at the time. Farwell J. decided that this was so, and allowed the action to stand over with leave to the defendants to apply to the court under section 19 of that Act.

7.41 Where the application for leave to amend had been made under section 18 of the 1883 Act, it was decided that the subsequent institution of legal proceedings did not suspend the application pending before the Comptroller,[94] and the amended specification was to be used in the trial of the action even when the action was brought in consequence of an action to restrain threats made on the strength of the unamended specification.[95] Where an action is settled between the parties but the terms of the settlement have not been made an order of the court by a

---

[89] *Hughes & Co.'s Appn.* (1931) 48 R.P.C. 125.
[90] Patents Rules (1978) s.103.
[91] *Temmler-Werke's Patent* [1966] R.P.C. 187. See *post*, §7.46.
[92] P.A. 1949, s.29(1).
[93] (1904) 21 R.P.C. 651.
[94] *Woolfe v. Automatica Picture Gallery Ltd.* (1903) 20 R.P.C. 177 (C.A.).
[95] *Stepney Spare Motor Wheel Ltd. v. Hull* (1911) 28 R.P.C. 381.

Consent Order or a Tomlin Order, proceedings are still pending for the purposes of section 30.[96] In *ICI Plc v. RAM Bathrooms Plc*[96a] the Patent Court has given guidelines as to the circumstances in which it will continue to entertain applications which were made in actions which have settled. Sections 29 and 30 create complementary and mutually exclusive jurisdictions.

Where notice of an intention to present a petition for revocation was **7.42** given to the proposed respondents, who thereupon made an application to amend to the Comptroller, before the fiat of the Attorney-General (which was then necesary before the petition could be presented) had been obtained, it was held that there were no "proceedings pending"; and the petition was ordered to stand over on an undertaking being given to proceed with due diligence with the application to amend.[97]

Practice under section 30

The practice on application to the court under section 30 is regulated **7.43** by Order 104, rule 3 of the Rules of the Supreme Court. The applicant must give notice to the Comptroller of his intention to apply, accompanied by a suitable draft advertisement, which the Comptroller must insert in the Official Journal (Patents). The advertisement must include identification of the pending proceedings in which leave to amend is proposed to be applied for and set out full particulars of the amendment sought.[98] Any person desiring to oppose the amendment must give notice within 28 days of the publication of the advertisement, and having done so is entitled to be heard upon the motion and to be served with the necessary papers. The applicant then proceeds by motion in the pending proceedings, 35 days after the advertisement has appeared.[99]

The Notice of Motion should ask for directions to be given for the hearing and determination thereof.[1] The Notice of Motion must be served with a copy of the specification as sought to be amended attached thereto.[2] On hearing the motion the court decides whether the application is to be allowed to proceed, and if so, upon what terms.[3] The directions normally given require the service by the patentee of a Statement of Reasons setting out the reasons for seeking the amendments and which should also identify the nature of the amendments sought, that is to say whether they are by way of disclaimer, explanation, etc. the Defendants and Opponents if any are ordered to file a

---

[96] *Critchley Bros. Ltd. v. Engleman & Buckham Ltd.* [1971] R.P.C. 346 and *Congoleum Industries Inc. v. Armstrong Cork co. Ltd.* [1977] R.P.C. 77. See also *Lever Bros. Patent* (1955) 72 R.P.C. 198. and *Cropper v. Smith and Hancock* (1884) 1 R.P.C. 254.
[96a] [1994] F.S.R. 181.
[97] *Re Western Electric Co. Ltd.'s Patent* (1933) 50 R.P.C. 59.
[98] R.S.C. Ord. 104 r.3(1).
[99] *Ibid.* r.3(2).
[1] *Ibid.* r.3(3).
[2] *Ibid.* r.3(2).
[3] *Ibid.* r.3(3).

Statement in Answer setting out their objections to the amendment with liberty to the patentee to file a reply if necessary.

The usual procedure in recent years has been for the court to order the motion and the trial of the action to be heard concurrently since this avoids duplication of evidence and the necessity to "educate" the court twice in the art. If there are a large number of opponents it may exceptionally be more convenient to hear the motion separately from the action but even in such cases it is usually more convenient to hear the trial immediately after the motion. Which course is to be adopted is entirely in the discretion of the judge before whom the motion comes, and the Court of Appeal will not review it.[4] If the motion is heard separately from the trial, affidavit evidence is almost invariably ordered with liberty to cross-examine. If the motion is heard at the trial it is not essential to file affidavit evidence but this is normally done, since it has the advantage of clarifying in advance of the hearing the respective cases as to the allowability of the amendment. Witnesses are normally cross-examined on their affidavits at the hearing of the motion to amend.[5] Provisions are normally made for discovery although this is probably not necessary so far as the patentee is concerned, in view of the onus on the patentee.[6]

7.44   The order made, if leave to proceed with the application is granted, often follows that settled in *Rheinische Gummi und Celluloid Fabrik v. British Xylonite Co. Ltd.*[7] It includes conditions that the patentee will not (pending the application) proceed with any other pending actions for infringement, or threaten other actions and will abide by any terms subsequently imposed as to costs, etc.

Where an injunction had been granted in an action for infringement, and the defendants subsequently petitioned for revocation and the patentees applied in the revocation proceedings for leave to amend, the injunction was dissolved as one of the terms of leave being given,[8] inasmuch as it would be highly inconvenient to try what might be a new issue on a motion to commit for breach of an injunction obtained before amendment.[9] An interlocutory injunction will not be granted if the patentee indicates that he intends to amend the patent in suit.[10]

---

[4] See *British Celanese Ltd. v. Courtaulds Ltd.* (1932) 49 R.P.C. 345.
[5] As to scope of cross-examination on affidavits filed in amendments proceedings at the trial of the action see *E.I. du Pont de Nemours v. Enka A.G.* [1987] R.P.C. 417.
[6] See *post*, §7.46.
[7] (1912) 29 R.P.C. 672 at p.673; see also *Hollandsche (N.V.) Glas-en Metaalbank v. Rockware Glass Syndicate Ltd.* (1931) 48 R.P.C..
[8] *Kennick and Jefferson's Patent* (1912) 29 R.P.C. 25.
[9] See *Dudgeon v. Thomson* (1877) 3 App.Cas. 34 and *PLG Research Ltd v. Ardon International Ltd.* [1993] F.S.R. 698.
[10] *Mölnlycke A.B. v. Proctor & Gamble Ltd.* [1990] R.P.C. 487.

Discretion of Court

The court has an inherent discretion whether or not to allow the **7.45** proceedings for amendment to proceed and as to any terms that should be imposed.[11] But in exercising that discretion a court must act judicially and, if it errs in principle or comes to a conclusion unsupported by the evidence or fails to give due weight to all relevant considerations, then an appellate court will exercise its own discretion.[12]

Duty of full disclosure

A patentee seeking amendment must set out fully all relevant facts in **7.46** the evidence filed in support of the application. In *Chevron Research Company's patent*[13] Mr. Justice Graham stated: "It is essential that those seeking amendment should realise that they have a heavy onus to discharge and can only expect to do so if they have full evidence to prove their case and put the whole story before the court."

It is usual for the patentee to disclose all relevant documents even though some (and in particular the file relating to the application for the patent being amended) are in fact the subject of privilege.[14] Failure to make full disclosure could result in refusal to allow amendments.

Challenging validity

As already mentioned, the court will not allow an amendment which **7.47** clearly does not cure invalidity.[15] However, it is not the normal practice on an application to amend (made other than at the trial of revocation proceedings) to allow the validity of the amended patent to be challenged.[16] Under the 1977 Act it has been held that it is not permissible when deleting claims to allege that the remaining unamended claims should never have been granted.[16a]

Altering amendment

The court or Comptroller may allow amendment in a different form to **7.48** that sought and advertised. If the alteration is substantial it should be re-advertised.[17] Where the amendments proposed (and allowed) on

---

[11] See *Strachan and Henshaw Ltd. v. Pakcel Ltd.* (1949) 66 R.P.C. 49 at p.58; as to costs, see *Leopold Rado v. John Tye & Sons* (1955) 72 R.P.C. 64.
[12] *Raleigh Cycle Co. Ltd. v. H. Miller & Co. Ltd.* (1950) 67 R.P.C. 226; *Van der Lely (C) N.V. v. Bamfords Ltd.* [1964] R.P.C. 54.
[13] [1970] R.P.C. 480 at p.586 approved by Court of Appeal in *S.C.M. Corp. Appn.* [1979] R.P.C. 341; see also *du Pont de Nemours Appn.* [1972] R.P.C. 545, *Smith Kline & French Lab.'s Ltd. v. Evans* [1989] F.S.R. and *Hsiung's Patents* [1992] R.P.C. 497.
[14] P.A. 1977, s.104. And see *Bonzel v. Intervention Ltd.* [1991] R.P.C. 231.
[15] See *ante*, §7.25.
[16] *Great Lake Carbon Corporation's Patent* [1971] R.P.C. 117 and cases cited therein.
[16a] *Chiron v. Organon* (Amendment) [1994] F.S.R. 458.
[17] See, *e.g. J. Lucas (Batteries) Ltd. and Another v. Gaedor Ltd. and Others* [1978] R.P.C. 297 at p.351.

appeal differed from those proposed before the Comptroller, the matter was referred back to the Comptroller to determine whether re-advertisement was necessary, in which case any opponent would have been "at liberty to argue the matter afresh."[18] Having advertised the deletion of certain claims a patentee may not be allowed to withdraw such deletion.[19]

Procedure on allowance of amendment

7.49   The amendment takes effect as from the date of the decision allowing the amendment. If the Comptroller allows amendment, the Patent Office deal with the formalities. If the patent is amended by Order of the Court, a copy of the Order should be lodged with the Comptroller.[20] If the amendment is made under section 30 of the 1949 Act but before trial, leave is usually granted to continue the action (or petition) on the specification as amended, and to make the amendments necessary in the pleadings for that purpose. The form of order usually made follows that settled in *Lilley v. Artistic Novelties.*[21]

Printing

7.50   Amended specifications were formerly printed with the deleted portions shown crossed through and the new wording in italics, but this is no longer done. A statement that the specification has been amended appears on the first page. If the amendments are substantial, the complete specification will be reprinted.

Amendment to delete invalid claims

7.51   As previously mentioned, under section 63 of the 1977 Act relief can be granted in an action in respect of any claim which is valid and infringed.[22] As a condition of granting relief the court may direct that the specification shall be amended upon an application made under section 30 and such an application may be made whether or not all other issues in the proceedings have been determined.[23] There have been cases where the Court of Appeal has itself ordered the amendment to be made, but where there is any difficulty an appellate court would presumably order the application to be made in the High Court, possibly accompanied by an indication of the general kind of amend-

---

[18] *Union Switch and Signal Co.'s Appn.* (1914) 31 R.P.C. 289 at p.293.
[19] *Quantel Ltd. v. Spaceward Microsystems Ltd.* [1990] R.P.C. 83.
[20] R.S.C. Ord. 104 r.3(4).
[21] (1913) 30 R.P.C. 18 at p.20; see also *Hollandsche (N.V.) Glas-en Metaalbank v. Rockware Glass Syndicate Ltd.* (1931) 48 R.P.C. 425; *Haslam Foundry and Engineering Co. v. Goodfellow* (1887) 37 Ch.D. 118 at p.123 and *Gillette Safety Razor Co. v. Luna Safety Razor Co. Ltd.* (1910) 27 R.P.C. 527.
[22] See *ante*, §7.27.
[23] P.A. 1977, s.63(3).

ment that the appellate court would regard as satisfactory.[24] As to procedure on a motion to amend under the corresponding section 62 of the 1949 Act see *David Kahn Inc. v. Conway Stewart & Co. Ltd.*[25]

Costs

Irrespective of whether the amendment sought is allowed or refused **7.52** it is the normal practice for the patentee to have to pay the costs of the defendants and/or opponents,[26] although costs are in the discretion of the court and the court might refuse costs or award reduced costs[27] to an opponent or defendant who made unnecessary and/or trivial objections. Exceptionally, costs may be awarded to the patentee.[27a]

Effect of amendment

Where leave is given to amend under either section 29 or section 30 of **7.53** the 1949 Act, two important consequences follow, *viz.* that the right of the patentee to make the amendment cannot be impeached, and that his right to the recovery of damages is limited in certain respects.

Leave to amend conclusive

Leave to amend granted by the Comptroller or the court is conclusive **7.54** except in the case of fraud.[28] Futhermore, the amendment, for all purposes, is deemed to form part of the specification,[29] so that the amended specification stands in the place of the specification as originally published. The latter may, however, be referred to for the purpose of construing the amended specification[30] and statements in the unamended specification may be relied on as admissions against the patentee's interests.[31]

In *Moser v. Marsden,*[32] Lord Watson said:

"In my opinion, the very object (of the corresponding provision) of the Act of 1883 was to make an amended claim, when admitted by the proper authorities, a complete substitute, to all effects and purposes, for the claim originally lodged by the patentee. The validity of the

---

[24] See *Van Der Lely v. Rustons* [1993] R.P.C. 45.
[25] [1974] R.P.C. 279.
[26] See, *e.g.* *British Thomson-Houston Company's Patent* (1936) 53 R.P.C. 225; *Mullard v. British Helmet Radio* (1938) 55 R.P.C. 197; *Matbro v. Michigan Ltd.* [1973] R.P.C. 823; *Bristol Meyers v. Manon Freres Ltd.* [1973] R.P.C. 836.
[27] See, *e.g.* *Wilkinson Sword v. Gillette Industries* [1975] R.P.C. 101 and *Redifusion Simulation v. Link* [1993] F.S.R. 743.
[27a] *Chiron v. Organon* (Amendment) [1994] F.S.R. 458.
[28] P.A. 1949, s.31(2). See *Trubenising Ltd. v. Steel & Glover Ltd.* (1945) 62 R.P.C. 1 at p.13.
[29] *Ibid.*
[30] *Ibid.* see *Multiform Displays Ltd. v. Whitmarley Display Ltd.* [1957] R.P.C. 260 at p.252 and *Dow Chemical A.G. v. Spence Bryson* [1984] R.P.C. 359.
[31] *Corning Glass Works* and *Corning Ltd.'s Appn.* [1984] R.P.C. 459.
[32] (1896) 13 R.P.C. 24 at p.31.

amended claim must, therefore, be determined in the same way, and on the same footing, as if it had formed part of the original specification; and the claim as it stood before amendment cannot be competently referred to, except as an aid in the construction of its language after amendment."

7.55　　The reasons for an amendment form no part of the amendment itself,[33] and evidence of proceedings on amendment is not admissible upon the question of the true construction of the amended specification.[34] Such evidence might however be relevant if, at a later date, the patentee gave different evidence on, for example, technical questions.

Damages

7.56　　Section 62(3) of the 1977 Act[35] provides that, where a specification is amended, no damages are awarded prior to the date of the decision allowing the amendment unless the court is satisfied that the specification as originally published was framed in good faith and with reasonable skill and knowledge. It was held by Lloyd-Jacob J. in *Ronson Products Ltd. v. Lewis & Co.* that:

"where the drafting of the specification departs in a material respect from the intention of the applicant for protection, and this despite the transmission by the applicant to his patent agent of all relevant information, an acknowledgment of such agent, that the way he expressed himself in the passage in question was wrong in view of the information he had received, must establish the absence of reasonable skill and knowledge."[36]

7.57　　In the *General Tire & Rubber Co. v. Firestone Tyre & Rubber Co. Ltd.,* the Court of Appeal stated:[37]

"Section 59(3) [of the 1949 Act) does not speak of 'reasonable care' but of 'reasonable skill and knowledge.' This we take to be limited to the field of expertise peculiar to those concerned with framing specifications, and in no way to refer to mere commonplace slips which are from time to time the fate of those in many fields remote from patent expertise. A particular lack of reasonable care may in any given case exhibit a lack of reasonable relevant skill, but not in every case by any means, and certainly not in the case suggested."

---

[33] *Cannington v. Nuttall* (1867) L.R. 5 H.L. 205 at pp.227, 228 and *Dow Chemicals v. Spence Bryson* [1984] R.P.C. 359.

[34] *Bowden Brake Co. v. Bowden Wire Ltd.* (1913) 30 R.P.C. 561 at p.571.

[35] By Sched. 4(3) of the 1977 Act, it is provided that s.62 of the 1977 Act not s.59 of the 1949 Act applies to acts carried out after the appointed day.

[36] [1963] R.P.C. 103 at p.138; see also *J. Lucas (Batteries) Ltd. and Another v. Gaedor Ltd. and Others* [1978] R.P.C. 289.

[37] [1975] R.P.C. at p.270.

In the same case, the court also stated:

"On this question of good faith in framing a specification one is, we apprehend, basically in a field of inquiry whether the patentee or his agent knew something detrimental to the patent, as applied for in the form in which the specification was framed, which escaped the eagle eye of the examining officer in the Patent Office. If a patent agent puts forward something of which he had no knowledge, which suffers from some fatal imperfection in the patent field we do not consider that, when the Patent Office accepts it without demur, it can be said that it was framed otherwise than in good faith. It is, after all, the function of a patent agent to argue in honesty for the width of the application."[38]

The fact that the original claim was not "framed in good faith and with reasonable skill and knowledge" does not, however, affect the validity of the patent, after it has been amended.[39] The question under section 62(3) of the 1977 Act is sometimes left to the hearing of any enquiry as to damages. However, at least in cases where amendment is sought in an infringement action it is submitted that it is better practice to hear this question as part of the amendment proceedings since usually the court has most of the relevant facts before it as part of the question of the allowability of the amendment.[40] To recover damages in proceedings where deletion of invalid claims is made pursuant to section 63 of the 1977 Act, the plaintiff must also prove good faith and reasonable skill and knowledge.[41] No mention is made in sections 62(3) and 63(2) of the 1977 Act of proving reasonable skill and knowledge as a prerequisite to obtaining an account of profits and an account will be ordered without reasonable skill and knowledge being proved.[42]   **7.58**

Onus of proof
The onus of proof that the original claim was framed in good faith and with reasonable skill and knowledge lies on the patentee,[43] but it has   **7.59**

---

[38] *Ibid.* at p.269. See also *J. Lucas (Batteries) Ltd. and Another v. Gaedor Ltd.* [1978] R.P.C. 289 *Redifusion Simulation v. Link* [1993] F.S.R. 743. *Hallen v. Brabantia* [1990] F.S.R. 134 and *Chiron v. Organon* (Amendment) [1994] F.S.R. 458. See also chap. 12, §12.251.

[39] See *British United Shoe Machinery Co. Ltd. v. A. Fussel & Sons Ltd.* (1908) 25 R.P.C. 631 at p.660.

[40] See, *e.g. Lucas* case cited above.

[41] P.A. 1949, s.62(2); P.A. 1977, s.63(2) and see *David Kahn Inc. v. Conway Stewart & Co. Ltd.* [1976] R.P.C. 279.

[42] *Codex Corp. v. Racal Milgo Ltd.* [1983] R.P.C. 369.

[43] See *British United Shoe Machinery Co. Ltd. v. A. Fussell & Sons Ltd.* (1908) 25 R.P.C. 368; *British United Shoe Machinery Co. Ltd. v. Gimson Shoe Machinery Co. Ltd. (No. 2)* (1929) 46 R.P.C. 137 at p.164. Relief was granted in the following cases: *Hopkinson v. St. James and Pall Mall Electric Light Co. Ltd.* (1893) 10 R.P.C. 46; *J.B. Brooks & Co. Ltd. v. E. Lycett Ltd.* (1903) 20 R.P.C. 390; *J.B. Brooks & Co. Ltd. v. Rendall, Underwood & Co. Ltd.* (1907) 24 R.P.C. 17.

been said by Greene M.R. that: "good faith and reasonable skill and knowledge would be assumed in the patentee's favour in the absence of internal or external evidence to the contrary."[44]

Correction of clerical errors

7.60   By section 76 of the 1949 Act the Comptroller has power to correct any clerical error in any patent, any application for a patent or any document filed in pursuance of such an application, or any error in the Register of Patents. The clerical error must have occurred in the course of preparation of a document filed in pursuance of an application for a patent and there is no jurisdiction under this section to correct clerical errors made prior to the preparation of such a document (for example, in a research report subsequently included in the body of the complete specification).[45] Thus, it has been held that, where a clerical error in a foreign specification led to the same error in the corresponding British specification, this could not be corrected under section 76.[46] If the Comptroller is of the opinion that the correction applied for would have a material effect on the meaning or scope of the document, and that it should not be made without notice to other persons, he may require notice of the application to be advertised. Any person may oppose, and if an opposition is entered the Comptroller shall give the parties an opportunity of being heard before making the correction. There is no provision in the Act for an appeal from the Comptroller's decision under this section. The procedure is regulated by rules 129 to 132 of the Patents Rules 1968.

2. Amendment Under the 1977 Act

7.61   The amendment of patents granted under the 1977 Act is covered by sections 17, 18, 19, 27, 62, 63, 72, 75, 76[47] and 117 of the 1977 Act. Generally speaking the 1977 Act follows the old law in the following aspects namely procedure, the retrospective effect of amendments, the existence of a discretion whether to allow amendment and in sections 62(3) and 63 discussed above. The major changes brought about by the 1977 Act are:

(a) that the allowability of amendments can be challenged after the decision allowing amendment and form a ground of invalidity,

(b) the requirement that the amendment must be by way of

---

[44] *Molins & Molins Machine Co. Ltd. v. Industrial Machinery Co. Ltd.* (1938) 55 R.P.C. 31 at p.33. See also *General Tire case* [1975] R.P.C. 203 at p.269.
[45] *Mobil Oil Corporation's Appn.* [1974] R.P.C. 507.
[46] *Maere's Appn.* [1962] R.P.C. 182.
[47] As amended by C.D.P.A. 1988 Sched. 5, para. 20.

disclaimer, correction or explanation has been abolished and replaced with a requirement that the amendment must not extend the disclosure of the patent,

(c) amendment of specifications prior to grant and after grant are placed on the same footing, and

(d) the Comptroller has been given wider powers to correct "mistakes" including obvious mistakes.

For the remainder of this chapter references to sections are to the 1977 Act unless otherwise stated.

Pre and post grant

By virtue of section 19 amendment prior to grant is placed on the same **7.62** footing as amendment after grant in that any amendment can be made whether before or after grant provided it complies with the requirements of section 76 dealt with below. There is one important exception to this general statement namely that the prohibition against an amendment which "extends the protection conferred by the patent" only relates to granted patents. It follows therefore that while the prohibition against extending the disclosure applies equally to amendment before and after grant the facility still remains for the patentee to submit different claims in pre-grant proceedings. Thus, in principle there appears to be no objection to a patentee seeking to delete narrow claims and substitute broader ones provided this is carried out before grant and provided new matter is not introduced.[48] Under the 1949 Act considerable latitude was given to the patentee in terms of amendment to the specification, and since the provision of section 76 as to not extending the disclosure is construed strictly there were certainly many instances under the old law where amendments were allowed which would now be contrary to the provisions of section 76. It follows that those preparing patent specifications must be much more careful in pre-grant proceedings as to the nature of the amendments which they seek and indeed should proceed on the basis that it will be impossible to rectify an inadequate disclosure [See *post* § 7.65].

Permissible amendments

As stated above, the 1977 Act has abandoned the requirement that an **7.63** amendment must fall within prescribed definitions and the scheme of the Act is that any amendment is allowable provided it complies with the provisions of section 76(2). By virtue of subsection 2 an amendment is not permissible if it results in the application for the patent "disclosing matter extending beyond that disclosed in the application as filed" or by virtue of subsection 76(3) in the case of a granted patent where the

---

[48] *Southco Inc. v. Dzus Fastener European Ltd.* [1992] R.P.C. 299 and see *post*, §7.65.

amendment "(a) results in the specification disclosing additional matter or (b) extends the protection conferred by the patent."

In addition to the requirements of section 76[49] the amended specification must continue to comply with the requirements of section 14(5) of the Act.[49a]

Section 76(3)(*b*)

7.64   At least on its face the requirement of section 76(3)(*b*) seems comparatively straightforward and would seem simply to be a prohibition against any amendment which widened the scope of the claims. Generally speaking in terms of practical effect it is submitted the section will be construed by the courts as having the same effect as the provisions against widening the claim under the 1949 Act. It should be borne in mind however, that if the provisions of section 125 of the Act referred to *ante*,[50] are interpreted so that the disclosure in the body of the specification affects the construction of the claims, amendment to the body of the specification could result in a widening of the scope of the claims. While in most cases an amendment to the body of the specification which could affect the construction of the claims in a widening manner would be contrary to the requirement that the disclosure should not extend beyond that disclosed in the unamended specification, there could be cases where deletion of matter, which was not prohibited as extending the disclosure, could widen the claims. Section 76 does not contain any requirement that the scope of the new claim should fall wholly within the scope of at least one unamended claim however it is submitted that such a claim, not meeting this requirement, must extend the protection conferred by the patent since it would make an infringement something which would not otherwise have been an infringement. It would seem therefore that apart from an amendment to clarify what was already claimed and correction of an obvious mistake discussed below,[51] a permissible amendment to the claims must necessarily be what is regarded as a "disclaimer" under the 1949 Act.

7.65   Section 76(2) and (3)(*a*)

The requirement that the amended application or specification should not disclose matter which extends beyond that previously disclosed has now been interpreted by the Court and the Patent Office in a number of decisions.[52] These decisions show that the section is to be

---

[49] See *post*, §7.65.
[49a] *Genentech Inc.'s Patent* [1989] R.P.C. 147, *Sheving Biotech Corp.'s Appn.* [1993] R.P.C. 249 and *Chiron v. Organon* (Amendment C.N.).
[50] See *ante*, §6.38.
[51] See *post*, §7.78.
[52] *Protoned's Appn.* [1983] R.P.C. 122, *B&R Relays Ltd.'s Appn.* [1985] R.P.C. 1, *RTL Contactor Holding's Appn.* [Unrep., Patents Court, 1983], *Raychem Ltd.'s Appn.* [1986] R.P.C. 547, *Van der Lely's Appn.* [1987] R.P.C. 61, *Southco v. Dzus Fasteners Ltd.* [1992] R.P.C. 299,

interpreted strictly and the crucial question is "whether any subject matter relevant to the invention has been added whether by deletion or addition".[53] Thus, in *Protoned's Application* an amendment to delete the requirement that a spring be a compression spring was held to be a widening amendment since the unamended specification did not disclose the possibility that any sort of spring other than a compression spring be used. Similarly, in *RTL Contactor* deletion of a requirement that a particular device had tie bars was held to be extending the disclosure since the unamended specification did not describe a device without tie bars. In *Raychem's Application* an amendment to omit the necessity of a final process step was disallowed since there was no disclosure in the overall process described that the last step could be omitted. In *Van der Lely's Application* an amendment to claim as a separate invention a part of a hay baling machine was refused since the specification did not disclose the existence of the particular feature independently of the total machine disclosed in the specification.

These decisions and the others referred to in the footnotes show that, apart from disclaiming amendments which limit the monopoly claimed and amendments to correct an obvious mistake, the power to amend is extremely limited and it is difficult to envisage how any amendment to make good any inadequacies of description or to introduce intermediate generalisations[54] can be made. It has, however, been held by the EPO that it is permissible to add references to prior art, although clearly even here there are dangers that new matter may be added, for example, by pointing out advantages of the invention over the prior art. It may also be possible to delete material such as a description of the prior art in circumstances where this would not have constituted a disclaimer or explanation under the 1949 Act [see *ante* § 7.09].

7.66 In view of the danger that the patent may be invalidated by a widening amendment [see *post*, § 7.69] clearly the greatest care will be necessary when seeking amendments. In *Hallen v. Brabantia*[55] the change of wording from a requirement that a first member be carried "on" a second member, to a requirement that the first member be carried "by" the second member was suggested to be a widening amendment. The Court held on the facts of the case that the skilled reader would attach no significance to the change of wording but the case illustrates the potential dangers of even comparatively innocuous amendments.

In *A.C. Edwards v. Acme Sign & Displays Ltd*[56] the Defendants unsuccessfully argued that amendments made to claim 1 of the patent in suit, which were generalisations on what was specifically described, constituted an extension of the disclosure in the application as filed. The

---

Bonzel v. Intervention [1991] R.P.C. 553, See also *Glatt's Appn.* [1983] R.P.C. 122, *Chinoin's Appn.* [1986] 39 and *Ward's Appn.* [1986] R.P.C. 50.

[53] *Bonzel v. Intervention* [1991] R.P.C. 553 at p.574.

[54] See *ante* §7.20.

[55] *Hallen Company v. Brabantia [U.K.] Ltd.* [1989] R.P.C. 307.

[56] [1992] R.P.C. 131.

decision can be explained by reference to one of the factual issues. The specification only disclosed an embodiment where there were two studs retaining a particular component. Originally the claim had no limitation to the presence of such studs but by amendment a limitation was introduced that the component was attached by "a stud". It was argued that since a requirement for "a stud" included within its scope a device having only one stud, the amendment to the claim had extended the disclosure of the patent by the additional information that there should be one stud per component. The Court of Appeal held that the mere fact that the amended claim covered such an arrangement within its monopoly did not mean that there was an extension of the disclosure.

Widening claims pre grant

7.67 The application of section 76(2) to pre-grant amendments of claims where the amendment widened the monopoly was considered in *Southco Inv. v. Dzus Fasteners Ltd.*[57] The Court of Appeal held that amendments to claims which deleted integers do not offend against section 76(2) where from the terms of the original disclosure it is quite apparent to the skilled reader that the matter sought to be omitted was not meant to be an essential feature of the inventions. In the same case in the Patents Court[58] Aldous J. held that:

> "it was not material whether pre-grant amendment had the effect of widening or narrowing the monopoly claimed, provided the invention in the amended claim was disclosed in the application when read as a whole. What the Act sought to prevent was a patentee altering his claim in such a way as to claim a different invention from that which was disclosed in the application. Section 76 did not prevent the granted patent claiming a different combination from that in the application if the amended claim had in it the essential elements required by both the application and the specification of the patent to achieve the objects of the invention. The section prevented the patentee disclosing either by deletion or addition any inventive concept which was not disclosed before, but did not prevent him claiming the same invention in a different way."

Approach to be adopted by the Court

7.68 In *Bonzel v. Intervention Ltd.* Aldous J. stated:[59]

> "The decision as to whether there was an extension of disclosure must

---

[57] [1992] R.P.C. 299.
[58] [1990] R.P.C. 587.
[59] *Bonzel v. Intervention* [1991] R.P.C. 553 at p.574.

be made on a comparison of the two documents read through the eyes of a skilled addressee. The task of the Court is threefold:

(a) To ascertain through the eyes of the skilled addressee what is disclosed, both explicitly and implicitly in the application.

(b) To do the same in respect of the patent as granted.

(c) To compare the two disclosures and decide whether any subject matter relevant to the invention has been added whether by deletion or addition.

The comparison is strict in the sense that subject matter will be added unless such matter is clearly and unambiguously disclosed in the application either explicitly or implicitly."

In considering the disclosure in the relevant specification in its original and amended form the claims are part of the relevant disclosures and the status of information in the claims is no different from that in the body of the specification.[60] The principle of there being an implicit disclosure has been recognised by the EPO[61] and has been followed by the Court of Appeal.[62]

Subsequent challenge to allowability of amendments

The Act does not provide for challenging the allowability of amend- **7.69** ments in the sense that if a successful challenge is made the amendments are cancelled and the specification reverts to its unamended form. It is, however, by section 72(1)(d) a ground of invalidity that the matter disclosed in the specification of a patent extends beyond that disclosed in the application for that patent. It is also by section 72(1)(e) a ground of invalidity that the protection conferred by the patent has been extended by an amendment which should not have been allowed. **7.70**

Apart from the question of what is meant by "extends beyond" discussed above, the wording of section 72(1)(d) seems clear and if the result of an amendment is that the disclosure does extend beyond that originally disclosed, the patent will be invalid. Thus, an amendment made at any stage pre or post grant even though allowed by the Office or conceivably the court might later be shown to have been unallowable because of extending the disclosure with the result that the patent will be invalid.[63]

The wording of section 72(1)(e) on the other hand presents difficulties **7.71** in that the wording has no exact counterpart in section 76. Clearly the section is aimed at amendments to a granted patent which widen the scope of the patent. However, the section is not at all clear (unlike section 76(3)(b)) as to whether it is concerned merely with amendments

---

[60] See P.A. 1977, s.130(3), and *Asahi Kasei Kogyo KK's Appns.* [1991] R.P.C. 585.

[61] Decision T 151/84 [1988] 1 E.P.O.R. 29 and *THOMSON-CSF/Spooling process* [1991] O.J. EPO 115.

[62] *A.C. Edwards Ltd. v. Acme Signs & Displays Ltd.* [1992] R.P.C. 131.

[63] See, *e.g. Hallen Company v. Brabantia* [1989] R.P.C. 307; *Bonzel v. Intervention Ltd.* [1991] R.P.C. 553; *Southco Inc. v. Dzush* [1992] R.P.C. 299; *A.C. Edwards v. Acme Signs & Displays Ltd.* [1992] R.P.C. 131.

made after grant or concerns any amendment made to the application which results in a wrongful extension of the protection. It is submitted that the wording is not very apt to cover pre-grant amendments and that the draftsman would have chosen more suitable language if this had been the intention. Further, the wording if strictly construed would appear to be limited to post-grant amendments since the protection conferred by a patent does not arise until after grant. It can thus be argued that extending the protection conferred by a patent can only arise by widening amendments after grant. The language is however certainly not clear enough to prevent a wider construction and only a decision of the court will make clear which construction is to be adopted.

7.72   The provision of subsection (*e*) in particular is somewhat unusual since it must be presupposing a wrong decision made by the Comptroller, the Patents Court or conceivably the Court of Appeal. Perhaps this subsection is directed towards cases where a patentee is allowed to amend in circumstances where the tribunal is not given the full facts or is given incorrect facts and at a later date the full facts are put before the tribunal. However, it is submitted the wording is wide enough to cover the case where say the patentee amends before the Comptroller without any third party opposition and the Comptroller wrongfully allows amendment even though the full facts are before him. If at a later date a higher court holds that the decision was wrong, for example because it was wrong in law, it would seem that the patent would be held invalid under subsection (*d*) or (*e*) depending whether the disclosure had been extended or the protection conferred extended.

Under the 1949 Act it was quite common for a patentee intending to sue for infringement to amend his patent before the Patent Office prior to commencing proceedings in the hope that potential defendants would not oppose the amendment thereby facilitating obtaining amendment. This course can still be followed but now the allowability of the amendment can be challenged in sense set out above, patentees will now have to run the risk that if they obtain a questionable amendment this could ultimately rebound on them by leading to the patent being invalidated.

Further amendment to cure invalidity under Section 72(1)

7.73   In many cases it will be impossible to re-amend the specification to remove matter which has created invalidity under Section 72(1)(*d*) or (*e*) without further contravening section 76. There may well, however, be situations where the wrong amendment [for example, a claim which had widened the monopoly] could be removed by amendment. Section 72(4) provides that rather than revoking a patent where it has been established that it is invalid "to a limited extent" the Comptroller may order that the patent be revoked unless within a specified time an application to amend under section 75 be made. In *Harding's Patent*[64] the Comptroller found a patent invalid under section 72(1)(*d*) but allowed the patentee to attempt to cure the invalidity by amendment. The Patents Court, whilst not dealing with the point, apparently upheld the decision by remitting the case back to the Comptroller to consider an application to amend. The Comptroller indicated that amendment would normally be allowed unless bad faith was established.

General practice of court

Many of the general principles as to amendment set out in relation to amendment under the old law will apply to amendment under the 1977 Act[65] thus the comments made in the following paragraphs will apply equally to amendment under the new act: **7.74**

§7.23 (vagueness or ambiguity of amendment)
§7.25 (amendment does not cure invalidity it is designed to cure)
§7.32 (adequacy of original drafting)
§7.34 (further amendments)
§7.35 (amendment after expiry)
§7.36 (amendment to subsidiary claims)

Discretion and condition

Both section 27 (amendment before the Comptroller) and section 75 (amendment before the court)[66] contain the word "may" and it is submitted that the general principles as to discretion set out in relation to amendment under the 1949 Act will continue to apply. Likewise, both sections would seem to allow the imposition of conditions (section 27 expressly makes provision whereas it would seem to be covered by the words "such terms as to costs, expenses or otherwise" in section 75) and again the principles set out in relation to 1949 Act amendments should continue to apply [see *ante* §§7.28, 7.31 and 7.33].   **7.75**

Amendment of partially valid patent

It is submitted that the difference in principle between merely allowing deletion of invalid claims and amendment to produce a valid claim mentioned in *ante* § 7.27 above apply equally to amendments under the 1977 Act.[67]   **7.76**

---

[64] [1988] R.P.C. 515.
[65] *Hallen v. Brabantia* [1990] F.S.R. 134.
[66] See *post*, §§7.87, 7.88.
[67] *Ibid.* and *Chiron v. Organon* (Amendment) [1994] F.S.R. 458.

Discretion where amendment cures invalidity

7.77   Since the grounds on which a patent can be revoked have been reduced by section 72 and objections such as inutility and false suggestion no longer are grounds of invalidity, it is suggested that the question discussed *ante* § 7.23 of whether an amendment which might cure internal deficiencies was allowable as a matter of discretion generally will not arise under the new law. However, the question whether the court will as a matter of discretion allow removal of embarrassing subject matter (normally an acknowledgment of prior art) will still continue unless the court accepts that the law on amendment has been liberalised. Only decisions of the court will show whether the attitude adopted 20 years ago in for example the *Union Carbide* case[68] will still continue.

Obvious mistake

7.78   For the reasons set out above, section 76 clearly prohibits any amendment which has the effect of widening the claims. It follows from this that on an application to amend under sections 27 or 75 even the most obvious mistake in the claims cannot be amended if its correction would result in a widening of the claims. Likewise, if the correction results in an extension of the disclosure contrary to subsection 2 of section 76 it will be prohibited no matter how obvious. The Act does appear however to have provided some facility for the correction of obvious mistakes under section 117 discussed in the next paragraph.

Section 117

7.79   This section provides that:

"the Comptroller may, subject to any provision of rules, correct any error of translation or transcription, clerical error or mistake in any specification of a patent or application for a patent or any document filed in connection with a patent or such an application."

The rules provided under this section are contained in rule 91 of the 1990 Patents Rules. Apart from setting out the procedure for an application under section 117, subrule (2) provides that where a request for the correction of an error relates to a specification of a patent "no correction shall be made therein unless the correction is obvious in the sense that it is immediately evident that nothing else would have been intended than what is offered as the correction." Subsections (2) and (3) of section 76 do not extend the effect of that section to section 117 and it would, therefore, seem to follow that provided the correction sought is obvious in the sense set out by subrule (2) provision is made in the Act for the

---

[68] [1972] R.P.C. 854.

correction of obvious mistakes including mistakes the correction of which would widen the claim.

Interpretation of subrule (2)

The subrule does not state to whom the mistake must be immediately **7.80** evident. However, it is submitted that, as with questions of obviousness, the person to whom the question should be directed is the notional addressee namely a person skilled in the relevant art. Further, the subrule does not make it clear as to what material can be considered in deciding whether a mistake is immediately evident. For example, if the question must be answered on the face of the specification alone, a given mistake may well not be self-evident but would be self-evident if the notional addressee could consider, for example, assuming an error of transcription had occurred the original document which had been wrongly transcribed.[69] The requirement that the mistake must be obvious only relates to correction of errors in the specification of a patent and it is submitted that the courts are likely to interpret the subrule on similar lines to obvious mistake under the old law namely that the mistake must be obvious on the face of the document.[70] If the subrule were to be construed broadly allowing amendment where a mistake was only immediately obvious having seen all relevant documents, the public would not be protected in that the error would not be immediately self-evident on considering the specification alone. It is to be noted that the requirement as to the obviousness of the mistake only relates to a granted patent and therefore all other mistakes presumably can be corrected merely on proof that a mistake has occurred.

Errors of translation or transciption

In so far as the section allows for correction of errors of translation or **7.81** transcription or clerical errors the jurisdiction seems clear in that the types of mistakes are identified. However, the reference to the word "mistake" is not qualified in any way and problems are likely to arise as to what other types of "mistake" can be corrected under this section. Insofar as the mistake can be corrected under section 27 or 75 being allowable under section 76 no difficulty will probably arise in practice. It is possible, however, that an attempt could be made under section 117 to obtain an amendment which would otherwise be prohibited as extending the disclosure or extending the protection. In such circumstances the question will arise as to the type of mistake that can be corrected. It is, therefore, possible that similar questions to those arising

---

[69] See *Antiphon A.B.'s Appn.* [1984] R.P.C. 1 where the Patent Office held that the question must be answered on the face of the specification alone; see also *Dukhouskoi's Appn.* [1985] R.P.C. 8 and *Celtrix Lab's Appn.* [1991] O.J. 3/1993, case 125.
[70] See *ante* §7.16.

under section 31 of the 1949 Act will arise as to whether matters such as errors of judgment can fairly be regarded as mistakes. Pending a decision of the court it is suggested that by "mistake" is meant the type of mistake which could be corrected as an obvious mistake under the old law. This is considered *ante* § 7.12.

The effect on third parties of an amendment under this section is discussed below. A new subsection (3A) has been added to section 15 allowing an application under sections 117(1) to correct errors or mistakes with respect to the filing of drawings.[71]

Translations

7.82   Apart from the general power under section 117 to correct errors of translation, the Act contains special provisions for correcting errors of translation of European Patents (U.K.) which are not processed in English. Section 77(6) provides that a European Patent (U.K.) published in French or German will not have validity in this country unless a translation of the specification into English is filed at the patent office. Likewise, section 78(7) requires filing of a translation into English of the claims of a European Patent application in French or German in the circumstances set out in that subsection. If errors in such translations occur, by section 80(3) provision is made for the filing of corrected translations. Section 80(4) contains provisions protecting persons whose action only became an infringement as a result of correction of a translation provided such acts were commenced prior to the publication of the corrected translation.

7.83   It is to be noted that section 117 contains the word "may" and it is suggested that the general principles of the application of discretion apply equally to amendment made under this section.

7.84   The power to revoke under section 72(1)(*e*) mentioned above does not make any exception for amendments made under section 117 and it is submitted that an unlawful amendment made under this section will, as with an unlawful amendment made under section 27 or 75, result in the patent being invalid.

3. Practice

7.85   As mentioned above, apart from amendment pre-grant the procedure in applying for amendment is generally similar to that under the 1949 Act and there are two routes for making amendments namely before the Comptroller or the court as under the 1949 Act. However, whereas under the old law application could not be made to the Comptroller if infringement or revocation proceedings were pending, under the new

---

[71] C.D.P.A. 1988, Sched. 5, para. 2, reversing the decision in *Autophon A.B.'s Appn.* [1984] R.P.C. 1.

Act, (under section 27(2)) application to the Comptroller is only prohibited if proceedings are pending before the Court or Comptroller "in which the validity of the patent may be put in issue". Strictly speaking, any proceedings prior to judgment for infringement are proceedings in which validity might be put in issue. However, section 75 only allows application to the court or Comptroller to amend an infringement proceedings in which validity is put in issue. It follows therefore that unless a common sense approach is adopted to the meaning of section 27(2) a patentee involved in an infringement action might find that he cannot amend under section 75 because validity is not in issue and likewise cannot amend under section 27 because validity could conceivably be put in issue. It is submitted that the only sensible interpretation must be that amendment can be made under section 27 as long as there are no proceedings in being in which validity has been challenged on the pleadings. There is a change in procedure under the provisions allowing the hearing of infringement and revocation pro-ceedings before the Comptroller in that by virtue of section 75 the Comptroller may allow an amendment in the course of the proceeding before him for infringement or revocation. This procedure did not exist under the old Act.

Subject to the difficulties of construction concerning section 27(2) it is submitted the general law in deciding whether proceedings are pending as set out *ante*, §§ 7.40–42 will still apply.

Amendment before grant

The procedure is governed by rule 36 of the 1990 Patents Rules. **7.86** Amendment cannot be made prior to being informed under section 17(5) of the Examiner's report unless required by the Comptroller. After receipt of the report under section 17(5) and before receipt of the first report of the Examiner under section 18 the applicant may amend the specification without formality. After receipt of the report under section 18 the applicant can amend once at the time of replying to a report under section 18(3) or within two months of a report under section 18(4) being sent to the applicant. Any further amendment may only be made with the consent of the Comptroller and the application must be made on form 11/77 which requires the applicant to give reasons for seeking the amendments sought. Applications to amend under rule 36 must be made before the issuing by the Patent Office of the letter notifying the applicant that the application was in order and that a patent had been granted.[72]

---

[72] Patents Rules 1990, r.40(1).

Practice under section 27

7.87   The procedure is governed by rule 40 of the 1990 Patents Rules. The application to amend is advertised by the Comptroller[73] and any person may oppose within two months from the date of the advertisement in the journal.[74] Neither the Act nor the rules appear to make any provision requiring an opponent to show that he has a locus standi.

The rules do not provide that reasons for seeking the amendment must be given, but form 14/77 which must be used to make the application does require a statement as to the reasons for making the amendment. The rules also require, in the case of an opposition, the filing of a statement setting out the grounds of opposition and a counterstatement by the applicant for amendment. It is suggested that the general principles set out in §§ 7.38 and 7.39 above continue to apply.

Practice under section 75 in Patents Court

7.88   The practice is governed by order 104 rule 3 of the rules of the Supreme Court and is identical to the practice under section 30 of the 1949 Act set out *ante* § 7.43.

Procedure under section 75 before Comptroller

7.89   Amendment before the Comptroller under section 75 is governed by rule 78 of the 1990 Patents Rules. The rule states that where a proposed amendment is advertised notice of opposition shall be filed within two months from the date of the advertisement accompanied by a statement setting out the grounds of opposition and that thereafter the Comptroller shall give such directions as he may think fit with regard to the subsequent procedure. The rule does not actually provide that the amendment be advertised. Presumably the application to the Comptroller should be made in accordance with the provisions of rule 40 although that rule is headed merely in relation to applications under section 27. Alternatively the general discretion given to the Comptroller in the conduct of infringement or revocation proceedings before him by rules 72 to 76 would allow the Comptroller to make a similar direction. Nevertheless, on the face of it the rules seem deficient in not specifically providing for procedural requirements such as advertisement in proceedings before the Comptroller under section 75.

General procedural practice

7.90   It is suggested that the general practice set out in relation to amendment under the old law will apply to amendment under the 1977

---

[73] *Ibid.*, s.78(1).

Act. Thus, the comments made in the following paragraphs will apply equally to amendment under the 1977 Act:

§7.43 (Directions given by court)
§7.45 (Discretion of court)
§7.46 (Duty of full disclosure)
§7.47 (Challenging validity)
§7.48 (Altering amendment)
§7.49 (Procedure on allowance)
§7.50 (Printing)
§7.52 (Costs)

Amendment to delete invalid claims

As previously mentioned, under section 63 of the Act relief can be **7.91** granted in an action in respect of a partially valid patent which is infringed. As a condition of granting relief the court may direct that the specification be amended upon an application made under section 75 and such an application may be made whether or not all other issues in the proceedings have been determined (section 75(3)). As to the general procedure see *ante* § 7.51.

Conclusiveness of leave to amend

As previously mentioned, under the Act amendment can be chal- **7.92** lenged if it results in the patent being invalidated on the grounds of making an unlawful amendment. Unless however it can be shown that the amendments were contrary to section 76, amendments made under section 27 or section 75 "shall have effect and be deemed always to have had effect from the grant of the patent".[74] Subject to the invalidity question it is suggested that the principles set out in §7.53 above likewise will apply after amendment of patents under the 1977 Act. The Act does not in terms state what is the effect of an amendment under section 117. However, it is submitted, that it will have the same effect as an amendment made under section 27 or 75.

Damages

Section 62(3) is in identical terms to section 59(3) of the 1949 Act and **7.93** the comments in §§7.56 to 7.59 above apply equally to the question of damages after amendment under the 1977 Act.

---

[74] P.A. 1977, s.27(3), 75(3).

Double Grant

7.94   An amendment can be made to overcome an objection of double grant under section 73 of the 1977 Act.[75]

Amendment of European Patent (U.K.)

7.95   After grant, European Patents (U.K.) are treated as if they had been granted in pursuance of an application made under the 1977 Act.[76] It follows that after grant European Patents in so far as they relate to the United Kingdom are amended in exactly the same way and with the same consequences as amendments of patents granted under the 1977 Act.

Amendments of European Patents and applications before EPO

7.96   Prior to grant European Patent applications can be amended in accordance with the same principles as amendment under the 1977 Act.[77] During the course of any opposition before the EPO[78] after grant a European Patent can also be amended.[79] If a European Patent is amended, the amendment takes effect in the United Kingdom as if it had been made under the 1977 Act and in particular the provisions of sections 62(3) and 63(1) and (2) will apply.[80] The procedure on applying to amend is governed by the E.P.C. Rules 49(3) and 86 to 88. After amendment in an opposition the European Patent is republished.[81] There are translation requirements where the amendment was made in French or German which must be complied with before any such amendment becomes effective in this country.[82]

---

[75] *Turner & Newall Ltd.'s Patent* [1984] R.P.C. 49.
[76] P.A. 1977, s.77(1).
[77] See E.P.C. Art. 123, and E.P.C. Rule 88, P.A. 1977, ss.76 and 117; and *Appeal Practice Decision No. 4* [1981] R.P.C. 80.
[78] See *ante* §7.05.
[79] E.P.C. Arts 102 and 103.
[80] P.A. 1977, s.77(4).
[81] E.P.C. Art. 103.
[82] P.A. 1977, ss.77(4) and (6) as amended by C.D.P.A. 1988, Sched. 5, para. 21.

CHAPTER 8

DEVOLUTION, ASSIGNMENTS AND LICENCES, CO–OWNERSHIP AND REGISTRATION

The provisions of the 1949 Act relating to the subjects covered by this **8.01** chapter have all been repealed and the statutory law is now contained in the provisions of the 1977 Act.

1. Devolution

The applicant and the patentee

Upon publication of the application for a patent the Comptroller **8.02** causes the name, etc., of the applicant or applicants to be entered in the Register of Patents, which is kept at the Patent Office,[1] and upon grant of the patent the Comptroller also causes the name, etc., of the grantee or grantees to be entered if different to that of the applicant.[2]

The Register is only prima facie evidence of anything required to be **8.03** registered under the Act.[3] Accordingly registration as applicant or as proprietor is not proof that the person registered is entitled to be granted a patent or is in fact the proprietor of the patent.[4] The right to sue for infringement of the patent is vested in the proprietor as opposed to the person registered as the proprietor.[5]

---

[1] Patents Rules 1990, r.44(2).
[2] Patents Rules 1990, r.44(3)(*d*).
[3] P.A. 1977, s.32(9), as amended by Patents, Designs and Trade Marks Act 1986 hereafter "P.D.M.A. 1986", s.1, Sched.1, para.4.
[4] See also P.A. 1977, s.7(4).
[5] P.A. 1977, s.61.

Devolution of patents and applications

8.04   Any patent or application for a patent is personal property (without being a thing in action)[6] and may be transferred by assignment[7] or vested by operation of law (as on death or bankruptcy) in the same way as any other personal property.[8]

8.05   Unlike the 1949 Act[9] the 1977 Act does not contain any provision to the effect that, subject to the equities, the person registered as proprietor of the patent has title to assign the same or grant rights under the patent. Protection of persons taking an assignment from the proprietor of a patent or from an applicant is provided for by the provisions relating to conflicting transactions set out below[10] which require that assignments of patents and applications be registered if the assignee is not to be prejudiced. It is to be noted that the Act contains no definition as to who is the proprietor of the patent and in particular the Act does not provide that the proprietor is the registered proprietor. It is suggested, however, that the proprietor of the patent can only be the original grantee or grantees or a person who obtains title to the patent by an assignment which meets the requirements of the Act.[11]

Devolution on death or dissolution

8.06   The property in a patent or application passes, by operation of law, when the proprietor or applicant dies, or becomes bankrupt, or, in the case of a company, is dissolved. Upon the death of a proprietor or applicant his interest in the property passes to his executors or administrators, as the case may be, in a like manner to the rest of his personal estate, that is to say, upon trust to fulfil the provisions of the will, or, in the case of intestacy, upon trust for sale with power to postpone such sale.[12] If, however, the proprietor or applicant dies intestate and without any next of kin the patent or application, as the case may be, vests in the Crown as *bona vacatia*.[13]

As to devolution on the death of a co–proprietor of a patent or application, see *post*, § 8.90.

8.07   Any step which by the Act is required to be taken by the proprietor of a patent or application may be taken by his Executor or Administrator; and an application for a patent may also be made by (and the patent granted to) the successor of any deceased person who, immediately before his death, was entitled to make such an application.[14] A patent or

---

[6] P.A. 1977, s.30(1).
[7] P.A. 1977, s.30(2).
[8] P.A. 1977, s.30(3).
[9] P.A. 1949, s.74(4).
[10] See *post*, §8.27.
[11] See *post*, §8.24.
[12] See Administration of Estates Act 1925, s.33(1).
[13] See Administration of Estates Act 1925, s.46(1)(vi), and Inheritance (Provision for Family and Dependants) Act 1975, s.24.
[14] P.A. 1977, ss.7(2)(c), 8(8), and 30(3).

an application may be vested by an assent of person representatives.[15] The assent will be void unless in writing.[16] The death of the proprietor of a patent or application and the vesting by an assent of personal representatives are events to which section 33 applies,[17] and should be registered without delay to prevent loss of rights in an infringement action.[18]

If a limited company is the proprietor of a patent or application (or a   8.08 patent or application is held in trust for it) and is dissolved without having assigned such property, it vests in the Crown as *bona vacantia*.[19] It has been held that in the case of a patent there is no merger in the Crown in these circumstances because the monopoly right given by the patent "is not a right against the Crown only; but is a right to prevent others from using the invention".[20] Where, however, the company at the time of its dissolution holds the patent or application as a trustee for some other person, the property does not vest in the Crown as *bona vacantia*,[21] and the court may make a vesting order vesting the rights in such person as the court may appoint.[22]

Charges on patents, or on licences under patents, by a limited   8.09 company will be void against the liquidator and the creditors unless such charges are registered with the Registrar of Companies within 21 days of being created.[23] If the charge is already in existence when the patent or licence is acquired by the company, the company must furnish particulars to the Registrar of Companies (for the purpose of registration) within 21 days of acquiring the patent or licence concerned.[24] As to the registration of mortgages, etc., in the Register of Patents, see *post*, §§ 8.93 to 8.95.

Bankruptcy

Patents and applications which are the property of a bankrupt pass on   8.10 his bankruptcy to his trustee in bankruptcy.[25] A secret process also has to be disclosed where it is part of the assets and goodwill of a business.[26] The trustee in bankruptcy is also entitled to call for after-acquired

---

[15] P.A. 1977, s.30(3).
[16] P.A. 1977, s.30(6).
[17] P.A. 1977, s.33(3)(*d*).
[18] P.A. 1977, ss.68 and 69(1).
[19] See Companies Act 1985, s.654.
[20] *Dutton's Patent* (1923) 40 R.P.C. 84 at p.86 (dissenting from *Re Taylor's Agreement Trusts* (1904) 21 R.P.C. 713); see also *Bates' Patent* (1921) 38 R.P.C. 385, and Law of Property Act 1925, s.185.
[21] See Companies Act 1985, s.654.
[22] See Trustee Act 1925, s.41; see also *ibid.* s.51(1)(ii) and Law of Property Act 1925, ss.9, 181. For vesting orders made under Trustee Act 1893 see, *e.g. Heath's Patent* (1912) 29 R.P.C. 389; *Dutton's Patent* (1923) 40 R.P.C. 84.
[23] Companies Act 1985, s.395(1) and s.396(1)(*j*) as amended by C.D.P.A. 1988, s.303(1), Sched.7, para.31. Note also the prospective amendment by Companies Act 1989, s.93.
[24] Companies Act 1985, s.400.
[25] Insolvency Act 1986, s.306.
[26] See *Re Keene* [1922] 2 Ch. 475; *Cotton v. Gillard* (1874) 44 L.J. Ch. 90.

patents[27] and royalties,[28] but if he fails to call for such patents a bona fide sale for value will be valid against him.[29] A patent held by a bankrupt patentee in trust for others does not pass upon his bankruptcy, even though the cirumstances be such that he is the reputed owner.[30]

Writ of fieri facias

8.11   Under the old law a patentee's right, being merely that of preventing others from working his invention, was a chose in action, and was incapable of seizure under a writ of *fieri facias*.[31] Now that it is specifically provided[32] that a patent is not a chose in action it must be doubtful whether this proposition is still correct. So also in respect of an application for a patent.[33] A receiver will not be appointed in execution of a judgment, at any rate where it is not shown that the patentee is in receipt of profits by way of royalties or otherwise.[34] The extent to which a patentee's right can be said to have "no locality" is, however, doubtful.[35]

Articles manufactured in accordance with a patent can be seized and sold under a writ of *fieri facias*, but such seizure and sale do not give to the purchaser any rights beyond those which he would have acquired in the ordinary way; thus, if a person in possession of a patented chattel has only a limited and personal licence to use it, a purchaser, with notice of such licence, from a sheriff who has seized the article, does not acquire any licence to use it.[36]

Devolution of licences and sub–licences

8.12   Any licence or sub–licence under a patent or application vests by operation of law in the same way as any other personal property and may be vested by an assent of personal representatives.[37]

8.13   The death of a licensee or sub–licensee under a patent or application is an event to which section 33(3) applies. So also is the vesting of any such licence or sub–licence by an assent of personal representatives.[38] It is particularly important to ensure that these events are registered in the

---

[27] Insolvency Act 1986, s.307(1); *Hesse v. Stevenson* (1803) 3 Bos. & Pul. 565 at p.577; approved in *Re Roberts* [1900] 1 Q.B. 122.
[28] See *Re Graydon, ex p. Official Receiver* [1896] 1 Q.B. 417 at p.419.
[29] Insolvency Act 1986, s.307(4); and see *Dyster v. Randall & Sons* [1926] Ch. 932.
[30] Insolvency Act 1986, s.283(3).
[31] *British Mutoscope and Biograph Co. v. Homer* (1901) 18 R.P.C. 177; and see *Edwards & Co. v. Picard* [1909] 2 K.B. 903 at p.905.
[32] P.A. 1977, s.30(1).
[33] *Ibid.*
[34] *Edwards & Co. v. Picard* [1909] 2 K.B. 903 (Moulton L.J. dissenting).
[35] See *English Scottish and Australian Bank Ltd. v. Inland Revenue Commissioners* [1932] A.C. 238, overruling *Smelting Co. of Australia Ltd. v. Commissioners of Inland Revenue* [1897] 1 Q.B. 175; and cases referred *ante*, note 31.
[36] *British Mutoscope and Biograph Co. v. Homer* (1901) 18 R.P.C. 177.
[37] P.A. 1977, s.30(4)(*a*).
[38] P.A. 1977, s.33(3)(*d*).

case of an exclusive licence for otherwise the right to relief in a subsequent infringement action may be prejudiced.[39]

In order to prevent licences from vesting in the manner referred to, it **8.14** is common to include express provisions in licence agreements providing for the automatic determination of the licence upon the death of the licensee or in the event that the licensee should be adjudicated bankrupt or, in the case of a company, go into receivership or liquidation (otherwise than for the purposes of amalgamation or reconstruction).

2. Assignments and Licences

At Common Law

It would appear that at common law a patentee could not assign his **8.15** rights unless power to do so was given by the Crown.[40] The wording of the recitals in the letters patent, *viz.* "... the said applicant (hereinafter together with his executors, administrators and assigns, or any of them, referred to as the patentee) ...", made it clear, however, that the grantee was to have power to assign his rights. The right to grant licences was also recognised by the wording of the parts of the letters patent which contained "the grant" and in "the prohibition".[41]

By Statute

By section 30(2) of the Act any patent or application or any right in a **8.16** patent or application may be assigned or mortgaged, and by section 30(4) licences may be granted under any patent or any application. To the extent that the licence so provides, a sub–licence may be granted thereunder, and any such licence or sub–licence may be assigned or mortgaged.[42]

An assignment of a patent or an application and an exclusive licence **8.17** granted under any patent or application may confer on the assignee or licensee, as the case may be, the right of the assignor or licensor to bring proceedings for a previous infringement.[43]

Under the old law[44] an assignment for a part only of the United **8.18** Kingdom could be made. The present Act contains no specific provisions but presumably such a limited assignment would be covered by the words "any right in it" in section 30(2). In any event the same practical effect could be achieved by granting an exclusive licence, see *post*, §§8.20 *et seq.*

---

[39] P.A. 1977, s.68.
[40] See *Duvergier v. Fellows* (1830) 10 B. & C. 826 at p.829.
[41] See Patents Rules 1968, Sched.4.
[42] P.A. 1977, s.30(4)(*a*).
[43] P.A. 1977, s.30(7).
[44] P.A. 1949, s.21(1).

The rights of co–owners to assign and grant licences are dealt with *post*, §8.89.

Difference between assignment and licence

8.19   There is a fundamental distinction between an assignment of a patent (or an application for a patent) and a licence. By the former the assignee stands in the shoes of the assignor, and is fully entitled to deal with the patent or application as he pleases, subject to the provisions of the Act as to the grant of compulsory licences.[45] A non–exclusive licensee, on the contrary, is merely permitted to do acts which would, but for the licence, be prohibited.[46] Other contractual rights as between the parties may be created by the licence, as in the case of an exclusive licence where the patentee or applicant contracts not to grant other licences.

Exclusive licence

8.20   The Act of 1949 gave to an exclusive licensee an important new statutory right, *viz.* to take proceedings in respect of infringement in his own name,[47] and this right has been continued by the 1977 Act.[48] Thus, an exclusive licensee has a right in relation to the patent or application which is more than contractual; nevertheless, an exclusive licence is a right under, not in, the patent or application.[49] An exclusive licensee under an application may also bring proceedings in his own name in respect of any infringement of the rights arising upon publication of the application.[50] An exclusive licence may also confer on the licensee the right to bring proceedings for a previous infringement.[51] If the patentee or applicant, as the case may be, does not join as a plaintiff, he must be added as a defendant.[52] Where both the proprietor and the exclusive licensee sue as co–Plaintiffs, each is entitled, if successful, to damages assessed on normal principles.[53]

8.21   As in the case of proprietorship, there is no requirement in the Act to the effect that the exclusive licence must be registered before proceedings are commenced. However, non–registration may affect the right to damages or an account.[54]

8.22   Exclusive licence is defined as meaning:[55]

---

[45] See *post*, Chap.9.

[46] This has been well settled since the eighteenth century, see, *per* Lord Diplock in *Allen & Hanburys v. Generics (U.K.) Ltd* [1986] R.P.C. 203, at p.246.

[47] P.A. 1949, s.63(1).

[48] P.A. 1977, s.67(1).

[49] *Instituform v. Inliner* [1992] R.P.C. 83 at p.105.

[50] P.A. 1977, ss.67 and 69, subject to the restrictions of s.69(2).

[51] P.A. 1977, s.30(7).

[52] P.A. 1977, s.67(3).

[53] *Optical Coating Laboratories Inc. v. Pilkington PE Ltd.* [1993] F.S.R. 310.

[54] P.A. s.68; and see *post*, §8.28, and the cases there cited.

[55] P.A. 1977, s.130.

"a licence from the proprietor of or applicant for a patent conferring on the licensee, or on him and persons authorised by him, to the exclusion of all other persons (including the proprietor or applicant), any right in respect of the invention to which the patent or application relates."

There may, therefore, be several exclusive licensees, each having an exclusive licence in his own field and each may sue in respect of an infringement committed in contravention of his particular right. An authorised agent of an exclusive licensee is not himself an exclusive licensee.[56] In the absence of evidence establishing that the Plaintiff is an exclusive licensee he will be non–suited, but there should be no additional finding to the effect that he is *not* in fact an exclusive licensee unless there is evidence to justify that finding.[57]

Where the exclusive licensee sues in respect of goods supplied by the   **8.23** proprietor of the patent, the Defendant will not be liable unless he acquired the goods with notice of the exclusive licence.[58] Where the proprietor is prevented from succeeding by virtue of an agreement which offends section 44, the exclusive licensee will be prevented from succeeding as well.[58a]

Form of assignment

Under the old law an assignment had to be by deed to convey the   **8.24** legal estate and thereby alter the proprietorship in a patent, as that which is created by deed can only be assigned by deed.[59] Under the present law however there is no need for an assignment to be under seal. By section 30(6) it is provided that any assignment or mortgage of a patent or any application, or any right in a patent or any application or any assent relating to any patent or any such application shall be void unless it is in writing and is signed on or behalf of the parties to the transaction. It is to be noted that all the parties to the transaction (normally two) should sign the document whereas under the old law with an assignment under seal it was only necessary for the assignor to sign the documents. However, a purported assignment which does not comply with the requirements of the Act will normally amount to an agreement to assign which would be specifically enforceable in equity as set out *post*, §8.26.

---

[56] *Bondax Carpets v. Advance Carpet Tiles* [1993] F.S.R. 162.
[57] *Proctor & Gamble v. Peaudouce (U.K.)* [1989] F.S.R. 180 (C.A.).
[58] *Heap v. Hartley* (1889) 6 R.P.C. 499; *Cochrane & Co. v. Martins* (1911) 28 R.P.C. 284; *Scottish Vacuum Cleaner Co. Ltd. v. Provincial Cinematograph Theatres Ltd.* (1915) 32 R.P.C. 353; *Christian Salvesen v. Odfjell Drilling* [1985] R.P.C. 569; see also *post*, §8.63.
[58a] *Chiron Corp. v. Organon Teknika (No. 3)* [1994] F.S.R. 202.
[59] Co. Litt 96, 172a; *Stewart v. Casey* (1892) 9 R.P.C. 9 at pp.11, 13.

Form of licence

8.25   The Act does not require that a licence whether exclusive or non–exclusive be in any particular form and, therefore, subject to proof of the existence of the same, an oral licence will be enforceable.[60] In view, however, of the problems of uncertainty with regard to an oral contract and the advisability of registering any licence, dealt with in *post*, §8.27 it is obviously sensible that any licence be in writing.

Agreements to assign or grant licences

8.26   Agreements, parol or otherwise, to assign or to grant licences are specifically enforceable in equity, and are governed by the ordinary rules relating to contract as to specific performance, consideration, etc. Such agreements must, however, be of the degree of definiteness required by law to constitute an enforceable contract; thus, an agreement to grant one for a definite period and on stated terms would be enforceable.[61] An agreement to assign does not alter the proprietorship of a patent, but gives right in equity to have the proprietorship altered in law.[62]

Agreements to assign or to grant licences may be made prior to the application for the patent concerned. Thus, an agreement relating to a subsisting patent may, subject to EC law,[63] contain provisions for the assignment of, or the grant of licences under, patents in respect of future improvements.

Effect of registration on rights in patents

8.27   Section 33 makes provision for the situation where a transaction, instrument or event in relation to a patent or application is incompatible with an earlier transaction, instrument or event relating to that patent or application. The section provides that a person claiming under the later transaction shall be entitled to the property in the patent or application as against the person claiming under the earlier transaction, if the earlier transaction was not registered or, in the case of an application which has not been published, notice of the earlier transaction had not been given to the Comptroller and in both cases the person claiming under the later transaction did not know of the earlier transaction. The provisions apply equally to the case where any person claims to have acquired any right in or under a patent or application by virtue of a transaction, instrument or event to which the section applies, and that right is incompatible with any such right acquired by virtue of an earlier transaction, instrument or event to which the section applies.[64]

---

[60] See *Morton-Norwich Products Inc. v. Intercen* [1981] F.S.R. 337.
[61] See, *e.g. Brake v. Radermacher* (1903) 20 R.P.C. 631.
[62] *Stewart v. Casey* (1892) 9 R.P.C. 9 at p.14 (C.A.).
[63] See *post*, §§8.73 *et seq.* particularly §8.78.
[64] P.A. 1977, s.33(2).

The transactions, instruments and events to which the provisions of section 33 extend are set out in subsection (3) of that section and cover, assignments of a patent or application for a patent or a right in a patent or application, the mortgage of a patent or application, the grant or assignment of a licence or sub–licence, mortgage of a licence or sub–licence, the death of a proprietor of a patent or application or any person having a right in or under a patent or application; the vesting of a patent or application by an assent of personal representatives, and any order of the court transferring a patent or application to any person or that an application should proceed in the name of any person.

It is submitted, that the intention of the section is that any person obtaining title to, property in, or any right in or under a patent or application can be certain that his claim will prevail over any conflicting claim provided he checks the register immediately before entering into the transaction and registers the transaction immediately afterwards.

Effect of non-registration on infringement proceedings

As previously mentioned *ante*, §8.03 non–registration of title to a patent does not prevent the proprietor or exclusive licensee commencing proceedings or from seeking interlocution relief,[65] however the right of an unregistered proprietor or exclusive licensee to recover damages or an account of profits could be effected. Section 68 of the Act provides that where a person becomes the proprietor or an exclusive licensee of a patent by a transaction covered by section 33 that person shall not be entitled to recover damages or an account of profits in respect of infringement subsequent to the transaction unless the transaction is registered within six months of its date or the court is satisfied that it was not practicable to register it in that period.[66]

In this context "practicable" means that the applicant for registration must take all the steps which the reasonable applicant acting on competent advice would take in the circumstances to secure registration.[66a]

The section is not directed to punishing the applicant for delay but to protecting the infringer from a claim to damages on an account at the suit of someone whose interest he could not have ascertained from an inspection of the register.[66b]

Section 68 of the Act also applies where relief is claimed in respect of infringement of the rights conferred by publication of the application.[67]

8.28

---

[65] *Christian Salvesen v. Odfjell Drilling* [1985] R.P.C. 569.

[66] *Ibid.; Instituform v. Inliner* [1992] R.P.C. 83; *Minnesota Mining & Manufacturing v. Rennicks* [1992] R.P.C. 331; [1992] F.S.R. 118. *Mölnlycke A.B. v. Proctor & Gamble Ltd.* [1994] R.P.C. 49.

[66a] *Mölnlycke A.B. v. Procter & Gamble Ltd.* [1994] R.P.C. 49.

[66b] *Ibid., per* Morritt J. at p. 109.

[67] P.A. 1977, s.69.

Notice of equitable interests

8.29   Section 33 only applies to some of the potential transactions relating to a patent and for example excludes an assignment which is invalid for lack of writing or signatures of both parties and acts merely as an agreement to assign. Such agreements to assign, and any other equitable right arising in relation to a patent not covered by section 33(3), are subject to the usual conditions of equitable assignments, and a person obtaining a legal assignment without notice of the equitable one can claim priority,[68] and can convey a good title, even though the subsequent purchaser from him may in fact have had notice.[69] Similarly, a licensee who before entering into a licence agreement has notice of a prior agreement to assign may be restrained from infringing by the new proprietor, as soon as the latter's title has been perfected by a legal assignment.[70] Thus, under the 1977 Act if a person taking an assignment of a patent had notice that the assignor was holding the patent on trust for a third party the assignment would not give the assignee priority as against the interest of the third party. The misdescription of the nature of a previous agreement, as where an assignment was described to a party as a licence, may not prevent such party's knowledge of its existence constituting constructive notice.[71]

In any event, early registration of licences or assignments or agreements conferring rights with regard to a patent or application is of great importance, the existence of such registration preventing the patentee from granting licences under or otherwise dealing with the patent in an incompatible manner.[72]

Covenants attaching to patents

8.30   Where an assignee of a patent covenants with the assignor for himself and his assigns that he will work the patent and pay certain royalties thereon to the assignor, a subsequent assignee with notice takes the patent subject to those covenants.[73] In such a case there is no privity of contract between the assignor and the second assignee, but the rights of the assignor are analogous to a vendor's lien, and the second assignee cannot hold the rights which he has acquired without also fulfilling the obligations which may be said to attach to those rights, and consequently the terms of the original assignment become a matter of great importance.

In *Dansk Rekylriffel Syndikat Aktieselskab v. Snell,*[74] Neville J. said:

---

[68] *e.g.* as in *Wapshare Tube Co. Ltd. v. Hyde Imperial Rubber Co.* (1901) 18 R.P.C. 374.
[69] *Actiengesellschaft für Cartonnagen Industrie v. Temler and Seeman* (1901) 18 R.P.C. 6.
[70] See, *e.g. New Ixion Tyre and Cycle Co. v. Spilsbury* (1898) 15 R.P.C. 380, 567.
[71] *Morey's Patent* (1858) 25 Beav. 581.
[72] P.A. 1977, s.33.
[73] *Werderman v. Société Générale d'Electricité* (1881) 19 Ch.D. 246 at pp.251, 252.
[74] [1908] 2 Ch. 127 at p.136.

"The obligation to fulfil the terms of the agreement, being with regard to the assignees not personal, but attached to the property which they acquired with notice on the terms upon which it was held by their assignor, disables them from holding the property without fulfilling the terms. It appears to me that such an interest of the vendor, if not properly described as a vendor's lien, is closely analogous to it.[75] The question involved is whether, upon the true construction of the original assignment, it was intended that the vendor should retain a charge upon the property, or that he should part with the property completely, looking solely to the personal liability of the purchaser to pay the consideration."[76]

In that case the existence of clauses in the original contract to the effect that the purchaser thereunder should keep the patent in force and should pay royalties, was held to indicate a reservation of interest in the vendor sufficient to bring the case within the above principle.

Assignor estopped from impeaching validity

When a patent has been assigned the new proprietor is entitled, in the **8.31** absence of any provision in the assignment to the contrary to prevent the assignor from manufacturing the patented article;[77] and in any action brought for that purpose by the assignee (or by any person deriving title through him) the assignor is estopped by his deed of assignment from impeaching the validity of the patent.[78] Similarly, the assignor of a licence is estopped from alleging as against his assignees that the patent is invalid.[79] The estoppel in such cases is of a personal nature, and does not extend to the partner of an assignor even in an action in which both are joined as co-defendants.[80] Estoppel can "only operate in the same transaction as that in which it arises";[81] it is limited to such implication of validity as may be contained in the deed to which the assignor has put his hand and seal, and does not exist, for example, where there is an assignment by operation of law, as upon bankruptcy of the patentee.[82] The former patentee is not estopped as against the new owner of the patent either by matter of record contained in the letters patent itself, or by statements contained in a specification (which professes only fully to declare the nature of the invention and how it is

---

[75] See also, *British Association of Glass Bottle Manufacturers v. Foster & Sons Ltd.* (1917) 34 R.P.C. 217 at p.224.
[76] See also *Bagot Pneumatic Tyre Co. v. Clipper Pneumatic Tyre Co.* (1902) 19 R.P.C. 69 at p.75; *Barker v. Stickney* [1919] 1 K.B. 121.
[77] See, *e.g. Franklin Hocking & Co. Ltd. v. Franklin Hocking* (1887) 4 R.P.C. 255.
[78] *Chambers v. Crichley* (1864) 33 Beav. 374.
[79] *Gonville v. Hay* (1904) 21 R.P.C. 49.
[80] *Heugh v. Chamberlain* (1877) 25 W.R. 742.
[81] *Fuel Economy Co. Ltd. v. Murray* (1930) 47 R.P.C. 346 at p.353; *V. D. Ltd. v. Boston Deep Sea Fishing, etc., Ltd.* (1935) 52 R.P.C. 303 at p.331; see also *Compania Naviera Vasconzada v. Churchill & Sim* [1906] 1 K.B. 237 at p.251.
[82] *Cropper v. Smith and Hancock* (1884) 1 R.P.C. 81.

to be carried into effect), or by representations contained in the application for letters patent unless it be shown that the other party relied upon such representations.[83] It is probable that there would be such estoppel against the patentee as between himself and the Crown.[84]

8.32   An assignor, where he is estopped from denying the validity of the patent, may, of course, contend for a construction of the specification which will exclude what he is in fact doing, and so long as it does not impugn the validity of the patent, may call evidence as to the state of the art in the light of which the specification must be construed.[85]

A person estopped from disputing the validity of a patent is, nevertheless, entitled to give evidence and assist in attacking its validity in proceedings to which he is not himself a party.[86]

8.33   It should be noted that the proposition of United Kingdom national law set out in this section might in certain circumstances be contrary to EC competition law. It is submitted that, if the European Court of Justice was to strike down a no–challenge clause in a patent assignment as contravening Article 85(1), then the Court would be unlikely to permit the same effect to be achieved through the national law of estoppel. The validity of no–challenge clauses under EC law is considered in greater detail *post*, §§8.73 *et seq.*

Estoppel against licensee

8.34   It is frequently said that a licensee is estopped from denying the validity of the patent.[87] There is not, however, "an absolute estoppel in all cases and in all circumstances ... but only an estoppel which is involved in and necessary to the exercise of the licence which the licensee has accepted."[88]

8.35   If the licence is limited in its scope, *e.g.* in area, and the patentee brings an action against the licensee, not under the licence, but for infringement of the patent in respect of acts done outside the licensed area, then the licensee would not be estopped in the action for infringement from disputing the validity of the patent.[89] It appears that a licensee would never be estopped from alleging that the patent is invalid, if the action brought against him is for infringement of patent, but only when an action is brought against him under the licence to enforce its provisions. As Luxmoore J. said in *Fuel Economy Co. Ltd. v. Murray*:[90]

---

[84] *Cropper v. Smith and Hancock* (1884) 1 R.P.C. 81 at p.96.

[85] *Franklin Hocking & Co. Ltd. v. Franklin Hocking* (1887) 4 R.P.C. 255, 434; (1889) 6 R.P.C. 69.

[86] *London and Leicester Hosiery Co. v. Griswold* (1886) 3 R.P.C. 251.

[87] See *Crossley v. Dixon* [1863] 10 H.L.C. 293 at p.304; *Adie v. Clark* (1876) 3 Ch.D. 134 at p.144 (C.A.); 2 App.Cas. 423 at p.425; *Cummings v. Stewart* (1913) 30 R.P.C. 1 at p.9.

[88] *Fuel Economy Co. Ltd. v. Murray* (1930) 47 R.P.C. 346 at p.358; see also *V. D. Ltd. v. Boston Deep Sea Fishing, etc., Ltd.* (1935) 52 R.P.C. 303 at p.331 and *Kerbing Consolidated Ltd. v. Dick* [1973] R.P.C. 68.

[89] *Fuel Economy Co. Ltd. v. Murray* (1930) 47 R.P.C. 346.

[90] *Ibid.* at p.353.

"A licensee cannot challenge the validity of a patent in an action under the licence, the licence being admitted by the licensee, because the title is not in issue. But in an action for infringement a different set of circumstances arises altogether. It is not an action under the licence at all, and in such a case, so far as my judgment goes, no estoppel arises."

Further, where there is in an agreement for sale, or for a licence, a covenant that the patent is valid, the question of validity is open to the assignee or licensee, and may go to the root of the consideration.[91] The real question to be decided in such cases is: "Did the defendant buy a good and indefeasible patent right, or was the contract merely to place the defendant in the same situation as the plaintiff was with reference to the alleged patent?"[92] Where a patentee contracted to give to the defendant the *exclusive right to sell* certain things for which patents had been obtained, it was held that if one of the patents was invalid the consideration failed as the patentee could not confer the privileges which he agreed to confer.[93] The decision upon this point might have been otherwise if he had refrained from inquiring into the validity and had worked the patent for a long time and subsequently, when called upon to pay royalty, refused upon the ground of invalidity.[95] In a case, however, where there was a covenant that payments should cease if the patent became void for lack of novelty, it was held that this referred to the patent being held void in proceedings between the patentee and other parties, and that the licensee was not entitled to put the validity of the patent in issue in an action upon the licence.[96] The above principles apply equally where there is a licence not under seal,[97] and where the licence is a verbal one.[98]

A licensee is entitled to contend that what he is doing is not within the terms of his licence, and where (as is ordinarily the case) such terms are defined by the claims of the specification, he is at liberty to adduce evidence of common knowledge in the light of which ambiguous claims will be construed. He is not, however, entitled, in an action brought under the licence, to prove facts which would be inconsistent with the validity of the patent,[99] though obviously he may plead that the patent

8.36

8.37

---

[91] *Nadel v. Martin* (1906) 23 R.P.C. 41; *Henderson v. Shiels* (1907) 24 R.P.C. 108.

[92] See *Hall v. Conder* (1857) 26 L.J.C.P. 138 at p.143. See also *Suhr v. Crofts (Engineers) Ltd.* (1932) 49 R.P.C. 359.

[93] *Chanter v. Leese* (1839) 5 Mee. & W. 698, as explained in *Hall v. Conder* (1857) 26 L.J.C.P. 138 at p.143.

[94] *Wilson v. Union Oil Mills Co. Ltd.* (1892) 9 R.P.C. 57.

[95] *Ibid.*; see also *Suhr v. Crofts (Engineers) Ltd.* (1932) 49 R.P.C. 359.

[96] *Mills v. Carson* (1892) 9 R.P.C. 9.

[97] *Lawes v. Purser* (1856) 6 El. & Bl. 930.

[98] *Crossley v. Dixon* [1863] 10 H.L.C. 293.

[99] See *Clark v. Adie* (1877) 2 App.Cas. 423 at pp.426, 436; *Young and Beilby v. Hermand Oil Co. Ltd.* (1892) 9 R.P.C. 373; *Jandus Arc Lamp etc. Co. Ltd. v. Johnson* (1900) 17 R.P.C. 361 at p.376; *Hay v. Gonville* (1907) 24 R.P.C. 213 at p.218.

has expired,[1] and also may dispute that the patent should be extended and the length of its extension.[2]

8.38   As with the estoppel against an assignor,[3] an estoppel against a licensee from challenging validity might, in certain circumstances, be contrary to EC competition law, see *post*, §§8.75 *et seq.*

Fraud

8.39   A licensee is, of course, entitled to repudiate his licence on the ground of fraud or common mistake, and the invalidity of the patent, if known to the licensor at the time of granting the licence, may be an element constituting fraud;[4] if the licensee proposes to take this course he must plead fraud in distinct terms.[5]

No estoppel against licensee

8.40   Where the licence has been determined prior to the expiration of the patent and the patentee consequently sues the other party for infringement instead of for royalties under the licence, the defendant may contest the validity of the patent, and, it appears, is not under any estoppel merely because he once was a licensee.[6]

If the agreement to assign or grant a licence is purely executory, there is no estoppel.[7]

It would appear that the mere purchase of a patented article from the patentee or a licensee does not compel the purchaser to assume the position of a licensee in respect of the article and in consequence to be estopped from attacking the validity of the patent.[8]

Implication of terms

8.41   The ordinary rules of construction apply to assignments and licences, and their meaning may be determined by the court in the same way as in the case of other documents.[9] Terms will not be implied unless "on considering the terms of the contract in a reasonable and businesslike manner, an implication necessarily arises that the parties must have

---

[1] *Muirhead v. Commercial Cable Co.* (1895) 12 R.P.C. 317 at p.325. (1895) 12 R.P.C. 39 (C.A.).
[2] *Bristol Repetition Ltd. v. Fomento* [1960] R.P.C. 163.
[3] See *ante*, §8.31 to 8.33.
[4] See *Lawes v. Purser* (1856) 6 El. & Bl. 930 at p.936.
[5] *McDougall Bros. v. Partington* (1890) 7 R.P.C. 216; *Ashworth v. Law* (1890) 7 R.P.C. 231 at p.234.
[6] *Crossley v. Dixon* [1863] 10 H.L.C. 293; *Axmann v. Lund* (1874) L.R. 18 Eq. 330 at pp.337, 338. See also *Neilson v. Fothergill* (1841) 1 W.P.C. 287; *Noton v. Brooks* (1861) 7 H. & N. 499; *Ashworth v. Law* (1890) 7 R.P.C. 231.
[7] See *Basset v. Graydon* (1897) 14 R.P.C. 701 at p.709; *Henderson v. Shiels* (1907) 24 R.P.C. 108 at pp.113, 115; *Suhr v. Crofts (Engineers) Ltd.* (1932) 49 R.P.C. 359 at p.365.
[8] See *Gillette Safety Razor Co. v. A. W. Gamage Ltd.* (1906) 23 R.P.C. 492 at p.500, *per* Warrington J.; 26 R.P.C. 745, *per* Parker J.
[9] See *E. I. du Pont de Nemours & Co. v. Imperial Chemical Industries Ltd.* (1950) 67 R.P.C. 144.

intended that the suggested stipulation should exist".[10] Thus, when a patent was assigned in consideration of royalties which were to continue to be payable while the patent was subsisting, and the assignee inadvertently allowed the patent to lapse by non-payment of a renewal fee, the court refused to imply into the contract a covenant that the assignee should keep the patent on foot.[11] The decision would probably be otherwise were the lapse of the patent due to a wilful act of the assignee. Where a patentee covenanted with his licensee "by all means in his power to protect and defend the said letters patent from all infringements", it was held that he was thereby bound to maintain the patent in force by payment of the renewal fees.[12]

In the absence of express warranty the maxim *caveat emptor* ordinarily   **8.42**
applies to the assignments of patents and the grant of licences and there is no implied warranty that the patent is valid; the invalidity of the patent is no defence to an action brought by the assignor or patentee for the purchase price or for royalties.[13] There is not ordinarily any implied warranty in an assignment of a patent or a licence under a patent that the manufacture or sale of articles made under the patent will not infringe any other patents. Knowledge of and concealment of such a fact by the patentee might, however, amount to fraud on his part, and entitle the assignee or licensee to rescission of the contract.

There is not ordinarily any implied covenant that the licensee shall work the invention;[14] express provisions are, therefore, commonly inserted in licence agreements whereby the licensee undertakes to pay a minimum royalty whether he manufactures or not; and in the case of an exclusive licence, where there may be danger of what was formerly called "Abuse of Monopoly",[15] it is often though desirable that the licensee should be bound actually to manufacture a certain number of articles each year.

"Best endeavours"

Some clauses of a commonly occurring kind have been interpreted,   **8.43**
e.g. an audit clause[16] and an obligation by licensees to use "all diligence" and their "best endeavours" to promote the sale of the patented

---

[10] *Mills v. Carson* (1893) 10 R.P.C. 9 at p.15, quoting from *Hamlyn & Co. v. Wood & Co.* [1891] 2 Q.B. 488; see also *Campbell v. G. Hopkins & Sons (Clerkenwell) Ltd.* (1931) 49 R.P.C. 38 at pp.44, 45; *The Moorcock* (1889) 14 P.D. 64 at p.68.

[11] *Re Railway and Electric Appliances Co.* (1888) 38 Ch.D. 597.

[12] *Lines v. Usher* (1897) 14 R.P.C. 206; see also *Cummings v. Stewart* (1913) 30 R.P.C. 1.

[13] *Hall v. Conder* (1857) 26 L.J.C.P. 138; *Smith v. Buckingham* (1870) 21 L.T. 819; *Liardet v. Hammond Electric Light & Power Co.* (1883) 31 W.R. 710; *Bessimer v. Wright* (1858) 31 L.T. (o.s.) 213; *Chanter v. Hopkins* 4 M & W 399; *cf. Chanter v. Leese* (1839) 4 M & W 295, 5 M & W 498 where it was held that the contract was for the sale of an exclusive right.

[14] See, *e.g. Re Railway and Electrical Appliances Co.* (1888) 38 Ch.D. 597 at p.608; *Cheetham v. Nuthall* (1893) 10 R.P.C. 321 at p.333.

[15] See Chap.9.

[16] *Fomento (Sterling Area) Ltd. v. Selsdon Fountain Pen Co. Ltd.* [1958] R.P.C. 8.

articles.[17] The last mentioned obligation is a particularly onerous one for a licensee.[18]

"Beneficial owner"

8.44   Where the assignor conveys as "beneficial owner" the covenants set out in the Second Schedule, Part I, of the Law of Property Act 1925 will be implied.[19]

Breach of licence

8.45   The general law relating to breach of contract is applicable to breaches of the terms contained in a licence.[20] It is, of course, open to a licensee to contend that no royalties are payable on the articles he is producing as they do not fall within the scope of the claims of the patent,[21] unless he is estopped from so contending by his previous conduct.[22]

Conflict of laws

8.46   Where there is an agreement between British nationals for the grant of a licence under British patents and an order of a foreign court purports to make such grant illegal, the matter must be resolved in accordance with the law relating to the comity of nations.[23]

On the other hand, it is no answer to a defence raised under section 44(3) of the Act (namely, that at the time of the infringement there was in force a contract containing a condition or term void under section 44(1) thereof) to say that the contract in question is governed by a foreign law which does not give effect to section 44(1).[24] For these purposes, the foreign law is irrelevant.[25]

Revocability of licences

8.47   The question of the rights of one or other party to terminate a licence has, where there has been no express provision in the agreement dealing with the matter, given rise to considerable difficulty, and it would seem

---

[17] *Terrell v. Mabie Todd & Co. Ltd.* (1952) 69 R.P.C. 234. See also *I.B.M. (U.K.) Ltd. v. Rockware Glass Ltd.* [1980] F.S.R. 335; *Transfield Pty. v. Arlo International* [1981] R.P.C. 141, Aust. High Ct.

[18] *Ibid.*

[19] Law of Property Act 1925, s.76.

[20] See *National Carbonising Co. Ltd. v. British Coal Distillation Ltd.* (1936) 54 R.P.C. 41.

[21] *Dobson v. Adie Bros. Ltd.* (1935) 52 R.P.C. 358; *Pytchley Autocar Co. Ltd. v. Vauxhall Motors Ltd.* (1941) 58 R.P.C. 287.

[22] *Lyle-Meller v. A. Lewis & Co. (Westminster) Ltd.* [1956] R.P.C. 14.

[23] *British Nylon Spinners Ltd. v. Imperial Chemical Industries Ltd.* (1952) 69 R.P.C. 288; [1954] 71 R.P.C. 327.

[24] *Chiron Corp. v. Organon Teknika Ltd. (No. 2)* [1993] F.S.R. 324; [1992] 3 C.M.L.R. 813; [1993] F.S.R. 567 (C.A.).

[25] *Ibid.*

that a certain amount of confusion has existed between equitable rights as arising from contract between licensor and licensee, and such purely legal rights as a licensor may in general possess to withdraw at his pleasure such permission as he may have given. The case of *Wood v. Leadbitter*,[26] which was heard at common law before the Judicature Act 1873, turned upon a technical point not of contract but of trespass upon land, and decided that a mere permission to go upon a person's land, unless accompanied by some transfer of interest or property, as where a right was conferred, for example, to cut and remove the hay upon the land, was revocable at the pleasure of the owner of the land. An attempt was made in *Ward v. Livesey*[27] to apply this doctrine to a case of a licence under a patent, and it was held that the revocability of a licence depended on whether it was or was not "coupled with an interest". It appears, however, not to have been realised that, since the fusion of law and equity by the Judicature Act, the real point at issue is not any purely legal right that an owner may have of revoking his licence, but whether, upon the true construction of the *contract* between the parties, one or the other is debarred in equity from the exercise of such legal right.[28]

It may be that one or the other party is entitled to terminate at pleasure or upon the happening of certain events, and inferences have been drawn as to this from the nature of the obligations imposed upon one or other of the parties by the contract.[29] For example, where a patentee by granting an exclusive licence debarred himself from working the invention and received a lump sum as part consideration for the grant of the licence, he was held not entitled to revoke it at his pleasure.[30] In an ordinary verbal licence, however, where nothing is said as to any precise duration of the term, the presumption is that the licence is terminable at the pleasure of either party.[31]

Where there are express provisions for termination upon certain specified events or by one of the parties to the contract, it will be inferred that there is no right of termination upon other events not so specified or by the other of the parties.[32] Thus, a breach of an independent covenant by the licensor to pay the renewal fees will not go to the root of the contract;[33] nor will the breach of a covenant to sue infringers,[34] or to give instruction as to the working of the invention.[35]

---

[26] (1845) 13 Mee. & W. 838.
[27] (1888) 5 R.P.C. 102.
[28] *Guyot v. Thomson* (1894) 11 R.P.C. 541 at p.552; and see *Kerrison v. Smith* [1897] 2 Q.B. 445; *Hurst v. Picture Theatres Ltd.* [1915] 1 K.B. 1; *British Actors Film Co. Ltd. v. Glover* [1918] 1 K.B. 299.
[29] *Guyot v. Thomson, ante.*
[30] *Ibid.*
[31] *Crossley v. Dixon* [1863] 10 H.L.C. 293; 32 L.J.Ch. 617; *Coppin v. Lloyd* (1898) 15 R.P.C. 373.
[32] *Guyot v. Thomson* (1894) 11 R.P.C. 541; *Cutlan v. Dawson* (1896) 13 R.P.C. 710; (1897) 14 R.P.C. 249; *Patchett v. Sterling Engineering Co. Ltd.* (1953) 70 R.P.C. 269.
[33] *Mills v. Carson* (1893) 10 R.P.C. 9.
[34] *Huntoon Co. v. Kolynos (Inc.)* (1930) 47 R.P.C. 403 at pp.416–429.
[35] *Campbell v. Jones* (1796) 6 Term Rep. 570.

Termination if patent held invalid

8.48   Provisions are frequently inserted providing for the termination of the licence in the event of the patent being held to be invalid by a court of competent jurisdiction. In such a case, where the decision of the court of first instance is against the patent, but is reversed upon appeal and the patent is eventually upheld, the licence is still in force and the licensee liable for royalties thereunder.[36] The simplest course is to provide that the licence shall continue so long as the patent remains subsisting.

Statutory determination

8.49   At any time after the patent or all the patents included in a licence has or have ceased to be in force, and, notwithstanding any provision in the licence or any contract to the contrary, either party may give three months' notice to determine the licence to the extent and only to the extent that the contract relates to the subject matter of the patents in question.[37] This right becomes exercisable as soon as all the patents or applications for patents originally included in the licence have expired and it is irrelevant that patents have subsequently been granted for improvements, to the benefit of which the licensee is entitled by reason of the "improvements" clause in the licence.[38] Where the court is satisfied in consequence of the patent or patents concerned ceasing to be in force, that it would be unjust to require the applicant to continue to comply with all the terms and conditions of the licence it may make such order varying those terms or conditions as it deems appropriate.[39] The provision that the contract is only determined to the extent that it related to the relevant product or invention protected by the expired patent may have avoided the difficulties arising under the previous section of the 1949 Act[40] where it was uncertain as to the effect of this section where the agreement was an international one containing foreign patents as well as United Kingdom patents.[41]

Where no express power to determine

8.50   In a case where the licence contained no provision as to the period for which it was to remain in force, it was held that the licence was determinable on reasonable notice.[42]

---

[36] *Cheetham v. Nuthall* (1893) 10 R.P.C. 321.
[37] P.A. 1977, s.45(1).
[38] *Advance Industries Ltd. v. Paul Frankfurther* [1958] R.P.C. 392.
[39] P.A. 1977, s.45(3).
[40] P.A. 1977, s.58(1).
[41] See *Hansen v. Magnavox* [1977] R.P.C. 301.
[42] *Martin Baker Aircraft Co. Ltd. v. Canadian Flight Equipment Ltd.* (1955) 72 R.P.C. 236.

Licences under several patents

Where licences are granted under several patents or a group of **8.51**
patents, care is necessary to define the state of affairs which is to prevail
when some but not all of the patents have expired. Such licences are
often drafted in such a way that the licensee remains liable to pay
royalties until the expiry of the last patent, even though he may be
working only under the patents which have expired and not under the
surviving ones at all.[43]

Notices

Where an assignment or licence was executed or came into operation **8.52**
after January 1, 1926, all notices required to be served thereunder must
be in writing, and will be deemed to have been sufficiently served if they
are left at, or sent by registered letter or by recorded delivery to, the
last-known address of the party to be served.[44] In all such assignments
and licences, the word "month" is to be deemed to mean "a calendar
month" unless the context requires otherwise.[45]

Ambit of licences

There are a number of acts specified in section 60 which constitute an **8.53**
infringement of the rights conferred by a patent and care should be
taken in drafting licence arrangements to ensure that the licence granted
is clearly defined. A licence to "use and exercise" conveys the fullest
rights, including that of importation.[46] A licence to "make" does not
imply a licence to use or vend.[47] But a purchaser from a person who is
licensed to "make and vend" has been held to be entitled to use and
vend the article so purchased.[48]

If it is intended to give all rights under the patent it is better to use
general wording rather than attempting to set out seriatim the various
permitted acts.

Assignment of licence and sub–licensing

By section 30(4)(*a*) of the Act, to the extent that the licence so provides, **8.54**
a sub–licence may be granted under the licence and any such licence or
sub–licence may be assigned. It is submitted, that the licence may so
provide either expressly or impliedly and that the extent to which

---

[43] See, *e.g. Siemens v. Taylor* (1892) 9 R.P.C. 393.
[44] Law of Property Act 1925, s.196(1), (3), (4), (5). Recorded Delivery Service Act 1962, ss.1, 2.
[45] Law of Property Act 1925, s.61.
[46] *Dunlop Pneumatic Tyre Co. v. North British Rubber Co.* (1904) 21 R.P.C. 161 at pp.181, 183.
[47] *Basset v. Graydon* (1897) 14 R.P.C. 701 at pp.708, 713; and see *Huntoon Co. v. Kolynos (Inc.)* (1930) 47 R.P.C. 403 at p.422.
[48] *Thomas v. Hunt* (1864) 17 C.B.(N.S.) 183. See also *National Phonograph Co. of Australia v. Menck* (1911) 28 R.P.C. 229.

sub–licences may be granted or the licence (or sub–licences) assigned is, therefore, essentially a matter of construction. This interpretation of the Act is in accordance with the position at Common Law where it has been held that a mere licence under a patent is personal only, and does not authorise the licensee to grant sub–licences or to assign his licence.[49] But if there is anything which shows that there was an intention that the licence should not be limited exclusively to the individual the result may be otherwise.[50] Thus, where a licence is expressed to be granted to a licensee and his assigns, or where provisions are made for the payment of royalties upon goods made by a sub–licensee, the licensee would clearly be entitled to assign or grant sub–licences as the case might be. In drafting a patent licence, therefore, care should be taken to make it clear by express language whether the licence is to be personal to the licensee or is to be assignable.

If a licensee is not entitled to assign, and the licensor knowingly accepts royalties from a purported assignee, the licensor is thereby estopped from disputing the assignment.[51]

Although a licensee under a personal licence is entitled to exercise his rights by his servants or agents, he is not entitled to exercise his rights in such a way that his "agents" are in substance "independent contractors".[52]

Where the benefit of a licence, in which the consideration is payable by way of a share of profits, is assigned by the licensor the assignee is entitled to an account from the licensee, provided that he puts himself into the position of the licensor by agreeing to pay any moneys due from the licensor to the licensee,[53] but if the assignment be of a share only of the benefit of the licence he must join the other persons entitled, as the licensee is not bound to account separately to several parties.[54]

If the licensee has power to grant sub–licences, such sub–licences will determine upon the determination of his own licence unless it appears from the terms of his own licence that the contrary is intended.[55]

Sub–licences or an assignment of a licence should be registered, see *ante*, §8.27 *et seq.*

Purchase of articles from patentee

8.55 The owner of a United Kingdom patent who, by himself or his agent, sells the patented article abroad without reservation or condition,

---

[49] Hindmarch, 242; *Lawson v. Donald Macpherson & Co. Ltd.* (1897) 14 R.P.C. 696; *Allen & Hanbury's (Salbutamol) Patent* [1987] R.P.C. 372, *per* Dillon L.J. at p.380.
[50] *Lawson v. Donald Macpherson & Co.* (1897) 14 R.P.C. 696; and see also *National Carbonising Co. Ltd. v. British Coal Distillation Ltd.* (1937) 54 R.P.C. 41.
[51] *Lawson v. Donald Macpherson & Co., loc. cit.*
[52] *Howard and Bullough Ltd. v. Tweedales and Smalley* (1895) 12 R.P.C. 519.
[53] *Bergmann v. Macmillan* (1881) 17 Ch.D. 423.
[54] *Ibid.*
[55] See *Austin Baldwin & Co. Ltd. v. Greenwood & Batley Ltd.*, (1925) 42 R.P.C. 454.

cannot restrain the importation of the article so sold in to this country,[56] as the unconditional sale of an article implies the grant of authority to use and sell it co-extensive with the right of the vendor at the date of the sale.[57] And a subsequent assignee of the patent is not entitled to restrain the further use or sale of goods sold under conditions such as to confer an absolute authority to use and sell so far as patent rights are concerned.[58] But if a patentee assigned his patent and subsequently continued to make the goods abroad the assignee could, no doubt, restrain their importation or sale,[59] unless in the case of imports from another Member State of the EC the doctrine of exhaustion of rights applies.[60]

Licence under foreign patent

A licence under a foreign patent to manufacture and sell, thereunder **8.56** granted by a patentee who also owns a British patent does not imply any licence to the purchase of articles so manufactured or sold to import the same into this country.[61]

Doctrine of Exhaustion of Rights

Under EC Law[62] the proprietor of a patent may not exercise his patent **8.57** rights to prevent the importation into the United Kingdom of a product put into circulation for the first time by him or with his consent in another Member State of the EC.[63] The theory is that Article 36 of the Treaty permits the exercise of patent rights against imports only insofar as the exercise of such rights is necessary to protect the specific subject matter of the patent. In this context, the specific subject matter is the exclusive right to use the invention to put the patented products into circulation for the first time. Thus, once that has been done by the patentee or with his consent, the patentee has "exhausted" his rights.[64] The doctrine of exhaustion applies even if there is no corresponding patent in the Member State where the product was first put into

---

[56] *Betts v. Willmott* (1871) L.R. 6 Ch.App.239.
[57] See *ibid.*; see also *Incandescent Gas Light Co. Ltd. v. Cantelo* (1895) 12 R.P.C. 262 at p.264; *National Phonograph Co. of Australia Ltd. v. Menck* (1911) 28 R.P.C. 229.
[58] *Ibid.*; see also *Gillette Safety Razor Co. Ltd. v. Gamage (A.W.) Ltd.* (1907) 24 R.P.C. 1.
[59] See *Betts v. Willmott* (1871) L.R. 6 Ch.App. 239 at p.244.
[60] See *post*, §8.57. Case C-10/89, *CNL-SUCAL v. HAG* [1990] 1 E.C.R. 3711, [1990] 3 C.M.L.R. 571, [1991] F.S.R. 99; Case C-9/93, *IHT Internationale v. Ideal-Standard GmbH*, *The Times*, 7 July, 1994.
[61] *Société Anonyme des Manufactures de Glaces v. Tilghman's Patent Sand Blast Co.* (1930) 25 Ch.D. 1 at p.9; and see *Beecham Group Ltd. v. International Products Ltd.* [1968] R.P.C. 129; *Minnesota Mining and Manufacturing Co. v. Geerpres Europe* [1974] R.P.C. 35; *Smith Kline & French v. Global Pharmaceuticals* [1986] R.P.C. 394; *Wellcome Foundation v. Discpharm Ltd.* [1993] F.S.R. 433.
[62] Treaty of Rome, Arts. 30–36. See also §§6.63 *ante*.
[63] Case 15/74, *Centrafarm BV v. Sterling Drug* [1974] E.C.R. 1147, [1974] 2 C.M.L.R. 480, [1975] F.S.R. 161.
[64] *Ibid.*

circulation by the patentee or with his consent.[65] The rule is that if a patentee decides to market his product in a Member State where patent protection does not exist, he must accept the consequences as regards free circulation of the product in the Common Market.[66]

On the other hand, the proprietor of a patent is entitled to exercise his patent rights against a product first put into circulation in another Member State by a third party *without* his consent.[67] Furthermore, the consent must be voluntary and thus the doctrine does not apply where the product in question was first put into circulation in a Member State under a compulsory licence from the proprietor.[68]

8.58   Special provisions apply in respect of the importation of certain products from Spain or Portugal.[69] The proprietor of a patent for a chemical or pharmaceutical product or a product relating to plant health filed at a time when a product patent could not be obtained for that product in Spain (or, as the case may be, Portugal) may rely on his patent rights to prevent the importation into the United Kingdom of that product, even if that product was first put on the market in Spain (or Portugal) for the first time by him or with his consent.[70] Where these provisions apply, their effect is to put Spain and Portugal in the same position as non–EC countries so far as concerns importation from either of them.[71]

Covenants for improvements

8.59   Covenants are frequently inserted in assignments and licences whereby the assignor or licensor undertakes to communicate to the other party any new discovery or invention which he may make or acquire connected with his invention and, if he obtains a patent for such new invention, to assign it to or to grant a licence to the other party. In other cases the covenants are mutual, each party communicating improvements to the other.

Such covenants require care in wording in order to ensure that there is no danger of their being in restraint of trade, and in order to avoid unnecessary difficulties in deciding what is and what is not an "improvement".

---

[65] Case 187/80, *Merck v. Stephar BV* [1981] E.C.R. 2063, [1981] 3 C.M.L.R. 463, [1982] F.S.R. 57.

[66] *Ibid.*, para.[11].

[67] Case 24/67, *Parke Davis v. Probel* [1968] C.M.L.R. 47; case 35/87 *Thetford v. Fiamma* [1989] F.S.R. 57; case 341/87, *EMI Electrola GmbH v. Patricia* [1989] E.C.R. 92, [1989] 2 C.M.L.R. 413, [1989] F.S.R. 544.

[68] Case 19/84, *Pharmon v. Hoechst* [1985] 3 C.M.L.R. 775, [1985] E.C.R. 2281, [1986] F.S.R. 108.

[69] Art. 47 and 209 of the Treaty of Accession of the Kingdom of Spain and the Portuguese Republic; European Communities (Spanish and Portuguese Accession) Act 1985.

[70] *Wellcome Foundation Ltd. v. Discpharm Ltd.* [1993] F.S.R. 433.

[71] Case C-191/90, *Generics (U.K.) Ltd. v. Smith Kline & French Laboratories Ltd.* [1993] R.P.C. 333, [1993] F.S.R. 592, [1992] I E.C.R. 5335, [1993] 1 C.M.L.R. 89 (ECJ); *Smith Kline & French Laboratories Ltd.'s (Cimetidine) Patents* [1990] R.P.C. 203 at pp.261–262 (C.A.).

Certain types of improvement clause may no longer be permissible, in certain circumstances, as contravening Article 85(1), see *post*, §§8.73 *et seq.*

Ambit of covenants for improvements

It is difficult to foretell at the time of making a contract the precise **8.60** nature of the "improvement" which it will be desired to cover. The ambit of the rights conferred depends entirely upon the construction of the contract.[73] Sometimes "improvements" are defined as being confined to articles or processes which would be an infringement of the patent in question; in other cases it may be desired to secure any further inventions relating to the particular art. The words "improvement upon", unless otherwise qualified, are ambiguous in that, for instance, in the case of a machine, they may relate to some alteration in its design which will enable it to perform its duty better or more cheaply, or they may relate to a different machine which performs the same duty in a different and better way; the former meaning is that usually adopted, and a separate and distinct invention, although relating to the same general subject-matter, cannot usually be described as an improvement.[74] Notwithstanding this ambiguity, it is usually best, when drafting a licence, merely to use the word "improvements", without attempting any more precise definition, as the parties are usually reluctant to agree to anything more detailed and even an elaborate and complicated clause often gives rise to disputes as to its true construction.

In *Linotype and Machinery Ltd. v. Hopkins*,[75] where the licensor covenanted to communicate "every improvement in or additon to the Hopkins machine or mode of applying the same or any discovery useful to the manufacture thereof", the Court of Appeal, having regard to those words, would not agree that any improvement of which the company was to have the benefit should necessarily be limited to something that was an infringement of the original patent assigned, and in the same case Lord Loreburn[76] said:

"I think that any part does constitute an improvement, if it can be adapted to this machine, and it would make it cheaper and more effective or in any way easier or more useful or valuable, or in any other way make it a preferable article in commerce."

In *National Broach etc. Co. v. Churchill Gear Machines Ltd.*[77] the licensee

---

[73] See *Valveless Gas Engine Syndicate Ltd. v. Day* (1899) 16 R.P.C. 97; *Osram-Robertson Lamp Works Ltd. v. Public Trustee* (1920) 37 R.P.C. 189; *Vislok Ltd. v. Peters* (1927) 44 R.P.C. 235.

[74] *Davies v. Davies Patent Boiler Ltd.* (1908) 25 R.P.C. 823; *Sadgrove v. Godfrey* (1920) 37 R.P.C. 7 at pp.20, 21; *Vislok Ltd. v. Peters* (1927) 44 R.P.C. 235. See also *Davies v. Curtis & Harvey Ltd.* (1903) 20 R.P.C. 561.

[75] (1908) 25 R.P.C. 349, 665; 27 R.P.C. 109.

[76] (1910) 27 R.P.C. at p.113.

[77] [1967] R.P.C. 99 at pp.110, 11. See also *Beecham v. Bristol Laboratories* [1978] R.P.C. 521 and *Regina Glass v. Schuler* [1972] R.P.C. 229.

covenanted to "communicate to [the licensor] all details of any improvements which may be developed during the subsistence" of the licence agreement and to apply for patents if so requested by the licensor. A question in the case was when the duty to communicate something which had been developed arose. The House of Lords held it was impossible to lay down any criterion and the court, looking at the matter through technical eyes, must answer the question in any particular case in all the circumstances of that case, but, if an idea has arisen which may lead to some patentable improvement, the obligation to communicate will arise at a very early stage as the licensor must have time to consider whether he wanted patents applied for.

Patents subsequently acquired

8.61   Agreements by the vendors of a patent to assign to the purchasers all patent rights that they may subsequently acquire of a like nature to the patent sold are not contrary to public policy, under United Kingdom national law[78] but may contravene Article 85(1). The danger to the purchasers of the destruction of the value of the rights which they have bought would otherwise be great, as inventors frequently continue to make inventions relating to the same art, and without such protection the purchasers would be exposed to competition from the vendors with the benefit of their previous experience.[79] The validity of such contracts at Common Law, as always where the question is one of restraint of trade, depends upon whether the restrictions extend further than is reasonably necessary to protect the legitimate interests of the parties in the circumstances of the case. The period over which the disability imposed is to last, and the area over which it is to extend are material factors to be considered in each case. Although covenants by a vendor not to make or sell the invention at all, or the product obtained by the patented or any similar process which would be in competition with it, may be perfectly valid under national law,[80] such covenants might well contravene Article 85(1).[81]

Limited licences

8.62   Licences frequently contain clauses limiting the licensee's right so that he is not entitled to work the patent in any way he chooses. Care is necessary that such licences do not contravene section 44 of the Act, and that terms are not included which are void under the Resale Prices Act 1976 or contrary to the public interest having regard to the Restrictive Trade Practices Act 1976, or contrary to Article 85(1) of the EC Treaty.

---

[78] *Printing and Numerical Registering Co. v. Sampson* (1875) L.R. 19 Eq. 462.
[79] *Ibid.*
[80] See *Nordenfelt v. Maxim Nordenfelt, etc., Co. Ltd.* [1894] A.C. 535; *Mouchel v. Cubitt & Co.* (1907) 24 R.P.C. 194.
[81] See *post*, §§8.73 *et seq.*

But, subject to those exceptions which will be referred to subsequently in this Chapter,

> "a patentee has a right, not merely by sale without reserve to give an unlimited right to the purchaser to use, and thereby to make in effect a grant which he cannot derogate, but may attach to it conditions, and if these conditions are broken, then there is no licence, because the licence is bound up with the observance of the conditions."[82]

Purchaser without notice of limited licence

A purchaser of patented goods without notice of restrictions affecting **8.63** such goods is free to use and sell them in any way he chooses.[83] But if at the time of his purchase he has notice of any restrictions affecting the patented goods (other than restrictions that are void) and contravenes such restrictions he is liable to be sued for infringement by the patentee, as the restrictions are "not contractual but are incident to and a limitation of the grant of the licence to use, so that, if the conditions are broken, there is no grant at all."[84]

The question of the knowledge of the defendant is one of fact in each case, as to which the passing of some leaflet or label with the goods at the time of sale may or may not be sufficient evidence according to the nature of the goods and the general circumstances. It is not essential that the purchaser should have knowledge of the precise restrictions concerned so long as he has knowledge of their nature and existence and means of knowledge of their exact extent.[85] Registration of the limited licence at the Patent Office is not in itself equivalent to notice of the limitations to a purchaser of an article.[86]

It is submitted that just as a patentee may impose restrictions on the **8.64** otherwise unlimited licence implied by the sale of a patented article, so a licensee may similarly impose restrictions upon articles made and sold

---

[82] *Per* Kennedy J. in *Incandescent Gas Light Co. Ltd. v. Brogden* (1899) 16 R.P.C. 179 at p.183; and see *Incandescent Gas Light Co. Ltd. v. Cantelo* (1895) 12 R.P.C. 262 at p.264. See also *Sterling Drug Inc. v. C. H. Beck Ltd.* [1973] R.P.C. 915.

[83] See *Betts v. Willmott* (1871) L.R. 6 Ch.App. 239 at p.245; *Incandescent Gas Light Co. Ltd. v. Cantelo* (1895) 12 R.P.C. 262; *Incandescent Gas Light Co. Ltd. v. Brogden* (1899) 16 R.P.C. 179; *Scottish Vacuum Cleaner Co. Ltd. v. Provincial Cinematograph Theatres Ltd.* (1915) 32 R.P.C. 353; *Hazeltine Corporation v. Lissen Ltd.* (1939) 56 R.P.C. 62.

[84] *Per* Farwell J. in *British Mutoscope and Biograph Co. Ltd. v. Homer* (1901) 18 R.P.C. 177 at p.179; see also *National Phonograph Co. of Australia Ltd. v. Menck* (1911) 28 R.P.C. 229 at p.248; see also *Columbia Graphophone Co. v. Vanner* (1916) 33 R.P.C. 104; *Columbia Graphophone Co. Ltd. v. Murray* (1922) 39 R.P.C. 239; *Columbia Graphophone Co. Ltd. v. Thoms* (1924) 41 R.P.C. 294; *Dunlop Rubber Co. Ltd. v. Longlife Battery Depot* [1958] R.P.C. 473; all cases decided prior to Resale Prices Act 1964 and 1976 and relating to breaches of restrictions as to the resale prices of articles.

[85] See *Columbia Graphophone Co. Ltd. v. Murray* (1922) 39 R.P.C. 239; *cf. Badische Anilin und Soda Fabrik v. Isler* (1906) 23 R.P.C. 633.

[86] *Heap v. Hartley* (1889) 42 Ch.D. 461; (1888) 5 R.P.C. 603 at p.608; (1889) 6 R.P.C. 495 (C.A.); *Scottish Vacuum Cleaner Co. v. Provincial Cinematograph Theatres Ltd.* (1915) 32 R.P.C. 353 (O.H.).

by him pursuant to his licence and provided these restrictions are not void and have been sufficiently brought to the notice of the purchaser any contravention of them constitutes an infringement in respect of which a patentee or an exclusive licensee[87] may take action. The contrary is suggested in one reported case,[88] but there the order of the court of first instance was discharged by the Court of Appeal[89] and in the subsequent proceedings the contention that the limitation of the licence was invalid appears to have been dropped.[90]

Conditions void under section 44 of the Patents Act 1977

8.65   A common type of limitation imposed before the Act of 1907 was that the patented article should not be used save in conjunction with some other article produced by the patentee, for example, that patented gas mantles should only be used in conjunction with the patentee's gas burners,[91] or that the patented machine alone should be used and that the user should purchase his raw materials from the patentee. Following section 57 of the 1949 Act conditions of this kind can, however, no longer be imposed, and by section 44(1) of the present Act any condition in a contract for the supply of a patented article, or in a licence to use or work a patented invention, is void which purports:

(a) to restrict the right of the licensee or person supplied to acquire where he pleases any article not protected by the patent, or

(b) to prohibit or restrict the licensee from using any article or process (whether patented or not) which does not belong to the licensor.[92]

Section 44(1) cannot be circumvented by providing that the contract is to be governed by a foreign law which does not give effect to the section.[93]

No bar to restrictions on sales by licensee

8.66   It is to be observed that the prohibition imposed by section 44 does not apply to selling[94] and, therefore, the licensor may impose a condition

---

[87] See *ante*, §8.20.
[88] *Gillette Safety Razor Co. Ltd. v. A. W. Gamage Ltd.* (1908) 25 R.P.C. 492. For a modern case see *Sterling Drug Inc. v. C. H. Beck Ltd.* [1973] R.P.C. 915.
[89] (1908) 25 R.P.C. 782; see also *Liverpool v. Irwin* [1977] A.C. 239.
[90] (1909) 26 R.P.C. 745.
[91] See, *e.g. Incandescent Gas Light Co. Ltd. v. Cantelo* (1895) 12 R.P.C. 262; *Incandescent Gas Light Co. Ltd. v. Brogden* (1899) 16 R.P.C. 179.
[92] See *Sarason v. Frenay* (1914) 31 R.P.C. 252, 330; *Huntoon Co. v. Kolynos (Inc.)* (1930) 47 R.P.C. 403; *Tool Metal Manufacturing Co. Ltd. v. Tungsten Electric Co. Ltd.* (1955) 72 R.P.C. 209 at p.218 (H.L.); *Thomas Hunter Ltd.'s Patent* [1965] R.P.C. 416 (an Irish case); *Transfield Pty. v. Arlo International* [1981] R.P.C. 141, Aust. High Ct.; *Fichera v. Flogates* [1984] R.P.C. 257 (C.A.); *Chiron Corporation v. Organon Teknika (No. 3)* [1994] F.S.R. 202.
[93] *Chiron Corporation v. Organon Teknika Ltd. (No. 2)* [1993] F.S.R. 324; [1992] 3 C.M.L.R. 813, [1993] F.S.R. 567 (C.A.).
[94] P.A. 1977, s.44(1).

that the licensee shall not sell any goods except such as are protected by the patent. Furthermore, it is expressly provided that a condition of a contract shall not be void by reason only that it prohibits any person from selling goods other than those supplied by a specified person.[95] Accordingly, a patentee can make it a condition of a grant of a selling agency that the agent shall not sell the goods of anyone else.

Spare parts

A licensor may reserve the right, in a contract for the use or hire of a **8.67** patented article, to supply such new parts as are required to keep it in repair.[96] A part needed to replace a worn part is a part required to keep the article in repair.[97]

Condition not necessarily invalid

Contracts of the kind referred to in subsection (1) of section 44 are not **8.68** invariably to be deemed invalid. The section is designed for the protection of persons such as repairers in a small way of business who (apart from its provisions) would practically be compelled to enter into contracts of that kind in order to obtain a lease of a necessary machine, and it was not the purpose of the section to interfere with contracts which had been voluntarily entered into by parties who had the opportunity clearly laid before them of purchasing or hiring upon different terms. Accordingly, subsection (4) provides that such a condition is not void provided:

(a) a contract without the condition on reasonable terms "specified in the contract or licence" was offered at the time when the actual contract was made, and

(b) the condition can be determined on three months' notice in writing and subject to the payment of compensation.

The onus of proving that an alternative contract, on reasonable terms and without the restriction, was offered to the other party is upon the vendor, lessor or licensor.[98]

Defence in infringement action

Subsection (1) of section 44 is of a penal nature, and subsection (3) **8.69** provides that in proceedings against any person for infringement of a patent it shall be a defence to prove that at the time of the infringement

---

[95] P.A. 1977, s.44(6).
[96] P.A. 1977, s.44(6).
[97] *Fichera v. Flogates* [1984] R.P.C. 257, (C.A.).
[98] P.A. 1977, s.44(5).

there was in force[99] a contract relating to that patent and containing a condition void under this section. The fact that the contract concerned was made with a third party and not with the defendant is not material.[1]

A plaintiff who has had to discontinue an action owing to the defendant pleading the existence of a contract containing unlawful conditions, may commence a fresh action against the same defendant for infringement of the same patent after the offending contract has been terminated,[2] but is not entitled to recover damages for infringements committed while the offending contract was in force.[3] Where a plaintiff failed at trial by reason of section 44, leave to amend the pleadings after judgment and removal of the offending provision from the contract was refused.[3a]

The section applies to all contracts made after January 1, 1950.[4]

Resale price maintenance conditions void under the Resale Prices Act

8.70   Formerly it was not uncommon for patented goods to be supplied subject to a condition as to the minimum price at which they could be resold retail. However, the Resale Prices Act 1964 was enacted with a view to abolishing resale price maintenance of goods except where the Restrictive Practices Court have ordered such goods to be exempted from the provisions of the Act. The law is now governed by the Resale Prices Act 1976.

By section 9(1) of this Act any term or conditions of a contract for the sale of goods by a supplier to a dealer, or of any agreement between a supplier and a dealer relating to such a sale, shall be void insofar as it purports to establish or provide for the establishment of minimum prices to be charged on the resale of the goods in the United Kingdom. (For the purposes of the Act a supplier is defined as "a person carrying on a business of selling goods other than a business in which goods are sold only by retail" and a dealer as "a person carrying on a business of selling goods, whether by wholesale or by retail".[5] Furthermore, it is unlawful for a supplier of goods to include any such term or condition in any contract of sale or agreement relating to the sale of goods, or to require, as a condition of supplying goods to a dealer, the inclusion in any contract or any agreement of any such term or condition, or to notify

---

[99] See *Trubenising Ltd. v. Steel and Glover Ltd.* (1945) 62 R.P.C. 1 at p.15.
[1] *Sarason v. Frenay* (1914) 31 R.P.C. 252, 330 (C.A.).
[2] *Aktiengesellschaft für Autogene Aluminium Schweissung v. London Aluminium Co. Ltd.* (1919) 36 R.P.C. 29.
[3] P.A. 1977, s.44(3) overruling *Aktiengesellschaft für Autogene Aluminium Schweissung v. London Aluminium Co. Ltd. (No.2)* (1923) 40 R.P.C. 107.
[3a] *Chiron Corporation v. Organon Teknika (No. 4)* [1994] F.S.R. 252.
[4] P.A. 1977, s.44(2).
[5] s.24(1).

to dealers, or publish in relation to goods, a minimum price for the goods on resale.[6]

Section 10(1) expressly enacts that section 9 of the Act applies to patented articles (including articles made by a patented process) as it applies to other goods; and that notice of any term or condition which is void by virtue of the section, or which would be so void if included in a contract of sale or agreement relating to the sale of any such article, shall be of no effect for the purpose of limiting the right of a dealer to dispose of that article without infringement of the patent. However, section 10(3) provides that nothing in section 9 of the Act shall affect the validity, as between the parties and their successors, of any term or condition of a licence granted by the proprietor of a patent or by a licensee under any such licence, or of any assignment of a patent, so far as it regulates the price at which articles produced or processed by the licensee or assignee may be sold by him.

It is to be noted that the foregoing provisions of section 9(1) of the Act have no application to any patented articles registered under the Act as an "exempt" class of goods, *i.e.* registered as exempt pursuant to an order of the Restrictive Practices Court under section 5 of the Act.[7]

It is also to be noted that the presence in any contract of sale or other agreement of a term or condition void by virtue of the provisions of section 9(1) of the Act does not affect the enforceability of the contract or agreement except in respect of the void term or condition.[8]

The effect of sections 9 and 10 of the Resale Prices Act 1976 in relation **8.71** to patented goods may be summarised as follows:

(a) A patent licence, including a licence granted by a licensee (*i.e.* a sub–licence), may lawfully include a term or condition which regulates the price at which the licensee (or sub–licensee) may sell the patented articles made or processed by him under the licence and such a term is not void under the Act.

(b) Similarly, a patent assignment may lawfully include a term or condition regulating the price at which the assignee may sell the patented articles made or processed by him.

(c) Where patented articles, not being articles within any exempted class of goods registered under the Act, are supplied to a dealer for resale (whether for resale, wholesale or retail) no term or condition which fixes the minimum resale price, wholesale or retail, may be imposed by the supplier. Any such term purported to be imposed by a supplier in respect of any such articles will be void and may be ignored by any dealer who acquires the articles for resale, whether he acquires the articles direct from that supplier or after they have passed through the hands of another

---

[6] s.9(2).
[7] s.14(1).
[8] s.9(2).

trader or other traders and even though he acquires them with notice of such purported term or condition.

Effect of the Restrictive Trade Practices Act

8.72   The Restrictive Trade Practices Act 1976 does not apply to patent licences or sub–licences or assignments of patents or the right to apply for patents, or to agreements to grant licences or sub–licences or to assign which contain restrictions only in respect of the use of the patented invention or articles made by the use of that invention (see section 28 and Schedule 3, para. 5). But, if there are restrictions other than the above and such restrictions fall within sections 6(1) or 11(2) of the Act, then the agreement will have to be registered under the Act. Further, the Restrictive Trade Practices Act provides in section 35 that agreements which are registrable, but are not registered shall be void in respect of all restrictions accepted and that it shall be unlawful to give effect to or enforce or purport to enforce such an agreement in respect of any such restrictions.

Effect of Article 85 of the EC Treaty on Assignments and Licences[9]

8.73   Article 85(1) prohibits as incompatible with the Common Market, *inter alia*, all agreements between undertakings which may affect trade between Member States and which have as their object or effect the prevention, restriction or distortion of competition within the Common Market. Any agreement prohibited by Article 85(1) is automatically void.[10] But the nullity applies only to those elements of the agreement which are subject to the prohibition unless those elements are not severable in which case the nullity will apply to the agreement as a whole.[11] The consequences of the nullity are determined by the National Law.[12] The Commission also has power to impose fines on the parties infringing Article 85.[13] Clauses commonly found in patent licence agreements which may contravene Article 85 are set out *post*, §8.78.

---

[9] A comprehensive study of the impact of Article 85 of the EC Treaty on patent assignments and licences is outside the scope of this work and the following paragraphs are intended only as a summary.

[10] EC Treaty, Art. 85(2).

[11] Case 56/65, *Technique Minière v. Maschinenbau Ulm G.m.b.H.* [1966] E.C.R. 235, [1966] C.M.L.R. 357.

[12] Case 10/86, *V.A.G. v. Magne* [1986] E.C.R. 4071, [1988] 4 C.M.L.R. 98 (E.C.J.); *Chemidus Wavin v. TERI* [1977] 3 C.M.L.R. 514, [1977] F.S.R. 181, (C.A.); *Inntrepreneur Estates v. Mason* [1993] 2 C.M.L.R. 293.

[13] Reg. 17, Art. 15. Fines may be up to 10 per cent of the undertaking's turnover in the preceding business year.

Degree of effect: The De Minimis Rule

An agreement may affect trade between Member States within the **8.74** meaning of Article 85(1) if it is capable of having that effect.[14] But an agreement will not fall within Article 85(1) where it is unlikely to affect trade between Member States or restrict competition to any appreciable extent.[15] What is "appreciable" is a question of fact to be decided in each case.[16] Previous decisions of the Commission and the European Court of Justice provide some guidance. The Commission's Notice of September 3, 1986 on Agreements of Minor Importance[17] may also assist. Agreements covered by the Notice need not be notified in accordance with Regulation 17. Where, due to exeptional circumstances, an agreement which is covered by the Notice nevertheless falls under Article 85(1), the Commission will not impose fines.[18] It should be noted that the Notice is for guidance only: it is not a Regulation and it is not binding on the courts of the United Kingdom or on the European Court.

The Notice states the Commission's view that agreements between undertakings engaged in the production or distribution of goods or in the provision of services generally do not fall under the prohibition of Article 85(1) if:

(i) the goods or services which are the subject of the agreement together with the participating undertakings' other goods or services which are considered by users to be equivalent in view of their characteristics, price and intended use, do not represent more than five per cent of the total market for such goods or services in the area of the Common Market affected by the agreement and

(ii) the aggregate annual turnover of the participating undertakings does not exceed 200 million ECU.[19]

Block Exemptions

Article 85(1) may be declared inapplicable in certain cases.[20] The **8.75** Commission has power to issue regulations granting block exemptions to certain agreements or category of agreements.[21] Currently there are two substantive regulations of particular relevance to patent licensing,

---

[14] Case 19/77, *Miller v. Commission* [1978] E.C.R. 131, [1978] 2 C.M.L.R. 334.
[15] Case 5/69, *Volk v. Vervaecke* [1969] E.C.R. 295, [1969] C.M.L.R. 273, *cf. Miller v. Commission* see *ante.*
[16] Commonly the lack of appreciable effect is due to the weakness of the parties on the market; but *cf.* case 30/78, *Distillers v. E.C. Commission* [1980] E.C.R. 229, [1980] 3 C.M.L.R. 121.
[17] [1986] O.J. C231/2, replacing the Notice of December 19, 1977 [1986] O.J. C231/2 ([1977] O.J. C313/3); see also the Notice of May 27, 1970 ([1970] O.J. C64/1).
[18] See the text of the Notice.
[19] The value of the ECU is published in the Official Journal and in the financial press, including *The Times.*
[20] EC Treaty, Art. 85(3).
[21] Reg. 19/65.

namely Regulation 2349/84 and Regulation 556/89.[22] Further Regulations deal with Exclusive Distribution Agreements (*i.e.* sales only),[23] Specialisation Agreements and Research and Development Agreements.[24]

Regulation 2349/84 applies to patent assignments[25] and licences and includes within its scope patent licensing agreements which also contain provisions assigning, or granting the right to use, non–patented technical knowledge (*i.e.* know–how). However, such mixed agreements are only covered by the Regulation where the know–how permits a better exploitation of the licensed patents and insofar as the licensed patents are necessary for achieving the objects of the licensed technology.[26] Thus, a know–how licensing agreement involving some patent licensing but only as a minor component was held not to fall within Regulation 2349/84.[27] The more recent Regulation 556/89 now covers that situation. These Regulations, particularly Regulation 2349/84, are dealt with in more detail below.[28]

Negative Clearance and individual exemption

8.76   If the agreement is outside the scope of the *De Minimis* Rule and neither of the block exemptions apply, then the agreement must be notified.[29] The Commission may grant negative clearance[30] or specific exemption.[31] If not, then it may require the parties to bring the infringement of Article 85(1) to an end.[32] The procedure to be followed on notification is set out in Regulation 27.[33]

8.77   In certain cases it may be possible to take advantage of the simplified procedure of notification provided by Article 4 of Regulation 2349/84 which extends the Block Exemption to cover agreements notified to the Commission and to which the Commission does not object within a period of six months. Article 4 applies where the agreement in question does not contain any obligations within Article 3 (the Black List) but which does contain obligations restrictive of competition not covered by Articles 1 and 2. It is essential to refer to Article 4 when notifying.[34] There is a similar provision in respect of Regulation 556/89.[35]

---

[22] The text of both regulations (as amended by Regulation 151/93) [1993] O.J. L21/8 is set out at [1993] 4 C.M.L.R. 151.

[23] Reg. 1983/83 [1983] O.J. L173/1 as amended by [1983] O.J. L281/24.

[24] Reg. 417/85 [1985] O.J. L53/1 and Reg. 418/85 [1985] O.J. L53/5; both as amended by Reg. 151/93 [1993] O.J. L21/8.

[25] Recital (6), and Art. 11(2).

[26] Recital (9).

[27] Boussois/Interpane [1987] O.J. L50/30, [1988] 4 C.M.L.R. 124, [1988] F.S.R. 215.

[28] See *post*, §8.79 *et seq.*

[29] Art. 4(1), Council Reg. No.17.

[30] Art. 2, *ibid.*

[31] Art. 6, *ibid.*

[32] Art. 3, *ibid.*

[33] As amended by Reg. 1699/75 [1975] O.J. L172/11 and Reg. 2526/85 [1985] O.J. L240/1.

[34] Art. 4(3)(*a*).

[35] See Art. 4.

Particular Clauses

Article 3 of Regulation 2349/84 (the Black List)[36] sets out a number of   **8.78**
obligations which it may be assumed the Commission regard as
contravening Article 85(1). These clauses are dealt with in more detail
below.[37] Previous decisions of the Commission (most of which were
made prior to the Block Exemptions) and of the European Court provide
further guidance. However, in reviewing the previous decisions it is
important to bear in mind that the decisions of the Commission are not
binding on the courts of the United Kingdom and on the basis of the
success rate of appeals from the Commission to the European Court it is
clear that it cannot necessarily be assumed that decisions of the
Commission are correct. European Competition Law is still in development and some of the decisions of the Commission, particularly the
early decisions, may overstate the ambit of Article 85(1). The European
Court is also capable of reversing itself.[38]

The following provisions of patent licence agreements have been held
by the Commission or the European Court to be contrary to Article
85(1): export prohibitions and obligations not to sell save in certain
specified States;[39] no challenge clauses;[40] an obligation to obtain the
licensor's approval in respect of non–patented components;[41] a prohibition on the sale of patented components alone and an obligation to sell
the patented components as part of a complete unpatented article;[42] an
obligation to mark the complete article with an attribution in respect of a
patent relating to a component;[43] an obligation to pay royalties after
termination or expiry of the original patents;[44] a post–termination ban
on the manufacture and marketing of the licensed products;[45] an
obligation to assign improvement patents to the licensor;[46] the grant of

---

[36] Similarly, Art. 3 of Reg. 556/89 [1989] O.J. L61/1, 4 C.M.L.R. 195.

[37] See *post*, §8.82.

[38] Case C-10/89, *CNL-SUCAL v. HAG* [1990] 1 E.C.R. 3711, [1990] 3 C.M.L.R. 571, [1991] F.S.R. 99, reversing case 192/73, *Van Zuylen Freres v. HAG* [1974] E.C.R. 731, [1974] 2 C.M.L.R. 127.

[39] *Nungesser* [1978] O.J. L286/23, [1978] 3 C.M.L.R. 434, a decision in respect of breeders rights; *Kabel Mettalwerke* [1975] O.J. L222/34, [1975] 2 C.M.L.R. D.40, [1976] F.S.R. 18; see also, for example, *A.I.O.P./Beyrard* [1976] O.J. L6/8, [1976] 1 C.M.L.R. D.14, [1976] F.S.R. 181; *Velcro/Aplix* [1985] O.J. L233/22, [1989] 4 C.M.L.R. 157. *cf.* Reg. 2349/84 [1984] O.J. L219/15, Art. 1(1)(3) to 1(1)(7), but see also Art. 3(10) and 3(11)(*a*).

[40] Case 193/83, *Windsurfing International v. Commission* [1986] E.C.R. 611, [1986] 3 C.M.L.R. 489, [1988] F.S.R. 139; *cf.* case 65/86 *Bayer A.G. v. Sullhoffer* [1988] E.C.R. 5249, [1990] 4 C.M.L.R. 429, [1990] F.S.R. 300. See also *Raymond/Nagoya* [1972] O.J. L143/39 [1972] C.M.L.R. D.45; *Re Davidson Rubber* [1972] O.J. L143/31 [1972] C.M.L.R. D.52; *Kabel Mettalwerke* [1975] O.J. L222/34 [1975] C.M.L.R. D.40. [1976] F.S.R. 18; A.I.O.P./Beyrard, *ante*; *Vaessen/Moris* [1979] O.J. L19/32 [1979] 1 C.M.L.R. 511, [1979] F.S.R. 259; ACC [1979] 3 C.M.L.R. 77. See also Reg. 2349/84 [1984] O.J. L219/15, Art. 3(1).

[41] *Windsurfer International v. Commission* see *ante*.

[42] *Ibid.*

[43] *Ibid.*

[44] Case 320/87, *Ottung v. Klee* [1989] E.C.R. 1177, [1990] 4 C.M.L.R. 915, [1991] F.S.R. 657; *A.I.O.P./Beyrard*, see *ante*.

[45] Case 320/87, *Ottung v. Klee*, see *ante*; *cf.* Reg. 2349/84 [1984] O.J. L219/15, Art. 2(1)(4).

[46] *Raymond/Nagoya* [1972] O.J. L143/39, [1972] C.M.L.R. D.45; *Kabel Mettalwerke*, see *ante*; *Velcro/Aplix*, see *ante*. See also Reg. 2349/84 [1984] O.J. 219/15, Art. 3(8); *cf.* Art. 2(1)(10).

an exclusive licence;[47] an obligation not to grant further licences without the agreement of existing licensees;[48] an obligation on the parties not to compete in any way;[49] an excessive purchasing obligation in respect of non–patented products or manufacturing equipment;[50] an obligation to pay royalties on non–patented products;[51] an agreement which continues after expiry of all the original patents licensed;[52] exchange of know–how;[53] quality standards peculiar to licensors equipment;[54] restrictions on parties to a joint research and development agreement exercising their patents with third parties;[55] cross–licensing pooling arrangements.[56]

Regulation 2349/84

8.79   Regulation 2349/84 applies only to agreements between two parties[57] but for these purposes connected undertakings[58] are treated as a single undertaking. The Block Exemption applies to licences issued in respect of national patents of Member States, Community patents or European patents granted for Member States, utility models and licences in respect of inventions for which a patent application is made within one year.[59] It also applies to licensing agreements which contain obligation relating to non–member countries.[60] Assignments and sub–licences also fall within the scope of the Regulation.[61] Agreements concerning sales alone are expressly excluded.[62] So too are patent pools, licensing agreements entered into in connection with joint ventures (save as mentioned in Article 5(2)(a)), and reciprocal licensing or distribution agreements (save for reciprocal agreements which do not involve any territorial restrictions within the Common Market).[63] As mentioned above, the Regulation extends to mixed patent and know–how licensing

---

[47] *Raymond/Nagoya* see *ante*; *Re Davidson Rubber*, see *ante*; *Kabel Mettalwerke* see *ante*; *A.I.O.P./Beyrard*, see *ante*; *cf.* Reg. 2349/84 [1984] O.J. 219/15, Recital (11) and Art. 1(11)(1) and (1)(1)(2).

[48] *Zuid Nederlandsche BV* [1975] O.J. L249/27, [1975] 2 C.M.L.R. D.67, [1976] F.S.R. 70. *cf.* Reg. 2349/84, Art. 1(1)(1).

[49] *A.I.O.P./Beyrard*, see *ante*. See also Reg. 2349/84 [1984] O.J. 219/15, Art. 3(3).

[50] *Vaessen/Moris*, see *ante*; *Velcro/Aplix*, see *ante*.

[51] *A.I.O.P./Beyrard*, see *ante*. See also Reg. 2349/84 [1984] O.J. L219/15, Art. 3(4).

[52] A.I.O.P./Beyrard, see *ante*; *Velcro/Aplix*, see *ante*. See also Reg. 2349/84 [1984] O.J. L219/15, Art. 3(2).

[53] *United Reprocessors* [1975] O.J. L51/7, [1976] 2 C.M.L.R. D.1, [1976] F.S.R. 542.

[54] *Re Agreements on Video Cassette Recorders* [1978] F.S.R. 376, *cf.* the Commission's view as set out in *Windsurfer International v. Commission*, see *ante*, at para.43; see also Reg. 2349/84 [1984] O.J. L219/15.

[55] *Re the Agreement of Sopelem* [1975] C.M.L.R. D.72, [1975] F.S.R. 269 and see *Vacuum Interrupters Ltd.* [1977] O.J. L48/32, [1977] 1 C.M.L.R. D.67, [1977] F.S.R. 340.

[56] *Re Agreement on Video Cassette Recorders*, see *ante*.

[57] See Art. 1(1) and Recital (2).

[58] See Art. 12.

[59] Recital (4) and Art. 10.

[60] *Ibid.* But note Recital (5).

[61] Recital (6) and Art. 11(2).

[62] Recital (7). These are covered by Reg. 1983/83.

[63] Recital (8) and Art. 5. Note the amendment made by Reg. 151/93 to Art. 5(2).

agreements but only in certain cases.[64] It also extends to patent licensing agreements containing ancillary provisions relating to trade marks.[65] Exclusive licensing agreements, and agreements containing certain export bans on the licensor or his licensees are within the scope of the Regulation, but this is stated to be "without prejudice to subsequent developments in the case law of the Court of Justice regarding the status of such agreements under Article 85(1)".[66] The Regulation applies until December 31, 1994.[67]

Article 1(1) of the Regulation is the substantive provision which **8.80** declares Article 85(1) inapplicable to patent licensing agreements and mixed agreements which include one or more of the following obligations: an obligation on the licensor not to licence other undertakings in the licensed territory;[68] an obligation on the licensor not to exploit the licensed invention in the licensed territory himself;[69] an obligation on the licensee not to exploit the licensed invention in territories reserved for the licensor (provided that parallel patents exist in those territories);[70] an obligation on the licensee not to manufacture or use the licensed product, or use the patented process or know–how, in territories licensed to others (provided that parallel patents exist in those territories);[71] an obligation not to pursue an active policy of putting the licensed product on the market in such territories, and in particular not to engage in advertising specifically aimed at those territories, or to establish any branch or maintain any distribution depot there;[72] an obligation on the licensee not to put the licensed product on the market in such territories for a period not exceeding five years from the date when the product is first put on the market within the Common Market by the licensor or a licensee;[73] an obligation on the licensee to use only the licensor's trade mark or get up provided that the licensee is not prevented from identifying himself as the manufacturer.[74] The exemption of the restriction on putting the licensed product on the market (which is inherent in the obligations in Articles 1(1), (2), (3), (5) and (6)) apply only if the licensee manufactures the licensed product.[75]

Article 2(1) is the White List. It sets out a number of permissible **8.81** obligations which do not generally restrict competition and which may be included in an agreement without jeopardising the exemption. These

---

[64] See Recital (9); *Boussois/Interpane* [1987] O.J. L50/30, [1988] 4 C.M.L.R. 124, [1988] F.S.R. 215; and *ante*, §8.75.
[65] See Recital (10).
[66] Recital (11).
[67] Art. 14.
[68] Art. 1(1)(1).
[69] Art. 1(1)(2).
[70] Art. 1(1)(3).
[71] Art. 1(1)(4). Note the difference in wording between Art. 1(1)(3) and 1(1)(4) which is developed further in Art. 1(1)(5) and 1(1)(6).
[72] Art. 1(1)(5).
[73] Art. 1(1)(6).
[74] Art. 1(1)(7).
[75] Art. 1(2).

obligations are exempted even if they are not accompanied by any of the obligations exempted by Article 1.[76] The White List includes[77] the following obligations on the licensee: to procure goods or services from the licensor and to observe specifications concerning minimum quality of the licensed products insofar as they are necessary for the technically satisfactory exploitation of the licensed invention;[78] to pay minimum royalties or to achieve minimum production levels;[79] to restrict exploitation to one or more fields of use;[80] not to exploit the patent after termination insofar as the patent is still in force;[81] not to grant sub–licences or assign the licence;[82] to mark the licence product with an attribution in respect of the licensor, the patent and the licence;[83] not to divulge the know–how;[84] to inform the licensor of infringements, to take legal action against infringers and to assist the licensor in legal action against infringer.[85] The White List also permits obligations on both parties to communicate to one another any experienced gain in exploiting the licensed invention and to grant one another non–exclusive licences in respect of improvements.[86] Finally, a most favoured licensee clause is also permitted.[87]

8.82   Article 3 is the Black List, so called because the inclusion of any of the obligations listed will result in the agreement falling outside the Block Exemption. The Black List includes the following: no challenge clauses;[88] automatic extension of the agreement beyond the life of the original patents by the inclusion of new patents subsequently obtained by the licensor;[89] non–competition clauses save as provided in Article 1;[90] an obligation to pay royalties on non–patented products or for use of know–how in the public domain;[91] manufacturing or sale quotas;[92] price

---

[76] Art. 2(2).
[77] The List is not exhaustive: see Recital (18).
[78] Art. 2(1)(1) and 2(1)(9).
[79] Art. 2(1)(1).
[80] Art. 2(1)(3).
[81] Art. 2(1)(4).
[82] Art. 2(1)(5).
[83] Art. 2(1)(6).
[84] Art. 2(1)(7). This obligation may continue even after the agreement has expired.
[85] Art. 2(1)(8). These obligations are expressed to be without prejudice to the licensee's right to challenge the validity of the patent, see also Art. 3(1).
[86] Art. 2(1)(10).
[87] Art. 2(1)(11).
[88] Art. 3(1). A clause may however be included entitling the licensor to terminate in the event of a challenge.
[89] Art. 3(2). But note that such a clause is acceptable if each party has a right to terminate at least annually after the expiry of the last of the original patents. Also this provision is without prejudice to the licensor's right to charge royalties for the use of know–how, even after expiry of the patents.
[90] Art. 3(3). This provision is expressed to be without prejudice to an obligation on the licensee to use his best endeavours to exploit the licensed invention.
[91] Art. 3(4). But without prejudice to those instances where, in order to facilitate payment, the royalty payments are spread over a period extending beyond the life of the patents or entry of the know–how into the public domain.
[92] Art. 3(5).

or discount restrictions;[93] customer restrictions or packaging restrictions aimed at customer sharing;[94] an obligation to assign improvement patents or patents for new uses;[95] agreements which are conditional on the licensee accepting or using licences, products or services which he does not want;[96] an obligation on the licensee not to put licensed product on the market in territories licensed to other licensees for a period exceeding five years from the date when the product is first put on the market within the Common Market by the licensor or a licensee;[97] clauses requiring either party to refuse to supply persons who may export to other Member States,[98] or to make it difficult for users or resellers to obtain supplies from elsewhere in the Common Market, particularly by the exercise of intellectual property rights or the taking of other measures so as to prevent parallel importing.[99]

Regulation 556/89

The structure of Regulation 556/89 is similar to Regulation 2349/84: **8.83** there is a long recital followed by the substantive declaratory provision,[1] a White List,[2] a Black List,[3] a simplified notification procedure,[4] exclusions,[5] and then various miscellaneous provisions.

Regulation 556/89 covers pure know–how agreements and mixed know–how and patent licensing agreements not covered by Regulation 2349/84.[6] The definitions in Article 1(7)(5) and 1(7)(6) make it clear that the two Regulations are mutually exclusive.[7] In particular Regulation 556/89 covers mixed agreements:

(a) in which the licensed patents are not necessary for the achievement of the objects of the licensed technology containing both patented and non–patented elements, and

(b) which contain obligations which restrict the exploitation of the

---

[93] Art. 3(6).
[94] Art. 3(7), save as provided in Art. 1(1)(7) (the obligation to use the licensor's trade mark or get up) and Art. 2(1)(3) (field of use restrictions).
[95] Art. 3(8).
[96] Art. 3(9), unless they are necessary for the technically satisfactory exploitation of the licensed invention.
[97] Art. 3(10). To put it another way, the five year period mentioned in Art. 1(1)(7) must be strictly observed. Nor must there be any concerted practice. There is an express saving for the permissible obligation of Art. 1(1)(5).
[98] Art. 3(11)(*a*).
[99] Art. 3(11)(*b*).
[1] Art. 1(1).
[2] Art. 2(1).
[3] Art. 3.
[4] Art. 4.
[5] Art. 5.
[6] Recitals (2) and (3).
[7] See also Art. 1(1).

relevant technology by the licensor or licensee in Member States without patent protection.[8]

Many of the provisions of Regulation 556/89 so far as concerns patents are the same as or similar to those of the earlier Regulation 2349/84 but, as Regulation 556/89 is primarily concerned with know–how agreements, a detailed exposition of the Regulation is not appropriate for this work. The Regulation applies until December 31, 1999.[9]

Refusal to license

8.84   It has been argued that it may be unlawful to refuse to grant a licence under a patent in certain circumstances, particularly where such refusal is an abuse of a dominant position and therefore contrary to Article 86 of the EC Treaty.[10] However, the European Court has ruled that the refusal by the proprietor of a Registered Design to grant a licence, even in return for a reasonable royalty, cannot in itself constitute an abuse of a dominant position.[11]

Statutory extension of licences

8.85   The 1977 Act extends the term of all new existing patents[12] granted under the 1949 Act to 20 instead of 16 years.[13] In order to protect the position of licensees under such patents, the Act further provides that any licence in force under the patent from immediately before the appointed day[14] until the end of the sixteenth year from the date of the patent[15] shall, together with any contract relating to the licence, continue in force so long as the patent remains in force but that, notwithstanding the terms of the licence, the licensee shall not be required to make any payment to the proprietor for working the invention in question after the end of the sixteenth year.[16] The Act further provides that, if it is an exclusive licence, it shall after the end of the sixteenth year be treated as a non–exclusive licence.[17]

---

[8] Recital (2).
[9] Art. 12.
[10] *Pitney Bowes Inc. v. Francotyp-postalia G.m.b.H.* [1991] F.S.R. 72, [1990] 3 C.M.L.R. 466; see also *Chiron Corp. v. Organon Teknika Ltd. (No. 2)* [1993] F.S.R. 324, [1992] 3 C.M.L.R. 813; *Chiron Corp. v. Murex Diagnostics Ltd. (No. 2)* [1994] F.S.R. 187, (C.A.), and see *ante*, §6.64.
[11] Case 238/87, *Volvo v. Erik Veng (U.K.) Ltd.* [1988] E.C.R. 6211, [1989] 4 C.M.L.R. 122, at para.8.
[12] *i.e.* patents with at least 5 years to run as at the appointed day June 1, 1978; see P.A. 1977, s.127, Sched.1, para.3(1).
[13] P.A. 1977, s.127, Sched.1, para.4.
[14] June 1, 1978.
[15] Being the date when the patent would have expired but for the extension of the term thereof.
[16] P.A. 1977, s.127, Sched.1, para.3(2)(*a*) & (*b*).
[17] P.A. 1977, s.127, Sched.1, para.4(2)(*a*).

3. Co-ownership

Ownership of patent for limited area

Assuming it is still possible to assign a patent for a limited part of the **8.86** United Kingdom or to achieve the same result by granting an exclusive licence[18] in such circumstances the "assignee" would be owner of his share of the patent in severalty, and could sue or grant licences in respect of acts done or to be done in the area to which his portion of the patent extended and would not, apart from contract, be liable to account in any way to the owner of the rest of the patent.

Co-ownership

Co-ownership of a patent, or an application for a patent may arise by **8.87** the patent being applied for by or granted to joint applicants or by assignment. The title of a co-owner should be entered in the register.[19] Apart from an agreement to the contrary, joint grantees are each entitled to an equal undivided share in the patent[20] and every registered co-owner is entitled, "by himself or his agents", to work the patented invention for his own benefit without accounting to the other or others.[21] It is submitted that the word "agents" in this connection must be narrowly interpreted and does not include an independent contractor.[22] The same provisions apply to applications.[23]

The right to sue

One co-owner can sue for infringement of the patent[24] or of the rights **8.88** arising on publication of the application,[25] but must join his fellow co-owners, either as co-plaintiff(s) or as defendant(s). If a co-owner joined as a defendant takes no part in the proceeding he shall not be liable for costs.[26]

Licence and assignment

Apart from an agreement to the contrary (and subject to the powers of **8.89** the Comptroller under the provisions of sections 8, 12 and 37 of the Act), no licence can be granted by one or more co-owners and no assignment or mortgage can be made of the share of any co-owner without the

---

[18] See *ante*, §8.18.
[19] See *ante*, §8.27.
[20] P.A. 1977, s.36(1). *Young v. Wilson* (1955) 72 R.P.C. 351.
[21] P.A. 1977, s.36(2), (4).
[22] See *Howard & Bullough Ltd. v. Tweedales and Smalley* (1895) 12 R.P.C. 519.
[23] P.A. 1977, s.36(7).
[24] P.A. 1977, s.66.
[25] P.A. 1977, s.69.
[26] P.A. 1977, s.66(2).

consent of all persons who are co–owners of the patent or application, as the case may be.[27] But the purchaser of an article sold by one co–owner becomes entitled to deal with it just as though it had been sold by a sole proprietor.[28]

Devolution of title

8.90   The rules of law applicable to the devolution of personal property generally apply in relation to co–owned patents and applications.[29] Accordingly, the undivided share of a co–owner of a patent or an application devolves upon his personal representatives.

Power of Comptroller

8.91   Any co–owner registered as joint proprietor may apply to the Comptroller for directions regarding whether any right in or under the patent should be transferred or granted to any other person.[30] This provision is to prevent the proper exploitation of a patent being unreasonably prevented by one or more co–owners. The procedure is governed by rule 54 of the Patents Rules 1990. If a person ordered to execute any instrument or do any other acts fails to do so within 14 days of being requested to do so, the Comptroller may, on an application made to him, give directions empowering some other person to perform such act.[31] The person in default must to be given notice of the application.[32] An appeal lies to the Patents Court and, with leave, from the Patents Court to the Court of Appeal.[33]

Trustees and personal representatives

8.92   The provisions of the Act as to co–ownership do not affect the mutual rights or obligations of trustees or personal representatives or their rights and obligations as such.[34]

---

[27] P.A. 1977, s.36(3) and s.36(7).
[28] P.A. 1977, s.36(5).
[29] P.A. 1977, s.36(6) and (7).
[30] P.A. 1977, s.37(1)(*c*) as amended by C.A.P.A. 1988, s.295, Sched.5, para.9(2). *Florey & Others' Patent* [1962] R.P.C. 186.
[31] P.A. 1977, s.37(3), Patents Rules 1990, r.55. *Florey & Others' Patent* [1962] R.P.C. 186 at p.194. See also *Cannings' United States Appn.* [1992] R.P.C. 459.
[32] Patents Rules 1990, r.55(2).
[33] P.A. 1977, s.97(1), (3).
[34] P.A. 1977, s.37(6).

4. Registration

Register of Patents

There is kept at the Patent Office a Register of Patents open to public **8.93**
inspection upon application and payment of the prescribed fee[35] in
which are entered particulars of published applications, patents,
assignments, licences and other matters in compliance with the Rules.[36]

Where a person becomes entitled to a patent or application, or a share
or interest in or under a patent or application, there is no requirement to
apply to have his title registered but registration is advisable.[37]
Omission to register may, however, be rectified at any time.[38] Until the
register is rectified, it is prima facie but rebuttable evidence of the right
of the person registered as proprietor to sue for infringement. The
practice is regulated by rules 44 to 53 of the Patents Rules 1990.

Nature of title registered

A person's interest or estate in a patent or application will only be **8.94**
registered as what it is; for example, a person will not be registered as
proprietor of a patent unless he has the legal estate in the patent.[39] A
mortgagee will be registered as mortgagee and not as proprietor even
though the mortgage be a legal one.[40] Provided, however, that documents are properly executed and are produced from the proper
custody, the Comptroller will not go into the question of whether there
was consideration or of the circumstances of their execution.[41]

Registrable documents, etc.

Although the Act provides the statutory framework for registration of **8.95**
all transactions, instruments or events affecting rights in or under
patents or applications,[42] the Rules are narrower and they only
expressly authorise registration of those transactions, etc., referred to in
section 33(3).[43] The Comptroller does, however, retain a discretion to
register such other particulars as he may think fit.[44] Nevertheless, no
notice of any trust whether express, implied or constructive may be
entered in the Register and the Comptroller is not affected by any such

---

[35] Patents Rules 1990, r.49.
[36] P.A. 1977, s.32 as amended by P.D.M.A. 1986, s.1, Sched.1, para.4; Patents Rules 1990,
r.44 and r.93.
[37] See *ante*, §8.27.
[38] P.A. 1977, ss.33, 34, Patents Rules 1990, r.46.
[39] (1910) 27 R.P.C. *Comptroller's Ruling E.*
[40] See *Van Gelder Apsimon & Co. Ltd. v. Sowerby Bridge Flour Society Ltd.* (1890) 7 R.P.C. 208.
[41] (1910) 27 R.P.C. *Comptroller's Ruling E.*
[42] P.A. 1977, s.32(2)(*b*) as amended by P.D.M.A. 1986, s.1, Sched.1, para.4.
[43] Patents Rules 1990, r.44(3)(f).
[44] Patents Rules 1990, r.44(4).

notice.[45] It has been held that a document which affects the proprietorship of a patent, whether by creating trusts or otherwise, is not excluded from the Register by this provision.[46] However, to be registrable documents containing an agreement must be complete and of such a nature that the agreement could be enforced by specific performance as otherwise no legal or equitable interest in the patent or proprietorship thereof would pass.[47]

The Comptroller may refuse to register documents if he is not satisfied that they are properly stamped.[48]

Certificate of the Comptroller

8.96   A certificate by the Comptroller as to any entry which he is authorised to make or as to any other thing which he is authorised to do is prima facie evidence of the matters so certified.[49] Certified copies of any entry will be furnished by the Comptroller on payment of the prescribed fee, and will be admitted in proceedings in all courts without further proof or production of the originals.[50]

Information. Caveat

8.97   Any person interested in a particular patent or application for a patent may, after publication of the application, leave a request at the Patent Office to be informed of certain matters, for example, of any attempt to register an assignment or other document in connection with the patent or application in question.[51] Notice will then be given to the person who has left the request and registration will be suspended for a few days so as to enable the person interested to apply to the courts for leave to serve notice of motion to prevent registration if he so desires.

The matters in respect of which information may be obtained are set out in Rule 92 of the Patents Rules 1990 and include when a request for substantive examination has been filed, when the specification of a patent or application for a patent has been published, when an application for a patent has been withdrawn or taken to be withdrawn or treated as withdrawn or refused or treated as refused, when a renewal fee has been paid within the period of six months referred to in section 25(4) of the Act, when a patent has ceased to have effect, and

---

[45] P.A. 1977, s.32(3) as amended by P.D.M.A. 1986, s.1, Sched.1, para.4.
[46] *Kakkar v. Szelke* [1989] F.S.R. 225 at p.237, following *Stewart v. Casey* (1892) 9 R.P.C. 9; see also (1910) 27 R.P.C. *Comptroller's Ruling E; cf. Haslett v. Hutchinson* (1891) 8 R.P.C. 457, *Svenska Aktiebolaget Gasaccumulator's App.* [1962] R.P.C. 106.
[47] *Haslett v. Hutchinson* (1891) 8 R.P.C. 457; *Fletcher's Patent* (1893) 10 R.P.C. 252; *Morey's Patent* (1858) 25 Beav. 581; *Parnell's Patent* (1888) 5 R.P.C. 126.
[48] See Stamp Act 1891, s.17; *cf. Maynard v. Consolidated Kent Collieries* [1903] 19 T.L.R. 448.
[49] P.A. 1977, s.35 as amended by P.D.M.A. 1986 s.3, Sched.3, Pt.1.
[50] P.A. 1977, s.35(3), Patents Rules 1990, r.52.
[51] P.A. 1977, s.118.

when an entry has been made in the register or an application has been made for making such an entry.

Inspection of documents

In addition to inspection of the Register,[52] it is also possible after the **8.98** date of publication of an application for a patent to inspect all documents filed or kept at the Patent Office in relation to the application or any patent granted in pursuance of it.[53] The procedure for such inspection is set out in the Rules.[54] There are special provisions in respect of documents which the applicant or proprietor has requested to be treated as confidential and the Comptroller has so directed.[55]

Where prior to the publication of an application for a patent the **8.99** applicant threatens a person with proceedings after publication of the application, a request may be made by that person for information and inspection of documents notwithstanding that the application has not been published.[56]

Rectification of register by the court

The court may, on the application of any person aggrieved, rectify the **8.100** register.[57]

The application must be made by originating motion[58] and is heard by one of the Patents Judges in the Patents Court.[59] The applicant must forthwith serve an office copy of the application on the Comptroller, who shall be entitled to appear and to be heard on the application.[60]

Clerical errors in the register may be corrected by the Comptroller on application made to him in the prescribed manner.[61]

Falsifying entries

It is an offence to make a false entry in the register or a writing falsely **8.101** purporting to be a copy of any entry, or to produce or tender in evidence any such writing knowing it to be false.[62]

---

[52] See *ante*, §8.93.
[53] P.A. 1977, s.118.
[54] Patents Rules 1990, r.93.
[55] Patents Rules 1990, r.94.
[56] P.A. 1977, s.118(4); Patents Rules 1990, r.96.
[57] P.A. 1977, s.34.
[58] Save where it is made in a petition for revocation or by way of counterclaim in proceedings for infringement, or in the case of an application for an order under s.51 of the Trustee Act 1925 where it is made by originating summons: R.S.C. Ord.104, r.22(1).
[59] R.S.C. 104, r.22(1).
[60] R.S.C. 104, r.22(2).
[61] P.A. 1977, s.32 as amended by P.D.M.A. 1986 s.1, Sched.1, para.4. Patents Rules 1978, r.47.
[62] P.A. 1977, s.109.

False use of "Patent Office"

8.102   If any person uses on his place of business, or on any document issued by him, the words "Patent Office" or any other words suggesting that his place of business is, or is officially connected with, the Patent Office, he is liable on summary conviction to a fine not exceeding level 4 on the standard scale.[63]

---

[63] P.A. 1977, s.112; "... not exceeding level 4 on the standard scale" means not exceeding £2,500; see Criminal Justice Act 1982, s.37(2) as substituted by Criminal Justice Act 1991, s.17.

CHAPTER 9

COMPULSORY LICENCES (ABUSE OF MONOPOLY) AND LICENCES OF RIGHT

The provisions of the 1949 Act relating to compulsory licences and   **9.01**
licences of right have been repealed by the 1977 Act[1] and the
corresponding provisions of the 1977 Act apply to both old and new Act
patents,[2] including all applications for licences of right made after the
appointed day.[3] Transitional provisions continue to apply the repealed
provisions of the 1949 Act to existing patents for certain limited
purposes.[4]

1. Compulsory Licence (Abuse of Monopoly)

A. History

As has already been stated, the early industrial "monopoly" patents   **9.02**
were granted with a view to establishing new industries in this country.
By the Statute of Monopolies a patent was void if hurtful to trade or
generally inconvenient. The common form of grant also provided for
revocation by the Privy Council if the grant was prejudicial or

---

[1] P.A. 1977, s.132(7), Sched. 6.
[2] P.A. 1977, s.127, Sched. 2.
[3] *Allen & Hanburys Ltd. v. Generics (U.K.) Ltd.* [1986] R.P.C. 203 (H.L.) at p.247.
[4] P.A. 1977, s.127, Sched. 4, para.8. *Glaverbel's Patent* [1987] R.P.C. 73, [1987] F.S.R. 153.

inconvenient to the King's subjects.[5] Many patents were in fact revoked for non-working during the seventeenth century;[6] but the courts later held that manufacture under the patent in this country was not essential,[7] and prior to the Act of 1883 there were no statutory provisions whereby a patentee could be forced to grant a licence if he abused his monopoly rights. By section 22 of that Act the Board of Trade was given power to order the grant of a compulsory licence where:

(a) the patent was not being worked in the United Kingdom; or
(b) the reasonable requirements of the public with respect to the invention were not satisfied; or
(c) any person was prevented from working or using an invention of which he was possessed.

There are only a few cases reported, however, of applications under this Act.[8]

9.03 By the Act of 1902 the jurisdiction of the Board of Trade was transferred to the Judicial Committee of the Privy Council, who might not only order a compulsory licence, but also revoke the patent if the granting of licences would be an inadequate remedy. No applications under this procedure are reported.

By section 24 of the Act of 1907 the jurisdiction was transferred to the court which was given power to order the grant of compulsory licences or to revoke the patent in cases where the reasonable requirements of the public in respect of the patented invention had not been satisfied; and by section 27 of that Act the Comptroller was given power (subject to an appeal to the court) to revoke the patent in cases where manufacture was carried on wholly or mainly abroad.

The Act of 1919 repealed sections 24 and 27 of the 1907 Act and substituted a new section 27, whereby the Comptroller was given jurisdiction in all cases where abuse of monopoly rights was alleged, his decision being subject to an appeal to the court. That section was subsequently amended and extended by the Acts of 1928 and 1932.

1949 Act

9.04 This Act further extended the grounds on which a compulsory licence could be obtained or the patent endorsed "licences of right",[9] or, in the last resort, the patent revoked. It had long been a popular misconception

---

[5] See Chap. 1, and *Hatschek's Patents* (1909), 26 R.P.C. 228.
[6] See Hulme, E. W., 13 L.Q.R. 313; 33 *ibid*, 71.
[7] See *Badische Anilin und Soda Fabrik v. W. G. Thompson Ltd. and Others* (1904) 21 R.P.C. 473.
[8] *Continental Gas Gluhlicht, etc., Petition* (1898) 15 R.P.C. 727; *Levenstein's Petition* (1898) 15 R.P.C. 732; *Hulton and Bleakley's Petition* (1898) 15 R.P.C. 749; *Bartlett's Patent* (1899) 16 R.P.C. 641; and see J. W. Gordon, *Compulsory Licences* (London 1899).
[9] P.A. 1949, s.37.

that patents were frequently applied for or purchased in order that the inventions covered thereby could be stifled for the benefit of rival commercial interests and in consequence of this belief the 1949 Act contained somewhat elaborate provisions designed to prevent "abuse of monopoly". In fact, no reliable evidence of even a single instance of such a suppression of an invention has ever been forthcoming, in spite of efforts of a Royal Commission to unearth it, if it in fact existed.

The 1949 Act allowed for the grant of compulsory licences in two cases firstly in respect of any patent where there had been inadequate working or oppressive conduct by the patentee[10] or secondly where the invention was concerned with food or medicine or a surgical or curative device.[11] The latter provision gave rise to a number of applications particularly in the pharmaceutical field,[12] however, the relevant provisions of the 1949 Act have been repealed and are not present in the 1977 Act. Apart from applications under section 41, there were very few applications for compulsory licences made under the 1949 Act.

1977 Act

Apart from the omission of special provisions relating to food, **9.05** medicines, etc., the Act in sections 48–51 has substantially re–enacted sections 37–40 of the 1949 Act.[12a] However, the European Court has held that by treating a case where demand for a patented product is satisfied on the domestic market by imports from other Member States as a case where a compulsory licence may be granted for insufficiency of exploitation of the patent, the United Kingdom has failed to fulfill its obligations under Article 30 of the EC Treaty.[13] Moreover, the European Court has held that it is also contrary to Article 30 of the EC Treaty for the Comptroller to exercise his discretion in granting licences of right so as to permit a licensee to import product from outside the EC if the patentee works the invention in another Member State but not if he works it within the United Kingdom.[14] Such an exercise of discretion discriminates against the patentee who decides to manufacture in another member State of the EC. The statutory provisions on compulsory licences and licences of right must be applied in the light of these rulings.[15]

There are special provisions for when the Community Patent

---

[10] *Ibid.*
[11] P.A. 1949, s.41.
[12] See, *e.g. Hoffman-La Roche Cases* [1965] R.P.C. 226 and [1969] R.P.C. 504.
[12a] Note that P.A. 1977, s.49(3) has now been deleted by C.D.P.A. 1988, Sched. 5, para. 13.
[13] *Re Compulsory Patent Licences: Case C-30/90, E.C. Commission v. United Kingdom* [1992] I E.C.R. 777 [1992] 2 C.M.L.R. 709, [1993] R.P.C. 283, [1993] F.S.R. 1.
[14] Case C-191/90, *Generics (U.K.) Ltd. v. Smith Kline & French Laboratories Ltd.* [1992] I E.C.R. 5335, [1993] 1 C.M.L.R. 89, [1993] R.P.C. 333, [1993] F.S.R. 592.
[15] See also Case 434/85, *Allen & Hanburys Ltd. v. Generics (U.K.) Ltd.* [1988] E.C.R. 1275, [1988] C.M.L.R. 701, [1988] F.S.R. 312, (E.C.J.).

Convention comes into force.[16] However, in view of the recent decisions of the European Court, these provisions may no longer be of any significance.[17]

As with the 1949 Act, there have to date been few applications for Compulsory Licences under the 1977 Act and most of the cases cited in this Chapter are pre–war. Unless otherwise stated, all references hereafter in this Chapter are to the 1977 Act.

B. Grounds for compulsory licence

9.06   The full grounds are set out in paragraph 9.09 *et seq., post*, but as stated above the right to obtain a compulsory licence arises where there has been inadequate working or oppressive conduct by the patentee. An application for a compulsory licence or to have the patent endorsed "licences of right", cannot be made until three years have elapsed from the date of the grant of the patent.[18] The Act states[19] that "any person" may apply for a compulsory licence, however the Act also requires the Comptroller to take account of the ability of the applicant to work the invention[20] so that in effect the applicant has to show a proper interest. As is dealt with below the applicant must make out a prima facie case before the Comptroller will allow the application to proceed.

Objects to be attained

9.07   By section 50, the Comptroller is to exercise his powers with a view to securing the following purposes:

(a) that inventions which can be worked on a commercial scale in the United Kingdom shall be worked there without undue delay and to the fullest practicable extent;

(b) that the inventor or other person entitled shall receive reasonable remuneration having regard to the invention;

(c) that the interests of any person working or developing an invention in the United Kingdom shall not be unfairly prejudiced.

---

[16] P.A. 1977, ss.53(1)and 86. C.P.C. Art.47 provides that it shall not be a ground of seeking a compulsory licence that the demand is being met by importation from another member state. Art.89 provides that signatory states are allowed to decline to be bound by Art.47 for a period up to 10 years.

[17] See, in particular, Case 30/90, *E.C. Commission v. United Kingdom* [1993] R.P.C. 283, [1993] F.S.R. 1 at p.49, para.32 where the E.C.J. stated that Art.89 of the C.P.C. may itself prove incompatible with Art.30 of the EC Treaty.

[18] P.A. 1977, s.48(1). See *Cathro's Appn.* (1934) 51 R.P.C. 75 at p.79.

[19] P.A. 1977, s.48(1).

[20] P.A. 1977, s.50(2)(*b*); see *J. R. Geigy S.A.'s Patent* [1964] R.P.C. 391; *Enviro-spray Systems Inc.'s Patents* [1986] R.P.C. 147.

These powers must be applied in the light of the EC Treaty which has the effect of prohibiting the grant of a compulsory licence which does not permit importation from another member state of the EC.[21] Nor may the Comptroller exercise his powers so as to discriminate against the patentee who decides to manufacture elsewhere in the EC.[22]

The Comptroller is also to take into account:

(a) the nature of the invention, how long the patent has been granted and the measures taken by the patentee or any licensee to make full use of the invention;
(b) the ability of a prospective licensee to work the invention; and
(c) the risks the latter must undertake;

but the Comptroller need not take into account matters arising subsequent to the application for a compulsory licence.[23]

Commercial scale

The Act of 1919 contained a special definition of "working on a **9.08** commercial scale",[24] but neither the 1949 Act nor the present Act provides any definition of "commercial scale" and these words must, therefore, be given their natural and ordinary meaning, *i.e.* "in contradistinction to research work or work in the laboratory".[25]

Grounds

There are five classes of cases in which the act or default of the **9.09** patentee can give rise to an application for a compulsory licence. These classes are not mutually exclusive; but unless the circumstances relied upon fall within one or other of the classes, no relief can be granted under the section.[26] The classes, particularly sections 48(3)(a)–(c), must be applied in the light of the ruling of the European Court of Justice that it is not legitimate under EC law to discriminate against commercial working of the invention by importation from another member state of

---

[21] Case 434/85 *Allen & Hanburys Ltd. v. Generics (U.K.) Ltd.* [1988] E.C.R. 1275, [1988] 1 C.M.L.R. 701, [1988] F.S.R. 312. But note the exception in EC law in respect of Spain and Portugal in certain circumstances: case C-191/90 *Generics (U.K.) Ltd. v. Smith Kline & French Laboratories* [1992] I E.C.R. 5335. [1993] 1 C.M.L.R. 89; *quare* whether U.K. national law now permits the prohibition of imports from Spain or Portugal in view of the amendments made to section 46(3)(c) by C.D.P.A. 1988, s.295, Sched. 5, para.12(2).
[22] Case C-191/90 *Generics (U.K.) Ltd. v. Smith Kline & French Laboratories Ltd.* [1992] I E.C.R. 5335, [1993] 1 C.M.L.R. 89; [1993] R.P.C. 333, [1993] F.S.R. 592. See also *Re Compulsory Patent Licences*: Case C-30/90 *EC Commission v. United Kingdom* [1992] E.C.R. 777, [1992] 2 C.M.L.R. 709, [1993] R.P.C. 283, [1993] F.S.R. 1.
[23] P.A. 1977, s.50(2).
[24] Act of 1919, s.93.
[25] *McKechnie Bros. Ltd.'s Appn.* (1934) 51 R.P.C. 461 at p.468.
[26] See *Brownie Wireless Co. Ltd.'s Appns.* (1928) 45 R.P.C. 457 at p.471.

the EC and in favour of production in the United Kingdom.[27] The classes are:

(a) Non-working in the United Kingdom, section 48(3)(a)

9.10 *"Where the patented invention is capable of being commercially worked in the United Kingdom, that it is not being so worked or is not being worked to the fullest extent that is reasonably practicable";*

The onus is upon the applicants to establish that the patented invention is not being worked to the fullest extent that is reasonably possible, *i.e.* at the rate of production which is practicable and necessary to meet the demand of the patented invention. In order to establish a case under this subsection it will normally be necessary for an applicant to bring evidence to show what the demand for the invention might reasonably be expected to be and how far short production in the United Kingdom or importation from another member state of the EC[28] fails to supply that demand.[29] Where the invention is not being worked to the fullest extent that is reasonably practicable whether by manufacture in the United Kingdom or by importation from another member state of the EC a compulsory licence may be granted.[30]

"Patented invention"

9.11   The meaning of the words "patented invention" requires some discussion in considering the obligation on the patentee to establish working on a commercial scale. In the case of an invention involving a small improvement in a complicated machine, a question arises as to the obligation on the patentee to manufacture. Again, if the patent is for the combination of old parts, there is the question whether the mere assembling in this country of parts made abroad is sufficient to comply with the section. In *Lakes' Patent*,[31] the Comptroller said:

"As a general rule a patentee ought not to be called upon to manufacture any mechanism or machine which he has not specific-ally described and claimed in his specification ... There may be, of course, cases in which it is impossible to sever the various elements

---

[27] Case C-30/90 *EC Commission v. United Kingdom* [1992] 1 E.C.R. 777 [1992] 2 C.M.L.R. 709, [1993] R.P.C. 283, [1993] F.S.R. 1; Case C-191/90 *Generics (U.K.) Ltd. v. Smith Kline & French Laboratories Ltd.* [1992]I E.C.R. 5335. [1993] 1 C.M.L.R. 89, [1993] R.P.C. 333, [1993] F.S.R. 592; and see *ante*, § 9.05.
[28] *Ibid.*
[29] *Kamborian's Patent* [1961] R.P.C. 403 at p.405.
[30] *Gebhardt's Patent* [1992] R.P.C. 1 at p.18. See also *Extrude Home Corp.'s Patent* [1982] R.P.C. 361 at p.383; that part of the judgment concerned with the EC Treaty cannot be sustained in the light of the subsequent rulings of the European Court, particularly *EC Commission v. United Kingdom*, see *ante*.
[31] (1909) 26 R.P.C. 443 at p.447.

claimed in combination, and in such cases different considerations may arise. If, however, the general principle stated is correct, the following general results would seem to follow, *viz*: if the patentee has claimed a wholly new machine or mechanism, he must manufacture that in this country or run the risk of coming within the provisions of the section ... If he claims a new improvement in a well-known machine, he must manufacture the improvement, and not necessarily the whole machine; but if he claims the improvement in combination with a machine consisting of well-known parts it may be that he must besides manufacturing the improvement put together the whole machine in this country, or at any rate the combination he claims. If his invention merely consists in a new combination of old and well-known elements, it would seem sufficient for him prima facie to put together the whole machine in this country, and it is not necessary for him to manufacture the old and well-known parts which are also possibly the subject-matter of prior patents; but different considerations may again arise where important alterations in the known parts are necessary for the new combination. Each case must, of course, be decided on its merits, and in each case it will have to be determined on a proper construction of the patentee's specification, what the patentee's invention really is, and what are its essential features.''[32]

In *Smith Kline & French Laboratories Ltd.'s (Cimetidine) Patents*,[33] Falconer J. said:

"...it seems to me that the mere formulation in the United Kingdom of cimetidine manufactured in Ireland and imported therefrom does not, as a matter of substance, amount to a commercial working of the patented invention of each of the patents to the fullest extent reasonably practicable in the United Kingdom. The patents contain product and process claims and it seems to me that, even for the formulation claim in each patent, commercial working in the United Kingdom to the fullest extent reasonably practicable of the invention so claimed is not obtained with the manufacture of the basic active ingredient in a foreign country."

Manufacture by infringers

The words "patented invention" are comparable with the words   **9.12** "patented article or process" in section 27 of the 1907 Act. It was held under that section that the words were descriptive of the manufacture itself, and that manufacture by infringers might be relied upon by the

---

[32] And see *Hill's Patent* (1915) 32 R.P.C. 475; *Wardwell's Patent* (1913) 30 R.P.C. 408; and *cf. Co-operative Union Ltd.'s Appns.* (1933) 50 R.P.C. 161.
[33] [1990] R.P.C. 203 at p.224.

patentee.[34] This would appear to be the case under the present law also. However, it is submitted, that it would be wrong to refuse a compulsory licence merely because the market was being met by infringers.

Relevant date

9.13   In *McKechnie Bros. Ltd.'s Application*[35] Luxmoore J. said:

> "the actual facts existing at the date of hearing may be considered as well as those existing at the date of the filing of the application . . . It is, of course, of first-class importance to consider the actual position at the date of the application; for if there is no actual working at that date, it may well be that the subsequent working has been arranged solely for the purpose of defeating the application and is not really bona fide."[36]

Commercial working discontinued

9.14   A patentee cannot resist an application for a compulsory licence merely on the ground that there has at one time been commercial working in this country if such working has been discontinued.[37]

Under section 27 of the 1907 Act an applicant had to show that the patented invention was worked exclusively or mainly abroad, and the patentee had to furnish satisfactory reasons why manufacture to an adequate extent was not carried on in the United Kongdom. The cases decided under that section may be of some assistance in construing the words "fullest extent that is reasonably practicable" of the present section.

9.15   In *Hatschek's Patent*[38] Parker J. said:

> "I do not think that any reasons can be satisfactory which do not account for the inadequacy of the extent to which the patented article is manufactured or the patented process is carried on in this country by causes operating irrespective of any abuse of the monopoly granted by the patent. The first thing, therefore, for the patentee to do is, by full disclosure of the manner in which he exercised his patent rights, to free himself from all suspicion of having done anything to hamper the industry of the United Kingdom."

The learned judge then dealt with the case of a patentee who had favoured foreign manufacturers to the disadvantage of British ones. Under the present section, although the British and foreign manufac-

---

[34] See Parker J. in *Mercedes Daimler Co.'s Patents* (1910) 27 R.P.C. 762 at p.768.
[35] (1934) 51 R.P.C. 461 at p.467.
[36] See also *Fabricmeter Co. Ltd.'s Appn.* (1936) 53 R.P.C. 307.
[37] *Cathro's Appn.* (1934) 51 R.P.C. 75 at p.79.
[38] [1909] 2 Ch. 68; 26 R.P.C. 228 at p.241.

turers may have been treated equally by the patentee, he is, nevertheless, under the obligation to furnish an explanation of the circumstances which have prevented the establishment of commercial manufacture in this country. On this point the further observations of the learned judge[39] are applicable:

"Certainly the fact that persons who were carrying on the industry in this country would make smaller profits than persons carrying it on abroad would, in my opinion, be no satisfactory reason at all. I can conceive cases in which a patentee ... may find it impossible to work ... in the United Kingdom because of the nature of the invention, or because of local conditions which prevail here but not in other countries, although these cases must, I think, be rare ... But it can never, in my opinion, be sufficient for a patentee, defending himself under the section, to prove that he cannot now start an industry with any chance of profit."

The last sentence of the learned judge needs further explanation: he went on to say that the reason for there being no chance of profit might be that the foreign manufacturers had become firmly established in consequence of the patentee having favoured foreign trade at the expense of home trade. It is suggested that, in the absence of circumstances of that kind, the fact that there was no hope of profit, or that a loss was to be expected, would constitute a defence to an application under the present section.[40]

Absence of demand
The proof of absence of any demand for the invention in this country **9.16**
is not itself a sufficient defence. In *Boult's Patent*[41] the Comptroller said:

"The consideration of the adequacy of manufacture in this country does, no doubt, depend to some extent upon the demand existing for the article here or in neutral markets, but it does not follow that, if there is no demand existing, there is no obligation on a patentee to start an industry here. If he does in fact manufacture in foreign countries, and if there is in fact a demand for the article or process abroad, the absence of any demand here does not seem to be a valid excuse. The patentee must, in such cases, make an effort to create a demand here, and the establishment of an industry will in itself help to create in many cases a demand for the article or process in question."

---

[39] [1909] 26 R.P.C. at p.243.
[40] And see *Boult's Patent* (1909) 26 R.P.C. 383 at p.387; also *Kent's Patent* (1909) 26 R.P.C. 666 at p.670.
[41] (1909) 26 R.P.C. 383 at p.387.

Where, however, the type of engine to which the invention was applicable had been almost superseded, so that it would not have been commercially advisable to establish a manufacture of the patented mechanism in this country, and the patentee had merely charged royalties on imported French machines of a special kind, containing the patented mechanism, it was held that he had furnished a sufficiently satisfactory reason to comply with the requirements of the former law.[42]

But it is not

"open to a patentee, who has already filled the bulk of a largely non-recurrent demand for a patented article in this country by importation from abroad and who then, under the stimulus of an application for a compulsory licence, has arranged for a manufacture to be started here, to say that such a manufacture must be considered to be 'adequate and reasonable under all the circumstances' for the purpose in question merely because it is sufficient, or he considers it sufficient, to meet so much of the demand as has remained unsupplied from abroad."[43]

The Comptroller will not usually consider whether the demand would be increased if a lower price were charged; but if the price asked for articles made in this country is higher than that charged for the imported article, it becomes necessary to inquire whether the price is a bona fide one, or one merely adopted for the purpose of checking and diminishing the demand for the home-manufactured article.[44]

Fear of infringement action

9.17   In *Taylor's Patent*[45] the patentee showed that he dared not establish manufacture in this country for fear of an infringement action under a master patent owned by the applicants for revocation, who had in fact refused the offer of a licence under the patent in question. Parker J. refused to revoke the patent, and held that the patentee was not bound, as the applicants contended, to apply for a voluntary or a compulsory licence under the applicants' patent. Had the applicants been able to show, however, that they had been ready and willing to grant the patentee a licence on reasonable terms the decision might have been otherwise.

Requisite skill exclusively foreign

9.18   It will not avail the patentee to allege that the special skill and experience necessary to enable the invention to be carried into effect can

---

[42] *Osborn's patent* (1909) 26 R.P.C. 819.
[43] *Fabricmeter Co. Ltd.'s Appn.* (1936) 53 R.P.C. 307, p.312.
[44] *Kent's Patent* (1909) 26 R.P.C. 666 at p.670.
[45] (1912) 29 R.P.C. 296.

only be found abroad,[46] although it may well be that an invention requiring special skill and the establishment of a factory with special tools may need a longer time to develop than one in which these features are not present. It is incumbent on the patentee to take steps to import the necessary tools and skilled labour to effect manufacture in this country.

In *Kent's Patent*[47] the Comptroller said:

"I shall always decline to accept, as a rule, any argument based on the impossibility of securing an efficient manufacture of special machinery in this country,[48] but I think it is natural for a patentee who desires to put the best possible machine upon the market to be somewhat over-scrupulous at first in obtaining his materials, and supervising the construction of his machine."

Circumstances beyond patentee's control

Under the 1907 Act, if the patentee could be shown to have done his best to establish a manufacture in the United Kingdom, and to have failed for reasons beyond his control, he was not held to have abused his monopoly. In *Bremer's Patent*,[49] Parker J. said: **9.19**

"In my opinion, the company have throughout used, and still are using, their best endeavours to fulfil the obligation arising under the Act of 1907 by establishing in this country an industry in the article, the subject of their patent, and they have further proved, to my satisfaction, that their want of success up to the present time has been due to circumstances beyond their own control, and not to the manner in which they have exercised the rights conferred upon them by the patent in question. The Act of 1907 was never meant to penalise want of success when the patentee has done his best, and I cannot, therefore, come to the conclusion that the patent ought to be revoked."

But having regard to the changed language of the present section[50] it is doubtful whether this decision would now be followed.

---

[46] *Johnson's Patent* (1909) 26 R.P.C. 52.
[47] (1909) 26 R.P.C. 666 at p.670.
[48] And see *Wardwell's Patent* (1913) 30 R.P.C. 408; *A. Hamson & Son (London) Ltd.'s Appn.* [1958] R.P.C. 88.
[49] (1909) 26 R.P.C. 449 at p.465.
[50] P.A. 1977, s.48(3)(*a*).

Power to adjourn the application

9.20   If the circumstances are such as to justify the Comptroller in affording the patentee more time to establish manufacture in this country, he may adjourn the application.[51]

(b) Unreasonable terms and importation, section 48(3)(b)

9.21   *"Where the patented invention is a product a demand for the product in the United Kingdom—(i) is not being met on reasonable terms, or (ii) is being met to a substantial extent by importation."*

Demand must be existing

9.22   The demand must be an actual one and not merely one which the applicant for a licence hopes and expects to create if and when he obtains a licence.[52]

Reasonable terms

9.23   The matters which have to be taken into consideration in determining what constitutes "reasonable terms" are similar to those which have to be considered under paragraph (d) in the case of licences, and are dealt with below.

In *Robin Electric Lamp Co. Ltd.'s Petition*[53] the patentees required an undertaking from their licensees not to sell articles (in which the patented invention was used) below a specified price. This resulted in the price of such articles being considerably higher in this country than abroad. The supply was adequate to meet the demands of the public, and there was no evidence that the price was "so high as to be a serious burden to the consumer or to be unreasonable"; and it was held that there had not been a default by the patentees.

In a Licence of Right case, *Research Corporation's (Carboplatin) Patent,*[54] Hoffman J. stated that if the price charged by a patentee was reasonable and demand at that price was being met then it was irrelevant to say that demand would have been greater at a lower price. The question was whether or not a given price was reasonable bearing in mind that patentees are entitled to recoup research costs, fund further research in the public interest, and make a profit from their monopoly.

---

[51] P.A. 1977, s.48(5).
[52] *Cathro's Appn.* (1934) 51 R.P.C 75 at p.82.
[53] (1915) 32 R.P.C. 202.
[54] [1990] R.P.C. 663.

Importation

With the rapid growth of international trade and the tendency of large **9.24** companies to centralise manufacture in a particular country, it is likely that there will be an increasing tendency for the demand for many patented products to be met solely by importation. In Case C-30/90, *E.C. Commission v. United Kingdom*,[55] the European Court held that Article 30 of the EC Treaty prohibited discrimination against an importer from another Member State of the EC in favour of a manufacturer in the United Kingdom and section 48(3)(*b*) of the Act must be applied in the light of that decision. It is submitted that the effect of the decision is that importation from another member state of the EC must now be regarded as equivalent to manufacture in the United Kingdom when considering whether the ground for a compulsory licence has been established.

Where the importation is from outside the EC it is submitted that a **9.25** compulsory licence should be granted to anybody willing to set up manufacture in this country.[56] There may be cases where there is some good reason (other than economics) for manufacture abroad but this will be rare and generally speaking if it can be shown the patentee is meeting the demand by importation from outside the EC a compulsory licence should be ordered. Such an approach would be consistent with section 50(1)(*a*). See also the older cases set out *ante* paragraphs 9.15 and 9.16. If the invention is actually being adequately worked in this country it is not necessarily a ground for granting a compulsory licence under this head that certain specialised applications of the invention are not being met by manufacture here.[57]

It would appear likely that the special provisions for when the C.P.C. **9.26** comes into force,[58] particularly the 10 year reservation provision[59] in respect of Article 47 (which provides that it shall not be a ground of seeking a compulsory licence that the demand is being met by imports from other Member States), will also infringe Article 30 of the EC Treaty if the United Kingdom seeks to avail itself of this facility.[60]

Section 54 provides that by Order in Council, the Comptroller may be **9.27** prevented from granting a compulsory licence under section 48 on the grounds of the demand being met by importation from Non-Member States specified in the Order. To date no such Order has been made.

---

[55] [1992]I E.C.R. 777, [1992] 2 C.M.L.R. 709, [1993] R.P.C. 283, [1993] F.S.R. 1. See also Case C-190/90 *Generics (U.K.) Ltd. v. Smith Kline & French Laboratories Ltd.* [1992]I E.C.R. 5335, [1993]I C.M.L.R. 89, [1993] R.P.C. 333, [1993] F.S.R. 592.

[56] The licence would also permit importation from the EC: See *Allen & Hanburys Ltd. v. Generics (U.K.) Ltd.* [1988] E.C.R. 1275 [1988] 1 C.M.L.R. 701, [1988] F.S.R. 312. But note the exception which may apply in certain circumstances in respect of imports from Spain and Portugal *ante*, §§ 8.57, 9.05 & 9.07 and *post*, § 9.58.

[57] *Cathro's Appn.* (1934) 51 R.P.C. 75 at p.81.

[58] P.A. 1977, ss.53(1) and 86. See also C.P.C. Articles 47 and 89.

[59] C.P.C. Article 89.

[60] Case C-30/90 *EC Commission v. United Kingdom* [1992]I E.C.R. 777, [1992] 2 C.M.L.R. 709, [1993] R.P.C. 283, [1993] F.S.R. 1, at para.32. See also *ante*, § 9.05, and the notes thereunder.

(c) Working prevented by importation

9.28 *"Where the patented invention is capable of being commercially worked in the United Kingdom, that it is being prevented or hindered from being so worked—*

> (*i*) where the invention is a product, by the importation of the product,
>
> (*ii*) where the invention is a process, by the importation of a product obtained directly by means of the process or to which the process has been applied."

Apart from the fact that section 48(3)(*c*)(ii) clearly extends to importation of a product made by a patented process it is not easy to envisage a likely commercial situation to which this subsection would apply but subsection 48(3)(*b*)(ii) would not. In applying the section, EC law must be taken into account so far as concerns imports from other Member States of the EC (see above).

(d) Refusal of reasonable terms, section 48(3)(d)

9.29 *"That by reason of the refusal of the proprietor of the patent to grant a licence or licences on reasonable terms—*

> (*i*) a market for the export of any patented product made in the United Kingdom is not being supplied; or
>
> (*ii*) the working or efficient working in the United Kingdom of any other patented invention which makes a substantial contribution to the art is prevented or hindered; or
>
> (*iii*) the establishment or development of commercial or industrial activities in the United Kingdom is unfairly prejudiced";

No order for endorsement of the patent "licences of right" is to be made on ground (i) above and any licence granted on that ground may restrict the countries in which the patented article may be sold or used by the licensee.[61] And no order is to be made on ground (ii) above unless the proprietor of the patent for the other invention is willing to grant a reciprocal licence on reasonable terms.[62]

It has been held that before any application could be made under the provisions of the 1907 Act corresponding to this paragraph there must have been either a complete refusal to grant a licence or the terms upon which it was offered must have been unreasonable.[63] It is submitted that this general principle will continue to be followed, but the applicant is now in no way prejudiced by the fact that he has already accepted a licence or made any admission in relation thereto.[64]

---

[61] P.A. 1977, s.48(6).
[62] P.A. 1977, s.48(7).
[63] *Loewe Radio Co. Ltd.'s Appns.* (1929) 46 R.P.C. 479 at pp.489, 490.
[64] P.A. 1977, s.48(8).

"Reasonable terms"

As to what constitutes "reasonable terms", Luxmoore J. in *Brownie* **9.30**
Wireless Co. Ltd.'s Applications[65] said:

> "The answer to the question must in each case depend on a careful
> consideration of all the surrounding circumstances. The nature of the
> invention ... the terms of the licences (if any) already granted, the
> expenditure and liabilities of the patentee in respect of the patent, the
> requirements of the purchasing public, and so on,"

It was argued that the royalty was out of proportion to the cost and
selling price, and that a reduction would result in a greatly increased
public demand. The learned judge held there was no evidence to
support the later contention, and said:[66]

> "There is in fact no necessary relationship between cost price or
> selling price ... and the royalty which a patentee is entitled to ask ...
> The best test of whether a royalty is reasonable in amount or the
> reverse is: How much are manufacturers who are anxious to make
> and deal with the patented article on commerical lines ready and
> willing to pay? ..."

He held on the evidence that the royalty was reasonable, that terms
prohibiting export and providing for payment of royalty on non-
patented articles were reasonable in the circumstances, and that in view
of the nature of the invention it was reasonable to require licensees to
take a licence under all patents belonging to a given group and to refuse
to grant licences under individual patents.

"Commercial or industrial activities"

Under the corresponding provisions of the 1919 Act it was held that **9.31**
the words "trade or industry of the United Kingdom" should be
construed in a wide sense.[67] It is submitted that the words "commercial
or industrial activities in the United Kingdom" are even wider than the
former words. The requirement under the 1907 Act under this ground
that "it is in the public interest that a licence or licences should be
granted"[68] has been abolished and this must be borne in mind when
considering cases decided under the earlier Acts.

---

[65] (1929) 46 R.P.C. 457 at p.473.
[66] (1929) 46 R.P.C. 457 at p.475; see also *Research Corp.'s Patent* [1991] R.P.C. 663.
[67] *Brownie Wireless Co. Ltd.'s Appns.* (1929) 46 R.P.C. 457 at p.478; and see *Robin Electric Lamp Co. Ltd.'s Petition* (1915) 32 R.P.C. 202 at p.213.
[68] Act of 1907, s.27(2)(*d*).

Export market

9.32   In *Penn Engineering & Manufacturing Corporation's Patent*[69] Mr. Justice Graham stated:

> "In my judgment, particularly at the present time, public interest does demand that exports from this country should be on as large a scale as possible. At the same time it would not be right to deprive the inventor of such reasonable remuneration as he may be able himself to get from his own exploitation of his patent.
>
> "If the patentee is already manufacturing in this country and exporting to foreign countries it might well be reasonable for him to ask that the grant of a compulsory licence should be restricted so as to prevent export by the licensee to those countries to which he (the patentee) is already exporting. If however the patentee is not manufacturing here and does not possess foreign patents in countries in which there is likely to be a market for export from this country, there seems very little, if any, reason to put restrictions on export in a compulsory licence to be granted. Any such restriction will prevent working 'to the fullest extent that is reasonably practicable', and it is, in my judgment, incumbent upon the patentee to ask for and justify such a restriction if he wishes to get it inserted in a compulsory licence order made against him."

(e) Unreasonable conditions, sections 48(3)(e)

9.33   *"That by reason of conditions imposed by the proprietor of the patent on the grant of licences under the patent, or on the disposal or use of the patented product or on use of the patented process, the manufacture, use or disposal of materials not protected by the patent,[70] or the establishment or development of commercial or industrial activities[71] in the United Kingdom is unfairly prejudiced"*

Where the patentee inserted in a limited licence conditions which prohibited the sale of the patented article to a specified class of retailers, it was held that such retailers were not "unfairly prejudiced" within the meaning of the provisions of the 1907 Act.[72]

Terms

9.34   In each case the terms upon which a compulsory licence will be granted will depend on the particular facts of the case.

In *Farmers Marketing & Supply Ltd.'s Patent*[73] a licence to manufacture

---

[69] [1973] R.P.C. 242.
[70] *Colbourne Engineering Co. Ltd.'s Appn.* (1955) 72 R.P.C. 169.
[71] See *ante*, § 9.31.
[72] *Co-operative Union Ltd.'s Appn.* (1933) 50 R.P.C. 161 at pp.164, 165.
[73] [1966] R.P.C. 546.

abroad and import was refused. However, a licence to import has been granted,[74] but in that case a bar was placed on the licensee to prevent export. The principles applied in these cases will be subject to the EC Treaty and if the country from which importation is to take place is a member state of the EC refusal of a licence to import would today be contrary to the Treaty.[75]

Guidance as to the financial terms can be obtained from the many licence of right decisions discussed *post*, § 9.61. In respect of mechanical inventions, royalty rates for compulsory licences have in the more modern cases been in the range 5–7 per cent.[76]

Application by Crown

A Government department may apply after the expiry of three years **9.35** from the date of sealing of a patent on any one or more of the grounds set out above that the patent shall be endorsed "licences of right" or that a licence may be granted to some specified person.[77]

Report on Monopolies

Under the Fair Trading Act 1973[78] the Monopolies and Mergers **9.36** Commission may lay a report before Parliament to the effect that a monopoly situation exists (or may be created by a merger) in relation to a description of goods which consist of or include patented products or in relation to services in which a patented product or process is used and that the same operates or may operate against the public interest. Similarly, under the Competition Act 1980[79] the Commission may lay a report before Parliament to the effect that any person is engaged in an anti-competitive practice in relation to a description of goods which consist of patented goods or services in which a patented process is used and that that practice operates or might be expected to operate against the public interest. In that event the Minister to whom the report is made may apply to the Comptroller for an order cancelling any restrictive conditions contained in an existing licence, or for the endorsement of the patent "licences of right," or both.[80]

---

[74] *Hoffman-La Roche & Co. A.G.'s Patent* [1969] R.P.C. 504 and also [1970] F.S.R. 225.
[75] Case 434/85 *Allen & Hanburys Ltd. v. Generics (U.K.) Ltd.* [1988] E.C.R. 1275, [1988] 1 C.M.L.R. 701, [1988] F.S.R. 312. See also *ante*, §§ 8.57, 9.05, 9.07 & 9.24, and *post*, § 9.58.
[76] *Kalle & Co. A.G.'s Patent* [1966] F.S.R. 112; *Penn Engineering Corp.'s Patent* [1973] R.P.C. 233; *Extrude Hone Corp.'s Patent* [1982] R.P.C. 361.
[77] P.A. 1977, s.48(1)(c).
[78] Fair Trading Act 1973, ss.50, 51, 64 and 75.
[79] 1980 Competition Act, ss.6 and 11.
[80] P.A. 1977, s.51, substituted by C.D.P.A. 1988, s.295, Sched. 5, para.14.

Alternative remedies

9.37   Where the Comptroller is satisfied that one or more of the conditions set out above is satisfied, he may order the patent to be endorsed "licences of right" (thus enabling any person interested thereafter to obtain a licence on reasonable terms as of right)[81] or he may order the grant of a licence to the applicant.[82] The Comptroller can not, however, order a patent to be endorsed "licence of right" where the only ground established is that set out in section 48(3)(*d*)(i) (export market not being supplied). The Act[83] does not appear to enable the Comptroller to give relief other than in respect of the specific relief requested and it may therefore be advisable in appropriate cases to seek relief in the alternative. If the Comptroller is satisfied that conditions imposed by the patentee on the grant of licences, or on the disposal or use of the patented product or process, unfairly prejudice the manufacture, use or disposal of materials not protected by the patent, he may also order the grant of licences to customers of the applicant.[84] If the applicant is already a licensee, the Comptroller may amend the existing licence or order it to be cancelled and grant a new licence.[85] The Comptroller will not, however, grant a compulsory licence if it would be futile to do so, .*e.g.* if manufacture under thatlicence would necessarily infringe another patent in respect of which no compulsory licence could be obtained.[86] The power to deprive the patentee of any right to work the invention or grant licences and to revoke existing licences has been repealed.[87]

C. Practice

9.38   The procedure to be followed is laid down in section 52 and is further provided for in rules 68–71 of the Patents Rules 1990. The application is made on Form 33/77 setting forth the facts and the relief asked for, and must be verified by declarations. If the Comptroller is not satisifed that a bona fide interest is disclosed, and a prima facie case for relief is made out, the application will be dismissed at this stage.[88] If, however, he is satisfied on these points, the Comptroller serves copies on the patentee and on all persons appearing, from the entries in the register, to be

---

[81] See *post*, § 9.48 et seq.
[82] P.A. 1977, s.48(4). For examples of compulsory licences, see *McKechnie Bros. Ltd.'s Appn.* (1934) 51 R.P.C. at pp.454, 472;; *Cathro's Appn.* (1934) 51 R.P.C. 475 at p.483 and *Zanetti-Streccia's Patent* [1973] R.P.C. 227.
[83] P.A. 1977, s.48(4).
[84] P.A. 1977, s.49(1).
[85] P.A. 1977, s.49(2).
[86] *Cathro's Appn.* (1934) 51 R.P.C. 475 at p.488.
[87] P.A. 1977, s.49(3) deleted by C.D.P.A. 1988 Sched. 5 para. 13.
[88] Patents Rules 1990, r.70(1); see *Co-operative Union Ltd.'s Appns.* (1933) 50 R.P.C. 161; and *Halcon SD Group Inc.'s Patents* [1989] R.P.C. 1.

interested. The application is also advertised in the *Official Journal*. The patentee, or any other person desiring to oppose the application, delivers a notice of opposition containing a statement, verified by declaration, setting out the grounds on which the application is opposed. The Comptroller normally decides the case after giving the applicant and the opponent an opportunity of being heard. Even if the Comptroller allows an application to proceed it will be struck out before discovery unless supported by sufficient evidence to make out a prima facie case.[89] However, if an applicant puts in evidence sufficient to make his case, it is immaterial that the evidence in question is not the best evidence.[90] The Comptroller may wish the applicant to file a draft licence prior to the determination of the application. Where a patentee did not oppose an application he was allowed to appeal against the decision granting a compulsory licence.[91] The Comptroller can order a licence to include the right to export even though the grounds for granting the licence are not based on an export market not being supplied.[92]

Unless the terms of the licence are agreed, they are settled by the Comptroller.[93] The Comptroller has no power to antedate the grant of a licence,[94] and the licence will run from the decision or order of the Comptroller which settles all the terms of the licence.[95]

Reference to Arbitrator

If the parties consent, or the proceedings require a "prolonged examination of documents or any scientific or local investigation", the Comptroller may refer the whole proceedings, or any issue of fact, to an arbitrator.[96]

9.39

Appeal

An appeal from any order of the Comptroller and from any award of the arbitrator (unless otherwise agreed before the award is made) lies to the Patents Court.[97]

9.40

---

[89] *Richco Plastic Co.'s Patent* [1989] R.P.C. 722; see also *Rhône Poulenc S.A.'s (Ketoprofen) Patent* [1989] R.P.C. 570.
[90] *Monsanto's C.C.P. Patent* [1990] F.I.R. 93, following *Fette's patent* [1961] R.P.C. 396.
[91] *Zanetti Streccia's Patent* [1973] R.P.C. 227.
[92] *Penn Engineering Patent* [1973] R.P.C. 233.
[93] See, *e.g. Zanetti*, case above.
[94] *Hoffman-La Roche & Co. A.G. v. Inter-Continental Pharmaceuticals Ltd.* [1965] R.P.C. 226.
[95] *Geigy S.A.'s Patent* [1966] R.P.C. 250.
[96] P.A. 1977, s.52(3).
[97] P.A. 1977, s.97.

Infringement or Revocation action pending

9.41   An application for a compulsory licence may be made to the Comptroller even though in parallel proceedings before the court the applicant denies infringement (and therefore denies he needs a compulsory licence) or asserts that the patent is invalid.[98] Even though a compulsory licence has been applied for an interlocutory injunction may be granted. Further, an action for infringement will not, in general, be stayed pending the outcome of an application for a compulsory licence.[99] However, an application for a compulsory licence may be stayed pending the final outcome of an infringement action.[1]

2. Licences of Right

A. The endorsement

Voluntary endorsement

9.42   By the provisions of section 46 of the Act a patentee may voluntarily throw his invention open to anyone who cares to ask for a licence on terms to be agreed with him or, in default of agreement, on terms to be settled by the Comptroller. In each case the terms will depend on the relevant facts of that case.[2] The patentee gains some advantages: he reduces the risk that he may be held at any time to have abused his monopoly; to some small extent to be advertised his invention and gives manufacturers or financiers the knowledge that the invention may be used on reasonable terms; and by subsection (3)(*d*) his renewal fees are reduced to a half of what they would otherwise have been. The patentee must satisfy the Comptroller that he is not precluded by contract from granting licences under the patent.[3] The Comptroller must give notice of the application to any person registered as having a right or interest in or under the patent[4] but, unlike the 1949 Act,[4] the Comptroller is not required to give any such person an opportunity to be heard. Doubtless the Comptroller will consider any observations which any such person may make. After the endorsement has been made, any person who claims that the patentee is precluded by a contract from granting licences (in which contract the claimant is interested) may apply to cancel the endorsement under section 47(3).[6]

---

[98] *Halcon SD Group Inc.'s Patents* [1989] R.P.C. 1.
[99] *Pfizer Corp. v. D.D.S.A. Pharmaceuticals Ltd.* [1966] R.P.C. 44.
[1] *Halcon SD Group Inc.'s Patents* [1989] R.P.C. 1.
[2] See *Casson's Patent* [1970] F.S.R. 433.
[3] P.A. 1977, s.46(2).
[4] P.A. 1977, s.46(2).
[5] P.A. 1949, s.35(1).
[6] See *post*, § 9.43.

Cancellation of endorsement

The patentee may apply at any time for cancellation of the endorse- **9.43** ment "licences of right" where the endorsement is voluntary and if the balance of renewal fees is paid as though there had been no endorsement and the Comptroller is satisfied that there is no existing licence, or that all licensees agree, the endorsement will be cancelled.[7] In that case the rights and liabilities of the patentee are as if no endorsement had been made.[8] However, where a patentee sought to cancel an endorsement after an application for a licence had been made, the cancellation was allowed subject to the grant of the licence for which application had been made.[9] The application for cancellation of the endorsement must be advertised,[10] and any person may give notice of opposition and the Comptroller shall, in considering the application, determine whether the opposition is justified.[11] The 1977 Act does not require that the opponent be a "person interested", but, it is submitted, that the interest of the opponent may be a factor in determining whether his opposition is justified.[12] It seems that the provisions of the 1949 Act relating to cancellation continue to apply where the endorsement was made under that Act.[13]

Any person who claims that the patentee is precluded by a contract from granting licences, in which contract the claimant is interested, may apply within two months of the endorsement for its cancellation.[14] The Comptroller must advertise the application[15] and give notice of it to the Patentee.[16] Only the patentee may oppose.[17]

Endorsement and patents of addition

Under the 1949 Act any application for the endorsement of a patent of **9.44** addition was to be treated as an application for the endorsement of the main patent also and any application for the endorsement of a patent was to be treated as an application in respect of all patents of addition also.[18] There is no similar provision under the 1977 Act and, therefore, presumably after the appointed day a patent of addition or a main patent can be endorsed without a similar endorsement being made to respectively the main patent or a patent or addition.

---

[7] P.A. 1977, s.47(2).
[8] P.A. 1977, s.47(5).
[9] *Casson's Patent* [1970] F.S.R. 433.
[10] Patents Rules 1990, r.65(1).
[11] P.A. 1977, s.47(6)(*a*).
[12] *cf.* P.A. 1949, s.36(5)(*a*). *Serengi's Patent* (1938) 55 R.P.C. 228. *Glaverbel's Patent* [1987] R.P.C. 73, [1987] F.S.R. 153.
[13] P.A. 1977, s.127, Sched. 4, para.8(1). *Glaverbel's Patent* [1987] R.P.C. 73, [1987] F.S.R. 153.
[14] P.A. 1977, s.47(3). *Patents Rules* 1990, r.64.
[15] *Patents Rules* 1990, r.65(1).
[16] *Ibid.* r.64(2).
[17] P.A. 1977, s.47(6)(*b*).
[18] P.A. 1949, s.35(5).

Statutory endorsement

9.45   The 1977 Act extends the terms of all new existing patents[19] granted under the 1949 Act to 20 instead of 16 years[20] but all such patents are to be treated as endorsed "licences of right" under section 35 of the 1949 Act for the period of the extension,[21] subject to the excepted uses mentioned below. Although stated to be endorsed under the 1949 Act, where an application is made for such a licence after the appointed day (June 1, 1978) the application is governed by the 1977 Act.[22]

Pharmaceutical and other excepted uses

9.46   Special provisions prohibit the grant of licences pursuant to the statutory endorsement of "licences of right" in respect of pharmaceutical use and such other uses as the Secretary of State may by order except.[23] The use of a product as a pesticide has been excepted by order.[24] The provisions may apply to any patent for an invention which is a product.[25] For the provisions to take effect the proprietor must file a declaration with the Patent Office in the prescribed form.[26] A declaration may not be filed in respect of a patent which has passed the end of its fifteenth year on January 15, 1989 or if, at the date of filing, there is an existing licence for any description of excepted use of the product or an outstanding application for a licence of right for any description of excepted use of the product.[27]

Patents of Addition

9.47   For the purposes of the provisions relating to statutory endorsement, the date of a patent of addition is defined as the date of the patent for the main invention. Thus, the patent for the main invention and the patent of addition will be treated as endorsed "licences of right" on the same date.[28]

Endorsement by order of Comptroller

9.48   If a case of abuse of monopoly is made out against a patentee under section 48 of the Act, the Comptroller may, as one of the remedies applicable, make an order throwing the invention open to licences of

---

[19] *i.e.* patents with at least 5 years to run as at the appointed day (June 1, 1978), see P.A. 1977, s.127, Sched. 1, para.3(1).
[20] P.A. 1977, s.127, Sched. 1, para.4(1).
[21] P.A. 1977, s.127, Sched. 1, para.4(2)(2).
[22] *Allen & Hanbury v. Generics (U.K.) Ltd.* [1986] R.P.C. 203 at p.247 (H.L.).
[23] P.A. 1977, s.127, Sched. 1, para.4a, inserted by C.D.P.A. 1988, s.293.
[24] The Patents (Licences of Right) (Exception of Pesticidal use) Order 1989, (S.I. 1989 No. 1202).
[25] P.A. 1977, s.127, Sched. 1, para.4a, inserted by C.D.P.A. 1988, 293.
[26] *Ibid.*; see also Patents Rules 1990, r.67.
[27] *Ibid.*
[28] P.A. 1977, s.127, Sched. 1, para.3(1)(*c*) and 4(2)(*c*).

right.[29] Also, under section 51(3) of the Act,[30] the Comptroller has power to make an entry in the Register to the effect that licences under a patent are to be available as of right in consequence of a report of the Monopolies and Mergers Commission.[31]

B. Consequences of endorsement

Licences of right

Where an entry is made in the Register to the effect that licences are **9.49** available as of right, any person shall, at any time after the entry is made, be entitled as of right to a licence under the patent on such terms as may be settled by agreement or, in default of agreement, by the Comptroller on the application of the proprietor or the person requiring the licence.[32] As to the earliest date of application and the date when the licence takes effect, see *post*, §§ 9.53 and 9.54.

Exchange of licence

After the endorsement "licences of right" has been made, any existing **9.50** licensee may apply to the Comptroller to exchange his licence for one granted pursuant to the endorsement.[33] In the case of statutory endorsement, the existing licensee should first consider whether he is able to take advantage of the statutory extension of licences which in effect provides for a royalty free licence during the period of the extension.[34]

Remedies for infringement after endorsement

An infringer of a patent endorsed "licences of right" may undertake **9.51** to accept a licence to be settled by the Comptroller, in which case no injunction will be granted against him and the damages will be limited to double what the royalties would have been if the licence had been granted before the earliest infringement.[35] This restriction on the remedies against an infringer does not apply to infringement by importation from a country which is not a Member State of the EC.[36] Nor does it apply in so far as the infringement consists of any excepted use of

---

[29] P.A. 1977, ss.48(1)(*b*) and 48(4)(*b*). See *ante* § 9.37.
[30] As substituted by C.D.P.A. 1988, s.295, Sched. 5, para.14.
[31] See *ante*, § 9.36.
[32] P.A. 1977, s.46(3)(*a*).
[33] P.A. 1977, s.46(3)(*b*).
[34] See *ante*, § 8.85.
[35] P.A. 1977, s.46(3)(*c*).
[36] *Ibid.*, as amended by C.D.P.A. 1988, s.295, Sched. 5, para.12(2) in consequence of the decision of the European Court in Case 434/85 *Allen & Hanburys v. Generics (U.K.) Ltd.* [1988] E.C.R. 1275, [1988] 1 C.M.L.R. 701, [1988] F.S.R. 312.

the product after the filing of a declaration.[37] The undertaking may be given at any time before final order in the proceedings, without any admission of liability.[38]

Renewal fees

9.52   The renewal fee payable in respect of a patent endorsed licences of right is half the fee which would be payable if the entry had not been made.[39]

C. Settlement of terms by Comptroller

Date when application can be made

9.53   In the case of statutory endorsement, the application for a licence of right may be made before the date when the patent is so endorsed.[40] But the licence may not be granted until after that date.[41] By a subsequent amendment to the Act, it is now provided that the application may not be made more than one year before the date of endorsement.[42] Applications in anticipation of a voluntary endorsement or endorsement by order of the Comptroller present practical difficulties because until such endorsements are actually made the potential applicants for licences of right will be unaware that they have any right to apply.[43]

There is no pre–requisite that the applicant must attempt to reach agreement with the patentee before applying for a licence of right.[44]

Date when licence takes effect

9.54   A licence granted by the Comptroller pursuant to the licence of right provisions takes effect from the date when terms are settled by the Comptroller, not from the date of application.[45] Terms are settled when the Comptroller gives his final decision or makes his order irrespective of any appeal[46] and the licensee may accept those terms without prejudice to any appeal.[47] Where the royalty is increased on appeal, it

---

[37] P.A. 1977, s.127, Sched. 1, para. 4A(7) inserted by C.D.P.A. 1988, s.293. See also *ante* §
[38] 9.46. 1977, s.46(3A) inserted by C.D.P.A. 1988, s.295, Sched. 5, para.12(3).
[39] P.A. 1977, s.46(3)(*d*).
[40] *Allen & Hanburys Ltd. v. Generics (U.K.) Ltd.* [1986] R.P.C. 203 at pp.251 & 253 (H.L.).
[41] *Ibid.*
[42] P.A. 1977, s.127, Sched. 1, para.4b, inserted by C.D.P.A. 1988, s.294.
[43] *Allen & Hanburys Ltd. v. Generics (U.K.) Ltd.* [1986] R.P.C. 203 (H.L.) at p.251.
[44] *Roussel-Uclaf (Clemence & Le Martret's) Patent* [1987] R.P.C. 109; *Rhône Poulenc S.A.'s (Ketoprofen) Patent* [1989] R.P.C. 570.
[45] *Allen & Hanburys Ltd. v. Generics (U.K.) Ltd.* [1986] R.P.C. 203 (H.L.) at p.252, overruling *R. v. Comptroller-General of Patents, Designs and Trade Marks, ex parte Gist Brocades NV* [1985] F.S.R. 379.
[46] *Allen & Hanburys Ltd. (Salbutamol) Patent* [1987] R.P.C. 327 (C.A.).
[47] *Ibid.*

will be backdated to the date of the original grant by the Comptroller by requiring a further royalty payment in respect of the increase.[48]

Applicant attacking validity

There is jurisdiction to entertain an application for a licence of right **9.55** under a patent, notwithstanding that the applicant is attacking the validity of the patent by way of defence to infringement proceedings.[49] The two courses of action are not inconsistent courses requiring an election.[50] An application for a licence of right does not amount to an admission of validity.[51] The application for a licence may, however, be stayed in an appropriate case but it will not be stayed where the applicant wishes to operate the licence pending the outcome of his invalidity attack.[52]

Non–trading applicant

There is also jurisdiction to entertain an application for a licence of **9.56** right from a non–trading company and application from such a company will not be summarily struck out or stayed.[53] But if as a practical matter the applicant would not be able to use the licence of right which he sought, the Comptroller may reject the application as an abuse of the process.[54]

Terms of licence

The Comptroller's discretion to impose limitations and conditions **9.57** upon what the licence of right authorises the licensee to do is a wide one and his jurisdiction is not limited to terms as to the amount of royalties and security for their payment.[55] The Comptroller cannot impose upon the licensee any positive obligation to do any of the acts so licenced. Nor can he settle terms which would have the effect of debarring future applications for a similar licence. But these are the only fetters on his jurisdiction to settle terms of licences of right.[56]

Since by section 53(4) of the Act a compulsory endorsement of a patent with the words "licences of right" has for all purposes the same effect as a voluntary endorsement under section 46, recourse may be had to the grounds on which the Comptroller is empowered to make a

---

[48] See Falconer J. in *Smith Kline & French Laboratories Ltd.'s (Cimetidine) Patents* [1990] R.P.C. 203 at p.230.

[49] *E.I. Du Pont (Blades') Patent* [1988] R.P.C. 479.

[50] Halcon S.D. Group Inc.'s Patent [1989] R.P.C. 1.

[51] *E.I. Du Pont (Blade's) Patent*, see *ante*; *Halcon S.D. Group Inc.'s Patent*, see *ante*.

[52] *Ibid.*

[53] *Roussel Uclaf (Clemence & Le Martret's) Patent* [1989] F.S.R. 405.

[54] *Rhone-Poulenc S.A.'s (Ketoprofen) Patent* [1989] R.P.C. 570.

[55] *Allen & Hanburys Ltd. v. Generics (U.K.) Ltd.* [1986] R.P.C. 203 (H.L.) at p.248.

[56] *Ibid.*

compulsory endorsement in order to identify the policy to the achievement of which Parliament intended the Comptroller's exercise of his discretion to be directed.[57]

9.58   The previous cases provide guidance as to the limitations and conditions which may be imposed by the Comptroller in the exercise of his discretion. These include: a prohibition on imports[58] (but, under EC law, there can be no prohibition on imports from other member States of the EC[59] except that the imports may be prohibited from Spain and Portugal in certain circumstances[60]); quality controls;[61] a clause allowing termination of the licence if the licensee comes under the control of any other company in the field[62] or if the licensee attacks the validity of the patent;[63] and a prohibition on assigning or sub-licensing.[64]

Under EC law the Comptroller may not, in settling the terms, discrimate against the patentee who manufactures in another member State of the EC and imports into the United Kingdom.[65] Accordingly in such cases the licence should contain the same terms (particularly as to importation from non-EC countries) as it would have done if the patentee had been manufacturing in the United Kingdom.[66]

9.59   The following clauses have been refused: Clauses aimed at preventing passing off by the licensee, the proprietor being left to his remedies in tort;[67] a most favoured nation clause;[68] an export ban, other than to countries where parallel patents are in force[69] or where such exports would significantly affect manufacture in the United Kingdom;[70] a clause allowing immediate termination of the licence without

---

[57] *Ibid.* at p.249. For such grounds, see P.A. 1977, ss.48–50 and see *ante* § 9.09 *et seq.*

[58] *Allen & Hanburys Ltd. v. Generics (U.K.) Ltd.* [1986] R.P.C. 203 (H.L.).

[59] Case 434/85 *Allen & Hanburys Ltd. v. Generics (U.K.) Ltd.* [1988]E.C.R. 1275, [1988]1 C.M.L.R. 701, [1988] F.S.R. 312 (E.C.J.); *Allen & Hanburys Ltd. (Salbutamol) Patent* [1987] R.P.C. 327; *Ciba Geigy A.G.'s Patent* [1986] R.P.C. 403; *American Cyanamid Co.'s (Fenbufen) Patent* [1990] R.P.C. 309, [1991] R.P.C. 409; *Research Corp.'s (Carboplatin) Patent* [1990] R.P.C. 663; *Smith Kline & French Laboratories Ltd. (Cimetidine) Patents* [1990] R.P.C. 203.

[60] Case C-191/90 *Generics (U.K.) Ltd. v. Smith Kline & French Laboratories Ltd.* [1992] 1 E.C.R. [1993] 1 C.M.L.R. 89, [1993] R.P.C. 333, [1993] F.S.R. 592; and see *ante*, §§ 8.57, 9.05 and 9.07.

[61] *Allen & Hanburys Ltd. v. Generics (U.K.) Ltd.* [1986] R.P.C. 203 (H.L.) at p.248; *cf. Cabot Safety Corp.'s Patent* [1992] R.P.C. 39.

[62] *Syntex Corp.'s Patent* [1986] R.P.C. 585; See also *Smith Kline & French v. Harris* [1992] F.S.R. 110.

[63] *E.I. Du Point (Blades) Patent* [1988] R.P.C. 479; *Cabot Safety Corp.'s Patent* [1992] R.P.C. 39.

[64] *Allen & Hanbury Ltd.'s (Salbutamol) Patent* [1987] R.P.C. 327 (C.A.); *cf. Cathro's Appn.* (1934) 51 R.P.C. 475; *Hilti A.G.'s Patent* [1988] R.P.C. 51.

[65] Case C-191/90 *Generics (U.K.) Ltd. v. Smith Kline & French Laboratories Ltd.* [1992] I E.C.R. 5385, [1993] 1 C.M.L.R. 89; [1993] R.P.C. 333, [1933] F.S.R. 592, (E.C.J.).

[66] *Ibid.*

[67] *Syntex Corp.'s Patent* [1986] R.P.C. 585; *Hilti A.G.'s Patent* [1988] R.P.C. 51; *Cabot Safety Corp.'s Patent* [1992] R.P.C. 39; *cf. Shiley Inc.'s Patent* [1988] R.P.C. 97; *Farbwerke Hoechst A.G. (Sturm's) Patent* [1973] R.P.C. 253.

[68] *Allen & Hanbury's Ltd.'s (Salbutamol) Patent* [1987] R.P.C. 327, *per* Whitford J.

[69] *Ibid.*; see also *Smith Kline & French Laboratories Ltd. (Cimetidine) Patent* [1990] R.P.C. 203.

[70] *American Cyanamid Co.'s (Fenbufen) Patent* [1990] R.P.C. 305, [1991] R.P.C. 409.

prior warning for even trivial or accidental breaches;[71] a clause requiring a patent attribution.[72]

In an appropriate case the Comptroller may order a grant by way of **9.60** sub–licence from an existing licensee with provision for it to become a licence from the patentee if the head licence is terminated.[73]

Financial terms

Royalties are commonly expressed as a fixed price per unit of product **9.61** rather than as a percentage of the sales price.[74] Royalties based on sales price may be unjust to the patentee because it enables the licensee to reduce the royalty payable by price cuts. Royalties based on a fixed price per unit enables both sides to know where they stand.[75] The price per unit may also be subject to indexing.[76] A bank guarantee may be required to secure payment.[77]

In assessing the level of royalty, the Comptroller must exercise his **9.62** powers with a view to securing that the patentee receives a reasonable remuneration having regard to the nature of the invention.[78] The effect of this provision is that the Comptroller must consider what a willing licensor and a willing licensee would have agreed upon as a reasonable royalty to be paid for the rights granted to the licensee under the licence of right.[79] The following approaches have been considered in the decided cases:

The "section 41" approach.

Under the section 41 approach,[80] the royalty should cover three **9.63** elements, namely allowances for the recovery by the patentee of the cost of discovering the product (usually a drug in the recently decided cases) and establishing its efficiency, for the recoupment to the patentee of the promotional expenses incurred in creating and maintaining the market for it, and a reward for the patentee for his contribution to the art

---

[71] *American Cyanamid Co.'s (Fenbufen) Patent see ante.*
[72] *Cabot Safety Corp.'s Patent* [1992] R.P.C. 39.
[73] *Research Corp.'s (Carboplatin) Patents* [1990] R.P.C. 663.
[74] *Syntex Corp.'s Patent* [1986] R.P.C. 585; *Allen & Hanburys Ltd.'s (Salbutamol) Patent* [1987] R.P.C. 327 (C.A.); *Smith Kline & French Laboratories Ltd.'s (Cimetidine) Patents* [1990] R.P.C. 203 at 245, 259 (C.A.); *Research Corp.'s (Carboplatin) Patent* [1990] R.P.C. 663; *American Cyanamid Co.'s (Fenbufen) Patent* [1990] R.P.C. 309, [1991] R.P.C. 409; *Cabots Safety Corp's Patent* [1992] R.P.C. 39.
[75] *Per* Whitford J. in *Allen & Hanbury's Ltd. (Salbutamol) Patent* [1987] R.P.C. 327.
[76] *Shiley Inc.'s Patent* [1988] R.P.C. 87.
[77] *Ibid.*
[78] P.A. 1977, s.50(1)(*b*).
[79] *Allen & Hanburys Ltd.'s (Salbutamol) Patent* [1987] R.P.C. 327; *Smith Kline & French Laboratories Ltd.'s (Cimetidines) Patent* [1990] R.P.C. 203 at p.236; *American Cyanamid Co.'s (Fenbufen) Patent* [1991] R.P.C. 409.
[80] So called because this was the approach adopted in proceedings under the Patents Act 1949, s.41.

secured by an appropriate measure of profit upon the capital investment he has been constrained to make in the project.[81] On the other hand, the patentee's position as manufacturer is not to be taken into account: The patentee is only entitled to remuneration *qua* patentee or inventor, not to remuneration *qua* manufacturer.[83]

9.64   For the purposes of the assessment of the research and development costs, it may be appropriate to treat the patentee and exclusive licensee as one.[83] Research and development do not include formulation work.[84] It is not necessary to reduce the promotion element in the section 41 calculation if part of the market created by the patentee is not available to the licensee because the licensee only pays royalties on the share of the market he actually obtains.[85] But the patentee is not entitled to recoup his promotional expenditure however large.[86] The appropriate measure of profit upon the capital investment may be the profit obtained by the patentee on his actual costs rather than the return on capital normally obtained in the industry.[87]

The "comparables" approach

9.65   Where there are comparable licences negotiated at arms length, the rate of royalty may provide an appropriate measure of remuneration. However, it is more usual that the "comparables" are not entirely comparable and, although it may still be appropriate to take such "comparables" into account, it may be necessary to make adjustments to the rate of royalty because of the differences.[88] What is or is not a comparable and how far it is a comparable is a question of fact.[89] Where the alleged comparability is not demonstrated in evidence, it will not be taken into account.[90] Either party may be required to give discovery of other patent licences.[91]

---

[81] *J.R. Geigy S.A.'s Patents* [1964] R.P.C. 391 at p.411; *Allen & Hanburys Ltd.'s (Salbutamol) Patent* [1987] R.P.C. 327 at p.376 (C.A.).

[82] *Allen & Hanburys Ltd.'s (Salbutamol) Patent* [1987] R.P.C. 327 (C.A.) at p.378, following *Patchett's Patent* [1967] R.P.C. 237 (C.A.), a case in respect of compensation for Crown user. See also *Shiley Inc.'s Patent* [1988] R.P.C. 97.

[83] *Research Corporation's (Carboplatin) Patent* [1990] R.P.C. 663.

[84] *Smith, Kline & French Laboratories Ltd.'s (Cimetidine) Patent* [1990] R.P.C. 203, following *Farbwerke Hoechst (Sturm's) Patent* [1973] R.P.C. 253.

[85] *Smith, Kline & French Laboratories Ltd.'s (Cimetidine) Patent* [1990] R.P.C. 203 (C.A.); *American Cyanamid Co.'s (Fenbufen) Patent* [1990] R.P.C. 309, [1991] R.P.C. 409 (C.A.).

[86] *American Cyanamid Co.'s (Fenbufen) Patent* [1990] R.P.C. 309, [1991] R.P.C. 409 (C.A.).

[87] *Smith, Kline & French Laboratories Ltd.'s (Cimetidine) Patent* [1990] R.P.C. 203 (C.A.).

[88] *Allen & Hanbury's Ltd.'s (Salbutamol) Patent* [1987] R.P.C. 327 (C.A.) at p.377; *Syntex Corp.'s Patent* [1986] R.P.C. 327; *American Cyanamid (Fenbufen) Patent* [1990] R.P.C. 309, [1991] R.P.C. 409.

[89] *American Cyanamid (Fenbufen) Patent* [1991] R.P.C. 409 (C.A.) at p.413; see also *Cabot Safety Corp.'s Patent* [1992] R.P.C. 39.

[90] *Research Corp.'s (Carboplatin) Patent* [1990] R.P.C. 663.

[91] *Smith Kline & French Laboratories Ltd.'s (Cimetidine) Patents* [1988] R.P.C. 148, a case where the potential licensee was required to give such discovery.

In cases of conflict between the section 41 approach and the "comparables" approach, the latter may be preferred.[92]

The "profits available" approach

If the profits which a licensee can expect to receive are high, that is a **9.66** factor which can properly be taken into account when fixing the amount of the patentee's remuneration.[93] But the approach has been criticised as contrary to section 50(1)(*b*) of the Act and one that should be used as a last resort.[94] The "profits available" approach does not assist if there is no clear evidence to show how the profits should be split.[95] Where price–cutting is likely, the profits-available calculation may cease to be useful.[96]

Prevarication by patentee

It has been recognised that the value of the endorsement "licence of **9.67** right", particularly in the case of statutory endorsement, can be significantly reduced if there is disagreement between the parties and the proceedings for settlement of the licence are lengthy.[97] But the patentee's delay in licence of right proceedings, even if culpable, is not relevant in settling the royalty rate.[98] The European Court has held that delay in licence of right proceedings may amount to an abuse of a dominant position under Article 86 of the EC Treaty.[99]

Licensee's right to sue for infringement

A licensee under a patent endorsed "licences of right" may, apart **9.68** from agreement to the contrary, call upon the patentee to take proceedings for infringement and if the patentee does not do so within two months the licensee may institute proceedings in his own name, joining the patentee as a defendant.[1] The patentee is not liable for costs unless he enters an appearance and takes part in the proceedings.[2]

---

[92] *American Cyanamid Co.'s (Fenbufen) Patent* [1990] R.P.C. 309, [1991] R.P.C. 409; *Smith Kline & French Laboratories Ltd.'s (Cimetidine) Patents* [1990] R.P.C. 203.
[93] *Smith Kline & French Laboratories Ltd.'s (Cimetidine) Patent* [1990] R.P.C. 203, *per* Nicholls L.J. at p.257.
[94] *Ibid., per* Lloyd L.J. at p.244.
[95] *American Cyanamid Co.'s (Fenbufen) Patent* [1990] R.P.C. 309. See also Lloyd L.J. in *Smith Kline & French Laboratories Ltd. (Cimetidine) Patent*, see *ante*, at p.244.
[96] *Research Corp.'s (Carboplatin) Patent* [1990] R.P.C. 663.
[97] *Allen & Hanburys Ltd. v. Generic (U.K.) Ltd.* [1986] R.P.C. 203 (H.L.) at p.252.
[98] *Cabot Safety Corp.'s Patent* [1992] R.P.C. 39.
[99] Case T-30/89 *Hilti A.G. v. E.C. Commission* [1991] 2 E.C.R. 1439, [1992] 4 C.M.L.R. 16; [1992] F.S.R. 210.
[1] P.A. 1977, s.46(4).
[2] P.A. 1977, s.46(5).

D. Procedure

The Application

9.69   The procedure for application to the Comptroller for settlement of the terms of a licence of right is governed by the Rules.[3] In the case of an application by a person other than the proprietor of the patent, the applicant is required to file the appropriate form[4] together with two copies of the draft licence which he seeks.[5] The Comptroller sends copies of these documents to the proprietor who is required within two months to file and send to the applicant a statement setting out fully the grounds of his objection.[6] Thereafter the applicant has two months to file and send to the proprietor a counter–statement.[7] Alternative provisions apply when the application is made by the proprietor.[8]

9.70   The pleadings should provide a clear statement of the facts which are to be relied on and which will be proved by evidence.[9] After the pleadings are filed, the Comptroller may give such directions as he may think fit with regard to the subsequent procedure.[10] Discovery may be, and often is, ordered.[11] Frequently licence of right applications will involve the disclosure of confidential information and, as in the case of litigation before the Court, the parties should first endeavour to agree the terms for such disclosure but in default of agreement the Comptroller will set the terms. No distinction is normally made between employee patent agents and those in private practice.[12]

Appeal

9.71   An appeal from the Comptroller in all matters relating to licences of right lies to the Patents Court.[13] The appeal is a full re-hearing.[14] With leave of the Court or of the Court of Appeal, an appeal lies from the Patents Court to the Court of Appeal where the ground of appeal is that the decision of the Patents Court is wrong in law.[15]

---

[3] Patents Rules 1990, r.62.
[4] Patents Form 29/77.
[5] *Ibid.*, r.62(1)(*b*).
[6] *Ibid.*, r.62(3)(*b*).
[7] *Ibid.*, r.62(4).
[8] *Ibid.* see r.62(1)(*a*) and r.62(3)(*a*).
[9] *Roussel-Uclaf (Clemence & Le Martret's) Patent* [1987] R.P.C. 109. See also *Rhone Poulenc S.A.'s Patent* [1989] R.P.C. 570.
[10] *Ibid.*, r.62(6).
[11] *Smith Kline & French Laboratories (Cimetidine) Patents* [1988] R.P.C. 148. *Merrell Dow Pharmaceuticals Inc.'s (Terfenadine) Patent* [1991] R.P.C. 221.
[12] *Schering A.G.'s Patent* [1986] R.P.C. 30.
[13] P.A. 1977, s.97(1).
[14] *Allen & Hanbury's Ltd.'s (Salbutamol) Patent* [1987] R.P.C. 327 (C.A.).
[15] P.A. 1977, s.97(3). See also *Smith Kline & French Laboratories (Cimetidine) Patents* [1990] R.P.C. 203 (C.A.); *American Cyanamid Co.'s (Fenbufen) Patent* [1990] R.P.C. 309, [1991] R.P.C. 409 (C.A.).

CHAPTER 10

REVOCATION PROCEEDINGS

Application for revocation

Section 32 of the 1949 Act provides that revocation of a patent may be **10.01** obtained by any person interested on petition to the court. This section still applies to existing patents granted under the 1949 Act. The grounds available to a petitioner are also available as defences to an action for infringement,[1] and are dealt with in detail in Chapter 5.[2] No preliminary formality is necessary before the petition is presented, but that it may be resisted on the ground that the petitioner has no bona fide interest in revoking the patent, *i.e.* no interest such as would have given him a *locus standi* in opposition proceedings.[3]

Section 72 of the 1977 Act provides for revocation of patent by any person. Thus, there is no requirement that the person applying for revocation must be interested. The application can be made before the High Court by petition,[4] before the County Court[5] or before the Comptroller.

Counterclaim in action for infringement

The defendant in an action for infringement may counterclaim for **10.02** revocation without presenting a petition. The grounds available are also available as defences.[6] The practice in such cases is dealt with in Chapter 12. A counterclaim for revocation may be proceeded with even though the action by the plaintiff is stayed, discontinued or dismissed.[7] In some circumstances concurrent proceedings by petition for the revocation of

---

[1] P.A. 1949, s.32(4) para. 12.01.
[2] See *post*, §§5.01 *et seq.*
[3] P.A. 1949, s.14(1). And see *White's Patent* [1957] R.P.C. 405.
[4] R.S.C. Ord. 104, r.4.
[5] Patents County Court (Designation and Jurisdiction) Order 1994 (S.I. 1994 No.1609).
[6] P.A. 1949, s.61 and P.A. 1977, s.74.
[7] See R.S.C. Ord. 15, r.2(3).

a patent may be allowed to proceed.[8] No provisions exist which permit a counterclaim for infringement to be brought in response to a petition for revocation and separate infringement proceedings must be instituted. Both the petition and the action may then be heard together.[9]

No declaration of invalidity

10.03   An action cannot be brought claiming a declaration that a patent is invalid,[10] the proper course being to petition for revocation. It is probable that a petition would lie for the revocation of a patent which had expired.[11]

1. Before the High Court by Petition

Parties

10.04   The person upon whom a petition should be served is the registered proprietor of the patent. It is customary also to serve any other persons who at the time the petition is presented appear upon the register as being beneficially interested in the patent.[12] Persons required to be served should be identified at the end of the petition.[13]

Where an assignment had been executed after the petition had been presented, the name of the assignee was ordered to be substituted for that of the original respondent to the petition.[14]

The Tribunal

10.05   Petitions for revocation in England come before the Patents Court.[15] In Scotland proceedings for revocation are in the form of an action of reduction,[16] and are heard by the Court of Session.[17]

---

[8] *Lever Bros. and Unilever Ltd.'s Patent* (1952) 69 R.P.C. 117.
[9] See *Genentech Inc.'s Patent* [1987] R.P.C. 553.
[10] P.A. 1977, s.74(2); *North-Eastern Marine Engineering Co. v. Leeds Forge Co.* (1906) 23 R.P.C. 529; *Traction Corp. v. Bennett* (1908) 25 R.P.C. 819 at p.822; *cf. Killen v. MacMillan* (1932) 49 R.P.C. 258 at p.260.
[11] *North-Eastern Marine Engineering Co. v. Leeds Forge Co.* (1906) 23 R.P.C. 529, at p.531. See also *John Summers & Sons Ltd. v. The Cold Metal Process Co. Ltd.* (1948) 65 R.P.C. 75 at p.91.
[12] See *Avery's Patent* (1887) 36 Ch.D. 307; (1887) 4 R.P.C. 152, 322.
[13] R.S.C. Ord. 9, r.2(2).
[14] *Haddan's Patent* (1885) 2 R.P.C. 218.
[15] R.S.C. Ord. 104, r.2.
[16] P.A. 1949, s.103(2).
[17] P.A. 1949, s.103(3); P.A. 1977, s.98.

Practice before trial

The practice is regulated by Order 104, rules 2, 4 and 6 to 14 of the **10.06** Rules of the Supreme Court, and is in most respects similar to or identical with the practice in actions for infringement.[18]

Service of petition

The proceedings are commenced by the presentation of a petition[19] to **10.07** the court, and its service upon the respondent in the same way as a writ. Particulars of the objections to the validity of the patent on which the petitioner is going to rely must be served with the petition.[20] The practice as to these particulars is the same as in the case of an action for infringement in which the issue of invalidity is raised.[21]

Persons out of jurisdiction

Where the patentee or other person interested in the patents is out of **10.08** the jurisdiction, leave to serve out of the jurisdiction is not required although under Order 10, rules 1 and 5 of the Rules of the Supreme Court, personal service must be effected.[22]

A respondent residing out of the jurisdiction will not be ordered to give security for costs.[23]

Application for directions

Order 104, rule 14, applies to petitions for revocation, and at any rate a **10.09** contested petition cannot be heard until an application for directions under this rule has been disposed of.

Discovery, interrogatories and inspection

The directions which have to be obtained under Order 104, rule 14,[24] **10.10** and the practice as to discovery of documents, interrogatories and inspection, are the same as in the case of an action for infringement.[25]

---

[18] See Chap. 12.
[19] R.S.C. Ord. 104, r.4.
[20] R.S.C. Ord. 104, r.6.
[21] See Chap. 12; R.S.C. Ord. 104, rr.6–8.
[22] *Napp Laboratories Ltd. v. Pfizer Incorporated* [1993] F.S.R. 150 and *Symbol Technologies Inc. v. Optican Sensors Europe B.V. (No.1)* [1993] R.P.C. 211.
[23] *Miller's Patent* (1894) 11 R.P.C. 55.
[24] See *post*, §§12.14 *et seq.*
[25] See Chap. 12; *Haddan's Patent* (1885) 54 L.J.Ch. 126. See also *Sommerfeld's Patent* [1956] R.P.C. 77; *Compania Uruguaya de Fomento Industrial S.A.'s Petition* [1957] R.P.C. 283, 314.

The trial

Right to begin

10.11 By Order 103, rule 18(3) of the Rules of the Supreme Court (now revoked), the respondent was entitled to begin and give evidence in support of the patent, and if the petitioner gave evidence impeaching the validity of the patent the respondent was entitled to reply. The revocation of this rule denotes a change of practice. As the onus is on the petitioner normally he will open the case and call his evidence first.[26] However, the court has complete power to give directions as to which party should begin.[27]

10.12 If the petitioner starts his counsel will open and then call evidence which must prove his case: a respondent need not call evidence and can thereby request the final speech. If the respondent calls evidence, as is usual, the petitioner has the right of reply.

The nature of the evidence required, and the procedure generally, at the trial is similar to that at the trial of an action for infringement.[28] Petitions for revocation are tried upon *viva voce* evidence,[29] unless the parties agree to the simplified trial procedure under which evidence is given by way of affidavits.[30]

Res judicata

10.13 Where a defendant in an action for infringement puts in issue the validity of the patent, but does not counterclaim for its revocation, the question arises whether the validity of the patent can be relitigated in subsequent proceedings for revocation. Under the previous law it was held that such former proceedings were not bar to a petitioner who had the Attorney-General's fiat to present the petition, on the ground that he was then acting as a member of the public and not as an individual.[31] Now that the necessity for the fiat has been abolished, it is submitted, that if the defendant failed to establish the invalidity of the patent in the action, he would thereafter be debarred from raising the same issue in a subsequent petition for revocation.[32] Likewise, it is submitted, that a contested petition will prevent the same issues from being relitigated in an infringement action by way of counterclaim.[33] Where the application

---

[26] As in *Genentech Inc.'s Patent* [1987] R.P.C. 553 and in *Genentech Inc.'s (Human Growth Hormone) Patent* [1989] R.P.C. 613.

[27] R.S.C. Ord. 35, r.7.

[28] See Chap. 12.

[29] *Gaulard and Gibb's Patent* (1889) 34 Ch.D. 396.

[30] See Practice Note on simplified trials; [1994] F.S.R. 334.

[31] *Shoe Machinery Co. Ltd. v. Cutlan* (1895) 12 R.P.C. 530; *Deeley's Patent* (1895) 12 R.P.C. 192; *Lewis and Stirkler's Patent* (1897) 14 R.P.C. 24; and see *Poulton's Patent* (1906) 23 R.P.C. 506 but *cf. Shoe Machinery Co. Ltd. v. Cutlan (No.2)* (1896) 13 R.P.C. 141.

[32] See *Jameson's Patent* (1896) 13 R.P.C. 246.

[33] But *quaere* whether they may nonetheless be raised in defence.

for revocation is made before the Comptroller section 72(5) expressly prevents an estoppel arising from his decision.

Amendment of specification

Section 30 of the 1949 Act and section 75 of the 1977 Act apply to petitions for revocation as well as to actions for infringement, and a patentee may be allowed, in certain circumstances, to amend his specification after revocation proceedings have been commenced.[36] The practice in such applications is dealt with in Chapter 8.   **10.14**

The remedy

If in any proceedings for revocation the court decides that the patent is invalid, the court may allow the specification to be amended instead of revoking the patent.[34]   **10.15**

An order for revocation will only be made in open court, and will not be made in chambers even though the patentee consents.[35]

Stay pending appeal

It is usual to stay the order for revocation pending an appeal.[36] The form of order made in such cases follows that made in *Cincinnati Grinders (Inc.) v. B.S.A. Tools Ltd.*.[37] An undertaking is, however, required that the patentees will not apply to the Comptroller to amend their specification pending the appeal.[38] An undertaking not to advertise or threaten has also been required.[39] Such orders are otherwise to be presented at the Patent Office forthwith by the person in whose favour they are made.[40]   **10.16**

Certificates

A successful petitioner should obtain a certificate that the various particulars of objections have been proved or were reasonable.[41]   **10.17**

If any claim whose validity is contested is found to be valid, the court may so certify, and in that case in any subsequent proceedings the party upholding the validity of the patent, if finally successful, may recover

---

[34] P.A. 1949, s.30(1); and P.A. 1977, s.72(4).
[35] *Clifton's Patent* (1904) 21 R.P.C. 515.
[36] See, *e.g. Klaber's Patent* (1905) 22 R.P.C. 405; *Waterhouse's Patent* (1906) 23 R.P.C. 470; *cf. Stahlwerk Becker A.G.'s Patent* (1918) 35 R.P.C. 81.
[37] (1931) 48 R.P.C. 33 at p.60.
[38] *Ibid.* and see also *Le Rasoir Apollo's Patent* (1932) 49 R.P.C. 1 at p.15.
[39] *Amalgamated Carburetters Ltd. v. Bowden Wire Ltd.* (1931) 48 R.P.C. 105 at p.122; see also *Klaber's Patent* (1905) 22 R.P.C. 405 at p.416.
[40] Patents Rules 1990 r.53.
[41] R.S.C. Ord. 62, Appendix 2, Part 1, para.3, and see Chap. 12.

his costs as between solicitor and client.[42] These are taxed on an indemnity basis subject to the presumptions set out in Order 62, rule 15 of the Rules of the Supreme Court.

Costs

10.18   The principles governing the award of costs are the same as in the case of actions for infringement.[43]

An order for revocation will usually include an order for the respondent to pay the petitioner's costs, and this is so even though the order is made by consent, and no previous notice of the intention to present a petition has been given to the patentee (which would enable the latter to surrender his patent).[44]

Appeals

10.19   Appeals upon petitions for revocation are to the Court of Appeal and (with leave) to the House of Lords as in ordinary actions.

2. Before the County Court

Jurisdiction

10.20   The Patents County Court has jurisdiction to hear any action or matter relating to patents over which the High Court would have jurisdiction (except appeals from the Comptroller).[45] This includes application for revocation for a patent.

Tribunal

At the time of writing one Patents County Court[46] has been designated only.

Procedure

An application for revocation in the Patents County Court is made by summons accompanied by a Statement of Case.[47] The same rules govern

---

[42] P.A. 1949, s.64, and P.A. 1977, s.65 and R.S.C. Ord. 62, r.15.
[43] See Chap. 12, §12.256 *et seq.*
[44] *Aylott's Patent* (1911) 28 R.P.C. 227; *Merryweather's Patent* (1912) 29 R.P.C. 64; *Berry's Patent* (1915) 32 R.P.C. 350.
[45] Patents County Court (Designation and Jurisdiction) Order 1994 (S.I. 1994 No.1609).
[46] Central London County Court; see S.I. 1994 No.1609 *ibid*, revoking S.I. 1990 No. 1496 in respect of Edmonton County Court.
[47] C.C.R. 1981, Ord. 48A, r.4.

applications for revocation as govern other actions in the Patents County Court.[48]

Appeals

Appeals from any determination of the judge in the Patents County Court are to the Court of Appeal.[49]

3. Before the Comptroller

Jurisdiction

The Comptroller has no power to hear applications for revocation **10.21** under the 1949 Act; but has the same powers as the Court upon an application made to him under the 1977 Act.[50] However, a decision of the Comptroller, or an appeal from such a decision, does not create an estoppel in proceedings for infringement.[51] If an application has been made to the Comptroller for revocation then no subsequent application can be made to the Court (except by way of appeal or by way of putting the validity of the patent in issue in an infringement action) without the leave of the court[52] or without a certificate from the Comptroller that the matters would more properly be determined by the Court.[53] If an application to the Comptroller for revocation has been refused then the applicant may not make a subsequent application to the Court (except by way of appeal or by putting validity in issue in an infringement action) without the leave of the Court.[54] If an application to the Comptroller for revocation is still pending the applicant may not make a subsequent application to revoke to the Court without either the agreement of the proprietor or a certificate from the Comptroller that the matters would be more properly dealt with by the Court.[55]

The Comptroller also has a limited jurisdiction to revoke a patent on his own initiative.[56]

Procedure

An application for revocation is made to the Comptroller in accord- **10.22** ance with the Patents Rules 1990, rules 75 to 77. The procedure is essentially the same as that under the Patents Rules 1978 and 1982 and is

---

[48] See Chap. 12, 12.162 *et seq.*
[49] C.C.A. 1984, s.77.
[50] P.A. 1977, s.72.
[51] P.A. 1977, s.72(5).
[52] P.A. 1977, s.72(6).
[53] P.A. 1977, s.72(7).
[54] See n.52.
[55] See n.53.
[56] P.A. 1977, s.73.

similar to that which was used in opposition and section 33 revocation proceedings under the 1949 Act. Thus, it would seem that many of the cases in such proceedings will be relevant in proceedings for revocation before the Comptroller.

Practice

10.23   The application for revocation must be made on Form No. 38/77 and be accompanied by a copy. It must be accompanied by a statement in duplicate setting out fully the grounds of revocation, the facts relied upon, and the relief sought. Further particulars of the statement may be sought and ordered.[57] A copy of such an application and statement is sent by the Comptroller to the proprietor.

The fact that the applicant's statement does not accompany the application is not necessarily fatal as the Comptroller has a complete discretion to enlarge the times under this rule.[58] The extent to which particulars of any allegation (*e.g.* prior user) must be given depends on the facts of each case.

10.24   If the proprietor desires to contest the application he must within two[59] months of the date of the application and statement being sent to him file a counter-statement in duplicate setting out fully the grounds upon which the application is contested. The Comptroller sends a copy to the applicant. Within two[60] months of the date when such copy was sent to him the applicant may file evidence in support of his case, and must deliver to the proprietor a copy thereof.

Within two[61] months from the date when a copy of the applicant's evidence was sent to him, the proprietor may file evidence in answer, a copy of which must be sent to the applicant. The applicant may file further evidence within two[62] months of the date when the proprietor's evidence was sent to him, a copy of which must be delivered to the proprietor; such last-mentioned evidence must be confined to matters strictly in reply.

No further evidence may be filed on either side except by leave of the Comptroller.[63] A degree of latitude is, however, given to admitting further evidence provided that it enables all issues fairly to be brought to the attention of the Comptroller and no undue prejudice is caused to either party.

The issues must be adequately defined by the statement and counter-statement, and not left to be made clear by the declarations filed

---

[57] *Morgan Refractories Ltd.'s Patent* [1968] R.P.C. 374.
[58] See *Morton and Others' Appn.* (1932) 49 R.P.C. 404; see also Patents Rules 1990 r.110.
[59] Under the Patents Rules 1978 and 1982 three months was allowed from the date of receipt.
[60] *Ibid.*
[61] *Ibid.*
[62] *Ibid.*
[63] *Bakelite Ltd.'s Patent* [1958] R.P.C. 152; *Ford Motor Co. Ltd.'s Appn.* [1968] R.P.C. 221. See also r.75(6), *Patents Rules 1982*.

at a later stage. A counter-statement which contains merely a bare denial of the applicant's allegations is not a sufficient compliance with the rules.[64] The counter-statement must contain replies in a reasonable manner to each of the matters pleaded in the statement by way of admission, denial or an offer to amend the complete specification and must set out any facts relied on.[65] If amendments are offered in the counter-statement and the opponents wish to rely upon matters not pleaded, an application should be made to amend the statement.[66]

A party filing declarations which are unnecessary, or which raise matters not relevant to the issues, may be penalised in costs.[67]

The application and statement may be amended so as to include all documents to which it is desired to refer[68] and all grounds on which it is proposed to rely,[69] but the addition of new grounds may be refused if made at a very late stage or after unreasonable delay.[70]

Hearing

The parties, if they so wish, are entitled to a hearing, which will be in **10.25** public unless the Comptroller, after consultation with the parties represented at the hearing, otherwise directs.[71]

Where in revocation proceedings pursuant to section 33 of the 1949 Act the patentees failed to file a counter-statement, notwithstanding repeated extensions of time it was held that the Comptroller had no duty to consider the merits of the case and the patent was revoked.[72] If a counter-statement is filed, but the applicant does not appear at the hearing nor file evidence, then the inference may be drawn that the applicant sees no effective answer to the case made against his application.[73]

It remains the practice in the Patent Office that the proprietor has the right to begin.[74]

Evidence

The requirements as to the form of evidence are governed by rules 103 **10.26** to 107 of the Patents Rules 1990. Normally such evidence will be by way of statutory declaration or affidavit.

The Comptroller has power to take oral evidence and shall allow any

---

[64] See (1929) 46 R.P.C., *Comptroller's Ruling B*; (1932) 49 R.P.C., *Comptroller's Ruling A*.
[65] *Marshall's Appn.* [1969] R.P.C. 83.
[66] *Horville Engineering Co. Ltd.'s Appn.* [1969] R.P.C. 266.
[67] *Brand's Appn.* (1895) 12 R.P.C. 102. See also *Hedges' Appn.* (1895) 12 R.P.C. 136.
[68] *Ibid.*; (1910) 27 R.P.C., *Comptroller's Ruling C*.
[69] *Linotype and Machinery Ltd.'s Appn.* (1937) 54 R.P.C. 228; Patents Rules 1990, r.100.
[70] *Phillips Petroleum Co.'s Appn.* [1964] R.P.C. 470.
[71] Patents Rules 1990, rr.88–89.
[72] *Fontaine Converting Works Inc.'s Patent* [1959] R.P.C. 72.
[73] *Eichengrun's Appn.*, (1932) 49 R.P.C. 435.
[74] But see *E.I. Du Pont De Nemours & Co. (Hull's) Appn.* [1979] F.S.R. 128.

witness to be cross-examined on his affidavit or declaration, unless he orders otherwise.

If cross-examination is desired, the party desiring to cross-examine should inform the Comptroller, who will, if he thinks the request reasonable, inquire of the other party whether he will produce the witnesses for cross-examination without any order for their attendance. A party cannot prevent a witness from being cross-examined by withdrawing his declaration.[75]

The Comptroller has all the powers of a judge of the High Court as regards the attendance and examination of witnesses and the discovery and production of documents except the power to punish summarily for contempt.[76] The attendance of witnesses, may, therefore, be enforced by subpoena under Order 39, rule 4 of the Rules of the Supreme Court; and the effect is that the Comptroller has the same powers in respect of discovery and production of documents as a judge of the High Court. Privilege can be claimed for documents, if the appropriate conditions are satisfied.[77]

Interim decision

10.27   It is likely that interim decisions, *i.e.* decisions that a patent needs amendment, will arise. If so, there does not seem to be any reason why the suggestions made in the past as to the best procedure should not be adopted.[78] However, an appeal should be entered unless all parties agree that a reasonable chance exists of resolving the matters in issue.[79]

Appeals

10.28   An appeal lies to the Patents Court both from an interlocutory and from a final Order.[80]

The procedure for an appeal is governed by Order 104, rule 19 of the Rules of the Supreme Court.

Notice of appeal by originating motion must be given within 14 days of the date of the decision appealed against in the case of a matter of procedure and within six weeks of the date of the decision in any other case. The Comptroller may, however, extend the period, but if the specified period has expired and no extension has been granted, special leave to appeal must be obtained.

The notice of appeal must state the nature of the decision, and the parts appealed against. A cross-appeal is necessary if a respondent desires to contend that the actual decision of the hearing officer should

---

[75] *Re Quartz Hill etc. Co.* (1882) 21 Ch.D. 642.
[76] Patents Rules 1990, r.103(3).
[77] *Cooper Mechanical Joints Ltd.'s Appn.* [1958] R.P.C. 459.
[78] *L. Oertling Ltd.'s Appn.* [1962] R.P.C. 148; *E.I. Du Pont's Appn.* [1962] R.P.C. 228.
[79] *Du Pont de Nemours & Co.'s Appn.* [1969] R.P.C. 271.
[80] P.A. 1977, s.97.

be varied or affirmed on grounds other than those set out in the decision. Thus, if the Comptroller decides that a patent will be revoked if the specification is not amended, the proprietor may appeal and contend that no amendment is necessary. If the Applicant wishes to argue that even if the amendments are made no patent should be granted, a cross-appeal is necessary. The subsequent proceedings set out in Order 104, rule 19 of the Rules of the Supreme Court.

The evidence at the hearing is the same as that used before the   **10.29**
Comptroller, and no further evidence can be given except by leave,[81] which will not usually be given unless the Tribunal can be satisfied:

(1) that the new evidence was not in the possession of the party seeking to introduce it at the time of the original hearing and
(2) that such party could not with the exercise of reasonable diligence have obtained such evidence for use at the original hearing.[82]

The appellant normally has the right to begin at the hearing, except that where there is an appeal and a cross-appeal the applicant for the patent normally begins.[83]

Security for costs

The Comptroller may order security for costs against any person who   **10.30**
invokes his litigious jurisdiction, if such person neither resides nor carries on business in the United Kingdom.[84]

Appeals to Court of Appeal

An appeal lies to the Court of Appeal from a decision of the Patents   **10.31**
Court acting in its appellate capacity when considering revocation.[85]

Costs

The Comptroller has power to award to any party such costs as he   **10.32**
thinks reasonable and any such order may be enforced.[86]

If an applicant does not succeed in obtaining the full amount of relief asked for he will not necessarily be deprived of costs;[87] but if, after having been offered by the proprietor substantially all that he ultimately is held entitled to, he persists in forcing the matter to a hearing he will

---

[81] R.S.C. Ord. 104, r.19(14).
[82] *Toyo Tsushinki Kabushiki Kaisha's Appn.* [1962] R.P.C. 9 at p.13. This passage was cited with approval in *Mediline A.G.'s Patent* [1973] R.P.C. 91. See also *Toyama Chemical Co.'s Appn.* [1990] R.P.C. 555.
[83] *Johnson & Johnson's Appn.* [1963] R.P.C. 40.
[84] P.A. 1977, s.107(4).
[85] P.A. 1977, s.97(3).
[86] P.A. 1977, s.107(1).
[87] (1910) 27 R.P.C., *Comptroller's Ruling H.*

get no costs.[88] Similarly, if the application is not contested by the proprietor or the patentee offers to surrender the patent,[89] the Comptroller in awarding costs will consider whether the proceedings might have been avoided if reasonable notice had been given to the applicant before the opposition or application for revocation was lodged.

Where an adjournment is necessary by reason of a party introducing an important document into the case at a late stage a special award of costs may also be made.[90] If a party, though successful, overloads the case with unnecessary documents, no costs may be awarded.[91]

An appellant who abandons an appeal before the hearing will be ordered to pay the costs,[92] and if fresh evidence is called on the appeal and the appeal is allowed in consequence, the appellant may be refused costs.[93]

4. Surrender of Patent

10.33   A patentee may at any time by notice to the Comptroller offer to surrender his patent.[94] The object of this provision is to enable a patentee to avoid having proceedings for revocation brought against him and thereby being made liable for costs. The offer is advertised and any person interested (*e.g.* a licensee) may oppose.[95] An appeal to the Patents Court lies from the decision of the Comptroller.[96]

The practice is governed by rule 43 of the Patents Rules 1990. The notice is advertised in the *Official Journal* and any person desirous of opposing must give notice of opposition within two months of the advertisement. Such notice is accompanied by a statement (in duplicate) setting out the full facts upon which he relies, and the relief he seeks.

---

[88] (1910) 27 R.P.C., *Comptroller's Ruling H.*
[89] See *post*, §12.32.
[90] See (1929) 46 R.P.C. (1929) *Comptroller's Ruling B.*
[91] *Metallgesellschaft A.G.'s Appn.* (1934) 51 R.P.C. 368.
[92] See *Knight's Appn.* (1887) Griff.P.C. 35; *Metallgesellschaft A.G.'s Appn.* (1934) 51 R.P.C. 368.
[93] See *Stubb's Patent* (1884) Griff.P.C. 298; *Chambers' Appn.* (1915) 32 R.P.C. 416 at p.420.
[94] P.A. 1977, s.29(1).
[95] P.A. 1977, s.29(2) and Patents Rules 1990, r.43.
[96] P.A. 1977, s.97.

CHAPTER 11

ACTION TO RESTRAIN THREATS

Contents   Para.

1. History

Prior to the Act of 1883 the proprietor of a patent might issue threats of **11.01** proceedings for infringement without rendering himself liable for any damage which he might occasion thereby, provided such threats were made bona fide. It was open to an injured person to apply for an injunction to restrain the patentee from continuing to threaten him, but he could be successful only by showing that the statements made were in fact untrue,[1] and that the defendant intended, even after they were found to be untrue, to repeat them.[2]

In the case of malicious threats an action for damages lay similar to that of slander of title, when the plaintiff had to show that the threat made by the defendant amounted to a "malicious attempt to injure the plaintiffs by asserting a claim of right against his own knowledge that it was without any foundation",[3] and that actual damage had resulted from the threats.[4] Such an action could, and may still, be maintained quite independently of any provisions of the Patents Acts.[5]

Statutes prior to the 1977 Act

Section 32 of the 1883 Act and section 36 of the 1907–1928 Acts gave a **11.02** statutory right of action, in certain limited cases, to any person who was damaged by groundless threats of infringement proceedings, whether

---

[1] *Halsey v. Brotherhood* (1880) 15 Ch.D. 514; 19 Ch.D. 386.
[2] *Sugg v. Bray* (1885) 2 R.P.C. 223 at p.246.
[3] *Per* Blackburn J. in *Wren v. Weild* (1869) L.R. 4 Q.B. 730 at p.727. See also *Halsey v. Brotherhood* (1881) 19 Ch.D. 386 at p.388.
[4] See, *e.g. Farr v. Weatherhead and Harding*, (1932) 49 R.P.C. 262 at p.267.
[5] See *Cars v. Bland Light Syndicate Ltd.* (1911) 28 R.P.C. 33; *Mentmore Manufacturing Co. Ltd. v. Fomento (Sterling Area) Ltd.* (1955) 72 R.P.C. 157; *Olin Mathieson Chemical Co. v. Biorex Laboratories Ltd.* [1970] R.P.C. 157.

such threats were made bona fide or not.[6] These sections did not apply if an action for infringement was "commenced and prosecuted with due diligence" and it was also held that section 36 of the 1907–1928 Acts had no application where no patents had in fact been sealed.[7] The Act of 1932 repealed section 36 of the 1907–1928 Acts and enacted a new section in its place which gave a remedy for groundless threats irrespective of whether the person making the threats did or did not have any interest in a patent. That section also revoked the previous statutory defence to an action for threats of commencing and prosecuting an action for infringement with due diligence.

11.03   Section 65 of the 1949 Act substantially re-enacted section 36 of the Act of 1932 but was more clearly drafted. Under section 65, if any person threatened any other person with proceedings for infringement of a patent, any person aggrieved could claim relief. Unless the defendant proved that the acts in respect of which the threats were made constituted an infringement of a patent or of rights arising from the publication of a complete specification in respect of a claim not shown by the plaintiff to be invalid, the plaintiff could obtain a declaration that the threats were unjustifiable, an injunction to restrain their continuance and damages. It was enacted that a mere notification of the existence of a patent did not constitute such a threat.

2. Threats Under the 1977 Act

11.04   The remedy of an aggrieved party for groundless threats of proceedings for infringement of patents and applications is governed by section 70 of the 1977 Act. The section substantially re-enacts section 65 of the 1949 Act with one significant limitation on the ambit of an actionable threat[8] and in proceedings under the 1977 Act the case law developed under preceding statutes continues to apply.

Under section 70, if any person (whether or not entitled to any right in a patent) by circulars, advertisements or otherwise threatens another person with proceedings for any infringement of a patent, a person aggrieved by the threats (whether or not the person to whom the threats are made) may bring proceedings against the person making the threats, provided that proceedings may not be brought for a threat to bring proceedings for infringement alleged to consist of making or importing a product for disposal or of using a process. If the threats and the plaintiff's status as a person aggrieved are proved then the plaintiff can obtain relief unless the defendant proves that the acts in respect of which proceedings were threatened constitute or would constitute an

---

[6] See, e.g. Day v. Foster (1890) 7 R.P.C. 54; Skinner & Co. v. Perry (1893) 10 R.P.C. 1; Diamond Coal Cutter Co. v. Mining Appliances Co. (1915) 32 R.P.C. 569.
[7] See Ellis & Sons Ltd. v. Pogson (1923) 40 R.P.C. 62, 179.
[8] See para. 11.09 below.

infringement of a patent and the patent alleged to be infringed is not shown by the plaintiff to be invalid. The plaintiff may claim relief by way of a declaration, injunction and damages. Mere notification of the existence of a patent does not constitute a threat of proceedings within the meaning of section 70. A person notified of an unpublished application may obtain information relating to that application from the Comptroller which would otherwise not be available until publication.[9]

Section 70 applies to threats made in respect of patents granted under the 1949 Act as well as those under the 1977 Act.[10]

Bona fides immaterial

It is no defence to an action for threats under section 70 that the threats   **11.05** were made in good faith in the honest belief that the act complained of was an infringement of a valid claim.[11] The right at common law to take proceedings for malicious threats remains unaffected by the statutory provisions as to threats.[12]

Must be within jurisdiction

The threat complained of must have been made within the jurisdiction in order to be actionable for otherwise no tort would have been committed within the jurisdiction.[13]

Nature of threats

The cause of action given by section 70 is not similar to libel, and there   **11.06** is no question of publication; the manner in which the threat was made is, therefore, not material. In *Skinner & Co. v. Perry*[14] the plaintiffs complained of two threats—one in the form of a letter to a third party, who had inquired of the defendants whether they thought that the plaintiff's article of manufacture infringed the defendants' patent; the other contained in a letter from the defendants to the plaintiffs themselves in reply to similar inquiries. It was held that the words "or otherwise" in the section were not to be construed *ejusdem generis* with the preceding words "circulars, advertisements".[15] In giving judgment for the plaintiffs, Bowen L.J. said:[16]

"Using language in its ordinary sense, it is difficult to see that an

---

[9] P.A. 1977, s.118(4).
[10] See *Therm-a-stor Ltd. v. Weatherseal Windows Ltd.* [1981] F.S.R. 579 and P.A. 1977, Sched. 4, para.3(2).
[11] See *Skinner & Co. v. Perry* (1893) 10 R.P.C. 1 at p.8.
[12] See *ante*, note 5.
[13] *Egg Fillers etc. Ltd. v. Holed-Tite Packing Corpn.* (1934) 51 R.P.C. 9.
[14] (1893) 10 R.P.C. 1.
[15] see also *Speedcranes Ltd. v. Thompson* [1978] R.P.C. 221.
[16] (1893) 10 R.P.C. 1 at p.5.

intimation ceases to be a threat because it is addressed to a third person in answer to an inquiry, or because it is addressed to the person himself. We are not dealing with libel or questions of publication—we are dealing with threats. If I threaten a man that I will bring an action against him, I threaten him nonetheless because I address that intimation to himself, and I threaten him nonetheless because I address the intimation to a third person."

Verbal statements can amount to threats[17] in appropriate cases, even when made in answer to inquiries.[18] A letter by a solicitor before issuing a writ, or in proposing a compromise, is a threat within the meaning of the subsection if it conveys an intimation that proceedings would be taken to restrain infringement,[19] and the fact that the interviews or letters were stated to be "without prejudice" does not affect the matter.[20]

Background to be considered

11.07   Regard has to be had to the background in which the alleged threat was made.[21] The threat of an action for infringement can thus be made indirectly or by implication. In *Luna Advertising Co. Ltd. v. Burnham & Co.*[22] a representative of the defendants called on a customer of the plaintiff's and stated that a sign exhibited outside the customer's premises was an infringement of his firm's patent and requested that it should be removed. Clauson J. granted an interlocutory injunction, and said:

"I think that an interview of this kind ... between business men, although nobody speaks of solicitors and writs, has no real meaning except to convey ... that the threatener has legal rights and means to enforce them ... in the way in which they are naturally enforced, *i.e.* by legal proceedings."

The *Luna Advertising* case was followed in *Bowden Controls v. Acco Cable Controls Ltd.*[23] where the threat was alleged to have been made in a letter to the plaintiff's customers which stated that the plaintiff's product had

---

[17] See *Kurtz v. Spence* (1887) 4 R.P.C. 161; *Ellis & Sons Ltd. v. Pogson* (1922) 39 R.P.C. 62; *Luna Advertising Co. Ltd. v. Burnham & Co.* (1928) 45 R.P.C. 258; *Farr v. Weatherhead and Harding* (1922) 39 R.P.C. 262.

[18] *Skinner & Co. v. Perry* (1893) 10 R.P.C. 1. But see *Alpi-Pietro E Figlio & Co. v. John wright & Sons (Veneers) Ltd.* [1972] R.P.C. 125.

[19] See, *e.g. Driffield Cake Co. v. Waterloo Mills Cake Co.* (1886) 3 R.P.C. 46; *Combined Weighting etc. Machine Co. v. Automatic Weighing Machine Co.* (1889) 6 R.P.C. 502; *Day v. Foster* (1890) 7 R.P.C. 54 at p.58; *Douglass v. Pintsch's Patent Lighting Co. Ltd.* (1897) 14 R.P.C. 673; *H.V.E. (Electric Ltd. v. Cufflin Holdings Ltd.* [1964] R.P.C. 149; and the cases referred to *ante* note 17.

[20] See *Kurtz v. Spence* (1887) 4 R.P.C. 161 at p.173.

[21] *Surridge's Patents Ltd. v. Trico-Folberth Ltd.* (1936) 53 R.P.C. 420 at pp.423, 424.

[22] (1928) 45 R.P.C. 258.

[23] [1990] R.P.C. 427.

been found by a German court to infringe a European patent (in Germany) and that the defendant had corresponding patents in all major European countries. The letter then said: "It is the intention of [the defendant] to enforce the rights arising by virtue of these patents in a realistic manner and will carefully ensure all current customers requirements are properly safeguarded". In considering whether to grant an interlocutory injunction, Aldous J. said:

"The letter does not explicitly threaten patent proceedings, but states that the first defendant will enforce its rights. The fact that it is not explicit that patent proceedings will be taken is in no way conclusive as a threat can be veiled or implied just as much as it can be explicit . . ."

The judge went on to decide:

"He [the reader] would realise that it contained a threat of patent proceedings. He would realise that there is nothing in the letter which explicitly excluded him from the threat. Even if he thought that suppliers did not consider it practical to sue manufacturers, I believe the recipient would consider what was the purpose of the letter. He would conclude that the purpose of the letter was to give him information and a warning. That requires the answer; a warning as to what?"

In *Olin Mathieson Chemical Co. v. Biorex Laboratories Ltd.*[24] it was held that writing a letter to the Ministry of Health with the object of ensuring that hospitals would not purchase the defendant's products amounted to a threat.[25]

"Threatens another person"

It is not necessary in order that the threat should be actionable that it **11.08** should have been communicated either directly or through an agent to the person threatened; the words "threaten another person" do not mean only "communicates a threat to any person" but include also the expression of a threat, by circulars, advertisements, or otherwise, "in relation to any person".[26]

---

[24] [1970] R.P.C. 157.
[25] See also *Willis & Bates Ltd. v. Tilley Lamp Co.* (1944) 61 R.P.C. 8; *Alpi Pietro E Figlio & Co. v. John Wright & Sons (Veneers) Ltd.* [1972] R.P.C. 125.
[26] *John Summers & Sons Ltd. v. The Cold Metal Process Co.* (1948) 65 R.P.C. 75 at p.96 and see *Bowden Controls v. Acco Cable Controls Ltd.* [1990] R.P.C. 427.

Threats to manufacturers or importers of products or users of processes

11.09   Section 70(4) provides that proceedings may not be brought under the section for a threat to bring proceedings for an infringement alleged to consist of making or importing a product for disposal or of using a process. It is submitted that the subsection means that threats in respect of making and importing products and using processes are permitted but threats (even to a manufacturer) in respect of other infringing acts (*e.g.* selling) are actionable. This view is supported by the *obiter dicta* of Oliver L.J. in *Therm-a-stor Ltd. v. Weatherseal Windows Ltd.*[27] where he said:

> "The word product is a perfectly general word apt to describe any article and there is nothing in subsection (4) of section 70 which indicates an intention to confine it to a product which is itself the subject of a patent. The intention of the legislature seems to have been to enable a person, whether a patentee or not, to threaten infringement proceedings with impunity under either subsections (1) or (2) of section 60 where what is complained of as infringement is the making of a product for disposal."[28]

The contrary view, that the subsection means manufacturers and importers of products and users of processes may be threatened with impunity has been advanced[29] but it is submitted that this is not the natural meaning of the words of the subsection.

Notification of patent

11.10   A mere notification of the existence of a patent does not constitute a threat.[30] But if words are added to the effect that what is complained of constituted an infringement of the patent, this constitutes a threat.[31]

General Warnings

11.11   By section 70(1), in order that a threat may be actionable under the 1977 Act, it must have been directed against "another person".

In *Challender v. Royle*[32] Bowen L.J. said:

> "Everybody, it seems to me, has still a right to issue a general warning

---

[27] [1981] F.S.R. 579 at 594.
[28] See also *Neild v. Rockley* [1986] F.S.R. 3.
[29] For example, in *Bowden Controls v. Acco Cable Controls Ltd.* [1990] R.P.C. 427 and *Johnson Electric Industrial Manufactory Ltd. v. Mabuchi–Motor K.K.* [1986] F.S.R. 280.
[30] P.A. 1977, s.70(5). *Paul Trading Co. Ltd. v. J. Marksmith & Co. Ltd.* (1952) 69 R.P.C. 301; *C. and P. Development Co. (London) Ltd. v. Sisabro Novelty Co. Ltd.* (1953) 70 R.P.C. 277.
[31] *Finkelstein v. Billig* (1930) 47 R.P.C. 516; *C. and P. Development Co. (London) Ltd. v. Sisabro Novelty Co. Ltd.* (1953) 70 R.P.C. 277.
[32] (1887) 4 R.P.C. 363 at p.375.

to pirates not to pirate, and to infringers not to infringe, and to warn the public that the patent to which the patentee is entitled, and under which he claims, is one which he intends to enforce."

"But my language must not be misunderstood on this point. It does not follow that because a threat is so worded as in mere language apparently and grammatically to apply only to the future that, therefore, it may not be in any particular case in substance, and, in fact, applicable to what has been done. Supposing, for a moment, that a manufacturer is making and issuing machines which the patentee considers to be infringements of his patent; if with reference to that act done, or to those machines made, the patentee endeavours to guard himself against this section by merely issuing a threat in the air, it seems to me he would not escape if the true gist of what he has done is to apply that threat to a particular person and to a particular act."

Thus, if, by issuing a general warning, it can be shown that a warning finger was pointed against the products of some other specific manufacturer, importer or vendor, the warning becomes an actionable threat.[33]

Threats as to the future

Threats that acts to be done in the future will constitute an infringement are actionable.[34] **11.12**

Abuse of monopoly when action pending

Once an action for infringement has been commenced, section 70 **11.13** provides no remedy for the defendant to that action for any injury suffered by reason of the existence or publication of the action. The courts have, however, sought to prevent such injury when inflicted by an abuse of the patentee's monopoly. Thus, a statement that an action for infringement has been commenced against a specific person, coupled with a general warning against dealing in infringing goods, may constitute a contempt of court if it suggests that the validity of the patent has been determined and that the defendant has in fact infringed,[35] or if it misrepresents what has in fact taken place in proceedings before the court.[36] The general principle is, however, that an application to commit for contempt of court should not be made "unless

---

[33] See *Weldrics Ltd. v. Quasi-Arc Co. Ltd.* (1922) 39 R.P.C. 323; *Cars v. Bland Light Syndicate Ltd.* (1911) 28 R.P.C. 33; *Boneham and Hart v. Hirst Bros. & Co. Ltd.* (1917) 34 R.P.C. 209; *Martin and Another v. Selsdon Fountain Pen Co. Ltd.* (1949) 66 R.P.C. 193 at p.215; *Alpi Pietro E Figlio & Co. v. John Wright & Sons (Veneers) Ltd.* [1972] R.P.C. 125 at 133.
[34] P.A. 1977, s.70(1) and (2).
[35] See *Goulard & Gibbs v. Sir Coutts Lindsay & Co. Ltd. and Ferranti* (1887) 4 R.P.C. 189 at p.190; *St. Mungo Mfg. Co. Ltd. v. Hutchinson, Main & Co. Ltd.* (1908), 25 R.P.C. 356 at p.360.
[36] See *Gillette Safety Razor Co. v. A. W. Gamage Ltd.* (1906) 23 R.P.C. 1; *Mentmore Manufacturing Co. Ltd. v. Fomento (Sterling Area) Ltd.* (1955) 72 R.P.C. 157. *Therma-Stor Ltd. v. Weatherseal Windows Ltd.* [1981] F.S.R. 579.

the thing done is of such a nature as to require the arbitrary and summary interference of the court in order to enable justice to be duly and properly administered without any interruption or interference. ...''[37] The courts have refused to consider as contempt of court advertisements which referred to certain specified goods as "infringing" goods or goods "offered for sale in infringement" of the letters patent, apparently upon the ground that a patentee was entitled to say: "The patent is a good one; I am going to maintain that it is a good patent and that you are infringing it".[38]

11.14 Similarly, where, having sued the manufacturer of a product, a patentee commences proceedings against the manufacturer's customers, so as to secure a collateral advantage, such proceedings may be stayed or restrictions placed on the commencement of further actions.[39]

11.15 The commencement of proceedings against one party does not prevent a third party bringing an action under section 70. Thus, it would appear that an advertisement which stated that an action for infringement had been commenced against a specified person and that others dealing in similar goods would also be proceeded against would be a threat which could be restrained under the provisions of section 70(1).

The plaintiff

A person aggrieved can sue

11.16 The statutory right of action is not merely limited to the person to whom the threats were directly made; any person aggrieved,[40] such as a rival patentee, to whom damage was occasioned by the issue of the threats is entitled to relief. Thus, in *Johnson v. Edge*[41] where circulars were issued to the trade intimating that the articles manufactured and sold by the plaintiff were infringements of the defendant's patent and that proceedings would be taken against any person dealing with such articles, and in consequence injury was done to the plaintiff's business, it was held that the plaintiff was a person aggrieved and could maintain an action, although no threats were made to him personally.[42] However, in

---

[37] *Hunt v. Clarke* (1919) 58 L.J.Q.B. 490 at p.493. *Re New Gold Coast Exploration Co.* [1901] 1 Ch. 860.

[38] See *Haskell Golf Ball Co. v. Hutchinson and Main* (1904) 21 R.P.C. 497 at p.500; see also *Fenner & Wilson Co. LTd.* (1893) 10 R.P.C. 283; *De Mare's Patent* (1899) 16 R.P.C. 528; *Dunlop Pneumatic Tyre Co. Ltd. v. Suction Cleaners Ltd.,* (1904) 21 R.P.C. 300; *Mullard Radio Valve Co. Ltd. v. Rothermel Corpn. Ltd.* (1934) 51 R.P.C. 1; *Selsdon Fountain Pen Co. Ltd. v. Miles Martin Pen Co. Ltd.* (1934) 51 R.P.C. 365 at p.367.

[39] *Landi den Hartog B.V. v. Sea Bird Ltd.* [1976] F.S.R. 489; *Jacey (Printers) v. Norton & Wright Group Ltd.* [1977] F.S.R. 475.

[40] P.A. 1977, s.70(1).

[41] (1892) 9 R.P.C. 142.

[42] And see, *e.g. Challender v. Royle* (1887) 4 R.P.C. 363 at p.371; *Kensington and Knightsbridge Electric Lighting Co. Ltd. v. Lane Fox Electrical Co. Ltd.* (1891), 8 R.P.C. 277; *Douglass v. Pintsch's Patent Lighting Co. Ltd.* (1897) 14 R.P.C. 673; *Hoffnung & Salsbury* (1899) 16

Reymes-Cole v. Elite Hosiery Co. Ltd.,[43] the defendants were held not to be persons aggrieved as they had ceased production of the type of stocking prior to the threat being made.

Defences

If there is a patent in existence, the defendant can defend the action on **11.17** the ground that the acts in respect of which the threats were made constituted an infringment of some claim and can (if so entitled) counterclaim for infringement. The onus then shifts to the plaintiff who can rebut the allegation of infringement and attack the validity of that claim in the same way as in an action for infringement.[44] It is to be observed, however, that the defendant does not have to be the proprietor of, or entitled to any right in the patent.

If the specification is amended after the threats and before the action, the issues of infringement and validity must presumably be tried with reference to the amended document and not the specification as it stood at the date when the threats were made.[45]

Where no patent has been granted

In proceedings brought under the 1949 Act it was also a defence that **11.18** the acts, in respect of which the infringement proceedings were threatened, constituted infringement of rights arising from the publica-tion (following acceptance) of the complete specification.[46] That defence has no counterpart in proceedings brought under the 1977 Act. It is submitted that if a person threatens another with proceedings for infringement of a patent then proceedings under the 1977 Act may be brought against them despite the fact that at the date of the threats there was no patent in existence or there was merely an application for a patent. In those circumstances the threats would be incapable of justification. The alternative view, that the words "of a patent" in section 70 require the existence of a granted patent before relief may be granted, would be contrary to the policy underlying section 70 and its predecessors, namely to discourage threats.

R.P.C. 375; *Luna Advertising Co. Ltd. v. Burnham & Co.* (1928) 45 R.P.C. 258; *Reymes-Cole v. Elite Hosiery Co. Ltd.* [1965] R.P.C. 102; *Bristol Myers v. Manon Freres Ltd.* [1973] R.P.C. 836; *Bowden Controls v. Acco Cable Controls Ltd.* [1990] R.P.C. 427.

[43] [1965] R.P.C. 102 at p.112.

[44] P.A. 1977, s.70(2) and see *John Summers & Sons Ltd. v. The Cold Metal Process Co.* (1948) 65 R.P.C. 75.

[45] See P.A. 1977, s.75(3) and *cf. Hall v. Stepney Spare Motor Wheel Ltd.* (1910) 27 R.P.C. 233; (1911) 28 R.P.C. 381.

[46] P.A. 1949, s.65(2).

Procedure

Right to begin

11.19   In *Lewis Falk Ltd. v. Jacobwitz*[47] Morton J.[48] said:

> "It is for a plaintiff in a 'threats' action first to prove the threat or threats and, once that has been done, the onus shifts to the defendant, and the burden is on him to prove that the acts, in respect of which proceedings are threatened, constitute, or if done would constitute, an infringement of a patent ... If the defendant succeeds in proving this, the burden then shifts again to the plaintiff to prove, if he can, that the patent ... is invalid. In the present case one threat is admitted, and it is, therefore, for the defendant to open his case first."[49]

Interlocutory injunction

11.20   The general principles upon which such an injunction will be granted are those set out in the opinion of Lord Diplock in *American Cyanamid Co. v. Ethicon Limited*[50] and old decisions[51] differing are not good law.[52] Accordingly, provided the court is satisfied that it is arguable that an actionable threat has been made, the granting or withholding of interlocutory relief will depend upon the ability of either party adequately to be compensated in monetary terms and ultimately on the balance of convenience. The fact that the defendant has counterclaimed for infringement is no bar to the granting of an interlocutory injunction and there is no analogy to be drawn with trade libel cases in that an assertion by a defendant that the threats will be justified will not provide a bar to interlocutory relief.[53-54]

If mala fides is relied on

11.21   If for any reason it is intended to rely upon mala fides on the part of the defendant, the fact has to be brought out upon the affidavits on any motion for an interlocutory injunction and not concealed until the actual trial.[55]

---

[47] (1944) 61 R.P.C. 116.
[48] *Ibid.* at p.118.
[49] See also *John Summers & Sons Ltd. v. The Cold Metal Process Co.* (1948) 65 R.P.C. 75; *Pearson v. Holden* (1948) 65 R.P.C. 424 at p.428.
[50] [1975] A.C. 396. See *Bowden Controls v. Acco Cable Controls Ltd.* [1990] R.P.C. 427.
[51] See, *e.g. Challender v. Royle* (1887) 4 R.P.C. 363; *Cerosa Ltd. v. Poseidon Industrie A.B.* [1973] R.P.C. 882.
[52] *Johnson Electric Industrial Manufactory v. Mabuchi–Motor K.K.* [1986] F.S.R. 280.
[53-54] *H.V.E. Electric Ltd. Cufflin Holdings Ltd.* [1964] R.P.C. 149; *Cerosa Ltd. v. Poseidon Industrie A.B.* [1973] R.P.C. 883. *Johnson Electric Industrial Manufactory v. Mabuchi–Motor K.K.* [1986] F.S.R. 280.
[55] See *English and American Machinery Co. Ltd. v. Gare Machine Co. Ltd.* (1894) 11 R.P.C. 627 at p.631.

Particulars

The defendant in an action under section 70 is entitled to particulars **11.22** of the threats upon which the plaintiff relies[56] and the plaintiff is entitled, if the defendant sought to justify, to particulars of the acts which are said to constitute infringement of the patent[57] and if the validity of the patent is put in question the general rules relating to particulars of objections apply.[58] Where there was a doubt upon which patents the defendants had based their threats, the court ordered that the defendants should deliver to the plaintiffs a list of such patents.[59] And where the plaintiffs alleged that the threats were made by the defendants' agents, it was held that the defendants were entitled to particulars of the names of those agents.[60]

Remedy

Declaration, injunction, damages

By the terms of section 70(3), the plaintiff, if successful, is entitled to: **11.23**

(1) a declaration that the threats were unjustifiable,
(2) an injunction against the continuance of the threats, and
(3) damages.

A declaration would not, however, be made by consent or in default of defence.[61] But the plaintiff is not entitled to any relief, even if he proves that the threat made in respect of infringement of a number of patents cannot be justified in respect of some of the patents, provided that the defendant can justify the threat in respect of one patent. In *Rosedale Associated Manufacturers Ltd. v. Carlton Tyre Saving Co. Ltd.,* Lord Evershed M.R. said:[62]

"Prima facie the right to relief which section 65(2) of the 1949 Act postulates depends upon the defendant in the action failing to prove that the acts in respect of which the threats were made did or would constitute an infringement of 'a patent.' Prima facie, therefore, the defendant's burden is discharged if he does prove infringement of 'a' that is any patent."

---

[56] *Law v. Ashworth* (1890) 7 R.P.C. 86.
[57] *Reymes-Cole v. Elite Hosiery Co. Ltd.* [1961] R.P.C. 277.
[58] *Law v. Ashworth* (1890) 7 R.P.C. 86; *Union Electrical Power etc. Co. v. Electrical Storage Co.,* (1888) 5 R.P.C. 329.
[59] *Union Electrical Power etc. Co. v. Electrical Storage Co.* (1888) 38 Ch.D. 325; (1888) 5 R.P.C. 329.
[60] *Downson-Taylor & Co. Ltd. v. The Drosophore Co. Ltd.* (1894) 11 R.P.C. 653.
[61] *Corn Products Co. Ltd. v. N.V. Schoeton* (1939) 56 R.P.C. 59; and *R. Demuth Ltd. v. Inter-Pan Ltd.* [1967] R.P.C. 75.
[62] [1960] R.P.C. 59 at p.62.

Where, however, no infringement is proved, the width of the injunction granted will in part depend upon the nature of the threat.[63]

11.24   The *quantum* of damage can be assessed by the judge at the trial,[64] but the ordinary form of order directs an inquiry.[65] The measure of damages is that ordinarily applicable in cases of tort, and damages can only be recovered if they are the natural and reasonable consequences of the threats,[66] and have to be due to the threats alone. In *Ungar v. Sugg*[67] Lord Esher M.R. said:

> "But then what is the liability? It must be for damage done by the threats—not damage done by anything else. They (*i.e.* the defendants) are not liable for the damage which is the result of any rumour getting about in the trade which is not their act. They are liable for the damages caused by their own act—the threats which they have made, and which they have caused to be made known to the people to whom their circulars were given."

The defendants will not be liable for damage caused by threats not authorised to be made by them (*ibid.*).

11.25   Damages suffered through the loss of a contract,[68] or the breaking off of negotiations for a contract[69] are recoverable. Where a plaintiff was not inconvenienced by the threat, the court in its discretion made no order in the action.[70]

Certificate of contested validity

11.26   Where validity is in issue and the patent is found wholly or partially valid a certificate of contested validity may be granted.[71] If such a certificate were granted it would not entitle a patentee to the increased allowance of costs in a subsequent threats action unless the threats action contained a counter–claim for infringment.

---

[63] *Mechanical Services (Trade Engineers) Ltd. v. Avon Rubber Co. Ltd.* [1977] R.P.C. 66.
[64] *E.g. Cars v. Bland Light Syndicate Ltd.* (1911) 28 R.P.C. 33; *Horne v. Johnston Bros.* (1921) 38 R.P.C. 366.
[65] *E.g. Hoffnung v. Salsbury* (1899) 16 R.P.C. 375; *Pittveil & Co. v. Brackelsberg Melting Process Ltd.* (1931) 50 R.P.C. 73; *Neild v. Rockley* [1986] F.S.R. 3.
[66] See *Horne v. Johnston Bros.* (1921) 38 R.P.C. 366 at p.372.
[67] (1892) 9 R.P.C. 114 at p.118.
[68] *Skinner & Co. v. Perry* (1894) 11 R.P.C. 406; see also *Hoffnung v. Salsbury* (1899) 16 R.P.C. 375.
[69] *Solanite Signs Ltd. v. Wood* (1933) 50 R.P.C. 315.
[70] *Tudor Associates Ltd. v. J.N. Somers Ltd.* [1960] R.P.C. 215.
[71] P.A. 1977, s.65(1).

CHAPTER 12

ACTION FOR INFRINGEMENT

An action for infringement is the method by which a patentee can in the **12.01** last resort enforce his patent privileges.

The courts are bound to take notice of the patent and to give legal effect to it to the extent of affording to the patentee a monopoly of the invention which he has claimed, subject, however, to the provisions of section 44(3) of the 1977 Act, and provided that it is not shown that the grant is invalid.

Expired patent

An action may be brought after the date of expiry of the patent[1-2] and **12.02** damages recovered in respect of infringements committed before such date.

[1-2] See, *e.g. Paterson Engineering Co. Ltd. v. Candy Filter Co. Ltd.* (1933) 50 R.P.C. 1.

1. Parties

The plaintiff

12.03   The plaintiff will normally be the patentee, *i.e.* the person or persons
for the time being entered on the register as grantee or proprietor of the
patent. Section 67 of the 1977 Act, however, enables an exclusive licensee to sue for infringement in his own name. The patentee must, unless
he consents to join as a plaintiff, be joined as a defendant, but he is not
liable for any costs unless he acknowledges service and takes part in the
proceedings.[3-4]

The patentee may have become such either by registration as grantee
upon grant of the patent, or by subsequent registration as proprietor
upon application made at the Patent Office after becoming entitled to
the patent by assignment, transmission, or other operation of law.[5]

The register is prima facie evidence of proprietorship.[6] By Section 68
of the 1977 Act no damages or an account of profits may be awarded to
the plaintiff in respect of infringement occurring before the plaintiff's
right is registered unless such right is registered within six months of
the date of acquisition of such right or unless the tribunal is satisfied that
it was not practicable so to register and that registration occurred as
soon as practicable thereafter. The section does not affect applications
for an injunction.[7]

An assignee of a patent or an exclusive licence may bring proceedings
in respect of infringements occurring prior to the date of such
assignment or licence provided that such right is included within the
relevant grant of title.[8]

After grant a patentee may sue in respect of acts of infringement
occurring prior to grant, but after publication of the complete
specification.[9]

Licensees under Patent Act 1977, s.46

12.04   In the cases of licences granted under a patent endorsed "licences
of right"[10] (except where the licence is settled by agreement or, in
default of agreement, by the Comptroller and expressly provides
otherwise) or granted compulsorily,[11] the licensee may call upon the
patentee to take proceedings for infringement and if the patentee

---

[3-4] P.A. 1977, s.67(3). See *British and International Proprietaries Ltd. v. Selcol Products Ltd.*
[1957] R.P.C. 1.
[5] See Chap. 8 and P.A. 1977, ss.33 to 38.
[6] P.A. 1977, s.32(9) as amended by Patents, Designs and Marks Act 1986.
[7] See *Christrian-Salvesen (O.T. Services) Ltd. v. Odfjell Drilling and Consulting Co. (U.K.) Ltd.*
[1985] R.P.C. 569.
[8] P.A. 1977, s.30(7).
[9] P.A. 1977, s.69.
[10] P.A. 1977, s.46.
[11] P.A. 1977, s.49(8).

refuses or neglects to do so within two months may institute such proceedings in his own name, making the patentee a defendant.[12] As in the case of an action by an exclusive licensee, the patentee is not liable for any costs unless he acknowledges service and takes part in the proceedings.[13]

Assignee

An assignment of a patent does not *per se* include an accrued right of **12.05** action for infringements committed prior to the assignment.[14] Where the patent has been assigned after the commencement of the action the assignee may be added as a necessary party.[15]

Proprietor of part of patent

A proprietor of a separate and distinct part of a patent has been held **12.06** entitled to sue for infringement of such part without joining the proprietors of the other parts of the patent.[16] Similarly, it is submitted, that a proprietor of a portion of a patent in respect of a certain territory can bring an action for infringements committed within his territory as sole plaintiff.

Co-owners

Where two or more persons are co-owners of a patent, one may sue **12.07** for infringement without the consent of the others, but the others must be parties to the proceedings.[17] If the others are joined as defendants, they are not liable for costs or expenses unless they acknowledge service and take part in the proceedings.

Alien enemies in time of war

An alien enemy cannot institute or maintain an action in the courts as **12.08** plaintiff,[18] nor as a co-plaintiff in a case of joint ownership of a patent,[19] unless he is merely a formal party.[20] He can, however, defend an action or appeal against a decision in a case in which he has been attacked;[21]

---

[12] P.A. 1977, ss.46(4).
[13] P.A. 1977, ss.46(5).
[14] P.A. 1977, s.30(7) and see *Wilderman v. F. W. Berk & Co. Ltd. v.* (1925) 42 R.P.C. 79 at p.90; see also *United Horse Shoe and Nail Co. Ltd. v. Stewart & Co.* (1888) 5 R.P.C. 260.
[15] See *Bates Valve Bag Co. v. B. Kershaw & Co. (1920) Ltd.* (1933) 50 R.P.C. 43, and R.S.C., Ord. 15, rr.6, 7, 8.
[16] *Dunnicliff v. Mallett* (1859) 7 C.B.(N.S.) 209; 29 L.J.C.P. 70.
[17] P.A. 1977, s.66(2).
[18] *Porter v. Freudenberg* [1915] 1 K.B. 857.
[19] *Actiengesellschaft für Anilin Fabrikation v. Levinstein Ltd.* (1915) 32 R.P.C. 140.
[20] *Mercedes Daimler Motor Co. Ltd. v. Maudslay Motor Co. Ltd.* (1915) 32 R.P.C. 149.
[21] *Mertern's Patent* (1915) 32 R.P.C. 109.

and as a defence to proceedings for revocation he can apply to the court for leave to amend his specification.[22-23]

The defendant
12.09   Any person infringing a patent by himself or by his servants or agents, is liable and may be made a defendant and sued for damages, and, if there be shown by act or word any threat or intent to continue to infringe, for an injunction. Any person who is a joint tortfeasor with such a person is similarly liable, but no other person is liable.

Assignee of infringer's business
12.10   Thus, an assignee of the business of a defendant, the assignment being subsequent to the issue of the writ, cannot be joined by the defendant as a co-defendant.[24]

Manufacturers
12.11   It has been held that the manufacturer and patentee of a machine, the use of which is claimed to be an infringement of another patent, cannot compel the plaintiff to join him as a co-defendant with the person by whom the machine is used and against whom the action for infringement is brought.[25] However this decision has probably been overruled by the Court of Appeal which allowed a manufacturer to be joined on appeal.[26] He would probably, however, be so entitled if the action were brought against his agent in respect of goods which were his property.[27]

Directors of company
12.12   Directors of a limited company are only liable in respect of infringements committed by the company if it be proved that the company committed the infringements as their agent, or that they expressly authorised or directed the acts of infringement.[28] In such a case particulars should be given of any facts on which the plaintiff intends to rely.[29]

[22-23] *Stahlwerk Becker A.G.'s Patent* (1917) 34 R.P.C. 332.
[24] *Briggs v. Lardeur* (1885) 2 R.P.C. 13.
[25] *Moser v. Marsden* (1892) 1 Ch. 487; (1892) 9 R.P.C. 214.
[26] *Tetra Molectric Ltd. v. Japan Imports Ltd.* [1976] R.P.C. 541.
[27] *Vavasseur v. Krupp* (1878) 9 Ch.D. 351.
[28] *British Thomson-Houston Co. Ltd. v. Sterling Accessories Ltd.* (1924) 2 Ch. 33; (1924) 41 R.P.C. 311; see also *Cropper Minerva Machines Co. Ltd. v. Cropper, Charlton & Co. Ltd.* (1906) 23 R.P.C. 388 at p.392; *Pritchard and Constance (Wholesale) Ltd. v. Amata Ltd.* (1925) 42 R.P.C. 63 (trade name); *Leggatt v. Hood* (1950) 67 R.P.C. 134; *Oertli A.G. v. E. J. Bowman Ltd. and Others* [1956] R.P.C. 282; [1957] R.P.C. 388; *White Horse Distillers Ltd. v. Gregson Associates Ltd.* [1984] R.P.C. 61; *C. Evans & Sons Ltd. v. Spritebrand Ltd.* [1985] F.S.R. 267. (Copyright)
[29] *British Thomson-Houston Co. Ltd. v. Irradiant Lamp Works Ltd.* (1924) 41 R.P.C. 338.

The existence of the relationship of principal and agent and the necessary degree of control or direction of the acts complained of is not to be inferred from the mere fact that the directors in question may be sole directors and sole shareholders of the company.[30] If, however, a company is formed for the express purpose of doing a wrongful act, or if, when formed, those in control expressly direct that a wrongful act be done, such individuals as well as the company are responsible.[31] In each case it is necessary to examine with care what part the director played personally in regard to the act or acts complained of.[32]

Proper course where infringers numerous

In the case of *Bovill v. Crate*[33] it was stated by Sir W. Page-Wood V.-C. **12.13** that in cases where there were numerous infringers a patentee might well:

"select that which he thought the best in order to try the question fairly, and proceed in that case to obtain his interlocutory injunction. He might write at the same time to all the others who were *in simili casu*, and say them them: 'Are you willing to take this as a notice to you that the present case is to determine yours? Otherwise I shall proceed against you by way of interlocutory injunction; and if you will not object on the ground of delay, I do not mean to file bills against all of you at once. Am I to understand that you make no objection of that kind? If you do not object I shall file a bill against only one of you.' I do not think any court could complain of a patentee for taking the course I am suggesting,"

and stated further that such conduct would not in itself debar the patentee (owing to the delay) from obtaining interlocutory injunctions.[34] Such a letter would however exceed the permitted notification under section 70(5) and the patentee would be committed to instituting proceedings if the offer were so treated.

The usual course is for the patentee to select the main sources of supply of infringing articles and to obtain a decision in an action against a representative infringer, and, if the decision on such action is in his favour, to proceed against the others. Where there were two actions on the same patent in which the issues and defences were substantially the same, the second action was stayed pending the trial of the first action,

---

[30] *Rainham Chemical Works v. Belvedere Fish Guano Co.* [1921] 2 A.C. 465.
[31] *Ibid.* See also *Middlemas and Wood v. Moliver & Co. Ltd.* (1921) 38 R.P.C. 97; *Performing Right Society Ltd. v. Ciryl Theatrical Syndicate Ltd.* [1924] 1 K.B. 1.
[32] *C. Evans & Sons Ltd. v. Spritebrand Ltd.* [1985] F.S.R. 267.
[33] (1865) L.R. 1 Eq. 388.
[34] See also *Foxwell v. Webster* (1863) 3 New Rep. 103; *North British Rubber Co. Ltd. v. Gormully and Jeffery Manufacturing Co.* (1894) 11 R.P.C. 17.

the defendant in the second action undertaking to submit to an order similar to any order which the plaintiff might obtain in the first action.[35]

Carriers

12.14   Under the 1949 Act, an action could properly be brought against innocent carriers who had infringed by importing articles to restrain them from dealing with or handing over such articles to other persons,[36] and on the discovery of the name of the consignee, such consignee was joined as a co-defendant in the action.[37] The carriers were absolved from all liability if they made full disclosure of the names of the consignors and consignees of the goods complained of. It has been held that the position is the same under the 1977 Act and that the word "keep" in section 60(1) of the Act does not cover mere carriers.[38]

Third party procedure

12.15   Where an indemnity was given to the defendants, after the commencement of the action, by a third party who had manufactured the infringing articles, it was held that the person giving such an indemnity should be joined as party under Order 16, rules 1 and 2.[39] Such third party will only be bound by the decision of the court in so far as the decision to appear, and if the plaintiffs neglect to amend by joining him as a defendant they will not be able to obtain an injunction against him as well as against the actual defendant.[40]

A defendant, however, is not entitled to compel the plaintiff to join as co-defendant a person who supplied the defendant with the machine, the use of which is alleged to be an infringement, and who, the defendant alleges, is a licensee of the plaintiff; the question of infringement can be properly and conveniently tried without such joinder.[41] Unless the defendant can join such person as a third party under Order 16, his only course is to commence a separate action against him.

---

[35] *Multiple Utilities Co. Ltd. v. Souch* (1929) 46 R.P.C. 402; *McCreath v. Mayor etc. of South Shields and Baker* (1932) 49 R.P.C.; *Gillette Industries Ltd. v. Albert* (1940) 57 R.P.C. 85; *White v. Glove (Industrial) Manufacturing Co. Ltd.* [1958] R.P.C. 142; *Reymes-Cole v. West Riding Hosiery Ltd.* [1961] R.P.C. 273.

[36] *Upman v. Elkan* (1871) L.R. 7 Ch. App. 130; *Washburn and Moen Manufacturing Co. v. Cunard Steamship Company* (1889) 6 R.P.C. 398.

[37] *Washburn and Moen Manufacturing Co. v. Cunard Steamship Co.* (1889) 6 R.P.C. 398.

[38] *Smith, Kline and French Laboratories Ltd. v. R. D. Harbottle (Mercantile) Ltd.* [1980] R.P.C. 363.

[39] *Edison and Swan Electric Light Co. v. Holland* (1886) 33 Ch.D. 497; (1886) 3 R.P.C. 395 (under R.S.C., Ord. 16, rr.1, 2).

[40] *Edison and Swan Electric Light Co. v. Holland* (1889) 41 Ch.D. 28; 6 R.P.C. 243 at p.286.

[41] *Evans v. Central Electric Supply Co. Ltd.* (1923) 40 R.P.C. 357.

Change of parties by death, etc.

The procedure where a change of parties is necessitated by death, **12.16** bankruptcy, etc. of one or other of them is regulated by Order 15 of the Rules of the Supreme Court.

2. The Tribunal

The 1977 Act established the Patents Court which is composed of the **12.17** Patents Judges who are puisne judges of the High Court.[42] The Copyright Designs and Patents Act 1988 provided power to designate any County Court as a Patents County Court and to nominate persons to sit there as patents judges. At the time of writing the Central London County Court has been designated.[43] The Comptroller has a limited jurisdiction to decide disputes as to infringement.

Patents judges of the High Court

The patents judges are nominated by the Lord Chancellor and are **12.18** attached to the Chancery Division of the High Court. By Order 104, rule 2 all patent proceedings in the High Court are assigned to the Chancery Division and taken by the Patents Court. The Patents Court may appoint scientific advisers to assist it.[44]

Patents judges of the Patents County Court

The patents judges of the Patents County Court, like those of the High **12.19** Court, are nominated by the Lord Chancellor.[45] The Patents County Court may also appoint scientific advisers to assist it.[46]

The maximum possible scope of the jurisdiction of a Patents County Court is set by section 287(1) of the 1988 Act; while the jurisdiction of a particular court (its "special jurisdiction") is set by the Order designating the court as such. The special jurisdiction of the Central London Patents County Court is defined as covering: "any action or matter relating to patents or designs over which the High Court would have jurisdiction, together with any claims or matters ancillary to, or arising from, such proceedings".[47] A claim for copyright infringement may be a claim ancillary to or arising from the action or matter relating to the plaintiff's patent and, as such, within the special jurisdiction.[48]

---

[42] Supreme Court Act 1981, s.6 and s.62.
[43] See C.D.P.A. 1988, s.287; The Central London County Court was designated by (S.I. 1994 No.1609) which came into force on July 11, 1994, revoking the designation of the Edmonton County Court (S.I. 1990 No. 1496). The Central London County Court is at the Central London Courthouse, 26/29 Park Crescent, London W1N 4HT.
[44] Supreme Court Act 1981, s.70.
[45] C.D.P.A. 1988, s.291(1); C.C.R., Ord. 48A, r.7.
[46] *Ibid.*
[47] See *ante*, (S.I. 1994 No.1609), Art 3. The words used are slightly different from those used in the previous Order and in the Act *sed quaere* whether the difference is material. *McDonald v. Graham* (Unrep.) C.A., December 16, 1993.
[48] *McDonald v. Graham, ante.*

Patents County Court has no jurisdiction to hear appeals from the Comptroller.[49] Under the Community Patent Convention only the High Court (in England and Wales) will have jurisdiction to hear actions in respect of community patents.[50]

Power exists to impose financial limits on the special jurisdiction,[51] but as yet no such limits have been set.

All proceedings within the special jurisdiction shall be dealt with by the Patents Judge (except urgent interlocutory matters when the Patents Judge is unavailable).[52]

Choice of tribunal between the High Court and the Patents County Court

12.20 The Plaintiff chooses the tribunal in which to bring an action by either issuing a writ in the High Court or a summons in the Patents County Court.[53]

The 1988 Act provided power to prescribe an amount such that if, in a High Court action which could have been commenced in the Patents County Court in which a claim for a pecuniary remedy is made, the plaintiff recovers less than the amount prescribed then the plaintiff shall not be entitled to any more costs than those he would have recovered in the County Court.[54] As yet no such amount has been prescribed and the provision has no effect. In its absence the choice of tribunal will depend on how the different procedures, particularly pleadings, discovery and costs to be incurred and recovered, are perceived to suit the case.

It is submitted, that the main effects of the differences between the two courts are that more work must be done earlier in an action in the Patents County Court than in the High Court and that a successful party risks failing to recover the same proportion of its costs in the Patents County Court as in the High Court.[55]

The ideal Patents County Court case is one in which the issues of fact are simple and not really in dispute and where the only real issue between the parties is one of construction of the patent. Cases in which discovery may be important, where there are real disputes as to facts, or where a significant amount of experimentation may be required are not suited to the County Court. Generally, the longer, heavier, more complex, more important and more valuable actions continue to belong in the High Court.[56-57]

---

[49] See *ante*, (S.I. 1994 No.1609), Art 4.
[50] Protocol on Litigation, Art 1.
[51] C.D.P.A. 1988, s.288.
[52] C.C.R., Ord. 48A, r.2.
[53] But see *post*, §12.32 and 12.187 on the question of transfers between the High Court and Patents County Court.
[54] C.D.P.A. 1988, s.290.
[55] Due to more restrictive County Court costs rules, although in practice the costs of any substantial matter in the Patents County Court are likely to be ordered on the High Court scale, see *The Wellcome Foundation v. Discpharm Ltd. (No. 2)* [1993] F.S.R. 444.
[56-57] *Per* Sir Thomas Bingham M.R. in *Chaplin Patents Holdings Co. Inc. v. Group Lotus plc and Lotus Car Ltd.* (Unrep.) C.A., December 17, 1993.

The Comptroller

Under the 1977 Act, the Comptroller's jurisdiction has been extended **12.21** from the limited jurisdiction under the 1949 Act[58] and the parties may by agreement refer infringement to the Comptroller.[59] The Comptroller may decline to deal with it, if the matters involved would more properly be determined by the court.[60] The Comptroller may decide whether damages and a declaration are appropriate.[61] However, the Comptroller can consider all matters of validity.[62] An appeal lies from any decision of the Comptroller on infringement or validity to the Patents Court and thereafter, with leave of the Patents Court or the Court of Appeal, to the Court of Appeal.[63]

Although the jurisdiction of the Comptroller has been extended to meet in part the criticisms of the jurisdiction under the 1949 Act, it is submitted, that questions of infringement should only in exceptional circumstances be referred to the Comptroller. Normally, an injunction is sought which necessitates going before the court. Further, in many cases, the costs will be increased by adding a further tribunal in the normal chain of possible appeals. If discovery or cross-examination is necessary, then this is best done before the court which has the machinery and experience to deal with disputes relating thereto.

Scotland, etc.

The 1977 Act applies to the United Kingdom. Actions in respect of **12.22** infringements committed in Scotland ar heard in the Court of Session which has power to hear proceedings for revocation of a patent.

The application of the Act to the Isle of Man is provided for by section 132.

3. Practice before Trial in the High Court

General

The practice of the High Court is regulated by Order 104 of the Rules **12.23** of the Supreme Court.

These rules do not apply to the Scottish courts.

---

[58] P.A. 1949, s.67.
[59] P.A. 1977, s.61(3).
[60] P.A. 1977, s.61(5).
[61] P.A. 1977, s.61(3).
[62] P.A. 1977, s.72.
[63] P.A. 1977, s.97(3).

The writ

Issue

12.24 Actions in the High Court in England are commenced by the issue of a writ from the Central Office or from a District Registry.[64]

Indorsement

12.25 In nearly all actions for infringement the writ is indorsed[65] with a claim for

(1) an injunction;
(2) damages or at the plaintiffs option an account of profits; and
(3) delivery up to the plaintiffs or destruction of all infringing articles in the possession of the defendants.[66]

More than one cause of action

12.26 Writs are frequently indorsed with claims in respect of infringements of more than one patent, and sometimes with claims with regard to analogous matters such as infringement of designs, trade marks, etc. The question of separate causes of action being dealt with in the same or in separate actions is regulated by Order 15 of the Rules of the Supreme Court.

Where the plaintiffs sued on 23 patents (all of which related to the process of making saccharin), the action was ordered to be limited to three patents to be selected by the plaintiffs.[67]

Service

12.27 Service of the writ is regulated by Orders 10, 11 and 65 of the Rules of the Supreme Court.

Service out of jurisdiction

12.28 The practice as to service out of the jurisdiction is regulated by Order 11 of the Rules of the Supreme Court. The Civil Jurisdiction and Judgments Act came into force on January 1, 1987, giving effect to the

---

[64] R.S.C., Ord. 5 and Ord. 104, r.5.
[65] See R.S.C., Ord. 6.
[66] See *post*, §14.02.
[67] *Saccharin Corp. Ltd. v. Wild & Co.* (1903) 20 R.P.C. 243; see also *Saccharin Corp. Ltd. v. R. White & Sons Ltd.* (1903) 20 R.P.C. 454 (C.A.); cf. *Saccharin Corp. Ltd. v. Alliance Chemical Co. Ltd.* (1905) 22 R.P.C. 175.

1968 Brussels Convention on civil jurisdiction and the enforcement of judgments. Under this Act leave to serve out of the jurisdiction is not required in many cases, either where the defendant is domiciled in a Contracting State or where one of the other bases of jurisdiction set out in Articles 5–18 of Schedule 1 apply. Under Article 5(3) a tort is actionable where the harmful event occurred, and by Article 16, in proceedings concerned with the registration or validity of patents, the Courts of the Contracting State in which the registration has been applied for, has taken place or is under the terms of an international convention deemed to have taken place have exclusive jurisdiction. By Schedule 4 leave to serve in Scotland or Northern Ireland is no longer required in all circumstances. These provisions are given effect to by R.S.C. Order 11, rule 1(2).

An application for leave must be supported by an affidavit stating *inter alia* the ground upon which the application is made,[68] and it should also state facts which, if proved, would be a sufficient foundation for the cause of action alleged.[69] The affidavit would be full and frank in its disclosure and must be sufficiently full to show that there is a good arguable case for the relief claimed,[70] a mere assertion of infringement is insufficient.[71]

Where leave to serve out is required, the usual grounds in patent actions are that:

(a) an injunction is sought to restrain a person from doing an act within the jurisdiction;[72]

(b) a person is a necessary and proper party to an action properly brought against some other person duly served within the jurisdiction,[73] as, for instance, upon the consignees of infringing goods in respect of which an action had been brought against the carriers thereof.[74]

(c) the claim is founded upon tort and the damage was sustained, or resulted from an act committed, within the jurisdiction.[75]

---

[68] R.S.C., Ord. 11, r.4.

[69] *Badische Anilin und Soda Fabrik v. Chemische Fabrik Vormals Sandoz* (1903) 20 R.P.C. 413; (1904) 21 R.P.C. 345, 533 at p.539; see also *Badische Anilin und Soda Fabrik v. W. G. Thompson Ltd.* (1903) 20 R.P.C. 422; *British Oxygen Co. Ltd. v. Gesellschaft für Industriegasverwertung M.B.H.* (1930) 47 R.P.C. 130.

[70] *Vitkovice Horni a Hutni Tezirstuo v. Korner* [1951] A.C. 869; *The Electric Furnace Co. v. Selas Corp. of America* [1987] R.P.C. 23; *Unilever v. Gillette U.K.* [1989] R.P.C. 583; *Molnlyke A.B. v. Proctor & Gamble Ltd. and others* [1992] R.P.C. 21 and *Lubrizol Corp. v. Esso Petroleum Co. Ltd.* [1992] R.P.C. 281 (High Ct) and 467 (C.A.).

[71] *Raychem Corp. v. Thermon (U.K.)* [1989] R.P.C. 423; *Puschner v. Tom Palmer (Scotland) Ltd.* [1989] R.P.C. 430.

[72] R.S.C., Ord. 11, r.1(1)(*h*).

[73] R.S.C., Ord. 11, r.1(1)(*c*); and see *Massey v. Haynes & Co.* (1888) 21 Q.B.D. 330.

[74] *Washburn and Moen Manufacturing Co. v. Cunard Steamship Co.* (1889) 6 R.P.C. 398.

[75] R.S.C., Ord. 11, r.1(1)(*f*).

Acknowledgement of service

12.29   The next step is ordinarily an acknowledgement of service by the defendant.[76] If the defendant is outside the jurisdiction, such acknowledgement is without prejudice to his right to contest the jurisdiction of the court provided that he does so within the time limited for service of a defence.[77]

Stay of High Court proceedings

12.30   In the case of United Kingdom National Patents an application may be made to stay the High Court proceedings pending the outcome of an application to the Comptroller either to revoke the patent or for a declaration of non-infringement. Such a stay will depend upon the circumstances of each case and an application was unsuccessful in *Ferro Corporation v. Escol Products*.[78] In *Hawker Siddeley Dynamics Engineering Limited v. Real Time Developments Limited*[79] a stay was granted, but that case has since been described as very unusual.[80] In particular the Patent Office proceedings had been commenced, the defendants could not afford High Court proceedings and agreed to be bound by the decision of the Patent Office.

12.31   The situation also arises in the case of a European Patent (U.K.) which is the subject of opposition proceedings in the EPO. The United Kingdom courts have so far declined to stay United Kingdom proceedings for infringement with a counterclaim for evocation,[81] but again each case turns on its facts and a petition for revocation in the United Kingdom of a European Patent (U.K.) is more likely to be stayed in appropriate circumstances.

Transfer to the Patents County Court

12.32   The Patents Court in the High Court has power to transfer any proceedings before it over which the Patents County Court would have jurisdiction to that court under section 40(2) of the County Courts Act 1984.[82] The High Court has a complete discretion as regards such transfers but there are certain criteria[83] to which the court must have regard namely:

    (a) the financial substance of the action, including the value of any counterclaim;

---

[76] R.S.C., Ord. 12.
[77] R.S.C., Ord. 12, r. 8.
[78] [1990] R.P.C. 651; and see *Gen Set Sp.A. v. Mosarc Ltd.* [1985] R.P.C. 302.
[79] [1983] R.P.C. 395.
[80] [1990] R.P.C. 651.
[81] *Amersham International plc v. Corning Ltd.* [1987] R.P.C. 53, and *Pall Corp. v. Commercial Hydraulics (Bedford) Ltd.* [1989] R.P.C. 703 (C.A.).
[82] As substituted by s.2(1) of the Court and Legal Services Act 1990.
[83] See The High Court and County Courts Jurisdiction Ord. 1991, Art. 7(5).

(b) whether the action is otherwise important and, in particular, whether it raises questions of importance to persons who are not parties or questions of general public interest;

(c) the complexity of the facts, legal issues, remedies or procedures involved; and

(d) whether transfer is likely to result in a more speedy trial of the action.

Section 289(2) of the 1988 Act also bears on the court's discretion; it provides that the court shall have regard to the financial position of the parties when considering transfer and that transfer may be ordered, notwithstanding that the proceedings are likely to raise an important question of fact or law. The latter part of this provision was more significant in the light of the previous section 40 of the County Courts Act 1984 which fettered the court's discretion in such cases.

The effect of the differences in procedure between the two tribunals on any individual case ought also to be borne in mind when considering transfer.

In *Memminger v. Trip-lite*,[84] decided prior to the amendment of section 40 of the County Courts Act 1984, the court had to consider a contested application by the defendants to transfer a case from the High Court to the Patents County Court. The court ordered transfer holding that the fact that the defendants intended to dispense with solicitors and counsel in the Patents County Court was the factor which tipped an otherwise even balance in favour of tranfer. In *GEC-Marconi v. Xyllyx Viewdata Terminals*[85] the court considered a similar case but refused to order transfer because there was no evidence that costs would be saved by the transfer. For the approach to be followed subsequent to the amendment of section 40 of the County Courts Act see, in particular, *Mannesmann Kienzle G.m.b.H. v. Microsystems Design Limited*[86] and *Symbol Technologies Inc. v. Opticon Sensors Europe B.V. (No.2)*.[87]

Failure to give notice of intention to defend

The procedure in case of failure to give notice of intention to defend **12.33** by the defendant is regulated by Order 13 of the Rules of the Supreme Court. Where, as is usually the case, there is a claim for an injunction and there is such default, upon the filing of an affidavit of service and of a statement of claim by the plaintiff the action proceeds in the ordinary way.[88] On motion for judgment in default of defence,[89] the Writ and Statement of Claim must show prima facie the entitlement to the relief

---

[84] [1992] R.P.C. 210.
[85] [1991] F.S.R. 319.
[86] [1992] R.P.C. 569.
[87] [1993] R.P.C. 232.
[88] R.S.C., Ord. 13, r.6.
[89] R.S.C., Ord. 19, r.7. 636 R.S.C., Ord. 12, r.8.

sought and the order for delivery up must identify the goods to be delivered up.[90]

Joinder of additional parties

12.34   The joinder of additional parties is regulated by Order 15, rules 6 and 8 of the Rules of the Supreme Court.[91]

Where one defendant only appears

12.35   A question has arisen as to what should be done if in an action against two defendants for the same infringement one of them fails to appear. If the cause of action was severable the plaintiff might move, under Order 19, rule 7, for judgment against the defendant who failed to give notice of an intention to defend.[92] The defendant who defended might, however, succeed in establishing the invalidity of the patent, and the difficulty arises as to the position of the other defendant.

On the whole it may be said that an injunction is an equitable remedy, and that it would be contrary to principle for the same tribunal which had pronounced a patent to be invalid to restrain a member of the public from doing what could not be an infringement. This might not, however, be the case where the reason for the lack of defence of the one defendant proves to be that he is unable to contest the validity of the patent owing to his being a licensee, as, under these circumstances, the plaintiff's rights against him would really be contractual and such defendant might have disentitled himself from working the invention save on a royalty basis, apart from any question of validity of the patent.

In *Actiengesellschaft für Cartonnagen Industrie v. Remus and Burgon*[93] one defendant had put the validity of the patent in issue and Chitty J. refused leave to set down the action on motion for judgment against the other defendant who had not delivered a defence, but did not consent to judgment.

In *Savage Brothers Ltd. v. Brindle and another*[94] a motion for judgment against one defendant stood over until the trial; after the hearing he consented to an injunction, but the other defendant succeeded in upsetting the patent. Farwell J. granted the injunction asked for, but *quaere* whether this practice would be followed today.

---

[90] *Paton Culvert & Co. Ltd. v. Rosedale Associated Manufacturers Ltd.* [1966] R.P.C. 61.
[91] See *Amon v. Raphael Tuck & Sons Ltd.* [1956] R.P.C. 29 although the narrow interpretation in that case of the predecessor to the current rule was criticised in *Gurtner v. Circuit* [1968] 2 Q.B. 587.
[92] See *Weinberg v. Balkan Sobranie Cigarettes Ltd.* (1923) 40 R.P.C. 399 (trade mark).
[93] (1896) 13 R.P.C. 94.
[94] (1900) 17 R.P.C. 228 at p.233.

Chancery Masters' Jurisdiction

Masters have no jurisdiction to make orders in proceedings in the **12.36**
Patents Court pursuant to Order 104, rule 2(1) except

    (i)   consent orders;
    (ii) orders on summonses for extensions of time;
    (iii) orders giving leave to serve out of the jurisdiction; and
    (iv) orders for security for costs.[95]

Interlocutory injunctions

Where it appears to the court "just or convenient" the plaintiff can **12.37**
obtain an injunction to restrain the defendant from infringing pending
the trial of the action.[96] Such application is made in the Chancery
Division to the Patents Court by motion normally after service of notice
of motion upon the defendant, or in rare cases *ex parte.*

Principle governing interlocutory injunctions

The House of Lords in *American Cyanamid Company v. Ethicon Limited*[97] **12.38**
laid down the principles upon which interlocutory injunctions should
be granted. Lord Diplock stated that:

> "the object of the interlocutory injunction is to protect the plaintiff
> against injury by violation of his right for which he could not be
> adequately compensated in damages recoverable in the action if the
> uncertainty were resolved in his favour at the trial; but the plaintiff's
> need for protection must be weighed against the corresponding need
> of the defendant to be protected against injury resulting from his hav-
> ing been prevented from exercising his own legal rights for which he
> could not be adequately compensated under the plaintiff's undertak-
> ing in damages if the uncertainty were resolved in the defendant's
> favour at the trial. The court must weigh one need against another
> and determine where 'the balance of convenience' lies."[98]

Lord Diplock, in a speech which was agreed with by the rest of the
House, laid down the following guidelines:

    (i)   There is no rule that a plaintiff must make out a prima facie case.
          "The court no doubt must be satisfied that the claim is not
          frivolous or vexatious; in other words, that there is a serious
          issue to be tried."[99] ... "So unless the material available to the

---

[95] Chancery Division Practice Direction April 9, 1991, see *White Book* (1994) Vol. 2, Pt. 3B,
    para. 854.
[96] Supreme Court Act 1981, s.37; R.S.C., Ord. 29.
[97] [1975] R.P.C. 513.
[98] *Ibid.* at p.540, 1.6.
[99] *Ibid.* at p.541, 1.13.

court at the hearing of the application for an interlocutory injunction fails to disclose that the plaintiff has any real prospect of succeeding in his claim for a permanent injunction at the trial, the court should go on to consider whether the balance of convenience lies in favour of granting or refusing the interlocutory relief that is sought."[1]

(ii) "It is no part of the court's function at this stage of the litigation to try to resolve conflicts of evidence on affidavit as to facts on which the claims of either party may ultimately depend nor to decide difficult questions of law which call for detailed agreement and mature considerations."[2]

(iii) "If damages in the measure recoverable at common law would be an adequate remedy and the defendant would be in a financial position to pay them, no interlocutory injunction should normally be granted, however strong the plaintiff's claim appeared to be at that stage."[3]

(iv) "If, on the other hand, damages would not provide an adequate remedy for the plaintiff..., the court should then consider whether, on the contrary hypothesis that the defendant were to succeed at the trial ... he would be adequately compensated under the plaintiff's undertaking as to damages for the loss he would have sustained by being prevented from doing so between the time of the application and the time of the trial. If damages in the measure recoverable under such an undertaking would be an adequate remedy and the plaintiff would be in a financial position to pay them, there would be no reason upon this ground to refuse an interlocutory injunction."[4]

(v) "It is where there is doubt as to the adequacy of the respective remedies in damages available to either party or to both, that the question of balance of convenience arises. It would be unwise to attempt even to list all the various matters which may need to be taken into consideration in deciding where the balance lies, let alone to suggest the relative weight to be attached to them. These will vary from case to case."[5]

(vi) "Where other factors appear to be evenly balanced it is a counsel of prudence to take such measures as are calculated to preserve the status quo."[6]

(vii) "If the extent of the uncompensatable disadvantage to each party would not differ widely, it may not be improper to take into account in tipping the balance the relative strength of each party's case as revealed by this affidavit evidence adduced on

---

[1] *Ibid.* at p.541, 1.23.
[2] *Ibid.* at p.541, 1.15. But see R.S.C., Ord. 14A.
[3] *Ibid.* at p.541, 1.32.
[4] *Ibid.* at p.541, 1.36.
[5] *Ibid.* at p.541, 1.46.
[6] *Ibid.* at p.542, 1.3.

the hearing of the application. This however should be done only where it is apparent upon the facts disclosed by evidence as to which there is no credible dispute that the strength of one party's case is disproportionate to that of the other party."[7]

In view of the speech of Lord Diplock most of the old cases on interlocutory injunctions are not applicable.

An interlocutory injunction may be granted if the defendant has applied for a compulsory licence, but he infringes that patent during a period when his application is still pending.[8] Further, an interlocutory injunction may be granted in respect of a valid claim even though other claims in the specification are not prima facie valid.[9]   **12.39**

Defendant with other business interests

The fact that a defendant may have other viable business interests to which it can turn its attention is not a strong ground for urging the grant of interlocutory relief.[10]   **12.40**

The "Snowball" effect

It is often argued that unless a plaintiff is seen quickly to prevent infringements of his patent, other persons will be encouraged to infringe. This may in a suitable case be a proper matter to be taken into account,[11] but it must be supported by cogent evidence.   **12.41**

The Springboard argument

In cases where a patent is reaching the end of its term no lesser protection should be afforded to a plaintiff.   **12.42**

"A patent monopoly not only entitles the holder to exploit the invention without competition during the period of patent protection, it also enables him to approach or enter on the period after the monopoly ceases in a strong position in the market place."[12]

A defendant should not, therefore, pre-empt the expiry of a patent and thereby acquire a valuable commercial bridgehead. Nor will a defendant if subject to an injunction be permitted to carry out those tests and

---

[7] *Ibid.* at p.542, 1.19. See also *N.W.L. v. Woods* [1979] 3 All E.R. 614.
[8] *Hoffman-La Roche & Co. A.G. v. Inter-Continental Pharmaceuticals Ltd.* [1965] R.P.C. 226.
[9] *Hoffman-La Roche & Co. A.G. v. D.D.S.A. Pharmaceuticals Ltd.* [1965] R.P.C. 503. See also §12.44 below where an application to amend the patent is made.
[10] *Condor International Ltd. v. Hibbing* [1984] R.P.C. 312.
[11] *Condor International Ltd. v. Hibbing ibid.* at p.315.
[12] Per Eichelbaum J. *Monsanto Co. v. Stauffer Chemical Co. (N.Z.)* [1984] F.S.R. 559; and *Monsanto Co. v. Stauffer Chemical Co.* [1984] F.S.R. 576.

trials necessary to secure the regulatory approvals needed to commence marketing once the patent has expired.[13]

Calculated Risk by Defendant

12.43   Where a defendant commences the commission of acts in full knowledge of the complaint against him limited consideration will be given to the effect of the injunction in relation to those acts in considering where the balance of convenience lies.[14]

Amendment pending

12.44   The court will not grant an injunction to restrain infringement of a patent, the scope of the monopoly of which could not be defined,[15] and if an interlocutory injunction had been granted before an application was made to amend, the court would discharge that injunction.[16]

Impecunious Defendant

12.45   Where damages are an adequate remedy to the plaintiff, but doubt exists as to the financial standing of the defendant the court may decline to grant an interlocutory injunction upon the undertaking of the Defendant to pay a reasonable sum into a suitable joint bank account, usually in the names of the parties' solicitors.[17]

Impecunious Plaintiff

12.46   The fact that a plaintiff may not be able to meet his liability on the cross–undertaking is not conclusive. The course to be taken is that which would involve the least risk of ultimate injustice.[18]

Interlocutory injunction to restrain threats.

12.47   The damage which can be caused by unjustified threats of patent infringement is such that an interlocutory injunction to restrain such threats represents a valuable remedy. The proviso in section 70(5) which permits the mere notification of the existence of a patent and the fact that proceedings to restrain threats may not be instituted in respect of threats to bring proceedings in respect of manufacture, use of a process or

---

[13] *Monsanto Co. v. Stauffer Chemical Co.* [1985] R.P.C. 515.
[14] *Improver Corp. v. Remington Consumer Products Ltd.* [1989] R.P.C. 82.
[15] *Molnlycke A.B. v. Proctor & Gamble* [1990] R.P.C. 487.
[16] *Ibid.*
[17] *Vernon & Co. (Pulp Products) Ltd. v. Universal Pulp Containers Ltd.* [1980] F.S.R. 179 and *Brupat Ltd. v. Sandford Marine Products Ltd.* [1983] R.P.C. 61.
[18] *Fleming Fabrications Ltd. v. Albion Cylinders Ltd.* [1989] R.P.C. 47; applying *Allen v. Jambo Holdings Ltd.* [1980] 1 W.L.R. 1252, and *Cayne v. Global Natural Resources* [1984] 1 All E.R. 225.

importation of a product[19] means that the balance of convenience will usually be in favour of restraining any threats which go outside of these categories. Furthermore, the onus is on the maker of the threats to justify them but such justification will not be a matter which can be resolved on motion unless validity and infringement are admitted.[20]

Ex parte injunctions
An *ex parte* injunction may be granted after the issue of the writ and **12.48** before service thereof, but normally only where it can be shown that great injury will accrue to the plaintiff by delay, that the plaintiff is the property person to sue, that the defendant committed the act complained of, and that such an act is prima facie an infringement. Such *ex parte* injunctions will normally be granted for a few days only.[21]

Interlocutory undertaking to deliver up
Where in interlocutory proceedings the defendants gave an under- **12.49** taking to deliver up confidential documents, an affidavit verifying compliance with the undertaking was ordered to be made.[22]

Notice of motion
Notice of motion may be served without leave with the writ, or at any **12.50** time subsequently.[23]

Practice
Applictions for interlocutory injunctions are heard and decided upon **12.51** affidavit evidence in open court. Motions in actions and matters relating to patents are made to the Patents Court.

Nature of affidavits
The plaintiff's affidavits should clearly point out the ownership and **12.52** registration of the patent and that it is in force. It should also identify what the alleged infringement consists of. Affidavits on "information and belief" must state the sources and grounds of the information.[24] An injunction granted prior to statement of claim will be dissolved if the

---

[19] P.A. 1977, s.70(4).
[20] *Johnson Electric Industrial Manufactory Ltd. v. Mabuchi-Motor K.K.* [1986] F.S.R. 280.
[21] See *British Thomson-Houston Co. Ltd. v. Philip Henry & Co. Ltd.* (1928) 45 R.P.C. 218; see also *Gardner v. Broadbent* (1856) 2 Jur.(N.S.) 1041; and Ord. 8, r.2.
[22] *Kangol Industries Ltd. v. Alfred Bray & Sons Ltd.* (1953) 70 R.P.C. 15.
[23] R.S.C., Ord. 8, r.4.
[24] R.S.C., Ord. 41, r.5(2).

statement of claim when delivered is not consistent with the affidavits upon which the injunction was granted.[25]

The defendant's affidavits should show that he seriously intends to resist the plaintiff's claim. He need not, however, give details of his defence and should not put in elaborate evidence on infringement and validity which cannot be assessed on motion.[26]

Delay will bar right

12.53   An interlocutory injunction will not be granted in cases where the plaintiff is guilty of delay after learning of the infringement.

In *North British Rubber Co. v. Gormully and Jeffery Co.*,[27] Chitty J. said:

"Now I am not aware, having regard to patents, that there is any substantial ground of distinction between an interlocutory injunction upon a patent right and upon any other. The principles appear to me to be substantially the same; and the general rule of the court is that a person who comes to ask for that remedy, which is granted with despatch and for the purposes of protecting rights until the trial, should come promptly."[28]

Whether or not such delay will deprive a plaintiff of an interlocutory injunction will be judged also by reference to any prejudice occasioned to the defendant.[29]

The amount of delay which will prevent the granting of an interlocutory injunction will, of course, vary with the nature of the patent and the circumstances of the trade.

The delay may, in some cases, be satisfactorily explained, as in a case where the plaintiffs' solicitors advised them not to commence an action until the defendants appeared to be in a condition of sufficient financial soundness to undertake manufacture of the infringing articles.[30]

Delay in proceeding against persons who are not parties to the application in question is no ground for refusing an injunction, if there has been no delay in proceeding against the defendant.[31]

---

[25] *Stocking v. Llewellyn* (1845–46) 3 L.T. 33.
[26] *T. J. Smith & Nephew Ltd. v. 3M United Kingdom* [1983] R.P.C. 92.
[27] (1894) 11 R.P.C. 17 at p.20.
[28] See also *Bovill v. Crate* (1865) L.R. 1 Eq. 388; *Aluminium Co. v. Domeiere* (1898) 15 R.P.C. 32; *Gillette Safety Razor Co. v. A. W. Gamage Ltd.* (1906) 23 R.P.C. 1; *Versil Ltd. v. Cork Insulation and Asbestos Co. Ltd.* [1966] R.P.C. 76.
[29] *Monsanto v. Stauffer (N.Z.)* [1984] F.S.R. 559 at 572; considering *Legg v. I.L.E.A.* [1972] 1 W.L.R. 1245.
[30] *United Telephone Co. v. Equitable Telephone Association* (1888) 5 R.P.C. 233.
[31] *Pneumatic Tyre Co. v. Warrilow* (1896) 13 R.P.C. 284.

Usual course on application

The plaintiff issues his writ and Notice of Motion and serves them **12.54** together with his evidence in chief. On the return date, if the parties have not come to terms, it is usual for the defendant to seek and obtain time for serving his evidence in answer. In such circumstances the court will normally give directions for the further conduct of the motion. If no undertaking is given, the plaintiff may move *ex parte* for relief. It is usual for the defendant to be heard upon such an application. On the hearing of the motion, the party seeking relief opens the case and reads his evidence in chief; thereafter the defendant reads his evidence, the plaintiff closes his case, the defendant opens and closes his case. The plaintiff has no right of reply but usually is heard in reply. If interlocutory relief is granted the plaintiff will be required to give an undertaking to pay any damages occasioned by an interlocutory injunction if it should appear subsequently that the defendant was in the right.[32] Where an undertaking is given to the court in lieu of an interlocutory injunction a cross-undertaking in damages will be inserted in the order unless the contrary is agreed and expressed at the time.[33] The discontinuance of the action will not prevent the cross-undertaking being enforced.[34] An undertaking in damages will normally be required from the Crown or anyone suing on the Crown's behalf.[35]

Form of Order

With any injunction or undertaking pending trial, it is desirable that **12.55** the defendant should know, with as much certainty as possible, what he may, or may not do. This is also in the plaintiff's interest as any breach is easier to identify and enforce. Accordingly the injunction should be directed towards restraining a specific act in relation to a particular product or process rather than infringing the plaintiff's patent generally.[36]

Costs

For a discussion of the factors to be taken into account when making **12.56** an order for costs of an abandoned motion for an interlocutory injunction see *Kickers International S.A. v. Paul Kettle Agencies.*[37] Where a

---

[32] See *Graham v. Campbell* (1877) 7 Ch.D. 490 (undertaking enforced).
[33] *Practice Note* [1904] W.N. 203, 208.
[34] *Newcomen v. Coulson* (1876) 7 Ch.D. 764; *Rothwell v. King* (1886) 3 R.P.C. 76.
[35] F. *Hoffmann-La Roche & Co. A.G. v. Secretary of State for Trade and Industry* [1975] A.C. 295, covering the practice in *Secretary of State for War v. Cope* (1919) 36 R.P.C. 273 (registered design).
[36] *The Staver Co. Inc. v. Digitext Display Ltd.* [1985] F.S.R. 512, and *Video Arts Ltd. v. Paget Industries Ltd.* [1986] F.S.R. 623.
[37] [1990] F.S.R. 436.

party causes the prolongation of interlocutory proceedings by argument of the merits of case in circumstances where this is unnecessary then a special order as to costs may be made, including the payment of costs in any event to be taxed and paid at once.[38]

Treating motion as trial of action

12.57 Where, as sometimes happens, during the proceedings for an interlocutory injunction, the parties come to terms, they can agree, subject to the consent of the court, to treat the hearing of the motion as the trial of the action and for an agreed form of judgment to be entered forthwith, the further expense of an action being thereby avoided.

Plaintiff entitled to order in court

12.58 Where the defendants offered to consent to judgment, the order to be made on a summons in Chambers, it was held that the plaintiffs were entitled to an order made in open court, and to the costs of the motion for judgment.[39]

Appeal from grant or refusal of interlocutory injunction

12.59 Leave to appeal to the Court of Appeal is required from a decision of the judge granting or refusing an interlocutory injunction.[40] In *Elan Digital Systems Ltd. v. Elan Computers Ltd.*[41] (a case decided before leave to appeal was required) the Master of the Rolls stated that:

> "I think it should be said, and said with great volume and clarity, that this court does not exist to provide a second bite at each interim cherry in the sense that it is open to parties, having failed in front of the learned judge, simply to start again and have a *de novo* hearing in the hope that they will succeed in front of the Court of Appeal. We are a court of appeal, and particularly in the field of interim injunctions it is primarily the trial judge who is appointed to decide whether or not an injunction should be granted. This is not of course to say that there is no right of appeal, but there is a heavy burden on the appellant to show that the learned judge has erred in principle, and that in exercising his discretion there is either an error of principle or—which is the same thing in a different form—he exercised his discretion in a way which no reasonable judge properly directing himself as to the relevant considerations could have exercised it."

---

[38] See, *e.g. Apple Corps. Ltd. v. Apple Computer Inc.* [1992] R.P.C. 70.

[39] *Smith and Jones Ltd. v. Service, Reeve & Co.* (1914) 31 R.P.C. 319.

[40] See S. 18(1) of the Supreme Court Act 1981 as amended by the Courts and Legal Services Act 1990, s.7 and Sched. 20 (with effect from October 1, 1993) and R.S.C., Ord. 59, r. 1B.

[41] [1984] F.S.R. 373 at 384; see also Browne-Wilkinson L.J. at 386.

In considering whether leave will be granted it is likely that this approach will apply.

Nature of pleadings

Pleadings generally are regulated by Order 18, rules 6 and 7 and **12.60** Order 104, rules 5 and 6 of the Rules of the Supreme Court, which requires all material facts to be pleaded and prohibits the pleading of evidence.

Statement of claim

The statement of claim may be served with the writ, or at any time **12.61** within 14 days after the defendant has given notice of intention to defend.[42] It should allege that the plaintiff is the registered proprietor of the letters patent sued on. It is not necessary to allege that the patent is valid, as "a patent is prima facie good as long as it stands",[43] nor is it necessary to set out facts material to the validity.[44] If the specification has been amended such facts should be pleaded together with an averment that the specification and claims as originally filed were framed in good faith and with reasonable skill and knowledge.[45]

If a certificate that validity was contested has been granted in a previous action so as to entitle the plaintiff to solicitor and client costs,[46] the certificate and the claim to such costs should be pleaded.[47]

A plaintiff is entitled to amend his statement of claim without leave once at any time before the pleadings are closed by serving the amended pleading upon the defendant or his solicitor.[48]

Particulars of infringements

In an action for infringement the plaintiff must serve "particulars of **12.62** infringements",[49] i.e. particulars of the times, places, occasions, and manner in which the plaintiff says the defendant has infringed his

---

[42] R.S.C., Ord. 18, r.1.

[43] *Halsey v. Brotherhood* (1880) 15 Ch.D. 514 at p.521; see also *Amory v. Brown* (1869) L.R. 8 Eq. 663 at p.664.

[44] See *Amory v. Brown* (1869) L.R. 8 Eq. 663; *Ward Bros. v. J. Hill & Son* (1901) 18 R.P.C. 481, *per* Wills J. at p.491, following *Young v. White* (1853) 23 L.J. Ch. 190, and *Harris v. Rothwell* (1887) 4 R.P.C. 225.

[45] See *Kane and Pattison v. Boyle* (1901) 18 R.P.C. 325 at p.337, P.A. 1949, s.62(2) and P.A. 1977, s.63(2).

[46] Under P.A. 1949, s.64 or P.A. 1977, s.65.

[47] *Pneumatic Tyre Co. Ltd. v. Chisholm* (1896) 13 R.P.C. 488.

[48] See R.S.C., Ord. 20, r.3 and Ord. 18.

[49] See Ord. 104, r.5. See also *Salopian Engineers Ltd. v. The Salop Trailer Co. Ltd.* (1954) 71 R.P.C. 223.

patent. The defendant must have full, fair, and distinct notice of the case to be made against him.[50]

Actionable infringement must be alleged

12.63   The particulars of infringements must allege an actionable infringement, *i.e.* an act committed subsequent to the date of publication of the complete specification or publication of the application,[51] or else the statement of claim may be struck out.[52] But a mere threat to infringe, if made after that date, is sufficient.[53] However, an allegation of infringement which is speculative, although disclosing a cause of action, may be struck out under the inherent jurisdiction of the court.[54]

Which claims infringed

12.64   The plaintiff will not be required to place a construction upon his patent in his particulars of infringements.[55] All he need do is to indicate which claims of his patent he relies upon and by what act he considers the defendant to have infringed, and if these two points be made clear without adducing specific instances, that will be sufficient.[56] There is no objection to a plaintiff stating that he relies on *all* the claims of his specification, and it is a matter of costs at the trial if this course has been taken unreasonably.[57]

Type of infringement should be specified

12.65   It is customary to state that the patent has been infringed and "in particular (*e.g.*) by the sale, on the____day of____, 19__, to one A B, of an aritcle constructed according to the invention described and claimed in claim No.__." This is for the purpose of identifying the type of act complained of; a plaintiff does not thereby limit his rights to damages to the specified example only.

Each type of infringement represents a separate course of action and a Plaintiff will not be allowed to amend to introduce a different type of infringement if such acts have become statute barred under the Limitation Act.[58]

---

[50] *Needham v. Oxley* (1863) 1 Hem. & M. 248; *Mandleberg v. Morley* (1893) 10 R.P.C. 256; *Batley v. Kynock* (No.2) (1874) L.R. 19 Eq. 229 at p.231.
[51] P.A. 1949, s.13(4); P.A. 1977, s.69.
[52] See *Schuster v. Hine, Parker & Co. Ltd.* (1935) 52 R.P.C. 345.
[53] *Bloom v. Shuylman* (1934) 51 R.P.C. 308.
[54] *Upjohn Co. v. Kerfoot & Co. Ltd.* [1988] 4 F.S.R. 1; considered in *Smith, Kline & French Laboratories Ltd. v. Evans Medical* [1989] F.S.R. 513 at 524.
[55] *Wenham Co. Ltd. v. Champion Gas Co. Ltd.* (1890) 7 R.P.C. 22.
[56] *Actiengesellschaft für Anilin Fabrikation v. Levinstein Ltd.* (1912) 29 R.P.C. 677; but *cf. Marsden v. Albrecht* (1910) 27 R.P.C. 785 (C.A.); *Actiengesellschaft für Autogene Aluminium Schweissung v. London Aluminium Co. Ltd.*(1919) 36 R.P.C. 199.
[57] *Haslam & Co. v. Hall* (1887) 4 R.P.C. 203 at p.206.
[58] *Sorata Ltd. v. Gardex Ltd.* [1984] R.P.C. 317.

Infringements after action brought

When an action is brought in respect of a particular type of **12.66** infringement, and to restrain the threatened infringement by continued manufacture of that type (the usual way in which an action is framed), the plaintiffs will be not allowed to give evidence of infringements of a different type, committed after action brought to justify the allegation of intention to infringe; the proper course is to apply to amend the particulars of infringements.[59]

Degrees of particularity required against vendor

Where an action is brought against a mere vendor of articles alleged to **12.67** have been made by a process which infringes the plaintiff's patent, a greater degree of precision is required in the particulars of infringements then if the defendant had been the manufacturer himself.

In *Mandleberg v. Morley*[60] Stirling J. said:

"Now if a manufacturer is attacked for infringing a patent by a particular process he does not want to be told in the shape of particulars, or otherwise, what the process is he is using. He knows what the process he is using is. But it is a very different thing with respect to a vendor. The vendor does not know with certainty what process is being used by the person from whom he himself buys, and who manufactures the article."

In that case the particulars of infringements alleged that:

"The plaintiffs complain that each of the said letters patent of the plaintiffs have been infringed by the sale and exposure for sale by the defendants of each of the said garments known as 'The Champion,' and 'The Distingué,' and by the sale and exposure for sale of other waterproof garments made by the manufacturers of 'The Champion', 'The Distingué,' and 'The Tropical Odourless,' but not bearing their distinguishing names, but which unnamed garments are manufactured by similar processes to the three named garments."

It was held that the reference to unnamed garments was not sufficiently specific, as it was not clear that the unnamed garments referred to were substantially the same as those which were specifically mentioned.

---

[59] *Shoe Machinery Co. Ltd. v. Cutlan* (1895) 12 R.P.C. 342 at p.358; *Welsbach Incandescent Gas Light Co. Ltd. v. Dowle* (1899) 16 R.P.C. 391.
[60] (1893) 10 R.P.C. 256 at p.260.

Further and better particulars

12.68   If the particulars served are too general, the defendant should apply
for further and better particulars under Order 104, rule 8; but "It lies on
the party who alleges that for the honest purpose of his litigation he
wants further information, to satisfy the court that he is really placed in
a difficulty by the particulars as they stand."[61] Further particulars of
infringements have sometimes been postponed until after discovery on
the ground that the defendant knew the breaches which he had
committed better than the plaintiff.[62] When a party consents to an order
for the giving of particulars that party waives the right to object to any of
the particulars sought and must comply so far as is possible with the
request.[63]

An order for further and better particulars of infringements before
defence was refused on the ground that they were unnecessary[64] where
the Plaintiff had given the best particulars that they could and the
relevant facts were in the knowledge of the Defendant.[65]

Evidence admitted if within particulars

12.69   Under Order 104, rule 16, evidence of matters not particularised is not
admissible except with leave of the court.

If at the trial evidence is tendered which comes within the literal
meaning of the particulars it wil be admitted, notwithstanding that the
particulars are too general, as the defendant should have objected to the
particulars, and not have waited until the trial to make his objection.

In *Sykes v. Howarth*[66] the plaintiff having delivered particulars of
infringements specifying certain sales by the defendant of rollers, and in
particular to Shaw and Smith, the defendant, in answer to interrogatories, admitted sales to Hirst. Fry J., in giving judgment, said:

"In this case I think I must admit the evidence tendered in respect of
Hirst's case. It is said that in respect of those cases which are not
mentioned by name in the particulars of breaches, the plaintiff cannot
give evidence. It may be that the particulars were not sufficient, or
tendered to embarrass. But the defendant did not apply for amended
particulars, according to the case of *Hull v. Bollard*.[67] It appears to me I
have to inquire what is the meaning of the particulars. I find the case
of Hirst is within the literal meaning of the particulars. If I had found
that the case of Hirst was likely to create surprise, or likley to
introduce any point not raised by Smith's or Shaw's case, I should

---

[61] *Per* Wills J. in *Haslam & Co. v. Hall* (1887) 4 R.P.C. 203 at 207; and see R.S.C., Ord. 18, r.12.
[62] *Russell v. Hatfield* (1885) Griff.P.C. 204; 2 R.P.C. 144. See also *Mullard Radio Valve Co. Ltd.
v. Tungsram Electric Lamp Works (Great Britain) Ltd.* (1932) 49 R.P.C. 299.
[63] *Fearis v. Davies and others* [1989] F.S.R. 555.
[64] R.S.C., Ord. 18, r.12(5).
[65] *Intel Corp. v. General Instrument Corp.* [1989] F.S.R. 640.
[66] (1879) 12 Ch.D. 826 at p.830.
[67] (1879) 25 L.J.Ex. 304 at p.306.

probably have given an opportunity to the defendant to bring fresh evidence. I have asked whether there is any witness not here whom the defendants would desire to bring in respect of Hirst's case, and have received no satisfactory answer on that point, and must assume that there is no such witness."

Conversely, where the particulars of infringements complained of infringement by user only, the court refused to enter into the question as to whether there had been infringement by manufacturing the articles complained of.[68]

Particulars of infringements may also be ordered in actions which, though not strictly actions for infringement, involve the question of infringement as an issue; this is done under the ordinary jurisdication of the court.[69]

Striking out the statement of claim

In *Anchor Building Products Ltd. v. Redland Roof Tiles Ltd.*[70] the Court of Appeal upheld the striking out by Whitford J. of a counterclaim alleging infringement of a patent on the ground that the patentee had been unable to put before the court any evidence of an arguable case of infringement. But in *Strix Ltd. v. Otter Controls Ltd.*[71] the Court of Appeal distinguished *Anchor v. Redland* and pointed out that it was not and never had been permissible, on a strike out application where the issues in an action included issues of fact, to conduct a mini-trial on affidavits. Accordingly the courts will only strike out claims for patent infringement in exceptional cases such as *Anchor v. Redland* which involved a very simple device.[72]   **12.70**

Defence

If a party alleges invalidity of the patent then the defence must be served within 42 days from the service of the statement of claim.[73] If validity is not put in issue, the defence must be served within 14 days from the time limited for acknowledgement of service, or from the service of the statement of claim (whichever is the later).[74]   **12.71**

The following defences are available in an action for infringement:

(1) Denial that the plaintiff is the registered grantee or proprietor, or an exclusive licensee, as the case may be.

---

[68] *Henser and Guignard v. Hardie* (1894) 11 R.P.C. 421 at p.427.
[69] R.S.C., Ord. 18, r.12; see, *e.g. Wren v. Weild* (1869) L.R. 4 Q.B. 213.
[70] [1990] R.P.C. 283.
[71] [1991] F.S.R. 354.
[72] *Per* Oliver L.J. [1991] F.S.R. 354 at 360.
[73] R.S.C., Ord. 104, r.6(C.A.).
[74] R.S.C., Ord. 18, r.2.

(2) Leave or licence of the patentee.

(3) Denial of infringement or, as a defence to a claim for an injunction, of any threat or intent to infringe.

(4) Allegation that all claims alleged to be infringed are invalid.

(5) Allegation of existence of contract offending against section 44 of the 1977 Act.

(6) As defence to claim for damages, allegation of innocent infringement or other special circumstances specified in sections 62 and 68 of the 1977 Act.

(7) Rights to continue prior use under section 64 of the 1977 Act.

(8) Laches, acquiescence or estoppel.

(9) Statute bar under Limitation Act.

(10) Right to repair or exhaustion of rights.[75]

(11) That the defendant is a person entitled to the grant of the patent.[76]

(12) That the relief sought by the plaintiff is contrary to European law.

Counterclaim for revocation

12.72   A defendant may counterclaim for revocation of the patent; where he does so, the plaintiff should serve a defence to such counterclaim. If the plaintiff discontinues the action the defendant may still proceed upon his counterclaim,[77] and if no defence thereto has been served may move for judgment in default of service of defence.[78]

Dealing with the above pleas in defence:

Title to sue

12.73   If, and so long as the plaintiff is registered as the proprietor of, or as an exclusive licensee under, the patent, it is submitted that his title to sue is thereby established for the purposes of an action for infringement.[79] If the defendant wishes to dispute the plaintiff's title to an existing patent, he must move the court for an order that the register may be rectified under section 34 of the 1977 Act. Under the 1977 Act limited rights are given to start an action for a declaration under section 72. Title to sue must be established as of the date of the writ.[80]

Leave or licence

12.74   Where a defendant pleads leave or licence of the patentee he should particularise the circumstances, stating, if the licence be alleged to have

---

[75] See *Dellareed Ltd. v. Delkim Developments* [1988] F.S.R. 329.

[76] See *Dolphin Showers Ltd. v. Farmiloe* [1989] F.S.R. 1.

[77] R.S.C., Ord. 15, r.2.

[78] E.g. *Coventry Radiator Co. Ltd. v. Coventry Motor Fittings Co. Ltd.* (1917) 34 R.P.C. 239.

[79] P.A. 1949, ss.73, 74, 101(1); P.A. 1977, s.32, *Martin and another v. Scrib Ltd.* (1950) 67 R.P.C. 127.

[80] *Proctor & Gamble Co. v. Peaudouce (U.K.) Ltd.* [1989] F.S.R. 180.

been verbal, the time and place at which it was given and by whom, or if alleged to be in writing, identifying the document by date and otherwise. The onus of proof is upon the defendant,[81] and subject to the overriding provisions of EC law a defendant relying on the existence of a licence cannot attack the validity of the patent.[82]

Denial of infringement

12.75 A mere denial of infringement, which need not be further particularised, puts the plaintiff to the proof:

(a) that the defendant has committed the acts complained of in the particulars of breaches;
(b) that such acts are in infringement of the patent, and in proving infringement with regard to goods purchased by the defendant it is incumbent upon the patentee to give evidence that such goods were not produced by himself or his agents.[83]

Where a defendant admitted importing the substance alleged to infringe, but denied knowledge of the process by which it was made and denied infringement, particulars of the method by which the substance was made were not ordered.[84]

Admission of certain infringements only

12.76 Where a statement of defence admitted infringement in 10 instances and no more, and the plaintiffs elected to move for judgment upon such admissions under Order 27, rule 3, it was held that they were entitled to an inquiry as to damages as to those 10 instances only, and that all evidence as to any other instances of infringement alleged to have been committed by the defendant must be excluded.[85-86]

Contract with void conditions

12.77 By section 44 of the 1977 Act, if there has been inserted into any contract, in force at the time of the infringement and made by or with the consent of the plaintiff, certain conditions specified in one section, this constitutes a defence to the action.

The nature of the conditions made void by the section is dealt with in Chapter 8 see §§8.65 *et seq.*

Order 104, rule 5(3) of the Rules of the Supreme Court, provides that a

---

[81] *British Thomson-Houston Co. Ltd. v. British Insulated and Helsby Cables Ltd.* (1924) 41 R.P.C. 345 at p.375; see also *Whitehead and Poole v. Farmer & Sons Ltd.* (1918) 35 R.P.C. 241.
[82] See Chap. 8.
[83] *Betts v. Willmott* (1871) L.R. 6 Ch.App. 239.
[84] *Parke, Davis & Co. v. Allen and Hanburys Ltd.* (1953) 70 R.P.C. 123.
[85-86] *United Telephone Co. v. Donohoe* (1886) 31 Ch.D. 399; (1886) 3 R.P.C. 45.

defendant relying on this defence must serve with his defence full particulars of the contract and the particular conditions thereon on which he relies, but provided that there appears to be some substance in the allegation and it is not put forward for the purpose of getting a 'fishing'' discovery, an application for further particulars may be ordered to stand over till after discovery.[87]

Ignorance of patent, defence as to damages

12.78   Section 62 of the 1977 Act provides that a patentee shall not be entitled to recover damages from a defendant who proves that he was not aware of the patent, and had no reasonable grounds for supposing it existed.[88]

Failure to pay renewal fee

12.79   Section 59(2) of the 1949 Act and section 62(2) of the 1977 Act provides that the court may refuse to award damages in respect of any infringement committed during any period in respect of which a renewal fee remained unpaid.

Amendment of specification

12.80   Subsections (3) of section 59 of the 1949 Act and section 62 of the 1977 Act provide that where the specification has been amended no damages shall be awarded before the date of amendment unless the court is satisfied that the specification as originally published was framed in good faith and with reasonable skill and knowledge. The restriction in either provision does not apply if the plaintiff opts to take an account of profits.[89]

Right to continue prior use

12.81   By section 64 of the 1977 Act a person who in the United Kingdom before the priority date of the invention does in good faith an act which would constitute an infringement of the patent if it were in force or makes in good faith effective and serious preparations to do such an act has the right to continue to do that act.

The effect of this section is dealt with in Chapter 6.

Such a defence is always specifically pleaded.[90]

---

[87] See, *e.g. Sarason v. Frenay* (1914) 31 R.P.C. 252; see also *Gerrard Industries Ltd. v. Box Wiring Co. Ltd.* (1933) 50 R.P.C. 125; *Soapless Foam Ltd. v. The Physical Treatments Institute Ltd.* (1935) 52 R.P.C. 256.
[88] See *post*, §14.05.
[89] *Codex Corp. v. Racal-Milgo Ltd.* [1983] R.P.C. 369.
[90] See, *e.g. Helitune v. Steward Hughes* [1991] F.S.R. 171 at 205.

Laches, Acquiescence or Estoppel

All facts relied upon as supporting these defences must be pleaded. **12.82**
For the principles to be considered see Oliver L.J. in *Habib Bank Ltd. v.
Habib Bank A.G. Zurich.*[91]

Estoppel

(i) by conduct

It is not every defendant who is entitled to attack the validity of a **12.83**
patent. The position in this respect of an assignor of, or a licensee under,
a patent is dealt with in Chapter 9.[92]

(ii) by record

Where judgment has been given in an action, and the record shows **12.84**
that some question has been put in issue and decided,[93] whether such
judgment be by consent or otherwise,[94] either party to the litigation is
thenceforth estopped in subsequent proceedings between the same
parties from alleging and proving facts inconsistent with the correctness
of such decision.

Thus, where judgment is given for a plaintiff in an action for
infringement, the patent being held to be valid and to have been
infringed, the defendant if sued again by the patentee will be estopped
from denying that the acts previously complained of were an infringement or that the patent is valid,[95] even though he seek to attack its
validity upon entirely new grounds.[96] Conversely, if the patent were
held to be invalid the patentee could not, unless the ground of invalidity
had been removed by amendment,[97] bring a fresh infringement action
against the same defendant.[98]

Estoppel personal only

Estoppel is personal, and exists only against those whose conduct **12.85**
gave rise to it, and persons claiming through them, or, in the case of
estoppel by record, only in proceedings between the same parties. Thus,
it does not run against the partner of a person estopped[99] nor against a

---

[91] [1982] R.P.C. 1 at p.36.
[92] See *ante*, §§9.20 *et seq.*
[93] See *Goucher v. Clayton* (1865) 11 Jur.(N.S.) 107; 34 L.J.Ch. 239; see also *Murex Welding Processes Ltd. v. Weldrics (1922) Ltd.,* (1933) 50 R.P.C. 178 at p.182.
[94] *Thomson v. Moore* (1889) 6 R.P.C. 426; (1890) 7 R.P.C. 325; *Brown v. Hastie & Co. Ltd.* (1906) 23 R.P.C. 361.
[95] *Thomson v. Moore* (1889) 6 R.P.C. 426; (1890) 7 R.P.C. 325.
[96] *Shoe Machinery Co. v. Cutlan (No.2)* [1896] 1 Ch. 667; (1896) 13 R.P.C. 141.
[97] See *Deeley's Patent* (1894) 11 R.P.C. 72.
[98] *Horrocks v. Stubbs* (1895) 12 R.P.C. 540.
[99] *Heugh v. Chamberlain* (1865) 25 W.R. 742; *Goucher v. Clayton* (1865) 11 Jur.(N.S.) 107; 34 L.J.Ch. 239.

person who was not actually a party to the previous action[1] even though he may have supported one of such parties by financing his defence under a contract of indemnity.[2] Where a question of infringement was submitted to an arbitrator, who found that the letters patent were not illegal or void, it was held in a subsequent action for infringement between the parties that such award did not estop the defendant from several pleas in which he alleged facts inconsistent with validity of the patent, it only being possible to gather by inference that the arbitrator must have considered such allegations in making his award.[3]

The discontinuance of an action by a plaintiff does not create any estoppel against him by record, and unless there be a term of the order allowing discontinuance that no fresh action shall be brought on the same patent against the defendant, the plaintiff is entitled to commence a fresh action in respect of the same infringement.[4]

Effect of decision between different parties

12.86   Where there has been a previous decision upon the validity of a patent by a court of co-ordinate or superior jurisdiction, which by reason of having been given in proceedings between different parties does not operate as an estoppel, strong additional evidence will be required in order to reverse the previous finding, and the court will usually hold itself bound by previous decisions on the question of the construction of the specification.[5]

Where a party produces evidence at the trial of an action to prove a certain fact and at the trial of a subsequent action against a different party produces other witnesses whose evidence is inconsistent with such fact, although the original evidence does not create any estoppel and is not admissible as evidence in the subsequent action,[6] the court will scrutinise the new evidence with great care, the more especially if the witnesses called in the first action do not give evidence in the second action to explain that the previous evidence was the result of some mistake.[7]

---

[1] *Ibid.*; Otto *v. Steel* (1885) 2 R.P.C. 109.
[2] *Gammons v. Singer Manufacturing Co.* (1904) 21 R.P.C. 452 at p.459 (C.A.).
[3] *Newall v. Elliot* (1863) 1 H. & C. 797; 32 L.J.Ex. 120.
[4] See, *e.g.* *Haskell Golf Ball Co. Ltd. v. Hutchinson* (1904) 21 R.P.C. 205; *Murex Welding Processes Ltd. v. Weldrics* (1922) *Ltd.* (1933) 50 R.P.C. 178 at p.183.
[5] *Otto v. Steel* (1886) 3 R.P.C. 109 at p.114; *Automatic Weighing Machine Co. v. Combined Weighing Machine Co.* (1889) 6 R.P.C. 367; *Edison v. Holland,* (1886) 3 R.P.C. 243; *Flour Oxidising Co. Ltd. v. Carr & Co. Ltd.* (1908) 25 R.P.C. 428 at p.448; *Higginson and Arundel v. Pyman* (1926) 43 R.P.C. 291 at p.300.
[6] *British Thomson-Houston Co. Ltd. v. British Insulated and Helsby Cables Ltd.* (1924) 41 R.P.C. 345 at pp.353–357, 376–390.
[7] *Ibid.* (1924) 41 R.P.C. 345 at p.408; (1925) 42 R.P.C. 180 at pp.199, 200.

Limitation Act

Reliance upon the Limitation Act 1980 as a defence in respect of any   **12.87**
acts committed more than six years prior to the issue of the writ must be
expressly pleaded.[8]

Right to repair

A defence based on a right to repair patented articles ought to be   **12.88**
specifically pleaded.

Defendant entitled to grant of patent

Such a defence should be specifically pleaded.[9]   **12.89**

Relief contrary to European Community law

In principle, EC law, based on Articles 30, 85 and 86 of the Treaty of   **12.90**
Rome, provides defences which can be used in patent infringement
actions. For example, in *Parke Davis v. Probel*[10] the European Court held,
in the context of a Dutch action, that Article 86 could restrict the right of
a proprietor of a patent to restrain infringements if that action
degenerated into an abuse of the proprietor's dominant position
(assuming the proprietor was in such a position).

Apart from those cases concerned with the doctrine of Exhaustion of
Rights (see *ante*, §8.57) in practice, at the time of writing, no such
"Eurodefence" has been ultimately successful in a patent action[11]
although they have been used in related cases to establish an arguable
defence for the purposes of avoiding summary judgment.[12]

"Gillette" defence

In *Gillette Safety Razor Co. v. Anglo-American Trading Co.*[13] Lord   **12.91**
Moulton used words that have sometimes been interpreted as suggesting a further defence, *viz.* that the alleged infringement was not
novel at the relevant date. These words have now been explained in *Page
v. Brent Toy Products*.[14] It is submitted, that particulars of objections
drafted in this manner would not comply with the requirements of
Order 104, rule 6,[15] and that, therefore, this plea can no longer be

---

[8] R.S.C., Ord. 18, r.8.
[9] See *Dolphin Showers v. Farmiloe* [1989] F.S.R. 1.
[10] Case 24/67 [1968] E.C.R. 55, [1958] C.M.L.R. 47.
[11] See *Quantel v. Electron Graphics* [1990] R.P.C. 272. See also case 238/87, *Volvo v. Erik Veng*
[1988] E.C.R. 6211, [1989] 4 C.M.L.R. 122; *Ransburg Gema v. Electrostatic Plant Systems*
[1989] 2 C.M.L.R. 712; *Pitney Bowes v. Francotype-postalia* [1991] F.S.R. 72.
[12] *E.g. Dymond v. Britton* [1976] 1 C.M.L.R. 133 (a contract case).
[13] (1913) 30 R.P.C. 465 at p.480.
[14] (1950) 67 R.P.C. 4 at p.33. See *ante*, §344.
[15] See *Hardaker v. Boucher & Co. Ltd.* (1934) 51 R.P.C. 278. See also *V. D. Ltd. v. Boston Deep
Sea Fishing Co. Ltd.* (1935) 52 R.P.C. 1.

regarded as sufficient, notwithstanding that it remains a useful test by which to judge the chances of success in the action and a basis for argument on behalf of the defendant. Where, however, a defendant had assigned the patent to the plaintiff (and was, therefore, estopped from denying its validity) and, when sued for infringement by the assignee, contended that on the true construction of the claims he had not infringed, but that if the claims were read more widely they would be invalid for anticipation, the court refused to strike out this plea, although it appeared to be unnecessary.[16]

Default of defence

12.92   Where the defendant makes default in serving a defence, the plaintiff may, under Order 19, rule 7 of the Rules of the Supreme Court, set down the action on motion for judgment in default of defence, or where one of several defendants makes such default and the cause of action is severable, the plaintiff may proceed in the same way with regard to such individual.[17]

Amendment of defence

12.93   The defence may be amended without leave once before the pleadings are closed but thereafter leave to amend is required.[18]

Particulars of Objections

12.94   If the defendant disputes validity he must deliver with his defence, and if he counterclaims for revocation he must deliver with his counterclaim adequate particulars of all the objections to validity on which he relies.[19] The requirements of particulars of objections differ materially from those of particulars of infringement, since in the case of the latter the specification tells the defendant what the patentee claims and the defendant well knows what he himself is doing.[20] Particulars of objections must give to the plaintiff such information as will inform him as to the case he has to meet, and enable him to prepare for trial by investigation or research without danger of surprise.

Particulars of a similar nature have been ordered under Order 18, rule 12, in actions, other than those for infringement, where the validity of a patent comes in issue.[21-22]

---

[16] *Hocking v. Hocking* (1886) 3 R.P.C. 291.
[17] R.S.C., Ord. 19, r.7.
[18] R.S.C., Ord. 20, rr.3, 5.
[19] R.S.C., Ord. 104, rr.6, 8, 9.
[20] See *Cheetham v. Oldham and Fogg* (1888) 5 R.P.C. 624 at p.626.
[21-22] See, *e.g. Hazlehurst v. Rylands* (1892) 9 R.P.C. 1. *Cf. Suhr v. Crofts (Engineers) Ltd.* (1932) 49 R.P.C. 359.

Grounds of invalidity under the 1949 and 1977 Acts

The grounds of invalidity which may be relied on as a defence to an **12.95** action for infringement, and also in a counterclaim for revocation, are set out in detail in section 32(1) of the 1949 Act and section 77 of the 1977 Act. Each ground relied upon must be separately specified. The grounds are as follows:

Prior grant (1949 Act)

"That the invention, so far as claimed in any claim of the complete **12.96** *specification, was claimed in a valid claim of earlier priority date contained in the complete specification of another patent granted in the United Kingdom."*

This objection is distinct from that of want of novelty, and must be pleaded separately.[23] The particulars should state the number of the prior patent, the name of the grantee thereof, and identify the relevant claim or claims. A patentee, who does not admit the validity of an alleged prior grant, will be ordered to give particulars of his objections to its validity.[24-25]

Applicant not entitled to apply (1949 Act)

"That the patent was granted on the application of a person not entitled **12.97** *under the provisions of this Act to apply therefor."*

The wording of this ground of objection has been enlarged in order to conform to the provisions of the Act whereby the patent may be applied for by the true and first inventor or by an assignee of the right to make the application. It is submitted, that just as under the previous practice it was necessary to give particulars as to whom the defendant alleged to be the true and first inventor, so now particulars should be given sufficient to identify the person alleged to have had the right to apply,[26] but that where fraud is not alleged, no further particulars need be given.[27-28]

An allegation of fraudulent conduct is not essential under this ground of invalidity, as the basis of the allegation is the deceit of the Crown by the claim made (on applciation for the patent) that the applicant was entitled to apply. Fraud, however, is usually involved, and where this is so, the particulars required are further governed by Order 18, rule 12 of the Rules of the Supreme Court.

Patent obtained in fraud (1949 Act)

"That the patent was obtained in contravention of the rights of the petitioner **12.98** *or any person under or through whom he claims."*

---

[23] See *Blackett v. Dickson and Mann Ltd.* (1909) 26 R.P.C. 73 at p.82 (O.H.).
[24-25] *Electric & Musical Industries Ltd. v. Radio & Allied Industries Ltd.* [1960] R.P.C. 115.
[26] See *Stroud v. Humber Ltd.* (1907) 24 R.P.C. 141 at p.151; *Smith's Patent* (1912) 29 R.P.C. 339.
[27-28] See *Sylow-Hansen v. June Hair etc. Ltd.* (1948) 65 R.P.C. 421.

In this case, also, if there is an allegation of fraudulent conduct, the particulars necessary are governed by Order 18, rule 12 of the Rules of the Supreme Court.[29]

If a patent is revoked on this ground, the Comptroller may direct that an application for a patent for the same invention by the rightful applicant shall be deemed to have the priority date of the revoked patent.[30]

Leave was given to amend the particulars of objections to raise new material where it was alleged to have been inserted into a complete specification before acceptance and this new matter originated from the defendants.[31-32]

Not within definition of invention (1949 Act)

12.99   *"That the subject of any claim of the complete specification is not an invention within the meaning of this Act."*

The issue which is intended to be raised by this plea is that the invention is not a "manner of ... manufacture the subject of letters patent and grant of privilege within section six of the Statute of Monopolies" or a "method or process of testing applicable to the improvement or control of manufacture".[33] Such objection need not be further particularised.[34] The definition of "invention" contains the word "new" and also "includes an alleged invention", but, it is submitted, that these latter considerations are not adequately raised by this plea.[35-38] Thus whether the invention is "new" must be dealt with under the following paragraph.

Not capable of industrial application (1977 Act)

12.100   This issue is in practice similar to the issue under the 1949 Act as to whether the claim related to an invention. It is submitted, that it is sufficient to allege the fact and no particulars are necessary.

The grant is excluded by section 1(2) or 1(3) of the 1977 Act

12.101   These sections exclude from patenting certain inventions including such matters as literary and artistic works and those relating to immoral purposes. The objection must be specifically pleaded and it must be

---

[29] See *Colthurst and Hyde Ltd. v. Stewart Engineering Co. Ltd.* (1950) 67 R.P.C. 87.
[30] P.A. 1949, s.53.
[31-32] *Sandoz Ltd. v. Roussel Laboratories Ltd.* [1966] R.P.C. 308.

[33] P.A. 1949, s.101(1).
[34] *Hardaker v. Boucher & Co. Ltd.* (1934) 51 R.P.C. 278.
[35-38] See *General Electric Co. Ltd. v. Thorn Electrical Industries Ltd.* (1947) 64 R.P.C. 22.

made clear as to why the patent in suit falls within the subsections of the Act.

Novelty (1949 and 1977 Acts)

1949 Act—*"That the invention, so far as claimed in any claim of the com-* 12.102 *plete specification, is not new having regard to what was known or used, before the priority date of the claim, in the United Kingdom."*

1977 Act—*That the invention is not new.*

Order 104, rule 6 requires detailed particulars to be given under this plea, stating the time and place of the previous publication or user alleged, and, in the case of the prior user, a sufficient identification of it, the names of those alleged to have made such prior user,[39] whether the same has continued down to the date of the patent, and, if not, the earliest and latest dates at which such prior user is alleged to have taken place.[40] In the case of machinery or apparatus the particulars must further state whether it is in existence and where it can be inspected. If it is in existence, unless the party relying on it offers, or uses his best endeavours to obtain, inspection of it, evidence relating to it cannot be given; nor can evidence be given which is at variance with any statement contained in the particulars.

Documentary publication

Prior documents must be pleaded specifically, together with the time 12.103 and place of their publication, the usual course with regard to patent specifications being to allege their publication by deposit upon or about some date upon the shelves of the National Library of Science and Invention, and with regard to books or newpapers to give similar details, so as to enable the plaintiff to find and identify them, and further to specify the pages or chapters relied upon.

Whether or not a defendant will be required to give particulars of the exact passages of the prior documents relied upon, or to point out specifically what part or parts of the plaintiff's specification he alleges to be affected thereby, will depend upon the circumstances of the case and the nature of the documents.[41] Where it appeared that the defendant had, figuratively speaking, "thrown at the head" of the plaintiff a large number of complicated specifications without any attempt at discrimination, further particulars were required.[42] If, however, the defendant bona fide relies upon the whole of one or more documents, and the

---

[39] See *Leggatt v. Hood* (1949) 66 R.P.C. 293.

[40] See *British Thomson-Houston Co. Ltd. v. Crompton Parkinson Ltd.* (1935) 52 R.P.C. 409.

[41] *Heathfield v. Greenway* (1893) 10 R.P.C. 17; *Marchant and Another v. J. A. Prestwich & Co. Ltd.* (1949) 66 R.P.C. 117.

[42] *Holliday v. Heppenstall Bros.* (1889) 6 R.P.C. 320; *Sidebottom v. Fielden* (1891) 8 R.P.C. 266 at p.270; *Heathfield v. Greenway* (1893) 10 R.P.C. 17.

subject-matter is simple, his particulars of objections will not be interfered with.[43]

Publication by prior user

12.104   In the case of prior user the requirements as to particulars are particularly stringent with respect to user of machinery and apparatus, as the defendant is required to do his best to procure inspection thereof for the plaintiff. But this does not necessarily apply to an alleged prior user of a process. In *Minerals Separation Ltd. v. Ore Concentration (1905) Ltd.*,[44] where the patent was a patent solely for a process, it was held, that the fact that machinery or apparatus may have been necessary in the carrying out of the alleged prior user did not entitle the plaintiff to particulars as to such apparatus or machinery, or to inspection thereof, and an order for the production of or information as to the existence of samples of the materials used in or resulting from the process was refused. Cozens-Hardy M.R. said:[45]

"It seems to me that we cannot impose upon the defendant in a patent action any greater liability than is justified by that rule (now rule 21) and it does not seem to me to be relevant to urge that something beyond and outside that rule will enable the plaintiffs better to prepare for trial and will minimise expense ... If the patent is one for machinery or apparatus, great detail is required by the rule ... drawings have to be furnished and experiments have to be permitted, always qualifying that statement by the fact that it must be within the power of defendants to furnish the drawings and allow the experiment. But when the patent is for a process, and merely for a process, no such detailed particulars are required. All that the rule exacts is a description sufficient to identify such alleged prior user ... The patent relates to a process, and there is nothing either in the body of the specification or in the claim at the end which justifies us in exacting from the defendants any further particulars as to the nature of the apparatus used in working the particular process; nor do I think it is within our jurisdiction to require the defendants to say whether they have any samples of the ores so treated, or to require them to say whether they will allow the plaintiffs to have inspection of such samples and to make test therefrom."

12.105   Where the apparatus alleged to constitue a prior user is in existence, the defendant is not required to supply any description further than is required merely to identify the prior user so as to enable the plaintiff, if

[43] *Siemens v. Karo, Barnett & Co.* (1891) 8 R.P.C. 376; *Nettlefolds Ltd. v. Reynolds* (1892) 9 R.P.C. 410; *Edison-Bell Consolidated Phonograph Co. v. Columbia Phonograph Co.* (1901) 18 R.P.C. 4.
[44] [1909] 1 Ch. 744; (1909) 26 R.P.C. 413.
[45] (1909) 26 R.P.C. at p.421.

inspection be obtainable, to inspect it, but where the apparatus is no longer in existence, the drawings or description must be sufficient to show what is going to be alleged at the trial to have been the nature of the article the user of which is relied on as a prior user,[46] and, it is submitted, that the same principle would apply as regards a process, that is to say, that, inspection not being required by the rule in such a case, the description of the prior user should identify it in the sense not only of when and where it took place, but also of, so far as it be relevant, what precisely it was that took place at the time and place alleged.[47]

The same reasoning applies where the patent is for a particular prescription of ingredients; in such circumstances particulars will only be ordered of the ingredients used in the alleged prior user.[48]

In *Avery v. Ashworth, Son & Co.*[49] the defendants in their particulars of **12.106** objections stated that they would rely "either by way of anticipation or as showing the scope of the claims ... upon matters known to the plaintiffs, in consequence of which the plaintiffs" at an earlier date had applied to amend their specification by disclaimer. The defendants were directed to deliver full particulars of the "matters" alleged. The further particulars delivered consisted of a statement that the defendants would rely upon all the matters contained in the particulars of objections which had been delivered in an action by the plaintiffs against other defendants upon another patent several years before. This, and the original paragraph, were ordered to be struck out.

Where the defendants pleaded a public use and sale of articles manufactured by certain specified machines, particulars were ordered of the names and addresses of persons to whom the articles were alleged to have been sold, and of the dates of such sales.[50]

Secret use irrelevant

Secret prior user cannot be relied on in support of this plea.[51-53] **12.107**

Oral disclosure

Under the 1977 Act, oral disclosure is relevant. Similar particulars will **12.108** be required as to disclosure by documents including the names of the parties, the place, time, circumstances and what was said.

---

[46] *Crosthwaite Fire Bar Syndicate Ltd. v. Senior* (1909) 26 R.P.C. 260 at p.263.
[47] See, *e.g. Minerals Separation Ltd. v. Ore Concentration Co. (1905) Ltd.* [1909] 1 Ch. 744; (1909) 26 R.P.C. 413 at p.423.
[48] *Stahlwerk Becker A.G.'s Patent* (1917) 34 R.P.C. 332.
[49] (1916) 33 R.P.C. 463, 560; (1916) 33 R.P.C. 235.
[50] See *British United Shoe Machinery Co. Ltd. v. Albert Pemberton & Co.* (1930) 47 R.P.C. 134 at p.141.
[51-53] P.A. 1949, s.32(2).

Obviousness (1949 and 1977 Acts)

12.109   1949—*"That the invention, so far as claimed in any claim of the complete specification, is obvious and does not involve any inventive step having regard to what was known or used, before the priority date of the claim, in the United Kingdom."*

1977—*The invention involves no inventive step.*

This ground of objection has been commonly, but most inappropriately, called "want of subject-matter". It must be specifically pleaded[54] and the same rules concerning particulars of prior publication and user that apply to novelty (above) apply to obviousness.[55-56]

Prior knowledge

12.110   The prior knowledge under the 1949 Act that can be relied upon in order to attack validity (sometimes called "public knowledge") may be of two kinds, *viz.*

(1) that contained in some particular document or documents or used by some particular individual or group, and

(2) common general knowledge.

In the case of the former, particulars of the publication of the document, or of the user, as the case may be, must be given, but provided that a document is proved to have been published, it is irrelevant that no person is proved to have seen or read it, or to have any knowledge of its contents. Similar considerations apply to a prior user, provided it is not secret. In that case it cannot be relied on in support of this plea.[57] "Common general knowledge", or, as it is sometimes termed, "common knowledge" or "public general knowledge", means "the information which, at the date of the patent in question, is common knowlege in the art or science to which the alleged invention relates, so as to be known to duly qualified persons engaged in that art or science";[58] in other words, it is part of the mental equipment necessary for competency in that art or science concerned. Under sections 1, 2 and 3 of the 1977 Act the "state of the art" may be relied upon. Full particulars must be given of where, when, to whom, and *in* what circumstances information was made available to the public.

---

[54] *Holliday v. Heppenstall Bros.* (1889) 6 R.P.C. 320 at p.327; 41 Ch.D. 109; *Phillips v. Ivel Cycle Co. Ltd.* (1890) 7 R.P.C. 77 at p.82.
[55-56] R.S.C., Ord. 104, r.6(3).
[57] P.A. 1949, s.32(2).
[58] *British Thomson-Houston Co. Ltd. v. Stonebridge Electrical Co. Ltd.* (1916) 33 R.P.C. 166 at p.171.

Common general knowledge

Proof of common knowledge is given by witnesses competent to **12.111** speak upon the matter, who, to supplement their own recollections, may refer to standard works upon the subject which were published at the time and which were known to them.[59] The publication at or before the relevant date of other documents such as patent specifications may be to some extent prima facie evidence tending to show that the statements contained in them were part of the common knowledge, but is far from complete proof, as the statements may well have been discredited or forgotten or merely ignored,[60] evidence may, however, be given to prove that such statements did become part of the common knowledge.[61]

In *British Celanese Ltd. v. Courtaulds Ltd.*[62] it was argued that evidence-in-chief could not prove common knowledge. Clauson J. said:

"I have a man properly informed in the art who knows so and so. I can infer that everybody properly informed in the art will have some knowledge because they have exactly the same opportunity as he has ... I must be satisfied that he has not an excess of any peculiar or special sort of knowledge, but that what he is telling me is what he has acquired in his ordinary practice as a man engaged in the art."

Particulars not ordinarily required

If the defendant proposes to rely on common general knowledge he **12.112** should state in general terms the nature of the prior knowledge relied on, but in a normal case detailed particulars will not be required.[63] The practice is that if such particulars are ordered they will be mutual, *i.e.* both parties will be required to state what they say was common general knowledge at the relevant time. The defendant may not rely, in support of an objection of common knowledge, upon documents of limited publicity (such as patent specifications) unless they have been particularised in some way before the trial.[64] A defendant may also be required to give disclosure of those documents relied upon as part of common general knowledge.[65]

---

[59] *Holliday v. Heppenstall Bros.* (1889) 41 Ch.D. 109; (1889) 6 R.P.C. 320 at p.326.
[60] *The Solvo Laundry Supply Co. Ltd. v. Mackie* (1893) 10 R.P.C. 68; *Holliday v. Heppenstall* (1889) 6 R.P.C. 320 at p.327; *Metropolitan-Vickers etc. Co. Ltd. v. British Thomson-Houston Co. Ltd.* (1925) 42 R.P.C. 76 at p.93.
[61] *Sutcliffe v. Thomas Abbott* (1903) 20 R.P.C. 50 at p.55.
[62] (1933) 50 R.P.C. 63 at p.90.
[63] *Holliday v. Heppenstall* (1889) 6 R.P.C. 320; *McCreath v. Mayor etc. of South Shields and Baker* (1932) 49 R.P.C. 349; *American Chain and Cable Co. Inc. v. Hall's Barton Ropery Co. Ltd.* (1938) 55 R.P.C. 287 at p.293; *Walton v. Hawtins Ltd.* (1948) 65 R.P.C. 69.
[64] *British Thomson-Houston Co. Ltd. v. Stonebridge Electrical Co. Ltd.* (1916) 33 R.P.C. 166 at p.171; *English and American Machinery Co. Ltd. v. Union Boot and Shoe Machine Co. Ltd.* (1894) 11 R.P.C. 367 at pp.373, 374. And see *Killick v. Pye Ltd.* [1958] R.P.C. 366 at p.376.
[65] *Aluma Systems Inc. v. Hunnebeck G.m.b.H.* [1982] F.S.R. 239.

Appeal on question of obviousness

12.113   The circumstances in which a finding of fact as to obviousness by the trial judge will be reversed on appeal were discussed in *Benmax v. Austin Motor Co. Ltd.* Lord Simonds said:[66]

> "Fifty years ago in *Montgomerie & Co. Ltd. v. Wallace James*[67-68] Lord Halsbury said:
>> 'But where no question arises as to truthfulness, and where the question is as to the proper inferences to be drawn from truthful evidence, then the original tribunal is in no better position to decide than the judges of an Appellate Court.'
>
> And in *Mersey Docks and Harbour Board v. Proctor* Lord Cave said:
>> 'The procedure on an appeal from a judge sitting without a jury is not governed by the rules applicable to a motion for a new trial after a verdict of a jury. In such a case it is the duty of the Court of Appeal to make up its own mind, not disregarding the judgment appealed from and giving special weight to that judgment in cases where the credibility of witnesses comes into question, but with full liberty to draw its own inference from the facts proved or admitted, and to decide accordingly.'
>
> It appears to me that these statements are consonant with the Rules of Court which prescribe that 'An appeal to the Court of Appeal shall be by way of re-hearing' and that 'the Court of Appeal shall have powers to draw inferences of fact and to give any judgment and make any order that ought to have been made.' This does not mean that an Appellate Court should lightly differ from the finding of a trial judge on a question of fact, and I would say that it would be difficult for it to do so where the finding turned solely on the credibility of a witness. But I cannot help thinking that some confusion may have arisen from failure to distinguish between the finding of a specific fact and a finding of fact which is really an inference from facts specifically found, or, as it has sometimes been said, between the perception and evaluation of facts. An example of this distinction may be seen in any case in which a plaintiff alleges negligence on the part of the defendant. Here it must first be determined what the defendant in fact did and, secondly, whether what he did amounted in the circumstances (which must also so far as relevant be found as specific facts) to negligence. A jury finds that the defendant has been negligent and that is an end of the matter, unless its verdict can be upset according to well-established rules. A judge sitting without a jury would fall short of his duty if he did not first find the facts and then draw from them the inference of fact whether or not the defendant had been

---

[66] [1904] A.C. 73.
[67-68] [1923] A.C. 253.

negligent. This is a simple illustration of a process in which it may often be difficult to say what is simple fact and what is inference from fact, or, to repeat what I have said, what is perception, what evaluation. Nor is it of any importance to do so except to explain why, as I think, different views have been expressed as to the duty of an Appellate Tribunal in relation to a finding by a trial judge. For I have found on the one hand universal reluctance to reject a finding of specific fact, particularly where the finding could be founded on the credibility or bearing of a witness, and on the other hand no less a willingness to form an independent opinion about the proper inference of fact, subject only to the weight which should as a matter of course be given to the opinion of the learned judge. But the statement of the proper function of the Appellate Court will be influenced by the extent to which the mind of the speaker is directed to the one or other of the two aspects of the problem. In a case like that under appeal where, so far as I can see, there can be no dispute about any relevant specific fact, much less any dispute arising out of the credibility of witnesses, but the sole question is whether the proper inference from those facts is tht the patent in suit disclosed an inventive step, I do not hesitate to say that an Appellate Court should form an independent opinion, though it will naturally attach importance to the judgment of the trial judge."

Utility (1949 Act)

"*That the invention, so far as claimed in any claim of the complete specification, is not useful.*" **12.114**

Where it is intended to rely on the fact that an example of the invention which is the subject of a claim of the patent in suit cannot be made to work, either at all or as described in the specification, particulars are required.[69-71]

Insufficiency (1949 and 1977 Acts)

1949 Act—"*That the complete specification does not sufficiently and fairly describe the invention and the method by which it is to be performed, or does not disclose the best method of performing it which was known to the applicant for the patent and for which he was entitled to claim protection.*" **12.115**

1977 Act—("*the specification of the patent does not disclose the invention clearly enough and completely enough for it to be performed by a person skilled in the art.*")

The objection of insufficiency should be accompanied where possible by particulars of the alleged defects and of the point at which a workman would meet with difficulty in carrying out the directions given.[72] Where, however, the objection is not that one cannot carry out

---

[69-71] R.S.C., Ord. 104, r.6(4).
[72] *Crompton v. Anglo-American Brush Corporation Ltd. (No.2)* (1887) 4 R.P.C. 197; *Heathfield v. Greenway* (1893) 10 R.P.C. 17.

the directions given, but that if one does carry them out the result described is not attained, further particulars are not required.[73]

Best method not disclosed (1949 Act)

12.116   In most cases it is unlikely that a defendant would be in a position to rely upon this ground. It may happen, however, during the course of the trial that evidence is given on behalf of the plaintiff which will allow of this objection being taken. In such a case an amendment of the pleadings would readily be granted,[74] but the application for leave to amend should be made at as early a stage as possible in order that the plaintiff may have an opportunity of considering the objection and calling further evidence on the point.[75]

Where this objection is pleaded it would appear necessary to give some particulars of what is alleged not to have been disclosed in order that the plaintiff may be informed as to the case he has to meet. However, the defendant is not bound to allege a particular method known to the patentee at the relevant date; it is sufficient to rely on inferences from pleaded matter, provided such inferences are made clear.[76] Further, it is permissible to plead this ground without giving such particulars if the defendant is only pleading a dilemma arising on proof of his particulars of insufficiency, *viz.*, that either the patentee did not know how to carry out the invention or alternatively, if he did know, he must have been aware of a method not described in his specification.[77-79]

Ambiguity, lack of fair basis (1949 Act)

12.117   *"That the scope of any claim of the complete specification is not sufficiently and clearly defined or that any claim of the complete specification is not fairly based on the matter disclosed in the specification."*

In a case decided under section 29 of the 1883 Act it was held that a plea that "The specification does not sufficiently define the extent or limits of the invention claimed" need not be further particularised,[80] and this is still the general practice.[81]

In *Natural Colour Kinematograph Co Ltd. v. Bioschemes Ltd.,*[82] Lord Loreburn said, in holding the patent bad for ambiguity, that a court might and should hold a patent to be invalid upon the ground of

---

[73] See, *e.g. "Z" Electric Lamp Manufacturing Co. Ltd. v. Marples, Leach & Co. Ltd.* (1909) 26 R.P.C. 762 (C.A.).

[74] *Franc-Strohmenger & Cowan Inc. v. Peter Robinson Ltd.* (1930) 47 R.P.C. 493 at p.502.

[75] *Ibid.*

[76] *Polaroid Corp.'s Patent* [1977] F.S.R. 233.

[77-79] *Anxionnaz v. Ministry of Aviation* [1966] R.P.C. 21.

[80] *Minerals Separation Ltd. v. British Ore Concentration Ltd.* (1907) 24 R.P.C. 790; *Marconi Wireless Telegraph Co. Ltd. v. Cramer & Co. Ltd.* (1932) 49 R.P.C. 400.

[81] *Raychem Corp. and others v. Thermon (U.K.) Ltd. and others* [1989] R.P.C. 578.

[82] (1915) 32 R.P.C. 256 at p.266.

ambiguity, even though such a point had not been raised upon the pleadings.[83] The absence of the plea might, however, prejudicially affect the defendant as regards costs, and it is advisable to include it specifically in the particulars of objections if it is to be taken.[84] What may be regarded as an instance where the second half of this plea was applicable is to be found in *Mullard Radio Valve Co. Ltd. v. Philco Radio and Television Corporation Ltd.*[85-86] This contention, like ambiguity, can be raised even if not specifically pleaded.

False suggestion or representation (1949 Act)

"That the patent was obtained on a false suggestion or representation"   **12.118**

In modern practice this plea is usually concerned with the allegation that some promise contained in the specification is not fulfilled even when the directions therein contained are properly followed, and in such cases the same matters may also constitute inutility. Obviously, particulars must be given sufficient to identify the false suggestion or represenation alleged.[87] There are, however, other cases in which this plea would be appropriate. Thus, where the patent sued on had been granted out of time under the provisions of the 1914 Patents, Designs and Trade Marks (Temporary Rules) Act, the defendants pleaded *inter alia* that such patents had been granted upon representations made on the application form, which were untrue. This being a plea of misrepresentation (and in fact of fraud on the Crown), appropriate particulars were ordered.[88]

Invention contrary to law (1949 Act)

"That the primary or intended use or exercise of the invention is contrary to   **12.119**
law."

This objection has only rarely been taken.[89] The only particulars which would seem to be necessary are in cases where it is contended that the use of the invention is contrary to the provisions of a particular statute.

Prior secret user (1949 Act)

"That the invention, so far as claimed in any claim of the complete   **12.120**
specification, was secretly used in the United Kingdom, otherwise than as

---

[83] And see *Safveans Aktie Bolag v. Ford Motor Co. (Eng.) Ltd.* (1927) 44 R.P.C. 49 at p.56, and *Franc-Strohmenger & Cowan Inc. v. Peter Robinson Ltd.* (1930) 47 R.P.C. 493 at p.500.
[84] See, *e.g. Heathfield v. Greenway* (1893) 10 R.P.C. 17 at p.20.
[85-86] (1936) 53 R.P.C. 323.
[87] And see *Godfrey L. Cabot Inc. v. Philblack Ltd.* [1961] R.P.C. 53.
[88] *E.g. Tecalemit Ltd. v. Ex-A-Gun Ltd.* (1927) 44 R.P.C. 62.
[89] See *Pessers and Moody v. Haydon & Co.* (1909) 26 R.P.C. 58.

mentioned in subsection (2) of this section [32], before the priority date of that claim."

Section 32(2) of the 1949 Act provides that no account shall be taken of any secret prior user which was:

(a) for the purpose of reasonable trial or experiment only;
(b) by or with the authority of a government department consequent upon a communication of the invention by the applicant or by a person from whom he derives title;
(c) by any other person, in consequence of such a communication, if made without consent.

Particulars must be given as in the case of a non-secret prior user.[90]

Extension by Amendment (1977 Act)

12.121   *"The protection conferred by the patent has been extended by an amendment which should not have been allowed."*

Particulars will be necessary as to the date of amendment, the nature of the extension of the protection and the reason why the amendment should not have been allowed.

Extension of disclosure (1977 Act)

12.122   *"The matter disclosed in the specification of the patent extends beyond that disclosed in the application for the patent, as filed, or, if the patent was granted on a new application filed under section 8(3), 12, or 37(4) above or as mentioned in section 15(4) above, in the earlier application, as filed."*

Particulars will be necessary to identify the relevant application and the extension alleged to have been included.

Extension granted null and void

12.123   In *Anxionnaz v. Rolls Royce Ltd.*[91] it was sought to plead that an extension which was obtained on the ground of fraud was null and void. Whether or not fraud vitiates an order for extension was not decided; but it is submitted that an order obtained by fraud is void.

Admissibility of evidence having regard to particulars

12.124   Order 104, rule 16 provides that no evidence may be admitted in proof of any alleged infringement or objection that is not raised in the particulars, except by leave of the court, to be given on suitable terms.

---

[90] See Ord. 104, r.6. And see *Stracham and Henshaw Ltd. v. Pakcel Ltd.* (1949) 66 R.P.C. 49 at p.55.
[91] [1965] R.P.C. 122.

The discretion of the court under this rule is separate and distinct from its discretion under Order 104, rule 7 as to amendment of particulars.[92] While the court would exercise its discretion so as to avoid an injustice, it would be unlikely to admit evidence, outside the particulars, relating to individual prior users or constructions. It might, however, admit evidence as to what was practically common knowledge.[93]

In *British United Shoe Machinery Co. Ltd. v. A. Fussell & Sons Ltd.*,[94] the specification had been amended, and the judge at the trial held that the original claims were not framed with reasonable skill and knowledge. The defendant, in the Court of Appeal, attempted to rely on this finding of fact as an additional ground of invalidity, but the court would not allow this course as the objection had not been pleaded, and they saw no grounds for going beyond the particulars of objections.

In *Cropper v. Smith and Hancock*[95] the defendants, who were partners, were sued in respect of a joint infringement. Owing to an unfounded fear that Hancock might be estopped from disputing the validity of the patent they severed their defences, and while Smith delivered particulars of objections to validity, Hancock did not do so. The patent was held to be invalid by the Court of Appeal, but owing to the lack of particulars judgment was given, nevertheless, against Hancock, restraining him from further infringement. The House of Lords, however, held that judgment should be given for Hancock as well as for Smith, and penalised the former merely by refusing him costs of the appeal. In the course of his judgment the Lord Chancellor (Earl of Selborne) said:[96]

"If it so happened ... that the defendants were persons whose cases were wholly distinct, who had nothing to do with each other, whose acts were acts for which each of them was severally and solely responsible, and in which the others of them had no interest, if that case arose, it might be that a court of justice, applying this section of the statute, might properly hold that one defendant who had not given full particulars should have no benefit from what had been done by another defendant, with whom he had no connection or concern, and whose case was entirely separate from his own. What the consequences of that might be it is not necessary at present to say. But where there is a case, as I said, not expressly noticed or provided for in terms by the section, of co-defendants who are sued as being jointly liable for their joint and common acts, whose cases on the face of the plaintiffs' pleadings and their own are not separate as to the substance, though they may sever in the conduct of their defences, then as to that case, if the substance of the statute and its substantial

---

[92] See *post*, § 12.125 *et seq.*
[93] *Britain v. Hirsch* (1888) 5 R.P.C. 226 at p.231.
[94] (1908) 25 R.P.C. 631 at pp.659, 660.
[95] (1885) 10 App.Cas. 249; (1885) 2 R.P.C. 17.
[96] (1885) 10 App.Cas. at p.254; (1885) 2 R.P.C. at p.22.

objects are complied with, I see no words in it which say that justice is not to be done in the case because one of the defendants has neglected or omitted or refused in point of form to put in the particulars which have been put in by the other, who is in *pari casu*."

Apart from the exercise of the discretion of the court, the same practice is applicable to actions for infringement as to other actions, *viz.*, that evidence is admissible if the wording of the particulars of objections is sufficiently wide to cover it, even though such wording be vague and general in its terms. The party aggrieved should apply before the hearing for further and better particulars so as to be sure of not being taken by surprise.[97]

In *Sugg v. Silber*[98] Mellish L.J. said:

"In my opinion there is a very large difference between a case where a judge has been applied to and has ordered further particulars in order to state an objection more specifically, and a case where at the trial the plaintiff asserts that the defendant ought to be prevented from availing himself of an objection. It is perfectly obvious that, if ... the two questions are the same, and that wherever the court would order further particulars because the objection had not been particularly specified, it would also hold that the party was precluded from raising it at the trial, nobody would be foolish enough to apply to a judge for further particulars."[99]

Amendment of particulars

12.125   Order 104, rule 7, provides that particulars of infringement and particulars of objections may from time to time be amended by leave of the court upon such terms as may be just.

Amendment of particulars of objections before trial

12.126   Amendments of particulars of objections under this rule are usually permitted upon application made before trial, the terms imposed being such that the plaintiff shall not be prejudiced by the defectiveness of the particulars as originally delivered. The form of order which is almost invariably followed[1] is that made in the case of *Baird v. Moule's Patent Earth Closet Co.*, which is set out in the report of *Edison Telephone Co. v. India Rubber Co.*[2] The effect of such order is to give to the plaintiff the

---

[97] See R.S.C., Ord. 18, r.12.
[98] (1877) 2 Q.B.D. 493 at p.495.
[99] And see *Neilson v. Harford* (1841) 1 W.P.C. 295 at p.370; *Hull v. Bollard* (1856) 25 L.J.Ex. 304.
[1] See, *e.g. Ehrlich v. Intec* (1887) 4 R.P.C. 115; *Wilson v. Wilson & Co. Ltd.* (1899) 16 R.P.C. 315; *Lusty & Sons v. G. W. Scott & Sons Ltd.* (1931) 48 R.P.C. 475.
[2] (1881) 17 Ch.D. 137 at p.139n.

option either of discontinuing the action or of proceeding therewith. If he discontinues, he has to pay the costs up to and including the original particulars of objections, the defendant paying the costs subsequent to that time. If he proceeds with the action the defendants have to pay the costs of the application to amend,[3] and in other respects the action proceeds in the ordinary way.

A similar form of order is made in the case of the particulars of objections in a counterclaim for revocation.[4]

The rationale behind the *Earth Closet* and *See v. Scott-Paine* form of orders was fully reviewed by the Court of Appeal in *Williamson v. Moldline*[5] in which it was held that a plaintiff was entitled to know the case he had to meet and that it was for the defendant who intended to attack the validity of a prima facie valid patent to make such investigations as might be required to enable him to formulate the appropriate particulars of objections at a relatively early stage of the proceedings. It follows from this that if a defendant later seeks leave to introduce a further objective, it is incumbent on the defendant to satisfy the court that he could not by reasonably diligent investigation have discovered the relevant information before, and could thus not have pleaded it at an earlier stage. This might be the case where the new ground of objection, for example, a prior use, was wholly within the knowledge of the plaintiff.[6] **12.127**

Where the particulars of objections were permitted to be amended a second time, it was ordered that if the plaintiff discontinued, the defendant should pay the costs as from the date when the amended particulars of objections were delivered.[7]

Where the defendants applied for leave to amend upon the eve of the trial, such leave was granted, and, the plaintiffs deciding to proceed, it was ordered that the defendants should pay the costs occasioned by the amendment and, also, the costs unnecessarily caused to the plaintiffs by the amendment being made so late.[8]

Amendment of particulars at the trial

Where the application to amend is made at the trial such leave may only be granted if the new matter has only been recently discovered, and could not with reasonable diligence have been discovered before.[9] **12.128**

---

[3] And see *Bloxham v. Kee-Less Clock Co.* (1922) 39 R.P.C. 195 at p.211.

[4] *See v. Scott-Paine* (1933) 50 R.P.C. 56; *Strachan and Henshaw Ltd. v. Pakcel Ltd.* (1949) 66 R.P.C. 49 at p.56; *Betts v. Ideal Capsules Ltd.* (1951) 68 R.P.C. 23.

[5] [1986] R.P.C. 556; See also *Behr-Thompson Dehnstoffrengler Verwattungs G.m.b.H. v. Western Thompson Controls* [1990] R.P.C. 569.

[6] See *Gill v. Chapman* [1987] R.P.C. 209; and *Helitune v. Stewart Hughes* [1991] R.P.C. 78.

[7] *Wilson v. Wilson & Co. Ltd.*(1899) 16 R.P.C. 315; *Lever Brothers and Unilever Ltd.'s Patent* (1953) 70 R.P.C. 275; *Williamson v. Modline* [1986] R.P.C. 556; *Behr-Thompson v. Weston Thompson* [1990] R.P.C. 569. See also *Ecdab Inc. v. Reddish Savilles Ltd.* [1993] F.S.R. 193.

[8] *Parker v. Maignen's Filtre Rapide Co.* (1888) 5 R.P.C. 207.

[9] *Moss v. Malings* (1886) 33 Ch.D. 603; (1886) 3 R.P.C. 373 at p.375; and see *British United Shoe Machinery Co. Ltd. v. A. Fussell & Sons Ltd.* (1908) 25 R.P.C. 631 at pp.659, 660.

However, the modern practice is to allow amendments subject to the right of any party affected to an adjournment and costs. A general discussion of the principles applicable to amendments is to be found in the judgment of Bowen L.J. in *Cropper v. Smith and Hancock.*[10]

Where the defendant wishes to add further objections in consequence of evidence given by the plaintiff's witnesses during the trial, the application to amend should be made at the earliest opportunity, in order that the plaintiff may have an opportunity to consider the matter and call further evidence if necessary.[11]

In *Badische Anilin und Soda Fabrik v. La Société Chimique*[12] it became clear during the course of the trial that the specification of the patent sued upon was insufficient, and the defendants applied for leave to amend the particulars by inserting an objection on this ground. Leave was granted to amend, the plaintiffs having a fortnight to elect whether they would continue the action, the terms upon which such leave should be granted being left for argument until the plaintiffs had elected. On the hearing the plaintiffs elected to continue, and the patent was declared invalid as a result of the new objection, but all costs of and occasioned by the application to amend, and all costs thrown away by reason of the amendment being made so late, were given to the plaintiffs.[13]

In *Helitune v. Stewart Hughes*[14] the defendants applied for leave to amend the particulars to allege a prior user after cross-examining one of the plaintiffs' witnesses. The court held, that since the defendants had known of the prior user after discovery they could have pleaded it nine months before the trial and so there should be an *Earth Closet* order with the date nine months before trial being the date from which the defendants would be liable to costs if the plaintiffs elected to discontinue. In view of the costs implication the defendants were allowed to withdraw their application to amend.

In *Birtwhistle v. Sumner Engineering Co. Ltd.*[15] the defendants at the trial desired to give evidence as to the use of an article (pleaded as a "prior user") by persons other than those mentioned in the particulars of objections. They were allowed to amend by adding the names of such persons upon the terms of the ordinary *Baird v. Moule* order.

The terms on which amendment will be allowed are a matter for the discretion of the court, and such terms will not, in general, be reviewed by the Court of Appeal.[16]

---

[10] (1884) 26 Ch.D. 700 at p.710; (1884) 1 R.P.C. 81 at p.95.
[11] See *Franc-Strohmenger & Crown Inc. v. Peter Robinson Ltd.* (1930) 47 R.P.C. 493 at p.502.
[12] (1899) 16 R.P.C. 875 at pp.881, 892.
[13] See also *Allen v. Horton* (1893) 10 R.P.C. 412; *Westley, Richards & Co. v. Perkes* (1893) 10 R.P.C. 181 at p.186.
[14] [1991] R.P.C. 78.
[15] (1928) 45 R.P.C. 59 at p.67.
[16] *Wilson v. Wilson & Co. Ltd.* (1899) 16 R.P.C. 315 (C.A.).

Amendment in Court of Appeal

12.129 In *Pirrie v. York Street Flax Spinning Co. Ltd.*[17] leave to amend particulars of objections was granted by the Court of Appeal in Ireland pending appeal.

In *Shoe Machinery Co. Ltd. v. Cutlan*[18] the Court of Appeal decided that they had jurisdiction to permit amendment of the particulars of objections although in that particular case they declined to do so, and the same rule has been held to apply to the Scottish Inner House.[19] The Court of Appeal is, however, very reluctant to permit such amendments.[20]

Reply

12.130 The plaintiff may deliver a reply setting out facts which may tend to negative some of the pleas raised by the particulars of objections, *e.g.* that the invention was obvious. Although evidence of such facts could be called at the trial without these being pleaded, to set them out in a reply may be advantageous from the point of view of obtaining a wider discovery.[21]

Where a party wishes to rely upon commercial success in defence to an allegation of deviousness Order 104, rule 6(5) of the Rules of the Supreme Court, requires the party to state the grounds upon which he relies. This has been interpreted as requiring the party to identify any defect in the prior act, how it was overcome, whether long felt want was being sought to be established and, if so, how it was going to be established.[22]

Admissions

12.131 Under Order 104, rule 10 of the Rules of the Supreme Court, where a party desires any other party to make any admission he shall 21 days after service of the Reply (as, if none is served 21 days after the time for service of the Reply) serve a notice requiring admissions of the facts stated in the notice. 21 days after service of the notice the party upon whom the notice is served must serve a notice stating in respect of each fact whether or not he admits it.

The importance of the notice to admit is two-fold. First, it enables the real issues in the action to be more closely defined. Secondly, it enables the court to order that the costs of issues needlessly put in issue shall be borne by the party refusing to make the admissions sought. Although

---

[17] (1894) 11 R.P.C. 429 at p.431.
[18] [1896] 1 Ch. 108; (1895) 12 R.P.C. 530.
[19] *Watson, Laidlaw & Co. Ltd. v. Pott, Cassels and Williamson* (1908) 25 R.P.C. 349 at p.360.
[20] See, *e.g. Alsop Flour Process Ltd. v. Flour Oxidising Co. Ltd.* (1907) 24 R.P.C. 349 (C.A.); (1908) 25 R.P.C. 477 (H.L.).
[21] See *Laurence Scott and Electronics Ltd. v. General Electric Co. Ltd.* (1938) 55 R.P.C. 233.
[22] *John Deks Ltd. v. Aztec Washer Co.* [1989] R.P.C. 413.

the provisions of Order 62, rule 6(7) apply to admissions sought under Order 27, rule 2 it is likely that the court in the exercise of its discretion will impose the same sanction in costs.

Discovery

Interrogatories

12.132 Order 26, rules 1 to 6 of the Rules of the Supreme Court, govern the procedure for interrogatories and provide that either party to an action may serve interrogatories on the other party not more than twice without leave of the court. Thereafter leave is required.

12.133 The interrogatories served must be necessary either:

(a) for disposing fairly of the cause or matter; or
(b) for the saving of costs.[23]

An interrogatory which does not relate to either, may not be served,[24] notwithstanding that it may be admissible in oral cross-examination of a witness.

At the end of the interrogatories there must be a note specifying:

(a) the period of time in which they are to be answered, being no less than 28 days from the date of service,[25]
(b) the officer, member, agent or servant of the defendant who is required to answer the interrogatories.[26]

A person who objects to the interrogatories served may, no later than 14 days after service apply to the court for them to be varied or withdrawn.[27] A person served may also object to answer on the ground of privilege. Save for these two exceptions a person is required to answer the interrogatories on affidavit.

Where the party from whom information is required is a company or corporation, interrogatories may be delivered to the proper officer, *e.g.* the secretary of such company or corporation, who answers on its behalf.[28]

---

[23] R.S.C., Ord. 26, r.1(1).
[24] R.S.C., Ord. 26, r.1(3).
[25] R.S.C., Ord. 26, r.2(1)(*a*).
[26] R.S.C., Ord. 26, rr.2(1)(*b*) & (*c*).
[27] R.S.C., Ord. 26, r.3(2).
[28] R.S.C., Ord. 26, r.2.

Documents

Under Order 104, rule 11 of the Rules of the Supreme Court, **12.134** automatic discovery provided for in Order 24, rules 1 and 2 applies to actions for infringement of patent. Such discovery is given by exchange of lists within 21 days after the time for service of notice of admissions under rule 10(2). Documents which are in the custody, possession, power or control of an associated company are not discoverable.[29]

Application may also be made by either party for discovery on oath of relevant[30] documents in the possession or power of the other party. The court thereupon will make such order as it may think fit, having regard to the necessity for such discovery for a fair trial or for saving costs.[31]

General principles as to discovery

Discovery, whether of documents or by interrogatories, is a powerful **12.135** weapon, which by its nature is particularly liable to abuse when actions between traders are concerned, and its utilisation is watched by the court with care lest, on the one hand, facts material to the dispute before it be concealed, or, on the other, immaterial facts be elicited with some ulterior motive. Discovery, as was stated by Lord Watson in *Ind, Coope & Co. v. Emmerson*,[32] is a "matter of remedy and not matter of right".

On discovery there exists an implied undertaking given that the **12.136** disclosed documents will only be used for the purpose of the action in which they are disclosed and that they will not be used for any collateral or ulterior motive.[33] Breach of that undertaking is a contempt of court. Only in exceptional circumstances will the court release a party from the implied undertaking.[34] The existance of a co-pending EPO opposition involving the same parties, subject matter and issues is not such a circumstance.[35]

This undertaking ceases to apply, however, to a document after it has been read to, or by the court, or referred to, in open court, unless the court for special reasons otherwise orders on the application of a party

---

[29] *Sommer Allibert (U.K.) Ltd. v. Flair Plastics Ltd.* [1987] R.P.C. 599 at 627; and *Unilever plc. v. Gillette U.K. Ltd.* [1988] R.P.C. 416.

[30] See *Martin v. Sarib Ltd.*, (1950) 67 R.P.C. 340; (1950) 67 R.P.C. 127; *Sonotone Corporation v. Multitone Electric Co. Ltd.* (1953) 70 R.P.C. 83; *Martin v. H. Millwood Ltd.*, (1955) 72 R.P.C. 316.

[31] R.S.C., Ord. 24, rr.3, 7, 8, 13, 14, 16.

[32] 12 App.Cas. 300 at p.309; and see *Martin v. Sarib Ltd.*, (1950) 67 R.P.C. 127.

[33] *Home Office v. Harman* [1983] A.C. 280; *Alterskye v. Scott* [1948] 1 All E.R. 469; *Halcon International Inc. v. Shell Transport and Trading Co.* [1979] R.P.C. 97; *Distillers Co. (Biochemicals) Ltd. v. Times Newspapers Ltd.* [1975] Q.B. 613; *Riddick v. Thames Board Mills* [1977] Q.B. 881; *Sybron Corp. v. Barclays Bank* [1984] 3 W.L.R. 1055; *Wilden Pumps v. Fusfield* [1985] F.S.R. 583; *Bayer v. Winter (No.2)* [1986] F.S.R. 357; *C.B.S. Songs Ltd. v. Amstrad Consumer Electronics plc.* [1987] R.P.C. 417; *Crest Homes plc. v. Marks* [1988] R.P.C. 21.

[34] See, *e.g. Crest Homes plc. v. Marks* [1988] R.P.C. 21; and *Dory v. Wolf G.m.b.H.* [1990] F.S.R. 266.

[35] *Bonzel v. Intervention* [1991] R.P.C. 43.

or of the person to whom the document belongs.[36]

Objection may be taken to answering interrogatories. Discovery of documents must be given completely as far as the mention of all relevant documents in the affidavit is concerned, privilege being claimed in respect of such documents so mentioned as the other party is not entitled to see.[37] The ordinary principles as to objections to answer interrogatories or to produce documents apply to patent cases.

There is no obligation upon a party giving discovery of a document in a foreign language to provide a translation.[38]

Time for discovery

12.137   Since it is not possible to say precisely what the issues between the parties are before the defence is delivered, neither party, except under special circumstances, will be allowed to interrogate, or obtain discovery of documents,[39] until that stage of the action has been reached. But thereafter discovery will not be delayed merely because it is inconvenient to a party to give it immediately.[40]

Nor will interrogatories be allowed or discovery of documents ordered before trial as to facts which will only become relevant after trial as, for instance, with regard to the extent of the defendant's infringements—a fact which is not material until the inquiry as to damages.[41] The practice as to discovery upon such inquiry as to damages is dealt with below.[42] The fact, however, that the question of validity of a patent may have to be decided before the plaintiff can enforce his rights as regards infringement does not render inadmissible interrogatories as to the acts of infringement as defined in the particulars of infringements, because, as a matter of convenience, the issues of validity and infringement are always heard together or in immediate succession.[43]

Where issues not properly defined

12.138   The issues in patent cases to which both interrogatories and discovery of documents must be relevant are not the broad issues of validity and infringement, but those issues as narrowed down by the particulars of objections or infringements.

---

[36] R.S.C., Ord. 24, r.14A.
[37] *Carnegie Steel Co. v. Bell Bros. Ltd.* (1907) 24 R.P.C. 82 at p.93.
[38] *Bayer A.G. v. Harris Pharaceuticals* [1991] F.S.R. 170.
[39] *Woolfe v. Automatic Picture Gallery Ltd.* (1902) 19 R.P.C. 161; *R.H.M. Foods Ltd. v. Bovril Ltd.* [1983] R.P.C. 275; *Intel Corp. v. General Instrument Corp.* [1989] F.S.R. 640.
[40] *British United Shoe Machinery Co. Ltd. v. Holdfast Boots Ltd.* (1934) 51 R.P.C. 489.
[41] *De La Rue v. Dickenson* (1857) 3 K. & J. 388; *Lea v. Saxby* (1875) 32 L.T.(N.S.) 731; *Fennessy v. Clark* (1887) 37 Ch.D. 184; but *cf.* R.S.C., Ord. 24, r.4.
[42] See *post*, §12.245.
[43] *Benno Jaffé und Darmstaedter Lanolin Fabrik v. John Richardson & Co. Ltd.* (1893) 10 R.P.C. 136; *cf. Rawes v. Chance* (1890) 7 R.P.C. 175.

Thus, where the particulars of infringements alleged infringement of a process in general terms, and also specified a particular instance of infringement, it was held that the plaintiff was only entitled to interrogate as to the particular act complained of.[44]

Similarly, where the defendant alleged invalidity by reason of certain facts within the knowledge of the plaintiff, it was held, that the issue was not the validity of the patent generally, but only as limited by the particulars of objections, and that a plaintiff should not be ordered to disclose every document which might suggest invalidity irrespective of whether it related to the particular grounds relied upon by the defendant.[45]

Documents not to be construed

Interrogatories the reply to which by either party would involve placing a construction upon the specification are not permissible.[46] Nor ordinarily will interrogatories be permitted, the determination of the relevance of which depends upon the construction of the specification.[47]   **12.139**

Issue of infringement

The plaintiff may interrogate the defendant or obtain discovery as to facts relevant to points in issue[48] with respect to the particular act instanced as an alleged infringement in the particulars of infringements, both as to whether the act was performed and as to the details which tend to show whether or not it was an infringement.   **12.140**

Thus, a plaintiff may administer interrogatories framed upon portions of his specification and ask the defendant whether he has used the processes described therein and forming part of his invention, taking them step by step,[49] but he may not go further and ask, "If you do not use that process, tell me what you do use";[50] nor is he entitled to interrogate the defendant in further detail than is given in the specification with the

---

[44] *Actiengesellschaft etc. Aluminium Schweissung v. London Aluminium Co. Ltd. (No.2)* (1919) 36 R.P.C. 199; but see *Alliance Flooring Co. Ltd. v. Winsorflor Ltd.* [1961] R.P.C. 375.

[45] *Avery Ltd. v. Ashworth, Son & Co. Ltd.* (1915) 32 R.P.C. 463, 560; *cf. Edison and Swan United Electric Light Co. v. Holland* (1888) 5 R.P.C. 213; *Belegying en Exploitatiemaatshappij Lavender B.V. v. Witten Industrial Diamonds* [1979] F.S.R. 59; *Intalite International N.V. v. Cellular Ceilings Ltd. (No.1)* [1987] R.P.C. 532; *Intel Corp. v. General Instrument Corp.* [1989] F.S.R. 640 at 646.

[46] *Wenham Co. Ltd. v. Champion Gas Lamp Co. Ltd.* (1890) 7 R.P.C. 22; *Bibby & Baron Ltd. v. Duerden* (1910) 27 R.P.C. 283 (C.A.); *Lux Traffic Controls v. Staffordshire Public Works Co.* [1991] R.P.C. 73.

[47] *Delta Metal Co. Ltd. v. Maxim Nordenfelt Guns and Ammunition Co. Ltd.* (1891) 8 R.P.C. 169.

[48] See *Marriott v. Chamberlain* (1886) 17 Q.B.D. 154 at p.163; *Nash v. Layton* [1911] 2 Ch. 71.

[49] *Benno Jaffé und Darmstaedter Lanolin Fabrik v. John Richardson & Co. Ltd.* (1893) 10 R.P.C. 136; and see *Sharpe & Dohme Inc. v. Boots Pure Drug Co. Ltd.* (1927) 44 R.P.C. 69.

[50] *Actiengesellschaft für Anilin Fabrikation v. Levinstein Ltd.* (1913) 30 R.P.C. 401 (C.A.); *Osram Lamp Works Ltd. v. Pope's Electric Lamp Co.* (1917) 34 R.P.C. 313.

object of meeting a possible objection to the sufficiency of the description in his specification.[51]

A plaintiff may be required to give discovery of documents generated in other jurisdictions which disclose the approach which may be taken on the issue of infringement.[52]

Names of defendant's customers

12.141   A defendant cannot conceal the name of hs customer in the case of the specific article complained of, and as regards that article may be interrogated as to whether he has supplied it to anybody and to whom, unless, of course, he has already admitted the sale thereof in his defence.[53] A plaintiff is not, however, entitled to discover before trial the names of the defendant's customers generally, as this only becomes relevant if he establishes his case and obtains an inquiry into damages.[54] Even upon an inquiry the matter is discretionary and the defendant may not be required to identify the names of his customers.[55]

Names of defendant's suppliers

12.142   The names of the persons who supplied the defendant with goods alleged to infringe are not normally relevant to any issue between the parties, although the names of such suppliers may be discoverable under the principles of *Norwich Pharmacal v. Customs and Excise Commissioners*,[56] even when the supplier is outside the jurisdiction.[57] Where the defendants dealt in a chemical product, all known processes for the manufacture of which were alleged to be covered by patents owned by the plaintiffs, interrogatories as to the sources of the defendants' supply were permitted by the Court of Appeal on the ground that the answers would probably enable the plaintiffs to ascertain whether the substance had been manufactured by an infringing process or not.[58]

Such a probability has also been held to exist where the plaintiffs alleged that they had knowledge of the processes employed at certain works and that, if informed as to the source of the defendants' goods, they would be enabled, utilising such knowledge, to prove infringement.[59]

---

[51] *Actiengesellschaft für Anilin Fabrikation v. Levinstein Ltd.* (1913) 30 R.P.C. 673.
[52] *Vickers v. Horsell Graphic Industries Ltd.* [1988] R.P.C. 421.
[53] See *Lister v. Norton Bros. & Co. Ltd.* (1886) 3 R.P.C. 68; see also *Stahlwerk Becker A.G.'s Patent* (1917) 34 R.P.C. 344.
[54] *Sega Enterprises Ltd. v. Alca Electronics* [1982] F.S.R. 516.
[55] *Murray v. Clayton* L.R. 15 Eq.Cas. 115; and *Smith, Kline & French Laboratories Ltd. v. Doncaster Pharmaceuticals Ltd. and others* [1989] F.S.R. 401 at pp.405–406.
[56] See *post*, §12.151.
[57] *Smith, Kline & French Laboratories Ltd. v. Global Pharmaceutics Ltd.* [1986] R.P.C. 394.
[58] *Saccharin Corporation v. Haines* (1898) 15 R.P.C. 344; and see *Stahlwerk Becker A.G.'s Patent* (1917) 34 R.P.C. 344.
[59] *Osram Lamp Works Ltd. v. Gabriel Lamp Co.* (1914) 31 R.P.C. 230 (C.A.).

An allegation by the defendant that his process is a secret one would not seem to render necessary any departure from the above principles with regard to interrogatories,[60] though, of course, it may have a material effect upon an application for inspection of the process.[61]

Discovery relating to issue of validity

Interrogatories or discovery of documents relating to the issue of validity may be obtained by either party. In *Sharpe & Dohme Inc. v. Boots Pure Drug Co. Ltd.*[62] the plaintiffs were allowed to interrogate as to whether the substance of the chemical composition and constitution set forth in their specification was "a new substance at the date of the patent", and whether it was "a substance produced by a chemical process". In *Haslam v. Hall*[63] the plaintiffs had, before becoming the owners, made preparations to dispute the validity of the patent. The defendants were given discovery of the documents in such proceedings except those which had come into existence for communication to the solicitors for the purposes of the litigation.[64] Documents generated in other jurisdictions which disclose potential lines of defences to a particular citation may be discoverable.[65]

12.143

Prior user

As regards prior user of machinery or apparatus the requirements with regard to particulars and inspection are so stringent that it is unlikely that further information could in most cases properly be obtained by interrogatories or discovery of documents. Where the prior user is of a process, the information afforded by the particulars may need supplementing. It was held, however, in *Delta Metal Co. Ltd. v. Maxim Nordenfelt Ltd.*,[66] where the plaintiff interrogated with respect to a prior user as to the precise process used, that an answer that the prior user was substantially the process as described in the plaintiff's specification was sufficient.

12.144

And in *Crossley v. Tomey*,[67] where the defendant was required to state whether he was not making articles in all respects identical with those of the plaintiff, and to set forth in what respects they differed, and by what process they were made, it was held that the defendant (who alleged

---

[60] See *Renard v. Levinstein* (1864) 3 New Rep. 665; 10 L.T.(N.S.) 94. See also *Reddanay & Co. Ltd. v. Flynn* (1923) 30 R.P.C. 16; *Helps v. Mayor etc. of Oldham* (1923) 40 R.P.C. 68. *Cf. Sorbo etc. Products Ltd. v. Defries* (1930) 47 R.P.C. 454 (secret process).

[61] See *post*, §14.152.

[62] (1927) 44 R.P.C. 69.

[63] (1988) 5 R.P.C. 1 at p.9.

[64] And see *Brown v. Sansom, Teale & Co.* (1888) 5 R.P.C. 510; *Edison and Swan United Electric Light Co. v. Holland* (1888) 5 R.P.C. 213; *Thomson v. Hughes* (1890) 7 R.P.C. 187; *Avery Ltd. v. Ashworth, Son & Co. Ltd.* (1915) 32 R.P.C. 463, 560.

[65] *Vickers plc. v. Horsell Graphic Industries Ltd. and others* [1988] R.P.C. 422.

[66] (1891) 8 R.P.C. 169.

[67] (1876) 2 Ch.D. 533.

prior user by himself and others) had sufficiently answered by stating that, save so far as the articles manufactured by him before the date of the patent were similar to those of the plaintiff, the articles he now made differed from those made by the plaintiff, but he could not show in what they differed without ocular demonstration.

12.145   In the past the interrogatory or application for discovery would not be allowed if it would disclose the evidence by which the other party will support its own case. In *Brown's Patent*[68] Buckley L.J. said: "The broad statement is still true that a party can only interrogate to support his own case and not to ascertain the evidence of his opponent in order to destroy his opponent's case."

Thus, in *Carnegie Steel Co. v. Bell Bros. Ltd.*,[69] the defendants objected to allow inspection of certain documents referred to in their affidavit of documents, which documents, they said, referred solely to certain prior users alleged in their particulars of objections. It was held that the documents were privileged, and Buckley L.J. said:[70]

"Particulars of prior user must be given; evidence of prior user need not be given; and it does not follow that every document relating to prior user is a particular of prior user; it may be something which may assist the defendant to prove the prior user, but that he is not bound to produce. I am not aware of any principle which in a patent action any more than any other action compels the defendant to produce documents of that description."[71]

It is submitted, that this is no longer the law and that discovery will be ordered of documents relevant to both parties' case.

Obviousness

12.146   Where obviousness is pleaded documents relating to the making of the invention, including the inventor's notebooks may be discoverable documents.[72] The correct test is to ask whether there is any way in which knowledge of the inventor's researches can assist the defendant's case on obviousness. If evidence of the inventor is to be given, the inventor's notes and experiments are relevant either as a part of, or for testing the inventor's evidence and are therefore relevant to the issue pleaded. An application for such discovery should, however, be carefully framed and an application for "all documents relating to the invention of the

---

[68] (1907) 24 R.P.C. 61 at p.64.
[69] (1906) 23 R.P.C. 82.
[70] (1906) 23 R.P.C. 82 at p.92.
[71] See also *Stahlwerk Becker A.G.'s Patent* (1917) 34 R.P.C. 332.
[72] See *Halcon International Inc. v. Shell Transport and Trading Co. Ltd.* [1979] R.P.C. 459 considered in *The Wellcome Foundation v. VR Laboratories (Australia) Pty. Ltd.* [1982] R.P.C. 343 and followed in *SKM SA and or. v. Wagner Spraytech (U.K.) Ltd. and ors.* [1982] R.P.C. 497.

plaintiff's patent" has been considered too wide.[73]

When commercial success is relied upon to rebut an allegation of obviousness, discovery of licences granted by the patentee in respect of the patent should be given.[74]

Interrogatories as to the state of mind of particular researchers in the field at the relevant time were found to be unnecessary in the context of obviousness and the court ordered their withdrawal.[75]

Objection of lack of utility

In *Rylands v. Ashley's Patent Bottle Co.,*[76] where the defendant pleaded   **12.147**
that the invention patented was not useful, the Court of Appeal allowed an interrogatory on behalf of the defendant asking whether it had not been found necessary to use some and what modifications in the process described in the specification; but Lindley L.J. said[77] that an answer which left out "the 'what' " might be sufficient.

Fair basis

The question of fair basis is entirely a matter of construction for the   **12.148**
court. The fact that foreign patents had claims which were more restricted is irrelevant and accordingly documents which related to the restriction of the claims in other jurisdictions are not discoverable.[78]

Claim of privilege

Communications between a litigant and his professional legal adviser   **12.149**
are privileged, whether at the time they are made litigation be pending or anticipated or not; similarly communications from some other person to such advisor are also privileged, but only if made when litigation is pending or contemplated. Documents called into existence for the purpose of litigation in another jurisdiction, are prima facie privileged, and use of such documents, while subject to a protection order, is a waive of the privilege.[79] Formerly, patent agents when performing their ordinary work were not considered as professional legal advisers and communications with them were not privileged.[80] However, the position of patent agents in this regard was altered by section 15 of the Civil Evidence Act 1968 and is now covered by section 280 of the 1988 Act.

---

[73] *Fuji Photo Film (U.K.) Ltd. v. Carr's Paper Ltd.* [1989] R.P.C. 713 and *Mölnlycke A.B. v. Proctor & Gamble Ltd. (No.3)* [1990] R.P.C. 498.
[74] *Mentor Corp. v. Hollister Inc.* [1990] F.S.R. 577.
[75] *Ibid.*
[76] (1890) 7 R.P.C. 175.
[77] (1890) 7 R.P.C. 175 at p.182.
[78] *Shering Agrochemicals v. ABM Chemicals Ltd.* [1987] R.P.C. 185.
[79] *Minnesota Mining & Manufacturing Co. v. Rennicks (U.K.) Ltd.* [1991] F.S.R. 97.
[80] *Moseley v. Victoria Rubber Co.* (1886) 3 R.P.C. 35.

The meaning of "contemplated proceedings" in the context of *inter partes* litigation has been explained as requiring that the person who was in the position to bring the proceedings has indicated in some way or other that proceedings might be brought.[81] Documents prepared by a party's solicitors for the purpose of obtaining the fiat of the Attorney-General to enable the party to counterclaim for revocation (as was then necessary) were held to be privileged documents.[82]

Secrecy of confidential documents

12.150   In cases where discoverable documents include trade secrets or other confidential information it is usual to limit the persons who may inspect such documents. There is no universal form of order as to who should be included and each case will turn on its own facts. The principles to be considered are set out in *Warner-Lambert Co. v. Glaxo Laboratories Ltd.*[83] and the cases therein referred to.

Action for discovery

12.151   A person may be made a defendant in an action brought specifically to obtain discovery of the identity of infringers where that person (whether knowingly or not) "has got mixed up in tortious acts of others so as to facilitate their wrong-doing".[84] The costs of an innocent defendant in providing such information will be borne by the plaintiff as will the costs of proceedings if the defendant properly doubts whether he should have to provide such information and submits the matter for determination by the court. The plaintiff may, however, be able to recover such costs from the infringer in subsequent proceedings.[85]

The court has jurisdiction to order the discovery of the name of a wrong-doer outside the jurisdiction even though such wrong-doing is under the laws of another country, provided it is shown that the transaction in which the defendant and the wrongdoer here involved related to the same subject matter.[86]

Inspection

12.152   By Order 104, rule 14, before an action for infringement is set down for trial, an application for directions under that rule must be made and disposed of; under paragraph 2(*h*) of the rule of the court may give directions for the making of experiments, tests, inspections or reports.

---

[81] *Rockwell International Corp. v. Serok Industries Ltd.* [1987] R.P.C. 89.
[82] *Vigneron-Dahl Ltd. v. Pettitt Ltd.* (1925) 42 R.P.C. 431.
[83] [1975] R.P.C. 354; see also *Roussel Uclaf v. Imperial Chemical Industries* [1990] F.S.R. 25, [1989] R.P.C. 59, [1990] R.P.C. 45.
[84] *Norwich Pharmacal Co. v. Customs & Excise Commissioners* [1974] A.C. 133.
[85] *Morton-Norwich Products Inc. v. Intercen (No.2)* [1981] F.S.R. 337.
[86] *Smith, Kline & French Laboratories Ltd. v. Global Pharmaceutics Ltd.* [1986] R.P.C. 394.

For inspection prior to the summons for directions an application may be made under Order 29, rule 2, or under the inherent jurisdiction of the court.[87] For the purposes of that Order, however, a manufacturing process is not "property" within rule 2 although machinery is property as to which a question may arise in the action.[88]

The power to order an inspection had previously been assumed by the courts. In *Bovill v. Moore*[89] Lord Eldon said:

"There is no use in this court directing an action to be brought, if it does not possess the power to have the action properly tried. The plaintiff has a patent for a machine used in making bobbin lace. The defendant is a manufacturer of that article; and, as the plaintiff alleges, he is making it with a machine constructed upon the principle of the machine protected by plaintiff's patent. Now the manufactory of the defendant is carried on in secret. The machine which the defendant uses to make bobbin lace, and which the plaintiff alleges to be a piracy of his invention, is in the defendant's own possession, and no one can have access to it without his permission. The evidence of the piracy, at present, is the bobbin lace made by the defendant. The witnesses say that this lace must have been manufactured by the plaintiff's machine, or by a machine similar to it in principle. This is obviously in a great measure conjecture. No court can be content with evidence of this description. There must be an order that plaintiff's witnesses shall be permitted before the trial of the action to inspect the defendant's machine and to see it work."[90]

The object which the court has in view in all cases, where an inspection is permitted is to ensure that the true facts of the case shall be carefully sifted,[91] but at the same time care will be taken that the process of the law is not abused, and that an action for infringement shall not be made a means and lever for the discovery of other persons' secrets.

Prima facie case of infringement necessary

An order for inspection will normally be made as of course if a prima **12.153** facie case of infringement has been made out. An order will also be made if the court is satisfied that there is a genuine and substantial issue to be tried.[92]

---

[87] See *Ash Buxted Poultry, per* Brooke J. (Unrep.) following *Christy v. Arthur Bell & Sons Ltd., per* Lord Cullen August 19, 1987 (Unrep.), Edinburgh Vacation Court.

[88] *Tudor Accumulator Co. Ltd. v. China Mutual Steam Navigation Co. Ltd.* (1930) W.N. 201; and *Unilever plc. v. Pearce* [1985] F.S.R. 475.

[89] (1815) 2 Coop.t.Cott. 56n.

[90] See also *McDougall Bros. v. Partington (No.2)* (1890) 7 R.P.C. 351 at p.357.

[91] See, *e.g. Osram Lamp Works Ltd. v. British Union Lamp Works Ltd.* (1914) 31 R.P.C. 309.

[92] See *British Xylonite Co. Ltd. v. Fibrenyle Ltd.* [1959] R.P.C. 252, followed in *Unilever plc. v. Pearce* [1985] F.S.R. 475.

May be limited

12.154   When the interests of justice require, the inspection will be limited to solicitors, counsel, patent agents independent as well as to scientific witnesses, who will be required to keep any secrets which they may have discovered and which do not affect the question of infringement.[93]

In *British Thomson-Houston Co. Ltd. v. Duram Ltd. (No.2)*,[94] the plaintiffs filed an affidavit of an expert who deposed that he had examined the defendant's products and believed that they could only have been produced by the aid of the plaintiffs' patented process. Inspection of defendants' process was asked for and the defendants swore that their process was a valuable secret. Astbury J. gave leave to the plaintiffs to administer interrogatories, and to ask for samples,[95] and refused to entertain the application for inspection until it should be shown that the answers by the defendants would be insufficient to enable the plaintiffs to present their case.

In a case where the plaintiff's right to inspection depended upon a contract, the construction of which was disputed, and he was unable to show that inspection was necessary to prepare his case, it was held that no inspection should be granted, on the ground that the right depended upon the question to be determined at the trial.[96]

And where the defendant delivered to the plaintiff specimens of the alleged infringing articles, the latter was not allowed to see those articles in actual use on the defendant's premises.[97]

Mutual inspection

12.155   Where it is necessary, the court will order the defendant and the plaintiff to give mutual inspection, and to show both the patented machine and the alleged infringement at work, and to permit either party to take away any of the work or samples of the work which has been done in their presence.[98]

Time for application

12.156   The usual practice is to make the application on the hearing of the summons under Order 104, rule 14 although it may be made at any time after commencement of proceedings (by a plaintiff) or after giving

---

[93] See, *e.g. Flower v. Lloyd* [1876] W.N. 169, 230; *Swai v. Edlin-Sinclair Tyre Co.* (1903) 20 R.P.C. 435; *British Celanese Ltd. v. Courtaulds Ltd.* (1935) 52 R.P.C. 63 at p.80; *Coloured Asphalt Co. Ltd. v. British Asphalt and Bitumen Ltd.* (1936) 53 R.P.C. 89. See also *British Syphon Co. Ltd. v. Homewood* [1956] R.P.C. 225. *British Xylonite Co. Ltd. v. Fibrenyle Ltd.* [1959] R.P.C. 252.
[94] (1920) 37 R.P.C. 121.
[95] See also *Patent Type Founding Co. v. Walter* (1860) 8 W.R. 353.
[96] *McDougall Bros. v. Partington (No.2)* (1890) 7 R.P.C. 351, 472.
[97] *Sidebottom v. Fielden* (1891) 8 R.P.C. 266.
[98] *Davenport v. Jepson* (1862) 1 New Rep. 307; *Amies v. Kelsey* (1852) 22 L.J.Q.B. 84; see also *Germ Milling Co. v. Robinson* (1884) 1 R.P.C. 11.

notice of intention to defend (by a defendant) under Order 29, rule 2. An order has been made before delivery of the statement of claim;[99] and also upon an application for an interlocutory injunction as a condition of the refusal of such injunction.[1] Any evidence in support must be on affidavit.

Notification of experts

Under Order 104, rule 13 of the Rules of the Supreme Court, a party **12.157** who intends to adduce oral expert evidence shall, no later than 14 days before the hearing of the summons for directions, notify each other party, and the court, of the name of each expert he intends to call as a witness. This requirement is without prejudice to the power of the court to restrict the number of expert witnesses.

Summons for directions

No action can be set down for trial until a summons under Order 104, **12.158** rule 14, has been disposed of. The plaintiff should issue such a summons within 21 days of the expiration of the period for responses to the Notices of Experiments under Order 104, rule 12(2), and if he fails to do so the defendant may do so. Each party may apply at the hearing of the summons for any directions which they desire and should notify the other party as to the directions for which it is proposed to ask.[2] The directions usually considered are as follows:

(a) For the service of further pleadings or particulars.

(b) For the discovery of documents and inspection, including the restriction (if required) of inspection to named persons where issues of confidentiality arise.

(c) For the service of any further interrogatories and of answers thereto.

(d) For the exchange of witness statements pursuant to Order 38, rule 2A. Such an order should include the date upon which such statements should be exchanged and whether such statements should stand as evidence in chief pursuant to Order 38, rule 2A(5)(*b*).[3]

(e) For the taking and giving of evidence relating to expert knowledge by affidavit and the attendance of any deponent for cross-examination.

(f) For the exchange of experts reports. The parties' experts may thereafter be requested to identify those purposes of the reports

---

[99] *Elder v. Victoria Press Manufacturing Co.*, (1910) 27 R.P.C. 114.
[1] *Webb v. Kynoch* (1899) 16 R.P.C. 269 at p.273.
[2] See *Solaflex Signs Amalgamated Ltd. v. Allan Manufacturing Co. Ltd.* (1931) 48 R.P.C. 577.
[3] See also Practice Direction (Chancery: Summons for Directions) No.1 of 1989 [1989] F.S.R. 400; see also *Black & Decker v. Flyne* [1991] F.S.R. 93.

which are not agreed and may be required to meet for this purpose and for agreeing a 'primer' of the technology concerned (see below).

(g) For the preparation of all agreed report or 'primer' on the state of the relevant art.[4]

(h) For the directions for the repetition of experiments notified under Order 104, rule 12 in the presence of representatives of the other party,[5] and for any experiments in reply thereto.

(i) For any inspections, sampling tests or reports.

(j) For the hearing of any preliminary issue.[6]

(k) For the mutual disclosure of models, drawings, photographs and films.[7]

(l) For the appointment of a scientific advisor.

Scientific advisers

12.159   In an action for infringement or in any other proceedings under the 1977 Act scientific advisers may be appointed to assist the court or to inquire and report upon any question of fact or opinion not involving questions of law or construction.[8] Experts have been called in the past where there is a conflict of evidence to make experiments and to report to the court.[9] The duty of an expert so appointed "is, instead of determining issues of fact, or of law, to find the materials upon which the court is to act".[10] It is the duty of the court to look at the expert's report and obtain from it (with or without cross-examination, as the case may be) whatever help it can, but the court is not bound to accept the report.[11] In a case in which an assessor was employed in the court of first instance his written statement was read to the Court of Appeal when the case came before it.[12]

Experiments

12.160   Under Order 104, rule 12 of the Rules of the Supreme Court where a party desires to establish any fact by experimental proof, he must serve

---

[4] See, e.g. Olin Mathieson Chemical Corp. v. Biovex Laboratories Ltd. [1970] R.P.C. 157; Valensi v. British Radio Corp. Ltd. [1972] R.P.C. 373; Genentech Inc.'s (Human Growth Hormone) Patent [1989] R.P.C. 613.

[5] See, e.g. Junkers v. Ford Motor Car Co. Ltd. (1932) 49 R.P.C. 345 at 348.

[6] See Minnesota Mining and Manufacturing Co. v. Johnson & Johnson [1976] F.S.R. 66, and post, §12.165.

[7] Photographs sought to be admitted at a late stage may well be excluded, see H & R Johnson Tiles Ltd. v. Candy Tiles Ltd. [1985] F.S.R. 253.

[8] P.A. 1977, s.96(4); R.S.C., Ord. 104, r.11; and see Marconi v. Helsby Wireless Telegraph Co. Ltd. (1914) 31 R.P.C. 121.

[9] See Badische Anilin und Soda Fabrik v. Levinstein (1883) 24 Ch.D. 156; Moore v. Bennett (1884) 1 R.P.C. 129; North British Rubber Co. Ltd. v. Macintosh & Co. Ltd. (1894) 11 R.P.C. 477.

[10] Per Bramwell L.J. in Mellin v. Monico (1877) 3 C.P.D. 142 at p.149.

[11] Non-Drip Measure Co. Ltd. v. Strangers Ltd. (1942) 59 R.P.C. 1 at p.24.

[12] Hattersley & Sons Ltd. v. Hodgson Ltd. (1905) 22 R.P.C. 229.

upon the other party a notice which states the facts which he desires to establish, and giving full particulars of the experiments proposed to establish them. Such a notice must be served within 21 days after service of lists of documents under Order 104, rule 11.[13] Within 21 days of service of the notice the party upon whom it is served must state in respect of each fact whether or not he admits it.[14] Where any fact is not admitted directions must be sought on the hearing of the summons for directions in respect of such experiments.[15]

It is the invariable practice to limit the evidence relating to experiments unless the procedure of notice and subsequent directions has been followed. It is usual to provide that each party shall demonstrate his experiments to the other party and permit the other party with an opportunity of securing drawings, photographs, samples and such other data as the party may reasonably require. It is also desirable to order that reports of the experiments be prepared and, where possible, agreed.[16]

Although Order 104, rule 12 requires details of the facts proposed to be established, if it comes to the attention of the party serving the notice that the experiments he has done establish some other facts he will be at liberty to amend the notice and, provided there is no prejudice or detriment to the other party, such an application to amend will be sympathetically received.[17] Experiments as to matters which arise in the course of a hearing of an action have also been allowed.[18]

It had previously been considered that an analysis to establish infringement was not an "experiment".[19] However, the wording of Order 104, rule 12 is now such as to require any fact which requires experimental proof to be subject to the notice procedure.

The costs of experiments can be considerable and these may be disallowed from a successful party unless the court considers that they were of assistance in resolving the issues before the court.[20]

Dismissal for Want of Prosecution

If the plaintiff unduly delays his application under rule 14 the **12.161** defendant may apply under Order 25, rule 1(4), to dismiss the action for want of prosecution.[21-22]

---

[13] R.S.C., Ord. 104, r.12(1).
[14] R.S.C., Ord. 104, r.12(2).
[15] R.S.C., Ord. 104, r.12(3).
[16] *Oak Manufacturing Co. Ltd. v. The Plessey Co. Ltd.* (1950) 67 R.P.C. 71.
[17] *Van der Lely N.V. v. Watveare Overseas Ltd.* [1982] R.P.C. 122 at 123.
[18] *British Celanese Ltd. v. Courtaulds Ltd.* (1933) 50 R.P.C. 63 at p.84.
[19] *International de Lavand Ltd. v. Stanton Ironworks Co. Ltd.* (1941) 58 R.P.C. 177 at p.198.
[20] *Pall v. Commercial Hydraulics* [1990] F.S.R. 329 at 358.
[21-22] *Baird Television Ltd. v. Gramophone Co. Ltd.* (1932) 49 R.P.C. 227; *White v. Glove (Industrial) Manufacturing Co. Ltd.* [1958] R.P.C. 142.

4. Practice before Trial in the Patents County Court

12.162   The practice of the Patents County Court is regulated by the County Court Rules, including in particular Order 48A thereof, in conjunction with parts of the Rules of the Supreme Court, in particular, parts of Order 104 of the Rules of the Supreme Court.

General practice

Time extensions

12.163 No time limit mentioned in Order 48A, rule 4 of the County Court Rules (relating to service of pleadings) may be extended more than once save by order of the court, that extension being limited to 42 days at the most.[23] All other time limits are governed by Order 13, rule 4 of the County Court Rules, which allows time limits to be extended or abridged by consent or order indefinitely; however, the Patents County Court has adopted a restrictive policy to ordering such extensions.

Outline arguments

12.164 Parties are encouraged to prepare written outlines of their arguments with references to the documents to be relied upon and lists of authorities and to lodge them with the court prior to any hearing.

The summons

Issue

12.165 Actions in the Patents County Court are commenced by the issue of a summons from the court.[24] Every summons must be accompanied by a statement of case.[25] See *post*, § 12.173, concerning the contents of the statement of case.

Service

12.166 Service of the summons and statement of case within and outside the jurisdiction is regulated by Orders 7 and 8[26] of the County Court Rules

---

[23] C.C.R., Ord. 48A, r.4(9).
[24] C.C.R., Ord. 3, Ord. 48A, r.3 and form N4P.
[25] C.C.R., Ord. 48A, r.4(1) and C.C.R., Ord. 3, r.3 as modified by Ord. 48A, r.9.
[26] See also C.C.R., Ord. 3, r.3(6).

respectively in the same way as in a usual County Court action, except that Order 7 is modified by Order 48A, rule 5 to allow service by posting by the plaintiff.

Acknowledgement of service

In the Patents County Court no acknowledgement of service as such **12.167** is required after receipt of the summons. If a defendant wishes to serve a defence (and counterclaim) he must do so within 42 days of service upon him of the summons.[27] Order 9 of the County Court Rules does not apply (apart from Order 9, rule 19).[28]

Stay of County Court proceedings

The principles concerning stays of High Court proceedings pending **12.168** actions in the U.K. or European Patent Offices will apply to the Patents County Court.

Joinder of additional parties

The joinder of additional parties is regulated by Order 5, rules 2 nd 4 **12.169** of the County Court Rules.

Interlocutory injunctions

The Patents County Court is able to grant both final and interlocutory **12.170** injunctions in actions within its special jurisdiction.[29] This includes both *Anton Piller* and *Mareva* relief which other County Courts have no power to grant.[30] An application for an injunction may be made at any stage in an action,[31] but applications prior to the issue of the summons are only allowed in cases of urgency.[32]. Applications are normally made on notice but may, in cases of urgency, be made *ex parte*.[33] Applications will normally be heard in open court and will be dealt with by the patents judge.[34] If the patents judge is unavailable the matter may be dealt with by another judge.[35]

---

[27] C.C.R., Ord. 48A, r.4(6).
[28] C.C.R., Ord. 48A, r.9(e).
[29] (S.I. 1994 No.1609) Art. 3 and C.C.A. 1984, s.38.
[30] County Court Remedies Regulations 1991 (S.I. 1991 No.1222 (L.8)). *McDonald v. Graham* (Unrep.), C.A., December 16, 1993.
[31] C.C.R., Ord. 13, r.6(1).
[32] C.C.R., Ord. 13, r.6(4).
[33] C.C.R., Ord. 13, rr.1 and 6(3).
[34] C.C.R., Ord. 13, r.6(5) and Ord. 48A, r.2(1).
[35] C.C.R. 1981, Ord. 48A, r.2(2). In this case the court would have no power under the County Courts Remedies Regulations 1991 to grant *Anton Piller* or *Mareva* relief (see para. 3(2) thereof).

Principles governing interlocutory injunctions

12.171   The principles governing the grant of interlocutory injunctions are the same as those in the High Court.[36]

Nature of pleadings

12.172   Pleadings are regulated by Order 48A, rule 4 and Order 6, rules 1 to 6 and 8 of the County Court Rules and Order 104, rule 6(2) to (4) of the Rules of the Supreme Court. These rules do not strictly knit together to make a coherent code of procedure but the intention is clear enough, namely that all facts, matters and arguments in support of a party's case must be set out in any pleading.[37] Where a pleading is served which refers to any document, a copy of the document together with an English translation of any foreign text, certified as being correct, must also be served.[38]

In a patent infringement action the usual order of pleadings will be:

(1) Plaintiff's Statement of Case with Summons.
(2) Defendant's Defence and Counterclaim.
(3) Plaintiff's Reply and Defence to Counterclaim.

Plaintiff's statement of case

12.173   Order 48A, rule 4(2) of the County Court Rules governs the contents of the plaintiff's statement of case in an action for infringement and provides that the pleading shall give full particulars of the infringement relied on (see *post*). Order 6, rules 1 to 6 and 8 of the County Court Rules also apply to the Patents County Court. Although they are expressed as relating to "Particulars of Claim", it is submitted, that a plaintiff is intended to produce one pleading complying with all the relevant rules.[39] Under Order 6 the plaintiff must, at the time of commencing an action, file particulars of his claim specifying his cause of action and the relief or remedy sought and stating briefly the material facts upon which he relies along with a claim for interest, if required.

Every statement of case must be signed by the plaintiff if he sues in his own name or by his solicitor or registered patent agent in his own name or the name of his firm and shall state the plaintiff's address for service.[40] In addition, if settled by Counsel, it must be signed by him and his name shall appear on every copy used in the proceedings.[41]

---

[36] See *ante*, §12.37 *et seq.*
[37] See, *e.g.* the Patents County Court Users' Guide, para.4.
[38] C.C.R., Ord. 48A, r.5(2).
[39] See also the amendment to C.C.R., Ord. 3, r.3(1) and (2)(*c*) by C.C.R., Ord. 48A, r.9(*a*).
[40] C.C.R., Ord. 48A, r.4(5), Ord. 6, r.8, and C.D.P.A. 1988 s.292.
[41] C.C.R., Ord. 50, r.6.

Particulars of infringements

In a statement of case full particulars of infringements must be given **12.174** setting out which claims are alleged to be infringed and in respect of each such claim the grounds supporting the allegations of infringement and all facts matters and arguments relied on as establishing those grounds including at least one example of each type of infringement.[42] This provision is analogous to Order 104, rule 5 of the Rules of the Supreme Court, (which does not apply to the Patents County Court) save that the grounds and all facts, matters and arguments relied upon in support must also be pleaded. High Court authorities relating to the pleading of actionable infringements and the pleading of types of infringements will be relevant.[43]

An important consequence of the requirement of pleading all facts, matters and arguments is that the plaintiff must place a construction on the patent at the pleading stage.

Defence and counterclaim

If a defendant wishes to serve a defence to any claim he shall serve it, **12.175** together with any counterclaim, upon the plaintiff within 42 days of service of the summons.[44] Every defence and counterclaim must be signed by the defendant if he acts in person or by his solicitor or registered patent agent in his own name or the name of his firm and shall state the defendant's address for service.[45] In addition, if settled by Counsel, it must be signed by him and his name shall appear on every copy used in the proceedings.[46]

For a discussion on the defences available in a patent infringement action see *ante*, §§ 12.171 *et seq*. If the validity of a patent is put in issue then a "statement of case"[47] is required which must give particulars of objections to validity (see below).[48] The rules do not express whether such a "statement of case" is intended to be a separate document from the defence and counterclaim. In practice, one pleading (a defence and counterclaim, including objections, to validity is convenient in most cases and is not contrary to the rules.[49]

The general practice in the Patents County Court is that all facts, matters and arguments generally relied upon must be pleaded,[50]

---

[42] C.C.R., Ord. 48A, r.4(2).
[43] See *ante*, §12.62 *et seq*.
[44] C.C.R., Ord. 48A, r.4(6).
[45] C.C.R., Ord. 9, r.19 as modified by Ord. 48A, r.9(*e*), and C.D.P.A. 1988 s.292.
[46] C.C.R., Ord. 50, r.6.
[47] Although the rules refer to a defendant's pleading on the issue of validity as a "statement of case"; for convenience and to distinguish the plaintiff's pleading this work will refer to a defence and counterclaim.
[48] C.C.R., Ord. 48A, r.4(3).
[49] Such an approach has been accepted so far in actions in the Patents County Court.
[50] See, *e.g.* the Patents County Court Users' Guide, para.4.

accordingly defences such as a denial of infringement must be supported by all facts, matters and arguments relied upon.

A copy of the defence and counterclaim does not need to be lodged at the court until the application for directions.

Objections to validity

12.176   The defendant must give particulars of the objections to validity relied upon and in particular must explain the relevance of every citation to each claim, with identification of the significant parts of each citation and must give all facts, matters and arguments relied upon for establishing the invalidity of the patent.[51] In addition the provisions of Order 104, rules 6(2) to (4) apply to such particulars.[52] For the application of these rules see *ante*, §§ 12.102, 12.109 and 12.114.

Default of defence and judgment on admissions

12.177   Since Order 9 of the County Court Rules (apart from rule 19 relating to signatures) does not apply to the Patents County Court the usual County Court procedure to deal with judgment in default or on admissions does not apply. If a defendant admits the plaintiff's claim the court could exercise its power under Order 21, rule 5 to enter judgment. If a defendant was in default of defence then, it is submitted, that the court could deem the plaintiff's claim to be admitted and enter judgment likewise. Under Order 21, rule 5, if the defendant fails to appear then the plaintiff must prove his claim to the satisfaction of the court before judgment may be given.

Reply

12.178   A plaintiff may wish to serve a reply and will wish to serve a defence to counterclaim if such is made. This must be done within 28 days of service of the defence (and counterclaim).[53] Although not expressed to apply to the Patents County Court, Order 104, rule 6(5) of the Rules of the Supreme Court provides that a party wishing to rely on commercial success to rebut a plea of invalidity by reason of obviousness must state the grounds upon which he so relies. This practice will be followed in the Patents County Court.[54]

A copy of the reply and defence to counterclaim does not need to be lodged at the court until the application for directions.

---

[51] C.C.R., Ord. 48A, r.4(3).
[52] C.C.R., Ord. 48A, r.4(4).
[53] C.C.R., Ord. 48A, r.4(7).
[54] See the Patents County Court Users' Guide, *ibid.*

Amendment of pleadings

Amendment of pleadings in the Patents County Court, including **12.179** particulars of infringement and objections to validity, is governed by Order 15 of the County Court Rules. These may either be ordered by the court or by consent, subject to the court's approval. The practice in the High Court concerning amendment of particulars based on *Baird v. Moule's Patent Earth Closet Co.*[55] will be followed.[56]

Further and better particulars

The normal County Court power to order a plaintiff to give further **12.180** and better particulars of his claim does not apply to the Patents County Court.[57] However, the procedure governing amendment of documents may be used to the same effect.

Preliminary consideration

Preparation for the preliminary consideration
Within 14 days of the close of pleadings (seven days after the expiry of **12.181** the time limited for service of a reply)[58] all parties shall file and serve an application for directions, signed by the person settling it.[59] Each application for directions shall:[60]

(a) summarise the outstanding issues in the proceedings;
(b) summarise the further steps necessary to prove the applicant's contentions in the proceedings and prepare his case for a hearing;
(c) give full particulars of any experiments the applicant intends to conduct, stating the facts which he intends to prove by them and the date by which he will submit a written report of the results; and
(d) set out all orders and directions the applicant will ask for at the preliminary consideration of the action.

Once the court has received all the parties applications a date is set for the preliminary consideration.

---

[55] (1881) 17 Ch.D. 137 at 139.
[56] See §12.126 *et seq.*
[57] C.C.R., Ord. 48A, r.9(*d*) disapplying Ord. 6, r.7.
[58] C.C.R., Ord. 48A, r.4(8).
[59] C.C.R., Ord. 48A, r.8(1).
[60] C.C.R., Ord. 48A, r.8(2).

Hearing of the preliminary consideration

12.182   At the hearing of the preliminary consideration the judge will review the case with the parties. The procedure is intended to encourage settlement of the litigation and failing that to progress the action in the most efficient and cost effective manner possible.[61] It is clearly the intention behind the rules setting up the Patents County Court that as many interlocutory procedural matters as possible should be dealt with at the preliminary consideration. By Order 48A, rule 8(5), the following matters shall be considered and directions concerning them given where appropriate:

(a) witnesses to be called;
(b) whether evidence should be given orally or in writing;
(c) exchange of witness statements;[62]
(d) provison of Patent Office Reports;
(e) use of assessors at the hearing;
(f) transfer to the High Court;
(g) reference to the Court of Justice of the European Communities;
(h) applications for discovery and inspection;
(i) application for leave under rule 6 (Notices to Admit and Interrogatories);
(j) written reports of experiments.

In addition the following further matters may be considered:

(k) any preliminary point of law;
(l) whether to strike out any point raised in the proceedings;
(m) applications to amend any documents.

Some of these matters are considered in more detail below.

Witnesses

12.183   Witness statements will be required in the Patents County Court. It is the court's policy to treat such statements as the evidence in chief of the witness and to discourage the calling of witnesses of fact on matters which are not "seriously contested".[63]

Although Order 104, rules 16(1) and (2) of the Rules of the Supreme Court does not apply to the Patents County Court (restricting the admission of evidence outside particulars), in the light of the rules requiring the pleading of all facts, matters and arguments to be relied on, the court will not readily allow evidence outside the particulars of infringements or objections to be admitted.

---

[61] See Patents County Court Users' Guide, para.12.
[62] See also C.C.R., Ord. 20, r.12A.
[63] Patents County Court Users' Guide, para.13.

Expert evidence

Order 38, rules 37 to 44 of the Rules of the Supreme Court govern the **12.184** admission of expert evidence in the Patents County Court[64] alongside the court's general power to supervise evidence via directions at the preliminary consideration. The policy of the Patents County Court is to limit the calling of expert witnesses at trial and to encourage the use of expert reports. Accordingly expert reports will invariably be exchanged prior to the trial.

Patent Office reports

The Patents County Court has power to order the Patent Office to **12.185** inquire into and report on any question of fact or opinion in an action.[65]

Scientific advisers and assessors

The Patents County Court has power to appoint scientific advisers **12.186** and assessors to assist the court.[66]

Transfer of proceedings to High Court

The Patents County Court has power[67] to transfer actions to the High **12.187** Court of its own motion or an application. At the preliminary consideration directions, where appropriate, shall be given concerning such a transfer. Applications for transfer must be made on notice stating the grounds relied on.[68] The Patents County Court has a complete discretion to order transfer.[69] In deciding whether to exercise its power the court must consider[70] the financial substance of the action and counterclaim, the general importance of the action, its complexity (factual, legal or procedural) and whether transfer is likely to result in a speedier trial.[71] Section 289(2) of the Copyright Designs and Patents Act 1988 also bears on the court's discretion in that the court must have regard to the financial position of the parties and may refuse transfer, notwithstanding the proceedings are likely to raise an important question of fact or law. The Court of Appeal will not interfere with the Judge's exercise of his direction unless he is shown to have misdirected himself or reached a manifestly untenable conclusion.[71a]

---

[64] See C.C.R., Ord. 20, rr.27 and 28.
[65] C.C.R., Ord. 48A, r.7(1)(*b*).
[66] C.C.R., Ord. 48A, r.7(1)(*a*).
[67] C.C.A. 1984, s.42.
[68] C.C.R., Ord. 16, r.9.
[69] C.C.A. 1984, s.42(2).
[70] The High Court and County Courts Jurisdiction Order 1991 (S.I. 1991 No.1724), para.7(5).
[71] Although no transfer may be made on this ground alone, see (S.I. 1991 No.1724) *ibid.*, para.7(5).
[71a] *Chaplin Patents Holdings Co. Inc. v. Group Lotus plc* (Unrep.) C.A., December 17, 1993.

Discovery and inspection of documents

12.188   There is no automatic discovery of documents in the Patents County Court although it may be ordered at the preliminary consideration. The policy, as stated in the Patents County Court Users Guide,[72] is that discovery on an issue will only be ordered if it is reasonably necessary for disposing fairly of the action and if the issue can be decided without any discovery then that should be done. The duty of full disclosure by a patentee seeking amendment of his patent is not affected by this policy.

    Order 14 of the County Court Rules sets out the governing procedure for discovery and inspection in the County Court.

Inspection of property

12.189   The procedure concerning inspection is governed by Order 29, rule 3 of the Rules of the Supreme Court.

Notices to admit

12.190   A notice to admit facts may be served without leave by either party provided it is served within 14 days of the close of pleadings. Otherwise, the leave of the court is required, an application for which may only be made at the preliminary consideration.[73]

Interrogatories

12.191   Interrogatories may not be served without leave, an application for which may only be made at the preliminary consideration.[74]

Experiments

12.192   The policy in the Patents County Court is to restrict experiments and inspection of property. A party intending to conduct experiments must serve a notice of the facts he intends to prove and the particulars of the experiments to be performed as part of the application for directions.[75]

5. The Trial in the High Court and Patents County Court

Date of trial

12.193   In the ordinary way the date of trial will not be altered because the validity of the patent is about to be considered in other proceedings,[76-77]

---

[72] Para.9.
[73] C.C.R., Ord. 48A, r.6, and Ord.20, r.2.
[74] C.C.R., Ord. 48A, r.6, and Ord.14, r.11.
[75] C.C.R., Ord. 48A, r.8(2)(*c*).
[76-77] See *Muntz v. Foster* (1843) 2 W.P.C. 93n.

but where there are several actions on the same patent and the issues and defences are similar, the practice is to stay them until the principal action has been heard.

Reading guide

No later than 7 days before the date fixed for trial in the High Court, **12.194** the plaintiff's solicitors must lodge the documents in a form to be used at trial together with a reading guide.[78] The reading guide should be short, non-contentious and agreed if possible. It should shortly set out the issues, the parts of the documents to be read on each issue and the most convenient order that they should be read. If thought appropriate the relevant passages in text books and cases should be referred to. In the Patents County Court the parties are encouraged to adopt a similar approach.[79]

Right to begin

The normal rule applies that unless the court directs to the contrary, **12.195** the person bearing the onus of proof should begin. Accordingly in patent actions, the patentee will normally begin, unless infringement is admitted and in proceedings for revocation the applicant for revocation should begin.[80]

Trial of preliminary issue

Where more than one issue is raised, directions may be given for the **12.196** trial of one of the issues as a preliminary point.[81] In general, however, this will only be done where it appears probable that the trial of such issue will decide the action.[82]

In *Sarason v. Frenay*[83] the defendant pleaded *inter alia* that the plaintiff had inserted into a contract a condition contravening the statutory provisions now re-enacted in section 44 of the 1977 Act. This point was ordered to be tried as a preliminary issue, and, being decided in favour of the defendant, the action was dismissed. In *Hanks v. Coombes*,[84] where the trial of the issue of infringement would have involved heavy

---

[78] Practice Direction (Patent Action: Reading Guide) [1990] R.P.C. 60.
[79] Patents County Court Users' Guide, para.14.
[80] As in *Genentech Inc.'s Patent* [1987] R.P.C. 553 at 558.
[81] See R.S.C., Ord. 18, r.11 and Ord. 33, r.3, and C.C.R., Ord. 13, r.2(2); *Toogood & Jones Ltd. v. Soccerette Ltd.* [1959] R.P.C. 265.
[82] See Jessel M.R. in *Emma Silver Mining Co. v. Grant* (1877) 11 Ch.D. 918 at p.927; *Piercy v. Young* (1879) 15 Ch.D. 475; see also *United Telephone Co. v. Mattishead* (1886) 3 R.P.C. 213; *Kurtz v. Spence* (1887) 4 R.P.C. 61; *Bescol (Electrics) Ltd. v. Merlin Mouldings Ltd.* (1952) 69 R.P.C. 159; *A/B Astra v. Pharmaceutical Mfg. Co.* (1952) 69 R.P.C. 312; [1956] R.P.C. 265.
[83] (1914) 31 R.P.C. 252, 330.
[84] (1927) 44 R.P.C. 305; 45 R.P.C. 237.

expense, and related to apparatus of a secret character, the issue of validity was ordered to be heard first.[85]

Trial in camera

12.197   Where the defendant alleged that his process was a secret, part of the hearing was conducted *in camera* and the shorthand notes were ordered to be impounded.[86]

Burden of proof of infringement

12.198   The burden of proving infringement (where it is denied) is on the plaintiff, and, if he is unable to prove it, there is no necessity for entering upon the question of validity, unless there is a counterclaim for revocation. It may, however, not be possible for the plaintiff to ascertain precisely what the defendant has done, especially where the defendant's manufacture is carried on abroad; and in such circumstances, if the plaintiff makes out a prima facie case which the defendant does not answer, it will probably be sufficient.[87] Evidence of experiments a defendant had adduced for the purposes of amendment proceedings in the Patent Office, is not subject to absolute privilege and can be used by a plaintiff to prove infringement.[88] Where the infringement complained of is the sale or user merely of a patented article, and the plaintiff manufactures such articles himself, he must, in order to throw the onus on to the defendant, prove that the article was not made by himself or his agent.[89]

Where the defendant does not appear at the trial but has disputed the validity of the patent in his defence, it is usual for the plaintiff to give prima facie proof of validity, but it has been doubted whether such proof is strictly necessary.[90-93]

Sequence of issues

12.199   In determining the issues raised in a patent action the court must first construe the specification and claims of the patent. Next it must be determined whether the claims, or some of them, are valid, having regard to the matters set out in the particulars of objections. The court must then consider the evidence relating to and the admissions

---

[85] And see, *e.g. Woolfe v. Automatic Picture Gallery Ltd.* (1902) 19 R.P.C. 425; *Stephenson, Blake & Co. v. Grant, Legros & Co. Ltd.* (1917) 34 R.P.C. 192 (registered design); *Murex Welding Processes Ltd. v. Weldrics (1922) Ltd.*, (1933) 50 R.P.C. 178.

[86] *Badische Anilin und Soda Fabrik v. Levinstein* (1885) 2 R.P.C. 73; 24 Ch.D. 156; see also the ruling of *Aldous J. in Bonzel v. Intervention* see *supra.*

[87] *British Thomson-Houston Co. Ltd. v. Charlesworth Peebles & Co.* (1923) 40 R.P.C. 426 at p.456.

[88] *Smith, Kline & French Laboratories v. Evans* [1989] 1 F.S.R. 513.

[89] *Betts v. Willmott* (1871) L.R. 6 Ch.App.239.

[90-93] See *Weber v. Xetal Products Ltd.* (1933) 50 R.P.C. 211.

concerning the alleged infringing act and come to a conclusion whether it falls within the ambit of one or more valid claims. Finally, the court must decide what relief shall be given.

Proof of title

The patentee must prove that he is the registered proprietor of the **12.200** patent in suit. This, where not admitted, is proved by the production of a certified copy of or extract from the register, which is admissible as evidence by virtue of section 77 of the 1949 Act and section 32 of the 1977 Act.

The plaintiff is never in practice required to prove the actual grant itself, or the specification, but this can, if required, be done by the production of the patent itself or a certified copy thereof, sealed with the seal of the Patent Office,[94] and of a certified copy of the specification.

If a defendant desires to prove the absence of an entry from the register he may do so by producing a certificate from the Comptroller.[95]

Issue of validity

The issue of validity is subdivided into the various objections pleaded **12.201** in the particulars of objections. The plaintiff usually gives prima facie evidence in support of his patent in respect of the objections taken because it is forensically advantageous for him to do so, but it is submitted that there is not need for him to do more than to establish his title to a subsisting patent, for the grant of a monopoly by the Crown must be deemed prima facie to be valid. Having proved this much, the onus is thereby shifted on to the defendant. In the case, however, of an objection that the applicant for the patent was not a person entitled under the 1949 Act to apply,[96] it is submitted, that the onus is upon the defendant from the start.[97] If the defendant succeeds in establishing a case against the plaintiff, the latter will be permitted, before the defendant's counsel sums up, to call rebutting evidence,[98] but the defendant will not be allowed, after his counsel has summed up, to adduce still further evidence to corroborate his own case.[99]

Where the objection is want of novelty by reason of publication in a written document, the actual publication of the document must, of course, be proved by the defendant, unless, as is usual, publication is admitted by the plaintiff. Similarly, the onus of proof of an alleged prior

---

[94] P.A. 1949, s.21(1); P.A. 1977, s.32.
[95] P.A. 1977, s.32(10).
[96] P.A. 1949, s.32(1)(*h*).
[97] See *Young v. White* (1853) 23 L.J.Ch. 190 at p.196; *Ward Bros. v. J. Hill & Sons* (1901) 18 R.P.C. 481 at p.490.
[98] *Penn v. Jack and Others* (1866) L.R. 2 Eq. 314.
[99] *Ibid.*

user is on the defendant and must be fully discharged.[1] Where publication was admitted by inadvertence, leave to withdraw the admission was granted on special terms as to costs.[2]

12.202 The construction of every document is for the court, following the ordinary rules of construction relating to written documents, guided by evidence as to the meaning of technical terms therein and as to the common knowledge at the material date. But this does not apply to photographs or presumably to drawings of any kind; as Lord Reid said in *Van der Lely (C.) N.V. v. Bamfords Ltd.*:[3]

> "There is no doubt that, where the matter alleged to amount to anticipation consists of a written description, the interpretation of that description is, like the interpretation of any document, a question for the court assisted where necessary by evidence regarding the meaning of technical language. It was argued that the same applies to a photograph. I do not think so. Lawyers are expected to be experts in the use of the English language, but we are not experts in the reading or interpretation of photographs. The question is what the eye of the man with appropriate engineering skill and experience would see in the photograph, and that appears to me to be a matter for evidence. Where the evidence is contradictory the judge must decide. But the judge ought not, in my opinion, to attempt to read or construe the photograph himself; he looks at the photograph in determining which of the explanations given by the witnesses appears to be most worthy of acceptance."

The decision as to the identity or otherwise of the process or apparatus disclosed by a prior document with that of the patent in suit is, however, one of fact, and where the identity is not obvious upon the face of the documents expert evidence is admissible to resolve the doubt,[4-5] but an expert must give his evidence upon some stated hypothesis as to the construction of the document, and must not purport to construe the document himself. The disclosure which a document (whether it be an alleged anticipation or a specification the sufficiency of which is in dispute) would make to a competent technician is sometimes tested by handing it to a suitable person who is ignorant of the points in issue in

---

[1] See *Dick v. Tallis & Sons* (1896) 13 R.P.C. 149 at p.162; *British United Shoe Machinery Co. Ltd. v. Albert Pemberton & Co.* (1930) 47 R.P.C. 134 at p.158; *Vax v. Hoover* [1991] F.S.R. 307 at 317.

[2] *Van der Lely N.V. v. Bamfords Ltd.* [1959] R.P.C. 99.

[3] [1963] R.P.C. 61 at p.71, followed in relation to video recordings in *Vax v. Hoover* (1991) F.S.R. 307.

[4-5] *Betts v. Menzies* (1957) 10 H.L.Cas. 117 at pp.153, 154; *British Thomson-Houston Co. Ltd. v. British Insulated and Helsby Cables Ltd.* (1925) 41 R.P.C. 345 at pp.399, 400. *British Celanese v. Courtalds* (1935) 52 R.P.C. 171 at p.196.

the case, and seeing what he does in endeavouring to follow its instructions and what results he arrives at.[6]

Expert evidence

The evidence usually given as to validity apart from that as to specific **12.203** facts, such as prior users or commercial success, is that of witnesses who have expert scientific knowledge and are well acquainted with the art to which the invention relates. Such evidence is admissible as to the intelligibility and sufficiency of the specification to a competent technician, as to the novelty and utility of the invention, as to the state of common knowledge in the art at material dates, and as to the meaning of technical terms. The principles as to the degrees of intelligibility, sufficiency, novelty and utility required are, of course, matters of law for the court, as also is the question of whether the alleged invention is inherently proper subject-matter for letters patent.

Experts cannot be asked to give their opinions directly upon the questions which are before the court for its decision, whether they be of law or fact; their evidence must be confined to the facts upon which such decision may be based. Thus, an expert cannot be asked whether or not there has been an infringement or whether or not an invention is obvious, but he may be asked as to the nature of the alleged infringing acts or as to the problem solved by the patentee and the nature of the difficulties involved in its solution.

The function of an expert was very clearly explained by Lindley L.J. in **12.204** *Brooks v. Steele and Currie*:[7]

"It is necessary to examine the patent, and to ascertain first what the patented invention really is; and, secondly, whether the defendants have used that invention. In this, as in all cases, the nature of the invention must be ascertained from the specification, the interpretation of which is for the judge, and not for any expert. The judge may, and, indeed, generally must, be assisted by expert evidence to explain technical terms, to show the practical working of machinery described or drawn, and to point out what is old and what is new in the specification. Expert evidence is also admissible and is often required to show the particulars in which an alleged invention has been used by an alleged infringer, and the real importance of whatever differences there may be between the plaintiff's invention and whatever is done by the defendant. But, after all, the nature of the invention for which a patent is granted must be ascertained from the specification, and has to be determined by the judge and not by a jury,

---

[6] See, *e.g. Actiengesellschaft für Autogene Schweissung v. London Aluminium Co. (No.2)* (1920) 37 R.P.C. 153 at p.164; 39 R.P.C. 296 at p.309; *British Thomson-Houston Co. Ltd. v. British Insulated and Helsby Cables Ltd.* (1924) 41 R.P.C. 345 at p.407.

[7] (1896) 13 R.P.C. 46 at p.73.

nor by any expert or other witness. This is familiar law, although apparently often disregarded when witnesses are being examined."[8]

As to the function of an expert in proving "common knowledge", see the observations of Clauson J. in *British Celanese Ltd. v. Courtaulds Ltd.*[9] As to the function of an expert in proving what a photograph or drawing discloses, see *ante*, §12.202.

12.205   A party is not bound in proceedings against one party by evidence given on its behalf by experts or others in previous proceedings against some other party, nor is such evidence admissible against it in the subsequent proceedings as an admission.[10] If, however, it be proved that such evidence was given, this fact may be very material as showing the previous conduct of the party or of the witnesses where such conduct throws light on any question in issue in the subsequent action.[11] Witnesses may, of course, always be cross-examined as to statements which they themselves have made in previous proceedings.[12] The plaintiff's witnesses can be cross-examined on documents contained in the Patent Office file of the application for the patent in suit, which file can be obtained by *subpoena duces tecum*.[13]

Number of experts

12.206   The number of experts (*i.e.* scientific witnesses entitled to give their opinion to the court) may be limited by order.[14]

Amendment of specification

12.207   Under section 30 of the 1949 Act, and section 75 of the 1977 Act, the court has power in an action for infringement or where the validity of the patent is put in issue to make an order allowing the patentee to amend his complete specification. The practice as to this is dealt with in Chapter 7.

---

[8] See also *Graphic Arts Co. v. Hunters Ltd.* (1910) 27 R.P.C. 677 at p.687; *Joseph Crosfield Ltd. v. Techno-Chemical Laboratories Ltd.* (1913) 30 R.P.C. 297 at p.309; *British Celanese v. Courtaulds* (1935) 52 R.P.C. 171 at p.196; *Glavenbel SA v. British Coal Corp. (No.2)* [1993] R.P.C. 90.
[9] (1933) 50 R.P.C. 63 at p.90.
[10] *British Thomson-Houston Co. Ltd. v. British Insulated and Helsby Cables Ltd.* (1924) 41 R.P.C. 345; (1925) 42 R.P.C. 180. But see Civil Evidence Act 1968.
[11] *Ibid.*
[12] See *British Hartford-Fairmont Syndicate Ltd. v. Jackson Bros. (Knottingly) Ltd.* (1932) 49 R.P.C. 495 at p.532.
[13] *Cascelloid Ltd. v. Milex Star Eng. Co. Ltd.* (1953) 70 R.P.C. 18 at p.35.
[14] R.S.C., Ord. 104, r.13; C.C.R., Ord. 48A, r.8(5)(a).

6. The Remedy

The remedy sought or granted in an action for infringement may **12.208** consist of an injunction, damages or, at the option of the plaintiff, an account of profits in lieu of damages,[15] and delivery up or destruction of all infringing articles in the possession or power of the defendant.

A. Injunction

Injunction based on threat to infringe

The basis of an injunction is the threat, actual or implied, on the part of **12.209** the defendant that he is about to do an act which is in violation of the plaintiff's right; so that not only must it be clear that the plaintiff has rights, but also that the defendant has done something which induces the court to believe that he is about to infringe those rights.

The fact that he has been guilty of an infringement of the patent rights will, in most circumstances, be sufficient evidence that he intends to continue his infringement, but, whether he has actually infringed the patent or not, it will be sufficient if he has threatened to infringe it. Actual infringement is merely evidence upon which the court implies an intention to continue in the same course.

In *Frearson v. Loe*,[16] Jessel M.R. said:

"I am not aware of my suit or action in the Court of Chancery which has been successful on the part of a patentee, without infringement having been proved; but in my opinion, on principle there is no reason why a patentee should not succeed in obtaining an injunction without proving actual infringement. I think, for this reason, where the defendant alleges an intention to infringe, and claims the right to infringe, the mischief done by the threatened infringement of the patent is very great, and I see no reason why a patentee should not be entitled to the same protection as every other person is entitled to claim from the court from threatened injury, where that threatened injury will be very serious. No part of the jurisdiction of the old Court of Chancery was considered more valuable than that exercise of jurisdiction which prevented material injury being inflicted, and no subject was more frequently the cause of bills for injunction than the class of cases which were brought to restrain threatened injury, as distinguished from injury which was already accomplished. It seems to me, when you consider the nature of a patent right, that where there is a deliberate intention expressed, and about to be carried into

---

[15] P.A. 1949, s.60; P.A. 1977, s.61.
[16] (1878) 9 Ch.D. 48 at p.65.

execution, to infringe certain letters patent under the claim of a right to use the invention patented, the plaintiff is entitled to come to this court to restrain that threatened injury. Of course, it must be plain that what is threatened to be done is an infringement."

In *Dowling v. Billington*[17] two acts which fell within the claims of the plaintiff's patent were proved, the first of which took place prior to the acceptance of the complete specification by the Comptroller, while the second was committed a few days after the commencement of the action. Chatterton V.-C. held that neither of these acts constituted an actionable infringement; but inasmuch as the conduct of the defendant showed a deliberate intention to infringe, the plaintiffs were entitled to an injunction upon the principle laid down by Jessel M.R. in *Frearson v. Loe, ante*; and this judgment was upheld by the Court of Appeal.

Evidence of acts after action brought

12.210   Evidence of acts after action brought is inadmissible, except for the purpose of showing that the defendant has an intention of infringing in the future. In *Welsbach Incandescent Gas Light Co. v. Dowle*[18] the plaintiffs attempted to call evidence of acts done since the issue of the writ, not in order to establish threatened infringement, but to strengthen and explain evidence of actual infringement before the writ. Bruce J. refused to admit such evidence.

Contrast of actual and threatened infringements

12.211   If what has been done since action brought differs in any way from what was done before, and is relied on as evidence of the intention to infringe, the defendant must have clear notice of the nature of the infringement which he is alleged to be contemplating. In *Shoe Machinery Co. Ltd. v. Cutlan*[19] Romer J. said:

"Two kinds of action may be brought by a plaintiff patentee. The one is based on this—that the defendant has infringed before action brought, and in respect of this the plaintiff is entitled to claim damages, or an account, and an injunction to prevent similar infringements in the future. The other action is based on the fact, not that the defendant has infringed, but that he threatens and intends to infringe; and in this case the plaintiff may claim an injunction to restrain the threatened infringement. Of course, you may find both kinds of action combined in one, but they are distinct in themselves in several respects. In the first, the plaintiff has to give particulars of

---

[17] (1890) 7 R.P.C. 191.
[18] (1899) 16 R.P.C. 391.
[19] (1895) 12 R.P.C. 342 at p.357.

breaches ... In the other, of necessity, there can be no particulars of breaches; but to avoid unfairness to the defendant, care is always taken that he shall have fair notice as to the nature and particulars of the special infringement he is alleged to be contemplating; and then, no doubt, if after action he commits that special infringement, or substantially that infringement, evidence of it can be given, as it is evidence to show that the plaintiff was right in his allegation that, at the date of action brought, the defendant was threatening and intending to infringe. I may add that if an action, as originally brought by a plaintiff patentee, is of the first class only, but he finds that the defendant has, since action brought, infringed in a way substantially different from his former infringements, leave would be given by the court to the plaintiff in a proper case, and on proper terms, to amend his action, and to bring these subsequent infringements before the court to be dealt with once and for all with the prior infringements."

In *3M v. Rennicks* October 1, 1990 (Unreported) Aldous J. in deciding **12.212** to disallow interrogatories as to how a defendant's process was alleged to have changed subsequent to the commencement of an infringement action, said:

"The third interrogatory is in this form:
'3. Is not the process set out in the Schedule hereto a correct description of the way in which the [defendants product] sold to the first and second defendants for sale in the United Kingdom is now made by the fourth defendants?'
As I understand it, it is quite clear (as far as the defendants are concerned) the material now sold is not made in the same way as the material alleged to infringe. On behalf of the plaintiffs it is said that the defendants threaten and intend to infringe and, therefore, it is relevant to know whether the alleged infringing material is made in the same way as current production and, in particular, to identify which parts of the process are not being used.
If the plaintiffs succeed at trial there will remain two issues:
(1) whether there should be an injunction after trial and
(2) the extent of damages, if any, on an enquiry as to damages.
I need not deal with the inquiry as to damages as the question of whether the current production infringes can be dealt with at that stage. As to whether there should be an injunction, the defendants have not pleaded a positive case that their process has changed. In those circumstances, there being continued marketing of this similar material, an injunction will follow unless the defendants plead and prove some material difference. The injunction would be to restrain infringement and therefore the defendants will incur difficulty in deciding whether their new product does infringe the patent."

Actual infringement evidence of intention

12.213   The actual infringement of the patent is taken by the court to imply an intention to continue the infringement, notwithstanding any promises not to do so, unless it be clear that there is in fact no intention to continue infringing, and an injunction will be granted. Shadwell V.-C. in *Losh v. Hague*[20] said:

> "If a threat had been used, and the defendant revokes the threat, that I can understand as making the plaintiff satisfied; but if once the thing complained of has been done, I apprehend this court interferes, notwithstanding any promise the defendant may make not to do the same thing again."[21]

Mere possession is not necessarily threat

12.214   Possession of an infringing machine may give rise to a presumption of a threat to infringe, but the presumption may be rebutted by evidence of non-user and of the absence of any such intention and in that case no injunction will be granted.[22]

In the case of *Adair v. Young*[23] the defendant was the captain of a ship which was fitted with certain pumps which were an infringement of the plaintiff's patent. No act of using the pumps was proved; but it was shown that the ship was not supplied with other pumps. It was held that the possession of the pumps under such circumstances, although not of itself amounting to an infringement, was evidence upon which the court would infer that the defendant intended to use the pumps should occasion require. And the court, Brett and Cotton L.JJ. (James L.J. dissenting), granted an injunction.

Abandoned user

12.215   In *Proctor v. Bayley & Son*[24] the infringement complained of took place six years before the trial of the action. It was proved that the user continued only for a few months, after which the machines were abandoned as unsatisfactory. It was held by the Court of Appeal, reversing the decision of Bristowe V.-C., that it was clear that the defendants had no intention whatever of continuing the wrongful act, and consequently that it was not a proper case in which an injunction should be granted. Cotton L.J. in his judgment said:[25]

> "There is no doubt that it was a good patent, and we must also take it

---

[20] (1838) 1 W.P.C. 200.
[21] See also *Geary v. Norton* (1846) 1 De G. & Sm. 9.
[22] *British United Shoe Machinery Co. Ltd. v. Simon Collier Ltd.* (1908) 25 R.P.C. 567.
[23] (1879) 12 Ch.D. 13.
[24] (1889) 42 Ch.D. 390; (1889) 6 R.P.C. 538.
[25] (1889) 6 R.P.C. 538 at p.541.

that the defendants have infringed; but the point is this: Is there any ground here which would justify the court in exercising the extraordinary jurisdiction of the Court of Chancery in granting an injunction? That, I think, has been a good deal lost sight of in the argument. It is not because a man has done a wrong that an injunction will be granted against him. If a man has done a wrong which will not be continued, at common law damages may be obtained for the wrong done, which the common law says is sufficient indemnity for that wrong; but then the Court of Chancery says this, in the exercise of its extraordinary jurisdiction: We will not be satisfied with that; we will grant an injunction, because a wrongful act has been done, in order to prevent that wrongful act; and they grant an injunction where a wrongful act has been done, and the court is satisfied of the probability of the continuance of the wrongful act ... But here, although the defendants did infringe the plaintiff's patent, we must consider all the circumstances of the case in order to guide us in the consideration of this: Ought the court to draw the inference that there will be a continuance of the wrongful act so as to justify the court in granting the extraordinary interference and the protection which is exercised by the court of equity?"[26]

Importation

In *Thetford v. Fiamma*[27] the European Court of Justice, observing that the right of a proprietor to prevent importation of products manufactured under a compulsory licence abroad is part of the substance of patent law,[28] held that a proprietor of a patent was entitled to an injunction to prevent importation of products manufactured by a third party in a country where a corresponding patent had never subsisted.   **12.216**

Acquiescence and delay

Positive acquiescence will bar the right of the patentee to an injunction if it amounts to a representation to the defendant that he is free to do what would otherwise be an infringement.[29] Thus, if a defendant constructed machinery, for instance, in ignorance of the existence of the plaintiff's patent, and the plaintiff, aware of such ignorance, lay by in silence and later attempted to obtain an injunction, such relief would probably be refused.[30] Otherwise, however, laches, while a bar to the obtaining of an interlocutory order, would not bar the   **12.217**

---

[26] See also *Hudson v. Chatteris Engineering Co.* (1898) 15 R.P.C. 438; *Wilderman v. E. W. Berk & Co. Ltd.* (1925) 42 R.P.C. 79 at p.90; 1 Ch.116.
[27] [1989] F.S.R. 57. See also Case 24/67 *Parke Davis v. Probel* [1968] C.M.L.R. 47.
[28] Case 19/84 *Pharmon v. Hoechst* [1985] E.C.R. 2281, [1985] 3 C.M.L.R. 775.
[29] *Proctor v. Bennis* (1887) 4 R.P.C. 333 at p.356; 36 Ch.D. 740.
[30] *Ibid.* See *Electrolux Ltd. v. Electrix Ltd.* (1954) 71 R.P.C. 23.

right to a perpetual injunction as "there must be more than mere delay to disentitle a man to his legal rights".[31]

Stay of injunction

12.218   Where the immediate operation of an injunction would cause great public inconvenience, such operation may be suspended for a time to minimise such inconvenience. Thus in *Hopkinson v. St. James' and Pall Mall Electric Light Co. Ltd.*[32] the injunction was suspended for six months on account of the exceptional public inconvenience which would be caused by suddenly stopping the use of the three-wire electric lighting system, the defendants undertaking to keep an account in the meantime. A stay has also been granted to avoid extensive unemployment.[33]

In the past it has been said that the operation of an injunction will not usually be suspended pending an appeal.[34] But the question whether or not a stay should be ordered is a matter for the discretion of the court. The correct approach to exercising that discretion is to be found in the judgment of Buckley L.J. in *Minnesota Mining and Manufacturing Co. v. Johnson & Johnson Ltd.*[35] In recent years it has become the practice to give to the patentee the chance of either giving a cross-undertaking as to damages to obtain an injunction or, if not given, granting a stay pending appeal. The usual order where a stay is granted is that the injunction[36] should be stayed for such time as to enable the defendants to give notice of, or present a petition of appeal, the stay to continue thereafter so long as the defendant prosecuted his appeal with due diligence, provided that the defendant undertook to keep an account or in some cases paid money into a joint account.[37]

Lifting of injunction

12.219   An injunction will not normally be lifted nor will a defendant be relieved from an enquiry as to damages where a patent is revoked at the

---

[31] *Van der Lely (C.) N.V. v. Bamfords* [1964] R.P.C. 54, *per* Harman L.J. at p.81 citing *Fullwood v. Fullwood* (1878) 9 Ch.D. 176.

[32] (1893) 10 R.P.C. 46 at p.62.

[33] See, *e.g. Leeds Forge Co. Ltd. v. Deighton's Patent Flue and Tube Co. Ltd.* (1901) 18 R.P.C. 233 at p.240; *British Thomson-Houston Co. Ltd. v. British Insulated and Helsby Cables Ltd.* (1925) 42 R.P.C. 345 at p.375; and see *Bonnard v. London General Omnibus Co. Ltd.* (1919) 36 R.P.C. 307.

[34] *E.g. Samuel Parkes & Co. Ltd. v. Cocker Bros. Ltd.* (1929) 46 R.P.C. 241.

[35] [1976] R.P.C. 671 at 676; see also *Minnesota Mining and Manufacturing Co. v. Rennicks (U.K.) Ltd.* [1992] R.P.C. 331 at 368.

[36] *Letraset Ltd. v. Dymo Ltd.* [1976] R.P.C. 65, *Minnesota Mining & Manufacturing Co. v. Johnson & Johnson Ltd.* [1976] R.P.C. 671; *E. Warnick B.V. v. J. Townsend & Sons Ltd.* [1980] R.P.C. 31.

[37] *Martin v. Selsdon Fountain Pen Co. Ltd.* (1949) 66 R.P.C. 193 at p.216; *Martin v. H. Millwood Ltd.* (1954) 71 R.P.C. 458 at p.472; *Rosendale Associated Manufacturers Ltd. v. Carlton Tyre Saving Co. Ltd.* [1959] R.P.C. 189 at pp.219, 220. *Bugges Insecticide Ltd. v. Herbon Ltd.* [1972] R.P.C. 197. *Illinois Tool Works Inc. v. Autobars Co. (Services) Ltd.* [1974] R.P.C. 337; *Quantel v. Spaceward Microsystems* [1990] R.P.C. 147.

subsequent application of some other person.[38] However, the defendants' acts cease to be infringing by reason of the revocation of the patent in respect of which the injunction is granted. It is likely that this would apply also to European patents found valid and infringed in the United Kingdom, but subsequently revoked in the EPO on a successful opposition.

An injunction was lifted where a change in the law meant that an injunction was no longer available.[39]

Form of injunction

The ordinary form in which injunctions are now granted is "that the defendants, by themselves, their servants or agents be restrained from infringing the plaintiffs' Letters Patent No.—." But however it is worded, an injunction not to infringe a patent cannot be effective after the patent has ceased to be in force.[40]   **12.220**

In *Saccharin Corporation v. Dawson*[41] and *Saccharin Corporation v. Jackson*[42] actions were brought upon several patents. It was impossible to say which patent had been infringed, but it was clear that one of them must have been. An injunction was granted in respect of all the patents for the life of the patent which would earliest expire.

In *Dunlop Pneumatic Tyre Co. Ltd. v. Clifton Rubber Co. Ltd.*,[43] where there was another action pending on the same patent against the defendants in which another type of infringement was alleged, the injunction was in general form but the plaintiffs undertook not to move to commit in respect of such other alleged infringement but to raise the issue in the other action.   **12.221**

Where an infringer was also a Crown contractor within the meaning of section 29 of the Act of 1907 (now replaced by section 46 of the 1949 Act and 55 of the 1977 Act) the injunction was granted "without prejudice to the rights of the Crown under section 29".[44]

Before the introduction of the practice of ordering delivery up to the plaintiff or destruction of all infringing articles in the defendant's power or possession, it was customary, where necessary, to grant an injunction to restrain the defendant from using or selling, after expiry of the patent, infringing goods manufactured during the term of the patent,[45] but such an order would not now be necessary.

---

[38] *Poulton v. Adjustable Cover & Boiler Block Co.* [1908] 2 Ca. 430, (1908) 25 R.P.C. 661.
[39] *E.I. Du Pont de Nemours & Co. v. Enka B.V.* [1988] R.P.C. 497.
[40] *Daw v. Eley* (1867) L.R. 3 Eq. 496 at p.508.
[41] (1902) 19 R.P.C. 169.
[42] (1903) 20 R.P.C. 611.
[43] (1903) 20 R.P.C. 393.
[44] *Commercial Solvents Corp. v. Synthetic Products Co. Ltd.* (1926) 43 R.P.C. 185 at p.238.
[45] See *Crossley v. Beverley* (1829) 1 W.P.C. 112.

Enforcement of injunction

12.222   A person against whom an injunction has been granted or who has given an undertaking in court is liable to be committed, should he be guilty of a breach of such injunction or undertaking, and a person aiding and abetting such a person and with knowledge of the injunction is also guilty of contempt,[46] but an application for committal, involving as it does the liberty of the subject, will require the strictest proof in its support.[47]

Where an injunction was granted against a limited liability company restraining it, its servants, agents and workmen from infringing a patent, and such injunction was broken by infringement, the injunction was enforced both against the company and its directors, though the enforcement was not pushed to the extent of an order for sequestration or committal.[48] It does not appear from the report precisely how the directors were concerned in the breach, but somewhat different considerations may be applicable in such a motion for contempt from those ordinarily applicable in the case of an action for infringement in which directors are made parties.[49]

Where an injunction is granted in the ordinary form and the patent is subsequently held in other proceedings to be invalid, it is suggested that the proper course is for the party against whom the injunction was made to apply for the injunction to be removed. Where the patent has actually been revoked such injunction ceases automatically and no such application is necessary.

Subsequent amendment of specification

12.223   In *Dudgeon v. Thomson*[50] the plaintiff had obtained an injunction. The specification was subsequently amended, and after this had been done he took proceedings to enforce the injunction. The House of Lords held that he should have brought a new action, since the new specification might be open to objection, and was not the same as the old specification.

Enforcement of undertaking

12.224   Where, in settlement of an action, a defendant offers undertakings to the court these are of identical effect to an injunction in the same terms. Where an undertaking is contractual in form a separate action is

---

[46] *Incandescent Gas Light Co. v. Sluce* (1900) 17 R.P.C. 173.
[47] *Dick v. Haslam* (1891) 8 R.P.C. 196.
[48] *Spencer v. Ancoats Vale Rubber Co. Ltd.* (1888) 5 R.P.C. 46; see also *Lancashire Explosives Co. Ltd. v. Roburite Explosives Co. Ltd.* (1896) 13 R.P.C. 429 at p.441; *Hattersley & Sons Ltd. v. Hodgson Ltd.* (1905) 22 R.P.C. 229 at p.239.
[49] See *ante*, §6.55, 12.12. See also *Multiform Displays v. Whitmarley Displays Ltd.* [1956] R.P.C. 143 (reversed in the House of Lords on other grounds [1957] R.P.C. 260); [1957] R.P.C. 401, and in *re Galvanised Tank Manufacturers Association's Agreement* [1965] 1 W.L.R. 1074.
[50] (1877) 3 App.Cas. 34.

required to secure compliance in the event of any breach. When the undertaking is in the form not to infringe a particular patent a defendant in an action for breach of the undertaking is not entitled to raise the validity of the patent in his defence. He may, however, argue that the acts complained of are different and do not fall within the claims of the patent.[51]

B. Damages

Damages or account of profits

A successful plaintiff is entitled to damages in respect of actual **12.225** infringements of his patent, or, at his option, an account of profits. This latter remedy was abolished by the Act of 1919, reintroduced by the 1949 Act and is kept in section 61 of the 1977 Act. It is to be noted that the profits, or, it may be, losses, made by the infringer are not of any relevance in computing the damage caused to the patentee by his infringements.[52]

The fact that contracts containing terms contrary to section 44 of the 1977 Act were in existence at the date of the infringements will prevent the plaintiff recovering damages for such infringements.

Stay of enquiry or account

The prosecution of the enquiry or account will not normally be stayed **12.226** pending an appeal although provision may be made to secure any sums which may be found due, for example, by an undertaking by the plaintiffs' solicitors to repay such sums, or by payment into an account in the parties' solicitors names.[53]

Principle on which damages assessed

The principle to be applied in assessing damages is that the plaintiff **12.227** should be restored by monetary compensation to the position which he would have occupied but for the wrongful acts of the defendant, provided always that such loss as he proves is "the natural and direct consequence of the defendant's acts".[54] Lord Wilberforce in the *General Tire Case*[55] stated the principle thus:

---

[51] *Heginbotham Bros. Ltd. v. Burne* (1942) 59 R.P.C. 399; and *Van der Lely NV v. Maulden Engineering Co. (Beds.) Ltd.* [1984] F.S.R. 157.

[52] *United Horse Shoe and Nail Co. Ltd. v. Steward & Co.* (1888) 13 App.Cas. 401; (1888) 5 R.P.C. 260 at p.267.

[53] See *J. Lucas (Batteries) Ltd. v. Gaedor Ltd.* [1978] R.P.C. 389; and *Minnesota Mining & Manufacturing Co. v. Rennicks (U.K.) Ltd.* [1992] R.P.C. 331 at 371.

[54] *Per* Lord Macnaghten, *United Horse Shoe and Nail Co. Ltd. v. Stewart & Co.* (1888) 13 App.Cas. 401; (1888) 5 R.P.C. 260 at p.268.

[55] [1976] R.P.C. at 212.

"As in the case of any other tort (leaving aside cases where exemplary damages can be given) the object of damages is to compensate for loss or injury. The general rule at any rate in relation to 'economic' torts is that the measure of damages is to be, so far as possible, that sum of money which will put the injured party in the same position as he would have been in if he had not sustained the wrong. (*Livingstone v. Rawyards Coal Co.* 5 A.C. 25, 39, *per* Lord Blackburn.)

In the case of infringement of a patent, an alternative remedy at the option of the plaintiff exists by way of an account of profits made by the infringer—see Patents Act 1949, section 60. The respondents did not elect to claim an account of profits: their claim was only for damages. There are two essential principles in valuing that claim: first, that the plaintiffs have the burden of proving their loss: second, that the defendants being wrongdoers, damages should be liberally assessed but that the object is to compensate the plaintiffs and not punish the defendants. (*Pneumatic Tyre Co. Ltd. v. Puncture Proof Pneumatic Tyre Co. Ltd.* (1899) 16 R.P.C. 209 at page 215.)"

12.228   Patentees derive their remuneration in respect of their inventions either by utilising their monopoly rights to enable them to obtain increased profits as manufacturers, or by permitting others to use their inventions under licence in consideration of royalty payments. In the latter case the determination of the damages accruing from infringements is usually a relatively simple matter, it being generally assumed that the damage is equal to the amount which the infringer would have had to pay had he had a licence upon the terms normally granted by the patentee.[56]

Where the patentee does not grant licences or makes his profit as manufacturer the court may assess the damages, if no other damage can be proved, upon a reasonable royalty basis. As Fletcher Moulton L.J. said in the *Meters Case*:[57]

"I am inclined to think that the court might in some cases, where there did not exist a quoted figure for a licence, estimate the damages in a way closely analogous to this. It is the duty of the defendant to respect the monopoly rights of the plaintiff. The reward to a patentee for his invention is that he shall have the exclusive right to use the invention, and if you want to use it your duty is to obtain his permission. I am inclined to think that it would be right for the court to consider what would have been the price which—although no price was actually

---

[56] See, *e.g. Penn v. Jack* (1866) L.R. 5 Eq. 81; *English and American Machinery Co. v. Union Boot and Shoe Machine Co.* (1895) 12 R.P.C. 64; *Pneumatic Tyre Co. Ltd. v. Puncture Proof Pneumatic Tyre Co. Ltd.*(1899) 16 R.P.C. 209; *British Motor Syndicate v. John Taylor & Sons Ltd.* [1901] 17 R.P.C. 723; *Meters Ltd. v. Metropolitan Gas Meters* (1911) 28 R.P.C. 157; *British Thomson-Houston Co. Ltd. v. Naamlooze Vennootschap Pope's Metaaldraadlampenfabriek* (1923) 40 R.P.C. 119 (C.S.) at p.127; *Catnic Components v. Hill & Smith Ltd.* [1983] F.S.R. 513.
[57] (1911) 28 R.P.C. 157 at 164–5. Approval in the *General Tire* Case [1976] R.P.C. at p.214.

quoted—could have reasonably been charged for that permission, and estimate the damage in that way. Indeed, I think that in many cases that would be the safest and best way to arrive at a sound conclusion as to the proper figure. But I am not going to say a word which will tie down future judges and prevent them from exercising their judgment, as best they can in all the circumstances of the case, so as to arrive at that which the plaintiff has lost by reason of the defendant doing certain acts wrongfully instead of either abstaining from doing them, or getting permission to do them rightfully.''

In *Catnic Components v. Hill & Smith Ltd.*[58] Falconer J. held that a proper notional rate was that which a potential licensee not yet in the market would pay, disregarding the possibility that he could make and sell non-infringing lintels.

Where the patentee makes his profits as manufacturer (whether or not **12.229** he grants licences in addition) rather more difficult questions arise, such as whether the infringement has deprived him of manufacturer's profits equivalent to those which he would have made had he had the sale of the infringing goods, and what, if any, other damage may have been occasioned to him by their unauthorised sale. In *Smith, Kline & French Laboratories v. Doncaster Pharmaceuticals*[59] damages were assessed on the basis of the difference between the price a parallel importer of infringing products actually paid for the products and the price he would have had to pay in order lawfully, to import the products. Other classes of damage which a manufacturer may well sustain by such illegal competition are loss of goodwill and business connection or losses due to the necessity to reduce the prices of his wares to meet such competition. The onus of proving damage is, of course, upon the plaintiff in each case, but the burden is greatly lightened by the readiness of the court to infer that the wrongful invasion of a patentee's monopoly will in the ordinary course of events cause damage to him, and, further, the court will not be deterred from awarding substantial sums in damages by reason of the difficulty or impossibility of proof of precise figures by means of which the amount of damage can be mathematically calculated.

In *Ungar v. Sugg*,[60] an action in respect of "threats", Wright J. said: "No one can doubt that in this case there was substantial damage, and the difficulty and impossibility of stating the precise ground for assessing it at any particular figure does not seem to be a sufficient reason for giving only a nominal sum." And Lord Esher M.R. in the Court of Appeal said:[61] "They were problematical damages, and had to be what is called guessed at: that is, not a mere guess, as if you were

---

[58] [1983] F.S.R. 513.
[59] [1989] F.S.R. 401.
[60] (1891) 8 R.P.C. 385 at p.388.
[61] (1892) 9 R.P.C. 114 at p.117.

tossing up for the thing, but it must come to a mere question of what, in the mind of the person who has to estimate them, was a fair sum."

12.230   The assessment of damages is especially difficult with regard to infringements which do not actually compete directly with the goods manufactured by the patentee; for instance, where they are of a totally different quality or price or where it is established that, for some other reason, the order in any case would not have gone to him. In such cases the defendant is not excused from the payment of substantial damages, but is compelled to pay what would, upon a reasonable estimate, be the royalty which the patentee could have fairly obtained under the circumstances.

In *Watson, Laidlaw & Co. Ltd. v. Pott, Cassels and Williamson*[62] Lord Shaw said:

> "If with regard to the general trade which was done, or would have been done by the plaintiffs within their ordinary range of trade, damages be assessed, these ought, of course, to enter the account and to stand. But in addition there remains that class of business which the plaintiffs would not have done; and in such case it appears to me that the correct and full measure is only reached by adding that a patentee is also entitled, on the principle of price or hire, to a royalty for the unauthorised sale or use of every one of the infringing machines in a market which the infringer, if left to himself, might not have reached. Otherwise, that property which consists in the monopoly of the patented articles granted to the patentee has been invaded, and indeed abstracted, and the law when appealed to would be standing by and allowing the invader or abstractor to go free. In such cases a royalty is an excellent key to unlock the difficulty, and I am in entire accord with the principle laid down by Lord Moulton in *Meters Ltd. v. Metropolitan Gas Meters Ltd.*[63] Each of the infringements was an actionable wrong, and although it may have been committed in a range of business or of territory which the patentee may not have reached, he is entitled to hire or royalty in respect of each unauthorised use of his property. Otherwise the remedy might fall unjustly short of the wrong."[64]

12.231   Where a manufacturer seeks to recover damages on account of reduction of his prices he must establish that the reduction was necessitated by the defendant's wrongful competition and was not the result of the ordinary exigencies of trade.[65]

---

[62] (1914) 31 R.P.C. 104 at p.120.
[63] (1911) 28 R.P.C. 157 at p.163.
[64] And see *British United Shoe Machinery Co. Ltd. v. A. Fussell & Sons Ltd.* (1910) 27 R.P.C. 205; *British Thomson-Houston Co. Ltd. v. Naamlooze Vennootshap Pope's Metaaldraadlampenfabriek* (1923) 40 R.P.C. 119 (C.S.) at pp.127, 128.
[65] *Alexander & Co. v. Henry & Co. and Others* (1895) 12 R.P.C. 360 at p.367; *United Horse Shoe and Nail Co. Ltd. v. Stewart & Co.* (1888) 13 App.Cas. 401; (1888) 5 R.P.C. 260.

In *American Braided Wire Co. v. Thomson*[66] the patent infringed was one for the manufacturer of a particular form of bustle; no one else being able to put a similar bustle on the market without infringing that patent, the plaintiffs did not reduce their prices until compelled to do so by the defendants, and then only reduced them to the level quoted by the defendants. The official referee came to the conclusion that the plaintiffs would have made, but for the infringement, all the sales that they did make and also the sales made by the defendants, in each case at the plaintiffs' original prices, and awarded damages accordingly. This assessment of damages was upheld by the Court of Appeal.[67]

Price reductions may, to some extent, counterbalance the loss of profit which they cause to the patentee on each article by the increased demand for such articles which they create among the public and this may be taken into consideration.[68]

Regard had to plaintiffs' establishment charges

In *Leeds Forge Co. Ltd. v. Deighton's Patent Flue Co.*,[69] it was held, that in **12.232** arriving at the damages due to competition, regard should be had to the fact that had the plaintiffs received the orders which in fact went to the defendants, they would have been able to make a profit larger than the profit actually made by themselves on similar articles, or by the defendants on the articles actually made in infringement, since the proportion borne on account of establishment charges by each article made would have been materially reduced.

Importance of invention irrelevant

The importance of the plaintiff's invention or of the portion of that **12.233** invention which the defendant has taken, or the ease with which the defendant could have manufactured his goods without infringing the plaintiff's patent, are not in themselves material upon the assessment of the damages suffered by the plaintiff. The principle is that if the defendant's acts are wrongful, the degree of their wrongfulness does not matter, and the defendant must pay such damage as is, in fact, occasioned to the plaintiff by his acts.[70]

Where the infringement is a mere accessory of the article manufactured and sold by the defendant, the plaintiff is only entitled to recover damages in respect of that accessory alone.[71] But where it is an integral part of a machine as a whole, damages may be based on the fact that the

---

[66] (1890) 7 R.P.C. 152.
[67] And see *Wellman and Others v. Burstinghaus* (1911) 28 R.P.C. 326.
[68] See, *e.g. American Braided Wire Co. v. Thomson* (1890) 44 Ch.D. 274; (1890) 7 R.P.C. 152.
[69] (1908) 25 R.P.C. 209.
[70] See *United Horse Shoe and Nail Co. Ltd. v. Stewart & Co.* (1888) 13 App.Cas. 401; (1886) 3 R.P.C. 139 (C.S.) at p.143; (1888) 5 R.P.C. 260 at p.267.
[71] *Clement Talbot Ltd. v. Wilson and Another* (1909) 26 R.P.C. 467; see also *United Telephone Co. v. Walker and Others* (1886) 3 R.P.C. 63.

plaintiff has lost an order for the whole machine, and the profits on the whole machine must be taken into account.[72]

Where a patentee sues a manufacturer of infringing articles and recovers damages for infringement the articles are thereafter free for use by the public if the damages have been assessed upon the basis of total loss of the profit which the patentee would have made had he supplied them himself.[73] Where, on the contrary, the patentee's custom was to hire out articles on an annual royalty basis, and he recovered an agreed sum by way of damages from the manufacturer of infringing articles, it was held that the articles were not "franked" thereby and that users were liable in respect of any use subsequent thereto.[74] Likewise, when an account of profits is taken, the articles subject of such an account do not become franked in the sense that further use and disposal of such items are no longer infringing acts.[75]

Types of infringement not fully determined

12.234   Where certain of the types of alleged infringement were not exemplified in the particulars of infringements and so were not the subject of any express findings, it was ordered that this question should be determined as a preliminary issue in the inquiry.[76]

Exemplary damages

12.235   In the absence of any authority that exemplary damages had been awarded for infringement of patent prior to the decision of the House of Lords in *Rookes v. Barnard*[77] it has been held that a claim for exemplary damages is not available to a plaintiff.[78]

Damages where exclusive licensee is plaintiff

12.236   In awarding damages or granting any other relief to an exclusive licensee who sues as plaintiff, the court must take into consideration only the loss suffered or likely to be suffered by the actual exclusive licensee. If the latter claims an account of profits in lieu of damages, the profits to be considered are those earned by means of the infringement

---

[72] *Meters Ltd. v. Metropolitan Gas Meters Ltd.* (1910) 27 R.P.C. 721; (1911) 28 R.P.C. 157.

[73] *United Telephone Co. v. Walker and Others* (1887) 4 R.P.C. 63; see also *Penn v. Bibby* (1966) L.R. 3 Eq. 308 at p.311, and *Catnic Components v. C. Evans & Co.* [1983] F.S.R. 401 at pp.420–423.

[74] *Ibid.*

[75] *Codex Corp. v. Racal-Milgo Ltd.* [1984] F.S.R. 87; considering *Neilson v. Betts* (1871) L.R. 5 H.L. 1; and *Watson v. Holiday* (1882) 20 Ch.D.

[76] *Cleveland Graphite Bronze Co. Ltd. v. Glacier Metal Co. Ltd.* (1951) 68 R.P.C. 181.

[77] [1964] A.C. 1129.

[78] *Catnic Components v. Hill & Smith Ltd.* [1983] F.S.R. 512 at p.539 to p.541 following *Morton-Norwich Products Inc. v. United Chemicals (London) Ltd.* [1981] F.S.R. 337.

so far as it constitutes an infringement of the rights of the exclusive licensee as such.[79]

Date from which damages are recoverable

The date from which damages should be reckoned in cases where a patent has been amended or where some of the claims are held to be invalid is dealt with in Chapter 7. In the case of 1949 Act patents, damages are recoverable (subject to the six years' limit of the Statute of Limitations) from the date of publication of the complete specification.[80] The court may, if it thinks fit, refuse to award damages in respect of infringements committed during any period in which the patentee is in default of payment of renewal fees.[81] Under section 69(1) of the 1977 Act, damages are recoverable from the date of publication of the application, but no action can be brought until the patent is granted.[82]

12.237

Interest

A successful plaintiff may recover simple interest on all sums payable.[83] Such interest may be awarded from the date of each infringement complained of at a rate which reflects the rate which the plaintiff would have had to have paid had it borrowed the amount payable by way of damages.[84] This should be objectively determined by reference to what it would cost plaintiffs in general to borrow money rather than the particular plaintiff of any one case. In *Catnic Components Ltd. v. Hill & Smith Ltd.*[85] this was taken to be 2 per cent above the clearing bank base rate.

12.238

Position of assignee

An assignment of a patent does not, *per se* transfer an accrued right of action for infringement[86] but such a right can be expressly assigned in the same manner as any other chose in action.[87]

12.239

Innocent infringers

Neither damages nor an account of profits may be awarded against a defendant who proves that at the date of the infringement he was not aware, and had no reasonable ground for supposing, that the patent

12.240

---

[79] P.A. 1977, s.67. See also §§8.20 *et seq.*
[80] P.A. 1949, s.13(4).
[81] P.A. 1977, s.62(2).
[82] P.A. 1977, s.69(2)(a); see also the conditions contained in s.69(2)(b).
[83] Supreme Court Act 1981, s.35A.
[84] *Tate & Lyle Food & Distribution Ltd. v. G.L.C.* [1981] 3 All E.R. 716 applied in *Catnic Components Ltd. v. Hill & Smith Ltd.* [1983] F.S.R. 513 at pp.542–544.
[85] [1983] F.S.R. 513.
[86] *Wilderman v. F. W. Berk & Co. Ltd.* (1925) 42 R.P.C. 79 at p.90.
[87] *Ibid.*

existed.[88] This special defence is not available to an infringer who has been informed of the existence of a patent application in respect of the article in question.[89] It was decided by Lloyd-Jacob J. in *Benmax v. Austin Motor Co. Ltd.*[90] that the protection given by section 59(1) of the 1949 Act:

"is absolute ... It is not in terms directed to the division of a continuing period of infringing use between a state of ignorance and a state of knowledge of the plaintiff's rights ... a defendant who seeks to avail himself of the protection afforded by section 59(1) must plead and prove a complete ignorance of the existence of the patent monopoly during the period in which the wrongful acts were being done."

12.241   Graham J. in *Lancer Boss Ltd. v. Henley Forklift Co. Ltd.*[91] said:

"Clearly the onus is on the defendant to prove that he is innocent at the date of the infringement. This must mean innocent at the date of each separate infringement of which he is accused. He must prove not only that he was not aware that the relevant patent existed, but also that 'he had no reasonable ground for supposing' that such patent existed. Furthermore, the concluding words of the section make it clear that marking goods with the word 'patent' or 'patented' without the actual number of the patent is not enough to justify the court in holding against him. The question, however, arises whether the words 'had no reasonable ground for supposing' are to be read as imposing a subjective or objective test. In particular, even if, as a matter of fact, the finding is that the particular defendant was not aware of the patent in question and did not know of any grounds for supposing it existed, can and should he be held guilty of infringement if there were in fact reasonable grounds for supposing that the patent did exist?"

Graham J. continued at page 317:

"It seems to me that the intention of the legislature in section 59(1) was to ensure that merely marking goods 'patent' or 'patented' without the number of the patent was not ever in itself alone to be conclusive against the infringer in the absence of actual knowledge on his part that such goods were patented. It would also have been expected that if it was intended that marking with the patent number was always to be conclusive against such infringer, the section would have said so. Quite clearly marking the goods with the patent number is a very important factor in gauging guilt or innocence if, as I hold it

---

[88] P.A. 1977, s.62(1).
[89] *Wilbec Plastics Ltd. v. Wilson Dawes Ltd.* [1966] R.P.C. 513.
[90] (1953) 70 R.P.C. 143 at p.156.
[91] [1975] R.P.C. 307 at p.314.

is, the test in the absence of actual knowledge is objective. Circumstances might however exist is which only a few examples of the plaintiffs' patented goods, though marked with a patent number, had been made and sold at the time of the infringement in question and the defendant might not have seen any of them. If so, it might well not be right to hold that at that time there had been sufficient notification to amount to the existence of reasonable grounds for supposing that a patent existed."

This provision does not affect the plaintiff's right to an injunction.

Patents indorsed "licences of right"

If a patent is indorsed "licences of right",[92] in proceedings for infringement (otherwise than by the importation of any article from a country which is not a member state of the European Economic Community) and if the defendant undertakes to take a licence to be settled by the Comptroller no injunction will be made and the damages will not exceed double the amount payable by him as licensee if the licence had been granted before the earliest infringement.[93] There is no such limitation in relation to an account of profits.

12.242

Form of order

Where damages are given, the usual form of order is to direct an inquiry as to damages, the costs thereof being reserved, with liberty to apply;[94] and where the action is in respect of certain claims of the patent only, the inquiry is limited as to infringement of the claims sued upon.[95] A person may not on the inquiry seek to re-open questions of infringement determined by the trial judge.[96] In a case where the evidence was available, and the parties consented, a liquidated sum was assessed at the end of a successful application for summary judgment rather than waiting for an enquiry.[97]

12.243

Where patent afterwards revoked

Where an injunction was obtained in an action, and an inquiry as to damages ordered, and after judgment, but before the inquiry, the patent was revoked on the petition of another person, who adduced further reasons for attacking its validity, it was held that this fact did not

12.244

---

[92] See *ante*, Chap. 9.
[93] P.A. 1977, s.46.
[94] *British Thomson-Houston Co. Ltd. v. G. and R. Agency* (1925) 42 R.P.C. 305.
[95] E.g. *Benjamin Electric Ltd. and Igranic Co. Ltd. v. Garnett Whiteley & Co. Ltd.* (1930) 47 R.P.C. 44.
[96] *Harrison v. Project & Design Co. (Redcar) Ltd.* [1987] R.P.C. 151, 146.
[97] *S.K. & F. Laboratories Ltd. v. Doncaster Pharmaceuticals Ltd.* [1989] F.S.R. 401.

preclude the inquiry from being prosecuted and the damages re-covered. Parker J. decided the case on the basis of an estoppel operating against the defendant. The Court of Appeal, in confirming the judg-ment, decided the case on the basis of *res judicata*.[98]

Discovery on inquiry as to damages

12.245   Where an inquiry as to damages is directed the same principles as to discovery of documents apply as in the case of any other issue which has to be tried between the parties.[99] The defendant must give full discovery, and will be required to set out the names and addresses of the persons to whom machines, made in infringement of the patent, have been sold[1] but not ordinarily the names of the agents concerned in the transaction.[2] The deliberate destruction of records or, in particular circumstances a failure to keep records, will raise an inference of infringement in favour of the plaintiff.[3]

The plaintiff may also be ordered to give discovery of his business books if he alleges a falling off of profits;[4] and of documents relating to prime cost of machinery.[5]

Costs of inquiry

12.246   If the defendant, before the inquiry, should offer a sum in satisfaction, that fact should be recited in the order so that it may be considered upon the question of costs when that question comes to be decided.[6] The costs of the inquiry are usually given to the plaintiff if the damages found due exceed the sum offered by the defendant; but they are usually given to the defendant if the damages do not exceed the sum offered.[7]

Order for delivery up or destruction

12.247   Under the modern practice a successful plaintiff can obtain an order for the destruction or delivery up of infringing goods in the possession

---

[98] *Poulton v. Adjustable Cover and Boiler Block Co.* (1908) 25 R.P.C. 529, 661.
[99] *British United Shoe Machinery Co. Ltd. v. Lambert Howarth & Sons Ltd.* (1929) 46 R.P.C. 315 at p.317.
[1] *Murray v. Clayton* (1872) L.R. 15 Eq. 115; *American Braided Wire Co. v. Thompson & Co. (No.2)* (1888) 5 R.P.C. 375; *Saccharin Corporation v. Chemicals & Drugs Co. Ltd.* (1900) 17 R.P.C. 612.
[2] *Murray v. Clayton* (1872) L.R. 15 Eq. 115.
[3] *Seager v. Copydex Ltd.* [1969] R.P.C. 250 at p.258; applied in *General Tire and Rubber Co. v. Firestone Tyre and Rubber Co. Ltd.* [1975] R.P.C. 203 at p.228 (*per* Graham J.) and p.267 (*per* Russell L.J.).
[4] *Hamilton & Co. v. Neilson* (1909) 26 R.P.C. 671.
[5] *British United Shoe Machinery Co. Ltd. v. Lambert Howarth & Sons Ltd.* (1929) 46 R.P.C. 315 at p.320.
[6] *Fettes v. Williams* (1908) 25 R.P.C. 511; *British Vacuum Co. v. Exton Hotels Co. Ltd.* (1908) 25 R.P.C. 617.
[7] *Clement Talbot Ltd. v. Wilson and Another* (1909) 26 R.P.C. 467.

of the defendant, so as to ensure that such goods are not retained in order to be placed upon the market after the expiry of the patent.

History of order

In the early case of *Crossley v. Beverley*,[8] the possibility above referred to was dealt with by the grant of an injunction perpetually restraining the defendant from selling infringing goods made during the continuance of the patent.[9] In *Betts v. De Vitre*[10] an inquiry was ordered as to what infringing goods the defendants had, and it was ordered that such goods should be destroyed in the plaintiff's presence.[11] In *Plimpton v. Malcolmson*[12] the defendant was ordered to deliver up or to destroy or render unfit for use infringing articles.

12.248

Form of order

The principle underlying the above cases (from which the practice of making the present form of order originated) seems to be the same in each case, namely that the court should protect the patentee from any use after the expiry of his patent of infringing articles made during its currency, and also that such destruction or delivery up would render still more effective the injunction ordinarily granted by the court prohibiting their use during the term of the patent. To this end, though the normal form of the order is for actual destruction or delivery up of infringing articles, it is modified in suitable cases, as, for instance, where an infringing article can be rendered non-infringing by some alteration or by the removal of some part.[13] Nor will an order be made for the delivery up of an article which is not itself an infringement but may be used as part of an infringing apparatus.[14] Careful attention should therefore be given to the exact form of the wording of any order for delivery up or destruction upon oath.[15]

12.249

The defendant is not entitled to any compensation for loss caused to him by such destruction or delivery up, and cannot set off the value of goods delivered up against a claim for damages.[16] But there is no question of confiscation of infringing articles, in the sense that the

---

[8] (1829) 1 W.P.C. 112.
[9] See also *Crossley v. The Derby Gas Light Co.* (1834) 4 L.T.Ch. 25; but see *Monsanto Co. v. Stauffer Chemicals* [1988] F.S.R. 57 at p.62.
[10] (1865) 34 L.J.Ch. 289.
[11] See also *Frearson v. Loe* (1878) 9 Ch.D. 48 at p.67.
[12] *Seton on Judgments* (7th Ed.), p.630.
[13] *Merganthaler Linotype Co. v. Intertype Ltd. and Others* (1926) 43 R.P.C. 381; see also *Siddell v. Vickers, Sons & Co. Ltd.* (1890) 7 R.P.C. 81 at p.101; *Howes and Burley v. Webber* (1895) 12 R.P.C. 465; *Aktiengesellschaft für Autogene Aluminium Schweissung v. London Aluminium Co. Ltd. (No. 2)* (1920) 37 R.P.C. 153 at p.170; *British United Shoe Machinery Co. Ltd. v. Gimson Shoe Machinery Co. Ltd.* (1927) 44 R.P.C. 85.
[14] *Electric and Musical Industries Ltd. v. Lissen Ltd.* (1937) 54 R.P.C. 5 at p.35.
[15] *Codex Corporation v. Racal-Milgo Ltd.* [1984] F.S.R. 87.
[16] *United Telephone Co. v. Walker* (1886) 3 R.P.C. 63 at p.67.

defendant is deprived of his property in them, the only purpose of the order being the rendering of the goods non-infringing to the satisfcation of the patentee.[17] The ordinary order, therefore, gives the infringer the choice between destruction or delivery up without any objection being made at the time by the defendant, it was held, upon a subsequent motion to vary the minutes so as to give the defendant the option, that the original order, not having been objected to, must stand.[18]

In aid of the above-mentioned order the defendant will be ordered to make discovery upon oath as to any infringing goods in his possession or power.[19]

Stay of order

12.250   The order for delivery up may be stayed pending an appeal.[20]

Relief for infringement of partially valid patent

12.251   If in proceedings for infringement one or more claims are held to be invalid but some claim is valid and infringed the court may always grant an injunction.[21] Indeed, once infringement of a valid claim is proved, the patentee is prima facie entitled under section 63 of the 1977 Act to an injunction. As Pearson L.J. said in *Van der Lely (C.) N.V. v. Bamfords Ltd.*[22] in respect of section 62 of the 1949 Act:

"Under these provisions ... it is clear that the claims can be considered separately, and the invalidity of some only of the claims does not invalidate the whole patent, and does not prevent the giving of relief in respect of the claims which are valid. Indeed, I think that the section gives to the patentee a prima facie right to relief subject to the qualifications provided. Under subsection (1) he can apply for an injunction and the court has the usual discretion with regard to the granting of an injunction. If a breach of a legal right is established and there is no equitable bar to the granting of an injunction, and no bar has arisen under subsection (3) of the section, the court will (or at any rate normally would) grant an injunction. It is to be noted that an injunction can be granted without any amendment of the patent."

This approach has been followed by Aldous J. in *Hallen Co. v. Brabantia (U.K.) Ltd.*[23] in relation to section 63 of the 1977 Act.

---

[17] *Vavasseur v. Krupp* (1878) 9 Ch.D. 351 at p.360; see *ante, Codex Corp. v. Racal-Milgo Ltd.*
[18] *British Westinghouse Electric and Manufacturing Co. Ltd. v. Electrical Co. Ltd.* (1911) 28 R.P.C. 517 at p.531.
[19] See, *e.g. British Thomson-Houston Co. Ltd. v. Irradiant Lamp Works Ltd.* (1923) 40 R.P.C. 243.
[20] *E.g. British United Shoe Machinery Co. Ltd. v. Lambert Howarth & Sons Ltd.* (1927) 44 R.P.C. 511; *Samual Parkes & Co. Ltd. v. Cocker Bros. Ltd.* (1929) 46 R.P.C. 241.
[21] P.A. 1977, s.63.
[22] [1964] R.P.C. 54 at p.73.
[23] [1990] F.S.R. 134. See also *Chiron v. Orgenon* [1994] F.S.R. 458; and Chap. 7, §7.27.

Where a valid claim has been infringed, the mere fact that there has been delay in seeking to amend is no ground for refusing an injunction. As Harman L.J. stated in *Van der Lely (C.) N.V. v. Bamfords Ltd.*:[24]

"If the relief asked be by way of injunction, on the ordinary principles well known in the Court of Chancery, where a man's legal rights have been invaded, mere delay will not deprive him of relief; that is stated by Fry J. in the well-known decision *Fullwood v. Fullwood*[25] where he said that there must be more than mere delay to disentitle a man to his legal rights."[25]

The court may also grant relief by way of damages and costs if the plaintiff proves that any valid claim was framed in good faith and with reasonable skill and knowledge;[26] but the court has a discretion as to the costs and to the date from which damages should be reckoned. Unless the plaintiff is blameworthy, it is submitted that the damages should run from the date of the infringement.[27] This imposes on the plaintiff a duty to prove on the balance of probabilities:

(a) that the specification was framed honestly with a view to obtaining a monopoly to which, as the material known to him, he believed he was entitled; and

(b) that as framed it was in the form which would be produced by a person with reasonable skill in drafting patent specifications and a knowledge of the law and practice relating thereto.[28]

The restriction on recovery of damages does not apply to an account of profits.[28a]

The court may, and no doubt normally will, direct that the specification shall be amended to its satisfaction upon an application made by the patentee. The amendments will have to be such as will validate the patent. Similar provisions have been applied where the patent has expired but was subsequently extended.[29] Cases decided under the law prior to 1949[30] are of doubtful authority and must in any case be read in relation to the language of the statutes in force at the time which can only be considered as background.[31]

---

[24] [1964] R.P.C. 54 at p.81.

[25] (1878) 9 Ch.D. 176.

[26] P.A. 1977, s.63(2).

[27] See *David Kahn Inc. v. Conway Stewart & Co. Ltd.* [1974] R.P.C. 279; see *ante, Hallen Co. v. Brabantia (U.K.) Ltd.* [1990] F.S.R. 134.

[28] *Hallen Co. v. Brabantia (U.K.) Ltd.* [1990] F.S.R. 134; following *General Tire & Rubber Co. v. Firestone Tyre & Rubber Co. Ltd.* [1975] R.P.C. 203 at pp.269–270; see also *Rediffusion Simulation Ltd. v. Link Miles Ltd.* [1993] F.S.R. 369 and Chap. 7, §§7.56 *et seq.*

[28a] *Codex Corporation v. Racal-Milgo Ltd.* [1982] R.P.C. 369.

[29] *Leggatt v. Hood's Original Darts Accessories Ltd.* (1951) 68 R.P.C. 3; but see *David Kahn Inc. v. Conway Stewart & Co. Ltd.* [1974] R.P.C. 279.

[30] See, *e.g. Tucker v. Wandsworth* (1925) 42 R.P.C. 480; *Eyres v. Grundy* (1939) 56 R.P.C. 253; *Raleigh Cycle Co. Ltd. v. H. Miller & Co. Ltd.* (1950) 67 R.P.C. 226.

[31] See *ante, Hallen Co. v. Brabantia (U.K.) Ltd.* [1990] F.S.R. 134.

The court may impose terms on allowing the patent to be amended, or some limitation ordered as to the date on which damages would be reckoned. Whether or not the court does so will depend upon the particular facts of each case. The defendant must establish:

(a) that he received reasonable advice that the patent was not infringed or was invalid;
(b) that he acted on that advice to his detriment; and
(c) that the advice given was based in some way upon the defect to be cured by the amendment.

The court should also consider in the public interest whether the defect could have caused persons not before the court to act to their detriment, when it might be proper to allow the amendment only subject ot conditions safeguarding the position of such persons.[32]

C. Certificate of contested validity

12.252   At the close of an action for infringement where the issue of validity is raised and the patent is upheld, the plaintiff should obtain a certificate of contested validity entitling him to a special privilege in subsequent actions. In order to prevent a patentee from being put repeatedly to the expense of defending successive attacks on the validity of his patent, it is enacted that a court may in any proceedings certify that validity of any claim[33] was contested in those proceedings and in that case, if in any subsequent proceedings for infringement or for revocation of the patent the patentee is successful, he is entitled to costs as between solicitor and client so far as that claim is concerned unless the court otherwise directs.[34]

Both as regards the grant of a certificate of contested validity and as regards the subsequent direction depriving a plaintiff of solicitor and client costs, the power conferred upon the court is purely discretionary, and is exercised upon the facts of the particular case before the court. It is difficult, therefore, to extract from the many reported decisions any guiding principles upon which such certificates or directions should be granted.[35]

In general, however, a certificate will not be granted unless there has

---

[32] *General Tire & Rubber Co. (Frost's) Patent* [1974] R.P.C. 207 at pp.227–228; considered in *Hallen Co. v. Brabantia (U.K.) Ltd.* [1990] F.S.R. 134.
[33] See *Ludlow Jute Co. Ltd. v. James Low & Co. Ltd.* (1953) 70 R.P.C. 69.
[34] P.A. 1977, s.65.
[35] See *Letraset International Ltd. v. Mecanorma Ltd.* [1975] F.S.R. 125.

been a real contest as to validity,[36] although in exceptional circumstances the court may depart from this rule.[37]

Where the question of validity was disputed upon a certain construction of a specification only, and not generally, a certificate has been
refused.[38]

When a certificate of validity has once been granted there is no need
for another in a subsequent action upon the same patent.[39] In one case,
however, a fresh certificate was granted where validity was attacked on
new grounds.[40]

If the specification is amended after the granting of the certificate, so
as to affect the claim or claims certified, the certificate will no longer
hold good, and a new one must be applied for in any subsequent
action.[41]

Certificates are granted in respect of any individual claims of a patent
which come into question.[42]

Certificate in threats action

Under the law prior to 1949, it was doubtful whether a certificate of **12.253**
contested validity could be granted in a threats action.[43] The words of
the 1949 and 1977 Acts[44] are plainly wide enough to enable this to be
done. Such certificates can also be granted by the Court of Appeal when
a decision by the court of first instance is reversed.[45]

Where a patent which has been held to be invalid in the lower courts is
held valid by the House of Lords, the practice is for the House of Lords
to remit the matter to the Chancery Division with a direction to grant a
certificate of validity and, where necessary such other certificates to
which the patentee may be entitled.[46]

It has been held that a certificate that the validity of a claim was
contested is not a judgment or order within section 19 of the Judicature
Act 1873 (now section 18(1) of the Supreme Court Act 1981; and no

---

[36] *Gillette Industries Ltd. v. Bernstein* (1941) 58 R.P.C. 271 at p.285; *Martin v. C.B. Projection
(Engineering) Ltd.* (1948) 65 R.P.C. 361. See also *British Thomson-Houston Co. Ltd. v. Corona
Lamp Works Ltd.* (1921) 38 R.P.C. 49 at p.93; *Auster Ltd. v. Perfect Motor Equipments Ltd.*
(1924) 41 R.P.C. 482 at p.498; *Brupat v. Smith* [1985] F.S.R. 156.
[37] *Gillette Industries Ltd. v. Bernstein* [1942] 58 R.P.C. 271 at p.285.
[38] *New Inverted Incandescent Gas Lamp Co. Ltd. v. Globe Light Ltd.* (1906) 23 R.P.C. 157; and
see *Morris and Bastert v. Young* (1895) 12 R.P.C. 455 at pp.464, 465.
[39] *Edison and Swan Electric Light Co. v. Holland* (1889) 6 R.P.C. 243 at p.287.
[40] See *Flour Oxidising Co. Ltd. v. J. and R. Hutchinson* (1909) 26 R.P.C. 597 at p.638.
[41] *Brooks & Co. Ltd. v. Rendall, Underwood & Co. Ltd.* (1906) 23 R.P.C. 17 at p.27.
[42] P.A. 1977, s.65; and see, *e.g.* *Marconi's Wireless Telegraph Co. Ltd. v. Mullard Radio Valve
Co. Ltd.* (1923) 40 R.P.C. 1 at p.27; *British United Shoe Machinery Co. Ltd. v. Gimson Shoe
Machinery Co. Ltd. (No.2)* (1929) 46 R.P.C. 137.
[43] See, *e.g.* *Crampton v. Patents Investments Co.* (1888) 5 R.P.C. 382; *Pittevil & Co. v.
Brackelsberg Melting Processes Ltd.* (1932) 49 R.P.C. 73.
[44] P.A. 1949, s.64; P.A. 1977, s.65. *Cannon K.K.'s Appn.* [1982] R.P.C. 550.
[45] See *Cole v. Saqui* (1888) 40 Ch.D. 132; (1888) 5 R.P.C. 41 at p.45.
[46] *British Thomson-Houston Co. Ltd. v. Corona Lamp Works Ltd.* (1922) 39 R.P.C. 49 at p.95;
Van der Lely v. Rustons [1993] R.P.C. 45.

appeal, therefore, lies from the decision of the judge granting or withholding the certificate.[47]

The subsequent action

12.254   Under the 1949 Act it was the law that a certificate of contested validity granted in one action will not affect the costs in another, although decided at a later date, provided that the latter proceedings were instituted before the grant of the certificate in the earlier action.[48] Under section 65(2) of the 1977 Act, however, it has been held that a party to existing proceedings who has challenged the validity of a patent may elect either to proceed with the challenge or accept the certificate. If he adopts the former course and loses he will be liable to pay the higher scale costs.[48a]

Discretion as to costs

12.255   The court in the subsequent action has an unlimited discretion, which it exercises in view of the facts of the particular case; thus, a direction depriving the plaintiffs of solicitor and client costs was made where the second action was vexatious[49] or where the issue of validity was not raised therein, and the defendants were innocent infringers[50] or had a plausible argument with respect to non-infringement.[51] The mere fact that validity is not disputed in the subsequent action is not, however, sufficient to cause such a direction to be made,[52] some special reason being required.[53]

Solicitor and client costs are refused in respect of the issue of validity where the plaintiff is successful upon that issue but fails owing to non-infringement, as the party relying on the validity of the patent must obtain a final order or judgment in his favour.[54]

The court has on occasion refused to go behind the certificate of validity and inquire as to the circumstances in which it was granted;[55] but the modern tendency is to order only party and party costs in cases

---

[47] *Haslam & Co. v. Hall (No.2)* (1888) 5 R.P.C. 144.

[48] *Automatic Weighing Machine Co. v. International Hygienic Society* (1889) 6 R.P.C. 475 at p.480; *Saccharin Corp. Ltd. v. Anglo-Continential Chemical Works Ltd.* [1901] 1 Ch. 414; (1900) 17 R.P.C. 307 at p.320. See *Letraset International Ltd. v. Mecanorma Ltd.* [1975] F.S.R. 125.

[48a] See *Mölnlycke AB v. Proctor & Gamble Ltd. (No. 5)* [1994] R.P.C. 49 at 140–141.

[49] *Proctor v. Sutton Lodge Chemical Co.* (1888) 5 R.P.C. 184.

[50] *Boyd v. Tootal Broadhurst Lee Co. Ltd.* (1894) 11 R.P.C. 175 at p.185.

[51] *Saccharin Corp. Ltd. v. Dawson* (1902) 19 R.P.C. 169 at p.173.

[52] *United Telephone Co. Ltd. v. Patterson* (1889) 6 R.P.C. 140; *British Vacuum Cleaner Co. v. Exton Hotels Ltd.* (1908) 25 R.P.C. 617 at p.629.

[53] *Welsbach Incandescent Gas Light Co. Ltd. v. Daylight Incandescent Mantle Co. Ltd.* (1899) 16 R.P.C. 344 at p.353.

[54] P.A. 1977, s.65(2) and see *Higginson and Arundel v. Pyman* (1926) 43 R.P.C. 113 at p.136.

[55] *Fabriques de Produits Chimique etc. v. Lafitte* (1899) 16 R.P.C. 61 at p.68; *Peter Pilkington Ltd. v. B. and S. Massey* (1904) 21 R.P.C. 421 at p.438; *Badische Anilin und Soda Fabrik v. W. G. Thompson & Co. Ltd.* (1904) 21 R.P.C. 473 at p.480.

where the real substantial trial of validity has taken place in the subsequent action.[56]

In *Otto v. Steel*[57] solicitor and client costs were refused on the ground that the validity of the patent was attacked on new grounds,[58] but it is unlikely that that case will be followed at the present time, save in exceptional circumstances.

Solicitor and client costs have also been refused where the patent has been amended since the certificate of validity was granted.[59]

D. Costs

The principles of apportionment of costs and those concerning partially valid patents apply to both the High Court and the Patents County Court.

12.256

Apportionment of costs

The issue typically arises when the plaintiff loses the action as a whole but succeeds either on the issue of infringement (the patent being invalid) or validity (but no infringement). In making orders apportioning the costs of an action and counterclaim, in the exercise of its discretion, the court has had to reconcile two competing principles, on the one hand, prima facie, the costs of litigation should follow the event,[60] but on the other hand the costs order ought to reflect the extent to which costs have been thrown away by one party raising and pursuing unsuccessful points.[61] This question was considered by Aldous J. in *Rediffusion Simulation Ltd. v. Link Miles Ltd.*[62] where he stated:

12.257

> "The general principles to be applied when ordering costs were set out by Nourse L.J. in *Re Elgindata Ltd.* [1992] T.L.R. 299. He said:
> 'The applicable principles were:
>   (1) Costs were in the discretion of the court.
>   (2) They should follow the event, except when it appeared that in the circumstances some other order should be made.
>   (3) The general rule did not cease to apply because the successful

---

[56] *British Thomson-Houston Co. Ltd. v. Corona Lamp Works Ltd.* (1922) 39 R.P.C. 49 at p.93; *Auster Ltd. v. Perfecta Motor Equipments Ltd.* (1924) 41 R.P.C. 482 at p.498.
[57] (1886) 3 R.P.C. 109 at p.120.
[58] See also *Flour Oxidising Co. Ltd. v. J. and R. Hutchinson* (1909) 26 R.P.C. 597 at p.638.
[59] *J. B. Brooks & Co. Ltd. v. Rendall, Underwood & Co. Ltd.* (1907) 24 R.P.C. 17 at p.27.
[60] See R.S.C., Ord. 62, r.3(3); and, in relation to the Patents Court, *Omron Tateisi Co.'s Appn.* [1981] R.P.C. 25; *Extrude Hone Corp.'s Patent* [1983] R.P.C. 361.
[61] The provision of certificates is an application of this principle.
[62] [1993] F.S.R. 369 at 410.

party raised issues or made allegations on which he failed, but that where that had caused a significant increase in the length of the proceedings he could be deprived of the whole or part of his costs.

(4) Where the successful party raised issues or allegations improperly or unreasonably the court could not only deprive him of his costs but might order him to pay the whole or a part of the unsuccessful party's costs.

A successful party who neither improperly nor unreasonably raised issues or made allegations on which he failed ought not to be ordered to pay any part of the unsuccessful party's costs.'

Those principles are in general applicable to patent actions, but it is necessary in patent actions to take into account the large number of issues involved and the very extensive costs that can be incurred. Therefore there should be added to the general principles set out by Nourse L.J., the further principle that the costs order in patent actions should, in appropriate cases, reflect the extent to which significant sums of costs have been thrown away by reason of one party, albeit successful, overall raising and pursuing unsuccessful points. (See the judgment of Nicholls L.J. in *Van der Lely N.V. v. Ruston's Engineering Company (No.2)* [1993] R.P.C. 45.) That principle is not new to patent actions.''

As Aldous J. observed, there is no settled way in which the discretion is exercised and the practice of the court has not been uniform.

12.258   In cases where the plaintiff has lost overall the defendant is normally awarded the general costs of the action. However, when the court has revoked a patent but found that it would have been infringed had it been valid, the increase in the plaintiff's costs caused by the defendant contesting infringement have been awarded to the plaintiff.[63] In *Badische Anilin und Soda Fabrik v. Levinstein*,[64] Bowen L.J. said:

"I am of opinion in this case that the plaintiffs should have the costs occasioned by the issues raised by the particulars of breaches, and that in respect of all the other costs the costs in the action should follow the usual result and be awarded to the successful party. It seems to me that without laying down any hard-and-fast line, or trying to fetter our discretion at a future period, in any other case, we are acting on a sensible and sound principle, namely, the principle that the parties ought not, even if right in the action, to add to the expenses of an action by fighting issues in which they are in the wrong. It may be very reasonable with regard to their own interest,

---

[63] See, *e.g. Badische Anilin und Soda Fabrik v. Levinstein* (1885) 29 Ch.D. 366 at p.418; (1885) 2 R.P.C. 73 at p.118; *Haslam Co. v. Hall* (1888) 5 R.P.C. 1 at p.25; *Cassel Gold Extracting Co. Ltd. v. Cyanide Gold Recovery Syndicate* (1894) 11 R.P.C. 638 at p.652; *Metropolitan-Vickers Electrical Co. Ltd. v. British Thomson-Houston Co. Ltd.* (1925) 42 R.P.C. 143 at p.178.

[64] (1885) 29 Ch.D. 366 at p.418; (1885) 2 R.P.C. 73 at p.118.

and may help them in the conduct of the action, that they should raise issues in which, in the end, they are defeated, but the defendant who does so does it in his own interest, and I think he ought to do it at his own expense. The order, therfore, I think ought to be as I have stated."[65]

In some cases where a patent is held to be invalid by reason of some only of the objections particularised against it and not of the others, the plaintiff has been granted the cost of the unsuccessful objections and the defendant that of the successful ones.[66]

Equally when the court has found the patent to be valid but not infringed the increase in the plaintiff's costs caused by the unsuccessful plea of invalidity have been awarded to the plaintiff.[67]

The same practice was followed in *Marconi's Wireless Telegraph Co. Ltd. v. Mullard Radio Valve Co. Ltd.*[68] the defendants being given amongst their costs upon the issue of infringement the cost of putting in evidence such of the matters referred to in their particulars of objections as were necessary for the purpose of explaining the scope and ambit of the plaintiff's patent.[69]

But in *Vaisey v. Toddlers Footwear (1954) Ltd.*,[70] where the defendants failed on the issue of validity but succeeded on the issue of infringement, a different course was adopted, the defendants being given the costs of the action less the costs incurred in respect of those particulars in the particulars of objections not certified as reasonable and proper.

In some cases the increased costs of the issue in respect of which the plaintiff was successful have been awarded to neither side.[71]

Thus, it may be said that when the issues of infringement and validity are sufficiently distinct and where the costs have been materially increased by the defendant fighting an issue in respect of which the plaintiff was successful the costs of that issue would normally be given to the plaintiff. In several cases, however, where patents were held invalid, it was held that the defendant had acted reasonably in pleading non-infringement, even though, save insofar as it might always be said that there could be no infringement of an invalid patent, he did not

---

[65] See also *No-Fume Ltd. v. Frank Pitchford & Co. Ltd.* (1935) 52 R.P.C. 231 at p.253 but see *Vaisey v. Toddlers Footwear (1954) Ltd.* [1957] R.P.C. 90 at pp. 103–104.

[66] *Lister v. Norton Bros. & Co.* (1886) 3 R.P.C. 199 at p.211.

[67] *Godfrey v. Hancock & Co. (Engineers) Ltd.* (1925) 42 R.P.C. 407 at p.431; *Higginson and Arundel v. Pyman* (1926) 43 R.P.C. 113 at 134; *N.V. Hollandsche Glas-en Metaalbank v. Rockware Glass Syndicate Ltd.* (1932) 49 R.P.C. 288 at p.323.

[68] (1923) 40 R.P.C. 1 at p.29; (1923) 40 R.P.C. 159 at p.178.

[69] See also *Brown v. Sperry Gyroscope Co. Ltd.* (1925) 42 R.P.C. 111 at p.141; and *Marconi Wireless Telegraph Co. Ltd. v. Philips Lamps Ltd.* (1933) 50 R.P.C. 287 at p.314.

[70] [1957] R.P.C. 90 at pp.103–104.

[71] See, *e.g. Needham and Kite v. Johnson & Co.* (1884) 1 R.P.C. 49 at p.59; *Peter Pilkington Ltd. v. Massey* (1904) 21 R.P.C. 696 at p.712; *Rondo Co. Ltd. v. Gramophone Co. Ltd.* (1929) 46 R.P.C. 378 at p.395.

succeed in establishing that plea, and costs of the issue of infringement were awarded to the defendant.[72]

If some only of the claims pleaded as having been infringed are found to be infringed while others are not infringed the plaintiff will normally get the whole of the costs.[73]

Costs where patent partially valid

12.259   If the patentee obtains relief in respect of some claim which is held valid and infringed in a case where one or more other claims are invalid,[74] no costs will be awarded to him unless he proves that the invalid claims were framed in good faith and with reasonable skill and knowledge.[75]

Where actions are brought upon more than one patent and the plaintiff is successful as to some but not all of the patents sued on, it is usual for the costs to be apportioned.[76]

Where apportionment would be very difficult and expensive the judge at the trial will, instead of making an order as to costs in the usual form, order that the entire taxed costs are to be divided between the parties in definite proportions,[77] or where it seems fair to him will award no costs at all.[78]

E. Costs in the High Court

Certificates as to particulars of infringement and of objections

12.260   Order 62, Appendix 2, Part 1, paragraph 3 of the Rules of the Supreme Court, provides that if an action, or petition or counterclaim for revocation, proceeds to trial, no costs shall be allowed in respect of any issues raised in the particulars of infringements or particulars of

---

[72] See, *e.g. Guibert-Martin v. Kerr and Jubb* (1887) 4 R.P.C. 18 at p.23; *Kaye v. Chubb & Sons Ltd.* (1887) 4 R.P.C. 289 at p.300; *Blakey & Co. v. Latham Co.* (1889) 6 R.P.C. 29 at p.38; 184 at p.190; *Westley, Richards & Co. v. Perkes* (1893) 10 R.P.C. 181 at p.194; *Haskell Golf Ball Co. Ltd. v. Hutchinson (No.2)* (1906) 23 R.P.C. 125; *Harris v. Brandreth* (1925) 42 R.P.C. 471 at p.479; *White v. Todd Oil Burners Ltd.* (1929) 46 R.P.C. 275 at p.293.

[73] See, *e.g. Auster Ltd. v. Perfecta Motor Equipments Ltd.* (1924) 41 R.P.C. 482 at p.498; *Mergenthaler Linotype Co. v. Intertype Ltd.* (1926) 43 R.P.C. 239 at p.270; but *cf. Mouchel v. Coignet* (1906) 23 R.P.C. 649.

[74] P.A. 1977, s.63(1).

[75] P.A. 1977, s.63(2) and see *Hale v. Coombes* (1925) 42 R.P.C. 328 at p.350; *Ronson Products Ltd. v. Lewis & Co.* [1963] R.P.C. 103 at p.138.

[76] See, *e.g. Hocking v. Fraser* (1886) 3 R.P.C. 3; *Brooks v. Lamplugh* (1898) 15 R.P.C. 33 at p.52.

[77] See, *e.g. Incandescent Gas Light Co. Ltd. v. Sunlight Incandescent Gas Lamp Co. Ltd.* (1896) 13 R.P.C. 333 at p.345; *Monnet v. Beck* (1897) 14 R.P.C. 777 at p.850; *Lektophone Corp. v. S. G. Brown Ltd.* (1929) 46 R.P.C. 203 at p.235; *Lister v. Thorp, Medley & Co.* (1930) 47 R.P.C. 99 at p.114; *Marconi Wireless Telegraph Co. Ltd. v. Philips Lamps Ltd.* (1933) 50 R.P.C. 287 at p.313; *Vaisey v. Toddlers Footwear (1954) Ltd.* [1957] R.P.C. 90 at p.103; *Birmingham Sound Reproducers Ltd. v. Collaro Ltd.* [1956] R.P.C. 53 at p.71.

[78] *Hale v. Coombes* (1923) 40 R.P.C. 283 at p.319; *Rondo Co. Ltd. v. Gramophone Co. Ltd.*(1929) 46 R.P.C. 378 at p.396.

objections unless the court certifies that such issues or particulars have been proven or were reasonable.[79] If the action does not proceed to trial, the costs of these matters are in the discretion of the Taxing Master. The time for obtaining such certificates is at the conclusion of the trial, and omission to apply then will subject the party to the costs of any later application to that end, though it will not preclude him from obtaining a certificate if he applies within a reasonable time.[80]

Infringements

Where the defendant does not appear at the trial the court will usually **12.261** certify for the particulars of infringements on the ground that the defendant's non-appearance is evidence that they are reasonable.[81]

A certificate as to particulars of infringements having been "reasonable and proper", but not that they have been "proved",[82] may be obtained where a plaintiff is awarded the costs of the issue of infringement even though he may have failed in is action on account of invalidity of his patent.[83]

Objections

As to the particulars of objections, the practice is now well settled that **12.262** when the action goes to trial, the court will not certify unless they have been proven or the defendants can actually show that they are reasonable and proper; and so, where the action came on for hearing, and the plaintiff's case broke down by reason of certain of the particulars being proven, the court would not go through the other particulars with a view to ascertaining whether they were reasonable and proper, and a certificate was granted only as to those upon which the action was decided,[84] but where a number of prior users were pleaded, some of which were put to the plaintiff's witnesses in cross-examination, a certificate was granted as to these latter, notwithstanding that it became unnecessary to prove them all.[85] And when the defendant succeeds on the issue of infringement and the issue of validity is not considered, the particulars of objections will not be certified.[86] Similarly, no certificate will be granted where the allegations in the particulars of objections were not successful and did not play any part in the successful defence of non-infringement.[87]

---

[79] See, *e.g. Reitzman v. Grahame-Chapman* (1950) 67 R.P.C. 178 at p.195.
[80] *Rawcliffe v. Morris* (1886) 3 R.P.C. 145; *Duckett v. Sankey* (1899) 16 R.P.C. 357.
[81] *Brooks v. Hall* (1904) 21 R.P.C. 29; *Saccharin Corp. Ltd. v. Skidmore* (1904) 21 R.P.C. 31.
[82] *United Telephone Co. v. Harrison, Cox-Walker & Co.* (1882) 21 Ch.D. 720 at p.747.
[83] *Kane v. Guest & Co.* (1899) 16 R.P.C. 433 at p.443.
[84] *Boyd v. Horrocks* (1889) 6 R.P.C. 152 at p.162; *Longbottom v. Shaw* (1889) 6 R.P.C. 143, 510; *Bowen v. Pearson & Sons Ltd.* (1925) 42 R.P.C. 101.
[85] *Franc-Strohmenger and Cowan Inc. v. Peter Robinson Ltd.* (1930) 47 R.P.C. 493 at p.515.
[86] *Peter Pilkington Ltd. v. Massey* (1904) 21 R.P.C. 696 at p.712.
[87] *Deere & Co. v. Archie Kidd Ltd.* [1975] R.P.C. 246.

12.263   Where the patent was held invalid for want of inventiveness, insufficiency and prior user, and the decision was upheld on appeal as to the first two grounds but not as to the last, the Court of Appeal refused to vary the certificate as to particulars of objections.[88]

In some cases it may be reasonable to put a number of specifications to a witness *en bloc*, and if thereupon he concedes the point, the certificate may allow each specification.[89]

Where one of the items in the particulars of objections is relied on as an anticipation, but fails in this capacity, the court may nevertheless, certify for it, if it has been useful in illustrating the state of the art of otherwise.[90]

And it may occur that costs incurred by a defendant in respect of an investigation into prior knowledge may be allowed as part of the costs of his defence in limiting the plaintiff's claim, although no certificate as to the particulars of the objections may have been granted.[91]

The rule does not, of course prevent a party *against* whom objections are paricularised from recovering his costs if successful upon such objections.[92]

12.264   If when a case is called on for hearing the plaintiff abandons it, or does not appear, the case is deemed not to have proceeded to trial, and no certificate as to particulars of objections will be granted; the costs of the particulars of objections are then in the discretion of the Taxing Master.[93] Similarly, if several patents are sued on in the same action, but some of them are abandoned at the trial, a certificate for the particulars of objections will be refused in respect of such patents.[94]

Where a certificate has been granted in respect of a few only out of numerous objections it appears to have been the practice upon taxation for the total cost in respect of all the objections to be apportioned among the number contained in each category. This practice appears clearly to be wrong, it being more proper for the costs connected with the certified objections to be taxed upon the same footing as if they had been the only

---

[88] *Wright and Eagle Range Ltd. v. General Gas Appliances Ltd.* (1928) 45 R.P.C. 346; (1929) 46 R.P.C. 169 at p.183.

[89] *Cooper Patent Anchor Rail Joint Co. Ltd. v. London County Council* (1906) 23 R.P.C. 289 at p.297.

[90] *Castner-Kellner Alkali Co. Ltd. v. Commercial Development Co. Ltd.* (1899) 16 R.P.C. 251 at p.276; and see *Nettlefolds Ltd. v. Reynolds* (1892) 9 R.P.C. 270 at p.290; *Cassel Gold Extracting Co. Ltd. v. Cyanide Gold Recovery Syndicate* (1895) 12 R.P.C. 303; *Birch v. Harrap & Co.* (1896) 13 R.P.C. 615 at p.622.

[91] *Piggott & Co. Ltd. v. Corporation of Hanley* (1906) 23 R.P.C. 639; *Marconi's Wireless Telegraph Co. Ltd. v. Mullard Radio Valve Co. Ltd.* (1923) 40 R.P.C. 1 at p.29.

[92] *Sunlight Incandescent Gas Lamp Co. Ltd. v. Incandescent Gas Light Co.* (1897) 14 R.P.C. 757 at pp.775, 776.

[93] *British Foreign and Colonial etc. Co. Ltd. v. Metropolitan Gas Meters Ltd.* [1912] 2 Ch. 82; (1912) 29 R.P.C. 303; *Babcock and Wilcox Ltd. v. Water Tube Boiler and Engineering Co.* (1910) 27 R.P.C. 626; *McCreath v. Mayor etc. of South Shields and Baker* (1933) 50 R.P.C. 119; see also R.S.C., Ord. 62, App. 2 Pt. X, 4(3).

[94] *Textile Patents Ltd. v. Weinbrenner* (1925) 42 R.P.C. 515; *Lamson Paragon Supply Co. Ltd. v. Carter-Davis Ltd.* (1931) 48 R.P.C. 133.

ones pleaded;[95] that is to say, an attempt should be made to ascertain the actual amount of costs incurred in respect of each.

Costs of inspection and experiments

The costs of an inspection are in the discretion of the court,[96] but if the **12.265** inspection was necessary and proper the costs thereof are recoverable even though it was made without an order of the court.[97] The costs of experiments may be disallowed if they are not properly conducted in accordance with the order of the court,[98] or if, at trial, they are found to be of no assistance to the court.

Costs on higher scale

There is no provision in Order 62 of the Rules of the Supreme Court **12.266** for the court certifying that costs should be on "the higher scale" or for "three counsel", but the Taxing Master would follow any such intimation by the court in exercising his discretion as to the fees allowable on taxation.

Costs on the higher scale are only certified in cases of exceptional difficulty,[99] and in recent years have seldom been certified except in chemical cases.[1]

Costs on the higher scale have been refused although the costs of three counsel have been allowed.[2]

Three counsel

The principle upon which costs on the higher scale and the costs of **12.267** briefing three counsel should be certified were discussed, and the authorities considered, by Buckley J. in *Dunlop Pneumatic Tyre Co. v. Wapshare Tube Co.*,[3] where both were certified.[4]

The question of allowing costs of three counsel is sometimes left to the

---

[95] *Clorious v. Tonner* (1922) 39 R.P.C. 242 at p.252.
[96] *Mitchell v. Darley Main Colliery Co.* (1883) 10 Q.B.D. 457.
[97] *Ashworth v. English Card Clothing Co. Ltd.* (1904) 21 R.P.C. 353.
[98] *Reitzman v. Grahame-Chapman* (1950) 67 R.P.C. 178 at p.195.
[99] See *General Signal Co. v. Westinghouse* (1939) 56 R.P.C. 295 at p.394.
[1] The following are the cases in which they have been allowed since 1907: *Andrews' Patent* (1907) 24 R.P.C. 349; *Max Müller's Patent* (1907) 24 R.P.C. 465; *Alsop's Patent* (1907) 24 R.P.C. 733; *Flour Oxidising Co. Ltd. v. Carr & Co. Ltd.* (1908) 25 R.P.C. 428; *British Liquid Air Co. Ltd. v. British Oxygen Co. Ltd.* (1908) 25 R.P.C. 218, 577; *Carnegie Steel Co. v. Bell Bros. Ltd.* (1909) 26 R.P.C. 265; *Vidal Dyes Syndicate Ltd. v. Levinstein Ltd.* (1911) 28 R.P.C. 541; *Joseph Crosfield & Sons Ltd. v. Techno-Chemical Laboratories Ltd.* (1913) 30 R.P.C. 297; *Commercial Solvents Corporation v. Synthetic Products Co. Ltd.* (1926) 43 R.P.C. 185; *I. G. Farbenindustrie A.G.'s Patents* (1930) 47 R.P.C. 289; *May and Baker's Patent* (1948) 65 R.P.C. 255 at p.304. Costs on the higher scale were refused in *John Summers & Sons Ltd. v. The Cold Metal Process Co.* (1948) 65 R.P.C. 75 at p.122.
[2] *Marconi v. British Radio Telegraph and Telephone Co. Ltd.* (1911) 28 R.P.C. 181. See also *Commercial Solvents Corporation v. Synthetic Products Co. Ltd.* (1926) 43 R.P.C. 185 at p.238; *Société Anonyme Servo-Frein Dewandre v. Citroen Cars Ltd.* (1930) 47 R.P.C. 221 at p.261; *John Summers & Sons Ltd. v. The Cold Metal Process Co.* (1948) 65 R.P.C. 75 at p.122.
[3] (1900) 17 R.P.C. 433 at p.459.
[4] See also *Bradford Dyers' Association Ltd. v. Bury* (1902) 19 R.P.C. 125.

Taxing Master with or without an intimation of the court's opinion upon the point.[5]

Costs of appeal to Patents Court from Patent Office

Such costs are to be taxed in accordance with any other proceeding in the High Court.[6] Counsel may be instructed by patent agents to appear, and the fees of counsel may be recovered on taxation.[7]

12.268 Costs of shorthand notes

The costs of transcripts of the shorthand notes are usually agreed between the parties before the trial commences, but in default of such an arrangement they will not be allowed unless they have been of material assistance to the court in shortening the amount of time the case has taken or otherwise.[8]

F. Costs in the Patents County Court

12.269

The general rule as to the entitlement of a party to costs in the Patents County Court is identical to that in the High Court, as it is for any County Court.[8a]

The actual amount of costs recoverable in the Patents County Court will depend on which scale is ordered. Where the Patents County Court is exercising essentially the same jurisdiction as the High Court, it is likely that the costs of any substantial patent matter will be ordered on the High Court Scale.[8b]

In other cases, Order 38 of the County Court Rules provides that from July 1, 1991, there are three County Court scales, namely the Lower Scale, Scale 1 and Scale 2. The appropriate County Court scale is determined in accordance with C.C.R. Order 38, rule 4. In an action for the recovery of a sum of money, the scales are linked to the amount recovered or, as regards the costs of a successful Defendant, to the amount claimed.[8c] But this rule does not apply to an action under equity jurisdiction where costs are on such a scale as the judge when awarding costs, or the registrar when taxing or assessing them, may determine.[8d]

---

[5] *British Thomson-Houston Co. Ltd. v. British Insulated and Helsby Cables Ltd.* (1925) 42 R.P.C. 345 at p.375; *Commercial Solvents Corporation v. Synthetic Products Co. Ltd.* (1926) 43 R.P.C. 185 at p.238.

[6] *Extrude Hone Corporation's Patent* [1982] R.P.C. 361.

[7] *Reiss Engineering Co. Ltd. v. Harris* [1987] R.P.C. 171.

[8] See, *e.g. Castner-Kellner Alkali Co. v. Commercial Development Co. Ltd.* (1899) 16 R.P.C. 251 at p.275; *Palmer Tyre Co. Ltd. v. Pneumatic Tyre Co. Ltd.* (1889) 6 R.P.C. 451 at p.496; *British Westinghouse Electric and Manufacturing Co. Ltd. v. Braulik* (1910) 27 R.P.C. 209 at p.233.

[8a] Supreme Court Act 1981, s.51, as substituted by Courts and Legal Services Act 1990, s.4; C.C.R. Ord. 38, r.1.

[8b] *The Wellcome Foundation Ltd. v. Discpharm Ltd. (No.2)* [1993] F.S.R. 444.

[8c] C.C.R. Ord. 38, r.3(3) & r.4(1). The scales are as follows:

    the Lower Scale .... over £25 but not exceeding £100

    Scale 2 .... £100 to £3000

    Scale 2 .... over £3000.

[8d] C.C.R. Ord. 38, r. 5(7).

Where costs are to be taxed on Scale 2 the amount of costs to be allowed are in the discretion of the taxing officer and, in exercising his discretion, he is required to have regard to all the relevant circumstances and in particular to the circumstances referred to in paragraph 1(2) of Part 1 of Appendix 2 to Order 62. of the Rules of the Supreme Court.[8e] The bill of costs is to consist of the items specified in Part II of Appendix 2 to Order 62 of the Rules of the Supreme Court.[8f] For all practical purposes, a party entitled to costs on Scale 2 should receive costs if the action had been conducted in the High Court.[8g]

Certificates

Unlike the High Court there is no specific provision in the County Court Rules regarding certificates that particulars of infringements or objections were proven or reasonable. However, the provisions of Part II of Order 62 of the rules of the Supreme Court relating to the entitlement of costs apply in relation to the costs of and incidental to any proceedings in a County Court as they apply in relation to the costs of any like proceedings to which that Order relates.[9] Accordingly, it is submitted, that certificates should be sought where appropriate in the Patents County Court.   **12.270**

Submissions as to costs

It is the practice in the Patents County Court that a party's submissions as to what order the court ought to make regarding costs should be made at the end of the hearing prior to the judge retiring to reserve judgment.   **12.271**

Comparison with patents agents fees

In assessing generally whether or not a particular level of costs[10] is appropriate in a Patents County Court action it is the practice of the court to consider how much a firm of patent agents would charge for such work.   **12.272**

G. Miscellaneous matters

Declaration as to non-infringement

Where an action is commenced for a declaration to be made under section 72 of the 1977 Act that a certain process or article does not infringe a claim of a patent, rule 3(3) of Order 62 of the Rules of the Supreme Court applies and *prima facie* costs will follow the event.[10a] This section alters the law as to costs from that of section 66 of the 1949 Act.   **12.273**

[8e] C.C.R., Ord. 38, r. 3(3B).
[8f] C.C.R., Ord. 38, r. 3(3C).
[8g] See the notes on p.1642, C.C.R. (1994).
[9] C.C.R., Ord. 38, rule 1(3).
[10] *E.g.* by way of security or in a specific order.
[10a] *Mölnlycke AB v. Procter & Gamble* [1990] R.P.C. 267.

Several defendants

12.274   Where an action is brought against two defendants and the case against one of them is settled, and the action proceeds against the other and judgment is recovered, then unless a special order as to costs is made no deduction on taxation will be made from the general costs of the action to represent the amount incurred as against the defendant whose case was settled.[11]

Minutes

12.275   Judgment having been recovered, minutes of judgment should be prepared. Care should be exercised, when an inquiry is directed, that provision be made for the payment of costs to the plaintiff up to and including the hearing, otherwise the payment of all costs may be delayed until the final account has been taken.[11a]

Undertaking to return costs

12.276   A common course with regard to costs is for the solicitor to the successful party to give an undertaking to return the costs in the event of a successful appeal.[12] In *Ackroyd and Best Ltd. v. Thomas and Williams*,[13] where the solicitors declined to give the undertaking, Joyce J. stayed the payment of costs, but refused to stay the taxation.

Interest of costs

12.277   The previous rule that interest on costs ran from the date of the Master's certificate on taxation[14] has been overruled and the current rule is that interest on costs should run from the date of judgment.[15]

No appeal as to costs

12.278   Section 18(1) of the Supreme Court Act 1981 (as amended) provides that without leave there shall be no appeal as to costs only which are by law left to the discretion of the court or tribunal. However, leave can now be granted either by the court below or by the Court of Appeal (Order 59, rule 1B(1)(b). Prior to amendment of the section an appeal did lie if upon a true view of the facts the judge had either not exercised his discretion at all, or had exercised it otherwise than judicially.[16] It is doubtful to what extent this principle will be relevant in the future now that both the Court below and the Court of Appeal can grant leave as to costs only: any case bad enough to fall within the principle will be granted leave at least by the Court of Appeal.

---

[11] *Kelly's Directories Ltd. v. Gavin and Lloyds* [1901] 2 Ch. 763; *Badische Anilin und Soda Fabrik v. Hickson* (1906) 23 R.P.C. 149.
[11a] *Mölnlycke AB v. Procter & Gamble Ltd.* [1993] F.S.R. 154.
[12] *Ticket Punch Register Co. Ltd. v. Colley's Patents Ltd.* (1895) 12 R.P.C. 1 at p.10.
[13] (1904) 21 R.P.C. 403 at p.412.
[14] *K. v. K.* [1977] Fam. D.39 followed in *Erven Warnink B.V. v. J. Townend & Sons (Hull) Ltd.* [1982] R.P.C. 511.
[15] *Hunt v. R. M. Douglas (Roofing) Ltd.* [1988] 3 W.L.R. 975.
[16] *Jones v. Mckie* [1964] 1 W.L.R. 960; *Scherer v. Counting Instruments Ltd.* [1977] F.S.R. 569; *Infabrics Ltd. v. Jaytex Ltd. (Costs Appeal)* [1987] F.S.R. 529.

Action based on undertaking or contract

If a defendant has given an undertaking or entered into a contract not **12.279** to infringe a patent (*e.g.* as part of the terms of settlement of a previous action or threatened action) such a bargain can be enforced, (subject to its enforceability under E.C. Competition Law) notwithstanding the invalidity of the patent.[17] Such an agreement or undertaking will normally be assumed to subsist for the life of the patent.[18]

Compromise of action affecting infant children

Where a patent action is continued by the personal representative of a **12.280** deceased patentee and the interests of infant children are involved, a compromise of the action must be sanctioned by the court.[19]

7. Appeals to the Court of Appeal

Appeals to the Court of Appeal are initiated by notice of motion, **12.281** otherwise referred to as a Notice of Appeal.[20] On appeals from the High Court the notice must be lodged within four weeks of the order "being signed, entered, or otherwise perfected".[21] On appeals from the County Court every notice of appeal must be served "not later than four weeks after the date of judgment or order of the court below".[22] The handing down of the reasons for the judgment is not the date of judgment. This occurs when the judge makes an order consequent upon his judgment.[23] The procedure on appeal in a patent action is the same as in any other action.[24]

In order that the Court of Appeal may entertain an appeal there must still be a real issue between the parties for determination when the matter comes before that court; otherwise the appeal will be dismissed.[25]

The costs of employing an expert to assist counsel in the Court of Appeal will not be allowed save under the most special circumstances.[26]

Costs may be awarded against a legally aided party to be paid by the legal aid fund.[27]

---

[17] *Heginbotham Bros. Ltd. v. Burne* (1939) 56 R.P.C. 399 at p.407.
[18] *Ibid.* And see *Bescol (Electric) Ltd. v. Merlin Mouldings Ltd.* (1952) 69 R.P.C. 297.
[19] *Schwank v. Radiant Heating Ltd.* [1958] R.P.C. 266.
[20] R.S.C., Ord. 59, r.3.
[21] R.S.C., Ord. 59, r.4.
[22] R.S.C., Ord. 59, r.19(3).
[23] *Pavel v. Sony Corp.* [1993] F.S.R. 177.
[24] But see R.S.C., Ord. 59, rr.17, 18.
[25] *Martin v. Selsdon Fountain Pen Co. Ltd.* (1949) 66 R.P.C. 294; *Sun Life Assurance Co. of Canada v. Jervis* [1944] A.C. 111. See also *Norton and Gregory v. Jacobs* (1937) 54 R.P.C. 271; *Manbré and Garton v. Albion Sugar Co.* (1937) 54 R.P.C. 243.
[26] *Consolidated Pneumatic Tool Co. v. Ingersoll Sergeant Drill Co.* (1908) 25 R.P.C. 574; *Société Anonyme Servo-Frein Dewandre v. Citroen Cars Ltd.* (1930) 47 R.P.C. 221 at p.282.
[27] *Tiefebrun's Appn.* [1979] F.S.R. 97.

CHAPTER 13

USE BY THE CROWN, INCOME TAX, STAMPS, ETC.

Contents

1. Use by the Crown

History

13.01   Prior to the Act of 1883 the Crown was entitled to use patented inventions without the assent of or compensation to the patentee,[1] though it was the practice to reward the patentee *ex gratia*. The exemption of the Crown did not, however, extend to protect contractors who supplied patented articles to the Crown,[2] as distinguished from servants or agents of the Crown, at any rate where such contractors could if they had so wished have supplied instead articles which were not patented.

Present law

13.02   Since the Act of 1883, and now under the present law, a patent has the same effect against the Crown as against a subject.[3] This, however, is subject to very wide rights of user by the Crown, as set out below. By section 3 of the Crown Proceedings Act 1947[4] a patentee is able to sue the Crown in civil proceedings for infringement, if the Crown purports to authorise any infringing act otherwise than in accordance with its statutory rights.

    By reason of paragraph 2 of Schedule 4 to the 1977 Act, just as with the

---

[1] *Feather v. R.* (1865), 6 B. & S. 257.
[2] *Dixon v. London Small Arms Co.* (1865), L.R. 10 Q.B. 130; 1 Q.B.D. 384; 1 App.Cas. (1875) 632.
[3] P.A. 1949, s.21(2); P.A. 1977, s.129.
[4] As substituted by C.D.P.A. 1988, s.303(1), Sched. 7, para.4(1).

question of infringement, the provisions of the 1977 Act regarding Crown user apply to existing patents and, subject to two minor differences[5] to patent applications under the 1949 Act insofar as concerns acts done on or after June 1, 1978 (the appointed day). As regards acts done before June 1, 1978 the 1949 Act applies and as regards an act commenced before such date which continues to be done thereafter, then if it did not amount to a use for services of the Crown under the 1949 Act its continuance will not amount to such use under the 1977 Act.[6]

Authorisation for Services of Crown

Any government department and any person authorised in writing by a government department may for the services of the Crown do any of the acts listed in section 55(1) of the 1977 Act.[7] The listed acts are similar to the infringing acts set out in section 60, the main difference being the qualified right of the Crown to sell other than for purposes of foreign defence or for production or supply of specified drugs and medicines. In so far as the provisions of section 55 are narrower than section 60, any act authorised by the Crown which is not covered by section 55 will constitute an infringing act—in such circumstances, although damages may be obtainable, no injunction will lie.[8]

13.03

The requirement that the authorisation must be in writing was first introduced by the Act of 1919. It would seem that such written authorisation need not be directed specifically to the use of the particular patent concerned, and that a written authorisation or requirement of a department that a contractor should supply apparatus of a certain type is sufficient if it is in fact impossible for the contractor to supply such apparatus without infringing the patent.[9]

In *Aktiengesellschaft für Aluminium Schweissung v. London Aluminium Co. Ltd. (No.2)*,[10] Sargant J. said:

13.04

"The origin of the section, of course, is well known; it is to be found undoubtedly in the decision of the House of Lords in *Dixon v. London Small Arms Co. Ltd.*,[11] where it was held that the right of the Crown to use a patented article or process could not extend to contractors who were employed as contractors by the Government. The difficulty that arises is this: In some cases it is clear that the defendants, who were the direct contractors with the Government, were told to use this particular process, and in those cases it is not questioned by counsel

---

[5] P.A. 1977, s.55(5)(*b*) and s.58(10) do not apply.
[6] See *Therm-a-Stor Ltd. v. Weatherseal Windows Ltd.*, [1981] F.S.R. 579.
[7] Under the 1949 Act it was "make use and exercise any patented invention". See P.A. 1949, s.46(1).
[8] See s.21 Crown Proceedings Act, 1947.
[9] See *Pyrene Co. Ltd. v. Webb Lamp Co. Ltd.* (1920) 37 R.P.C. 57.
[10] (1923) 40 R.P.C. 107 at p.116.
[11] (1876) 1 App.Cas. 632.

for the plaintiffs that no damages can be assessed. The right of the patentees in that case will be under section 29 [now section 55] ... But there are a number of cases where the facts are nothing like so simple, cases where the company, the defendants, have not been contracting directly with the Government, but have been, for instance, supplying persons who themselves were the direct contractors with the Government; in those cases it is said that the protection of the section does not apply and that the patentees accordingly are entitled to the ordinary remedy against the defendant company. It seems to me really that it is impossible to deal as a whole with the various contracts that are now in question. In my judgment, the section is primarily an agency section; that is to say, protection is afforded to the government department, and to any person or persons, contractors or others, who are acting as agents for, or by the express or implied authority of, a government department. In each case it will have to be ascertained, if the parties think fit to fight out each individual case, whether the acts of the defendant company in that particular case were acts done for the purposes of the Crown, and with the authority or by the direction of the Crown. In that case they will not be liable; but where the acts that they have done have not been done by virtue of some express or implied authority from the Crown, then it seems to me they will be liable. It may be in many cases that, where they are sub-contractors, there will have been such a relation between them and their contractors, such a direction given by the Government to the contractors, or such a direct supervision over the employers by the Government, as will amount to an implied authority sufficient to make the company in that individual case an agent acting by the authority, and for the purposes, of the Crown."

Services of the Crown

13.05   Use for the services of the Crown is use by members of such services in the course of their duties. Thus, the use of patented drugs in the treatment of National Health Service hospital patients has been held to be use for the services of the Crown.[12]

As Diplock L.J. (as he then was) said in the Court of Appeal in the *Pfizer case*:

"An act is done for 'the services (or service) of the Crown' if it is done for the purpose of the performance of a duty or the exercise of a power which is imposed upon or vested in the executive government of the United Kingdom by statute or by the prerogative. Where there is no explicit agency between the persons performing the act and the executive government, difficult questions may arise as to whether the

---

[12] *Pfizer Corp. v. Minister of Health* [1965] R.P.C. 261; [1965] A.C. 512; see also *Dory v. Sheffield Health Authority* [1991] F.S.R. 221.

duty or power, the performance or exercise of which is the purpose of the act, is one which is imposed upon or vested in the executive government of the United Kingdom and not upon some other person or authority; but this problem does not arise where the act is done by an agent for a government department itself."[13]

Section 56(2) of the 1977 Act lists three matters that are included within the meaning of "the services of the Crown", namely the supply for foreign defence purposes,[14] the production or supply of specific drugs and medicines[15] and matter relating to the production or use of atomic energy or research connected therewith.

Scope of authority

The right to authorise given by the 1977 Act applies to a patented **13.06** invention or to an alleged invention that is the subject of a patent application.[16] It also applies to European patents (U.K.)[17] and applications therefor.[18] The authority may be given either before or after the patent is granted and either before or after the acts authorised are done.[19] Retrospective authority takes away any cause of action which may have existed and substitutes a right of remuneration under section 55(4).[20] The sale of a patented article to a government department for the services of the Crown is a "use" of the patented invention which may be authorised by that department.[21] The Crown may also sell to anybody patented articles made pursuant to an authority given by a government department when these are no longer required for the purpose for which they were made,[22] and the purchaser of such articles and any person claiming through him may deal with such articles freely, as though the patent were held by the Crown.[23] During a period of emergency very wide powers are conferred on the Crown.[24]

---

[13] [1965] R.P.C. at 276.
[14] See P.A. 1977, s.56(3) as to meaning of foreign defence purposes.
[15] See P.A. 1977, s.56(4) as to meaning of specified drugs and medicines.
[16] P.A. 1949, s.56(1); see also *American Flange and Manufacturing Co. Inc. v. Van Leer,* (1948) 65 R.P.C. 305 at p.318.
[17] P.A. 1977, s.77.
[18] P.A. 1977, s.78.
[19] P.A. 1977, s.55(6).
[20] *Dory v. Sheffield Health Authority* [1991] F.S.R. 221.
[21] *Pfizer Corp. v. Minister of Health* [1965] R.P.C. 261, [1965] A.C. 512; *Dory v. Sheffield Health Authority* [1991] F.S.R. 221.
[22] P.A. 1977, s.55(1)(*e*).
[23] P.A. 1977, s.55(8).
[24] P.A. 1977, s.59.

Use for foreign defence purposes and health services

13.07　　Under section 55(1)(*a*) of the 1977 Act[25] the powers exercisable for the services of the Crown in respect of foreign defence and health include the power to sell or offer to sell without qualification in contrast to the more limited powers of sale in respect of other Crown services which can only be exercised where the sale or offer for sale would be incidental or ancillary to making, using, importing or keeping the patented product.

As regards health services the powers exercisable under section 55(1) are in respects of drugs and medicines specified in regulations made by the Secretary of State for services under Part II of the National Health Service Act 1977, Part II of the National Health Service (Scotland) Act 1978 or corresponding provisions in Northern Ireland or the Isle of Man.[26]

Compensation for Crown use

13.08　　If the invention has been recorded by or tried by or on behalf of a government department[27] before the relevant priority date otherwise than in consequence of a communication made in confidence directly or indirectly from the patentee or a predecessor in title, any use of the invention may be made free of any royalty or other payment.[28] But if the invention has not been so recorded or tried, any use made after the publication of the application or in consequence of such a communication of the invention is to be on terms to be agreed between the government department and the patentees with the approval of the Treasury or in default of agreement to be settled by the High Court,[29] which may refer the whole proceedings or any issue of fact to a special or official referee or an arbitrator.[30]

The sum payable by way of compensation under section 55(4) of the 1977 Act is in the nature of remuneration payable to the inventor or his successor in title for the use made by the Crown of his invention pursuant to that concurrent right; he is not entitled under section 55(4) to compensation on any other basis, for instance, in his status as a manufacturer for loss of chance to manufacture.[31] However, section 57A of the Act[32] now provides for compensation to the proprietor or the exclusive licensee for loss of profit resulting from his not being awarded a contract. Compensation is payable only to the extent that such a contract could have been fulfilled from his existing manufacturing or

---

[25] See also P.A. 1977, s.55(1)(c) for power to sell drugs and medicines.
[26] P.A. 1977, s.56(4).
[27] See *Re Carbonit A.G.*(1923) 40 R.P.C. 360.
[28] P.A. 1977, s.55(3), (9); P.A. 1949, s.46(2).
[29] P.A. 1977, s.55(4), s.58.
[30] P.A. 1977, s.58(12).
[31] *Patchett's Patent* [1967] R.P.C. 237 at pp.246, 251, 257; see also *Allen & Hanburys (Salbutamol) Patent* [1987] R.P.C. 327 at p.328.
[32] Added by C.D.P.A. 1988, s.295, Sched. 5, para.16(1).

other capacity.[33] The amount payable is in addition to any amount payable under sections 55 or 57.[34]

Date from which compensation runs

It is to be noted that compensation is payable in respect of use either   **13.09**
from the date of publication of the application or the date of communication of the invention. The reason for this is that the Crown may require the patent to be kept secret,[35] and, if the date of publication were the relevant date, the patentee could thereby be deprived of compensation altogether.

The court may order interest to be paid to the patentee on the compensation sum.[36]

Information as to use to be given

Where the use of an invention is authorised by a government   **13.10**
department the latter must notify the patentee as soon as practicable after the use has begun and give information from time to time as to the extent of the use, unless it would be contrary to the public interest to do so.[37]

Terms of any licence, etc., to be inoperative

A government department may authorise a licensee of the patentee   **13.11**
make use of the invention for the services of the Crown and in such a case the terms of any licence or agreement (other than one made with a government department) are inoperative as regards such user.[38] Similarly, the patentee may be authorised to use or supply the patented invention for the services of the Crown, nowithstanding the terms of any assignment or agreement which purport to debar him from so doing.[39] And any provisions which restrict or regulate the use of the invention or of any model, document, or information relating to the invention are inoperative.[40] Furthermore, the reproduction or publication of any model or document in connection with such use is not to be deemed an infringement of copyright.[41]

---

[33] P.A. 1977, s.57A(2).

[34] P.A. 1977, s.57A(5).

[35] P.A. 1977, s. 22; see *ante*, § 3.69.

[36] *Patchett's Patent* [1967] R.P.C. 237.

[37] P.A. 1977, s.55(7).

[38] P.A. 1977, s.57(1). See *No-Nail Cases Proprietary Ltd. v. No-Nail Boxes Ltd.* (1944) 61 R.P.C. 94.

[39] P.A. 1977, s.57(1), overruling *Foster Wheeler Ltd. v. E. Green & Son Ltd.* (1946) 63 R.P.C. 10.

[40] P.A. 1977, s.57(1).

[41] *Ibid.*

Compensation to licensee or assignor

13.12   An exclusive licensee whose licence was granted for a consideration other than a royalty assessed by reference to use can claim compensation for Crown user,[42] including user by the patentee for the services of the Crown. Similarly, where a patent or the right to apply for a patent has been assigned in consideration of the payment of royalties the assignor can claim compensation and any sum payable is to be divided between assignor and patentee as may be agreed or be settled by reference to the court.[43] An exclusive licensee whose licence was granted in consideration of the payment of royalties can recover such proportion of any payment made to the patentee as may be agreed or determined by the court.[44]

Where co-owners of a patent have previously agreed on the proportions in which they will divide any royalties or other proceeds from exploitation of the patent, the court will apportion in those proportions any compensation awarded in respect of Crown use of the patent.[45]

Procedure

13.13   The procedure on reference to the High Court is by way of originating notice of motion assigned to the Patents Court.[46] On the first hearing of the motion the usual practice is to order pleadings and give other directions, such as discovery.[47]

Validity may be challenged

13.14   In proceedings for the assessment of compensation for Crown user, if the patentee is a party the government department may apply for revocation of the patent and in any case may put validity in issue without applying for revocation.[48]

Where the Crown puts validity in issue and there is also concurrently an action for infringement of the patent against a third party who has also put validity in issue, the Crown proceedings and the action may be ordered to be heard together so far as they raise common issues.[49]

Confidential disclosure

13.15   If any question arises as to whether or not an invention has been recorded or tried by a government department and any disclosure

---

[42] P.A. 1977, s.57(3)(*a*).
[43] P.A. 1977, s.57(4).
[44] P.A. 1977, s.57(5), (7), (8).
[45] *Patchett's Patent* [1967] R.P.C. 237.
[46] R.S.C., Ord. 104, r.21.
[47] See, *e.g. Re Carbonit* (1924) 41 R.P.C. 203 at p.209 and *Sageb's Claim* (1952) 69 R.P.C. 73 at p.77.
[48] P.A. 1977, s.74(1)(*e*).
[49] *Anxionnaz v. Ministry of Aviation* [1966] R.P.C. 510.

would be contrary to the public interest, such disclosure may be made confidentially to counsel or to an independent expert mutually agreed on.[50]

Factors taken into account in determining terms

13.16 Any benefit or compensation that the claimant or his predecessor in title may have received or be entitled to receive directly or indirectly from any government department in respect of the invention is to be taken into account in assessing compensation.[51] Furthermore, the court shall have regard to whether the claimant or his predecessor in title has without reasonable cause failed to comply with a request of the department to use the invention for the services of the Crown on reasonable terms.[52] If, during the course of proceedings for the assessment of compensation for Crown user, amendment of the patent specification is sought and allowed, the court may consider limitation of the period of compensation as a term of allowing the amendment.[53]

Costs in proceedings against the Crown

13.17 In any civil proceedings, or arbitration, to which the Crown (or a government department) is a party, the court, or arbitrator, may make *"an order for the payment of costs by or to the Crown"*.[54]

Articles forfeited under customs law

13.18 Section 122 of the 1977 Act says: *"Nothing in this Act shall affect the right of the Crown or of any person deriving title directly or indirectly from the Crown to dispose of or use articles forfeited under the laws relating to customs or excise."*

This section does not confer any rights upon the Crown or persons deriving title from the Crown, but merely states that existing rights are not affected. It is a matter of doubt whether purchasers from the Crown of articles manufactured in infringement of a patent and forfeited under the laws relating to the customs or excise are entitled to use them without the licence of the patentee.[55]

---

[50] P.A. 1977, s.58(2).
[51] P.A. 1977, s.58(3)(*a*).
[52] P.A. 1977, s.58(3)(*b*).
[53] *Electric and Musical Industries' Patent* [1963] R.P.C. 241; see also s.58(6) of the 1977 Act.
[54] See Administration of Justice (Miscellaneous Provisions) Act 1933, s.7(1), (2); and see *Patchett's Patent* [1967] R.P.C. 237 at p.259.
[55] See *British Mutoscope and Biograph Co. Ltd. v. Homer* (1901) 18 R.P.C. 177.

2. Stamp Duty

13.19   The question of the stamping of documents is of importance in view of the provisions of section 33 of the 1977 Act whereby patentees, licensees, and others who fail to register the documents under which they derive their title are placed under certain disabilities.[56] The Comptroller is liable to a penalty of £10 if he registers a document which is not duly stamped,[57] and he may, therefore, refuse to register a document where he is not satisfied that the true consideration is stated on the face of the document.[58] The proper mode of questioning the legality of his refusal is to obtain the opinion of the Commissioners of Inland Revenue.[59] An appeal from their decision lies to the High Court.

13.20   By reason of sections 1, 54 and 59 and Schedule 1 to the Stamp Act 1891 an assignment or contract for the sale of a patent requires to be stamped as a conveyance or transfer on sale at the *ad valorem* rates imposed by section 55(1) of the Finance Act 1963 as amended by section 109(1) of the Finance Act 1984. The rates are as follows:

(a) where the amount or value of the consideration is £30,000 or under and the instrument is certified, as described in section 34(4) of the Finance Act 1958,[60] at £30,000, nil;

(b) where paragraph (a) above does not apply and the amount or value of the consideration does not exceed £500, the rate of 50p for every £50 or part of £50 of the consideration; and

(c) where paragraph (a) above does not apply and the amount or value of the consideration exceeds £500, the rate of £1 for every £100 or part of £100 of the consideration.

13.21   An irrevocable licence to use and vend is also liable to conveyance duty on sums reserved by way of fixed royalties during the life of the patent, but if the licence contains a power of revocation no conveyance duty is payable in practice. Licences which are not liable to coveyance duty because they are revocable are no longer liable to covenant duty.[61] For the purposes of conveyance duty it is immaterial whether a conveyance is under hand or under seal. The obligatory 50p stamp for a deed has been abolished.[62]

---

[56] §§8.27 and 8.28 (*ante*). See also Stamp Act 1891, s.14.
[57] Stamp Act 1891, s.17.
[58] *Maynard v. Consolidated Kent Collieries* (1902) 19 T.L.R. 448.
[59] *R. v. Registrar of Joint Stock Companies* 21 Q.B.D. 131; and see Stamp Act 1891, s.12.
[60] S.34(4) states: "References in this section to an instrument being certified at a particular amount means that it contains a statement certifying that the transaction effected by the instrument does not form part of a larger transaction or series of transactions in respect of which the amount or value or aggregate amount or value, of the consideration exceeds that amount...."
[61] See Finance Act 1971, s.64(1) and (2).
[62] See Finance Act 1985, s.85, Sched. 24.

It was held in *Smelting Company of Australia v. Commissioners of Inland* **13.22**
Revenue[63] that a share in a patent and sole licence to use the patented
invention are "property" within section 59, subsection (1) of the Stamp
Act 1891; and this part of the decision does not appear to be affected by
the decision in *English, Scottish and Australian Bank v. Inland Revenue*
Commissioners.[64]

In view of the decision in the latter case, however, an interest in a
foreign or colonial patent is an interest in "property locally situate out of
the United Kingdom", and, therefore, an agreement relating to such
rights is not liable to "conveyance duty".

An instrument relating to a Community patent or an application for a **13.23**
European patent is not chargeable with stamp duty if, under the
Community Patent Convention, it is designated to have effect throughout the territories to which the Convention applies or is treated as a
national patent of the contracting state in which the applicant's
representative has a place of business.[65]

Stamp Duty on a conveyance or transfer on sale may shortly be **13.24**
abolished. The statutory framework is in place.[66] The abolition day is
such a day as may be appointed under s.111(1) of the Finance Act 1990
(abolution of stamp duty for securities, etc.).[67]

3. Income Tax and Corporation Tax

There are two basic and quite separate inquiries underlying the **13.25**
taxation of patent rights. One is to determine what allowances one is
entitled to in respect of monies expended on such rights and the other is
to determine what monies received in respect of such rights are liable to
tax. However, before either of these questions can be determined it is
first of all necessary to decide whether such monies expended or
received in respect of patent rights are of an income or capital nature.

Income or capital nature

The distinction between capital and income monies is a question of **13.26**
fact.[68] As Lord Denning M.R. said in *Murray (Inspector of Taxes) v.*
Imperial Chemical Industries:[69]

"I see no difference in this regard between an assignment of patent

---

[63] [1897] 1 Q.B. 175 at p.181.
[64] [1932] A.C. 238.
[65] P.A. 1977, s.126.
[66] Finance Act 1991, s.110.
[67] *Ibid.*, s.110(7).
[68] *Inland Revenue Commissioners v. British Salmson Aero Engines Ltd.* [1938] 2 K.B. 482; 22
T.C. 29.
[69] [1967] Ch. 1038 at p.1052; [1967] R.P.C. 216.

rights and the grant of an exclusive licence for the period of the patent. It is the disposal of a capital asset. But this does not determine the quality of the money received. A man may dispose of a capital asset for a lump sum which is then a capital receipt. Or he may dispose of it in return for an annuity, in which case the annual payments are revenue receipts. Or he may dispose of it in part for one and in part for the other. Each case must depend on its own circumstances. But it seems to me fairly clear that if, and in so far as, a man disposes of patent rights outright (for example by an assignment of his patent, or by the grant of an exclusive licence) and receives in return *royalties* calculated by reference to the actual user, the royalties are clearly revenue receipts. If, and in so far as, he disposes of them for *annual payments* over the period, which can fairly be regarded as compensation for the user during the period, then those also are revenue receipts. If, and in so far as, he disposes of the patent rights outright for a *lump sum*, which is arrived at by reference to some anticipated quantum of user, it will normally be income in the hands of the recipient (see the judgment of Lord Greene M.R. in *Withers v. Nethersole*[70] approved by Lord Simon in the House of Lords).[71] But if, and in so far as, he disposes of them outright for a lump sum which has no reference to anticipated user, it will normally be capital. It is different when a man does not dispose of his patent rights, but retains them and grants a non-exclusive licence. He does not then dispose of a capital asset. He retains the asset and he uses it to bring in money for him. A lump sum may in those cases be a revenue receipt; see *Rustproof Metal Window Co. Ltd. v. Inland Revenue Commissioners.*"[72]

Capital expenditure and capital sums do not include sums which are treated as revenue expenditure or receipts nor do they include sums on which a deduction of tax falls or may fall to be made by the payer other than a capital sum in respect of a United Kingdom patent paid to a person not resident in the United Kingdom.[73]

Persons entitled to allowances and liable to tax

13.27   Persons entitled to allowances in respect of expenditure on patent rights and liable to tax on sums received in respect of such rights are as follows:[74]

---

[70] [1946] 1 All E.R. 711 at p.716; 28 T.C. 501.
[71] [1948] 1 All E.R. 400 (H.L.).
[72] [1947] 2 All E.R. 454 at p.459; (1947) 29 T.C. 243; see also *Constantinesco v. R.,* (1927) 11 T.C. 730; *Mills v. Jones,* (1929) 14 T.C. 769; affirmed 14 T.C. 785 (H.L.) and *Industrial Combustion Ltd. v. Revenue Commissioners* (1932) 16 T.C. 532 royalties in respect of foreign patent.
[73] Capital Allowances Act 1990, s.159(1); Income and Corporation Taxes Act 1988 (referred to hereafter as the I.C.T.A. 1988) s.532. See *post,* § 13.41.
[74] I.C.T.A. 1988, s.18(1)(*a*)(i)–(iii).

(a) Any person residing in the United Kingdom in respect of any patent rights (whether situate in the United Kingdom or elsewhere).

(b) Any person residing in the United Kingdom and carrying on a business or trade (whether in the United Kingdom or elsewhere), in respect of patent rights used or acquired for that person's trade.

(c) Any person whether a British subject or not, not resident in the United Kingdom, in respect of United Kingdom patent rights or of any trade or business carried on in the United Kingdom in respect of patent rights used or acquired for that trade.[75]

A. Allowances

Expenditure in respect of which allowances may be claimed may be divided as follows: **13.28**

(a) Expenses incurred in devising an invention and patenting it.

(b) Expenditure on purchase of patent rights.

(a) Expenses incurred in devising an invention and patenting it

Patent rights used or to be used for the purposes of a trade
In the case of a trader (whether an individual or a firm) whose profits or gains are chargeable to tax under Case I of Schedule D, expenses incurred in devising an invention and patenting it (or attempting to patent it in the case of a rejected or abandoned application) are normally incurred wholly and exclusively for the purposes of the trade and accordingly such expenses may be deducted in the normal way in computing the profits or gains of the trade for income tax purposes.[76] In the case of a corporate trader, the same principles apply in computing the profit for corporation tax purposes.[77] If after deducting expenses there is a loss, the normal rules for loss relief apply and, for example, the loss may be carried forward to the following year to be deducted from or set off against profits or gains in respect of the same trade, and so on for succeeding years.[78] **13.29**

---

[75] See *Inland Revenue Commissioners v. Marine Steam Turbine Co.* [1920] 1 K.B. 193; 12 T.C. 174; a company sold its business for a royalty for a term of years was held not to be carrying on a business.

[76] I.C.T.A. 1988, ss.1, 18 and 70; see also ss.74(*a*) and 83, the latter provision being required for it might otherwise be said that the application fees, etc, are paid to acquire a capital asset.

[77] I.C.T.A. 1988, s.9.

[78] I.C.T.A. 1988, s.385 and, for companies, s.393.

Patents rights held by non–trader

13.30   In the case of a non–trader allowances are to be made in respect of fees paid or expenses incurred in connection with the grant or maintenance of a patent, or the obtaining of an extension of a term of a patent or a rejected or abandoned application for a patent.[79] The manner in which such allowances are made is by way of deduction or set off against income from patents for the year of assessment.[80] Where the allowance is more than the patent income for the year in which the allowance becomes due, then any balance may be carried forward and is available against income from patents in succeeding years.[81] Similar provisions also apply in the case of a non-trading corporation.[82]

13.31   Income from patents is defined as (a) any royalty or other sum paid in respect of the user of a patent, and (b) any amount on which tax is payable for any accounting period of a company or any year of assessment by virtue of sections 520(6), 523(3), 524 or 525 of the Income and Corporation Taxes Act 1988[83] and therefore is deemed to include both royalties and other sums payable in respect of the user of a patent and capital sums received for the sale of patent rights chargeable to tax by reason of the above sections.

The individual inventor

13.32   Where a patent is granted, the individual who actually devised the invention may claim an allowance equal to the net amount of any expenses incurred by him (whether he was the sole or joint inventor)[84] except where an allowance falls to be made under some other provision of the Income Tax Acts 1988 (*e.g.* as a deduction when computing trading profits). The allowance is set off against income from patents.[85]

(b) Expenditure on purchase of patent rights

Capital payments post March 31, 1986

13.33   Capital Expenditure incurred after March 31, 1986, on the acquisition of patent rights is written off against tax in a manner which is broadly similar to that applicable in respect of expenditure on plant. A writing–down allowance is given each year at the rate of 25 per cent of

---

[79] I.C.T.A. 1988, s.526(1).
[80] I.C.T.A. 1988, s.528(2)(*a*).
[81] I.C.T.A. 1988, s.528(2)(*b*).
[82] I.C.T.A. 1988, s.528(3)(*a*) & (*b*).
[83] I.C.T.A. 1988, s.533(1).
[84] I.C.T.A. 1988, s.526(2).
[85] I.C.T.A. 1988, s.528(2). See also the definition of "income from patents", §13.31 *ante*.

the outstanding amount of the expenditure.[86] The outstanding amount is reduced each year by the allowance given.

There is a balancing charge if the rights are disposed of for an amount which is more than the written-down value.[87] The balancing charge applies up to the amount of the expenditure originally incurred.[88] Any excess is taxed as a capital receipt from the sale of patent rights.[89] Conversely there is a balancing allowance if there is any unallowed expenditure remaining on permanent discontinuance of trade or on the last of the patent rights coming to an end.[90]

Capital payments pre March 31, 1986

Capital expenditure incurred on or before March 31, 1986, is written **13.34** off against tax on a straight–line basis over a fixed period, that is to say a writing–down allowance is calculated by dividing the capital expenditure by the writing–down period and an equal amount is allowed end year.[91] The writing–down period for patent rights is normally 17 years beginning with the chargeable period related to the expenditure.[92] If the rights are purchased for a specified period less than 17 years or if the remaining life of the patent is less than 17 years, then the writing down period is the number of years comprised within that lesser period.[93] If the patent has already been in existence for 17 complete years, then the whole of the expenditure is given for the year in which it was incurred.[94]

Where a person who has purchased patent rights before April 1, 1986, either sells all the patent rights before the end of the writing–down period (or sells any part of them for a sum equal to or greater than the amount of capital expenditure remaining unallowed) or where the rights come to an end before the end of such period, he will receive no further writing–down allowances.[95]

If all of such rights are sold and the net proceeds of the sale (so far as they consist of capital sums) are less than the amount of the capital expenditure remaining unallowed or if the rights come to an end, then a balancing allowance equal to the amount of capital expenditure remaining unallowed (less the net proceeds of the sale in the case of a sale) is made.[96]

Where all or any part of the patent rights are sold and the net proceeds of sale (so far as they consist of capital sums) exceed the amount of

---

[86] I.C.T.A. s.520.
[87] I.C.T.A. s.520(6).
[88] I.C.T.A. 1988, s.521(3)
[89] I.C.T.A. 1988, s.524.
[90] I.C.T.A. 1988, s.520(4).
[91] I.C.T.A. 1988, s.522. Capital Allowances Act 1990, s.146.
[92] I.C.T.A. 1988, s.522(3).
[93] I.C.T.A. 1988, s.522(4) & (5).
[94] I.C.T.A. 1988, s.522(5).
[95] I.C.T.A. 1988, s.523(1).
[96] I.C.T.A. 1988, s.523(2).

capital expenditure remaining unallowed, then a balancing charge equal to the excess is made for the chargeable period relating to the sale.[97] In addition to such a balancing charge, there may be a capital gain which will be liable to tax as a capital receipt from the sale of patent rights.[98]

If on sale of any part of the patent rights the preceding paragraph does not apply, then the writing–down allowance for the chargeable period related to the sale and subsequent periods is adjusted by dividing the difference between the sale price and the unallowed sum by the number of complete years of writing–down period remaining at the beginning of the chargeable period related to the sale.[99]

Manner of making allowances

13.35   Any allowance or charge in respect of capital expenditure on purchase of patent rights is made to or on a person in taxing his trade if he is carrying on trade and the patent rights in question were or were to be used for the purposes of that trade.[1] Thus, any allowance would be made against the profits or gains of the trade.

Where the allowance or charge is not to be made in taxing a trade, the amount of the allowance is deducted from or set off against income from patents[2] for the year of assessment, with any balance being carried forward to subsequent years.[3] Effect is given to any balancing charge by an assessment under Case VI of Schedule D.[4]

Royalty payments

13.36   Royalty payments[5] in respect of the user of a patent are not a deductible expense in computing the profits or gains of a trade.[6] However, where any such royalty is paid wholly out of profits or gains brought into change to income tax, the person making the payment is entitled on making it to deduct and retain a sum representing the amount of the income tax thereon at the standard rate.[7] But, if the royalty is not paid or is not paid wholly out of profits or gains bought into change to income tax, the person by, or through whom the payment

---

[97] I.C.T.A. 1988, s.523(3).
[98] I.C.T.A. 1988, s.524.
[99] I.C.T.A. 1988, s.523(4).
[1] I.C.T.A. 1988, s.528(1).
[2] See *post*, § 13.31.
[3] I.C.T.A. 1988, s.528(2). See also s.528(3) in respect of corporations.
[4] I.C.T.A. 1988, s.528(4)(*a*). See also s.528(4)(*b*) in respect of corporations.
[5] *i.e.* payments which are income, not capital, payments, see *ante*.
[6] I.C.T.A. s.74(*p*); see *Paterson Engineering Co. Ltd. v. Dutt*, 25 T.C. 43, royalty relating to the use of secret processes, advice and use of trade marks held to be deductible but royalty relating to use of patents not deductible.
[7] I.C.T.A. s.348(2)(*a*); see *Desoutter Brothers Ltd. v. Hanger & Co. Ltd and Artificial Limb Makers Ltd.* [1936] 1 All E.R. 535, installment of lump sum paid in advance for anticipated user held to be capital sum—income tax therefore not deductible.

is made must make the deduction[8] and must forthwith deliver to his Inspector of Taxes an account of the payment, on which he is assessable to income tax at the basic rate[9] even if he had failed to make the deduction.[10] If the recipient requests it, the payer must furnish him with a certificate of deduction of tax.[11]

Thus, the payer, in effect, acts as collector for the Crown of tax due from the recipient,[12] but, if he is paying tax on profits himself, he also secures a recoupment of tax in respect of his royalty payments.

B. Taxation of receipts

Taxation of sums received in respect of patent rights may be **13.37** considered as follows:

(a) Tax on capital sums received for sale of patent rights;
(b) Tax on royalties received in respect of patent rights;
(c) Miscellaneous.

(a) Sale of patent rights

Capital sums received for the sale of all or any part of any patent **13.38** rights[13] (which includes any assignment or licence)[14] or any sum received for a right to acquire, in the future, patent rights as respects any invention in respect of which the patent has not yet been granted,[15] are chargeable to tax as follows:

(i) Vendor resident in U.K.

Where the vendor is resident in the United Kingdom he will normally **13.39** be charged to tax under Case VI of Schedule D on one-sixth of the sum liable to tax for the accounting period or year of assessment in which such capital sum is received and for each of the succeeding five years.[16] However, the vendor may elect to be charged upon the whole sum for the accounting period or year of assessment in which it is received, in which case he must give notice in writing to the Inspector of Taxes not later than two years after the end of the chargeable period in which the capital sum was received.[17]

---

[8] I.C.T.A. s.349(1)(*b*).
[9] I.C.T.A. s.350. For companies, see s.350(4), and Sched. 16.
[10] *Edinburgh Life Assurance Co. v. Lord Advocate* [1910] A.C. 143.
[11] I.C.T.A. 1988, s.352.
[12] See the explanation of the Scheme in *Allchin v. Coulthard* [1943] A.C. 607 at p.619, *per* Viscount Simond L.C.
[13] I.C.T.A. 1988, s.533(1).
[14] I.C.T.A. 1988, s.533(2).
[15] I.C.T.A. 1988, s.533(5) and (6).
[16] I.C.T.A. 1988, s.524(1).
[17] I.C.T.A. 1988, s.524(2).

Where the patent rights to be sold were acquired by the vendor by payment of a capital sum, the vendor will be charged on the net capital gain. The net proceeds of sale when the vendor sells the patent rights are reduced by the amount the vendor paid for the patent rights for the purposes of assessment for tax.[18] There is no capital gain in respect of any gain charged to income tax.[19]

Deaths, windings up and partnership changes

13.40   If the vendor dies or the trade of a partnership is discontinued or being a body corporate is wound up before the beginning of the last six years, no sums will be charged for any year subsequent to the year in which the death or discontinuance takes place or the winding up commences, but the amount to be charged for the year or accounting period in which the death or discontinuance takes place or winding up commences will be that total amount which, but for the death or discontinuance or winding up, would be charged for subsequent years.[23]

In the case of a death, the personal respresentatives are entitled to have the income tax payable out of the deceased's estate reduced so as not to exceed the total amount of income tax which would have been payable by the deceased if the charge had been spread over the period of years from when the capital sum was received until the year of death.[21]

In the case of the discontinuance of a partnership, the additional amount on which tax is chargeable is to be apportioned among the members of the partnership according to their respective shares in the partnership profits, immediately before the discontinuance. Each partner (or, if dead, his personal representatives) has the same right to reduction of income tax payable as in the case of a death.[22]

(ii) Vendor non-resident

13.41   Where the vendor is not resident in the United Kingdom and sells United Kingdom patent rights, the vendor is assessable under Case VI of Schedule D.[23] Provision is made for deduction of the tax by the person by, or through whom any payment of capital sum is made at the standard rate in force at the time of payment and for paying over the tax to the Inland Revenue.[24]

The non–resident vendor may elect (by notice in writing to the Commissioners of Inland Revenue to be given not later than two years

---

[18] I.C.T.A. 1988, s.524(7).
[19] Taxation of Chargeable Gains Act 1992, s.37(1).
[20] I.C.T.A. 1988, s.525(1).
[21] I.C.T.A. 1988, s.525(2).
[22] I.C.T.A. 1988, s.525(3) and (4).
[23] I.C.T.A. 1988, s.524(3).
[24] I.C.T.A. 1988, ss.349 and 350.

after the end of the year of assessment in which the sum is paid) to spread the capital sum over six years.[25] But this does not affect the obligation on the person by, or through whom the payment is made to deduct tax.[26] Any adjustments and repayments of tax are then made year by year.[27]

Sale of patent rights not at arm's length

Transactions after March 31, 1988, between connected persons or **13.42** where it appears that the sole or main benefit of the transaction was the obtaining of an allowance under section 520(4) are subject to special provisions.[28] Transactions on or before March 31, 1986, are subject to similar provisions.[29] Thus, if the vendor or purchaser has control over the other (*e.g.* as in the case of a purchase or sale by a majority shareholder in a company) or if they are under common control (*e.g.* a subsidiary company controlled by a parent company) then the value of the patent rights in the open market may be substituted for the actual sale price.

(a) Tax on Royalties

The scheme for the payment of royalties and the deduction of tax **13.43** therefrom by the payer is described above.[30] The effect of the scheme is that the recipient of royalty payments will normally receive the amount due by way of royalties less income tax at the basic rate. The payer, in effect, acts as collector for the Crown of the tax due.

As Lord Green M.R. said in *Inland Revenue Commissions v. British Salmson Aero Engines Limited*[31]

> "... where a business is being carried on with the use of the patents in respect of which royalties or other sums fall to be paid, the person carrying on the business, in computing his profits, cannot deduct the sums in question. On the other hand, he is entitled under rule 19 (now section 52(2)) and bound under rule 21 (now section 53) when he comes to make the payment, to deduct the tax."

Deduction of income tax on royalties at the source secures the collection of the tax on the profits derived from the working of patents in the United Kingdom payable to patentees who reside abroad and have no

---

[25] I.C.T.A. 1988, s.524(4). for corporations, see s.524(6).
[26] I.C.T.A. 1988, s.524(4)(*a*).
[27] I.C.T.A. 1988, s.524(4)(*b*) and (*c*).
[28] I.C.T.A. 1988, ss.520(5) and (6) as amended and substituted by Finance Act 1989, ss.121, 187(1), Sched. 13, para.27, Sched. 17, Pt.VI.
[29] I.C.T.A. 1988, s.532(2); Capital Allowances Act 1990, ss.157 and 158.
[30] See *ante*, § 13.36.
[31] [1938] 2 K.B. 482 at p.497; 22 T.C. 29.

agent resident in this country; an agreement to pay the full amount of a royalty without any deduction is void.[32]

In cases of failure to deduct the tax the Revenue may assess the recipient direct under Case III of Schedule D.[33]

13.44 Where a person received a royalty or other non-capital payment in respect of the past user of a patent which extended over six or more years, that person may require that the income tax or corporation tax payable shall be reduced so as not to exceed the total amount of income or corporation tax which would have been payable if the payment had been made in six equal instalments at yearly intervals, the last of which being made on the date on which the payment was in fact made.[34] If such payment is in respect of at least two years but less than six years' user the patentee may claim an adjustment so that his liability is spread over the number of complete years in the period of user.[35]

(b) Miscellaneous

13.45 *Invention income*

An individual's income derived from an invention actually devised and patented by him whether alone or jointly is treated as earned income for the purposes of earned income relief.[36]

Compensation awards

Under section 40 of the 1977 Act the court or the comptroller may award compensation to be paid by an employer to an employee who has made an invention belonging to the employer. Such compensation may be awarded where the employee has made an invention for which a patent has been granted and the patent is of outstanding benefit to the employer. It is to be noted that it is the patent (not the invention itself or the work done by the inventor) which must be of outstanding benefit.[36a] It may be, therefore, that the compensation paid is not directly related to the employment and thus not taxable under Schedule E.

---

[32] Taxes Management Act 1970, s.106(2).
[33] *Wild v. Ionides*, 9 T.C. 392; *Grosvenor Place Estates v. Roberts* [1961] Ch.148.
[34] I.C.T.A. 1988, s.527(1).
[35] I.C.T.A. 1988, s.527(2).
[36] I.C.T.A. 1988, s.529.
[36a] *Memco-Med Ltd.'s Patent* [1992] R.P.C. 403 at pp. 412–413; see also *GEC Avionics Ltd.'s Patent* [1992] R.P.C. 107, and *British Steel Plc's Patent* [1992] R.P.C. 117.

Double taxation agreements[37]

Sums on the sale of patent rights and patent royalties arising in one country and payable to a resident of another country may be exempt from tax.

4. VAT

Value added tax is charged on any supply of services made in the United Kingdom where it is a taxable supply made by a taxable person in the course or furtherance of any business carried on by him.[38] The term "supply" includes all forms of supply (but not anything done otherwise than for consideration) and anything which is not a supply of goods but is done for a consideration (including, if so done, the granting, assignment or surrender of any right) is a supply of services.[39] The term "a taxable person" includes any person registered for VAT.[40]

13.46

Where there is a transfer or assignment of patents, licences or similar rights by a person who belongs in a country other than the United Kingdom and received by a person who belongs in the United Kingdom for the purposes of any business carried on by him, a reverse charge (*i.e.* a charge on the recipient) applies.[41] A recipient who is registered for VAT is, however, entitled to credit for input tax.[42]

As patent proprietors are commonly registered for VAT, it follows that VAT will normally be payable on most transactions involving patents. Accordingly, it is prudent to ensure that patent licences and other transactions involving patents expressly provide for VAT, insofar as it may be payable, to be paid in addition to the agreed royalty or other sum by way of consideration.[43] The proprietor may be required to provide a VAT invoice or receipt to enable the payer to obtain credit as input tax for the VAT paid.

---

[37] I.C.T.A. 1988, Pt. XVIII.
[38] VAT Act 1983, s.2(1).
[39] *Ibid.*, s.3(2).
[40] *Ibid.*, s.2(5).
[41] *Ibid.*, s.7, and see Sched. 3, para.1.
[42] *Ibid.*, ss.14 and 15; but note s.7(3).
[43] The consideration paid on settlement of legal proceedings may also be subject to V.A.T., see *Cooper Chagney Ltd. v. Commissioners of Customs and Excise* [1992] F.S.R. 298.

CHAPTER 14

PRECEDENTS AND PLEADINGS

Contents   *Para.*

1. High Court

A. General High Court Heading   14.01

IN THE HIGH COURT OF JUSTICE   CH 199 – – No. .
CHANCERY DIVISION
PATENTS COURT

[Writ issued the ____ day of _____]¹

BETWEEN

_____

                                                    Plaintiff

              and

_____

                                                    Defendant

---

¹ To be included on a Statement of Claim not endorsed on Writ.

B. Indorsement of Writ

THE PLAINTIFF CLAIMS:

1. A declaration that United Kingdom Patent No. _____:

   (a) is valid; and
   (b) has been infringed by the Defendant.

2. An injunction to restrain the Defendant, whether acting by its [directors, officers,] [partners,] servants or agents or otherwise howsoever, from infringing United Kingdom Patent No. _____.

3. The delivery up or the destruction upon oath of all material in the possession, custody, power or control of the Defendant the keeping or disposal of which would infringe the foregoing injunction.

4. An enquiry as to damages, or, at the Plaintiff's option, an account of profits by reason of the Defendant's acts of infringements of the United Kingdom Patent No. _____.

5. An Order that the Defendants do pay to the Plaintiff all the sums found due on taking such account and/or enquiry, together with interest to be assessed thereon pursuant to Section 35A of the Supreme Court Act 1981 and/or the equitable jurisdiction of the Court.

6. Further or other relief.

7. Costs.

C. Statement of Claim   14.03

1. The Plaintiff is the Registered Proprietor of United Kingdom Patent No. _____ entitled "_____" (hereinunder referred to as "the Patent").

2. The Patent is in force.

3. [(*where the specification has been amended*) The complete specification of the Patent was amended pursuant to and in accordance with, the decision of (*state whom*) dated ____ day of _____. The specification as originally published was framed in good faith with reasonable skill and knowledge].[2]

4. The Defendant has carried out the acts referred to in the Particulars of Infringement served herewith.

5. By carrying out the acts referred to in the Particulars of Infringement the Defendant has infringed the Patent.

6. By reason of the Defendant's acts of infringement of the Patent the Plaintiff has suffered loss and damage.

7. Further, unless restrained by an order of this Honourable Court, the Defendant threatens and intends to continue the acts complained of herein whereby the Plaintiff will suffer further loss and damage.

8. The Plaintiff is not at present able to give particulars of all the Defendant's acts of infringement but at the trial of this action the Plaintiff will seek relief in respect of all such acts.

9. Further, the Plaintiff seeks an order for interest upon all sums found due herein pursuant to section 35A of the Supreme Court Act 1981 and/or the equitable jurisdiction of the Court such interest to be awarded at the rate of ____ per cent from the date of each act of infringement complained of herein or at such rate and for such period as shall to this Honourable Court seem fit.

10. [Further a certificate of contested validity was granted on _____ by _____ in respect of the Patent. In the premises the Plaintiff in this action is entitled to its solicitor and client costs pursuant to section 65(2) of the Patents Act 1977].

AND THE PLAINTIFF CLAIMS:

(*continue as for writ above*)

---

[2] P.A. 1977, s.62(3).

14.04 ### D. Particulars of Infringement[3]

The following are the Particulars of Infringement of United Kingdom Patent No. _____ referred to in paragraphs 4 and 5 of the Statement of Claim herein:

1. Prior to the date of the issue of the Writ herein but subsequent to the date of publication of the application for United Kingdom Patent No. _____ the Defendant has infringed the said Patent by doing the following acts[4] that is to say:

(a)[5] —
    (i)   making;
    (ii) disposing of;
    (iii) offering to dispose of;
    (iv) using;
    (v) importing; and/or
    (vi) keeping in the United Kingdom (whether for disposal or otherwise)

(*state product*) as claimed in claims _____ of the said Patent.

(b)[6] —
    (i)   using; and/or offering to use in the United Kingdom

(*state process*) as claimed in claims _____ of the said Patent.

(c)[7] —
    (i)   disposing of;
    (ii) offering to dispose of;
    (iii) using;
    (iv) importing; and/or
    (v) keeping (whether for disposal or otherwise)

(*state product*) obtained directly by means of (*state process*) as claimed in claims _____ of the said Patent.

(d)[8] —
    (i)   supplying; and/or
    (ii) offering to supply in the United Kingdom a person other than a licensee or other person entitled to work the invention with

---

[3] See R.S.C., Ord. 104, r.5.
[4] Acts restrained are specified with reference to P.A. 1977, s.60(1).
[5] Where infringement complained of is a product; see P.A. 1977, s.60(1)(*a*).
[6] Where infringment complained of is a process; see P.A. 1977, s.60(1)(*b*).
[7] Where infringement complained of is a product by process; see P.A. 1977, s.60(1)(*c*).
[8] Contributory infringement; see P.A. 1977, s.60(2).

means relating to an essential element of the invention, for putting the invention into effect in the United Kingdom when he knew, or when it was obvious to a reasonable person in the circumstances, that those means were suitable for putting, and were intended to put, the invention into effect in the United Kingdom.

2. In particular the Plaintiff complains of the doing of the aforesaid acts[9] by (*state particulars of alleged infringing acts identifying date, place and relevant product/process*)

3.[10] [Further each of the acts complained of would, if the patent had been granted on the date of the publication of the application, have infringed claims ⸻ in the form in which they were contained in the application immediately before preparation for its publication were completed by the Patent Office].

4. [The Plaintiff is not at present able to state the precise dates of when such acts were undertaken by the Defendant, such particulars being only within the Defendant's knowledge].

---

[9] R.S.C., Ord. 104, r.5(2): the Plaintiff must give at least one instance of each type of infringement relied upon.

[10] Where acts complained of took place in the period between the date of publication of the application and the grant of the patent; see P.A. 1977, s.69.

E. Defence and Counterclaim

DEFENCE[11]

1. Paragraph 1 of the Statement of Claim is admitted.

2. It is admitted that the said Patent is in force, however, it is averred that the said Patent is and has at all times been invalid for the reasons set out in the Particulars of Objections served herewith.

3. [It is admitted that the said Patent was amended in accordance with the decision of ___ dated ___ day of _____. It is denied that the specification as originally published was framed in good faith with reasonable skill and knowledge.]

4. It is admitted that the Defendant committed the following acts referred to in the Particulars of Infringement, namely: _____. Save as aforesaid paragraph 4 of the Statement of Claim is denied.

5. It is denied that the Defendant has infringed the patent by reason of the acts specified in the Particulars of Infringement or at all.

6. If, which is denied, the Defendant has infringed the Patent as alleged or at all, in defence to this action there was in force at the time of such infringement [a contract relating to the Patent made by or with the consent of the Plaintiff/a licence under the Patent granted by him or with his consent] containing a condition or term void by virtue of section 44 of the Patents Act 1977.

Particulars

Give particulars

7. If, which is denied, the Defendant has infringed the Patent as alleged or at all, in defence to the claim for damages or an account of profits, at the date of the infringements complained of, the Defendant was not aware, and had no reasonable grounds for supposing that the Patent existed.[12]

Particulars

Give particulars of grounds relied on

8. If, which is denied, the Defendant has infringed the Patent as alleged or at all, in defence to any damages or any other order in respect of the alleged infringement, a further period under section 25(4) of the

---

[11] See also the defences available other than under the Patents Act set out at §12.71 *supra*.
[12] P.A. 1977, s.62(1).

Patents Act 1977 existed during which the renewal fees for the patent were unpaid.[13]

Particulars

Give particulars of period relied upon

9. If, which is denied, the Defendant has infringed the Patent as alleged or at all, in defence to any claim for damages in respect of any acts before the date of the decision to amend the Patent, the Patent was not framed in good faith and with reasonable skill and knowledge.[14]

Particulars

Give particulars of lack of good faith and reasonable skill and knowledge

10. The Defendant has the right to continue the acts complained of herein in that before the priority date of the patent it (a) did in good faith the said acts; and/or (b) made in good faith effective and serious preparations to do such acts.[15]

Particulars

Give particulars of facts and matters relied upon

11. If, which is denied, the Defendant has infringed the Patent as alleged or at all, the Plaintiff became the [co-]proprietor/exclusive licensee of the Patent by virtue of an instrument which was registrable under section 33 but which was not registered within 6 months of its date. In the premises, the Plaintiff is not entitled to any damages or an account of profits prior to the said date.[16]

Particulars

Give particulars of unregistered transaction relied upon.

12. The Patent was granted to a person who was not entitled to be granted the Patent and, in the premises, the Patent is invalid on this

---

[13] See P.A. 1977, s.62(2).
[14] See P.A. 1977, s.62(3).
[15] See P.A. 1977, s.64.
[16] See P.A. 1977, s.68.

ground and may be relied on in defence of this action under section 74(1)(*a*) of the Patents Act 1977.[17]

13. Paragraph 6 of the Statement of Claim is denied.

14. It is admitted that the Defendant intends lawfully to continue the acts admitted in paragraphs 4 and 6 above. Save as aforesaid paragraph 7 of the Statement of Claim is denied.

15. In the premises the Plaintiff is not entitled to the relief sought or any relief.

COUNTERCLAIM

16. Paragraph 2 of the Defence is repeated.

AND THE DEFENDANT COUNTERCLAIMS FOR:

(1) An Order that United Kingdom Patent No. _____ be revoked.
(2) Further or other relief.
(3) Costs.

---

[17] Only a person who was entitled may raise this plea: see *Dolphin Showers Ltd. v. Farmiloe* [1989] F.S.R. 1. Further, the proceedings must have commenced within two years of the date of grant of the Patent unless entitlement has already been determined in separate entitlement proceedings: P.A. 1977, s.74(4)(*b*).

F. Particulars of Objection[18]   14.06

The following are the Particulars of Objection to the validity of United Kingdom Patent No. _____ ("the Patent") referred to in the Defence and Counterclaim herein.

1. None of the claims of the Patent is in respect of a patentable invention in that the subject matter thereof was not new as of the priority date of the Patent having regard to the state of the art which comprised the following matter which was made available to the public prior thereto.

Particulars[19]
Hereunder the Defendant relies upon the following:

(a) *(Give particulars of prior publications)*.
(b) *(Give particulars of prior use, etc.)*[20]

2. None of the claims of the Patent is in respect of a patentable invention in that the subject matter thereof did not involve an inventive step as of the priority date of the Patent in that the same was obvious to a man skilled in the art having regard to the state of the art which comprised the following matter which was made available to the public prior thereto.

Particulars
Hereunder the Defendant relies upon:

(a) the publications referred to in paragraph (a) above.
(b) the facts and matters pleaded in paragraph 1 (b) above.
(c) *(give further particulars of publication or use)*.
(d) common general knowledge.[21]

3. None of the claims of the Patent is in respect of a patentable invention in that none is in respect of an invention capable of industrial application.

---

[18] R.S.C., Ord. 104, r.6.
[19] R.S.C., Ord. 104, r.6(3) requires the manner, time and place of every prior publication and user to be stated.
[20] See R.S.C., Ord. 104, r.6(3)(*a*) to 6(3)(*d*).
[21] In respect of the requirement to plead common general knowledge see notes to R.S.C., Ord. 104, r.6 at 104/6/4 of the *Supreme Court Practice, 1993*.

Particulars

(Give particulars)

4. None of the claims of the Patent is in respect of a patentable invention in that none is in respect of an "invention" within the meaning of the Patents Act 1977.

Particulars

(Give particulars relied upon under Patents Act 1977, section 1(2) or 1(3))

5. The Patent was granted to a person who was not entitled to the grant of the patent.[22]

Particulars

(Give particulars)

6. The specification of the patent does not disclose the alleged invention clearly enough and completely enough for it to be performed by a person skilled in the art.

Particulars

(Give particulars)

7. The matter disclosed in the specification of the Patent extends beyond that disclosed in the application as filed.[23]

Particulars

(Give particulars)

---

[22] This plea is only open to a party found to be entitled to the grant of that Patent, P.A. 1977, s.72(1)(b). *Dolphin Showers Ltd. v. Farmiloe* [1989] F.S.R. 1.
[23] See P.A. 1977, s.72(1)(c).

8. The protection conferred by the Patent has been extended by an amendment which should not have been allowed.[24]

Particulars

(Give particulars)

---

[24] See P.A. 1977, s.72(1)(*e*).

G. Reply and Defence to Counterclaim

Reply

1. The Plaintiff joins issue with the Defendant upon the Defence save insofar as it contains admissions.

2. It is denied that United Kingdom Patent No. _____ is invalid as alleged in paragraph 2 of the Defence or at all.

3. In response to the allegation that the invention of the Patent is obvious the Plaintiff will rely upon the commercial success of the invention.

Particulars of commercial success

(Give particulars of long felt want in particular the defect in the prior art that was overcome by the invention. Give particulars of sales[25])

Defence to counterclaim

4. Paragraph 15 of the Counterclaim is denied and paragraphs 2 and 3 of the Reply are repeated. The Defendant is not entitled to the relief for which it counterclaims nor any relief.

---

[25] R.S.C., Ord. 104, r.6(5); *John Deks Ltd. v. Aztec Washer Company* [1989] R.P.C. 413.

H. Notice of Motion for Interlocutory Injunction to Restrain Infringement of a Patent

14.08

TAKE NOTICE THAT this Honourable Court will be moved before the Chancery Patents Judge sitting at the Royal Courts of Justice, Strand, London, WC2 2LL on _____ day the ___ day of _____ at 10.30 o'clock in the forenoon (or soon thereafter as Counsel can be heard) by Counsel on behalf of the Plaintiff.
FOR AN ORDER THAT:[26]

The Defendant be restrained until after judgment or further order whether acting by its directors, officers, servants, agents or otherwise howsoever from doing the following acts[27] or any of them namely:

(i) importing, making, disposing of, offering to dispose of, using and/or keeping (whether for disposal or otherwise) (*state product (s)*).
(ii) using or offering to use in the United Kingdom (*state process*).
(iii) disposing of, offering to dispose of, using, importing, and/or keeping (whether for disposal or otherwise) any product obtained directly by means of (*state process*).
(iv) supplying or offering to supply (*state products*).

AND FOR such further or other order as shall to the Court seem fit including an Order providing for the costs of this application.

---

[26] Acts restrained are specified with reference to P.A. 1977, ss.60(1) and (2).
[27] Interlocutory junctions should be limited to specific acts and should not be as broad as "infringement of Patent No. ____". See the comments of Falconer J. in *Mölnlycke A.B. v. Proctor & Gamble Ltd.* [1990] R.P.C. 487 at 494. See also *Staver Company Inc. v. Digitext Display Ltd.* [1985] F.S.R. 521; *Video Arts Ltd. v. Paget Ltd.* [1986] F.S.R. 623.

14.09   I. Interlocutory Injunction to Restrain Infringement of a Patent

UPON MOTION made by Counsel for the Plaintiff

AND UPON HEARING Counsel for the Plaintiff and Counsel for the Defendant

AND UPON READING the documents recorded on the Court File as having been read

AND UPON the Plaintiff by its Counsel undertaking to abide by any Order this Court may make as to damages in the event this Court shall hereafter be of the opinion that the Defendant shall have sustained any by reason of the Order which the Plaintiff ought to pay.

IT IS ORDERED THAT

(For form of relief see Notice of Motion above)

J. Notice of Experiments[28]   14.10

TAKE NOTICE that the Defendant proposes to establish the facts set out below by experimental proof and that the Plaintiff is requested within ____ days to state whether or not it admits each such fact.

FACTS TO BE PROVED

1. Fact A
2. Fact B

PARTICULARS OF EXPERIMENTS

Experiment 1
(Give experimental protocol)

Experiment 2
(Give experimental protocol)

---

[28] Ord. 104, r.12.

14.11   **K. Order Pursuant to Judgment**

THIS ACTION AND COUNTERCLAIM coming on for trial before this Honourable Court on _____

AND UPON READING the documents recorded in the Court file as having been read

THIS COURT DOTH ORDER THAT this Action and Counterclaim do stand for judgment.

[AND UPON the Plaintiff by its Counsel undertaking to amend United Kingdom Patent _____ to delete claim _____ therefrom and to make any necessary amendments consequential thereupon]

THIS COURT DOTH ORDER THAT

1. The Defendant be restrained whether acting by its directors, officers servants or agents or otherwise howsoever from infringing U.K. Patent No. _____.

2. The Defendant does within 14 days [destroy/deliver up to the Plaintiff] all material in its possession, custody, or control which infringes U.K. Patent No. _____ and does within ____ days thereafter by its proper officer made swear and serve upon the Plaintiff an affidavit verifying that it has [destroyed/delivered up] all such material.

[AND THIS COURT DOTH ORDER THAT paragraphs 1 and 2 be stayed pending an appeal to the Court of Appeal provided that the said Appeal is prosecuted with due diligence]

AND THIS COURT DOTH ORDER THAT [an enquiry be taken as to whether the specification of U.K. Patent No. _____ was drafted in good faith with reasonable skill and knowledge and, if it is so held, it is order that]

(a) The following enquiry be taken, that is to say an enquiry as to the damage suffered by the Plaintiff by reason of the Defendant's infringement of Patent No. _____.

(b) The Defendant does pay to the Plaintiff all sums found due on the taking of the said enquiry together with interest thereon pursuant to section 35A of the Supreme Court Act 1981.

(c) The Plaintiff the costs of this action and counterclaim to be taxed forthwith if not agreed.

(d) The costs of the enquiry be reserved.

AND THIS COURT DOTH DECLARE THAT

(i) Claims _____ of U.K. Patent No. _____ are valid [and have been infringed by the Defendant].

(ii) Claim _____ of U.K. Patent No. _____ is invalid.

AND THIS COURT DOTH CERTIFY THAT

(1) The Particulars of Infringement in respect of U.K. Patent No. _____ were reasonable and were proved.

(2) The validity of claims of U.K. Patent No. _____ were unsuccessfully contested.[29]

---

[29] P.A. 1977, s.65.

14.12   **L. Statement of Claim for a Declaration of Non-Infringement**

1. The Plaintiff carries on business as _____.

2. The Defendant is the proprietor of U.K. Patent No. _____ entitled "_____" ("the Patent"). The Patent is in force.

3. The Plaintiff avers that the manufacture of _____ would not constitute an infringement of any of the claims of the Patent.

4. The Plaintiff wrote to the Defendant on _____ requesting written acknowledgement that the manufacture of _____ would not infringe the said Patent. Full particulars of the aforesaid manufacture were given. The Defendants have failed and/or refused to give such acknowledgement.

5.[30] Further, the Defendant has asserted that the said acts of the Plaintiff infringe the Patent.

Particulars

(Give particulars)

AND THE PLAINTIFF CLAIMS:

1. A declaration pursuant to section 71(1) of the Patents Act 1977 and/or the inherent jurisdiction of the Court that the manufacture of _____ would not constitute an infringement of any of the claims of U.K. Patent No. _____.

2. Further or other relief.

3. Costs.

---

[30] Where relief under inherent jurisdiction sought.

M. Minute of Order for Directions 14.13

The draft order is reproduced in the notes of Order 104 of the Rules of the Supreme Court at 104/14/4.

The following, which was prepared with the assistance of the Patents Court Users Committee, has the approval of the Senior Patents Judge. It is intended only as a guide and may need adaptation for particular circumstances.

*indicates a provision which may be necessary when a rule, e.g. for automatic discovery, has not been complied with.

[UPON THE SUMMONS FOR DIRECTIONS in this Action and Counterclaim].

AND UPON HEARING Counsel for the Plaintiffs and for the Defendants.

[AND UPON THE PLAINTIFFS by their Counsel undertaking forthwith to issue a pro-forma summons for directions and treating that summons as before the Court].

AND UPON READING the documents marked in the Court file as having been read

THIS COURT ORDERS THAT

[Transfer
1. This Action and Counterclaim be transferred to the Patents County Court].
(If this order is made, no other order will generally be necessary)

Proof of Documents
2. Legible copies of the specification of the Patent in suit [and any Patent specifications or other documents cited in the Particulars of Objections] may be used at the trial without further proof thereof or of their contents.

Amendments to Pleadings
3. The Plaintiffs have leave to amend their Writ herein by [ ] and that service of the Writ and the Defendants' acknowledgement of service stand and that that the costs of and occasioned by the amendments be the Defendants in any event.
4. The Plaintiffs have leave to amend their Statement of Claim [and

Particulars of Infringement] as shown in red on the copy [annexed to the Summons for Directions/as signed by the solicitors for the parties/ annexed hereto] and [to re–serve the same on or before [ ]/and that re-service be dispensed with] and that the Defendants have leave to serve a consequentially amended Defence within [ ] days [thereafter/ hereafter] and that the Plaintiffs have leave to serve a consequentially amended Reply (if so advised) within [ ] days thereafter.

5. —

(a) The Defendants have leave to amend their Defence [and Counter-claim and Particulars of Objections] as shown in red on the copy [annexed to the Summons for Directions/as signed by the solicitors for the parties/annexed hereto] and [to reserve the same within [ ] days/on or before][and that re–service be dispensed with] and that the Plaintiffs have leave to serve a consequentially amended Reply (if so advised) within [ ] days thereafter.

(b) The Plaintiffs do on or before [ ] elect whether they will discontinue this Action and withdraw their Defence to Counter-claim and consent to an Order for the revocation of Patent No. [ ] ("the patent in suit") AND IF the Plaintiffs shall so elect and give notice thereof in the time aforesaid IT IS ORDERED THAT the patent in suit be revoked and that it be referred to the taxing master to tax the costs of the Defendants of this Action and Counterclaim up to and including [ ] being the date of delivery of the [amended] Particulars of Objections and Counterclaim to the date of this Order [except so far as the same have been increased by the failure of the Defendants originally to deliver the Defence and Counterclaim in its amended form], and to tax the costs of the Plaintiffs in this Action and Counterclaim from [ ] [insofar as they have been increased by the failure of the Defendants aforesaid] AND IT IS ORDERED that the said taxing officer is to set off the costs of the Defendants and of the Plaintiffs when so taxed as aforesaid and to certify to which of them the balance after such set–off is due.

Further and Better Particulars

6. —

(a) The [Plaintiffs/Defendants] do on or before [ ] serve on the [Defendants/Plaintiffs] the Further and Better Particulars of the [ ] as requested by the [Plaintiffs/Defendants] by their Request served on the [Defendants/Plaintiffs] on [ ] [and/or]

(b) The [Plaintiffs/Defendants] do on or before [ ] serve on the [Defendants/Plaintiffs] a response to their Request for Further and Better Particulars of the [ ] served on the [Defendants/ Plaintiffs] on [ ].

Admissions*

7. The [Plaintiffs/Defendants] do on or before [ ] state in writing whether or not they admit the facts specified in the [Defendants'/ Plaintiffs'] Notice to Admit facts dated [ ] and that the said Notice shall stand as a Notice to Admit within the meaning of Order 27, rule 2 and Order 62, rule 7 of the Rules of the Supreme Court.

Security

8. The Plaintiffs do provide security for the Defendants' costs in the sum of £ by [paying the said sum into Court and giving notice of such payment in to the Defendants] [paying the said sum into an account at [ ] Bank of [ ] in the joint names of solicitors for the parties] [giving the Defendants a bond securing the said sum [in the terms annexed hereto] on or before [ ] and that in the meantime all further proceedings be stayed.

Lists of Documents*

9. —
 (a) The Plaintiffs and the Defendants respectively do on or before [ ] make and serve on the other of them a list of the documents which are or have been in their possession, custody, power or control relating to the matters in question in this Action and Counter-claim and on request file an affidavit verifying such list.
 (b) In respect of those issues identified in Schedule [ ] hereto discovery shall be limited to those [documents/categories of documents] listed in Schedule [ ].

Inspection*

10. If any party wishes to inspect or have copies of such documents as are in another party's possession, power, custody or control it shall give notice in writing that it wishes to do so and such inspection shall be allowed at all reasonable times upon reasonable notice and any copies shall be provided within [ ] working days of the request upon the undertaking of the party requesting the copies to pay the reasonable copying charges.

Experiments*

11. —
 (a) If any party shall wish to establish any fact by experimental proof that party shall on or before [ ] serve on all the other parties a notice stating the facts which it desires to establish and giving full particulars of the experiments proposed to establish them.
 (b) A party upon whom a notice is served under the preceding

subparagraph shall within 21 days serve on the party serving the notice a notice stating in respect of each fact whether or not that party admits it.

(c) Where any fact which a party wishes to establish by experimental proof is not admitted that party may apply to the Court for further directions in respect of such experiments.

[or, where Order 104, rule 11 has been complied with]

(a) The Plaintiffs/Defendants are to afford to the other parties an opportunity, if so requested, of inspecting a repetition of the experiments identified in paragraphs [ ] of the Notice[s] of Experiments served on [ ]. Any such inspection must be requested within [ ] days of the date of this Order and shall take place within [ ] days of the date of the request.

(b) If any party shall wish to establish any fact in reply by experimental proof that party shall on or before [ ] serve on all the other parties a notice stating the facts which it desires to establish and giving full particulars of the experiments proposed to establish them.

(c) A party upon whom a notice is served under the preceding subparagraph shall within 21 days serve on the party serving the notice a notice stating in respect of each fact whether or not that party admits it.

(d) Where any fact which a party wishes to establish by experimental proof in reply is not admitted that party may apply to the Court for further directions in respect of such experiments.

Notice of Models, etc.

12. —

(a) If any party wishes to rely at the trial of this action upon any model, apparatus, drawing, photographs, cinematograph or video film that party shall on or before [ ] give notice thereof to all the other parties; shall afford the other parties an opportunity within 14 days of the service of such notice of inspecting the same and shall, if so requested, furnish the other party with copies of any such drawing or photograph and a sufficient drawing, photograph or other illustration of any model or apparatus.

(b) If any party wishes to rely upon any such materials in reply to any matter of which notice was given under subparagraph (a) of this paragraph, that party shall within 14 days after the last inspection to be made in pursuance of the said subparagraph (a) give to the other parties a like notice; if so requested within seven days of delivery of such notice shall afford like opportunities of inspection which shall take place within seven days of such request; and shall in like manner furnish copies of any drawing or photograph and illustration of any such model or apparatus.

(c) No further or other model, apparatus, drawing, photograph, cinematograph or video film shall be relied upon in evidence by either party save with mutual consent or leave of the Court.

Written evidence

13. —

(a) Each party may call up to [ ] expert witnesses in this Action and Counterclaim provided that the said party

  (i) supplies the name of such expert to the other parties and to the Court on or before [ ]; and

  (ii) no later than [(date)/[ ] days before the date set for the hearing of this Action and Counterclaim] serve upon the other parties a report of each such expert comprising the evidence which that expert intends to give at trial.

(b) Each party shall on or before [ ] serve on the other parties [signed] written statements of the oral evidence which the party intends to lead on any issues of fact to be decided at the trial, such statements to stand as the evidence in chief of the witness unless the Court otherwise directs;

(c) The parties shall ... (*here insert the particular directions sought, e.g. within 21 days after service of the other party's expert reports and written statements state in writing the facts and matters in those reports and statements which are admitted*).

Admissibility of evidence

14. A party who objects to any statement of any witness being read by the judge prior to the hearing of the trial, shall serve upon each other party a notice in writing to that effect setting out the grounds of the objection.

Non-compliance

15. Where either party fails to comply with the directions relating to experiments and written evidence it shall not be entitled to adduce evidence to which such directions relate without the leave of the Court.

Trial Bundles

16. Each party shall no later than [28] days before the date fixed for the trial of this Action and Counterclaim serve upon the parties a list of all the documents to be included in the trial bundles. The Plaintiffs shall no later than [21] days before the date fixed for trial serve upon the Defendants index of the bundles for use at trial.

Trial

17. The trial of these proceedings shall be before an Assigned Judge alone in London, estimated length [ ] days and a pre–reading estimate for the Judge of [ ] days.

Setting Down

18. Any party may set this Action and Counterclaim down for trial [after [date]/forthwith] [to heard not before [ ] [with liberty to apply for an earlier date].

Liberty to Apply

19. The parties are to be at liberty on two days notice to apply for further directions and generally.

Costs

20. The costs of this Application are to be costs in the Action and Counterclaim.

N. Petition for Revocation   14.14

IN THE HIGH COURT OF JUSTICE   CH 1993 No.
CHANCERY DIVISION
PATENTS COURT

IN THE MATTER OF United Kingdom Patent No. _____
in the name of _____ ("the Respondent")

AND IN THE MATTER OF the Patents Act 1977

AND IN THE MATTER OF a Petition by _____ ("the
Petitioner") to revoke the said Patent

To Her Majesty's High Court of Justice

_____

PETITION

_____

The humble petition of _____ SHEWETH as follows:

1. The Respondent is the proprietor of United Kingdon Patent
No._____ (hereinafter referred to as "the Patent") entitled "_____".
2. The Patent is in force.
3. The Patent is invalid for the reasons set out in the Particulars of
Objection accompanying this petition.[31]

AND your Petitioner therefore humbly prays for an Order that:

---

[31] Particulars of objections similar to those served in an action for infringement must
accompany the petition.

(a) United Kingdom Patent No. _____ be revoked;
(b) The Respondent does pay your Petitioner's costs

AND such further or other Order as shall to the Court seems just.

AND your Petitioner shall ever pray, etc.

TAKE notice that this Petition is intended to be served on _____ whose address for service is _____

AND further take notice that your Petitioner's solicitors are _____.

O. Notice of Motion for Leave to Amend Specification Where Action 14.15 for Infringement, or Petition for Revocation Pending[32]

(Title of action or petition)

TAKE NOTICE THAT this Honourable Court will be moved by Counsel on behalf of the Plaintiff that it may be granted leave to amend the specification of United Kingdom Patent No. _____ as indicated in red ink on the copy of the specification certified by the Comptroller–General of Patents served herewith and advertised in the Official Journal on _____.

AND THAT for the purposes of the application for leave to amend direction may be given for the hearing and determination thereof in terms of the minute of order served herewith.

---

[32] P.A. 1977, s.75. Procedure is governed by R.S.C., Ord 104, r.3.

14.16   P. Minute of Order on Application for Directions for Amendment in the Course of an Action

----

MINUTE OF ORDER

UPON MOTION made by Counsel for the Plaintiff

AND UPON HEARING Counsel for the Plaintiff and for the Defendant

AND UPON READING the documents recorded in the Court file as having been read

IT IS ORDERED THAT:

1. The Plaintiff be at liberty to proceed with its Motion for leave to amend United Kingdom Patent No. _____ ("The Patent") upon the directions hereafter set out.

2. The Plaintiff does serve upon the Defendant within 21 days its Statement of Reasons for the amendments.

3. The Defendant does within 21 days of service of the Statement of Reasons serve upon the Plaintiff its Statement in Answer thereto.

4. The Plaintiff does within 14 days of the service of the Statement in Answer serve its Statement in Reply thereto if so advised.

5. The evidence in chief to be adduced at the hearing of the Motion is to be way of affidavit.

6. The Plaintiff does serve its evidence in support of the application to amend on or before [ ] and at the same time does disclose any documents relating to the matters in issue on the said application. If any privilege is claimed in any documents such claim to privilege is to be stated in the affidavit.

7. The Defendant does serve its evidence (if any) in opposition of the application to amend on or before [ ] and at the same time does disclose any documents relating to the matters in issue on the said application. If any privilege is claimed in any documents such claim to privilege is to be stated in the affidavit.

8. The Plaintiff does serve its evidence in reply to the evidence of the Defendant on or before [ ].

9. Where either party wishes to cross-examine any deponent upon the contents of his or her affidavit that party shall serve on the other a notice to that effect no later than 28 days before the time fixed for the hearing of the application to amend. If any person of whom notice has been given

fails to attend for cross-examination that person's affidavit shall not be admitted save by consent or with the leave of the Court.

10. The hearing of this application to amend shall be heard at the same time as the action for infringement of the Patent.

14.17 Q. Statement of Reasons for Amendment of Patent Where Action for Infringement, or Petition for Revocation Pending[33]

(*Title of action or petition*)

STATEMENT OF REASONS

---

1. The following are the Plaintiff's reasons for seeking the amendments to United Kingdom Patent No. _____ ("the Patent") as shown in red ink on the copy of the specification certified by the Comptroller-General of Patents served herewith and advertised in the Official Journal on _____.

2. The following amendments, namely

(*state amendments*)

are each by way of (*disclaimer and/or explanation*) and relate to (*state feature of invention disclaimed and/or explained*). The purpose of these amendments is [further] to distinguish the Patent over the prior art cited by the Defendant in these proceedings.

3. The following amendments, namely

(*state amendments*)

are each consequential on the amendment (*state triggering amendment*)

4. The following amendments, namely

(*state amendments*)

are each by way of the correction of an obvious mistake.

5. The following amendments, namely

(*state amendments*)

are each to make clear and to emphasise that particular inventive step resides in (*state inventive step*). The said amendments strengthen the validity of the Patent over the prior art cited by the Defendant in these proceedings none of which discloses such (*state inventive step*).

---

[33] P.A. 1977, s.75; for procedure see R.S.C., Ord. 104, r.3.

R. Statement of Claim, Action to Restrain Threats[34] 14.18

(Title of action or petition)

1. The Plaintiff carries on business, *inter alia*, as _____.
2. The Defendant is the registered proprietor of United Kingdom Patent No. _____ entitled "_____" ("the Patent").
3. Prior to the issue of the writ herein the Defendant has threatened another person with proceedings for infringement of the Patent.

Particulars

Pending discovery and/or interrogatories herein the Plaintiff relies upon the following facts and matters:

(Here give details of threats relied on)

4. The Plaintiff is a person aggrieved by the said threats.

Particulars

(Here give grounds on which the Plaintiff is aggrieved)

5. The Defendant threatens and intends to continue the acts complained of.
6. By reason of the matters aforesaid the Plaintiff has suffered and will suffer loss and damage.

Particulars

(Where special damage claimed)

7. The Plaintiff is not aware of all the Defendant's threats complained of but at the trial the Plaintiff will seek relief in respect of all such acts.
8. The Plaintiff is entitled to interest on all sums found to be due pursuant to section 35A of the Supreme Court Act 1981 and/or the equitable jurisdiction of the Court.

---

[34] P.A. 1977, s.70.

AND THE PLAINTIFF CLAIMS:

1. A declaration that the Defendant's threats of proceedings for infringement of United Kingdom Patent No. _____ are unjustifiable.

2. An injunction to restrain the Defendant whether acting by its directors, officers, servants or agents or otherwise howsoever from threatening any other person with proceedings for infringement of United Kingdom Patent No. _____.

3. An inquiry as to the damages sustained by the Plaintiff by reason of the threats made by the Defendant.

4. An order for the payment of all sums found to be due to the Plaintiff upon taking such inquiry together with interest thereon pursuant to section 35A of the Supreme Court Act 1981 and/or the equitable jurisdiction of the Court.

5. An order that the Defendant does within 14 days identify by affidavit the names and addresses of all persons to whom the Defendant has made threats of proceedings for infringement of United Kingdom Patent No. _____.

6. Further to other relief.

7. Costs.

2. Patents County Court

A. Patents County Court Heading   14.19

IN THE PATENTS COUNTY COURT   CASE No. _____
B E T W E E N:

(1) _____

(2) _____

Plaintiffs

-and-

_____

Defendant

14.20 **B. Statement of Case (Patents County Court)**

1. The First Plaintiff is the proprietor of United Kingdom Patent No. _____ ("_____") in respect of _____. The Patent was granted on _____ [to (*original grantee*) and assigned to the First Plaintiff on _____. The assignment was registered at the Patent Office on _____].[35] The Second Plaintiff is the exclusive licensee under the patent by a licence dated _____ and registered at the Patent Office on _____. The specification of the Patent, the assignment and the licence are annexed hereto as Appendices 1, 2 and 3 respectively.

2. The Patent is in force. [The Patent expired on _____].[36]

3. Both the Plaintiffs and the Defendant carry on business _____.

4. Without the consent of the Plaintiffs [or *original grantee*] the Defendant has in the United Kingdom made, disposed of, offered to dispose of and kept _____ prior to the issue of the summons in this action and after the date of grant of the patent [and before the date of expiry thereof].

Particulars

In particular the Plaintiffs complain of:

4.1 the offer for sale of the Defendant's _____ by the Defendant in its advertisement on page _____ of the _____ edition of _____. A copy of the advertisement is annexed hereto as Appendix 4;

4.2 the sale of one of the Defendant's _____ by the Defendant to _____ of _____ on _____. The receipt for the sale is annexed hereto as Appendix 5;

4.3 the making and keeping of the _____ sold to _____ at the Defendant's factory in _____ on a date unknown to the Plaintiff but prior to the sale.

The _____ sold to _____ is available for inspection by arrangement with the Plaintiff's solicitors.

5. By reason of the acts set out above the Defendant has infringed claims 1 and 2 of the Patent pursuant to section 60(1) of the Patents Act 1977.

---

[35] Where the original grantee has assigned the Patent.
[36] Where the Patent has expired.

Particulars

The Defendant's _____ is illustrated in the drawing annexed hereto as Appendix 6.

Claim 1
5.1 (*State how the Defendant's product infringes claim 1*)

Claim 2
5.2 (*State how the Defendant's product infringes claim 2*)

6. Further or alternatively, without the consent of the Plaintiffs [or _____] the Defendant has, prior to the issue of the summons in this action and after the date of grant of the patent [and before the date of expiry thereof], supplied or offered to supply in the United Kingdom a person other than a licensee or other person entitled to work the invention with a means relating to an essential element of the invention the subject of the Patent in suit for putting the invention into effect when the Defendant knew or it was obvious to a reasonable person in the circumstances that those means were suitable for putting and were intended to put the invention into effect in the United Kingdom. Accordingly the Defendant has infringed the Patent pursuant to section 60(2) of the Patents Act 1977.

Particulars

Of Acts
6.1 In particular the Plaintiffs complain of the offer for sale and subsequent sale of (*state item complained of*) by the Defendant to _____ of _____ on _____. The receipt for the sale is annexed hereto as Appendix 7.

Of Knowledge
6.2 The Plaintiffs will rely on (*state facts and matters relied on*).

Of the item complained of
6.3 The _____ is illustrated in the drawing annexed hereto as Appendix 6, and is present on the Defendant's _____ (shown marked C in Appendix 6). It is a means relating to an essential element of the invention because the _____ is an essential element of the invention. The Plaintiffs will rely upon the passage at _____ of the Patent in suit. Without the _____ the Defendant's _____ would not be _____ in accordance with the Patent. The _____ has no other use than _____ in accordance with the Patent.
The _____ sold to _____ is available for inspection by arrangement with the Plaintiff's solicitors.

7. Further the Defendant threatens and intends to continue the infringements complained of. The Plaintiffs will rely on its letter before action dated _____ and the reply thereto by the Defendant dated _____ stating that the Defendant would not cease to make and sell its _____.

8. By reason of the foregoing the Plaintiffs have suffered and will continue to suffer loss and damage.

9. The Plaintiffs claim interest pursuant to section 69 of the County Courts Act 1984 and/or the inherent jurisdiction of the Court at such rate and for such period as the Court thinks fit.

AND the Plaintiffs claim:

1. A declaration that United Kingdom Patent No. _____ is valid and has been infringed by the Defendant.

2. An injunction to restrain the Defendant, whether acting by its [directors, officers] servants or agents or otherwise howsoever from infringing United Kingdom Patent No. _____.

3. Delivery up or destruction upon oath of all infringing material in the Defendant's possession, power, custody or control the keeping, use or disposal of which would breach the foregoing injunction.

4. An inquiry as to damages or at the Plaintiffs' option an account of profits by reason of the Defendant's acts of infringement of United Kingdom Patent No. _____.

5. An order that the Defendant pay to the Plaintiff all sums found due on taking such enquiry or account together with interest thereon pursuant to section 69 of the County Courts Act 1984 and/or the inherent jurisdiction of the Court.

6. Further or other relief.

7. Costs.

C. Defence and Counterclaim (Patents County Court)   14.21

DEFENCE

1. References to numbered paragraphs are references to the Statement of Case. Paragraphs 1, 2, 3 and 4 are admitted. [Save that it is denied that the Second Plaintiff's licence was registered at the Patent Office, paragraphs 1, 2, 3 and 4 are admitted.]

2. The Patent is invalid for the reasons set out in the Particulars of Objections served herewith.

3. It is admitted that the Defendant's _____ is a _____ as described in Claim 1 of the Patent. It is denied that the Defendant's _____ falls within the scope of Claim 2 of the Patent.

4. The Defendant intends to continue lawfully to make and sell its _____. Save as aforesaid paragraph 6 is denied.

5. It is denied that the Defendant has caused the Plaintiff any loss and damage. The extent of any loss and damage and interest is not admitted.

[6. At the date of any alleged infringement prior to _____ the Defendant was not aware and had no reasonable grounds for supposing that the patent existed.[37]]

COUNTERCLAIM

7. Paragraph 2 above is repeated.

AND the Defendant Counterclaims:

1. An Order that United Kingdom Patent No. _____ be revoked.
2. Further or other relief.
3. Costs.

---

[37] P.A. 1977, s.62.

14.22   **D. Particulars of Objections (Patents County Court)**

The following are the Particulars of Objections to the validity of United Kingdom Patent No. _____ ("_____"). The Patent is and has at all material times been invalid for lack of novelty, lack of inventive step and insufficiently clear and complete disclosure of the alleged invention. The Defendant's facts, matters and arguments in support of these contentions are set out below:

Lack of novelty (section 72(1)(a) of the Patents Act 1977)

1. On _____ (the priority date) the alleged invention was not new having regard to the matter which was available to the public from each of the following prior publications:

Disclosure	Date of publication
(a) _____ ("_____")	_____
(b) _____ ("_____")	_____
(c) _____ ("_____")	_____

The Defendant's facts, matters and arguments in support of these contentions are set out below:

(a) _____ ("_____")

1.1 This discloses a clear anticipation of claim 1 of the Patent in suit. In particular the Defendant relies upon _____.

(b) _____ ("_____")

1.2 This anticipates claim 2 of the Patent in suit. In particular the Defendant relies upon _____.

(c) _____ ("_____")

1.3 This discloses all the features of the Patent in suit. In this disclosure the "_____" correspond to the _____ of the Patent in suit.

2. Further the alleged invention was anticipated by the sale by the First Plaintiff of its _____ on a date unknown to the Defendant but before _____ (the priority date) to _____. Photographs of the _____ are annexed hereto as Appendix 2. This _____ anticipates the Plaintiff's _____ as claimed in claims 1 and 2 as can be seen from the photograph.

Lack of inventive step (section 72(1)(a) 1977 Act

3. On _____ (the priority date) the alleged invention did not involve any inventive step having regard to the matter which was available to the public set out above and to common general knowledge.

The Defendant's facts, matters and arguments in support of these contentions are set out below:

(a) _____ ("_____")

3.1 Common general knowledge in the art included an understanding of _____. Also in the art at the priority date was a trend to _____. Accordingly it would have been obvious to the skilled man, when faced with the _____, to _____. The result would be a _____ in accordance with the Patent in suit.

(b) _____ ("_____")

3.2 Common general knowledge in the art included a knowledge of _____ which operates in a way in all material respects the same as that described in the Patent. Faced with _____ it would have been obvious to the skilled man that _____.

(c) _____ ("_____")

3.3 It was obvious to the skilled addressee at the relevant time that _____ (as described in this disclosure) could easily be replaced by _____ without any substantial effect on _____.

Anticipation

4. Any differences (which are not admitted) between the (*product claimed as anticipating claim*) and the _____ the subject of the Patent in suit are so minor as to be trivial and unable to constitute an inventive step.

Insufficiently clear and complete disclosure (section 72(1)(c) 1977 Act

5. The specification of the Patent in suit does not disclose the alleged invention clearly and completely enough for it to be performed by a person skilled in the art, in that a person skilled in the art cannot determine from the Patent specification how to _____.

6. [Other objections – see High Court Particulars under §14.06 above.]

Served, etc.

14.23   **E. Reply and Defence to Counterclaim (Patents County Court)**

REPLY

1. Save insofar as the same consists of admissions the Plaintiffs join issue with the Defendant upon its Defence and Counterclaim.

DEFENCE TO COUNTERCLAIM

2. It is denied that the Patent in suit is invalid as alleged in paragraph 2 of the Defence and Counterclaim and in the Particulars of Objections or at all. Further, claims 1, 2 and 4 of the Patent in suit are independently valid.

3. Without prejudice to the generality of the denial in paragraph 2 hereof it is denied that any _____ was sold by the Plaintiff before the priority date of the Patent in suit. The Plaintiff did not even start to manufacture such _____ until _____, after the priority date.

Commercial success

4. Further, in answer to the allegation that the Patent in suit lacks inventive step the Plaintiffs will rely on the fact that for many years prior to _____ (the priority date) there was a long felt want for _____ and upon the introduction of the commercial embodiment of the invention, the _____, it enjoyed substantial commercial success. Such commercial success was wholly or substantially attributable to the inventive features of the _____.

Particulars

The Plaintiffs will rely on the following matters in support of the plea of commercial success:

Long felt want

4.1 In order to establish a long felt want for _____ the Plaintiffs will rely on the following patents, applications, and other publications which claimed to provide a solution to the said long felt want but which failed to do so.

Patent/publication   Date

_____ ("_____")   _____
_____ ("_____")   _____

These documents are annexed hereto as Appendix 1.

(The product for which commercial success is claimed)

4.2 The _____ is the commercial embodiment of the Patent in suit in that it falls within the scope of claim 1 of the Patent. Annexed hereto as Appendix 2 is a drawing illustrating the _____.

Commercial success of the (product)

4.3 Since _____ the _____ has accounted for a very substantial portion of the market for _____ in the United Kingdom. Attached hereto as Confidential Appendix 3 is a schedule of sales figures for the _____ upon which the Plaintiffs will rely. The schedule will be made available to the Defendant upon the receipt of suitable undertakings as to confidentiality.

Served, etc.

APPENDICES

Contents

PATENTS ACT 1977

(1977 c. 37 as amended)

ARRANGEMENTS OF SECTIONS

PART I. NEW DOMESTIC LAW

Patentability

Right to apply for and obtain a patent and be mentioned as inventor

Applications

Examination and search

APPENDICES

Patents Act 1977

Part III. Miscellaneous and General

Legal proceedings

Offences

Patent agents

Immunity of department

Administrative provisions

Supplemental

SCHEDULES:

GENERAL NOTE

Textual additions and amendments to the 1977 Act are printed in bold, while the original version appears within square brackets and in italics.

An Act to establish a new law of patents applicable to future patents and applications for patents; to amend the law of patents applicable to existing patents and applications for patents; to give effect to certain international conventions on patents; and for connected purposes.

[29th July 1977]

Part I

New Domestic Law

Patentability

Patentable inventions

1.—(1) A patent may be granted only for an invention in respect of **15.01** which the following conditions are satisfied, that is to say—
  (a) the invention is new;
  (b) it involves an inventive step;
  (c) it is capable of industrial application;
  (d) the grant of a patent for it is not excluded by subsections (2) and
      (3) below;
and references in this Act to a patentable invention shall be construed accordingly.

(2) It is hereby declared that the following (among other things) are not inventions for the purposes of this Act, that is to say, anything which consists of—
  (a) a discovery, scientific theory or mathematical method;
  (b) a literary, dramatic, musical or artistic work or any other aesthetic
      creation whatsoever;
  (c) a scheme, rule or method for performing a mental act, playing a
      game or doing business, or a program for a computer;
  (d) the presentation of information;
but the foregoing provision shall prevent anything from being treated as an invention for the purposes of this Act only to the extent that a patent or application for a patent relates to that thing as such.

(3) A patent shall not be granted—
  (a) for an invention the publication or exploitation of which would
      be generally expected to encourage offensive, immoral or anti-
      social behaviour;
  (b) for any variety of animal or plant or any essentially biological
      process for the production of animals or plants, not being a
      micro-biological process or the product of such a process.

(4) For the purposes of subsection (3) above behaviour shall not be regarded as offensive, immoral or anti-social only because it is prohibited by any law in force in the United Kingdom or any part of it.

(5) The Secretary of State may by order vary the provisions of subsection (2) above for the purpose of maintaining them in conformity with developments in science and technology; and no such order shall

be made unless a draft of the order has been laid before, and approved by resolution of, each House of Parliament.

Novelty

15.02   **2.**—(1) An invention shall be taken to be new if it does not form part of the state of the art.

(2) The state of the art in the case of an invention shall be taken to comprise all matter (whether a product, a process, information about either, or anything else) which has at any time before the priority date of that invention been made available to the public (whether in the United Kingdom or elsewhere) by written or oral description, by use or in any other way.

(3) The state of the art in the case of an invention to which an application for a patent or a patent relates shall be taken also to compromise matter contained in an application for another patent which was published on or after the priority date of that invention, if the following conditions are satisfied, that is to say—

    (a) that matter was contained in the application for that other patent both as filed and as published; and

    (b) the priority date of that matter is earlier than that of the invention.

(4) For the purposes of this section the disclosure of matter constituting an invention shall be disregarded in the case of a patent or an application for a patent if occurring later than the beginning of the period of six months immediately preceding the date of filing the application for the patent and either—

    (a) the disclosure was due to, or made in consequence of, the matter having been obtained unlawfully or in breach of confidence by any person—

        (i) from the inventor or from any other person to whom the matter was made available in confidence by the inventor or who obtained it from the inventor because he or the inventor believed that he was entitled to obtain it; or

        (ii) from any other person to whom the matter was made available in confidence by any person mentioned in sub-paragraph (i) above or in this sub-paragraph or who obtained it from any person so mentioned because he or the person from whom he obtained it believed that he was entitled to obtain it;

    (b) the disclosure was made in breach of confidence by any person who obtained the matter in confidence from the inventor or from any other person to whom it was made available, or who obtained it from the inventor; or

    (c) the disclosure was due to, or made in consequence of the inventor displaying the invention at an international exhibition and the applicant states, on filing the application, that the invention has been so displayed and also, within the prescribed period, files written evidence in support of the statement complying with any prescribed conditions.

(5) In this section references to the inventor include references to any proprietor of the invention for the time being.

(6) In the case of an invention consisting of a substance or composition for use in a method of treatment of the human or animal body by surgery or therapy or of diagnosis practised on the human or animal body, the fact that the substance or composition forms part of the state of the art shall not prevent the invention from being taken to be new if the use of the substance or composition in any such method does not form part of the state of the art.

Inventive step

3. An invention shall be taken to involve an inventive step if it is not obvious to a person skilled in the art, having regard to any matter which forms part of the state of the art by virtue only of section 2(2) above (and disregarding section 2(3) (above). **15.03**

Industrial application

4.—(1) Subject to subsection (2) below, an invention shall be taken to be capable of industrial application if it can be made or used in any kind of industry, including agriculture. **15.04**

(2) An invention of a method of treatment of the human or animal body by surgery or therapy or of diagnosis practised on the human or animal body shall not be taken to be capable of industrial application.

(3) Subsection (2) above shall not prevent a product consisting of a substance or composition being treated as capable of industrial application merely because it is invented for use in any such method.

Priority date

5.—(1) For the purposes of this Act the priority date of an invention to which an application for a patent relates and also of any matter (whether or not the same as the invention) contained in any such application is, except as provided by the following provisions of this Act, the date of filing the application. **15.05**

(2) If in or in connection with an application for a patent (the application in suit) a declaration is made, whether by the applicant or any predecessor in title of his, complying with the relevant requirements of rules and specifying one or more earlier relevant applications for the purposes of this section made by the applicant or a predecessor in title of his and each having a date of filing during the period of twelve

months immediately preceding the date of filing the application in suit, then—

(a) if an invention to which the application in suit relates is supported by matter disclosed in the earlier relevant application or applications, the priority date of that invention shall instead of being the date of filing the application in suit be the date of filing the relevant application in which that matter was disclosed or, if it was disclosed in more than one relevant application, the earliest of them;

(b) the priority date of any matter contained in the application in suit which was also disclosed in the earlier relevant application or applications shall be the date of filing the relevant application in which that matter was disclosed or, if it was disclosed in more than one relevant application, the earliest of them.

(3) Where an invention or other matter contained in the application in suit was also disclosed in two earlier relevant applications filed by the same applicant as in the case of the application in suit or a predecessor in title of his and the second of those relevant applications was specified in or in connection with the application in suit, the second of those relevant applications shall, so far as concerns that invention or matter, be disregarded unless—

(a) it was filed in or in respect of the same country as the first; and

(b) not later than the date of filing the second, the first (whether or not so specified) was unconditionally withdrawn, or was abandoned or refused, without—

(i) having been made available to the public (whether in the United Kingdom or elsewhere);

(ii) leaving any rights outstanding; and

(iii) having served to establish a priority date in relation to another application, wherever made.

(4) The foregoing provisions of this section shall apply for determining the priority date of an invention for which a patent has been granted as they apply for determining the priority date of an invention to which an application for that patent relates.

(5) In this section "relevant application" means any of the following applications which has a date of filing, namely—

(a) an application for a patent under this Act;

(b) an application in or for a convention country (specified under section 90 below) for protection in respect of an invention or an application which, in accordance with the law of a convention country or a treaty or international convention to which a convention country is a party, is equivalent to such an application.

Disclosure of matter, etc., between earlier and later applications

6.—(1) It is hereby declared for the avoidance of doubt that where an **15.06** application (the application in suit) is made for a patent and a declaration is made in accordance with section 5(2) above in or in connection with that application specifying an earlier relevant application, the application in suit and any patent granted in pursuance of it shall not be invalidated by reason only of relevant intervening acts.

(2) In this section—

"relevant application" has the same meaning as in section 5 above; and

"relevant intervening acts" means acts done in relation to matter disclosed in an earlier relevant application between the dates of the earlier relevant application and the application in suit, as for example, filing another application for the invention for which the earlier relevant application was made, making information available to the public about that invention or that matter or working that invention, but disregarding any application, or the disclosure to the public of matter contained in any application, which is itself to be disregarded for the purposes of section 5(3) above.

Right to apply for and obtain a patent and be mentioned as inventor

Right to apply for and obtain a patent

7.—(1) Any person may make an application for a patent either alone **15.07** or jointly with another.

(2) A patent for an invention may be granted—

(a) primarily to the inventor or joint inventors;

(b) in preference to the foregoing, to any person or persons who, by virtue of an enactment or rule of law, or any foreign law or treaty or international convention, or by virtue of an enforceable term of any agreement entered into with the inventor before the making of the invention, was or were at the time of the making of the invention entitled to the whole of the property in it (other than equitable interests) in the United Kingdom;

(c) in any event, to the successor or successors in title of any person or person mentioned in paragraph (*a*) or (*b*) above or any person so mentioned and the successor or successors in title of another person so mentioned;

and to no other person.

(3) In this Act "inventor" in relation to an invention means the actual devisor of the invention and "joint inventor" shall be construed accordingly.

(4) Except so far as the contrary is established, a person who makes an application for a patent shall be taken to be the person who is entitled under subsection (2) above to be granted a patent and two or more persons who make such an application jointly shall be taken to be the persons so entitled.

Determination before grant of questions about entitlement to patents, etc.

15.08   8.—(1) At any time before a patent has been granted for an invention (whether or not an application has been made for it)—
  (a) any person may refer to the comptroller the question whether he is entitled to be granted (alone or with any other persons) a patent for that invention or has or would have any right in or under any patent so granted or any application for such a patent; or
  (b) any of two or more co-proprietors of an application for a patent for that invention may so refer the question whether any right in or under the application should be transferred or granted to any other person;
and the comptroller shall determine the question and may make such order as he thinks fit to give effect to the determination.
     (2) Where a person refers a question relating to an invention under subsection (1)(a) above to the comptroller after an application for a patent for the invention has been filed and before a patent is granted in pursuance of the application, then, unless the application is refused or withdrawn before the reference is disposed of by the comptroller, the comptroller may, without prejudice to the generality of subsection (1) above and subject to subsection (6) below,—
  (a) order that the application shall proceed in the name of that person, either solely or jointly with that of any other applicant, instead of in the name of the applicant or any specified applicant;
  (b) where the reference was made by two or more persons, order that the application shall proceed in all their names jointly;
  (c) refuse to grant a patent in pursuance of the application or order the application to be amended so as to exclude any of the matter in respect of which the question was referred;
  (d) make an order transferring or granting any licence or other right in or under the application and give directions to any person for carrying out the provisions of any such order.
     (3) Where a question is referred to the comptroller under subsection (1)(a) above and—
  (a) the comptroller orders an application for a patent for the invention to which the question relates to be so amended;
  (b) any such application is refused under subsection (2)(c) above before the comptroller has disposed of the reference (whether the

reference was made before or after the publication of the application); or

(c) any such application is refused under any other provision of this Act or is withdrawn before the comptroller has disposed of the reference, but after the publication of the application;

the comptroller may order that any person by whom the reference was made may within the prescribed period make a new application for a patent for the whole or part of any matter comprised in the earlier application or, as the case may be, for all or any of the matter excluded from the earlier application, subject in either case to section 76 below, and in either case that, if such a new application is made, it shall be treated as having been filed on the date of filing the earlier application.

(4) Where a person refers a question under subsection (1)(*b*) above relating to an application, any order under subsection (1) above may contain directions to any person for transferring or granting any right in or under the application.

(5) If any person to whom directions have been given under subsection (2)(*d*) or (4) above fails to do anything necessary for carrying out any such directions within 14 days after the date of the directions, the comptroller may on application made to him by any person in whose favour or on whose reference the directions were given authorise him to do that thing on behalf of the person to whom the directions were given.

(6) Where on a reference under this section it is alleged that, by virtue of any transaction, instrument or event relating to an invention or an application for a patent, any person other than the inventor or the applicant for the patent has become entitled to be granted (whether alone or with any other persons) a patent for the invention or has or would have any right in or under any patent so granted or any application for any such patent, an order shall not be made under subsection (2)(*a*), (*b*) or (*d*) above on the reference unless notice of the reference is given to the applicant and any such person, except any of them who is a party to the reference.

(7) If it appears to the comptroller on a reference of a question under this section that the question involves matters which would more properly be determined by the court, he may decline to deal with it and, without prejudice to the court's jurisdiction to determine any such question and make a declaration, or any declaratory jurisdiction of the court in Scotland, the court shall have jurisdiction to do so.

(8) No directions shall be given under this section so as to the affect the mutual rights or obligations of trustees or of the personal representatives of deceased persons, or their rights or obligations as such.

Determination after grant of questions referred before grant

15.09   9. If a question with respect to a patent or application is referred by any person to the comptroller under section 8 above, whether before or after the making of an application for the patent, and it is not determined before the time when the application is first in order for a grant of a patent in pursuance of the application, that fact shall not prevent the grant of a patent, but on its grant that person shall be treated as having referred to the comptroller under section 37 below any question mentioned in that section which the comptroller thinks appropriate.

Handling of application by joint applicants

15.10   10. If any dispute arises between joint applicants for a patent whether or in what manner the application should be proceeded with, the comptroller may, on a request made by any of the parties, give such directions as he thinks fit for enabling the application to proceed in the name of one or more of the parties alone or for regulating the manner in which it shall be proceeded with, or for both those purposes, according as the case may require.

Effect of transfer of application under s.8 or 10

15.11   11.—(1) Where an order is made or directions are given under section 8 or 10 above that an application for a patent shall proceed in the name of one or some of the original applicants (whether or not it is also to proceed in the name of some other person), any licenses or other rights in or under the application shall, subject to the provisions of the order and any directions under either of those sections, continue in force and be treated as granted by the persons in whose name the application is to proceed.

(2) Where an order is made or directions are given under section 8 above that an application for a patent shall proceed in the name of one or more persons none of whom was an original applicant (on the ground that the original applicant or applicants was or were not entitled to be granted the patent), any licences or other rights in or under the application shall, subject to the provisions of the order and any directions under that section and subject to subsection (3) below, lapse on the registration of that person or those persons as the applicant or applicants or, where the application has not been published, on the making of the order.

(3) If before registration of a reference under section 8 above resulting in the making of any order mentioned in subsection (2) above—

(a) the original applicant or any of the applicants, acting in good faith, worked the invention in question in the United Kingdom or made effective and serious preparations to do so; or

(b) a licensee of the applicant, acting in good faith, worked the invention in the United Kingom or made effective and serious preparations to do so;

that or those original applicant or applicants or the licensee shall, on making a request within the prescribed period to the person in whose name the application is to proceed, be entitled to be granted a licence (but not an exclusive licence) to continue working or, as the case may be, to work the invention.

(4) Any such licence shall be granted for a reasonable period and on reasonable terms.

(5) Where an order is made as mentioned in subsection (2) above, the person in whose name the application is to proceed or any person claiming that he is entitled to be granted any such licence may refer to the comptroller the question whether the latter is so entitled and whether any such period is or terms are reasonable, and the comptroller shall determine the question and may, if he considers it appropriate, order the grant of such a licence.

Determination of questions about entitlement to foreign and convention patents. etc.

12.—(1) At any time before a patent is granted for an invention in **15.12** pursuance of an application made under the law of any country other than the United Kingdom or under any treaty or international convention (whether or not that application has been made)—

(a) any person may refer to the comptroller the question whether he is entitled to be granted (alone or with any other persons) any such patent for that invention or has or would have any right in or under any such patent or an application for such a patent; or

(b) any of two or more co-proprietors of an application for such a patent for that invention may so refer the question whether any right in or under the application should be transferred or granted to any other person;

and the comptroller shall determine the question so far as he is able to and may make such order as he thinks fit to give effect to the determination.

(2) If it appears to the comptroller on a reference of a question under this section that the question involves matters which would more properly be determined by the court, he may decline to deal with it and, without prejudice to the court's jurisdiction to determine any such question and make a declaration, or any declaratory jurisdiction of the court in Scotland, the court shall have jurisdiction to do so.

(3) Subsection (1) above, in its application to a European patent and an

application for any such patent, shall have effect subject to section 82 below.

(4) Section 10 above, except so much of it as enables the comptroller to regulate the manner in which the application is to proceed, shall apply to disputes between joint applicants for any such patent as is mentioned in subsection (1) above as it applies to joint applicants for a patent under this Act.

(5) Section 11 above shall apply in relation to—

(a) any orders made under subsection (1) above and any directions given under section 10 above by virtue of subsection (4) above; and

(b) any orders made and directions given by the relevant convention court with respect to a question corresponding to any question which may be determined under subsection (1) above as it applies to orders made and directions given apart from this section under section 8 or 10 above.

(6) In the following cases, that is to say—

(a) where an application for a European patent (U.K.) is refused or withdrawn, or the designation of the United Kingdom in the application is withdrawn, after publication of the application but before a question relating to the right to the patent has been referred to the comptroller under subsection (1) above or before proceedings relating to that right have begun before the relevant convention court;

(b) where an application has been made for a European patent (and on a reference under subsection (1) above or any such proceedings as are mentioned in paragraph (a) above, the comptroller, the court or the relevant convention court determines by a final decision (whether before or after publication of the application) that a person other than the applicant has the right to the patent, but that person requests the European Patent Office that the application for the patent shoud be refused; or

(c) where an international application for a patent (U.K.) is withdrawn, or the designation of the United Kingdom in the application is withdrawn, whether before or after the making of any reference under subsection (1) above but after publication of the application;

the comptroller may order that any person (other than the applicant) appearing to him to be entitled to be granted a patent under the Act may within the prescribed period make an application for such a patent for the whole or part of any matter comprised in the earlier application (subject, however, to section 76 below) and that if the application for a patent under this Act is filed, it shall be treated as having been filed on the date of filing the earlier application.

(7) In this section—

(a) references to a patent and an application for a patent include respectively references to protection in respect of an invention and an application which, in accordance with the law of any country other than the United Kingdom or any treaty or international convention, is equivalent to an application for a patent or for such protection; and

(b) a decision shall be taken to be final for the purposes of this section when the time for appealing from it has expired without an appeal being brought or, where an appeal is brought, when it is finally disposed of.

Mention of inventor

13.—(1) The inventor or joint inventors of an invention shall have a right to be mentioned as such in any patent granted for the invention and shall also have a right to be so mentioned if possible in any published application for a patent for the invention and, if not so mentioned, a right to be so mentioned in accordance with the rules in a prescribed document.   **15.13**

(2) Unless he has already given the Patent Office the information hereinafter mentioned, an applicant for a patent shall within the prescribed period file with the Patent Office a statement—

(a) identifying the person or persons whom he believes to be the inventor or inventors; and

(b) where the applicant is not the sole inventor or the applicants are not the joint inventors, indicating the derivation of his or their right to be granted the patent;

and, if he fails to do so, the application shall be taken to be withdrawn.

(3) Where a person has been mentioned as sole or joint inventor in pursuance of this section, any other person who alleges that the former ought not to have been so mentioned may at any time apply to the comptroller for a certificate to that effect, and the comptroller may issue such a certificate; and if he does so, he shall accordingly rectify any undistributed copies of the patent and of any documents prescribed for the purposes of subsection (1) above.

Applications

Making an application

14.—(1) Every application for a patent—   **15.14**

(a) shall be made in the prescribed form and shall be filed at the Patent Office in the prescribed manner; and

(b) shall be accompanied by the fee prescribed for the purposes of this subsection (hereafter in this Act referred to as the filing fee).

(2) Every application for a patent shall contain—

(a) a request for the grant of a patent;

(b) a specification containing a description of the invention, a claim or claims and any drawing referred to in the description or any claim; and

(c) an abstract;

but the foregoing provision shall not prevent an application being initiated by documents complying with section 15(1) below.

(3) The specification of an application shall disclose the invention in a manner which is clear enough and complete enough for the invention to be performed by a person skilled in the art.

[(4) Without prejudice to subsection (3) above, rules may prescribe the circumstances in which the specification of an application which requires for its performance the use of a micro-organism is to be treated for the purposes of this Act as complying with that subsection.]

(5) The claim or claims shall—

(a) define the matter for which the applicant seeks protection;

(b) be clear and concise;

(c) be supported by the description; and

(d) relate to one invention or to a group of inventions which are so linked as to form a single inventive concept.

(6) Without prejudice to the generality of subsection (5)(d) above, rules may provide for treating two or more inventions as being so linked as to form a single inventive concept for the purpose of this Act.

(7) The purpose of the abstract is to give technical information and on publication it shall not form part of the state of the art by virtue of section 2(3) above, and the comptroller may determine whether the abstract adequately fulfils its purpose and, if it does not, may reframe it so that it does.

[(8) Rules may require a person who has made an application for a patent for an invention which requires for its performance the use of a micro-organism not to impose or maintain in the prescribed circumstances any restrictions on the availability to the public of samples of the micro-organism and the uses to which they may be put, subject, however, to any prescribed exceptions, and rules may provide that in the event of a contravention of any provision included in the rules by virtue of this subsection the specification shall be treated for the purposes of this Act as not disclosing the invention in a manner required by subsection (3) above.]

(9) An application for a patent may be withdrawn at any time before the patent is granted and any withdrawal of such an application may not be revoked.

Subss. (4) and (8) repealed by C.D.P.A. 1988, s.303(2) and Sched. 8.

Date of filing applications

15.—(1) The date of filing an application for a patent shall, subject to 15.15
the following provisions of this Act, be taken to be the earliest date on
which the following conditions are satisfied in relation to the application, that is to say—
  (a) the documents filed at the Patent Office contain an indication that
      a patent is sought in pursuance of the application;
  (b) those documents identify the applicant or applicants for the
      patent;
  (c) those documents contain a description of the invention for which
      a patent is sought (whether or not the description complies with
      the other provisions of this Act and with any relevant rules); and
  (d) the applicant pays the filing fee.

(2) If any drawing referred to in any such application is filed later than
the date which by virtue of subsection (1) above is to be treated as the
date of filing the application, but before the beginning of the preliminary examination of the application under section 17 below, the
comptroller shall give the applicant an opportunity of requesting within
the prescribed period that the date on which the drawing is filed shall be
treated for the purposes of this Act as the date of filing the application,
and—
  (a) if the applicant makes any such request, the date of filing the
      drawing shall be so treated; but
  (b) otherwise any reference to the drawing in the application shall be
      treated as omitted.

(3) If on the preliminary examination of an application under section
17 below it is found that any drawing referred to in the application has
not been filed, then—
  (a) if the drawing is subsequently filed within the prescribed period,
      the date on which it is filed shall be treated for the purposes of this
      Act as the date of filing the application; but
  (b) otherwise any reference to the drawing in the application shall be
      treated as omitted.

**(3A) Nothing in subsection (2) or (3) above shall be construed as
affecting the power of the comptroller under section 117(1) below to
correct errors or mistakes with respect to the filing of drawings.**

(4) Where, after an application for a patent has been filed and before
the patent is granted, a new application is filed by the original applicant
or his successor in title in accordance with rules in respect of any part of
the matter contained in the earlier application and the conditions
mentioned in subsection (1) above are satisfied in relation to the new

application (without the new application contravening section 76 below) the new application shall be treated as having, as its date of filing, the date of filing the earlier application.

(5) An application which has a date of filing by virtue of the foregoing provisions of this section shall be taken to be withdrawn at the end of the relevant prescribed period, unless before that end the applicant—

    (a) files at the Patent Office one or more claims for the purposes of the application and also the abstract; and

    (b) makes a request for a preliminary examination and search under the following provisions of this Act and pays the search fee.

NOTE

    Subs. (3A) inserted by C.D.P.A. 1988, Sched. 5, para.2. It applies only to applications filed after commencement of that paragraph. With effect from January 7, 1991 (S.I. 1990, No.2168).

Publication of application

15.16   **16.**—(1) Subject to section 22 below, where an application has a date of filing, then, as soon as possible after the end of the prescribed period, the comptroller shall, unless the application is withdrawn or refused before preparations for its publication have been completed by the Patent Office, publish it as filed (including not only the original claims but also any amendments of those claims and new claims subsisting immediately before the completion of those preparations) and he may, if so requested by the applicant, publish it as aforesaid during that period, and in either event shall advertise the fact and date of its publication in the journal.

(2) The comptroller may omit from the specification of a published application for a patent any matter—

    (a) which in his opinion, disparages any person in a way likely to damage him, or

    (b) the publication or exploitation of which would in his opinion be generally expected to encourage offensive, immoral or anti-social behaviour.

Examination and search

Preliminary examination and search

15.17   **17.**—(1) Where an application for a patent has a date of filing and is not withdrawn, and before the end of the prescribed period—

(a)   a request is made by the applicant to the Patent Office in the prescribed form for a preliminary examination and a search; and

(b)   the prescribed fee is paid for the examination and search (the seach fee);

the comptroller shall refer the application to an examiner for a preliminary examination and search, except that he shall not refer the application for a search until it includes one or more claims.

(2) On a preliminary examination of an application the examiner shall determine whether the application complies with those requirements of this Act and the rules which are designated by the rules as formal requirements for the purposes of this Act and shall report his determination to the comptroller.

(3) If it is reported to the comptroller under subsection (2) above that not all the formal requirements are complied with, he shall give the applicant an opportunity to make observations on the report and to amend the application within a specified period (subject to section 15(5) above) so as to comply with those requirements (subject, however, to section 76 below), and if the applicant fails to do so the comptroller may refuse the application.

(4) Subject to subsections (5) and (6) below, on a search requested under this section, the examiner shall make such investigation as in his opinion is reasonably practicable and necessary for him to identify the documents which he thinks will be needed to decide, on a substantive examination under section 18 below, whether the invention for which a patent is sought is new and involves an inventive step.

(5) On any such search the examiner shall determine whether or not the search would serve any useful purpose on the application as for the time being constituted and—

(a)   if he determines that it would serve a purpose in relation to the whole or part of the application, he shall proceed to conduct the search so far as it would serve such a purpose and shall report on the results of the search to the comptroller; and

(b)   if he determines that the search would not serve such a purpose in relation to the whole or part of the application, he shall report accordingly to the comptroller.

and in either event the applicant shall be informed of the examiner's report.

(6) If it appears to the examiner, either before or on conducting a search under this section, that an application relates to two or more inventions, but they are not so linked as to form a single inventive concept, he shall initially only conduct a search in relation to the first invention specified in the claims of the application, but may proceed to conduct a search in relation to another invention so specified if the applicant pays the search fee in respect of the application so far as it relates to that other invention.

(7) After a search has been requested under this section for an application the comptroller may at any time refer the application to an

examiner for a supplementary search, and subsections (4) **and** (5) above shall apply in relation to a supplementary search as [*it applies*] **they apply** in relation to any other search under this section.

(8) **A reference for a supplementary search in consequence of—**

(a) **an amendment of the application made by the applicant under section 18(3) or 19(1) below, or**

(b) **a correction of the application, or of a document filed in connection with the application, under section 117 below,**

shall be made only on payment of the prescribed fee, unless the comptroller directs otherwise.

NOTE

Subs. (7) amended and Subs. (8) inserted by C.D.P.A. 1988, Sched. 5, para.3, with effect from January 7, 1991 (S.I. 1990, No.2168).

Substantive examination and grant or refusal of patent

15.18   18.—(1) Where the conditions imposed by section 17(1) above for the comptroller to refer an application to an examiner for a preliminary examination and search are satisfied and at the time of the request under that subsection or within the prescribed period—

(a) a request is made by the applicant to the Patent Office in the prescribed form for a substantive examination; and

(b) the prescribed fee is paid for the examination;

the comptroller shall refer the application to an examiner for a substantive examination; and if no such request is made or the prescribed fee is not paid within that period, the application shall be treated as having been withdrawn at the end of that period.

(1A) If the examiner forms the view that a supplementary search under section 17 above is required for which a fee is payable, he shall inform the comptroller, who may decide that the substantive examination should not proceed until the fee is paid; and if he so decides, then unless within such period as he may allow—

(a) **the fee is paid, or**

(b) **the application is amended so as to render the supplementary search unnecessary,**

he may refuse the application.

(2) On a substantive examination of an application the examiner shall investigate, to such extent as he considers necessary in view of any examination and search carried out under section 17 above, whether the application complies with the requirements of this Act and the rules and shall determine that question and report his determination to the comptroller.

(3) If the examiner reports that any of those requirements are not

complied with, the comptroller shall give the applicant an opportunity within a specified period to make observations on the report and to amend the application so as to comply with those requirements (subject, however, to section 76 below), and if the applicant fails to satisfy the comptroller that those requirements are complied with, or to amend the application so as to comply with them, the comptroller may refuse the application.

(4) If the examiner reports that the application, whether as originally filed or as amended in pursuance of section 17 above, this section or section 19 below, complies with those requirements at any time before the end of the prescribed period, the comptroller shall notify the applicant of that fact and, subject to subsection (5) and sections 19 and 22 below and on payment within the prescribed period of any fee prescribed for the grant, grant him a patent.

(5) Where two or more applications for a patent for the same invention having the same priority date are filed by the same applicant or his successor in title, the comptroller may on that ground refuse to grant a patent in pursuance of more than one of the applications.

NOTE

Subs. (1A) inserted by C.D.P.A. 1988, Sched. 5, para.4. In force January 7, 1991 (S.I. 1990, No.2168).

General power to amend application before grant

19.—(1) At any time before a patent is granted in pursuance of an application the applicant may, in accordance with the prescribed conditions and subject to section 76 below, amend the application of his own volition. **15.19**

(2) The comptroller may, without an application being made to him for the purpose, amend the specification and abstract contained in an application for a patent so as to acknowledge a registered trade mark.

Failure of application

20.—(1) If it is not determined that an application for a patent complies before the end of the prescribed period with all the requirements of this Act and the rules, the application shall be treated as having been refused by the comptroller at the end of that period, and section 97 below shall apply accordingly. **15.20**

(2) If at the end of that period an appeal to the court is pending in respect of the application or the time within which such an appeal could be brought has not expired, that period—

(a) where such an appeal is pending, or is brought within the said time or before the expiration of any extension of that time granted (in the case of a first extension) on an application made within that time or (in the case of a subsequent extension) on an application made before the expiration of the last previous extension, shall be extended until such date as the court may determine;

(b) Where no such appeal is pending or is so brought, shall continue until the end of the said time, or if any extension of that time is so granted, until the expiration of the extension or last extension so granted.

Observations by third party on patentability

15.21   **21.**—(1) Where an application for a patent has been published but a patent has not been granted to the applicant, any other person may make observations in writing to the comptroller on the question whether the invention is a patentable invention, stating reasons for the observations, and the comptroller shall consider the observations in accordance with rules.

(2) It is hereby declared that a person does not become a party to any proceedings under this Act before the comptroller by reason only that he makes observations under this section.

Security and safety

Information prejudicial to defence of realm or safety of public

15.22   **22.**—(1) Where an application for a patent is filed in the Patent Office (whether under this Act or any treaty or international convention to which the United Kingdom is a party and whether before or after the appointed day) and it appears to the comptroller that the applicant contains information of a description notified to him by the Secretary of State as being information the publication of which might be prejudicial to the defence of the realm, the comptroller may give directions prohibiting or restricting the publication of that information or its communication to any specified person or description of persons.

(2) If it appears to the comptroller that any application so filed contains information the publication of which might be prejudicial to the safety of the public, he may give directions prohibiting or restricting the publication of that information or its communication to any specified person or description of persons until the end of a period not exceeding three months from the end of the period prescribed for the purposes of section 16 above.

(3) While directions are in force under this section with respect to an application—

(a) if the application is made under this Act, it may proceed to the stage where it is in order for the grant of a patent, but it shall not be published and that information shall not be so communicated and no patent shall be granted in pursuance of the application;

(b) if it is an application for a European patent, it shall not be sent to the European Patent Office; and

(c) if it is an international application for a patent, a copy of it shall not be sent to the International Bureau or any international searching authority appointed under the Patent Co-operation Treaty.

(4) Subsection (3)(b) above shall not prevent the comptroller from sending the European Patent Office any information which it is his duty to send that office under the European Patent Convention.

(5) Where the comptroller gives directions under this section with respect to any application, he shall give notice of the application and of the directions to the Secretary of State, and the following provisions shall then have effect:—

(a) The Secretary of State shall, on receipt of the notice, consider whether the publication of the application or the publication or communication of the information in question would be prejudicial to the defence of the realm or the safety of the public;

(b) if the Secretary of State determines under paragraph (a) above that the publication of the application or the publication or communication of that information would be prejudicial to the safety of the public, he shall notify the comptroller who shall continue his directions under subsection (2) above until they are revoked under paragraph (e) below;

(c) if the Secretary of State determines under paragraph (a) above that the publication of the application or the publication or communication of that information would be prejudicial to the defence of the realm or the safety of the public, he shall (unless a notice under paragraph (d) below has previously been given by the Secretary of State to the comptroller) reconsider that question during the period of nine months from the date of filing the applications and at least once in every subsequent period of twelve months;

(d) if on consideration of an application at any time it appears to the Secretary of State that the publication of the application or the publication or communication of the information contained in it would not, or would no longer, be prejudicial to the defence of the realm or the safety of the public, he shall give notice to the comptroller to that effect; and

(e) on receipt of such a notice the comptroller shall revoke the directions and may, subject to such conditions (if any) as he thinks fit, extend the time for doing anything required or authorised to be done by or under this Act in connection with the application, whether or not that time has previously expired.

(6) The Secretary of State may do the following for the purpose of enabling him to decide the question referred to in subsection (5)(c) above—

(a) where the application contains information relating to the production or use of atomic energy or research into matters connected with such production or use, he may at any time do one or both of the following, that is to say, inspect and authorise the United Kingdom Atomic Energy Authority to inspect the application and any documents sent to the comptroller in connection with it; and

(b) in any other case, he may at any time after (or, with the applicant's consent, before) the end of the period prescribed for the purposes of section 16 above inspect the application and any such documents;

and where that Authority are authorised under paragraph (a) above they shall as soon as practicable report on their inspection to the Secretary of State.

(7) Where directions have been given under this section in respect of an application for a patent for an invention and, before the directions are revoked, that prescribed period expires and the application is brought in order for the grant of a patent then—

(a) if while the directions are in force the invention is worked by (or with the written authorisation of or to the order of) a government department, the provisions of sections 55 to 59 below shall apply as if—

(i) the working were use made by section 55;

(ii) the application had been published at the end of that period; and

(iii) a patent had been granted for the invention at the time the application is brought in order for the grant of a patent (taking the terms of the patent to be those of the application as it stood at the time it was so brought in order); and

(b) if it appears to the Secretary of State that the applicant for the patent has suffered hardship by reason of the continuance in force of the directions, the Secretary of State may, with the consent of the Treasury, make such payments (if any) by way of compensation to the applicant as appears to the Secretary of State and the Treasury to be reasonable having regard to the inventive merit and utility of the invention, the purpose for which it is designed and any other relevant circumstances.

(8) Where a patent is granted in pursuance of an application in respect of which directions have been given under this section, no renewal fees shall be payable in respect of any period during which those directions were in force.

(9) A person who fails to comply with any direction under this section shall be liable—

(a) on summary conviction, to a fine not exceeding £1,000; or

(b) on conviction on indictment, to imprisonment for a term not exceeding two years or a fine, or both.

Restrictions on applications abroad by United Kingdom residents

23.—(1) Subject to the following provisions of this section, no person resident in the United Kingdom shall, without written authority granted by the comptroller, file or cause to be filed outside the United Kingdom an application for a patent for an invention unless— **15.23**

(a) an application for a patent for the same invention has been filed in the Patent Office (whether before, on or after the appointed day) not less than six weeks before the application outside the United Kingdom; and

(b) either no directions have been given under section 22 above in relation to the application in the United Kingdom or all such directions have been revoked.

(2) Subsection (1) above does not apply to an application for a patent for an invention for which an application for a patent has first been filed (whether before or after the appointed day) in a country outside the United Kingdom by a person resident outside the United Kingdom.

(3) A person who files or causes to be filed an application for the grant of a patent in contravention of this section shall be liable—

(a) on summary conviction, to a fine not exceeding £1,000; or

(b) on conviction on indictment, to imprisonment for a term not exceeding two years or a fine, or both.

(4) In this section—

(a) any reference to an application for a patent includes a reference to an application for other protection for an invention;

(b) any reference to either kind of application is a reference to an application under this Act, under the law of any country other than the United Kingdom or under any treaty or international convention to which the United Kingdom is a party.

Provisions as to patents after grant

Publication and certificate of grant

24.—(1) As soon as practicable after a patent has been granted under this Act the comptroller shall publish in the journal a notice that it has been granted. **15.24**

(2) The comptroller shall, as soon as practicable after he publishes a

notice under subsection (1) above, send the proprietor of the patent a certificate in the prescribed form that the patent has been granted to the proprietor.

(3) The comptroller shall, at the same time as he publishes a notice under subsection (1) above in relation to a patent publish the specification of the patent, the names of the proprietor and (if different) the inventor and any other matters constituting, or relating to the patent which, in the comptroller's opinion it is desirable to publish.

Term of patent

15.25   25.—(1) A patent under this Act shall be treated for the purposes of the following provisions of this Act as having been granted, and shall take effect, on the date on which notice of its grant is published in the journal and, subject to subsection (3) below, shall continue in force until the end of the period of 20 years beginning with the date of filing the application for the patent or with such other date as may be prescribed.

(2) A rule prescribing any such other date under this section shall not be made unless a draft of the rule has been laid before, and approved by resolution of, each House of Parliament.

(3) A patent shall cease to have effect at the end of the period prescribed for the payment of any renewal fee if it is not paid within that period.

(4) If during the period of six months immediately following the end of the prescribed period the renewal fee and any prescribed additional fee is paid, the patent shall be treated for the purposes of this Act as if it had never expired, and accordingly—

(a) anything done under or in relation to it during that further period shall be valid;

(b) an act which would constitute an infringement of it if it had not expired shall constitute such an infringement; and

(c) an act which would constitute the use of the patented invention for the services of the Crown if the patent had not expired shall constitute that use.

(5) Rules shall not include provision requiring the comptroller to notify the registered proprietor of a patent that a renewal fee has not been received from him in the Patent Office before the end of the prescribed period and before the framing of the notification.

Patent not to be impugned for lack of unity

15.26   26. No person may in any proceedings object to a patent or to an amendment of a specification of a patent on the ground that the claims contained in the specification of the patent, as they stand or, as the case may be, as proposed to be amended, relate—

(a) to more than one invention; or

(b) to a group of inventions which are not so linked as to form a single inventive concept.

General power to amend specification after grant

27.—(1) Subject to the following provisions of this section and to section 76 below, the comptroller may, on an application made by the proprietor of a patent, allow the specification of the patent to be amended subject to such conditions, if any, as he thinks fit.

(2) No such amendments shall be allowed under this section where there are pending before the court or the comptroller proceedings in which the validity of the patent may be put in issue.

(3) An amendment of a specification of a patent under this section shall have effect and be deemed always to have had effect from the grant of the patent.

(4) The comptroller may, without an application being made to him for the purpose, amend the specification of a patent so as to acknowledge a registered trade-mark.

(5) A person may give notice to the comptroller of his opposition to an application under this section by the proprietor of a patent, and if he does so the comptroller shall notify the proprietor and consider the opposition in deciding whether to grant the application.

15.27

Restoration of lapsed patents

28.—[(1) *Where a patent has ceased to have effect by reason of a failure to pay any renewal fee within the prescribed period, an application for the restoration of the patent may be made to the comptroller under this section within one year from the date on which the patent ceased to have effect.*]

(1) Where a patent has ceased to have effect by reason of a failure to pay any renewal fee, an application for the restoration of the patent may be made to the comptroller within the prescribed period.

(1A) Rules prescribing that period may contain such transitional provisions and savings as appear to the Secretary of State to be necessary or expedient.

(2) An application under this section may be made by the person who was the proprietor of the patent or by any other person who would have been entitled to the patent if it had not ceased to have effect; and where the patent was held by two or more persons jointly, the application may, with the leave of the comptroller, be made by one or more of them without joining the others.

(2A) Notice of the application shall be published by the comptroller in the prescribed manner.

(3) If the comptroller is satisfied that—

15.28

(a) the proprietor of the patent took reasonable care to see that any renewal fee was paid within the prescribed period or that that fee and any prescribed additional fee were paid within the six months immediately following the end of that period, [*and*

(b) *those fees were not so paid because of circumstances beyond his control,*] the comptroller shall by order restore the patent on payment of any unpaid renewal fee and any prescribed additional fee.

(4) An order under this section may be made subject to such conditions as the comptroller thinks fit (including a condition requiring compliance with any provisions of the rules relating to registration which have not been complied with), and if the proprietor of the patent does not comply with any condition of such an order the comptroller may revoke the order and give such directions consequential on the revocation as he thinks fit.

[*(5) where an order is made under this section and, between the end of the period of six months beginning with the date when the patent concerned ceased to have effect and the date of the application under this section,—*

(a) a person continued to do or did again an act which would have constituted an infringement of the patent if it had not expired and which he first did before the end of that period, that act shall constitute such an infringement; or

(b) a person began in good faith to do an act which would consistute an infringement of the patent if it had been in force or made in good faith effective and serious preparations to do such an act, he shall, after the order comes into force, have the rights conferred by subsection (6) below.

(6) Any such person shall have the right—

(a) to continue to do or, as the case may be, to do the act himself; and

(b) if it was done or preparations had been made to do it in the course of a business, to assign the right to do it or to transmit that right on his death or, in the case of a body corporate on its dissolution, to any person who acquires that part of the business in the course of which the act was done or preparations had been made to do it, or to authorise it to be done by any partners of his for the time being in that business;

and the doing of that act of this subsection shall not amount to an infringement of the patent concerned.

(7) The rights mentioned in subsection (6) above shall not include the right to grant a licence to any person to do an act so mentioned.

(8) Where a patented product is disposed of by any person to another in exercise of a right conferred by subsection (6) above, that other and any other person claiming through him shall be entitled to deal with the product in the same way as if it had been disposed of by a sole registered proprietor.

(9) Subsections (5) to (7) above shall apply in relation to an act which would constitute the use of a patented invention for the services of the Crown if the patent had been in force as they apply in relation to an act which would constitute an infringement of the patent if it had been in force, and subsection (8) above shall apply accordingly to the disposal of a patented product in the

exercise of a right conferred by subsection (6) above as applied by the foregoing provision.]

NOTE

S.28 amended by C.D.P.A. 1988, Sched. 5, para.6, with effect from January 7, 1991 (S.I. 1990, No.2168).

Effect of order for restoration of patent

28A.—(1) The effect of an order for the restoration of a patent is as follows.   15.28A

(2) Anything done under or in relation to the patent during the period between expiry and restoration shall be treated as valid.

(3) Anything done during that period which would have constituted an infringement if the patent had not expired shall be treated as an infringement—

(a) if done at a time when it was possible for the patent to be renewed under section 25(4), or

(b) if it was a continuation or repetition of an earlier infringing act.

(4) If after it was no longer possible for the patent to be so renewed, and before publication of notice of the application for restoration, a person—

(a) began in good faith to do an act which would have constituted an infringement of the patent if it had not expired, or

(b) made in good faith effective and serious preparations to do such an act,

he has the right to continue to do the act or, as the case may be, to do the act, notwithstanding the restoration of the patent; but this right does not extend to granting a licence to another person to do the act.

(5) If the act was done, or the preparations were made, in the course of a business, the person entitled to the right conferred by subsection (4) may—

(a) authorise the doing of that act by any partners of his for the time being in that business, and

(b) assign that right, or transmit it on death (or in the case of a body corporate on its dissolution), to any person who acquires that part of the business in the course of which the act was done or the preparations were made.

(6) Where a produce is disposed of to another in exercise of the rights conferred by subsection (4) or (5), that other and any person claiming through him may deal with the product in the same way as if it had been disposed of by the registered proprietor of the patent.

(7) The above provisions apply in relation to the use of a patent for

the services of the Crown as they apply in relation to infringement of the patent.

NOTE

S.28A inserted by C.D.P.A. 88, Sched. 5, para. 7, with effect from January 7, 1991 (S.I. 1990, No.2168).

Surrender of patents

15.29   **29.**—(1) The proprietor of a patent may at any time by notice given to the comptroller offer to surrender his patent.

(2) A person may give notice to the comptroller of his opposition to the surrender of a patent under this section, and if he does so the comptroller shall notify the proprietor of the patent and determine the question.

(3) If the comptroller is satisfied that the patent may properly be surrendered, he may accept the offer and, as from the date when notice of his acceptance is published in the journal, the patent shall cease to have effect, but no action for infringement shall lie in respect of any act done before that date and no right to compensation shall accrue for any use of the patented invention before that date for the services of the Crown.

Property in patents and applications, and registration

Nature of, and transactions in, patents and applications for patents

15.30   **30.**—(1) Any patent or application for a patent is personal property (without being a thing in action), and any patent or any such application and rights in or under it may be transferred, created or granted in accordance with subsection (2) to (7) below.

(2) Subject to section 36(3) below, any patent or any such application, or any right in it, may be assigned or mortgaged.

(3) Any patent or any such application or right shall vest by operation of law in the same way as any other personal property and may be vested by an assent of personal representatives.

(4) Subject to section 36(3) below, a licence may be granted under any patent or any such application for working the invention which is the subject of the patent or the application; and—

    (a) to the extent that the licence so provides, a sub-licence may be granted under any such licence and any such licence or sub-licence may be assigned or mortgaged; and

(b) any such licence or sub-licence shall vest by operation of law in the same way as any other personal property and may be vested by an assent of personal representatives.

(5) Subsections (2) to (4) above shall have effect subject to the following provisions of this Act.

(6) Any of the following transactions, that is to say—

(a) any assignment or mortgage of a patent or any such application, or any right in a patent or any such application;

(b) any assent relating to any patent or any such application or right; shall be void unless it is in writing and is signed by or on behalf of the parties to the transaction (or, in the case of an assent or other transaction by a personal representative, by or on behalf of the personal representative) or in the case of a body corporate is so signed or is under the seal of that body.

(7) An assignment of a patent or any such application or a share in it, and an exclusive licence granted under any patent or any such application, may confer on the assignee or licensee the right of the assignor or licensor to bring proceedings by virtue of section 61 or 69 below for a previous infringement or to bring proceedings under section 58 below for a previous act.

Nature of, and transactions in, patents and applications for patents in Scotland

31.—(1) Section 30 above shall not extend to Scotland, but instead the following provisions of this section shall apply there. **15.31**

(2) Any patent or application for a patent, and any right in or under any patent or any such application, is incorporeal moveable property, and the provisions of the following subsections and of section 36(3) below shall apply to any grant of licences, assignations and securities in relation to such property.

(3) Any patent or any such application, or any right in it, may be assigned and security may be granted over a patent or any such application or right.

(4) A licence may be granted, under any patent or any application for a patent, for working the invention which is the subject of the patent or the application.

(5) To the extent that any licence granted under subsection (4) above so provides, a sub-licence may be granted under any such licence and any such licence or sub-licence may be assigned and security may be granted over it.

(6) Any assignation or grant of security under this section may be carried out by writing probative or holograph of the parties to the transaction.

(7) An assignation of a patent or application for a patent or a share in it, and an exclusive licence granted under any patent or any such

application, may confer on the assignee or licensee the right of the assignor or licensor to bring proceedings by virtue of section 61 or 69 below for a previous infringement or to bring proceedings under section 58 below for a previous act.

Register of patents, etc.

15.32 [*32.—(1) There shall continue to be a register kept at the Patent Office and known as the register of patents which shall comply with rules made by virtue of this section and shall be kept in accordance with such rules; and in this Act, except so far as the context otherwise requires—*

"register," as a noun, means the register of patents;

"register", as a verb, means in relation to any thing, to register or register particulars, or enter notice, of that thing in the register and, in relation to a person, means to enter his name in the register;

and cognate expressions shall be construed accordingly.

(2) Without prejudice to any other provision of this Act or rules, rules may make provision with respect to the following matters, including provision imposing requirements as to any of those matters, that is to say—

(a) Registration of patents and of published applications for patents;

(b) the registration of transactions, instruments or events affecting rights in or under patents and applications;

(c) the furnishing to the comptroller of any prescribed documents or description of documents in connection with any matter which is required to be registered;

(d) the correction of errors in the register and in any documents filed at the Patent Office in connection with registration;

(e) making the register or entries or reproductions of entries in it available for inspection by the public;

(f) supplying certified copies of any such entries or reproductions to persons requiring them; and

(g) the publication and advertisement of anything done under this Act or rules in relation to the register.

(3) Notwithstanding anything in subsection (2)(b) above, no notice of any trust, whether express, implied or constructive, shall be entered in the register and the comptroller shall not be affected by any such notice.]

32.—(1) The comptroller shall maintain the register of patents, which shall comply with rules made by virtue of this section and shall be kept in accordance with such rules.

(2) Without prejudice to any other provision of this Act or rules, rules may make provision with respect to the following matters, including provision imposing requirements as to any of those matters—

(a) the registration of patents and of published applications for patents;

(b) the registration of transactions, instruments or events affecting rights in or under patents and applications;

(c) the furnishing to the comptroller of any prescribed documents or description of documents in connection with any matter which is required to be registered;

(d) the correction of errors in the register and in any documents filed at the Patents Office in connection with registration; and

(e) the publication and advertisement of anything done under this Act or rules in relation to the register.

(3) Notwithstanding anything in subsection (2)(b) above, no notice of any trust, whether express, implied or constructive, shall be entered in the register and the comptroller shall not be affected by any such notice.

(4) The register need not be kept in documentary form.

(5) Subject to rules, the public shall have a right to inspect the register at the Patent Office at all convenient times.

(6) Any person who applies for a certified copy of an entry in the register or a certified extract from the register shall be entitled to obtain such a copy or extract on payment of a fee prescribed in relation to certified copies and extracts; and rules may provide that any person who applies for an uncertified copy or extract shall be entitled to such a copy or extract on payment of a fee prescribed in relation to uncertified copies and extracts.

(7) Applications under subsection (6) above or rules made by virtue of that subsection shall be made in such manner as may be prescribed.

(8) In relation to any portion of the register kept otherwise than in documentary form—

(a) the right of inspection conferred by subsection (5) above is a right to inspect the material on the register; and

(b) the right to a copy or extract conferred by subsection (6) above or rules is a right to a copy or extract in a form in which it can be taken away and in which it is visible and legible.

(9) Subject to subsection (12) below, the register shall be prima facie evidence of anything required or authorised by this Act or rules to be registered and in Scotland shall be sufficient evidence of any such thing.

(10) A certificate purporting to be signed by the comptroller and certifying that any entry which he is authorised by this Act or rules to make has or has not been made, or that any other thing which he is so authorised to do has or has not been done, shall be prima facie evidence, and in Scotland shall be sufficient evidence, of the matters so certified.

(11) Each of the following, that is to say—

(a) a copy of an entry in the register or an extract from the register which is supplied under subsection (6) above;

(b) a copy of any document kept in the Patent Office or an extract

from any such document, any specification of a patent or any
application for a patent which has been published.

which purports to be a certified copy or a certified extract shall, subject
to subsection (12) below, be admitted in evidence without further
proof and without production of any original; and in Scotland such
evidence shall be sufficient evidence.

(12) In the application of this section to England and Wales nothing
in it shall be taken as detracting from section 69 or 70 of the Police and
Criminal Evidence Act 1984 or any provision made by virtue of either
of them.

(13) In this section "certified copy" and "certified extract" mean a
copy and extract certified by the comptroller and sealed with the seal
of the Patent Office.

(14) In this Act, except so far as the context otherwise requires—

"register," as a noun, means the register of patents;

"register", as a verb, means in relation to any thing, to register or
register particulars, or enter notice of that thing in the register
and, in relation to a person, means to enter his name in the
register;

and cognate expressions shall be construed accordingly.

Note

S.32 substituted by Patents, Designs and Marks Act 1986, s.1 and Sched. 1.

Effect of registration etc. on rights in patents

15.33   33.—(1) Any person who claims to have acquired the property in a
patent or application for a patent by virtue of any transaction,
instrument or event to which this section applies shall be entitled as
against any other person who claims to have acquired that property by
virtue of an earlier transaction, instrument or event to which this section
applies, if, at any time of the later transaction, instrument or event—

(a) the earlier transaction, instrument or event was not registered, or

(b) in the case of any application which has not been published,
notice of the earlier transaction, instrument or event has not been
given to the comptroller, and

(c) in any case, the person claiming under the later transaction,
instrument or event, did not know of the earlier transaction,
instrument or event.

(2) Subsection (1) above shall apply equally to the case where any
person claims to have acquired any right in or under a patent or
application for a patent, by virtue of a transaction, instrument or event
to which this section applies, and that right is incompatible with any

such right acquired by virtue of an earlier transaction, instrument or event to which this section applies.

(3) This section applies to the following transactions, instruments and events:—

(a) the assignment or assignation of a patent or application for a patent, or a right in it;

(b) the mortgage of a patent or application or the granting of security over it;

(c) the grant, assignment or assignation of a licence or sub-licence or mortgage of a licence or sub-licence under a patent or application;

(d) the death of the proprietor or one of the proprietors of any such patent or application or any person having a right in or under a patent or application and the vesting by an assent of personal representatives of a patent, application or any such right; and

(e) any order or directions of a court or other competent authority—

(i) transferring a patent or application or any right in or under it to any person; or

(ii) that an application should proceed in the name of any person;

and in either case the event by virtue of which the court or authority had power to make any such order or give any such directions.

(4) Where an applicant for the registration of a transaction, instrument or event has been made, but the transaction, instrument or event has not been registered, then, for the purposes of subsection (1)(a) above, registration of the application shall be treated as registration of the transaction, instrument or event.

Rectification of register

34.—(1) The court may, on the application of any person aggrieved, **15.34** order the register to be rectified by the making, or the variation or deletion, of any entry in it.

(2) In proceedings under this section the court may determine any question which it may be necessary or expedient to decide in connection with the rectification of the register.

(3) Rules of court may provide for the notification of any application under this section to the comptroller and for his appearance on the application and for giving effect to any order of the court on the application.

[*Evidence of register, documents, etc.*

35.—(1) *The register shall be prima facie evidence of anything required or* **15.35** *authorised by this Act or rules to be registered and in Scotland shall be admissible and sufficient evidence of any such thing.*

(2) A certificate purporting to be signed by the comptroller and certifying that any entry which he is authorised by this Act or rules to make has not been made, or that any other thing which he is so authorised to do has or has not been done, shall be prima facie evidence, and in Scotland shall be admissible, and sufficient evidence, of the matters so certified.

(3) Each of the following, that is to say—

(a) a copy of any entry in the register or of any document kept in the Patent Office, any specification of a patent or any application for a patent which has been published.

(b) a document reproducing in legible form an entry made in the register otherwise than in legible form; or

(c) an extract from the register or of any document mentioned in paragraph (a) or (b) above;

purporting to be certified by the comptroller and to be sealed with the seal of the Patent Office shall be admitted in evidence without further proof and without production of the original, and in Scotland such evidence shall be sufficient evidence.]

NOTE

S.35 repealed by Patents, Designs and Marks Act 1986, Sched. 3, Pt.1.

Co-ownership of patents and applications for patent

15.36   **36.**—(1) Where a patent is granted to two or more persons each of them shall, subject to any agreement to the contrary, be entitled to an equal undivided share in the patent.

(2) Where two or more persons are proprietors of a patent, then, subject to the provisions of this section and subject to any agreement to the contrary—

(a) each of them shall be entitled, by himself or his agents, to do in respect of the invention concerned, for his own benefit and without the consent of or the need to account to the other or others, any act which would apart from this subsection and section 55 below, amount to an infringement of the patent concerned; and

(b) any such act shall not amount to an infringement of the patent concerned.

(3) Subject to the provisions of section 8 and 12 above and section 37 below and to any agreement for the time being in force, where two or more persons are proprietors of a patent one of them shall not without the consent of the other or others grant a licence under the patent or assign or mortgage a share in the patent or in Scotland cause or permit security to be granted over it.

(4) Subject to the provisions of those sections, where two or more

persons are proprietors of a patent, anyone else may supply one of those persons with the means, relating to an essential element of the invention, for putting the invention into effect, and the supply of those means by virtue of this subsection shall not amount to an infringement of the patent.

(5) Where a patented product is disposed of by any of two or more proprietors to any person, that person and any other person claiming through him shall be entitled to deal with the product in the same way as if it had been disposed of by a sole registered proprietor.

(6) Nothing in subsection (1) or (2) above shall affect the mutual rights or obligations or trustees or of the personal representatives of a deceased person, or their rights or obligations as such.

(7) The foregoing provisions of this section shall have effect in relation to an application for a patent which is filed as they have effect in relation to a patent and—

(a) references to a patent and a patent being granted shall accordingly include references respectively to any such application and to the application being filed; and

(b) the reference in subsection (5) above to a patented product shall be construed accordingly.

Determination of right to patent after grant

37.—[(1) *After a patent has been granted for an invention—*   **15.37**

(a) *any person may refer to the comptroller the question whether he is the true proprietor of the patent or whether the patent should have been granted to him (in either case alone or jointly with any other persons) or whether the patent or any right in or under it should be transferred to him (alone or jointly with any other persons); and*

(b) *any of two or more persons registered as joint proprietors of the patent may refer to the comptroller the question whether any right in or under the patent should be transferred or granted to any other person;*

and the comptroller shall determine the question and make such order as he thinks fit to give effect to the determination.]

(1) After a patent has been granted for an invention any person having or claiming a proprietary interest in or under the patent may refer to the comptroller the question—

(a) who is or are the true proprietor or proprietors of the patent,

(b) whether the patent should have been granted to the person or persons to whom it was granted, or

(c) whether any right in or under the patent should be transferred or granted to any other person or persons;

and the comptroller shall determine the question and make such order as he thinks fit to give effect to the determination.

(2) Without prejudice to the generality of subsection (1) above, an order under that subsection may contain provision—

(a) directing that the person by whom the reference is made under that subsection shall be included (whether or not to the exclusion of any other person) among the persons registered as proprietors of the patent;

(b) directing the registration of a transaction, instrument or event by virtue of which that person has acquired any right in or under the patent;

(c) granting any licence or other right in or under the patent;

(d) directing the proprietor of the patent or any person having any right in or under the patent to do anything specified in the order as necessary to carry out the other provisions of the order.

(3) If any person to whom directions have been given under subsection (2)(d) above fails to do anything necessary for carrying out any such directions within 14 days after the date of the order containing the directions, the comptroller may, on application made to him by any person in whose favour or on whose reference the order containing the directions was made, authorise him to do that thing on behalf of the persons to whom the directions were given.

(4) Where the comptroller finds on a reference under **this section** [*subsection (1)(a) above*] that the patent was granted to a person not entitled to be granted that patent (whether alone or with other persons) and on an application made under section 72 below makes an order on that ground for the conditional or unconditional revocation of the patent, the comptroller may order that the person by whom the application was made or his successor in title may, subject to section 76 below, make a new application for a patent—

(a) in the case of unconditional revocation, for the whole of the matter comprised in the specification of that patent; and

(b) in the case of conditional revocation, for the matter which in the opinion of the comptroller should be excluded from that specification by amendment under 75 below:

and where such a new application is made, it shall be treated as having been filed on the date of filing the application for the patent to which the reference relates.

(5) On any such reference no order shall be made under this section transferring the patent to which the reference relates on the ground that the patent was granted to a person not so entitled, and no order shall be made under subsection (4) above on that ground, if the reference was made after the end of the period of two years beginning with the date of the grant, unless it is shown that any person registered as a proprietor of the patent knew at the time of the grant or, as the case may be, of the transfer of the patent to him that he was not entitled to the patent.

(6) An order under this section shall not be so made as to affect the mutual rights or obligations of trustees or of the personal representatives of a deceased person, or their rights or obligations as such.

(7) Where a question is referred to the comptroller under **this section** [*subsection (1)(a) above*] an order shall not be made by virtue of

subsection (2) or under subsection (4) above on the reference unless notice of the reference is given to all persons registered as proprietor of the patent or as having a right in or under the patent except those who are parties to the reference.

(8) If it appears to the comptroller on a reference under **this section** [*subsection (1) above*] that the question referred to him would more properly be determined by the court, he may decline to deal with it and, without prejudice to the court's jurisdiction to determine any such question and make a declaration, or any declaratory jurisdiction of the court in Scotland, the court shall have jurisdiction to do so.

(9) The court shall not in the exercise of any such declaratory jurisdiction determine a question whether a patent was granted to a person not entitled to be granted the patent if the proceedings in which the jurisdiction is invoked were commenced after the end of the period of two years beginning with the date of the grant of the patent, unless it is shown that any person registered as a proprietor of the patent knew at the time of the grant or, as the case may be, of the transfer of the patent to him that he was not entitled to the patent.

NOTE

Subs. (1) substituted and (4), (7) and (8) amended by C.D.P.A. 1988, Sched. 5, para.9, with effect from January 7, 1991 (S.I. 1990, No.2168).

Effect of transfer of patent under s.37

38.—(1) Where an order is made under section 37 above that a patent **15.38** shall be transferred from any person or persons (the old proprietor or proprietors) to one or more persons (whether or not including an old proprietor) then except in a case falling within subsection (2) below, any licences or other rights granted or created by the old proprietor or proprietors shall subject to section 33 above and to the provisions of the order, continue in force and be treated as granted by the person or persons to whom the patent is ordered to be transferred (the new proprietor or proprietors).

(2) Where an order is so made that a patent shall be transferred from the old proprietor or proprietors to one or more persons none of whom was an old proprietor (on the ground that the patent was granted to a person not entitled to be granted the patent), any licences or other rights in or under the patent shall, subject to the provisions of the order and subsection (3) below, lapse on the registration of that person or those persons as the new proprietor or proprietors of the patent.

(3) Where an order is so made that a patent shall be transferred as mentioned in subsection (2) above or that a person other than an old proprietor may make a new application for a patent and before the

reference of the question under that section resulting in the making of any such order is registered, the old proprietor or proprietors or a licensee of the patent, acting in good faith, worked the invention in question in the United Kingdom or made effective and serious preparations to do so, the old proprietor or proprietors or the licensee shall on making a request to the new proprietor or proprietors within the prescribed period be entitled to be granted a licence (but not an exclusive licence) to continue working or, as the case may be, to work the invention, so far as it is the subject of the new application.

(4) Any such licence shall be granted for a reasonable period and on reasonable terms.

(5) The new proprietor or proprietors of the patent or any person claiming that he is entitled to be granted any such licence may refer to the comptroller the question whether that person is so entitled and whether any such period is or terms are reasonable, and the comptroller shall determine the question and may, if he considers it appropriate, order the grant of such a licence.

Employees' inventions

Right to employees' inventions

15.39   39.—(1) Notwithstanding anything in any rule of law, an invention made by an employee shall, as between him and his employer, be taken to belong to his employer for the purposes of this Act and all other purposes if—

(a) it was made in the course of the normal duties of the employee or in the course of duties falling outside his normal duties, but specifically assigned to him, and the circumstances in either case were such that an invention might reasonably be expected to result from the carrying out of his duties; or

(b) the invention was made in the course of the duties of the employee and, at the time of making the invention, because of the nature of his duties and the particular responsibilities arising from the nature of his duties he had a special obligation to further the interests of the employer's undertaking.

(2) Any other invention made by an employee shall, as between him and his employer, be taken for those purposes to belong to the employee.

(3) Where by virtue of this section an invention belongs, as between him and his employer, to an employee, nothing done—

(a) by or on behalf of the employee or any person claiming under him for the purposes of pursuing an application for a patent, or

(b) by any person for the purpose of performing or working the invention,

shall be taken to infringe any copyright or design right to which, as between him and his employer, his employer is entitled in any model or document relating to the invention.

NOTE

Subs. (3) inserted by C.D.P.A. 1988, Sched. 5, para.11, with effect from January 7, 1991 (S.I. 1990, No.2168).

Compensation of employees for certain inventions

40.—(1) Where it appears to the court of the comptroller on an application made by an employee within the prescribed period that the employee has made an invention belonging to the employer for which a patent has been granted, that the patent is (having regard among other things to the size and nature of the employer's undertaking) of outstanding benefit to the employer and that by reason of those facts it is just that the employee should be awarded compensation to be paid by the employer, the court or the comptroller may award him such compensation of an amount determined under section 41 below.   **15.40**

(2) Where it appears to the court or the comptroller on an application made by an employee within the prescribed period that—

(a) a patent has been granted for an invention made by and belonging to the employee;

(b) his rights in the invention, or in any patent or application for a patent for the invention, have since the appointed day been assigned to the employer or an exclusive licence under the patent or application, has since the appointed day been granted to the employer;

(c) the benefit derived by the employee from the contract of assignment, assignation or grant or any ancillary contract ("as the relevant contract") is inadequate in relation to the benefit derived by the employer from the patent; and

(d) by reason of those facts it is just that the employee should be awarded compensation to be paid by the employer in addition to the benefit derived from the relevant contract;

the court or the comptroller may award him such compensation of an amount determined under section 41 below.

(3) Subsections (1) and (2) above shall not apply to the invention of an employee where a relevant collective agreement provides for the payment of compensation in respect of inventions of the same description as that invention to employees of the same description as that employee.

(4) Subsection (2) above shall have effect notwithstanding anything in

the relevant contract or any agreement applicable to the invention (other than any such collective agreement).

(5) If it appears to the comptroller on an application under this section that the application involves matters which would more properly be determined by the court, he may decline to deal with it.

(6) In this section—

"the prescribed period", in relation to proceedings before the court, means the period prescribed by rules of court, and

"relevant collective agreement" means a collective agreement within the meaning of the Trade Union and Labour Relations **(Consolidation) Act 1992**[*Act 1974*], made by or on behalf of a trade union to which the employee belongs, and by the employer or an employer's association to which the employer belongs which is in force at the time of the making of the invention.

(7) References in this section to an invention belonging to an employer of an employee are references to it so belonging as between the employer and the employee.

NOTE

Subs. (6) amended by Trade Union and Labour Relations (Consolidation) Act 1992, Sched. 2.

Amount of compensation

15.41   **41.**—(1) An award of compensation to an employee under section 40(1) or (2) above in relation to a patent for an invention shall be such as will secure for the employee a fair share (having regard to all the circumstances) of the benefit which the employee has derived, or may reasonably be expected to derive, from the patent or from the assignment, assignation or grant to a person connected with the employer of the property or any right in the invention or the property in, or any right in or under, an application for that patent.

(2) For the purposes of subsection (1) above the amount of any benefit derived or expected to be derived by an employer from the assignment, assignation or grant of—

(a) the property in, or any right in or under, a patent for the invention or an application for such a patent; or

(b) the property or any right in the invention;

to a person connected with him shall be taken to be the amount which could reasonably be expected to be so derived by the employer if that person had not been connected with him.

(3) Where the Crown or a Research Council in its capacity as employer assigns or grants the property in, or any right in or under, an invention, patent or application for a patent to a body having among its functions

PATENTS ACT 1977

that of developing or exploiting inventions resulting from public research and does so for no consideration or only a nominal consideration, any benefit derived from the invention, patent or application by that body shall be treated for the purposes of the foregoing provisions of this section as so derived by the Crown or, as the case may be, Research Council.

In this subsection "Research Council" means a body which is a Research Council for the purposes of the Science and Technology Act 1965.

(4) In determining the fair share of the benefit to be secured for an employee in respect of a patent for an invention which has always belonged to an employer, the court or the comptroller shall, among other things, take the following matters into account, that is to say—

(a) the nature of the employee's duties, his remuneration and the other advantages he derives or has derived from his employment or has derived in relation to the invention under this Act;

(b) the effort and skill which the employee has devoted to making the invention;

(c) the effort and skill which any other person has devoted to making the invention jointly with the employee concerned, and the advice and other assistance contributed by any other employee who is not a joint inventor of the invention; and

(d) the contribution made by the employer to the making, developing and working of the invention by the provision of advice, facilities and other assistance, by the provisions of opportunities and by his managerial and commercial skill and activities.

(5) In determining the fair share of the benefit to be secured for an employee in respect of a patent for an invention which originally belonged to him, the court or the comptroller shall, among other things, take the following matters into account, that is to say—

(a) any conditions in licence or licences granted under this Act or otherwise in respect of the invention or the patent;

(b) the extent to which the invention was made jointly by the employee with any other person; and

(c) the contribution made by the employer to the making, developing and working of the invention as mentioned in subsection (4)(d) above.

(6) Any order for the payment of compensation under section 40 above may be an order for the payment of a lump sum or for periodical payment, or both.

(7) Without prejudice to section 32 of the Interpretation Act 1889 (which provides that a statutory power may in general be exercised from time to time), the refusal of the court or the comptroller to make any such order on an application made by an employee under section 40 above shall not prevent a further application being made under that section by him or any successor in title of his.

(8) Where the court or the comptroller has made any such order, the

court or he may on the application of either the employer or the employee vary or discharge it or suspend any provision of the order and revive any provision so suspended, and section 40(5) above shall apply to the application as it applies to an application under that section.

(9) In England and Wales any sums awarded by the comptroller under section 40 above shall, if a county court so orders, be recoverable by execution issued from the county court or otherwise as if they were payable under an order of that court.

(10) In Scotland an order made under section 40 above by the comptroller for the payment of any sums may be enforced in like manner as a recorded decree arbitral.

(11) In Northern Ireland an order made under section 40 above by the comptroller for the payment of any sums may be enforced as if it were a money judgment.

Enforceability of contracts relating to employee's inventions

15.42   42.—(1) This section applies to any contract (whenever made) relating to inventions made by an employee, being a contract entered into by him—

(a) with the employer (alone or with another); or

(b) with some other person at the request of the employer or in pursuance of the employee's contract of employment.

(2) Any term in a contract to which this section applies which diminishes the employee's rights in inventions of any description made by him after the appointed day and the date of the contract, or in or under patents for those inventions or applications for such patents, shall be unenforceable against him to the extent that it diminishes his rights in an invention of that description so made, or in or under a patent for such an invention or an application for any such patent.

(3) Subsection (2) above shall not be construed as derogating from any duty of confidentiality owed to his employer by an employee by virtue of any rule of law or otherwise.

(4) This section applies to any arrangement made with a Crown employee by or on behalf of the Crown as his employer as it applies to any contract made between an employee and an employer other than the Crown, and for the purpose of this section "Crown employee" means a person employed under or for the purposes of a Government department or any officer or body exercising on behalf of the Crown functions conferred by any enactment **or a person serving in the naval, military or air forces of the Crown.**

NOTE

The addition to s.42(4) was made by the Armed Forces Act 1981, s.22.

Supplementary

43.—(1) Sections 39 to 42 above shall not apply to an invention made
before the appointed day.   **15.43**

(2) Sections 39 to 42 above shall not apply to an invention made by an employee unless at the time he made the invention one of the following conditions was satisfied in his case, that is to say—

(a) he was mainly employed in the United Kingdom; or

(b) he was not mainly employed anywhere or his place of employment could not be determined, but his employer had a place of business in the United Kingdom to which the employee was attached, whether or not he was also attached elsewhere.

(3) In sections 39 to 42 above and this section, except so far as the context otherwise requires, references to the making of an invention by an employee are references to his making it alone or jointly with any other person, but do not include references to his merely contributing advice or other assistance in the making of an invention by another employee.

(4) Any references in sections **39** [*40*] to 42 above to a patent and to a patent being granted are respectively references to a patent or other protection and to its being granted whether under the law of the United Kingdom or the law in force in any other country or under any treaty or international convention.

(5) For the purposes of section 40 and 41 above the benefit derived or expected to be derived by an employer from a patent shall, where he dies before any award is made under section 40 above in respect of the patent, include any benefit derived or expected to be derived from the patent by his personal representatives or by any person in whom it was vested by their assent.

(6) Where an employee dies before an award is made under section 40 above in respect of a patented invention made by him, his personal representatives or their successors in title may exercise his right to make or proceed with an application for compensation under subsection (1) or (2) of that section.

(7) In sections 40 and 41 above and this section "benefit" means benefit in money or money's worth.

(8) Section 533 of the Income and Corporation Taxes Act 1970 (definition of connected persons) shall apply for determining for the purposes of section 41(2) above whether one person is connected with another as it applies for determining that question for the purposes of the Tax Acts.

Subs. (4) amended by C.D.P.A. 1988, Sched. 5, para.11, with effect from January 7, 1991 (S.I. 1990, No.2168).

Contracts as to patented products, etc.

Avoidance of certain restrictive conditions

15.44   **44.**—(1) Subject to the provisions of this section, any conditions or term of a contract for the supply of a patented product or of a licence to work a patented invention, or of a contract relating to any such supply or licence, shall be void in so far it purports—

(a) in the case of a contract for supply, to require the person supplied to acquire from the supplier, or his nominee, or prohibit him from acquiring from any specified person, or from acquiring except from the supplier or his nominee, anything other than the patented product;

(b) in the case of a licence to work a patented invention, to require the licensee to acquire from the licensor or his nominee, or prohibit him from acquiring from any specified person, or from acquiring except from the licensor or his nominee, anything other than the product which is the patented invention or (if it is a process) other than any product obtained directly by means of the process or to which the process has been applied;

(c) in either case, to prohibit the person supplied or licensee from using articles (whether patented products or not) which are not supplied by, or any patented process which does not belong to, the supplier or licensor, or his nominee, or to restrict the right of the person supplied or licensee to use any such articles or process.

(2) Subsection (1) above applies to contracts and licences whether made or granted before or after the appointed day, but not to those made or granted before January 1, 1950.

(3) In proceedings against any person for infringement of a patent it shall be a defence to prove that at the time of the infringement there was in force a contract relating to the patent made by or with the consent of the plaintiff or pursuer or a licence under the patent granted by him or with his consent and containing in either case a condition or term void by virtue of this section.

(4) A condition or term of a contract or licence shall not be void by virtue of this section if—

(a) at the time of the making of the contract or granting of the licence the supplier or licensor was willing to supply the product, or grant a licence to work the invention, as the case may be, to the person supplied or licensee, on reasonable terms specified in the contract or licence and without any such condition or term as is mentioned in subsection (1) above; and

(b) the person supplied or licensee is entitled under the contract or licence to relieve himself of his ability to observe the condition or term on giving to the other party three months' notice in writing and subject to payment to that other party of such compensation (being, in the case of a contract to supply, a lump sum or rent for the residue of the term of the contract and, in the case of a licence, a royalty for the residue of the term of the licence) as may be determined by an arbitrator or arbiter appointed by the Secretary of State.

(5) If in any proceeding it is alleged that any condition or term of a contract or licence is void by virtue of this section it shall lie on the supplier or licensor to prove the matters set out in paragraph (*a*) of subsection (4) above.

(6) A condition or term of a contract or licence shall not be void by virtue of this section by reason only that it prohibits any person from selling goods other than those supplied by a specific person or, in the case of a contract for the hiring of or licence to use a patented product, that it reserves to the bailor (or, in Scotland, hirer) or licensor, or his nominee, the right to supply such new parts of the patented product as may be required to put or keep it in repair.

Determination of parts of certain contracts

45.—(1) Any contract for the supply of a patented product or licence **15.45** to work a patented invention, or contract relating to any such supply or licence, may at anytime after the patent or all the patents by which the product or invention was protected at the time of the making of the contract or granting of the licence has or have ceased to be in force, and notwithstanding anything to the contrary in the contract or licence or in any other contract, be determined, to the extent (and only to the extent) that the contract or licence relates to the product or invention, by either party on giving three months' notice in writing to the other party.

(2) In subsection (1) above "patented product" and "patented invention" include respectively a product and an invention which is the subject of an application for a patent, and that subsection shall apply in relation to a patent by which any such product or invention was protected and which was granted after the time or the making of the contract or granting of the licence in question, on an application which had been filed before that time, as it applies to a patent in force at that time.

(3) If, on an application under this subsection made by either party to a contract or licence falling within subsection (1) above, the court is satisfied that, in consequence of the patent or patents concerned ceasing to be in force, it would be unjust to require the applicant to continue to

comply with all terms and conditions of the contract or licence, it may make such order varying those terms or conditions, as, having regard to all the circumstances of the case, it thinks just as between the parties.

(4) Without prejudice to any other right of recovery, nothing in subsection (1) above shall be taken to entitle any person to recover property bailed under a hire-purchase agreement (within the meaning of the Consumer Credit Act 1974).

(5) The foregoing provisions of this section apply to contracts and licences whether made before or after the appointed day.

(6) The provisions of this section shall be without prejudice to any rule or law relating to the frustration of contracts and any right of determining a contract or licence exercisable apart from this section.

Licences of right and compulsory licences

Patentee's application for entry in register that licences are available as of right

15.46   46.—(1) At any time after the grant of a patent its proprietor may apply to the comptroller for an entry to be made in the register to the effect that licences under the patent are to be available as of right.

(2) Where such an application is made, the comptroller shall give notice of the application to any person registered as having a right in or under the patent and, if satisfied that the proprietor of the patent is not precluded by contract from granting licences under the patent, shall make that entry.

(3) Where such an entry is made in respect of a patent—

(a) any person shall, at any time after the entry is made, be entitled as of right to a licence under the patent on such terms as may be settled by agreement or, in default of agreement, by the comptroller on the application of the proprietor of the patent or the person requiring the licence;

(b) the comptroller may, on the application of the holder of any licence granted under the patent before the entry was made, order the licence to be exchanged for a licence of right on terms so settled;

(c) if in proceedings for infringement of the patent (otherwise than by the importation of any article **from a country which is not a member State of the European Economic Community)** the defendant or defender undertakes to take a licence on such terms, no injunction or interdict shall be granted against him and the amount (if any) recoverable against him by way of damages shall not exceed double the amount which would have been payable by him as licensee if such a licence on those terms had been granted before the earliest infringement;

(d) the renewal fee payable in respect of the patent after the date of the entry shall be half the fee which would be payable if the entry had not been made.

(3A) An undertaking under subsection (3)(c) above may be given at any time before final order in the proceedings, without any admission of liability.

(4) The licensee under a licence of right may (unless, in the case of a licence the terms of which are settled by agreement, the licence otherwise expressly provides) request the proprietor of the patent to take proceedings to prevent any infringement of the patent; and if the proprietor refuses or neglects to do so within two months after being so requested, the licensee may institute proceedings for the infringement in his own name as if he were proprietor, making the proprietor a defendant or defender.

(5) A proprietor so added as defendant or defender shall not be liable for any costs or expenses unless he enters an appearance and takes part in the proceedings.

NOTE

Subs. (3)(c) amended and subs. (3A) inserted by C.D.P.A. 1988, Sched. 5, para.12.

Cancellation of entry made under section 46

47.—(1) At any time after an entry has been made under section 46 **15.47** above in respect of a patent, the proprietor of the patent may apply to the comptroller for cancellation of the entry.

(2) Where such an application is made and the balance paid of all renewal fees which would have been payable if the entry had not been made, the comptroller may cancel the entry, if satisfied that there is no existing licence under the patent or that all licences under the patent consent to the application.

(3) Within the prescribed period after an entry has been made under section 46 above in respect of a patent, any person who claims that the proprietor of the patent is, and was at the time of the entry, precluded by a contract in which the claimant is interested from granting licences under the patent may apply to the comptroller for cancellation of the entry.

(4) Where the comptroller is satisfied, on an application under subsection (3) above, that the proprietor of the patent is and was so precluded, he shall cancel the entry; and the proprietor shall then be liable to pay, within a period specified by the comptroller, a sum equal to the balance of all renewal fees which would have been payable if the entry had not been made, and the patent shall cease to have effect at the expiration of that period if that sum is not so paid.

(5) Where an entry is cancelled under this section, the rights and liabilities of the proprietor of the patent shall afterwards be the same as if the entry had not been made.

(6) Where an application has been made under this section, then—

(a) in the case of an application under subsection (1) above, any person, and

(b) in the case of an application under subsection (3) above, the proprietor of the patent,

may within the prescribed period give notice to the comptroller of opposition to the cancellation; and the comptroller shall, in considering the application, determine whether the opposition is justified.

Compulsory licences

15.48   48.—(1) At any time after the expiration of three years, or of such other period as may be prescribed, from the date of the grant of a patent any person may apply to the comptroller on one or more of the grounds specified in subsection (3) below—

(a) for a licence under a patent,

(b) for an entry to be made in the register to the effect that licences under the patent are to be available as of right, or

(c) where the applicant is a government department, for the grant to any person specified in the application of a licence under the patent.

(2) A rule prescribing any such other period under subsection (1) above shall not be made unless a draft of the rule has been laid before, and approved by resolution of, each House of Parliament.

(3) The grounds are:—

(a) where the patented invention is capable of being commercially worked in the United Kingdom, that it is not being so worked or is not being so worked to the fullest extent that is reasonably practicable;

(b) where the patented invention is a product, that a demand for the product in the United Kingdom—

(i)   is not being met on reasonable terms, or

(ii) is being met to a substantial extent by importation;

(c) where the patented invention is capable of being commercially worked in the United Kingdom, that it is being prevented or hindered from being so worked—

(i)   where the invention is a product, by the importation of the product,

(ii) where the invention is a process by the importation of a product obtained directly by means of the process or to which the process has been applied;

(d) that by reason of the refusal of the proprietor of the patent to grant a licence or licences on reasonable terms—

(i) a market for the export of any patented product made in the United Kingdom is not being supplied, or

(ii) the working or efficient working in the United Kingdom of any other patented invention which makes a substantial contribution to the art is prevented or hindered, or

(iii) the establishment or development of commercial or industrial activities in the United Kingdom is unfairly prejudiced;

(e) that by reason of conditions imposed by the proprietor of the patent on the grant of licences under the patent, or on the disposal or use of the patented product or on the use of the patented process, the manufacture, use or disposal of materials not protected by the patent, or the establishment or development of commercial or industrial activities in the United Kingdom, is unfairly prejudiced.

(4) Subject to the provisions of subsections (5) to (7) below, if he is satisfied that any of those grounds are established, the comptroller may—

(a) where the application is under subsection (1)(a) above, order the grant of licence to the applicant, on such terms as the comptroller thinks fit;

(b) where the application is under subsection (1)(b) above, make such an entry as it there mentioned;

(c) where the application is under subsection (1)(c) above, order the grant of a licence to the person specified in the application on such terms as the comptroller thinks fit.

(5) Where the application is made on the ground that the patented invention is not being commercially worked in the United Kingdom or is not being worked to the fullest extent that is reasonably practicable, and it appears to the comptroller that the time which has elapsed since the publication in the journal of a notice of the grant of the patent has for any reason been insufficient to enable the invention to be so worked, he may by order adjourn the application for such period as will in his opinion give sufficient time for the invention to be so worked.

(6) No entry shall be made in the register under this section on the ground mentioned in subsection (3)(d)(i) above, and any licence granted under this section on that ground shall contain such provisions as appear to the comptroller to be expedient for restricting the countries in which any product concerned may be disposed of or used by the licensee.

(7) No order or entry shall be made under this section in respect of a patent (the patent concerned) on the ground mentioned in subsection (3)(d)(i) above unless the comptroller is satisfied that the proprietor of the patent for the other invention is able and willing to grant to the proprietor of the patent concerned and his licencees a licence under the patent for the other invention or reasonable terms.

(8) An application may be made under this section in respect of a patent notwithstanding that the applicant is already the holder of a

licence under the patent; and no person shall be estopped or barred from alleging any of the matters specified in subsection (3) above by reason of any admission made by him, whether in such a licence or otherwise, or by reason of his having accepted such a licence.

Provisions about licences under s.48

15.49   49.—(1) Where the comptroller is satisfied, on an application made under section 48 above in respect of a patent, that the manufacture, use or disposal of materials not protected by the patent is unfairly prejudiced by reason of conditions imposed by the proprietor of the patent on the grant of licences under the patent, or on the disposal or use of the patented product or the use of the patented process, he may (subject to the provisions of that section) order the grant of licences under the patent to such customers of the applicant as he thinks fit as well as to the applicant.

(2) Where an application under section 48 above is made in respect of a patent by a person who holds a licence under the patent, the comptroller—

    (a) may, if he orders the grant of a licence to the applicant, order the existing licence to be cancelled, or

    (b) may, instead of ordering the grant of a licence to the applicant, order the existing licence to be amended.

[*(3) Where, on an application under section 48, above in respect of a patent, the comptroller orders the grant of a licence, he may direct that the licence shall operate—*

    (a) to deprive the proprietor of the patent of any right he has to work the invention concerned or grant licences under the patent:

    (b) to revoke all existing licences granted under the patent.]

(4) Section 46(4) and (5) above shall apply to a licence granted in pursuance of an order under section 48 above and to a licence granted by virtue of an entry, under that section as it applies to a licence granted by virtue of an entry under section 46 above.

NOTE

Subs. (3) deleted by C.D.P.A. 1988, Sched. 5 para.13, with effect from August 1, 1989 (S.I. 1989, No.816).

Exercise of powers on applications under s.48

15.50   50.—(1) The powers of the comptroller on an application under section 48 above in respect of a patent shall be exercised with a view to securing the following general purposes:—

(a) that inventions which can be worked on a commercial scale in the United Kingdom and which should in the public interest be so worked shall be worked there without undue delay and to the fullest extent that is reasonably practicable;

(b) that the inventor or other person beneficially entitled to a patent shall receive reasonable remuneration having regard to the nature of the invention;

(c) that the interests of any person for the time being working or developing an invention in the United Kingdom under the protection of a patent shall not be unfairly prejudiced.

(2) Subject to subsection (1) above, the comptroller shall, in determining whether to make an order or entry in pursuance of such an application, take account of the following matters, that is to say—

(a) the nature of the invention, the time which has elapsed since the publication in the journal of a notice of the grant of the patent and the measures already taken by the proprietor of the patent or any licensee to make full use of the invention;

(b) the ability of any person to whom a licence would be granted under the order concerned to work the invention to the public advantage; and

(c) the risks to be undertaken by that person in providing capital and working the invention if the application for an order is granted.

but shall not be required to take account of matters subsequent to the making of the application.

[Application by Crown in cases of monopoly or merger

51.—(1) Where, on a reference under section 50 or 51 of the Fair Trading Act **15.51**
1973 (the 1973 Act), a report of the Monopolies and Mergers Commission (the Commission), as laid before Parliament, contains conclusions to the effect—

(a) *that a monopoly situation (within the meaning of the 1973 Act) exists in relation to a description of goods which consist of or include patented products or in relation to a description of services in which a patented product or process is used, and*

(b) *that facts found by the Commission in pursuance of their investigations under section 49 of the 1973 Act operate, or may be expected to operate, against the public interest,*

the appropriate Minister or Ministers may, subject to subsection (3) below, apply to the comptroller for relief under subsection (4) below in respect of the patent.

(2) Where, on a reference under section 64 or 75 of the 1973 Act, a report of the Commission, as laid before Parliament, contains conclusions to the effect—

(a) *that a merger situation qualifying for investigation has been created;*

(b) *that one of the elements which constitute the creation of that situation is that the condition specified in section 64(2) or (3) of the 1973 Act prevails (or does so to a greater extent) in respect of a description of goods which consist of or include patented products or in respect of a description of services in which a patented product or process is used; and*

(c) *that the creation of that situation, or particular elements in or consequences of it specified in the report, operate, or may be expected to operate, against the public interest,*

the Secretary of State may, subject to subsection (3) below, apply to the comptroller for relief under subsection (5) below in respect of the patent.

(2A) Where—

(a) *on a reference under section 5 of the Competition Act 1980, a report of the Commission, as laid before Parliament, contains conclusions to the effect that—*

    (i) *any person was engaged in an anti-competitive practice in relation to a description of goods which consist of or include patented products or in relation to a description of services in which a patented product or process is used, and*

    (ii) *that practice operated or might be expected to operate against the public interest; or*

(b) *on a reference under section 11 of that Act, such a report contains conclusions to the effect that—*

    (i) *any person is pursuing a course of conduct in relation to such a description of goods or services, and*

    (ii) *that course of conduct operates against the public interest,*

the appropriate Minister or Ministers may, subject to subsection (3) below, apply to the comptroller for relief under subsection (5A) below in respect of the patent.

(3) Before making an application under subsection (1) (2) or (2A) above, the appropriate Minister or Ministers shall publish, in such manner as he or they think appropriate, a notice describing the nature of the proposed application, and shall consider any representations which, within the period of thirty days from the date of publication of the notice, may be made to him or them by persons whose interests appear to the appropriate Minister or Ministers to be likely to be affected by the proposed application.

(4) If on an application under subsection (1) above it appears to the comptroller that the facts specified in the Commission's report as being those which, in the Commission's opinion, operate or may be expected to operate against the public interest include—

(a) *any conditions in a licence or licences granted under the patent by its proprietor restricting the use of the invention concerned by the licensee or the right of the proprietor to grant other licences under the patent, or*

(b) *a refusal by the proprietor to grant licences under the patent on reasonable terms;*

the comptroller may by order cancel or modify any such condition or may, instead or in addition, make an entry in the register to the effect that licences under the patent are to be available as of right.

(5) If on an application under subsection (2) above it appears to the comptroller that the particular matters indicated in the Commission's report as

being those which, in the Commission's opinion, operate or may be expected to operate against the public interest (whether those matters are so indicated in pursuance of a requirement imposed under section 69(4) or 75(3) of the 1973 Act or otherwise) include any such condition or refusal as is mentioned in paragraph (a) or (b) of subsection (4) above, the comptroller may by order cancel or modify any such condition or may, instead or in addition, make an entry in the register to the effect that licences under the patent are to be available as of right.

(5A) If on an application under subsection (2A) above it appears to the comptroller that the practice of course of conduct in question involved or involves the imposition of any such condition as is mentioned in paragraph (a) of subsection (4) above or such a refusal as is mentioned in paragraph (b) of that subsection, the comptroller may by order cancel or modify any such condition or may, instead or in addition, make an entry in the register to the effect that licences under the patent are to be available as of right.

(6) In this section "the appropriate Minister or Ministers", in relation to a report of the Commission, means the Minister or Ministers to whom the report is made.]

Powers exercisable in consequence of report of Monopolies and Mergers Commission

51.—(1) Where a report of the Monopolies and Mergers Commission has been laid before Parliament containing conclusions to the effect—

(a) on a monopoly reference, that a monopoly situation exists and facts found by the Commission operate or may be expected to operate against the public interest.

(b) on a merger reference, that a merger situation qualifying for investigation has been created and the creation of the situation, or particular elements in or consequences of it specified in the report, operate or may be expected to operate against the public interest,

(c) on a competition reference, that a person was engaged in an anti-competitive practice which operated or may be expected to operate against the public interest, or

(d) on a reference under section 11 of the Competition Act 1980 (reference of public bodies and certain other persons), that a person is pursuing a course of conduct which operates against the public interest,

the appropriate Minister or Ministers may apply to the comptroller to take action under this section.

(2) Before making an application the appropriate Minister or Ministers shall publish, in such manner as he or they think appropriate, a notice describing the nature of the proposed application and shall consider any representations which may be made within 30 days

of such publication by persons whose interests appear to him or them to be affected.

(3) If on an application under this section it appears to the comptroller that the matters specified in the Commission's report as being those which in the Commission's opinion operate, or operated or may be expected to operate, against the public interest include—

(a) conditions in licences granted under a patent by its proprietor restricting the use of the invention by the licensee or the right of the proprietor to grant other licences, or

(b) a refusal by the proprietor of a patent to grant licences on reasonable terms.

he may by order cancel or modify any such condition or may, instead or in addition, make an entry in the register to the effect that licences under the patent are to be available as of right.

(4) In this section "the appropriate Minister or Ministers" means the Minister or Ministers to whom the report of the Commission was made.

NOTE

S.51 substituted by C.D.P.A 1988, Sched. 5, para.14.

Opposition, appeal and arbitration

15.52   52.—(1) The proprietor of the patent concerned or any other person wishing to oppose an application under sections 48 to 51 above may, in accordance with rules, give to the comptroller notice of opposition; and the comptroller shall consider the opposition in deciding whether to grant the application.

(2) Where an appeal is brought from an order made by the comptroller in pursuance of an application under section 48 to 51 above or from a decision of his to make an entry in the register in pursuance of such an application or from a refusal of his to make such an order or entry, the Attorney General, Lord Advocate or Attorney General for Northern Ireland, or such other counsel as any of them may appoint, shall be entitled to appear and be heard.

(3) Where an application under sections 48 to 51 above is opposed under subsection (1) above, and either—

(a) the parties consent, or

(b) the proceedings require a prolonged examination of documents or any scientific or local investigation which cannot in the opinion of the comptroller conveniently be made before him,

the comptroller may at any time order the whole proceedings, or any question or issue of fact arising in them, to be referred to an arbitrator or arbiter agreed on by the parties or, in default of agreement, appointed by the comptroller.

(4) Where the whole proceedings are so referred, section 21 of the Arbitration Act 1950 or, as the case may be, section 22 of the Arbitration Act (Northern Ireland) 1937 (statement of cases by arbitrators) shall not apply to the arbitration; but unless the parties otherwise agree before the award of the arbitrator or arbiter is made an appeal shall lie from the award to the court.

(5) Where a question or issue of fact is so referred, the arbitrator or arbiter shall report his findings to the comptroller.

Compulsory licences; supplementary provisions

53.—(1) Without prejudice to section 86 below (by virtue of which the **15.53** Community Patent Convention has effect in the United Kingdom), sections 48 to 51 above shall have effect subject to any provision of that convention relating to the grant of compulsory licences for lack or insufficiency of exploitation, as that provision applies by virtue of that section.

(2) In any proceedings on an **application made under section 48 above in respect of a patent** [*application made in relation to a patent under sections 48 to 51 above*], any statement with respect to any activity in relation to the patented invention, or with respect to the grant or refusal of licences under the patent, contained in a report of the Monopolies and Mergers Commission laid before Parliament under Part VII of the Fair Trading Act 1973 **or section 17 of the Competition Act, 1980** shall be prima facie evidence of the matters stated, and in Scotland shall be sufficient evidence of those matters.

(3) The comptroller may make an entry in the register under sections 48 to 51 above notwithstanding any contract which would have precluded the entry on the application of the proprietor of the patent under section 46 above.

(4) An entry made in the register under sections 48 to 51 above shall for all purposes have the same effect as an entry made under section 46 above.

(5) No order or entry shall be made in pursuance of an application under sections 48 to 51 above which would be at variance with any treaty or international convention to which the United Kingdom is a party.

NOTE

Subs. (2) amended by C.D.P.A. 1988, Sched. 5, para.15, with effect from August 1, 1989 (S.I. 1989, No.816).

Special provisions where patented invention is being worked abroad

15.54   54.—(1) Her Majesty may by Order in Council provide that the comptroller may not (otherwise than for purposes of the public interest) make an order or entry in respect of a patent in pursuance of an application under sections 48 to 51 above if the invention concerned is being commercially worked in any relevant country specified in the Order and demand in the United Kingdom for any patented product resulting from that working is being met by importation from that country.

(2) In subsection (1) above "relevant country" means a country other than a member state whose law in the opinion of Her Majesty in Council incorporates or will incorporate provisions treating the working of an invention in, and importation from, the United Kingdom in a similar way to which the Order in Council would (if made) treat the working of an invention in, and importation from, the country.

Use of patented inventions for services of the Crown

Use of patented inventions for services of the Crown

15.55   55.—(1) Notwithstanding anything in this Act, any government department and any person authorised in writing by a government department may, for the services of the Crown and in accordance with this section, do any of the following acts in the United Kingdom in relation to a patented invention without the consent of the proprietor of the patent, that is to say—
  (a) where the invention is a product, may—
      (i)   make, use, import or keep the product, or sell or offer to sell it where to do so would be incidental or ancillary to making, using, importing or keeping it; or
      (ii) in any event, sell or offer to sell it for foreign defence purposes or for the production or supply of specified drugs and medicines, or dispose or offer to dispose of it (otherwise than by selling it) for any purpose whatever;
  (b) where the invention is a process, may use it or do in relation to any product obtained directly by means of the process anything mentioned in paragraph (a) above;
  (c) without prejudice to the foregoing, where the invention or any product obtained directly by means of the invention is a specified drug or medicine, may sell or offer to sell the drug or medicine;
  (d) may supply or offer to supply to any person any of the means, relating to an essential element of the invention, for putting the invention into effect;

(e) may dispose or offer to dispose of anything which was made, used, imported or kept in the exercise of the powers conferred by this section and which is no longer required for the purpose for which it was made, used, imported or kept (as the case may be),

and anything done by virtue of this subsection shall not amount to an infringement of the patent concerned.

(2) Any act done in relation to an invention by virtue of this section is in the following provisions of this section referred to as use of the invention; and "use", in relation to an invention, in sections 56 to 58 below shall be construed accordingly.

(3) So far as the invention has before its priority date been duly recorded by or tried by or on behalf of a government department or the United Kingdom Atomic Energy Authority otherwise than in consequence of a relevant communication made in confidence, any use of the invention by virtue of this section may be made free of any royalty or other payment to the proprietor.

(4) So far as the invention has not been so recorded or tried, any use of it made by virtue of this section at any time either—

(a) after the publication of the application for the patent for the invention; or

(b) without prejudice to paragraph (a) above, in consequence of a relevant communication made after the priority date of the invention otherwise than in confidence;

shall be made on such terms as may be agreed either before or after the user by the government department and the proprietor of the patent with the approval of the Treasury or as may in default of agreement be determined by the court on a reference under section 58 below.

(5) Where an invention is used by virtue of this section at any time after publication of an application for a patent for the invention but before such a patent is granted, and the terms for its use agreed or determined as mentioned in subsection (4) above include terms as to payment for the use, then (notwithstanding anything in those terms) any such payment shall be recoverable only—

(a) after such a patent is granted; and

(b) if (apart from this section) the use would, if the patent had been granted on the date of the publication of the application, have infringed not only the patent but also the claims (as interpreted by the description and any drawings referred to in the description or claims) in the form in which they were contained in the application immediately before the preparations for its publication were completed by the Patent Office.

(6) The authority of a government department in respect of an invention may be given under this section before or after the patent is granted and either before or after the use in respect of which the authority is given is made, and may be given to any person whether or not he is authorised directly or indirectly by the proprietor of the patent to do anything in relation to the invention.

(7) Where any use of an invention is made by or with the authority of a government department under this section, then, unless it appears to the department that it would be contrary to the public interest to do so, the department shall notify the proprietor of the patent as soon as practicable after the second of the following events, that is to say, the use is begun and the patent is granted and furnish him with such information as to the extent of the use as he may from time to time require.

(8) A person acquiring anything disposed of in the exercise of powers conferred by this section, and any person claiming through him, may deal with it in the same manner as if the patent were held on behalf of the Crown.

(9) In this section "relevant communication" in relation to an invention, means a communication of the invention directly or indirectly by the proprietor of the patent or any person from whom he derives title.

(10) Subsection (4) above is without prejudice to any rule of law relating to the confidentiality of information.

(11) In the application of this section to Northern Ireland, the reference in subsection (4) above to the Treasury shall, where the government department referred to in that subsection is a department of the Government of Northern Ireland, be construed as a reference to the Department of Finance for Northern Ireland.

Interpretation, etc., of provisions about Crown use

15.56   56.—(1) Any reference in section 55 above to a patented invention, in relation to any time, is a reference to an invention for which a patent has before that time been, or is subsequently, granted.

(2) In this Act, except so far as the context otherwise requires, "the services of the Crown" includes—

(a) the supply of anything for foreign defence purposes;

(b) the production or supply of specified drugs and medicines; and

(c) such purposes relating to the production or use of atomic energy or research into matters connected therewith as the Secretary of State thinks necessary or expedient;

and "use for the services of the Crown" shall be construed accordingly.

(3) In section 55(1)(a) above and subsection (2)(a) above, references to a sale or supply of anything for foreign defence purposes are references to a sale or supply of the thing—

(a) to the government of any country outside the United Kingdom, in pursuance of an agreement or arrangement between Her Majesty's Government in the United Kingdom and the government of that country, where the thing is required for the defence of that country or of any other country whose government is party to any agreement or arrangement with Her Majesty's Government in respect of defence matters; or

(b) to the United Nations, or to the government of any country belonging to that organisation, in pursuance of an agreement or arrangement between Her Majesty's Government and that organisation or government, where the thing is required for any armed forces operating in pursuance of a resolution of that organisation or any organ of that organisation.

(4) For the purposes of section 55(1)(a) and (c) above and subsection (2)(b) above, specified drugs and medicines are drugs and medicines which are both—

(a) required for the provision of pharmaceutical services, general medical services or general dental services, that is to say, services of those respective kinds under Part II of the National Heath Service Act 1977, [*Part IV of the National Health Service (Scotland) Act 1947*], **Part II of the National Health Service (Scotland) Act 1978,** or the corresponding provisions of the law in force in Northern Ireland or the Isle of Man, and

(b) specified for the purposes of this subsection in regulations made by the Secretary of State.

NOTE

S.56(4)(a) amended by National Health Service (Scotland) Act 1978, Sched. 16.

Rights of third parties in respect of Crown use

57.—(1) In relation to—   **15.57**

(a) any use made for the services of the Crown of an invention by a government department, or a person authorised by a government department, by virtue of section 55 above, or

(b) anything done for the services of the Crown to the order of a government department by the proprietor of a patent in respect of a patented invention or by the proprietor of an application in respect of an invention for which an application for a patent has been filed and is still pending,

the provisions of any licence, assignment, assignation or agreement to which this subsection applies shall be of no effect so far as those provisions restrict or regulate the working of the invention, or the use of any model, document or information relating to it, or provide for the making of payments in respect of, or calculated by reference to, such working or use; and the reproduction or publication of any model or document in connection with the said working or use shall not be deemed to be an infringement of any copyright **or design right** subsisting in the model or document.

(2) Subsection (1) above applies to a licence, assignment, assignation or agreement which is made, whether before or after the appointed day, between (on the one hand) any person who is a proprietor of or an applicant for the patent, or anyone who derives title from any such person or from whom such person derives title, and (on the other hand) any person whatever other than a government department.

(3) Where an exclusive licence granted otherwise than for royalties or other benefits determined by reference to the working of the invention is in force under the patent or application concerned, then—

    (a) in relation to anything done in respect of the invention which, but for the provisions of this section and section 55 above, would constitute an infringement of the rights of the licensee, subsection (4) of that section shall have effect as if for the reference to the proprietor of the patent there were substituted a reference to the licensee; and

    (b) in relation to anything done in respect of the invention by the licensee by virtue of an authority given under that section, that section shall have effect as if the said subsection (4) were omitted.

(4) Subject to the provisions of subsection (3) above, where the patent or the right to the grant of the patent, has been assigned to the proprietor of the patent on application in consideration of royalties or other benefits determined by reference to the working of the invention, then—

    (a) in relation to any use of the invention by virtue of section 55 above, subsection (4) of that section shall have effect as if the reference to the proprietor of the patent included a reference to the assignor, and any sum payable by virtue of that subsection shall be divided between the proprietor of the patent or application and the assignor in such proportion as may be agreed on by them or as may in default of agreement be determined by the court on a reference under section 58 below; and

    (b) in relation to any act done in respect of the invention for the services of the Crown by the proprietor of the patent or application to the order of a government department, section 55(4) above shall have effect as if that act were use made by virtue of an authority given under that section.

(5) Where section 55(4) above applies to any use of an invention and a person holds an exclusive licence under the patent or application concerned (other than such a licence as is mentioned in subsection (3) above) authorising him to work the invention, then subsections (7) and (8) below shall apply.

(6) In those subsections "the section 55(4)" payment means such payment (if any) as the proprietor of the patent or application and the department agree under section 55 above, or the court determines under section 58 below, should be made by the department to the proprietor in respect of the use of the invention.

(7) The licensee shall be entitled to recover from the proprietor of the patent or application such part (if any) of the section 55(4) payment as

may be agreed on by them or as may in default of agreement be determined by the court under section 58 below to be just having regard to any expenditure incurred by the licensee—

(a) in developing the invention, or

(b) in making payments to the proprietor in consideration of the licence, other than royalties or other payments determined by reference to the use of the invention

(8) Any agreement by the proprietor of the patent or application and the department under section 55(4) above as to the amount of the section 55(4) payment shall be of no effect unless the licensee consents to the agreement; and any determination by the court under section 55(4) above as to the amount of that payment shall be of no effect unless the licensee has been informed of the reference to the court and is given an opportunity to be heard.

(9) Where any models, documents or information relating to an invention are used in connection with any use of the invention which falls within subsection (1)(a) above, or with anything done in respect of the invention which falls within subsection (1)(b) above, subsection (4) of section 55 above shall (whether or not it applies to any such use of the invention) apply to the use of the models, documents or information as if for the reference in it to the proprietor of the patent there were substituted a reference to the person entitled to the benefit of any provision of an agreement which is rendered inoperative by this section in relation to that use; and in section 58 below the references to terms for the use of an invention shall be construed accordingly.

(10) Nothing in this section shall be construed as authorising the disclosure to a government department or any other person of any model, document or information to the use of which this section applies in contravention of any such licence, assignment, assignation or agreement as is mentioned in this section.

NOTE

Subs. (1) amended by C.D.P.A 1988, Sched. 7, para.20, with effect from August 1, 1989.

Compensation for loss of profit

57A.—(1) Where use is made of an invention for the services of the Crown, the government department concerned shall pay—   15.57A

(a) to the proprietor of the patent, or

(b) if there is an exclusive licence in force in respect of the patent, to the exclusive licensee,

compensation for any loss resulting from his not being awarded a contract to supply the patent product or, as the case may be, to perform

the patented process or supply a thing made by means of the patented process.

(2) Compensation is payable only to the extent that such a contract could have been fulfilled from his existing manufacturing or other capacity; but is payable notwithstanding the existence of circumstances rendering him ineligible for the award of such a contract.

(3) In determining the loss, regard shall be had to the profit which would have been made on such a contract and to the extent to which any manufacturing or other capacity was under-used.

(4) No compensation is payable in respect of any failure to secure contracts to supply the patented product or, as the case may be, to perform the patented process or supply a thing made by means of the patented process, otherwise than for the service of the Crown.

(5) The amount payable shall, if not agreed between the proprietor or licensee and the government department concerned with the approval of the Treasury, be determined by the court on a reference under section 58, and is in addition to any amount payable under section 55 or 57.

(6) In this section "the government department concerned," in relation to any use of an invention for the services of the Crown, means the government department by whom or on whose authority the use was made.

(7) In the application of this section to Northern Ireland, the reference in subsection (5) above to the Treasury shall, where the government department concerned is a department of the Government of Northern Ireland, be construed as a reference to the Department of Finance and Personnel.

NOTE

S.57A inserted by C.D.P.A. 1988, Sched. 5, para.16.

References of disputes as to Crown use

15.58   58.—[(1) Any dispute as to the exercise by a government department or a person authorised by a government department of the powers conferred by section 55 above, or as to terms for the use of an invention for the services of the Crown thereunder, or as to the right of any person to receive any part of a payment made or agreed to be made in pursuance of subsection (4) of that section or determined by the court in pursuance of that subsection and this section, may be referred to the court by either party to the dispute after a patent has been granted for the invention.]

(1) Any dispute as to—

(a) the exercise by a government department, or a person author-

ised by a government department, of the powers conferred by
section 55 above,

(b) terms for the use of an invention for the services of the Crown
under that section,

(c) the right of any person to receive any part of a payment made in
pursuance of subsection (4) of that section, or

(d) the right of any person to receive a payment under section 57A,

may be referred to the court by either party to the dispute after a
patent has been granted for the invention.

(2) If in such proceedings any question arises whether an invention
has been recorded or tried as mentioned in section 55 above, and the
disclosure of any document recording the invention, or of any evidence
of the trial thereof, would in the opinion of the department be
prejudicial to the public interest, the disclosure may be made confidentially to counsel for the other party or to an independent expert
mutually agreed upon.

(3) In determining under this section any dispute between a government department and any person as to the terms for the use of an
invention for the services of the Crown, the court shall have regard—

(a) to any benefit or compensation which that person or any person
from whom he derives title may have received or may be entitled
to receive directly or indirectly from any government department
in respect of the invention in question;

(b) to whether that person or any person from whom he derives title
has in the court's opinion without reasonable cause failed to
comply with a request of the department to use the invention for
the services of the Crown on reasonable terms.

(4) In determining whether or not to grant any relief **under subsection (1)(a), (b) or (c) above,** [*under this section*] and the nature and extent
of the relief granted the court shall, subject to the following provisions of
this section, apply the principles applied by the court immediately
before the appointed day to the granting of relief under section 48 of the
1949 Act.

(5) On a reference under this section the court may refuse to grant
relief by way of compensation in respect of the use of an invention for
the services of the Crown during any further period specified under
section 25(4) above, but before the payment of the renewal fee and any
additional fee prescribed for the purposes of that section.

(6) Where an amendment of the specification of a patent has been
allowed under any of the provisions of this Act, the court shall not grant
relief by way of compensation under this section in respect of any such
use before the decision to allow the amendment unless the court is
satisfied that the specification of the patent as published was framed in
good faith and with reasonable skill and knowledge.

(7) If the validity of a patent is put in issue in proceedings under this
section and it is found that the patent is only partially valid, the court
may, subject to subsection (8) below, grant relief to the proprietor of the

patent in respect of that part of the patent which is found to be valid and to have been used for the services of the Crown.

(8) Where in any such proceedings it is found that a patent is only partially valid, the court shall not grant relief by way of compensation, costs or expenses except where the proprietor of the patent proves that the specification of the patent was framed in good faith and with reasonable skill and knowledge, and in that event the court may grant relief in respect of that part of the patent which is valid and has been so used, subject to the discretion of the court as to costs and expenses and as to the date from which compensation should be awarded.

(9) As a condition of any such relief the court may direct that the specification of the patent shall be amended to its satisfaction upon an application made for that purpose under section 75 below, and an application may be so made accordingly, whether or not all other issues in the proceedings have been determined.

(10) In considering the amount of any compensation for the use of an invention for the services of the Crown after publication of an application for a patent for the invention and before such a patent is granted, the court shall consider whether or not it would have been reasonable to expect, from a consideration of the application as published under section 16 above, that a patent would be granted conferring on the proprietor of the patent protection for an act of the same description as that found to constitute that use, and if the court finds that it would not have been reasonable, it shall reduce the compensation to such amount as it thinks just.

(11) Where by virtue of a transaction, instrument or event to which section 33 above applies a person becomes the proprietor or one of the proprietors or an exclusive licensee of a patent (the new proprietor or licensee) and a government department or a person authorised by a government department subsequently makes use under section 55 above of the patented invention, the new proprietor or licensee shall not be entitled to any compensation under section 55(4) above (as it stands or as modified by section 57(3) above) **or to any compensation under section 57A above** in respect of a subsequent use of the invention before the transaction, instrument or event is registered unless—

(a) the transaction, instrument or event is registered within the period of six months beginning with its date; or

(b) the court is satisfied that it was not practicable to register the transaction, instrument or event before the end of that period and that it was registered as soon as practicable thereafter.

(12) In any proceedings under this section the court may at any time order the whole proceedings or any question or issue of fact arising in them to be referred, on such terms as the court may direct, to a Circuit judge discharging the functions of an official referee or an arbitrator in England and Wales or Northern Ireland, or to an arbiter in Scotland; and references to the court in the foregoing provisions of this section shall be construed accordingly.

(13) One of two or more joint proprietors of a patent or application for a patent may without the concurrence of the others refer a dispute to the court under this section, but shall not do so unless the others are made parties to the proceedings; but any of the others made a defendant or defender shall not be liable for any costs or expenses unless he enters an appearance and takes part in the proceedings.

NOTE

Subs. (1) substituted and Subss. (4) and (11) amended by C.D.P.A. 1988, Sched. 5, para.16.

Special provisions as to Crown use during emergency

59.—(1) During any period of emergency within the meaning of this   **15.59**
section the powers exercisable in relation to an invention by a government department or a person authorised by a government department under section 55 above shall include power to use the invention for any purpose which appears to the department necessary or expedient—
  (a) for the efficient prosecution of any war in which Her Majesty may be engaged;
  (b) for the maintenance of supplies and services essential to the life of the community;
  (c) for securing a sufficiency of supplies and services essential to the well-being of the community;
  (d) for promoting the productivity of industry, commerce and agriculture;
  (e) for fostering and directing exports and reducing imports, or imports of any classes, from all or any countries and for redressing the balance of trade;
  (f) generally for ensuring that the whole resources of the community are available for use, and are used, in a manner best calculated to serve the interests of the community; or
  (g) for assisting the relief of suffering and the restoration and distribution of essential supplies and services in any country or territory outside the United Kingdom which is in grave distress as the result of war;
and any reference in this Act to the services of the Crown shall as respects any period of emergency, include a reference to those purposes.
  (2) In this section the use of an invention includes, in addition to any act constituting such use by virtue of section 55 above, any act which would, apart from that section and this section, amount to an infringement of the patent concerned or, as the case may be, give rise to a right

under section 69 below to bring proceedings in respect of the application concerned, and any reference in this Act to "use for the services of the Crown" shall, as respects any period of emergency, be construed accordingly.

(3) In this section "period of emergency" means any period beginning with such date as may be declared by Order in Council to be the commencement, and ending with such date as may be so declared to be the termination, of a period of emergency for the purposes of this section.

(4) A draft of an Order under this section shall not be submitted to Her Majesty unless it has been laid before, and approved by resolution of, each House of Parliament.

Infringement

Meaning of infringement

15.60 **60.**—(1) Subject to the provisions of this section, a person infringes a patent for an invention if, but only if, while the patent is in force, he does any of the following things in the United Kingdom in relation to the invention without the consent of the proprietor of the patent, that is to say—

(a) where the invention is a product, he makes, disposes of, offers to dispose of, uses or imports the product or keeps it whether for disposal or otherwise;

(b) where the invention is a process, he uses the process or he offers it for use in the United Kingdom when he knows, or it is obvious to a reasonable person in the circumstances, that its use there without the consent of the proprietor would be an infringement of the patent;

(c) where the invention is a process, he disposes of, offers to dispose of, uses or imports any product obtained directly by means of that process or keeps any such product whether for disposal or otherwise.

(2) Subject to the following provisions of this section, a person (other than the proprietor of the patent) also infringes a patent for an invention if, while the patent is in force and without the consent of the proprietor, he supplies or offers to supply in the United Kingdom a person other than a licensee or other person entitled to work the invention with any of the means, relating to an essential element of the invention, for putting the invention into effect when he knows, or it is obvious to a reasonable person in the circumstances, that those means are suitable for putting, and are intended to put, the invention into effect in the United Kingdom.

(3) Subsection (2) above shall not apply to the supply or offer of a

staple commercial product unless the supply or the offer is made for the purpose of inducing the person supplied or, as the case may be, the person to whom the offer is made to do an act which constitutes an infringement of the patent by virtue of subsection (1) above.

(4) Without prejudice to section 86 below, subsections (1) and (2) above shall not apply to any act which, under any provision of the Community Patent Convention relating to the exhaustion of the rights of the proprietor of a patent, as that provision applies by virtue of that section, cannot be prevented by the proprietor of the patent.

(5) An act which, apart from this subsection, would constitute an infringement of a patent for an invention shall not do so if—

(a) it is done privately and for purposes which are not commercial;

(b) it is done for experimental purposes relating to the subject-matter of the invention;

(c) it consists of the extemporaneous preparation in a pharmacy of a medicine for an individual in accordance with a prescription given by a registered medical or dental practitioner or consists of dealing with a medicine so prepared;

(d) it consists of the use, exclusively for the needs of a relevant ship, of a product or process in the body of such a ship or in its machinery, tackle, apparatus or other accessories, in a case where the ship has temporarily or accidentally entered the internal or territorial waters of the United Kingdom;

(e) it consists of the use of a product or process in the body or operation of a relevant aircraft, hovercraft or vehicle which has temporarily or accidentally entered or is crossing the United Kingdom (including the air space above it and its territorial waters) or the use of accessories for such a relevant aircraft, hovercraft or vehicle;

(f) it consists of the use of an exempted aircraft which has lawfully entered or is lawfully crossing the United Kingdom as aforesaid or of the importation into the United Kingdom, or the use or storage there, of any part or accessory for such an aircraft.

(6) For the purposes of subsection (2) above a person who does an act in relation to an invention which is prevented only by virtue of paragraph (a), (b) or (c) of subsection (5) above from constituting an infringement of a patent for the invention shall not be treated as a person entitled to work the invention, but—

(a) the reference in that subsection to a person entitled to work an invention includes a reference to a person so entitled by virtue of section 55 above, and

(b) a person who by virtue of **section 28A(4) or (5)** [*section 28(6)*] above or section 64 below is entitled to do an act in relation to the invention without it constituting such an infringement shall, so far as concerns that act, be treated as a person entitled to work the invention.

(7) In this section—

"relevant ship" and "relevant aircraft, hovercraft or vehicle" mean respectively a ship and an aircraft, hovercraft or vehicle registered in, or belonging to, any country, other than the United Kingdom, which is a party to the Convention for the Protection of Industrial Property signed at Paris on 20th March 1883; and

"exempted aircraft" means an aircraft to which section 53 of the Civil Aviation Act 1949 (aircraft exempted from seizure in respect of patent claims) applies.

NOTE

S.60(6)(b) amended by C.D.P.A. 1988, Sched. 5, para.8(a), with effect from January 7, 1991 (S.I. 1990, No.2168).

Proceedings for infringement of patent

15.61   61.—(1) Subject to the following provisions of this Part of this Act, civil proceedings may be brought in the court by the proprietor of a patent in respect of any act alleged to infringe the patent and (without prejudice to any other jurisdiction of the court) in those proceedings a claim may be made—

(a) for an injunction or interdict restraining the defendant or defender from any apprehended acts of infringement;

(b) for an order for him to deliver up or destroy any patented product in relation to which the patent is infringed or any article in which that product is inextricably comprised;

(c) for damages in respect of the infringement;

(d) for an account of the profits derived by him from the infringement;

(e) for a declaration or declarator that the patent is valid and has been infringed by him.

(2) The court shall not, in respect of the same infringement, both award the proprietor of a patent damages and order that he shall be given an account of the profits.

(3) The proprietor of a patent and any other person may by agreement with each other refer to the comptroller the question whether that other person has infringed the patent and on the reference of the proprietor of the patent may make any claim mentioned in subsection (1)(c) or (e) above.

(4) Except so far as the context requires, in the following provisions of this Act—

(a) any references to proceedings for infringement and the bringing of such proceedings includes a reference to a reference under subsection (3) above and the making of such a reference;

(b) any reference to a plaintiff or pursuer includes a reference to the proprietor of the patent; and

(c) any reference to a defendant or defender includes a reference to any other party to the reference.

(5) If it appears to the comptroller on a reference under subsection (3) above that the question referred to him would more properly be determined by the court, he may decline to deal with it and the court shall have jurisdiction to determine the question as if the reference were proceedings brought in the court.

(6) Subject to the following provisions of this Part of this Act, in determining whether or not to grant any kind of relief claimed under this section and the extent of the relief granted the court or the comptroller shall apply the principles applied by the court in relation to that kind of relief immediately before the appointed day.

Restrictions on recovery of damages for infringement

62.—(1) In proceedings for infringement of a patent damages shall not **15.62** be awarded, and no order shall be made for an account of profits, against a defendant or defender who proves that at the date of the infringement he was not aware, and had no reasonable grounds for supposing, that the patent existed; and a person shall not be taken to have been so aware or to have had reasonable grounds for so supposing by reason only of the application to a product of the word "patent" or "patented," or any word or words expressing or implying that a patent has been obtained for the product, unless the number of the patent accompanied the word or words in question.

(2) In proceedings for infringement of a patent the court or the comptroller may, if it or he thinks fit, refuse to award any damages or make any such order in respect of an infringement committed during any further period specified under section 25(4) above, but before the payment of the renewal fee and any additional fee prescribed for the purposes of that subsection.

(3) Where an amendment of the specification of a patent has been allowed under any of the provisions of this Act, no damages shall be awarded in proceedings for an infringement of the patent committed before the decision to allow the amendment unless the court or the comptroller is satisfied that the specification of the patent as published was framed in good faith and with reasonable skill and knowledge.

Relief for infringement of partially valid patent

63.—(1) If the validity of a patent is put in issue in proceedings for **15.63** infringement of the patent and it is found that the patent is only partially valid, the court or the comptroller may, subject to subsection (2) below, grant relief in respect of that part of the patent which is found to be valid and infringed.

(2) Where in any such proceedings it is found that a patent is only partially valid, the court or the comptroller shall not grant relief by way of damages, costs or expenses, except where the plaintiff or pursuer proves that the specification for the patent was framed in good faith and with reasonable skill and knowledge, and in that event the court or the comptroller may grant relief in respect of that part of the patent which is valid and infringed, subject to the discretion of the court or the comptroller as to costs or expenses and as to the date from which damages should be reckoned.

(3) As a condition of relief under this section the court or the comptroller may direct that the specification of the patent shall be amended to its or his satisfaction upon an application made for that purpose under section 75 below, and an application may be so made accordingly, whether or not all other issues in the proceedings have been determined.

Right to continue use begun before priority date

15.64   **64.**—[*(1) Where a patent is granted for an invention, a person who in the United Kingdom before the priority date of the invention does in good faith an act which would constitute an infringement of the patent if it were in force, or makes in good faith effective and serious preparations to do such an act, shall have the rights conferred by subsection (2) below.*

(2) Any such person shall have the right—

(a) to continue to do or, as the case may be, to do that act himself; and

(b) if it was done or preparations had been made to do it in the course of a business, to assign the right to do it or to transmit that right on his death or, in the case of a body corporate on its dissolution, to any person who acquires that part of the business in the course of which the act was done or preparations had been made to do it, or to authorise it to be done by any partners of his for the time being in that business;

and the doing of that act by virtue of this subsection shall not amount to an infringement of the patent concerned.

(3) The rights mentioned in subsection (2) above shall not include the right to grant a licence to any person to do an act so mentioned.

(4) Where a patented product is disposed of by any person to another in exercise of a right conferred by subsection (2) above, that other and any person claiming through him shall be entitled to deal with the product in the same way as if it had been disposed of by a sole registered proprietor.]

64.—**(1) Where a patent is granted for an invention, a person who in the United Kingdom before the priority date of the invention—**

(a) does in good faith an act which would constitute an infringement of the patent if it were in force, or

(b) makes in good faith effective and serious preparation to do such an act,

has the right to continue to do the act or, as the case may be, to do the act, notwithstanding the grant of the patent; but his right does not extend to granting a licence to another person to do the act.

(2) If the act was done, or the preparations were made, in the course of a business, the person entitled to the right conferred by subsection (1) may—

(a) authorise the doing of that act by any partners of his for the time being in that business, and

(b) assign that right, or transmit it on death (or in the case of a body corporate on its dissolution), to any person who acquires that part of the business in the course of which the act was done or the preparations were made.

(3) Where a product is disposed of to another in exercise of the rights conferred by subsection (1) or (2), that other and any person claiming through him may deal with the product in the same way as if it had been disposed of by the registered proprietor of the patent.

Note

S.64 substituted by C.D.P.A. 1988, Sched. 5, para.17, with effect from January 7, 1991 (S.I. 1990, No.2168).

Certificate of contested validity of patent

65.—(1) If in any proceedings before the court or the comptroller the **15.65** validity of a patent to any extent is contested and that patent is found by the court or the comptroller to be wholly or partially valid, the court or the comptroller may certify the finding and the fact that the validity of the patent was so contested.

(2) Where a certificate is granted under this section, then, if in any subsequent proceedings before the court or the comptroller for infringement of the patent concerned or for revocation of the patent a final order or judgment or interlocutor is made or given in favour of the party relying on the validity of the patent as found in the earlier proceedings, that party shall, unless the court or the comptroller otherwise directs, be entitled to his costs or expenses as between solicitor and own client (other than the costs or expenses of any appeal in any such proceedings).

Proceedings for infringement by a co-owner

15.66   66.—(1) In the application of section 60 above to a patent of which there are two or more proprietors the reference to the proprietor shall be construed—

(a) in relation to any act, as a reference to that proprietor or those proprietors who, by virtue of section 36 above or any agreement referred to in that section, is or are entitled to do that act without its amounting to an infringement; and

(b) in relation to any consent, as a reference to that proprietor or those proprietors who, by virtue of section 36 above or any such agreement, is or are the proper person or persons to give the requisite consent.

(2) One of two or more joint proprietors of a patent may without the concurrence of the others bring proceedings in respect of an act alleged to infringe the patent, but shall not do so unless the others are made parties to the proceedings, but any of the others made a defendant or defender shall not be liable for any costs or expenses unless he enters an appearance and takes part in the proceedings.

Proceedings for infringement by exclusive licensee

15.67   67.—(1) Subject to the provisions of this section, the holder of an exclusive licence under a patent shall have the same right as the proprietor of the patent to bring proceedings in respect of any infringement of the patent committed after the date of the licence; and references to the proprietor of the patent in the provisions of this Act relating to infringement shall be construed accordingly.

(2) In awarding damages or granting any other relief in any such proceedings the court or the comptroller shall take into consideration any loss suffered or likely to be suffered by the exclusive licensee as such as a result of the infringement, or, as the case may be, the profits derived from the infringement, so far as it constitutes an infringement of the rights of the exclusive licensee as such.

(3) In any proceedings taken by an exclusive licensee by virtue of this section the proprietor of the patent shall be made a party to the proceedings, but if made a defendant or defender shall not be liable for any costs or expenses unless he enters an appearance and takes part in the proceedings.

Effect of non-registration on infringement proceedings

15.68   68. Where by virtue of a transaction, instrument or event to which section 33 above applies a person becomes the proprietor or one of the proprietors or an exclusive licensee of a patent and the patent is subsequently infringed, the court or the comptroller shall not award him damages or order that he be given an account of the profits in respect of such a subsequent infringement occurring before the transaction, instrument or event is registered unless—

(a) the transaction, instrument or event is registered within the period of six months beginning with its date; or

(b) the court or the comptroller is satisfied that it was not practicable to register the transaction, instrument or event before the end of that period and that it was registered as soon as practicable thereafter.

Infringement of rights conferred by publication of application

69.—(1) Where an application for a patent for an invention is **15.69** published, then, subject to subsections (2) and (3) below, the applicant shall have, as from the publication and until the grant of the patent, the same right as he would have had, if the patent had been granted on the date of the publication of the application, to bring proceedings in the court or before the comptroller for damages in respect of any act which would have infringed the patent; and (subject to subsections (2) and (3) below) references to sections 60 to 62 and 66 to 68 above to a patent and the proprietor of a patent shall be respectively construed as including references to any such application and the applicant, and references to a patent being in force, being granted, being valid or existing shall be construed accordingly.

(2) The applicant shall be entitled to bring proceedings by virtue of this section in respect of any act only—

(a) after the patent has been granted; and

(b) if the act would, if the patent had been granted on the date of the publication of the application, have infringed not only the patent, but also the claims (as interpreted by the description and any drawings referred to in the description or claims) in the form in which they were contained in the application immediately before the preparations for its publication were completed by the Patent Office.

(3) Section 62(2) and (3) above shall not apply to an infringement of the rights conferred by this section, but in considering the amount of any damages for such an infringement, the court or the comptroller shall consider whether or not it would have been reasonable to expect, from a consideration of the application as published under section 16 above, that a patent would be granted conferring on the proprietor of the patent protection from an act of the same description as that found to infringe those rights, and if the court or the comptroller finds that it would not have been reasonable, it or he shall reduce the damages to such an amount as it or he thinks just.

Remedy for groundless threats of infringement proceedings

15.70   **70.**—(1) Where a person (whether or not the proprietor of, or entitled to any right in, a patent) by circulars, advertisements or otherwise threatens another person with proceedings for any infringement of a patent, a person aggrieved by the threats (whether or not he is the person to whom the threats are made) may, subject to subsection (4) below, bring proceedings in the court against the person making the threats, claiming any relief mentioned in subsection (3) below.

(2) In any such proceedings the plaintiff or pursuer shall, if he proves that the threats were so made and satisfies the court that he is a person aggrieved by them, be entitled to the relief claimed unless—

    (a) the defendant or defender proves that the acts in respect of which proceedings were threatened constitute or, if done, would constitute an infringement of a patent; and

    (b) the patent alleged to be infringed is not shown by the plaintiff or pursuer to be invalid in a relevant respect.

(3) The said relief is—

    (a) a declaration or declarator to the effect that the threats are unjustifiable;

    (b) an injunction or interdict against the continuance of the threats; and

    (c) damages in respect of any loss which the plaintiff or pursuer has sustained by the threats.

(4) Proceedings may not be brought under this section for a threat to bring proceedings for an infringement alleged to consist of making or importing a product for disposal or of using a process.

(5) It is hereby declared that a mere notification of the existence of a patent does not constitute a threat of proceedings within the meaning of this section.

Declaration or declarator as to non-infringement

15.71   **71.**—(1) Without prejudice to the court's jurisdiction to make a declaration or declarator apart from this section, a declaration or declarator that an act does not, or a proposed act would not, constitute an infringement of a patent may be made by the court or the comptroller in proceedings between the person doing or proposing to do the act and the proprietor of the patent, notwithstanding that no assertion to the contrary has been made by the proprietor, if it is shown—

    (a) that that person has applied in writing to the proprietor for a written acknowledgment to the effect of the declaration or declarator claimed, and has furnished him with full particulars in writing of the act in question; and

    (b) that the proprietor has refused or failed to give any such acknowledgment.

(2) Subject to section 72(5) below, a declaration made by the comptroller under this section shall have the same effect as a declaration or declarator by the court.

Revocation of patents

Power to revoke patents on application

72.—(1) Subject to the following provisions of this Act, the court or the comptroller may on the application of any person by order revoke a patent for an invention on (but only on) any of the following grounds, that is to say— **15.72**

(a) the invention is not a patentable invention;

[*(b) the patent was granted to a person who was not the only person entitled under section 7(2) above to be granted that patent or to two or more persons who were not the only persons so entitled;*]

(b)) that the patent was granted to a person who was not entitled to be granted that patent;

(c) the specification of the patent does not disclose the invention clearly enough and completely enough for it to be performed by a person skilled in the art;

(d) the matter disclosed in the specification of the patent extends beyond that disclosed in the application for the patent, as filed, or, if the patent was granted on a new application filed under section 8(3), 12, or 37(4) above or as mentioned in section 15(4) above, in the earlier application, as filed;

(e) the protection conferred by the patent has been extended by an amendment which should not have been allowed.

(2) An application for the revocation of a patent on the ground mentioned in subsection (1)(*b*) above—

(a) may only be made by a person found by the court in an action for a declaration or declarator, or found by the court or the comptroller on a reference under section 37 above, to be entitled to be granted that patent or to be granted a patent for part of the matter comprised in the specification of the patent sought to be revoked; and

(b) may not be made if that action was commenced or that reference was made after the end of the period of two years beginning with the date of the grant of the patent sought to be revoked, unless it is shown that any person registered as a proprietor of the patent knew at the time of the grant or of the transfer of the patent to him that he was not entitled to the patent.

(3) Rules under section 14(4) and (8) above shall, with any necessary modifications, apply for the purposes of subsection (1)(*c*) above as they apply for the purposes of section 14(3) above.

(4) An order under this section may be an order for the unconditional revocation of the patent or, where the court or the comptroller determines that one of the grounds mentioned in subsection (1) above has been established, but only so as to invalidate the patent to a limited extent, an order that the patent should be revoked unless within a specified time the specification is amended under section 75 below to the satisfaction of the court or the comptroller, as the case may be.

(5) A decision of the comptroller or on appeal from the comptroller shall not estop any party to civil proceedings in which infringement of a patent is in issue from alleging invalidity of the patent on any of the grounds referred to in subsection (1) above, whether or not any of the issues involved were decided in the said decision.

(6) Where the comptroller refuses to grant an application made to him by any person under this section, no application (otherwise than by way of appeal or by way of putting validity in issue in proceedings for infringement) may be made to the court by that person under this section in relation to the patent concerned, without the leave of the court.

(7) Where the comptroller has not disposed of an application made to him under this section, the applicant may not apply to the court under this section in respect of the patent concerned unless either—

(a) the proprietor of the patent agres that the applicant may so apply, or

(b) the comptroller certifies in writing that it appears to him that the question whether the patent should be revoked is one which would more properly be determined by the court.

NOTE

Subs. (1)(b) substituted by C.D.P.A. 1988, Sched. 5, para.18, with effect from January 7, 1991 (S.I. 1990, No.2168).

Comptroller's power to revoke patents on his own initiative

15.73   73.—(1) If it appears to the comptroller that an invention for which a patent has been granted formed part of the state of the art by virtue only of section 2(3) above, he may on his own initiative by order revoke the patent, but shall not do so without giving the proprietor of the patent an opportunity of making any observations and of amending the specification of the patent so as to exclude any matter which formed part of the state of the art as aforesaid without contravening section 76 below.

[(2) If it appears to the comptroller that a patent under this Act and a European patent (U.K.) have been granted for the same invention having the same priority date and that the applications for both patents were filed by the same applicant or his successor in title, the comptroller may, on his own *initiative but only after the relevant date, consider whether to revoke the patent granted under this Act and may, after giving the proprietor of the patent an opportunity of making any observations and of amending the specification of the patent, revoke the patent.*]

(2) If it appears to the comptroller that a patent under this Act and a European patent (U.K.) have been granted for the same invention having the same priority date, and that the applications for the patents were filed by the same applicant or his successor in title, he shall give the proprietor of the patent under this Act an opportunity of making observations and of amending the specification of the patent, and if the proprietor fails to satisfy the comptroller that there are not two patents in respect of the same invention, or to amend the specification so as to prevent there being two patents in respect of the same invention, the comptroller shall revoke the patent.

[*(3) In this section "the relevant date" means whichever of the following dates is relevant, that is to say—*

(a) *the date on which the period for filing an opposition to patent under the European Patent Convention expires without an opposition being filed;*

(b) *the date when any opposition proceedings under that convention are finally disposed of by a decision to maintain the European patent;*

(c) *if later than either of the foregoing dates, the date when the patent under this Act is granted.*]

(3) The comptroller shall not take action under subsection (2) above before—

(a) **the end of the period for filing an opposition to the European patent (U.K.) under the European Patent Convention, or**

(b) **if later, the date on which opposition proceedings are finally disposed of;**

and he shall not then take any action if the decision is not to maintain the European patent or if it is amended so that there are not two patents in respect of the same invention.

(4) The comptroller shall not take action under subsection (2) above if the European patent (U.K.) has been surrendered under section 29(1) above before the date on which by virtue of section 25(1) above the patent under this Act is to be treated as having been granted or, if proceedings for the surrender of the European patent (U.K.) have been begun before that date, until those proceedings are finally disposed of; and he shall not then take any action if the decision is to accept the surrender of the European patent.

NOTE

Subs. (2) and (3) substituted and subs. (4) added by C.D.P.A. 1988, Sched. 5, para.19, with effect from January 7, 1991 (S.I. 1990, No.2168).

Putting validity in issue

Proceedings in which validity of patent may be put in issue

15.74   74.—(1) Subject to the following provisions of this section, the validity of a patent may be put in issue—

   (a) by way of defence, in proceedings for infringement of the patent under section 61 above or proceedings under section 69 above for infringement of rights conferred by the publication of an application;
   (b) in proceedings under section 70 above;
   (c) in proceedings in which a declaration in relation to the patent is sought under section 71 above;
   (d) in proceedings before the court or the comptroller under section 72 above for the revocation of the patent;
   (e) in proceedings under section 58 above.

   (2) The validity of a patent may not be put in issue in any other proceedings and, in particular, no proceedings may be instituted (whether under this Act or otherwise) seeking only a declaration as to the validity or invalidity of a patent.

   (3) The only grounds on which the validity of a patent may be put in issue (whether in proceedings for revocation under section 72 above or otherwise) are the grounds on which the patent may be revoked under that section.

   (4) No determination shall be made in any proceedings mentioned in subsection (1) above on the validity of a patent which any person puts in issue on the ground mentioned in section 72(1)(b) above unless—

   (a) it has been determined in entitlement proceedings commenced by that person or in the proceedings in which the validity of the patent is in issue that the patent should have been granted to him and not some other person; and
   (b) except where it had been so determined in entitlement proceedings, the proceedings in which the validity of the patent is in issue are commenced before the end of the period of two years beginning with the date of the grant of the patent or it is shown that any person registered as a proprietor of the patent knew at the time of the grant or of the transfer of the patent to him that he was not entitled to the patent.

   (5) Where the validity of a patent is put in issue by way of defence or counterclaim the court or the comptroller shall, if it or he thinks it just to do so, give the defendant an opportunity to comply with the condition in subsection (4)(a) above.

   (6) In subsection (4) above "entitlement proceedings," in relation to a patent, means a reference under [*section 37(1)(a)*] **section 37(1)** above on the ground that the patent was granted to a person not entitled to it or proceedings for a declaration or declarator that it was so granted.

(7) Where proceedings with respect to a patent are pending in the court under any provision of this Act mentioned in subsection (1) above, no proceedings may be instituted without the leave of the court before the comptroller with respect to that patent under section 61(3), 69, 71 or 72 above.

(8) It is hereby declared that for the purposes of this Act the validity of a patent is not put in issue merely because the comptroller is considering its validity in order to decide whether to revoke it under section 73 above.

Note

Subs. (6) amended by C.D.P.A. 1988, Sched. 5, para.10, with effect from January 7, 1991 (S.I. 1990, No.2168).

General provisions as to amendment of patents and applications

Amendment of patent in infringement or revocation proceedings

75.—(1) In any proceedings before the court or the comptroller in   **15.75**
which the validity of a patent is put in issue the court or, as the case may be, the comptroller may, subject to section 76 below, allow the proprietor of the patent to amend the specification of the patent in such manner, and subject to such terms as to advertising the proposed amendment and as to costs, expenses or otherwise, as the court or comptroller thinks fit.

(2) A person may give notice to the court or the comptroller of his opposition to an amendment proposed by the proprietor of the patent under this section, and if he does so the court or the comptroller shall notify the proprietor and consider the opposition in deciding whether the amendment or any amendment should be allowed.

(3) An amendment of a specification of a patent under this section shall have effect and be deemed always to have had effect from the grant of the patent.

(4) Where an application for an order under this section is made to the court, the applicant shall notify the comptroller, who shall be entitled to appear and be heard and shall appear if so directed by the court.

Amendments of applications and patents not to include added matter

[**76.**—*(1) An application for a patent (the later application) shall not be*   **15.76**
allowed to be filed under section 8(3), 12 or 37(4) above or as mentioned in

section 15(4) above, in respect of any matter disclosed in an earlier application or the specification of a patent which has been granted if the later application discloses matter which extends beyond that disclosed in the earlier application, as filed, or the application for the patent, as filed.

(2) No amendment of an application or the specification of a patent shall be allowed under any of the provisions of this Act to which this subsection applies if it—

(a) results in the application or specification disclosing any such matter, or

(b) (where a patent has been granted) extends the protection conferred by the patent.

(3) Subsection (2) above applies to the following provisions of this Act namely, section 17(3), 18(3) 19(1) 27(1), 73 and 75.]

76.—(1) An application for a patent which—

(a) is made in respect of matter disclosed in an earlier application, or in the specification of a patent which has been granted, and

(b) discloses additional matter, that is, matter extending beyond that disclosed in the earlier application, as filed, or the application for the patent, as filed.

may be filed under section 8(3), 12 or 37(4) above, or as mentioned in section 15(4) above, but shall not be allowed to proceed unless it is amended so as to exclude the additional matter.

(2) No amendment of an application for a patent shall be allowed under section 17(3), 18(3) or 19(1) if it results in the application disclosing matter extending beyond that disclosed in the application as filed.

(3) No amendment of the specification of a patent shall be allowed under section 27(1), 73 or 75 if it—

(a) results in the specification disclosing additional matter, or

(b) extends the protection conferred by the patent.

NOTE

S.76 replaced by C.D.P.A. 1988, Sched. 5, para.20, with effect from January 7, 1991 (S.I. 1990, No.2168).

European patents and patent applications

Effect of European patent (U.K.)

77.—(1) Subject to the provisions of this Act, a European patent (U.K.) **15.77** shall, as from the publication of the mention of its grant in the European Patent Bulletin, be treated for the purposes of Parts I and III of this Act as if it were a patent under this Act granted in pursuance of an application made under this Act and as if notice of the grant of the patent had, on the date of that publication, been published under section 24 above in the journal; and—

(a) the proprietor of a European patent (U.K.) shall accordingly as respects the United Kingdom have the same rights and remedies, subject to the same conditions, as the proprietor of a patent under this Act;

(b) references in Parts I and III of this Act to a patent shall be construed accordingly; and

(c) any statement made and any certificate filed for the purposes of the provision of the convention corresponding to section 2(4)(*c*) above shall be respectively treated as a statement made and written evidence filed for the purposes of the said paragraph (*c*).

(2) Subsection (1) above shall not affect the operation in relation to a European patent (U.K.) of any provisions of the European Patent Convention relating to the amendment or revocation of such a patent in proceedings before the European Patent Office.

[*(3) Section 58(7) to (9) and 63 above shall apply to the case where, after proceedings for the infringement of a European patent have been commenced before the court or the comptroller but have not been finally disposed of, it is established in proceedings before the European Patent Office that the patent is only partially valid as those provisions apply to proceedings in which the validity of a patent is put in issue and in which it is found that the patent is only partially valid.*]

(3) Where in the case of a European patent (U.K.)—

(a) proceedings for infringement, or proceedings under section 58 above, have been commenced before the court or the comptroller and have not been finally disposed of, and

(b) it is established in proceedings before the European Patent Office that the patent is only partially valid,

the provisions of section 63 or, as the case may be, of subsection (7) to (9) of section 58 apply as they apply to proceedings in which the validity of a patent is put in issue and in which it is found that the patent is only partially valid.

[*(4) Subject to subsection (6) below, where a European patent (U.K.) is amended or revoked in accordance with the European Patent Convention, the amendment shall be treated for the purposes of Parts I and III of this Act as if it had been made, or as the case may be the patent shall be treated for those purposes as having been revoked, under this Act.*]

(4) Where a European patent (U.K.) is amended in accordance with the European Patent Convention, the amendment shall have effect for the purposes of Parts I and III of this Act as if the specification of the patent had been amended under this Act; but subject to subsection (6)(b) below.

(4A) Where a European patent (U.K.) is revoked in accordance with the European Patent Convention, the patent shall be treated for the purposes of Parts I and III of this Act as having been revoked under this Act.

(5) Where—

(a) under the European Patent Convention a European patent (U.K.) is revoked for failure to observe a time limit and is subsequently restored; and

(b) between revocation and publication of the fact that it has been restored a person begins in good faith to do an act which would, apart from section 55 above, constitute an infringement of the patent or makes in good faith effective and serious preparations to do such an act;

he shall have the rights conferred by [*section 28(6) above, and subsections (8) and (9) of that section shall apply accordingly*] **section 28A(4) and (5) above, and subsection (6) and (7) of that section shall apply accordingly.**

(6) While this subsection is in force—

(a) subsection (1) above shall not apply to a European patent (U.K.) the specification of which was published in French or German, unless a translation of the specification into English is filed at the Patent Office and the prescribed fee is paid before the end of the prescribed period;

(b) subsection (4) above shall not apply to an amendment made in French or German unless a translation of *the amendment* into English **of the specification as amended** is filed at the Patent Office and the prescribed fee is paid before the end of the prescribed period.

(7) Where such a translation *of a specification or amendment into English* is not filed *in accordance with subsection (6)(a) or (b) above*, the patent shall be treated as always having been void.

(8) The comptroller shall publish any translation filed at the Patent Office under subsection (6) above.

(9) Subsection (6) above shall come into force on a day appointed for the purpose by rules and shall cease to have effect on a day so

appointed, without prejudice, however, to the power to bring it into force again.

NOTE

Subs. (3) and (4) replaced, subs. (4A) inserted and changes to subs. (6) and (7) by C.D.P.A. 1988, Sched. 5, para.21, with effect from January 7, 1991 (S.I. 1990, No.2168).

Effect of filing an application for a European patent (U.K.)

78.—(1) Subject to the provisions of this Act, an application for a European patent (U.K.) having a date of filing under the European Patent Convention shall be treated for the purposes of the provisions of this Act to which this section applies as an application for a patent under this Act having that date as its date of filing and having the other incidents listed in subsection (3) below, but subject to the modifications mentioned in the following provisions of this section.   **15.78**

(2) This section applies to the following provisions of this Act:—

section 2(3) and so much of section 14(7) as relates to section 2(3);

section 5;

section 6;

so much of section 13(3) as relates to an application for and issue of a certificate under that subsection;

sections 30 to 33;

sections 36;

sectins 55 to 69;

section 74, so far as relevant to any of the provisions mentioned above;

section 111; and

section 125.

(3) The incidents referred to in subsection (1) above in relation to an application for a European patent (U.K.) are as follows:—

(a) any declaration of priority made in connection with the application under the European Patent Convention shall be treated for the purposes of this Act as a declaration made under section 5(2) above;

(b) where a period of time relevant to priority is extended under that convention, the period of 12 months specified in section 5(2) above shall be so treated as altered correspondingly;

(c) where the date of filing an application is re-dated under that convention to a later date, that date shall be so treated as the date of filing the application;

(d) the application, if published in accordance with that convention, shall, subject to subsection (7) and section 79 below, be so treated as published under section 16 above;

(e) any designation of the inventor under that convention or any statement under it indicating the origin of the right to a European patent shall be treated for the purposes of section 13(3) above as a statement filed under section 13(2) above;

(f) registration of the application in the register of European patents shall be treated as registration under this Act.

(4) Rules under section 32 above may not impose any requirements as to the registration of applications for European patents (U.K.) but may provide for the registration of copies of entries relating to such applications in the European register of patents.

[*(5) Subsections (1) to (3) above shall cease to apply to an application for a European patent (U.K.) when the application is refused or withdrawn or deemed to be withdrawn, or the designation of the United Kingdom in the application is withdrawn or deemed to be withdrawn, but if the rights of the applicant are re-established under the European Patent Convention, subsection (1) to (3) above shall as from the re-establishment of those rights again apply to the application.*]

(5) Subsections (1) to (3) above shall cease to apply to an application for a European patent (U.K.), except as mentioned in subsection (5A) below, if—

> **(a) the application is refused or withdrawn or deemed to be withdrawn, or**
>
> **(b) the designation of the United Kingdom in the application is withdrawn or deemed to be withdrawn,**

but shall apply again if the rights of the applicant are re-established under the European Patent Convention, as from their re-establishment.

(5A) The occurrence of any of the events mentioned in subsection (5)(a) or (b) shall not affect the continued operation of section 2(3) above in relation to matter contained in an application for a European patent (U.K.) which by virtue of that provision has become part of the state of the art as regards other inventions.

(6) Where between those subsections ceasing to apply to any such application and the re-establishment of the rights of the applicant a person begins in good faith to do an act which would, apart from section 55 above, constitute an infringement of the application if those subsections then applied, or makes in good faith effective and serious preparations to do such an act, he shall have the rights conferred by [*section 28(6) above, and section 28(8) and (9) above shall apply to the exercise of any such right accordingly*] **section 28A(4) and (5) above, and subsections (6) and (7) of that section shall apply accordingly.**

(7) While this subsection is in force, an application for a European patent (U.K.) published by the European Patent Office under the European Patent Convention in French or German shall be treated for the purposes of sections 55 and 69 above as published under section 16 above when a translation into English of the claims of the specification of the application has been filed at and published by the Patent Office and the prescribed fee has been paid, but an applicant—

(a) may recover a payment by virtue of section 55(5) above in respect of the use of the invention in question before publication of that translation; or

(b) may bring proceedings by virtue of section 69 above in respect of an act mentioned in that section which is done before publication of that translation;

if before that use or the doing of that act he has sent by post or delivered to the government department who made use or authorised the use of the invention, or, as the case may be, to the person alleged to have done the act, a translation into English of those claims.

(8) Subsection (7) above shall come into force on a day appointed for the purpose by rules and shall cease to have effect on a day so appointed, without prejudice, however, to the power to bring it into force again.

NOTE

Subs. (5) substituted and subs. (5A) inserted by C.D.P.A. 1988, Sched. 5, para.22, with effect from January 7, 1991 (S.I. 1990, No.2168).

Operation of section 78 in relation to certain European patent applications

79.—(1) Subject to the following provisions of this section, section 78 **15.79** above, in its operation in relation to an international application for a patent (U.K.) which is treated by virtue of the European Patent Covention as an application for a European patent (U.K.), shall have effect as if any reference in that section to anything done in relation to the application under the European Patent Convention included a reference to the corresponding thing done under the Patent Co-operation Treaty.

(2) Any such international application which is published under that treaty shall be treated for the purposes of section 2(3) above as published only when a copy of the application has been supplied to the European Patent Office in English, French or German and the relevant fee has been paid under that convention.

(3) Any such international application which is published under that treaty in a language other than English, French or German shall, subject to section 78(7) above, be treated for the purposes of sections 55 and 69 above as published only when it is re-published in English, French or German by the European Patent Office under that convention.

Authentic text of European patents and patent applications

15.80   80.—(1) Subject to subsection (2) below, the text of a European patent or application for such a patent in the language of the proceedings, that is to say, the language in which proceedings relating to the patent or the application are to be conducted before the European Patent Office, shall be the authentic text for the purposes of any domestic proceedings, that is to say, any proceedings relating to the patent or application before the comptroller or the court.

(2) Where the language of the proceedings is French or German, a translation into English of the specification of the patent under section 77 above or of the claims of the application under section 78 above shall be treated as the authentic text for the purpose of any domestic proceedings other than proceedings for the revocation of the patent, if the patent or application as translated into English confers protection which is narrower than that conferred by it in French or German.

(3) If any such translation results in a European patent or application conferring the narrower protection, the proprietor of or applicant for the patent may file a corrected translation with the Patent Office and, if he pays the prescribed fee within the prescribed period, the Patent Office shall publish it, but—

> (a) any payment for any use of the invention which (apart from section 55 above) would have infringed the patent as correctly translated, but not as originally translated, or in the case of an application would have infringed it as aforesaid if the patent had been granted, shall not be recoverable under that section,
>
> (b) the proprietor or applicant shall not be entitled to bring proceedings in respect of an act which infringed the patent as correctly translated, but not as originally translated, or in the case of an application would have infringed it as aforesaid if the patent had been granted.

unless before that use or the doing of the act the corrected translation has been published by the Patent Office or the proprietor or applicant has sent the corrected translation by post or delivered it to the government department who made use or authorised use of the invention or, as the case may be, to the person alleged to have done that act.

(4) Where a correction of a translation is published under subsection (3) above and before it is so published a person begins in good faith to do an act which would not constitute an infringement of the patent or application as originally translated but would (apart from section 55 above) constitute an infringement of it under the amended translation, or makes in good faith effective and serious preparations to do such an act, he shall have the rights conferred by [*section 28(6) above, and section 28(8) and (9) above shall apply to the exercise of any such right accordingly*] **section 28A(4) and (5) above, and subsections (6) and (7) of that section shall apply accordingly.**

NOTE

S.80 amended by C.D.P.A. 1988, Sched. 5, para.8, with effect from January 7, 1991 (S.I. 1990, No.2168).

Conversion of European patent applications

81.—(1) The comptroller may direct that on compliance with the **15.81** relevant conditions mentioned in subsection (2) below an application for a European patent (U.K.) shall be treated as an application for a patent under this Act in the following cases:—
  (a) where the application is deemed to be withdrawn under the provisions of the European Patent Convention relating to the restriction of the processing of applications;
  (b) where under the convention the application is deemed to be withdrawn because it has not, within the period required by the convention, been received by the European Patent Office.
(2) The relevant conditions referred to above are that—
  (a) in the case of an application falling within subsection (1)(a) above, the European Patent Office transmits a request of the applicant to the Patent Office that his application should be converted into an application under this Act, together with a copy of the files relating to the application.
  (b) in the case of an application falling within subsection (1)(b) above,—
    (i) the applicant requests the comptroller within the relevant prescribed period (where the application was filed with the Patent Office) to give a direction under this section, or
    (ii) the central industrial property office of a country which is party to the convention, other than the United Kingdom, with which the application was filed transmits within the relevant prescribed period a request that the application should be converted into an application under this Act, together with a copy of the application; and
  (c) in either case the applicant within the relevant prescribed period pays the filing fee and if the application is in a language other than English, files a translation into English of the application and of any amendments previously made in accordance with the convention.
(3) Where an application for a European patent falls to be treated as an application for a patent under this Act by virtue of a direction under this section—
  (a) the date which is the date of filing the application under the European Patent Convention shall be treated as its date of filing for the purposes of this Act, but if that date is re-dated under the

convention to a later date, the later date shall be treated for those purposes as the date of filing the application;

(b) if the application satisfies a requirement of the convention corresponding to any of the requirements of this Act or rules designated as formal requirements, it shall be treated as satisfying that formal requirement;

(c) any document filed with the European Patent Office under any provision of the convention corresponding to any of the following provisions of this Act, that is to say, section 2(4) (c), 5, 13(2) and 14, or any rule made for the purposes of any of those provisions shall be treated as filed with the Patent Office under that provision or rule; and

(d) the comptroller shall refer the application for only so much of the examination and search required by sections 17 and 18 above as he considers appropriate in view of any examination and search carried out under the convention and those sections shall apply with any necessary modifications accordingly.

Jurisdiction to determine questions as to right to a patent

15.82 82.—(1) The court shall not have jurisdiction to determine a question to which this section applies except in accordance with the following provisions of this section.

(2) Section 12 above shall not confer jurisdiction on the comptroller to determine a question to which this section applies except in accordance with the following provisions of this section.

(3) This section applies to a question arising before the grant of a European patent whether a person has a right to be granted a European patent, or a share in any such patent, and in this section "employer-employee question" means any such question between an employer and an employee, or their successors in title, arising out of an application for a European patent for an invention made by the Employee.

(4) The court and the comptroller shall have jurisdiction to determine any question to which this section applies, other than an employer-employee question, if either of the following conditions is satisfied, that is to say—

(a) the applicant has his residence or principal place of business in the United Kingdom; or

(b) the other party claims that the patent should be granted to him and he has his residence or principal place of business in the United Kingdom and the applicant does not have his residence or principal place of business in any of the relevant contracting states;

and also if in either of those cases there is no written evidence that the parties have agreed to submit to the jurisdiction of the competent authority of a relevant contracting state other than the United Kingdom.

(5) The court and the comptroller shall have jurisdiction to determine an employer-employee question if one of the following conditions is satisfied, that is to say—

(a) the employee is mainly employed in the United Kingdom; or

(b) the employee is not mainly employed anywhere or his place of main employment cannot be determined, but the employer has a place of business in the United Kingdom to which the employee is attached (whether or not he is also attached elsewhere);

and also if in either of those cases there is no written evidence that the parties have agreed to submit to the jurisdiction of the competent authority of a relevant contracting state other than the United Kingdom or, where there is such evidence of such an agreement, if the [*proper law of*] **law applicable to** the contract of employment does not recognise the validity of the agreement.

(6) Without prejudice to subsections (2) to (5) above, the court and the comptroller shall have jurisdiction to determine any question to which this section applies if there is written evidence that the parties have agreed to submit to the jurisdiction of the court or the comptroller, as the case may be, and, in the case of an employer-employee question, the [*proper law of*] **law applicable to** the contract of employment recognises the validity of the agreement.

(7) If after proceedings to determine a question to which this section applies have been brought before the competent authority of a relevant contracting state other than the United Kingdom proceedings are begun before the court or a reference is made to the comptroller under section 12 above to determine that question, the court or the comptroller, as the case may be, shall stay or sist the proceedings before the court or the comptroller unless or until the competent authority of that other state either—

(a) determines to decline jurisdiction and no appeal lies from the determination or the time for appealing expires, or

(b) makes a determination which the court or the comptroller refuses to recognise under section 83 below.

(8) References in this section to the determination of a question include respectively references to—

(a) the making of a declaration or the grant of a declarator with respect to that question (in the case of the court); and

(b) the making of an order under section 12 above in relation to that question (in the case of the court or the comptroller).

(9) In this section and section 83 below "relevant contracting state" means a country which is a party to the European Patent Convention and has not exercised its right under the convention to exclude the application of the protocol to the convention known as the Protocol on Recognition.

NOTE

Subs. (5) and (6) amended by Contracts (Applicable Law) Act 1990, Sched. 4.

Effect of patent decisions of competent authorities of other states

15.83   83.—(1) A determination of a question to which section 82 above applies by the competent authority of a relevant contracting state other than the United Kingdom shall, if no appeal lies from the determination or the time for appealing has expired, be recognised in the United Kingdom as if it had been made by the court or the comptroller unless the court or he refuses to recognise it under subsection (2) below.

(2) The court or the comptroller may refuse to recognise any such determination that the applicant for a European patent had no right to be granted the patent, or any share in it, if either—

(a) the applicant did not contest the proceedings in question because he was not notified of them at all or in the proper manner or was not notified of them in time for him to contest the proceedings; or

(b) the determination in the proceedings in question conflicts with the determination of the competent authority of any relevant contracting state in proceedings instituted earlier between the same parties as in the proceedings in question.

Patent agents and other representatives

15.84   *84.—(1) No individual shall carry on for gain in the United Kingdom alone or in partnership with any other person, the business of acting as agent or other representative of other persons for the purpose of conducting proceedings in relation to applications for or otherwise in connection with such patents before the European Patent Office or the comptroller or hold himself out, or permit himself to be held out, as so carrying on such a business unless he satisfies the condition that his name and that of each of his partners appears on the European list.*

(2) Subsection (1) above shall not prohibit a barrister, advocate or solicitor of any part of the United Kingdom from conducting or otherwise taking part in any proceedings in connection with European patents before the European Patent Office or the comptroller to the same extent as he is entitled to take part in the corresponding proceedings in connection with patents under this Act before the Patent Office or the comptroller.

(3) A body corporate shall not for gain act or describe itself or hold itself out as entitled to act as agent or other representative of other persons for any purpose mentioned in subsection (1) above unless permitted to do so under the European Patent Convention.

(3A) In so far as it imposes any prohibition in relation to the business of acting as agent of other persons for the purpose of conducting proceedings

before the comptroller in connection with European patents (U.K.) to which section 77(1) above for the time being applies—

   (a) *subsection (1) above does not apply to any individual who carries on such a business alone if he is registered as a patent agent in the register of patent agents, or to an individual who carries on such a business in partnership if he and each of his partners is so registered; and*

   (b) *subsection (3) above does not apply to any body corporate which satisfies the condition specified in paragraph (a) or (b) of section 114(2) below (as the case may require).*

(4) Any person who contravenes subsection (1) or (3) above shall be liable on summary conviction to a fine not exceeding £1,000.

(5) Proceedings for an offence under this section may be begun at any time within twelve months from the date of the offence.

(6) A person who does any act mentioned in subsection (1) above, but satisfies the condition mentioned in that subsection, shall not be treated as contravening section 114 below so long as he does not describe himself as a patent agent without qualification and does not hold himself out or permit himself to be held out as carrying on any business other than one mentioned in that subsection.

(7) In this section "the European list" means the list of professional representatives maintained by the European Patent Office in pursuance of the European Patent Convention.]

Note

S.84 repealed by C.D.P.A. 1988, Sched. 8 with effect from August 13, 1990 (S.I. 1990, No. 1400).

[European patent attorneys

85.—(1) For the avoidance of doubt, it is hereby declared that any person **15.85** *whose name appears on the European list shall not be guilty of an offence under section 21 of the Solicitors Act 1974 or Article 22 of the Solicitors (Northern Ireland) Order 1976 by reason only of his describing himself as a European patent attorney.*

(2) A person whose name appears on the European list shall not be guilty of an offence under any of the enactments mentioned in subsection (3) below by reason only for the preparation by him of any document (other than a deed) for use in proceedings before the comptroller under this Act, in relation to a European patent or application for such a patent.

(3) The enactments referred to in subsection (2) above (which prohibit the preparation for reward of certain instruments or writs by persons not legally qualified) are—

   (a) *section 22 of the Solicitors Act 1974;*

   (b) *section 39 of the Solicitors (Scotland) act 1933; and*

(c) Article 23 of the Solicitors (Northern Ireland) Order 1976.

(4) In this section "the European list" means the list of professional representatives maintained by the European Patent Office in pursuance of the European Patent Convention.]

NOTE

S.85 repealed by C.D.P.A. 1988, Sched 8, with effect from August 13, 1990 (S.I. 1990, No.1400).

Implementation of Community Patent Convention

15.86   **86.**—(1) All rights, powers, liabilities, obligations and restrictions from time to time created or arising by or under the Community Patent Convention and all remedies and procedures from time to time provided for by or under that convention shall by virtue of this section have legal effect in the United Kingdom and shall be used there, be recognised and available in law and be enforced, allowed and followed accordingly.

(2) The Secretary of State may by regulations make provision—

(a) for implementing any obligation imposed by that convention on a domestic institution or enabling any such obligation to be implemented or enabling any rights or powers conferred on any such institution to be exercised; and

(b) otherwise for giving effect to subsection (1) above and dealing with matters arising out of its commencement or operation.

(3) Regulations under this section may include any incidental, consequential, transitional or supplementary provision appearing to the Secretary of State to be necessary or expedient, including provision amending any enactment, whenever passed, other than an enactment contained in this Part of this Act, and provision for the application of any provision of the regulations outside the United Kingdom.

(4) Sections 12, 73(2), 77 to 80, 82 and 83 above shall not apply to any application for a European Patent which under the Community patent Convention is treated as an application for a Community patent, or to a Community patent (since any such application or patent falls within the foregoing provisions of this section).

(5) In this section "domestic institution" means the court, the comptroller or the Patent Office, as the case may require.

Decisions on Community Patent Convention

15.87   **87.**—(1) For the purposes of all legal proceedings, including proceedings before the comptroller, any question as to the meaning or effect of the Community Patent Convention, or as to the validity, meaning and effect of any instrument made under or in implementation of that convention by any relevant convention institution shall be treated as a question of law (and if not referred to the relevant convention court, be for determination as such in accordance with the principles laid down by any relevant decision of that court).

(2) In this section—

"relevant convention institution" means any institution established by or having functions under the Community Patent Convention, not being an institution of the United Kingdom or any other member state, and

"relevant convention court" does not include—

(a) the European Patent Office or one of its departments; or

(b) a court of the United Kingdom or of any other member state.

[Jurisdiction in legal proceedings in connection with Community Patent Convention

88.—(1) For the purposes of the application in the United Kingdom of Article 69 of the Community Patent Convention (residence of a party as founding jurisdiction in actions for infringement, etc.) the residence of a party shall be determined in accordance with the following provisions of this section until such date as the Secretary of State may by order appoint for the repeal of those provisions.   **15.88**

(2) For the purpose of determining whether a person is resident in any part of the United Kingdom the court shall apply the law of that part of the United Kingdom.

(3) A company within the meaning of the Companies Act 1948 shall be treated for the purposes of subsection (2) above as resident in that part of the United Kingdom where its registered office is situated or where it has a principal place of business.

(4) Any other body corporate or any unincorporated body of persons shall be so treated as resident in that part of the United Kingdom where it has a principal place of business.

(5) Where any body has a principal place of business in two or more parts of the United Kingdom it shall be so treated as resident in all those parts.

(6) If the court determines that a person is not resident in the United Kingdom, then, in order to determine whether he is resident in a country which is a party to the Community Patent Convention the court shall, except in a case falling within subsection (7) below, apply the law which would be applied by the courts of that country in order to found jurisdiction under that convention.

(7) The question whether a person is to be taken for the purposes of this section as resident in the United Kingdom or any other country shall be determined in accordance with the law of that country of which he is a citizen if by that law his residence depends on that of another person or on the location of an authority.]

NOTE

S.88 repealed by C.D.P.A. 1988, Sched. 5, para.23 with effect from January 7, 1991 (S.I. 1990, No.2168).

International applications for patents

[Effect of filing international application for a patent

15.89   **89.**—*(1) Subject to the provisions of this Act, an international application for a patent (U.K.) for which a date of filing has been accorded (whether by the Patent Office or by any other body) under the Patent Co-operation Treaty (in this section referred to as the Treaty) shall, until this subsection ceases to apply to the application be treated for the purposes of Parts I and III of this Act as an application for a patent under this Act having that date as its date of filing and—*

(a) *the application, if published in accordance with the Treaty and if it satisfies relevant conditions, shall be so treated as published under section 16 above, subject, however, to subsection (7) below;*

(b) *where the date of filing an application is re-dated under the Treaty to a later date, that date shall be so treated as the date of filing the application;*

(c) *any declaration of priority made under the Treaty shall be so treated as a declaration made under section 5(2) above;*

(d) *where a period of time relevant to priority is extended under the Treaty, the period of 12 months specified in section 5(2) above shall be treated as altered correspondingly;*

(e) *any statement of the name of the inventor under the Treaty shall be so treated as a statement filed under section 13(2) above; and*

(f) *an amendment of the application made in accordance with the Treaty shall, if it satisfies the relevant conditions, be so treated as made under this Act.*

(2) Accordingly until subsection (1) above ceases to apply to an application filed or published in accordance with the Treaty the applicant shall, subject to subsection (7) below, have the same rights and remedies in relation to the application as an applicant for a patent under this Act has in relation to a filed or, as the case may be, a published application for such a patent.

(3) Notwithstanding anything in subsection (1) above, the provisions of the Treaty and not those of this Act relating to publication, search, examination and amendment shall apply to any such application until all the relevant conditions are satisfied and, if those conditions are not satisfied before the end of the prescribed period, the application shall be taken to be withdrawn.

(3A) If the relevant conditions are satisfied with respect to an application which is amended in accordance with the Treaty and the relevant conditions are not satisfied with respect to any amendment, that amendment shall be disregarded.

(4) The relevant conditions—

(a) in the case of an application, are that a copy of the application and, if it is not in English, a translation into English have been filed at the Patent Office and the filing fee has been paid to the Patent Office by the applicant; and

(b) in the case of an amendment, are that a copy of the amendment and, if it is not in English, a translation into English have been filed at the Patent Office.

(4A) In subsection (4)(a) "a copy of the application" includes a copy of the application published in accordance with the Treaty in a language other than that in which it was filed.

(5) The comptroller shall on payment of the prescribed fee publish any translation filed at the Patent Office under subsection (4) above.

(6) Before the relevant conditions are satisfied, subsection (1) above shall not operate so as to secure that an international application for a patent (U.K.) is to be treated for the purposes of section 8 above as an application for a patent under this Act and shall not affect the application of section 12 above to an invention for which an international application of a patent is made or proposed to be made, but when the relevant conditions are satisfied the international application shall be so treated and accordingly section 12 above shall not apply to it.

(7) For the purposes of sections 55 and 69 above an international application for a patent (U.K.) published in accordance with the Treaty—

(a) shall, if published in English, be treated as published under section 16 above on its publication in accordance with the Treaty;

(b) shall, if published in any other language and if the relevant conditions are satisfied, be treated as published under section 16 above on the publication of a translation of the application under subsection (5) above;

but, if the application is published in a language other than English, the applicant may recover a payment by virtue of section 55 above in respect of the use of the invention in question before publication of that translation, or may bring proceedings by virtue of section 69 above in respect of an act mentioned in that section which is done before publication of that translation, if before that use or the doing of that act he has sent by post or delivered to the government department who made use or authorised the use of the invention, or, as the case may be, to the person alleged to have done the act, a translation into English of the specification of the application.

(8) Subsection (1) above shall cease to apply to an international application for a patent (U.K.) if—

(a) the application is withdrawn or deemed to be withdrawn; or

(b) the designation of the United Kingdom in the application is withdrawn or deemed to be withdrawn;

except where the application or the designation of the United Kingdom in the application is deemed to be withdrawn under the Treaty because of an error or ommission in the Patent Office or any other institution having functions under the Treaty or of an application not being received by the International Bureau, owing to circumstances outside the applicant's control, before the end of the time limited for that purpose by the Treaty.

(9) Where the relevant conditions are satisfied before the end of the prescribed period, the comptroller shall refer the application for so much of the examination and search as is required by sections 17 and 18 above as he considers appropriate in view of any examination and search carried out under the Treaty, and those sections shall apply with any necessary modifications accordingly.

(10) The foregoing provisions of this section do not apply to an application which falls to be treated as an international application for a patent (U.K.) by reason only of its containing an indication that the applicant wishes to obtain a European patent (U.K.); but without prejudice to the application of those provisions to an application which also separately designates the United Kingdom.

(11) If an international application for a patent which purports to designate the United Kingdom is refused a filing date under the Treaty and the comptroller determines that the refusal was caused by an error or omission in the Patent Office or any other institution having functions under the Treaty; he may direct that that application shall be treated as an application under this Act.]

NOTE

S.89 repealed by C.D.P.A. 1988, Sched. 5, para. 25, with effect from January 7, 1991 (S.I. 1990, No.2168)

Effect of international application for patent

89.—(1) An international application for a patent (U.K.) for which a date of filing has been accorded under the Patent Co-operation Treaty shall, subject to—

> section 89A (international and national phases of application), and
>
> section 89B (adaptation of provisions in relation to international application),

be treated for the purposes of Parts I and III of this Act as an application for a patent under this Act.

(2) If the application, or the designation of the United Kingdom in it, is withdrawn or (except as mentioned in subsection (3)) deemed to be withdrawn under the Treaty, it shall be treated as withdrawn under this Act.

(3) An application shall not be treated as withdrawn under this Act if it, or the designation of the United Kingdom in it, is deemed to be withdrawn under the Treaty—

> (a) because of an error or omission in an institution having functions under the Treaty, or

(b) because, owing to circumstances outside the applicant's control, a copy of the application was not received by the International Bureau before the end of the time limited for that purpose under the Treaty,

or in such other circumstances as may be prescribed.

(4) For the purposes of the above provisions an application shall not be treated as an international application for a patent (U.K.) by reason only of its containing an indication that the applicant wishes to obtain a European patent (U.K.), but an application shall be so treated if it also separately designates the United Kingdom.

(5) If an international application for a patent which designates the United Kingdom is refused a filing date under the Treaty and the comptroller determines that the refusal was caused by an error or omission in an institution having functions under the Treaty, he may direct that the application shall be treated as an application under this Act, having such date of filing as he may direct.

NOTE

S.89 substituted by C.D.P.A. 1988, Sched. 5, para.25, with effect from January 5, 1991 (S.I. 1990, No.2168).

International and national phases of application

89A.—(1) The provisions of the Patent Co-operative Treaty relating to publication, search, examination and amendment and not those of this Act, apply to an international application for a patent (U.K.) during the international phase of the application.   15.89A

(2) The international phase of the application means the period from the filing of the application in accordance with the Treaty until the national phase of the application begins.

(3) The national phase of the application begins—
(a) when the prescribed period expires, provided any necessary translation of the application into English has been filed at the Patent Office and the prescribed fee has been paid by the applicant; or
(b) on the applicant expressly requesting the comptroller to proceed earlier with the national phase of the application, filing at the Patent Office—
  (i) a copy of the application, if none has yet been sent to the Patent Office in accordance with the Treaty, and
  (ii) any necessary translation of the application into English, and paying the prescribed fee.
For this purpose a "copy of the application" includes a copy

published in accordance with the Treaty in a language other than that in which it was originally filed.

(4) If the prescribed period expires without the conditions mentioned in subsection (3)(a) being satisfied, the application shall be taken to be withdrawn.

(5) Where during the international phase the application is amended in accordance with the Treaty, the amendment shall be treated as made under this Act if—

(a) when the prescribed period expires, any necessary translation of the amendment into English has been filed at the Patent Office, or

(b) where the applicant expressly requests the comptroller to proceed earlier with the national phase of the application, there is then filed at the Patent Office—

(i) a copy of the amendment, if none has yet been sent to the Patent Office in accordance with the Treaty, and

(ii) any necessary translation of the amendment into English;

(6) The comptroller shall on payment of the prescribed fee publish any translation filed at the Patent Office under subsection (3) or (5) above.

NOTE

S.89A inserted by C.D.P.A. 1988, Sched. 5, para.25 with effect from January 7, 1991 (S.I. 1990, No.2168).

Adaption of provisions in relation to international application

15.89B   89B.—(1) Where an international application for a patent (U.K.) is accorded a filing date under the Patent Co-operation Treaty—

(a) that date, or if the application is re-dated under the Treaty to a later date that later date, shall be treated as the date of filing the application under this Act.

(b) any declaration of priority made under the Treaty shall be treated as made under section 5(2) above, and where in accordance with the Treaty any extra days are allowed, the period of 12 months specified in section 5(2) shall be treated as altered accordingly, and

(c) any statement of the name of the inventor under the Treaty shall be treated as a statement filed under section 13(2) above.

(2) If the application, not having been published under this Act, is published in accordance with the Treaty it shall be treated, for purposes other than those mentioned in subsection (3), as published under section 16 above when the conditions mentioned in section 89A(3)(a) are complied with.

(3) For the purpose of section 55 (use of invention for service of the Crown) and section 69 (infringement of rights conferred by publication) the application, not having been published under this Act, shall be treated as published under section 16 above—

(a) if it is published in accordance with the Treaty in English, on its being so published; and

(b) if it is so published in a language other than English—

    (i)   on the publication of a translation of the application in accordance with section 89A(6) above, or

    (ii) on the service by the applicant of a translation into English of the specification of the application on the government department concerned or, as the case may be, on the person committing the infringing act.

The reference in paragraph (b)(ii) to the service of a translation on a government department or other person is to its being sent by post or delivered to that department or person.

(4) During the international phase of the application, section 8, above does not apply (determination of questions of entitlement in relation to application under this Act) and section 12 above (determination of entitlement in relation to foreign and convention patents) applies notwithstanding the application; but after the end of the international phase, section 8 applies and section 12 does not.

(5) When the national phase begins the comptroller shall refer the application for so much of the examination and search under section 17 and 18 above as he considers appropriate in view of any examination or search carried out under the Treaty.

NOTE

S.89B inserted by C.D.P.A. 1988, Sched. 5, para.25, with effect from January 7, 1991 (S.I. 1990, No.2168).

Convention countries

Orders in Council as to convention countries

90.—(1) Her Majesty may with a view to the fulfilment of a treaty or international convention, arrangement or engagement, by Order in Council declare that any country specified in the Order is a convention country for the purposes of section 5 above.   **15.90**

(2) Her Majesty may by Order in Council direct that any of the Channel Islands, any colony *or any British protectorate or protected state* shall be taken to be a convention country for those purposes.

(3) For the purposes of subsection (1) above every colony, protectorate, and territory subject to the authority or under the suzerainty of another country, and every territory administered by another country under the trusteeship system of the United Nations shall be taken to be a country in the case of which a declaration may be made under that subsection.

NOTE

Subs. (2) words repealed by Statute Law (Repeals) Act 1986, s.1 and Sched. 1, Pt.VI.

Miscellaneous

Evidence of conventions and instruments under conventions

15.91   91.—(1) Judicial notice shall be taken of the following, that is to say—
  (a) the European Patent Convention, the Community Patent Convention and the Patent Co-operation Treaty (each of which is hereafter in this section referred to as the relevant convention);
  (b) any bulletin, journal or gazette published under the relevant convention and the register of European or Community patents kept under it; and
  (c)   any decision of, or expression of opinion by, the relevant convention court on any question arising under or in connection with the relevant convention.

(2) Any document mentioned in subsection (1)(b) above shall be admissible as evidence of any instrument or other act thereby communicated of any convention institution.

(3) Evidence of any instrument issued under the relevant convention by any such institution, including any judgment or order of the relevant convention court, or of any document in the custody of any such institution or reproducing in legible form any information in such custody otherwise than in legible form, or any entry in or extract from such a document, may be given in any legal proceedings by production of a copy certified as a true copy by an official of that institution; and any document purporting to be such a copy shall be received in evidence without proof of the official position or handwriting of the person signing the certificate.

(4) Evidence of any such instrument may also be given in any legal proceedings—
  (a) by production of a copy purporting to be printed by the Queen's Printer;
  (b)   where the instrument is in the custody of a government department, by production of a copy certified on behalf of the

department to be a true copy by an officer of the department generally or specially authorised to do so;

and any document purporting to be such a copy as is mentioned in paragraph (b) above of an instrument in the custody of a department shall be received without proof of the official position or handwriting of the person signing the certificate, or of his authority to do so, or of the document being in the custody of the department.

(5) In any legal proceedings in Scotland evidence of any matter given in a manner authorised by this section shall be sufficient evidence of it.

(6) In this section—

"convention institutions" means an institution established by or having functions under the relevant convention;

"relevant convention court" does not include a court of the United Kingdom or of any other country which is a party to the relevant convention; and

"legal proceedings," in relation to the United Kingdom, includes proceedings before the comptroller.

Obtaining evidence for proceedings under the European Patent Convention

92.—(1) Sections 1 to 3 of the Evidence (Proceedings in Other Jurisdictions) Act 1975 (provisions enabling United Kingdom courts to assist in obtaining evidence for foreign courts) shall apply for the purpose of proceedings before a relevant convention court under the European Patent Convention as they apply for the purposes of civil proceedings in a court exercising jurisdiction in a country outside the United Kingdom. **15.92**

(2) In the application of those sections by virtue of this section any reference to the High Court the Court of Session or the High Court of Justice in Northern Ireland shall include a reference to the comptroller.

(3) Rules under this Act may include provision—

(a) as to the manner in which an application under section 1 of the said Act of 1975 is to be made to the comptroller for the purpose of proceedings before a relevant convention court under the European Patent Convention; and

(b) subject to the provisions of that Act, as to the circumstances in which an order can be made under section 2 of that Act on any such application.

(4) Rules of court and rules under this Act may provide for an officer of the European Patent Office to attend the hearing of an application under section 1 of that Act before the court or the comptroller, as the case may be, and examine the witnesses or request the court or comptroller to put specified questions to the witnesses.

(5) Section 1(4) of the Perjury Act 1911 and section 1(4) of the Perjury Act (Northern Ireland) 1946 (statements made for the purposes, among

others, of judicial proceedings in a tribunal of a foreign state) shall apply in relation to proceedings before a relevant convention court under the European Patent Convention as they apply to a judicial proceeding in a tribunal of a foreign state.

Enforcement of orders for costs

15.93   93. If the European Patent Office orders the payment of costs in any proceedings before it—
  (a) in England and Wales the costs shall, if a county court so orders, be recoverable by execution issued from the county court or otherwise as if they were payable under an order of that court;
  (b) in Scotland the order may be enforced in like manner as [*a recorded decree arbitral*] **an extract registered decree arbitral bearing a warrant for execution issued by the sheriff court of any sheriffdom in Scotland;**
  (c) in Northern Ireland the order may be enforced as if it were a money judgment.

Note

S.93 (b) amended by Debtors (Scotland) Act 1987 (c.18), Sched. 6.

Communication of information to the European Patent Office, etc.

15.94   94. It shall not be unlawful by virtue of any enactment to communic- ate the following information in pursuance of the European Patent Convention to the European Patent Office or the competent authority of any country which is party to the Convention, that is to say—
  (a) information in the files of the court which, in accordance with rules of court, the court authorises to be so communicated;
  (b) information in the files of the Patent Office which, in accordance with rules under this Act, the comptroller authorises to be so communicated.

Financial provisions

15.95   95.—(1) There shall be paid out of moneys provided by Parliament any sums required by any Minister of the Crown or government department to meet any financial obligation of the United Kingdom under the European Patent Convention, the Community Patent Con- vention or the Patent Co-operation Treaty.
    (2) Any sums received by any Minister of the Crown or government

department in pursuance of either of those conventions or that treaty shall be paid into the Consolidated Fund.

PART III

MISCELLANEOUS AND GENERAL

Legal Proceedings

[The Patents Court

96.—(1) *There shall be constituted, as part of the Chancery Division of the* **15.96** *High Court, a Patents Court to take such proceedings relating to patents and other matters as may be prescribed by rules of court.*

(2) *The judges of the Patents Court shall be such of the puisne judges of the High Court as the Lord Chancellor may from time to time nominate.*

(3) *The foregoing provisions of this section shall not be taken as prejudicing the provisions of the Supreme Court of Judicature (Consolidation) Act 1925 which enable the whole jurisdiction of the High Court to be exercised by any judge of that court.*

(4) *Rules of court shall make provision for the appointment of scientific advisers to assist the Patents Court in proceedings under this Act and for regulating the functions of such advisers.*

(5) *The remuneration of any such adviser shall be determined by the Lord Chancellor with the consent of the Minister for the Civil Service and shall be defrayed out of moneys provided by Parliament.]*

NOTE

S.96 repealed by Supreme Court Act 1981, S.152 (4) and Sched. 4.

Appeals from the comptroller

97.—(1) Except as provided by subsection (4) below, an appeal shall **15.97** lie to the Patents Court from any decision of the comptroller under this Act or rules except any of the following decisions, that is to say—
  (a) a decision falling within section 14(7) above;
  (b) a decision under section 16(2) above to omit matter from a specification;
  (c) a decision to give directions under subsection (1) or (2) of section 22 above;

(d) a decision under rules which is excepted by rules from the right of appeal conferred by this section.

(2) For the purpose of hearing appeals under this section the Patents Court may consist of one or more judges of that court in accordance with directions given by or on behalf of the Lord Chancellor; and the Patents Court shall not be treated as a divisional court for the purposes of section 31(1)(*f*) of the Supreme Court of Judicature (Consolidation) Act 1925 (appeals from divisional courts).

(3) An appeal shall not lie to the Court of Appeal from a decision of the Patents Court on appeal from a decision of the comptroller under this Act or rules—

(a) except where the comptroller's decision was given under section 8, 12, 18, 20, 27, 37, 40, 61, 72, 73 or 75 above; or

(b) except where the ground of appeal is that the decision of the Patents Court is wrong in law;

but an appeal shall only lie to the Court of Appeal under this section if leave to appeal is given by the Patents Court or the Court of Appeal.

(4) An appeal shall lie to the Court of Session from any decision of the comptroller in proceedings which under rules are held in Scotland, except any decision mentioned in paragraphs (a) to (d) of subsection (1) above.

(5) An appeal shall not lie to the Inner House of the Court of Session from a decision of an Outer House judge on appeal from a decision of the comptroller under this Act or rules—

(a) except where the comptroller's decision was given under section 8, 12, 18, 20, 27, 37, 40, 61, 72, 73 or 75 above; or

(b) except where the ground of appeal is that the decision of the Outer House judge is wrong in law.

Proceedings in Scotland

15.98   98.—(1) In Scotland proceedings relating primarily to patents (other than proceedings before the comptroller) shall be competent in the Court of Session only and any jurisdiction of the sheriff court relating to patents is hereby abolished except in relation to questions which are incidental to the issue in proceedings which are otherwise competent there.

(2) The remuneration of any assessor appointed to assist the court in proceedings under this Act in the Court of Session shall be determined by the Lord President of the Court of Session with the consent of the Minister for the Civil Service and shall be defrayed out of moneys provided by Parliament.

General powers of the court

99. The court may, for the purpose of determining any question in the **15.99**
exercise of its original or appellate jurisdiction under this Act or any
treaty or international convention to which the United Kingdom is a
party, make any order or exercise any other power which the comptroller could have made or exercised for the purpose of determining that
question.

Power of Patents Court to order report

99A.—(1) Rules of court shall make provisions empowering the **15.99A**
Patents Court in any proceedings before it under this Act, on or
without the application of any party, to order the Patent Office to
inquire into and report on any question of fact or opinion.

(2) Where the court makes such an order on the application of a
party, the fee payable to the Patent Office shall be at such rate as may
be determined in accordance with rules of court and shall be costs of
the proceedings unless otherwise ordered by the court.

(3) Where the court makes such an order of its own motion, the fee
payable to the Patent Office shall be at such rate as may be determined
by the Lord Chancellor with the approval of the Treasury and shall be
paid out of money provided by Parliament.

NOTE

S.99A inserted by C.D.P.A. 1988, Sched. 5, para.26, with effect from January 7, 1991 (S.I.
1990, No.2168).

Power of Court of Session to order report

99B.—(1) In any proceedings before the Court of Session under this **15.99B**
Act the court may, either of its own volition or on the application of
any party, order the Patent Office to inquire into the report on any
question of fact or opinion.

(2) Where the court makes an order under subsection (1) above of its
own volition the fee payable to the Patent Office shall be at such rate
as may be determined by the Lord President of the Court of Session
with the consent of the Treasury and shall be defrayed out of moneys
provided by Parliament.

(3) Where the court makes an order under subsection (1) above on
the application of a party, the fee payable to the Patent Office shall be
at such rate as may be provided for in rules of court and shall be
treated as expenses in the cause.

NOTE

S.99B inserted by C.D.P.A 1988, Sched. 5, para.26, with effect from January 7, 1991 (S.I. 1990, No.2168).

Burden of proof in certain cases

15.100   **100.**—(1) If the invention for which a patent is granted is a process for obtaining a new product, the same product produced by a person other than the proprietor of the patent or a licensee of his shall, unless the contrary is proved, be taken in any proceedings to have been obtained by that process.

(2) In considering whether a party has discharged the burden imposed upon him by this section, the court shall not require him to disclose any manufacturing or commercial secrets if it appears to the court that it would be unreasonable to do so.

Exercise of comptroller's discretionary powers

15.101   **101.** Without prejudice to any rule of law, the comptroller shall give any party to a proceeding before him an opportunity of being heard before exercising adversely to that party any discretion vested in the comptroller by this Act or rules.

[Right of audience in patent proceedings

15.102   *102.*—(1) *Any party to any proceedings before the comptroller under this Act or any treaty or international convention to which the United Kingdom is a party, may appear before the comptroller in person or be represented by counsel or a solicitor (of any part of the United Kingdom) or a patent agent or, subject to rules under section 115 below, by any other person whom he desires to represent him.*

(2) Subsection (1) above, in its application to proceedings under any such treaty or convention in relation to applications for, or otherwise in connection with, European patents, shall have effect subject to section 84(1) or (3) above.

(3) Without prejudice to the right of counsel to appear before the High Court, a member of the Bar of England and Wales who is not in actual practice, a solicitor of the Supreme Court and a patent agent shall each have the right to appear and be heard on behalf of any party to an appeal under this Act from the comptroller to the Patents Court.]

Right of audience, &c. in proceedings before comptroller

102.—(1) A party to proceedings before the comptroller under this Act, or under any treaty or international convention to which the United Kingdom is a party, may appear before the comptroller in person or be represented by any person whom he desires to represent him.

(2) No offence is committed under the enactments relating to the preparation of documents by persons not legally qualified by reason only of the preparation by any person of a document other than a deed, for use in such proceedings.

(3) Subjection (1) has effect subject to rules made under section 281 of the Copyright, Designs and Patents Act 1988 (power of comptroller to refuse to recognise certain agents).

(4) In its application to proceedings in relation to applications for, or otherwise in connection with, European patents, this section has effect subject to any restrictions imposed by or under the European Patent Convention.

(5) Nothing in this section shall be taken to limit the right to draw or prepare deeds given to a registered patent agent by section 68 of the Courts and Legal Services Act 1990.

NOTE

S.102 substituted by C.D.P.A. 1988, Sched. 5, para.27, with effect from August 13, 1990 (S.I. 1990, No.1400).
Subs. (5) added by Courts and Legal Services Act 1990, Sched. 18.

Right of audience, &c. in proceedings on appeal from the comptroller

102A.—(1) A solicitor of the Supreme Court may appear and be heard on behalf of any party to an appeal under this Act from the comptroller to the Patents Court.   15.102A

(2) A registered patent agent or a member of the Bar not in actual practice may do, in or in connection with preceedings on an appeal under this Act from the comptroller to the Patents Court, anything which a solicitor of the Supreme Court might do, other than prepare a deed.

(3) The Lord Chancellor may by regulations—

(a) provide that the right conferred by subsection (2) shall be subject to such conditions and restrictions as appear to the Lord Chancellor to be necessary or expedient, and

(b) apply to persons exercising that right such statutory provisions, rules of court and other rules of law and practice applying to solicitors as may be specified in the regulations;

and different provisions may be made for different descriptions of proceedings.

(4) Regulations under this section shall be made by statutory instrument which shall be subject to annulment in pursuance of a resolution of either House of Parliament.

(5) This section is without prejudice to the right of counsel to appeal before the High Court.

(6) Nothing in this section shall be taken to limit the right to draw and prepare deeds given to a registered patent agent by section 68 of the Courts and Legal Services Act 1990.

NOTE

S.102A inserted by C.D.P.A. 1988, Sched. 5, para.27, with effect from August 13, 1990 (S.I. 1990, No.1400).
Subs. (6) added by the Courts and Legal Services Act 1990, Sched. 18.

Extension of privilege for communications with solicitors relating to patent proceedings

15.103   103.—(1) It is hereby declared that the rule of law which confers privilege from disclosure in legal proceedings in respect of communications made with a solicitor or a person acting on his behalf, or in relation to information obtained or supplied for submission to a solicitor or a person acting on his behalf, for the purpose of any pending or contemplated proceedings before a court in the United Kingdom extends to such communications so made for the purpose of any pending or contemplated—

(a) proceedings before the comptroller under this Act or any of the relevant conventions, or

(b) proceedings before the relevant convention court under any of those conventions.

(2) In this section—

"legal proceedings" includes proceedings before the comptroller; the references to legal proceedings and pending or contemplated proceedings include references to applications for a patent or a European patent and to international applications for a patent; and

"the relevant conventions" means the European Patent Convention, the Community Patent Convention and the Patent Co-operation Treaty.

(3) This section shall not extend to Scotland.

[Privilege for communications with patent agents relating to patent proceedings

104.—(1) *This section applies to any communication made for the purpose of* **15.104**
any pending or contemplated patent proceedings, being either—

(a) *a communication between the patent agent of a party to those proceedings and that party or any other person; or*

(b) *a communication between a party to those proceedings and a person other than his patent agent made for the purpose of obtaining, or in response to a request for, information which that party is seeking for the purpose of submitting it to his patent agent.*

(2) *For the purposes of subsection (1) above a communication made by or to a person acting—*

(i) *on behalf of a patent agent; or*

(ii) *on behalf of a party to any pending or contemplated proceedings, shall be treated as made by or to that patent agent or party, as the case may be.*

(3) *In any legal proceedings other than criminal proceedings a communication to which this section applies shall be privileged from disclosure in like manner as if any proceedings before the comptroller or the relevant convention court for the purpose of which the communication was made were proceedings before the court (within the meaning of this Act) and the patent agent in question had been the solicitor of the party concerned.*

(4) *In this section—*

"legal proceedings" includes proceedings before the comptroller; "patent agent" means an individual registered as a patent agent in the register of patent agents, a company lawfully practising as a patent agent in the United Kingdom or a person who satisifes the condition mentioned in section 84(1) or (3) above;

"patent proceedings" means proceedings under this Act or any of the relevant conventions before the court, the comptroller or the relevant convention court, whether contested or uncontested and including an application for a patent;

"party," in relation to any contemplated proceedings, means a prospective party to the proceedings; and

"the relevant conventions" means the European Patent Convention, the Community Patent Convention and the Patent Co-operation Treaty.

(5) *This section shall not extend to Scotland.]*

NOTE

S.104 repealed by C.D.P.A. 1988, Sched. 8, with effect from August 13, 1990 (S.I. 1990, No.1400).

Extension of privilege in Scotland for communications relating to patent proceedings

15.105   105.—(1) It is hereby declared that in Scotland the rules of law which confer privilege from disclosure in legal proceedings in respect of communications, reports or other documents (by whomsoever made) made for the purpose of any pending or contemplated proceedings in a court in the United Kingdom extends to communications, reports or other documents made for the purpose of patent proceedings [*within the meaning of section 104 above*].

    (2) In this section—

> "patent proceedings" means proceedings under this Act or any of the relevant conventions, before the court, the comptroller or the relevant convention court, whether contested or uncontested and including an application for a patent; and

> "the relevant conventions" means the European Patent Convention, the Community Patent Convention and the Patent Cooperation Treaty.

NOTE

S.105 words repealed by C.D.P.A. 1988, Sched. 8, with effect from August 13, 1990 (S.I. 1990, No.1400).
Subs. (2) added by C.D.P.A. 1988, Sched. 7, para.21

Costs and expenses in proceedings before the Court under s.40

15.106   106.—(1) In proceedings before the court under section 40 above (whether on an application or on appeal to the court), the court, in determining whether to award costs or expenses to any party and what costs or expenses to award, shall have regard to all the relevant circumstances, including the financial position of the parties.

    (2) If in any such proceedings the Patents Court directs that any costs of one party shall be paid by another party, the court may settle the amount of the costs by fixing a lump sum or may direct that the costs shall be taxed on a scale specified by the court, being a scale of costs prescribed by the Rules of the Supreme Court or by the County Court Rules.

Costs and expenses in proceedings before the comptroller

15.107   107.—(1) The comptroller may, in proceedings before him under this Act, by order award to any party such costs or, in Scotland, such expenses as he may consider reasonable and direct how and by what parties they are to be paid.

(2) In England and Wales any costs awarded under this section shall, if a county court so orders, be recoverable by execution issued from the county court or otherwise as if they were payable under an order of that court.

(3) In Scotland any order under this section for the payment of expenses may be enforced in like manner as [*a recorded decree arbitral*] **an extract registered decree arbitral bearing a warrant for execution issued by the sheriff court of any sheriffdom in Scotland.**

(4) If any of the following persons, that is to say—

(a) any person by whom a reference is made to the comptroller under section 8, 12 or 37 above;

(b) any person by whom a reference is made to the comptroller for the revocation of a patent;

(c) any person by whom notice of opposition is given to the comptroller under section 27(5), 29(2), 47(6), or 52(1) above, or section 117(2) below;

neither resides nor carries on business in the United Kingdom, the comptroller may require him to give security for the costs or expenses of the proceedings and in default of such security being given may treat the reference of application as abandoned.

(5) In Northern Ireland any order under this section for the payment of costs may be enforced as if it were a money judgment.

NOTE

S.107(3) amended by Debtors (Scotland) Act 1987 (c.18) Sched. 6.

Licences granted by order of comptroller

108. Any order for the grant of a licence under section 11, 38, 48 or 49 above shall, without prejudice to any other method of enforcement, have effect as if it were a deed, executed by the proprietor of the patent and all other necessary parties, granting a licence in accordance with the order.   **15.108**

Offences

Falsification of register, etc.

109. If a person makes or causes to be made a false entry in any register kept under this Act, or a writing falsely purporting to be a copy   **15.109**

or reproduction of an entry in any such register, or produces or tenders or causes to be produced or tendered in evidence any such writing, knowing the entry or writing to be false, he shall be liable—
(a) on summary conviction, to a fine not exceeding £1,000;
(b) on conviction on indictment, to imprisonment for a term not exceeding two years or a fine, or both.

Unauthorised claim of patent rights

15.110 110.—(1) If a person falsely represents that anything disposed of by him for value is a patented product he shall, subject to the following provisions of this section, be liable on summary conviction to a fine not exceeding £200.

(2) For the purposes of subsection (1) above a person who for value disposes of an article having stamped, engraved or impressed on it or otherwise applied to it the word "patent" or "patented" or anything expressing or implying that the article is a patented product, shall be taken to represent that the article is a patented product.

(3) Subsection (1) above does not apply where the representation is made in respect of a product after the patent for that product or, as the case may be, the process in question has expired or been revoked and before the end of a period which is reasonably sufficient to enable the accused to take steps to ensure that the representation is not made (or does not continue to be made).

(4) In proceedings for an offence under this section it shall be a defence for the accused to prove that he used diligence to prevent the commission of the offence.

Unauthorised claim that patent has been applied for

15.111 111.—(1) If a person represents that a patent has been applied for in respect of any article disposed of for value by him and—
(a) no such application has been made, or
(b) any such application has been refused or withdrawn.
he shall, subject to the following provisions of this section, be liable on summary conviction to a fine not exceeding £200.

(2) Subsection (1)(b) above does not apply where the representation is made (or continues to be made) before the expiry of a period which commences with the refusal or withdrawal and which is reasonably sufficient to enable the accused to take steps to ensure that the representation is not made (or does not continue to be made).

(3) For the purposes of subsection (1) above person who for value disposes of an article having stamped, engraved or impressed on it or otherwise applied to it the words "patent applied for" or "patent pending," or anything expressing or implying that a patent has been

applied for in respect of the article, shall be taken to represent that such a patent has been applied for.

(4) In any proceedings for an offence under this section it shall be a defence for the accused to prove that he used due diligence to prevent the commission of such an offence.

Misuse of the title "Patent Office"

112. If any person uses on his place of business, or any document   **15.112** issued by him, or otherwise, the words "Patent Office" or any other words suggesting that his place of business is, or is officially connected with, the Patent Office, he shall be liable on summary conviction to a fine not exceeding £500.

Offences by corporations

113.—(1) Where an offence under this Act which has been committed   **15.113** by a body corporate is proved to have been committed with the consent or connivance of, or to be attributable to any neglect on the part of, a director, manager, secretary or other similar officer of the body corporate, or any person who was purporting to act in any such capacity, he, as well as the body corporate, shall be guilty of that offence and shall be liable to be proceeded against and punished accordingly.

(2) Where the affairs of a body corporate are managed by its members, subsection (1) above shall apply in relation to the acts and defaults of a member in connection with his functions of management as if he were a director of the body corporate.

Patent agents

[Restrictions on practice as patent agent

114.—*(1) An individual shall not, either alone or in partnership with any*   **15.114** *other person, practise, describe himself or hold himself out as a patent agent, or permit himself to be so described or held out, unless he is registered as a patent agent in the register of patent agents or (as the case may be) unless he and all his partners are so registered.*

(2) A body corporate shall not practise, describe itself or hold itself out or permit itself to be described or held out as mentioned in subsection (1) above unless—

(a) in the case of a company within the meaning of the Companies Act 1948 which began to carry on business as a patent agent before 17th November 1917, a director or the manager of the company is registered as a patent

agent in the register of patent agents and the name of that director or manager is mentioned as being so registered in all professional advertisements, circulars or letters issued by or with the consent of the company in which the name of the company appears;

   (b) in any other case, every director or, where the body's affairs are managed by its members, every member of the body and in any event, if it has a manager who is not a director or member, that manager, is so registered.

(2A) Notwithstanding the definition of "patent agent" in section 130(1) below, subsections (1) and (2) above do not impose any prohibition in relation to the business of acting as agent for other persons for the purpose of conducting proceedings before the comptroller in connection with European patents (U.K.) to which section 77(1) above for the time being applies.

(3) Any person who contravenes the provisions of this section shall be liable on summary conviction to a fine not exceeding £1,000.

(4) Proceedings for an offence under this section may be begun at any time within twelve months from the date of the offence.

(5) This section shall not be construed as prohibiting solicitors from taking such part in proceedings relating to patents and applications for patents as has heretofore been taken by solicitors and, in particular, shall not derogate from the provisions of section 102 above as it applies to solicitors.

(6) A patent agent shall not be guilty of an offence under section 22 of the Solicitors Act 1974 or section 39 of the Solicitors (Scotland) Act 1933 (which prohibit the preparation for reward of certain instruments or writs by persons not legally qualified) by reason only of the preparation by him for use in proceedings under this Act before the comptroller or on appeal under this Act to the Patents Court from the comptroller of any document other than a deed.

(7) For Article 23(2)(d) of the Solicitors (Northern Ireland) Order 1976 there shall be substituted the following paragraph—

   "(d) a patent agent within the meaning of the Patents Act 1977 preparing, for use in proceedings under that Act or the Patents Act 1949 before the comptroller (as defined in the former Act) or on appeal under either of those Acts to the Patents Court from the comptroller, any document other than a deed;".]

NOTE

   S.114 repealed by C.D.P.A. 1988, Sched. 8, with effect from August 13, 1990 (S.I. 1990, No.1400).

[Power of comptroller to refuse to deal with certain agents

15.115   *115.—(1) Rules may authorise the comptroller to refuse to recognise as agent in respect of any business under this Act—*

   (a) any individual whose name has been erased from, and not restored to, the

register of patent agents, or who is for the time being suspended from acting as a patent agent;

(b) any person who has been convicted of an offence under section 114 above or section 88 of the 1949 Act (which is replaced by section 114);

(c) any person who is found by the Secretary of State to have been convicted of any offence or to have been guilty of any such misconduct as, in the case of an individual registered in the register of patent agents, would render him liable to have his name erased from it;

(d) any person, not being registered as a patent agent, who in the opinion of the comptroller is engaged wholly or mainly in acting as agent in applying for patents in the United Kingdom or elsewhere in the name or for the benefit of a person by whom he is employed;

(e) any company or firm, if any person whom the comptroller could refuse to recognise as agent in respect of any business under this Act is acting as director or manager of the company or is a partner in the firm.

(2) The comptroller shall refuse to recognise as agent in respect of any business under this Act any person who neither resides nor has a place of business in the United Kingdom.

(3) Rules may authorise the comptroller to refuse to recognise as agent or other representative for the purpose of applying for European patents any person who does not satisfy the condition mentioned in section 84(1) above and does not fall within the exemption in subsection (2) of that section.]

NOTE

S.115 repealed by C.D.P.A. 1988, Sched. 8, with effect from August 13, 1990 (S.I. 1990, No.1400).

Immunity of department

Immunity of department as regards official acts

116. Neither the Secretary of State nor any officer of his— **15.116**

(a) shall be taken to warrant the validity of any patent granted under this Act or any treaty or international convention to which the United Kingdom is a party; or

(b) shall incur any liability by reason of or in connection with any examination or investigation required or authorised by this Act or any such treaty or convention, or any report or other proceedings consequent on any such examination or investigation.

Administrative provisions

Correction of errors in patents and applications

15.117   117.—(1) The comptroller may, subject to any provision of rules, correct any error of translation or transcription, clerical error or mistake in any specification of a patent or application for a patent or any document filed in connection with a patent or such an application.

(2) Where the comptroller is requested to correct such an error or mistake any person may in accordance with rules give the comptroller notice of opposition to the request and the comptroller shall determine the matter.

Information about patent applications and patents, and inspection of documents

15.118   118.—(1) After publication of an application for a patent in accordance with section 16 above the comptroller shall on a request being made to him in the prescribed manner and on payment of the prescribed fee (if any) give the person making the request such information, and permit him to inspect such documents, relating to the application or any patent granted in pursuance of the application as may be specified in the request, subject, however, to any prescribed restrictions.

(2) Subject to the following provisions of this section, until an application for a patent is so published documents or information constituting or relating to the application shall not, without the consent of the applicant, be published or communicated to any person by the comptroller.

(3) Subsection (2) above shall not prevent the comptroller from—

(a) sending the European Patent Office information which it is his duty to send that office in accordance with any provision of the European Patent Convention; or

(b) publishing or communicating to others any prescribed bibliographic information about an unpublished application for a patent;

nor shall that subsection prevent the Secretary of State from inspecting or authorising the inspection of an application for a patent or any connected documents under section [*22(6)(a)*] **22(6)** above.

(4) Where a person is notified that an application for a patent has been made, but not published in accordance with section 16 above, and that the applicant will, if the patent is granted, bring proceedings against that person in the event of his doing an act specified in the notification after the application is so published, that person may make a request under subsection (1) above, notwithstanding that the application has not been published, and that subsection shall apply accordingly.

(5) Where an application for a patent is filed, but not published, and a new application is filed in respect of any part of the subject-matter of the earlier application (either in accordance with rules or in pursuance of an order under section 8 above) and is published, any person may make a request under subsection (1) above relating to the earlier application and on payment of the prescribed fee the comptroller shall give him such information and permit him to inspect such documents as could have been given or inspected if the earlier application had been published.

NOTE

S.118 amended by C.D.P.A. 1988, Sched. 5, para.28, with effect from January 7, 1991, (S.I. 1990, No.2168).

Service by post

119.—Any notice required or authorised to be given by this Act or rules, and any application or other document so authorised or required to be made or filed, may be given, made or filed by post.   **15.119**

Hours of business and excluded days

120.—(1) Rules may specify the hour at which the Patent Office shall be taken to be closed on any day for purposes of the transaction by the public of business under this Act or of any class of such business, and may specify days as excluded days for any such purposes.   **15.120**

(2) Any business done under this Act on any day after the hour so specified in relation to business of that class, or on a day which is an excluded day in relation to business of that class, shall be taken to have been done on the next following day not being an excluded day; and where the time for doing anything under this Act expires on an excluded day that time shall be extended to the next following day not being an excluded day.

Comptroller's annual report

121.—Before the 1st June in every year the comptroller shall cause to be laid before both Houses of Parliament a report with respect to the execution of this Act and the discharge of his functions under the European Patent Convention, the Community Patent Convention and the Patent Co-operation Treaty, and every such report shall include an account of all fees, salaries and allowances, and other money received   **15.121** and paid by him under this Act, those conventions and that treaty during the previous year.

Supplemental

Crown's right to sell forfeited articles

15.122   **122.**—Nothing in this Act affects the right of the Crown or any person deriving title directly or indirectly from the Crown to dispose of or use articles forfeited under the laws relating to customs or excise.

Rules

15.123   **123.**—(1) The Secretary of State may make such rules as he thinks expedient for regulating the business of the Patent Office in relation to patents and applications for patents (including European patents, applications for European patents and international applications for patents) and for regulating all matters placed by this Act under the direction or control of the comptroller; and in this Act, except so far as the context otherwise requires, "prescribed" means prescribed by rules and "rules" means rules made under this section.

(2) Without prejudice to the generality of the subsection (1) above, rules may make provision—

   (a) prescribing the form and contents of applications for patents and other documents which may be filed at the Patent Office and requiring copies to be furnished of any such documents;

   (b) regulating the procedure to be followed in connection with any proceeding or other matter before the comptroller or the Patent Office and authorising the rectification or irregularities of procedure;

   (c) requiring fees to be paid in connection with any such proceeding or matter or in connection with the provision of any service by the Patent Office and providing for the remission of fees in the prescribed circumstances;

   (d) regulating the mode of giving evidence in any such proceeding and empowering the comptroller to compel the attendance of witnesses and the discovery of and production of documents;

   (e) requiring the comptroller to advertise any proposed amendments of patents and any other prescribed matters, including any prescribed steps in any such proceeding;

   (f) requiring the comptroller to hold proceedings in Scotland in such circumstances as may be specified in the order where there is more than one party to proceedings under section 8, 12, 37, 40(1) or (2), 41(8), 61(3), 71 or 72 above;

(g) providing for the appointment of advisers to assist the comptroller in any proceedings before him;

(h) prescribing time limits for doing anything required to be done in connection with any such proceeding by this Act or the rules and providing for the alteration of any period of time specified in this Act or the rules;

(i) giving effect to the right of an inventor of an invention to be mentioned in an application for a patent for the invention;

(j) without prejudice to any other provision of this Act, requiring and regulating the translation of documents in connection with an application for a patent or a European patent or an international application for a patent and the filing and authentication of any such translations;

[(k) *requiring the keeping of a register of patent agents and regulating the registration of patent agents and authorising in prescribed cases the erasure from the register of patent agents of the name of any person registered therein or the suspension of the right of any such person to act as a patent agent;*]

(l) providing for the publication and sale of documents in the Patent Office and of information about such documents.

(3) Rules may make different provision for different cases.

(3A) It is hereby declared that rules—

(a) authorising the rectification of irregularities of procedure, or

(b) providing for the alteration of any period of time,

may authorise the comptroller to extend or further extend any period notwithstanding that the period has already expired.

(4) Rules prescribing fees shall not be made except with the consent of the Treasury.

(5) The remuneration of any adviser appointed under rules to assist the comptroller in any proceeding shall be determined by the Secretary of State with the consent of the Minister for the Civil Service and shall be defrayed out of moneys provided by Parliament.

(6) Rules shall provide for the publication by the comptroller of a journal; (in this Act referred to as "the journal") containing particulars of applications for and grants of patents, and of other proceedings under this Act.

(7) Rules shall require or authorise the comptroller to make arrangements for the publication of reports of cases relating to patents, trade marks *and* registered designs **and design right** decided by him and of cases relating to patents (whether under this Act or otherwise) trade marks, registered designs *and* copyright **and design right** decided by any court or body (whether in the United Kingdom or elsewhere).

Note

Subs. (2)(k) repealed by C.D.P.A. 1988, Sched. 8, with effect from August 13, 1990 (S.I. 1990, No.1400).

Subs. (3A) inserted by C.D.P.A. 1988, Sched. 5, para.29, with effect from November 15, 1988.

Rules, regulations and orders; supplementary

15.124 **124.**—(1) Any power conferred on the Secretary of State by this Act to make rules, regulations or orders shall be exercisable by statutory instrument.

(2) Any Order in Council and any statutory instrument containing an order, rules or regulations under this Act, other than an order or rule required to be laid before Parliament in draft or an order under section 132(5) below, shall be subject to annulment in pursuance of a resolution of either House of Parliament.

(3) Any Order in Council or order under any provision of this Act may be varied or revoked by a subsequent order.

Extent of invention

15.125 **125.**—(1) For the purpose of this Act an invention for a patent for which an application has been made or for which a patent has been granted shall, unless the context otherwise requires, be taken to be that specified in a claim of the specification of the application or patent, as the case may be, as interpreted by the description and any drawings contained in that specification, and the extent of the protection conferred by a patent or application for a patent shall be determined accordingly.

(2) It is hereby declared for the avoidance of doubt that where more than one invention is specified in any such claim, each invention may have a different priority date under section 5 above.

(3) The Protocol on the Interpretation of Article 69 of the European Patent Convention (which Article contains a provision corresponding to subsection (1) above) shall, as for the time being in force, apply for the purposes of subsection (1) above as it applies for the purposes of that Article.

Disclosure of invention by specification: availability of samples of micro-organisms

15.125A **125A.**—(1) Provision may be made by rules prescribing the circumstances in which the specification of an application for a patent, or of a patent, for an invention which requires for its performance the use of a micro-organism is to be treated as disclosing the invention in a manner which is clear enough and complete enough for the invention to be performed by a person skilled in the art.

(2) The rules may in particular require the applicant or patentee—

(a) to take such steps as may be prescribed for the purposes of making available to the public samples of the micro-organism, and

(b) not to impose or maintain restrictions on the uses to which such samples may be put, except as may be prescribed.

(3) The rules may provide that, in such cases as may be prescribed, samples need only be made available to such persons or descriptions of persons as may be prescribed; and the rules may identify a description of persons by reference to whether the comptroller has given his certificate as to any matter.

(4) An application for revocation of the patent under section 72(1)(c) above may be made if any of the requirements of the rules cease to be complied with.

NOTE

S.125A inserted by C.D.P.A. 1988, Sched. 5, para.30, with effect from January 7, 1991 (S.I. 1990, No.2168).

Stamp duty

126.—(1) An instrument relating to a Community patent or to an **15.126** application for a European patent shall not be chargeable with stamp duty by reason only of all or any of the provisions of the Community Patent Convention mentioned in subsection (2) below.

(2) The said provisions are—

(a) Article 2.2 (Community patent and application for European patent in which the contracting states are designated to have effect throughout the territories to which the Convention applies);

(b) Article 39.1(c) (Community patent treated as national patent of contracting state in which applicant's representative has place of business);

(c) Article 39.1(c) as applied by Article 45 to an application for a European patent in which the contracting states are designated.

Existing patents and applications

127.—(1) No application for a patent may be made under the 1949 Act **15.127** on or after the appointed day.

(2) Schedule 1 to this Act shall have effect for securing that certain provisions of the 1949 Act shall continue to apply on and after the appointed day to—

(a) a patent granted before that day;

(b) an application for a patent which is filed before that day, and which is accompanied by a complete specification or in respect of which a complete specification is filed before that day;

(c) a patent granted in pursuance of such an application.

(3) Schedule 2 to this Act shall have effect for securing that (subject to the provision of that Schedule) certain provisions of this Act shall apply on and after the appointed day to any patent and application to which subsection (2) above relates, but, except as provided by the following provisions of this Act, this Act shall not apply to any such patent or application.

(4) An application for a patent which is made before the appointed day, but which does not comply with subsection (2)(b) above, shall be taken to have been abandoned immediately before that day, but, notwithstanding anything in section 5(3) above, the application may nevertheless serve to establish a priority date in relation to a later application for a patent under this Act if the date of filing the abandoned application falls within the period of fifteen months immediately preceding the filing of the later application.

(5) Schedule 3 to this Act shall have effect for repealing certain provisions of the 1949 Act.

(6) The transitional provisions and savings in Schedule 4 to this Act shall have effect.

(7) In Schedules 1 to 4 to this Act "existing patent" means a patent mentioned in subsection (2)(a) and (c) above, "existing application" means an application mentioned in subsection (2)(b) above, and expressions used in the 1949 Act and those Schedules have the same meanings in those Schedules as in that Act.

Priorities between patents and applications under 1949 Act and this Act

15.128   128.—(1) The following provisions of this section shall have effect for the purpose of resolving questions of priority arising between patents and applications for patents under the 1949 Act and patents and applications for patents under this Act.

(2) A complete specification under the 1949 Act shall be treated for the purposes of sections 2(3) and 5(2) above—

(a) if published under that Act, as a published application for a patent under this Act;

(b) if it has a date of filing under that Act, as an application for a patent under this Act which has a date of filing under this Act;

and in the said section 2(3), as it applies by virtue of this subsection in relation to any such specification, the words "both as filed and" shall be omitted.

(3) In section 8(1), (2) and (4) of the 1949 Act (search for anticipation by

prior claim) the references to any claim of a complete specification, other than the applicant's, published and filed as mentioned in section 8(1) shall include references to any claim contained in an application made and published under this Act or in the specification of a patent granted under this Act, being a claim in respect of an invention having a priority date earlier than the date of filing the complete specification under the 1949 Act.

(4) In section 32(1)(a) of the 1949 Act (which specifies, as one of the grounds of revoking a patent, that the invention was claimed in a valid claim of earlier priority date contained in the complete specification of another patent), the reference to such a claim shall include a reference to a claim contained in the specification of a patent granted under this Act (a new claim) which satisfies the following conditions:—

(a) the new claim must be in respect of an invention having an earlier priority date than that of the relevant claim of the complete specification of the patent sought to be revoked; and

(b) the patent containing the new claim must be wholly valid or be valid in those respects which have a bearing on that relevant claim.

(5) For the purposes of this section and the provisions of the 1949 Act mentioned in this section the date of filing an application for a patent under that Act and the priority date of a claim of a complete specification under that Act shall be determined in accordance with the provisions of that Act, and the priority date for an invention which is the subject of a patent or application for a patent under this Act shall be determined in accordance with the provisions of this Act.

Application of Act to Crown

129. This Act does not affect Her Majesty in her private capacity but, subject to that, it binds the Crown.   **15.129**

Interpretation

130.—(1) In this Act, except so far as the context otherwise requires—   **15.130**
"application for a European patent (U.K.)" and "international application for a patent (U.K.)" each mean an application of the relevant description which, on its date of filing, designates the United Kingdom;

"appointed day", in any provision of this Act, means the day appointed under section 132 below for the coming into operation of that provision;

"Community Patent Convention" means the Convention for the European Patent for the Common Market and "Community patent" means a patent granted under that convention;

"comptroller" means the Comptroller-General of Patents, Designs and Trade Marks;

"Convention on International Exhibitions" means the Convention relating to International Exhibitions signed in Paris on 22nd November 1928, as amended or supplemented by any protocol to that convention which is for the time being in force;

"court"means

[(a) *as respects England and Wales, the High Court;*]

   (a) **as respects England and Wales, the High Court or any patents county court having jurisdiction by virtue of an order under section 287 of the Copyright, Designs and Patents Act 1988.**

   (b) as respects Scotland, the Court of Session;

   (c) as respects Northern Ireland, the High Court in Northern Ireland;

"date of filing" means—

   (a) in relation to an application for a patent made under this Act, the date which is the date of filing that application by virtue of section 15 above; and

   (b) in relation to any other application the date which, under the law of the country where the application was made or in accordance with the terms of a treaty or convention to which that country is a party, is to be treated as the date of filing that application or is equivalent to the date of filing an application in that country (whatever the outcome of the application);

"designate" in relation to an application or a patent, means designate the country or countries (in pursuance of the European Patent Convention or the Patent Co-operation Treaty) in which protection is sought for the invention which is the subject of the application or patent;

"employee"means a person who works or (where the employment has ceased) worked under a contract of employment or in employment under or for the purposes of a government department **or a person who serves (or served) in the naval, military or air forces of the Crown;**

"employer", in relation to an employee, means the person by whom the employee is or was employed;

"European Patent Convention" means the Convention on the Grant of European Patents, "European patent" means a patent granted under that convention, "European patent (U.K.)" means a European patent designating the United Kingdom, "European Patent Bulletin" means the bulletin of that name published under that convention, and "European Patent Office" means the office of that name established by that convention;

"exclusive licence" means a licence from the proprietor of or applicant for a patent conferring on the licensee, or on him and persons authorised by him, to the exclusion of all other persons (including the proprietor or applicant), any right in respect of the invention to which the patent or application relates, and "exclusive licensee" and "non-exclusive licence" shall be construed accordingly;

"filing fee" means the fee prescribed for the purposes of section 14 above;

"formal requirements" means those requirements designated as such by rules made for the purposes of section 17 above;

"international application for a patent" means an application made under the Patent Co-operation Treaty;

"International Bureau" means the secretariat of the World Intellectual Property Organisation established by a convention signed at Stockholm on 14th July 1967;

"international exhibition" means an official or officially recognised international exhibition falling within the terms of the Convention of International Exhibitions or falling within the terms of any subsequent treaty or convention replacing that convention;

"inventor" has the meaning assigned to it by section 7 above;

"journal" has the meaning assigned to it by section 123(6) above;

"mortgage" when used as a noun, includes a charge for securing money or money's worth and, when used as a verb, shall be construed accordingly;

"1949 Act" means the Patents Act 1949;

"patent" means a patent under this Act;

["patent agent" means a person carrying on for gain in the United Kingdom the business of acting as agent for other persons for the purpose of applying for or obtaining patents (other than European patents) in the United Kingdom or elsewhere or for the purpose of conducting proceedings in connection with such patents before the comptroller—

> *(a) in relation to applications for, or otherwise in connection with, such patents, or*
>
> *(b) in connection with European patents (U.K.) to which section 77(1) above for the time being applies;"]*

"Patent Co-operation Treaty" means the treaty of that name signed at Washington on 19th June 1970;

"patented invention" means an invention for which a patent is granted and "patented process" shall be construed accordingly;

"patented product" means a product which is a patented invention or, in relation to a patented process, a product obtained directly by means of the process or to which the process has been applied;

"prescribed" and "rules" have the meanings assigned to them by section 123 above;

"priority date" means the date determined as such under section 5 above;

"published" means made available to the public (whether in the

United Kingdom or elsewhere) and a document shall be taken to be published under any provision of this Act if it can be inspected as of right at any place in the United Kingdom by members of the public, whether on payment of a fee or not; and "republished" shall be construed accordingly;

"register" and cognate expressions have the meanings assigned to them by section 32 above;

"relevant convention court", in relation to any proceedings under the European Patent Convention, the Community Patent Convention or the Patent Co-operation Treaty, means that court or other body which under that convention or treaty has jurisdiction over those proceedings, including (where it has such jurisdiction) any department of the European Patent Office;

"right", in relation to any patent or application, includes an interest in the patent or application and without prejudice to the foregoing, any reference to a right in a patent includes a reference to a share in the patent;

"search fee" means the fee prescribed for the purposes of section 17(1) above;

"services of the Crown" and "use for the services of the Crown" have the meanings assigned to them by section 56(2) above, including, as respects any period of emergency within the meaning of section 59 above, the meanings assigned to them by the said section 59.

(2) Rules may provide for stating in the journal that an exhibition falls within the definition of international exhibition in subsection (1) above and any such statement shall be conclusive evidence that the exhibition falls within that definition.

(3) For the purposes of this Act matter shall be taken to have been disclosed in any relevant application within the meaning of section 5 above or in the specification of a patent if it was either claimed or disclosed (otherwise than by way of disclaimer or acknowledgment of prior art) in that application or specification.

(4) References in this Act to an application for a patent, as filed, are references to such an application in the state it was on the date of filing.

(5) References in this Act to an application for a patent being published are references to its being published under section 16 above.

(6) References in this Act to any of the following conventions, that is to say—

(a) The European Patent Convention;
(b) The Community Patent Convention;
(c) The Patent Co-operation Treaty;

are references to that convention or any other international convention or agreement replacing it, as amended or supplemented by any convention or international agreement (including in either case any protocol or annex), or in accordance with the terms of any such convention or agreement, and include references to any instrument made under any such convention or agreement.

(7) Whereas by a resolution made, on the signature of the Community Patent Convention the governments of the member states of the European Economic Community resolved to adjust their laws relating to patents so as (among other things) to bring those laws into conformity with the corresponding provisions of the European Patent Convention, the Community Patent Convention and the Patent Co-operation Treaty, it is hereby declared that the following provisions of this Act, that is to say, sections 1(1) to (4), 2 to 6, 14(3), (5) and (6), 37(5), 54, 60, 69, 72(1) and (2), 74(4), 82, 83, [*88(6) and (7)*,] 100 and 125, are so framed as to have, as nearly as practicable, the same effects in the United Kingdom as the corresponding provisions of the European Patent Convention, the Community Patent Convention and the Patent Co-operation Treaty have in the territories to which those Conventions apply.

(8) The Arbitration Act 1950 shall not apply to any proceedings before the comptroller under this Act.

(9) Except so far as the context otherwise requires, any reference in this Act to any enactment shall be construed as a reference to that enactment as amended or extended by or under any other enactment, including this Act.

Northern Ireland

131. In the application of this Act to Northern Ireland— 15.131
   (a) "enactment" includes an enactment of the Parliament of Northern Ireland and a Measure of the Northern Ireland Assembly;
   (b) any reference to a government department includes a reference to a Department of the Government of Northern Ireland;
   (c) any reference to the Crown includes a reference to the Crown in right of Her Majesty's Government in Northern Ireland;
   (d) any reference to the Companies Act 1948 includes a reference to the corresponding enactments in force in Northern Ireland; and
   (e) the Arbitration Act (Northern Ireland) 1937 shall apply in relation to an arbitration in pursuance of this Act as if this Act related to a matter in respect of which the Parliament of Northern Ireland had power to make laws.

Short title, extent, commencement, consequential amendments and repeals

132.—(1) This Act may be cited as the Patents Act 1977. 15.132

(2) This Act shall extend to the Isle of Man, subject to any modifications contained in an Order made by Her Majesty in Council, and accordingly, subject to any such order, references in this Act to the

United Kingdom shall be construed as including references to the Isle of Man.

(3) For the purposes of this Act the territorial waters of the United Kingdom shall be treated as part of the United Kingdom.

(4) This Act applies to acts done in an area designated by order under section 1(7) of the Continental Shelf Act 1964, [*in connection with the exploration of the sea bed or subsoil or exploitation of their natural resources*], **or specified by Order under section 22(5) of the Oil and Gas (Enterprise) Act 1982 (c.23) in connection with any activity falling within section 23(2) of that Act,** as it applies to acts done in the United Kingdom.

(5) This Act (except section 77(6), (7) and (9), 78(7) and (8), this subsection and the repeal of section 41 of the 1949 Act) shall come into operation on such day as may be appointed by the Secretary of State by order, any different days may be appointed under this subsection for different purposes.

(6) The consequential amendments in Schedule 5 shall have effect.

(7) Subject to the provisions of Schedule 4 to this Act, the enactments specified in Schedule 6 to this Act (which include certain enactments which were spent before the passing of this Act) are hereby repealed to the extent specified in column 3 of that Schedule.

NOTE

Subs. (4) amended by Oil and Gas (Enterprise) Act 1982 (c.23), Sched. 3, para.39.

SCHEDULES

SCHEDULE 1

APPLICATION OF 1949 ACT TO EXISTING PATENTS AND APPLICATIONS

Section 127

15.133   1.—(1) The provisions of the 1949 Act referred to in sub-paragraph (2) below shall continue to apply on and after the appointed day in relation to existing patents and applications (but not in relation to patents and applications for patents under this Act).

(2) The provisions are sections 1 to 10, 11(1) and (2), 12, 13, 15 to 17, 19 to 21, 22(1) to (3), 23 to 26, 28 to 33, 46 to 53, 55, 56, 59 to 67, 76, 80, 87(2), 92(1), 96, 101, 102(1) and 103 to 107.

(3) Sub-paragraph (1) above shall have effect subject to the following provisions of this Schedule, paragraph (2)(b) of Schedule 3 below and the provisions of Schedule 4 below.

2.—(1) In section 6 of the 1949 Act, at the end of the proviso to subsection (3) (post-dating of application) there shall be inserted "and—

(c) no application shall, on or after the appointed day, be post-dated under this subsection to a date which is that of the appointed day or which falls after it,"

and there shall be inserted at the end of subsection (4)"; but no application shall on or after the appointed day be post-dated under this subsection to a date which is that of the appointed day or which falls after it."

(2) At the end of subsection (5) of the section (ante-dating) there shall be inserted"; but a fresh application or specification may not be filed on or after the appointed day in accordance with this subsection and those rules unless the comptroller agrees that he will direct that the application or specification shall be ante-dated to a date which falls before the appointed day."

3.—(1) This paragraph and paragraph 4 below shall have effect with respect to the duration of existing patents after the appointed day, and in those paragraphs—

(a) "old existing patent" means an existing patent the date of which fell eleven years or more before the appointed day and also any patent of addition where the patent for the main invention is, or was at any time, an old existing patent by virtue of the foregoing provision;

(b) "new existing patent" means any existing patent not falling within paragraph (a) above; and

(c) any reference to the date of a patent shall, in relation to a patent of addition, be construed as a reference to the date of the patent for the main invention.

(2) Sections 23 to 25 of the 1949 Act (extension of patents on grounds of inadequate remuneration and war loss) shall not apply to a new existing patent.

(3) The period for which the term of an old existing patent may be extended under section 23 or 24 of that Act shall not exceed in the aggregate four years, except where an application for an order under the relevant section has been made before the appointed day and has not been disposed of before that day.

4.—(1) The term of every new existing patent under section 22(3) of the 1949 Act shall be twenty instead of sixteen years from the date of the patent, but—

(a) the foregoing provision shall have effect subject to subsections 25(3) to (5) above; and

(b) on and after the end of the sixteenth year from that date a patent shall not be renewed under section 25(3) to (5) above except by or with the consent of the proprietor of the patent.

(2) Where the term of a new existing patent is extended by this paragraph—

(a) any licence in force under the patent from immediately before the appointed day until the end of the sixteenth year from the date of the patent shall, together with any contract relating to the licence, continue in force so long as the patent remains in force (unless determined otherwise than in accordance with this sub-paragraph), but, if it is an exclusive licence, it shall after the end of that year be treated as a non-exclusive licence;

(b) notwithstanding the terms of the licence, the licensee shall not be required to make any payment to the proprietor for working the invention in question after the end of that year;

(c) every such patent shall after the end of that year be treated as endorsed under section 35 of the 1949 Act (licences of right) **but subject to paragraph 4A below**.

(3) Where the term of a new existing patent is extended by this paragraph and any government department or any person authorised by a government department—

(a) has before the appointed day, used the invention in question for the services of the Crown; and

(b) continues to so use it until the end of the sixteenth year from the date of the patent, any such use of the invention by any government department or person so authorised, after the end of that year, may be made free of any payment to the proprietor of the patent.

(4) Without prejudice to any rule of law about the frustration of contracts, where any person suffers loss or is subjected to liability by reason of the extension of the term of a patent by this paragraph, the court may on the application of that person determine how and by whom the loss or liability is to be borne and make such order as it thinks fit to give effect to the determination.

(5) No order shall be made on an application under sub-paragraph (4) above which has the effect of imposing liability on any person other than the applicant unless notification of the application is given to that person.

4A.—(1) If the proprietor of a patent for an invention which is a product files a   **15.134**

declaration with the Patent Office in accordance with this paragraph, the licences to which persons are entitled by virtue of paragraph (4(2)(c) above shall not extend to a use of the product which is excepted by or under this paragraph.

(2) Pharmaceutical use is excepted, that is—
(a) use as a medicinal product within the meaning of the Medicines Act 1968, and
(b) the doing of any other act mentioned in section 60(1)(a) above with a view to such use.

(3) The Secretary of State may by order except such other uses as he thinks fit; and an order may—
(a) specify as an excepted use any act mentioned in section 60(1)(a) above, and
(b) make different provision with respect to acts done in different circumstances or for different purposes.

(4) For the purposes of this paragraph the question what uses are excepted, so far as that depends on —
(a) orders under section 130 of the Medicines Act 1968 (meaning of "medicinal product"), or
(b) orders under sub-paragraph (3) above,
shall be determined in relation to a patent at the beginning of the sixteenth year of the patent.

(5) A declaration under this paragraph shall be in the prescribed form and shall be filed in the prescribed manner and within the prescribed time limits.

(6) A declaration may not be filed—
(a) in respect of a patent which has at the commencement of section 293 of the Copyright, Designs and Patent Act 1988 passed the end of its fifteenth year; or
(b) if at the date of filing there is—
(i) an existing licence for any description of excepted use of the product, or
(ii) an outstanding application under section 46(3)(a) or (b) above for the settlement by the comptroller of the terms of a licence for any description of excepted use of the product,
and, in either case, the licence took or is to take effect at or after the end of the sixteenth year of the patent.

(7) Where a declaration has been filed under this paragraph in respect of a patent—
(a) section 46(3)(c) above (restriction of remedies for infringement where licences available as of right) does not apply to an infringement of the patent in so far as it consists of the excepted use of the product after the filing of the declaration; and
(b) section 46(3)(d) above (abatement of renewal fee if licences available as of right) does not apply to the patent.

4B.—(1) An application under section 46(3)(a) or (b) above for the settlement by the comptroller of the terms on which a person is entitled to a licence by virtue of paragraph 4(2)(c) above is ineffective if made before the beginning of the sixteenth year of the patent.

(2) This paragraph applies to applications made after the commencement of section 294 of the Copyright, Designs and Patents Act 1988 and to any application made before the commencement of that section in respect of a patent which has not at the commencement of that section passed the end of its fifteenth year.

15.135   5. In section 26(3) of the 1949 Act (no patent of addition unless date of filing of complete specification was the same as or later than the date of filing of complete specification in respect of main invention) after "main invention" there shall be inserted "and was earlier than the date of the appointed day."

6. Notwithstanding anything in section 32(1)(j) of the 1949 Act (ground for revocation that patent was obtained on a false suggestion or representation), it shall not be a ground of revoking a patent under that subsection that the patent was obtained on a false suggestion or representation that a claim of the complete specification of the patent had a priority date earlier than the date of filing the application for the patent, but if it is shown—
(a) on a petition under that section or an application under section 33 of that Act; or
(b) by way of defence or on a counterclaim on an action for infringement;
that such a suggestion or representation was falsely made, the priority date of the claim shall be taken to be the date of filing the application for that patent.

7.—(1) In section 33 of the 1949 Act (revocation of patent by comptroller), in subsection (1) for the words preceding the proviso there shall be substituted—
"(1) Subject to the provisions of this Act, a patent may, on the application of any

person interested, be revoked by the comptroller on any of the grounds set out in section 32(1) of this Act;".

(2) At the end of the said section 33 there shall be added the following subsection—

"(5) A decision of the comptroller or on appeal from the comptroller shall not estop any party to civil proceedings in which infringement of a patent is in issue from alleging that any claim of the specification is invalid on any of the grounds set out in section 32(1) of this Act, whether or not any of the issues involved were decided in that decision."

8. In section 101(1) of the 1949 Act (interpretation) there shall be inserted in the appropriate place—

"appointed day" means the day appointed under section 132 of the Patents Act 1977 for the coming into operation of Schedule 1 to that Act;".

NOTE

Paras.4A and 4B inserted by C.D.P.A. 1988, s.293–4, with effect from January 15, 1989.

SCHEDULE 2

APPLICATIONS OF THIS ACT TO EXISTING PATENTS AND APPLICATIONS

Section 127

1.—(1) Without prejudice to those provisions of Schedule 4 below which apply (in **15.136** certain circumstances) provisions of this Act in relation to existing patents and applications, the provisions of this Act referred to in sub-paragraph (2) below shall apply in relation to existing patents and applications on and after the appointed day subject to the following provisions of this Schedule and the provisions of Schedule 4 below.

(2) The provisions are sections 22, 23, 25(3) to (5), 28 to 36, 44 to 54, 86, 96, 98, 99, 101 to 105, 107 to 111, 113 to 116, 118(1) to (3), 119 to 124, 130 and 132(2), (3) and (4).

2. In those provisions as they apply by virtue of this Schedule—

(a) a reference to this Act includes a reference to the 1949 Act;

(b) a reference to a specified provision of this Act other than one of those provisions shall be construed as a reference to the corresponding provision of the 1949 Act (any provision of that Act being treated as corresponding to a provision of this Act if it was enacted for purposes which are the same as or similar to that provision of this Act);

(c) a reference to rules include a reference to rules under the 1949 Act;

(d) references to a patent under this Act and to an application for such a patent include respectively a reference to an existing patent and application;

(e) references to the grant of a patent under this Act includes a reference to the sealing and grant of an existing patent;

(f) a reference to a patented product and to a patented invention include respectively a reference to a product and invention patented under an existing patent;

(g) references to a published application for a patent under this Act, and to publication of such an application, include respectively references to a complete specification which has been published under the 1949 Act and to publication of such a specification (and a reference to an application for a patent under this Act which has not been published shall be construed accordingly);

(h) a reference to the publication in the journal of a notice of the grant of a patent includes a reference to the date of an existing patent;

(i) a reference to the priority date of an invention includes a reference to the priority date of the relevant claim of the complete specification.

SCHEDULE 3

REPEALS OF PROVISIONS OF 1949 ACT

Section 127

15.137   1.—(1) Subject to the provisions of Schedule 4 below, the provisions of the 1949 Act referred to in paragraph 2 below (which have no counterpart in the new law of patents established by this Act in relation to future patents and applications) shall cease to have effect.

(2) The provisions are:—
(a) section 14 (opposition to grant of patent);
(b) section 32(3) (revocation for refusal to comply with Crown request to use invention);
(c) section 41 (inventions relating to food or medicine, etc.);
(d) section 42 (comptroller's power to revoke patent after expiry of two years from grant of compulsory licence);
(e) section 71 (extension of time for certain convention applications);
(f) section 72 (protection of inventions communicated under international agreements);

SCHEDULE 4

TRANSITIONAL PROVISIONS

General

Section 127

15.138   1. In so far as any instrument made or other thing done under any provision of the 1949 Act which is repealed by virtue of this Act could have been made or done under a corresponding provision of this Act, it shall not be invalidated by the repeals made by virtue of this Act but shall have effect as if made or done under that corresponding provision.

Use of patented invention for services of the Crown

2.—(1) Any question whether—
(a) an act done before the appointed day by a government department or a person authorised in writing by a government department amounts to the use of an invention for the services of the Crown; or
(b) any payment falls to be made in respect of any such use (whether to a person entitled to apply for a patent for the invention, to the patentee, or to an exclusive licensee);
shall be determined under sections 46 to 49 of that Act and those sections shall apply accordingly.

(2) Sections 55 to 59 above shall apply to an act so done on or after the appointed day in relation to an invention—

(a) for which an existing patent has been granted or an existing application for a patent has been made; or

(b) which was communicated before that day to a government department or any person authorised in writing by a government department by the proprietor of the patent or any person from whom he derives title;

and shall so apply subject to sub-paragraph (3) below, the modifications contained in paragraph 2 of Schedule 2 above and the further modification that sections 55(5)(b) and 58(10) above shall not apply in relation to an existing application.

(3) Where an act is commenced before the appointed day and continues to be done on or after that day, then, if it would not amount to the use of an invention for the services of the Crown under the 1949 Act, its continuance on or after that day shall not amount to such use under this Act.

Infringement

3.—(1) Any question whether an act done before the appointed day infringes an existing patent or the privileges or rights arising under a complete specification which has been published shall be determined in accordance with the law relating to infringement in force immediately before that day and, in addition to those provisions of the 1949 Act which continue to apply by virtue of Schedule 1 above, section 70 of that Act shall apply accordingly.

(2) Sections 60 to 71 above shall apply to an act done on or after the appointed day which infringes an existing patent or the privileges or rights arising under a complete specification which has been published (whether before, on or after the appointed day) as they apply to infringements of a patent under this Act or the rights conferred by an application for such a patent, and shall so apply subject to sub-paragraph (3) below, the modifications contained in paragraph 2 of Schedule 2 above and the further modification that section 69(2) and (3) above shall not apply in relation to an existing application.

(3) Where an act is commenced before the appointed day and continues to be done on or after that day, then, if it would not, under the law in force immediately before that day, amount to an infringement of an existing patent or the privileges or rights arising under a complete specification, its continuance on or after that day shall not amount to the infringement of that patent or those privileges or rights.

Notice of opposition

4.—(1) Where notice of opposition to the grant of a patent has been given under section **15.139** 14 of the 1949 Act before the appointed day, the following provisions shall apply:—

(a) if issue has been joined on the notice before the appointed day, the opposition, any appeal from the comptroller's decision on it and any further appeal shall be prosecuted under the old law, but as if references in the 1949 Act and rules made under it to the Appeal Tribunal were references to the Patents Court;

(b) in any other case, the notice shall be taken to have abated immediately before the appointed day.

(2) Sub-paragraph (1)(a) above shall have effect subject to paragraph 12(2) below.

Secrecy

5.—(1) Where directions given under section 18 of the 1949 Act in respect of an existing application (directions restricting publication of information about inventions) are in force immediately before the appointed day, they shall continue in force on and after that day and that section shall continue to apply accordingly.

(2) Where sub-paragraph (1) above does not apply in the case of an existing application section 18 of the 1949 Act shall not apply to the application but section 20 of this Act shall.

(3) Where the comptroller has before the appointed day served a notice under section 12 of the Atomic Energy Act 1946 (restrictions on publication of information about atomic energy etc.) in respect of an existing application that section shall continue to apply to the application on and after that day; but where no such notice has been so served that section shall not apply to the application on and after that day.

Revocation

6.—(1) Where before the appointed day an application has been made under section 33 of the 1949 Act for the revocation of a patent (the original application), the following provisions shall apply:—

(a) if issue has been joined on the application before the appointed day, the application, any appeal from the comptroller's decision on it and any further appeal shall be prosecuted under the old law, but as if references in the 1949 Act and rules made under it to the Appeal Tribunal were references to the Patents Court;

(b) if issue has not been so joined, the original application shall be taken to be an application under section 33 of the 1949 Act for the revocation of the patent on whichever of the grounds referred to in section 32(1) of that Act corresponds (in the comptroller's opinion) to the ground on which the original application was made, or, if there is no ground which so corresponds, shall be taken to have abated immediately before the appointed day.

(2) Sub-paragraph (1)(a) above shall have effect subject to paragraph 11(3) below.

7.—(1) This paragraph applies where an application has been made before the appointed day under section 42 of the 1949 Act for the revocation of a patent.

(2) Where the comptroller has made no order before that day for the revocation of the patent under that section, the application shall be taken to have abated immediately before that day.

(3) Where the comptroller has made such an order before that day, then, without prejudice to section 38 of the Interpretation Act 1889, section 42 shall continue to apply to the patent concerned on and after that day as if this Act had not been enacted.

Licences of right and compulsory licences

15.140 8.—(1) Sections 35 to 41 and 43 to 45 of the 1949 Act shall continue to apply on and after the relevant day—

(a) to any endorsement or order made or licence granted under sections 35 to 41 which is in force immediately before that day; and

(b) to any application made before that day under section 35 to 41.

(2) Any appeal from a decision or oder of the comptroller instituted under sections 35 to 41 or 43 to 45 on or after the relevant day (and any further appeal) shall be prosecuted under the old law, but as if references in the 1949 Act and rules made under it to the Appeal Tribunal were references to the Patents Court.

(3) In this paragraph "the relevant day" means, in relation to section 41, the date of the passing of this Act and, in relation to sections 35 to 40 and 43 to 45, the appointed day.

Convention countries

9.—(1) Without prejudice to paragraph 1 above, an Order in Council declaring any country to be a convention country for all purposes of the 1949 Act or for the purposes of section 1(2) of that Act and in force immediately before the appointed day shall be treated as an Order in Council under section 90 above declaring that country to be a convention country for the purposes of section 5 above.

(2) Where an Order in Council declaring any country to be a convention country for all purposes of the 1949 Act or for the purposes of section 70 of that Act is in force immediately before the appointed day, a vessel registered in that country (whether before, on or after that day) shall be treated for the purposes of section 60 above, as it applies by virtue of paragraph 3(2) above to an existing patent or existing application, as a relevant ship and an aircraft so registered and a land vehicle owned by a person ordinarily resident in that country shall be so treated respectively as a relevant aircraft and a relevant vehicle.

Appeals from court on certain petitions for revocation

10. Where the court has given judgment on a petition under section 32(1)(*j*) of the 1949 Act before the appointed day, any appeal from the judgment (whether instituted before, on or after that day) shall be continued or instituted and be disposed of under the old law.　　　**15.141**

Appeals from comptroller under continuing provisions of 1949 Act

11.—(1) In this paragraph "the continuing 1949 Act provisions" means the provisions of the 1949 Act which continue to apply on and after the appointed day as mentioned in paragraph 1 of Schedule 1 above.

(2) This paragraph applies where—
(a) the comptroller gives a decision or direction (whether before or on or after the appointed day) under any of the continuing 1949 Act provisions, and
(b) an appeal lies under those provisions from the decision or direction;
but this paragraph applies subject to the foregoing provisions of this Schedule.

(3) Where such an appeal has been instituted before the Appeal Tribunal before the appointed day, and the hearing of the appeal has begun but has not been completed before that day, the appeal (and any further appeal) shall be continued and disposed of under the old law.

(4) Where such an appeal has been so instituted, but the hearing of it has not begun before the appointed day, it shall be transferred by virtue of this subparagraph to the Patents Court on that day and the appeal (and any further appeal) shall be prosecuted under the old law, but as if references in the 1949 Act and rules made under it to the Appeal Tribunal were references to the Patents Court.

(5) Any such appeal instituted on or after the appointed day shall lie to the Patents Court or, where the proceedings appealed against were held in Scotland, the Court of Session; and accordingly, the reference to the Appeal of Tribunal in section 31(2) of the 1949 Act shall be taken to include a reference to the Patents Court or (as the case may be) the Court of Session.

(6) Section 97(3) of this Act shall apply to any decision of the Patents Court on appeal instituted on or after the appointed day from a decision or direction of the comptroller under any of the continuing 1949 Act provisions as it applies to a decision of that Court referred to in that subsection, except that for references to the sections mentioned in paragraph (a) of that subsection there shall be substituted references to sections 33, 55 and 56 of the 1949 Act.

Appeals from comptroller under repealed provisions of 1949 Act

12.—(1) This paragraph applies where an appeal to the Appeal Tribunal has been instituted before the appointed day under any provision of the 1949 Act repealed by this Act.　　　**15.142**

(2) Where the hearing of such an appeal has begun but has not been completed before that day, the appeal (and any further appeal) shall be continued and disposed of under the old law.

(3) Where the hearing of such an appeal has not begun before that day, it shall be

transferred by virtue of this sub-paragraph to the Patents Court on that day and the appeal (and any further appeal) shall be prosecuted under the old law, but as if references in the 1949 Act and rules made under it to the Appeal Tribunal were references to the Patents Court.

Appeals from Appeal Tribunal to Court of Appeal

13. Section 87(1) of the 1949 Act shall continue to apply on and after the appointed day to any decision of the Appeal Tribunal given before that day, and any appeal by virtue of this paragraph (and any further appeal) shall be prosecuted under the old law.

Rules

14. The power to make rules under section 123 of this Act shall include power to make rules for any purpose mentioned in section 94 of the 1949 Act.

Supplementary

15. Section 97(2) of this Act applies to—
(a) any appeal to the Patents Court by virtue of paragraph 4(1)(*a*), 6(1)(*a*), 8(2) or 11(5) above, and
(b) any appeal which is transferred to that Court by virtue of paragraph 11(4) or 12(3) above,
as it applies to an appeal under that section; and section 97 of this Act shall apply for the purposes of any such appeal instead of section 85 of the 1949 Act.
16. In this Schedule "the old law" means the 1949 Act, any rules made under it and any relevant rule of law as it was or they were immediately before the appointed day.
17. For the purposes of this Schedule—
(a) issue is joined on a notice of opposition to the grant of a patent under section 14 of the 1949 Act when the applicant for the patent files a counter-statement fully setting out the grounds on which the opposition is contested;
(b) issue is joined on an application for the revocation of a patent under section 33 of that Act when the patentee files a counter-statement fully setting out the grounds on which the application is contested.
18.—(1) Nothing in the repeals made by this Act in sections 23 and 24 of the 1949 Act shall have effect as respects any such application as is mentioned in paragraph 3(3) of Schedule 1 above.
(2) Nothing in the repeal by this Act of the Patents Act 1957 shall have effect as respects existing applications.
(3) Section 69 of the 1949 Act (which is not repealed by this Act) and section 70 of that Act (which continues to have effect for certain purposes by virtue of paragraph 3 above) shall apply as if section 68 of that Act has not been repealed by this Act and as if paragraph 9 above had not been enacted.

PATENTS ACT 1977

SCHEDULE 5

CONSEQUENTIAL AMENDMENTS

Crown Proceedings Act 1947 (c. 44)

[*1. In section 3 of the Crown Proceedings Act 1947, for subsection (2) there shall be substituted—* **15.143**
"(2) *Nothing in the preceding subsection or in any other provision of this Act shall affect the
rights of any Government department under Schedule 1 to the Registered Designs Act 1949
or section 55 of the Patents Act 1977, or the rights of the Secretary of State under section 22
of the said Act of 1977.*"]

2. In section 32(1) of the Registered Designs Act 1949—
(a) in paragraph (a), for "the Patents Act 1949" there shall be substituted "the Patents
Act 1977"; and
(b) in paragraph (c), after "1949" there shall be inserted "or section 114 of the Patents
Act 1977".

[*3. In sections 42 and 44(1) of the Registered Designs Act 1949, for "the Patents Act 1949" there
shall be substituted, in each case, "the Patents Act 1977".*]

Defence Contracts Act 1958 (c. 38)

4.—In subsectioin (4) of section 4 of the Defence Contracts Act 1958, for the words from
"Patents Act 1949" to the end there shall be substituted "Patents Act 1977".

Administration of Justice Act 1970 (c. 31)

5.—(1) In subsections (2) and (3) of section 10 of the Administration of Justice Act 1970
for "either" there shall be substituted, in each case, "the".
(2) In subsection (4) of the said section 10, for "(as so amended)" there shall be
substituted "(as amended by section 24 of the Administration of Justice Act 1969)".
(3) For subsection (5) of the said section 10, there shall be substituted:—
"(5) In subsection (8) of the said section 28 (which confers power on the Tribunal to
make rules about procedure etc.), there shall be inserted at end of the subsection the
words "including right of audience".

Atomic Energy Authority (Weapons Group) Act 1973 (c. 4)

6. In section 5(2) of the Atomic Energy Authority (Weapons Group) Act 1973—
(a) after the first "Patents Act 1949" there shall be inserted, "the Patents Act 1977"; and
(b) after the second "Patents Act 1949" there shall be inserted "section 55(4) of the
Patents Act 1977".

Fair Trading Act 1973 (c. 41)

7.—(1) In paragraph 10 of Schedule 4 to the Fair Trading Act 1973 for "Patents Act 1949"
there shall be substituted "Patents Act 1977".
(2) After the said paragraph 10 there shall be inserted—

"10A. The services of persons carrying on for gain in the United Kingdom the business of acting as agents or other representatives of other persons for the purpose of applying for or obtaining European patents or for the purpose of conducting proceedings in connection with such patents before the European Patent Office or the comptroller and whose names appear on the European list (within the meaning of section 84(7) fo the Patents Act 1977) in their capacity as such persons."

Restrictive Trade Practices Act 1976 (c. 34)

8.—(1) In paragraph 10 of Schedule 1 to the Restrictive Trade Practices Act 1976, for "the Patents Act 1949" there shall be substituted "the Patents Act 1977".

(2) After the said paragraph 10 there shall be inserted—

"10A. The services of persons carrying on for gain in the United Kingdom the business of acting as agents or other representatives of other persons for the purpose of applying for or obtaining European patents or for the purpose of conducting proceedings in connection with such patents before the European Patent Office or the comptroller and whose names appear on the European list (within the meaning of section 84(7) of the Patents Act 1977), in their capacity as such persons."

NOTE

Paras.1 and 3 deleted by C.D.P.A. 1988 Sched. 8, with effect from August 1, 1989 (S.I. 1989, No.816).

SCHEDULE 6

ENACTMENTS REPEALED

Section 132

15.144

Chapter	Short title	Extent of repeal
7 Edw. 7. 3.29	The Patents and Designs Act 1907	Section 47(2).
9 & 10 Geo. 6, c. 80. 12, 13 & 14 Geo. 6, c. 87	The Atomic Energy Act 1946	In section 12, subsections (1) to (7).
	The Patents Act 1949.	Section 11(3). Section 14. Section 16(6). Section 18. Sections 22(4) and (5). In section 23(1), the words from "(not exceeding" to "ten years)".

Chapter	Short title	Extent of repeal
		In section 24, in subsection (1) the words "(not exceeding ten years)" and, in subsection (7), the words from "but" to the end.
		Section 27.
		In section 32, subsection (3).
		In section 33(3), the proviso.
		Sections 34 to 35.
		Sections 54, 57 and 58.
		Section 68.
		Sections 70 to 75.
		Sections 77 to 79.
		Section 81 to 86.
		Section 87(1) and (3).
		Sections 88 to 91.
		Sections 93 to 95.
		Sections 97 to 100.
		Section 102(2).
		Schedule 1.
		Schedule 3, except paragraphs 1 and 26.
5 & 6 Eliz. 2, c. 13	The Patents Act 1957.	The whole Act, except in relation to existing applications.
9 & 10 Eliz. 2, c. 25	The Patents and Designs (Renewals, Extensions and Fees) Act 1961.	In section 1(1), the words from "subsection (5)" to "and in". Section 2.
10 & 11 Eliz. 2, c. 30.	The Northern Ireland Act 1962.	In Schedule 1, the entries relating to section 61 of the Patents Act 1949.
1967, c.80	The Criminal Justice Act 1967.	In Schedule 3, in Parts I and IV, the entries relating to the Patents Act 1949.
1968, c. 80.	The Civil Evidence Act 1968.	Section 15.
1969, c. 58.	The Administration of Justice Act 1969.	In section 24, in subsection (1), the words "85 of the Patents Act 1949 and section" and "each of", in subsection (2), (3) and (4) the words "of each of those sections" and in subsection (1))" to "and" and the words "in the case of the said section 28".
1970, c. 31.	The Administration of Justice Act 1970.	In section 10, in subsection (1), the words "Patents Appeal Tribunal or the" and in subsection (4), the words from "the Patents Appeal" to "and".
1971, c.23.	The Courts Act 1971.	Section 46.
1971, c. 36 (N.I.)	The Civil Evidence Act (Northern Ireland) Act 1971.	Section 11.
1973, c. 41.	The Fair Trading Act 1973.	Section 126. In Schedule 3, in paragraph 16(2), the words from "of section 40" to "Commission)", where first occurring.
1974, c. 47.	The Solicitors Act 1974.	In Schedule 12, the entry relating to the Patents Act 1949. In Schedule 3, paragraph 3.

THE PATENTS RULES 1990

(S.I. 1990 No.2384, as amended.)

Made ....*29th November 1990*
Laid before Parliament...*6th December 1990*
Coming into force..*7th January 1991*

ARRANGEMENT OF RULES

Preliminary

SECTION

Right to apply for and obtain a patent

Inventors

Applications for patents

Examination and search

Grant, amendment and continuation of patent

Registration

Appendices

Entitlement to patent

Employees' inventions

Licences of right

Compulsory licences

Infringement proceedings before comptroller

Revocation of patents

Amendment of patents in infringement or revocation proceedings

International applications

SCHEDULES

GENERAL NOTE

These rules were amended by The Patents (Amendment) Rules 1992 (S.I. 1992, No. 1142) and The Patents (Amendment) Rules 1993 (S.I. 1993, No. 2423). Text which has been inserted is shown in bold, while text which has been replaced or deleted is shown in italics. The amendments effected by S.I. 1992, No. 1142 came into force on June 1, 1992 except for those to Rules 85 and 118 which came into force on July 1, 1992. The amendments made by S.I. 1993, No. 2423 came into force on November 1, 1993.

The Secretary of State, in exercise of the powers conferred upon him by sections 5(2), 8(3), 12(6), 13(1) and (3), 14(1) and (6), 15(2), (3) and (5), 16(1), 17(1), (2) and (8), 18(1) and (4), 19(1), 20(1), 21(1), 24(2), 25(3) and (5), 28(1), (1A) and (2A), 32(2), (6) and (7), 40(1) and (2), 47(3) and (6), 52(1), 77(6), 78(4), 80(3), 81(2)(*b*) and (2)(*c*), 89, 89A, 92(3) and (4), 97(1)(*d*), 118(1) and (3)(*b*), 120(1), 123(1) to (3A), (6) and (7), 124, 125A(1), (2) and (3), 127(6) and 130(2) of, and paragraph 4A(5) of Schedule 1 and paragraph 14 of Schedule 4 to, the Patents Act 1977, after consultation with the Council on Tribunals pursuant to section 10(1) of the Tribunals and Inquiries Act 1971, hereby makes the following Rules:

Preliminary

Citation and commencement

16.01   **1.** These Rules may be cited as the Patents Rules 1990 and shall come into force on January 7, 1991.

Interpretation

2. In these Rules—   16.02

"the Act" means the Patents Act 1977;

"the 1949 Act" means the Patents Act 1949;

"declared priority date" means—

(a) the date of filing of the earliest relevant application specified in a declaration made for the purposes of section 5 where the priority date claimed in the declaration has not been withdrawn before preparations for the publication of the application in suit have been completed by the Patent Office in accordance with section 16;

(b) the date of filing of any such application for a patent as is referred to in section 127(4) which is specified in a declaration made for the purposes of that section;

(c) where an application for a European patent (U.K.) is, by virtue of section 81(1), to be treated as an application for a patent under the Act, the date of filing of the earliest previous application mentioned in the declaration of priority filed by the applicant in respect of the application for a European patent (U.K.) under Article 88(1) of the European Patent Convention where the priority date claimed in the declaration has not been lost or abandoned and where the declaration has not been withdrawn before the comptroller directs that the application for a European patent (U.K.) shall be so treated; or

(d) where an international application for a patent (U.K.) is to be treated as an application for a patent under the Act, the date of filing of the earliest application filed in or for a State which is a party to the Convention for the Protection of Industrial Property signed at Paris on March 20, 1883 the priority of which is claimed in a declaration filed for the purposes of Article 8 of the Patent Co-operation Treaty, provided that such priority claim has not been lost or abandoned under the provisions of that Treaty;

"Journal" means the Official Journal (Patents) published in accordance with rule 115.

Construction

3. In these Rules, save where otherwise indicated—   16.03

(a) references to a section are references to that section of the Act;

(b) references to a rule are references to that rule in these Rules;

(c) references to a Schedule are references to that Schedule to these Rules;

(d) references to a form are references to that form as set out in Schedule 1;

and references to the filing of a form or other document are references to filing it at the Patent Office.

Forms

16.04 4.—(1) The forms of which the use is required by these Rules (except the forms mentioned in rule 123(1)) are those set out in Schedule 1.

(2) A requirement under these Rules to use such a form is satisfied by the use either of a replica of that form or of a form which is acceptable to the comptroller and contains the information required by the form set out in that Schedule.

International exhibitions

16.05 5.—(1) An applicant for a patent who wishes the disclosure of matter constituting an invention to be disregarded in accordance with section 2(4)(c) shall, at the time of filing the application for the patent, inform the comptroller in writing that the invention has been displayed at an international exhibition.

(2) The applicant shall, within four months of filing the application, file a certificate, issued at the exhibition by the authority responsible for the exhibition, stating that the invention was in fact exhibited and, where the first disclosure of the invention did not take place on the opening date, the date of the first disclosure. The certificate shall be accompanied by an identification of the invention duly authenticated by the authority.

(3) For the purposes of section 130(2) a statement may be published in the Journal that an exhibition described in the statement falls within the definition of international exhibition in subsection (1) of that section.

(4) In the case of an international application for a patent (U.K.), the application of this rule shall be subject to the provisions of rule 85(3).

Declaration of priority for the purposes of section 5

16.06 6.—(1) A declaration for the purposes of section 5 shall be made at the time of filing the application for a patent ("the application in suit") and shall state the date of filing of any application specified in the declaration and the country in or for which it was made.

(2) Subject to the provisions of rule 26 and paragraphs (3), (4) and (5) below, where the application in suit is for a patent under the Act, the applicant shall, within the period of 16 months after the declared priority date, furnish to the Patent Office in respect of every application specified in the declaration—

(a) its file number; and

(b) except where paragraph (3) below has effect, a copy of that application duly certified by the authority with which it was filed or otherwise verified to the satisfaction of the comptroller.

(3) Where an application specified in the declaration is an application for a patent under the Act or an international application for a patent which is filed at the Patent Office,—

(a) if the application is filed under section 15(4), the applicant shall, at the time of filing the application, file—

(i) a request that a copy of the application specified in the declaration be prepared for use in the Patent Office; and

(ii) Patents Form 24/77 requesting the comptroller to certify the same; or

(b) if the application is filed otherwise than under section 15(4), the applicant shall file that request and that form in compliance with any request made by the comptroller.

(4) Where the application in suit is an application for a European patent (U.K.) which, by virtue of section 81, is to be treated as an application for a patent under the Act, the requirements of paragraphs (1) and (2) above shall be treated as having been complied with to the extent that the requirements of rule 38(1) to (3) of the Implementing Regulations to the European Patent Convention have been fulfilled.

(5) Where the application in suit is an international application for a patent (U.K.) which is to be treated as an application for a patent under the Act, the requirements of paragraphs (1) and (2) above shall be treated as having been complied with to the extent that the requirements of rules 4.10(a) and (c) and 17.1(a) or (b) of the Regulations made under the Patent Co-operation Treaty have been fulfilled.

(6) Where a copy of an application is filed or treated as having been filed under paragraph (2)(b), (3), (4) or (5) above and that application is in a language other than English, subject to rule 85(3)(c) and (d), a translation thereof into English verified to the satisfaction of the comptroller as corresponding to the original text shall be filed within the period of 21 months after the declared priority date.

(7) In the case of an international application for a patent (U.K.), the application of paragraph (6) above shall be subject to the provisions of rule 85(3)(c) and (d).

Right to apply for and obtain a patent

References under section 8(1)(a) or 12(1)(a)

7.—(1) A reference under section 8(1)(a) or 12(1)(a) shall be made on **16.07**
Patents Form 2/77 and shall be accompanied by a copy thereof and a statement in duplicate setting out fully the nature of the question, the

facts upon which the person making the reference relies and the order or other relief which he is seeking.

(2) The comptroller shall send a copy of the reference and statement to—

(a) any person (other than the person referred to in paragraph (1) above) alleged in the reference to be entitled to be granted a patent for the invention;

(b) any person, not being a party to the reference, who is shown in the register as having a right in or under the patent application;

(c) where the application for the patent has not been published, any person (not being a party to the reference) who is an applicant for the patent or has given notice to the comptroller of a relevant transaction, instrument or event; and

(d) every person who has been identified in the patent application or a statement filed under section 13(2)(a) as being, or being believed to be, the inventor or joint inventor of the invention.

(3) If any person who is sent a copy of the reference and statement under paragraph (2) above wishes to oppose the making of the order or the granting of the relief sought, he ("the opponent") shall, within the period of two months beginning on the date the copies are sent to him, file in duplicate a counter-statement setting out fully the grounds of his opposition and the comptroller shall send a copy of the counter-statement to the person making the reference and to those recipients of the copy of the reference and statement who are not party to the counter-statement.

(4) The person making the reference or any such recipient may, within the period of two months beginning on the date when the copy of the counter-statement is sent to him, file evidence in support of his case and shall send a copy of the evidence,—

(a) in any case, to the opponent; and

(b) in the case of evidence filed by such a recipient, to the person making the reference.

(5) Within the period of two months beginning on the date when the copy of such evidence is sent to him or, if no such evidence is filed, within two months of the expiration of the time within which it might have been filed, the opponent may file evidence in support of his case and shall send a copy of the evidence so filed to the person making the reference and those recipients; and within the period of two months beginning on the date when the copy of the opponent's evidence is sent to him, that person or any of those recipients may file further evidence confined to matters strictly in reply and shall send a copy of it to the persons mentioned in sub-paragraphs (a) and (b) of paragraph (4) above.

(6) No further evidence shall be filed except by leave or direction of the comptroller.

(7) The comptroller may give such directions as he may think fit with regard to the subsequent procedure.

References by co-proprietors under section 8(1)(b) or 12(1)(b)

8.—(1) A reference under section 8(1)(b) or 12(1)(b) shall be made on **16.08**
Patents Form 2/77 and shall be accompanied by a copy thereof and a
statement in duplicate setting out fully the nature of the question, the
facts relied upon by the co-proprietor making the reference and the
order which he is seeking.

(2) The comptroller shall send a copy of the reference and statement
to—

(a) each co-proprietor who is not a party to the reference and who has
not otherwise indicated his consent to the making of the order
sought;

(b) any person to whom it is alleged in the reference that any right in
or under an application for a patent should be transferred or
granted;

(c) any person, not being a party to the reference, who is shown in the
register as having a right in or under the patent application;

(d) where the application for the patent has not been published, any
person (not being a party to the reference) who has given notice to
the comptroller of a relevant transaction, instrument or event;
and

(e) every person who has been identified in the patent application or
a statement filed under section 13(2)(a) as being, or being believed
to be, the inventor or joint inventor of the invention.

(3) Any person who received a copy of the reference and statement
and who wishes to oppose the order sought may, within the period of
two months beginning on the date when the copies are sent to him, file a
counter-statement in duplicate setting out fully the grounds of his
opposition.

(4) The comptroller shall, as appropriate, send a copy of any
counter-statement to—

(a) each co-proprietor who is a party to the reference; and

(b) any person to whom a copy of the reference and statement were
sent pursuant to paragraph (2) above.

(5) Any person who receives a copy of the counter-statement may,
within the period of two months beginning on the date when the copy is
sent to him, file evidence in support of his case and shall send a copy of
the evidence so filed to the co-proprietor making the reference and to
each person who has filed a counter-statement.

(6) Any person entitled to receive a copy of the evidence filed under
paragraph (5) above may, within the period of two months beginning
on the date when the copy is sent to him or, if no such evidence is filed,
within two months of the expiration of the period within which it might
have been filed, file evidence in support of his case and shall send a copy
of the evidence so filed to each of the other parties listed in paragraph (4)
above.

(7) Any person who receives a copy of the evidence filed under

paragraph (6) above may, within the period of two months of the date when the copy is sent to him, file further evidence confined to matters strictly in reply and shall as appropriate send a copy of the evidence so filed to the parties listed in paragraph (4) above.

(8) No further evidence shall be filed by any party except by leave or direction of the comptroller.

(9) The comptroller may give such directions as he may think fit with regard to the subsequent procedure.

Orders under section 8 or 12

16.09   9.—(1) Where an order is made under section 8 or section 12 that an application for a patent shall proceed in the name of one or more persons none of whom was an original applicant, the comptroller shall notify all original applicants and their licensees of whom he is aware of the making of the order.

(2) A person notified under paragraph (1) above may make a request under section 11(3) or under that section as applied by section 12(5),—

    (a) in the case of a request by the original applicant or any of the original applicants, within the period of two months beginning on the date when the notification is sent to him; or

    (b) in the case of a request by a licensee, within the period of four months beginning on the date when the notification is sent to him.

Prescribed period for new applications under section 8(3) or 12(6)

16.10   10. The prescribed period for the purposes of sections 8(3) and 12(6) shall be three months calculated from the day on which the time for appealing from an order made under either of those subsections expires without an appeal being brought or, where an appeal is brought, from the day on which it is finally disposed of.

Authorisation under section 8(5)

16.11   11.—(1) An application under section 8(5) for authority to do anything on behalf of a person to whom directions have been given under section 8(2)(d) or (4) shall be made on Patents Form 3/77 and shall be accompanied by a copy thereof and a statement in duplicate setting out fully the facts upon which the applicant relies and the nature of the authorisation sought.

(2) The comptroller shall send a copy of the application and statement to the person alleged to have failed to comply with the directions.

(3) The comptroller may give such directions as he may think fit with regard to the subsequent procedure.

Request by joint applicant under section 10 or 12(4)

12.—(1) A request under section 10 or section 12(4) by a joint applicant   **16.12**
shall be made on Patents Form 4/77 and shall be accompanied by a copy
thereof and a statement in duplicate setting out fully the facts upon
which he relies and the directions which he seeks.

(2) The comptroller shall send a copy of the request and statement to
each other joint applicant who shall, if he wishes to oppose the request,
within the period of two months beginning on the date when such
copies are sent to him, file in duplicate a counter-statement setting out
fully the grounds of his opposition; and the comptroller shall send a
copy of the counter-statement to the person making the request and to
each other joint applicant who is not party to the counter-statement.

(3) The comptroller may give such directions as he may think fit with
regard to the subsequent procedure.

Referral to the comptroller under section 11(5)

13.—(1) Where, following the making of such an order as is   **16.13**
mentioned in section 11(2), a question is referred to the comptroller
under subsection (5) of section 11 or that subsection as applied by
section 12(5) as to whether any person is entitled to be granted a licence
or whether the period or terms of a licence are reasonable, the reference
shall be made on Patents Form 5/77 and shall be accompanied by a copy
thereof and a statement in duplicate setting out fully the facts upon
which the person making the reference relies and the terms of the licence
which he is prepared to accept or grant.

(2) The comptroller shall send a copy of the reference and statement to
every person in whose name the application is to proceed or, as the case
may be, every person claiming to be entitled to be granted a licence, in
either case not being the person who makes the reference, and if any
recipient does not agree to grant or accept a licence for such period and
upon such terms, he shall, within the period of two months beginning
on the date when the copies are sent to him, file a counter-statement in
duplicate setting out fully the grounds of his objection and the
comptroller shall send a copy of the counter-statement to the person
making the reference.

(3) The comptroller may give such directions as he may think fit with
regard to the subsequent procedure.

Inventors

Mention of inventor under section 13

16.14   14.—(1) An application to the comptroller under section 13(1) or (3) by any person who alleges—
  (a) that he ought to have been mentioned as the inventor or joint inventor of an invention in any patent granted or published application for a patent for the invention; or
  (b) that any person mentioned as sole or joint inventor in any patent granted or published application for the invention ought not to have been so mentioned,
shall be made on Patents Form 6/77 and shall be accompanied by a copy thereof and a statement in duplicate setting out fully the facts relied upon.

(2) The comptroller shall send a copy of any such application and statement to—
  (a) every person registered as proprietor of, or applicant for, the patent (other than the applicant under section 13 himself);
  (b) every person who has been identified in the patent application or a statement filed under section 13(2)(*a*) as being, or being believed to be, the inventor or joint inventor of the invention; and
  (c) every other person whose interests the comptroller considers may be affected by the application.

(3) Any recipient of such a copy of an application and statement who wishes to oppose the application shall, within the period of two months beginning on the date when the copies are sent to him, file a counter-statement in duplicate setting out fully the grounds of his objection and the comptroller shall send a copy of the counter-statement to each of the persons described in this rule other than any person who is party to the counter-statement.

(4) The comptroller may give such directions as he may think fit with regard to the subsequent procedure.

(5) The document prescribed for the purposes of section 13(1) shall be an addendum or erratum slip.

Procedure where applicant is not the inventor or sole inventor

16.15   15.—(1) Subject to the provisions of rules 26, 81(3), 82(3) and 85(7)(a), if the applicant or applicants are not the inventor or inventors, a statement under section 13(2) identifying the inventor or inventors and, where required by section 13(2)(b), the derivation of the right of the applicant or applicants to be granted the patent shall be made on Patents Form 7/77, within the period of sixteen months after the declared priority date or, where there is no declared priority date, the date of filing the application.

(2) Where the applicant is not the sole inventor or the applicants are not the joint inventors of the invention the subject of the application and the application does not contain a declared priority date which relates to an earlier relevant application as defined in section 5(5)(b), a sufficient number of copies of Patents Form 7/77 shall be filed by the applicant or applicants within the said period to enable the comptroller to send one to each inventor who is not one of the applicants.

(3) Where the application is an application for a European patent (U.K.) which by virtue of section 81 is to be treated as an application for a patent under the Act, the requirements of paragraphs (1) and (2) above shall be treated as having been complied with to the extent that the requirements of rule 17 of the Implementing Regulations to the European Patent Convention have been fulfilled.

(4) Where the application is an international application for a patent (U.K.), the requirements of paragraphs (1) and (2) above shall be treated as having been complied with if the provisions of rules 4.1(a)(v) and 4.6 of the Regulations made under the Patent Co-operation Treaty have been complied with, whether or not there was any requirement that they be complied with.

Applications for patents

Applications for the grant of patents under sections 14 and 15

16.—(1) A request for the grant of a patent shall be made on Patents Form 1/77.   **16.16**

(2) The specification contained in an application for a patent made under section 14 shall state the title of the invention and continue with the description and the claim or claims and drawings, if any, in that order.

(3) The title shall be short and indicate the matter to which the invention relates.

(4) The description shall include a list briefly describing the figures in the drawings, if any.

Micro-organisms

17. Schedule 2 shall have effect in relation to certain applications for   **16.17**
patents, and patents, for inventions which require for their performance the use of micro-organisms.

Drawings

16.18   **18.**—(1) Drawings forming part of an application for a patent made under section 14 shall be on sheets the usable surface area of which shall not exceed 26.2 cm by 17 cm. The sheets shall not contain frames round the usable or used surface. The minimum margins shall be as follows—

top	2.5 cm
left side	2.5 cm
right side	1.5 cm
bottom	1.0 cm

(2) Drawings shall be executed as follows—

(a) without colouring in durable, black, sufficiently dense and dark, uniformly thick and well-defined lines and strokes to permit satisfactory reproduction;

(b) cross-sections shall be indicated by hatching which does not impede the clear reading of the reference signs and leading lines;

(c) the scale of the drawings and the distinctness of their graphical execution shall be such that a photographic reproduction with a linear reduction in size to two-thirds would enable all details to be distinguished without difficulty. If, as an exception, the scale is given on a drawing, it shall be represented graphically;

(d) all numbers, letters, and reference signs, appearing on the drawings shall be simple and clear and brackets, circles and inverted commas shall not be used in association with numbers and letters;

(e) elements of the same figure shall be in proportion to each other, unless a difference in proportion is indispensable for the clarity of the figure;

(f) the height of the numbers and letters shall not be less than 0.32 cm and for the lettering of drawings, the Latin and, where customary, the Greek alphabets shall be used;

(g) the same sheet of drawings may contain several figures. Where figures drawn on two or more sheets are intended to form one whole figure, the figures on the several sheets shall be so arranged that the whole figure can be assembled without concealing any part of the partial figures. The different figures shall be arranged without wasting space, clearly separated from one another. The different figures shall be numbered consecutively in arabic numerals, independently of the numbering of the sheets;

(h) reference signs not mentioned in the description or claims shall not appear in the drawings, and vice versa. The same features, when denoted by reference signs, shall, throughout the application, be denoted by the same signs;

(i) the drawings shall not contain textual matter, except, when required for the understanding of the drawings, a single word or words such as "water," "steam," "open," "closed," "section on

AA,'' and, in the case of electric circuits and block schematic or flow sheet diagrams, a few short catchwords; and

(j) the sheets of the drawings shall be numbered in accordance with rule 20(9).

(3) Flow sheets and diagrams shall be considered to be drawings for the purposes of these Rules.

The abstract

19.—(1) The abstract shall commence with a title for the invention.   **16.19**

(2) The abstract shall contain a concise summary of the matter contained in the specification. The summary shall indicate the technical field to which the invention belongs and be drafted in a way which allows a clear understanding of the technical problem to which the invention relates, the gist of the solution to that problem through the invention and the principal use or uses of the invention. Where appropriate, the abstract shall also contain the chemical formula which, among those contained in the specification, best characterises the invention. It shall not contain statements on the alleged merits or value of the invention or on its speculative application.

(3) The abstract shall normally contain more than 150 words.

(4) If the specification contains any drawings, the applicant shall indicate on the abstract the figure or, exceptionally, the figures of the drawings which he suggests should accompany the abstract when published. The comptroller may decide to publish one or more other figures if he considers that they better characterise the invention. Each main feature mentioned in the abstract and illustrated by a drawing shall be followed by the reference sign used in that drawing.

(5) The abstract shall be so drafted that it constitutes an efficient instrument for the purposes of searching in the particular technical field, in particular by making it possible to assess whether there is a need to consult the specification itself.

Size and presentation of documents

20.—(1) All documents (including drawings) making up an applica-   **16.20** tion for a patent or replacing such documents shall be in the English language.

(2) The specification, abstract and any replacement sheet thereof shall be filed in duplicate.

(3) All documents referred to in paragraph (1) above shall be so presented as to permit of direct reproduction by photography, electrostatic processes, photo offset and micro-filming, in an unlimited number of copies. All sheets shall be free from cracks, creases and folds. Only

one side of the sheet shall be used, except in the case of a request for the grant of a patent.

(4) All documents referred to in paragraph (1) above shall be on A4 paper (29.7 cm × 21 cm) which shall be pliable, strong, white, smooth, matt and durable. Each sheet (other than drawings) shall be used with its short sides at the top and bottom (upright position).

(5) The request for the grant of a patent and the description, claims, drawings and abstract shall each commence on a new sheet. The sheets shall be connected in such a way that they can easily be turned over, separated and joined together again.

(6) Subject to rule 18(1), the minimum margins shall be as follows:

top	2.0 cm
left side	2.5 cm
right side	2.0 cm
bottom	2.0 cm

(7) The margins of the documents making up the application and of any replacement documents must be completely blank.

(8) In the application, except in the drawings—

(a) all sheets in the request shall be numbered consecutively; and

(b) all other sheets shall be numbered consecutively as a separate series,

and all such numbering shall be in arabic numerals placed at the top of the sheet, in the middle, but not in the top margin.

(9) All sheets of drawings contained in the application shall be numbered consecutively as a separate series. Such numbering shall be in arabic numerals placed at the top of the sheet, in the middle, but not in the top margin.

(10) Every document (other than drawings) referred to in paragraph (1) above shall be typed or printed in a dark, indelible colour in at least 1½ line spacing and in characters of which the capital letters are not less than 0.21 cm high:

Provided that Patents Form 1/77 may be completed in writing, and that graphic symbols and characters and chemical and mathematical formulae may be written or drawn, in a dark indelible colour.

(11) The request for the grant of a patent, the description, the claims and the abstract shall not contain drawings. The description, the claims and the abstract may contain chemical or mathematical formulae. The description and the abstract may contain tables. The claims may contain tables only if their subject-matter makes the use of tables desirable.

(12) In all documents referred to in paragraph (1) above units of weight and measures shall be expressed in terms of the metric system. If a different system is used they shall also be expressed in terms of the metric system. Temperatures shall be expressed in degrees Celsius. For the other physical values, the units recognised in international practice shall be used, for mathematical formulae the symbols in general use, and for chemical formulae the symbols, atomic weights and molecular formulae in general use shall be employed. In general, use should be

made of technical terms, signs and symbols generally accepted in the field in question.

(13) If a formula or symbol is used in the specification a copy thereof, prepared in the same manner as drawings, shall be furnished if the comptroller so directs.

(14) The terminology and the signs shall be consistent throughout the application.

(15) All documents referred to in paragraph (1) above shall be reasonably free from deletions and other alterations, overwritings and interlineations and shall, in any event, be legible.

Form of statements, counter-statements and evidence

21. Any statement, counter-statement or evidence filed shall, unless the comptroller otherwise directs, comply with the requirements of rule 20(1) and (4) and, except that both sides of the sheet may be used in the case of statutory declarations and affidavits, with the requirements of rule 20(3).

16.21

[Claims in different categories

22. *Without prejudice to the generality of section 14(5)(d), an application for a patent which includes,—*

(a) *in addition to an independent claim for a product, an independent claim for a process specially adapted for the manufacture of the product, and an independent claim for a use of the product;*

(b) *in addition to an independent claim for a process, an independent claim for an apparatus or means specifically designed for carrying out the process; or*

(c) *in addition to an independent claim for a product, an independent claim for a process specially adapted for the manufacture of the product, and an independent claim for an apparatus or means specifically designed for carrying out the process,*

shall be treated as relating to a group of inventions which are so linked as to form a single inventive concept.]

16.22

Unity of invention

22.—(1) Without prejudice to the generality of section 14(5)(*d*), where two or more inventions are claimed (whether in a single claim or in separate claims), and there exists between or among those inventions a technical relationship which involves one or more of the same or corresponding special technical features, then those

inventions shall be treated as being so linked as to form a single inventive concept for the purposes of the Act.

(2) In this rule, "special technical features" means those technical features which define a contribution which each of the claimed inventions, considered as a whole, makes over the prior art.

NOTE

Rule 22 substituted by The Patents (Amendment) Rules 1992, with effect from June 1, 1992 (S.I. 1992, No.1142).

Late filed drawings

16.23   23. The period prescribed for the purposes of section 15(2) and (3) shall be one month calculated from the date on which the comptroller sends out notification to the applicant that the drawing has been filed later than the date which is, by virtue of section 15(1), to be treated as the date of filing the application or, as the case may be, that it has not been filed.

New applications under section 15(4)

16.24   24.—(1) Subject to paragraph (2) below, a new application for a patent, which includes a request that it shall be treated as having as its date of filing the date of filing of an earlier application, may be filed in accordance with section 15(4) not later than the latest of—

(a) the beginning of the sixth month before the end of the period ascertained under rule 34 in relation to the earlier application as altered, if that be the case, under rule 100 or rule 110 ("the rule 34 period");

(b) where the earlier application is amended as provided by section 18(3) so as to comply with section 14(5)(d), the expiry of the period of two months beginning on the day that the amendment is filed; and

(c) where the first report of the examiner under section 18 is made under subsection (3), the expiry of the period specified for reply to that report:

Provided that, where the first report of the examiner under section 18 is made under subsection (4) and the comptroller notifies the applicant that the earlier application complies with the requirements of the Act and these Rules, notwithstanding the foregoing provisions of this paragraph but subject to paragraph (2) below, a new application may be filed not later than the expiry of the period of two months beginning on the day that the notification is sent.

(2) Where any of the following dates falls before the date ascertained under paragraph (1) above, a new application may only be filed before that date instead of the date so ascertained—

(a) the date when the earlier application is refused, is withdrawn, is treated has having been withdrawn or is taken to be withdrawn;

(b) the expiry of the rule 34 period ascertained in relation to the earlier application; and

(c) the date when a patent is granted on the earlier application.

(3) Where possible, the description and drawings of the earlier application and the new application shall respectively relate only to the matter for which protection is sought by that application. However, when it is necessary for an application to describe the matter for which protection is sought by another application, it shall include a reference by number to that other application and shall indicate the matter for which protection is claimed in the other application.

Periods prescribed under section 15(5)(a) and (b) and 17(1) for filing claims, abstract and request for preliminary examination and search

25.—(1) The period prescribed for the purposes of section 15(5)(a) shall be,— **16.25**

(a) if the application contains no declared priority date, the period of twelve months calculated from its date of filing; or

(b) if the application does contain a declared priority date, the last to expire of the period of twelve months calculated from the declared priority date and period of one month calculated from the date of filing the application.

(2) Subject to the provisions of rules 81(3), 82(3) and 85(7)(a), the period prescribed for the purposes of sections 15(5)(b) and 17(1) shall be,—

(a) if the application contains no declared priority date, the period of twelve months calculated from its date of filing; or

(b) if the application does contain a declared priority date, the period of twelve months calculated from the declared priority date.

(3) Where a new application is filed under section 8(3), 12(6), 15(4) or 37(4) after the end of the period prescribed in paragraph (1) or (2) above, as the case may be, the period prescribed for the purposes of sections 15(5) and 17(1) shall be the period which expires on the actual date of filing of the new application.

Extensions for new applications

26.—(1) Where a new application is filed under section 8(3), 12(6), **16.26** 15(4) or 37(4) after the period of sixteen months prescribed in either rule 6 or rule 15, then, subject to the following provisions of this rule,—

(a) the requirements of those rules shall be complied with at the time of filing the new application; and

(b) the requirement of paragraph 1(2)(a)(ii) and (3) of Schedule 2, in a case to which they apply, shall be complied with not later than the later of the time ascertained under the said paragraph 1(3) and the time of filing the new application.

(2) Where a new application is filed under any of those sections—

(a) within the period prescribed in paragraph (6) of rule 6 as modified, in the case of an international application, by rule 85(3), the requirement of that paragraph shall have effect as provided therein; or

(b) after that period, the requirements of that paragraph shall be complied with at the time of filing.

subject, in either case, to paragraph (3) below.

(3) Where a new application is filed under section 15(4) after—

(a) the period of sixteen months prescribed in rule 6(2) or rule 15(1); or

(b) the period prescribed in rule 6(6) as modified, in the case of an international application, by rule 85(3),

but within an extension of that period under rule 110(3) or (4) in respect of the earlier application, the requirements of rule 6(2) and (3), rule 6(6) or rule 15, as the case may be, shall be complied with before the end of the extended period.

Period for publication of application

16.27   27. The period prescribed for the purposes of section 16 shall be the period of eighteen months calculated from the declared priority date or, where there is no declared priority date, the date of filing the application.

Examination and search

Preliminary examination and search under section 17

16.28   28.—(1) A request under section 17(1)(a) for a preliminary examination and search shall be made on Patents Form 9/77.

(2) On a preliminary examination the examiner shall determine, not only whether the application ("the application in suit") complies with those requirements of the Act and these Rules which are designated by rule 31 as formal requirements for the purposes of the Act, but also whether the requirements of rules 6(1) and (2) and 15(1) and the provisions of section 15(3) have been complied with.

(3) The comptroller may, if he thinks fit, send to the applicant a copy

of any document (or any part thereof) referred to in the examiner's report under section 17(5).

Procedure where earlier application made

29. Where the preliminary examination under rule 28 reveals that an **16.29** earlier relevant application declared for the purposes of section 5 has been stated in the application in suit to have a date of filing more than 12 months before the date of filing of the application in suit, the Patent Office shall notify the applicant that the earlier relevant application will be disregarded unless, within one month, he supplies the Patent Office with a corrected date, being one which falls within those twelve months.

Address for service

[30. Every person concerned in any proceedings to which these Rules relate **16.30** *and every proprietor of a patent shall furnish to the comptroller an address for service in the United Kingdom; and that address may be treated for all purposes connected with such proceedings or patent (as appropriate) as the address of the person concerned in the proceedings or of the proprietor of the patent.]*
    30.—(1) There shall be furnished to the comptroller—
    (a) **by every applicant for the grant of a patent, an address for service in the United Kingdom for the purpose of his application, and**
    (b) **notwithstanding the provisions of paragraphs (2) to (4) below, by every person (including the applicant for, or the proprietor of, a patent, as the case may be) concerned in any proceedings to which any of these Rules relate, an address for service in the United Kingdom,**
and the address so furnished or, where another address (being an address in the United Kingdom) has been furnished in place thereof, that address shall be treated for the purposes of that application or those proceedings, as appropriate, as the address of that applicant or, as the case may be, of that person.
    (2) Upon the grant of an application for a patent (not being an application for a European patent (U.K.)), the applicant's address for service as shown in the register shall be treated as the address for service of the proprietor of the patent unless an alternative address is furnished.
    (3) As from publication of the mention of the grant of every European patent (U.K.) in the European Patent Bulletin, the address for service of the proprietor shall be the address for service notified to the comptroller by or on behalf of the proprietor, whether before or after the said mention of the grant, and in the absence of any such

notification the proprietor's address on the register shall be treated as the address for service.

(4) An address for service for an applicant for, or a proprietor of, a patent may be withdrawn by the applicant or the proprietor or the person providing the address for service, as the case may be, by notice to the comptroller; and upon such notification the comptroller may treat the address of the applicant or the proprietor previously notified to him, or the address shown in the register, as the address for service until such time as an alternative address is furnished.

NOTE

Rule 30 substituted by The Patents (Amendment) Rules 1993, with effect from November 1, 1993 (S.I. 1993, No.2423).

Formal requirements

16.31   **31.**—(1) The requirements of rules 16(1), 18(1) and (2) (other than those contained in paragraph (2)(*h*)), 20 (other than those contained in the last sentence of paragraph (11) and in paragraphs (12) and (14)) and 30**(1)(a)** shall be formal requirements for the purposes of the Act.

(2) Where the application is—

(a) an application for a European patent (U.K.); or

(b) an international application for a patent (U.K.)

which, by virtue of section 81 or 89, as the case may be, is to be treated as an application for a patent under the Act, the said requirements of rules 16(1), 18(1) and (2) and 20 shall be treated as having been complied with to the extent that the requirements of the corresponding provisions of the Implementing Regulations to the European Patent Convention or, as the case may be, of the Regulations made under the Patent Co-operation Treaty, have been fulfilled.

NOTE

Para. (1) amended by The Patents (Amendment) Rules 1993, with effect from November 1, 1993 (S.I. 1993, No.2423).

Searches under section 17(6) and (8)

16.32   **32.**—(1) Where an examiner conducts a search under section 17(6) in relation to the first only of two or more inventions specified in the claims of an application, the Patent Office shall notify the applicant of that fact.

(2) If the applicant desires a search to be conducted under section

17(6) in relation to a second or subsequent invention specified in the claims, he shall, before the expiry of the period specified for the making of observations on the report made under section 18(3), request the Patent Office on Patents Form 9/77 to conduct such a search and pay the search fee for each invention in respect of which the search is to be made.

(3) The fee for a supplementary search under section 17(8) shall be accompanied by Patents Form 9/77.

(4) The comptroller may, if he thinks fit, send to the applicant a copy of any document (or any part thereof) referred to in the examiner's report under section 17 pursuant to subsection (6) or (8) thereof.

Request for substantive examination under section 18

33.—(1) A request for a substantive examination of an application for **16.33** a patent shall be made on Patents Form 10/77.

(2) Subject to the provisions of rules 83(1), 85(7)(*b*) [*and paragraphs (3) and (4) below*] **and paragraphs (3) and (5) below** the request shall be made and the fee for the examination paid within six months of the date of publication of the application in accordance with section 16.

(3) Where an application is subject to directions under section 22(1) or (2), the request shall be made and the fee paid within two years of the declared priority date or, where there is no declared priority date, from the date of filing the application except in the case of a new application made under section 8(3), 12(6) or 15(4) after the expiry of the said two years, when the request shall be made and the fee paid at the time of filing the new application.

(4) When he gives the applicant the opportunity under section 18(3) to make observations on the examiner's report under subsection (2) of that section, the comptroller may, if he thinks fit, send to the applicant a copy of any document (or part thereof) referred to in the report.

(5) Where a new application is filed under section 8(3), 12(6), 15(4) or 37(4) then,—
   (a) if the new application is filed within two years calculated from the declared priority date or, where there is no declared priority date, from the date treated as its date of filing, the request shall be made and the fee for the examination paid within those two years; and
   (b) if the new application is filed after the expiration of those two years, the request shall be made and the fee for the examination paid at the time of filing the new application.

NOTE

Para. (2) amended by The Patents (Amendment) Rules 1992, with effect from June 1, 1992 (S.I. 1992, No.1142).

Period for putting application in order

16.34   34.—[(1) *Subject to the provisions of paragraph (2) below and of rule 83(3), for the purposes of sections 18(4) and 20(1), the period within which an application for a patent shall comply with the Act and these Rules,—*

(a) *subject to the following provisions of this paragraph, shall be the period of four years and six months calculated from its declared priority date or, where there is no declared priority date, from the date of filing of the application; and*

(b) *in the case of an application under section 8(3), 12(6) or 37(4), shall be—*

(i) *the period of four years and six months calculated from the declared priority date for the earlier application or, where there is no such declared priority date, the date of filing of the earlier application; or*

(ii) *the period of 18 months calculated from the actual date of filing of the application,*

whichever expires the later.]

(1) Subject to the provisions of paragraph (2) below and of rule 83(3), for the purposes of sections 18(4) and 20(1), the period within which an application for a patent shall comply with the Act and these Rules—

(a) subject to sub-paragraphs (b) and (c) hereof and paragraph (1A) below, shall be—

(i) the period of four years and six months calculated from its declared priority date or, where there is no declared priority date, from the date of filing of the application; or

(ii) the period of twelve months calculated from the date the first report under section 18 in respect of that application is sent to the applicant,

whichever expires the later;

(b) in the case of a new application for a patent arising from and made in accordance with an order of the comptroller under section 8(3), 12(6) or 37(4), shall be—

(i) the period of four years and six months calculated from the declared priority date for the earlier application or, where there is no such declared priority date, the date of filing of the earlier application; or

(ii) the period of eighteen months calculated from the actual date of filing of the application,

whichever expires the later;

(c) subject to paragraph (1A) below, in the case of a new application under section 15(4), shall be—

(i) the period of four years and six months calculated from its declared priority date or, where there is no declared priority date, from the date of filing of the earlier application; or

(ii) the period of twelve months calculated from the date the first report under section 18 in respect of the earlier application is sent to the applicant, whichever expires the later.

(1A) Where the first report under section 18 is not sent to the applicant before the expiry of the period prescribed by sub-paragraphs (a)(i) and (c)(i) of paragraph (1) above, those periods shall be extended to the date that report is sent to the applicant and the periods specified by sub-paragraphs (a)(ii) and (c)(ii) of paragraph (1) shall then apply.

(2) In a case where,—

(a) before or after these Rules come into force, a third party makes observations under section 21 on an application;

(b) the examiner, for the first time in a report under section 18(3), relies upon the substance of those observations to report that the patentability requirements of the Act are not met; and

(c) following that report, and within the last three months of the period ascertained under paragraph (1) above (including any alteration thereof under rule 100 or rule 110 or an alteration thereof previously made under this paragraph) but after these Rules come into force, the comptroller gives the applicant the opportunity under section 18(3) to make observations on the report and to amend the application,

the period within which an application for a patent shall comply with the Act and these Rules shall expire at the end of the period of three months beginning on the date when the comptroller sends notification to the applicant of that opportunity.

NOTE

Paras. (1) and (1A) substituted by The Patents (Amendment) Rules 1992, with effect from June 1, 1992 (S.I. 1992, No.1142).

Amendment of request for grant

35. Subject to rule 45(3), an application for amendment of the request **16.35** for the grant of a patent shall be made on Patents Form 11/77 and shall be accompanied by a document clearly identifying the proposed amendment.

Amendment of application before grant

36.—(1) Unless the comptroller so requires, the applicant may not **16.36** amend the description, claims and drawings contained in his application before the comptroller sends to the applicant the examiner's report under section 17(5).

(2) An applicant may of his own volition amend his application in accordance with the following provisions of this rule but not otherwise.

(3) After the comptroller has sent to the applicant the examiner's report under section 17(5) and before he sends to the applicant the first report of the examiner under section 18, the applicant may of his own volition amend the description, claims and drawings contained in his application.

(4) After the applicant has been sent the first report of the examiner under section 18, in addition to his right under section 18(3) to amend the application so as to comply with the requirements of the Act and these Rules, the applicant may of his own volition amend once the description, claims or drawings of the application: provided that, if the examiner's first report is made under section 18(3), the amendment shall be filed at the same time as the applicant replies to that report or, if the examiner's first report is made under section 18(4), the amendment shall be filed within two months of that report being sent to the applicant.

(5) Any further amendment to the description, claims or drawings which the applicant desires to make of his own volition may only be made with the consent of the comptroller following the filing of Patents Form 11/77 accompanied by a document clearly identifying the proposed amendment.

Observations on patentability under section 21

16.37   37.—(1) Subject to paragraph (2) below, the comptroller shall send to the applicant a copy of—

    (a) any document containing observations which he receives under section 21 in connection with the application; and

    (b) any document referred to in any such observations being a document which he receives from the person making them.

(2) Nothing in paragraph (1) above shall impose any duty on the comptroller in relation to any document—

    (a) a copy of which it appears to the comptroller is readily available for retention by the applicant; or

    (b) which in his opinion is not suitable for photocopying, whether on account of size or for any other reason.

(3) If the period ascertained under rule 34 (as altered, if that be the case, under rule 100 or rule 110) has not expired and the comptroller has not sent to the applicant notice in accordance with section 18(4) that the application complies with the requirements of the Act and these Rules, the observations shall be referred to the examiner conducting a substantive examination of the application under section 18; and the examiner shall consider and comment upon them as he thinks fit in his report under that section.

Grant, amendment and continuation of patent

Certificates of grant

38. A certificate that a patent has been granted shall be in the form set out in Schedule 3. **16.38**

Renewal of patents

39.—(1) If, except in the case of a European patent (U.K.), it is desired **16.39** to keep a patent in force for a further year after the expiration of the fourth or any succeeding year from the date of filing an application for that patent as determined in accordance with section 15, Patents Form 12/77, in respect of the next succeeding year, accompanied by the prescribed renewal fee for that year, shall be filed in the three months ending with the fourth or, as the case may be, succeeding anniversary of the date of filing:

Provided that, where a patent is granted in the three months ending with the fourth of any succeeding anniversary as so determined or at any time thereafter, Patents Form 12/77, accompanied by the prescribed renewal fee, in respect of the fifth or succeeding year may be filed not more than three months before the expiration of the fourth or relevant succeeding year but before the expiration of three months from the date on which the patent is granted.

(2) If it is desired, at the expiration of the fourth or any succeeding year from the date of filing an application for a European patent (U.K.), as determined in accordance with Article 80 of the European Patent Convention, and provided that mention of the grant of the patent is, or has been, published in the European Patent Bulletin, to keep the patent in force, Patents Form 12/77, accompanied by the prescribed renewal fee, shall be filed in the three months ending with the fourth or, as the case may be, succeeding anniversary of the date of filing as so determined:

Provided that, where any renewal fee is due on, or within the period of three months after, the date of publication in the European Patent Bulletin of the mention of the grant of the patent, being a date on or after that on which these Rules come into force, that renewal fee may be paid within those three months; but, where the date of such publication is before that on which these Rules come into force, the proviso to rule 39(2) of the Patents Rules 1982 shall continue to apply.

(3) On receipt of the prescribed renewal fee accompanied by Patents

Form 12/77 duly completed, the comptroller shall (if the patent has been granted) issue a certificate of payment on the appropriate portion of that form.

(4) Where the period for payment of a renewal fee pursuant to paragraph (1) or (2) above has expired, the comptroller shall, not later than six weeks after the last date for payment under that paragraph and if the fee still remains unpaid, send to the proprietor of the patent a notice reminding him that payment is overdue and of the consequences of non-payment.

(5) The comptroller shall send a notice under paragraph (4) above to—

(a) the address in the United Kingdom specified by the proprietor on payment of the last renewal fee; or

(b) where another address in the United Kingdom has been notified to him for that purpose by the proprietor since the last renewal, that address,

and, in any other case, the address for service entered in the register.

(6) A request for extending the period for payment of a renewal fee shall be made on Patents Form 12/77 and shall be accompanied by the prescribed renewal fee and the prescribed additional fee for late payment.

Amendment of specification after grant

16.40 40.—(1) An application to the comptroller for leave to amend the specification of a patent shall be made on Patents Form 14/77 and shall be advertised by publication of the application and the nature of the proposed amendment in the Journal and in such other manner, if any, as the comptroller may direct.

(2) Any person wishing to oppose the application to amend shall, within two months from the date of the advertisement in the Journal, give notice to the comptroller on Patents Form 15/77.

(3) Such notice shall be accompanied by a copy thereof and be supported by a statement in duplicate setting out fully the facts upon which the opponent relies and the relief which he seeks. The comptroller shall send a copy of the notice and of the statement to the applicant.

(4) Within the period of two months beginning on the date when such copies are sent to him, the applicant shall, if he wishes to continue with the application, file a counter-statement in duplicate setting out fully the grounds upon which the opposition is resisted; and the comptroller shall send a copy of the counter-statement to the opponent.

(5) The comptroller may give such directions as he may think fit with regard to the subsequent procedure.

(6) An application under this rule shall be accompanied by—

(a) a copy of the specification as published on which the proposed amendment is clearly identified;
(b) if the specification as published is not in English, a document containing a translation into English of the part of the specification proposed to be amended verified to the satisfaction of the comptroller as corresponding to the original text; and
(c) in the case of an application for amendment of a European patent (U.K.), a copy of the specification for that patent is published,
and, if the specification as published is not in English, the applicant shall, if the comptroller so requests, supply a translation thereof into English verified to his satisfaction as corresponding to the original text.

(7) Where leave to amend a specification is given, the applicant shall, if the comptroller so requires, and within a time to be fixed by him, file a new specification as amended, which shall be prepared in accordance with rules 16, 18 and 20.

Restoration of lapsed patents under section 28

41.—(1) An application under section 28 for the restoration of a **16.41** patent, including an application for restoration of a patent which lapsed not more than 12 months before these Rules came into force (being in any case a patent which has lapsed by reason of a failure to pay any renewal fee),—
(a) may be made at any time within the period of 19 months beginning on the day on which it ceased to have effect; and
(b) shall be made on Patents Form 16/77 supported by evidence of the statements made in it;
and the comptroller shall publish in the Journal notice of the making of the application.

(2) If, upon consideration of the evidence, the comptroller is not satisfied that a case for an order under section 28 has been made out, he shall notify the applicant accordingly and, unless within one month the applicant requests to be heard in the matter, the comptroller shall refuse the application.

(3) If the applicant requests a hearing within the time allowed, the comptroller shall, after giving the applicant an opportunity of being heard, determine whether the application shall be allowed or refused.

(4) If the comptroller decides to allow the application, he shall notify the applicant accordingly and require him, within two months after the notification is sent to him, to file Patents Form 17/77, together with Patents Form 12/77, duly completed, and the amount of any unpaid renewal fee, upon receipt of which the comptroller shall order the restoration of the patent and advertise the fact in the Journal:

Provided that, in a case where a notification under this paragraph is sent to the applicant before these Rules come into force, this paragraph shall have effect as if the words "within two months after the notification is sent to him" were omitted.

Notification of lapsed patent

16.42   42. Where a patent has ceased to have effect because a renewal fee has not been paid within the period prescribed in rule 39(1) or (2) and the extended period specified in section 25(4) has expired without the renewal fee and prescribed additional fee having been paid, the comptroller shall, within six weeks after the expiration of the extended period, notify the proprietor of the patent of the fact and draw his attention to the provisions of section 28.

Surrender of patents

16.43   43.—(1) A notice of an offer by a proprietor of a patent under section 29 to surrender his patent shall be given on Patents Form 18/77 and shall be advertised by the comptroller in the Journal.

(2) At any time within two months from the advertisement any person may give notice of opposition to the surrender to the comptroller on Patents Form 19/77.

(3) Such notice shall be accompanied by a copy thereof and be supported by a statement in duplicate setting out fully the facts upon which the opponent relies and the relief which he seeks. The comptroller shall send a copy of the notice and of the statement to the proprietor of the patent.

(4) Within the period of two months beginning on the date when such copies are sent to him, the proprietor of the patent shall, if he wishes to continue with the surrender, file a counter-statement in duplicate setting out fully the grounds upon which the opposition is resisted; and the comptroller shall send a copy of the counter-statement to the opponent.

(5) The comptroller may give such directions as he may think fit with regard to the subsequent procedure.

Registration

Entries in the register

16.44   44.—(1) No entry shall be made in the register in respect of any application for a patent before the application has been published in accordance with section 16.

(2) Upon such publication, the comptroller shall cause to be entered in the register—

(a) the name and address of the applicant or applicants;

(b) the name and address of the person or persons stated by the applicant or applicants to be believed to be the inventor or inventors;

(c) the title of the invention;

(d) the date of filing and the file number of the application for the patent;

(e) the date of filing and the file number of any application declared for the purposes of section 5(2) or 127(4) and the country in or for which the application was made;

(f) the date on which the application was published; and

(g) the address for service of the applicant or applicants.

(3) The comptroller shall also cause to be entered in the register—

(a) the date of filing of the request for substantive examination;

(b) the date on which the application is withdrawn, taken to be withdrawn, treated as having been withdrawn, refused or treated as having been refused;

(c) the date on which the patent is granted;

(d) the name and address of the person or persons to whom the patent is granted if different to the entries made in accordance with paragraph (2)(a) above;

(e) the address for service if different to the entry made in accordance with paragraph (2)(g) above; and

(f) notice of any transaction, instrument or event referred to in section 33(3).

(4) The comptroller may at any time enter in the register such other particulars as he may think fit.

Alteration of name or address

45.—(1) A request by any person, upon the alteration of his name, for that alteration to be entered in the register or on any application or other document filed at the Patent Office shall be made on Patents Form 20/77.   **16.45**

(2) Before acting on a request to alter a name, the comptroller may require such proof of the alteration as he thinks fit.

(3) A request by any person for the alteration or correction of his address or address for service entered in the register or on any application or other document filed at the Patent Office shall, if not made on a form filed under any provision of these Rules, be made in writing and shall identify any relevant application or patent.

(4) If the comptroller is satisfied that a request to alter a name or to alter or correct an address or address for service may be allowed, he

shall cause the register, application or other document to be altered accordingly.

Registrations under section 33

16.46   46.—(1) An application to register, or to give notice to the comptroller of, any transaction, instrument or event to which section 33 applies shall be made on Patents Form 21/77.

(2) Unless the comptroller otherwise directs, an application under paragraph (1) above shall be accompanied by—
   (a) a certified copy of any document which establishes the transaction, instrument or event; or
   (b) a certified copy of such extracts from such document as suffice to establish the transaction, instrument or event.

Request for correction of error

16.47   47.—(1) Without prejudice to rule 45(3), a request for the correction of an error in the register or in any document filed at the Patent Office in connection with registration shall be made on Patents Form 22/77; and the correction shall be clearly identified on a document annexed to the form or, if not, on the form itself.

(2) The comptroller may call for such written explanation of the reasons for the request or evidence in support of it as he may require in order to satisfy himself that there is an error and, upon being so satisfied, shall make such correction as may be agreed between the proprietor of the patent or applicant and the comptroller.

16.48   ### Request as to payment of renewal fee

48. A request for information about the date of payment of any renewal fee shall be made on Patents Form 23/77 and shall be accompanied by [*the appropriate fee*] **the prescribed fee, if any.**

NOTE

Amended by The Patents (Amendment) Rules 1992, with effect from June 1, 1992 (S.I. 1992, No.1142).

Inspection of register

49.—(1) The register or entries or reproductions of entries in it shall be   **16.49**
made available for inspection by the public on payment of the
prescribed fee, **if any**, between the hours of 10.00 am and 4.00 pm on
weekdays, other than Saturdays and days which are specified as
excluded days for the purposes of section 120.
(2) A request to be allowed to inspect the register shall be made on
Patents Form 23/77 and shall be accompanied by [*the appropriate fee*] **the
prescribed fee, if any.**

NOTE

Paras. (1) and (2) amended by The Patents (Amendment) Rules 1992, with effect from
June 1, 1992 (S.I. 1992, No.1142).

Advertisements in relation to register

50. The comptroller may arrange for the publication and advertise-   **16.50**
ment of such things done under the Act or these Rules in relation to the
register as he may think fit.

Entries relating to sections 8(1), 12(1) and 37(1)

51. On the reference to the comptroller of a question under section   **16.51**
8(1), 12(1) or 37(1), he shall, subject to rule 44(1), cause an entry to be
made in the register of the fact and of such other information relating to
the reference as he may think fit.

Certificates and copies supplied by comptroller

52.—(1) Upon request made on Patents Form 24/77 and payment of   **16.52**
the appropriate fee, but subject to paragraph (3) below, the comptroller
shall supply—
  (a) a certified copy or certified extract falling within section 32(11);
  (b) a copy of an entry in or an extract from the register or a copy of or
       an extract from anything referred to in section 32(11)(b), certified
       by the impression of a rubber stamp;
  (c) a certificate for the purposes of section 32(10).
(2) Upon request made on Patents Form 23/77 and payment of [*the
appropriate fee*] **the prescribed fee, if any,** but subject to paragraph (3)
below, the comptroller shall supply an uncertified copy of an entry in or

an uncertified extract from the register or an uncertified copy of or an uncertified extract from anything referred to in section 32(11)(b).

(3) The restrictions on making documents available for inspection contained in rule 93(4) shall apply equally to the supply by the comptroller under this rule of copies of or extracts from such documents or requests as are referred to in rule 93(4); and nothing in this rule shall be construed as imposing upon the comptroller the duty of supplying copies of or extracts from any document or file of a description referred to in rule 93(5).

NOTE

Para. (2) amended by The Patents (Amendment) Rules 1992, with effect from June 1, 1992 (S.I. 1992, No.1142).

Order or direction by court

16.53   53. Where any order or direction has been made or given by the court—
   (a) transferring a patent or application or any right in or under it to any person;
   (b) that an application should proceed in the name of any person;
   (c) allowing the proprietor of a patent to amend the specification; or
   (d) revoking a patent;
the person in whose favour the order is made or the direction is given—
      (i) shall file Patents Form 25/77 accompanied by an office copy of the order or direction; and
      (ii) if the comptroller so requires and before a time fixed by him, shall file a specification as amended (prepared in accordance with rules 16, 18 and 20),
and thereupon the specification shall be amended or the register rectified or altered, as the case may require.

Entitlement to patent

Reference of question to the comptroller under section 37(1)

16.54   54.—(1) A reference under section 37(1) shall be made on Patents Form 2/77 and shall be accompanied by a copy thereof and a statement in duplicate setting out fully the nature of the question, the facts upon which the person making the reference relies and the order which he is seeking.

(2) The comptroller shall send a copy of the reference and statement to every person who is not a party to the reference being—

(a) a person who is shown on the register as having any right in or under the patent; or

(b) a person who is alleged in the reference to be entitled to a right in or under the patent.

(3) If any person who is sent a copy of the reference and statement under paragraph (2) above wishes to oppose the making of the order sought ("the opponent"), he shall, within the period of two months beginning on the date when such copies are sent to him, file in duplicate a counter-statement setting out fully the grounds of his opposition and the comptroller shall send a copy of the counter-statement to the person making the reference and to those recipients of the copy of the reference and statement who are not party to the counter-statement.

(4) The person making the reference or any such recipient may, within the period of two months beginning on the date when the copy of the counter-statement is sent to him, file evidence in support of his case and shall send a copy of the evidence,—

(a) in any case, to the opponent; and

(b) in the case of evidence filed by such a recipient, to the person making the reference.

(5) Within the period of two months after the copy of such evidence is sent to him or, if no such evidence is filed, within two months of the expiration of the time within which it might have been filed, the opponent may file evidence in support of his case and shall send a copy of that evidence to the person making the reference and to those recipients; and within the period of two months after the copy of the opponent's evidence is sent to him, that person or any of those recipients may file further evidence confined to matters strictly in reply and shall send a copy of it to the persons mentioned in sub-paragraph (a) and (b) of paragraph (4) above.

(6) No further evidence shall be filed by any party except by leave or direction of the comptroller.

(7) The comptroller may give such directions as he may think fit with regard to the subsequent procedure.

Applications under section 37(3)

55.—(1) An application under section 37(3) for authority to do anything on behalf of a person to whom directions have been given under section 37(2)(d) shall be made on Patents Form 3/77 and shall be accompanied by a copy thereof and a statement in duplicate setting out fully the facts upon which the applicant relies and the nature of the authorisation sought. **16.55**

(2) The comptroller shall send a copy of the application and statement to the person alleged to have failed to comply with the directions.

(3) The comptroller may give such directions as he may think fit with regard to the subsequent procedure.

Time limit for new application

16.56   56. Where the comptroller orders that a new application may be made under section 37(4), it shall be made within three months calculated from the day on which the time for appealing from that order expires without an appeal being brought or, where an appeal is brought, from the day on which it is finally disposed of.

Request under section 38(3)

16.57   57.—(1) Where an order is made under section 37 that a patent shall be transferred to one or more persons none of whom was an old proprietor of it or that a person other than an old proprietor may make a new application for a patent, a request under section 38(3) for the grant of licence to continue working or, as the case may be, to work the invention shall, in the case of any of the old proprietors, be made within two months, and in the case of a licensee, four months, of his being notified by the comptroller of the making of the order.

(2) Where such an order is made, the comptroller shall notify the old proprietor or proprietors and their licensees of whom he is aware, of the making of the order.

Reference to comptroller under section 38(5)

16.58   58.—(1) Where a question is referred to the comptroller under section 38(5) as to whether any person is entitled to be granted a licence or whether the period or terms of a licence are reasonable, the reference shall be made on Patents Form 5/77 and shall be accompanied by a copy thereof and a statement in duplicate setting out fully the facts upon which the person making the reference relies and the terms of the licence which he is prepared to accept or grant.

(2) The comptroller shall send a copy of the reference and statement to the new proprietor or proprietors and every person claiming to be entitled to be granted a licence, in either case not being the person who makes the reference, and if any recipient does not agree to grant or accept a licence for such period and upon such terms, he shall, within the period of two months beginning on the date when such copies are sent to him, file a counter-statement in duplicate setting out fully the ground of his objection and the comptroller shall send a copy of the counter-statement to the person making the reference.

(3) The comptroller may give such directions as he may think fit with regard to the subsequent procedure.

Employees inventions

Application under section 40 for compensation

59.—(1) An application to the comptroller under section 40 for an **16.59** award of compensation shall be made on Patents Form 26/77 and shall be accompanied by a copy thereof and a statement in duplicate setting out fully the facts relied upon.

(2) The prescribed period for the purposes of section 40(1) and (2) shall, in relation to proceedings before the comptroller, be that period which begins when the relevant patent is granted and which expires one year after it has ceased to have effect:

Provided that, where a patent has ceased to have effect by reason of a failure to pay any renewal fee within the period prescribed for the payment thereof and an application for restoration is made to the comptroller under section 28, the said period shall,—

(a) if restoration is ordered, continue as if the patent has remained continuously in effect; or

(b) if restoration is refused, be treated as expiring one year after the patent ceased to have effect or six months after the refusal, whichever is the later.

(3) The comptroller shall send a copy of the application and statement to the employer who, if he wishes to contest the application, shall within the period of two months beginning on the date when such copies are sent to him, file a counter-statement in duplicate setting out fully the grounds on which he disputes the employee's right to the award sought, and the comptroller shall send a copy of the counter-statement to the employee.

(4) The employee may, within the period of two months beginning on the date when the copy of the counter-statement is sent to him, file evidence in support of his case and shall send a copy of the evidence to the employer.

(5) Within the period of two months beginning on the date when the copy of the employee's evidence is sent to him or, if the employee does not file any evidence, within two months of the expiration of the time within which the employee's evidence might have been filed, the employer may file evidence in support of his case and shall send a copy of the evidence to the employee; and within the period of two months beginning on the date when the copy of the employer's evidence is sent to him, the employee may file evidence confined to matters strictly in reply and shall send a copy of that evidence to the employer.

(6) No further evidence shall be filed by either party except by leave or direction of the comptroller.

(7) The comptroller may give such directions as he may think fit with regard to the subsequent procedure.

Application under section 41(8) to vary etc. awards of compensation

16.60   **60.**—(1) Where an award of compensation has been made to an employee under section 40(1) or (2) an application under section 41(8) to vary, discharge, suspend or revive any provision of the order shall be made on Patents Form 27/77 and shall be accompanied by a copy thereof and a statement in duplicate setting out fully the facts relied upon and the relief which is sought.

(2) Thereafter the provisions of rule 59(3) to (7) shall apply to an application made under section 41(8) by an employee as they apply to an application referred to in that rule and to an application made under section 41(8) by an employer as if references in those paragraphs to the employee were references to the employer and references to the employer were references to the employee.

Licences of right

Application under section 46(1) for entry in the register

16.61   **61.**—(1) An application under section 46(1) shall be made on Patents Form 28/77.

(2) Every entry made in the register consequent upon such an application shall be published in the Journal and in such other manner (if any) as the comptroller thinks necessary.

Application under section 46(3) to settle licences of right

16.62   **62.**—(1) An application under section 46(3)(a) or (b) (made on or after the date on which these Rules come into force) shall be made on Patents Form 29/77 which shall be filed in duplicate together with,—

(a) in the case of an application by the proprietor of the patent, two copies of a draft of the licence he proposes and of a statement of the facts he relies on; and

(b) in the case of an application by any other person, two copies of a draft of the licence he seeks.

(2) The comptroller shall,—

(a) in the case of an application by the proprietor, send a copy of Patents Form 29/77 and a copy of the documents filed under sub-paragraph (a) of paragraph (1) above to the person to whom the proprietor proposes to grant the licence; and

(b) in the case of an application by any other person, send a copy of Patents Form 29/77 and a copy of the documents filed under sub-paragraph (b) of that paragraph to the proprietor.

(3) Within the period of two months beginning on the date when the documents are sent to him under paragraph (2) above,—

(a) in the case of an application by the proprietor, the person referred to in paragraph (2)(a) above may file a counter-statement setting out fully the grounds of his objection; and

(b) in the case of an application by any other person, the proprietor may file a statement setting out fully the grounds of his objection, and, if he does so, at the same time shall send a copy of the statement or counter-statement, as the case may be, to the other party.

(4) Within the period of two months beginning on the date when a statement under paragraph (3)(b) above is sent to him, the person therein referred to may file a counter-statement; and, if he does so, he shall at the same time send a copy of the counter-statement to the proprietor.

(5) No further statement or counter-statement shall be served by either party without the leave or direction of the comptroller.

(6) The comptroller may give such directions as he may think fit with regard to the subsequent procedure.

(7) Notwithstanding its repeal by rule 123(3), rule 63 of the Patents Rules 1982 shall continue to apply to an application made under it before these Rules come into force.

Application by proprietor under section 47(1) for cancellation of entry

63. An application under section 47(1) shall be made on Patents Form 30/77 and shall be accompanied by Patents Form 12/77 and fees to the amount of the balance of all renewal fees which would have been payable if the entry had not been made.   **16.63**

Application under section 47(3)

64.—(1) An application under section 47(3) shall be made on Patents Form 31/77 within two months after the making of the relevant entry and shall be accompanied by a copy of the application supported by a statement in duplicate setting out fully the nature of the claimant's interest and the facts upon which he relies.   **16.64**

(2) The comptroller shall send a copy of the application and statement to the proprietor of the patent.

Procedure on receipt of application made under section 47

16.65   **65.**—(1) Every application under section 47(1) or (3) shall be advertised in the Journal and the period within which notice of opposition to the cancellation of an entry may be given under section 47(6) shall be two months after the advertisement.

(2) Such notice shall be given on Patents Form 32/77 and shall be accompanied by a copy thereof and supported by a statement in duplicate setting out fully the facts upon which the opponent relies.

(3) The comptroller shall send a copy of the notice and statement to the applicant for cancellation of the entry who, if he desires to proceed with the application, shall, within the period of two months beginning on the date when such copies are sent to him, file a counter-statement in duplicate setting out fully the grounds on which the opposition is contested and the comptroller shall send a copy of the counter-statement to the opponent.

(4) The comptroller may give such directions as he may think fit with regard to the subsequent procedure.

Procedure after cancellation of entry pursuant to section 47(3)

16.66   **66.** Where the comptroller cancels an entry in the register pursuant to section 47(3), he shall inform the proprietor of the patent who shall, within such period as the comptroller specifies, file Patents Form 12/77, accompanied by fees to the amount of the balance of all renewal fees which would have been payable if the entry had not been made.

Declaration under paragraph 4A of Schedule 1 to the Act

16.67   **67.**—(1) A declaration under paragraph 4A of Schedule 1 to the Act shall be made on Patents Form 58/77.

(2) The comptroller shall cause to be entered in the register notice of any declaration filed under the said paragraph 4A and the entry in the register shall be published in the Journal and in such other manner (if any) as the comptroller thinks necessary.

Compulsory licences

Application under section 48(1) for compulsory licence

16.68   **68.** An application under section 48(1) shall be made on Patents Form 33/77 and shall be accompanied by a statement in duplicate of the facts upon which the applicant relies and evidence in duplicate verifying the statement.

Application by Crown under section 51

69. An application under section 51(1) for an order or entry under section 51(3) shall be made on Patents Form 34/77 and shall be accompanied by a statement of the facts upon which the applicant relies and evidence verifying the statement.

16.69

Procedure on receipt of application under section 48 or 51

70.—(1) If upon consideration of the evidence submitted with Patents Form 33/77 or 34/77, the comptroller is not satisfied that a prima facie case has been made out for the making of an order or entry, he shall notify the applicant accordingly, and unless, within one month of such notification, the application requests to be heard in the matter, the comptroller shall refuse the application.

16.70

(2) Where the applicant requests a hearing within the time allowed, the comptroller, after giving the applicant an opportunity of being heard, shall determine whether the application may proceed or whether it shall be refused.

(3) If upon consideration of the evidence the comptroller is satisfied that a prima facie case has been made out for the making of the order or entry, or if, after hearing the applicant, he so determines, he shall direct that the application shall be advertised in the Journal and shall send a copy of the application, the statement and the evidence filed in support thereof to the proprietor of the patent and any other person shown on the register as having any right in or under the patent.

Opposition under section 52(1)

71.—(1) The time within which notice of opposition under section 52(1) may be given shall be two months after the advertisement of the application in accordance with rule 70.

16.71

(2) Such notice shall be given on Patents Form 35/77 and shall be accompanied by a copy thereof and supported by a statement in duplicate setting out fully the facts upon which the opponent relies and evidence in duplicate verifying the statement.

(3) The comptroller shall send a copy of the notice, the statement and the evidence to the applicant who, if he desires to proceed with the application, shall within the period of two months beginning on the date when such copies are sent to him, file evidence in duplicate confined to

matters strictly in reply and the comptroller shall send a copy thereof to the opponent.

(4) No further evidence shall be filed by either party except by leave or direction of the comptroller.

(5) The comptroller may give such directions as he may think fit with regard to the subsequent procedure.

Infringement proceedings before comptroller

Procedure on reference to comptroller under section 61(3)

16.72   72.—(1) Where a reference is made to the comptroller under section 61(3), the parties thereto shall make it on Patents Form 36/77, accompanied by a joint statement giving full particulars of the matters which are in dispute and of those on which they are in agreement.

(2) The procedure set out in this rule shall apply unless the only matter stated in the reference to be in dispute is the validity of any patent or part of a patent.

(3) The party to the dispute who is the proprietor of the patent or an exclusive licensee of the patent (such party being referred to in this and the next following rule as the plaintiff) shall within fourteen days of making the reference file a statement in duplicate giving full particulars of his case on the matters in dispute.

(4) The comptroller shall send a copy of the plaintiff's statement to the other party to the dispute (referred to in this and the next following rule as the defendant), who shall, within the period of two months beginning on the date when such copy is sent to him, file a counter-statement in duplicate setting out fully the grounds on which he contests the plaintiff's case and the comptroller shall send a copy of the counter-statement to the plaintiff.

(5) If the defendant alleges in his counter-statement that the patent or any part of it alleged by the plaintiff to have been infringed is not valid, the plaintiff shall, within the period of two months beginning on the date when the counter-statement is sent to him, file a further statement in duplicate setting out fully the grounds on which he contests the defendant's allegation; and the comptroller shall send a copy of the further statement to the defendant.

(6) Subject to such directions as the comptroller may give, the plaintiff may, within the period of two months beginning on the date when the counter-statement is sent to him, or, if he has filed a further statement under paragraph (5) above, within the period of two months thereof, file evidence in support of his case and shall send a copy thereof direct to the defendant.

(7) Within the period of two months beginning on the date when the copy of the plaintiff's evidence is sent to him or, if the plaintiff does not

file any evidence, within two months of the expiration of the time within which such evidence might have been filed, the defendant may file evidence in support of his case and shall send a copy of it to the plaintiff; and, within the period of two months beginning on the date when the copy of the defendant's evidence is sent to him, the plaintiff may file further evidence confined to matters strictly in reply and shall send a copy of it direct to the defendant.

(8) No further evidence shall be filed by either party except by leave or direction of the comptroller.

(9) The comptroller may give such directions as he may think fit with regard to the subsequent procedure.

Procedure where validity of patent in dispute

73.—(1) Where the only matter stated in the reference made under   **16.73** section 61(3) to be in dispute is the validity of any patent or part of a patent, the procedure set out in this rule shall apply.

(2) The defendant shall, within fourteen days of making the reference, file a statement in duplicate giving full particulars of the grounds on which he alleges that the patent or part of the patent is invalid.

(3) The comptroller shall send a copy of the defendant's statement to the plaintiff, who shall, within the period of two months beginning on the date when the copy is sent to him, file a counter-statement in duplicate giving full particulars of the grounds on which he contests the defendant's allegations, and the comptroller shall send a copy of it to the defendant.

(4) Subject to such directions as the comptroller may think fit to give, the defendant may, within the period of two months beginning on the date when the copy of the plaintiff's counter-statement is sent to him, file evidence in support of his case, and shall send a copy of it to the plaintiff.

(5) Within the period of two months beginning on the date when the copy of the defendant's evidence is sent to him or, if the defendant does not file any evidence within two months of the expiration of the time within which such evidence might have been filed, the plaintiff may file evidence in support of his case and shall send a copy of it to the defendant; and, within the period of two months beginning on the date when the copy of the plaintiff's evidence is sent to him, the defendant may file further evidence confined to matters strictly in reply and shall send a copy of it to the plaintiff.

(6) No further evidence shall be filed by either party except by leave or direction of the comptroller.

(7) The comptroller may give such directions as he may think fit with regard to the subsequent procedure.

Procedure on application under section 71

16.74   74.—(1) An application to the comptroller under section 71 for a declaration that an act does not, or a proposed act would not, constitute an infringement of a patent shall be made on Patents Form 37/77 and shall be accompanied by a copy thereof and a statement in duplicate, setting out fully the facts upon which the applicant relies as showing that sub-paragraphs (*a*) and (*b*) of section 71(1) have been complied with and the relief which he seeks.

(2) The comptroller shall send a copy of the statement to the proprietor of the patent who shall, if he wishes to contest the application, within the period of two months beginning on the date when the copy is sent to him, file a counter-statement in duplicate setting out fully the grounds on which he contests the applicant's case; and the comptroller shall send a copy thereof to the applicant.

(3) Subject to such directions as the comptroller may think fit to give, the applicant may, within the period of two months beginning on the date when the copy of the counter-statement is sent to him, file evidence in support of his application and send a copy thereof to the proprietor of the patent.

(4) Within the period of two months beginning on the date when the copy of the applicant's evidence is sent to him or, if the applicant does not file any evidence, within two months of the expiration of the time within which such evidence might have been filed, the proprietor of the patent may file evidence in support of his case and shall send a copy of that evidence to the applicant; and, within the period of two months beginning on the date when the copy of the proprietor's evidence is sent to him, the applicant may file further evidence confined to matters strictly in reply and shall send a copy of it to the proprietor.

(5) No further evidence shall be filed by either party except by leave or direction of the comptroller.

(6) The comptroller may give such directions as he may think fit with regard to the subsequent procedure.

Revocation of patents

Procedure on application for revocation under section 71

16.75   75.—(1) An application to the comptroller for the revocation of a patent shall be made on Patents Form 38/77 and shall be accompanied by a copy thereof and a statement in duplicate setting out fully the grounds of revocation, the facts upon which the applicant relies and the relief which he seeks.

(2) The comptroller shall send a copy of the application and statement to the proprietor of the patent.

(3) Within the period of two months beginning on the date when such copies are sent to him, the proprietor of the patent shall, if he wishes to contest the application, file a counter-statement in duplicate setting out fully the grounds upon which the application is contested; and the comptroller shall send a copy of the counter-statement to the applicant.

(4) The applicant may, within the period of two months beginning on the date when the copy of the counter-statement is sent to him, file evidence in support of his case and shall send a copy of the evidence to the proprietor.

(5) Within the period of two months beginning on the date when the copy of the applicant's evidence is sent to him or, if the applicant does not file any evidence, within two months of the expiration of the time within which such evidence might have been filed, the proprietor of the patent may file evidence in support of his case and shall send a copy of that evidence to the applicant; and, within the period of two months beginning on the date when the copy of the proprietor's evidence is sent to him, the applicant may file further evidence confined to matters strictly in reply and shall send a copy of it to the proprietor.

(6) No further evidence shall be filed by either party except by leave or direction of the comptroller.

(7) The comptroller may give such directions as he may think fit with regard to the subsequent procedure.

Award of costs

76. If, in proceedings before the comptroller under section 72, the proprietor of a patent offers to surrender it under section 29, the comptroller shall, in deciding whether costs should be awarded to the applicant for revocation, consider whether proceedings might have been avoided if the applicant had given reasonable notice to the proprietor before the application was filed.   **16.76**

Revocation and amendment of patents under section 73

77.—(1) The opportunity to be given by the comptroller under subsection (1) or (2) of section 73, to the proprietor of a patent to make observations and to amend the specification of the patent shall be given by the comptroller sending to the proprietor notice informing him that he may make the observations and amend the specification and that, if he wishes to do so, he must do so within three months after the notice is sent to him.   **16.77**

(2) Where the comptroller gives leave under section 73 for the specification of the patent to be amended, he may, before the specification is amended, require the applicant to file a new specification as amended, prepared in accordance with rules 16, 18 and 20.

Amendment of patents in infringement or revocation proceedings

Amendment of patent under section 75

16.78   **78.**—(1) Where in proceedings before the comptroller a proposed amendment under section 75 is advertised, notice of opposition to such an amendment shall, within the period of two months from the date of advertisement in the Journal, be filed on Patents Form 15/77.

(2) Such notice shall be accompanied by a copy thereof and be supported by a statement in duplicate setting out fully the facts upon which the opponent relies and the relief which he seeks. The comptroller shall send a copy of the notice and statement to the proprietor of the patent and any other party to the proceedings before the comptroller.

(3) The comptroller may give such directions as he may think fit with regard to the subsequent procedure.

(4) Where the comptroller gives leave under section 75 for the specification of the patent to be amended, he may, before the specification is amended, require the applicant to file a new specification as amended, prepared in accordance with rules 16, 18 and 20.

European patents and patent applications and national processing of international applications

Entries in the register

16.79   **79.**—(1) Upon publication of an application for a European patent (U.K.) under Article 93 of the European Patent Convention, the comptroller shall cause to be entered in the register a copy of every entry which, at the date of such publication, has been made in the Register of European Patents kept under Article 127 of that Convention in respect of that application.

(2) The comptroller shall also cause to be entered in the register in respect of an application for a European patent (U.K.) which has been published under Article 93 of the Convention copies of any entry made in the Register of European Patents following such publication, provided that an application to that effect is made to the comptroller on Patents Form 39/77, accompanied by a copy of the relevant entry in the Register duly certified to the satisfaction of the comptroller.

European patents and applications (U.K.): translations

80. Schedule 4 shall have effect in cases where translations are   16.80
required by the Act to be filed in connection with applications for, and
with, European patents (U.K.).

Procedure for making request under section 81(2)(b)(i)

81.—(1) A request referred to in section 81(2)(b)(i) shall be made on   16.81
Patents Form 41/77 and the period within which such a request may be
made shall be three months from the date on which the applicant is
notified by the European Patent Office that his application for a
European patent (U.K.) has been deemed to be withdrawn.

(2) In such a case, the applicant shall file Patents Form 40/77, and,
where necessary, a translation in duplicate into English of the application, within a period of two months from the date on which the
comptroller receives the request mentioned in paragraph (1) above.

(3) The applicant shall also, within the period referred to in paragraph
(2) above, for the purposes of section 15(5)(b), file Patents Form 9/77,
and, for the purposes of section 13(2), file Patents Form 7/77.

Procedure where section 81(2)(b)(ii) applies

82.—(1) Where section 81(2)(b)(ii) applies, the period within which a   16.82
request may be transmitted to the comptroller shall be the twenty
months calculated from the declared priority date or, where there is no
declared priority date, the date of filing of the application for the
European patent (U.K.).

(2) Upon receipt of the request, the comptroller shall notify the
applicant thereof and Patents Form 40/77 and, where necessary, a
translation in duplicate into English of the application shall be filed by
the applicant within the period of four months calculated from the date
of the notification.

(3) The applicant shall also, within the period referred to in paragraph
(2) above, for the purposes of section 15(5)(b), file Patents Form 9/77
and, for the purposes of section 13(2), file Patents Form 7/77.

Procedures for making request for substantive examination where section 81(2) applies

83.—(1) The period within which a request may be made to the   16.83
comptroller for substantive examination of any application for a patent
to which section 81(2) applies shall be two years from the declared

priority date or, where there is no declared priority date, the date of filing of the application for the European patent (U.K.).

(2) The request shall be made on Patents Form 10/77.

[*(3) Where an application for a European patent (U.K.) is to be treated as an application for a patent under the Act, the period prescribed for the purposes of sections 18(4) and 20(1) shall be the period which expires four years and six months after the declared priority date, or where there is no declared priority date, the date of filing of the application for the European patent (U.K.).*]

(3) The periods prescribed for the purposes of sections 18(4) and 20(1) by paragraphs (1)(*a*), (1A) (insofar as paragraph (1A) applies to paragraphs (1)(a)) and (2) of rule 34 above shall also apply to an application for a European patent (U.K.) which is to be treated as an application for a patent under the Act, except that any reference to the date of filing of the application in paragraph (1)(a) of the said rule 34 shall be taken to refer to the date of filing of the application for the European patent (U.K.).

NOTE

The paragraph (3) was substituted by The Patents (Amendment) Rules 1992, with effect from June 1, 1992 (S.I. 1992, No.1142).

Recognition of determinations in proceedings before comptroller

16.84   84. Any person seeking recognition in proceedings before the comptroller of a determination by a competent authority of a relevant contracting state other than the United Kingdom of a question to which section 82 applies shall furnish the comptroller with a copy thereof certified as a true copy by an official of the said authority.

International applications for patents: section 89

16.85   85.—(1) Subject to the provisions of this rule, in relation to an international application for a patent (U.K.) which is, under section 89, to be treated as an application for a patent under the Act, the prescribed periods for the purposes of section 89A(3) and (5) are—

(a) the period of twenty months calculated from the date which, by virtue of section 89B(1)(b), is to be treated as the declared priority date or, where there is no declared priority date, the date of filing of the international application for a patent (U.K.); or

(b) in a case where the United Kingdom has been elected in accordance with Chapter II of the Patent Co-operation Treaty—

(i)   before the expiry of nineteen months calculated from the declared priority date, the period of thirty months calculated from the declared priority date; or

(ii) where there is no declared priority date and the United Kingdom has been so elected before the expiry of nineteen months calculated from the date of filing of the international application for a patent (U.K.), the period of thirty months calculated from the date of filing of that international application.

(2) Where, in accordance with paragraph 1 of Schedule 2, the information specified in sub-paragraph (2)(a)(ii) of that paragraph is added to an international application for a patent (U.K.) **after the international filing date**, rule 113(1) shall not apply in respect of that information; and where the translation of the information, the filing of which is required to satisfy the relevant conditions of section 89A(3), has not been filed at the Patent Office before the end of the relevant period referred to in paragraph (1) above,—

(a) the comptroller shall give notice to the applicant at the address furnished by the applicant in accordance with rule 30 requiring the applicant to file the translation within the period of two months commencing on the day on which the notice is sent; and

(b) the relevant period shall be treated in respect of the translation as not expiring until the end of the period specified in the notice given under sub-paragraph (a) above.

(3) In the case of an international application for a patent (U.K.),—

(a) rule 5(1) shall not apply if the applicant, on filing the application, states in writing to the receiving office that the invention has been displayed at an international exhibition;

(b) rule 5(2) may be complied with—

(i) where sub-paragraph (b) of paragraph (1) above applies, at any time before the end of the period of twenty-two months, or

(ii) where sub-paragraph (b) of paragraph (1) above applies, at any time before the end of the period of thirty-two months,

after the declared priority date or, if there is no declared priority date, the date of filing of the international application for a patent (U.K.);

(c) rule 6(6) shall have effect with the substitution, for the reference to the period of twnety-one months after the declared priority date, of a reference to the period of twenty-two months after that date;

(d) where the United Kingdom has been elected in accordance with Chapter II of the Patent Co-operation Treaty before the expiry of the nineteenth month after the declared priority date, rule 6(6) shall have effect with the substitution, for the reference to the period of twenty-one months after the declared priority date, of a reference to the period of thirty-two months after that date; and

(e) where a translation into English of a document or part of a document is required by the Act or these Rules to be filed—

(i)   before the end of the relevant period referred to in paragraph (1)(a) above, verification of the translation, as required by rule 113(1), may be given to the comptroller at any time before the end of the period of twenty-two months, or

(ii) before the end of the relevant period referred to in paragraph (1)(b) above, verification of the translation, as required by rule 113(1), may be given to the comptroller at any time before the end of the period of thirty-two months,

after the declared priority date or, if there is no declared priority date, the date of filing of the international application for a patent (U.K.).

(4) Where the relevant period referred to in paragraph (1) above has been extended under **paragraph (5A) below**, rule 100 or rule 110 so as to expire later than one month before the end of a period prescribed by paragraph (3) above or (7) below, paragraphs (3) above and (7) below shall have effect with the substitution for the period so prescribed of a period ending one month later than the relevant period referred to in paragraph (1) above as so extended.

(5) For the purposes of section 89A(3) and (5), to the extent that the application and any amendment as published under the Patent Co-operation Treaty and any amendment annexed to the international preliminary examination report under Chapter II of the Treaty are not in English, a translation into English of the application as originally filed or, as the case may be, of the application as originally filed and of the amendment is necessary; however, the translation—

(a) shall exclude the request and abstract unless—

(i)   the applicant expressly requests the comptroller to proceed earlier than the expiry of the period prescribed in paragraph (1) above; and

(ii) a copy of the application published by the International Bureau has not yet been sent to the Patent Office in accordance with the Treaty; and

(b) shall include any textual matter in the drawings in a form which complies with rule 49.5(d) of the Patent Co-operation Treaty; **and,**

(c) **where a title has been established by the International Searching Authority under rule 37.2 of the Regulations under the Patent Co-operation Treaty which differs from the title included in the application as originally filed, shall include the former title in place of the latter.**

(5A) Where an applicant is required to file a translation into English both of an application as originally filed and of the amendment to it, in accordance with paragraph (5) above, in order to satisfy the relevant conditions of section 89A(3) and (5) and at the expiry of the relevant period referred to in paragraph (1) above the prescribed fee has been paid and one but not both of the necessary translations has been filed—

(a) the comptroller shall give notice to the applicant at the address furnished by the applicant in accordance with rule 30 requiring the applicant to file the required translation within the period of one month commencing on the day on which the notice is sent; and

(b) the relevant period shall be treated in respect of that translation as not expiring until the end of the period specified in the notice given under sub-paragraph (a) above.

(6) The comptroller shall publish any translation supplied in accordance with section 89A(3) or (5) following the filing of Patents Form 43/77 and payment of the prescribed fee.

(7) In the case of an international application for a patent (U.K.) in respect of which the conditions specified in section 89A(3)(*a*) are satisfied, the period prescribed—

(a) for the purposes of sections 13(2), 15(5)(b) and 17(1),—
  (i) where sub-paragraph (a) of paragraph (1) above has effect, shall be the period which expires 22 months; or
  (ii) where sub-paragraph (b) of paragraph (1) above, has effect, shall be the period which expires 32 months; and

(b) for the purposes of section 18(1),—
  (i) where sub-paragraph (a) of paragraph (1) above applies, shall be the period which expires two years; or
  (ii) where sub-paragraph (b) of paragraph (1) above applies, shall be the period which expires 32 months,

after the declared priority date or, if there is no declared priority date, the date of filing of the international application for a patent (U.K.).

(8) Where, in relation to an international application for a patent (U.K.), the applicant desires that section 89(1) shall not cease to apply to the application by virtue of the operation of section 89(3), application shall be made to the comptroller on Patents Form 44/77, accompanied by a statement of the facts upon which the applicant relies.

(9) An international application for a patent (U.K.) shall not be treated as withdrawn under the Act if it, or the designation of the United Kingdom in it, is deemed to be withdrawn under the Patent Co-operation Treaty where, in the same or comparable circumstances in relation to an application under the Act (other than an international application)—

[*(a) the comptroller could have directed that an irregularity be rectified under rule 100 or that an extension be granted under rule 110; and*]

(a) the comptroller could have directed that an irregularity be rectified under rule 100, or could have been granted a dispensation for the doing of any act or thing, or the production or filing of any document under rule 101, or could have granted an extension of time under rule 110, or could have extended the time or determined the times or periods under rule 111; and

(b) the comptroller determines that the application would not have been treated as withdrawn under the Act.

(10) Where under section 89(3) an application is not to be treated as withdrawn and the applicant wishes to proceed—

    (a) the comptroller may amend any document received by the Patent Office from the receiving office or the International Bureau and alter any period or time which is specified in the Act or these Rules upon such terms (including payment of any appropriate prescribed fee) as he may direct; and

    (b) the fee prescribed under section 89A(3) shall not be payable.

(11) Where the applicant satisfies the comptroller that,—

    (a) because of an error made by the receiving office, an international application for a patent (U.K.) has been accorded a date of filing which is not correct; or

    (b) the declaration made under Article 8(1) of the Patent Co-operation Treaty has been cancelled or corrected by the receiving office or the International Bureau because of an error made by the office or the Bureau,

the comptroller may amend any document received by the Patent Office from the receiving office or the International Bureau or alter any period or time which is specified in the Act or these Rules as if the error were an error on the part of the Patent Office.

(12) Where—

    (a) an international application for a patent (U.K.) purports to designate the United Kingdom; and

    (b) the applicant alleges that he has been refused a filing date under the said Treaty on account of an error or omission in any institution having functions under the said Treaty,

the applicant may apply to the comptroller for it to be treated as an application under the Act by filing Patents Form 44/77, accompanied by a statement of the facts upon which he relies; and the comptroller may amend any document filed by the applicant and alter any period or time which is specified in the Act or these Rules upon such terms as he may direct.

(13) In this rule "receiving office" has the same meaning as in the Patent Co-operation Treaty.

NOTE

Paras. (4) and (5) amended and (5A) inserted by The Patents (Amendment) Rules 1992, with effect from July 1, 1992 (S.I. 1992, No.1142).

Para. 2 amended by The Patent (Amendment) Rules 1993, with effect from November 1, 1993 (S.I. 1993, No.2423).

Para. (9)(*a*) substituted by The Patents (Amendment) Rules 1993, with effect from November 1, 1993 (S.I. 1993, No.2423).

Obtaining evidence for proceedings under European Patent Convention

86.—(1) An application to the comptroller under section 1 of the **16.86**
Evidence (Proceedings in Other Jurisdictions) Act 1975, as applied by
section 92 of the Act, for an order for evidence to be obtained in the
United Kingdom shall be made *ex parte* on Patents Form 45/77 and shall
be accompanied by an affidavit made by a person duly authorised in
that behalf by the relevant convention court, evidencing that the request
is made in pursuance of a request issued by or on behalf of that court
and that the evidence to which the application relates is to be obtained
for the purposes of civil proceedings before it.

(2) After such an application as is mentioned in paragraph (1) above
has been made, an *ex parte* application for a further order or directions in
relation to the same matter may be made to the comptroller in writing.

(3) The comptroller may allow an officer of the European Patent
Office to attend the hearing of such an application as is mentioned in
paragraph (1) above and examine the witnesses or request the comptroller to put specified questions to them.

Communication of information to European Patent Office

87. The comptroller may authorise the communication to the Euro- **16.87**
pean Patent Office or the competent authority of any country which is
party to the European Patent Convention of such information in the files
of the Patent Office as may be disclosed in accordance with section 118
and rule 93.

Hearings, agents and correction of errors

Comptroller's discretionary powers

88.—(1) Before exercising any discretionary power vested in him by **16.88**
or under the Act adversely to any party to a proceeding before him, the
comptroller shall, unless the party concerned consents to shorter notice,
give that party at least 14 days' notice of the time when he may be heard.

(2) If, in *inter partes* proceedings, a party desires to be heard, he shall
give notice in writing to the comptroller; and the comptroller may refuse
to hear any party who has not given such notice before the day
appointed for the hearing.

(3) In *inter partes* proceedings, any party who intends to refer at the
hearing to any document (other than a report of a decision of any court
or of the comptroller) not already mentioned in the proceedings shall,
unless the comptroller consents and the other party agrees, give at least

14 days' notice of his intention with details of, or a copy of, the document to the comptroller and the other party.

(4) After hearing the party or parties desiring to be heard or, if no party so desires, without a hearing, the comptroller shall decide the matter and shall notify all parties of his decision and, if any party so desires, shall give his reasons for the decision.

Admittance to hearings before comptroller

16.89   **89.**—(1) Subject to the following provisions of this rule, where a hearing before the comptroller of any dispute between two or more parties relating to any matter in connection with a patent or an application for a patent takes place after the publication of the application under section 16, the hearing of the dispute shall be in public.

(2) After consulting those parties to the dispute who appear in person or are represented at a hearing to which paragraph (1) above applies, the comptroller may direct that the hearing be not held in public, but without prejudice to paragraph (3) below.

(3) A member of the Council on Tribunals or of its Scottish Committee may, in his capacity as such, attend such a hearing or any other hearing before the comptroller under these Rules.

Agents

16.90   **90.**—(1) Unless the comptroller otherwise directs in any particular case—
  (a) all attendances upon him may be made by or through an agent; and
  (b) every notice, application or other document filed under the Act may be signed by an agent.

(2) Where after a person has become a party to proceedings before the comptroller he appoints an agent for the first time or appoints one agent in substitution for another, the newly appointed agent shall file Patents Form 51/77 in duplicate on or before the first occasion when he acts as agent.

Correction of errors in patents and applications

16.91   **91.**—(1) Except where rule 45(3) or paragraph 4 of Schedule 4 has effect, a request for the correction of an error of translation or transcription or of a clerical error or mistake in any specification of a patent, in an application for a patent or in any document filed in connection with a patent or such an application shall be made on Patents

Form 47/77 and shall be accompanied by a document clearly identifying the proposed correction; and the comptroller may, if he thinks fit, require that the correction be shown on a copy of the document of which correction is sought.

(2) Where such a request relates to a specification, no correction shall be made therein unless the correction is obvious in the sense that it is immediately evident that nothing else would have been intended than what is offered as the correction.

(3) Where the comptroller requires notice of the proposed correction to be advertised, the advertisement shall be made by publication of the request and the nature of the proposed correction in the Journal and in such other manner (if any) as the comptroller may direct.

(4) Any person may, at any time within two months after the date of the advertisement, give notice to the comptroller of opposition to the request on Patents Form 48/77.

(5) Such notice shall be accompanied by a copy thereof and be supported by a statement in duplicate setting out fully the facts on which the opponent relies and the relief which he seeks. The comptroller shall send a copy of the notice and the statement to the person making the request who, if he desires to proceed with the request, shall within the period of two months beginning on the date when the copies are sent to him, file a counter-statement in duplicate setting out fully the grounds on which he contests the opposition and the comptroller shall send a copy of the counter-statement to the opponent.

(6) The comptroller may give such directions as he may think fit with regard to the subsequent procedure.

Information and inspection

Request for information under section 118

92.—(1) A request under section 118 for information relating to any **16.92** patent or application for a patent may be made—

(a) as to when a request for substantive examination has been filed or the prescribed period for doing so has expired without the request having been filed;

(b) as to when the specification of a patent or application for a patent has been published;

(c) as to when an application for a patent has been withdrawn, has been taken to be withdrawn, has been treated as having been withdrawn, has been refused or has been treated as having been refused;

(d) as to when a renewal fee has not been paid within the period prescribed for the purposes of section 25(3);

(e) as to when a renewal fee has been paid within the period of six months referred to in section 25(4);

(f) as to when a patent has ceased to have effect and/or an application for restoration of a patent has been filed;

(g) as to when an entry has been made in the register or an application has been made for the making of such entry;

(h) as to when any application or request is made or action taken involving an entry in the register or advertisement in the Journal, if the nature of the application, request or action is specified in the request; and

(i) as to when any document may be inspected in accordance with the provisions of rule 93 or 94.

(2) As regards information relating to any existing patent or existing application for a patent, a request may also be made—

(a) as to when a complete specification following a provisional specification has been filed or when the period of 15 months from the date of the application has expired and a complete specification has not been filed;

(b) as to when a complete specification is or will be published, or when an application for a patent has become void; and

(c) as to when a patent has been sealed or when the time for requesting sealing has expired.

(3) Any such request shall be made on Patents Form 49/77 and a separate form shall be used in respect of each item of information required.

(4) In this rule, "existing patent" means a patent mentioned in section 127(2)(a) and (c) and "existing application" means an application mentioned in section 127(2)(b).

Inspection of documents under section 118

16.93 93.—(1) Subject to paragraph (5) below, and to the restrictions prescribed in paragraph (4) below, after the date of publication of an application for a patent in accordance with section 16, the comptroller shall, upon request made on Patents Form 23/77 and payment of [*the appropriate prescribed fee*] **the prescribed fee, if any,** permit all documents filed or kept at the Patent Office in relation to the application or any patent granted in pursuance of it, to be inspected at the Patent Office.

(2) Subject to the same restrictions and to rule 96, where the circumstances specified in section 118(4) or (5) exist, the comptroller shall, upon request made on Patents Form 23/77, and payment of [*the appropriate fee*] **the prescribed fee, if any,** permit inspection of such documents before the publication in accordance with section 16.

(3) Where a declaration has been made in accordance with section 5(2) or 127(4), inspection of any application referred to therein and of any

translation thereof shall be permitted upon request under paragraph (1) or (2) above without payment of any fee.

(4) The restrictions referred to in paragraph (1) above are—

(a) that no document shall be open to inspection until fourteen days after it has been filed at the Patent Office;

(b) that documents prepared in the Patent Office solely for use therein shall not be open to inspection;

(c) that any document sent to the Patent Office, at its request or otherwise, for inspection and subsequent return to the sender, shall not be open to inspection;

(d) that no document filed at the Patent Office in connection with an application under section 40(1) or (2) or section 41(8) shall be open to inspection unless the comptroller otherwise directs;

(e) that no request made under rule 48, 49(2), 52(2) or 92 or this rule shall be open to inspection; [*and*]

(f) that documents in respect of which the comptroller issues directions under rule 94 that they are to be treated as confidential shall not be open to inspection, save as permitted in accordance with that rule; **and**

(g) that any documents issued by the Patent Office which the comptroller considers should be treated as confidential shall not be open to inspection unless the comptroller otherwise directs.

(5) Nothing in this rule shall be construed as imposing on the comptroller any duty of making available for public inspection—

(a) any document or any part of a document—

  (i) which in his opinion disparages any person in a way likely to damage him; or

  (ii) the publication or exploitation of which would in his opinion be generally expected to encourage offensive, immoral or antisocial behaviour; or

(b) the file (but not the report) of the international preliminary examination of an international application under the Patent Co-operation Treaty; or

(c) any document filed with or sent to **or by** the Patent Office before June 1, 1978.

(6) No appeal shall lie from a decision of the comptroller under paragraph (5)(a) above not to make a document or part of a document available for public inspection.

NOTE

Paras. (1) and (2) amended by The Patents (Amendment) Rules 1992, with effect from June 1, 1992 (S.I. 1992, No.1142).

Paras. (3)(e) and (5)(c) amended and (4)(g) inserted by The Patents (Amendment) Rules 1993, with effect from November 1, 1993 (S.I. 1993, No.2423).

Confidential documents

16.94   **94.**—[*(1) Where a document other than a Patents Form is filed at, or sent to, the Patent Office, and the person filing or sending it to any party to the proceedings to which the document relates so requests, giving his reasons, within fourteen days of the filing or sending of the document, the comptroller may direct that it be treated as confidential, and the document shall not be open to public inspection while the matter is being determined by the comptroller.*]

(1) A person filing at, or sending to, the Patent Office a document other than a Patents Form , or any party to any proceedings to which the document relates, may, within fourteen days of the filing or sending of the document, request the comptroller (giving reasons for the request) to direct that the document or any part of it specified by him be treated as confidential, and the comptroller may, at his discretion, so direct; and while the request is being considered by the comptroller, that document or part thereof (hereinafter referred to as the relevant document) shall not be open to public inspection.

(2) Where such a direction has been given and not withdrawn, nothing in this rule shall be taken to authorise or require any person to be allowed to inspect the **relevant** document to which the direction relates except by leave of the comptroller.

(3) The comptroller shall not withdraw any direction given under this rule nor shall he give leave for any person to inspect any **relevant** document to which a direction which has not been withdrawn relates without prior consultation with the person at whose request the direction was given, unless the comptroller is satisfied that such prior consultation is not reasonably practicable.

(4) Where such a direction is given or withdrawn a record of the fact shall be filed with the **relevant** document to which it relates.

(5) Where the period referred to in paragraph (1) above is extended under rule 110, the relevant document shall not be, or, if the period is extended after it has expired, shall cease to be, open to public inspection until the expiry of the extended period, and if a request for a direction is made the **relevant** document shall not be open to public inspection while the matter is being determined by the comptroller.

NOTE

Para. (1) substituted and paras. (2)–(5) amended by The Patents (Amendment) Rules 1993, with effect from November 1, 1993 (S.I. 1993, No.2423).

Bibliographic data for purposes of section 118(3)(b)

16.95   **95.** The following bibliographic data is prescribed for the purposes of section 118(3)(b)—

(a) the number of the application;

(b) the date of filing of the application and, where a declaration has been made under section 5(2) or 127(4), the filing date, country and file number when available of each application referred to in that declaration;

(c) the name of the applicant or applicants;

(d) the title of the invention; and

(e) if the application has been withdrawn, has been taken to be withdrawn, has been treated as having been withdrawn, has been refused or is treated as having been refused, that fact.

Request for information where section 118(4) applies

96.—(1) Where the circumstances specified in section 118(4) exist, a **16.96** request under section 118(1) shall be accompanied by a statutory declaration verifying their existence and such documentary evidence (if any) supporting the request as the comptroller may require.

(2) The comptroller shall send a copy of the request, the declaration and the evidence (if any) to the applicant for the patent and shall not comply with the request until the expiry of fourteen days thereafter.

Miscellaneous

Service by post

97. Any notice, application or other document sent to the Patent Office **16.97** by posting it in the United Kingdom shall be deemed to have been given, made or filed at the time when the letter containing it would be delivered in the ordinary course of post.

Hours of business

98. The Patent Office shall be deemed to be closed at the following **16.98** hours for the transaction of business of the classes specified—

(a) on weekdays other than Saturdays, at midnight for the filing of applications, forms and other documents, and at 4 pm for all other business; and

(b) on Saturdays, at 1 pm for the filing of new applications for patents in respect of which no declaration for the purposes of section 5(2) or 127(4) is made.

Excluded days

16.99 99.—(1) The following shall be excluded days for all purposes under the Act—

(a) all Sundays;

(b) Good Friday and Christmas Day;

(c) any day specified as or proclaimed to be a bank holiday in Englnd in or under section 1 of the Banking and Financial Dealings Act 1971 and

(d) any Saturday immediately preceded by one of the above.

(2) Saturdays not falling within paragraph (1) above shall be excluded days for all purposes except the filing of applications in respect of which no declaration for the purposes of section 5(2) is made.

Correction of irregularities

16.100 100.—(1) Subject to paragraph (2) below, any document filed in any proceedings before the comptroller may, if he thinks fit, be amended, and any irregularity in procedure in or before the Patent Office may be rectified, on such terms as he may direct.

(2) In the case of an irregularity or prospective irregularity—

(a) which consists of a failure to comply with any limitation as to times or periods specified in the Act or the 1949 Act or prescribed in these Rules or the Patents Rules 1968 as they continue to apply which has occurred, or appears to the comptroller is likely to occur in the absence of a direction under this rule;

(b) which is attributable wholly or in part to an error, default or omission on the part of the Patent Office; and

(c) which it appears to the comptroller should be rectified,

the comptroller may direct that the time or period in question shall be altered but not otherwise.

(3) Paragraph (2) above is without prejudice to the comptroller's power to extend any times or periods under rule 110 or 111.

Dispensation by comptroller

16.101 101. Where, under these Rules, any person is required to do any act or thing, or any document or evidence is required to be produced or filed, and it is shown to the satisfaction of the comptroller that from any reasonable cause that person in unable to do that act or thing, or that document or evidence cannot be produced or filed, the comptroller may, upon the production of such evidence and subject to such terms as he thinks fit, dispense with the doing of any such act or thing, or the production or filing of such document or evidence.

Remission of fees

102.—(1) The comptroller may emit the whole or part of a search fee in **16.102**
the following cases—
  (a) where an international application for a patent (U.K.) which has
      already been the subject of a search by the International Searching
      Authority in accordance with the Patent Co-operation Treaty falls
      to be treated as an application for a patent under the Act; and
  (b) where a new application is filed in accordance with section 15(4)
      for a patent for an invention in relation to which the applicant has
      previously paid the search fee in connection with the earlier
      application referred to in that subsection.
(2) In a case governed by Chapter II of the Patent Co-operation Treaty,
the comptroller may remit the whole or part of the fee for the
substantive examination of the international application where its
preliminary examination has been carried out by the Patent Office
acting as the International Preliminary Examining Authority under
Article 32 of the said Treaty.
(3) In cases falling within paragraph (1)(*b*) above the request for
remission of the whole or part of the fee shall be made in writing.
(4) No appeal shall lie from any decision of the comptroller under this
rule.

Evidence

103.—(1) Where under these Rules evidence may be filed, it shall be **16.103**
by statutory declaration or affidavit.
(2) The comptroller may if he thinks fit in any particular case take oral
evidence in lieu of or in addition to such evidence and shall allow any
witness to be cross-examined on his affidavit or declaration, unless he
directs otherwise.
(3) In England and Wales, the comptroller shall, in relation to the
giving of evidence (including evidence on oath), the attendance of
witnesses and the discovery and production of documents, have all the
powers of a judge of the High Court, other than the power to punish
summarily for contempt of court.
(4) In Scotland, the comptroller shall, in relation to the giving of
evidence (including evidence on oath), have all the powers which a
Lord Ordinary of the Court of Session has in an action before him, other
than the power to punish summarily for contempt of court, and, in
relation to the attendance of witnesses and the recovery and production
of documents, have all the powers of the Court of Session.

Statutory declarations and affidavits

16.104   104. Any statutory declaration or affidavit filed under the Act or these Rules shall be made and subscribed as follows,—
(a) in the United Kingdom, before any justice of the peace, or any commissioner or other officer authorised by law in any part of the United Kingdom to administer an oath for the purpose of any legal proceedings;
(b) in any other part of Her Majesty's dominions or in the Republic of Ireland, before any court, judge, justice of the peace, or any officer authorised by law to administer an oath for the purpose of any legal proceedings; and
(c) elsewhere, before a British Minister, or person exercising the functions of a British Minister, or a Consul, Vice-Consul, or other person exercising the functions of a British Consul, or before a notary public, judge or magistrate.

Admission of documents

16.105   105. Any document purporting to have affixed, impressed or sub-scribed thereto or thereon the seal or signature of any person authorised by the last foregoing rule to take a declaration, in testimony that the declaration was made and subscribed before him, may be admitted by the comptroller without proof of the genuineness of the seal or signature or of the official character of the person or his authority to take the declaration.

Directions as to the furnishing of documents etc.

16.106   106. At any stage of any proceedings before the comptroller he may direct that such documents, information or evidence as he may require shall be furnished within such period as he may fix.

Supporting statements or evidence

16.107   107.—(1) Where by virtue of any of the rules mentioned in paragraph (2) of this rule, any notice or application is required to be supported by a statement or evidence, such a statement or evidence shall be filed on, or within fourteen days after, the date on which the notice is given or the application is made.
(2) The rules referred to in paragraph (1) above are rules 40(3), 41(1), 43(3), 64(1), 65(2), 71(2), 78(2) and 91(5).

Proceedings in Scotland

108.—(1) Where there is more than one party to the proceedings **16.108**
under section 8, 12, 37, 40(1) or (2), 41(8), 61(3), 71 or 72, any party
thereto may request the comptroller to direct that any hearing in such
proceedings shall be held in Scotland and—
  (a) the comptroller shall so direct in the following cases—
    (i) where one party resides in Scotland and all parties to the
         proceedings agree to a hearing being held there; or
    (ii) where all the parties to the proceedings reside in Scotland and
          one of them requests a hearing there, unless it is shown to the
          comptroller's satisfaction that it would be unduly burdensome
          to any other party to hold the hearing there; and
  (b) the comptroller may direct that a hearing be held in Scotland
       (even where none of the parties resides in Scotland) where one
       party to the proceedings requests it and the balance of conveni-
       ence is in favour of holding the hearing there.
  (2) A request under paragraph (1) above shall be made in duplicate
and shall—
  (a) be in writing;
  (b) be accompanied by a statement of facts in duplicate setting out
       the grounds upon which the request is made; and
  (c) be filed at any time before the comptroller issues notification to
       the parties that a hearing has been appointed, or, with the leave of
       the comptroller, within 14 days thereafter.
  (3) The comptroller, upon a request being made under paragraph (1)
above, shall send a copy of the request and the statement to any party to
the proceedings who has not indicated that he consents to the request.
  (4) Any party or parties to the proceedings having objection to a
request made under paragraph (1) above may, [*within two months*]
within one month after notification of the request is sent to him, file at
the Patent Office a counter-statement in duplicate setting out the
grounds upon which objection is taken, and the comptroller shall send a
copy of the counter-statement to any person who is not party to it.
  (5) The comptroller may give such directions as he may think fit with
regard to the subsequent procedure.
  (6) Where the comptroller, after consideration of a request made
under paragraph (1)(a)(ii) or (*b*) above, is satisfied that any hearing
thereon should be held in Scotland, he shall grant the request and issue
such directions as shall seem to him appropriate.
  (7) No appeal shall lie from any decision of the comptroller under this
rule.

NOTE

Para. (4) amended by The Patents (Amendment) Rules 1992, with effect from June 1, 1992 (S.I. 1992, No.1142).

Appointment of advisers

16.109   109. The comptroller may appoint an adviser to assist him in any proceeding before the comptroller and shall settle the question or instructions to be submitted or given to such adviser.

Alteration of time limits

16.110   110.—(1) The times or periods prescribed by these Rules for doing any act or taking any proceedings thereunder, other than times or periods prescribed in the provisions mentioned in paragraph (2) below, and subject to paragraphs (3) and (4) below, may be extended by the comptroller if he thinks fit, upon such notice to the parties and upon such terms as he may direct; and such extension may be granted notwithstanding that the time or period for doing such act or taking such proceedings has expired.

(2) The provisions referred to in paragraph (1) above are rules 6(1), 26 (so far as it relates to rule 6(1)), 39(1) and (2), 40(2), 41(1), 43(2), 59(2), 64(1), 65(1), 71(1), 78(1), 81(1), 82(1) and 91(4) and paragraphs 4(2) of Schedule 2.

(3) A time or period prescribed in rules 6(2) and (6) (including the period therein prescribed as substituted by rule 85(3)(c) and (d)), 15(1), 23, 25(2) and (3) (except so far as it relates to the filing of claims for the purposes of the application and filing of the abstract), 26 (except so far as it relates to rule 6(1)), 33(2), (3) and (5), 34, 41(4), 81(2) and (3), 82(2) and (3), 83(3) and [*85(1) and (7)*] **85(1), (5A) and (7)**, [*paragraph (6) below*], paragraph 1(3) of Schedule 2 and paragraph 2 of Schedule 4 shall, if not previously extended, be extended for one month upon filing Patents Form 50/77 before the end of that month; and where in any proceedings more than one such time or period expires on the same day (but not otherwise), those times or periods may be extended upon the filing of a single such form.

(4) Without prejudice to paragraph (3) above, a time or period (other than any time or period expiring before March 24, 1987) prescribed in the rules referred to in that paragraph may, upon request made on Patents Form 52/77, be extended or further extended if the comptroller thinks fit, whether or not the time or period (including any extension obtained under paragraph (3) above) has expired; and the comptroller may allow an extension or further extension, under this paragraph on such terms as he may direct and subject, unless he otherwise directs, to

the furnishing of a statutory declaration or affidavit verifying the grounds for the request.

(5) A single request may be made under paragraph (4) above for the extension of more than one time or period in the same proceedings if the extensions are to be made to a common date (but not otherwise).

(6) If on consideration of a request under paragraph (4) above the comptroller decides that the extension requested (or, in a case falling within paragraph (5) above, any or all of the extensions requested) may be granted he shall notify the applicant accordingly and invite him, within two months after the notification is sent to him, to file Patents Form 53/77, upon receipt of which the comptroller shall effect the extension or extensions in accordance with the decision:

> Provided that, in a case where a notification under this paragraph is sent to the applicant before these Rules come into force, this paragraph shall have effect as if the words "within two months after the notification is sent to him" were omitted.

(7) Where the period within which any party to a dispute may file evidence under these Rules is to begin after the expiry of any period in which any other party may file evidence under these Rules and that other party notifies the comptroller that he does not wish to file any, or any further, evidence, the comptroller may direct that the period within which the first-mentioned party may file evidence shall begin on such date as may be specified in the direction and shall notify all parties to the dispute of that date.

NOTE

Para. (3) amended by The Patents (Amendment) Rules 1992, with effect from June 1, 1992 (S.I. 1992, No.1142).

Calculation of times or periods

111.—(1) Where, on any day, there is—   16.111
(a) a general interruption or subsequent dislocation in the postal services of the United Kingdom; or
(b) an event or circumstances causing an interruption in the normal operation of the Patent Office,
the comptroller may certify the day as being one on which there is an "interruption" and, where any period of time specified in the Act or these Rules for the giving, making or filing of any notice, application or other document expires on a day so certified the period shall be extended to the first day next following (not being an excluded day) which is not so certified.

(2) Any certificate of the comptroller given pursuant to this rule shall be posted in the Patent Office.

(3) Where, in or in connection with an application for a patent ("the application in suit"), it is desired to make a declaration specifying for the purposes of section 5(2) an earlier relevant application and the period of 12 months immediately following the date of filing the earlier relevant application ends on a day which is an excluded day for the purposes of section 120, such period shall, if the declaration is made on the first following day on which the Patent Office is open for the transaction of such business, be altered so as to include both the day of filing of the earlier relevant application and the day on which the declaration is made in or in connection with the application in suit.

(4) Where it is desired to make such a declaration and the said period of 12 months immediately following the date of filing the earlier relevant application ends on a day certified under paragraph (1) above as being one on which there is an interruption, the period shall, if the declaration is made on the first day following the end of the interruption, be altered so as to include both the day of filing of the earlier relevant application and day on which the declaration is made in or in connection with the application in suit.

(5) Where an application for a patent is filed upon the day immediately following a day which is certified under paragraph (1) above as being one on which there is an interruption or which is an excluded day for the purposes of section 120, the period of six months specified in section 2(4) shall be computed from the day following the next preceding day which is neither so certified nor so excluded.

(6) If in any particular case the comptroller is satisfied that the failure to give, make or file any notice, application or other document within—

    (a) any period of time specified in the Act or these Rules for such giving, making or filing;

    (b) the period of six months following a disclosure of matter constituting an invention falling within paragraph (a), (b) or (c) of section 2(4); or

    (c) the period of 12 months referred to in paragraph (3) above,

was wholly or mainly attributable to a failure or undue delay in the postal services in the United Kingdom, the comptroller may, if he thinks fit—

    (i) extend the period of time for the giving, making or filing so that it ends on the day of the receipt by the addressee of the notice, application or other document (or, if the day of such receipt is an excluded day, on the first following day which is not an excluded day);

    (ii) determine that the period of six months referred to in sub-paragraph (*b*) above shall be altered so that it begins on the day of the disclosure and ends on the day of receipt by the Patent Office of the application for the patent (or, if the day of

such receipt is an excluded day, on the first following day
which is not an excluded day); or

(iii) determine that the period of 12 months referred to in paragraph (3) above shall be altered so as to include both the day of
filing of the earlier relevant application and the day on which
the declaration specifying that application is received by the
Patent Office (or, if the day of such receipt is an excluded day,
the first following day which is not an excluded day);

as the case may be, in each case upon such notice to other parties and
upon such terms as he may direct.

Copies of documents

112. Where a document, other than a published United Kingdom   **16.112**
specification or application, is referred to in any reference, notice,
statement, counter-statement or evidence required by the Act or these
Rules to be filed at the Patent Office or sent to the comptroller, copies of
the document shall be furnished to the Patent Office within the same
period as the reference, notice, statement, counter-statement or evidence in which they are first referred to may be filed and in the following
number,—

(a) where the document in which they were so referred to had to be
filed or sent in duplicate or the original document had to be
accompanied by a copy thereof, in duplicate; and

(b) in all other cases, one:

Provided that where a copy of any evidence is required by the Act or
these Rules to be sent direct to any person, a copy of any document
referred to in that document shall also be sent direct to that person.

Translations

113.—(1) Subject to the provisions of rules 6, 40, 81, 82 and 85,   **16.113**
paragraph (3) below and paragraph 5 of Schedule 4, where any
document or part of a document which is in a language other than
English is filed at the Patent Office or sent to the comptroller in
pursuance of the Act or these Rules, it shall be accompanied by a
translation into English of the document or that part, verified to the
satisfaction of the comptroller as corresponding to the original text.
Where the document is or forms part of an application for a patent, the
Patent Office shall not, in the absence of such a translation, take any
further action in relation to that document, unless the comptroller
otherwise directs.

(2) Where more than one copy of that document is required to be so
filed or sent, a corresponding number of copies of the translation shall
accompany it.

(3) Where any document which, or any part of which, is in a language other than English—

    (a) is referred to in a search report drawn up under Article 18 of the Patent Co-operation Treaty; or

    (b) is cited in the statement contained in an international preliminary examination report established under Article 35 of that Treaty,

and any such report is filed at the Patent Office in relation to the provisions of section 89A, a translation into English of that document or part verified to the satisfaction of the comptroller as corresponding to the original text thereof shall, if the comptroller so directs, be filed within two months of the date on which such direction is given.

(4) Where proceedings are instituted before the comptroller in relation to a European patent (U.K.) the specification of which was published in French or German, the party who institutes those proceedings shall furnish to the Patent Office a translation into English of the specification of the patent verified to the satisfaction of the comptroller as corresponding to the original text thereof unless—

    (a) such a translation has already been filed under section 77(6); or

    (b) the comptroller determines that it is not necessary.

(5) If, in the course of such proceedings, leave is given for the amendment of the specification of the European patent (U.K.), the party given leave to amend shall furnish to the Patent Office a translation of the amendment into the language in which the specification of the patent was published, verified to the satisfaction of the comptroller as corresponding to the original text thereof.

(6) The comptroller may refuse to accept any translation which is in his opinion inaccurate and thereupon another translation of the document in question verified as aforesaid shall be furnished, together with the appropriate number of copies thereof.

Publication and sale of documents

16.114   114. The comptroller may arrange for the publication and sale of copies of specifications and other documents in the Patent Office and of indexes to, and abridgements or abstracts of, such documents.

The Journal

16.115   115.—(1) The comptroller shall publish a journal containing particulars of applications for patents and other proceedings under the Act and any other information that he may deem to be generally useful or important.

(2) The journal shall be entitled "The Official Journal (Patents)."

(3) Unless the comptroller otherwise directs, the Journal shall be published weekly.

Reports of cases

116. The comptroller shall from time to time publish reports of—   **16.116**
(a) cases relating to patents, trade marks, registered designs and design right decided by him; and
(b) cases relating to patents (whether under the Act or otherwise), trade marks, registered designs, copyright and design right decided by any court or body (whether in the United Kingdom or elsewhere),
being cases which he considers to be generally useful or important.

International applications

Filing of applications

117.—(1) Where the Patent Office is the competent receiving office   **16.117**
under the Patent Co-operation Treaty, an international application shall be filed at it in English in triplicate.

(2) If less than three copies of the international application are so filed, upon preparation by the Patent Office of the number of copies of it required to bring the total to three, the applicant shall on demand pay to the Patent Office the appropriate charge.

Transmittal, international and search fees

118.—(1) [*Payment*] **Subject to paragraph (4) below, payment** of the   **16.118**
prescribed transmittal fee and the basic fee referred to in rule 15.1(i) of the Regulations under the Patent Co-operation Treaty shall be made to the Patent Office not later than one month after the date on which the application to which they relate is filed at the Patent Office.

(2) [*Payment*] **Subject to paragraph (4) below, payment** of designation fees referred to in rule 15.1(ii) of the said Regulations shall be made to the Patent Office in the amount provided for in rule 15.2(b) thereof not later than—
(a) one year after the date on which the application to which they relate is filed at the Patent Office in a case in which there is no date to be treated by virtue of section 89B(1)(b) as the declared priority date; and
(b) one month after that date or, if later, one year after the date to be treated by virtue of section 89B(1)(b) as the declared priority date in any other case.

(2A) Payment of designation fees and of confirmation fees referred to in rule 15.5(a) in respect of designations made under rule 4.9(b) of the said Regulations shall be made to the Patent Office in the

respective amounts provided for in rule 15.2(b) and rule 15.5(a) thereof not later than 15 months after the date to be treated by virtue of section 89B(1)(b) as the declared priority date, or, where there is no declared priority date, the date on which the application to which they related is filed at the Patent Office.

(3) *[Payment]* **Subject to paragraph (4) below, payment** of the search fee referred to in rule 16.1 of the said Regulations shall be made to the Patent Office in the amount fixed by the Administrative Council of the European Patent Organisation and published in the Journal.

(4) Where payment of a fee pursuant to paragraphs (1), (2) and (3) above has not been made to the Patent Office, in the case of transmittal, basic and designation fees, within the periods prescribed by paragraphs (1) and (2) above, and in the case of search fees, within the period referred to in rule 16.1(f) of the said Regulations ("the specified period")—

    (a) **the Patent Office shall give notice to the applicant requiring the applicant to pay the Patent Office the outstanding fee and a late payment fee calculated in accordance with rule 16bis.2 of the said Regulations within the period of one month commencing on the date on which the notice is sent to the applicant; and**

    (b) **the specified period shall be treated in respect of the outstanding fee as not expiring until the end of the one month period referred to in sub-paragraph (a) above.**

NOTE

    Paras. (1), (2) and (3) amended and paras. (2A) and (4) inserted by The Patents (Amendment) Rules 1992, with effect from July 1, 1992 (S.I. 1992, No.1142).

Certified copies

16.119   119. A request under rule 20.9 of those Regulations for a certified copy of an international application as filed with the Patent Office as receiving office and of any corrections thereto shall be made on Patents Form 24/77 and shall be accompanied by the appropriate fee.

Fees for international preliminary examination

16.120   120. Where an applicant makes a demand to the Patent Office, as International Preliminary Examining Authority, for international preliminary examination under Article 31 of the said Treaty, he shall—

    (a) in accordance with rule 58 of those Regulations, pay the appropriate prescribed preliminary examination fee;

(b) in accordance with rule 57 of those Regulations, pay the handling fee therein referred to; and

(c) upon request by the Patent Office, pay to it an amount which is the equivalent in sterling of the search fee referred to in rule 118(3).

Additional fees for further inventions

121. Where under rule 68.2 of those Regulations the Patent Office, as International Preliminary Examining Authority, reports to the applicant that the requirement of unity of invention is not complied with and the applicant decides to pay an additional fee payable to the Patent Office in respect of each invention shall not exceed the appropriate prescribed preliminary examination fee.   **16.121**

Fees to be paid in sterling

122. The fees referred to in rules 118 to 121 shall be paid in sterling.   **16.122**

Transitional provisions and revocations

123.—(1) The reference to Schedule 2 to the Patents Rules 1968 in paragraph (a) of the proviso to rule 124 of the Patents Rules 1978 shall be construed as a reference to that Schedule with the substitution for forms 7, 9, 14 to 21, 23, 32 to 36, 38, 39, 43, 44, 46, 53 to 55, 63 to 65 and 69 of the correspondingly numbered forms in Schedule 5.   **16.123**

(2) In rule 124 of the Patents Rules 1978—

(a) for the words "the Patents Rules 1982" in each place where they occur, there shall be substituted the words "the Patents Rules 1990";

(b) for paragraph (*d*) of the proviso to paragraph (1), there shall be substituted—

"(*d*) subject to sub-rule (3) below, rules 30, 39(1) and (3) to (6), 41 to 50, 52, 61 to 66, 68 to 74, 76, 88(1), 90, 92 to 95, 97 to 101, 103 to 108, and 114 to 116 of the Patents Rules 1990 shall apply."

and

(c) for the words "in rule 39(1)" in paragraph (4) there shall be substituted the words "in rule 39(1) of the Patents Rules 1990."

(3) The rules described in column 1 of Schedule 6 are hereby revoked to the extent specified in column 3 thereof.

(4) Where—

(a) immediately before these Rules come into force, any time or period prescribed by the Rules hereby revoked has effect in relation to any act or proceeding and has not expired; and

(b) the corresponding time or period prescribed by these Rules would have expired or would expire earlier,

the time or period prescribed by those Rules and not by these Rules shall apply to that act or proceeding.

29th November 1990

SCHEDULE 1

16.124 [The Forms are not reproduced here. See Vitoria *et al.*, ed., *Encyclopedia of U.K. and European Patent Law* where they are reproduced in full.]

SCHEDULE 2

MICRO-ORGANISMS

Applications

16.125 1.—(1) The specification of an application for a patent, or of a patent, for an invention which requires for its performance the use of a micro-organism—
   (a) which is not available to the public at the date of filing of the application; and
   (b) which cannot be described in the specification in such a manner as to enable the invention to be performed by a person skilled in the art,
shall, in relation to the micro-organism itself, be treated for the purposes of the Act as disclosing the invention in such a manner only if one of the conditions set out in sub-paragraph (2) below is satisfied.
   (2) The conditions referred to in sub-paragraph (1) above are—
   (a) a condition that,—
      (i) not later than the date of filing of the application, a culture of the micro-organism has been deposited in a depositary institution which is able to furnish a sample of the micro-organism; and
      (ii) the name of the depositary institution, the date when the culture was deposited and the accession number of the deposit are given in the specification of the application; and
   (b) a condition, in the case of a European patent (U.K.), an application for a European patent (U.K.) or an international application for a patent (U.K.) which is treated, by virtue of section 77, 81 or 89 as a patent under the Act, or, as the case may be, an application for a patent under the Act, that the corresponding provisions of the Implementing Regulations to the European Patent Convention or, as the case may require, the Patent Co-operation Treaty have been complied with,
and, where a new deposit is made under paragraph 4 below, a further condition that the applicant or proprietor makes a new deposit in accordance with that paragraph.
   (3) Where the information specified in sub-paragraph (2)(a)(ii) above is not contained in an application for a patent as filed, it shall be added to the application—
   (a) before the end of the period of sixteen months after the declared priority date or, where there is no declared priority date, the date of filing of the application;
   (b) where, in a request made by the applicant, the comptroller publishes the application before the end of the period prescribed for the purposes of section 16(1), before the date of the request; or
   (c) where the comptroller sends notification to the applicant that, in accordance with

subsection (4) of section 118, he has received a request by any person for information and inspection of documents under subsection (1) of that section, before the end of one month after his sending to the applicant notification of his receipt of the request,

whichever is the earliest.

(4) The giving of the information specified in sub-paragraph (2)(a)(ii) above shall constitute the unreserved and irrevocable consent of the applicant to the depositary institution with which a culture (including a deposit which is to be treated as having always been available by virtue of paragraph 4(2) below) is from time to time deposited making the culture available on receipt of the comptroller's certificate authorising the release to the person who is named therein as a person to whom the culture may be made available and who makes a valid request therefor to the institution.

(5) The specification of an application for a patent described in paragraph (1) above shall mention any international agreement under which the micro-organism concerned is deposited.

(6) In relation to an application for a patent filed before this paragraph and paragraphs 2, 3 and 4 below come into force, rule 17 of the Patents Rules 1982 shall continue to have effect notwithstanding its revocation by rule 123(3) of these Rules.

Availability of cultures

2.—(1) Save where paragraph 3 below has effect, a request that the comptroller certify a **16.126** person as a person to whom a depositary institution may make available a sample of a micro-organism—
- (a) before publication of the application for a patent, to a person who has made a request under section 118(1) in the circumstances mentioned in paragraph 1(3)(c) above; and
- (b) at any later time, to any person,

shall be made on Patents Form 8/77 (which shall be filed in duplicate) together, in the case of a micro-organism of which a culture is deposited under the Budapest Treaty with an international depositary authority, with the form provided for by the Regulations under the Treaty.

(2) The comptroller shall send a copy of any form lodged with him under sub-paragraph (1) above and of his certificate authorising the release of the sample—
- (a) to the applicant for, or proprietor of, the patent;
- (b) to the depositary institution; and
- (c) to the person making the request.

(3) A request under sub-paragraph (1) above shall comprise, on the part of the person to whom the request relates, undertakings for the benefit of the applicant for, or proprietor of, the patent—
- (a) not to make the culture, or any culture derived from it, available to any other person; and
- (b) not to use the culture, or any culture derived from it, otherwise than for experimental purposes relating to the subject matter of the invention,

and—
- (i) subject to (iii) below, both undertakings shall have effect during any period before the application for a patent has been withdrawn, has been taken to be withdrawn, has been treated as having been withdrawn, has been refused or is treated as having been refused (incuding any further period allowed under rule 100 or rule 110(1) or (4) but excluding, where an application is reinstated under either of those rules, the period before it is reinstated);
- (ii) if a patent is granted on the application, the undertaking set out in sub-paragraph (1) above shall also have effect during any period for which the patent is in force and during the period of six months referred to in section 25(4); and
- (iii) the undertaking set out in paragraph (b) shall not have effect after the date of publication in the Journal of a notice that the patent has been granted,

and, in this sub-paragraph, references to a culture derived from a deposited culture of a micro-organism are references to a culture so derived which exhibits those characteristics of the deposited culture essential for the performance of the invention.

(4) For the purpose of enabling any act specified in section 55 to be done in relation to the

culture for the services of the Crown, the undertakings specified in sub-paragraph (3) above—

    (a) shall not be required from any government department or person authorised in writing by a government department for the purposes of this paragraph; and

    (b) shall not have effect in relation to any such person who has already given them.

(5) An undertaking given pursuant to sub-paragraph (3) above may be varied by way of derogation by agreement between the applicant or proprietor and the person by whom it is given.

(6) Where, in respect of a patent to which the undertaking set out in sub-paragraph 3(a) has effect,—

    (a) an entry is made in the register under section 46 to the effect that licences are to be available as of right; or

    (b) a compulsory licence is granted under section 48,

that undertaking shall not have effect to the extent necessary for effect to be given to any such licence.

Availability of cultures to experts

16.127   3.—(1) [*Where,*] **Subject to sub-paragraph (2A) below, where,** before the preparations for publication under section 16 of an application for a patent have been completed, the applicant gives notice to the comptroller on Patents Form 8A/77 of his intention that a sample of the micro-organism should be made available only to an expert, the provisions of this paragraph shall have effect.

(2) The comptroller—

    (a) shall publish with the application notice that the provisions of this paragraph have effect; and

    (b) notwithstanding paragraph 2 above, shall not, until the patent is granted or the application has been withdrawn, has been taken to be withdrawn, has been treated as having been withdrawn, has been refused or is treated as having been refused, issue any certificate authorising release of a sample otherwise than under this paragraph.

(2A) Where, for the purpose set out in sub-paragraph (1) above, an applicant for an international application for a patent (U.K.) gives notice in writing to the International Bureau under rule 13bis.3 of the Regulations under the Patent Co-operation Treaty before the technical preparations for international publication of the application are complete of his intention that a sample of the micro-organism should be made available only to an expert, he shall be treated by the comptroller for the purposes of this paragraph as having complied with the conditions in sub-paragraph (1) above and sub-paragraph (2)(a) above shall not apply.

(3) Any person wishing to have a sample of the micro-organism made available ("the requester")—

    (a) shall apply to the comptroller on Patents Form 8B/77 (which shall be filed in duplicate together, in the case of a micro-organism of which a culture is deposited under the Budapest Treaty with an international depositary authority, with the form provided for by the Regulations under that Treaty) nominating the person ("the expert") to whom he wishes the sample to be made available; and

    (b) shall at the same time file undertakings by the expert as set out in sub-paragraph (3) of paragraph 2 above in accordance with the provisions of that paragraph.

16.128   (4) The comptroller shall send a copy of Patents Form 8B/77 filed under sub-paragraph (3) above to the applicant for the patent and shall specify the period within which the applicant may object, in accordance with sub-paragraph (5) below, to a sample of the micro-organism being made available to the expert.

(5) Unless, within the period specified by the comptroller under sub-paragraph (4) above (or within such longer period as the comptroller may, on application made to him within that period, allow), the applicant for the patent sends notice in writing to the comptroller that he objects to a sample of the micro-organism being made available to the expert and gives his reasons for his objection, the comptroller shall send a copy of any form lodged with him under sub-paragraph (3)(*a*) above and of his certificate authorising the release of the sample—

    (a) to the applicant for the patent,

(b) to the depositary institution concerned,

(c) to the requester, and

(d) to the expert.

(6) Where, in accordance with sub-paragraph (5) above, the applicant for the patent sends notice to the comptroller of his objection to the issue of a certificate in favour of the expert, the comptroller—

(a) shall decide, having regard to the knowledge, experience and technical qualifications of the expert and to any other factors he considers relevant, whether to issue his certificate in favour of the expert; and

(b) if he decides to authorise the release of the sample to the expert, shall send to the persons referred to in sub-paragraph (5) above a copy of any form lodged with him under sub-paragraph (3)(a) above and of his certificate authorising the release of the sample to the expert.

(7) Before making a decision in accordance with sub-paragraph (6) above, the comptroller shall afford the applicant and the requester the opportunity of being heard.

(8) If the comptroller decides under sub-paragraph (6) above not to issue his certificate in favour of the expert, the requester may, by notice in writing to the comptroller and the applicant, nominate another person as the expert for the purposes of this paragraph; and the comptroller shall give such directions as he shall think fit with regard to the subsequent procedure.

(9) Nothing in this paragraph shall affect the rights under section 55 of any government department or any person authorised in writing by a government department.

NOTE

Sub-para. (1) amended and sub-para. (2A) inserted by The Patents (Amendment) Rules 1992, with effect from June 1, 1992 (S.I. 1992, No.1142).

New deposits

4.—(1) Where the depositary institution with which a deposit or a new deposit of a   **16.129**
culture has been made under this Schedule—

(a) notifies the applicant or proprietor that it—

(i) cannot satisfy a request made in accordance with paragraph 2(1) or 3(3) above, or

(ii) is not able lawfully, to satisfy such a request,

for the culture to be made available;

(b) ceases temporarily or permanently to carry out the functions of a depositary institution; or

(c) ceases for any reason to conduct its activities as a depositary institution in an objective and impartial manner,

subject to sub-paragraph (3) below, the applicant or proprietor may, unless the culture has been transferred to another depositary institution which is able to make it available, make a new deposit of a culture of that micro-organism.

(2) For the purposes of paragraph 1 above and of this paragraph, the deposit shall be treated as always having been available if, within three months of the receipt of such notification or of the depositary institution ceasing to perform the functions of a depositary institution or to conduct its activities as such an institution in an objective and impartial manner, the applicant or proprietor,—

(a) in a case where the deposit has not already been transferred, makes the new deposit;

(b) furnishes to the depositary institution with which the new deposit is made a declaration that the culture so deposited is of the same micro-organism as was the culture originally deposited; and

(c) requests amendment of the specification under section 19 or section 27, as the case may be, so as to indicate the accession number of the transferred or new deposit and, where applicable, the name of the depositary institution with which the deposit has been made.

(3) the new deposit referred to in sub-paragraph (1) above—

(a) shall, save as provided in sub-paragraph (b) below, be made with the same depositary institution as was the original deposit; or

(b) in the cases referred to in sub-paragraphs (1)(a)(ii), (b) and (c) above, shall be made with another depositary institution which is able to satisfy the request.

Interpretation of Schedule

16.130   5.—(1) In this Schedule—

"the Budapest Treaty" means the Treaty on the International Recognition of the Deposit of Micro-organisms for the purposes of Patent Procedure done at Budapest in 1977; and "international depositary authority" means a depositary institution which has acquired the status of international depositary authority as provided in Article 7 of the Budapest Treaty.

(2) For the purposes of this Schedule a "depositary institution" is an institution which, at all relevant times,—

(a) carries out the functions of receiving, accepting and storing micro-organisms and the furnishing of samples thereof; and

(b) conducts its affairs insofar as they relate to the carrying out of those functions in an objective and impartial manner.

SCHEDULE 3

FORM OF CERTIFICATE OF GRANT OF PATENT

16.131   In accordance with section 24(2) of the Patents Act 1977, it is hereby certified that a patent having the specification No.   has been granted to   in respect of an invention disclosed in an application for that patent having a date of filing of being an invention for

Dated this   day of   19

Comptroller-General of Patents,
Designs and Trade Marks.

SCHEDULE 4

EUROPEAN PATENTS AND APPLICATIONS (U.K.): TRANSLATIONS

Translations of European patents (U.K.) filed under section 77(6)

16.132   **1.**—(1) A translation filed under section 77(6) shall be filed in duplicate and shall be accompanied by—

(a) Patents Form 54/77 in duplicate, in the case of a translation filed under section 77(6)(a), or

(b) Patents Form 55/77 in duplicate, in the case of a translation filed under section 77(6)(b).

(2) A translation filed under section 77(6) shall comprise a translation of the entirety of the published specification of the patent (including the claims), irrespective of whether a translation of all or any part of the claims contained in the specification has previously been filed under section 78(7) but subject to sub-paragraph (5) below, and shall include any drawings in the specification, irrespective of whether the drawings contain textual matter.

(3) A translation filed under section 77(6) shall comply with the following requirements as to presentation, subject to sub-paragraph (4) below in the case of any drawings—

(a) it shall permit of direct reproduction by photography, electrostatic processes, photo-offset and micro-filming, in an unlimited number of copies;

(b) it shall be on A4 paper (29.7 cm × 21 cm) which shall be pliable, strong, white, smooth, matt and durable;

(c) each sheet of paper shall be free from cracks, creases and folds and used on one side only;

(d) each sheet shall be used with its short sides at the top and bottom (upright position);

(e) the minimum margins shall be—

top	2.0 cm
left side	2.5 cm
right side	2.0 cm
bottom	2.0 cm

(f) the margins of the sheets shall be completely blank;

(g) the translation shall be typed or printed in single-line spacing (unless the comptroller otherwise permits), in a dark, indelible colour and in characters of which the capital letters are not less than 0.21 cm high, save that graphic symbols and characters and chemical and mathematical formulae may, instead of being typed or printed, be written or drawn;

(h) the translation shall be reasonably free from extraneous matter and also from deletions and other alterations, overwritings and interlineations and shall, in any event, be legible; and

(i) each sheet (other than a sheet of drawings) shall be numbered consecutively in arabic numerals.

(4) Where a translation including any drawings is filed, the sheets of drawings shall correspond exactly in content and presentation to the sheets of drawings which were published by the European Patent Office, except that—

(a) each sheet shall be numbered consecutively in arabic numerals, as a separate series from that used for the other sheets of the translation, if not so numbered when published by the European Patent Office; and

(b) any textual matter contained in the published drawings shall be replaced with a translation into English.

(5) For the purposes of sub-paragraph (2) above, the published specification of the patent shall be taken not to include—

(a) anything which does not consist of, or form part of, the description of the invention, the claims or the drawings referred to in the description or the claims;

(b) any claim not having effect in the United Kingdom; or

(c) anything published in a language other than the language of the proceedings (within the meaning of Article 14 of the European Patent Convention).

Periods prescribed under section 77(6)

2.—(1) The period prescribed under section 77(6)(a) for filing a translation of the specification of a European patent (U.K.) and paying the prescribed fee shall be three months from the date of publication of the mention of the grant of the patent in the European Patent Bulletin.   **16.133**

(2) The period prescribed under section 77(6)(b) for filing a translation of the specification as amended of a European patent (U.K.) and paying the prescribed fee shall

be three months from the date of publication by the European Patent Office of the specification of the patent as amended.

Translations of claims of applications for European patents (U.K.) filed under section 78(7)

16.134   3.—(1) A translation of the claims of an application for a European patent (U.K.),—
(a) in the case of an application which has been published by the European Patent Office, may be filed under subsection (7) of section 78 after the application has been so published; and
(b) in the case of an application which has not been so published but which is the subject of proceedings before the European Patent Office by virtue of Article 150 of the European Patent Convention, may be filed under that subsection after the application has been published under Article 21 of the Patent Co-operation Treaty.
(2) A translation filed by virtue of sub-paragraph (1) above shall be filed in duplicate and shall be accompanied by Patents Form 56/77, also filed in duplicate.
(3) The translation shall comply with the requirements contained in paragraph 1(3) above.

Corrected translations filed under section 80(3)

16.135   4.—(1) A corrected translation filed under section 80(3) shall be filed in duplicate.
(2) The corrected translation shall comply with the requirements contained in paragraph 1(3) and (4) above.
(3) Publication of the corrected translation shall be requested on Patents Form 57/77, which shall be filed in duplicate.
(4) The period prescribed under section 80(3) for payment of the prescribed fee shall be fourteen days from the day on which the corrected translation is filed.

Verification of translation

16.136   5. A translation shall be verified to the satisfaction of the comptroller as corresponding to the original text of—
(a) the specification, in the case of a translation filed under section 77(6)(a);
(b) the specification as amended, in the case of translation filed under section 77(6)(b);
(c) the claims of the specification of the application, in the case of a translation filed under section 78(7); or
(d) the specification of the patent or the claims of the application, as the case may be, in the case of a translation filed under section 80(3),
and if such verification does not accompany the translation when filed it shall be filed within one month of the sending by the comptroller of a written request for such verification.

Inspection of translations

6. A request for inspection of a translation published under section 77(8), 78(7) or 80(3)   **16.137**
shall be made on Patents Form 23/77.

SCHEDULE 5

[The Patents Act 1949 Forms are not reproduced here. See Vitoria *et al.*, ed., *Encyclopedia*   **16.138**
of U.K. and European Patent Law where they are reproduced in full.]

PATENTS ACT 1949

(as amended; only those sections that are still likely to be relevant are reproduced)

ARRANGEMENT OF SECTIONS

Application, investigation, opposition, etc.

SECTION

Grant, effect and term of patent

Restoration of lapsed patents and patet applications

Amendment of specifications

Revocation and surrender of patents

Voluntary endorsement of patent

Compulsory licenses etc.

Use of patented inventions for services of the Crown

Anticipation, etc.

The Court and the Appeal Tribunal

Patent Agents

Offences

Rules, etc.

Supplemental

SCHEDULES:

An Act to consolidate certain enactments relating to patents.

[16th December, 1949.]

Application, investigation, opposition, etc.

Persons entitled to make application

17.01   1.—(1) Application for a patent for an invention may be made by any of the following persons, that is to say:—
  (a) by any person claiming to be the true and first inventor of the invention;
  (b) by any person being the assignee of the person claiming to be the true and first inventor in respect of the right to make such an application;
and may be made by that person either alone or jointly with any other person.

(2) Without prejudice to the foregoing provisions of this section, an application for a patent for an invention in respect of which protection has been applied for in a convention country may be made by the person by whom the application for protection was made or by the assignee of that person:

Provided that no application shall be made by virtue of this subsection after the expiration of twelve months from the date of the application for protection in a convention country or, where more than one such application for protection has been made, from the date of the first application.

(3) An application for a patent may be made under subsection (1) or subsection (2) of this section by the personal representative of any deceased person who, immediately before his death, was entitled to make such an application.

(4) An application for a patent made by virtue of subsection (2) of this section is in this Act referred to as a convention application.

Application

17.02   2.—(1) Every application for a patent shall be made in the prescribed form and shall be filed at the Patent Office in the prescribed manner.

(2) If the application (not being a convention application) is made by virtue of an assignment of the right to apply for a patent for the invention, there shall be furnished with the application or within such period as may be prescribed after the filing of the application a declaration, signed by the person claiming to be the true and first inventor or his personal representative, stating that he assents to the making of the application.

(3) Every application (other than a convention application) shall state that the applicant is in possession of the invention and shall name the person claiming to be the true and first inventor; and where the person so claiming is not the applicant or one of the applicants, the application shall contain a declaration that the applicant believes him to be the true and first inventor.

(4) Every convention application shall specify the date on which and the convention country in which the application for protection, or the first such application, was made, and shall state that no application for protection in respect of the invention had been made in a convention country before that date by the applicant or any person from whom he derives title.

(5) Where applications for protection have been made in one or more convention countries in respect of two or more inventions which are cognate or of which one is a modification of another, a single convention application may, subject to the provisions of section four of this Act, be made in respect of those inventions at any time within twelve months from the date of the earliest of the said applications for protection:

> Provided that the fee payable on the making of any such application shall be the same as if separate applications had been made in respect of each of the said inventions; and the requirements of the last foregoing subsection shall in the case of any such application apply separately to the applications for protection in respect of each of the said inventions.

Complete and provisional specifications

3.—(1) Every application for a patent (other than a convention **17.03** application) shall be accompanied by either a complete specification or a provisional specification; and every convention application shall be accompanied by a complete specification.

(2) Where an application for a patent is accompanied by a provisional specification, a complete specification shall be filed within twelve months from the date of filing of the application and if the complete specification is not so filed the application shall be deemed to be abandoned:

> Provided that the complete specification may be filed at any time after twelve months but within fifteen months from the date aforesaid if a request to that effect is made to the comptroller and the prescribed fee paid on or before the date on which the specification is filed.

(3) Where two or more applications accompanied by provisional specifications have been filed in respect of inventions which are cognate or of which one is a modification of another, a single complete

specification may, subject to the provisions of this and the next following section, be filed in pursuance of those applications, or, if more than one complete specification has been filed, may with the leave of the comptroller be proceeded with in respect of those applications.

(4) Where an application for a patent (not being a convention application) is accompanied by a specification purporting to be a complete specification, the comptroller may, if the applicant so requests at any time before the acceptance of the specification, direct that it shall be treated for the purposes of this Act as a provisional specification, and proceed with the application accordingly.

(5) Where a complete specification has been filed in pursuance of an application for a patent accompanied by a provisional specification or by a specification treated by virtue of a direction under the last foregoing subsection as a provisional specification, the comptroller may, if the applicant so requests at any time before the acceptance of the complete specification, cancel the provisional specification and post-date the application to the date of filing of the complete specification.

Contents of specification

17.04   4.—(1) Every specification, whether complete or provisional, shall describe the invention, and shall begin with a title indicating the subject to which the invention relates.

(2) Subject to any rules made by the Department of Trade and Industry under this Act, drawings may, and shall if the comptroller so requires, be supplied for the purposes of any specification, whether complete or provisional; and any drawings so supplied shall, unless the comptroller otherwise directs, be deemed to form part of the specification, and references in this Act to a specification shall be construed accordingly.

(3) Every complete specification—

(a) shall particularly describe the invention and the method by which it is to be performed;

(b) shall disclose the best method of performing the invention which is known to the applicant and for which he is entitled to claim protection; and

(c) shall end with a claim or claims defining the scope of the invention claimed.

(4) The claim or claims of a complete specification must relate to a single invention, must be clear and succinct, and must be fairly based on the matter disclosed in the specification.

(5) Rules made by the Department of Trade and Industry under this Act may require that in such cases as may be prescribed by the rules, a declaration as to the inventorship of the invention, in such form as may be so prescribed, shall be furnished with the complete specification or

within such period as may be so prescribed after the filing of that specification.

(6) Subject to the foregoing provisions of this section, a complete specification filed after a provisional specification, or filed with a convention application, may include claims in respect of developments of or additions to the invention which was described in the provisional specification or, as the case may be, the invention in respect of which the application for protection was made in a convention country, being developments or additions in respect of which the applicant would be entitled under the provisions of section one of this Act to make a separate application for a patent.

(7) Where a complete specification claims a new substance, the claim shall be construed as not extending to that substance when found in nature.

Priority date of claims of complete specification

5.—(1) Every claim of a complete specification shall have effect from **17.05** the date prescribed by this section in relation to that claim (in this Act referred to as the priority date); and a patent shall not be invalidated by reason only of the publication or use of the invention, so far as claimed in any claim of the complete specification, on or after the priority date of that claim, or by the grant of another patent upon a specification claiming the same invention in a claim of the same or later priority date.

(2) Where the complete specification is filed in pursuance of a single application accompanied by a provisional specification or by a specification which is treated by virtue of a direction under subsection (4) of section three of this Act as a provisional specification, and the claim is fairly based on the matter disclosed in that specification, the priority date of that claim shall be the date of filing of the application.

(3) Where the complete specification is filed or proceeded with in pursuance of two or more applications accompanied by such specifications as are mentioned in the last foregoing subsection, and the claim is fairly based on the matter disclosed in one of those specifications, the priority date of that claim shall be the date of filing of the application accompanied by that specification.

(4) Where the complete specification is filed in pursuance of a convention application and the claim is fairly based on the matter disclosed in the application for protection in a convention country or, where the convention application is founded upon more than one such application for protection, in one of those applications, the priority date of that claim shall be the date of the relevant application for protection.

(5) Where, under the foregoing provisions of this section, any claim of a complete specification would, but for this provision, have two or more priority dates, the priority date of that claim shall be the earlier or earliest of those dates.

(6) In any case to which subsections (2) to (5) of this section do not apply, the priority date of a claim shall be the date of filing of the complete specification.

* * *

Reference in case of potential infringement

17.06 9.—(1) If, in consequence of the investigations required by the foregoing provisions of this Act or of proceedings under section fourteen or section thirty-three of this Act, it appears to the comptroller that an invention in respect of which application for a patent has been made cannot be performed without substantial risk of infringement of a claim of any other patent, he may direct that a reference to that other patent shall be inserted in the applicant's complete specification by way of notice to the public unless within such time as may be prescribed either—

 (a) the applicant shows to the satisfaction of the comptroller that there are reasonable grounds for contesting the validity of the said claim of the other patent; or

 (b) the complete specification is amended to the satisfaction of the comptroller.

(2) Where, after a reference to another patent has been inserted in a complete specification in pursuance of a direction under the foregoing subsection,—

 (a) that other patent is revoked or otherwise ceases to be in force; or

 (b) the specification of that other patent is amended by the deletion of the relevant claim; or

 (c) it is found, in proceedings before the court or the comptroller, that the relevant claim of that other patent is invalid or is not infringed by any working of the applicant's invention;

the comptroller may, on the application of the applicant, delete the reference to that other patent.

(3) An appeal shall lie from any decision or direction of the comptroller under this section.

* * *

Grant, effect and term of patent

Amendment of patent granted to deceased applicant

17.07 20. Where, at any time after a patent has been sealed in pursuance of an application under this Act, the comptroller is satisfied that the person to whom the patent was granted has died, or (in the case of a body corporate) has ceased to exist, before the patent was sealed, he may amend the patent by substituting for the name of that person the name of the person to whom the patent ought to have been granted; and the patent shall have effect, and shall be deemed always to have had effect, accordingly.

Extent, effect and form of patent

21.—(1) A patent sealed with the seal of the Patent Office shall have   **17.08**
the same effect as if it were sealed with the Great Seal of the United Kingdom, and shall have effect throughout the United Kingdom and the Isle of Man:

Provided that a patent may be assigned for any place in or part of the United Kingdom or Isle of Man as effectually as if it were granted so as to extend to that place or part only.

(2) Subject to the provisions of this Act and of subsection (3) of section 3 of the Crown Proceedings Act 1947, a patent shall have the same effect against the crown as it has against a subject.

(3) A patent shall be in such form as may be authorised by rules made by the Department of Trade and Industry under this Act.

(4) A patent shall be granted for one invention only; but it shall not be competent for any person in an action or other proceeding to take any objection to a patent on the ground that it has been granted for more than one invention.

Date and term of patent

22.—(1) Every patent shall be dated with the date of filing of the   **17.09**
complete specification:

Provided that no proceeding shall be taken in respect of an infringement committed before the date of the publication of the complete specification.

(2) The date of every patent shall be entered in the register of patents.

(3) Except as otherwise expressly provided by this Act, the term of every patent shall be sixteen years from the date of the patent.

* * *

Patents of addition

17.10 26.—(1) Subject to the provisions of this section, where application is made for a patent in respect of any improvement in or modification of an invention (in this Act referred to as "the main invention") and the applicant also applies or has applied for a patent for that invention or is the patentee in respect thereof, the comptroller may, if the applicant so requests, grant the patent for the improvement or modification as a patent of addition.

(2) Subject to the provisions of this section, where an invention, being an improvement in or modification of another invention, is the subject of an independent patent and the patentee in respect of that patent is also the patentee in respect of the patent for the main invention, the comptroller may, if the patentee so requests, by order revoke the patent for the improvement or modification and grant to the patentee a patent of addition in respect thereof, bearing the same date as the date of the patent so revoked.

(3) A patent shall not be granted as a patent of addition unless the date of filing of the complete specification was the same as or later than the date of filing of the complete specification in respect of the main invention and was earlier than the appointed day.

(4) A patent of addition shall not be sealed before the sealing of the patent for the main invention; and if the period within which, but for this provision, a request for the sealing of a patent of addition could be made under section nineteen of this Act expires before the period within which a request for the sealing of the patent for the main invention may be so made, the request for the sealing of the patent of addition may be made at any time within the last-mentioned period.

(5) A patent of addition shall be granted for a term equal to that of the patent for the main invention, or so much thereof as is unexpired, and shall remain in force during that term or until the previous cesser of the patent for the main invention and no longer:

Provided that
- (a) if the term of the patent for the main invention is extended under the foregoing provisions of this Act, the term of the patent of addition may also be extended accordingly; and
- (b) if the patent for the main invention is revoked under this Act, the court or comptroller, as the case may be, may order that the patent of addition shall become an independent patent for the remainder of the term of the patent for the main invention, and thereupon the patent shall continue in force as an independent patent accordingly.

(6) No renewal fees shall be payable in respect of a patent of addition; but, if any such patent becomes an independent patent by virtue of an order under the last foregoing subsection, the same fees shall thereafter

be payable, upon the same dates, as if the patent had been originally granted as an independent patent.

(7) The grant of a patent of addition shall not be refused, and a patent granted as a patent of addition shall not be revoked or invalidated, on the ground only that the invention claimed in the complete specification does not involve any inventive step having regard to any publication or use of—

(a) the main invention described in the complete specification relating thereto; or

(b) any improvement in or modification of the main invention described in the complete specification of a patent of addition to the patent for the main invention or of an application for such a patent of addition;

and the validity of a patent of addition shall not be questioned on the ground that the invention ought to have been the subject of an independent patent.

(8) An appeal shall lie from any decision of the comptroller under this section.

* * *

Amendment of specifications

Amendment of specification with leave of comptroller

29.—(1) Subject to the provisions of section thirty-one of this Act, the **17.11** comptroller may, upon application made under this section by a patentee, or by an applicant for a patent at any time after the acceptance of the complete specification, allow the complete specification to be amended subject to such conditions, if any, as the comptroller thinks fit:

Provided that the comptroller shall not allow a specification to be amended under this section upon an application made while any action before the court for infringement of the patent or any proceeding before the court for the revocation of the patent is pending.

(2) Every application for leave to amend a specification under this section shall state the nature of the proposed amendment and shall give full particulars of the reasons for which the application is made.

(3) Any application for leave to amend a specification under this section, and the nature of the proposed amendment, shall be advertised in the prescribed manner:

Provided that where the application is made before the publication of the complete specification, the comptroller may, if he thinks fit, dispense with advertisement under this subsection or direct that advertisement shall be postponed until the complete specification is published.

(4) Within the prescribed period after the advertisement of an application under this section, any person may give notice to the comptroller of opposition thereto; and where such a notice is given within the period aforesaid, the comptroller shall notify the person by whom the application under this section is made and shall give to that person and to the opponent an opportunity to be heard before he decides the case.

(5) An appeal shall lie from any decision of the comptroller under this section.

(6) This section shall not apply in relation to any amendment of a specification effected in proceedings in opposition to the grant of a patent or on a reference to the comptroller of a dispute as to the infringement or validity of a claim, or effected in pursuance of any provision of this Act authorising the comptroller to direct a reference to another specification or patent to be inserted, or to refuse to grant a patent, or to revoke a patent, unless the specification is amended to his satisfaction.

Amendment of specification with leave of the court

17.12   30.—(1) In any action for infringement of a patent or any proceeding before the court for the revocation of a patent, the court may, subject to the provisions of the next following section, by order allow the patentee to amend his complete specification in such manner, and subject to such terms as to costs, advertisements or otherwise, as the court may think fit; and if in any such proceedings for revocation the court decides that the patent is invalid, the court may allow the specification to be amended under this section instead of revoking the patent.

(2) Where an application for an order under this section is made to the court, the applicant shall give notice of the application to the comptroller, and the comptroller shall be entitled to appear and be heard, and shall appear if so directed by the court.

Supplementary provisions as to amendment of specification

17.13   31.—(1) After the acceptance of a complete specification, no amendment thereof shall be effected except by way of disclaimer, correction or explanation, and no amendment thereof shall be allowed, except for the purpose of correcting an obvious mistake, the effect of which would be that the specification as amended would claim or describe matter not in substance disclosed in the specification before the amendment, or that any claim of the specification as amended would not fall wholly within the scope of a claim of the specification before the amendment.

(2) Where, after the date of the publication of a complete specification, any amendment of the specification is allowed or approved by the comptroller, the court or the Appeal Tribunal under this Act, the right of the patentee or applicant to make the amendment shall not be called in question except on the ground of fraud; and the amendment shall in all courts and for all purposes be deemed to form part of the specification:

Provided that in construing the specification as amended reference may be made to the specification as originally published.

(3) Where, after the date of the publication of a complete specification, any amendment of the specification is allowed or approved as aforesaid, the fact that the specification has been amended shall be advertised in the Journal.

Revocation and surrender of patents

Revocation of patent by court

32.—(1) Subject to the provisions of this Act, a patent may, on the petition of any person interested, be revoked by the court on any of the following grounds, that is to say,—

   17.14

(a) that the invention, so far as claimed in any claim of the complete specification, was claimed in a valid claim of earlier priority date contained in the complete specification of another patent granted in the United Kingdom;

(b) that the patent was granted on the application of a person not entitled under the provisions of this Act to apply therefor;

(c) that the patent was obtained in contravention of the rights of the petitioner or any person under or through whom he claims;

(d) that the subject of any claim of the complete specification is not an invention within the meaning of this Act;

(e) that the invention, so far as claimed in any claim of the complete specification, is not new having regard to what was known or used, before the priority date of the claim, in the United Kingdom;

(f) that the invention, so far as claimed in any claim of the complete specification, is obvious and does not involve any inventive step having regard to what was known or used, before the priority date of the claim, in the United Kingdom;

(g) that the invention, so far as claimed in any claim of the complete specification, is not useful;

(h) that the complete specification does not sufficiently and fairly describe the invention and the method by which it is to be performed, or does not disclose the best method of performing it which was known to the applicant for the patent and for which he was entitled to claim protection;

(i) that the scope of any claim of the complete specification is not sufficiently and clearly defined or that any claim of the complete specification is not fairly based on the matter disclosed in the specification;

(j) that the patent was obtained on a false suggestion or representation;

(k) that the primary or intended use or exercise of the invention is contrary to law;

(l) that the invention, so far as claimed in any claim of the complete specification, was secretly used in the United Kingdom, otherwise than as mentioned in subsection (2) of this section, before the priority date of that claim.

(2) For the purposes of paragraph (*l*) of subsection (1) of this section, no account shall be taken of any use of the invention—

(a) for the purpose of reasonable trial or experiment only; or

(b) by a Government department or any person authorised by a Government department, in consequence of the applicant for the patent or any person from whom he derives title having communicated or disclosed the invention directly or indirectly to a Government department or person authorised as aforesaid; or

(c) by any other person, in consequence of the applicant for the patent or any person from whom he derives title having communicated or disclosed the invention, and without the consent or acquiescence of the applicant or of any person from whom he derives title;

and for the purposes of paragraph (*e*) or paragraph (*f*) of the said subsection (1) no account shall be taken of any secret use.

(4) Every ground on which a patent may be revoked shall be available as a ground of defence in any proceeding for the infringement of the patent.

Revocation of patent by comptroller

17.15   33.—(1) Subject to the provision of this Act, a patent may, on the application of any person interested, be revoked by the comptroller on any of the grounds set out in section 32(1) of this Act:

Provided that when an action for infringement, or proceedings for the revocation, of a patent are pending in any court, an application to the comptroller under this section shall not be made except with the leave of the court.

(2) Where an application is made under this section, the comptroller shall notify the patentee and shall give to the applicant and the patentee an opportunity to be heard before deciding the case.

(3) If on an application under this section the comptroller is satisfied that any of the grounds aforesaid are established, he may by order direct that the patent shall be revoked either unconditionally or unless within such time as may be specified in the order the complete specification is amended to his satisfaction.

(4) An appeal shall lie from any decision of the comptroller under this section.

(5) A decision of the comptroller or on appeal from the comptroller shall not estop any party to civil proceedings in which infringement of a patent is in issue from alleging that any claim of the specification is invalid on any of the grounds set out in section 32(1) of this Act, whether or not any of the issues involved were decided in that decision.

* * *

Anticipation, etc.

Previous publication

50.—(1) An invention claimed in a complete specification shall not be   **17.16**
deemed to have been anticipated by reason only that the invention was published in the United Kingdom—

(a) in a specification filed in pursuance of an application for a patent made in the United Kingdom and dated more than fifty years before the date of filing of the first-mentioned specification;

(b) in a specification describing the invention for the purposes of an application for protection in any country outside the United Kingdom made more than fifty years before that date; or

(c) in any abridgment of or extract from any such specification published under the authority of the comptroller or of the government of any country outside the United Kingdom.

(2) Subject as hereinafter provided, an invention claimed in a complete specification shall not be deemed to have been anticipated by reason only that the invention was published before the priority date of the relevant claim of the specification, if the patentee or applicant for the patent proves—

(a) that the matter published was obtained from him or (where he is not himself the true and first inventor) from any person from whom he derives title, and was published without his consent or the consent of any such person; and

(b) where the patentee or applicant for the patent or any person from whom he derives title learned of the publication before the date of the application for the patent or (in the case of a convention application) before the date of the application for protection in a convention country, that the application or the application in a convention country, as the case may be, was made as soon as reasonably practicable thereafter:

Provided that this subsection shall not apply if the invention was before the priority date of the claim commercially worked in the United Kingdom, otherwise than for the purpose of reasonable trial, either by the patentee or applicant for the patent or any person from whom he derives title or by any other person with the consent of the patentee or applicant for the patent or any person from whom he derives title.

(3) Where a complete specification is filed in pursuance of an application for a patent made by a person being the true and first inventor or deriving title from him, an invention claimed in that specification shall not be deemed to have been anticipated by reason only of any other application for a patent in respect of the same invention, made in contravention of the rights of that person, or by reason only that after the date of filing of that other application the invention was used or published, without the consent of that person, by the applicant in respect of that other application, or by any other person in consequence of any disclosure of the invention by that applicant.

(4) Notwithstanding anything in this Act, the comptroller shall not refuse to accept a complete specification or to grant a patent, and a patent shall not be revoked or invalidated, by reason only of any circumstances which, by virtue of this section, do not constitute an anticipation of the invention claimed in the specification.

Previous communication, display or working

17.17   **51.**—(1) An invention claimed in a complete specification shall not be deemed to have been anticipated by reason only of the communication of the invention to a Government department or to any person authorised by a Government department to investigate the invention or its merits, or of anything done, in consequence of such a communication, for the purpose of the investigation.

(2) An invention claimed in a complete specification shall not be deemed to have been anticipated by reason only of—

    (a) the display of the invention with the consent of the true and first inventor at an exhibition certified by the Board of Trade for the purposes of this section, or the use thereof with his consent for the purposes of such an exhibition in the place where it is held;

    (b) the publication of any description of the invention in consequence of the display or use of the invention at any such exhibition as aforesaid;

(c) the use of the invention, after it has been displayed or used at any such exhibition as aforesaid and during the period of the exhibition, by any person without the consent of the true and first inventor; or

(d) the description of the invention in a paper read by the true and first inventor before a learned society or published with his consent in the transactions of such a society,

if the application for the patent is made by the true and first inventor or a person deriving title from him not later than six months after the opening of the exhibition or the reading or publication of the paper as the case may be.

(3) An invention claimed in a complete specification shall not be deemed to have been anticipated by reason only that, at any time within one year before the priority date of the relevant claim of the specification, the invention was publicly worked in the United Kingdom—

(a) by the patentee or applicant for the patent or any person from whom he derives title; or

(b) by any other person with the consent of the patentee or applicant for the patent or any person from whom he derives title,

if the working was affected for the purpose of reasonable trial only and if it was reasonably necessary, having regard to the nature of the invention, that the working for that purpose should be effected in public.

(4) Notwithstanding anything in this Act, the comptroller shall not refuse to accept a complete specification or to grant a patent, and a patent shall not be revoked or invalidated, by reason only of any circumstances which, by virtue of this section, do not constitute an anticipation of the invention claimed in the specification.

Use and publication after provisional specification or foreign application

52.—(1) Where a complete specification is filed or proceeded with in   **17.18** pursuance of an application which was accompanied by a provisional specification or by a specification treated by virtue of a direction under subsection (4) of section three of this Act as a provisional specification, then, notwithstanding anything in this Act, the comptroller shall not refuse to grant the patent, and the patent shall not be revoked or invalidated by reason only that any matter described in the provisional specification or in the specification treated as aforesaid as a provisional specification was used or published at any time after the date of filing of that specification.

(2) Where a complete specification is filed in pursuance of a convention application, then, notwithstanding anything in this Act, the

comptroller shall not refuse to grant the patent, and the patent shall not be revoked or invalidated by reason only that any matter disclosed in any application for protection in a convention country upon which the convention application is founded was used or published at any time after the date of that application for protection.

Power of comptroller to give directions to co-owners

17.19   **55.**—(1) Where two or more persons are registered as grantee or proprietor of a patent, the comptroller may, upon application made to him in the prescribed manner by any of those persons, give such directions in accordance with the application as to the sale or lease of the patent or any interest therein, the grant of licences under the patent, or the exercise of any right under the last foregoing section in relation thereto, as he thinks fit.

(2) If any person registered as grantee or proprietor of the patent fails to execute any instrument or to do any other thing required for the carrying out of any direction given under this section within fourteen days after being requested in writing so to do by any of the other persons so registered, the comptroller may, upon application made to him in the prescribed manner by any such other person, give directions empowering any person to execute that instrument or to do that thing in the name and on behalf of the person in default.

(3) Before giving directions in pursuance of an application under this section, the comptroller shall give an opportunity to be heard—

(a) in the case of an application under subsection (1) of this section, to the other person or persons registered as grantee or proprietor of the patent;

(b) in the case of an application under subsection (2) of this section, to the person in default.

(4) An appeal shall lie from any decision or direction of the comptroller under this section.

(5) No directions shall be given under this section so as to affect the mutual rights or obligations of trustees or of the personal representatives of a deceased person, or their rights or obligations as such.

Disputes as to inventions made by employees

17.20   **56.**—(1) Where a dispute arises between an employer and a person who is or was at the material time his employee as to the rights of the parties in respect of an invention made by the employee either alone or jointly with other employees or in respect of any patent granted or to be granted in respect thereof, the comptroller may, upon application made to him in the prescribed manner by either of the parties, and after giving to each of them an opportunity to be heard, determine the matter in dispute, and may make such orders for giving effect to his decision as he considers expedient:

Provided that if it appears to the comptroller upon any application under this section that the matter in dispute involves questions which would more properly be determined by the court, he may decline to deal therewith.

(2) In proceedings before the court between an employer and a person who is or was at the material time his employee, or upon an application made to the comptroller under subsection (1) of this section, the court or comptroller may, unless satisfied that one or other of the parties is entitled, to the exclusion of the other, to the benefit of an invention made by the employee, by order provide for the apportionment between them of the benefit of the invention, and of any patent or to be granted in respect thereof, in such manner as the court or comptroller considers just.

(3) A decision of the comptroller under this section shall have the same effect as between the parties and persons claiming under them as a decision of the court.

(4) An appeal shall lie from any decision of the comptroller under this section.

International Agreements, etc.

Supplementary provisions as to convention applications

69.—(1) Where a person has applied for protection for an invention by an application which— **17.21**

(a) in accordance with the terms of a treaty subsisting between any two or more convention countries, is equivalent to an application duly made in any one of those convention countries, or

(b) in accordance with the law of any convention country, is equivalent to an application duly made in that convention country,

he shall be deemed for the purposes of this Act to have applied in that convention country.

(2) For the purpose of this Act, matter shall be deemed to have been disclosed in an application for protection in a convention country if it was claimed or disclosed (otherwise than by way of disclaimer or acknowledgment of prior art) in that application or in documents submitted by the applicant for protection in support of and at the same time as that application; but no account shall be taken of any disclosure effected by any such document unless a copy of the document is filed at

the Patent Office with the convention application or within such period as may be prescribed after the filing of that application.

Register of patents, etc.

Power to correct clerical errors, etc.

17.22   **76.**—(1) The comptroller may, in accordance with the provisions of this section, correct any clerical error in any patent, any application for a patent or any document filed in pursuance of such an application, or any error in the register of patents.

(2) A correction may be made in pursuance of this section either upon a request in writing made by any person interested and accompanied by the prescribed fee, or without such a request.

(3) Where the comptroller proposes to make any such correction as aforesaid otherwise than in pursuance of a request made under this section, he shall give notice of the proposal to the patentee or the applicant for the patent, as the case may be, and to any other person who appears to him to be concerned, and shall give them an opportunity to be heard before making the correction.

(4) Where a request is made under this section for the correction of any error in a patent or application for a patent or any document filed in pursuance of such an application, and it appears to the comptroller that the correction would materially alter the meaning or scope of the document to which the request relates, and ought not to be made without notice to persons affected thereby, he shall require notice of the nature of the proposed correction to be advertised in the prescribed manner.

(5) Within the prescribed time after any such advertisement as aforesaid any person interested may give notice to the comptroller of opposition to the request, and where such notice of opposition is given the comptroller shall give notice thereof to the person by whom the request was made, and shall give to him and to the opponent an opportunity to be heard before he decides the case.

* * *

Loss or destruction of patent

17.23   **80.** Where the comptroller is satisfied that a patent has been lost or destroyed or cannot be produced, he may at any time cause a duplicate thereof to be sealed.

Offences

Unauthorised assumption of Royal Arms

92.—(1) The grant of a patent under this Act shall not be deemed to **17.24** authorise the patentee to use the Royal Arms or to place the Royal Arms on any patented article.

(2) If any person, without the authority of His Majesty, uses in connection with any business, trade, calling or profession the Royal Arms (or Arms so nearly resembling them as to be calculated to deceive) in such manner as to be calculated to lead to the belief that he is duly authorised to use the Royal Arms, then, without prejudice to any proceedings which may be taken against him under section sixty-one of the Trade Marks Act, 1938, he shall be liable on summary conviction to a fine not exceeding twenty pounds:

> Provided that this section shall not affect the right, if any, of the proprietor of a trade mark containing such Arms to continue to use that trade mark.

Proceedings of Board of Trade

96.—(2) All documents purporting to be orders made by the **17.25** Department of Trade and Industry and to be sealed with the seal of the Department, or to be signed by a secretary, under-secretary or assistant secretary of the Department, or by any person authorised in that behalf by the Secretary of State for the Department of Trade and Industry, shall be received in evidence, and shall be deemed to be such orders without further proof, unless the contrary is shown.

(3) A certificate, signed by the Secretary of State for the Department of Trade and Industry, that any order made or act done is the order or act of the Department, shall be conclusive evidence of the fact so certified.

Supplemental

* * *

Interpretation

101.—(1) In this Act, except where the context otherwise requires, the **17.26** following expressions have the meanings hereby respectively assigned to them, that is to say—

"Appeal Tribunal" means the Appeal Tribunal constituted and acting in accordance with section 85 of this Act as amended by the Administration of Justice Act 1969;

"applicant" includes a person in whose favour a direction has been given under section seventeen of this Act, and the personal representative of a deceased applicant;

"appointed day" means the day appointed under section 132 of the Patents Act 1977 for the coming into operation of Schedule 1 of that Act;

"article" includes any substance or material, and any plant, machinery or apparatus, whether affixed to land or not;

"assignee" includes the personal representative of a deceased assignee, and reference to the assignee of any person include references to the assignee of the personal representative or assignee of that person;

"comptroller" means the Comptroller-General of Patents, Designs and Trade Marks;

"convention application" has the meaning assigned to it by subsection (4) of section one of this Act;

"court" means the High Court;

"date of filing", in relation to any document filed under this Act, means the date on which the document is filed or, where it is deemed by virtue of any provision of this Act or of rules made thereunder to have been filed on any different date, means the date on which it is deemed to be filed;

"exclusive licence" means a licence from a patentee which confers on the licensee, or on the licensee and persons authorised by him, to the exclusion of all other persons (including the patentee), any right in respect of the patented invention, and "exclusive licensee" shall be construed accordingly;

"invention" means any manner of new manufacture the subject of letters patent and grant of privilege within section six of the Statute of Monopolies and any new method or process of testing applicable to the improvement or control of manufacture, and includes an alleged invention;

"Journal" has the meaning assigned to it by subsection (2) of section ninety-four of this Act;

"patent" means Letters Patent for an invention;

"patent agent" means a person carrying on for gain in the United Kingdom the business of acting as agent for other persons for the purpose of applying for or obtaining patents in the United Kingdom or elsewhere;

"patent of addition" means a patent granted in accordance with section twenty-six of this Act;

"patentee" means the person or persons for the time being entered on the register of patents as grantee or proprietor of the patent;

"prescribed" means prescribed by rules made by the Department of Trade and Industry under this Act;

"priority date" has the meaning assigned to it by section five of this Act;

"published", except in relation to a complete specification, means made available to the public; and without prejudice to the generality of the foregoing provision a document shall be deemed for the purposes of this Act to be published if it can be inspected as of right at any place in the United Kingdom by members of the public, whether upon payment of a fee or otherwise;

"The Statute of Monopolies" means the Act of the twenty-first year of the reign of King James the First, chapter three, intituled "An Act concerning monopolies and dispensations with penal laws and the forfeiture thereof".

(2) For the purposes of subsection (3) of section one, so far as it relates to a convention application, and for the purposes of section seventy-two of this Act, the expression "personal representative", in relation to a deceased person, includes the legal representative of the deceased appointed in any country outside the United Kingdom.

* * *

Application to Scotland

103. In the application of this Act to Scotland—　　　　　　17.27

(1) In any action for infringment of a patent in Scotland the action shall be tried without a jury unless the court otherwise direct, but otherwise nothing shall affect the jurisdiction and forms of process of the courts in Scotland in such an action or in any action or proceeding respecting a patent hitherto competent to those courts:

(2) Proceedings for revocation of a patent shall be in the form of an action of reduction, and service of all writs and summonses in that action shall be made according to the forms and practice existing immediately before the commencement of the Patents and Designs Act 1907:

(3) The provisions of this Act conferring a special jurisdiction on the court as defined by this Act shall not, except so far as the jurisdiction extends, affect the jurisdiction of any court in Scotland in any proceedings relating to patents; and with reference to any such proceedings, the term "the Court" shall mean the Court of Session;

(4) Notwithstanding anything in this Act, the expression "the Court" shall in reference to proceedings in Scotland for the extension of the term of a patent mean the Court of Session:

(5) If any rectification of a register under this Act is required in pursuance of any proceedings in a court, a copy of the order, decree, or other authority for the rectification shall be served on the comptroller, and he shall rectify the register accordingly:

(6) The expression "injunction" means "interdict"; the expression "chose in action" means a right of action or an incorporeal moveable; the expression "in account of profits" means "an accounting and payment of profits"; the expression "arbitrator" means "arbiter"; the expression "plaintiff" means "pursuer"; the expression "defendant" means "defender".

Application to Northern Ireland

17.28 104. In the application of this Act to Northern Ireland—

(1) All parties shall, notwithstanding anything in this Act, have in Northern Ireland their remedies under or in respect of a patent as if the same had been granted to extend to Northern Ireland only:

(2) The provisions of this Act conferring a special jurisdiction on the court, as defined by this Act, shall not, except so far as the jurisdiction extends, affect the jurisdiction of any court in Northern Ireland in any proceedings relating to patents; and with reference to any such proceedings the term "the Court" means the High Court in Northern Ireland:

(3) If any rectification of a register under this Act is required in pursuance of any proceedings in a court, a copy of the order, decree, or other authority for the rectification shall be served on the comptroller, and he shall rectify the register accordingly:

(4) Reference to enactments of the Parliament of the United Kingdom shall be construed as references to those enactments as they apply in Northern Ireland:

(5) References to a Government department shall be construed as including references to a department of the Government of Northern Ireland:

(6) The expression "summary conviction" shall be construed as meaning conviction subject to, and in accordance with, the Petty Sessions (Ireland) Act 1851 and any Act (including any Act of the Parliament of Northern Ireland) amending that Act.

Isle of Man

17.29 105. This Act shall extend to the Isle of Man, subject to the following modifications:—

(1) Nothing in this Act shall affect the jurisdiction of the courts in the Isle of Man in proceedings for infringement, or in any action or proceeding respecting a patent competent to those courts:

(2) The punishment for a misdemeanour under this Act in the Isle of Man shall be imprisonment for any term not exceeding two years, with or without hard labour, and with or without a fine not exceeding one hundred pounds, at the discretion of the court:

(3) Any offence under this Act committed in the Isle of Man which would in England be punishable on summary conviction may be prosecuted, and any fine in respect thereof recovered, at the instance of any person aggrieved, in the manner in which offences punishable on summary conviction may for the time being be prosecuted.

Repeals, transitional provisions and amendment

106.—(1) Subject to the provisions of this section, the enactments specified in the Second Schedule to this Act are hereby repealed to the extent specified in the third column of that Schedule.   **17.30**

(2) Without prejudice to the provisions of the Interpretation Act 1889, with respect to repeals, the transitional provisions set out in the Third Schedule to this Act shall have effect for the purposes of the transition to the provisions of this Act from the law in force before the commencement of the Patents and Designs Act 1949.

(3) *Now spent and superseded by P.A. 77, s.56(2).*

Short title and commencement

107.—(1) This Act may be cited as the Patents Act 1949.   **17.31**

(2) This Act shall come into operation on the first day of January, nineteen hundred and fifty, immediately after the coming into operation of the Patents and Designs Act 1949.

* * *

Section 106   THIRD SCHEDULE

TRANSITIONAL PROVISIONS

1.—Subject to the provisions of this Schedule, any Order in Council, rule, order,   **17.32**
requirement, certificate, notice, decision, direction, authorisation, consent, application,
request or thing made, issued, given or done under any enactment repealed by this Act
shall, if in force at the commencement of this Act, and so far as it could have been made,
issued, given or done under this Act, continues in force and have effect as if made, issued,
given or done under the corresponding enactment of this Act.

* * *

26.—Any document referring to any enactment repealed by this Act shall be construed
as referring to the corresponding enactment of this Act.

EUROPEAN PATENT CONVENTION

CONTENTS OF CONVENTION

Chapter II. Persons entitled to apply for and obtain European
patents—Mention of the inventor

Chapter III. Effects of the European patent and the European patent application

Chapter IV. The European patent application as an object of property

PART III. APPLICATION FOR EUROPEAN PATENTS

Chapter I. Filing and requirements of the European patent application

Chapter II. Priority

PART IV. PROCEDURE UP TO GRANT

PART V. OPPOSITION PROCEDURE

PART VI. APPEALS PROCEDURE

PART VII. COMMON PROVISIONS

Chapter I. Common provisions governing procedure

Chapter II. Information to the public or official authorities

Chapter III. Representation

PART VIII. IMPACT ON NATIONAL LAW

Chapter I. Conversion into a national patent application

Chapter II. Revocation and prior rights

Chapter III. Miscellaneous effects

PART IX. SPECIAL AGREEMENTS

PART X. INTERNATIONAL APPLICATION PURSUANT TO THE PATENT CO-OPERATION TREATY

PART XI. TRANSITIONAL PROVISIONS

PART XII. FINAL PROVISIONS

EUROPEAN PATENT CONVENTION
CONVENTION ON THE GRANT OF EUROPEAN PATENTS
(EUROPEAN PATENT CONVENTION)

Munich, 5 October 1973

[The Convention has been ratified by the United Kingdom]

PREAMBLE

The Contracting States,   **18.00**
    Desiring to strengthen co-operation between the States of Europe in respect of the protection of inventions,
    Desiring that such protection may be obtained in those States by a single procedure for the grant of patents, and by the establishment of certain standard rules governing patents so granted,
    Desiring, for this purpose, to conclude a Convention which establishes a European Patent Organisation and which constitutes a special agreement within the meaning of Article 19 of the Convention for the Protection of Industrial Property, signed in Paris on 20 March 1883 and last revised on 14 July 1967, and a regional patent treaty within the meaning of Article 45, paragraph 1, of the Patent Co-operation Treaty of 19 June 1970,
    Have agreed on the following provisions:

PART I. GENERAL AND INSTITUTIONAL PROVISIONS

Chapter I. General provisions

Article 1

European law for the grant of patents

A system of law, common to the Contracting States, for the grant of   **18.01**
patents for invention is hereby established.

Article 2

European patent

18.02 (1) Patents granted by virtue of this Convention shall be called European patents.

(2) The European patent shall, in each of the Contracting States for which it is granted, have the effect of and be subject to the same conditions as a national patent granted by that State, unless otherwise provided in this Convention.

Article 3

Territorial effect

18.03 The grant of a European patent may be requested for one or more of the Contracting States.

Article 4

European Patent Organisation

18.04 (1) A European Patent Organisation, hereinafter referred to as the Organisation, is established by this Convention. It shall have administrative and financial autonomy.

(2) The organs of the Organisation shall be:

(a) a European Patent Office;

(b) an Administrative Council.

(3) The task of the Organisation shall be to grant European patents. This shall be carried out by the European Patent Office supervised by the Administrative Council.

Chapter II. The European Patent Organisation

Article 5

Legal status

(1) The Organisation shall have legal personality. **18.05**
(2) In each of the Contracting States, the Organisation shall enjoy the most extensive legal capacity accorded to legal persons under the national law of that State; it may in particular acquire or dispose of movable and immovable property and may be a party to legal proceedings.
(3) The President of the European Patent Office shall represent the Organisation.

Article 6

Seat

(1) The Organisation shall have its seat at Munich. **18.06**
(2) The European Patent Office shall be set up at Munich. It shall have a branch at The Hague.

Article 7

Sub-offices of the European Patent Office

By decision of the Administrative Council, sub-offices of the Euro- **18.07**
pean Patent Office may be created if need be, for the purpose of information and liaison, in the Contracting States and with inter-governmental organisations in the field of industrial property, subject to the approval of the Contracting State or organisation concerned.

Article 8

Privileges and immunities

18.08   The Protocol on Privileges and Immunities annexed to this Convention shall define the conditions under which the Organisation, the
members of the Administrative Council, the employees of the European
Patent Office and such other persons specified in that Protocol as take
part in the work of the Organisation, shall enjoy, in the territory of each
Contracting State, the privileges and immunities necessary for the
performance of their duties.

Article 9

Liability

18.09   (1) The contractual liability of the Organisation shall be governed by
the law applicable to the relevant contract.

(2) The non-contractual liability of the Organisation in respect of any
damage caused by it or by the employees of the European Patent Office
in the performance of their duties shall be governed by the provisions of
the law of the Federal Republic of Germany. Where the damage is
caused by the branch at The Hague or a sub-office or employees
attached thereto, the provisions of the law of the Contracting State in
which such branch or sub-office is located shall apply.

(3) The personal liability of the employees of the European Patent
Office towards the Organisation shall be laid down in their Service
Regulations or conditions of employment.

(4) The courts with jurisdiction to settle disputes under paragraphs 1
and 2 shall be:

(a) for disputes under paragraph 1, the courts of competent jurisdiction in the Federal Republic of Germany, unless the contract
concluded between the parties designates the courts of another
State;

(b) for disputes under paragraph 2, either the courts of competent
jurisdiction in the Federal Republic of Germany, or the courts of
competent jurisdiction in the State in which the branch or
sub-office is located.

Chapter III. The European Patent Office

Article 10

Direction

(1) The European Patent Office shall be directed by the President who **18.10** shall be responsible for its activities to the Administrative Council.

(2) To this end, the President shall have in particular the following functions and powers:

(a) he shall take all necessary steps, including the adoption of internal administrative instructions and the publication of guidance for the public, to ensure the functioning of the European Patent Office;

(b) insofar as this Convention contains no provisions in this respect, he shall prescribe which transactions are to be carried out at the European Patent Office at Munich and its branch at The Hague respectively;

(c) he may place before the Administrative Council any proposal for amending this Convention and any proposal for general regulations or decisions which come within the competence of the Administrative Council;

(d) he shall prepare and implement the budget and any amending or supplementary budget;

(e) he shall submit a management report to the Administrative Council each year;

(f) he shall exercise supervisory authority over the personnel;

(g) subject to the provisions of Article 11, he shall appoint and promote the employees;

(h) he shall exercise disciplinary authority over the employees other than those referred to in Article 11, and may propose disciplinary action to the Administrative Council with regard to employees referred to in Article 11, paragraphs 2 and 3;

(i) he may delegate his functions and powers.

(3) The President shall be assisted by a number of Vice-Presidents. If the President is absent or indisposed, of the Vice-Presidents shall take his place in accordance with the procedure laid down by the Administrative Council.

Article 11

Appointment of senior employees

18.11   (1) The President of the European Patent Office shall be appointed by decision of the Administrative Council.

(2) The Vice-Presidents shall be appointed by decision of the Administrative Council after the President has been consulted.

(3) The members, including the Chairman, of the Boards of Appeal and of the Enlarged Board of Appeal shall be appointed by decision of the Administrative Council, taken on a proposal from the President of the European Patent Office. They may be re-appointed by decision of the Administrative Council after the President of the European Patent Office has been consulted.

(4) The Administrative Council shall exercise disciplinary authority over the employees referred to in paragraphs 1 to 3.

Article 12

Duties of office

18.12   The employees of the European Patent Office shall be bound, even after the termination of their employment, neither to disclose nor to make use of information which by its nature is a professional secret.

Article 13

Disputes between the Organisation and the employees of the European Patent Office

18.13   (1) Employees and former employees of the European Patent Office or their successors in title may apply to the Administrative Tribunal of the International Labour Organisation in the case of disputes with the European Patent Organisation in accordance with the Statute of the Tribunal and within the limits and subject to the conditions laid down in the Service Regulations for permanent employees or the Pension Scheme Regulations or arising from the conditions of employement of other employees.

(2) An appeal shall only be admissible if the person concerned has

exhausted such other means of appeal as are available to him under the Service Regulations, the Pension Scheme Regulations or the conditions of employment, as the case may be.

Article 14

Languages of the European Patent Office

(1) The official languages of the European Patent Office shall be **18.14** English, French and German. European patent applications must be filed in one of these languages.

(2) However, natural or legal persons having their residence or principal place of business within the territory of the Contracting State having a language other than English, French or German as an official language, and nationals of that State who are resident abroad, may file European patent applications in an official language of that State. Nevertheless, a translation in one of the official languages of the European Patent Office must be filed within the time limit prescribed in the Implementing Regulations; throughout the proceedings before the European Patent Office, such translation may be brought into conformity with the original text of the application.

(3) The official language of the European Patent Office in which the European patent application is filed or, in the case referred to in paragraph 2, that of the translation, shall be used as the language of the proceedings in all proceedings before the European Patent Office concerning the application or the resulting patent, unless otherwise provided in the Implementing Regulations.

(4) The persons referred to in paragraph 2 may also file documents which have to be filed within a time limit in an official language of the Contracting State concerned. They must however file a translation in the language of the proceedings within the time limit prescribed in the Implementing Regulations; in the cases provided for in the Implementing Regulations, they may file a translation in a different official language of the European Patent Office.

(5) If any document, other than those making up the European patent application, is not filed in the language prescribed by this Convention, or if any translation required by virtue of this Convention is not filed in due time, the document shall be deemed not to have been received.

(6) European patent applications shall be published in the language of the proceedings.

(7) The specifications of European patents shall be published in the language of the proceedings; they shall include a translation of the claims in the two other official languages of the European Patent Office.

(8) There shall be published in the three official languages of the European Patent Office:

(a) the European Patent Bulletin;

(b) the Official Journal of the European Patent Office.

(9) Entries in the Register of European Patents shall be made in the three official languages of the European Patent Office. In cases of doubt, the entry in the language of the proceedings shall be authentic.

Article 15

The departments charged with the procedure

18.15 For implementing the procedures laid down in this Convention, there shall be set up within the European Patent Office:

(a) a Receiving Section;

(b) Search Divisions;

(c) Examining Divisions;

(d) Opposition Divisions;

(e) a Legal Division;

(f) Boards of Appeal;

(g) an Enlarged Board of Appeal.

Article 16

Receiving Section

18.16 The Receiving Section shall be in the branch at The Hague. It shall be responsible for the examination on filing and the examination as to formal requirements of each European patent application up to the time when a request for examination has been made or the applicant has indicated under Article 96, paragraph 1, that he desires to proceed further with his application. It shall also be responsible for the publication of the European patent application and of the European search report.

Article 17

Search Divisions

The Search Divisions shall be in the branch at The Hague. They shall **18.17** be responsible for drawing up European search reports.

Article 18

Examining Divisions

(1) An Examining Division shall be responsible for the examination of **18.18** each European patent application from the time when the Receiving Section ceases to be responsible.

(2) An Examining Division shall consist of three technical examiners. Nevertheless, the examination prior to a final decision shall, as a general rule, be entrusted to one member of the Division. Oral proceedings shall be before the Examining Division itself. If the Examining Division considers that the nature of the decision so requires, it shall be enlarged by the addition of a legally qualified examiner. In the event of parity of votes, the vote of the Chairman of the Division shall be decisive.

Article 19

Opposition Divisions

(1) An Opposition Division shall be responsible for the examination of **18.19** oppositions against any European patent.

(2) An Opposition Division shall consist of three technical examiners, at least two of whom shall not have taken part in the proceedings for grant of the patent to which the opposition relates. An examiner who has taken part in the proceedings for the grant of the European patent shall not be the Chairman. Prior to the taking of a final decision on the opposition, the Opposition Division may entrust the examination of the opposition to one of its members. Oral proceedings shall be before the Opposition Division itself. If the Opposition Division considers that the nature of the decision so requires, it shall be enlarged by the addition of a legally qualified examiner who shall not have taken part in the

proceedings for grant of the patent. In the event of parity of votes, the vote of the Chairman of the Division shall be decisive.

Article 20

Legal Division

18.20   (1) The Legal Division shall be responsible for decisions in respect of entries in the Register of European Patents and in respect of registration on, and deletion from, the list of professional representatives.

(2) Decisions of the Legal Division shall be taken by one legally qualified member.

Article 21

Boards of Appeal

18.21   (1) The Boards of Appeal shall be responsible for the examination of appeals from the decisions of the Receiving Section, Examining Divisions, Opposition Divisions and of the Legal Division.

(2) For appeals from a decision of the Receiving Section or the Legal Division, a Board of Appeal shall consist of three legally qualified members.

(3) For appeals from a decision of an Examining Division, a Board of Appeal shall consist of:

(a) two technically qualified members and one legally qualified member, when the decision concerns the refusal of a European patent application or the grant of a European patent and was taken by an Examining Division consisting of less than four members;

(b) three technically qualified members and two legally qualified members, when the decision was taken by an Examining Division consisting of four members or when the Board of Appeal considers that the nature of the appeal so requires;

(c) three legally qualified members in all other cases.

(4) For appeals from a decision of an Opposition Division, a Board of Appeal shall consist of:

(a) two technically qualified members and one legally qualified member, when the decision was taken by an Opposition Division consisting of three members;

(b) three technically qualified members and two legally qualified members, when the decision was taken by an Opposition Division consisting of four members or when the Board of Appeal considers that the nature of the appeal so requires.

Article 22

Enlarged Board of Appeal

(1) The Enlarged Board of Appeal shall be responsible for: **18.22**
(a) deciding points of law referred to it by Boards of Appeal;
(b) giving opinions on points of law referred to it by the President of the European Patent Office under the conditions laid down in Article 112.
(2) For giving decisions or opinions, the Enlarged Board of Appeal shall consist of five legally qualified members and two technically qualified members. One of the legally qualified members shall be the Chairman.

Article 23

Independence of the members of the Boards

(1) The members of the Enlarged Board of Appeal and of the Boards of **18.23**
Appeal shall be appointed for a term of five years and may not be removed from office during this term, except if there are serious grounds for such removal and if the Administrative Council, on a proposal from the Enlarged Board of Appeal, takes a decision to this effect.
(2) The members of the Boards may not be members of the Receiving Section, Examining Divisions, Opposition Divisions or of the Legal Division.
(3) In their decisions the members of the Boards shall not be bound by any instructions and shall comply only with the provisions of this Convention.
(4) The Rules of Procedure of the Boards of Appeal and the Enlarged Board of Appeal shall be adopted in accordance with the provisions of the Implementing Regulations. They shall be subject to the approval of the Administrative Council.

Article 24

Exclusion and objection

18.24   (1) Members of the Boards of Appeal or of the Enlarged Board of Appeal may not take part in any appeal if they have any personal interest therein, if they have previously been involved as representatives of one of the parties, or if they participated in the decision under appeal.

(2) If, for one of the reaons mentioned in paragraph 1, or for any other reason, a member of a Board of Appeal or of the Enlarged Board of Appeal considers that he should not take part in any appeal, he shall inform the Board accordingly.

(3) Members of a Board of Appeal or of the Enlarged Board of Appeal may be objected to by any party for one of the reasons mentioned in paragraph 1, or if suspected of partiality. An objection shall not be admissible if, while being aware of a reason for objection, the party has taken a procedural step. No objection may be based upon the nationality of members.

(4) The Boards of Appeal and the Enlarged Board of Appeal shall decide as to the action to be taken in the cases specified in paragraphs 2 and 3 without the participation of the member concerned. For the purposes of taking this decision the member objected to shall be replaced by his alternate.

Article 25

Technical opinion

18.25   At the request of the competent national court trying an infringement or revocation action, the European Patent Office shall be obliged, against payment of an appropriate fee, to give a technical opinion concerning the European patent which is the subject of the action. The Examining Divisions shall be responsible for the issue of such opinions.

Chapter IV. The Administrative Council

Article 26

Membership

(1) The Administrative Council shall be composed of the Representa- **18.26** tives and the alternate Representatives of the Contracting States. Each Contracting State shall be entitled to appoint one Representative and one alternate Representative to the Administrative Council.

(2) The members of the Administrative Council may, subject to the provisions of its Rules of Procedure, be assisted by advisers or experts.

Article 27

Chairmanship

(1) The Administrative Council shall elect a Chairman and a Deputy **18.27** Chairman from among the Representatives and alternate Representatives of the Contracting States. The Deputy Chairman shall *ex officio* replace the Chairman in the event of his being prevented from attending to his duties.

(2) The duration of the terms of office of the Chairman and the Deputy Chairman shall be three years. The terms of office shall be renewable.

Article 28

Board

(1) When there are at least eight Contracting States, the Administra- **18.28** tive Council may set up a Board composed of five of its members.

(2) The Chairman and the Deputy Chairman of the Administrative Council shall be members of the Board *ex officio*; the other three members shall be elected by the Administrative Council.

(3) The term of office of the members elected by the Administrative Council shall be three years. This term of office shall not be renewable.

(4) The Board shall perform the duties given to it by the Administrative Council in accordance with the Rules of Procedure.

Article 29

Meetings

18.29 (1) Meetings of the Administrative Council shall be convened by its Chairman.

(2) The President of the European Patent Office shall take part in the deliberations of the Administrative Council.

(3) The Administrative Council shall hold an ordinary meeting once each year. In addition, it shall meet on the initiative of its Chairman or at the request of one-third of the Contracting States.

(4) The deliberations of the Administrative Council shall be based on an agenda, and shall be held in accordance with its Rules of Procedure.

(5) The provisional agenda shall contain any question whose inclusion is requested by any Contracting State in accordance with the Rules of Procedure.

Article 30

Attendance of observers

18.30 (1) The World Intellectual Property Organization shall be represented at the meetings of the Administrative Council, in accordance with the provisions of an agreement to be concluded between the European Patent Organisation and the world Intellectual Property Organization.

(2) Any other inter-governmental organisation charged with the implementation of international procedures in the field of patents with which the Organisation has concluded an agreement shall be represented at the meetings of the Administrative Council, in accordance with any provisions contained in such agreement.

(3) Any other inter-governmental and international non-governmental organisations exercising an activity of interest to the Organisation may be invited by the Administrative Council to arrange to be represented at its meetings during any discussion of matters of mutual interest.

Article 31

Languages of the Administrative Council

(1) The languages in use in the deliberations of the Administrative   **18.31**
Council shall be English, French and German.

(2) Documents submitted to the Administrative Council, and the
minutes of its deliberations, shall be drawn up in the three languages
mentioned in paragraph 1.

Article 32

Staff, premises and equipment

The European Patent Office shall place at the disposal of the   **18.32**
Administrative Council and any body established by it such staff,
premises and equipment as may be necessary for the performance of
their duties.

Article 33

Competence of the Administrative Council in certain cases

(1) The Administrative Council shall be competent to amend the   **18.33**
following provisions of this Convention:
- (a) the time limits laid down in this Convention; this shall apply to
  the time limit laid down in Article 94 only in the conditions laid
  down in Article 95;
- (b) the Implementing Regulations.

(2) The Administrative Council shall be competent, in conformity
with this Convention, to adopt or amend the following provisions:
- (a) the Financial Regulations;
- (b) the Service Regulations for permanent employees and the conditions of employment of other employees of the European Patent
  Office, the salary scales of the said permanent and other
  employees, and also the nature, and rules for the grant, of any
  supplementary benefits;
- (c) the Pension Scheme Regulations and any appropriate increases in
  existing pensions to correspond to increases in salaries;

(d) the Rules relating to Fees;

(e) its Rules of Procedure.

(3) Notwithstanding Article 18, paragraph 2, the Administrative Council shall be competent to decide, in the light of experience, that in certain categories of cases Examining Divisions shall consist of one technical examiner. Such decisions may be rescinded.

(4) The Administrative Council shall be competent to authorise the President of the European Patent Office to negotiate and, with its approval, to conclude agreements on behalf of the European Patent Organisation with States, with inter-governmental organisations and with documentation centres set up by virtue of agreements with such organisation.

Article 34

Voting rights

18.34 (1) The right to vote in the Administrative Council shall be restricted to the Contracting States.

(2) Each Contracting State shall have one vote, subject to the application of the provisions of Article 36.

Article 35

Voting rules

18.35 (1) The Administrative Council shall take its decisions other than those referred to in paragraph 2 by a simple majority of the Contracting States represented and voting.

(2) A majority of three-quarters of the votes of the Contracting States represented and voting shall be required for the decisions which the Administrative Council is empowered to take under Article 7, Article 11, paragraph 1, Article 33, Article 39, paragraph 1, Article 40, paragraphs 2 and 4, Article 46, Article 87, Article 95, Article 134, Article 151, paragraph 3, Article 154, paragraph 2, Article 155, paragraph 2, Article 156, Article 157, paragraphs 2 to 4, Article 160, paragraph 1, second sentence, Article 162, Article 163, Article 166, Article 167 and Article 172.

(3) Abstentions shall not be considered as votes.

Article 36

Weighting of votes

(1) In respect of the adoption or amendment of the Rules relating to **18.36** Fees and, if the financial contribution to be made by the Contracting States would thereby be increased, the adoption of the budget of the Organisation and of any amending or supplementary budget, any Contracting State may require, following a first ballot in which each Contracting State shall have one vote, and whatever the result of this ballot, that a second ballot be taken immediately, in which votes shall be given to the States in accordance with paragraph 2. The decision shall be determined by the result of this second ballot.

(2) The number of votes that each Contracting State shall have in the second ballot shall be calculated as follows:
   (a) the percentage obtained for each Contracting State in respect of the scale for the special financial contributions, pursuant to Article 40, paragraphs 3 and 4, shall be multiplied by the number of Contracting States and divided by five;
   (b) the number of votes thus given shall be rounded upwards to the next higher whole number;
   (c) five additional votes shall be added to this number;
   (d) nevertheless no Contracting State shall have more than 30 votes.

Chapter V. Financial provisons

Article 37

Cover for expenditure

The expenditure of the Organisation shall be covered: **18.37**
   (a) by the Organisation's own resources;
   (b) by payments made by the Contracting States in respect of renewal fees for European patents levied in these States;
   (c) where necessary, by special financial contributions made by the Contracting States;
   (d) where appropriate, by the revenue provided for in Article 146.

Article 38

The Organisation's own resources

18.38   The Organisation's own resources shall be the yield from the fees laid down in this Convention, and also all receipts, whatever their nature.

Article 39

Payments by the Contracting States in respect of renewal fees for European patents

18.39   (1) Each Contracting State shall pay to the Organisation in respect of each renewal fee received for a European patent in that State an amount equal to a proportion of that fee, to be fixed by the Administrative Council; the proportion shall not exceed 75 per cent and shall be the same for all Contracting States. However, if the said proportion corresponds to an amount which is less than a uniform minimum amount fixed by the Administrative Council, the Contracting State shall pay that minimum to the Organisation.

(2) Each Contracting State shall communicate to the Organisation such information as the Administrative Council considers to be necessary to determine the amount of its payments.

(3) The due dates for these payments shall be determined by the Administrative Council.

(4) If a payment is not remitted fully by the due date, the Contracting State shall pay interest from the due date on the amount remaining unpaid.

Article 40

Level of fees and payments—Special financial contributions

18.40   (1) The amounts of the fees referred to under Article 38 and the proportion referred to under Article 39 shall be fixed at such a level as to ensure that the revenue in respect thereof is sufficient for the budget of the Organisation to be balanced.

(2) However, if the Organisation is unable to balance its budget under the conditions laid down in paragraph 1, the Contracting States shall

remit to the Organisation special financial contributions, the amount of which shall be determined by the Administrative Council for the accounting period in question.

(3) These special financial contributions shall be determined in respect of any Contracting State on the basis of the number of patent applications filed in the last year but one prior to that of entry into force of this Convention, and calculated in the following manner:

    (a) one half in proportion to the number of patent applications filed in that Contracting State;

    (b) one half in proportion to the second highest number of patent applications filed in the order Contracting States by natural or legal persons having their residence or principal place of business in that Contracting State.

However, the amount to be contributed by States in which the number of patent applications filed exceeds 25,000 shall then be taken as a whole and a new scale drawn up determined in proportion to the total number of patent applications filed in these States.

(4) Where, in respect of any Contracting State, its scale position cannot be established in accordance with paragraph 3, the Administrative Council shall, with the consent of that State, decide its scale position.

(5) Article 39, paragraphs 3 and 4, shall apply *mutatis mutandis* to the special financial contributions.

(6) The special financial contributions shall be repaid together with interst at a rate which shall be the same for all Contracting States. Repayments shall be made in so far as it is possible to provide for this purpose in the budget; the amount thus provided shall be distributed among the Contracting States in accordance with the scale mentioned in paragraphs 3 and 4 above.

(7) The special financial contributions remitted in any accounting period shall be wholly repaid before any such contributions or parts thereof remitted in any subsequent accounting period are repaid.

Article 41

Advances

(1) At the request of the President of the European Patent Office, the   **18.41** Contracting States shall make advances to the Organisation, on account of their payments and contributions, within the limit of the amount fixed by the Administrative Council. Such advances shall be apportioned in proportion to the amounts due by the Contracting States for the accounting period in question.

(2) Article 39, paragraphs 3 and 4, shall apply *mutatis mutandis* to the advances.

Article 42

Budget

18.42   (1) Income and expenditure of the Organisation shall form the subject of estimates in respect of each accounting period and shall be shown in the budget. If necessary, there may be amending or supplementary budgets.

(2) The budget shall be balanced as between income and expenditure.

(3) The budget shall be drawn up in the unit of account fixed in the Financial Regulations.

Article 43

Authorisation for expenditure

18.43   (1) The expenditure entered in the budget shall be authorised for the duration of one accounting period, unless any provisions to the contrary are contained in the Financial Regulations.

(2) Subject to the conditions to be laid down in the Financial Regulations, any appropriations, other than those relating to staff costs, which are unexpended at the end of the accounting period may be carried forward, but not beyond the end of the following accounting period.

(3) Appropriations shall be set out under different headings according to type and purpose of the expenditure and subdivided, as far as necessary, in accordance with the Financial Regulations.

Article 44

Appropriations of unforeseeable expenditure

18.44   (1) The budget of the Organisation may contain appropriations for unforeseeable expenditure.

(2) The employment of these appropriations by the Organisation shall be subject to the prior approval of the Administrative Council.

Article 45

Accounting period

The accounting period shall commence on 1 January and end on 31 **18.45**
December.

Article 46

Preparation and adoption of the budget

(1) The President of the European Patent Office shall lay the draft **18.46**
budget before the Administrative Council not later than the date
prescribed in the Financial Regulations.

(2) The budget and any amending or supplementary budget shall be
adopted by the Administrative Council.

Article 47

Provisional budget

(1) If, at the beginning of the accounting period, the budget has not **18.47**
been adopted by the Administrative Council, expenditures may be
effected on a monthly basis per heading or other division of the budget,
according to the provisions of the Financial Regulations, up to one-
twelfth of the budget appropriations for the preceding accounting
period, provided that the appropriations thus made available to the
President of the European Patent Office shall not exceed one-twelfth of
those provided for in the draft budget.

(2) The Administrative Council may, subject to the observance of the
other provisions laid down in paragraph 1, authorise expenditure in
excess of one-twelfth of the appropriations.

(3) The payments referred to in Article 37, sub-paragraph (b), shall
continue to be made, on a provisional basis, under the conditions
determined under Article 39 for the year preceding that to which the
draft budget relates.

(4) The Contracting States shall pay each month, on a provisional
basis and in accordance with the scale referred to in Article 40,
paragraphs 3 and 4, any special financial contributions necessary to

ensure implementation of paragraphs 1 and 2 above. Article 39, paragraph 4, shall apply *mutatis mutandis* to these contributions.

Article 48

Budget implementation

18.48   (1) The President of the European Patent Office shall implement the budget and any amending or supplementary budget on his own responsibility and within the limits of the allocated appropriations.

(2) Within the budget, the President of the European Patent Office may, subject to the limits and conditions laid down in the Financial Regulations, transfer funds as between the various headings or sub-headings.

Article 49

Auditing of accounts

18.49   (1) The income and expenditure account and a balance sheet of the Organisation shall be examined by auditors whose independence is beyond doubt, appointed by the Administrative Council for a period of five years, which shall be renewable or extensible.

(2) The audit, which shall be based on vouchers and shall take place, if necessary, *in situ*, shall ascertain that all income has been received and all expenditure effected in a lawful and proper manner and that the financial management is sound. The auditors shall draw up a report after the end of each accounting period.

(3) The President of the European Patent Office shall annually submit to the Administrative Council the accounts of the preceding accounting period in respect of the budget and the balance sheet showing the assets and liabilities of the Organisation together with the report of the auditors.

(4) The Administrative Council shall approve the annual accounts together with the report of the auditors and shall give the President of the European Patent Office a discharge in respect of the implementation of the budget.

Article 50

Financial Regulations

The Financial Regulations shall in particular establish: 18.50
(a) the procedure relating to the establishment and implementation of the budget and for the rendering and auditing of accounts;
(b) the method and procedure whereby the payments and contributions provided for in Article 37 and the advances provided for in Article 41 are to be made available to the Organisation by the Contracting States;
(c) the rules concerning the responsibilities of accounting and paying officers and the arrangements for their supervision;
(d) the rates of interest provided for in Articles 39, 40 and 47;
(e) the method of calculating the contributions payable by virtue of Article 146;
(f) the composition of an duties to be assigned to a Budget and Finance Committee which should be set up by the Administrative Council.

Article 51

Rules relating to Fees

The Rules relating to Fees shall determine in particular the amounts of   18.51
the fees and the ways in which they are to be paid.

PART II. SUBSTANTIVE PATENT LAW

Chapter I. Patentability

Article 52

Patentable inventions

18.52   (1) European patents shall be granted for any inventions which are susceptible of industrial application, which are new and which involve an inventive step.

(2) The following in particular shall not be regarded as inventions within the meaning of paragraph 1:

(a) discoveries, scientific theories and mathematical methods;

(b) aesthetic creations;

(c) schemes, rules and methods for performing mental acts, playing games or doing business, and programs for computers;

(d) presentations of information.

(3) The provisions of paragraph 2 shall exclude patentability of the subject-matter or activities referred to in that provision only to the extent to which a European patent application or European patent relates to such subject-matter or activities as such.

(4) Methods for treatment of the human or animal body by surgery or therapy and diagnostic methods practised on the human or animal body shall not be regarded as inventions which are susceptible of industrial application within the meaning of paragraph 1. This provision shall not apply to products, in particular substances or compositions, for use in any of these methods.

Article 53

Exceptions to patentability

18.53   European patents shall not be granted in respect of:

(a) inventions the publication or exploitation of which would be contrary to "ordre public" or morality, provided that the exploitation shall not be deemed to be so contrary merely because it is prohibited by law or regulation in some or all of the Contracting States;

(b) plant or animal varieties or essentially biological processes for the production of plants or animals; this provision does not apply to microbiological processes or the products thereof.

Article 54

Novelty

(1) An invention shall be considered to be new if it does not form part of the state of the art. **18.54**

(2) The state of the art shall be held to comprise everything made available to the public by means of a written or oral description, by use, or in any other way, before the date of filing of the European patent application.

(3) Additionally, the content of European patent applications as filed, of which the dates of filing are prior to the date referred to in paragraph 2 and which were published under Article 93 on or after that date, shall be considered as comprised in the state of the art.

(4) Paragraph 3 shall be applied only insofar as a Contracting State designated in respect of the later application, was also designated in respect of the earlier application as published.

(5) The provisions of paragraphs 1 to 4 shall not exclude the patentability of any substance or composition, comprised in the state of the art, for use in a method referred to in Article 52, paragraph 4, provided that its use for any method referred to in that paragraph is not comprised in the state of the art.

Article 55

Non-prejudicial disclosures

(1) For the application of Article 54 a disclosure of the invention shall not be taken into consideration if it occurred no earlier than six months preceding the filing of the European patent application and if it was due to, or in consequence of: **18.55**

(a) an evident abuse in relation to the applicant or his legal predecessor, or

(b) the fact that the applicant or his legal predecessor has displayed the invention at an official, or officially recognised, international exhibition falling within the terms of the Convention on international exhibitions signed at Paris on 22 November 1928 and last revised on 30 November 1972.

(2) In the case of paragraph 1(b), paragraph 1 shall apply only if the applicant states, when filing the European patent application, that the invention has been so displayed and files a supporting certificate within the period and under the conditions laid down in the Implementing Regulations.

Article 56

Inventive step

18.56   An invention shall be considered as involving an inventive step if, having regard to the state of the art, it is not obvious to a person skilled in the art. If the state of the art also includes documents within the meaning of Article 54, paragraph 3, these documents are not to be considered in deciding whether there has been an inventive step.

Article 57

Industrial application

18.57   An invention shall be considered as susceptible of industrial application if it can be made or used in any kind of industry, including agriculture.

Chapter II. Persons entitled to apply for and obtain European patents—Mention of the inventor

Article 58

Entitlement to file a European patent application

18.58   A European patent application may be filed by any natural or legal person, or any body equivalent to a legal person by virtue of the law governing it.

820

Article 59

Multiple applicants

A European patent application may also be filed either by joint **18.59**
applicants or by two or more applicants designating different Contracting States.

Article 60

Right to a European patent

(1) The right to a European patent shall belong to the inventor or his **18.60**
successor in title. If the inventor is an employee the right to the
European patent shall be determined in accordance with the law of the
State in which the employee is mainly employed; if the State in which
the employee is mainly employed cannot be determined, the law to be
applied shall be that of the State in which the employer has his place of
business to which the employee is attached.

(2) If two or more persons have made an invention independently of
each other, the right to the European patent shall belong to the person
whose European patent application has the earliest date of filing;
however, this provision shall apply only if this first application has been
published under Article 93 and shall only have effect in respect of the
Contracting States designated in that application as published.

(3) For the purposes of proceedings before the European Patent
Office, the applicant shall be deemed to be entitled to exercise the right
to the European patent.

Article 61

European patent applications by persons not having the right to a
European patent

(1) If by a final decision it is adjudged that a person referred to in **18.61**
Article 60, paragraph 1, other than the applicant, is entitled to the grant
of a European patent, that person may, within a period of three months
after the decision has become final, provided that the European patent
has not yet been granted, in respect of those Contracting States

designated in the European patent application in which the decision has been taken or recognised, or has to be recognised on the basis of the Protocol on Recognition annexed to this Convention:

(a) prosecute the application as his own application in place of the applicant,

(b) file a new European patent application in respect of the same invention, or

(c) request that the application be refused.

(2) The provision of Article 76, paragraph 1, shall apply *mutatis mutandis* to a new application filed under paragraph 1.

(3) The procedure to be followed in carrying out the provisions of paragraph 1, the special conditions applying to a new application filed under paragraph 1 and the time limit for paying the filing, search and designation fees on it are laid down in the Implementing Regulations.

Article 62

Right of the inventor to be mentioned

18.62   The inventor shall have the right, *vis-à-vis* the applicant for or proprietor of a European patent, to be mentioned as such before the European Patent Office.

Chapter III. Effects of the European patent and the European patent application

Article 63

Term of the European patent

18.63   (1) The term of the European patent shall be 20 years as from the date of filing of the application.

(2) Nothing in the preceding paragraph shall limit the right of a Contracting State to extend the term of a European patent under the same conditions as those applying to its national patents, in order to take into account a state of war or similar emergency conditions affecting that State.

Article 64

Rights conferred by a European patent

(1) A European patent shall, subject to the provisions of paragraph 2, **18.64** confer on its proprietor from the date of publication of the mention of its grant, in each Contracting State in respect of which it is granted, the same rights as would be conferred by a national patent granted in that State.

(2) If the subject-matter of the European patent is a process, the protection conferred by the patent shall extend to the products directly obtained by such process.

(3) Any infringement of a European patent shall be dealt with by national law.

Article 65

Translation of the specification of the European patent

(1) Any Contracting State may prescribe that if the text, in which the **18.65** European Patent Office intends to grant a European patent or maintain a European patent as amended for that State, is not drawn up in one of its official languages, the applicant for or proprietor of the patent shall supply to its central industrial property office a translation of this text in one of its official languages at his option or, where that State has prescribed the use of one specific official language, in that language. The period for supplying the translation shall be three months after the start of the time limit referred to in Article 97, paragraph 2(b), or Article 102, paragraph 3(b), unless the State concerned prescribes a longer period.

(2) Any Contracting State which has adopted provisions pursuant to paragraph 1 may prescribe that the applicant for or proprietor of the patent must pay all or part of the costs of publication of such translation within a period laid down by that State.

(3) Any Contracting State may prescribe that in the event of failure to observe the provisions adopted in accordance with paragraphs 1 and 2, the European patent shall be deemed to be void *ab initio* in that State.

Article 66

Equivalence of European filing with national filing

18.66   A European patent application which has been accorded a date of filing shall, in the designated Contracting States, be equivalent to a regular national filing, where appropriate with the priority claimed for the European patent application.

Article 67

Rights conferred by a European patent application after publication

18.67   (1) A European patent application shall, from the date of its publication under Article 93, provisionally confer upon the applicant such protection as is conferred by Article 64, in the Contracting States designated in the application as published.

(2) Any Contracting State may prescribe that a European patent application shall not confer such protection as is conferred by Article 64. However, the protection attached to the publication of the European patent application may not be less than that which the laws of the State concerned attach to the compulsory publication of unexamined national patent applications. In any event, every State shall ensure at least that, from the date of publication of a European patent application, the applicant can claim compensation reasonable in the circumstances from any person who has used the invention in the said State in circumstances where that person would be liable under national law for infringement of a national patent.

(3) Any Contracting State which does not have as an official language the language of the proceedings, may prescribe that provisional protection in accordance with paragraphs 1 and 2 above shall not be effective until such time as a translation of the claims in one of its official languages at the option of the applicant or, where that State has prescribed the use of one specific official language, in that language:

    (a) has been made available to the public in the manner prescribed by national law, or

    (b) has been communicated to the person using the invention in the said State.

(4) The European patent application shall be deemed never to have had the effects set out in paragraphs 1 and 2 above when it has been withdrawn, deemed to be withdrawn or finally refused. The same shall apply in respect of the effects of the European patent application in a

Contracting State the designation of which is withdrawn or deemed to be withdrawn.

Article 68

Effect of revocation of the European patent

The European patent application and the resulting patent shall be **18.68** deemed not to have had, as from the outset, the effects specified in Articles 64 and 67, to the extent that the patent has been revoked in opposition proceedings.

Article 69

Extent of protection

(1) The extent of the protection conferred by a European patent or a **18.69** European patent application shall be determined by the terms of the claims. Nevertheless, the description and drawings shall be used to interpret the claims.

(2) For the period up to grant of the European patent, the extent of the protection conferred by the European patent application shall be determined by the latest filed claims contained in the publication under Article 93. However, the European patent as granted or as amended in opposition proceedings shall determine retroactively the protection conferred by the European patent application, insofar as such protection is not thereby extended.

Article 70

Authentic text of a European patent application or European patent

(1) The text of a European patent application or a European patent in **18.70** the language of the proceedings shall be the authentic text in any proceedings before the European Patent Office and in any Contracting State.

(2) However, in the case referred to in Article 14, paragraph 2, the original text shall, in proceedings before the European Patent Office,

constitute the basis for determining whether the subject-matter of the application or patent extends beyond the content of the application as filed.

(3) Any Contracting State may provide that a translation, as provided for in this Convention, in an official language of that State, shall in that State be regarded as authentic, except for revocation proceedings, in the event of the application or patent in the language of the translation conferring protection which is narrower than that conferred by it in the language of the proceedings.

(4) Any Contracting State which adopts a provision under paragraph 3:

(a) must allow the applicant for or proprietor of the patent to file a corrected translation of the European patent application or European patent. Such corrected translation shall not have any legal effect until any conditions established by the Contracting State under Article 65, paragraph 2, and Article 67, paragraph 3, have been complied with *mutatis mutandis*;

(b) may prescribe that any person who, in that State, in good faith is using or has made effective and serious preparations for using an invention the use of which would not constitute infringement of the application or patent in the original translation may, after the corrected translation takes effect, continue such use in the course of his business or for the needs thereof without payment.

Chapter IV. The European patent application as an object of property

Article 71

Transfer and constitution of rights

18.71 A European patent application may be transferred or give rise to rights for one or more of the designated Contracting States.

Article 72

Assignment

18.72 An assignment of a European patent application shall be made in writing and shall require the signature of the parties to the contract.

Article 73

Contractual licensing

A European patent application may be licensed in whole or in part for   **18.73**
the whole or part of the territories of the designated Contracting States.

Article 74

Law applicable

Unless otherwise specified in this Convention, the European patent   **18.74**
application as an object of property shall, in each designated Contracting State and with effect for such State, be subject to the law
applicable in that State to national patent applications.

PART III. APPLICATION FOR EUROPEAN PATENTS

Chapter I. Filing and requirements of the European patent application

Article 75

Filing of the European patent application

(1) A European patent application may be filed: **18.75**
(a) at the European Patent Office at Munich or its branch at The
    Hague, or
(b) if the law of the Contracting State so permits, at the central
    industrial property office or other competent authority of that
    State. An application filed in this way shall have the same effect as
    if it had been filed on the same date at the European Patent Office.
(2) The provisions of paragraph 1 shall not preclude the application of
legislative or regulatory provisions which, in any Contracting State:
(a) govern inventions which, owing to the nature of their subject-
    matter may not be communicated abroad without the prior
    authorisation of the competent authorities of that State, or
(b) prescribe that each application is to be filed initially with a

national authority or make direct filing with another authority subject to prior authorisation.

(3) No Contracting State may provide for or allow the filing of European divisional applications with an authority referred to in paragraph 1(b).

Article 76

European divisional applications

18.76 (1) A European divisional application must be filed directly with the European Patent Office at Munich or its branch at The Hague. It may be filed only in respect of subject-matter which does not extend beyond the content of the earlier application as filed; insofar as this provision is complied with, the divisional application shall be deemed to have been filed on the date of filing of the earlier application and shall have the benefit of any right to priority.

(2) The European divisional application shall not designate Contracting States which were not designated in the earlier application.

(3) The procedure to be followed in carrying out the provisions of paragraph 1, the special conditions to be complied with by a divisional application and the time limit for paying the filing, search and designation fees are laid down in the Implementing Regulations.

Article 77

Forwarding of European patent applications

18.77 (1) The central industrial property office of a Contracting State shall be obliged to forward to the European Patent Office, in the shortest time compatible with the application of national law concerning the secrecy of inventions in the interests of the State, any European patent applications which have been filed with that office or with other competent authorities in that State.

(2) The Contracting States shall take all appropriate steps to ensure that European patent applications, the subject of which is obviously not liable to secrecy by virtue of the law referred to in paragraph 1, shall be forwarded to the European Patent Office within six weeks after filing.

(3) European patent applications which require further examination as to their liability to secrecy shall be forwarded in such manner as to reach the European Patent Office within four months after filing, or,

where priority has been claimed, fourteen months after the date of priority.

(4) A European patent application, the subject of which has been made secret, shall not be forwarded to the European Patent Office.

(5) European patent applications which do not reach the European Patent Office before the end of the fourteenth month after filing or, if priority has been claimed, after the date of priority, shall be deemed to be withdrawn. The filing, search and designation fees shall be refunded.

Article 78

Requirements of the European patent application

(1) A European patent application shall contain: **18.78**
(a) a request for the grant of a European patent;
(b) a description of the invention;
(c) one or more claims;
(d) any drawings referred to in the description or the claims;
(e) an abstract.
(2) A European patent application shall be subject to the payment of the filing fee and the search fee within one month after the filing of the application.
(3) A European patent application must satisfy the conditions laid down in the Implementing Regulations.

Article 79

Designation of Contracting States

(1) The request for the grant of a European patent shall contain the   **18.79** designation of the Contracting State or States in which protection for the invention is desired.

(2) The designation of a Contracting State shall be subject to the payment of the designation fee. The designation fees shall be paid within twelve months after filing the European patent application or, if priority has been claimed, after the date of priority; in the latter case, payment may still be made up to the expiry of the period specified in Article 78, paragraph 2, if that period expires later.

(3) The designation of a Contracting State may be withdrawn at any time up to the grant of the European patent. Withdrawal of the designation of all the Contracting States shall be deemed to be a

withdrawal of the European patent application. Designation fees shall not be refunded.

Article 80

Date of filing

18.80   The date of filing of a European patent application shall be the date on which documents filed by the applicant contain:
(a) an indication that a European patent is sought;
(b) the designation of at least one Contracting State;
(c) information identifying the applicant;
(d) a description and one or more claims in one of the languages referred to in Article 14, paragraphs 1 and 2, even though the description and the claims do not comply with the other requirements of this Convention.

Article 81

Designation of the inventor

18.81   The European patent application shall designate the inventor. If the applicant is not the inventor or is not the sole inventor, the designation shall contain a statement indicating the origin of the right to the European patent.

Article 82

Unity of invention

18.82   The European patent application shall relate to one invention only or to a group of inventions so linked as to form a single general inventive concept.

Article 83

Disclosure of the invention

The European patent application must disclose the invention in a manner sufficiently clear and complete for it to be carried out by a person skilled in the art. **18.83**

Article 84

The claims

The claims shall define the matter for which protection is sought. They shall be clear and concise and be supported by the description. **18.84**

Article 85

The abstract

The abstract shall merely serve for use as technical information; it may not be taken into account for any other purpose, in particular not for the purpose of interpreting the scope of the protection sought nor for the purpose of applying Article 54, paragraph 3. **18.85**

Article 86

Renewal fees for European patent applications

(1) Renewal fees shall be paid to the European Patent Office in accordance with the Implementing Regulations in respect of European patent applications. These fees shall be due in respect of the third year and each subsequent year, calculated from the date of filing of the application. **18.86**

(2) When a renwal fee has not been paid on or before the due date, the fee may be validly paid within six months of the said date, provided that the additional fee is paid at the same time.

(3) If the renewal fee and any additional fee have not been paid in due time the European patent application shall be deemed to be withdrawn. The European Patent Office alone shall be competent to decide this.

(4) The obligation to pay renewal fees shall terminate with the payment of the renewal fee due in respect of the year in which the mention of the grant of the European patent is published.

Chapter II. Priority

Article 87

Priority right

18.87 (1) A person who has duly filed in or for any State party to the Paris Convention for the Protection of Industrial Property, an application for a patent or for the registration of a utility model or for a utility certificate or for an inventor's certificate, or his successors in title, shall enjoy, for the purpose of filing a European patent application in respect of the same invention, a right of priority during a period of twelve months from the date of filing of the first application.

(2) Every filing that is equivalent to a regular national filing under the national law of the State where it was made or under bilateral or multilateral agreements, including this Convention, shall be recognised as giving rise to a right of priority.

(3) By a regular national filing is meant any filing that is sufficient to establish the date on which the application was filed, whatever may be the outcome of the application.

(4) A subsequent application for the same subject-matter as a previous first application and filed in or in respect of the same State shall be considered as the first application for the purposes of determining priority, provided that, at the date of filing the subsequent application, the previous application has been withdrawn, abandoned or refused, without being open to public inspection and without leaving any rights outstanding, and has not served as a basis for claiming a right of priority. The previous application may not thereafter serve as a basis for claiming a right of priority.

(5) If the first filing has been made in a State which is not a party to the Paris Convention for the Protection of Industrial Property, paragraphs 1 to 4 shall apply only insofar as that State, according to a notification published by the Administrative Council, and by virtue of bilateral or multilateral agreements, grants on the basis of a first filing made at the European Patent Office as well as on the basis of a first filing made in or for any Contracting State and subject to conditions equivalent to those

laid down in the Paris Convention, a right of priority having equivalent effect.

Article 88

Claiming priority

(1) An applicant for a European patent desiring to take advantage of **18.88** the priority of a previous application shall file a declaration of priority, a copy of the previous application and, if the language of the latter is not one of the official languages of the European Patent Office, a translation of it in one of such official languages. The procedure to be followed in carrying out these provisions is laid down in the Implementing Regulations.

(2) Multiple priorities may be claimed in respect of a European patent application, notwithstanding the fact that they originated in different countries. Where appropriate, multiple priorities may be claimed for any one claim. Where multiple priorities are claimed, time limits which run from the date of priority shall run from the earliest date of priority.

(3) If one or more priorities are claimed in respect of a European patent application, the right of priority shall cover only those elements of the European patent application which are included in the application or applications whose priority is claimed.

(4) If certain elements of the invention for which priority is claimed do not appear among the claims formulated in the previous application, priority may nonetheless be granted, provided that the documents of the previous application as a whole specifically disclose such elements.

Article 89

Effect of priority right

The right of priority shall have the effect that the date of priority shall **18.89** count as the date of filing of the European patent application for the purposes of Article 54, paragraphs 2 and 3, and Article 60, paragraph 2.

PART IV. PROCEDURE UP TO GRANT

Article 90

Examination on filing

18.90   (1) The Receiving Section shall examine whether:
  (a) the European patent application satisfies the requirements for the accordance of a date of filing;
  (b) the filing fee and the search fee have been paid in due time;
  (c) in the case provided for in Article 14, paragraph 2, the translation of the European patent application in the language of the proceedings has been filed in due time.
  (2) If a date of filing cannot be accorded, the Receiving Section shall give the applicant an opportunity to correct the deficiencies in accordance with the Implementing Regulations. If the deficiencies are not remedied in due time, the application shall not be dealt with as a European patent application.
  (3) If the filing fee and the search fee have not been paid in due time or, in the case provided for in Article 14, paragraph 2, the translation of the application in the language of the proceedings has not been filed in due time, the application shall be deemed to be withdrawn.

Article 91

Examination as to formal requirements

18.91   (1) If a European patent application has been accorded a date of filing, and is not deemed to be withdrawn by virtue of Article 90, paragraph 3, the Receiving Section shall examine whether:
  (a) the requirements of Article 133, paragraph 2, have been satisfied;
  (b) the application meets the physical requirements laid down in the Implementing Regulations for the implementation of this provision;
  (c) the abstract has been filed;
  (d) the request for the grant of a European patent satisfies the mandatory provisions of the Implementing Regulations concerning its content and, where appropriate, whether the requirements of this Convention concerning the claim to priority have been satisfied;
  (e) the designation fees have been paid;

(f) the designation of the inventor has been made in accordance with Article 81;

(g) the drawing referred to in Article 78, paragraph 1(d), were filed on the date of filing of the application.

(2) Where the Receiving Section notes that there are deficiencies which may be corrected, it shall give the applicant an opportunity to correct them in accordance with the Implementing Regulations.

(3) If any deficiencies noted in the examination under paragraph 1(a) to (d) are not corrected in accordance with the Implementing Regulations, the application shall be refused; where the provisions referred to in paragraph 1 (d) concern the right of priority, this right shall be lost for the application.

(4) Where, in the case referred to in paragraph 1(e), the designation fee has not been paid in due time in respect of any designated State, the designation of that State shall be deemed to be withdrawn.

(5) Where, in the case referred to in paragraph 1(f), the omission of the designation of the inventor is not, in accordance with the Implementing Regulations and subject to the exceptions laid down therein, corrected within 16 months after the date of filing of the European patent application or, if priority is claimed, after the date of priority, the application shall be deemed to be withdrawn.

(6) Where, in the case referred to in paragraph 1(g), the drawings were not filed on the date of filing of the application and no steps have been taken to correct the deficiency in accordance with the Implementing Regulations, either the application shall be re-dated to the date of filing of the drawings or any reference to the drawings in the application shall be deemed to be deleted, according to the choice exercised by the applicant in accordance with the Implementing Regulations.

Article 92

The drawing up of the European search report

(1) If a European patent application has been accorded a date of filing and is not deemed to be withdrawn by virtue of Article 90, paragraph 3, the Search Division shall draw up the European search report on the basis of the claims, with due regard to the description and any drawings, in the form prescribed in the Implementing Regulations. **18.92**

(2) Immediately after it has been drawn up, the European search report shall be transmitted to the applicant together with copies of any cited documents.

Article 93

Publication of a European patent application

18.93 (1) A European patent application shall be published as soon as possible after the expiry of a period of eighteen months from the date of filing or, if priority has been claimed, as from the date of priority. Nevertheless, at the request of the applicant the application may be published before the expiry of the period referred to above. It shall be published simultaneously with the publication of the specification of the European patent when the grant of the patent has become effective before the expiry of the period referred to above.

(2) The publication shall contain the description, the claims and any drawings as filed and, in an annex, the European search report and the abstract, insofar as the latter are available before the termination of the technical preparations for publication. If the European search report and the abstract have not been published at the same time as the application, they shall be published separately.

Article 94

Request for examination

18.94 (1) The European Patent Office shall examine, on written request, whether a European patent application and the invention to which it relates meet the requirements of this Convention.

(2) A request for examination may be filed by the applicant up to the end of six months after the date on which the European Patent Bulletin mentions the publication of the European search report. The request shall not be deemed to be filed until after the examination fee has been paid. The request may not be withdrawn.

(3) If no request for examination has been filed by the end of the period referred to in paragraph 2, the application shall be deemed to be withdrawn.

Article 95

Extension of the period within which requests for examination may be filed

(1) The Administrative Council may extend the period within which **18.95** requests for examination may be filed if it is established that European patent applications cannot be examined in due time.

(2) If the Administrative Council extends the period, it may decide that third parties will be entitled to make requests for examination. In such cases, it shall determine the appropriate rules in the Implementing Regulations.

(3) Any decision of the Administrative Council to extend the period shall apply only in respect of applications filed after the publication of such decision in the Official Journal of the European Patent Office.

(4) If the Administrative Council extends the period, it must lay down measures with a view to restoring the original period as soon as possible.

Article 96

Examination of the European patent application

(1) If the applicant for a European patent has filed the request for **18.96** examination before the European search report has been transmitted to him, the European Patent Office shall invite him after the transmission of the report to indicate, within a period to be determined, whether he desires to proceed further with the European patent application.

(2) If the examination of a European patent application reveals that the application or the invention to which it relates does not meet the requirements of this Convention, the Examining Division shall invite the applicant, in accordance with the Implementing Regulations and as often as necessary, to file his observations within a period to be fixed by the Examining Division.

(3) If the applicant fails to reply in due time to any invitation under paragraph 1 or paragraph 2, the application shall be deemed to be withdrawn.

Article 97

Refusal or grant

18.97 (1) The Examining Division shall refuse a European patent application if it is of the opinion that such application or the invention to which it relates does not meet the requirements of this Convention, except where a different sanction is provided for by this Convention.

(2) If the Examining Division is of the opinion that the application and the invention to which it relates meet the requirements of this Convention, it shall decide to grant the European patent for the designated Contracting States provided that:

    (a) it is established, in accordance with the provisions of the Implementing Regulations, that the applicant approves the text in which the Examining Division intends to grant the patent;

    (b) the fees for grant and printing are paid within the time limit prescribed in the Implementing Regulations;

    (c) the renewal fees and any additional fees already due have been paid.

(3) If the fees for grant and printing are not paid in due time, the application shall be deemed to be withdrawn.

(4) The decision to grant a European patent shall not take effect until the date on which the European Patent Bulletin mentions the grant. This mention shall be published at least 3 months after the start of the time limit referred to in paragraph 2(b).

(5) Provision may be made in the Implementing Regulations for the applicant to file a translation, in the two official languages of the European Patent Office other than the language of the proceedings, of the claims appearing in the text in which the Examining Division intends to grant the patent. In such case, the period laid down in paragraph 4 shall be at least five months. If the translation has not been filed in due time, the application shall be deemed to be withdrawn.

Article 98

Publication of a specification of the European patent

18.98 At the same time as it publishes the mention of the grant of the European patent, the European Patent Office shall publish a specification of the European patent containing the description, the claims and any drawings.

Article 99

Opposition

(1) Within nine months from the publication of the mention of the   **18.99**
grant of the European patent, any person may give notice to the
European Patent Office of opposition to the European patent granted.
Notice of opposition shall be filed in a written reasoned statement. It
shall not be deemed to have been filed until the opposition fee has been
paid.

(2) The opposition shall apply to the European patent in all the
Contracting States in which that patent has effect.

(3) An opposition may be filed even if the European patent has been
surrendered or has lapsed for all the designated States.

(4) Opponents shall be parties to the opposition proceedings as well
as the proprietor of the patent.

(5) Where a person provides evidence that in a Contracting State,
following a final decision, he has been entered in the patent register of
such State instead of the previous proprietor, such person shall, at his
request, replace the previous proprietor in respect of such State. By
derogation from Article 118, the previous proprietor and the person
making the request shall not be deemed to be joint proprietors unless
both so request.

Article 100

Grounds for opposition

Opposition may only be filed on the grounds that: **18.100**
(a)   the subject-matter of the European patent is not patentable within
the terms of Articles 52 to 57;
(b)   the European patent does not disclose the invention in a manner
sufficiently clear and complete for it to be carried out by a person
skilled in the art;
(c)   the subject-matter of the European patent extends beyond the
content of the application as filed, or, if the patent was granted on
a divisional application or on a new application filed in accordance with Article 61, beyond the content of the earlier application
as filed.

Article 101

Examination of the opposition

18.101   (1) If the opposition is admissible, the Opposition Division shall examine whether the grounds for opposition laid down in Article 100 prejudice the maintenance of the European patent.

(2) In the examination of the opposition, which shall be conducted in accordance with the provisions of the Implementing Regulations, the Opposition Division shall invite the parties, as often as necessary, to file observations, within a period to be fixed by the Opposition Division, on communications from another party or issued by itself.

Article 102

Revocation or maintenance of the European patent

18.102   (1) If the Opposition Division is of the opinion that the grounds for opposition mentioned in Article 100 prejudice the maintenance of the European patent, it shall revoke the patent.

(2) If the Opposition Division is of the opinion that the grounds for opposition mentioned in Article 100 do not prejudice the maintenance of the patent unamended, it shall reject the opposition.

(3) If the Opposition Division is of the opinion that, taking into consideration the amendments made by the proprietor of the patent during the opposition proceedings, the patent and the invention to which it relates meet the requirements of this Convention, it shall decide to maintain the patent as amended, provided that:

(a) it is established, in accordance with the provisions of the Implementing Regulations, that the proprietor of the patent approves the text in which the Opposition Division intends to maintain the patent;

(b) the fee for the printing of a new specification of the European patent is paid within the time limit prescribed in the Implementing Regulations.

(4) If the fee for the printing of a new specification is not paid in due time, the patent shall be revoked.

(5) Provision may be made in the Implementing Regulations for the proprietor of the patent to file a translation of any amended claims in the two official languages of the European Patent Office other than the language of the proceedings. If the translation has not been filed in due time the patent shall be revoked.

Article 103

Publication of a new specification of the European patent

If a European patent is amended under Article 102, paragraph 3, the **18.103** European Patent Office shall, at the same time as it publishes the mention of the opposition decision, publish a new specification of the European patent containing the description, the claims and any drawings, in the amended form.

Article 104

Costs

(1) Each party to the proceedings shall meet the costs he has incurred **18.104** unless a decision of an Opposition Division or Board of Appeal, for reasons of equity, orders, in accordance with the Implementing Regulations, a different apportionment of costs incurred during taking of evidence or in oral proceedings.

(2) On request, the registry of the Opposition Division shall fix the amount of the costs to be paid under a decision apportioning them. The fixing of the costs by the registry may be reviewed by a decision of the Opposition Division on a request filed within the period laid down in the Implementing Regulations.

(3) Any final decision of the European Patent Office fixing the amount of costs shall be dealt with, for the purpose of enforcement in the Contracting States, in the same way as a final decision given by a civil court of the State in the territory of which enforcement is to be carried out. Verification of such decisions shall be limited to its authenticity.

Article 105

Intervention of the assumed infringer

(1) In the event of an opposition to a European patent being filed, any **18.105** third party who proves that proceedings for infringement of the same patent have been instituted against him may, after the opposition period has expired, intervene in the opposition proceedings, if he gives notice

of intervention within three months of the date on which the infringement proceedings were instituted. The same shall apply in respect of any third party who proves both that the proprietor of the patent has requested that he cease alleged infringement of the patent and that he has instituted proceedings for a court ruling that he is not infringing the patent.

(2) Notice of intervention shall be filed in a written reasoned statement. It shall not be deemed to have been filed until the opposition fee has been paid. Thereafter the intervention shall, subject to any exceptions laid down in the Implementing Regulations, be treated as opposition.

PART VI. APPEALS PROCEDURE

Article 106

Decisions subject to appeal

18.106   (1) An appeal shall lie from decisions of the Receiving Section, Examining Divisions, Opposition Divisions and the Legal Division. It shall have suspensive effect.

(2) An appeal may be filed against the decision of the Opposition Division even if the European patent has been surrendered or has lapsed for all the designated States.

(3) A decision which does not terminate proceedings as regards one of the parties can only be appealed together with the final decision, unless the decision allows separate appeal.

(4) The apportionment of costs of opposition proceedings cannot be the sole subject of an appeal.

(5) A decision fixing the amount of costs of opposition proceedings cannot be appealed unless the amount is in excess of that laid down in the Rules relating to Fees.

Article 107

Persons entitled to appeal and to be parties to appeal proceedings

18.107   Any party to proceedings adversely affected by a decision may appeal. Any other parties to the proceedings shall be parties to the appeal proceedings as of right.

Article 108

Time limit and form of appeal

Notice of appeal must be filed in writing at the European Patent Office **18.108** within two months after the date of notification of the decision appealed from. The notice shall not be deemed to have been filed until after the fee for appeal has been paid. Within four months after the date of notification of the decision, a written statement setting out the grounds of appeal must be filed.

Article 109

Interlocutory revision

(1) If the department whose decision is contested considers the appeal **18.109** to be admissible and well founded, it shall rectify its decision. This shall not apply where the appellant is opposed by another party to the proceedings.

If the appeal is not allowed within one month after receipt of the statement of grounds, it shall be remitted to the Board of Appeal without delay, and without comment as to its merit.

Article 110

Examination of appeals

(1) If the appeal is admissible, the Board of Appeal shall examine **18.110** whether the appeal is allowable.

(2) In the examination of the appeal, which shall be conducted in accordance with the provisions of the Implementing Regulations, the Board of Appeal shall invite the parties, as often as necessary, to file observations, within a period to be fixed by the Board of Appeal, on communications from another party or issued by itself.

(3) If the applicant fails to reply in due time to an invitation under paragraph 2, the European patent application shall be deemed to be withdrawn, unless the decision under appeal was taken by the Legal Division.

Article 111

Decision in respect of appeals

18.111   (1) Following the examination as to the allowability of the appeal, the Board of Appeal shall decide on the appeal. The Board of Appeal may either exercise any power within the competence of the department which was responsible for the decision appealed or remit the case to that department for further prosecution.

(2) If the Board of Appeal remits the case for further prosecution to the department whose decision was appealed, that department shall be bound by the *ratio decidendi* of the Board of Appeal, insofar as the facts are the same. If the decision which was appealed emanated from the Receiving Section, the Examining Division shall similarly be bound by the *ratio decidendi* of the Board of Appeal.

Article 112

Decision or opinion of the Enlarged Board of Appeal

18.112   (1) In order to ensure uniform application of the law, or if an important point of law arises:
  (a) the Board of Appeal shall, during proceedings on a case and either of its own motion or following a request from a party to the appeal, refer any question to the Enlarged Board of Appeal if it considers that a decision is required for the above purposes. If the Board of Appeal rejects the request, it shall give the reasons in its final decision;
  (b) the President of the European Patent Office may refer a point of law to the Enlarged Board of Appeal where two Boards of Appeal have given different decisions on that question.

(2) In the cases covered by paragraph 1(a) the parties to the appeal proceedings shall be parties to the proceedings before the Enlarged Board of Appeal.

(3) The decision of the Enlarged Board of Appeal referred to in paragraph 1(a) shall be binding on the Board of Appeal in respect of the appeal in question.

PART VII. COMMON PROVISIONS

Chapter I. Common provisions governing procedure

Article 113

Basis of decisions

(1) The decisions of the European Patent Office may only be based on **18.113** grounds or evidence on which the parties concerned have had an opportunity to present their comments.

(2) The European Patent Office shall consider and decide upon the European patent application or the European patent only in the text submitted to it, or agreed, by the applicant for or proprietor of the patent.

Article 114

Examination by the European Patent Office of its own motion

(1) In proceedings before it, the European Patent Office shall examine **18.114** the facts of its own motion; it shall not be restricted in this examination to the facts, evidence and arguments provided by the parties and the relief sought.

(2) The European Patent Office may disregard facts or evidence which are not submitted in due time by the parties concerned.

Article 115

Observations by third parties

(1) Following the publication of the European patent application, any **18.115** person may present observations concerning the patentability of the invention in respect of which the application has been filed. Such observations must be filed in writing and must include a statement of the grounds on which they are based. That person shall not be a party to the proceedings before the European Patent Office.

(2) The observations referred to in paragraph 1 shall be communicated to the applicant for or proprietor of the patent who may comment on them.

Article 116

Oral proceedings

18.116 (1) Oral proceedings shall take place either at the instance of the European Patent Office if it considers this to be expedient or at the request of any party to the proceedings. However, the European Patent Office may reject a request for further oral proceedings before the same department where the parties and the subject of the proceedings are the same.

(2) Nevertheless, oral proceedings shall take place before the Receiving Section at the request of the applicant only where the Receiving Section considers this to be expedient or where it envisages refusing the European patent application.

(3) Oral proceedings before the Receiving Section, the Examining Divisions and the Legal Division shall not be public.

(4) Oral proceedings, including delivery of the decision, shall be public, as regards the Boards of Appeal and the Enlarged Board of Appeal, after publication of the European patent application, and also before the Opposition Divisions, insofar as the department before which the proceedings are taking place does not decide otherwise in cases where admission of the public could have serious and unjustified disadvantages, in particular for a party to the proceedings.

Article 117

Taking of evidence

18.117 (1) In any proceedings before an Examining Division, an Opposition Division, the Legal Division or a Board of Appeal the means of giving or obtaining evidence shall include the following:
    (a) hearing the parties;
    (b) requests for information;
    (c) the production of documents;
    (d) hearing the witnesses;
    (e) opinions by experts;
    (f) inspection;

(g) sworn statements in writing.

(2) The Examining Division, Opposition Division or Board of Appeal may commission one of its members to examine the evidence adduced.

(3) If the European Patent Office considers it necessary for a party, witness or expert to give evidence orally, it shall either:

(a) issue a summons to the person concerned to appear before it, or

(b) request, in accordance with the provisions of Article 131, paragraph 2, the competent court in the country of residence of the person concerned to take such evidence.

(4) A party, witness or expert who is summoned before the European Patent Office may request the latter to allow his evidence to be heard by a competent court in his country of residence. On receipt of such a request, or if there has been no reply to the summons by the expiry of a period fixed by the European Patent Office in the summons, the European Patent Office may, in accordance with the provisions of Article 131, paragraph 2, request the competent court to hear the person concerned.

(5) If a party, witness or expert gives evidence before the European Patent Office, the latter may, if it considers it advisable for the evidence to be given on oath or in an equally binding form, request the competent court in the country of residence of the person concerned to re-examine his evidence under such conditions.

(6) When the European Patent Office requests a competent court to take evidence, it may request the court to take the evidence on oath or in an equally binding form and to permit a member of the department concerned to attend the hearing and question the party, witness or expert either through the intermediary of the court or directly.

Article 118

Unity of the European patent application or European patent

Where the applicants for or proprietors of a European patent are not   **18.118**
the same in respect of different designated Contracting States, they shall be regarded as joint applicants or proprietors for the purposes of proceedings before the European Patent Office. The unity of the application or patent in these proceedings shall not be affected; in particular the text of the application or patent shall be uniform for all designated Contracting States unless otherwise provided for in this Convention.

Article 119

Notification

18.119   The European Patent Office shall, as a matter of course, notify those concerned of decisions and summonses, and of any notice or other communication from which a time limit is reckoned, or of which those concerned must be notified under other provisions of this Convention, or of which notification has been ordered by the President of the European Patent Office. Notifications may, where exceptional circumstances so require, be given through the intermediary of the central industrial property offices of the Contracting States.

Article 120

Time limits

18.120   The Implementing Regulations shall specify:
(a) the manner of computation of time limits and the conditions under which such time limits may be extended, either because the European Patent Office or the authorities referred to in Article 75, paragraph 1(b), are not open to receive documents or because mail is not delivered in the localities in whch the European Patent Office or such authorities are situated or because postal services are generally interrupted or subsequently dislocated;
(b) the minima and maxima for time limits to be determined by the European Patent Office.

Article 121

Further processing of the European patent application

18.121   (1) If the European patent application is to be refused or is refused or deemed to be withdrawn following failure to reply within a time limit set by the European Patent Office, the legal consequence provided for shall not ensue or, if it has already ensued, shall be retracted if the applicant requests further processing of the application.
(2) The request shall be filed in writing within two months of the date on which either the decision to refuse the application or the communica-

tion that the application is deemed to be withdrawn was notified. The omitted act must be completed within this time limit. The request shall not be deemed to have been filed until the fee for further processing has been paid.

(3) The department competent to decide on the omitted act shall decide on the request.

Article 122

Restitutio in integrum

(1) The applicant for or proprietor of a European patent who, in spite **18.122** of all due care required by the circumstances having been taken, was unable to observe a time limit *vis-à-vis* the European Patent Office shall, upon application, have his rights re-established if the non-observance in question has the direct consequence, by virtue of this Convention, of causing the refusal of the European patent application, or of a request, or the deeming of the European patent application to have been withdrawn, or the revocation of the European patent, or the loss of any other right or means of redress.

(2) The application must be filed in writing within two months from the removal of the cause of non-compliance with the time limit. The omitted act must be completed within this period. The application shall only be admissible within the year immediately following the expiry of the unobserved time limit. In the case of non-payment of a renewal fee, the period specified in Article 86, paragraph 2, shall be deducted from the period of one year.

(3) The application must state the grounds on which it is based, and must set out the facts on which it relies. It shall not be deemed to be filed until after the fee for re-establishment of rights has been paid.

(4) The department competent to decide on the omitted act shall decide upon the application.

(5) The provisions of this Article shall not be applicable to the time limits referred to in paragraph 2 of this Article, Article 61, paragraph 3, Article 76, paragraph 3, Article 78, paragraph 2, Article 79, paragraph 2, Article 87, paragraph 1, and Article 94, paragraph 2.

(6) Any person who, in a designated Contracting State, in good faith has used or made effective and serious preparations for using an invention which is the subject of a published European patent application or a European patent in the course of the period between the loss of rights referred to in paragraph 1 and publication of the mention of re-establishment of those rights, may without payment continue such use in the course of his business or for the needs thereof.

(7) Nothing in this Article shall limit the right of a Contracting State to

grant *restitutio in integrum* in respect of time limits provided for in this Convention and to be observed *vis-à-vis* the authorities of such State.

Article 123

Amendments

18.123 (1) The conditions under which a European patent application or a European patent may be amended in proceedings before the European Patent Office are laid down in the Implementing Regulations. In any case, an applicant shall be allowed at least one opportunity of amending the description, claims and drawings of his own volition.

(2) A European patent application or a European patent may not be amended in such a way that it contains subject-matter which extends beyond the content of the application as filed.

(3) The claims of the European patent may not be amended during opposition proceedings in such a way as to extend the protection conferred.

Article 124

Information concerning national patent applications

18.124 (1) The Examining Division or the Board of Appeal may invite the applicant to indicate, within a period to be determined by it, the States in which he has made applications for national patents for the whole or part of the invention to which the European patent application relates, and to give the reference numbers of the said applications.

(2) If the applicant fails to reply in due time to an invitation under paragraph 1, the European patent application shall be deemed to be withdrawn.

Article 125

Reference to general principles

In the absence of procedural provisions in this Convention, the **18.125** European Patent Office shall take into account the principles of procedural law generally recognised in the Contracting States.

Article 126

Termination of financial obligations

(1) Rights of the Organisation to the payment of a fee to the European **18.126** Patent Office shall be extinguished after four years from the end of the calendar year in which the fee fell due.

(2) Rights against the Organisation for the refunding by the European Patent Office of fees or sums of money paid in excess of a fee shall be extinguished after four years from the end of the calendar year in which the right arose.

(3) The period laid down in paragraphs 1 and 2 shall be interrupted in the case covered by paragraph 1 by a request for payment of the fee and in the case covered by paragraph 2 by a reasoned claim in writing. On interruption it shall begin again immediately and shall end at the latest six years after the end of the year in which it originally began, unless, in the meantime, judicial proceedings to enforce the right have begun; in this case the period shall end at the earliest one year after the judgment enters into force.

Chapter II. Information to the public or official authorities

Article 127

Register of European Patents

The European Patent Office shall keep a register, to be known as the **18.127** Register of European Patents, which shall contain those particulars the registration of which is provided for by this Convention. No entry shall be made in the Register prior to the publication of the European patent application. The Register shall be open to public inspection.

Article 128

Inspection of files

18.128 (1) The files relating to European patent applications, which have not yet been published, shall not be made available for inspection without the consent of the applicant.

(2) Any person who can prove that the applicant for a European patent has invoked the rights under the application against him may obtain inspection of the files prior to the publication of that application and without the consent of the applicant.

(3) Where a European divisional application or a new European patent application filed under Article 61, paragraph 1, is published, any person may obtain inspection of the files of the earlier application prior to the publication of that application and without the consent of the relevant applicant.

(4) Subsequent to the publication of the European patent application, the files relating to such application and the resulting European patent may be inspected on request, subject to the restrictions laid down in the Implementing Regulations.

(5) Even prior to the publication of the European patent application, the European Patent Office may communicate the following bibliographic data to third parties or publish them:

(a) the number of the European patent application;

(b) the date of filing of the European patent application and, where the priority of a previous application is claimed, the date, State and file number of the previous application;

(c) the name of the applicant;

(d) the title of the invention;

(e) the Contracting States designated.

Article 129

Periodical publications

18.129 The European Patent Office shall periodically publish:

(a) a European Patent Bulletin containing entries made in the

Register of European Patents, as well as other particulars the publication of which is prescribed by this Convention;

(b) an Official Journal of the European Patent Office, containing notices and information of a general character issued by the President of the European Patent Office, as well as any other information relevant to this Convention or its implementation.

Article 130

Exchanges of information

(1) The European Patent Office and, subject to the application of the **18.130** legislative or regulatory provisions referred to in Article 75, paragraph 2, the central industrial property office of any Contracting State shall, on request, communicate to each other any useful information regarding the filing of European or national patent applications and regarding any proceedings concerning such applications and the resulting patents.

(2) The provisions of paragraph 1 shall apply to the communication of information by virtue of working agreements between the European Patent Office and:

(a) the central industrial property office of any State which is not a party to this Convention;

(b) any inter-governmental organisation entrusted with the task of granting patents;

(c) any other organisation.

(3) The communications under paragraphs 1 and 2(a) and (b) shall not be subject to the restrictions laid down in Article 128. The Administrative Council may decide that communications under paragraph 2(c) shall not be subject to such restrictions, provided that the organisation concerned shall treat the information communicated as confidential until the European patent application has been published.

Article 131

Administrative and legal co-operation

(1) Unless otherwise provided in this Convention or in national laws, **18.131** the European Patent Office and the courts or authorities of Contracting States shall on request give assistance to each other by communicating information or opening files for inspection. Where the European Patent Office lays files open to inspection by courts, Public Prosecutors' Offices

or central industrial property offices, the inspection shall not be subject to the restrictions laid down in Article 128.

(2) Upon receipt of letters rogatory from the European Patent Office, the courts or other competent authorities of Contracting States shall undertake, on behalf of that Office and within the limits of their jurisdiction, any necessary enquiries or other legal measures.

Article 132

Exchange of publications

18.132 (1) The European Patent Office and the central industrial property offices of the Contracting States shall despatch to each other on request and for their own use one or more copies of their respective publications free of charge.

(2) The European Patent Office may conclude agreements relating to the exchange or supply of publications.

Chapter III. Representation

Article 133

General principles of representation

18.133 (1) Subject to the provisions of paragraph 2, no person shall be compelled to be represented by a professional representative in proceedings established by this Convention.

(2) Natural or legal persons not having either a residence or their principal place of buisness within the territory of one of the Contracting States must be represented by a professional representative and act through him in all proceedings established by this Convention, other than in filing the European patent application; the Implementing Regulations may permit other exceptions.

(3) Natural or legal persons having their residence or principal place of business within the territory of one of the Contracting States may be represented in proceedings established by this Convention by an employee, who need not be a professional representative but who must be authorised in accordance with the Implementing Regulations. The Implementing Regulations may provide whether and under what conditions an employee of such a legal person may also represent other

legal persons which have their principal place of business within the territory of one of the Contracting States and which have economic connections with the first legal person.

(4) The Implementing Regulations may prescribe special provisions concerning the common representation of parties acting in common.

Article 134

Professional representatives

(1) Professional representation of natural or legal persons in proceed- **18.134** ings established by this Convention may only be undertaken by professional representatives whose names appear on a list maintained for this purpose by the European Patent Office.

(2) Any natural person who fulfils the following conditions may be entered on the list of professional representatives:

    (a) he must be a national of one of the Contracting States;

    (b) he must have his place of business or employement within the territory of one of the Contracting States;

    (c) he must have passed the European qualifying examination.

(3) Entry shall be effected upon request, accompanied by certificates which must indicate that the conditions laid down in paragraph 2 are fulfilled.

(4) Persons whose names appear on the list of professional representatives shall be entitled to act in all proceedings established by this Convention.

(5) For the purpose of acting as a professional representative, any person whose name appears on the list referred to in paragraph 1 shall be entitled to establish a place of business in any Contracting State in which proceedings established by this Convention may be conducted, having regard to the Protocol on Centralisation annexed to this Convention. The authorities of such State may remove that entitlement in individual cases only in application of legal provisions adopted for the purpose of protecting public security and law and order. Before such action is taken, the President of the European Patent Office shall be consulted.

(6) The President of the European Patent Office may, in special circumstances, grant exemption from the requirement of paragraph 2(a).

(7) Professional representation in proceedings established by this Convention may also be undertaken, in the same way as by a professional representative, by any legal practitioner qualified in one of the Contracting States and having his place of business within such State, to the extent that he is entitled, within the said State, to act as a

professional representative in patent matters. Paragraph 5 shall apply *mutatis mutandis*.

(8) The Administrative Council may adopt provisions governing:

(a) the qualifications and training required of a person for admission to the European qualifying examination and the conduct of such examination;

(b) the establishment or recognition of an institute constituted by the persons entitled to act as professional representatives by virtue of either the European qualifying examination or the provisions of Article 163, paragraph 7;

(c) any disciplinary power to be exercised by that institute or the European Patent Office on such persons.

PART VIII. IMPACT ON NATIONAL LAW

Chapter I. Conversion into a national patent application

Article 135

Request for the application of national procedure

18.135 (1) The central industrial property office of a designated Contracting State shall apply the procedure for the grant of a national patent only at the request of the applicant for or proprietor of a European patent, and in the following circumstances:

(a) when the European patent application is deemed to be withdrawn pursuant to Article 77, paragraph 5, or Article 162, paragraph 4;

(b) in such other cases as are provided for by the national law in which the European patent application is refused or withdrawn or deemed to be withdrawn, or the European patent is revoked under this Convention.

(2) The request for conversion shall be filed within three months after the European patent application has been withdrawn or after notification has been made that the application is deemed to be withdrawn, or after a decision has been notified refusing the application or revoking the European patent. The effect referred to in Article 66 shall lapse if the request is not filed in due time.

Article 136

Submission and transmission of the request

(1) A request for conversion shall be filed with the European Patent **18.136** Office and shall specify the Contracting States in which application of the procedure for the grant of a national patent is desired. The request shall not be deemed to be filed until the conversion fee has been paid. The European Patent Office shall transmit the request to the central industrial property offices of the Contracting States specified therein, accompanied by a copy of the files relating to the European patent application or the European patent.

(2) However, if the applicant is notified that the European patent application has been deemed to be withdrawn pursuant to Article 77, paragraph 5, the request shall be filed with the central industrial property office with which the application has been filed. That office shall, subject to the provisions of national security, transmit the request, together with a copy of the European patent application, directly to the central industrial property offices of the Contracting States specified by the applicant in the request. The effect referred to in Article 66 shall lapse if such transmission is not made within twenty months after the date of filing or, if a priority has been claimed, after the date of priority.

Article 137

Formal requirements for conversion

(1) A European patent application transmitted in accordance with **18.137** Article 136 shall not be subjected to formal requirements of national law which are different from or additional to those provided for in this Convention.

(2) Any central industrial property office to which the application is transmitted may require that the applicant shall, within not less than two months:

(a) pay the national application fee;

(b) file a translation in one of the official languages of the State in question of the original text of the European patent application and, where appropriate, of the text, as amended during proceedings before the European Patent Office, which the applicant wishes to submit to the national procedure.

Chapter II. Revocation and prior rights

Article 138

Grounds for revocation

18.138   (1) Subject to the provisions of Article 139, a European patent may only be revoked under the law of a Contracting State, with effect for its territory, on the following grounds:

    (a) if the subject-matter of the European patent is not patentable within the terms of Articles 52 to 57;

    (b) if the European patent does not disclose the invention in a manner sufficiently clear and complete for it to be carried out by a person skilled in the art;

    (c) if the subject-matter of the European patent extends beyond the content of the application as filed or, if the patent was granted on a divisional application or on a new application filed in accordance with Article 61, beyond the content of the earlier application as filed;

    (d) if the protection conferred by the European patent has been extended;

    (e) if the proprietor of the European patent is not entitled under Article 60, paragraph 1.

(2) If the grounds for revocation only affect the European patent in part, revocation shall be pronounced in the form of a corresponding limitation of the said patent. If the national law so allows, the limitation may be effected in the form of an amendment to the claims, the description or the drawings.

Article 139

Rights of earlier date or the same date

18.139   (1) In any designated Contracting State a European patent application and a European patent shall have with regard to a national patent application and a national patent the same prior right effect as a national patent application and a national patent.

(2) A national patent application and a national patent in a Contracting State shall have with regard to a European patent in which that Contracting State is designated the same prior right effect as they have with regard to a national patent.

(3) Any Contracting State may prescribe whether and on what terms an invention disclosed in both a European patent application or patent and a national application or patent having the same date of filing or, where priority is claimed, the same date of priority, may be protected simultaneously by both applications or patents.

Chapter III. Miscellaneous effects

Article 140

National utility models and utility certificates

Article 66, Article 124, Articles 135 to 137 and Article 139 shall apply to **18.140** utility models and utility certificates and to applications for utility models and utility certificates registered or deposited in the Contracting States whose laws make provision for such models or certificates.

Article 141

Renewal fees for European patents

(1) Renewal fees in respect of a European patent may only be imposed **18.141** for the years which follow that referred to in Article 86, paragraph 4.

(2) Any renewal fees falling due within two months after the publication of the mention of the grant of the European patent shall be deemed to have been validly paid if they are paid within that period. Any additional fee provided for under national law shall not be charged.

PART IX. SPECIAL AGREEMENTS

Article 142

Unitary patents

18.142   (1) Any group of Contracting States, which has provided by a special agreement that a European patent granted for those States has a unitary character throughout their territories, may provide that a European patent may only be granted jointly in respect of all those States.

(2) Where any group of Contracting States has availed itself of the authorisation given in paragraph 1, the provisions of this Part shall apply.

Article 143

Special departments of the European Patent Office

18.143   (1) The group of Contracting States may give additional tasks to the European Patent Office.

(2) Special departments common to the Contracting States in the group may be set up within the European Patent Office in order to carry out the additional tasks. The President of the European Patent Office shall direct such special departments; Article 10, paragraphs 2 and 3, shall apply *mutatis mutandis*.

Article 144

Representation before special departments

18.144   The group of Contracting States may lay down special provisions to govern representation of parties before the departments referred to in Article 143, paragraph 2.

Article 145

Select committee of the Administrative Council

(1) The group of Contracting States may set up a select committee of **18.145**
the Administrative Council for the purpose of supervising the activities
of the special departments set up under Article 143, paragraph 2; the
European Patent Office shall place at its disposal such staff, premises
and equipment as may be necessary for the performance of duties. The
President of the European Patent Office shall be responsible for the
activities of the special departments to the select committee of the
Administrative Council.

(2) The composition, powers and functions of the select committee
shall be determined by the group of Contracting States.

Article 146

Cover for expenditure for carrying out special tasks

Where additional tasks have been given to the European Patent Office **18.146**
under Article 143, the group of Contracting States shall bear the
expenses incurred by the Organisation in carrying out these tasks.
Where special departments have been set up in the European Patent
Office to carry out these additional tasks, the group shall bear the
expenditure on staff, premises and equipment chargeable in respect of
these departments. Article 39, paragraphs 3 and 4, Article 41 and Article
47 shall apply *mutatis mutandis.*

Article 147

Payments in respect of renewal fees for unitary patents

If the group of Contracting States has fixed a common scale of renewal **18.147**
fees in respect of European patents the proportion referred to in Article
39, paragraph 1, shall be calculated on the basis of the common scale; the
minimum amount referred to in Article 39, paragraph 1, shall apply to
the unitary patent. Article 39, paragraphs 3 and 4, shall apply *mutatis
mutandis.*

Article 148

The European patent application as an object of property

18.148 (1) Article 74 shall apply unless the group of Contracting States has specified otherwise.

(2) The group of Contracting States may provide that a European patent application for which these Contracting States are designated may only be transferred, mortgaged or subjected to any legal means of execution in respect of all the Contracting States of the group and in accordance with the provisions of the special agreement.

Article 149

Joint designation

18.149 (1) The group of Contracting States may provide that these States may only be designated jointly, and that the designation of one or some only of such States shall be deemed to constitute the designation of all the States of the group.

(2) Where the European Patent Office acts as a designated Office under Article 153, paragraph 1, paragraph 1 shall apply if the applicant has indicated in the international application that he wishes to obtain a European patent for one or more of the designated States of the group. The same shall apply if the applicant designates in the international application one of the Contracting States in the group, whose national law provides that the designation of that State shall have the effect of the application being for a European patent.

PART X. INTERNATIONAL APPLICATION PURSUANT TO THE PATENT
CO-OPERATION TREATY

Article 150

Application of the Patent Co-operation Treaty

18.150 (1) The Patent Co-operation Treaty of 19 June 1970, hereinafter referred to as the Co-operation Treaty, shall be applied in accordance with the provisions of this Part.

(2) International applications filed under the Co-operation Treaty may be the subject of proceedings before the European Patent Office. In such proceedings, the provisions of that Treaty shall be applied, supplemented by the provisions of this Convention. In case of conflict, the provisions of the Co-operation Treaty shall prevail. In particular, for an international application the time limit within which a request for examination must be filed under Article 94, paragraph 2, of this Convention shall not expire before the time prescribed by Article 22 or Article 39 of the Co-operation Treaty as the case may be.

(3) An international application, for which the European Patent Office acts as designated Office or elected Office, shall be deemed to be a European patent application.

(4) Where reference is made in this Convention to the Co-operation Treaty, such reference shall include the Regulations under that Treaty.

Article 151

The European Patent Office as a receiving Office

(1) The European Patent Office may act as a receiving Office within **18.151** the meaning of Article 2(xv) of the Co-operation Treaty if the applicant is a resident or national of a Contracting State to this Convention in respect of which the Co-operation Treaty has entered into force.

(2) The European Patent Office may also act as a receiving Office if the applicant is a resident or national of a State which is not a Contracting State to this Convention, but which is a Contracting State to the Co-operation Treaty and which has concluded an agreement with the Organisation whereby the European Patent Office acts as a receiving Office, in accordance with the provisions of the Co-operation Treaty, in place of the national office of that State.

(3) Subject to the prior approval of the Administrative Council, the European Patent Office may also act as a receiving Office for any other applicant, in accordance with an agreement concluded beween the Organisation and the International Bureau of the World Intellectual Property Organization.

Article 152

Filing and transmittal of the international application

18.152   (1) If the applicant chooses the European Patent Office as a receiving Office for his international application, he shall file it directly with the European Patent Office. Article 75, paragraph 2, shall nevertheless apply *mutatis mutandis.*

(2) In the event of an international application being filed with the European Patent Office through the intermediary of the competent central industrial property office, the Contracting State concerned shall take all necessary measures to ensure that the application is transmitted to the European Patent Office in time for the latter to be able to comply in due time with the conditions for transmittal under the Co-operation Treaty.

(3) Each international application shall be subject to the payment of the transmittal fee, which shall be payable *on the filing of the application,* **within one month after receipt of the application.**

Article 153

The European Patent Office as a designated Office

18.153   (1) The European Patent Office shall act as a designated Office within the meaning of Article 2(xiii) of the Co-operation Treaty for those Contracting States to this Convention in respect of which the Co-operation Treaty has entered into force and which are designated in the international application if the applicant informs the receiving Office in the international application that he wishes to obtain a European patent for these States. The same shall apply if, in the international application, the applicant designates a Contracting State of which the national law provides that designation of that State shall have the effect of the application being for a European patent.

(2) When the European Patent Office acts as a designated Office, the Examining Division shall be competent to take decisions which are required under Article 25, paragraph 2(a), of the Co-operation Treaty.

Article 154

The European Patent Office as an International Searching Authority

(1) The European Patent Office shall act as an International Searching **18.154** Authority within the meaning of Chapter I of the Co-operation Treaty for applicants who are residents or nationals of a Contracting State in respect of which the Co-operation Treaty has entered into force, subject to the conclusion of an agreement between the Organisation and the International Bureau of the World Intellectual Property Organization.

(2) Subject to the prior approval of the Administrative Council, the European Patent Office shall also act as an International Searching Authority for any other applicant, in accordance with an agreement concluded between the Organisation and the International Bureau of the World Intellectual Property Organization.

(3) The Boards of Appeal shall be responsible for deciding on a protest made by an applicant against an additional fee charged by the European Patent Office under the provisions of Article 17, paragraph 3(a), of the Co-operation Treaty.

Article 155

The European Patent Office as an International Preliminary Examining Authority

(1) The European Patent Office shall act as an International Prelimin- **18.155** ary Examining Authority within the meaning of Chapter II of the Co-operation Treaty for applicants who are residents or nationals of a Contracting State bound by that Chapter, subject to the conclusion of an agreement between the Organisation and the International Bureau of the World Intellectual Property Organization.

(2) Subject to the prior approval of the Administrative Council, the European Patent Office shall also act as an International Preliminary Examining Authority for any other applicant, in accordance with an agreement concluded between the Organisation and the International Bureau of the World Intellectual Property Organization.

(3) The Boards of Appeal shall be responsible for deciding on a protest made by an applicant against an additional fee charged by the European Patent Office under the provisions of Article 34, paragraph 3(a), of the Co-operation Treaty.

Article 156

The European Patent Office as an elected Office

18.156   The European Patent Office shall act as an elected Office within the meaning of Article 2(xiv) of the Co-operation Treaty if the applicant has elected any of the designated States referred to in Article 153, paragraph 1, or Article 149, paragraph 2, for which Chapter II of that Treaty has become binding. Subject to the prior approval of the Administrative Council, the same shall apply where the applicant is a resident or national of a State which is not a party to that Treaty or which is not bound by Chapter II of that Treaty, provided that he is one of the persons whom the Assembly of the International Patent Co-operation Union has decided to allow, pursuant to Article 31, paragraph 2(b), of the Co-operation Treaty, to make a demand for international preliminary examination.

Article 157

International search report

18.157   (1) Without prejudice to the provisions of paragraphs 2 to 4, the international search report under Article 18 of the Co-operation Treaty or any declaration under Article 17, paragraph 2(a), of that Treaty and their publication under Article 21 of that Treaty shall take the place of the European search report and the mention of its publication in the European Patent Bulletin.

(2) Subject to the decisions of the Administrative Council referred to in paragraph 3:

(a) a supplementary European search report shall be drawn up in respect of all international applications;

(b) the applicant shall pay the search fee, which shall be paid at the same time as the national fee provided for in Article 22, paragraph 1, or Article 39, paragraph 1, of the Co-operation Treaty. If the search fee is not paid in due time the application shall be deemed to be withdrawn.

(3) The Administrative Council may decide under what conditions and to what extent:

(a) the supplementary European search report is to be dispensed with;

(b) the search fee is to be reduced.

(4) The Administrative Council may at any time rescind the decisions taken pursuant to paragraph 3.

Article 158

Publication of the international application and its supply to the European Patent Office

(1) Publication under Article 21 of the Co-operation Treaty of an international application for which the European Patent Office is a designated Office shall, subject to paragraph 3, take the place of the publication of a European patent application and shall be mentioned in the European Patent Bulletin. Such an application shall not however be considered as comprised in the state of the art in accordance with Article 54, paragraph 3, if the conditions laid down in paragraph 2 are not fulfilled.   **18.158**

(2) The international application shall be supplied to the European Patent Office in one of its official languages. The applicant shall pay to the European Patent Office the national fee provided for in Article 22, paragraph 1, or Article 39, paragraph 1, of the Co-operation Treaty.

(3) If the international application is published in a language other than one of the official languages of the European Patent Office, that Office shall publish the international application, supplied as specified in paragraph 2. Subject to the provisions of Article 67, paragraph 3, the provisional protection in accordance with Article 67, paragraphs 1 and 2, shall be effective from the date of that publication.

PART XI. TRANSITIONAL PROVISIONS

Article 159

Administrative Council during a transitional period

(1) The States referred to in Article 169, paragraph 1, shall appoint their representatives to the Administrative Council; on the invitation of the Government of the Federal Republic of Germany, the Administrative Council shall meet no later than two months after the entry into force of this Convention, particularly for the purpose of appointing the President of the European Patent Office.   **18.159**

(2) The duration of the term of office of the first Chairman of the

Administrative Council appointed after the entry into force of this Convention shall be four years.

(3) The term of office of two of the elected members of the first Board of the Administrative Council set up after the entry into force of this Convention shall be five and four years respectively.

Article 160

Appointment of employees during a transitional period

18.160   (1) Until such time as the Service Regulations for permanent employees and the conditions of employment of other employees of the European Patent Office have been adopted, the Administrative Council and the President of the European Patent Office, each within their respective powers, shall recruit the necessary employees and shall conclude short-term contracts to that effect. The Administrative Council may lay down general principles in respect of recruitment.

(2) During the transitional period, the expiry of which shall be determined by the Administrative Council, the Administrative Council, after consulting the President of the European Patent Office, may appoint as members of the Enlarged Board of Appeal or of the Boards of Appeal technically or legally qualified members of national courts and authorities of Contracting States who may continue their activities in their national courts or authorities. They may be appointed for a term of less than five years, though this shall not be less than one year, and may be reappointed.

Article 161

First accounting period

18.161   (1) The first accounting period of the Organisation shall extend from the date of entry into force of this Convention to 31 December of the same year. If that date falls within the second half of the year, the accounting period shall extend until 31 December of the following year.

(2) The budget for the first accounting period shall be drawn up as soon as possible after the entry into force of this Convention. Until contributions provided for in Article 40 due in accordance with the first budget are received by the Organisation, the Contracting States shall, upon the request of and within the limit of the amount fixed by the Administrative Council, make advances which shall be deducted from

their contributions in respect of that budget. The advances shall be determined in accordance with the scale referred to in Article 40. Article 39, paragraphs 3 and 4, shall apply *mutatis mutandis* to the advances.

Article 162

Progressive expansion of the field of activity of the European Patent Office

(1) European patent applications may be filed with the European **18.162** Patent Office from the date fixed by the Administrative Council on the recommendation of the President of the European Patent Office.

(2) The Administrative Council may, on the recommendation of the President of the European Patent Office, decide that, as from the date referred to in paragraph 1, the processing of European patent applications may be restricted. Such restriction may be in respect of certain areas of technology. However, examination shall in any event be made as to whether European patent applications can be accorded a date of filing.

(3) If a decision has been taken under paragraph 2, the Administrative Council may not subsequently further restrict the processing of European patent applications.

(4) Where, as a result of the procedure being restricted under paragraph 2, a European patent application cannot be further processed, the European Patent Office shall communicate this to the applicant and shall point out that he may make a request for conversion. The European patent application shall be deemed to be withdrawn on receipt of such communication.

Article 163

Professional representatives during a transitional period

(1) During a transitional period, the expiry of which shall be **18.163** determined by the Administrative Council, notwithstanding the provisions of Article 134, paragraph 2, any natural person who fulfils the following conditions may be entered on the list of professional representatives:

(a) he must be a national of a Contracting State;
(b) he must have his place of business or employment within the territory of one of the Contracting States;

(c) he must be entitled to represent natural or legal persons in patent matters before the central industrial property office of the Contracting State in which he has his place of business or employment.

(2) Entry shall be effected upon request, accompanied by a certificate, furnished by the central industrial property office, which must indicate that the conditions laid down in paragraph 1 are fulfilled.

(3) When, in any Contracting State, the entitlement referred to in paragraph 1(c) is not conditional upon the requirement of special professional qualifications, persons applying to be entered on the list who act in patent matters before the central industrial property office of the said State must have habitually so acted for at least five years. However, persons whose professional qualification to represent natural or legal persons in patent matters before the central industrial property office of one of the Contracting States is officially recognised in accordance with the regulations laid down by such State shall not be subject to the condition of having exercised the profession. The certificate furnished by the central industrial property office must indicate that the applicant satisfies one of the conditions referred to in the present paragraph.

(4) The President of the European Patent Office may grant exemption from:

(a) the requirement of paragraph 3, first sentence, if the applicant furnishes proof that he has acquired the requisite qualification in another way;

(b) the requirement of paragraph 1(a) in special circumstances

(5) The President of the European Patent Office shall grant exemption from the requirement of paragraph 1(a) if on 5 October 1973 the applicant fulfilled the requirements of paragraph 1(b) and (c).

(6) Persons having their places of business or employment in a State which acceded to this Convention less than one year before the expiry of the transitional period referred to in paragraph 1 or after the expiry of the transitional period may, under the conditions laid down in paragraphs 1 to 5, during a period of one year calculated from the date of entry into force of the accession of that State, be entered on the list of professional representatives.

(7) After the expiry of the transitional period, any person whose name was entered on the list of professional representatives during that period shall, without prejudice to any disciplinary measures taken under Article 134, paragraph 8(c), remain thereon, or, on request, be restored thereto, provided that he then fulfils the requirement of paragraph 1(b).

Part XII. Final Provisions

Article 164

Implementing Regulations and Protocols

(1) The Implementing Regulations, the Protocol on Recognition, the   **18.164**
Protocol on Privileges and Immunities, the Protocol on Centralisation
and the Protocol on the Interpretation of Article 69 shall be integral parts
of this Convention.

(2) In the case of conflict between the provisions of this Convention
and those of the Implementing Regulations, the provisions of this
Convention shall prevail.

Article 165

Signature—Ratification

(1) This Convention shall be open for signature until 5 April 1974 by   **18.165**
the States which took part in the Inter-Governmental Conference for the
setting up of a European System for the Grant of Patents or were
informed of the holding of that conference and offered the option of
taking part therein.

(2) This Convention shall be subject to ratification; instruments of
ratification shall be deposited with the government of the Federal
Republic of Germany.

Article 166

Accession

(1) This Convention shall be open to accession by: **18.166**

(a) the States referred to in Article 165, paragraph 1;

(b) any other European State at the invitation of the Administrative
Council.

(2) Any State which has been a party to the Convention and has
ceased so to be as a result of the application of Article 172, paragraph 4,
may again become a party to the Convention by acceding to it.

(3) Instruments of accession shall be deposited with the Government
of the Federal Republic of Germany.

Article 167

Reservations

18.167   (1) Each Contracting State may, at the time of signature or when depositing its instrument of ratification or accession, make only the reservations specified in paragraph 2.

(2) Each Contracting State may reserve the right to provide that:

(a) European patents, insofar as they confer protection on chemical, pharmaceutical or food products, as such, shall, in accordance with the provisions applicable to national patents, be ineffective or revocable; this reservation shall not affect protection conferred by the patent insofar as it involves a process of manufacture or use of a chemical product or a process of manufacture of a pharmaceutical or food product;

(b) European patents, insofar as they confer protection on agricultural or horticultural processes other than those to which Article 53, sub-paragraph (b), applies, shall, in accordance with the provisions applicable to national patents, be ineffective or revocable;

(c) European patents shall have a term shorter than twenty years, in accordance with the provisions applicable to national patents;

(d) it shall not be bound by the Protocol on Recognition.

(3) Any reservation made by a Contracting State shall have effect for a period of not more than ten years from the entry into force of this Convention. However, where a Contracting State has made any of the reservations referred to in paragraph 2(a) and (b), the Administrative Council may, in respect of such State, extend the period by not more than five years for all or part of any reservation made, if that State submits, at the latest one year before the end of the ten-year period, a reasoned request which satisfies the Administrative Council that the State is not in a position to dispense with that reservation by the expiry of the ten-year period.

(4) Any Contracting State that has made a reservation shall withdraw this reservation as soon as circumstances permit. Such withdrawal shall be made by notification addressed to the Government of the Federal Republic of Germany and shall take effect one month from the date of receipt of such notification.

(5) Any reservation made in accordance with paragraph 2(a), (b) or (c) shall apply to European patents granted on European patent applications filed during the period in which the reservation has effect. The effect of the reservation shall continue for the term of the patent.

(6) Without prejudice to paragraphs 4 and 5, any reservation shall cease to have effect on expiry of the period referred to in paragraph 3,

first sentence, or, if the period is extended, on expiry of the extended period.

Article 168

Territorial field of application

(1) Any Contracting State may declare in its instrument of ratification **18.168** or accession, or may inform the government of the Federal Republic of Germany by written notification any time thereafter, that this Convention shall be applicable to one or more of the territories for the external relations of which it is responsible. European patents granted for that Contracting State shall also have effect in the territories for which such a declaration has taken effect.

(2) If the declaration referred to in paragraph 1 is contained in the instrument of ratification or accession, it shall take effect on the same date as the ratification or accession; if the declaration is made in a notification after the deposit of the instrument of ratification or accession, such notification shall take effect six months after the date of its receipt by the Government of the Federal Republic of Germany.

(3) Any Contracting State may at any time declare that the Convention shall cease to apply to some or to all of the territories in respect of which it has given a notification pursuant to paragraph 1. Such declaration shall take effect one year after the date on which the Government of the Federal Republic of Germany received notification thereof.

Article 169

Entry into force

(1) This Convention shall enter into force three months after the **18.169** deposit of the last instrument of ratification or accession by six States on whose territory the total number of patent applications filed in 1970 amounted to at least 180,000 for all the said States.

(2) Any ratification or accession after the entry into force of this Convention shall take effect on the first day of the third month after the deposit of the instrument of ratification or accession.

Article 170

Initial contribution

18.170   (1) Any State which ratifies or accedes to this Convention after its entry into force shall pay to the Organisation an initial contribution, which shall not be refunded.

(2) The initial contribution shall be 5 per cent of an amount calculated by applying the percentage obtained for the State in question, on the date on which ratification or accession takes effect, in accordance with the scale provided for in Article 40, paragraphs 3 and 4, to the sum of the special financial contributions due from the other Contracting States in respect of the accounting periods preceding the date referred to above.

(3) In the event that special financial contributions were not required in respect of the accounting period immediately preceding the date referred to in paragraph 2, the scale of contributions referred to in that paragraph shall be the scale that would have been applicable to the State concerned in respect of the last year for which financial contributions were required.

Article 171

Duration of the Convention

18.171   The present Convention shall be of unlimited duration.

Article 172

Revision

18.172   (1) This Convention may be revised by a Conference of the Contracting States.

(2) The Conference shall be prepared and convened by the Administrative Council. The Conference shall not be deemed to be validly constituted unless at least three-quarters of the Contracting States are represented at it. In order to adopt the revised text there must be a majority of three-quarters of the Contracting States represented and voting at the Conference. Abstentions shall not be considered as votes.

(3) The revised text shall enter into force when it has been ratified or

acceded to by the number of Contracting States specified by the Conference, and at the time specified by that Conference.

(4) Such States as have not ratified or acceded to the revised text of the Convention at the time of its entry into force shall cease to be parties to this Convention as from that time.

Article 173

Disputes between Contracting States

(1) Any dispute between Contracting States concerning the inter-   **18.173** pretation or application of the present Convention which is not settled by negotiation shall be submitted, at the request of one of the States concerned, to the Administrative Council, which shall endeavour to bring about agreement between the States concerned.

(2) If such agreement is not reached within six months from the date when the Administrative Council was seized of the dispute, any one of the States concerned may submit the dispute to the International Court of Justice for a binding decision.

Article 174

Denunciation

Any Contracting State may at any time denounce this Convention.   **18.174** Notification of denunciation shall be given to the Government of the Federal Republic of Germany. Denunciation shall take effect one year after the date of receipt of such notification.

Article 175

Preservation of acquired rights

(1) In the event of a State ceasing to be party to this Convention in   **18.175** accordance with Article 172, paragraph 4, or Article 174, rights already acquired pursuant to this Convention shall not be impaired.

(2) A European patent application which is pending when a designated State ceases to be party to the Convention shall be processed by

the European Patent Office, insofar as that State is concerned, as if the Convention in force thereafter were applicable to that State.

(3) The provisions of paragraph 2 shall apply to European patents in respect of which, on the date mentioned in that paragraph, an opposition is pending or the opposition period has not expired.

(4) Nothing in this Article shall affect the right of any State that has ceased to be a party to this Convention to treat any European patent in accordance with the text to which it was a party.

Article 176

Financial rights and obligations of a former Contracting State

18.176   (1) Any State which has ceased to be a party to this Convention in accordance with Article 172, paragraph 4, or Article 174, shall have the special financial contributions which it has paid pursuant to Article 40, paragraph 2, refunded to it by the Organisation only at the time and under the conditions whereby the Organisation refunds special financial contributions paid by other States during the same accounting period.

(2) The State referred to in paragraph 1 shall, even after ceasing to be a party to this Convention, continue to pay the proportion pursuant to Article 39 of renewal fees in respect of European patents remaining in force in that State, at the rate current on the date on which it ceased to be a party.

Article 177

Languages of the Convention

18.177   (1) This Convention, drawn up in a single original, in the English, French and German languages, shall be deposited in the archives of the Government of the Federal Republic of Germany, the three texts being equally authentic.

(2) The texts of this Convention drawn up in official languages of Contracting States other than those referred to in paragraph 1 shall, if they have been approved by the Administrative Council, be considered as official texts. In the event of conflict on the interpretation of the various texts, the texts referred to in paragraph 1 shall be authentic.

Article 178

Transmission and notifications

(1) The Government of the Federal Republic of Germany shall draw **18.178** up certified true copies of this Convention and shall transmit them to the Governments of all signatory or acceding States.

(2) The Government of the Federal Republic of Germany shall notify to the Governments of the States referred to in paragraph 1:

(a) any signature;

(b) the deposit of any instrument of ratification or accession;

(c) any reservation or withdrawal of reservation pursuant to the provisions of Article 167;

(d) any declaration or notification received pursuant to the provisions of Article 168;

(e) the date of entry into force of this Convention;

(f) any denunciation received pursuant to the provisions of Article 174 and the date on which such denunciation comes into force.

(3) The Government of the Federal Republic of Germany shall register this Convention with the Secretariat of the United Nations.

In witness whereof, the Plenipotentiaries authorised thereto, having presented their Full Powers, found to be in good and due form, have signed this Convention.

Done at Munich this fifth day of October one thousand nine hundred and seventy-three.

SIGNATURES

Belgium
Denmark
France
Germany, Federal Republic of
Greece*
Ireland, Republic of
Italy
Liechtenstein
Luxembourg
Netherlands
Norway
Sweden
Switzerland

United Kingdom

*Subject to the reservations permitted under Article 167.

PROTOCOL ON JURISDICTION AND THE RECOGNITION OF DECISIONS IN
RESPECT OF THE RIGHT TO THE GRANT OF A EUROPEAN PATENT
(PROTOCOL ON RECOGNITION)

Section I. Jurisdiction

Article 1

18.179   (1) The courts of the Contracting States shall, in accordance with
Articles 2 to 6, have jurisdiction to decide claims, against the applicant,
to the right to the grant of a European patent in respect of one or more of
the Contracting States designated in the European patent application.
(2) For the purposes of this Protocol, the term "courts" shall include
authorities which, under the national law of a Contracting State, have
jurisdiction to decide the claims referred to in paragraph 1. Any
Contracting State shall notify the European Patent Office of the identity
of any authority on which such a jurisdiction is conferred, and the
European Patent Office shall inform the other Contracting States
accordingly.
(3) For the purposes of this Protocol, the term "Contracting State"
refers to a Contracting State which has not excluded application of this
Protocol pursuant to Article 167 of the Convention.

Article 2

18.180   Subject to Articles 4 and 5, if an applicant for a European patent has
his residence or principal place of business within one of the Contracting States, proceedings shall be brought against him in the courts of
that Contracting State.

Article 3

18.181   Subject to Articles 4 and 5, if an applicant for a European patent has
his residence or principal place of business outside the Contracting
States, and if the party claiming the right to the grant of the European

patent has his residence or principal place of business within one of the Contracting States, the courts of the latter State shall have exclusive jurisdiction.

Article 4

Subject to Article 5, if the subject-matter of a European patent application is the invention of an employee, the courts of the Contracting State, if any, whose law determines the right to the European patent pursuant to Article 60, paragraph 1, second sentence, of the Convention, shall have exclusive jurisdiction over proceedings between the employee and the employer. **18.182**

Article 5

(1) If the parties to a dispute concerning the right to the grant of a European patent have concluded an agreement, either in writing or verbally with written confirmation, to the effect that a court or the courts of a particular Contracting State shall decide on such a dispute, the court or courts of that State shall have exclusive jurisdiction. **18.183**

(2) However, if the parties are an employee and his employer, paragraph 1 shall only apply insofar as the national law governing the contract of employment allows the agreement in question.

Article 6

In cases where neither Articles 2 to 4 nor Article 5, paragraph 1, apply, the courts of the Federal Republic of Germany shall have exclusive jurisdiction. **18.184**

Article 7

The courts of Contracting States before which claims referred to in Article 1 are brought shall of their own motion decide whether or not they have jurisdiction pursuant to Articles 2 to 6. **18.185**

Article 8

18.186 (1) In the event of proceedings based on the same claim and between the same parties being brought before courts of different Contracting States, the court to which a later application is made shall of its own motion decline jurisdiction in favour of the court to which an earlier application was made.

(2) In the event of the jurisdiction of the court to which an earlier application is made being challenged, the court to which a later application is made shall stay the proceedings until the other court takes a final decision.

Section II. Recognition

Article 9

18.187 (1) Subject to the provisions of Article 11, paragraph 2, final decisions given in any Contracting State on the right to the grant of a European patent in respect of one or more of the Contracting States designated in the European patent application shall be recognised without requiring a special procedure in the other Contracting States.

(2) The jurisdiction of the court whose decision is to be recognised and the validity of such decision may not be reviewed.

Article 10

18.188 Article 9, paragraph 1, shall not be applicable where:

(a) an applicant for a European patent who has not contested a claim proves that the document initiating the proceedings was not notified to him regularly and sufficiently early for him to defend himself; or

(b) an applicant proves that the decision is incompatible with another decision given in a Contracting State in proceedings between the same parties which were started before those in which the decision to be recognised was given.

Article 11

(1) In relations between any Contracting States the Provisions of this **18.189**
Protocol shall prevail over any conflicting provisions of other agreements on jurisdiction or the recognition of judgments.

(2) This Protocol shall not affect the implementation of any agreement
between a Contracting State and a State which is not bound by the
Protocol.

PROTOCOL ON PRIVILEGES AND IMMUNITIES OF THE EUROPEAN PATENT
ORGANISATION

(PROTOCOL ON PRIVILEGES AND IMMUNITIES)

Article 1

(1) The premises of the Organisation shall be inviolable.   **18.190**

(2) The authorities of the States in which the Organisation has its
premises shall not enter those premises except with the consent of the
President of the European Patent Office. Such consent shall be assumed
in the case of fire or other disaster requiring prompt protective action.

(3) Service of process at the premises of the Organisation and of any
other procedural instruments relating to a cause of action against the
Organisation shall not constitute breach of inviolability.

Article 2

The archives of the Organisation and any documents belonging to or **18.191**
held by it shall be inviolable.

Article 3

(1) Within the scope of its official activities the Organisation shall **18.192**
have immunity from jurisdiction and execution, except:
  (a) to the extent that the Organisation shall have expressly waived
       such immunity in a particular case;
  (b) in the case of a civil action brought by a third party for damage
       resulting from an accident caused by a motor vehicle belonging

to, or operated on behalf of, the Organisation, or in respect of a motor traffic offence involving such a vehicle;

(c) in respect of the enforcement of an arbitration award made under Article 23.

(2) The property and assets of the Organisation, wherever situated, shall be immune from any form of requisition, confiscation, expropriation and sequestration.

(3) The property and assets of the Organisation shall also be immune from any form of administrative or provisional judicial constraint, except insofar as may be temporarily necessary in connection with the prevention of, and investigation into, accidents involving motor vehicles belonging to or operated on behalf of the Organisation.

(4) The official activities of the Organisation shall, for the purposes of this Protocol, be such as are strictly necessary for its administrative and technical operation, as set out in the Convention.

Article 4

18.193 (1) Within the scope of its official activities the Organisation and its property and income shall be exempt from all direct taxes.

(2) Where substantial purchases for the exercise of its official activities, and in the price of which taxes or duties are included, are made by the Organisation, appropriate measures shall, whenever possible, be taken by the Contracting States to remit or reimburse to the Organisation the amount of such taxes or duties.

(3) No exemption shall be accorded in respect of duties and taxes which are no more than charges for public utility services.

Article 5

18.194 Goods imported or exported by the Organisation for the exercise of its official activities shall be exempt from duties and charges on import or export other than fees or taxes representing services rendered, and from all prohibitions and restrictions on import or export.

Article 6

18.195 No exemption shall be granted under Articles 4 and 5 in respect of goods purchased or imported for the personal benefit of the employees of the European Patent Office.

Article 7

(1) Goods belonging to the Organisation which have been acquired or **18.196** imported under Article 4 or Article 5 shall not be sold or given away except in accordance with conditions laid down by the Contracting States which have granted the exemptions.

(2) The transfer of goods and provision of services between the various buildings of the Organisation shall be exempt from charges or restrictions of any kind; where appropriate, the Contracting States shall take all the necessary measures to remit or reimburse the amount of such charges or to lift such restrictions.

Article 8

The transmission of publications and other information material by or **18.197** to the Organisation shall not be restricted in any way.

Article 9

The Contracting States shall accord the Organisation the currency **18.198** exemptions which are necessary for the exercise of its official activities.

Article 10

(1) With regard to its official communications and the transfer of all its **18.199** documents, the Organisation shall in each Contracting State enjoy the most favourable treatment accorded by that State to any other international organisation.

(2) No censorship shall be applied to official communications of the Organisation by whatever means of communication.

Article 11

The Contracting States shall take all appropriate measures to facilitate **18.200** the entry, stay and departure of the employees of the European Patent Office.

Article 12

18.201 (1) Representatives of Contracting States, alternate Representatives and their advisers or experts, if any, shall enjoy, while attending meetings of the Administrative Council and of any body established by it, and in the course of their journeys to and from the place of meeting, the following privileges and immunities:

(a) immunity from arrest or detention and from seizure of their personal luggage, except when found committing, attempting to commit, or just having committed an offence;

(b) immunity from jurisdiction, even after the termination of their mission, in respect of acts, including words written and spoken, done by them in the exercise of their functions; this immunity shall not apply, however, in the case of a motor traffic offence committed by one of the persons referred to above, nor in the case of damage caused by a motor vehicle belonging to or driven by such a person;

(c) inviolability for all their official papers and documents;

(d) the right to use codes and to receive documents or correspondence by special courier or sealed bag;

(e) exemption for themselves and their spouses from all measures restricting entry and from aliens' registration formalities;

(f) the same facilities in the matter of currency and exchange control as are accorded to the representatives of foreign Governments on temporary official missions.

(2) Privileges and immunities are accorded to the persons referred to in paragraph 1, not for their personal advantage, but in order to ensure complete independence in the exercise of their functions in connection with the Organisation. Consequently, a Contracting State has the duty to waive the immunity in all cases where, in the opinion of that State, such immunity would impede the course of justice and where it can be waived without prejudicing the purposes for which it was accorded.

Article 13

18.202 (1) Subject to the provisions of Article 6, the President of the European Patent Office shall enjoy the privileges and immunities accorded to diplomatic agents under the Vienna Convention on Diplomatic Relations of 18 April 1961.

(2) However, immunity from jurisdiction shall not apply in the case of a motor traffic offence committed by the President of the European Patent Office or damage caused by a motor vehicle belonging to or driven by him.

Article 14

The employees of the European Patent Office:

    18.203

(a) shall, even after their service has terminated, have immunity from jurisdiction in respect of acts, including words written and spoken, done in the exercise of their functions; this immunity shall not apply, however, in the case of a motor traffic offence committed by an employee of the European Patent Office, nor in the case of damage caused by a motor vehicle belonging to or driven by an employee;

(b) shall be exempt from all obligations in respect of military service;

(c) shall enjoy inviolability for all their official papers and documents;

(d) shall enjoy the same facilities as regards exemption from all measures restricting immigration and governing aliens' registration as are normally accorded to staff members of international organisations, as shall members of their families forming part of their household;

(e) shall enjoy the same privileges in respect of exchange regulations as are normally accorded to the staff members of international organisations;

(f) shall enjoy the same facilities as to repatriation as diplomatic agents in time of international crises, as shall the members of their families forming part of their household;

(g) shall have the right to import duty-free their furniture and personal effects at the time of first taking up their post in the State concerned and the right on the termination of their functions in that State to export free of duty their furniture and personal effects, subject to the conditions considered necessary by the Government of the State in whose territory the right is exercised and with the exception of property acquired in that State which is subject to an export prohibition therein.

Article 15

Experts performing functions on behalf of, or carrying out missions   **18.204** for, the Organisation shall enjoy the following privileges and immunities, to the extent that they are necessary for the carrying out of their functions, including during journeys made in carrying out their functions and in the course of such missions:

(a) immunity from jurisdiction in respect of acts done by them in the exercise of their functions, including words written or spoken, except in the case of a motor traffic offence committed by an expert or in the case of damage caused by a motor vehicle belonging to or driven by him; experts shall continue to enjoy this immunity after they have ceased to be employed by the Organisation;

(b) inviolability for all their official papers and documents;

(c) the exchange facilities necessary for the transfer of their remuneration.

Article 16

18.205 (1) The persons referred to in Articles 13 and 14 shall be subject to a tax for the benefit of the Organisation on salaries and emoluments paid by the Organisation, subject to the conditions and rules laid down by the Administrative Council within a period of one year from the date of the entry into force of the Convention. From the date on which this tax is applied, such salaries and emoluments shall be exempt from national income tax. The Contracting States may, however, take into account the salaries and emoluments thus exempt when assessing the amount of tax to be applied to income from other sources.

(2) Paragraph 1 shall not apply to pensions and annuities paid by the Organisation to the former employees of the European Patent Office.

Article 17

18.206 The Administrative Council shall decide the categories of employees to whom the provisions of Article 14, in whole or in part, and Article 16 shall apply and the categories of experts to whom the provisions of Article 15 shall apply. The names, titles and addresses of the employees and experts incuded in such categories shall be communicated from time to time to the Contracting States.

Article 18

18.207 In the event of the Organisation establishing its own social security scheme, the Organisation and the employees of the European Patent Office shall be exempt from all compulsory contributions to national social security schemes, subject to the agreements made with the Contracting States in accordance with the provisions of Article 25.

Article 19

(1) The privileges and immunities provided for in this Protocol are not **18.208** designed to give to employees of the European Patent Office or experts performing functions for or on behalf of the Organisation personal advantage. They are provided solely to ensure, in all circumstances, the unimpeded functioning of the Organisation and the complete independence of the persons to whom they are accorded.

(2) The President of the European Patent Office has the duty to waive immunity where he considers that such immunity prevents the normal course of justice and that it is possible to dispense with such immunity without prejudicing the interests of the Organisation. The Administrative Council may waive immunity of the President for the same reasons.

Article 20

(1) The Organisation shall co-operate at all times with the competent **18.209** authorities of the Contracting States in order to facilitate the proper administration of justice, to ensure the observance of police regulations and regulations concerning public health, labour inspection or other similar national legislation, and to prevent any abuse of the privileges, immunities and facilities provided for in this Protocol.

(2) The procedure of co-operation mentioned in paragraph 1 may be laid down in the complementary agreements referred to in Article 25.

Article 21

Each Contracting State retains the right to take all precautions **18.210** necessary in the interests of its security.

Article 22

No Contracting State is obliged to extend the privileges and immun- **18.211** ities referred to in Article 12, Article 13, Article 14, sub-paragraphs (b), (e) and (g) and Article 15, sub-paragraph (c) to:
  (a) its own nationals;
  (b) any person who at the time of taking up his functions with the Organisation has his permanent residence in that State and is not an employee of any other inter-governmental organisation whose staff is incorporated into the Organisation.

Article 23

18.212 (1) Any Contracting State may submit to an international arbitration tribunal any dispute concerning the Organisation or an employee of the European Patent Office or an expert performing functions for or on its behalf, insofar as the Organisation or the employees and experts have claimed a privilege or an immunity under this Protocol in circumstances where that immunity has not been waived.

(2) If a Contracting State intends to submit a dispute to arbitration, it shall notify the Chairman of the Administrative Council, who shall forthwith inform each Contracting State of such notification.

(3) The procedure laid down in paragraph 1 of this Article shall not apply to disputes between the Organisation and the employees or experts in respect of the Service Regulations or conditions of employment or, with regard to the employees, the Pension Scheme Regulations.

(4) No appeal shall lie against the award of the arbitration tribunal, which shall be final; it shall be binding on the parties. In case of dispute concerning the import or scope of the award, it shall be incumbent upon the arbitration tribunal to interpret it on request by either party.

Article 24

18.213 (1) The arbitration tribunal referred to in Article 23 shall consist of three members, one arbitrator nominated by the State or States party to the arbitration, one arbitrator nominated by the Administrative Council and a third arbitrator, who shall be the chairman, nominated by the said two arbitrators.

(2) The arbitrators shall be nominated from a panel comprising no more than six arbitrators appointed by each Contracting State and six arbitrators appointed by the Administrative Council. This panel shall be established as soon as possible after the Protocol enters into force and shall be revised each time this proves necessary.

(3) If, within three months from the date of the notification referred to in Article 23, paragraph 2, either party fails to make the nomination referred to in paragraph 1 above, the choice of the arbitrator shall, on request of the other party, be made by the President of the International Court of Justice from the persons included in the said panel. This shall also apply, when so requested by either party, if within one month from the date of appointment of the second arbitrator, the first two arbitrators are unable to agree on the nomination of the third arbitrator. However, if, in these two cases, the President of the International Court of Justice is prevented from making the choice, or if he is a national of one of the States parties to the dispute, the Vice-President of the International Court of Justice shall make the afore-mentioned appointments, pro-

vided that he himself is not a national of one of the States parties to the dispute; if such is the case, the member of the International Court of Justice who is not a national of one of the States parties to the dispute and who has been chosen by the President or Vice-President shall make the appointments. A national of the State applying for arbitration may not be chosen to fill the post of the arbitrator whose appointment devolves on the Administrative Council nor may a person included in the panel and appointed by the Administrative Council be chosen to fill the post of an arbitrator whose appointment devolves on the State which is the claimant. Nor may a person of either of these categories be chosen as chairman of the Tribunal.

(4) The arbitration tribunal shall draw up its own rules of procedure.

Article 25

The Organisation may, on a decision of the Administrative Council, conclude with one or more Contracting States complementary agreements to give effect to the provisions of this Protocol as regards such State or States, and other arrangements to ensure the efficient functioning of the Organisation and the safeguarding of its interests.   **18.214**

PROTOCOL ON THE CENTRALISATION OF THE EUROPEAN PATENT SYSTEM
AND ON ITS INTRODUCTION
(PROTOCOL ON CENTRALISATION)

Section I

(1)—   **18.215**

(a) Upon entry into force of the Convention, States parties thereto which are also members of the International Patent Institute set up by The Hague Agreement of 6 June 1947 shall take all necessary steps to ensure the transfer to the European Patent Office no later than the date referred to in Article 162, paragraph 1, of the Convention of all assets and liabilities and all staff members of the International Patent Institute. Such transfer shall be effected by an agreement between the International Patent Institute and the European Patent Organisation. The above States and the other States parties to the Convention shall take all necessary steps to ensure that that agreement shall be implemented no later than the date referred to in Article 162, paragraph 1, of the Convention. Upon implementation of the agreement, those Member States of the International Patent Institute which are also parties to the Convention further undertake to terminate their participation in The Hague Agreement.

(b) The States parties to the Convention shall take all necessary steps to ensure that all the assets and liabilities and all the staff members of the International Patent Institute are taken into the European Patent Office in accordance with the agreement referred to in sub-paragraph (a). After the implementation of that agreement the tasks incumbent upon the International Patent Institute at the date on which the Convention is opened for signature, and in particular those carried out *vis-à-vis* its Member States, whether or not they become parties to the Convention, and such tasks as it has undertaken at the time of the entry into force of the Convention to carry out *vis-à-vis* States which, at that date, are both members of the International Patent Institute and parties to the Convention, shall be assumed by the branch located at The Hague. In addition, the Administrative Council of the European Patent Organisation may allocate further duties in the field of searching to that branch.

(c) The above obligations shall also apply *mutatis mutandis* to the sub-office set up under The Hague Agreement under the conditions set out in the agreement between the International Patent Institute and the Government of the Contracting State concerned. This Government hereby undertakes to make a new agreement with the European Patent Organisation in place of the one already made with the International Patent Institute to harmonise the clauses concerning the organisation, operation and financing of the sub-office with the provisions of this Protocol.

(2) Subject to the provisions of Section III, the States parties to the Convention shall, on behalf of their central industrial property offices, renounce in favour of the European Patent Office any activities as International Searching Authorities under the Patent Co-operation Treaty as from the date referred to in Article 162, paragraph 1, of the Convention.

(3)—

(a) A sub-office of the European Patent Office for searching European patent applications shall be set up in Berlin (West) as from the date referred to in Article 162, paragraph 1, of the Convention. It shall operate under the direction of the branch at The Hague.

(b) The Administrative Council shall determine the duties to be allocated to the sub-office in Berlin in the light of general considerations and of the requirements of the European Patent Office with regard to searching.

(c) At least at the beginning of the period following the progressive expansion of the field of activity of the European Patent Office, the amount of work assigned to that sub-office shall be sufficient to enable the examining staff of the Berlin Annex of the German

Patent Office, as it stands at the date on which the Convention is opened for signature, to be fully employed.

(d) The Federal Republic of Germany shall bear any additional costs incurred by the European Patent Organisation in setting up and maintaining the sub-office in Berlin.

Section II

Subject to the provisions of Sections III and IV, the States parties to the Convention shall, on behalf of their central industrial property offices, renounce in favour of the European Patent Office any activities as International Preliminary Examining Authorities under the Patent Co-operation Treaty. This obligation shall apply only to the extent to which the European Patent Office may examine European patent applications in accordance with Article 162, paragraph 2, of the Convention and shall not apply until two years after the date on which the European Patent Office has begun examining activities in the areas of technology concerned, on the basis of a five-year plan which shall progressively extend the activities of the European Patent Office to all areas of technology and which may be amended only by decision of the Administrative Council. The procedures for implementing this obligation shall be determined by decision of the Administrative Council. **18.216**

Section III

(1) The central industrial property office of any State party to the Convention in which the official language is not one of the offical languages of the European Patent Office, shall be authorised to act as an International Searching Authority and as an International Preliminary Examining Authority under the Patent Co-operation Treaty. Such authorisation shall be subject to an undertaking by the State concerned to restrict such activities to international applications filed by nationals or residents of such State and by nationals or residents of States parties to the Convention which are adjacent to that State. The Administrative Council may decide to authorise the central industrial property office of any State party to the Convention to extend such activities to cover such international applications as may be filed by nationals or residents of any non-Contracting State having the same official language as the Contracting State in question and drawn up in that language. **18.217**

(2) For the purpose of harmonising search activities under the Patent Co-operation Treaty within the framework of the European system for the grant of patents, co-operation shall be established between the European Patent Office and any central industrial property office

authorised under this Section. Such co-operation shall be based on a special agreement which may cover *e.g.* search procedures and methods, qualifications required for the recruitment and training of examiners, guidelines for the exchange of search and other services between the offices as well as other measures needed to establish the required control and supervision.

Section IV

18.218   (1)—

(a) For the purpose of facilitating the adaptation of the national patent offices of the States parties to the Convention to the European patent system, the Administrative Council may, if it considers it desirable, and subject to the conditions set out below, entrust the central industrial property offices of such of those States in which it is possible to conduct the proceedings in one of the official languages of the European Patent Office with tasks concerning the examination of European patent applications drawn up in that language, which pursuant to Article 18, paragraph 2, of the Convention, shall, as a general rule, be entrusted to a member of the Examining Division. Such tasks shall be carried out within the framework of the proceedings for grant laid down in the Convention; decisions on such applications shall be taken by the Examining Division composed in accordance with Article 18, paragraph 2.

(b) Tasks entrusted under sub-paragraph (a) shall not be in respect of more than 40% of the total number of European patent applications filed; tasks entrusted to any one State shall not be in respect of more than one-third of the total number of European patent applications filed. These tasks shall be entrusted for a period of 15 years from the opening of the European Patent Office and shall be reduced progressively (in principle by 20% a year) to zero during the last 5 years of the period.

(c) The Administrative Council shall decide, while taking into account the provisions of sub-paragraph (b), upon the nature, origin and number of the European patent applications in respect of which examining tasks may be entrusted to the central industrial property office of each of the Contracting States mentioned above.

(d) The above implementing procedures shall be set out in a special agreement between the central industrial property office of the Contracting State concerned and the European Patent Organisation.

(e) An office with which such a special agreement has been concluded may act as an International Preliminary Examining

Authority under the Patent Co-operation Treaty, until the expiry of the period of 15 years.

(2)—

(a) If the Administrative Council considers that it is compatible with the proper functioning of the European Patent Office, and in order to alleviate the difficulties which may arise for certain Contracting States from the application of Section I, paragraph 2, it may entrust searching in respect of European patent applications to the central industrial property offices of those States in which the official language is one of the official languages of the European Patent Office, provided that these offices possess the necessary qualifications for appointment as an International Searching Authority in accordance with the conditions laid down in the Patent Co-operation Treaty.

(b) In carrying out such work, undertaken under the responsibility of the European Patent Office, the central industrial property offices concerned shall adhere to the guidelines applicable to the drawing up of the European search report.

(c) The provisions of paragraph 1(b), second sentence, and sub-paragraph (d) of this Section shall apply to this paragraph.

Section V

(1) The sub-office referred to in Section I, paragraph 1(c), shall be **18.219** authorised to carry out searches, among the documentation which is at its disposal and which is in the official language of the State in which the sub-office is located, in respect of European patent applications filed by nationals and residents of that State. This authorisation shall be on the understanding that the procedure for the grant of European patents will not be delayed and that additional costs will not be incurred for the European Patent Organisation.

(2) The sub-office referred to in paragraph 1 shall be authorised to carry out, at the option of an applicant for a European patent and at his expense, a search on his patent application among the documentation referred to in paragraph 1. This authorisation shall be effective until the search provided for in Article 92 of the Convention has been extended, in accordance with Section VI, to cover such documentation and shall be on the understanding that the procedure for the grant of European patents will not be delayed.

(3) The Administrative Council may also extend the authorisations provided for in paragraphs 1 and 2, under the conditions of those paragraphs, to the central industrial property office of a Contracting State which does not have as an official language one of the official languages of the European Patent Office.

Section VI

18.220   The search provided for in Article 92 of the Convention shall, in principle, be extended, in respect of all European patent applications, to published patents, published patent applications and other relevant documents not included in the search documentation of the European Patent Office on the date referred to in Article 162, paragraph 1, of the Convention. The extent, conditions and timing of any such extention shall be determined by the Administrative Council on the basis of a study concerning particularly the technical and financial aspects.

Section VII

18.221   The provisions of this Protocol shall prevail over any contradictory provisions of the Convention.

Section VIII

18.222   The decision of the Administrative Council provided for in this Protocol shall require a three-quarters majority (Article 35, paragraph 2, of the Convention). The provisions governing the weighting of votes (Article 36 of the Convention) shall apply.

PROTOCOL ON THE INTERPRETATION OF ARTICLE 69 OF THE CONVENTION

18.223   Article 69 should not be interpreted in the sense that the extent of the protection conferred by a European patent is to be understood as that defined by the strict, literal meaning of the wording used in the claims, the description and drawings being employed only for the purpose of resolving an ambiguity found in the claims. Neither should it be interpreted in the sense that the claims serve only as a guideline and that the actual protection conferred may extend to what, from a consideration of the description and drawings by a person skilled in the art, the patentee has contemplated. On the contrary, it is to be interpreted as defining a position betwen these extremes which combines a fair protection for the patentee with a reasonable degree of certainty for third parties.

PATENT CO-OPERATION TREATY

ARRANGEMENT OF ARTICLES

Introductory Provisions

Chapter I. International application and international search

Chapter II. International preliminary examination

Chapter III. Common provisions

Chapter IV. Technical services

Chapter V. Administrative provisions

Chapter VI. Disputes

Chapter VII. Revision and amendment

Chapter VIII. Final provisions

Introductory Provisions

Article 1

Establishment of a Union

(1) The States party to this Treaty (hereinafter called "the Contracting   **19.01**
States") constitute a Union for cooperation in the filing, searching, and
examination, of applications for the protection of inventions, and for
rendering special technical services. The Union shall be known as the
International Patent Cooperation Union.

(2) No provision of this Treaty shall be interpreted as diminishing the
rights under the Paris Convention for the Protection of Industrial
Property of any national or resident of any country party to that
Convention.

Article 2

Definitions

19.02   For the purposes of this Treaty and the Regulations and unless expressly stated otherwise:

(i)   "application" means an application for the protection of an invention; references to an "application" shall be construed as references to applications for patents for inventions, inventors' certificates, utility certificates, utility models, patents or certificates of addition, inventors' certificates of addition, and utility certificates of addition;

(ii)   references to a "patent" shall be construed as references to patents for inventions, inventors' certificates, utility certificates, utility models, patents or certificates of addition, inventors' certificates of addition, and utility certificates of addition;

(iii)   "national patent" means a patent granted by a national authority;

(iv)   "regional patent" means a patent granted by a national or an intergovernmental authority having the power to grant patents effective in more than one State;

(v)   "regional application" means an application for a regional patent;

(vi)   references to a "national application" shall be construed as references to applications for national patents and regional patents, other than applications filed under this Treaty;

(vii)   "international applications" means an application filed under this Treaty;

(viii)   references to an "application" shall be construed as references to international applications and national applications;

(ix)   references to a "patent" shall be construed as references to national patents and regional patents;

(x)   references to "national law" shall be construed as references to the national law of a Contracting State or, where a regional application or a regional patent is involved, to the treaty providing for the filing of regional applications or the granting of regional patents;

(xi)   "priority date", for the purposes of computing time limits; means:

(a) where the international application contains a priority claim under Article 8, the filing date of the application whose priority is so claimed;

(b) where the international application contains several priority claims under Article 8, the filing date of the earliest application whose priority is so claimed;

(c) where the international application does not contain any priority claim under Article 8, the international filing date of such applications;

(xii) "national Office" means the government authority of a Contracting State entrusted with the granting of patents; references to a "national Office" shall be construed as referring also to any intergovernmental authority which several States have entrusted with the task of granting regional patents, provided that at least one of those States is a Contracting State, and provided that the said States have authorised that authority to assume the obligations and exercises the powers which this Treaty and the Regulations provide for in respect of national Offices;

(xiii) "designated Office" means the national Office of or acting for the State designated by the applicant under Chapter I of this Treaty;

(xiv) "elected Office" means the national Office of or acting for the State elected by the applicant under Chapter II of this Treaty;

(xv) "receiving Office" means the national Office or the intergovernmental organization with which the international application has been filed;

(xvi) "Union" means the International Patent Cooperation Union;

(xvii) "Assembly" means the Assembly of the Union;

(xviii) "Organization" means the World Intellectual Property Organization;

(xix) "International Bureau" means the International Bureaux of the Organization and, as long as it subsists, the United International Bureaux for the Protection of Intellectual Property (BIRPI);

(xx) "Director General" means the Director General of the Organization and, as long as BIRPI subsists, the Director of BIRPI.

Chapter I. International application and international search

Article 3

The International application

(1) Applications for the protection of inventions in any of the **19.03** Contracting States may be filed as international applications under this Treaty.

(2) An international application shall contain, as specified in this Treaty and the Regulations, a request, a description, one or more claims, one or more drawings (where required), and an abstract.

(3) The abstract merely serves the purpose of technical information and cannot be taken into account for any other purpose, particularly not for the purpose of interpreting the scope of the protection sought.

(4) The international application shall:

(i)   be in a prescribed language;

(ii) comply with the prescribed physical requirements;

(iii) comply with the prescribed requirement of unity of invention;

(iv) be subject to the payment of the prescribed fees.

Article 4

The request

19.04   (1) The request shall contain:

(i)   a petition to the effect that the international application be processed according to this Treaty;

(ii) the designation of the Contracting State or States in which protection for the invention is desired on the basis of the international application ("designated States"); if for any designated State a regional patent is available and the applicant wishes to obtain a regional patent rather than a national patent, the request shall so indicate; if, under a treaty concerning a regional patent, the applicant cannot limit his application to certain of the States party to that treaty, designation of one of those States and the indication of the wish to obtain the regional patent shall be treated as designation of all the States party to that treaty; if, under the national law of the designated State, the designation of that State has the effect of an application for a regional patent, the designation of the said State shall be treated as an indication of the wish to obtain the regional patent;

(iii) the name of and other prescribed data concerning the applicant and the agent (if any);

(iv) the title of the invention;

(v)   the name of and other prescribed data concerning the inventor where the national law of at least one of the designated States requires that these indications be furnished at the time of filing a national application. Otherwise, the said indications may be furnished either in the request or in separate notices addressed to each designated Office whose national law requires the furnishing of the said indications but allows that they be furnished at a time later than that of the filing of a national application.

(2) Every designation shall be subject to the payment of the prescribed fee within the prescribed time limit.

(3) Unless the applicant asks for any of the other kinds of protection referred to in Article 43, designation shall mean that the desired protection consists of the grant of a patent by or for the designated State. For the purposes of this paragraph, Article 2(ii) shall not apply.

(4) Failure to indicate in the request the name and other prescribed data concerning the inventor shall have no consequences in any designated State whose national law requires the furnishing of the said indications but allows that they be furnished at a time later than that of the filing of a national application. Failure to furnish the said indications in a separate notice shall have no consequence in any designated State whose national law does not require the furnishing of the said indications.

Article 5

The description

The description shall disclose the invention in a manner sufficiently clear and complete for the invention to be carried out by a person skilled in the art.　　**19.05**

Article 6

The claims

The claim or claims shall define the matter for which protection is sought. Claims shall be clear and concise. They shall be fully supported by the description.　　**19.06**

Article 7

The drawings

(1) Subject to the provisions of paragraph (2)(ii), drawings shall be required when they are necessary for the understanding of the invention.　　**19.07**

(2) Where, without being necessary for the understanding of the invention, the nature of the invention admits of illustration by drawings:

    (i) the applicant may include such drawings in the international application when filed,

    (ii) any designated Office may require that the applicant file such drawings with it within the prescribed time limit.

Article 8

Claiming priority

19.08   (1) The international application may contain a declaration, as prescribed in the Regulations, claiming the priority of one or more earlier applications filed in or for any country party to the Paris Convention for the Protection of Industrial Property.

    (2)—

    (a) Subject to the provisions of sub-paragraph (*b*), the conditions for, and the effect of, any priority claim declared under paragraph (1) shall be as provided in Article 4 of the Stockholm Act of the Paris Convention for the Protection of Industrial Property.

    (b) The international application for which the priority of one or more earlier applications filed in or for a Contracting State is claimed may contain the designation of that State. Where, in the international application, the priority of one or more national applications filed in or for a designated State is claimed, or where the priority of an international application having designated only one State is claimed, the conditions for, and the effect of, the priority claim in that State shall be governed by the national law of that State.

Article 9

The applicant

19.09   (1) Any resident or national of a Contracting State may file an international application.

    (2) The Assembly may decide to allow the residents and the nationals of any country party to the Paris Convention for the Protection of Industrial Property which is not party to this Treaty to file international applications.

(3) The concepts of residence and nationality, and the application of those concepts in cases where there are several applicants or where the applicants are not the same for all the designated States, are defined in the Regulations.

Article 10

The receiving Office

The international application shall be filed with the prescribed **19.10** receiving Office, which will check and process it as provided in this Treaty and the Regulations.

Article 11

Filing date and effects of the international application

(1) The receiving Office shall accord as the international filing date the **19.11** date of receipt of the international application, provided that that Office has found that, at the time of receipt:
   (i) the applicant does not obviously lack, for reasons of residence or nationality, the right to file an international application with the receiving Office,
   (ii) the international application is in the prescribed language,
   (iii) the international application contains at least the following elements:
      (a) an indication that it is intended as an international application,
      (b) the designation of at least one Contracting State,
      (c) the name of the applicant, as prescribed,
      (d) a part which on the face of it appears to be a description,
      (e) a part which on the face of it appears to be a claim or claims.
(2)—
   (a) If the receiving Office finds that the international application did not, at the time of receipt, fulfil the requirements listed in paragraph (1), it shall, as provided in the Regulations, invite the applicant to file the required correction.
   (b) If the applicant complies with the invitation, as provided in the Regulations, the receiving Office shall accord as the international filing date the date of receipt of the required correction.
(3) Subject to Article 64(4), any international application fulfilling the requirements listed in items (i) to (iii) of paragraph (1) and accorded an

international filing date shall have the effect of a regular national application in each designated State as of the internatonal filing date, which date shall be considered to be the actual filing date in each designated State.

(4) Any international application fulfilling the requirements listed in items (i) to (iii) of paragraph (1) shall be equivalent to a regular national filing within the meaning of the Paris Convention for the Protection of Industrial Property.

Article 12

Transmittal of the international application to the International Bureau and the International Searching Authority

19.12 (1) One copy of the international application shall be kept by the receiving Office ("home copy"), one copy ("record copy") shall be transmitted to the International Bureau, and another copy ("search copy") shall be transmitted to the competent International Searching Authority referred to in Article 16, as provided in the Regulations.

(2) The record copy shall be considered the true copy of the international application.

(3) The international application shall be considered withdrawn if the record copy has not been received by the International Bureau within the prescribed time limit.

Article 13

Availability of copy of the international application to designated Offices

19.13 (1) Any designated Office may ask the International Bureau to transmit to it a copy of the international application prior to the communication provided for in Article 20, and the International Bureau shall transmit such copy to the designated Office as soon as possible after the expiration of one year from the priority date.

(2)—
 (a) The applicant may, at any time, transmit a copy of his international application to any designated Office,
 (b) The applicant may, at any time, ask the International Bureau to transmit a copy of his international application to any designated

Office, and the International Bureau shall transmit such copy to the designated Office as soon as possible.

(c) Any national Office may notify the International Bureau that it does not wish to receive copies as provided for in sub-paragraph (b), in which case that sub-paragraph shall not be applicable in respect of that Office.

Article 14

Certain defects in the international application

(1)—   19.14

(a) The receiving Office shall check whether the international application contains any of the following defects, that is to say:
   (i)   it is not signed as provided in the Regulations;
   (ii) it does not contain the prescribed indications concerning the applicant;
   (iii) it does not contain a title;
   (iv) it does not contain an abstract;
   (v)   it does not comply to the extent provided in the Regulations with the prescribed physical requirements.

(b) If the receiving Office finds any of the said defects, it shall invite the applicant to correct the international application within the prescribed time limit, failing which that application shall be considered withdrawn and the receiving Office shall so declare.

(2) If the international application refers to drawings which, in fact, are not included in that application, the receiving Office shall notify the applicant accordingly and he may furnish them within the prescribed time limit and, if he does, the international filing date shall be the date on which the drawings are received by the receiving Office. Otherwise, any reference to the said drawings shall be considered non-existent.

(3)—

(a) If the receiving Office finds that, within the prescribed time limits, the fees prescribed under Article 3(4)(iv) have not been paid, or no fee prescribed under Article 4(2) has been paid in respect of any of the designated States, the international application shall be considered withdrawn and the receiving Office shall so declare.

(b) If the receiving Office finds that the fee prescribed under Article 4(2) has been paid in respect of one or more (but less than all) designated States within the prescribed time limit, the designation of those States in respect of which it has not been paid within the prescribed time limit shall be considered withdrawn and the receiving Office shall so declare.

(4) If, after having accorded an international filing date to the

international application, the receiving Office finds, within the prescribed time limit, that any of the requirements listed in items (i) to (iii) of Article 11(1) was not complied with at that date, the said application shall be considered withdrawn and the receiving Office shall so declare.

Article 15

The international search

19.15 (1) Each international application shall be the subject of international search.

(2) The objective of the international search is to discover relevant prior art.

(3) International search shall be made on the basis of the claims, with due regard to the description and the drawings (if any).

(4) The International Searching Authority referred to in Article 16 shall endeavour to discover as much of the relevant prior art as its facilities permit, and shall, in any case, consult the documentation specified in the Regulations.

(5)—

(a) If the national law of the Contracting State so permits, the applicant who files a national application with the national Office of or acting for such State may, subject to the conditions provided for in such law, request that a search similar to an international search ("international-type search") be carried out on such application.

(b) If the national law of the Contracting State so permits, the national Office of or acting for such State may subject any national application filed with it to an international-type search.

(c) The international-type search shall be carried out by the International Searching Authority referred to in Article 16 which would be competent for an international search if the national application were an international application and were filed with the Office referred to in sub-paragraphs (a) and (b). If the national application is in a language which the International Searching Authority considers it is not equipped to handle, the international-type search shall be carried out on a translation prepared by the applicant in a language prescribed for international applications and which the International Searching Authority has undertaken to accept for international applications. The national application and the translation, when required, shall be presented in the form prescribed for international applications.

Article 16

The International Searching Authority

(1) International search shall be carried out by an International 19.16
Searching Authority, which may be either a national Office or an inter-
governmental organisation, such as the International Patent Institute,
whose tasks include the establishing of documentary search reports on
prior art with respect to inventions which are the subject of applications.

(2) If, pending the establishment of a single International Searching
Authority, there are several International Searching Authorities, each
receiving Office shall, in accordance with the provisions of the
applicable agreement referred to in paragraph (3)(b), specify the
International Searching Authority or Authorities competent for the
searching of international applications filed with such Office.

(3)—

(a) International Searching Authorities shall be appointed by the
Assembly. Any national Office and any intergovernmental
organisation satisfying the requirements referred to in sub-
paragraph (c) may be appointed as International Searching
Authority.

(b) Appointment shall be conditional on the consent of the national
Office or intergovernmental organisation to be appointed and the
conclusion of an agreement, subject to approval by the Assembly,
between such Office or organisation and the International Bureau. The agreement shall specify the rights and obligations of the
parties, in particular, the formal undertaking by the said Office or
organisation to apply and observe all the common rules of
international search.

(c) The Regulations prescribe the minimum requirements, particularly as to manpower and documentation, which any Office or
organisation must satisfy before it can be appointed and must
continue to satisfy while it remains appointed.

(d) Appointment shall be for a fixed period of time and may be
extended for further periods.

(e) Before the Assembly makes a decision on the appointment of any
national Office or intergovernmental organisation, or on the
extension of its appointment, or before it allows any such
appointment to lapse, the Assembly shall hear the interested
Office or organisation and seek the advice of the Committee for
Technical Co-operation referred to in Article 56 once that
Committee has been established.

Article 17

Procedure before the International Searching Authority

19.17   (1) Procedure before the International Searching Authority shall be governed by the provisions of this Treaty, the Regulations, and the agreement which the International Bureau shall conclude, subject to this Treaty and the Regulations, with the said Authority.

(2)—

(a) If the International Searching Authority considers:

    (i) that the international application relates to a subject-matter which the International Searching Authority is not required, under the Regulations, to search, and in the particular case decides not to search, or

    (ii) that the description, the claims, or the drawings, fail to comply with the prescribed requirements to such an extent that a meaningful search could not be carried out,

the said Authority shall so declare and shall notify the applicant and the International Bureau that no international search report will be established.

(b) If any of the situations referred to in sub-paragraph (a) are found to exist in connection with certain claims only, the international search report shall so indicate in respect of such claims, whereas, for the other claims, the said report shall be established as provided in Article 18.

(3)—

(a) If the International Searching Authority considers that the international application does not comply with the requirement of unity of invention as set forth in the Regulations, it shall invite the applicant to pay additional fees. The International Searching Authority shall establish the international search report on those parts of the international application which relate to the invention first mentioned in the claims ("main invention") and, provided the required additional fees have been paid within the prescribed time limit, on those parts of the international application which relate to inventions in respect of which the said fees were paid.

(b) The national law of any designated State may provide that, where the national Office of that State finds the invitation, referred to in sub-paragraph (a), of the International Searching Authority justified and where the applicant has not paid all additional fees, those parts of the international application which consequently have not been searched shall, as far as effects in that State are concerned, be considered withdrawn unless a special fee is paid by the applicant to the national Office of that State.

Article 18

The international search report

(1) The international search report shall be established within the prescribed time limit and in the prescribed form.

19.18

(2) The international search report shall, as soon as it has been established, be transmitted by the International Searching Authority to the applicant and the International Bureau.

(3) The international search report or the declaration referred to in Article 17(2)(a) shall be translated as provided in the Regulations. The translations shall be prepared by or under the responsibility of the International Bureau.

Article 19

Amendment of the claims before the International Bureau

(1) The applicant shall, after having received the international search report, be entitled to one opportunity to amend the claims of the international application by filing amendments with the International Bureau within the prescribed time limit. He may, at the same time, file a brief statement, as provided in the Regulations, explaining the amendments and indicating any impact that such amendments might have on the description and the drawings.

19.19

(2) The amendments shall not go beyond the disclosure in the international application as filed.

(3) If the national law of any designated State permits amendments to go beyond the said disclosure, failure to comply with paragraph (2) shall have no consequence in that State.

Article 20

Communication to designated Offices

(1)—

19.20

(a) The international application, together with the international search report (including any indication referred to in Article 17(2)(b) or the declaration referred to Article 17(2)(a), shall be communicated to each designated Office, as provided in the Regulations, unless the designated Office waives such requirements in its entirety or in part.

(b) The communication shall include the translation (as prescribed) of the said report or declaration.

(2) If the claims have been amended by virtue of Article 19(1), the communication shall either contain the full text of the claims both as filed and as amended or shall contain the full text of the claims as filed and specify the amendments, and shall include the statements, if any, referred to in Article 19(1).

(3) At the request of the designated Office or the applicant, the International Searching Authority shall send to the said Office or the applicant, respectively, copies of the documents cited in the international search report, as provided in the Regulations.

Article 21

International publication

19.21   (1) The International Bureau shall publish international publications.

(2)—

(a) Subject to the exceptions provided for in sub-paragraph (b) and in Article 64(3), the international publication of the international application shall be effected promptly after the expiration of 18 months from the priority date of that application.

(b) The applicant may ask the International Bureau to publish his international application any time before the expiration of the time limit referred to in sub-paragraph (a). The International Bureau shall proceed accordingly, as provided in the Regulations.

(3) The international search report or the declaration referred to in Article 17(2)(a) shall be published as prescribed in the Regulations.

(4) The language and form of the international publication and other details are governed by the Regulations.

(5) There shall be no international publication if the international application is withdrawn or is considered withdrawn before the technical preparations for publication have been completed.

(6) If the international application contains expressions or drawings which, in the opinion of the International Bureau, are contrary to morality or public order, or if, in its opinion, the international application contains disparaging statements as defined in the Regulations, it may omit such expressions, drawings, and statements, from its publications, indicating the place and number of words or drawings

omitted, and furnishing, upon request, individual copies of the passages omitted.

Article 22

Copy, translation, and fee, to designated Offices

(1) The applicant shall furnish a copy of the international application **19.22** (unless the communication provided for in Article 20 has already taken place) and a translation thereof (as prescribed), and pay the national fee (if any), to each designated Office not later than at the expiration of 20 months from the priority date. Where the national law of the designated State requires the indication of the name of and other prescribed data concerning the inventor but allows that these indications be furnished at a time later than that of the filing of a national application, the applicant shall, unless they were contained in the request, furnish the said indications to the national Office of or acting for that State not later than at the expiration of 20 months from the priority date.

(2) Notwithstanding the provisions of paragraph (1), where the International Searching Authority makes a declaration, under Article 17(2)(a), that no international search report will be established, the time limit for performing the acts referred to in paragraph (1) of this Article shall be the same as that provided for in paragraph (1).

(3) Any national law may, for performing the acts referred to in paragraphs (1) or (2), fix time limits which expire later than the time limit provided for in those paragraphs.

Article 23

Delaying of national procedure

(1) No designated Office shall process or examine the international **19.23** application prior to the expiration of the applicable time limit under Article 22.

(2) Notwithstanding the provisions of paragraph (1), any designated Office may, on the express request of the applicant, process or examine the international application at any time.

911

Article 24

Possible loss of effect in designated States

19.24 (1) Subject, in case (ii) below, to the provisions of Article 25, the effect of the international application provided for in Article 11(3) shall cease in any designated State with the same consequences as the withdrawal of any national application in that State:

  (i) if the applicant withdraws his international application or the designation of that State;

  (ii) if the international application is considered withdrawn by virtue of Articles 12(3), 14(1)(b), 14(3)(a), or 14(4), or if the designation of that State is considered withdrawn by virtue of Article 14(3)(b);

  (iii) if the applicant fails to perform the acts referred to in Article 22 within the applicable time limit.

(2) Notwithstanding the provisions of paragraph (1), any designated Office may maintain the effect provided for in Article 11(3) even where such effect is not required to be maintained by virtue of Article 25(2).

Article 25

Review by designated Offices

19.25 (1)—

  (a) Where the receiving Office has refused to accord an international filing date or has declared that the international application is considered withdrawn, or where the International Bureau has made a finding under Article 12(3), the International Bureau shall promptly send, at the request of the applicant, copies of any document in the file to any of the designated Offices named by the applicant.

  (b) Where the receiving Office has declared that the designation of any given State is considered withdrawn, the International Bureau shall promptly send, at the request of the applicant, copies of any document in the file to the national Office of such State.

  (c) The request under sub-paragraphs (a) or (b) shall be presented within the prescribed time limit.

(2)—

  (a) Subject to the provisions of sub-paragraph (b), each designated Office shall, provided that the national fee (if any) has been paid and the appropriate translation (as prescribed) has been furnished within the prescribed time limit, decide whether the refusal, declaration, or finding, referred to in paragraph (1) was justified under the provisions of this Treaty and the Regulations, and, if it finds that the refusal or declaration was the result of an error or omission on the part of the receiving Office or that the finding was the result of an error or omission on the part of the International Bureau, it shall, as far as effects in the State of the designated Office are concerned, treat the international application as if such error or omission had not occurred.

(b) Where the record copy has reached the International Bureau after the expiration of the time limit prescribed under Article 12(3) on account of any error or omission on the part of the applicant, the provisions of sub-paragraph (a) shall apply only under the circumstances referred to in Article 48(2).

Article 26

Opportunity to correct before designated Offices

No designated Office shall reject an international application on the **19.26** grounds of non-compliance with the requirements of this Treaty and the Regulations without first giving the applicant the opportunity to correct the said application to the extent and according to the procedure provided by the national law for the same or comparable situations in respect of national applications.

Article 27

National requirements

(1) No national law shall require compliance with requirements **19.27** relating to the form or contents of the international application different from or additional to those which are provided for in this Treaty and the Regulations.

(2) The provisions of paragraph (1) neither affect the application of the provisions of Article 7(2) nor preclude any national law from requiring, once the processing of the international application has started in the designated Office, the furnishing:

(i) when the applicant is a legal entity, of the name of an officer entitled to represent such legal entity,

(ii) of documents not part of the international application but which constitute proof of allegations or statements made in that application, including the confirmation of the international application by the signature of the applicant when that application, as filed, was signed by his representative or agent.

(3) Where the applicant, for the purposes of any designated State, is not qualified according to the national law of that State to file a national application because he is not the inventor, the international application may be rejected by the designated Office.

(4) Where the national law provides, in respect of the form or contents of national applications, for requirements which, from the viewpoint of applicants, are more favourable than the requirements provided for by this Treaty and the Regulations in respect of international applications, the national Office, the courts and any other competent organs of or acting for the designated State may apply the former requirements, instead of the latter requirements, to international applications, except where the applicant insists that the requirements provided for by this Treaty and the Regulations be applied to his international application.

(5) Nothing in this Treaty and the Regulations is intended to be construed as prescribing anything that would limit the freedom of each Contracting State to prescribe such substantive conditions of patentability as it desires. In particular, any provision in this Treaty and the Regulations concerning the definition of prior art is exclusively for the purposes of the international procedure and, consequently, any Contracting State is free to apply, when determining the patentability of an invention claimed in an international application, the criteria of its national law in respect of prior art and other conditions of patentability not constituting requirements as to the form and contents of applications.

(6) The national law may require that the applicant furnish evidence in respect of any substantive condition of patentability prescribed by such law.

(7) Any receiving Office or, once the processing of the international application has started in the designated Office, that Office may apply the national law as far as it relates to any requirement that the applicant be represented by an agent having the right to represent applicants before the said Office and/or that the applicant have an address in the designated State for the purpose of receiving notifications.

(8) Nothing in this Treaty and the Regulations is intended to be construed as limiting the freedom of any Contracting State to apply measures deemed necessary for the preservation of its national security or to limit, for the protection of the general economic interests of that State, the right of its own residents or nationals to file international applications.

Article 28

Amendment of the claims, the description, and the drawings, before designated Offices

(1) The applicant shall be given the opportunity to amend the claims, **19.28** the description, and the drawings, before each designated Office within the prescribed time limit. No designated Office shall grant a patent, or refuse the grant of a patent, before such time limit has expired except with the express consent of the applicant.

(2) The amendments shall not go beyond the disclosure in the international application as filed unless the national law of the designated State permits them to go beyond the said disclosure.

(3) The amendments shall be in accordance with the national law of the designated State in all respects not provided for in this Treaty and the Regulations.

(4) Where the designated Office requires a translation of the international application, the amendments shall be in the language of the translation.

Article 29

Effects of the international publication

(1) As far as the protection of any rights of the applicant in a **19.29** designated State is concerned, the effects, in that State, of the international publication of an international application shall, subject to the provisions of paragraphs (2) to (4), be the same as those which the national law of the designated State provides for the compulsory national publication of unexamined national applications as such.

(2) If the language in which the international publication has been effected is different from the language in which publications under the national law are effected in the designated State, the said national law may provide that the effects provided for in paragraph (1) shall be applicable only from such time as:

(i) a translation into the latter language has been published as provided by the national law, or

(ii) a translation into the latter language has been made available to the public, by laying open for public inspection as provided by the national law, or

(iii) a translation into the latter language has been transmitted by the applicant to the actual or prospective unauthorised user of the invention claimed in the international application, or

(iv) both the acts described in (i) and (iii), or both the acts described in (ii) and (iii), have taken place.

(3) The national law of any designated State may provide that, where the international publication has been effected, on the request of the applicant, before the expiration of 18 months from the priority date, the effects provided for in paragraph (1) shall be applicable only from the expiration of 18 months from the priority date.

(4) The national law of any designated State may provide that the effects provided for in paragraph (1) shall be applicable only from the date on which a copy of the international application as published under Article 21 has been received in the national Office of or acting for such State. The said Office shall publish the date of receipt in its gazette as soon as possible.

Article 30

Confidential nature of the international application

19.30 (1)—

(a) Subject to the provisions of sub-paragraph (b), the International Bureau and the International Searching Authorities shall not allow access by any person or authority to the international application before the international publication of that application, unless requested or authorized by the applicant.

(b) The provisions of sub-paragraph (a) shall not apply to any transmittal to the competent International Searching Authority, to transmittals provided for under Article 13, and to communications provided for under Article 20.

(2)

(a) No national Office shall allow access to the international application by third parties, unless requested or authorised by the applicant, before the earliest of the following dates:

(i) date of the international publication of the international application,

(ii) date of the receipt of the communication of the international application under Article 20,

(iii) date of the receipt of a copy of the international application under Article 22.

(b) The provisions of sub-paragraph (a) shall not prevent any national Office from informing third parties that it has been designated, or from publishing that fact. Such information or publication may, however, contain only the following data:

identification of the receiving Office, name of the applicant, international filing date, international application number, and title of the invention.

(c) The provisions of sub-paragraph (a) shall not prevent any designated Office from allowing access to the international application for the purposes of the judicial authorities.

(3) The provisions of paragraph (2)(a) shall apply to any receiving Office except as far as transmittals provided for under Article 12(1) are concerned.

(4) For the purposes of this Article, the term "access" covers any means by which third parties may acquire cognizance, including individual communication and general publication, provided, however, that no national Office shall generally publish an international application or its translation before the international publication or, if international publication has not taken place by the expiration of 20 months from the priority date, before the expiration of 20 months from the said priority date.

Chapter II. International preliminary examination

Article 31

Demand for international preliminary examination

(1) On the demand of the applicant, his international application shall **19.31** be the subject of an international preliminary examination as provided in the following provisions and the Regulations.

(2)—

(a) Any applicant who is a resident or national, as defined in the Regulations, of a Contracting State bound by Chapter II, and whose international application has been filed with the receiving Office of or acting for such State, may make a demand for international preliminary examination.

(b) The Assembly may decide to allow persons entitled to file international applications to make a demand for international preliminary examination even if they are residents or nationals of a State not party to this Treaty or not bound by Chapter II.

(3) The demand for international preliminary examination shall be made separately from the international application. The demand shall contain the prescribed particulars and shall be in the prescribed language and form.

(4)—

(a) The demand shall indicate the Contracting State or States in which the applicant intends to use the results of the international preliminary examination ("elected States"). Additional Contracting States may be elected later. Election may relate only to Contracting States already designated under Article 4.

(b) Applicants referred to in paragraph (2)(a) may elect any Contracting State bound by Chapter II. Applicants referred to in paragraph (2)(b) may elect only such Contracting States bound by Chapter II as have declared that they are prepared to be elected by such applicants.

(5) The demand shall be subject to the payment of the prescribed fees within the prescribed time limit.

(6)—

(a) The demand shall be submitted to the competent International Preliminary Examining Authority referred to in Article 32.

(b) Any later election shall be submitted to the International Bureau.

(7) Each elected Office shall be notified of its election.

Article 32

The International Preliminary Examining Authority

19.32 (1) International preliminary examination shall be carried out by the International Preliminary Examining Authority.

(2) In the case of demands referred to in Article 31(2)(a), the receiving Office, and, in the case of demands referred to in Article 31(2)(b), the Assembly, shall, in accordance with the applicable agreement between the interested International Preliminary Examining Authority or Authorities and the International Bureau, specify the International Preliminary Examining Authority or Authorities competent for the preliminary examination.

(3) The provisions of Article 16(3) shall apply, *mutatis mutandis*, in respect of International Preliminary Examining Authorities.

Article 33

The international preliminary examination

19.33 (1) The objective of the international preliminary examination is to formulate a preliminary and non-binding opinion on the questions whether the claimed invention appears to be novel, to involve an inventive step (to be non-obvious), and to be industrially applicable.

(2) For the purposes of the international preliminary examination, a claimed invention shall be considered novel if it is not anticipated by the prior art as defined in the Regulations.

(3) For the purposes of the international preliminary examination, a claimed invention shall be considered to involve an inventive step if, having regard to the prior art as defined in the Regulations, it is not, at the prescribed relevant date, obvious to a person skilled in the art.

(4) For the purposes of the international preliminary examination, a claimed invention shall be considered industrially applicable if, according to its nature, it can be made or used (in the technological sense) in any kind of industry. "Industry" shall be understood in its broadest sense, as in the Paris Convention for the Protection of Industrial Property.

(5) The criteria described above merely serve the purposes of international preliminary examination. Any Contracting State may apply additional or different criteria for the purposes of deciding whether, in that State, the claimed invention is patentable or not.

(6) The international preliminary examination shall take into consideration all the documents cited in the international search report. It may take into consideration any additional documents considered to be relevant in the particular case.

Article 34

Procedure before the International Preliminary Examining Authority

(1) Procedure before the International Preliminary Examining Authority shall be governed by the provisions of this Treaty, the Regulations, and the agreement which the International Bureau shall conclude, subject to this Treaty and the Regulations, with the said Authority. **19.34**

(2)—

(a) The applicant shall have a right to communicate orally and in writing with the International Preliminary Examining Authority.

(b) The applicant shall have a right to amend the claims, the description, and the drawings, in the prescribed manner and within the prescribed time limit, before the international preliminary examination report is established. The amendment shall not go beyond the disclosure in the international application as filed.

(c) The applicant shall receive at least one written opinion from the International Preliminary Examining Authority unless such Authority considers that all of the following conditions are fulfilled:

  (i) the invention satisfies the criteria set forth in Article 33(1).

  (ii) the international application complies with the requirements of this Treaty and the Regulations insofar as checked by that Authority.

(iii) no observations are intended to be made under Article 35(2), last sentence.

(d) The applicant may respond to the written opinion.

(3)—

(a) If the International Preliminary Examining Authority considers that the international application does not comply with the requirement of unity of invention as set forth in the Regulations, it may invite the applicant, at his option, to restrict the claims so as to comply with the requirement or to pay additional fees.

(b) The national law of any elected State may provide that, where the applicant chooses to restrict the claims under sub-paragraph (a), those parts of the international application which, as a consequence of the restriction, are not to be the subject of international preliminary examination shall, as far as effects in that State are concerned, be considered withdrawn unless a special fee is paid by the applicant to the national Office of that State.

(c) If the applicant does not comply with the invitation referred to in sub-paragraph (a) within the prescribed time limit, the International Preliminary Examining Authority shall establish an international preliminary examination report on those parts of the international application which relate to what appears to be the main invention and shall indicate the relevant facts in the said report. The national law of any elected State may provide that, where its national Office finds the invitation of the International Preliminary Examining Authority justified, those parts of the international application which do not relate to the main invention shall, as far as effects in that State are concerned, be considered withdrawn unless a special fee is paid by the applicant to that Office.

(4)—

(a) If the International Preliminary Examining Authority considers

(i) that the international application relates to a subject matter on which the International Preliminary Examining Authority is not required, under the Regulations, to carry out an international preliminary examination, and in the particular case decides not to carry out such examination, or

(ii) that the description, the claims, or the drawings, are so unclear, or the claims are so inadequately supported by the description, that no meaningful opinion can be formed on the novelty, inventive step (non-obviousness), or industrial applicability, of the claimed invention,

the said Authority shall not go into the questions referred to in Article 33(1) and shall inform the applicant of this opinion and the reasons therefor.

(b) If any of the situations referred to in sub-paragraph (a) are found to exist in, or in connection with, certain claims only, the provisions of that sub-paragraph shall apply only to the said claims.

Article 35

The international preliminary examination report

(1) The international preliminary examination report shall be estab- **19.35**
lished within the prescribed time limit and in the prescribed form.

(2) The international preliminary examination report shall not contain any statement on the question whether the claimed invention is or seems to be patentable or unpatentable according to any national law. It shall state, subject to the provisions of paragraph (3), in relation to each claim, whether the claim appears to satisfy the criteria of novelty, inventive step (non-obviousness), and industrial applicability, as defined for the purposes of the international preliminary examination in Article 33(1) to (4). The statement shall be accompanied by the citation of the documents believed to support the stated conclusion with such explanations as the circumstances of the case may require. The statement shall also be accompanied by such other observations as the Regulations provide for.

(3)—

(a) If, at the time of establishing the international preliminary examination report, the International Preliminary Examining Authority considers that any of the situations referred to in Article 34(4)(a) exists, that report shall state this opinion and the reasons therefor. It shall not contain any statement as provided in paragraph (2).

(b) If a situation under Article 34(4)(b) is found to exist, the international preliminary examination report shall, in relation to the claims in question, contain the statement as provided in sub-paragraph (a), whereas, in relation to the other claims, it shall contain the statement as provided in paragraph (2).

Article 36

Transmittal, translation and communication of the international preliminary examination report

19.36 (1) The international preliminary examination report, together with the prescribed annexes, shall be transmitted to the applicant and to the International Bureau.

(2)—

(a) The international preliminary examination report and its annexes shall be translated into the prescribed languages.

(b) Any translation of the said report shall be prepared by or under the responsibility of the International Bureau, whereas any translation of the said annexes shall be prepared by the applicant.

(3)—

(a) The international preliminary examination report, together with its translation (as prescribed) and its annexes (in the original language), shall be communicated by the International Bureau to each elected Office.

(b) The prescribed translation of the annexes shall be transmitted within the prescribed time limit by the applicant to the elected Offices.

(4) The provisions of Article 20(3) shall apply, *mutatis mutandis*, to copies of any document which is cited in the international preliminary examination report and which was not cited in the international search report.

Article 37

Withdrawal of demand or election

19.37 (1) The applicant may withdraw any or all elections.

(2) If the election of all elected States is withdrawn, the demand shall be considered withdrawn.

(3)—

(a) Any withdrawal shall be notified to the International Bureau.

(b) The elected Offices concerned and the International Preliminary Examining Authority concerned shall be notified accordingly by the International Bureau.

(4)—

(a) Subject to the provisions of sub-paragraph (b), withdrawal of the demand or of the election of a Contracting State shall, unless the national law of that State provides otherwise, be considered to be withdrawal of the international application as far as that State is concerned.

(b) Withdrawal of the demand or of the election shall not be considered to be withdrawal of the international application if such withdrawal is effected prior to the expiration of the applicable time limit under Article 22; however, any Contracting State may provide in its national law that the aforesaid shall apply only if its national Office has received, within the said time limit, a copy of the international application, together with a translation (as prescribed), and the national fee.

Article 38

Confidential nature of the international preliminary examination

(1) Neither the International Bureau nor the International Preliminary   **19.38**
Examining Authority shall, unless requested or authorized by the applicant, allow access within the meaning, and with the proviso, of Article 30(4) to the file of the international preliminary examination by any person or authority at any time, except by the elected Offices once the international preliminary examination report has been established.

(2) Subject to the provisions of paragraph (1) and Articles 36(1) and (3) and 37(3)(b), neither the International Bureau nor the International Preliminary Examining Authority shall, unless requested or authorized by the applicant, give information on the issuance or non-issuance of an international preliminary examination report and on the withdrawal or non-withdrawal of the demand or of any election.

Article 39

Copy, translation and fee, to elected Offices

(1)—   **19.39**

(a) If the election of any Contracting State has been effected prior to the expiration of the 19th month from the priority date, the provisions of Article 22 shall not apply to such State and the applicant shall furnish a copy of the international application (unless the communication under Article 20 has already taken place) and a translation thereof (as prescribed), and pay the national fee (if any), to each elected Office not later than at the expiration of 30 months from the priority date.

(b) Any national law may, for performing the acts referred to in sub-paragraph (a), fix time limits which expire later than the time limit provided for in that sub-paragraph.

(2) The effect provided for in Article 11(3) shall cease in the elected State with the same consequences as the withdrawal of any national application in that State if the applicant fails to perform the acts referred to in paragraph (1)(a) within the time limit applicable under paragraph (1)(a) or (b).

(3) Any elected Office may maintain the effect provided for in Article 11(3) even where the applicant does not comply with the requirements provided for in paragraph 1(a) or (b).

Article 40

Delaying of national examination and other processing

19.40 (1) If the election of any Contracting State has been effected prior to the expiration of the 19th month from the priority date the provisions of Article 23 shall not apply to such State and the national Office of or acting for that State shall not proceed, subject to the provisions of paragraph (2), to the examination and other processing of the international application prior to the expiration of the applicable time limit under Article 39.

(2) Notwithstanding the provisions of paragraph (1), any elected Office may, on the express request of the applicant, proceed to the examination and other processing of the international application at any time.

Article 41

Amendment of the claims, the description, and the drawings, before elected Office

19.41 (1) The applicant shall be given the opportunity to amend the claims, the description, and the drawings, before each elected Office within the prescribed time limit. No elected Office shall grant a patent, or refuse the grant of a patent, before such time limit has expired, except with the express consent of the applicant.

(2) The amendments shall not go beyond the disclosure in the

international application as filed, unless the national law of the elected State permits them to go beyond the said disclosure.

(3) The amendments shall be in accordance with the national law of the elected State in all respects not provided for in this Treaty and the Regulations.

(4) Where an elected Office requires a translation of the international application, the amendments shall be in the language of the translation.

Article 42

Results of national examination in elected Offices

No elected Office receiving the international preliminary examina- **19.42** tion report may require that the applicant furnish copies, or information on the contents, of any papers connected with the examination relating to the same international application in any other elected Office.

Chapter III. Common provisions

Article 43

Seeking certain kinds of protection

In respect of any designated or elected State whose law provides for **19.43** the grant of inventors' certificate, utility certificates, utility models, patents or certificates of addition, inventors' certificates of addition, or utility certificates of addition, the applicant may indicate, as prescribed in the Regulations, that his international application is for the grant, as far as that State is concerned, of an inventor's certificate, or a utility model, rather than a patent, or that it is for the grant of a patent of certificate of addition, an inventor's certificate of addition, or a utility certificate of addition, and the ensuing effect shall be governed by the applicant's choice. For the purposes of this Article and any Rule thereunder, Article 2(ii) shall not apply.

Article 44

Seeking two kinds of protection

19.44   In respect of any designated or elected State whose law permits an application, while being for the grant of a patent or one of the other kinds of protection referred to in Article 43, to be also for the grant of another of the said kinds of protection, the applicant may indicate, as prescribed in the Regulations, the two kinds of protection he is seeking, and the ensuing effect shall be governed by the applicant's indications. For the purposes of this Article, Article 2(ii) shall not apply.

Article 45

Regional patent treaties

19.45   (1) Any treaty providing for the grant of regional patents ("regional patent treaty"), and giving to all persons who, according to Article 9, are entitled to file international applications the right to file applications for such patents, may provide that International applications designating or electing a State party to both the regional patent treaty and the present Treaty may be filed as applications for such patents.
(2) The national law of the said designated or elected State may provide that any designation or election of such State in the international application shall have the effect of an indication of the wish to obtain a regional patent under the regional patent treaty.

Article 46

Incorrect translation of the international application

19.46   If, because of an incorrect translation of the international application, the scope of any patent granted on that application exceeds the scope of the international application in its original language, the competent authorities of the Contracting State concerned may accordingly and retroactively limit the scope of the patent, and declare it null and void to the extent that its scope has exceeded the scope of the international application in its original language.

Article 47

Time limits

(1) The details for computing time limits referred to in this Treaty are **19.47**
governed by the Regulations.

(2)—

(a) All time limits fixed in Chapters I and II of this Treaty may,
outside any revision under Article 60, be modified by a decision
of the Contracting States.

(b) Such decisions shall be made in the Assembly or through voting
by correspondence and must be unanimous.

(c) The details of the procedure are governed by the Regulations.

Article 48

Delay in meeting certain time limits

(1) Where any time limit fixed in this Treaty or the Regulations is not **19.48**
met because of interruption in the mail service or unavoidable loss or
delay in the mail, the time limit shall be deemed to be met in the cases
and subject to the proof and other conditions prescribed in the
Regulations.

(2)—

(a) Any Contracting State shall, as far as that State is concerned,
excuse, for reasons admitted under its national law, any delay in
meeting any time limit.

(b) Any Contracting State may, as far as that State is concerned,
excuse, for reasons other than those referred to in sub-paragraph
(a), any delay in meeting any time limit.

Article 49

Right to practice before international authorities

Any attorney, patent agent, or other person, having the right to **19.49**
practice before the national Office with which the international application was filed, shall be entitled to practice before the International
Bureau and the competent International Searching Authority and

competent International Preliminary Examining Authority in respect of that application.

Chapter IV. Technical services

Article 50

Patent information services

19.50   (1) The International Bureau may furnish services by providing technical and any other pertinent information available to it on the basis of published documents, primarily patents and published applications (referred to in this Article as "the information services").

(2) The International Bureau may provide these information services either directly or through one or more International Searching Authorities or other national or international specialized institutions, with which the International Bureau may reach agreement.

(3) The information services shall be operated in a way particularly facilitating the acquisition by Contracting States which are developing countries of technical knowledge and technology, including available published know-how.

(4) The information services shall be available to Governments of Contracting States and their nationals and residents. The Assembly may decide to make these services available also to others.

(5)—

(a) Any service to Governments of Contracting States shall be furnished at cost, provided that, when the Government is that of a Contracting State which is a developing country, the service shall be furnished below cost if the difference can be covered from profit made on services furnished to others than Governments of Contracting States or from the sources referred to in Article 51(4).

(b) The cost referred to in sub-paragraph (*a*) is to be understood as cost over and above costs normally incident to the performance of the services of a national Office or the obligations of an International Searching Authority.

(6) The details concerning the implementation of the provisions of this Article shall be governed by decisions of the Assembly and, within the limits to be fixed by the Assembly, such working groups as the Assembly may set up for that purpose.

(7) The Assembly shall, when it considers it necessary, recommend methods of providing financing supplementary to those referred to in paragraph (5).

Article 51

Technical assistance

(1) The Assembly shall establish a Committee for Technical Assist- **19.51**
ance referred to in this Article as "the Committee".

(2)—

(a) The members of the Committee shall be elected among the
Contracting States, with due regard to the representation of
developing countries.

(b) The Director General shall, on his own initiative or at the request
of the Committee, invite representatives of intergovernmental
organizations concerned with technical assistance to developing
countries to participate in the work of the Committee.

(3)—

(a) The task of the Committee shall be to organize and supervize
technical assistance for Contracting States which are developing
countries in developing their patent systems individually or on a
regional basis.

(b) The technical assistance shall comprise, among other things, the
training of specialists, the loaning of experts, and the supply of
equipment both for demonstration and for operational purposes.

(4) The International Bureau shall seek to enter into agreements, on
the one hand, with international financing organizations and intergovernmental organizations, particularly the United Nations, the
agencies of the United Nations, and the Specialized Agencies connected
with the United Nations concerned with the technical assistance, and,
on the other hand, with the Governments of the States receiving the
technical assistance, for the financing of projects pursuant to this Article.

(5) The details concerning the implementation of the provisions of
this Article shall be governed by decisions of the Assembly and, within
the limits to be fixed by the Assembly, such working groups as the
Assembly may set up for that purpose.

Article 52

Relations with other provisions of the Treaty

Nothing in this Chapter shall affect the financial provisions contained **19.52**
in any other Chapter of this Treaty. Such provisions are not applicable to
the present Chapter or to its implementation.

Chapter V. Administrative provisions

Article 53

Assembly

19.53   (1)—

(a) The Assembly shall, subject to Article 57(8), consist of the Contracting States.

(b) The Government of each Contracting State shall be represented by one delegate, who may be assisted by alternate delegates, advisors, and experts.

(2)—

(a) The Assembly shall:

  (i)   deal with all matters concerning the maintenance and development of the Union and the implementation of this Treaty;

  (ii)   perform such tasks as are specifically assigned to it under other provisions of this Treaty;

  (iii)   give directions to the International Bureau concerning the preparation for revision conferences;

  (iv)   review and approve the reports and activities of the Director General concerning the Union, and give him all necessary instructions concerning matters within the competence of the Union;

  (v)   review and approve the reports and activities of the Executive Committee established under paragraph (9), and give instructions to such Committee;

  (vi)   determine the program and adopt the triennial budget of the Union and approve its final accounts;

  (vii)   adopt the financial regulations of the Union;

  (viii)   establish such committees and working groups as it deems appropriate to achieve the objectives of the Union;

  (ix)   determine which States other than Contracting States and, subject to the provisions of paragraph (8), which intergovernmental and international non-governmental organizations shall be admitted to its meetings as observers;

  (x)   take any other appropriate action designed to further the objectives of the Union and perform such other functions as are appropriate under this Treaty.

(b) With respect to matters which are of interest also to other Unions administered by the Organization, the Assembly shall make its decisions after having heard the advice of the Coordination Committee of the Organization.

(3) A delegate may represent, and vote in the name of, one State only.

(4) Each Contracting State shall have one vote.

(5)—

(a) One-half of the Contracting States shall constitute a quorum.

(b) In the absence of the quorum, the Assembly may make decisions but, with the exception of decisions concerning its own procedure, all such decisions shall take effect only if the quorum and the required majority are attained through voting by correspondence as provided in the Regulations.

(6)—

(a) Subject to the provisions of Articles 47(2)(b), 58(2)(b), 58(3) and 61(2)(b), the decisions of the Assembly shall require two-thirds of the votes cast.

(b) Abstentions shall not be considered as votes.

(7) In connection with matters of exclusive interest to States bound by Chapter II, any reference to Contracting States in paragraphs (4), (5), and (6), shall be considered as applying only to States bound by Chapter II.

(8) Any intergovernmental organization appointed as International Searching or Preliminary Examining Authority shall be admitted as observer to the Assembly.

(9) When the number of Contracting States exceeds forty, the Assembly shall establish an Executive Committee. Any reference to the Executive Committee in this Treaty and the Regulations shall be construed as references to such Committee once it has been established.

(10) Until the Executive Committee has been established, the Assembly shall approve, within the limits of the program and triennial budget, the annual programs and budgets prepared by the Director General.

(11)—

(a) The Assembly shall meet in every second calendar year in ordinary session upon convocation by the Director General and, in the absence of exceptional circumstances, during the same period and at the same place as the General Assembly of the Organisation.

(b) The Assembly shall meet in extraordinary session upon convocation by the Director General, at the request of the Executive Committee, or at the request of one-fourth of the Contracting States.

(12) The Assembly shall adopt its own rules of procedure.

Article 54

Executive Committee

19.54 (1) When the Assembly has established an Executive Committee, that Committee shall be subject to the provisions set forth hereinafter.

(2)—

(a) The Executive Committee shall, subject to Article 57(8), consist of States elected by the Assembly from among States members of the Assembly.

(b) The Government of each State member of the Executive Committee shall be represented by one delegate, who may be assisted by alternate delegates, advisors, and experts.

(3) The number of States members of the Executive Committee shall correspond to one-fourth of the number of States members of the Assembly. In establishing the number of seats to be filled, remainders after division by four shall be disregarded.

(4) In electing the members of the Executive Committee, the Assembly shall have due regard to an equitable geographical distribution.

(5)—

(a) Each member of the Executive Committee shall serve from the close of the session of the Assembly which elected it to the close of the next ordinary session of the Assembly.

(b) Members of the Executive Committee may be re-elected but only up to a maximum of two-thirds of such members.

(c) The Assembly shall establish the details of the rules governing the election and possible re-election of the members of the Executive Committee.

(6)—

(a) The Executive Committee shall:

(i) prepare the draft agenda of the Assembly;

(ii) submit proposals to the Assembly in respect of the draft program and biennial budget of the Union prepared by the Director General;

(iii) submit, with appropriate comments, to the Assembly the periodical reports of the Director General and the yearly audit reports on the accounts;

(iv) take all necessary measures to ensure the execution of the program of the Union by the Director General, in accordance with the decisions of the Assembly and having regard to circumstances arising between two ordinary sessions of the Assembly;

(v) perform such other functions as are allocated to it under this Treaty.

(b) With respect to matters which are of interest also to other Unions administered by the Organization, the Executive Committee shall make its decisions after having heard the advice of the Coordination Committee of the Organization.

(7)—

(a) The Executive Committee shall meet once a year in ordinary session upon convocation by the Director General, preferably during the same period and at the same place as the Coordination Committee of the Organization.

(b) The Executive Committee shall meet in extraordinary session upon convocation by the Director General, either on his own initiative or at the request of its Chairman or one-fourth of its members.

(8)—

(a) Each State member of the Executive Committee shall have one vote.

(b) One-half of the members of the Executive Committee shall constitute a quorum.

(c) Decisions shall be made by a simple majority of the votes cast.

(d) Abstentions shall not be considered as votes.

(e) A delegate may represent, and vote in the name of, one State only.

(9) Contracting States not members of the Executive Committee shall be admitted to its meetings as observers, as well as any intergovernmental organisztion appointed as International Searching or Preliminary Examining Authority.

(10) The Executive Committee shall adopt its own rules of procedure.

Article 55

International Bureau

(1) Administrative tasks concerning the Union shall be performed by **19.55** the International Bureau.

(2) The International Bureau shall provide the secretariat of the various organs of the Union.

(3) The Director General shall be the chief executive of the Union and shall represent the Union.

(4) The International Bureau shall publish a Gazette and other publications provided for by the Regulations or required by the Assembly.

(5) The Regulations shall specify the services that national Offices shall perform in order to assist the International Bureau and the International Searching and Preliminary Examining Authorities in carrying out their tasks under this Treaty.

(6) The Director General and any staff member designated by him

shall participate, without the right to vote, in all meetings of the Assembly, the Executive Committee and any other committee or working group established under this Treaty or the Regulations. The Director General, or a staff member designated by him, shall be ex officio secretary of these bodies.

(7)—

(a) The International Bureau shall, in accordance with the directions of the Assembly and in cooperation with the Executive Committee, make the preparations for the revision conferences.

(b) The International Bureau may consult with intergovernmental and international non-governmental organizations concerning preparations for revision conferences.

(c) The Director General and persons designated by him shall take part, without the right to vote, in the discussions at revision conferences.

(8) The International Bureau shall carry out any other tasks assigned to it.

Article 56

Committee for Technical Co-operation

19.56   (1) The Assembly shall establish a Committee for Technical Co-operation (referred to in this Article as ''the Committee'').

(2)—

(a) The Assembly shall determine the composition of the Committee and appoint its members, with due regard to an equitable representation of developing countries.

(b) The International Searching and Preliminary Examining Authorities shall be ex officio members of the Committee. In the case where such an Authority is the national Office of a Contracting State, that State shall not be additionally represented on the Committee.

(c) If the number of Contracting States so allows, the total number of members of the Committee shall be more than double the number of ex officio members.

(d) The Director General shall, on his own initiative or at the request of the Committee, invite representatives of interested organizations to participate in discussions of interest to them.

(3) The aim of the Committee shall be to contribute, by advice and recommendations:

(i) to the constant improvement of the services provided for under this Treaty,

(ii) to the securing, so long as there are several International

Searching Authorities and several International Preliminary Examining Authorities, of the maximum degree of uniformity in their documentation and working methods and the maximum degree of uniformly high quality in their reports, and

(iii) on the initiative of the Assembly or the Executive Committee, to the solution of the technical problems specifically involved in the establishment of a single International Searching Authority.

(4) Any Contracting State and any interested international organization may approach the Committee in writing on questions which fall within the competence of the Committee.

(5) The Committee may address its advice and recommendations to the Director General or, through him, to the Assembly, the Executive Committee, all or some of the International Searching and International Preliminary Examining Authorities, and all or some of the receiving Offices.

(6)—

(a) In any case, the Director General shall transmit to the Executive Committee the texts of all the advice and recommendations of the Committee. He may comment on such texts.

(b) The Executive Committee may express its views on any advice, recommendation, or other activity of the Committee, and may invite the Committee to study and report on questions falling within its competence. The Executive Committee may submit to the Assembly, with appropriate comments, the advice, recommendations and report of the Committee.

(7) Until the Executive Committee has been established, references in paragraph (6) to the Executive Committee shall be construed as references to the Assembly.

(8) The details of the procedure of the Committee shall be governed by the decisions of the Assembly.

Article 57

Finances

(1)—   19.57

(a) The Union shall have a budget.

(b) The budget of the Union shall include the income and expenses proper to the Union and its contribution to the budget of expenses common to the Unions administered by the Organization.

(c) Expenses not attributable exclusively to the Union but also to one or more other Unions administered by the Organization shall be considered as expenses common to the Unions. The share of the

Union in such common expenses shall be in proportion to the interest the Union has in them.

(2) The budget of the Union shall be established with due regard to the requirements of coordination with the budgets of the other Unions administered by the Organization.

(3) Subject to the provisions of paragraph (5), the budget of the Union shall be financed from the following sources:

(i)   fees and charges due for services rendered by the International Bureau in relation to the Union;

(ii) sale of, or royalties on, the publications of the International Bureau concerning the Union;

(iii) gifts, bequests, and subventions;

(iv) rents, interests, and other miscellaneous income.

(4) The amounts of fees and charges due to the International Bureau and the prices of its publications shall be so fixed that they should, under normal circumstances, be sufficient to cover all the expenses of the International Bureau connected with the administration of this Treaty.

(5)—

(a) Should any financial year close with a deficit, the Contracting States shall, subject to the provisions of sub-paragraphs (b) and (c), pay contributions to cover such deficit.

(b) The amount of the contribution of each Contracting State shall be decided by the Assembly with due regard to the number of international applications which has emanated from each of them in the relevant year.

(c) If other means of provisionally covering any deficit or any part thereof are secured, the Assembly may decide that such deficit be carried forward and that the Contracting States should not be asked to pay contributions.

(d) If the financial situation of the Union so permits, the Assembly may decide that any contributions paid under sub-paragraph (a) be reimbursed to the Contracting States which have paid them.

(e) A Contracting State which has not paid, within two years of the due date as established by the Assembly, its contribution under sub-paragraph (b) may not exercise its right to vote in any of the organs of the Union. However, any organ of the Union may allow such a State to continue to exercise its right to vote in that organ so long as it is satisfied that the delay in payment is due to exceptional and unavoidable circumstances.

(6) If the budget is not adopted before the beginning of a new financial period, it shall be at the same level as the budget of the previous year, as provided in the financial regulations.

(7)—

(a) The Union shall have a working capital fund which shall be constituted by a single payment made by each Contracting State. If the fund becomes insufficient, the Assembly shall arrange to increase it. If part of the fund is no longer needed, it shall be reimbursed.

(b) The amount of the initial payment of each Contracting State to the said fund or of its participation in the increase thereof shall be decided by the Assembly on the basis of principles similar to those provided for under paragraph (5)(b).

(c) The terms of payment shall be fixed by the Assembly on the proposal of the Director General and after it has heard the advice of the Coordination Committee of the Organization.

(d) Any reimbursement shall be proportionate to the amounts paid by each Contracting State, taking into account the dates at which they were paid.

(8)—

(a) In the headquarters agreement concluded with the State on the territory of which the Organization has its headquarters, it shall be provided that, whenever the working capital fund is insufficient, such State shall grant advances. The amount of these advances and the conditions on which they are granted shall be the subject of separate agreements, in each case, between such State and the Organization. As long as it remains under the obligation to grant advances, such State shall have an ex officio seat in the Assembly and on the Executive Committee.

(b) The State referred to in sub-paragraph (a) and the Organization shall each have the right to denounce the obligation to grant advances, by written notification. Denunciation shall take effect three years after the end of the year in which it has been notified.

(9) The auditing of the accounts shall be effected by one or more of the Contracting States or by external auditors, as provided in the financial regulations. They shall be designated, with their agreement, by the Assembly.

Article 58

Regulations

(1) The Regulations annexed to this Treaty provide Rules: **19.58**

(i) concerning matters in respect of which this Treaty expressly refers to the Regulations or expressly provides that they are or shall be prescribed,

(ii) concerning any administrative requirements, matters or procedures,

(iii) concerning any details useful in the implementation of the provisions of this Treaty.

(2)—

(a) The Assembly may amend the Regulations.

(b) Subject to the provisions of paragraph (3), amendments shall require three-fourths of the votes cast.

(3)—

(a) The Regulations specify the Rules which may be amended
  (i) only by unanimous consent, or
  (ii) only if none of the Contracting States whose national Office acts as an International Searching or International Preliminary Examining Authority dissents, and, where such Authority is an intergovernmental organisation, if the Contracting State member of that organisation authorised for that purpose by the other member States within the competent body of such organisation does not dissent.

(b) Exclusion, for the future, of any such Rules from the applicable requirement shall require fulfilment of the conditions referred to in sub-paragraph (a)(i) or (a)(ii), respectively.

(c) Inclusion, for the future, of any Rule in one or the other of the requirements referred to in sub-paragraph (a) shall require unanimous consent.

(4) The Regulations provide for the establishment, under the control of the Assembly, of Administrative Instructions by the Director General.

(5) In the case of conflict between the provisions of the Treaty and those of the Regulations, the provisions of the Treaty shall prevail.

Chapter VI. Disputes

Article 59

Disputes

19.59   Subject to Article 64(5), any dispute between two or more Contracting States concerning the interpretation or application of this Treaty or the Regulations, not settled by negotiations, may, by any of the States concerned, be brought before the International Court of Justice by application in conformity with the Statute of the Court, unless the States concerned agree on some other method of settlement. The Contracting State bringing the dispute before the Court shall inform the International Bureau; the International Bureau shall bring the matter to the attention of the other Contracting States.

Chapter VII. Revision and amendment

Article 60

Revision of the Treaty

(1) This Treaty may be revised from time to time by a special **19.60**
conference of the Contracting States.

(2) The convocation of any revision conference shall be decided by the
Assembly.

(3) Any intergovernmental organisation appointed as International
Searching or Preliminary Examining Authority shall be admitted as
observer to any revision conference.

(4) Articles 53(5), (9) and (11), 54, 55(4) to (8), 56, and 57, may be
amended either by a revision conference or according to the provisions
of Article 61.

Article 61

Amendment of certain provisions of the Treaty

(1)— **19.61**
(a) Proposals for the amendment of Articles 53(5), (9) and (11), 54,
55(4) to (8), 56, and 57, may be initiated by any State member of
the Assembly, by the Executive Committee, or by the Director
General.
(b) Such proposals shall be communicated by the Director General to
the Contracting States at least six months in advance of their
consideration by the Assembly.

(2)—
(a) Amendments to the Articles referred to in paragraph (1) shall be
adopted by the Assembly.
(b) Adoption shall require three-fourths of the votes cast.

(3)—
(a) Any amendment to the Articles referred to in paragraph (1) shall
enter into force one month after written notifications of acceptance, effected in accordance with their respective constitutional
processes, have been received by the Director General from
three-fourths of the States members of the Assembly at the time it
adopted the amendment.
(b) Any amendment to the said Articles thus accepted shall bind all

the States which are members of the Assembly at the time the amendment enters into force, provided that the amendment increasing the financial obligations of the Contracting States shall bind only those States which have notified their acceptance of such amendment.

(c) Any amendment accepted in accordance with the provisions of sub-paragraph (a) shall bind all States which become members of the Assembly after the date on which the amendment entered into force in accordance with the provisions of sub-paragraph (a).

Chapter VIII. Final provisions

Article 62

Becoming party to the Treaty

19.62   (1) Any State member of the International Union for the Protection of Industrial Property may become party to this Treaty by:
(i) signature followed by the deposit of an instrument of ratification, or
(ii) deposit of an instrument of accession.
(2) Instruments of ratification or accession shall be deposited with the Director General.
(3) The provisions of Article 24 of the Stockholm Act of the Paris Convention for the Protection of Industrial Property shall apply to this Treaty.
(4) Paragraph (3) shall in no way be understood as implying the recognition or tacit acceptance by a Contracting State of the factual situation concerning a territory to which this Treaty is made applicable by another Contracting State by virtue of the said paragraph.

Article 63

Entry into force of the Treaty

19.63   (1)—
(a) Subject to the provisions of paragraph (3), this Treaty shall enter into force three months after eight States have deposited their instruments of ratification or accession, provided that at least four of those States each fulfill any of the following conditions:

  (i) the number of applications filed in the State has exceeded
       40,000 according to the most recent annual statistics published
       by the International Bureau,
  (ii) the nationals or residents of the State have filed at least 1,000
       applications in one foreign country according to the most
       recent annual statistics published by the International Bureau,
  (iii) the national Office of the State has received at least 10,000
       applications from nationals or residents of foreign countries
       according to the most recent annual statistics published by the
       International Bureau.
  (b) For the purposes of this paragraph, the term "applications" does
      not include applications for utility models.
  (2) Subject to the provisions of paragraph (3), any State which does
not become party to this Treaty upon entry into force under paragraph
(1) shall become bound by this Treaty three months after the date on
which such State has deposited its instrument of ratification or
accession.
  (3) The provisions of Chapter II and the corresponding provisions of
the Regulations annexed to this Treaty shall become applicable,
however, only on the date on which three States each of which fulfill at
least one of the three requirements specified in paragraph (1) have
become party to this Treaty without declaring, as provided in Article
64(1), that they do not intend to be bound by the provisions of Chapter
II. That date shall not, however, be prior to that of the initial entry into
force under paragraph (1).

Article 64

Reservations

(1)—   19.64
(a) Any State may declare that it shall not be bound by the provisions
    of Chapter II.
(b) States making a declaration under sub-paragraph (a) shall not be
    bound by the provisions of Chapter II and the corresponding
    provisions of the Regulations.
(2)—
(a) Any State not having made a declaration under paragraph (1)(a)
    may declare that:
  (i) it shall not be bound by the provisions of Article 39(1) with
      respect to the furnishing of a copy of the international
      application and a translation thereof (as prescribed),
  (ii) the obligation to delay national processing, as provided for
       under Article 40, shall not prevent publication, by or through

its national Office, of the international application or a translation thereof, it being understood, however, that it is not
exempted from the limitations provided for in Articles 30 and
38.

(b) States making such a declaration shall be bound accordingly.

(3)—

(a) Any State may declare that, as far as it is concerned, international
publication of international applications is not required.

(b) Where, at the expiration of 18 months from the priority date, the
international application contains the designation only of such
States as have made declarations under sub-paragraph (a), the
international application shall not be published by virtue of
Article 21(2).

(c) Where the provisions of sub-paragraph (b) apply, the international application shall nevertheless be published by the International Bureau:

   (i) at the request of the applicant, as provided in the Regulations,

   (ii) when a national application or a patent based on the international application is published by or on behalf of the national
Office of any designated State having made a declaration under
sub-paragraph (a), promptly after such publication but not
before the expiration of 18 months from the priority date.

(4)—

(a) Any State whose national law provides for prior art effect of its
patents as from a date before publication, but does not equate for
prior art purposes the priority date claimed under the Paris
Convention for the Protection of Industrial Property to the actual
filing date in that State, may declare that the filing outside that
State of an international application designating that State is not
equated to an actual filing in that State for prior art purposes.

(b) Any State making declaration under sub-paragraph (a) shall to
that extent not be bound by the provisions of Article 11(3).

(c) Any State making a declaration under sub-paragraph (a) shall, at
the same time, state in writing the date from which, and the
conditions under which, the prior art effect of any international
application designating that State becomes effective in that State.
This statement may be modified at any time by notification
addressed to the Director General.

(5) Each State may declare that it does not consider itself bound by
Article 59. With regard to any dispute between any Contracting State
having made such a declaration and any other Contracting State,
provisions of Article 59 shall not apply.

(6)—

(a) Any declaration made under this Article shall be made in writing.
It may be made at the time of signing this Treaty, at the time of
depositing the instrument of ratification or accession, or, except in
the case referred to in paragraph (5), at any later time by

notification addressed to the Director General. In the case of the said notification, the declaration shall take effect six months after the day on which the Director General has received the notification, and shall not affect international applications filed prior to the expiration of the said six-month period.

(b) Any declaration made under this Article may be withdrawn at any time by notification addressed to the Director General. Such withdrawal shall take effect three months after the day on which the Director General has received the notification and, in the case of the withdrawal of a declaration made under paragraph (3), shall not affect international applications filed prior to the expiration of the said three-month period.

(7) No reservations to this Treaty other than the reservations under paragraph (1) to (5) are permitted.

Article 65

Gradual application

(1) If the agreement with any International Searching or Preliminary **19.65** Examining Authority provides, transitionally, for limits on the number or kind of international applications that such Authority undertakes to process, the Assembly shall adopt the measures necessary for the gradual application of this Treaty and the Regulations in respect of given categories of international applications. This provision shall also apply to requests for an international-type search under Article 15(5).

(2) The Assembly shall fix the dates from which, subject to the provision of paragraph (1), international applications may be filed and demands for international preliminary examination may be submitted. Such dates shall not be later than six months after this Treaty has entered into force according to the provisions of Article 63(1), or after Chapter II has become applicable under Article 63(3), respectively.

Article 66

Denunciation

(1) Any Contracting State may denounce this Treaty by notification **19.66** addressed to the Director General.

(2) Denunciation shall take effect six months after receipt of the said notification by the Director General. It shall not affect the effects of the

international application in the denouncing State if the international application was filed, and, where the denouncing State has been elected, the election was made, prior to the expiration of the said six-month period.

Article 67

Signature and languages

19.67   (1)—
(a) This Treaty shall be signed in a single original in the English and French languages, both texts being equally authentic.
(b) Official texts shall be established by the Director General, after consultation with the interested Governments, in the German, Japanese, Portuguese, Russian and Spanish languages, and such other languages as the Assembly may designate.
(2) This Treaty shall remain open for signature at Washington until December 31, 1970.

Article 68

Depository functions

19.68   (1) The original of this Treaty, when no longer open for signature, shall be deposited with the Director General.

(2) The Director General shall transmit two copies, certified by him, of this Treaty and the Regulations annexed hereto to the Governments of all States party to the Paris Convention for the Protection of Industrial Property and, on request, to the Government of any other State.

(3) The Director General shall register this Treaty with the Secretariat of the United Nations.

(4) The Director General shall transmit two copies, certified by him, of any amendment to this Treaty and the Regulations to the Governments of all Contracting States and, on request, to the Government of any other State.

Article 69

Notifications

The Director General shall notify the Governments of all States party **19.69**
to the Paris Convention for the Protection of Industrial Property of:
  (i)   signatures under Article 62,
  (ii) deposits of instruments of ratification or accession under Article
        62,
  (iii) the date of entry into force of this Treaty and the date from
        which Chapter II is applicable in accordance with Article 63(3),
  (iv) any declarations made under Article 64(1) to (5),
  (v)   withdrawals of any declarations made under Article 64(6)(b),
  (vi) denunciations received under Article 66, and
  (vii) any declarations made under Article 31(4).

RULES OF THE SUPREME COURT

(S.I. 1978 No. 579 (L.11), as amended)

ORDER 59

Appeals to the Court of Appeal

Appeal against order for revocation of patent

20.01 17.—(1) The following provisions of this rule shall apply to any appeal to the Court of Appeal from an order for the revocation of a patent.

(2) The notice of appeal must be served on the Comptroller-General of Patents, Designs and Trade Marks (in this rule referred to as "the Comptroller") as well as on the party or parties required to be served under rule 3.

(3) If, at any time before the appeal comes on for hearing, the respondent decides not to appear on the appeal or not to oppose it, he must forthwith serve notice of his decision on the Comptroller and the appellant, and any such notice served on the Comptroller must be accompanied by a copy of the petition or of the pleadings in the action and the affidavits filed therein.

(4) The Comptroller must, within 14 days after receiving notice of the respondent's decision, serve on the appellant a notice stating whether or not he intends to appear on the appeal.

(5) The Comptroller may appear and be heard in opposition to the appeal—

(a) in any case where he has given notice under paragraph (4) of his intention to appear, and

(b) in any other case (including, in particular, a case where the respondent withdraws his opposition to the appeal during the hearing) if the Court of Appeal so directs or allows.

(6) The Court of Appeal may make such orders for the postponement or adjournment of the hearing of the appeal as may appear to the Court necessary for the purpose of giving effect to the foregoing provisions of this rule.

Appeal from Patents Court on appeal from Comptroller

18. In the case of an appeal to the Court of Appeal from a decision of **20.02**
the Patents Court on an appeal from a decision of the Comptroller-
General of Patents, Designs and Trade Marks the notice of appeal must
be served on the Comptroller-General as well as on the party or parties
required to be served under rule 3.

ORDER 104

The Patents Act 1949 to 1961 and 1977;
The Registered Designs Acts 1949 to 1971;
The Defence Contracts Act 1958.

Definitions

1. In this Order—   **20.03**
   "the 1949 Act" means the Patents Act 1949;
   "the 1977 Act" means the Patents Act 1977;
   "the Comptroller" means the Comptroller-General of Patents,
      Designs and Trade Marks;
   "the Court," without prejudice to Order 1, rule 4(2) means the
      Patents Court;
   "existing patent" means a patent mentioned in section 127(2)(a) or
      (c) of the 1977 Act;
   "the journal" means the journal published pursuant to rules made
      under section 123(6) of the 1977 Act;
   "1977 Act patent" means a patent under the 1977 Act;
   "patent" means an existing patent or a 1977 Act patent.

Assignment of proceedings

2.—(1) All proceedings in the High Court under the Patents Acts 1949 **20.04**
to 1961 and 1977, the Registered Designs Acts 1949 to 1961 and the
Defence Contracts Act 1958, and all proceedings for the determination
of a question or the making of a declaration relating to a patent under
the inherent jurisdiction of the High Court, shall be assigned to the
Chancery Division and taken by the Court.
   (2) Nothing in Order 4, rule 1, shall apply in relation to any
proceedings mentioned in paragraph (1) but every writ, summons,
petition, notice, pleading, affidavit or other document relating to such
proceedings must be marked in the top left-hand corner with the words
"Patents Court".

Application for leave to amend specification under s.30 of the 1949 Act or s.75 of the 1977 Act

20.05   3.—(1) A patentee or the proprietor of a patent intending to apply under section 30 of the 1949 Act or under section 75 of the 1977 Act for leave to amend his specification must give notice of his intention to the Comptroller accompanied by a copy of an advertisement—

(a) identifying the proceedings pending before the Court in which it is intended to apply for such leave;

(b) giving particulars of the amendment sought;

(c) stating the applicant's address for service within the United Kingdom, and

(d) stating that any person intending to oppose the amendment who is not a party to the proceedings must within 28 days after the appearance of the advertisement give written notice to his intention to the applicant;

and the Comptroller shall insert the advertisement once in the journal.

A person who gives notice in accordance with the advertisement shall be entitled to be heard on the application subject to any direction of the Court as to costs.

(2) As soon as may be after the expiration of 35 days from the appearance of the advertisement the applicant must make his application under the said section 30 or 75, as the case may be, by motion in the proceedings pending before the Court; and notice of the motion, together with a copy of the specification certified by the Comptroller and showing in coloured ink the amendment sought, must be served on the Comptroller, the parties to the proceedings and any person who has given notice of his intention to oppose the amendment.

(3) On the hearing of the motion the Court shall give such directions for the further conduct of the proceedings on the motion as it thinks necesary or expedient and, in particular, directions—

(a) requiring the applicant and any party or person opposing the amendment sought to exchange statements of the grounds for allowing the amendment and of objections to the amendment;

(b) determining whether the motion shall be heard with the other proceedings relating to the patent in question or separately and, if separately, fixing the date of hearing thereof;

(c) as to the manner in which the evidence shall be given and, if the evidence is to be given by affidavit, fixing the times within which the affidavits must be filed.

(4) Where the Court allows a specification to be amended, the applicant must forthwith lodge with the Comptroller an office copy of the order made by the court and, if so required by the Court or Comptroller, leave at the Patent Office a new specification and drawings as amended, prepared in compliance with the 1949 or 1977 Act, whichever is applicable, and the rules made under those Acts respectively.

The Comptroller shall cause a copy of the order to be inserted at least once in the journal.

Application for revocation of a patent

4.—(1) An application under section 72 of the 1977 Act for the **20.06** revocation of a patent shall be made by petition.

This paragraph does not apply to an application made in pending proceedings.

(2) The respondent to a petition under section 32 of the 1949 Act or section 72 of the 1977 Act must serve an answer on the petitioner within 21 days after service of the petition on him.

Action for infringement

5.—(1) Notwithstanding anything in Order 5, rule 4, proceedings in **20.07** which a claim is made by the plaintiff in respect of the infringement of a patent shall be begun by writ.

(2) The plaintiff in such an action must serve with his statement of claim particulars of the infringement relied on, showing which of the claims in the specification of the patent are alleged to be infringed and giving at least one instance of each type of infringement alleged.

(3) If a defendant in such an action alleges, as a defence to the action, that at the time of the infringement there was in force a contract or licence relating to the patent made by or with the consent of the plaintiff and containing a condition or term void by virtue of section 44 of the 1977 Act, he must serve on the plaintiff particulars of the date of, and parties to, each such contract or licence and particulars of each such condition or term.

Objections to validity of patent

6.—(1) A person who presents a petition under section 32 of the 1949 **20.08** Act or section 72 of the 1977 Act for the revocation of a patent must serve with his petition particulars of the objections to the validity of the patent on which he relies.

(1A) A party to an action concerning a patent who either challenges the validity of the patent or applies by counterclaim in the action for revocation of the patent must, notwithstanding Order 18, rule 2, serve his defence or counterclaim (as the case may be), together with particulars of the objections to the validity of the patent on which he relies, within 42 days after service upon him of the statement of claim.

(2) Particulars given pursuant to paragraph (1) or (1A) must state every ground on which the validity of the patent is challenged and must

include such particulars as will clearly define every issue which it is intended to raise.

(3) If the grounds stated in the particulars of objections include want of novelty or want of any inventive step, the particulars must state the manner, time and place of every prior publication or user relied upon and, if prior user is alleged, must—

(a) specify the name of every person alleged to have made such user,

(b) state whether such user is alleged to have continued until the priority date of the claim in question or of the invention, as may be appropriate, and, if not, the earliest and latest date on which such user is alleged to have taken place,

(c) contain a description accompanied by drawings, if necessary, sufficient to identify such user, and

(d) if such user relates to machinery or apparatus, state whether the machinery or apparatus is in existence and where it can be inspected.

(4) If in the case of an existing patent—

(a) one of the grounds stated in the particulars of objections is that the invention, so far as claimed in any claim of the complete specification, is not useful, and

(b) it is intended, in connection with that ground, to rely on the fact that an example of the invention which is the subject of any such claim cannot be made to work, either at all or as described in the specification,

the particulars must state that fact and identify each such claim and must include particulars of each such example, specifying the respect in which it is alleged that it does not work or does not work as described.

(5) In any action or other proceedings relating to a patent in which the validity of the patent has been put in issue on the ground of obviousness a party who wishes to rely on the commercial success of the patent must state in his answer or in his pleadings the grounds upon which he so relies.

Amendment of particulars

20.09   7. Without prejudice to Order 20, rule 5, the Court may at any stage of the proceedings allow a party to amend any particulars served by him under the foregoing provisions of this Order on such terms as to costs or otherwise as may be just.

Further particulars

20.10   8. The Court may at any stage of the proceedings order a party to serve on any other party further or better particulars of infringements or of objections.

Application of rules 10 to 14

9. Rules 10 to 14 of this Order apply to any action for infringement of a **20.11** patent (whether or not any other relief is claimed) and to any proceedings by petition for the revocation of a patent.

Admissions

10.—(1) Notwithstanding anything in Order 27, where a party desires **20.12** any other party to admit any facts, he shall, within 21 days after service of a reply or answer or after the expiration of the period fixed for the service thereof, serve on that other party a notice requiring him to admit for the purpose of the action or proceedings the facts specified in the notice.

(2) A party upon whom a notice under paragraph (1) is served shall within 21 days after service thereof serve upon the party making the request a notice stating in respect of each fact specified in the notice whether or not he admits it.

Discovery of documents

11.—(1) Order 24, rules 1 and 2 shall apply in an action for **20.13** infringement of a patent except that the list of documents must be served by each party within 21 days after service of the notice of admissions under rule 10(2), or within 21 days after the close of pleadings.

(2) Order 24, rules 1 and 2 shall apply in proceedings for the revocation of a patent as they apply to actions begun by writ except that the period prescribed by rule 2(1) shall be that which is prescribed by paragraph (1) of this rule.

Experiments

12.—(1) Where a party desires to establish any fact by experimental **20.14** proof he shall within 21 days after service of the lists of documents under rule 11 serve on the other party a notice stating the facts which he desires to establish and giving full particulars of the experiments proposed to establish them.

(2) A party upon whom a notice under paragraph (1) is served shall, within 21 days after service thereof, serve upon the other party a notice stating in respect of each fact whether or not he admits it.

(3) Where any fact which a party desires to establish by experimental proof is not admitted he may at the hearing of the summons for directions apply for directions in respect of such experiments.

Experts

20.15   13. Where a party intends to adduce oral expert evidence he shall not later than 14 days before the hearing of the summons for directions under rule 14 give notice to every other party and to the Court of the name of each expert he intends to call as witness.

This rule is without prejudice to the power of the Court to restrict the number of expert witnesses.

Summons for directions

20.16   14.—(1) The plaintiff or petitioner must, within 21 days after the expiration of all the periods specified in rules 10 to 12, take out a summons for directions as to the place and mode of trial returnable before a judge of the Patents Court in not less than 21 days, accompanied by minutes of the order proposed, a copy of the specification of any patent in issue, copies of the pleadings and of any documents referred to therein and copies of all documents served under rules 10 and 12 and if the plaintiff or petitioner does not take out such a summons in accordance with this paragraph, the defendant or respondent, as the case may be, may do so.

(2) The judge hearing a summons under this rule may give such directions:

(a) for the service of further pleadings or particulars;

(b) for the discovery of documents;

(c) for securing the making of admissions;

(d) for the service of interrogatories and of answers thereto;

(e) for the taking by affidavit of evidence relating to matters requiring expert knowledge, and for the filing of such affidavits and the service of copies thereof on the other parties;

(f) for the holding of a meeting of such experts as the judge may specify, for the purpose of producing a joint report on the state of the relevant art;

(g) for the exchanging of experts' reports, in respect of those matters on which they are not agreed;

(h) for the making of experiments, tests, inspections or reports;

(i) for the hearing, as a preliminary issue, of any question that may arise (including any questions as to the construction of the specification or other documents)

and otherwise as the judge thinks necessary or expedient for the purpose of defining and limiting the issues to be tried, restricting the number of witnesses to be called at the trial of any particular issue and otherwise securing that the case shall be disposed of, consistently with adequate hearing, in the most expeditious manner. Where the evidence is directed to be given by affidavit, the deponents must attend at the trial for cross-examination unless, with the concurrence of the Court, the parties otherwise agree.

(3) On the hearing of a summons under this rule the judge shall consider, if necessary of his own motion, whether:

(a) the parties' advisers should be required to meet for the purpose of agreeing which documents will be required at the trial and of paginating such documents;

(b) an independent scientific adviser should be appointed under rule 15 to assist the court.

(4) Part IV of Order 38 shall not apply to an action or proceedings to which this rule applies.

(5) No action or petition to which this rule applies shall be set down for trial unless and until a summons under this rule in the action or proceedings has been taken out and the directions given on the summons have been carried out or the time fixed by the judge for carrying them out has expired.

Appointment of a scientific adviser

15.—(1) In any proceedings under the 1949 or 1977 Act the Court may **20.17** at any time, and on or without the application of any party, appoint an independent scientific adviser to assist the Court, either—

(a) by sitting with the judge at the trial or hearing of the proceedings, or

(b) by inquiring and reporting on any question of fact or of opinion not involving a question of law or construction,

according as the Court may direct.

(2) The Court may nominate the scientific adviser and, where appropriate, settle any question or instructions to be submitted or given to him.

(3) Where the Court appoints a scientific adviser to inquire and report under paragraph (1)(b) Order 40, rules 2, 3, 4 and 6 shall apply in relation to his report as they apply in relation to a report made by a Court expert.

Restrictions on admissions of evidence

16.—(1) Except with the leave of the judge hearing any action or other **20.18** proceedings relating to a patent, no evidence shall be admissible in proof of any alleged infringement, or of any objection to the validity, of the patent, if the infringement or objection was not raised in the particulars of infringements or objections, as the case may be.

(2) In any action or other proceeding relating to a patent, evidence which is not in accordance with a statement contained in particulars of objections to the validity of the patent shall not be admissible in support

of such an objection unless the judge hearing the proceeding allows the evidence to be admitted.

(3) If any machinery or apparatus alleged to have been used before the priority date mentioned in rule 6(3)(b) is in existence at the date of service of the particulars of objections, no evidence of its user before that date shall be admissible unless it is proved that the party relying on such user offered, where the machinery or apparatus is in his possession, inspection of it to the other parties to the proceedings or, where it is not, used all reasonable endeavours to obtain inspection of it for those parties.

Determination of question or application where Comptroller declines to deal with it

20.19   **17.** Where the Comptroller—

(a) declines to deal with a question under section 8(7), 12(2), 37(8) or 61(5) of the 1977 Act;

(b) declines to deal with an application under section 40(5) of that Act, or

(c) certifies under section 72(7)(b) of that Act that the question whether a patent should be revoked is one which would more properly be determined by the Court,

any person entitled to do so may, within 28 days after the Comptroller's decision apply to the Court by originating summons to determine the question or application.

Application by employee for compensation under section 40 of the 1977 Act

20.20   **18.**—(1) An application by an employee for compensation under section 40(1) or (2) of the 1977 Act shall be made by originating summons issued within the period which begins when the relevant patent is granted and which expires one year after it has ceased to have effect:

Provided that, where a patent has ceased to have effect by reason of a failure to pay any renewal fee within the period prescribed for the payment thereof and an application for restoration is made to the Comptroller under section 28 of the said Act, the said period shall—

(a) if restoration is ordered, continue as if the patent had remained continuously in effect, or

(b) if restoration is refused, be treated as expiring one year after the patent ceased to have effect or six months after the refusal, whichever is the later.

(2) On the day fixed for the hearing of the originating summons under Order 28, rule 2, the Court shall, without prejudice to the generality of

Order 28, rule 4, give directions as to the manner in which the evidence (including any accounts of expenditure and receipts relating to the claim) shall be given at the hearing of the summons and, if the evidence is to be given by affidavit, specify the period within which the affidavit must be filed.

(3) The Court shall also give directions as to the provision by the defendant to the plaintiff, or a person deputed by him for the purpose, of reasonable facilities for inspecting and taking extracts from the books of account by which the defendant proposes to verify the accounts mentioned in paragraph (2) or from which those accounts have been derived.

Appeals from the Comptroller

19.—(1) An appeal to the Court from a decision of the Comptroller in any case in which a right of appeal is given by the 1949 or 1977 Act must be brought by originating motion and the notice of motion is referred to in this rule as "notice of appeal". **20.21**

(2) Notice of appeal shall be lodged with the proper officer—

(a) in the case of a decision on a matter of procedure, within 14 days after the date of the decision; and

(b) in any other case, within six weeks after the date of the decision.

(3) The Comptroller may determine whether any decision is on a matter of procedure and any such determination shall itself be a decision on a matter of procedure.

(4) Notice of appeal may be given in respect of the whole or any specific part of the decision of the Comptroller and must specify the grounds of the appeal and the relief which the appellant seeks.

(5) Except with the leave of the Court the appellant shall not be entitled on the hearing of the appeal to rely on any ground of appeal or to apply for any relief not specified in the notice of appeal.

(6) The appellant shall, within 5 days of lodging notice of appeal, serve a copy thereof on the Comptroller and other party to the proceedings before the Comptroller.

(7) On receiving notice of appeal the Comptroller shall forthwith transmit to the proper officer all the papers relating to the matter which is the subject of the appeal.

(8) Except by leave of the Court, no appeal shall be entertained unless notice of appeal has been given within the period specified in paragraph (2) or within such further time as the Comptroller may allow upon request made to him prior to the expiry of that period.

(9) A respondent who, not having appealed from the decision of the Comptroller, desires to contend on the appeal that the decision should be varied, either in any event or in the event of the appeal being allowed in whole or in part, must give notice to that effect, specifying the grounds of that contention and the relief which he seeks from the Court.

(10) A respondent who desires to contend on the appeal that the decision of the Comptroller should be affirmed on grounds other than those set out in the decision must give notice to that effect specifying the grounds of that contention.

(11) A respondent's notice shall be served on the Comptroller and on the appellant and every other party to the proceedings before the Comptroller within 14 days after receipt of notice of appeal by the respondent, or within such further time as the Court may direct.

(12) A party by whom a respondent's notice is given must within 5 days after service of the notice on the appellant, furnish 2 copies of the notice to the proper officer.

(13) The proper officer shall give to the Comptroller and to the appellant and every other party to the proceedings before the Comptroller not less than seven days' notice of the date appointed for the hearing of the appeal, unless the Court directs shorter notice to be given.

(14) An appeal shall be by way of rehearing and the evidence used on appeal shall be the same as that used before the Comptroller and except with the leave of the Court, no further evidence shall be given.

(15) *Deleted.*

(16) Any notice given in proceedings under this rule may be signed by or served on any patent agent, or member of the Bar of England and Wales not in actual practice, who is acting for the person giving the notice or, as the case may be, the person on whom the notice is to be served, as if the patent agent or member of the Bar were a solicitor.

(17) *Deleted.*

(18) Nothing in Order 42, rule 7 (except paragraph (1)), Order 55 (except rule 7(2) and (3) and (5) to (7)), or Order 57 shall apply in relation to an appeal under this rule.

Communication of information to the European Patent Office

20.22   **20.**—(1) The Court may authorise the communication to the European Patent Office or the competent authority of any country which is a party to the European Patent Convention of any such information in the files of the court as the Court thinks fit.

(2) Before complying with a request for the disclosure of information under paragraph (1) the Court shall afford to any party appearing to be affected by the request the opportunity of making representations, in writing or otherwise, on the question whether the information should be disclosed.

Proceedings for determination of certain disputes

20.23   **21.**—(1) The following proceedings must be begun by originating motion, that is to say—

(a) proceedings for the determination of any dispute referred to the Court under—
  (i) section 48 of the 1949 Act or section 58 of the 1977 Act;
  (ii) paragraph 3 of Schedule 1 to the Registered Designs Act 1949, or
  (iii) section 4 of the Defence Contracts Act 1958;
(b) any application under section 45(3) of the 1977 Act.

(2) There must be at least 10 clear days between the serving of notice of a motion under this rule and the day named in the notice for hearing the motion.

(3) On the hearing of a motion under this rule the Court shall give such directions for the further conduct of the proceedings as it thinks necessary or expedient and, in particular, directions for the service of particulars and as to the manner in which the evidence shall be given and as to the date of the hearing.

Application for rectification of register of patents or designs

22.—(1) An application to the Court for an order that the register of patents or the register of designs be rectified must be made by originating motion, except where it is made in a petition for the revocation of a patent or by way of counterclaim in proceedings for infringement or by originating summons in proceedings for an order under section 51 of the Trustee Act 1925.   **20.24**

(2) Where the application relates to the register of patents, the application shall forthwith serve an office copy of the application on the Comptroller, who shall be entitled to appear and to be heard on the application.

Counterclaim for rectification of register of designs

23.—(1) Where in any proceedings a claim is made for relief for infringement of the copyright in a registered design, the party against whom the claim is made may in his defence put in issue the validity of the registration of that design or may counterclaim for an order that the register of designs be rectified by cancelling or varying the registration or may do both those things.   **20.25**

(2) A party to any such proceedings who in his pleading (whether a defence or counterclaim) disputes the validity of the registration of a registered design must serve with the pleading particulars of the objections to the validity of the registration on which he relies in support of the allegation of invalidity.

(3) A party to any such proceedings who counterclaims for an order that the register of designs be rectified must serve on the comptroller a copy of the counterclaim together with a copy of the particulars

mentioned in paragraph (2); and the Comptroller shall be entitled to take such part in the proceedings as he thinks fit but need not serve a defence or other pleading unless ordered to do so by the Court.

PATENTS COURT: PRACTICE EXPLANATIONS

1. General

All originating notices of motion, notices of motion and summonses **21.01**
concerned with proceedings governed by Ord. 104 are issued in
accordance with Ord. 104/2/3.

Before issuing a notice of motion or summons, the applicant should
apply to the clerk in charge of the Patents Court List (Court 54, Tel: 071
936 6263) for a return date.

2. Appeals from the Comptroller

These are governed by Ord 104, r. 19. The Order refers to the "proper
officer." He is the clerk in charge of the Chancery List (Room TM813,
Tel: 071 936 6690/6778). In practice, the file is passed to the clerk in
charge of the Patents Court List (Court 54, Tel: 071 936 6263) who carries
out the duties of the Proper Officer.

3. Consent orders

Consent orders can be made by the Patents Court without the
attendance of solicitors or counsel.

To ensure that the public interest is safeguarded and the order
complies with the practice of the Chancery Division and the Patents
Court, the application, a minute of order and a document signifying the
consent of the parties must be lodged with the clerk in charge of the
Patents Court List (Court 54) by noon two clear days before the date on
which the application is to be heard.

Normally attendance in court will be required if a final order is sought
or the summons for directions is to be considered.

4. Ex parte *applications*

A party wishing to apply *ex parte* should contact the clerk in charge of
the Patents Court List.

5. Documents

It is the responsibility of both parties to any application to the Patents Court to ensure that all relevant documents are lodged with the clerk in charge of the Patents Court List (Court 54) by noon two days before the date fixed for hearing.

6. Summons for directions

The attention of practitioners is directed to the new precedent in the White Book (at the moment in the Third Supplement, Ord. 104/14/4).

14 January 1994   Mr. Justice Aldous

Simplified Trial

21.02   Attention is drawn to the ability and willingness of the Patents Court to hear actions on affidavit evidence, if that is the wish of the parties. It is suggested that in appropriate cases solicitors acting for one of the parties should, after close of pleadings, write to the solicitors acting for the other party requesting agreement to a "Simplified Trial". That letter should point out that refusal may be brought to the attention of the judge after judgment and could result in an adverse order on costs.

If the parties agree to a Simplified Trial, one of them should within 14 days after close of pleadings apply for directions which should include:
(1) the filing of evidence by affidavit,
(2) the trial to be heard on affidavit evidence,
(3) limitation of experts,
(4) setting down.

If agreed directions are sought, no attendance at Court is necessary.

A Simplified Trial would not be suitable where cross-examination is likely on any issue of substance nor where any substantial discovery is needed.

21 March 1994   Mr. Justice Aldous

COPYRIGHT, DESIGNS AND PATENTS ACT 1988 (extracts)

PART VI

PATENTS

Patents County Courts

Patents County Courts: special jurisdiction

287.—(1) The Lord Chancellor may by order made by statutory **22.01**
instrument designate any County Court as a Patents County Court and
confer on it jurisdiction (its "special jurisdiction") to hear and determine
such descriptions of proceedings—
  (a) relating to patents or designs, or
  (b) ancillary to, or arising out of the same subject matter as,
      proceedings relating to patents or designs,
as may be specified in the order.

(2) The special jurisdiction of a Patents County Court is exercisable
throughout England and Wales, but rules of court may provide for a
matter pending in one such court to be heard and determined in another
or partly in that and partly in another.

(3) A Patents County Court may entertain proceedings within its
special jurisdiction notwithstanding that no pecuniary remedy is
sought.

(4) An order under this section providing for the discontinuance of
any of the special jurisdiction of a Patents County Court may make
provision as to proceedings pending in the court when the order comes
into operation.

(5) Nothing in this section shall be construed as affecting the ordinary
jurisdiction of a County Court.

Financial limits in relation to proceedings within special jurisdiction of Patents County Court

22.02   288.—(1) Her Majesty may by Order in Council provide for limits of amount or value in relation to any description of proceedings within the special jurisdiction of a Patents County Court.

(2) If a limit is imposed on the amount of a claim of any description and the plaintiff has a cause of action for more than that amount, he may abandon the excess; in which case a patents county court shall have jurisdiction to hear and determine the action, but the plaintiff may not recover more than that amount.

(3) Where the court has jurisdiction to hear and determine an action by virtue of subsection (2), the judgment of the court in the action is in full discharge of all demands in respect of the cause of action, and entry of the judgment shall be made accordingly.

(4) If the parties agree, by a memorandum signed by them or by their respective solicitors or other agents, that a Patents County Court shall have jurisdiction in any proceedings, that court shall have jurisdiction to hear and determine the proceedings notwithstanding any limit imposed under this section.

(5) No recommendation shall be made to Her Majesty to make an Order under this section unless a draft of the Order has been laid before and approved by a resolution of each House of Parliament.

Transfer of proceedings between High Court and Patents County Court

22.03   289.—(1) No order shall be made under section 41 of the County Courts Act 1984 (power of High Court to order proceedings to be transferred from the County Court) in respect of proceedings within the special jurisdiction of a Patents County Court.

(2) In considering in relation to proceedings within the special jurisdiction of a Patents County Court whether an order should be made under section 40 or 42 of the County Courts Act 1984 (transfer of proceedings from or to the High Court), the court shall have regard to the financial position of the parties and may order the transfer of the proceedings to a Patents County Court or, as the case may be, refrain from ordering their transfer to the High Court notwithstanding that the proceedings are likely to raise an important question of fact or law.

Limitation of costs where pecuniary claim could have been brought in Patents County Court

22.04   290.—(1) Where an action is commenced in the High Court which could have been commenced in a Patents County Court and in which a claim for a pecuniary remedy is made, then, subject to the provisions of this section, if the plaintiff recovers less than the prescribed amount, he is not entitled to recover any more costs than those to which he would have been entitled if the action had been brought in the County Court.

(2) For this purpose a plaintiff shall be treated as recovering the full amount recoverable in respect of his claim without regard to any deduction made in respect of matters not falling to be taken into account in determining whether the action could have been commenced in a Patents County Court.

(3) This section does not affect any question as to costs if it appears to the High Court that there was reasonable ground for supposing the amount recoverable in respect of the plaintiff's claim to be in excess of the prescribed amount.

(4) The High Court, if satisfied that there was sufficient reason for bringing the action in the High Court, may make an order allowing the costs or any part of the costs on the High Court scale or on such one of the County Court scales as it may direct.

(5) This section does not apply to proceedings brought by the Crown.

(6) In this section "the prescribed amount" means such amount as may be prescribed by Her Majesty for the purposes of this section by Order in Council.

(7) No recommendation shall be made to Her Majesty to make an Order under this section unless a draft of the Order has been laid before and approved by a resolution of each House of Parliament.

Proceedings in Patents County Court

291.—(1) Where a County Court is designated a Patents County **22.05** Court, the Lord Chancellor shall nominate a person entitled to sit as a judge of that court as the patents judge.

(2) County Court rules shall make provision for securing that, so far as is practicable and appropriate—

(a) proceedings within the special jurisdiction of a Patents County Court are dealt with by the patents judge, and

(b) the judge, rather than a registrar or other officer of the court, deals with interlocutory matters in the proceedings.

(3) County Court rules shall make provision empowering a Patents County Court in proceedings within its special jurisdiction, on or without the application of any party—

(a) to appoint scientific advisers or assessors to assist the court, or

(b) to order the Patent Office to inquire into and report on any question of fact or opinion.

(4) Where the court exercises either of those powers on the application of a party, the remuneration or fees payable to the Patent Office shall be at such rate as may be determined in accordance with County Court

rules and shall be costs of the proceedings unless otherwise ordered by the judge.

(5) Where the court exercises either of those powers of its own motion, the remuneration or fees payable to the Patent Office shall be at such rate as may be determined by the Lord Chancellor with the approval of the Treasury and shall be paid out of money provided by Parliament.

Rights and duties of registered patent agents in relation to proceedings in Patents County Court

22.06   **292.**—(1) A registered patent agent may do, in or in connection with proceedings in a Patents County Court which are within the special jurisdiction of that court, anything which a solicitor of the Supreme Court might do, other than prepare a deed.

(2) The Lord Chancellor may by regulations provide that the right conferred by subsection (1) shall be subject to such conditions and restrictions as appear to the Lord Chancellor to be necessary or expedient; and different provision may be made for different descriptions of proceedings.

(3) A Patents County Court has the same power to enforce an undertaking given by a registered patent agent acting in pursuance of this section as it has, by virtue of section 142 of the County Courts Act 1984, in relation to a solicitor.

(4) Nothing in section 143 of the County Courts Act 1984 (prohibition on persons other than solicitors receiving remuneration) applies to a registered patent agent acting in pursuance of this section.

(5) The provisions of County Court rules prescribing scales of costs to be paid to solicitors apply in relation to registered patent agents acting in pursuance to this section.

(6) Regulations under this section shall be made by statutory instrument which shall be subject to annulment in pursuance of a resolution of either House of Parliament.

On p. 965, the heading should read
"Patents County Court (Designation
and Jurisdiction) Order **1994** (S.I. **1994** No. 1609)".

PATENTS COUNTY COURT (DESIGNATION AND JURISDICTION) ORDER 1990

(S.I. 1990 No.1609)

The Lord Chancellor, in exercise of the powers conferred upon him by **23.00** section 287 of the Copyright, Designs and Patents Act 1988, hereby makes the following Order:

Citation and Commencement

1. This Order may be cited as the Patents County Court (Designation **23.01** and Jurisdiction) Order 1994 and shall come into force on 11th July 1994.

Designation as Patents County Court

2. The Central London County Court is hereby designated as a patents **23.02** county court.

3. As a patents county court, the Central London County Court shall have jurisdiction, subject to article 4 below, to hear and determine any action or matter relating to patents or designs over which the High Court would have jurisdiction, together with any claims or matters ancillary to or arising from, such proceedings.

4. The jurisdiction conferred by article 3 above shall not include jurisdiction to hear appeals from the comptroller.

Discontinuance and transitional provision

5.—(1) The Edmonton County Court shall cease to be a patents county court and accordingly the Patents County Court (Designation and Jurisdiction) Order 1990 is hereby revoked.

(2) The patents county court at the Central London County Court shall have jurisdiction in proceedings commenced in the patents county court at the Edmonton County Court before coming into force this Order.

COUNTY COURT RULES 1981

ORDER 48A

PATENTS AND DESIGNS

Application and Interpretation

24.01   **1.**—(1) This Order applies to proceedings in respect of which Patents County Courts have jurisdiction under section 287(1) of the 1988 Act.
    (2) In this Order:
> "The 1988 Act" means the Copyright, Designs and Patents Act 1988;
> "Patents County Court" means a County Court designated as a Patents County Court under section 287(1) of the 1988 Act;
> "patents judge" means a person nominated under section 291(1) of the 1988 Act as the patents judge of a Patents County Court.

Patents Judge

24.02   **2.**—(1) Subject to paragraph (2), proceedings which this Order applies shall be dealt with by the patents judge.
    (2) When an interlocutory matter needs to be dealt with urgently and the patents judge is not available, the matter may be dealt with by another judge.

Commencement

24.03   **3.** Every summons, notice, pleading, affidavit or other document relating to proceedings to which this Order applies must be marked in the top left hand corner with the words "Patents County Court".

Pleadings

24.04   **4.**—(1) Every summons issued in accordance with rule 3 above shall be endorsed with or accompanied by a statement of case.
    (2) Where a claim is made by the plaintiff in respect of the

infringement of a patent, the statement of case shall give full particulars
of the infringement relied on, setting out:
  (a) which of the claims in the specification of the patent are alleged to
      be infringed; and
  (b) in respect of each claim alleged to be infringed the grounds relied
      on in support of the allegations that such claim has been
      infringed; and all facts, matters and arguments relied on as
      establishing those grounds, including at least one example of
      each type of infringement alleged.

(3) Where, in any proceedings, the validity of a patent is put in issue,
the statement of case shall give particulars of the objections to the
validity of the patent which are relied on; and in particular shall explain
the relevance of every citation to each claim, with identification of the
significant parts of each citation, and shall give all facts, matters and
arguments which are relied on for establishing the invalidity of the
patent.

(4) Without prejudice to paragraph (3) above, RSC Order 104, rule 6(2)
to (4) shall apply to particulars of objections given under paragraph (3)
as they apply to particulars given under paragraph (1) of that rule.

(5) Every statement of case shall be signed:
  (a) by the plaintiff, if he sues in person; or
  (b) by the plaintiff's solicitor in his own name or the name of his firm;
and shall state the plaintiff's address for service.

(6) Where a defendant wishes to serve a defence to any claim he shall
serve it, together with any counterclaim including a statement of case
under paragraph (2) or (3) above, upon the plaintiff within 42 days of
service upon him of the summons.

(7) Where a party wishes to serve a reply or a defence to counterclaim,
he shall do so within 28 days of the service of the previous pleading
upon him.

(8) Pleadings will close seven days after the expiry of the time for
service of a reply.

(9) No time limit mentioned in this rule may be extended more than
once (and then by no more than 42 days) save by order of the court; and
such order shall, in the first place, be applied for in writing, whereupon
the judge shall either grant the application, refuse it, or order a hearing.

(10) The parties to proceedings shall notify the court of any agreed
extension of any time limit mentioned in this rule.

Service

5.—(1) In their application to proceedings to which this Order applies,   **24.05**
rules 10 and 13 of Order 7 shall apply as if:
  (a) before the words "an officer" in paragraph (1)(b) of each rule
      there were inserted the words "the plaintiff or"; and
  (b) in paragraph (4) of rule 10 (and in that paragraph as applied by

rule 13) after the words "sent by post" there were inserted the words "by an officer of the court".

(2) Where a pleading is served which refers to any document, the party serving the pleading must also serve with it a copy of any such document together with an English translation of any foreign language text, certified as being accurate.

Interrogatories and notices to admit facts

24.06   6.—(1)
(a) Interrogatories under Order 14, rule 11, and
(b) a notice to admit facts under Order 20, rule 2,
may not be served without the leave of the court unless (in the case of a notice to admit facts) it is served within 14 days of the close of pleadings; and accordingly those provisions of Order 14, rule 11 (and of the RSC which are applied by that rule) which relate only to interrogatories without order shall not apply to proceedings under this Order.

(2) An application for leave to serve interrogatories or a notice to admit facts may only be made on notice at the preliminary consideration under rule 8.

Scientific advisers, assessors and Patent Office reports

24.07   7.—(1) The court may at any time, on or without the application of any party:
(a) appoint scientific advisers or assessors to assist the court; or
(b) order the Patent Office to inquire into and report on any question of fact or opinion.

(2) RSC Order 104, rule 15 shall apply to the appointment of a scientific adviser under this rule.

(3) Where the court appoints an assessor under this rule without the application of a party, paragraphs (3) and (6) of Order 13, rule 11 shall apply, and paragraph (4) of that rule shall apply with the omission of the words from "the applicant shall" to "and thereupon" inclusive.

Preliminary consideration

24.08   8.—(1) Within fourteen days of the close of pleadings, all parties shall file and serve an application for directions, signed by the person settling it.
(2) Each application for directions shall:
(a) summarise the outstanding issues in the proceedings;
(b) summarise the further steps necessary to prove the applicant's contentions in the proceedings and prepare his case for a hearing;

(c) give full particulars of any experiments the applicant intends to conduct, stating the facts which he intends to prove by them and the date by which he will submit a written report of the results; and

(d) set out all orders and directions the applicant will ask for at the preliminary consideration of the action.

(3) As soon as is practicable after receipt of each party's application for directions, the proper officer shall set a date for the preliminary consideration.

(4) On the preliminary consideration the judge may, with or without the application of any party and either after a consideration of the papers or having adjudicated upon a point of law strike out any point raised in the proceedings.

(5) On the preliminary consideration, the judge shall give directions as are necessary to prepare the proceedings for hearing and in particular shall consider and (where appropriate) give directions in respect of each or any of the following matters, namely:

(a) the witnesses who may be called;

(b) whether their evidence should be given orally or in writing or any combination of the two;

(c) the exchange of witness statements;

(d) the provision of Patent Office Reports;

(e) the use of assessors at the hearing;

(f) transfer to the High Court;

(g) reference to the Court of Justice of the European Communities;

(h) applications for discovery and inspection;

(i) applications for leave under rule 6 above; and

(j) written reports of the results of any experiments of which particulars have been given under rule 8(2)(c).

General modification of County Court rules

9. In their application to proceedings to which this Order applies, **24.09** County Court rules shall be subject to the following modifications:

(a) Order 3 rules 3(1) and (2)(c) shall have effect as if for the words "particulars of claim" there are substituted the words "statement of case".

(b) in Order 3, rule 3(2)(a), the words from "and in the case" to "return day" inclusive shall be omitted;

(c) Order 3, rule 3(3) shall not apply;

(d) Order 6, rule 7 shall not apply;

(e) Order 9 shall not apply, with the exception of Order 9, rule 19, which shall apply to every defence or counterclaim delivered under rule 4(6) above as it applies to those delivered under Order 9, rule 2.

Application of rules of the Supreme Court

24.10   **10.**—(1) RSC Order 104, rule 3 shall apply to applications by a patentee or the proprietor of a patent intending to apply under section 30 of the Patents Act 1949 or section 75 of the Patents Act 1977 for leave to amend his specification, save that references therein to an application by motion shall be construed, for the purposes of an application to a Patents County Court, as an application on notice to the patents judge.

(2) RSC Order 104, rule 17 shall apply to actions to which this Order applies, with the omission of the words "by originating summons".

(3) RSC Order 104, rule 16(3), rule 20 and rule 23 shall apply to actions to which this Order applies.

PATENTS COUNTY COURT USERS' GUIDE

(Extracts)

1. Jurisdiction

Ordinary jurisdiction

Most users of the Patents County Court will be concerned only with   **25.01**
its special jurisdiction indicated below but, as its ordinary jurisdiction as
a County Court is unaffected (*cf.* s.287(5) Copyright, Designs and
Patents Act 1988), there may be other causes of action (*e.g.* contractual
disputes, passing off) which can appropriately be brought before it. In
all such cases, however, the normal rules as to representation, jurisdiction, venue and limit of amount apply: for details, reference should be
made to the *County Court Practice* (the "Green Book") and, in case of
doubt, to the Chief Clerk of the Court.

It should not be forgotten that every County Court has general
ancillary jurisdiction to give the same relief, redress or remedy as the
High Court (s.38(1) County Courts Act 1984). In particular it can grant,
ex parte or on notice, interlocutory relief, including injunctions and
Anton Piller orders.

Special jurisdiction

Since the special jurisdiction of a designated Patents County Court
relating to patents and designs covers any action or matter over which
the High Court would have jurisdiction other than appeals from the
Comptroller, without regard to the normal venue and financial limit
rules, the Patents County Court may hear and determine actions and
counterclaims for:

   patent, design right and/or registered design infringement;
   revocation of patent and/or rectification of the register of designs;
   amendment of patent;
   declaration of non-infringement of patent, design right and/or
      registered design;
   determination of entitlement to patent, design right and/or regis-
      tered design;
   employee's compensation in respect of a patented invention;
   disputes as to Crown use of a patented invention, design right
      and/or registered design;

unjustified threats of proceedings for infringement of patent,
design right and/or registered design;
claims or matters ancillary to any of the above or arising therefrom.

It should be noted that, unlike an ordinary County Court, a Patents
County Court may entertain proceedings within its special jurisdiction
notwithstanding that no pecuniary remedy is sought (Section 287(3)
Copyright, Designs and Patents Act 1988).

Transferred Actions

In order to ensure access to justice for parties with limited financial
resources, s.289 Copyright, Designs and Patents Act 1988 contains
special provisions concerning transfer of proceedings between the High
Court and a Patents County Court.

Actions within the special jurisdiction of a Patents County Court may
be ordered to be transferred to such a court by the High Court either of
its own motion or on the application of any party to the proceedings. In
considering whether to make such an order, the High Court shall have
regard to the financial position of the parties and may order transfer
notwithstanding that the proceedings are likely to raise an important
question of law or fact.

Such actions may also be ordered to be transferred from a Patents
County Court to the High Court by the County Court either of its own
motion or on the application of any party to the proceedings. The county
court is required to have regard to the financial position of the parties
and may refrain from ordering transfer notwithstanding that the
proceedings are likely to raise an important question of law or fact.

The High Court does not have the power to order proceedings within
the special jurisdiction of a Patents County Court to be transferred from
the Patents County Court.

When an action is transferred to the Patents County Court, the court
will, after consultation with the parties, give any directions deemed
appropriate for the purpose of bringing the pleadings and any other
documents in the case and outstanding procedural steps into conformity with its own procedures.

2. Starting an action

Summons

25.02　All actions in a Patents County Court within its special jurisdiction
must be started by summons. Copies of the prescribed Form of
Summons (N4P) are available from the court. Prospective plaintiffs who
wish to prepare their own summons, using, *e.g.* a word processor, must

follow the text and layout of the prescribed form and must submit the draft summons to be embossed with the royal arms and sealed with the seal of the court.

When filed with the court the summons must be endorsed with or accompanied by a statement of case and the court fee must be paid at the time of filing. One copy of the summons and statement of case (including a copy of each document referred to therein) must be supplied for the court file. The number of additional copies of the summons and statement of case filed must equal the number of defendants to be served but further copies of documents referred to in the statement of case need only be filed if the court is being asked to effect postal service on the defendants.

Statement of case

The statement of case should be full but concise. It must set out all facts, matters and arguments relied on as establishing the allegations made and justifying the relief sought.

Attention is drawn to the following provisions: CCR Order 48A, r.4(2) and (3) and RSC Order 104, r.6(2), (3) and (4) and r.23. [The text of these rules is set out in full in the Guide.]

Signature of statement of case

Every statement of case must be signed by the plaintiff if he sues in person. Otherwise it must be signed by the plaintiff's solicitor or registered patent agent in his own name or in the name of his firm.

Additionally, if it has been settled by counsel, it must be signed by him and his name must appear on the copies filed by the solicitor or patent agent.

The statement of case must state the plaintiff's address for service.

Service of process

Service of the summons and statement of case must be effected in person or by post. The court cannot effect personal service for a plaintiff but can send documents by post to defendants within the jurisdiction. [Concerning service out of the jurisdiction see paragraph 18 below.]

3. Defending an action and serving a counterclaim

A statement of case must be served with every defence and with every counterclaim. It must set out all facts, matters and arguments relied on **25.03** and comply, as appropriate, with the requirements of CCR Order 48A r.4(2) and (3), RSC Order 104, r.6(2) to (5) and r.23.

Copies of documents referred to in the statement of case must be supplied to the parties served.

Signature of defence and counterclaim and statement of case

Every defence and counterclaim and every statement of case served therewith must be signed by the defendant if he is acting in person, otherwise it must be signed by his solicitor or registered patent agent in his own name or in the name of this firm. Additionally, if it has been settled by counsel, it must be signed by him and his name must appear on the copies filed by the solicitor or patent agent.

Every defence and counterclaim and every statement of case served therewith must state the defendant's address for service.

Copies of a defence and counterclaim and accompanying statement of case do not have to be filed with the court until the stage of applying for directions.

4. Reply and defence to counterclaim

25.04   The CCR do not provide expressly for the sevice of a reply to a defence but High Court practice is followed and CCR Order 48A, r.4(7) and (8) recognise this. If no counterclaim is served, it is generally unnecessary to serve a reply. A reply and a defence to counterclaim should be included in the same document and the rules and practice applying to a statement of case served with a defence should be followed in drafting the statement of case to be served with the defence to counterclaim.

The provisions of RSC Order 104, r.6(5) should not be overlooked: if the validity of a patent has been put in issue on the ground of obviousness, a party who wishes to rely on the commercial success of the patent must state the grounds on which he so relies. Furthermore, in accordance with the general rule for Patents County Court procedure, all facts, matters and arguments relied on in support of such grounds must be set out.

Copies of a reply and defence to counterclaim and accompanying statement of case do not have to be filed with the court until the stage of applying for directions.

5. Accompanying documents

25.05   See CCR Order 48A, r.5(2). [This is set out in full in the Guide.]

A party who is aggrieved by noncompliance or only partial compliance with this rule should immediately request compliance. If this request is not complied with within a short but reasonable time, application should be made to the court for an order directing compliance.

6. Further and better particulars

The normal County Court rule allowing the court to order the plaintiff to give the defendant further particulars of his claim (CCR Order 6, r.7) does not apply to proceedings to which CCR Order 48A applies (*ibid.* r.9(d)). **25.06**

The court may, however, by order allow or direct any summons, pleading or other document in the proceedings to be amended (CCR Order 15, r.1) and a party may amend any pleading of his by consent of the other parties, subject to the court's power to disallow such an amendment if it would have refused leave on an application under Order 15, r.1 (CCR Order 15, r.2 see esp. (3)).

7. Times and extensions of time

Special rules

The special rules as to times for service of pleadings in CCR Order 48A should be carefully noted. **25.07**

Extending time generally

Adjournments and general extensions of time are subject to the normal County Court rules (CCR Order 13, r.3(4)).

8. Interrogatories and notices to admit facts

Interrogatories may not be served in proceedings to which CCR Order 48A applies without the leave of the court (*ibid.* r.6(1)). **25.08**

A notice to admit facts may only be served in such proceedings without the leave of the court within 14 days of the close of pleadings (*ibid.*). An application for leave to serve interrogatories or (where required) a notice to admit facts may only be made on notice at the preliminary consideration of the case by the judge (*ibid.* r.6(2)).

9. Discovery

Discovery and inspection of documents is not ordered automatically **25.09** in proceedings in a Patents County Court. It should be asked for only insofar as it is reasonably necessary for disposing fairly of the action. If an issue can be decided without any discovery or any substantial discovery, this should be done. Discovery should not be asked for prematurely on an issue which can be postponed (*e.g.* an enquiry as to damages).

10. Scientific advisers and assessors

25.10 The court may at any time—though normally it will do so, if at all, at the stage of the preliminary consideration—appoint scientific advisers or assessors to assist it. Parties should give careful consideration to this possibility as a means of significantly reducing the need for technical instruction of the court and expert evidence, particularly in complex cases.

An independent scientific adviser may be appointed to assist the court either by sitting with the judge at the trial or by enquiring and reporting on any question of fact or opinion not involving a question of law or construction (CCR Order 48A, r.7(1)(a); RSC Order 104, r.15).

An assessor may be summoned to assist the judge at the hearing, normally on the application of a party. Notice of intention to summon an assessor must be given to all other parties who have the right to give notice of objection and to be heard on their objection. A party applying for an assessor to be summoned is required to deposit a sum considered reasonable in respect of the assessor's fee (CCR Order 13, r.11).

An independent scientific adviser or an assessor has only an advisory function. The decision of the court is that of the judge alone.

11. Patent Office reports

25.11 An additional or alternative method of reducing the need for technical instruction of the court and expert evidence is provided by the rule (CCR Order 48A, r.7(1)(b)) under which the court can order the United Kingdom Patent Office to inquire into and report on any question of fact or opinion. Parties will be given the opportunity before trial to comment upon any report made by the Patent Office.

The Patent Office has stated that it will report impartially, considering the question fully from all sides. The Office has commented as follows:

A request for a report should formulate the questions on which the Patent Office is to report as clearly and precisely as is practicable. The type of question will vary from case to case. On technically complex or detailed subject matter an explanation of the technical background might be sought to assist the court in understanding the technical issues. An appraisal of the background art might be considered useful in some cases. Since the Patent Office has extensive search files and wide experience of online searching the appraisal could include a search if requested. In involved cases an analysis of the issues in dispute might assist the court. An opinion on the interpretation of technical documents could be given.

It is the practice when an application to amend a patent is made to the Patents Court (of the High Court) for a report to be prepared in the Patent Office for the benefit of the court on the question as to whether the Office considers the amendments allowable. Since rule 10(1) of CCR Order 48A applies RSC Order 104, r.3 to Patents County Court procedures, a similar report on applications to the Patents County Court to amend a patent would be appropriate.

Fees charged by the Patent Office will be based on hourly rates.

12. Preliminary consideration

Applications for directions

Within 14 days of the close of pleadings in an action to which CCR   **25.12** Order 48A applies, every party must file with the court and serve on every other party an application for directions signed by the person settling it (*ibid.* r.8(1)).

In accordance with CCR Order 48A, r.8(2), each application for directions shall:

summarise the outstanding issues in the proceedings;

summarise the further steps necessary to prove the applicant's contentions in the proceedings and prepare his case for hearing;

give full particulars of any experiments the applicant intends to conduct, stating the facts which he intends to prove by them and the date by which he will submit a written report of the results;

set to all orders and directions the applicant will ask for at the preliminary consideration of the action.

When preparing an application for directions, the person settling it should consider in particular:

whether there is any preliminary point of law to be adjudicated;

whether any application is to be made for amendment of any document filed or served in the action;

whether any application is to be made on notice to the patents judge for leave to amend the specification of a patent;

whether any application is to be made on notice to the patents judge for rectification of the register of designs:

whether a scientific adviser should be appointed or an assessor should be summoned;

whether the United Kingdom Patent Office should be requested to provide a report;

the witnesses who may be called and whether their evidence should be given orally or in writing or any combination of the two;

the exchange of witness statements;

applications for discovery and inspection;

application for leave to administer interrogatories or to serve (more than 14 days after the close of pleadings) a notice to admit facts;

provision of written reports of the results of experiments of which particulars have been given under CCR Order 48A, r.8(2)(c);

reference of any point of law to the Court of Justice of the European Communities;

transfer of the action to the High Court;

date and place of trial;

whether any issue of damages should be dealt with at the trial or left for subsequent enquiry.

Preliminary consideration

As soon as is practicable after receipt by the court of each party's application for directions, the court will set a date for the preliminary consideration of the case by the patents judge. This date will be set after consultation with the parties. An estimate of time required should be given by each party and agreed if possible. Provided the total time estimated is not more than 2–2½ hours it should normally be possible to fix a date at short notice.

At the preliminary consideration, the patents judge will review the case with the parties, relatively informally. By this stage, each party should be aware of the relevant issues of law and fact and of the real strength of the case of his opponent. The procedure of preliminary consideration should, therefore, assist the parties in seeing if there is any realistic possibility of settlement and, if not, to progress the action further in the most efficient and cost-effective manner possible.

13. Preparation and exchange of written evidence

Factual evidence

25.13   Written evidence on a question of fact should be expressed in the witness's own words and the statement should be signed by him. A witness who does not command sufficient fluency in English to make his statement substantially unaided and, if required, to be further examined and/or cross-examined upon it orally in court, should use a language in which he is sufficiently fluent and a certified translation should be provided.

Although the statement should be expressed in the witness's own words, it should be logically structured and not include matter which is clearly irrelevant or inadmissible in accordance with English laws of evidence.

Any party on whom a witness statement is served who takes objection to the relevance or admissibility of the evidence should notify the party serving the statement of this as soon as possible after service and the parties concerned should attempt to resolve the matter before the statement is filed with the court. If it is not possible to resolve the matter, the party filing the statement should notify the court of the objections raised. Any party may request the court not to read in advance of the trial the whole or any identified part of a statement which has been filed. Such a request should be made promptly.

Unless otherwise ordered, a statement filed will be treated as the evidence in chief of the witness if he is called but the witness may be allowed to amend or supplement his statement orally at the trial before submitting to cross-examination.

Every reasonable attempt should be made to avoid calling witnesses of fact at the trial on matters which are not seriously contested.

Expert evidence

It is very desirable to limit the amount and extent of expert evidence by narrowing the technical issues in dispute and by agreeing technical facts, by relying on independent reports, by using the services of scientific advisers and assessors, by restricting experiments and inspection and by limiting the calling of expert witnesses at the trial. Informal "without prejudice" meetings between experts before trial may help to resolve disputed points.

As much expert evidence as possible should be presented in the form of reports.

14. Other preparations for trial

Bundles of documents

The main responsibility for the preparation of bundles lies with the   **25.14** plaintiff's representative but the parties should co-operate as fully as possible. Bundles should include copies of any pleadings and other documents already filed with the court.

Bundles should be paginated and copies of documents should be checked for legibility, clearly labelled and indexed. Any transcription or translation should be clearly identified as such and placed in the bundle adjacent to the document to which it relates.

Ring binders are a preferred method of keeping documents together.

Witness statements and documents referred to only in them should be bundled separately from other documents.

Documents relied on as citations in patent or registered design actions should be bundled separately from other documents and preferably

identified by letters and/or document numbers for general convenience. Plaintiffs', defendants' and third parties' documents (other than
citation) should be kept in separate bundles.

Outline arguments, lists of authorities, etc.

In a case which is particularly complex or in which the area of dispute
appears to have shifted significantly since the parties' pleadings were
originally served, it may be of assistance if each party prepares an
outline of its argument with references to the documents relied on and
lodges this with the court in advance of the trial. Lists of authorities and
of witnesses whom it is intended to call are helpful to the court in all
cases.

Pre-trial check list

A form of pre-trial check list is set out in Appendix 2 [see p.92 below].
It is important that such a check list be completed and lodged with the
court not less than seven working days before the date fixed for trial.

15. Trial

25.15   The trial, like the procedures before trial, is intended to ensure that
justice is done between the parties thoroughly but cost-effectively.

The more the parties do to enable the court to study the case in
advance of the trial, the greater will be the saving in time and costs. At
the hearing, there should be concentration on essentials with—in
particular—the minimum of reading out aloud of documents.

Shorthand notes will normally be taken of evidence given orally but
not of other parts of the proceedings.

Parties must make their own notes of the argument. The requests of
parties will be clarified with each to the conclusion of the oral argument
and judgments will usually be handed down.

16. Procedures after trial

25.16   Unless the judge otherwise orders, enquiries as to damages and
taxation of costs (the latter undertaken by the registrar) will be dealt
with in subsequent, essentially written, proceedings after the main trial.

17. *Ex parte* applications

A careful study should be made of the general procedural require-   **25.17**
ments for *ex parte* applications in the *Supreme Court Practice* (the "White
Book") and the *County Court Practice* (the "Green Book").

As the court is only being presented with one side of the story when
an *ex parte* application is made, there must be *complete disclosure of all
material facts*. Failure to make disclosure of matters which are or may be
adverse to the party making the application may result in any order
made being subsequently set aside on the ground of non-disclosure. It
may also have serious consequences for any person who has made an
affidavit in support of the application and any professional person
representing the applicant.

Ex parte applications within the special jurisdiction of a Patents
County Court will normally be dealt with by the patents judge.

Notice of an *ex parte* application must be filed a reasonable time before
the application is heard, unless the court otherwise directs (CCR Order
13, r.1(3)). All affidavits and other documents relied on should be filed at
the same time.

Ex parte applications should not be made when the applicant has
already issued a summons in proceedings under CCR ORder 48A.

In any case in which proceedings should be started by summons the
applicant for an *ex parte* order must be prepared to show that the
application is so urgent that it is not practical to issue and serve the
summons first.

Except in the case of an Anton Piller order or a Mareva injunction, the
court may require notice to be given to any person affected by the
application.

18. Service out of the jurisdiction

The rules relating to service out of the jurisdiction are very complicat-   **25.18**
ed. Reference should be made to the "White Book" and the "Green
Book". Attention is drawn in particular to CCR Order 8 and Order 3,
r.3(6).

Where leave is required, supporting evidence should state that in the
belief of the deponent the applicant has a good cause of action; where
the respondent is; whether or not he is a United Kingdom national; the
grounds for the application; and, if applicable, why he is a necessary or
proper party to proceedings brought against another party who has
been duly served. An application for leave is subject to the strict rules of
full disclosure already discussed above. A draft of the order sought
should be submitted.

19. Security for costs

25.19   The general principle is that parties to proceeedings are not required to give security for the costs of other parties. However, a plaintiff or a counterclaiming defendant (except a defendant in a patent or design action whose counterclaim raises only the invalidity of the patent or design) may be ordered to give such security if ordinarily resident out of England and Wales or if it is a limited company and there is credible evidence that there is reason to believe that it will be unable to pay the other side's costs.

Affidavit evidence in support of an application for security of costs should deal *inter alia* with any alleged practical difficulties of enforcing an order for costs.

Successive applications for security can be made. However, applications should always be made at the earliest possible moment: delay is a ground for refusal. The assistance of the registrar may be sought in assessing the amount of costs likely to be awarded on taxation.

20. Application for leave to amend a patent specification

25.20   A patentee or the proprietor of a patent intending to apply for leave to amend his specification must give notice of his intention to the Comptroller accompanied by a copy of an advertisement complying with RSC Order 104, r.3(1).

An application to the Patents County Court is made on notice to the patents judge (CCR Order 48A, r.10(1)) using County Court form N.244, and not as in the High Court by notice of motion. The application should include a request for directions for the further conduct of the amendment proceedings. Together with a copy of the patent specification certified by the Comptroller and showing in coloured ink the amendment sought, the notice must be served on the Comptroller, the parties to the proceedings and any person who has given notice of his intention to oppose the amendment. RSC Order 104, r.3 applies, *mutatis mutandis*, to the procedure. Attention is drawn to the duty of full disclosure of all relevant facts which is imposed on the party seeking amendment.

[Appendix 1 is not reproduced here]

APPENDIX 2-

PATENTS COUNTY COURT	CASE NO.

PRE-TRIAL CHECK LIST

BETWEEN _____ Plaintiff

AND _____ Defendant

AND _____ Third Party

Date fixed for Trial: _____ Estimated length of Trial: ____ days

This check list lodged on behalf of ☐ Plaintiff ☐ Defendant ☐ Third Party

Who will be represented at the trial by:

1. **PLEADINGS**
   Amendments have been made to my/our pleading
   by consent of the other party/parties. ☐ Yes ☐ No

   It is intended to ask for leave to amend
   my/our pleading ☐ Yes ☐ No

2. **ADMISSIONS, DISCOVERY, INTERROGATORIES**
   All notices to admit facts served on me/us
   have been complied with ☐ Yes ☐ No

   All orders to answer interrogatories
   served on me/us have been complied with ☐ Yes ☐ No

   All orders for discovery served on me/us
   have been complied with ☐ Yes ☐ No

3. **REPORTS**
   A report requested from the Patent Office
   has been received ☐ Yes ☐ No ☐ Not applicable

   Other technical opinions have been received ☐ Yes ☐ No ☐ Not applicable

4. **EVIDENCE**
   All orders relating to factual evidence have
   been complied with ☐ Yes ☐ No ☐ Not applicable

   All orders relating to hearsay evidence
   have been complied with ☐ Yes ☐ No ☐ Not applicable

   All orders relating to expert evidence
   have been complied with ☐ Yes ☐ No ☐ Not applicable

5. **WITNESSES**
   A list of witnesses of fact I/we intend to call ☐ has/ ☐ has not been filed.

   A list of expert witnesses I/we intend to call ☐ has/ ☐ has not been filed.

   Interpreters ☐ are required ☐ are not required for the following witness(es)

   Name   Foreign language

6. **EXCHANGE OF WITNESS STATEMENTS AND REPORTS**
   All witness statements ☐ have/ ☐ have not been exchanged

   All experts' reports ☐ have/ ☐ have not been exchanged

7. **BUNDLES OF DOCUMENTS etc.**
   Paginated bundles of documents ☐ have/ ☐ have not been lodged

   An outline argument ☐ has/ ☐ has not been lodged

   A list of authorities ☐ has/ ☐ has not been lodged

SIGNED: _____

DATE: _____

35

TREATY OF ROME

Article 30

26.01   Quantitative restrictions on imports and all measures having equivalent effect shall, without prejudice to the following provisions, be prohibited between Member States.

Article 31

26.02   Member States shall refrain from introducing between themselves any new quantitative restrictions or measures having equivalent effect.

This obligation shall, however, relate only to the degree of liberalisation attained in pursuance of the decisions of the Council of the Organisation for European Economic Cooperation of 14 January 1955. Member States shall supply the Commission, not later than six months after the entry into force of this Treaty, with lists of the products liberalised by them in pursuance of these decisions. These lists shall be consolidated between Member States.

Article 32

26.03   In their trade with one another Member States shall refrain from making more restrictive the quotas and measures having equivalent effect existing at the date of the entry into force of this Treaty.

These quotas shall be abolished by the end of the transitional period at the latest. During that period, they shall be progressively abolished in accordance with the following provisions.

Article 33

26.04   **1.** One year after the entry into force of this Treaty, each Member State shall convert any bilateral quotas open to any other Member States into global quotas open without discrimination to all other Member States.

On the same date, Member States shall increase the aggregate of the global quotas so established in such a manner as to bring about an

984

increase of not less than 20 per cent in their total value as compared with the preceding year. The global quota for each product, however, shall be increased by not less than 10 per cent.

The quotas shall be increased annually in accordance with the same rules and in the same proportions in relation to the preceding year.

The fourth increase shall take place at the end of the fourth year after the entry into force of this Treaty; the fifth, one year after the beginning of the second stage.

2. Where, in the case of a product which has not been liberalised, the global quota does not amount to 3 per cent of the national production of the State concerned, a quota equal to not less than 3 per cent of such national production shall be introduced not later than one year after the entry into force of this Treaty. This quota shall be raised to 4 per cent at the end of the second year, and to 5 per cent at the end of the third. Thereafter, the Member State concerned shall increase the quota by not less than 15 per cent annually.

Where there is no such national production, the Commission shall take a decision establishing an appropriate quota.

3. At the end of the tenth year, each quota shall be equal to not less than 20 per cent of the national production.

4. If the Commission finds by means of a decision that during two successive years the imports of any products have been below the level of the quota opened, this global quota shall not be taken into account in calculating the total value of the global quotas. In such case, the Member State shall abolish quota restrictions on the product concerned.

5. In the case of quotas representing more than 20 per cent of the national production of the product concerned, the Council may, acting by a qualified majority on a proposal from the Commission, reduce the minimum percentage of 10 per cent laid down in paragraph 1. This alteration shall not, however, affect the obligation to increase the total value of global quotas by 20 per cent annually.

6. Member States which have exceeded their obligations as regards the degree of liberalisation attained in pursuance of the decisions of the Council of the Organisation for European Economic Cooperation of 14 January 1955 shall be entitled, when calculating the annual total increase of 20 per cent provided for in paragraph 1, to take into account the amount of imports liberalised by autonomous action. Such calculation shall be submitted to the Commission for its prior approval.

7. The Commission shall issue directives establishing the procedure and timetable in accordance with which Member States shall abolish, as between themselves, any measures in existence when this Treaty enters into force which have an effect equivalent to quotas.

8. If the Commission finds that the application of the provisions of this Article, and in particular of the provisions concerning percentages, makes it impossible to ensure that the abolition of quotas provided for in the second paragraph of Article 32 is carried out progressively, the Council may, on a proposal from the Commission, acting unanimously

during the first stage and by a qualified majority thereafter, amend the procedure laid down in the Article and may, in particular, increase the percentages fixed.

Article 34

26.05   1. Quantitative restrictions on exports, and all measures having equivalent effect, shall be prohibited between Member States.

2. Member States shall, by the end of the first stage at the latest, abolish all quantitative restrictions on exports and any measures having equivalent effect which are in existence when this Treaty enters into force.

Article 35

26.06   The Member States declare their readiness to abolish quantitative restrictions on imports from and exports to other Member States more rapidly than is provided for in the preceding Articles, if their general economic situation and the situation of the economic sector concerned so permit.

To this end, the Commission shall make recommendations to the States concerned.

Article 36

26.07   The provisions of Articles 30 to 34 shall not preclude prohibitions or restrictions on imports, exports or goods in transit justified on grounds of public morality, public policy or public security; the protection of health and life of humans, animals or plants; the protection of national treasures possessing artistic, historic or archaeological value; or the protection of industrial and commercial property. Such prohibitions or restrictions shall not, however, constitute a means of arbitrary discrimination or a disguised restriction on trade between Member States.

Article 85

26.08   1. The following shall be prohibited as incompatible with the common market: all agreements between undertakings, decisions by associations of undertakings and concerted practices which may affect trade between Member States and which have as their object or effect the prevention, restriction or distortion of competition within the common market, and in particular those which:

(a) directly or indirectly fix purchase or selling prices or any other trading conditions;
(b) limit or control production, markets, technical development, or investment;
(c) share markets or sources of supply;
(d) apply dissimilar conditions to equivalent transactions with other trading parties, thereby placing them at a competitive disadvantage;
(e) make the conclusion of contracts subject to acceptance by the other parties of supplementary obligations which, by their nature or according to commercial usage, have no connection with the subject of such contracts.

2. Any agreements or decisions prohibited pursuant to this Article shall be automatically void.

3. The provisions of paragraph 1 may, however, be declared inapplicable in the case of:
—any agreement or category of agreements between undertakings;
—any decision or category of decisions by associations of undertakings;
—any concerted practice or category of concerted practices;
which contributes to improving the production or distribution of goods or to promoting technical or economic progress, while allowing consumers a fair share of the resulting benefit, and which does not:

(a) impose on the undertakings concerned restrictions which are not indispensable to the attainment of these objectives;
(b) afford such undertakings the possibility of eliminating competition in respect of a substantial part of the products in question.

Article 86

Any abuse by one or more undertakings of a dominant position within the common market or in a substantial part of it shall be prohibited as incompatible with the common market insofar as it may affect trade between Member States. Such abuse may, in particular, consist in: **26.09**

(a) directly or indirectly imposing unfair purchase or selling prices or other unfair trading conditions;
(b) limiting production, markets or technical development to the prejudice of consumers;
(c) applying dissimilar conditions to equivalent transactions with

other trading parties, thereby placing them at a competitive disadvantage;

(d) making the conclusion of contracts subject to acceptance by the other parties of supplementary obligations which, by their nature or according to commercial usage, have no connection with the subject of such contracts.

Article 177

26.10　The Court of Justice shall have jurisdiction to give preliminary rulings concerning:

(a) the interpretation of this Treaty;

(b) the validity and interpretation of acts of the institutions of the Community;

(c) the interpretation of the statues of bodies established by an act of the Council, where those statutes so provide.

Where such a question is raised before any court or tribunal of a Member State, that court or tribunal may, if it considers that a decision on the question is necessary to enable it to give judgment, request the Court of Justice to give a ruling thereon.

Where any such question is raised in a case pending before a court or tribunal of a Member State, against whose decisions there is no judicial remedy under national law, that court or tribunal shall bring the matter before the Court of Justice.

ACT OF ACCESSION OF THE KINGDOM OF SPAIN AND THE PORTUGUESE REPUBLIC

Article 47

1. Notwithstanding Article 42, the holder, or his beneficiary, of a **27.01** patent for a chemical or pharmaceutical product or a product relating to plant health, filed in a Member State at a time when a product patent could not be obtained in Spain for that product may rely upon the rights granted by that patent in order to prevent the import and marketing of that product in the present Member State or States where that product enjoys patent protection even if that product was put on the market in Spain for the first time by him or with his consent.

2. This right may be invoked for the products referred to in paragraph (1) until the end of the third year after Spain has made these products patentable.

Article 209

1. Notwithstanding Article 202, the holder, or his beneficiary, of a **27.02** patent for a chemical or pharmaceutical product or a product relating to plant health, filed in a Member State at a time when a product patent could not be obtained in Portugal for that product may rely upon the rights granted by that patent in order to prevent the import and marketing of that product in the Member State or States where that product enjoys patent protection even if that product was put on the market in Portugal for the first time by him or with his consent.

2. This right may be invoked for the products referred to in paragraph (1) until the end of the third year after Portugal has made these products patentable.

PATENTS (SUPPLEMENTARY PROTECTION CERTIFICATE FOR MEDICINAL PRODUCTS) REGULATIONS 1992

(S.I. 1992 No. 3091)

28.00   The Secretary of State, being a Minister designated for the purposes of section 2(2) of the European Communities Act 1972 in relation to measures concerning the creation of a supplementary protection certificate for medicinal products, in exercise of powers conferred by section 2(2) of the said Act of 1972 and of all other powers enabling him in that behalf, hereby makes the following Regulations:

Citation, commencement and extent

28.01   **1.**—(1) These Regulations may be cited as the Patents (Supplementary Protection Certificate for Medicinal Products) Regulations 1992 and shall come into force for the purposes of regulations 1, 2 and 4(2) on 10th December 1992 and for all other purposes on 2nd January 1993.
    (2) These Regulations extend to Great Britain and Northern Ireland.

Definitions

28.02   **2.** In these Regulations—
    "the 1977 Act" means the Patents Act 1977;
    "certificate" has the meaning assigned to it by Article 1(d) of the EC Regulation;
    "the court" has the same meaning as it has in the 1977 Act; and
    "the EC Regulation" means Council Regulation (EEC) No. 1768/92 of 18th June 1992 concerning the creation of a supplementary protection certificate for medicinal products and any reference in these Regulations to an article followed by a number is a reference to the article so numbered in the EEC Regulation.

Competent industrial property office (Article 9(1))

3. The competent industrial property office for the purposes of **28.03** lodging an application for a certificate in the United Kingdom shall be the Patent Office.

Extension of powers under the Patents Act 1977

4.—(1) For the purposes of section 123(1) of the Patents Act 1977 **28.04** matters relating to certificates and applications for certificates shall be the business of the Patent Office and, accordingly, shall be under the direction and control of the Comptroller-General of Patents, Designs and Trade Marks.

(2) The power of the Secretary of State to make rules under section 123 of the 1977 Act shall include power to make rules regulating the business of the Patent Office and matters relating to certificates and applications for certificates and subsections (2) to (7) of section 123 and section 124 shall apply accordingly.

Extension of existing provisions of the Patents Act 1977 and the Patents Act 1949 to certificates (Articles 5, 17 and 18)

5. Subject to any rules made by the Secretary of State under section 123 **28.05** of the 1977 Act relating to certificates, applications for certificates or matters relating to the same, the provisions of that Act and where they continue to apply, the provisions of the Patents Act 1949 and any rules made thereunder in respect of patents, applications for patents, existing patents or existing applications shall, in accordance with the provisions of Articles 5, 17 and 18 of the EC Regulation, extend and apply to, and be taken to make, as appropriate and with the necessary changes, corresponding provision, including corresponding provision relating to fees, forms and to the jurisdiction of and proceedings before the comptroller and the court, for certificates, applications for certificates and matter relating thereto, as they apply to, and make provision for, patents and applications for patents and matters relating thereto.

PATENTS (SUPPLEMENTARY PROTECTION CERTIFICATE FOR MEDICINAL PRODUCTS) RULES 1992

(S.I. 1992 No. 3162)

29.00   The Secretary of State, in exercise of powers conferred by section 123 of, and paragraph 14 of Schedule 4 to, the Patents Act 1977, of the power conferred upon him by the Department of Trade and Industry (Fees) Order 1988, and of all other powers enabling him in that behalf, after consultation with the Council on Tribunals pursuant to section 8(1) of the Tribunals and Enquiries Act 1992 and with the consent of the Treasury pursuant to subsection (4) of the said section 123, hereby makes the following Rules:

PART I. GENERAL

Citation, commencement and extent

29.01   1.—(1) These Rules may be cited as the Patents (Supplementary Protection Certificate for Medicinal Products) Rules 1992 and shall come into force on January 2, 1993.
(2) These Rules extend to Great Britain and Northern Ireland.

Interpretation

29.02   2.—(1) In these Rules—
"the 1977 Act" means the Patents Act 1977;
"basic patent" has the meaning assigned to it by paragraph (c) of Article 1 of the EC Regulation;
"certificate" has the meaning assigned to it in paragraph (d) of Article 1 of the EC Regulation;
"the Comptroller" and "the journal" have the same meanings as they have in the 1977 Act;
"the court" has the same meaning as it has in the 1977 Act;
"the EC Regulation" means Council Regulation (EEC) No. 1768/92 of June 18, 1992 concerning the creation of a supplementary protection certificate for medicinal products, the English lan-

guage version of which is set out in Schedule 1 to these Rules, and any reference in these Rules to an Article followed by a number is a reference to the Article so numbered in the EC Regulation; and "register of patents" means the register of patents maintained pursuant to section 32 of the 1977 Act.

(2) Subject to paragraph (3), the forms of which the use is required by these Rules are those set out in Schedule 2 to these Rules.

(3) A requirement under these Rules to use such a form is satisfied by the use either of a replica of that form or of a form which is acceptable to the Comptroller and contains the information required by the form set out in Schedule 2 to these Rules.

(4) The fees to be paid in respect of any matter arising under these Rules shall be those (if any) prescribed in relation to such matter in Schedule 4 to these Rules; and any reference to "prescribed fee" and "fees" in these Rules shall be construed accordingly.

PART II. PROVISIONS RELATING TO ARTICLES 4 TO 16 OF THE EC REGULATION

Application and fee in respect of application (Article 8 and 9(1))

3.—(1) The application for a certificate shall be—　　　　　　　29.03
(a) subject to the payment to the Patent Office of a prescribed fee; and
(b) lodged with the Patent Office accompanied by the prescribed fee.
(2) A request for the grant of a certificate shall be made on Form SP1.

Certificate of grant (Article 10)

4. A certificate shall be in the form set out in Schedule 3 to these Rules.　29.04

Fees in respect of effective period of certificate (Article 12)

5.—(1) A reference in this rule to—　　　　　　　　　　　29.05
(a) "due date" means the date on which a certificate, subject to the requirement to pay fees, would take effect at the end of the lawful term of the basic patent; and
(b) "maximum period" means the maximum possible period of duration of a certificate as determined in accordance with Article 13.

(2) A certificate shall not take effect, and its actual duration shall not be determined, until payment is made of the fees prescribed in accordance with paragraphs (3) to (10) below.

(3) Subject to paragraph (9), the amount of fees payable in order for a

certificate to take effect in respect of any period ("the appropriate fees") shall be the amount calculated by reference to the length of the maximum period, less, if any, such period deducted from the end of the maximum period during which it is desired by the holder of a certificate that the certificate shall not have effect, the resulting period, whether reduced from the maximum period or not, being referred to hereafter as the "effective period".

(4) The appropriate fees payable in respect of any effective period shall be the cumulative amount of fees prescribed—

(a) by reference to the successive 12 month periods of which an effective period is made up (any period of less than 12 months being treated as a 12 month period of which that lesser period forms part); the first such period shall commence on the due date ("the first year"); the second shall commence immediately upon expiry of the first ("the second year"), with corresponding provision in respect of each successive year up to a maximum of five years ("the fifth year") which years shall be referred to herein generally as "effective years"; and

(b) in respect of each of the effective years, by the prescribed fees in force—

(i) where payment is made before the due date, on the date on which payment is made;

(ii) in any other case, on the due date.

(5) Subject to paragraphs (7) and (9), the appropriate fees in respect of an effective period shall be paid not later than the due date but may not be paid earlier than three months preceding the due date.

(6) Without prejudice to the provisions of paragraphs (2) and (5), the Comptroller shall write to the holder of a certificate not later than two months before the due date—

(a) notifying him of the due date;

(b) indicating the prescribed fees applicable in respect of each of the effective years of which the maximum period of the certificate is made up; and

(c) specifying the period within which fees must be paid to the Patent Office in order for the certificate to take effect;

and the holder of the certificate shall, within the period specified under paragraph (c), notify the Patent Office on Form SP2 of the effective period of the certificate, which notification shall be accompanied by the appropriate fees payable in respect of that period.

(7) Where a certificate is granted later than three months before the end of the lawful term of the basic patent, the provisions of paragraphs (5) and (6) shall be modified as follows—

(a) the due date for the purposes of payment of the appropriate fees shall be the date three months after the date of grant of the certificate; and

(b) the Comptroller shall write to the applicant for the certificate in the terms prescribed by paragraph (6), subject to sub-paragraph

(a) of this paragraph, on the date on which he notifies him of the grant thereof.

(8) Where the effective period is less than the maximum period of the certificate it shall not subsequently be extended.

(9) Where the period for payment of fees under paragraph (5) or (7), as the case may be, has expired—

(a) the Comptroller shall, not later than six weeks after the applicable due date and if the fees remain unpaid, notify the holder of the certificate—
  (i) that the fees remain unpaid; and
  (ii) of the consequences of non-payment; and
  (iii) of the provisions of sub-paragraph (b);

(b) the holder, subject to the payment within a period of six months after the applicable due date of the unpaid fees and an additional late payment fee of an amount equal to one half of the amount of the unpaid fees, shall be treated as having paid the fees on the applicable due date.

(10) The notices under paragraphs (6) and (9) of this rule shall be sent by the Comptroller to—

(a) the address for service furnished in writing by the applicant for a certificate or any address replacing it, and,

(b) in relation to the basic patent in respect of which the certificate is granted, where it differs from the address referred to in sub-paragraph (a),
  (i) the address in the United Kingdom to which any renewal reminder is to be sent as specified by the proprietor on payment of the last renewal fee or any address replacing it, or
  (ii) where no such address is specified, the address for service (if any) entered in the register of patents.

6. If the certificate is surrendered or declared invalid on or with effect **29.06** from a date earlier ("the earlier date") than the date of the expiry of the effective period, where the appropriate fees in respect of that period have been paid, the Comptroller shall remit the fee paid in respect of any effective year which falls after the end of the effective year (if any) into which the earlier date falls.

Declaration of lapse or invalidity of certificate (Articles 14(d) and 15(1)(a) and (c))

7.—(1) On the application of any person, the Comptroller may, as the **29.07** case may be, declare—

(a) that a certificate has lapsed on the ground set out in Article 14(d); or

(b) that the ground for lapse under Article 14(d) no longer exists.

(2) The court or the Comptroller may declare that a certificate is invalid in accordance with the provisions of Article 15.

(3) An application to the Comptroller for a declaration under paragraph (1)(a) or paragraph (2) shall be made on Form SP3 and shall be accompanied by a copy thereof and a statement in duplicate setting out fully the facts upon which the applicant relies and the relief which he seeks.

(4) The Comptroller shall send a copy of the application and the statement to the holder of the certificate.

(5) Within the period of two months beginning on the date on which such copies are sent to him, the holder of the certificate shall, if he wishes to contest the application, file a counter-statement in duplicate at the Patent Office setting out fully the grounds on which the application is contested; and the Comptroller shall send a copy of the counter-statement to the applicant.

(6) No further statement or counter-statement shall be served by either party without the leave or direction of the Comptroller.

(7) The Comptroller may give such directions as he may think fit with regard to the subsequent procedure.

29.08　　8. If it appears to the Comptroller that a certificate has lapsed in accordance with Article 14(d) he may on his own initiative declare that the certificate has lapsed but shall not do so without giving the holder of the certificate notice of his intention to make such a declaration and affording him an opportunity to make representations within two months of the date of the notice.

Forms for use in connection with certificates or applications for certificates (Article 18(1))

29.09　　9. Those forms of which use is required by any provision of the 1977 Act or any rules made thereunder in relation to patents or applications for patents, except where replaced by the forms set out in Schedule 2 to these Rules, shall also be used, with the necessary changes, in the corresponding circumstances in relation to certificates or applications for certificates.

Publication of: application, grant of certificate, rejection of application, declaration of lapse or of invalidity or of termination of grounds for lapse of certificate (Articles 9(2), 11(1) and (2) and 16)

29.10　　10. Notification of—
(a) the application for a certificate;
(b) the fact that a certificate has been granted;
(c) the fact that the application for a certificate has been rejected;

(d) lapse of a certificate;

(e) invalidity of a certificate;

(f) termination of grounds for lapse of a certificate under Article 14(d),

shall be published by the Comptroller in the journal.

SCHEDULE 1   REGULATION 2(2)

Council Regulation (EEC) No. 1768/92 of June 18, 1992 concerning the creation of a
supplementary protection certificate for medicinal products

THE COUNCIL OF THE EUROPEAN COMMUNITIES,   **29.11**

Having regard to the Treaty establishing the European Economic Community, and in particular Article 100a thereof,

In co-operation with the European Parliament,

Having regard to the opinion of the Economic and Social Committee,

Whereas pharmaceutical research plays a decisive role in the continuing improvement in public health;

Whereas medicinal products, especially those that are the result of long, costly research will not continue to be developed in the Community and in Europe unless they are covered by favourable rules that provide for sufficient protection to encourage such research;

Whereas at the moment the period that elapses between the filing of an application for a patent for a new medicinal product and authorisation to place the medicinal product on the market makes the period of effective protection under the patent insufficient to cover the investment put into the research;

Whereas this situation leads to a lack of protection which penalises pharmaceutical research;

Whereas the current situation is creating the risk of research centres situated in the Member States relocating to countries that already offer greater protection;

Whereas a uniform solution at Community level should be provided for, thereby preventing the heterogeneous development of natural laws leading to further disparities which would be likely to create obstacles to the free movement of medicinal products within the Community and thus directly affect the establishment and the functioning of the internal market;

Whereas, therefore, the creation of a supplementary protection certificate granted, under the same conditions, by each of the Member States at the request of the holder of a national or European patent relating to a medicinal product for which marketing authorisation has been granted is necessary; whereas a Regulation is therefore the most appropriate legal instrument;

Whereas the duration of the protection granted by the certificate should be such as to provide adequate effective protection; whereas, for this purpose, the holder of both a patent and a certificate should be able to enjoy an overall maximum of 15 years of exclusively from the time the medicinal product in question first obtains authorisation to be placed on the market in the Community;

Whereas all the interests at stake, including those of public health, in a sector as complex and sensitive as the pharmaceutical sector must nevertheless be taken into account; whereas, for this purpose, the certificate cannot be granted for a period exceeding five years; whereas the protection granted should furthermore be strictly confined to the product which obtained authorisation to be placed on the market as a medicinal product;

Whereas a fair balance should also be struck with regard to the determination of the transitional arrangements; whereas such arrangements should enable the Community pharmaceutical industry to catch up to some extent with its main competitors who, for a number of years, have been covered by laws guaranteeing them more adequate protection, while making sure that the arrangements do not compromise the achievement of other legitimate objectives concerning the health policies pursued both at national and Community level;

Whereas the transitional arrangements applicable to applications for certificates filed and to certificates granted under national legislation prior to the entry into force of this Regulation should be defined;

Whereas special arrangements should be allowed in Member States whose laws introduced the patentability of pharmaceutical products only very recently;

Whereas provision should be made for appropriate limitation of the duration of the certificate in the special case where a patent term has already been extended under a specific national law,

HAS ADOPTED THIS REGULATION:

Article 1

Definitions

29.12 For the purposes of this Regulation:
(a) 'medicinal product' means any substance or combination of substances presented for treating or preventing disease in human beings or animals and any substance or combination of substances which may be administered to human beings or animals with a view to making a medical diagnosis or to restoring, correcting or modifying physiological functions in humans or in animals;
(b) 'product' means the active ingredient or combination of active ingredients of a medicinal product;
(c) 'basic patent' means a patent which protects a product as defined in (b) as such, a process to obtain a product or an application of a product, and which is designated by its holder for the purpose of the procedure for grant of a certificate;
(d) 'certificate' means the supplementary protection certificate.

Article 2

Scope

29.13 Any product protected by a patent in the territory of a Member State and subject, prior to being placed on the market as a medicinal product, to an administrative authorisation procedure as laid down in Council Directive 65/65/EEC or Directive 81/851/EEC may, under the terms and conditions provided for in this Regulation, be the subject of a certificate.

Article 3

Conditions for obtaining a certificate

29.14 A certificate shall be granted if, in the Member State in which the application referred to in Article 7 is submitted and at the date of that application:
(a) the product is protected by a basic patent in force;
(b) a valid authorisation to place the product on the market as a medicinal product has been granted in accordance with Directive 65/65/EEC or Directive 81/851/EEC, as appropriate;
(c) the product has not already been the subject of a certificate;
(d) the authorisation referred to in (b) is the first authorisation to place the product on the market as a medicinal product.

Article 4

Subject-matter of protection

Within the limits of the protection conferred by the basic patent, the protection conferred by a certificate shall extend only to the product covered by the authorisation to place the corresponding medicinal product on the market and for any use of the product as a medicinal product that has been authorised before the expiry of the certificate.   **29.15**

Article 5

Effects of the certificate

Subject to the provisions of Article 4, the certificate shall confer the same rights as conferred by the basic patent and shall be subject to the same limitations and the same obligations.   **29.16**

Article 6

Entitlement to the certificate

The certificate shall be granted to the holder of the basic patent or his successor in title.   **29.17**

Article 7

Application for a certificate

1. The application for a certificate shall be lodged within six months of the date on which the authorisation referred to in Article 3(b) to place the product on the market as a medicinal product was granted.   **29.18**
2. Notwithstanding paragraph 1, where the authorisation to place the product on the market is granted before the basic patent is granted, the application for a certificate shall be lodged within six months of the date on which the patent is granted.

Article 8

Content of the application for a certificate

1. The application for a certificate shall contain: **29.19**
(a) a request for the grant of a certificate, stating in particular:
   (i) the name and address of the applicant;
   (ii) if he has appointed a representative, the name and address of the representative;
   (iii) the number of the basic patent and the title of the invention;
   (iv) the number and date of the first authorisation to place the product on the market, as referred to in Article 3(b) and, if this authorisation is not the first authorisation for placing the product on the market in the Community, the number and date of that authorisation;

(b) a copy of the authorisation to place the product on the market, as referred to in Article 3(b), in which the product is identified, containing in particular the number and date of the authorisation and the summary of the product characteristics listed in Article 4a of Directive 65/65/EEC or Article 5a of Directive 81/851/EEC;

(c) if the authorisation referred to in (b) is not the first authorisation for placing the product on the market as a medicinal product in the Community, information regarding the identity of the product thus authorised and the legal provision under which the authorisation procedure took place, together with a copy of the notice publishing the authorisation in the appropriate official publication.

2. Member States may provide that a fee is to be payable upon application for a certificate.

Article 9

Lodging of an application for a certificate

29.20 **1.** The application for a certificate shall be lodged with the competent industrial property office of the Member State which granted the basic patent or on whose behalf it was granted and in which the authorisation referred to in Article 3(b) to place the product on the market was obtained, unless the Member State designates another authority for the purpose.

2. Notification of the application for a certificate shall be published by the authority referred to in paragraph 1. The notification shall contain at least the following information:

(a) the name and address of the applicant;
(b) the number of the basic patent;
(c) the title of the invention;
(d) the number and date of the authorisation to place the product on the market, referred to in Article 3(b), and the product identified in that authorisation;
(e) where relevant, the number and date of the first authorisation to place the product on the market in the Community.

Article 10

Grant of the certificate or rejection of the application

29.21 **1.** Where the application for a certificate and the product to which it relates meet the conditions laid down in this Regulation, the authority referred to in Article 9(1) shall grant the certificate.

2. The authority referred to in Article 9(1) shall, subject to paragraph 3, reject the application for a certificate if the application or the product to which it relates does not meet the conditions laid down in this Regulation.

3. Where the application for a certificate does not meet the conditions laid down in Article 8, the authority referred to in Article 9(1) shall ask the applicant to rectify the irregularity, or to settle the fee, within a stated time.

4. If the irregularity is not rectified or the fee is not settled under paragraph 3 within the stated time, the authority shall reject the application.

5. Member States may provide that the authority referred to in Article 9(1) is to grant certificates without verifying that the conditions laid down in Article 3(c) and (d) are met.

Article 11

Publication

1. Notification of the fact that a certificate has been granted shall be published by the authority referred to in Article 9(1). The notification shall contain at least the following information:
  (a) the name and address of the holder of the certificate;
  (b) the number of the basic patent;
  (c) the title of the invention;
  (d) the number and date of the authorisation to place the product on the market referred to in Article 3(b) and the product identified in that authorisation;
  (e) where relevant, the number and date of the first authorisation to place the product on the market in the Community;
  (f) the duration of the certificate.
2. Notification of the fact that the application for a certificate has been rejected shall be published by the authority referred to in Article 9(1). The notification shall contain at least the information listed in Article 9(2).

29.22

Article 12

Annual fees

Member States may require that the certificate be subject to the payment of annual fees.

29.23

Article 13

Duration of the certificate

1. The certificate shall take effect at the end of the lawful term of the basic patent for a period equal to the period which elapsed between the date on which the application for a basic patent was lodged and the date of the first authorisation to place the product on the market in the Community reduced by a period of five years.
2. Notwithstanding paragraph 1, the duration of the certificate may not exceed five years from the date on which it takes effect.

29.24

Article 14

Expiry of the certificate

The certificate shall lapse:
  (a) at the end of the period provided for in Article 13;
  (b) if the certificate holder surrenders it;
  (c) if the annual fee laid down in accordance with Article 12 is not paid in time;
  (d) if and as long as the product covered by the certificate may no longer be placed on the market following the withdrawal of the appropriate authorisation or authorisations to place on the market in accordance with Directive 65/65/EEC or Directive 81/851/EEC. The authority referred to in Article 9(1) may decide on the lapse of the certificate either of its own motion or at the request of a third party.

29.25

Article 15

Invalidity of the certificate

29.26   1. The certificate shall be invalid if:
(a) it was granted contrary to the provisions of Article 3;
(b) the basic patent has lapsed before its lawful term expires;
(c) the basic patent is revoked or limited to the extent that the product for which the certificate was granted would no longer be protected by the claims of the basic patent or, after the basic patent has expired, grounds for revocation exist which would have justified such revocation or limitation.

2. Any person may submit an application or bring an action for a declaration of invalidity of the certificate before the body responsible under national law for the renovation of the corresponding basic patent.

Article 16

Notification of lapse or invalidity

29.27   If the certificate lapses in accordance with Article 14(b), (c) or (d) or is invalid in accordance with Article 15, notification thereof shall be published by the authority referred to in Article 9(1).

Article 17

Appeals

29.28   The decisions of the authority referred to in Article 9(1) or of the body referred to in Article 15(2) taken under this Regulation shall be open to the same appeals as those provided for in national law against similar decisions taken in respect of national patents.

Article 18

Procedure

29.29   1. In the absence of procedural provisions in this Regulation, the procedural provisions applicable under national law to the corresponding basic patent shall apply to the certificate, unless that law lays down special procedural provisions for certificates.

2. Notwithstanding paragraph 1, the procedure for opposition to the granting of a certificate shall be excluded.

Article 19

Transitional provisions

29.30   1. Any product which, on the date on which this Regulation enters into force, is protected by a valid basic patent and for which the first authorisation to place it on the market as a medicinal product in the Community was obtained after January 1, 1985 may be granted a certificate.

In the case of certificates to be granted in Denmark and in Germany, the date of January 1, 1985 shall be replaced by that of January 1, 1988.

In the case of certificates to be granted in Belgium and in Italy, the date of January 1, 1985 shall be replaced by that of January 1, 1982.

2. An application for a certificate as referred to in paragraph 1 shall be submitted within six months of the date on which this Regulation enters into force.

Article 20

This Regulation shall not apply to certificates granted in accordance with the national **29.31** legislation of a Member State before the date on which this Regulation enters into force or to applications for a certificate filed in accordance with that legislation before the date of publication of this Regulation in the *Official Journal of the European Communities.*

Article 21

In those Member States whose national law did not on January 1, 1990 provide for the **29.32** patentability of pharmaceutical products, this Regulation shall apply five years after the entry into force of this Regulation.

Article 19 shall not apply in those Member States.

Article 22

Where a certificate is granted for a product protected by a patent which, before the date **29.33** on which this Regulation enters into force, has had its term extended or for which such extension was applied for, under national patent law, the term of protection to be afforded under this certificate shall be reduced by the number of years by which the term of the patent exceeds 20 years.

FINAL PROVISION

Article 23

Entry into force

This Regulation shall enter into force six months after its publication in the *Official* **29.34** *Journal of the European Communities.*

This Regulation shall be binding in its entirety and directly applicable in all Member States.

Done at Luxembourg, June 18, 1992.

Schedule 2

GENERAL FORMS

Form SP1*

The Patent Office	**Request for grant of Supplementary Protection Certificate**
	Form SP1

The Patents (Supplementary Protection Certificate for Medicinal Products) Rules 1992

---

1 Applicant

Name

Please provide details of further applicants on a separate sheet

Address and Postcode

ADP Number

---

2 Name of Agent (if any)

---

3 Address for Service in the United Kingdom
(to which all correspondence will be sent)

Name

Address and postcode

☎

ADP Number   Your reference

---

* Form reprinted as corrected (O.J. February 24, 1993).

(FORM SP1 CONTINUED)

4 Product for which protection is sought	**Reminder** Have you enclosed the following? ☐ Prescribed fee
5 Basic Patent (GB or EP(UK)) Number Title Expiry date Grant date (if after first authorisation under 6a below)	☐ Copy of authorisation identified at 6a. The authorisation must contain a summary of the product characteristics listed in Art 4a of Directive 65/65/EEC or Art 5a of Directive 81/851/EEC
6 Authorisation 6a. First authorisation in accordance with Directive 65/65/EEC or Directive 81/851/EEC to place the product on the market in the UK Number Date 6b. If this is not the first authorisation to place the product on the market in the Community, please give the following information concerning the first such authorisation State and Number Date Identity of product thus authorised Legal provision under which the authorisation took place	☐ Information concerning the product to enable the Comptroller to confirm that the product is protected by the basic patent (eg derivation of product from general formula; indication of reference to product in text) ☐ Copy of notice publishing any earlier authorisation (identified at 6b) in the appropriate official publication (if necessary) ☐ Translation (if necessary) of any notice of earlier authorisation identified at 6b, such translation to be verified to the satisfaction of the Comptroller
7 Signature and Date	

1005

Form SP2

The **Patent Office**	**Payment of annual fees (and additional fee for late payment)** Form SP2

The Patents (Supplementary Protection Certificate for Medicinal Products) Rules 1992

1 Supplementary Protection Certificate Number

Rule 5 is the main rule governing the completion and filing of this form.

2 Name of holder(s)

3 Due date for payment of annual fees

4 Desired effective period

5 Amount of fees

a Annual fees

£

b Late payment fee (if any)

£

6 Person paying fees

Name

Address and Postcode

Your reference

7 Do you want the certificate of payment of fees to be sent to the address at 6?

☐ **YES**

☐ **NO**

If NO, please give on a separate sheet the name and address to which it is to be sent.

1006

Form SP3

The Patent Office	**Application for decision of lapse or declaration of invalidity of a Supplementary Protection Certificate** **Form SP3**

The Patents (Supplementary Protection Certificate for Medicinal Products) Rules 1992

---

1 Name of Applicant(s)

This form and accompanying statement are to be filed in duplicate.

The statement should set out

2 Details of Certificate
Number

- whether decision of lapse or declaration of invalidity is sought

Name of holder(s)

- which of the grounds in Articles 14(d) and 15 is being relied on

- the full facts upon which the applicant relies in support of his case

3 Name of Agent (if any)

- the relief sought

---

4 Address for Service in the United Kingdom (to which all correspondence will be sent)

Name

Address and Postcode

☎

ADP Number   Your reference

---

5 Signature and Date

Schedule 3 *Rule 4*

CERTIFICATE

"EEC REGULATION No. 1768/92

SUPPLEMENTARY PROTECTION CERTIFICATE

In accordance with Article 10(1) of the above Regulation,

Supplementary Protection Certificate No. ....

is hereby granted to ....

in respect of the product ....

protected by basic patent no. ....

entitled ....

This certificate will take effect (subject to the payment of the prescribed fees) at the end of the lawful term of the basic patent and its maximum period of duration in accordance with Article 13 will expire on .... subject to the provisions of Articles 14 and 15.

Dated this day of 19

Comptroller-General of Patents, Designs and Trade Marks."

Schedule 4   *Rule 2(4)*

FEES

Number of corresponding Supplementary Protection Certificate Form	*Item*	*Amount*
		£
SP1	Application for grant of certificate under Article 8 and rule 3	250
SP2	Annual fees under Article 12 and rule 5:	
	— for first year or part thereof ...	600
	— for second year or part thereof	700
	— for third year or part thereof ..	800
	— for fourth year or part thereof	900
	— for fifth year or part thereof ..	1000
SP3	Application for declation of lapse or invalidity under Articles 14 and 15	—

INDEX

All references are to paragraph numbers

Abuse of Monopoly. *See* **Compulsory Licence.**
Account of Profits,
   generally, 12.225
   innocent infringers, and, 12.240–12.241
   licences of right, and, 12.242
   stay of, 12.226
Action for Infringement,
   appeals in,
     costs, on, 12.278
     generally, 12.281
   choice of court for, 12.20
   compulsory licence, grant of, pending, 9.41
   Crown, against, 13.02
   defendant in,
     assignee of infringers business, 12.10
     calculated risk by, 12.43
     carriers, 12.14
     company directors, 12.12
     generally, 12.09
     failure to appear by one, 12.35
     failure to notify intention to defend by, 12.33
     impecunious, 12.45
     indemnifier, 12.15
     manufacturers, 12.11, 12.15
     numerous infringers, 12.13
     patentee as, 12.03
     supplier as licensee of Plaintiff, 12.15
   expired patent and, 12.02
   High Court, in. *See* High Court.
   infants in, 12.280
   injunction in, 12.37 *et seq. See* **Injunctions.**
   Isle of Man, in, 12.22
   joinder of parties in. *See* parties *supra*
   licence of right, of, 9.51
   obligations of court in, 12.01
   parties in,
     change of, 12.16
     defendant, 12.09–12.14